THE GREEN GUIDE

# Japan

Five-story pagoda, Haguro-san, Mount Haguro, Yamagata, Tohoku © JNTO

**Special thanks** goes to the Visit Japan Campaign of the Japan National Tourism Organization (JNTO) and the International Tourism Center of Japan (ITCJ) for their help in the creation of this guide

**Editor** Clive Hebard

**Editorial** Jo Murray, Jackie Strachan, Yoshimi Kanazawa, Alison Coupe, Catherine Guégan, Geneviève Clastres, Floriane Charron, Akihiro Nishida, Clive Hebard

**Principal Writers** JMS Books (Howard Curtis, Barbara Beeby, Elsi Pichel-Juan, Simon Knight, Malcolm Garrard, Jenni Davis, Sheila Murphy)

**Special Features Writers** *Understanding Japan*: P. Pons (Journalist); J.-M. Butel (Senior Lecturer, INALCO); P. Pataud Célérier (Journalist); É. Barral (Journalist); J-L. Toula-Breysse (Journalist); Ch. Polak (Historian); B. Delmas (Michelin Japan); Ch. Vendredi-Auzanneau (Assistant Professor of History of Architecture, Keio University, Tokyo); M. Tardits (Architect, Mikan group); C. Brisset (Senior Lecturer, University of Paris Diderot-Paris 7); M. Lucken (INALCO); M. Inoue (Journalist); H. Kelmachter (Cultural Attachée, French Embassy, Tokyo); S. Sarrazin (Journalist); P. Duval (Journalist); M. Wasserman (Professor at Ritsumeikan University, Kyoto); F. Moréchand (Lifestyle Journalist); J-F. Mesplède (Michelin); G. Maucout (Michelin). *Discovering Japan*: P. Pataud Célérier (Tokyo and surroundings, Kyoto, Tohoku, and Hokkaido); J. Saglio (Kansai, Chugoku, Shikoku, Kyushu, Okinawa, and Chubu); S. Guillot (Kansai); Ph. Orain (Hokkaido); M. Fonovich

**Production Manager** Natasha G. George

**Cartography** ©2009 Cartographic data Shobunsha/Michelin
Stéphane Anton, Michèle Cana, Véronique Aissani

**Photo Editor** Yoshimi Kanazawa

**Proofreader**

**Interior Design**

**Cover Design**

**Layout**

**Cover Layout**

**Contact Us**



travelpubsales@uk.michelin.com

**Special Sales** For information regarding bulk sales, customized editions and premium sales, please contact our Customer Service Departments:

| | |
|---|---|
| USA | 1-800-432-6277 |
| UK | 01923 205240 |
| Canada | 1-800-361-8236 |

**Note to the reader** Addresses, phone numbers, opening hours and prices published in this guide are accurate at the time of press. We welcome corrections and suggestions that may assist us in preparing the next edition. While every effort is made to ensure that all information printed in this guide is correct and up-to-date, Michelin Apa Publications Ltd. accepts no liability for any direct, indirect or consequential losses howsoever caused so far as such can be excluded by law.

# HOW TO USE THIS GUIDE

## PLANNING YOUR TRIP

The blue-tabbed PLANNING YOUR TRIP section at the front of the guide gives you **ideas for your trip** and **practical information** to organise it. You'll find tours, practical information, a host of outdoor activities, a calendar of events, information on shopping, sightseeing, children's activities and more.

## INTRODUCTION

The orange-tabbed INTRODUCTION section explores Japan's **Nature**, geography and geology. The **History** section spans the Jomon era through today. The **Art and Culture** sections cover architecture, the visual arts, literature and music, while **A Way of Life** delves into modern Japanese lifestyle and culture.

## DISCOVERING

The green-tabbed DISCOVERING section features Principal Sights by region, featuring the most interesting local **Sights** and **Walking Tours**. Admission prices shown are normally for a single adult.

# ADDRESSES

We've selected the best hotels, restaurants, cafés, shops, nightlife and entertainment to fit all budgets. See the Legend on the cover flap for an explanation of the price categories. See the back of the guide for an index of where to find hotels and restaurants.

### Sidebars

Throughout the guide you will find blue, orange and green-coloured text boxes with lively anecdotes, detailed history and background information.

### A Bit of Advice

Green advice boxes found in this guide contain practical tips and handy information relevant to your visit or to a sight in the Discovering section.

## STAR RATINGS★★★

Michelin has given star ratings for more than 100 years. If you're pressed for time, we recommend you visit the ★★★, or ★★ sights first:

★★★ **Highly recommended**
★★ **Recommended**
★ **Interesting**

## MAPS

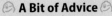

- Country map
- Principal Sights map
- Region maps
- Maps for cities and villages
- Local tour maps
- Subway map

All maps in this guide are oriented north, unless otherwise indicated by a directional arrow. The term "Local Map" refers to a map within the chapter or Tourism Region.
A complete list of the maps found in the guide appears at the back of this book. In the guide, subway station names spelt with an "n" before consonants (e.g. Jinbocho) are spelt with an "m" on the subway map (e.g. Jimbocho).

# PLANNING YOUR TRIP

© José Fuste Raga/AGE/Photononstop

# INTRODUCTION TO JAPAN

© Jochen Tack/age fotostock

# DISCOVERING JAPAN

# Welcome to Japan

**Japan's image is often limited to one of hypermodern cities of bustling consumerism, packed trains and tireless workers. Explore beyond that, however, and a stay in this complex, contradictory country will deepen you. The Japanese call this capacity *uskuji*, or the ability to live one's inner life beyond appearances. As architect Tadao Ando has said: "In Japan a temple is made of wood. The divine spirit inside the building is eternal, so the enclosure doesn't have to be." In other words, here you may get more than just an interesting visit abroad; you may also learn a new kind of intuition, to see past even the ugly to the astonishing, quiet beauty within.**

## TOKYO AND SURROUNDINGS *(pp118–229)*

Multifaceted Tokyo expresses a very different personality with each of its 23 wards. If you love the contemporary, you will find that after Akihabara's latest electronic gadgets and Ginza's elegant shopping, you will be ready for nightlife in Shinjuku, where neon turns night into day. Yet there is Tokyo's other side: incense-scented Akusaka temples, old bookstores in Jimbocho and the cup of hot sake a fellow patron in a Shibuya bar cheerfully pours you to make friends.

## CENTRAL HONSHU (CHUBU) *(pp230–281)*

Chubu, or central Honshu Island, lets you touch old Japan. Takayama, built by the carpenters who made Kyoto, dresses up the dark wood of its streets at festival time with colorful banners. The Japan Alps offer deep gorges and thick, fir-scented forests. Warm up after a glorious crisp day on the slopes at the village hot spring, your fellow bathers' wooden clogs echoing on the cobblestones. Feudal Japan lives on in this region: 16C Matsumoto Castle keeps dark watch, while Ise Shrine, Japan's most holy site, guards the sacred mirror of sun goddess Amaterasu; yet you dine simply, at the hearth of a centuries-old inn, frogs croaking in the night.

## KYOTO AND KANSAI *(pp282–370)*

For 11 centuries Kyoto aristocracy brought cultural pursuits to the highest possible degree of delicate refinement. Today, almost a quarter of Japan's National Treasures are here in temples, shrines, and museums. You can glimpse this Golden Age in the pigeon-toed gait of a young trainee geisha. In Nara, the sacred deer of the gods wander freely among temples and eat from your hand; yet a vibrantly contemporary world welcomes you warmly in Osaka, Kansai's economic capital.

## WESTERN HONSHU (CHUGOKU) *(pp371–401)*

In Chigoku you can visit Japan's second most important shrine, Izumo Taisha. Here, young women pray for a husband to Okuninushi, god of the earth, who is believed to bring joyous harmony to marriage. In Hiroshima is remembrance, but also hope, echoed in the peace you feel contemplating Koraku-en, one of Japan's three loveliest old gardens, where you can sit in its old tea-house, a cup of *matcha* warming your hand. At Isukushima Shrine the goddess of the sea is worshipped; you reach the celebrated vermillion-lacquered "floating torii" by waiting for low tide, at its most enchanting at dusk when lanterns illuminate one of Japan's most beautiful views.

## NORTHERN HONSHU (TOHOKU) *(pp402–421)*

Tohoku, the northeastern part of Honshu, is Japan's largest region after Hokkaido and an original homeland of the Ainu people. Expansive rice fields abut orchards and the rugged coastline around deep blue Matsushima Bay, whose 260-some pine-clad islands are considered one of the country's most beautiful views. From here you can take the magnificent trail to Mount Haguro and relax in a stone-slabbed sauna. Your old inn's inner garden has a tiny shrine to Inari, the fox-god.

## HOKKAIDO *(pp422–451)*

Hokkaido Island is Japan's northernmost and largest region. Here, the Ainu people settled before the Jomon era (10,000–300 BC). Visit in February to see the celebrated Snow Festival and admire the astounding talent of artists creating gigantic ice sculptures in the open air. A "Genghis Khan" dinner of barbecued mutton and vegetables will ward off the deep chill or winter, while a foaming Sapporo beer from the local brewery cheers the soul. Even in the depths of winter, hot-water Lake Shikotsu never freezes; it has been in this volcano crater for 40,000 years.

## SHIKOKU *(pp452–469)*

Japan's smallest and least-populated region is Shikoku. Its tranquillity has long been a source of comfort and inspiration, with 17C Kikugestu-tei the tea house where feudal lords performed the Tea Ceremony and composed *haiku*. In the surrounding stroll garden of Ritsurin-koen, twisted black pines have been shaped over five generations to suggest dragons or cranes in flight. Before leaving to hike the wild countryside of the Iya Valley or watch the 100,000 dancers of the Awa Odori festival in their brilliantly-hued kimonos, make time to visit the 19C Dogo *Onsen* bathhouse, formerly frequented by the Imperial Family: choose between the Bath of the Gods or the Bath of the Spirits for your afternoon relaxation.

## KYUSHU *(pp470–507)*

With its intense volcanic activity, Kyushu, "land of fire," has been Japan's main point of contact with other cultures. In dynamic Fukuoka, you'll get a good look at the modern and the contemporary at the Asian Art Museum before Tenjin shopping and Nakasu nightlife; dinner is on the wooden bench of a street-side *yatai*, eating noodles in thick pork broth. When you're ready for a different pace, explore mist-shrouded Yakushima Island's rainforest, or a volcanic-sand treatment in Ibusuki, with the water-fall bath to massage your shoulders.

## OKINAWA ARCHIPELAGO *(pp508–519)*

*Colorful Okinawa costume*



Here, some 60 islands stretch in an arc across the East China Sea, each a tropical paradise of its own. On Okinawa-honto, spry old ladies will try to sell you fish and exotic fruits at the covered market, and a boat trip takes you to see humpback whales. A short plane ride, and on Ishigaki-jima you will be diving at the coral reefs and coming face-to-face with manta rays, before heading for your little inn on the beach and dinner overlooking the blue-green sea.

Kabira Bay, Ishigaki-jima, Okinawa

# PLANNING YOUR TRIP

# When and Where to Go

## WHEN TO GO

**Spring** (*Mar–May*) and **Fall** (*Sept–Nov*) are the best seasons to visit Japan: the temperatures are mild and constant, and the countryside looks beautiful. Spring is famous for the luxuriant cherry blossom trees, which burst into flower first at Kyushu in the south in March, and then further north across Honshu throughout April. In the Fall, the forests and gardens are ablaze with magnificent gold and purple hues. The humid heat of summer (*mid-Jun–mid-Jul*) can be hard to take, accompanied as it is by incessant rain and sometimes even typhoons (end Aug). But it is the ideal season for enjoying the beaches, hiking on Hokkaido or in the mountains of Honshu, and attending the festivals and firework displays that are held in these regions. In winter (*Dec–Feb),* on Hokkaido, and on the coasts of the Sea of Japan, traveling can be difficult, as the roads and railways are sometimes blocked by snow. The cold is not all that severe, however, and often interspersed with fine sunny days that are perfect for skiing at the winter sports resorts on Hokkaido and in the Japan Alps. In addition, some towns and regions (*Kyoto, for example, with its "Kyoto Winter Special"*) offer special terms to winter visitors.
In contrast to the cold weather of Honshu, beach lovers and diving enthusiasts will find October to April the best time to visit the islands of Okinawa.

### SEASONS

Generally speaking, whichever region you decide to visit, watch out for the tourist **high seasons**, which coincide with the Japanese public holidays. During New Year (*Dec 29–Jan 3*), Golden Week (*Apr 29–May 5*), and the Bon Festival (*around Aug 15*), the temples and most famous places of interest are overwhelmed by vast crowds of visitors. Buying a ticket for a train or plane and finding a hotel to stay at becomes problematic, the more so because the prices increase significantly during these periods.
*See Making Reservations p31.*

## WHAT TO PACK

### CLOTHES

In spring (*Mar–May*) and in the Fall (*Sept–Nov*), take lightweight jackets and sweaters. In summer (*Jun–Aug*), choose loose, light clothes, and in winter (*Dec–Mar*), coats, fleeces, or warm sweaters, and thick socks. Your choice of clothing should also take account the region you are visiting: in spring it is still cold in Sapporo and Sendai, mild in Tokyo, Kyoto, and Fukuoka, and quite hot on Okinawa. Whenever you travel, it is advisable to pack warm clothes for the evenings and in mountainous areas. Take also a light raincoat or an umbrella and comfortable shoes that are easily removed (shoes need to be constantly taken off in Japan).

### OTHER ITEMS

A small compass is invaluable to help orient yourself in large towns, particularly when coming out of the subway and in districts where signs are only written in Japanese.
A suitcase on wheels saves unnecessary effort and a small knapsack for excursions is also a must.
A plug adapter is useful too.
Avoid taking a very large suitcase; baggage racks in trains and lockers of rooms in stations are very small.
Think to bring any necessary medications; Japanese pharmacies rarely dispense them without prescriptions. A bilingual dictionary is also a good idea, as English is not spoken much.

## WHERE TO GO

This multifacted country is so rich and offers so much to discover it can feel overwhelming when organizing your trip. How can you decide where to go, to feel you have seen the essential, especially if your time there is limited? It seems modern Japan cannot be experienced without its ancient traditions; city life takes on meaning when contrasted with life in the villages; even Tokyo seems to need to be offset by the Kyoto experience. The answer is to first let your budget, energy level, and the time you have available, define the limits on your plans; then let your curiosity take you where it will. Japan's uniqueness is that even a small taste of its complexity will give you some understanding of it as a whole.

## CHOOSE YOUR ROUTE

On the inside front cover, the **Principal Sights map** gives a general picture of the places featured and the star-rated areas.

The beginning of the section for **each Japanese region** includes a detailed map to help you get your bearings, a description of the places of interest, what to do with children, and advice on how best to organize your time and plan your trip. *See also UNESCO World Heritage Sites p12.*

## IDEAS FOR YOUR VISIT

Most tourists begin with the vast and varied city of Tokyo; if your time is limited, don't miss Asakusa's temples, Akihabara's electronics shopping, Jinbocho's bookselling, and Shinjuku's nightlife. With more time you can make day trips to Nikko, Kamakura, or Yokohama. If you have a few more days, take the Shinkansen bullet train from Tokyo to make a combined trip to Kyoto, Nara, and Mt. Fuji.

Hiroshima is an important destination owing not only to its Peace Park and Memorial Museum, but also for its castle, art museum, and gardens; while there, visit nearby Miyajima (*Shrine Island*), considered one of the most beautiful places in Japan.

## GUIDED TOURS

Several Japanese agencies organize guided tours for visitors. Package tours, including transport, hotels, meals, and visits, are often good value and offer a speedy visit to a town or region. Another option is the "free plan," which is a little more flexible for those who prefer not to be part of a group.

**JTB Sunrise Tours** – *03-5796-5454 in Tokyo; www.jtbgmt.com/sunrisetour.* For visits to Tokyo, Nikko, Ise, Kyoto, Nara, and Hiroshima, this reliable and reputable agency offers a wide range of tours lasting 2–3 days or longer at attractive prices. For something a little different, try the **Sumo Tour** in Tokyo during the Sumo Championships, or the visit to the Toyota factory at Nagoya. Half-day excursions are also available.

**Nippon Travel Agency** – *03-3572-8744 in Tokyo; www.nta.co.jp.* Another of the tourism sector's heavyweights, this agency organizes individual or group tours to Tokyo, Kamakura, Koya-san, and Hiroshima, as well as guided cycle tours in Kyoto.

## NATIONAL PARKS

Visitors to Japan often think first of its cities mingling modern and traditional; yet Japan is also a country offering nature lovers a multitude of extraordinarily beautiful sites to be enjoyed in every season. Serene lakes reflect ancient temples in their surfaces; craggy ravines become dramatic in the Fall when dressed in autumnal color; tropical fish dart around coral reefs off the coastline, while lofty peaks are snow-capped giants against the hard blue of winter skies.

Japan has designated a total of 29 National Parks, overseen by the Ministry of the Environment, with a view to preserving these superb examples of the natural beauty the country has to offer for the enjoyment of those who take the trouble to seek them out.

The Kanto National Parks include those of Nikko (*famous for being the site of the Toshogu Shrine and other shrines and temples*); Oze (*Mt. Shibutsu*

Konjiki-do, Chuson-ji, Hiraizumi

Chuson-ji

## UNESCO World Heritage Sites

In 1972, the United Nations Educational, Scientific, and Cultural Organization adopted a Convention for the preservation of cultural and natural sites. More than 900 sites "of outstanding universal value" are on the World Heritage List. The protected cultural heritage may be monuments (buildings, sculptures, archaeological structures, etc.) with unique historical, artistic or scientific features; groups of buildings (such as religious communities, ancient cities); or sites (human settlements, examples of exceptional landscape, cultural landscape) which are the combined works of nature and man of exceptional beauty. Natural sites may be testimony to the stages of the earth's geological history or to the development of human cultures and creative genius, or represent significant ongoing ecological processes, contain superlative natural phenomena or provide a habitat for threatened species. There are 16 World Heritage Sites in Japan: 12 of them **Cultural Heritage Sites**:

- Buddhist monuments at the temple of Horyu-ji (*see p336)* Himeji Castle (*see p366)*
- Temples, gardens and archaeological sites representing the Buddhist Pure Land at Hiraizumi(*see p410)*
- Historic monuments of old Kyoto (towns of Kyoto, Uji, and Otsu) (*see p284)*
- Historic villages of Shirakawa-go and Gokayama (*see p250 and p252)*
- Shinto shrine at Itsukushima (*see p383 and p388)*
- Peace memorial at Hiroshima (Genbaku Domu) (*see p384)*
- Historic monuments of old Nara (*see p327)*
- Shrines and temples of Nikko (*see p201)*
- Sites at Gusuku and related estates of the kingdom of Ryukyu (*see p508)*
- Sacred sites and pilgrimage routes in the Kii Peninsula (*see p346)*
- Iwami Ginzan Silver Mine and its cultural landscape (*see p388)*—and four sites listed as **Natural Heritage Sites**:
  - Yakushima (*see p114 and p420)*
  - Shirakami-sanchi (*see pp420 – 421)*
  - Shiretoko National Park (*see p437 and p438)* and the Ogasawara Islands.

*and other peaks surrounding one of Japan's largest moors*); Chichibu-Tama-Kai (*natural forests, mountains and gorges*); Ogasawara (*over 30 large and small subtropical islands*); Fuji-Hakone-Izu (*Mt. Fuji, Fujigoko Lakes, woodland*); and Miinami Alps (*mountains including Mt. Kita-dake, Japan's second-highest peak*).

On the island of Hokkaido, there are the parks of Rishiri-Rebun-Sarobetsu (*Japan's northernmost park*); Shiretoko (*Shiretoko Mountains, lakes*); Akan (*volcanoes and Lake Akan, one of the world's clearest lakes*); Kushiroshitsugen (*the country's largest extent of marshland*); Daisetsuzan (*Japan's largest park, known as the Roof of Hokkaido*); Shikotsu-Toya (*two large lakes, active volcanoes*).

On Kyushu, Setonaikai National Park offers a sweeping **view** of islands floating in an inland sea; Sakai consists of over 400 islands; Unzen-Amakusa includes a resort around the active volcano of Mt. Fugen-dake; Aso-Kuju contains many volcanoes and the world's largest caldera basin; Kirishima-Yaku has over 20 volcanoes and is famous for its cedars (*over 1,000 years old*) and Iriomote-Ishigaki includes islands and subtropical forests, as well as Japan's largest coral reef.

On the island of Tohoku lies the National Parks of Towada-Hachimantal (*Lake Towada and the Oirase River, as well as hot springs and volcanoes*); Rikuchukaigan (*rugged coastline of sharp cliffs, known as the Sea Alps*); and Bandai-Asahi (*lakes, forest, and peaks, including Mt. Dewa-Sanzan, famous as a site for mountain worship*).

The island of Chubu offers the National Parks of Joshin'etsukogen (*Japan's second-largest National Park, consisting of mountains and well-known volcanoes including Mt. Asama and Mt. Myoko*); Chubusangaku (*some of Japan's most famous mountains, as well as ravines and mountain streams; an important ptarmigan habitat*); Hakusan (*a destination for climbers, as Hakusan, with Mt. Fuji and Mt. Tateyama, is one of Japan's three sacred mountains*); and Ise-Shima (*vistas of islets and deep coves; home to the famous Ise-Jingu Shrine*).

On Kinki are found the National Parks of Yoshino-Kumano (*Mt. Yoshino, noted for its cherry blossoms and historic sites, and Mt. Omine, long worshipped by ascetics*); and San'inkaigan (*a marine park extending across the seacoast to the sand dunes of Tottori*).

Last, the Chugoku-Shikoku National Parks include Daisen-Oki (*famous for being the site of Mt. Daisen and the Oki Archipelago*) and Ashizuri-Uwakai, which includes the Ashizuri Promontory and the Tatsukushi Marine Park.

For detailed information look to the *Discovering Japan* pages.

## TEMPLES AND SHRINES

Temples are Buddhist places of worship and for quiet reflection. Show respect by putting a coin in the offering box before saying a brief prayer. If you buy incense, light it and let it burn a few seconds, extinguishing the flame by waving your hand rather than blowing it out. Then place the incense in the burner and fan the smoke toward yourself – it is believed to have healing powers. You may be asked to take off your shoes. Leave them on the shelves at the entrance or take them with you, if plastic bags are provided. Be sure to wear socks!

Shrines are places of worship and the dwellings of the *kami*, or Shinto gods. People visit to pay their respects to the *kami* or to pray for good fortune, coming especially during festivals, to present new babies, or to hold wedding ceremonies.

Traditionally, those ill or with an open wound or those in mourning may not visit, as these are considered causes of impurity.

At the purification fountain at the entrance, use the ladle to rinse both hands with water, then transfer some water into your cupped hand, rinse your mouth, and spit the water out beside the fountain. You are not supposed to drink directly from the ladle or to swallow the water. Many visitors skip the purification ritual altogether. Once inside, throw a coin in the offering box, bow deeply twice, clap twice, bow deeply once more, and then pray for a few seconds.

# What to See and Do

## OUTDOOR FUN
## SPORTS AND RECREATION

### Martial arts and sumo

Japan is well known for its martial arts such as judo, aikido, karate, kendo (two-handed sword-fighting), and kyudo (Japanese archery), which are all widely practiced across the country. Sports enthusiasts will find plenty of opportunities to see martial arts demonstrations and to watch contests while in Japan, though visitors are unlikely to be able to take part in training sessions. Sumo tournaments last 15 days and are held six times a year: in January, May, and September in Tokyo; in March in Osaka; in July in Nagoya; and in November in Fukuoka. If you cannot make it to a live bout, they are normally televized, often in the late afternoon.

A brochure published by the JNTO (Japan National Tourism Organization) entitled *Traditional Sports* can be downloaded from their website (*www.jnto.go.jp*). It lists the dojo (places where martial arts are practiced) for the different martial arts in Tokyo and gives details of the dates and locations of sumo tournaments. Otherwise, contact the following sports federations:

**International Aikido Federation** – 03-3203-9236, www.aikikai.or.jp.

**All Japan Judo Federation** – 03-3818-4199, www.judo.co.jp.

**Japan Karatedo Federation** – 03-3503-6637, www.karatedo.co.jp.

**All Japan Kendo Federation** – 03-3211-5804, www.kendo.or.jp.

**All Nippon Kyudo Federation** – 03-3481-2387, www.kyudo.jp.

**Nihon Sumo Kyokai** – 03-3623-5111, www.sumo.or.jp.

*See also Martial Arts and Sumo pp107–108.*

### Baseball

Introduced to Japan during the Meiji era, known as *yakyu* in Japanese, baseball is extremely popular in Japan. The championships take place between April and October. There are two professional leagues, the **Central League** and the **Pacific League**, with six teams in each. Matches are transmitted live on television. The university championships also have a considerable following. In Tokyo, the giant Tokyo Dome on the site of the old Koraku-en Stadium is home to the famous Yomiuri Giants baseball team.

### Golf

Some 17 million Japanese play golf, but the number of golf courses is limited and green fees are consequently high (around ¥10,000). However, you can keep your handicap

Watching base ball at Tokyo Dome

up by playing on one of the urban driving ranges, often found on the top of multistory buildings, and surrounded by protective netting. (*A complete list of golf courses in Japan, giving descriptions, prices, and addresses, appears on the website www.golf-in-japan.com*).

### Hiking

The many footpaths crisscrossing the valleys and mountainous regions of Japan lead through some exceptionally beautiful countryside and are accessible and well-signposted. The Japan Alps around Nagano and Kamikochi, the "pilgrimage" to the 88 temples of Shikoku, the National Parks of Hokkaido, the walk up Mount Fuji, trails around Kyoto, Nara, or Nikko … the choice for walkers is wide and varied (*information and suggestions for itineraries are given on www.outdoorjapan.com*). *Hiking in Japan*, published by Kodansha, gives detailed descriptions of many routes.

### Skiing

Japan boasts several ski slopes, all well equipped with ski lifts. The resorts of Hokkaido, Tohoku, and those in the center and to the west of Honshu are best for powder snow. Niseko, also on Hokkaido, has some superb pistes and is very lively in the evenings. Hakuba (*see pp258–259*), near Nagano, hosted a number of events during the Winter Olympics of 1998. Gala Yuzawa, near Niigata, is just 90 minutes from Tokyo by Shinkansen. During vacation periods and winter weekends, the resorts are packed, so it is best to reserve accommodation in advance. The Japanese ski slopes are neither steep nor long, but many of the hotels include *onsen* (hot springs), which are pleasant and relaxing after a day's skiing. (*Expect to pay around ¥4,500 for use of the ski lift and ¥5,000 for equipment rental*). The JNTO brochure *Skiing in Japan* lists the main resorts of Honshu and Hokkaido, how to get to there, and the accommodation offered. You will find more information on www.snowjapan.com, an excellent source of information for skiers and snowboarders.

### Water sports

**Diving** is popular mainly among the splendid coral reefs around the tropical islands of Okinawa (*see p508*), and in the clear, temperate waters of the islands of the Izu Peninsula, south of Tokyo. Expert and more intrepid divers might like to try diving under the ice in mid-winter, in the Sea of Okhotsk, off Hokkaido! The choice of dives available is wide, but prices are high. Two dives, plus boat and equipment rental, can easily cost ¥20,000. **Bathing at the beaches**, however, costs nothing. The beaches at Chiba, near Tokyo, those between Kobe and Himeji in the Kansai area, at Kamakura, on the Izu Peninsula (*see p224*), and those on Okinawa, with their superb white sand (*see p508*), attract large crowds during the summer. Some offer excellent conditions for surfing and **windsurfing**. But, apart from Okinawa, a few protected areas of Izu, and the south of Shikoku and Kyushu, the Japanese coastline rarely comes up to expectations; the detractions include polluted seawater near towns, swarms of jellyfish from mid-August onward, beaches piled with concrete tetrapods, and large blocks designed to prevent coastal erosion. *For details about surfing and windsurfing, see www.outdoorjapan.com.*

## ENTERTAINMENT

### THEME PARKS

The Japanese are crazy about theme parks, which are springing up all over the country. **History theme parks**, built to resemble villages from the samurai era; parks containing **models** of monuments from the world's capital cities; **leisure parks**, such as Disneyland or Sanrio Puroland in Tokyo, and Fuji-Q Highland near Mount Fuji; **science parks** like Space World at Fukuoka; **water parks** such as Ocean Dome in Miyazaki, DisneySea in Tokyo, or Hakkeijima Sea Paradise at Yokohama, etc. For many Japanese, these parks have become substitutes for the long-haul vacations that they can no longer afford. (*see p166*).

## ONSEN

Hot springs of volcanic origin are found in many parts of the Japanese archipelago. They are visited as much for rest and relaxation as for health reasons (*see The Onsen Ritual p 102*). The varying types of onsen are differentiated by the mineral composition and color of the water; the size, number and the type of bath provided and whether they are made of wood or stone; also whether the baths are indoor or outdoor *(rotenburo)*. Outdoor onsen are often found in river valleys at the foot of mountains, or in caves by the sea. Indoor onsen can be found in small, tranquil ryokan (*a traditional Japanese inn*), or as part of vast hotel complexes. A free brochure from JNTO, *Japanese Hot Springs*, gives a list of the 20 best onsen in the country, with opening times, prices, and directions.

## SHOWS, CINEMAS, AND CONCERTS

Despite the language barrier, a visit to a classic Japanese theater is recommended. Kabuki, *bunraku*, and Noh theater productions are performed regularly in the large theaters in Tokyo (*see pp99–100*), Kyoto (*see p326*), and Osaka (*see p357*). For opera, dance, musical comedies, concerts, and cinema, consult local magazines such as *Metropolis* (*www.metropolis.co.jp*) for Tokyo and *Kansai Time Out* for Osaka and Kyoto (*www.kto.co.jp*). Reduced rate tickets for shows (*and also train and plane journeys*) are offered by **discount ticket shops** *(kinken shoppu)*. These small stores are found just about everywhere in the big towns, but the vendors rarely speak any English.

## PACHINKO

*Pachinko* is a flourishing industry that arouses deep passions in the Japanese. The popular *pachinko parlors* (*pachinko* gaming halls), with endless rows of machines and flashing lights, are wreathed in clouds of smoke and ring to the cacophony of the metal balls dropping down through the machines. *Pachinko* is a cross between a pinball and a slot machine. By pressing a lever, a steel ball shoots upward and then drops down the machine, passing through an array of pins. If a ball falls into a "gate", the payout is in the form of more metal balls, which can be exchanged for small prizes. Playing for money is forbidden by law, but by happy coincidence, the prizes can be sold in a nearby shop. The real *pachinko* pros spend their days combing the parlors, trying to identify the machines that pay out most often.

## KARAOKE

If a Japanese person should invite you out for the evening, there is little hope of avoiding karaoke at some stage in the proceedings, where amateurs sing along to a musical backing track, following the lyrics flashed up on a screen. In Japan, this far outstrips clubbing as the nighttime entertainment of choice. A brash symbol of Japanese pop culture, karaoke was invented in 1971 and since then has spread throughout the world. The karaoke halls in Japan are made up of a series of little rooms ("boxes"), furnished with couches and a television set, that may be reserved by the hour or by the night (*for a fixed rate of around ¥2,000 from midnight to 10am*). Drinks and food can also be ordered.

The one saving grace is that karaoke catalogs offer thousands of songs, many of which are in English, so pick your number and Broadway, here you come!

## ACTIVITIES FOR KIDS

Japan is an ideal place for a vacation with children, with its reputation for cleanliness and for being relatively crime-free. Jars of baby and toddler food, milk formula for infants, and diapers are readily available in *depa-to* (department stores) and *conbini* (local convenience stores). Most public places, such as big stores, railway stations, and trains, have restrooms with changing areas for babies. The majority of most hotels have cribs for small children and some offer a baby-sitting service. (*To find a list of baby-sitters in Tokyo, consult the English website www.tokyowithkids.com*).

In terms of activities for children—apart from discovering the natural world—Japan offers a wide range of attractions, including theme parks (*such as Universal Studios in Osaka*), shops selling toys and electronic games, zoos, aquariums, etc.

We have made a selection of activities and places to visit that might appeal to children in each of Japan's regions (*see Family Activities below*). You will find them in the *Discovering Japan* section, identified by this symbol.

### FAMILY ACTIVITIES

**Tokyo:** Ghibli Museum; Harajuku Bridge; Yoyogi Park; monorail trip to Odaiba and Decks shopping mall; Inokashira Park.
**Yokohama:** Marine Museum; the Landmark Tower.
**Mount Fuji:** Museum of the Little Prince; old Hakone Checkpoint; Tenzan Open-Air Spa.
**Izu Peninsula:** Walk from Wakano-Ura to Shimoda or from Chikurin no Komichi to Shuzenji.
**Nikko:** Avenue lined with *Jizo* statues; watch *yabusame* archery contests on May 17–18.
**Kyoto:** Sail down the Hozu River to Arashiyama; Kyoto International Manga Museum; stroll through the Gion district; watch an *odori*.
**Nara:** Feed the deer in the park.
**Osaka:** Aquarium; Ferris Wheel and Universal Studios Theme Park.
**Kobe:** Bathing at Suma Beach; Kawasaki Maritime Museum.
**San-yo Coast:** Visit the Tottori sand dunes on a camel or by horse-drawn carriage; Vogel Park at Matsue; boat trip around castle moat.
**San-yo Coast, Okayama:** Bathing at the beaches of Nao-shima Island; Toy Museum at Kurashiki.
**San-yo Coast, Hiroshima:** Walks on Miyajima Island; Peace Memorial Museum (for older children).
**Matsuyama:** Trip on the small steam train, *Botchan Ressha*, from Dogo Onsen.
**Iya Valley:** Take a boat trip along Oboke Gorge.
**Kochi and the Pacific Coast:** Beach at Katsurahama; Makino Botanical Garden (*Kochi*).
**Fukuoka:** Hakata Machiya Folk Museum; Kyushu National Museum at Dazaifu; Sky Dream giant wheel and Robosquare (*Monochi*).
**Kumuamoto and Mount Aso:** Dolphins at Amakusa; pony-ride at Mount Aso.
**Kagoshima:** Beach at Ibusuki; Aquarium at Kagoshima.
**Okinawa archipelago:** Take a ride in buffalo-drawn cart on Iriomote-jima and Taketomi-jima islands; Okinawa-honto: Botanical Gardens in the southeast; Aquarium; Ocena Expo Park beaches.
**Sado Island:** *Bunya Ningyo* puppet show.
**Sendai:** Matushima Bay.
**Tsuruoka:** Trip to Mount Haguro and a night in its shukubo; Mummy of Churen-ji.
**Hirosaki:** Shirakami Forest; Neputa-mura.
**Sapporo:** Dai-ichi Takimoto-kan at Noboribetsu Onsen; Snow Festival (*Feb*).
**Daisetsu-zan National Park:** Excursion to Mount Asahi-dake with a night in a youth hostel.

## SHOPPING

### CRAFT ITEMS AND ANTIQUES

#### Amulets

Shops and stands selling good-luck charms and *ema* (votive plaques in wood from Shinto shrines) abound at the entrances to temples and shrines.

#### Engravings

Original engravings are sold in specialist shops (see Asakusa and Ueno Address Book p174). Prices depend on their rarity, quality, and state of conservation. You may be able to find a beautiful old *ukiyo-e* for less than ¥15,000, but if your budget is limited, there are some good-quality reproductions available.

#### Lacquerware, wood, bamboo

There is a vast range of goods on sale made of these materials, from useful everyday items (bowls, chopsticks, trays, combs) to decorative ones (statuettes, dolls, boxes). Prices are generally affordable for small items, but for larger or superior-quality lacquerware or antique wood furniture, the cost can be pretty extortionate.

#### Paper and calligraphy

Handmade Japanese paper *(washi)* is of excellent quality. It is often brightly colored and sometimes speckled or encrusted with flower petals. Washi is used to make many items, such as notebooks and exercise books, boxes, and fans, and is also used in origami. Stores specializing in paper often sell incense too, along with materials for calligraphy: brushes, ink, and ink-stones. These all make good presents.

Shopping for ceramics in Kamakura

©Yasufumi Nishi/JNTO

#### Umbrellas

Made from bamboo and oiled paper, the highly decorative traditional umbrellas *(kasa)* are sold in craft shops.

#### Pottery and ceramics

There are many potters working in Japan. Stores selling bowls, plates, cups, and bottles can be found in all villages, while ceramics may be found in the large stores and craft centers in the towns. Each region has its own style of earthenware or porcelain and its own specialties. The finest examples of Bizen, Arita, or Imari can cost millions of yen. However, pieces at a reduced price and cheaper items suitable for gifts can often be found in the big stores.

#### Dolls

Japanese dolls *(ningyo)* are beautifully made, particularly those from Kyoto and Kyushu, and as such are not toys but rather collectable pieces. During the Hina Matsuri Festival (*Mar 3*), dolls are given to girls and on Children's Day (*May 5*), boys receive samurai dolls. All these dolls make interesting souvenirs or gifts to take home.

#### Swords

The mythical Japanese swords *(katana)* carried by the samurai of the past now command colossal prices due to the amount of work that goes into making them. If an original, authentic sword from an antique shop is out of the question, you can still find good-quality imitations for a reasonable price in the big stores.

### OTHER PURCHASES

#### Foodstuffs

**Candy and cakes** – These are bought as much for their containers—delightful little boxes and colored

packaging that make perfect gifts—as for their contents (the red-bean cakes especially have a very strange flavor).
**Sake** – As with wine, there are hundreds of types of sake—some of the bottles bear labels written in ornate calligraphy. If you are not sure which to choose or have a particular budget, a cellarman is normally on hand to help in the large stores.
**Tea** – Since you are in the kingdom of green tea and the formal Tea Ceremony, taking a small box or two home with you is a must. You may like to buy a teapot too, but the cast-iron ones are rather heavy to carry.

## ELECTRONIC AND PHOTOGRAPHIC EQUIPMENT

In the cities, the stores selling electronic goods tend to be grouped together in certain districts, such as Akihabara in Tokyo (*see p135*) and Den Den Town in Osaka, where the prices are often quite reasonable. Big chains such as Bic Camera or Yodobashi also offer a wide choice at **fairly competitive prices**. The prices are much the same as those charged in Hong Kong or Singapore, but you are more likely to get a genuine deal. Japanese stores also stock the very latest in electronic novelties and high-tech gadgets. It is worth asking for a discount; some stores will respond and you might be able to knock down the price by as much as 10 percent. Be careful, however, to check for compatibility—in particular with regard to software and voltage—before buying a product and make sure that a user manual in English is included. If you have the choice, buy models made for export.

## MUSIC AND VIDEOS

The big chains such as HMV, Tower Records, or Virgin Megastore offer a good choice of foreign CDs and DVDs. There are also a number of shops that sell them secondhand. Remember, however, if you are tempted to buy secondhand DVDs, that the onscreen menu will be in Japanese.

## CLOTHES AND TEXTILES

The big stores offer a wide range of superb silk kimonos but often at prohibitive prices. Better deals can be obtained from secondhand shops, where kimonos are generally priced between ¥5,000 and ¥20,000. New *yukata* (light cotton kimonos) are cheaper at around ¥4,000. For conventional clothing, chains like Uniqlo (the Japanese equivalent of Gap) offer moderate prices. The top Japanese fashion houses (Yamamoto, Miyake) on the other hand are very expensive but prices do fall during the **sales**, generally held in January and July.

## WHERE TO SHOP

### Larger stores

The big department store chains such as Daimaru, Seibu, Takashimaya, Mitsukoshi, and Isetan are all crammed with a wide variety of high-quality goods. If time is tight, they offer an excellent, practical solution. The service is excellent and many of the staff speak English. A further advantage is that most of them accept credit cards. On the whole, however, they tend to be quite expensive.

### Conbini

You will find *conbini*, local convenience stores, on every street corner; the main chains include Lawson, FamilyMart and 7-Eleven. Open 24 hours, these handy minisupermarkets stock an amazing range of products crammed into a small area, from underwear to food, alongside magazines, cosmetics, batteries, etc. They are practical for everyday items and small impulse buys, but are not usually a particularly good source for gifts and souvenirs.

### 100 Yen shops

These stores are everywhere, particularly near railway stations, in shopping arcades, and hypermarkets. *Hyakuen shoppu* are discount shops that, as their name implies, sell all kinds of goods for the bargain price of ¥100 per item. Among the household and everyday goods, you will find a number of typical Japanese items such as chopsticks, toys, fans, dishes, etc., so they are a useful source for inexpensive souvenirs and gifts.

### Specialist stores

Specialist stores and craft workshops may be found in the shopping districts of the larger towns. They sell high-quality craft items, including the rare and unusual. If you are pressed for time, however, visit one of the big craft centers designed especially for tourists, such as the Oriental Bazaar in Tokyo (*see p160)* or the Kyoto Antiques Center (*see p325)*.

### Flea markets

Called *nomi-no-ichi* in Japanese, flea markets are lively affairs, generally held in the mornings in the grounds of temples and shrines, such as at the Hanazono Jinja on Sundays in Tokyo (*see p180)*. It is usually possible to find something interesting to take home, such as a secondhand kimono, and inexpensive souvenirs.

## TAX REFUNDS

A consumption tax of 5 percent is levied on every purchase and is generally included in the marked price. However, visitors from abroad can obtain a tax refund on purchases valued at more than ¥10,000. The tax can either be deducted at the point of sale or refunded on completion of a form. In either case a passport must be produced. Tax refunds are not given for everyday items (food, cosmetics, alcohol, cigarettes, medicines, or batteries and films), but can be claimed for electronic items and photographic equipment. There are duty-free counters in most big stores, and tax-free stores are marked with the logo "tax free". However, prices in the latter are often high. In practice, any shop selling electronic items can process a tax refund on request.

## MAILING YOUR PURCHASES

If you want to send a package home by mail, use the Express Mail Service **(EMS)** rather than the cheaper, slower Economy Air (SAL) Service. EMS offers better insurance terms and you can track the item on www.ems-post.jp.

## BOOKS

### CIVILIZATION AND SOCIETY

CRAIG, Albert M., *The Heritage of Japanese Civilization*, Prentice Hall, 2002. A short survey of Japan's rich and long history.

GOLDEN, Arthur, *Memoirs of a Geisha*, Knopf, 1997. Bestselling novel following the life of Sayuri, the most celebrated geisha in Gion, before and after World War II.

KOMOMO (author) and OGINO, Naoyuki (photographer), *A Geisha's Journey: My Life as a Kyoto Apprentice*, Kodansha International, 2008. Illustrated autobiography of a contemporary Japanese teenager's seven-year apprenticeship to become a geisha.

KURE, Mitsuo, *Samurai: An Illustrated History*, Tuttle, 2002. A chronological account of Samurai history.

MACKIE, Vera, *Feminism in Modern Japan*, Cambridge University Press, 2003. An account of the history of feminism in Japan from the end of the 19C to the present day.

NENZI, Laura, *Excursions in Identity: Travel and the Intersection of Place, Gender, and Status in Edo Japan*, University of Hawaii Press, 2008. An account of how travel changed the lives of people, in particular women, in the Japanese Edo period, 1600–1868.

SCHIROKAUER, Conrad, LURIE, David, and GAY, Suzanne, *A Brief History of Japanese Civilization*, Wadsworth, 2006. A clear and accessible account of all aspects of Japanese history.

## HISTORY

BEASLEY, W.G., *The Japanese Experience: A Short History of Japan*, University of California Press, 2000. A concise but comprehensive and authoritative history of Japan.

HARTSHORNE, Anna, *Japan and Her People*, Jetlag Press, 2007. Written in 1902 and republished, this book describes life in late–19C Japan.

HENSHALL, Kenneth G., *A History of Japan: From Stone Age to Superpower*, Palgrave Macmillan, 2001. A well-balanced overview of pre-modern and modern Japan.

HERSEY, John, *Hiroshima*, Vintage, 1989. First-hand accounts from those who survived the Hiroshima bomb.

NISHIMURA, Shigeo, *Illustrated History of Japan*, Tuttle, 2005. Aimed at children, this book highlights events in Japanese history through panoramic paintings with brief captions.

SCOTT MORTON, W., OLENIK, J. Kenneth, and LEWIS Charlton, *Japan: Its History and Culture*, McGraw-Hill, 2004. The history of Japan from its earliest-known civilization to the present day.

TOLAND, John, *The Rising Sun: The Decline and Fall of the Japanese Empire, 1936–1945*, Modern Library, 2003. An accessible but informative account of the Pacific War.

## ART, CULTURE, AND RELIGION

DAVIES, Roger J. and IKENO, Osamu, *The Japanese Mind: Understanding Contemporary Japanese Culture*, Tuttle, 2002. An exploration of the unique aspects of Japanese culture and what makes the Japanese tick.

EARLE, Joe (editor), *Japanese Art and Design*, V&A Publishing, 2009. An illustrated overview of Japanese art from the last four centuries.

HIBI, Sadao, *Japanese Detail: Architecture*, Chronicle Books, 2002. An exploration of the essential elements of the Japanese architectural aesthetic.

JESPERSEN, Bo M. and ALEXANDER, George W., *Dictionary of Japanese Martial Arts*, Yamazato, 2002. A guide to martial arts and weaponry.

KASAHARA, Kazuo, *A History of Japanese Religion*, Kosei, 2002. An overview of the history and development of Japan's major spiritual traditions.

OKAKURA, Kakuzo, *The Book of Tea: The Classic Work on the Japanese Tea Ceremony and the Value of Beauty*, Kodansha, 2006. The history and rules of the quintessentially Japanese Tea Ceremony.

ROSCOE, Bruce, *Windows on Japan: A Walk through Place and Perception*, Algora, 2007. An account of a walk through rural Japan.

SOSNOSKI, Daniel, *Introduction to Japanese Culture*, Tuttle, 1996. Illustrated guide to the country's customs and culture.

YOUNG, David, YOUNG, Michico, and YEW, Tan Hong, *The Art of the Japanese Garden*, Tuttle, 2005. The philosophy behind the various styles of Japanese garden.

## TRAVEL WRITING

BEATON, Hamish, *Under the Osakan Sun*, Awa Press, 2008. An account of living, traveling, and teaching in Japan.

CLANCY, Judith, *Exploring Kyoto: On Foot in the Ancient Capital*, Stone Bridge Press, 2008. Thirty routes around Kyoto.

DE MENTE, Boyé Lafayette, *The Dining Guide to Japan*, Tuttle, 2007. A guide to what to expect, how to order, what to eat, and dining etiquette in Japan.

REYNOLDS, Betty, *Clueless in Tokyo*, Weatherhill 1997; *Still Clueless in Tokyo*, Weatherhill, 2003. Sketchbooks of watercolors to guide the first-time visitor.

TANAKA, Brandia, *Five Great Days in Tokyo—An Insider's Day to Day Walking Guide*, CreateSpace,

2008. Five planned days out in Tokyo.

WILLIAMSON, Kate T., *A Year in Japan*, Princeton Architectural Press, 2006. Journal with watercolor illustrations by the author.

ZARIFEH, Ramsey, *Japan by Rail*, Trailblazer, 2007. A guide to exploring Japan with the Japan Rail Pass.

## JAPANESE LITERATURE

ABE, Kobo, *The Woman in the Dunes*, Vintage, 1991.

DAZAI, Osamu, *The Setting Sun*, New Directions, 1968.

IBUSE, Masuji, *Black Rain: A Novel*, Kodansha, 1988.

INOUE, Yasushi, *The Hunting Gun*, Peter Owen, 2004.

KAWABATA, Yasunari, *The Master of Go*, Vintage, Kodansha 1996; *Thousand Cranes*, Vintage, Kodansha 1996; *House of Sleeping Beauties*, Kodansha, 2004.

KEENE, Donald (editor), *Anthology of Japanese Literature*, Grove Press, 1994.

McALPINE, Helen and William, *Tales from Japan*, Oxford University Press USA, 2002. Illustrated myths, legends, and folk stories for children.

MISHIMA, Yukio, *Confessions of a Mask*, New Directions, 1958; *Spring Snow*, Vintage, 1990; *The Sailor Who Fell From Grace with the Sea*, Vintage, 1994; *After the Banquet*, Vintage, 1999.

MURAKAMI, Haruki, *The Wind-up Bird Chronicle*, Vintage, 1998; *A Wild Sheep Chase*, Vintage, 2002; *What I Talk About When I Talk About Running*, Vintage, 2009.

MURAKAMI, Ryu, *Coin Locker Babies*, Kodansha, 2002; *In the Miso Soup*, Penguin, 2006; *Piercing*, Penguin, 2007.

MURASAKI, Shikibu, *The Tale of Genji*, Penguin, 2002.

NAGAI, Kafu, *American Stories*, Columbia University Press, 2000; *Rivalry: A Geisha's Tale*, Columbia University Press, 2007.

OE, Kenzaburo, *Nip the Buds, Shoot the Kids*, Grove Press, 1996; *Seventeen and J*, Foxrock, 2002. Two novels by the Nobel Prize-winning author, both about psychologically disturbed young men.

OGAWA, Yoko, *The Diving Pool: Three Novellas*, Picador, 2008; *The Housekeeper and the Professor: A Novel*, Picador, 2009.

OOKA, Shohei, *Taken Captive: A Japanese POW's Story*, Wiley, 1996.

SOSEKI, Natsume, *I Am a Cat*, Tuttle, 2001; *Kokoro*, Dover, 2006; *Botchan: A Modern Classic*, Kodansha, 2007; *Kusamakura*, Penguin, 2008.

TANIZAKI, Junichiro, *In Praise of Shadows*, Leete's Island Books, 1977; *Naomi: A Novel*, Vintage, 2001; *The Key & Diary of a Mad Old Man*, Vintage, 2004.

YOSHIMOTO, Banana, *Goodbye Tsugumi*, Grove Press, 2003; *Kitchen*, Grove Press, 2006; *Hardboiled and Hard Luck*, Grove Press, 2006.

YOSHIMURA, Akira, *Shipwrecks*, Harvest Books, 2000.

## MANGA

JOSO, Estudio and CASAUS, Fernando, *The Monster Book of Manga: Draw Like the Experts*, Collins Design, 2006. Step-by-step instructions on creating manga illustrations.

TAKARI, Saori, *Manga Moods*, Japanime, 2006. How to transform the mood of a manga character in a stroke.

TSUKAMOTO, Hiroyoshi, *Manga Matrix: Create Unique Characters Using the Japanese Matrix System*, Collins Design, 2006. Creating manga illustrations using the grid method.

## PHOTOGRAPHY

MARCH, Philipp and DELANK, Claudia (editors), *The Adventure of Japanese Photography*

*1860–1890*, Kehrer Verlag, 2003. Images of Japan by the pioneering photographers Felice Beato and Adolpho Fasari.

NAKANO, Masataka, *Tokyo Nobody*, Trucatriche, 2000. A collection of photographs taken in and around Tokyo.

RUBINFIEN, Leo, PHILLIPS, Sandra S., DOWER, John W. and TOMATSU, Shomei, *Skin of the Nation*, Yale University Press, 2004. The career of the photographer Tomatsu Shomei.

TUCKER, Anne, *The History of Japanese Photography*, Yale University Press, 2003. Collection of photographs, including rare vintage images.

## FILMS

### FOREIGN DIRECTORS

COPPOLA, Sofia, *Lost in Translation*, 2003.

ESTENBERG, Erik, *Monster*, 2008.

KRAWCZYK, Gérard, *Wasabi*, 2001.

MARSHALL, Rob, *Memoirs of a Geisha*, 2005.

MORRISON, Christopher, *Into the Sun*, 2005.

SHIMIZU, Takashi, *The Grudge*, 2004.

ZWICK, Edward, *The Last Samurai*, 2003.

### JAPANESE DIRECTORS

FUKASAKU, Kinji, *Battle Royale*, 2000. Fukasaku also directed the Japanese section of *Tora! Tora! Tora!* (1970).

IMAMURA, Shohei, *The Eel*, 1997; *The Ballad of Narayama*, 1983.

ITAMI, Juzo, *Tampopo*, 1987.

KAWASE, Naomi, *The Mourning Forest*, 2007.

KITANO, Takeshi, *Dolls*, 2003; *Brother*, 2000; *Kids Return*, 1997.

KOBAYASHI, Masaki, *Hara Kiri*, 1963; *Human Condition*, 1959.

KOIZUMI, Takashi, *After the Rain*, 2000.

KUROSAWA, Akira, *Ran*, 1985; *The Seven Samurai*, 1954.

MIYAZAKI, Hayao, *Howl's Moving Castle*, 2005; *Spirited Away*, 2002..

MIZOGUCHI, Kenji, *The Crucified Lovers*, 1954; *Sisters of the Gion*, 1936.

OSHIMA, Nagisa, *Taboo*, 2000; *Cruel Story of Youth*, 1960.

OTOMO, Katsuhiro, *Steamboy*, 2004; *Metropolis*, 2001; *Memories*, 1995.

OZU, Yasujiro, *An Autumn Afternoon*, 1962; *Tokyo Story*, 1953.

TESHIGARA, Hiroshi, *The Face of Another*, 1966; *Woman in the Dunes*, 1963; *Pitfall*, 1962.

YOSHIDA, Kiju, *Impasse*, 1967; *Akitsu Springs*, 1962.

## MUSIC

### TRADITIONAL

*Flower Dance: Japanese Folk Melodies*, Explorer series: East Asia/ Japan, Nonesuch 2008.

*The Very Best of Japanese Music*, various artists, Arc Music 2004.

*Traditional Japanese Music*, Yoshikazu Iwamoto Shakuhachi, 2003.

### J-POP AND J-ROCK

AMURO, Namie, *Queen of the Hip-hop*, Avex Dd, 2006.

ASIAN KUN FU GENERATION, *Fan Club*, Sony, 2006.

B'Z, *The Best Pleasure*, Jb, 1998; *Circle*, Phantoms Import, 2005.

EVERY LITTLE THING, *4 force*, Import, 2001.

GLAY, *Pure Soul*, Universal, 1999; *The Frustrated*, Toshiba Emi, 2006.

HAMASAKI, Ayumi, *Miss-Understood*, Avex Dd, 2006.

HIRAI, Ken, *Fakin' Pop*, 2008.

SAZAN ALL STARS, *Dirty Old Man*, 2006.

SMAP, *Shake*, 1996; *Pop up Smap*, 2006.

UTADA, Hikaru, *Ultra Blue*, Toshiba Emi, 2006.

## JAPANESE CULTURE OVERSEAS

### CULTURAL CENTERS

**Japan Society**
333 East 47th Street
New York, NY 10017
✆212 832 1155
www.japansociety.org

*Cinema, theater, dance, popular culture, exhibitions, events, lectures, language center, gallery, and shop.*

**Japanese American Cultural & Community Center**
244 S. San Pedro Street, Suite 505
Los Angeles, CA 90012
☏213 628 2725
www.jaccc.org
*Promotes Japanese and Japanese American arts and culture. Exhibitions, film screenings, conferences, and Japanese garden.*

**Japanese Canadian Cultural Centre**
6 Garamond Court
Toronto, ON M3C 1Z5
☏416 441 2345
www.jccc.on.ca
*Cultural and martial arts classes and workshops; festivals; annual Nostalgia Night devoted to Japanese-Canadian culture and traditions.*

**The Japan Foundation**
Russell Square House
10-12 Russell Square
London WC1B 5EH
☏020 7436 6695
www.jpf.org.uk

Shop 23, Level 1 Chifley Plaza
2 Chifley Square
Sydney NSW 2000
☏02 8239 0055
www.jpf.org.au
*Arts and culture, Japanese studies, language department, and cinema.*

**Japanese Information and Cultural Centre**
Level 18 The Majestic Centre
100 Willis Street,
Wellington 6011
New Zealand
☏4 472 7808
www.asianz.org.nz
*Programs to promote Japanese culture and movie screenings.*

## MUSEUMS

**Japanese American National Museum**
369 East First Street
Los Angeles, CA 90012
☏213 625 0414
www.janm.org
*Permanent and temporary exhibitions; literary and film festivals; family festivals, workshops, and guided walks.*

**Japanese Canadian National Museum**
120-6688 Southoaks Crescent
Burnaby, BC V5E 4M7
☏604 777 7000
www.jcnm.ca
*Permanent and temporary exhibitions; lectures, workshops, and concerts.*

**V&A South Kensington**
Cromwell Road
London SW7 2RL
☏020 7942 2000
www.vam.ac.uk
*Art and artifacts from the 6C to the present day in the Japan gallery.*

## FESTIVALS

### US

**Japanese Street Festival**
Japan-America Society of Washington Annual exhibition of Japanese culture.

### Canada

**Powell Street Festival**
(Vancouver)
Annual festival to celebrate Japanese-Canadian arts, culture, and heritage.

### Australia

**Japan Festival**
(Melbourne)
Annual festival with performances, displays, demonstrations, and stands.

# Calendar of Events

**Japan has three main holiday seasons: the first is Shogatsu, the New Year period from Jan 1–3; the second is Golden Week, grouping four national holidays in one week in late April and early May; and the third is the week of Obon, an annual Buddhist event during which Japanese families gather, as it is believed ancestors' spirits return to this world to visit their relatives. Obon is in mid-August in many regions, and in mid-July in others. Try to avoid these periods, or book well in advance.**

*Also see box* Matsuri *p60.*

### JANUARY

**Jan 1** – National holiday of Shogatsu, New Year. Family celebrations and visits to temples or shrines, the most important holiday in Japan.

**Jan 6** – Tokyo (Kanto). Dezomeshiki. Big parade with firefighting demonstrations, put on by the Tokyo Fire Department.

**Second Mon of Jan** – National holiday of Seijin No Hi, Coming of Age Day. Young people turning 20 turn out in formal dress for town celebrations.

**Jan 9–11** – Osaka (Kansai). Ebisu Festival. People come to pray to the god of business and good fortune.

**Mid-Jan** – Tokyo (Kanto). First Sumo Tournament, lasting 15 days.

**Jan 14** – Sendai (Tohoku). Hachiman Matsuri. New Year parade to the Hachiman Shrine.

**Jan 15** – Nara (Kansai). Yamayaki. Dry grass on the Wakakusa hill is set on fire.

### FEBRUARY

**Beginning of Feb** – Sapporo (Hokkaido). Yuki Matsuri (Snow Festival), lasting 7 days.

**Feb 3** – Throughout Japan. Setsubun. Festival during which beans are scattered in the temples.

**Feb 3** – Nara (Kansai). Lantern Festival at the Kasuga Shrine. It also takes place on Aug 14–15.

**Feb 11** – National holiday of Kenkoku Kinenbi, National Foundation Day. First Japanese emperor said to be crowned on this day in 660 BC.

### MARCH

**Mar 1–14** – Nara (Kansai). Omizutori (Water-drawing Festival) at the temple of Todai-ji.

**Mar 3** – Throughout Japan. Hina Matsuri (Doll Festival) for young girls. Also called Girls' Day.

**Mid-Mar** – Osaka (Kansai). Second Sumo Tournament, lasting 15 days.

**About Mar 20** – National holiday of Shunbun No Hi, Spring Equinox Day. Visits to family graves.

### APRIL

**Apr 1–30** – Kyoto (Kansai). Miyako Odori (Spring Dance Festival). Dance performances by apprentice geishas.

**Apr 8** – Throughout Japan. Hana Matsuri (Flower Festival) in the temples.

**Apr 14–15** – Takayama (Chubu). Sanno Matsuri. Parade of *yatai* (giant floats) dedicated to the Hie-Jinja, the shrine in the southern part of the town.

**Apr 16–17** – Nikko (Kanto). Yayoi Matsuri in the Futarasan Shrine.

**Apr 29** – National holiday of Showa No Hi, birthday of former Emperor Showa.

### MAY

**May 3** – National holiday of Kenpo Kinenbi, Constitution Day. Remembrance of new constitution put into effect after World War II.

**May 4** – National holiday of Midori No Hi, Greenery Day, celebrating former Emperor Showa's love of plants and nature.

**May 5** – National holiday of Kodomo No Hi, Children's or Boys' Day.

Colored banners in the shape of carp *(koi nobori)*, made of paper or fabric, are hung everywhere.

**May 11** – Gifu (Chubu). Start of nocturnal fishing with cormorants season, which lasts until Oct 15 (*see p239*).

**May 15** – Kyoto (Kansai). Aoi Matsuri. Grand parade in costumes of the Heian era.

**Mid-May** – Tokyo (Kanto). Third Sumo Tournament, lasting 15 days.

**May 17–18** – Nikko (Kanto). Grand Festival of the Tosho-gu shrine. Spectacular parade.

**3rd weekend in May** – Tokyo (Kanto). Sanja Matsuri. Religious festival held at the Asakusa Shrine.

### JUNE

**Jun 1–2** – Kyoto (Kansai). Open-air Noh theater performance lit by torches and lanterns at the Heian Shrine.

### JULY

**Jul 1–15** – Fukuoka (Kyushu). The largest of Fukuoka's summer *matsuri*, the Yamagasa Festival, sets out from the Kushida-jinja.

**Mid-Jul** – Nagoya (Chubu). Fourth Sumo Tournament, lasting 15 days.

**Jul 14** – Nachi (Kansai). Hi Matsuri (Fire Festival) staged at the Nachi Shrine.

**3rd Mon of Jul** – National holiday of Umi No Hi, Ocean Day. Marks return of Emperor Meiji from 1876 boat trip to Hokkaido.

**Jul 16–17** – Kyoto (Kansai). Gion Matsuri. Parade of floats from the Yasaka Shrine.

### AUGUST

**Aug 1–7** – Hirosaki (Tohoku). Neputa Matsuri. Parade of floats decorated with papier mâché figures of people and animals.

**Aug 6–8** – Sendai (Tohoku). The Tanabata Matsuri celebrates summer.

**Mid-Aug** – Throughout Japan. The Bon (Festival of the Dead). It also takes place in mid-July.

**Aug 12–15** – Tokushima (Shikoku). Awa Odori. Largest parade of popular dance in Japan, held during the Festival of the Dead (*see pp60 and 61*).

### SEPTEMBER

**Mid-Sept** – Tokyo (Kanto). Fifth Sumo Tournament, lasting 15 days.

**Sep 16** – Kamakura (Kanto). Tournament and displays of archery on horseback at the Hachiman-gu Shrine.

**3rd Mon of Sep** – National holiday of Keiro No Hi, Respect for the Aged Day, celebrating age and longevity.

**About Sept 23** – National holiday of Shubun No Hi, Fall Equinox Day. Family graves visited.

### OCTOBER

**Oct 9–10** – Takayama (Chubu). Hachiman Matsuri. Parade of *yatai* (giant floats) in honor of Sakurayama, divine guardian of the northern part of the town.

**2nd Mon of Oct** – National holiday of Taiiku No Hi, Health and Sports day.

**Mid-Oct** – Nagoya (Chubu). Nagoya Matsuri. Town festival with processions of people dressed in feudal costume.

**Oct 17** – Nikko (Kanto). Fall Festival at the Tosho-gu Shrine.

**Oct 22** – Kyoto (Kansai). Jidai Matsuri (Festival of the Ages). Historical parade with people dressed in the costume of various eras.

### NOVEMBER

**Nov 3** – National holiday of Bunka No Hi, Culture Day.

**Mid-Nov** – Fukuoka (Kyushu). Sixth Sumo Tournament, lasting 15 days.

**Nov 23** – National holiday of Kinro Kansha No Hi, Labour Thanksgiving Day.

### DECEMBER

**Dec 15–18** – Nara (Kansai). On-Matsuri at Kasuga Taisha Grand Shrine. Festival, including a procession of characters in historical costume.

**Dec 31** – Kyoto (Kansai). Okera Mairi ceremony (the lighting of a sacred fire) at the Yasaka Shrine.

# Know Before You Go

## USEFUL WEBSITES

**www.jnto.go.jp**
The official site of the Japan National Tourism Organization, providing comprehensive information on all aspects of the country, including transport, accommodation, sport, and leisure activities.

**www.seejapan.co.uk**
The Japan National Tourism Organization's site for UK visitors.

**www.japantravelinfo.com**
The Japan National Tourism Organization's site for US visitors.

**www.jnto.go.jp/canada**
The Japan National Tourism Organization's site for Canadian visitors.

**www.jnto.org.au**
The Japan National Tourism Organization's site for visitors from Australia and New Zealand.

**www.fco.gov.uk**
The British Government's Foreign and Commonwealth Office website provides up-to-date information on travel.

**www.japan-guide.com**
Excellent source of travel information. All in English.

**www.state.gov**
American visitors may check the US State Department website for travel advice.

**www.smartraveller.gov.au**
Australian Government website with information and advice on travel.

**http://newzealand.govt.nz**
New Zealand Government website with information and advice on travel.

**www.jma.go.jp**
The Japanese weather service website, with an English link for forecasts.

**http://web-japan.org**
The Japanese Ministry for Foreign Affairs' "Introduction to Japan" website.

**www.yellowpage-jp.com and http://english.itp.ne.jp**
English version of the two Japanese Yellow Pages directories.

**www.kunaicho.go.jp/eindex.html**
Website of the Imperial Household Agency, giving information on visiting royal palaces and public events.

## TOURIST OFFICES

### THE JAPAN NATIONAL TOURISM ORGANIZATION (JNTO)

- **JNTO London**
  5th floor, 12 Nicholas Lane,
  London, EC4N 7BN
  ✆020-7398-5678
- **JNTO New York**
  One Rockefeller Plaza, Suite 1250,
  New York, NY 10020
  ✆212-757-5640
- **JNTO Los Angeles**
  Little Tokyo Plaza,
  340 E. 2nd Street, Suite 302,
  Los Angeles, CA 90012
  ✆213-623-1952
- **JNTO Toronto**
  481 University Avenue, Suite 306,
  Toronto, ON M5G 2E9
  ✆416-366-7140

## INTERNATIONAL VISITORS

### EMBASSIES AND CONSULATES

**US Embassy**
1-10-5 Akasaka, Minato-ku,
Tokyo, 107-8420
✆03-3224-5000
http://tokyo.usembassy.gov

**US Consular Offices:**

**Osaka**
ATTN ACS Unit 11-5 Nishitenma
2-chome, Kita-ku,
Osaka, 530-8543
☏06-6315-5900
http://osaka.usconsulate.gov

**Nagoya**
Nagoya International Center Bldg.
6th floor
1-47-1 Nagono, Nakamura-ku,
Nagoya, 450-0001
☏052-581-4501
http://nagoya.usconsulate.gov

**Fukuoka**
5-26 Ohori 2-chome, Chuo-ku,
Fukuoka, 810-0052
☏092-751-9331
http://fukuoka.usconsulate.gov

**Sapporo**
Kita 1-jo Nishi 28-chome
Chuo-ku, Sapporo, 064-0821
☏011-641-1115
http://sapporo.usconsulate.gov

**Naha**
2-1-1 Toyama, Urasoe City,
Okinawa 901-2104
☏098-876-4211
http://naha.usconsulate.gov

**Australian Embassy**
2-1-14 Mita, Minato-Ku,
Tokyo,108-8361
☏03-5232-4111
www.australia.or.jp

**Australian Consular Offices:**

**Osaka**
16F Twin 21 MID Tower 2-1-61
Shiromi, Chuo-ku,
Osaka, 540-6116
☏06-6941-9448
http://consular.australia.or.jp/osaka

**Nagoya**
Level 13, AMMNAT Bldg., 1-3-3
Sakae, Nakaku, Nagoya, 460-0008
☏052-211-0630
http://consular.australia.or.jp/Nagoya

**Fukuoka**
7th Floor, Tenjin Twin Building,
1-6-8 Tenjin, Chuo-ku,
Fukuoka, 810-0001
☏092-734-5055
http://consular.australia.or.jp/fukuoka

**Sapporo**
17th Floor, Sapporo Centre
Building, North 5, West 6-2,
Chuo-ku, Sapporo, 060-0005
☏011-242-4381
http://consular.australia.or.jp/sapporo

**British Embassy**
No 1 Ichiban-cho, Chiyoda-ku
Tokyo, 102-8381
☏03-5211-1100
http://ukinjapan.fco.gov.uk

**British Consulate**
Epson Osaka Building 19,
3-5-1 Bakuro-machi, Chuo-ku,
Osaka, 541-0059
☏06-6120-5600
http://ukinjapan.fco.gov.uk

**Canadian Embassy**
7-3-38 Akasaka, Minato-ku,
Tokyo, 107-8503
☏03-5412-6200
www.japan.gc.ca

**Canadian Consulate**
Nakato Marunouchi Bldg., 6F,
3-17-6 Marunouchi, Naka-ku,
Nagoya, 460-0002
☏052-972-0450
http://www.canadainternational.gc.ca/japan-japon/offices-bureaux/nagoya.aspx?lang=eng

**Embassy of Ireland**
Ireland House, 2-10-7, Kojimachi,
Chiyoda-ku, Tokyo, 102-0083
☏03-3263-0695
www.irishembassy.jp

**Honorary Irish Consulate**
c/o Takeda Pharmaceutical
Company Limited,
1-1 Dosho-machi, 4-Chome,

Chuo-ku, Osaka, 540-8645
☎06-6204-2024
www.irishembassy.jp

## TOURIST OFFICES

The **Tourist Information Centers** (TIC) in Tokyo and at the airports of Narita and Kansai have a wealth of information and will suggest itineraries for traveling around the country. They give out free brochures in English published by the Japan National Tourism Organization (JNTO) and will help to reserve a room in the network of Welcome Inns, hotels, and reasonably priced ryokan. Otherwise, most towns and villages have **local Tourist Offices**, generally situated in or near the railway station. One hundred of them have multilingual staff and booklets in English. In rural areas and small locations, few employees speak English, or have no more than a rudimentary knowledge, so the best policy is to be patient and courteous. You can ask the Tourist Offices to put you in contact with the local **Goodwill Guides**, volunteer bilingual guides who will take you to the places you wish to see. This is a free service, apart from the cost of transport, meals, and entry to sites.

## ENTRY REQUIREMENTS

### PASSPORTS AND VISAS

A valid passport is essential for entry into Japan. Citizens of the US, Canada, Australia, New Zealand, and Ireland do not need a visa for a stay of up to 90 days. They are automatically given a temporary visa for this period of time upon arrival in Japan. UK citizens may stay up to six months. However, after 90 days they must apply to the town hall of the area where they live for a registration card for foreign residents. Since November 2007, new formalities concerning all foreigners entering Japan have been put in place for security reasons: when passing through passport control, you will be photographed and finger-printed by the immigration services.

### CUSTOMS REGULATIONS

Those over 20 years of age may import, tax-free, 400 cigarettes or 100 cigars, 3 bottles of alcohol, 2fl oz/60ml of perfume, and gifts and souvenirs to a total value not exceeding ¥200,000 ($2,100). Unlimited amounts of foreign currency may be imported.

### VACCINATIONS

No vaccination certificate is required.

## HEALTH

All the usual medicines are sold in Japanese pharmacies, but take the precaution of packing a small first-aid kit: aspirin or paracetamol, anti-inflammatory remedies, dressings, antiseptic, anti-diarrhea products, sunscreen, and mosquito repellent if heading for rural areas in summer.
*See also Basic Information pp49–50.*

## INSURANCE

Before taking out insurance, check whether there is an aid and repatriation policy included in the price of your ticket. This is often the case if travel is booked through a tour operator or paid for using certain credit or bank cards. However, it is advisable to examine the clauses of any contract to check their contents and for any possible exclusions. If necessary, take out a travel policy that covers the cost of canceling the trip, sickness, repatriation in case of accident, and loss or theft of baggage. Keep the details of your insurer and the reference number of the policy with you during the trip.

**Travel Guard** – ☎+1-800-826-4919 (US toll free) or ☎+1-715-345-0505 (international collect), www.travelguard.com.

**AAA** – www.travel.aaa.com.

**Travelex** – ☎+1-800-228-9792, www.travelex-insurance.com.

**Mondial Assistance** – www.mondial-assistance.com.

## BUDGET

To help plan your trip, you will find below, as a rough guide, four examples of a daily budget. The price has been calculated for one person, based on two people staying together. It does not include flights or Japan Rail Passes. Local transportation is expensive, as are tickets to visit temples, especially if seeing several of them in one day.

**Mini budget** with accommodation in a youth hostel dormitory, shared travel and transportation, a bowl of noodles or a *bento* (lunch box) at noon, a low-priced menu at dinner, and two visits to temples or museums: allow $70 (£45) per day.

**Low budget** with accommodation at a modest hotel or ryokan, shared travel and transportation, low-priced menu at lunch, dinner in a small restaurant, four cultural visits, and a coffee: allow $120 (£75) per day.

**Average budget** with accommodation in a comfortable hotel or ryokan, shared transport and a taxi in the evening, two restaurants each day, one purchase, one coffee, and an outing to a bar: allow $210 (£130) per day.

**High budget** with accommodation in luxury hotels or very sophisticated ryokan, travel by taxi or rental car, and meals in fashionable or gastronomic restaurants: allow around $365 (£225) per day.

## MONEY

### CURRENCY

The Japanese unit of currency is the yen (¥). It comes in bills of ¥1,000, ¥5,000, and ¥10,000. Coins are valued at ¥1, 5, 10, 50, 100, or 500.

### EXCHANGE RATE

At the time of publication of this guide the exchange rate is approximately $1 = ¥80 and ¥100 = around $1.30 (0.82 GBP; 0.94 EUR; 1.26 AUD; 1.63 NZD; 1.30 CAD). It could be useful to buy a small quantity of yen from a bank or foreign exchange office before your trip. During your stay in Japan, foreign money can be changed in banks, foreign exchange offices, main post offices, and some hotels and department stores.

Bear in mind, however, that many Japanese banks will only change US dollars, and that these operations can be lengthy. To avoid this, or to exchange other currencies, go to foreign exchange offices, located in large towns or at airports. If you are likely to visit rural areas, it may be advisable to change a substantial amount of money in advance.

### TRAVELER'S CHECKS

These are not widely used in Japan and apart from big hotels, few smaller establishments and stores will accept them. Banks, foreign exchange offices, main post offices, and large hotels have no problem changing them (though they prefer those made out in dollars), but it is simpler and cheaper to pay cash. Japan is a country where cash is king, it is also one of the safest countries in the world and you run almost no risk of being robbed.

### CREDIT CARDS

International credit cards are very useful in Japan. The most readily accepted is Visa, followed by MasterCard. Payment by credit card is becoming much more widely accepted in large towns, where many hotels, restaurants, and shops now accept them. But in small establishments and in rural areas, you are less likely to find places willing to take them, so always have an adequate supply of yen with you.

It is possible to withdraw money on international cards everywhere in Japan, thanks to a network of 24,000 **post offices** equipped with automated cash machines (ATMs).

All the ATMs belonging to **Citibank** and some of those at Sumitomo Mitsui and Shinsei Banks also accept foreign cards. The Citibank ATMs in large towns are available 24 hours, while those in the post offices often only work until 7pm during the week and are closed on Sundays, (*the website www.citibank.co.jp/en gives a list of Citibank ATMs*).

Please note that the ATMs of other Japanese banks do not accept foreign cards, even foreign Visa cards. If a card is refused, do not try again: after three attempts the card will be retained. Since 2008, it has also been possible to withdraw money with international credit cards (Visa or MasterCard) from all the ATMs in the Japanese **7-Eleven** convenience stores, which are open 24 hours (*12,000 shops throughout the country, including 1,500 in Tokyo*). Note also that, generally speaking, you are only allowed to withdraw about $421 (*around ¥34,438*) over a 7-day period, which is not a great deal. Check this amount with your bank and if necessary, ask for an increase for the duration of your stay; otherwise take an adequate cash reserve with you.
In the event that a card is lost or stolen while in Japan:
**Visa:** 00531-11-1555
**MasterCard:** 00531-11-3886
**American Express:** 0120-02-012

## MAKING RESERVATIONS

Generally speaking, the Japanese are very organized and rarely do anything on the spur of the moment. In addition, many hoteliers and officials at railway and bus stations are not comfortable with spoken English, though they have a better understanding of written English. **Advance reservation**, especially for accommodation, is strongly recommended. Send applications by e-mail or, failing that, fax them, or use online reservation services or those of a tour operator. Some hotels give a discount for reservations made over the Internet.
If traveling during the 3 weeks the **high season** (*Dec 27–Jan 4, Apr 29–May 5, and the week of Aug 15*), or during the preceding or following weekends, it is essential to reserve hotels and transportation **at least one month in advance**.
The period when the cherry trees are in bloom in Kyoto (*first 2 weeks in April*) is also very busy. *See also Where to Stay pp42–45.*

## ACCESSIBILITY

Since Japan's enactment of the Fundamental Law for Disabled Persons in 1993, it has made real efforts to facilitate daily life for those with disabilities. At major train stations, hotels, and airports, and most new shopping centers and theaters, disabled travelers should have little trouble. About 35 percent of Japan's train stations are completely accessible and barrier-free toilets are in half of all train stations and most newer buildings. Smaller business hotels and more traditional Japanese-style inns may not be accessible. If you have special needs, check with your travel agent or directly with the facility before making reservations.
**Accessible Japan** – www.tesco-premium.co.jp./aj/.
**Accessible Tokyo** – http://accessible.jp.org/tokyo/en/index.html.

## MANNERS

### BASIC PRINCIPLES

The Japanese attach great importance to respect for etiquette and convention, which they regard as indispensable for maintaining harmonious and peaceful social relationships. The group takes precedence over the individual, imposing on everyone the correct attitude to be observed.
For the Japanese, it is good manners to respect the hierarchy within the group and to show consideration toward others. It is good manners to use respectful language and show politeness and humility; to dress smartly; observe strict punctuality when keeping appointments; take care never to express opinions or feelings openly and to apologize repeatedly should a problem arise. Don't be surprised therefore if, in the course of discussions with Japanese people, they express what appear to be banal or conformist ideas: these are not necessarily a true reflection of what they actually think.
Japanese politeness is very subtle and codified. In order to refuse something,

a Japanese person will never say "no," which would be terribly crass. Instead, they will say in a seemingly embarrassed way, "I'm sorry, it is difficult" or "I will think about it." In public, the Japanese behave discreetly and disapprove of such ostentatious behavior as shouting, laughing out loud, or, in the case of couples, kissing intimately. These rules, however, are not absolutely inflexible and are often broken, notably in the course of an evening of drinking.

*See p102 for information about onsen (hot bath) sento (public bath) and o-furo (ryokan communal bath) etiquette.*

## WHEN MEETING SOMEONE

### Greeting

It is not customary in Japan to make any physical contact when meeting someone, such as shaking hands or kissing. The correct form of greeting is to bow from the waist, keeping the arms down beside the body, or held forward in the case of a woman; the depth of the bow and the length of time it is held should be judged according to the age and hierarchical position of the person being greeted. The bow is also used to express thanks, an apology, to ask for help or a favor, and to say "goodbye."

### Names and courtesies

In Japan, the family name is normally placed before the given name, but many Japanese reverse the order when making introductions to foreigners. Check if possible, if you are not sure. People are normally addressed by their surname, with the addition of the word *san* as the equivalent of Mr. or Mrs. (for example, Smith-*san*, meaning Mr. Smith). The title of *sensei* (Master) is reserved for professors, doctors, and other professional people.

### Visiting cards

On a business trip to Japan a good supply of visiting cards *(meishi)* is a must, as these are essential for establishing credibility. To give or receive a visiting card, use two hands preferably, or if not, the right hand only. A person's visiting card is regarded as an extension of their personality. Accept it respectfully, read it attentively, place it face up on the table beside you, and when the meeting is over, avoid folding it or slipping it into the rear pocket of your pants—place it in your wallet or somewhere equally respectful.

### Gifts

It is customary for the Japanese to give each other small gifts when meeting or visiting. If invited to a Japanese home, always take a gift. This does not need to be expensive, but it must be beautifully wrapped. Wine, small cakes, or chocolates are all suitable offerings. Never take four gifts at the same time, because the figure 4 symbolizes death for those who are superstitious.

Offer the gift with both hands, while making light of it, uttering the time-honored formula that "it is nothing of consequence," but always give profuse thanks for any gifts that you receive.

### Shoes and Japanese interiors

The rule is not to contaminate a clean interior with dirt that may be brought in from outside. Before entering a house, temple, ryokan, or traditional restaurant, remove your shoes and leave them on the rack that is normally by the door. Put on any slippers that are provided or, if the floor is covered with tatami mats, enter in your bare or stockinged feet. Never walk on tatamis wearing slippers and remember, also, to take them off when entering the bedroom in a ryokan. Special slippers are provided for use in bathrooms. Even if you are already wearing slippers, they should be exchanged for bathroom slippers before entering and then changed back again upon leaving the bathroom. Umbrellas should also be left at the entrance to houses, temples, museums, hotels, and stores, or slipped into a plastic case so they do not drip on the floor.

Kyoto
Tokyo
Nara
奈良
NARA
Nara Visitors Bureau
http://www.pref.nara.jp/
©Hase-dera temple

## BEHAVIOR AT TABLE

### Before the meal

When taking a meal or tea on a tatami mat, the ideal posture is to kneel. But even on a pillow, this position soon becomes uncomfortable. Alternatively, men may sit cross-legged and women with their legs folded to one side. Before beginning the meal, the guests say: *"Itadakimasu"* ("Thank you for the meal") and at the end, *"Gochisosama deshita!"* ("That was a real feast!") If offered a small, wet towel *(oshibori)* before the meal, remember it is intended strictly for wiping the hands; do not wipe your face or neck with it.

### Chopstick taboos

Using chopsticks correctly requires some practice and a degree of dexterity. Nevertheless, there are certain faux pas that must be avoided at all costs. For instance, do not stand chopsticks upright in a bowl of rice, as this forms part of a funeral rite. Never pass food from your chopsticks onto those of someone else, never use your chopsticks to point at something or someone, and never play with them. Chopsticks should only be used to pick up food from your own plate or tray, but not to help yourself to food from serving dishes (separate, usually longer chopsticks are normally provided for that purpose). Finally, when you have finished eating, place the chopsticks on the holder provided, or side by side on the table but not on the plate or in the bowl.

### Other good and bad manners

Blowing one's nose or sniffing at table is considered impolite, but it is perfectly acceptable (and even desirable) to "slurp" soup or noodles noisily, as the Japanese do. Never sprinkle soy sauce on a bowl of rice; it is eaten plain. Last, when drinking alcohol, serve others but never yourself, and say *"kampai!"* to say "cheers".

# Getting There and Getting Around

## GETTING THERE

## BY PLANE

### Regular airlines – Direct flights

- **Air Canada** – ✆1-888-247-2262, www.aircanada.jp.
- **Air New Zealand** – ✆800-262-1234, www.airnewzealand.co.nz.
- **All Nippon Airways (ANA)** – www.ana.co.jp
- **American Airlines** –www.aa.com.
- **British Airways** – ✆0844 493 0 787, www.britishairways.com.
- **Japan Airlines (JAL)** – www.uk.jal.com, www.jal.com.
- **Qantas** – ✆5 800-227-4500, www.qantas.com.au.

Most travelers opt to fly to Tokyo, but if you want to go to Kansai and the west of Japan, there are plenty of domestic flights available.

A direct New York–Tokyo flight lasts about 13 hours. Ticket prices vary considerably according to the airline, the time you fly, and the day of the week. The most advantageous flight-only fares are to be found on websites and with tour operators.

### Airports

Flights for Tokyo land at Narita (NRT) and Haneda (HND) International Airports. Flights to Osaka land at Kansai (KIX) International. Some airlines, mainly Asian, also serve the international airports at Nagoya (Honshu), Fukuoka (Kyushu), Naha (Okinawa), and Sapporo (Hokkaido). Airport taxes are included in the price of your ticket.

## GETTING AROUND

Japan undoubtedly possesses the finest public transport network in the world, being both extensive and well organized. The rail network alone covers just about every possible destination. The speed, punctuality, and frequency of the trains make it the best method of traveling to all destinations. Bus and boat travel should not be discounted. However, they may take longer but are sometimes more economical. Air travel is also a good way of covering the long distances between the islands.

While traveling in Japan, try making use of that inspired Japanese invention, the express delivery service for baggage, or **takkyubin**. Check in cases the evening before your departure and, for about ¥1,800 per item, the express delivery service undertakes to deliver them the next day to the hotel or ryokan at your next stopover, whatever the distance. Avoiding the need to carry heavy cases around, this is particularly useful if you are moving from place to place. *Takkyubin* offices are found at airports and in most *conbini* (local convenience stores of the Lawson or 7-Eleven type). You can also ask the hotel receptionist to take care of it.

## INTERNAL FLIGHTS

### Airlines

**JAL** and **ANA** airlines cover the essential internal services, but they have competition from low-cost airlines like **Skymark** *(flights between Tokyo and Fukuoka, Kobe, Sapporo)*, **Air Do** *(flights between Tokyo and the large towns on Hokkaido)*, **Skynet Asia** *(flights between Tokyo and the large towns on Kyushu)*, **IBEX** *(flights between Osaka, Sendai, Akita)*, and **Starflyer** *(flights between Tokyo and Kitakyushu)*. This fierce competition has done much to lower prices. Thanks to discounts and special offers, some flights cost less than making the same journey by Shinkansen (*see below*).

### Passes and reduced fares

JAL and ANA airlines both offer a **pass** that allows 2–5 internal journeys for a flat fare of ¥12,600 per journey. It has to be bought abroad in advance from the airlines or tour operators specializing in Japanese trips (*see Know Before You Go p27*). Both airlines offer other **passes**, including the Yokoso Japan (JAL) and the Star Alliance Japan Air Pass (ANA), a little cheaper *(¥10,800 and ¥11,500 per journey respectively)*, but they are reserved for those who take international flights and are not valid during certain holiday periods, notably at Christmas and New Year. Both airlines offer multiple **reduction** options on flights reserved in advance *(from 25 to 70 percent for a reservation made more than one month in advance)*. Low-cost airlines also make similar reductions but at even lower prices, their normal fares being in general 20 percent lower than those of JAL and ANA.

- **JAL** – 0120-2559-71, www.jal.co.jp.
- **ANA** – 120-029-709, www.ana.co.jp.
- **Skymark** – 050-3116-7370, www.skymark.co.jp.
- **Air Do** – 0120-057-333, www.airdo.jp.
- **Skynet** – 0120-737-283, www.skynetasia.co.jp.
- **IBEX** – 0120-686-009, www.ibexair.co.jp.
- **Starflyer** – 03-5641-1489, www.starflyer.jp.

## BY TRAIN

Rapid, frequent, punctual, reliable, clean, and comfortable, Japanese trains are great. The national company **Japan Railways** (**JR**) runs about 70 percent of the rail network; various private companies run the rest, operating above all in large urban areas.

### Using the trains

Trains are in several categories from the fastest to the slowest: The **Shinkansen**, or super-express trains, are on the fastest lines. they run especially on the Tokaido Line *(Tokyo to Osaka)*, Sanyo Line *(Osaka to Fukuoka)*, Nagano Line *(Tokyo to Nagano)*, Joetsu Line *(Tokyo to Niigata)*, and Tohoku Line *(Tokyo to Hachinohe)*. A supplement *(¥800–8,000 according to the train, the*

We'll capture your heart in the sky.
JAPAN AIRLINES
JAL
JAPAN AIRLINES

## \ Unlimited Rail Travel /

# JR-WEST RAIL PASS

Kansai Airport Express "Haruka"    Sanyo Shinkansen "Bullet Train" (Super Express) "Nozomi" N700    Sanyo / Kyushu Shinkansen "Bullet Train" (Super Express) "Mizuho" / "Sakura" N700

## Kansai Area Pass: Excursion Pass for Kyoto, Osaka, Kobe, Nara, and Himeji

This pass can be used to visit the main sightseeing destinations in the Kansai area such as Kyoto, Osaka, Kobe, Nara, and Himeji by using local trains (including JR special rapid trains and rapid trains). You can also go to Universal-City station to visit Universal Studios Japan.®

**■Rate** *The child rate is applicable to children 6 to 11 years old.

| 1day | 2days | 3days | 4days |
|---|---|---|---|
| 2,000 YEN (Children: half price) Valid for one day | 4,000 YEN (Children: half price) Valid for two consecutive days | 5,000 YEN (Children: half price) Valid for three consecutive days | 6,000 YEN (Children: half price) Valid for four consecutive days |

**■Terms and conditions**

◎This pass allows unlimited travel on local trains (including JR special rapid trains and rapid trains) and non-reserved seats on Kansai Airport Express "Haruka" within the West Japan Railway Company (JR-West) network.

*This pass cannot be used for Shinkansen "Bullet Train" (Super Express) trains. If you use the pass for limited express trains or ordinary express trains other than non-reserved seats on Kansai Airport Express "Haruka," you will need to pay an extra charge for limited express services, ordinary express services, or any other applicable fees.

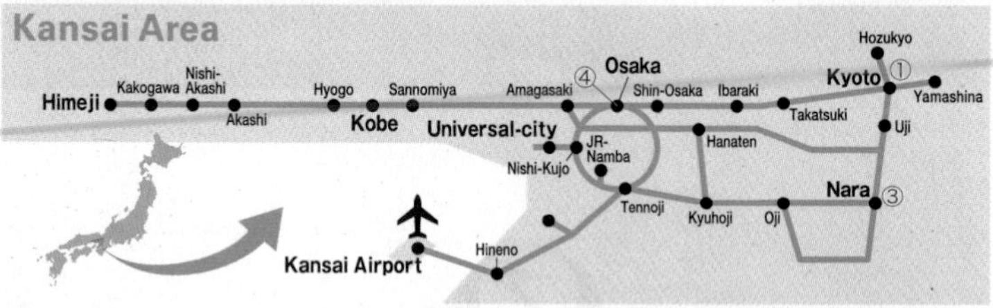


The contents above are correct as of August, 2011.
Visit our website for the latest information about the JR-West Rail Pass

**The JR-West Rail Pass can be reserved online!**

® Universal Studios. CR11-2421/SA11-696

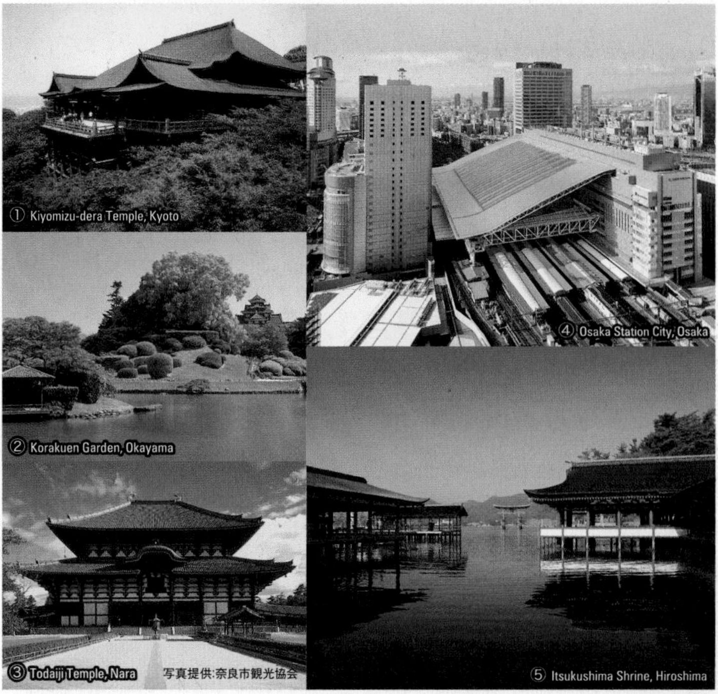

① Kiyomizu-dera Temple, Kyoto
② Korakuen Garden, Okayama
③ Todaiji Temple, Nara　写真提供:奈良市観光協会
④ Osaka Station City, Osaka
⑤ Itsukushima Shrine, Hiroshima

## Sanyo Area Pass: Excursion Pass for Osaka, Okayama, Hiroshima, and Hakata

This pass can be used to visit the main sightseeing destinations in the Sanyo area such as Osaka, Okayama, Hiroshima, and Hakata by using Sanyo Shinkansen "Bullet Train" (Super Express) trains including "Nozomi" and "Mizuho."

**■Rate** *The child rate is applicable to children 6 to 11 years old.

| 4days | 8days |
|---|---|
| 20,000 YEN (Children: half price)<br>Valid for four consecutive days | 30,000 YEN (Children: half price)<br>Valid for eight consecutive days |

**■Terms and conditions**

◎This pass allows unlimited travel on Sanyo Shinkansen "Bullet Train" (Super Express) trains, Kansai Airport Express "Haruka," local trains (reserved seats and non-reserved seats except Green Cars(First Class Car)), and JR-West Miyajima Ferry (Hiroshima) within the West Japan Railway Company (JR-West) network.

*Reserved seats are available only when a reserved ticket is issued (no extra charge is applicable) at JR-West Ticket offices before boarding.

### Sanyo Area

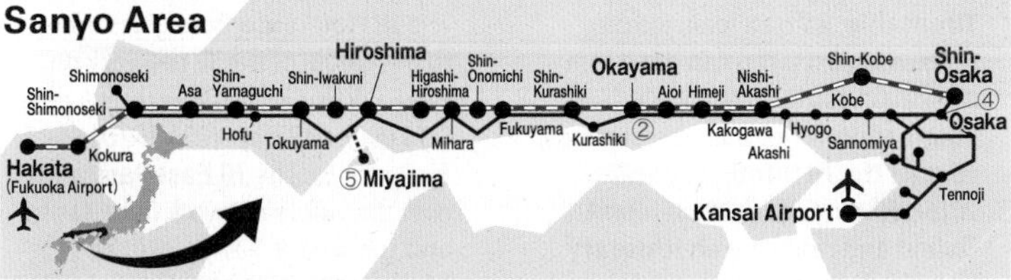


Sanyo Shinkansen "Bullet Train" (Super Express) services　JR-West Miyajima Ferry

**Visit our website!**

**URL:http//www.jr-odekake.net/en/jwrp/**

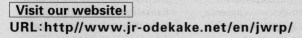

*most expensive being the Nozomi)* is added to the ticket price.
**Limited Express** trains *tokkyu* or *shinkaisoku* are fast trains stopping only at main stations. The supplement is between ¥500 and ¥4,000 depending on distance traveled. **Express trains** *(kyuko)* stop only at some stations and also carry a supplement. **Rapid trains** *(kaisoku)* stop a bit more often than the expresses and there are no supplements. Finally, **local trains** *futsu* or *kakueki-teisha*, stop at all the stations.
The trains consist of normal cars *(ordinary)* and green compartments *(green car)* for first class, accessible on paying a supplement. Reservations require supplements too, but all trains have cars with nonreserved seats *(jiyu-seki)*. Night trains also include sleeping cars with couchettes, also with a supplement. Buy your tickets from the automatic ticket machines *(for short distances)* or from station ticket offices, writing down in English anything you want to tell or ask the vendor. If you cannot find the exact fare listed on the machines, take the next cheapest. You can always pay the supplement to the train inspector with no penalty or extra cost. If necessary, pay the difference at the *fare adjustment machine* or at the window located near the platform exits.
Note that while unfailingly punctual, the trains only stop briefly in stations. Be there well in advance to find your platform and your car's position, marked on the ground.
The JR Company publishes a useful booklet in English, the **Railway Timetable**, with all main journey times and costs. You can get it free in all main stations. For all kinds of information, other than reservations, contact the **JR Infoline** *(℘050-2016-1603, in English 10am–6pm)*.
To find and calculate an **itinerary** by train *(timetables, length of journey, price)*, consult one of the following websites: www.hyperdia.com or www.jorudan.co.jp. Both include an English version.

### The Japan Rail Pass

Reserved for foreign visitors, the JR Pass is a real bargain that greatly simplifies life. Valid on the JR network, except for the Shinkansen Nozomi trains, it allows travel anywhere without having to buy a ticket over a period of 7, 14, or 21 days. The JR Pass can only be bought outside Japan from specialist tour operators. When purchasing, you will be given a reservation voucher.
On arrival in Japan the voucher can be exchanged for a pass in one of the JR Travel Service Centers, which can be found in all main stations and at Narita and Kansai International Airports.
The pass should be marked with the date on which you intend to begin using it. There is no point in dating the pass immediately if, for example, you will be staying a few days in Tokyo: the date, once entered, cannot be changed.
The cost of the JR Pass is generally quickly absorbed. For example, with the 7-day JR Pass *(¥28,300)*, if you travel from Tokyo to Kyoto return on Shinkansen *(¥26,440)* and the transfer between Tokyo and Narita Airport return *(¥5,880)*, you save ¥4,000. The 14-day JR Pass costs ¥45,100 and the 21-day pass ¥57,700; children under 11 travel half-fare. For more details about the JR Pass and the regional passes, consult www.japanrail.com.

### Other passes and reductions

Depending on your itinerary, other, cheaper passes may be better for your needs and these can be bought on the spot.
The **JR Hokkaido Pass** gives access to the whole of the JR network on Hokkaido for 3 days *(¥14,000)*, 5 days *(¥18,000)*, or 7 days *(¥23,750 or ¥43,220 for 2 people)*. The **JR East Pass** is valid over the whole network from Kanto and Tohoku for 5 days *(¥20,000)*, 10 days *(¥32,000)*, or 4 days spread over one month *(¥20,000)*. The **JR West Kansai Pass** is valid on the whole of the JR from Kansai for a period of 1 day *(¥2,000)* to 4 days *(¥6,000)*.

The **JR Sanyo Pass** covers the Osaka region and the Sanyo Line as far as Fukuoka *(Hakata)* for 4 days *(¥20,000)* or 8 days *(¥30,000)*. The **JR Kyushu Pass** covers the whole of the JR network from Kyushu for 5 days *(¥16,000)*.
Other options: the **JR Seishun Juhachi Kippu**—this card, on sale in most stations, allows unlimited travel on the JR network for 5 days for only ¥11,500. It may be used for several people and on different days but is only valid for local, rapid, or express trains *(not on the Limited Express and Shinkansen)*, and only during certain periods of the year *(Mar 1–Apr 10, Jul 20–Sept 10, Dec 10–Jan 20)*.
The **JR Shuyu Kippu** is an open ticket that gives a 20 percent reduction for a round trip on JR trains, buses, or ferries to a given region *(Kanto, Hokkaido, Kansai, Shikoku, Kyushu)*, and unlimited travel on JR trains in that region for 4 or 5 days. It is sold, according to the region, for ¥3,300–28,000.
*For passes specific to certain towns and regions, see also the Transport section in the Address Book panels in each Discovering Japan chapter.*

## BY BUS

Many tourists are unaware of the long-distance buses that cross Japan, but they are a cheap way of traveling. Night buses, for the most part with comfortable reclining seats, also save the cost of a night in a hotel. Journeys, however, take much longer than by train. Seats have to be reserved in advance at bus stations or local travel agencies. Travel on JR buses may also be reserved at station ticket offices. Telephone reservations can only be made in Japanese.
**www.bus.or.jp/e** – This website contains basic information about some 1,500 long-distance bus lines, with timetables, length, and price of journeys. Indicate the point of departure and arrival, then click on the name of the companies to get the details.
**www.jrbuskanto.co.jp** – This website gives information about the network of JR long-distance buses.
**Orion Tour** – ☏03-5725-2155, www.orion-tour.co.jp. Agency selling tickets at reduced prices for the night buses leaving from Tokyo. Its switchboard is English-speaking.

### The Japan Bus Pass

This pass, to be purchased outside Japan, permits travel anywhere on the Willer Express long-distance bus network for three days *(¥10,000)*, four days *(¥12,000)* or five days *(¥14,000)*.
A maximum of 2 trips may be reserved per day; days of use need not be consecutive. The pass is valid for 2 months. *(Information, reservations and sample itineraries: http//willer express.com/bus/pc/3/top.)*

## BY BOAT

*Routes described by region in Discovering Japan.*
An armada of ferries links the islands of Japan, especially the smallest ones, which can often only be reached by sea. While the large islands of Hokkaido, Honshu, Kyushu, and Shikoku are linked by tunnels and bridges, traveling by boat is a good option both to keep costs down and enjoy pleasant **views** of coastal scenery. The large long-route ferries can take passengers, vehicles, and goods. They have many services aboard, such as restaurants, boutiques, casinos, and bathing facilities. Cheaper tickets give access to a communal room with *tatami* flooring (matting made from straw), where you can put down your sleeping bag. Dormitory beds in second class cost a little more *(20–40 percent more)*. The first-class cabins cost around double the basic fare. Reserve a ticket through a hotel, a travel agency, or the local Tourist Office as shipping company personnel rarely speak English. The **Japan Long Distance Ferry Association** publishes a free brochure in English with ferry line timetables and prices (*in most Tourist Offices*). The ferry routes are not included in the JR pass, except for the JR Miyajima ferry near

Hiroshima. Boats in Japan are above all a means of transport; for the moment there are no tour cruises, except for tours lasting a few hours.

## BY CAR

The efficient public transport system means car rental in large towns is quite unnecessary, as it is for taking major routes such as the Tokyo–Nagoya–Kyoto–Osaka–Hiroshima roads, all well served by train. Yet a car is very practical way of seeing rural or mountainous areas, or remote islands, where public transport is often limited. A good compromise is to travel by train to your destination and rent a car locally.

### Road network

There is no problem about driving in Japan: the roads are reliable, the signs are clear *(on major roads the signs carry a translation in the Roman alphabet)*, and Japanese drivers are quite prudent and respectful. In addition, many rental cars come with GPS satellite navigation. The screen maps are in Japanese but have Arabic road numbers so that, with an English road atlas to hand, the GPS makes orientation easy.

In Japan they drive on the **left**. The speed limit is 25mph/40kph in towns and 37mph/60kph on country roads; 50–62mph/80–100kph on freeways and expressways. Freeways and expressways are **toll** roads at a fixed rate (*¥2000 per journey*) aside from motorways to Tokyo. There are plenty of gas stations (*Esso, Jomo, etc.*) and gas costs about ¥660 per gal *(¥145 per l)*. Large towns are often congested, so prepare the route in advance, noting street names and road numbers. Towns charge for parking *(at parking meters or car parks)*, but hotels offer free or reduced rate parking to guests. You may find a bilingual road atlas useful, the most complete being the *Japan Road Atlas* from Shobunsha, on sale in Japan or from store.maplink.com *($49.95)*. Less specific for roads but with good town plans, train lines, and subway details is the *Japan Atlas* from Kodansha. If you need breakdown assistance, ring the **Japan Automobile Federation's 24-hour emergency line**, in English on ✆0570-0-8139.

### Driving license

Citizens from English-speaking countries who intend to drive in Japan must carry an **international driving permit** (issued by your national automobile association) as well as a **national driving license**.

**Japan Automobile Federation** – 2-2-17 Shiba, Minato-ku, Tokyo 105-8562, ✆03-6833-9100. A list of offices in the provinces and further information is at www.jaf.or.jp/e.

### Car rental

Car rental agencies, mostly near rail stations and in airports, rent by the half-day, day, or week, often inclusive of unlimited mileage and insurance. An excess must, however, be deposited in case of accident. There is also a mileage supplement if vehicles are returned at a different location.

**Prices** vary little between small and large agencies. That said, international companies such as Avis, Hertz, or Budget are generally more expensive than national ones like Nissan Rent-A-Car, Toyota Rent-A-Car, Nippon Rent-A-Car, or Orix Rent-A-Car. For an economy-class car, the price is around ¥7,000 per day and around ¥50,000 for a week. Japanese car rental agencies do not generally have English websites and in most agencies the personnel do not speak English. Based in Tokyo and accustomed to foreign travelers, the **ToCoo! Agency** *(✆03-5333-0246)* offers cheap rates right across Japan. Reserve online at its English website: www2.tocoo.jp.

**Child car seats** – Japanese legislation requires car rental agencies to offer child car seats, but some have only a very few; check beforehand as to availability.

**GPS** – While all Japanese cars come with GPS, very few of them have it in English. Reserve your English-language GPS in advance to be sure of having one. The great innovation of Japanese GPS is the option of choosing your destination by telephone number. To be sure, ask the agency personnel to show you how the GPS works; you can also operate a Japanese GPS, which has road and motorway numbers in Roman numerals with a good road atlas.

## ON TWO WHEELS

You can rent small 50cc scooters at most places of interest, but you may not use them on the roads. Very few car rental agencies offer motorcycles larger than 125cc for hire and those that do rarely have English-speakers on their staff. As for touring Japan by bicycle, it is possible, but only if you are very fit and have plenty of time as the roads can be rather steep. Take a good road atlas to discover small, secondary roads and know enough Japanese to be able to read the road sign *kanji (chinese idiograms)*.
The regions best for cycling excursions are the center of Honshu, Hokkaido, Shikoku, and the south of Kyushu. To avoid the difficult exit from large towns, use the train. Bikes must be put in special bags *(rinko baggu)* to go on trains; these are sold in cycle accessory shops. For more details, see www.japancycling.org and www.outdoorjapan.com.
(*See also* Bicycles)

## IN TOWNS

### Subways and trains

Big cities such as Tokyo, Yokohama, Kyoto, Osaka, Fukuoka, or Sapporo have a network of subways, privately owned railways, and, in some cities, monorails, independent of the JR network. These are often the fastest means of urban transport. Buy your ticket from the automated ticket machines after checking the price for your destination on the information board, posted high for visibility; press the corresponding machine button and insert the money. If the exact fare is not indicated on the board, take a cheaper ticket and pay the balance when you leave at the fare adjustment machine, near the exit gates. One-day subway passes are also good value.

### Buses and trams

Trams are easy and still run in many cities, including Hiroshima, Matsuyama, and Nagasaki. Like buses, they are boarded at the back *(at the front in Tokyo)*; at the machine, take a ticket with your boarding area number. At each stop a sign lights at the front with the cost for each route section; you pay into the small machine near the driver on getting off. The Tokyo and Kyoto buses charge a flat fare whatever the distance covered.

### Taxis

Taxis are expensive in Japan, but trains and subways stop after midnight and bus service is limited in small towns. The big taxi stands are near railway stations and you can expect to pay ¥600–700 for the first 1.2mi/2km, and then ¥100 per 1,640ft/500m. It costs extra to take a taxi at night or to phone for one. Available taxis have a red light behind the windshield, which is green when the taxi is taken. Taxi doors open and close automatically; the drivers are smartly dressed and wear white gloves but generally don't speak English. Show where you want to go on a map, with a business card or with the *kanji* for your destination *(like those in this guide)*. Tips are unnecessary, being included in the fare.

### Bicycles

The Japanese cycle everywhere and tourists can easily rent bikes for a day near tourist sites for about ¥1,000. Lock them up, though, as theft happens. Cyclists should ride on the road and park in special parking lots, but in practice they often ride on sidewalks and park anywhere. The police tolerate this, but a badly parked bike can be impounded resulting in a heavy fine.

# Where to Stay and Eat

## WHERE TO STAY

### ADDRESSES IN THE GUIDE

In the Discovery section the **Address Books** list a selection of accommodation addresses in or near the towns or places of interest. To make it easy for you to find these addresses on the town maps (where given), we have marked each hotel (and restaurant) with a colored number.

**Price categories** *(see cover flap)*
To help you make your choice, we have given a **range of prices**: for accommodation, the prices indicated are calculated for **two people excluding meals** in high season; for dorms, prices indicate the cost per person. For restaurants, the prices are based on a standard menu or an à la carte meal consisting of two dishes *(starter and main course)*, but do not include drinks. The addresses are classed according to four price categories to meet all budgets:
⊖ **Lowest price** – These include *minshuku (see opposite)*, business hotels, and, in some regions, youth hostels.
⊖⊖ **Average price** – In this category you will find ryokan, hotels noted for their charm and atmosphere *(often offering a choice of Japanese or Western-style rooms)*, and small specialty restaurants.
⊖⊖⊖/⊖⊖⊖⊖ **Top of the range** – If you want to spoil yourself, try one of the historic ryokan (such as the Arai at Shuzenji, *see p229*), or one of the more contemporary hotels such the Hyatt Regency at Kyoto (*see p321*). Or splash out on a *kaiseki* meal (*see p46*) in a famous restaurant.

### CAMPSITES

Camping is popular and well catered for in Japan. It is the most economical form of accommodation and also an excellent way of visiting the National Parks of Hokkaido, Tohoku, and Okinawa. Unfortunately, most of the campsites are only open during the summer vacation, in July and August, and so get extremely crowded. Equipment available on site is often limited, so it is advisable to take your own tent and equipment. The JNTO publishes a free brochure, *Camping in Japan*, which lists the main campsites on the Japanese archipelago, with details of prices, facilities, and means of access *(it can be downloaded from www.jnto.go.jp/eng/location/rtg)*. Information in English is also available on the **Outdoor Japan** website *(www.outdoorjapan.com)*.

### YOUTH HOSTELS

There are almost 360 youth hostels in Japan, offering clean, cheap dormitories and sometimes a few individual rooms as well. A night in a dormitory costs around ¥3,000, breakfast is about ¥500, and dinner ¥1,000. The appeal of these hostels varies greatly. Some are housed in ugly, downtown buildings; others are found in smart areas or idyllic rural settings. There is no age limit for access to youth hostels, but the rather strict regulations and boarding-school atmosphere are not to everybody's taste. It is not necessary to be affiliated to the Federation of Youth Hostels, but if planning to stay in these hostels, it is a good idea to take out a membership card before traveling as nonmembers are charged a supplement of ¥1,000 a night. The prices quoted in this guide are those payable by nonmembers. The website of the **Japan Youth Hostel Association** (*www.jyh.or.jp*) lists all the youth hostels in Japan by region, with a description of each and whether or not it is possible to make reservations online. During the high season and the summer vacation it is essential to book a long time in advance. For the rest of the time, make reservations at least 2 days before. You can also book online for a selection of hostels through the Hostelling International website, www.hihostels.

com, and the JNTO publishes a free *Japan Youth Hostel Map*, available in the main Tourist Offices.

## CAPSULE HOTELS

A typical Japanese invention, *capsule hotels* are intended for male office workers who, having missed the last train home, or finding themselves too tired or drunk to go back to their suburban homes, need an **inexpensive place** *(¥3,000–4,000 per capsule)* in which to spend the night. Located close to railway stations or in districts filled with bars and clubs, these hotels rarely admit women. The capsules set in rows, one above the other, along corridors are like tiny cabins on a ship. Measuring 6.6ft/2m by 3.3ft/1m wide and 2.6ft/80cm high, they are sparsely furnished with just a bed, but are well equipped with air-conditioning, television, radio, alarm clock, and bedside lamp. C*apsule hotels* provide lockers, automatic dispensers *(razors, drinks)*, a communal bathroom, and sometimes a sauna. Visitors to Japan may find a night in a capsule hotel an interesting experience, but only providing they do not suffer from claustrophobia.

## LOVE HOTELS

Another Japanese curiosity, these hotels welcome couples wishing to spend some time together in discreet anonymity. They are recognizable by their outrageously kitsch façades. The rooms offer a wide choice of themes: jungle, dolls' house, Venetian or Parisian decor, even prison cell! ... not forgetting the mirrors on the ceiling, soft lighting and a choice of music, movies, and other accessories on demand. Rooms are rented for a 2- to 3-hour period during the day *(around ¥4,000)* or for the whole night *(around ¥8,000)*.

## BUSINESS HOTELS

These Western-style hotels, often located near railway stations, are intended for travelers on a reduced budget. For tourists, they have the advantage of providing **comfort at a modest price**. The rooms are similar to those in an American motel, but smaller: twin beds, molded plastic bathroom fittings, simple and functional equipment. Despite their small size, they are always clean and well equipped *(air-conditioning, television, hair dryer, yukata [loose cotton robe], etc.)*. In the lowest-priced *business hotels (¥6,000–10,000 for a double room)*, the minimal service is taken care of by a range of automatic vending machines.

## CLASSIC WESTERN HOTELS

There are a great many Western-style hotels in the large towns, belonging to Japanese or international chains. They are generally high-capacity (*more than 100 rooms*), with extensive facilities (*parking, restaurants, bars, boutiques*). Most of them also have a few Japanese-style rooms, with tatamis and futons, but the bulk of the accommodation is in wall-to-wall carpeted rooms with Western-style beds. The degree of luxury varies, ranging from middle-category hotels *(¥12,000–18,000 for a double room)* to luxurious four-star hotels *(¥30,000–60,000 for a double room)*. The staff speak impeccable English. A tax of 10–15 percent is added for service, while a buffet-style breakfast costs ¥1,000–2,500. Double rooms (with a big bed) are often cheaper than twin rooms (two beds).

## MINSHUKU

These **family-run** bed-and-breakfast style guesthouses are to be found all over Japan, but mostly in rural areas. As in the ryokan, guests sleep in Japanese tatami rooms. Accommodation in a *minshuku* is usually a little simpler than in a ryokan, but the price is correspondingly cheaper. Guests unroll and arrange the futons themselves, share a communal bathroom, and a supplement is sometimes charged for towels.

As in all traditional Japanese accommodation, the prices are quoted per person. You can generally expect to pay around ¥6,000 per night, ¥500 for breakfast *(Japanese)*, and ¥1,500 for dinner. A long list of *minshuku* may be found on the website www.minshuku.jp, on which reservations can also be made.

## SHUKUBO

Certain Buddhist **temples** also serving as inns are called *shukubo*. They traditionally offered bed and board to passing pilgrims, but some now take in travelers. For tourists it is a great opportunity to discover something of Japanese monastic life by joining in the morning prayers and Zen meditation sessions. Most of the temples serve a delicious vegetarian cuisine *(shojin ryori)*. Japan's most famous *shukubo* are found in Koya-san *(see pp340–343)*, the great sacred city of Kansai.
The average price is around ¥10,000 per person, including meals. Couples or families may normally stay in *shukubo (children's price: sometimes 30 to 50 percent less)*, but it is wise to check with the temple beforehand.

## RYOKAN

Ryokan are **traditional Japanese inns**, where meals are served and guests sleep in tatami rooms. There is a wide range, from the traditional to the more modern, and from modest, family-run establishments to the more luxurious. They all offer an elegant but relaxing atmosphere. To experience some authentic Japanese-style accommodation, visitors should spend at least one night in a ryokan.
Entered via sliding partitions, the furnishings are minimal: a low table, a few cushions, and a *tokonoma* – an alcove decorated with flowers or calligraphy (do not walk or stow suitcases in these alcoves). A futon (*a mattress and a quilt*) is rolled out on the floor for the night and then put away in a cupboard by the staff next morning. A *yukata* (light cotton kimono) is also supplied for guests and may be worn anywhere within the ryokan. Apart from in the most modest ryokan, all rooms have a bathroom, but there is always a communal bathroom for the hot bath *(o-furo)*, sometimes fed by a thermal spring, with separate access for men and women. Some ryokan also allow the reservation of the *o-furo* for private use for an hour or so.
Ryokan prices are per person, including meals *(breakfast and dinner)*, served in the dining room and sometimes in your room. It is generally not possible to rent a room without also taking meals. Expect to pay ¥6,000 per person for the most basic ryokan, ¥15,000–20,000 for one that is middle of the range, and ¥30,000–80,000 for top of the range. The **Japan Ryokan Association's website,** www.ryokan.or.jp, provides a long list of ryokan, classified by region, with addresses and phone numbers.

## LONG-TERM ACCOMMODATION

If you are staying for some time in Japan, the most economic way is to rent a **gaijin house**. These are fully-equipped studios or apartments found in the major cities such as Tokyo or Kyoto, which foreign visitors may rent in their entirety or just by the room *(about ¥50,000 per month)*; in the latter case the communal parts of the apartment etc. are shared with the other occupants. Addresses of gaijin houses can be found on the Internet, in magazines such as **Tokyo Classified** or through agencies such as **Sakura House**, www.sakura-house.com.

## WHERE TO EAT

*Also see Gastronomy p109.*
Restaurants in Japan may not have a menu in English, nor any English-speaking staff, but you can often make yourself understood by pointing at the wax models of the dishes displayed in the window. Apart from in the large towns, meals are usually served from 11.30am to 2pm and from 6 to 10pm. Wherever you go you will be greeted

by a resounding *"Irashaimase!"* ("Welcome!") before being seated at a table or a counter. The majority of restaurants specialize in a **single type of cuisine**: skewers, noodles, sushi, etc. Many offer a cheap lunchtime menu *(teishoku)*, though the evening menu is often more expensive. There is no service charge—other than in the grander restaurants, where a supplement of 10–15 percent is added to the bill—and there is no need to tip *(see p53)*. Take the check to the cash desk and pay when you leave.

## INFORMATION AND RESERVATIONS ONLINE

Apart from the websites already indicated, here are a few more useful links to consult:

**www.itcj.jp** – The Welcome Inn website, a network of hotels and ryokan accustomed to catering for foreign visitors, where the price of a double room is no more than ¥13,000.

**www.jpinn.com** – The Japanese Inn network includes a hundred or so inexpensive small ryokan and *minshuku* throughout Japan.

**www.nikkanren.or.jp/english** – The Japan Tourist Hotel Association website, with detailed information about hotels and ryokan by region.

**www.j-hotel.or.jp** – The Japan Hotel Association groups together good-quality hotels.

**www.japanhotel.net** – A wide choice of various categories of hotels and ryokan, classified by region and described in detail.

**www.itravel.jp** – Website for reserving hotels and various kinds of ryokan online.

**www.travel.rakuten.co.jp** – Rakuten Travel is the biggest agency for online hotel reservations in Japan, sometimes offering reductions on the price of the rooms.

**www.japaneseguesthouses.com** – This website offers almost 500 traditional ryokan, classified by region, with descriptive information for each.

**www.toho.net** – A network of small rural hotels, notably on Hokkaido, which charge very low prices *(about ¥5,000 per person)*.

## SPECIALIST RESTAURANTS

**Kare-ya** – Small, cheap eating places serving curry and rice *(kare raisu)* at unbeatably low prices, generally located near railway stations.

**Kushikatsu-ya** – Restaurants serving deep-fried skewers of meat.

**Okonomiyaki-ya** – Inexpensive cafes where *okonomiyaki* (savory pancake) is prepared on a griddle *(see p111)*.

**Ramen-ya** – Restaurants serving low-priced *ramen* dishes *(see p111)*.

**Soba-ya** – Restaurants specializing in *soba* and *udon*, Japanese noodles *(see p111)*.

**Sukiyaki-ya** – Chic and very expensive restaurants, since good beef is a luxury in Japan. *Sukiyaki* is a dish containing meat and vegetables cooked on a griddle *(see p410)*.

**Sushi-ya** – Restaurants serving *sushi* and *sashimi*, often in bars where you sit at a counter and watch the chef preparing the food. A good sushi restaurant can be expensive, but there are many low-priced versions, *kaiten-sushi*, where the plates of sushi are set out on a rotating belt and you help yourself as the dishes pass in front of you. Price is indicated by the color of the plate.

**Tempura-ya** – Sometimes very expensive, these serve an assortment of tempura *(see p111)*.

**Tonkatsu-ya** – These restaurants serve *tonkatsu* *(see p112)* and *korokke* (potato croquettes—also available at most other eateries).

**Unagi-ya** – Restaurants specializing in grilled eels *(unagi)*, which are carefully prepared.

**Yakiniku-ya** – Generally quite low-priced, these restaurants specialize in Korean barbecues, where diners grill strips of marinated meat and shellfish at the table.

**Yakitori-ya** – Restaurants serving *yakitori* (chicken skewers).

### OTHER TYPES OF RESTAURANT

**Izakaya,** a type of very popular bar or tavern serving small dishes and light snacks such as pickles, salads, sashimi, and grill for snacking with drinks. Most offer **nomihoudai**, an attractive all-you-can-drink happy hour fixed price *(about ¥2,500)* appreciated by businessmen and students.

**Shokudo** and **famiresu** *(family restaurant)* are low-priced and near railway stations or in the basements of large buildings. They offer various dishes, sometimes Western food, and cheap set menus *(teishoku)*.

**Kaiseki ryori** have the best Japanese haute cuisine. Some offer *kaiseki* menus for tourists at affordable prices *(¥5,000–8,000)*, but the best *kaiseki* cuisine is found in the *ryotei* in Kyoto, restaurants with wonderful gardens, patronized by the elite. The prices can be colossal *(more than ¥50,000)*.

**Temple restaurants**, especially in Kyoto, produce a vegetarian cuisine *(shojin ryori)*, often based on tofu and *yuba* (skin of boiled soy milk).

There are plenty of restaurants serving **Western** cuisine in the large towns, but a host of often-mediocre Italian restaurants and the ever-present American fast-food outlets rarely do them any favors. French cuisine, which takes pride of place in large hotels, is for the most part, both meager and rather pretentious. It is better to choose restaurants serving the food of other **Asian** countries, such as Chinese, Thai, Indonesian, and Vietnamese, which are very often good value, or Japanese restaurants serving hybrid dishes inspired by Southeast Asia.

In the **coffee shops** (*kissaten*), you can have a Western-style breakfast *(morning set)* consisting of toast, fried eggs, salad, and coffee, for about ¥500. Some of them also offer a cheap breakfast menu *(around ¥1,000)*, consisting of one dish, a salad, a bowl of rice, and a drink.

If you are on a tight budget, go for a *bento* (lunch box) from a *conbini*. In the shopping streets in the evenings, the **yatai** (food stands) offer quick snacks *(ramen, takoyaki)*. In Tokyo, Kyoto, Osaka, or Sapporo, some sushi restaurants, the *yakiniku*, and the *kushikatsu* occasionally display a tempting "**All you can eat**" sign. You have 90 minutes in which to eat as much as you want for around ¥2,500.

# Useful Words and Phrases

Written Japanese is a combination of *kanji* (Chinese ideograms) and two alphabets, *hiragana* (for Japanese words) and *katakana* (words of foreign origin). A simplified phonetic script is used for writing Japanese in *romaji* (Roman alphabet). The pronunciation is much the same as in English. Diphthongs are pronounced separately. "Ai" is pronounced "aï" as in "high." "U" is pronounced either as "oo" or as a short and barely audible "ew," as in "few." The letter "e" is pronounced "eh;" "g" is hard, as in "goose" and the "j" as in "judge." "Ch" is pronounced as in "church." "R" is rolled and sounds almost like "l." "S" is always pronounced as if it were double: "ss." "W" is the same as in English.

### Glossary of Place Names

| | Translation |
|---|---|
| bridge | -bashi or -hashi |
| district | -chome |
| peak | -dake or -take |
| waterfall | -daki or -taki |
| valley | -dani or -tani |
| temple | -dera or -tera |
| hall in a temple | -do |
| street | -dori or -tori |
| garden | -en |
| river | -gawa or -kawa |
| beach | -hama |

| | |
|---|---|
| peninsula | -hanto |
| east | -higashi |
| temple | -in or -ji |
| rock | -iwa |
| island | -jima or -shima |
| Shinto shrine | -jinja or -jingu |
| castle | -jo |
| sea | -kai |
| coast | -kaigan |
| prefecture | -ken |
| north | -kita |
| lake | -ko |
| park, garden | -koen |
| ward (subdivision of a department) | -ku |
| district, town | -machi |
| south | -minami |
| port | -minato or -ko |
| gate | -mon |
| village | -mura |
| west | -nishi |
| thermal spring | -onsen |
| slope | -saka or -zaka |
| town, city | -shi |
| Shinto shrine | -taisha |
| pagoda/tower | -to |
| gate | -torii |
| bay, creek | -ura or -wan |
| mountain | -yama, -zan or -san |

## Basic Conversation

**Yes/no** hai/iie
**Good morning** ohayo gozaimasu
**Good day** konnichiwa
**Good evening** konban wa
**Good night** oyasumi nasai
**Goodbye** sayonara
**How are you?** ogenki desuka?
**Very well, thank you**
hai, genki desu
**Thank you very much**
arigato (gozaimasu)/domo arigato
**No, thank you** iie, kekko desu
**Don't mention it** doitashimashite
**Please (come in, help yourself)**
dozo
**Excuse me** sumimasen/gomennasai
**If you please** onegai shimasu
**Delighted to meet you**
hajime mashite
**What is your name?**
o namae wa nan desuka?
**My name is …** watashi wa … desu
**What is your nationality?**
nani jin desuka?
**I am American**
watashi wa amerika-jin desu
**I am English** wastashi wa
igirisu-jin desu
**Do you speak English?**
eigo ga hanasemasuka?
**I understand/don't understand**
wakarimasu/wakarimasen
**Would you repeat that?**
mo ichido itte kudasai?
**What is the Japanese for …?**
nihongo de … wa nan to iimasuka?
**Could you write it in English?**
eigo de kaite kudasai?
**Please give me a moment**
chotto matte kudasai
**I like/do not like …**
… ga suki desu/… ga kirai desu

## Orienting Yourself

**Right/to the right** migi/migi ni
**Left/to the left** hidari/hidari ni
**Straight on** massugu
**In front/behind** mae/ushiro
**I want to go to …** … ni ikitai desu
**Whereabouts is …?**
… wa doko desuka?
**Where is it?/Is it here?**
doko desuka?/koko desuka?
**Is it near?/Is it far?**
chikai desuka?/toi desuka?
**Can I get there on foot?**
aruite wa ikemasuka?
**Could you draw me a plan?**
chizu o kaite kudasai?
**I am lost** mayoimashita

## Money and Purchases

**Bank** ginko
**Could you change some money?**
ryogae ga dekimasuka?
**How much is it?** ikura desuka?
**Do you take credit cards?**
kurejitto kado wa tsukaemasuka?
**Expensive/cheap** takai/yasui
**Do you have …?** … wa arimasuka?
**What is this?** kore wa nan desuka?
**Can I try this on?**
kite mite mo ii desuka?
**Small/large** chiisai/okii
**I'll take this** kore o kudasai

### At the Hotel

**Have you a room available?**
heya ha arimasuka?
**I would like to reserve a room**
heya o yoyaku shitai desu
**I have/haven't a reservation**
yoyaku o shimashita/yoyaku wa shite imasen
**Single room/double/twin**
shinguru/daburu/tsuin
**Japanese room/Western-type room**
washitsu/yoshitsu
**Room with bathroom**
ofuro tsuki no heya
**What does it cost per night?**
ippaku ikura desuka?
**I will stay for 1/2/3 nights**
ippaku/nihaku/sanpaku tomarimasu
**Do you have Internet access?**
netto akusesu wa arimasuka?
**May I leave my baggage?**
nimotsu o azukatte moraemasuka?
**I will be leaving the hotel tomorrow**
asu shuppatsu shimasu
**Please call me a taxi**
takushi o yonde kudasai
**Key/passport/reception**
kagi/pasupoto/furonto

### In a Restaurant

**A table for two, please**
futari onegaishimasu
**Have you a menu in English?**
eigo no menu wa arimasuka?
**Give me ... please** ... o kudasai
**The same thing as my neighbor**
tonari no hito to onaji mono o kudasai
**Breakfast/lunch/dinner**
choshoku/chushoku/yushoku
**Hot/cold** atsui/tsumetai
**I'm hungry/I'm not hungry** onaka ga sukimashita/onaka wa suite imasen
**That is good** oishii desu
**Waiter, the check please!** sumimasen, okanjoonegaishimasu!

### Emergencies and Health

**I have a headache/stomachache/toothache** atama/onaka/ha ga itai desu
**Help!** tasukete!
**Call an ambulance** kyukyusha o yonde kudasai
**Call the police** keisatsu o yonde kudasai
**I need a doctor** isha ga hitsuyo desu
**Where is the nearest hospital?**
byoin wa doko ni arimasuka?
**I've lost my passport**
pasupoto o nakushimashita
**Embassy** taishi kan
**Police booth/drugstore**
koban/kusuriya

## TRANSPORTATION

**Aircraft/airport** hikoki/kuko
**Station/train** eki/densha
**Subway/tram** chikatetsu/romen densha
**Boat** fune, boto
**Bus/bus stop** basu/basu-tei
**Bicycle/rental** jitensha/kashi-jitensha or renta-saikuru
**Car/driver's license** kuruma/unten-menkyo
**Taxi stand** takushi noriba
**Stop here, please**
koko de tomatte kudasai
**A ticket to ... please**
... yuki no kippu o kudasai
**One-way/return trip** katamichi kippu/ofuku kippu
**Reserved seat/seat not reserved**
shitei seki/jiyu seki
**Second class/first class** nito/itto
**Ticket office/baggage room**
kippu uriba/nimotsu azukarijo
**What time does the bus for ... leave?**
... iki no basu wa nanji ni demasuka?
**What time do we arrive?**
nanji ni tsukimasuka?
**How long does it take?**
donogurai kakarimasuka?
**Which platform does the train for ... leave from?** ... yuki wa nanban ... homu desuka?
**Is this the train for ...?** ... yuki no densha wa kore desuka?
**Which station have we arrived at?**
kono eki wa doko desuka?
**Let me know when we arrive at ...**
... ni tsuitara oshiete kudasai

### Figures and Numbers

| | Translation |
|---|---|
| 0 | zero, rei |
| 1 | ichi |

| | |
|---|---|
| 2 | ni |
| 3 | san |
| 4 | yon |
| 5 | go |
| 6 | roku |
| 7 | nana |
| 8 | hachi |
| 9 | kyu |
| 10 | ju |
| 11 | ju-ichi |
| 100 | hyaku |
| 200 | ni-hyaku |
| 1,000 | sen |
| 10,000 | ichi-man |
| 100,000 | ju-man |
| 1 million | hyaku-man |
| 1 person | hitori |
| 2 people | futari |
| 3 people | sannin |
| 4 people | yonin |

### How to order in a sushi-ya

**Abalone**: awabi
**Bonito**: katsuo
**Bream**: tai
**Crab**: kani
**Cuttlefish**: ika
**Eel**: anago (sea), unagi (freshwater)
**Ginger**: gari
**Mackerel**: saba
**Octopus**: tako
**Omelet**: tamago
**Raw shrimp**: nama ebi
**Salmon roe**: ikura
**Sardine**: iwashi
**Scallop**: hotate
**Sea bass**: suzuki
**Sea urchin**: uni
**Shrimp**: ebi
**Soy sauce**: shoyu
**Tuna belly**: toro
**Tuna**: maguro

# Basic Information

## DRINKING WATER

It is safe to drink the tap water throughout the whole of Japan. Mineral water can be bought from vending machines or in *conbini* and other stores.

## ELECTRICITY

The electrical current is 100V, 50 to 60Hz AC. Japanese plugs generally have two flat pins, like American ones; occasionally they have three pins (*two flat and one rounded*). Though the two-pin plugs look very similar to American plugs, visitors from North America may need an adapter. North American visitors may also need a converter for larger appliances such as irons and hairdryers, but should have no problem with cell phones and digital cameras. Visitors from other countries may need a converter for devices that are not 100–200V, such as kettles or hairdryers, or, if there is no battery adapter or dual voltage AC charger available, a transformer may be needed for devices such as computers.

## IN CASE OF EMERGENCY

**Police:** ✆110.
**Fire brigade or ambulance:** ✆119.
**Japan Helpline:** ✆570-000-911 or 120-461-997.
There is no charge for assistance in English, 24 hours.

## HEALTH

### ILLNESSES

The high standard of hygiene in Japan makes the risk of contracting an illness fairly small. Some precautions should be taken: there are many mosquitoes and packing some insect repellent would not go amiss.
*See also medications p10.*

### MEDICAL SERVICES

Japan has good hospitals and clinics (at least in large towns), but they are expensive. You are strongly advised to take out an insurance policy covering medical care abroad in case a problem occurs. In an **emergency** *(fire or ambulance)*, dial 119.

Ask your hotel to call a doctor or an ambulance, or tourist information centers may have a list of English-speaking doctors. To find an English-speaking doctor, you can also contact the **Amda** International Medical Information Center in Tokyo *(☎03-5285-8088, http://homepage3.nifty.com/amdack/english/E-index.html, or in Osaka, ☎06-4395-0555).* A list of general hospitals in Tokyo with English-speaking staff available appears on the website of the US Embassy, *(http://tokyo.usembassy.gov)*, under American Citizens Services: A–Z (Medical Resources).

*See also Health p29.*

## INTERNET

Japan offers high-speed *(30–100Mbps)* Internet connections. One particularly inspired Japanese invention is the **manga cafe** *(manga kissa)*, cybercafes that offer unlimited manga comics and drinks, in addition to booths equipped for surfing the net, watching DVDs, or playing video games. Some also have showers and sofas, so you can even spend the night. There are many cybercafes in big towns, but they are not always easy to find as their signs are generally written in *kanji* and the staff may not speak English.

Computer keyboards have both *kana* (Japanese script) and Roman letters arranged in the QWERTY layout. One key normally switches between the Roman and Japanese characters *(prices are around ¥500 per hour)*. The manga cafes also offer packages for 3 hours, 5 hours *(around ¥1,000)*, even a whole night. There are also many other places where the Internet can be accessed **at no cost** to check e-mails: in youth hostels, ryokan, hotels, and bars *(customers only)*; in public libraries, town halls, and Tourist Offices, and also in large computer stores (Bic Camera, Yodobashi), where computers are used for demonstration purposes.

## LAUNDRY

Coin-operated laundrettes are often located in or near *sento*, the local public baths, and dry cleaners can be found in shopping centers. Otherwise, hotels generally offer a laundry service *(prices correspond to the class of hotel)*. Youth hostels, ryokan, and business hotels normally provide washing machines for customers to use. *(Expect to pay ¥200 to use the washing machine, ¥50 for the detergent, and ¥200 to use a dryer.)*

## MAIL/POST

The Japanese mail service is efficient, reliable, and fast, with little risk of an item mailed from Japan going astray, whether for delivery locally or abroad. The cost of mailing a postcard to the USA, Canada, the UK, Australia, and New Zealand is ¥70; for a letter ¥110. Post offices are recognizable by their logo, a red T topped by a horizontal bar (〒). They also sell boxes and bags for mailing parcels.

## MEDIA

### NEWSPAPERS AND MAGAZINES

The Japanese press is noted for the huge circulation figures of its daily newspapers: 12 million for the *Yomiuri Shimbun*, 8.2 million for the *Asahi Shimbun*. English versions of these papers, as well as the *Japan Times*, are sold in bookshops in the larger towns and from kiosks at railway stations. They are also available on the Internet in English *(www.asahi.com/english and www.japantimes.co.jp)*. The *International Herald Tribune* is also widely available. A list of magazines published monthly or weekly runs to some 3,000, including journals in English, such as *Newsweek*, *Time*, *Kansai Time Out* (www.kto.co.jp) or *Weekender* (www.weekenderjapan.com).

### TELEVISION AND RADIO

Apart from the two public television channels of NHK *(the main state broadcaster)*, many commercial channels are also available *(NTV, TBS, Fuji-TV, TV-Asahi, TV-Tokyo)*, with regional and specialist versions. Some films and imported programs are broadcast in the original versions. It's also possible to tune in to an English language commentary for the NHK evening news on some TVs, and you may be able to access a bilingual soundtrack for other shows. CNN, BBC, or BS1 are normally received in the large hotels. You can hear the news in English on the radio via InterFM *(76.1)* broadcast from Tokyo and FM Cocolo *(76.5)* from Kansai. The BBC World Service is broadcast throughout Japan *(www.bbc.co.uk/worldservice)* and the AFN-TOKYO *(American Forces Network)* provides 24-hour radio services to its principle military audience across Japan *(www.yokota.af.mil/afn)*. AFN's Eagle 810 broadcasts throughout the Kanto Plain on 90.3 FM.

## MUSEUM, MONUMENT, AND SITE TARIFFS

Entry charges vary according to the nature and importance of the attraction or site. The cost of entry to temples ranges from ¥200 to ¥600, and for museums from ¥300 to ¥1,000.

## NAMES OF STREETS

Finding an address in large towns can sometimes prove difficult, for the Japanese inhabitants as well as for visitors, as most of the streets do not display a name. To make it even more complicated, the numbers of the buildings are not consecutive, but allocated according to the date they were built. Instead of indicating the street, addresses generally include the area *(ku)*, the district *(cho* or *machi)*, accompanied by a series of three figures indicating the number of the ward, the number of the block, and the number of the building. For example: Sony Building, 8 F, 3-6-2 Tenjin-cho, Chuo-ku. 8 F indicates the *floor*, in this case the seventh floor, since the ground floor is 1 F.

## OPENING HOURS

### BANKS

Banks are open 9am–3pm Monday to Friday. Foreign exchange offices keep more flexible hours. ATMs in banks and post offices are almost always inaccessible when these are closed in the evening and at weekends.

### OFFICES, GOVERNMENT OFFICES, AND POST OFFICES

Offices and government offices open 9am–5pm, except at weekends. Small post offices open 9am–5pm, Monday to Friday, and large post offices 9am–7pm during the week and up to 3pm on Saturdays. Only the main post offices in the very larger towns have a counter open on Sundays.

### STORES

Shops: 10am–8pm, every day. Department stores: 10am–7.30pm *(Sunday 7pm)*. Some stores, including *conbini* (local convenience stores), stay open 24 hours, 7 days a week.

### MUSEUMS, MONUMENTS, AND SITES

Museums generally open 10am–5pm, except on Monday. When Monday falls on a public holiday, they close on the Tuesday that follows. Temples and castles open every day, 9am–5pm. In most cases the last admissions are 30 minutes before closing time. Many sites are closed from Dec 28 to Jan 3.

### RESTAURANTS

Restaurants open every day, usually 11.30am–10.30pm, but generally speaking, they stop serving between 2.30 and 6pm, and again after 10pm.

## PHOTOGRAPHY

Memory cards and camera batteries are widely available and prices are reasonable, as you would expect in a country where photography is so popular. Shops that develop and print photos *(minilabs)* are found everywhere and do a fast and excellent job. Automatic machines print digital photos in next to no time. Traditional photographic film for prints or slides is also widely available.

## PUBLIC HOLIDAYS

When a public holiday falls on a Sunday, it is celebrated on the following day.

**Jan 1**: New Year's Day
**2nd Mon in Jan**: Coming of Age Day
**Feb 11**: National Foundation Day
**Around Mar 21**: Spring Equinox
**Apr 29**: Showa Day
**May 3:** Constitution Memorial Day
**May 4**: Greenery Day
**May 5**: Children's Day
**3rd Mon in Jul**: Marine Day
**3rd Mon in Sept**: Respect for the Aged Day
**Around Sept 23**: Fall Equinox
**2nd Mon in Oct**: Health and Sports Day
**Nov 3**: Culture Day
**Nov 23**: Labor Thanksgiving Day
**Dec 23**: The Emperor's Birthday

## PUBLIC TOILETS

There are public toilets everywhere in Japan—including in places of interest—that are free to use. The most common are the traditional toilets, normally found in public places, consisting of seat-less pans over which you squat, with your back to the door. Slippers are sometimes left by the door, which should be put on before entering and removed on leaving. The toilets in hotels and private homes are generally modern and very high-tech, with heated seats, illuminated push buttons, discreet background music, and extra fittings such as bidets that shoot jets of hot water and air.

## SECURITY

While muggings and crime in general are pretty rare, theft does sometimes occur especially in big cities and in busy areas such as railway stations. If you are in any kind of difficulty, or are simply lost and looking for an address, the easiest solution is to go to the nearest **koban**, the local police booth. They are recognizable by the small red lamp at the front.

## EARTHQUAKES AND NATURAL DISASTERS

**Earthquakes** are quite frequent in Japan. Fortunately most of them are only minor and cause minimal damage since buildings are designed to resist tremors. Should an earthquake occur when you are inside a building, keep away from windows, furniture and anything that is likely to topple over, and take shelter under a solid table or stand under a door frame. If out in the open, find a clear place well away from debris and dangerous objects (signboards, electric cables) that could fall from buildings. Don't panic and follow the evacuation instructions given by the person responsible for security. The **typhoon** season occurs between the end of August and the beginning of September. The impending arrival of these violent tropical storms is announced in warning bulletins on radio and television. They are not dangerous provided you keep under cover in some form of strong and durable shelter until they pass. Alerts are also put out for **tidal waves** *(tsunami)*. In the event of an alert, if you are on a beach, leave immediately and take refuge on high ground. Don't panic and, if necessary, get in contact with your embassy or consulate.

## SMOKING

Cigarettes may be bought from the local *conbini* or from the cigarette vending machines that are located more or less everywhere in the streets, stores, bars, and hotels. However, in 2008, the **Taspo system**, aimed at reducing underage smoking, was introduced. To buy cigarettes from a vending machine, the consumer needs a Taspo card proving they are over the age of 20. Since the card has to be applied for in writing, it does not make sense for short-term visitors who will have to rely on the other outlets. Both Japanese and American brands sell for around ¥270–300 a packet. The Japanese are heavy smokers and little effort was made by the authorities to reduce consumption until the arrival of the Taspo card. Nevertheless, for some years now, laws protecting nonsmokers in public places have been applied with increasing strictness. In Tokyo, especially, smoking in the street is prohibited in certain districts.

## TELEPHONES

### CALLING JAPAN FROM ABROAD

To call Japan from the USA/Canada, dial 011 + 81 + the regional code, omitting the first 0, + the number; from the UK/Ireland/New Zealand, dial 00 + 81, etc; from Australia dial 0011 + 81 etc.

### INTERNATIONAL CALLS FROM JAPAN

International calls can be made directly *(with ¥100 coins)* from public telephones marked International & Domestic Card/Coin Phone. Unfortunately there are not many of them. They can usually be found in the lobbies of big hotels, airports, large railway stations, and city centers. For international calls from Japan, dial 010, then dial the country code *(1 for the US and Canada, 44 for the UK, 353 for Ireland, 61 for Australia, 64 for New Zealand)*, followed by the area code *(minus the first 0 of the STD code when dialling the UK)*, and then the number.

### LOCAL CALLS WITHIN JAPAN

Even though there are fewer of them than there used to be, the gray or green **public telephones** are still fairly ubiquitous. They take ¥10 and ¥100 coins as well as prepaid telephone cards. A local call costs ¥10 per minute. They will not, however, give change for ¥100 coins. To avoid a constant search for the necessary coins, buy a **telephone card**. Cards with a value of ¥500 or ¥1,000 are sold from kiosks in railway stations, in *conbini,* and from automatic machines; they are often beautifully decorated. To call a number within the town or region in which you are located, dial the number omitting the regional code that is shown in brackets. To telephone from one town or region to another, dial the number preceded by the regional code.

**Free Numbers** – There is no charge for numbers that begin with 0120.

**Directory Information** – For national information, dial 104.

### CELL TELEPHONES

Unless you have a 3G cell phone, your cell phone will not work on the Japanese network, where the operators do not use GSM. It is possible, however, to **rent** a cell phone during your stay from a number of private telecommunications companies. Most of them have a counter at Narita or Kansai airports, or may deliver direct to your hotel. NTT Docomo, the biggest Japanese cell phone company, offers numerous services and products. Before deciding, compare the offers (price of rental, cost of calls) on the following websites: www.vodafonerental.com/Japanese-Phone-Rental.aspx, www.cellularabroad.com, www.pupuru.com, www.rentafonejapan.com, www.g-call.com, www.telecomsquare.co.jp/en/index/html.

## TIME DIFFERENCE

Compared to the US East Coast, the time difference in Japan is +13 hours (i.e., when it is 11am in New York, it is midnight in Tokyo); US West Coast: +16 hours; UK/Ireland: +9 hours; Eastern Australia: -1 hour; Western Australia: +1 hour; New Zealand: -3 hours. Time differences vary when DST is in operation.

## TIPPING

Tipping is not customary in Japan, but a service charge is automatically added to the bill by the main hotels and ryokan, and in luxury restaurants (10–15 percent).

## WEATHER

Weather forecasts are given on television and in the newspapers. For a forecast in English by phone, dial **177** *(for local forecasts, dial the code for the region–such as 03 for Tokyo –then 177)*. The website of the Japanese National Weather Service is also available in English: www.jma.go.jp.

*See also When to Go p10.*

*Torii, Itsukushima Shrine, Miyajima, Hiroshima*

常夜燈

# Understanding Japan

**At the end of the 19C, Lafcadio Hearn (1871–1904), one of the first Westerners to write about Japan, said: "One must learn how to understand," which is the best advice that can be given to any new visitor. But "learning how to understand" takes time—time to get to know both the people and the country at first hand, and not simply through books—and for the traveler, time is something that is often in short supply. However, awareness of what lies beneath the surface will enable foreigners to avoid basing their views of Japan on the usual clichés, and on Japan's reputation for being "Westernized." Japan has its own rich history—it cannot be understood simply by reference to the culture of the West. The WW II period (and its string of atrocities) aside, Westerners have generally formed their view of Japan from a cultural angle—usually by focusing on the stereotypes of the samurai and the geisha at the expense of ordinary Japanese people. Consequently, Western ideas of the "Japanese spirit" tend to ignore the country's complex history, its social structures, and the values and traditions of the majority of the population. As a result, with images of the samurai and geisha to the fore, many people's concept of Japan fluctuates confusedly between the mawkish and twee, an aggressive nation, and a highly technologically productive country.**

## A CONFUSING MODERNITY

Japan's modern society is not just a simple carbon copy of the West's. Japanese democracy is not an American import. The Occupation (1945–52, see p71) facilitated democratization but by the end of the 19C, liberal, even socialist ideas, had already begun to take root and despite the drift toward militarism, political thinking continued to evolve. This is why the Japanese "embraced" their defeat in World War II so well, to paraphrase the title of one of the most enlightening books on the Japanese postwar recovery, *Embracing Defeat,* by the American historian John Dower. And, though Japan was in ruins in 1945, it had been a world power: in 1905, the Japanese Navy sank the Russian fleet, a victory that gave it a place among the world's great powers less than 50 years after the Meiji reforms.

Contact with the West was the spur to modernize, but it was not the only stimulus. When Japan abandoned its isolationist policy in the middle of the 19C, it was regarded by the West as being politically and economically "backward" in comparison to Europe, though not in terms of its "civilization." Urban culture (popular literature, the press), the development of cities, and the standard of literacy were all on a par with Europe. With a population of 1 million, Edo—as Tokyo was originally known—was as densely populated as London.

The modernization of Japan was therefore the outcome of Japanese heritage coming into contact with foreign countries, with mutually beneficial and productive results.

If visitors can successfully distance themselves from the cliché that within every Japanese man lurks a potential samurai, that every Japanese woman is a submissive housewife waiting hand and foot on her "captain of industry" husband, the reality of Japanese culture will become apparent. In the end, the best way to gain an understanding of Japan is to explore it, and the best place to start is with its cities.

## ON FOOT IN THE CITY

In a city such as Tokyo, the real Japan can be discovered in small, everyday things just as much as in its wealth of cultural heritage or ultramodern architecture. A stroll around the urban landscape of Japan's capital city will reveal a vast architectural collage in a patchwork of styles and pastiches. By Western standards of urbanization, however, the

© Axiom/hemis.fr

large Japanese cities might be regarded as "ugly" and lacking in the harmony that gives European cities their beauty, even a city such as Kyoto. Unlike Florence, Kyoto's beauty is not immediately on show, but rather hidden in its temples and gardens, and in the old districts that lie sandwiched between a grid of wide, bland highways.

With its jumble of highrise buildings, architectural styles, and power lines, confusion seems to reign supreme in Tokyo. Due to the earthquake of 1923, the firebombing of World War II, and the financial speculation of the 1980s, its historic legacy is not as rich as Kyoto's. And yet, take a detour into a small street squeezed in between two apartment blocks and you will soon find another side to the city: suddenly the tempo shifts from the throbbing pulse of a metropolis to the peace and quiet of a village.

The charm of a Japanese city, especially Tokyo, lies in its network of little streets and one-way alleys. It's a way of life that owes less to materialism than to the neighborliness of its inhabitants. Here, cars are an intrusion and pedestrians and bicycles rule. Individual houses, little gardens, and small shops—nothing that is architecturally striking, but a genuine sense of community prevails in these urban villages.

So, where are these "urban villages"? The answer is almost everywhere—in the Hongo, Ueno, Uguisudani, and Yanaka districts, in the area that used to be called the "town below" *(shitamachi)* or "downtown," where the ordinary city folk lived. But this dual urban identity, which encompasses a whole galaxy of universes that coexist and interweave with each other, can also be found in the wealthier districts, where a certain social fluidity still exists.

Potted plants, flowering shrubs, and bamboos proliferate in the small streets, and this patchwork of traditional greenery lends the streets a particular gaiety. Paradoxically, in the middle of the city it's a glimpse of the special relationship that the Japanese have with nature, a relationship that has been raised to an aesthetic level, though it did not prevent the city from being ravaged during the period of huge economic growth from 1960 to 1980.

Attuned to the cycles of nature, the Japanese are highly respectful of their effects and mindful of the fragility of the natural world. This awareness of the passing of time and the seasons encourages them to live in the moment, be open-minded, and enjoy the pleasures of the here-and-now, as is evident as when night falls in the easygoing atmosphere of innumerable bistros and little bars. Another of Tokyo's charms, particularly for night owls, male or female, is the sense of security at night.

**Philippe Pons**

# Japan Today

**Japan is often considered to be the non-Western country whose practices and institutions are closest to those of the West. It is admired for the quality of its products and services, and its artistic, technological, and scientific creativity; its youth have embraced Western street culture, turning it into something unique of their own. However, Japan's originality or idiosyncracy tends to be too readily explained by reference to its religious system. In the following portrait of a young couple and a brief survey of Japan's religions, we aim to show Japan as it is today resolutely modern, but in its own way.**

## THE JAPANESE

Eiko closes her cell phone. Taka has just called; he's having dinner with clients for the second time in a week so she doesn't have to prepare the evening meal. Tonight, she'll make do with a bowl of rice and miso soup.

### THE WOMAN'S WORLD

Eiko is happy. She can swap text messages with Mari-chan, her best friend who married and moved away, or contact Secchan, a former office colleague who recently had a baby. They know that they will not lose touch, despite the distance. Their long-standing friendships will form an active, supportive network that will endure even when they are older. Eiko tidies the kitchen while waiting for Taka to come home. When he does arrive he often falls asleep at the dining-room table, but she likes to wait for him, to make sure he arrives safely.

### THE MAN'S WORLD

Taka arranges to eat out two or three times a week to help out his young wife. However, his colleagues often tease him: "Since you got married, we never see you; it's impossible to have a drink together after work." Taka wants to keep a good balance between home and work, but work also involves lively all-male outings and weekend golf. He can't get out of it; everyone does it to network and create a bond between work colleagues.

Besides, being married shouldn't deprive him of his liberty, which is what the Japanese bachelor fears most about marriage.

### HOME AND ITS CHOICES

Eiko enjoys the calm of being at home and not working. But Eiko's nonworking status is relative—despite the exhortations of the media, angry demands from women since the 1980s, and a growing number of more "modern" relationships, a Japanese man spends on average 26 minutes a day on household tasks, a figure that has hardly varied for 40 years. Although his conscience pricks him more than his father's did, Taka still depends almost entirely on his wife. It's a way of telling her that she is essential. Home, diet, clothing, finances—she decides everything, down to the amount of pocket money she gives him each month from his salary. She will also choose the children's school, their after-school activities, and very probably the retirement home for their respective parents and their last resting place.

Like most of her friends, Eiko stopped working shortly before she got married, just like her mother, in the model nuclear family that emerged during Japan's economic regeneration between 1950 and 1980. It's a way of life she is lucky to be able to follow today: wages are not what they were and the future is uncertain—women are increasingly forced to take up paid work. However 70 percent of mothers with a child under six do not work. Eiko enjoyed the time she spent working after her two-year higher education course (young men generally spend four years at university). Women aged between 20 and 29 form the group that is most highly satisfied with their present life (78 percent, as opposed to 67 percent of men of the same age range). But after 14 years in positions of little responsibility, aware that advancement in her social stratum is almost exclusively reserved for men, she longed to move on.

## THE IMPORTANCE OF MARRIAGE

Eiko's dislike of being a lowly employee without prospects was just one factor in her desire to marry. Like 90 percent of Japanese women under 30 and more than 92 percent of Japanese men, she hoped to get married one day (the figures for women who have never married remain very low, though they seem to be increasing), but she quietly passed her 30th birthday still single. The average age at which women marry in Japan is 28.2 years, and for men it's 30, among the highest ages in the world. Although she had had affairs (like one-fifth of young Japanese women; slightly higher for men), she had never lived with a man until now (less than 1 percent of Japanese couples live together outside marriage). After a year's courtship, she had done everything she could, albeit wordlessly, to get Taka to propose. One Saturday he took Eiko on a surprise visit to his parents and after the meal his mother said, "Thank you for being willing to take care of our son." And so the marriage was settled.

### The ceremony

Like more than 60 percent of Japanese couples, Eiko wanted a white wedding, in a chapel. The hotel arranged everything, from hiring the priest to the honeymoon, the reception, the *son et lumière* show, the rental of kimonos and tailcoats, and the gifts for the guests. It cost 3 million yen ($11,000/£7,500) but everything was perfect on the day.

### The Japanese family

At 1.39 children per woman, the Japanese birth rate is the lowest in the world. However, fewer than 5 percent of couples are childless, the first child arriving soon after marriage. The number of abortions is very high, more than 340,000 a year. A significant percentage of abortions occur within marriage; less than 1 percent of births occur outside marriage, whereas in 10 to 20 percent of marriages the bride is already pregnant.

## MIXED MARRIAGES

Eiko's sister flew in for the ceremony from Europe, where she lives with her husband, a foreigner. Highly educated, with experience in the international marketplace, she scared off her male compatriots, who were afraid they would be overshadowed by her. Her parents had long thought that she was in danger of being left on the shelf, like many highly qualified "career women." For Eiko, the idea of living abroad still seems like an aberration, but her attachment to her new brother-in-law is deeply sincere.

*Wedding taking place at Meiji-jingu, Tokyo*

©Yasufumi Nishi/JNTO

## RELIGION OR SPIRITUALITY

It soon becomes apparent to Western visitors that just below the surface of this modern, materialistic society, Japan remains a deeply spiritual nation. After all, this is the country that gave us Zen meditation, the haiku (a strictly defined form of Japanese poetry containing 17 syllables, often describing the most prosaic of things), and the martial arts. This is not how the Japanese see themselves, however.

Surveys conducted by the Japanese on the Japanese confirm that they are not religious, are not interested in religion, and even distrust religion. This conviction has been reinforced by the criminal acivitities of some cult movements such as the sarin gas attack carried out by the Aum cult in the Tokyo subway on March 20, 1995 (12 dead and more than 5,000 injured). Though exceptional, this attack was a shock that saw a hardening of public opinion and later the law with regard to religion.

Even before that, more than 80 percent of Japanese claimed to distrust religious organizations, barely 10 percent of parents considered that religion was an important aspect of education, and religion was ranked ninth in a list of the 10 "most important elements in life." Perhaps more astonishingly, only 10 percent of Japanese say they believe in the "other world." As a result, people never talk about their religious convictions, differentiating Japan from some Western countries.

The few tourists who take the time to talk with a monk or priest will realize their immense loneliness. Although Japan has not developed a tradition of militant atheism, the country considers itself deeply irreligious.

### The official figures

For all that, a look at the number of adherents claimed by various religious bodies, who have no interest in inflating their figures (the taxman would soon make them regret it), is dizzying. There are 112 million "Shintoists," 93 million Buddhists, 1.5 million Christians, and 11.5 million who belong to other religions (including large sectarian groups). Japan has 218 million believers, 1.8 times the population! The population may claim to be largely irreligious but it is still affiliated to its religious institutions. A primary factor for this may be the ambiguity of the words used in relation to religion (*see box p62*), or it may be due to a difference between people's practices and convictions.

Fewer than 40 percent of Japanese claim to believe in Buddha, and fewer still (35 percent) in the Shinto deities (although the figures show more Shinto faithful than Buddhists). In daily worship the Japanese may go through the motions, but the full spiritual meaning behind the rituals is generally ignored.

### Matsuri

The term *matsuri* ("festival") comes from the verb *matsuru*, which means "respecting and invoking the gods." The origins of the *matsuri* are essentially religious, a way of pacifying the *kami*, omnipresent divinities that make their presence felt through volcanic eruptions, earthquakes, or tidal waves. To ensure good harvests and therefore the survival of a community, the *matsuri* originally coincided with the two most important times of the agricultural year: sowing in spring and the harvest in the Fall. Since the *kami* are very demanding, other rites were added: the Festival of the New Year Fire (Hi-no-Matsuri), the essential period of purification during which the year's impurities are symbolically burned, and the Buddhist Festival of the Dead (Bon), celebrated throughout the country in July and August. Matsuri evolved over the centuries as festivals, adapting and acquiring new elements to suit individual communities. For the Japanese, there is always an excuse for a good-humored festival and for revisiting one's *furusato* (village or place of origin).

*Also see Aoi Matsuri p297, Yamagasa Matsuri p473, and Awa Odori p464.*

### The right ritual at the right time

The Japanese visit their ancestral tombs on certain days of the year and especially during **Bon, The Festival of the Dead**, usually held around August 15. Due to the large numbers of people traveling on such days, the roads and railways get very busy. It is therefore wise to avoid traveling then if possible.

The summer is also when many festivals *(matsuri,* *see box opposite)* are held in the villages and districts around the big cities. For the 60 percent of Japanese who take advantage of high-summer public holidays to honor the spirits of their ancestors, it means a return to their roots, as well as cheerful reunions with family and friends, dances that can take a year to organize, meals with plenty of liquor and food that harks back to childhood, the exchange of gifts, fireworks, and lanterns swaying in the wind. No one gives a thought to the history of Bon with its Indian origins, or to its religious roots (it is strongly Buddhist in character), or to the festival's implication that the dead live on in another world.

The Festival of the Dead is an extreme example perhaps, and its religious aspect is quite prominent, but a quick run through the year's other major festivals illustrates that Japanese life is organized along largely secular lines. Experts have suggested the term "communal religion" to describe the collection of miscellaneous rites that mark the Japanese calendar and cannot be classified within any existing system, but this is just another attempt to construct a coherent framework where one does not exist.

The Japanese cheerfully admit "**In Japan, you are born Shinto, married Christian, and die Buddhist,**" a reminder that principal birth ceremonies take place in Shinto shrines, two-thirds of marriages are celebrated in Christian chapels, and funeral rites are organized by Buddhist monks.

In addition, social ties such as those in business or at school have long been based on Confucian principles; the organization of time (the horoscope or almanacs) and space (the construction of houses) is often based on "Taoist" wisdom; and politics is conducted along democratic, atheist principles. Although there have been tensions, in general this easygoing mix can be explained by a generalized refusal to accept exclusive faith systems, allied to a belief in the efficacy of the right gesture made at the right moment and according to the right protocol, regardless of the religion that generated it.

## SHINTO

Shinto, "the way of the gods," is often held as Japan's indigenous religion. The preceding paragraph shows why it is wrong to see it as the Japanese religion as religious practice here often combines many beliefs. Nevertheless, over 90 percent of the 81,500 shrines in the country belong to the same Association of Shinto Shrines. All Shinto priests train in one of two Shinto study centers, and practices differ little from one shrine to another: they chiefly honor a local divinity who also has national status, give thanks on behalf of the community, and submit requests for the future. This homogenized Shintoism is, however, fairly recent and in fact results from a late 19C move to harmonize religion in Japan. Intellectuals and politicians then came to the fore with the restoration of imperial power in lieu of the shogunate (1867), and sought to establish a nationalistic religion (State Shinto, *Kokka Shinto*). This was seen as an essential component of a strong state capable of rivaling Western empires. Shinto and Buddhism, which had previously coexisted, were forceably separated; cult objects thought to encourage popular superstition or to offend public morals (especially phallic objects) were destroyed, shrines reorganized, and some temples demolished. As a result, Buddhism was suppressed and Shinto became the official religion of Japan. Promoting veneration of the emperor and valuing loyalty, inner strength, and self-denial, it was taught in schools and became a model for its Asiatic neighbors (shrines were built in the

## Shinto and Buddhism

These two religious movements are so inextricably intertwined that it may seem arbitrary to use a separate vocabulary when speaking of either, but some usages are now well established in Japan and elsewhere. In the context of Shinto, followers worship at a "shrine" (*jinja*, "pavilion of the gods," of which there are more than 80,000); it is a "priest" or "shrine priest" (*kan-nushi*, who serves the divinities—there are nearly 60,000 priests), or a "head priest" (*guji*) who officiates. Buddhists worship at a "temple" (*o-tera*, of which there are around 80,000); the temples are staffed by "monks" (*o-bo-san*—nearly 300,000, including just under 100,000 women), and a "superior" (*hoshi*, "master of the law"). The functions of Shinto priests and Buddhist monks are hereditary, some of them claiming descent through 74 generations.

As meditation does not feature strongly in Shinto practices, there are no monasteries. New converts who wish to become priests (the figures have increased recently) are brought into the administation of a shrine, where they are often confined to humble tasks, like sweeping the courtyard. In contrast, Buddhism has many institutions for monks and nuns, and also welcomes non-Japanese adherents into its ranks.

new colonies, starting with Taiwan). The suppression of Buddhism finally ended in 1946 when the Allies ordered the Japanese government to adopt a new constitution incorporating religious freedom and the separation of state and religion.

Despite this period of enforced homogenization lasting nearly 60 years, Shintoism remains diverse, encompassing beliefs and customs derived from tradition and different social strata. **"Primitive Shinto"** is an all-purpose term for religious practices from prehistory (i.e. before the 6C) identified through archeology and some Chinese writings. **"Folk Shinto"** derives from traditional peasant customs still practised widely at the beginning of the 1970s, and is based on annual observances involving respect for the earth's fertility, the sea, and the fecundity of women. While Folk Shinto can be seen as deriving from Primitive Shinto in the sense that peasants can trace their ancestry back to their prehistoric forebears, it shows that recent schisms in belief systems in Japan are nothing new. The **"Shinto of myths"** deals with the representation of the world as revealed in the divine saga *Kojiki (The Records of Ancient Matters)*, written in the 8C by members of the elite who sought to preserve knowledge threatened by the introduction of Chinese culture. **"Schools Shinto"** is a syncretic merging of teachings by one master, which developed chiefly between the 15C and 19C, while **"Shrine Shinto"** focuses on worship in important public shrines (from the 14C missionaries traveled through Japan praising the magical power of the divinity venerated in their sanctuary).

Finally, **Imperial Household Shinto** is performed by the Emperor at shrines in the grounds of the Imperial Palace.

Shinto is therefore a general term covering a range of different concepts, practices, outlooks, and perspectives linked only in that they were developed in the same part of the world, initially existing before Buddhism and subsequently refined in reaction to it. It is therefore difficult to define Shinto in precise and concise terms. It applies to a series of places, rites, and attitudes that the Japanese hold specific to their culture and which they are delighted to display to visitors as evidence of their profound and distinctive cultural identity.

Though Shinto has left few traces in art history, it is recognizable in the architecture of its shrines and in the joyful dynamism of its festivals. The discovery of this many-faceted religion is one of the great pleasures of traveling in Japan.

## BUDDHISM

Mahayana ("Great Vehicle") Buddhism arrived in Japan in the 6C, along with writing, science, the practice of divination, and the structuring of the state around a system of codes and the existence of an elite class.

Over 14 centuries, it formed part of the iconographic, literary, and philosophical advances made in Japan. When, in the 19C, it was necessary to understand Western concepts, they were explained in terms of the Buddhist vocabulary.

Buddhism developed in many forms, often in different but concurrent schools, which variously emphasized esoteric learning and a complex liturgy (Tendai, Shingon), an ascetic, mountain-dwelling lifestyle (the syncretic Buddhism of Shugendo), salvation for all, including women (Pure Land), or meditation (chiefly Zen schools). To some degree Buddhism's worldview penetrated every level and aspect of society, from the warrior elite to peasants and merchants, and from court poetry to street shows. It was strictly monitored by the ruling class who, when necessary, moved temples to more easily controlled localities. Buddhism was a network that reached throughout the whole country, playing a defining role in the creation of a national culture.

Today a large part of Japan's national heritage can be found in the treasuries and storehouses of Buddhist temples.

## THE NEW RELIGIONS

The freedom of worship imposed by the Americans following World War II sparked the blossoming of a multitude of religious organizations of every kind. Some 180,000 groups are legally recognized, of which over 500 are considered "new religions" (*shin-shukyo; shukyo* = "religion"). They claim more than 30 million adherents and some have spread overseas, with branches in Europe and the US, such as **Soka Gakkai** or **Tenri-kyo**, both founded before the war.

The 1970s saw the emergence of new religions, energetically proselytizing sects capable of recruiting thousands in a short time. They generally focused on mystical experiences and an exaggerated apocalyptic vision laid over previously distinct religious traditions. These sects tend to exacerbate the distrust with which most Japanese regard "religious institutions."

**Jean-Michel Butel**

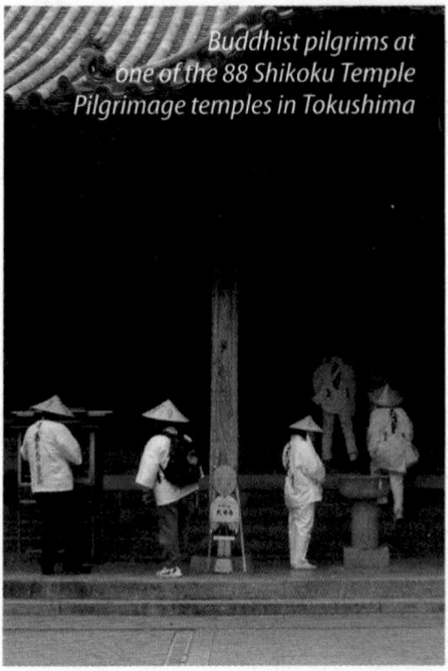

*Buddhist pilgrims at one of the 88 Shikoku Temple Pilgrimage temples in Tokushima*

©Yasufumi Nishi/JNTO

### Words of the religions

The literal meaning of *Bukkyo*, or Buddhism, is "the teaching *(kyo)* of the Buddha *(butsu).*"

The concept of religion as wisdom passed from master to disciple can also be found in the names of other movements in Japan: "teaching of the man of good will" (*jukyo*, Confucianism), "teaching of the way" (*dokyo*, Taoism), "the teaching of Christ" (*kurisuto-kyo*, Christianity), etc. Shinto constitutes a special case as the term, first used in the 15C, means the "way (*to*, another pronunciation of the Taoist *do*) of the gods" (*shin* for "gods," though *kami* is used when singular). This use of *do* is not unique to religion—*on-myo-do* is the "way of yin and yang," *ju-do* is "the way of suppleness," and *ken-do* "the way of the sword."

© Steve Vidler/Photoshot

*Computer game and comic shop in Akihabara*

# The Otaku Phenomenon

As the obligatory hangout for all *otaku* (addicts of video games, manga, and anime) the Akihabara district of Tokyo has become a magnet for a whole generation of curious young Westerners. Since they first appeared at the beginning of the 1980s, the Japanese *otaku* have met with criticism for what older Japanese see as antisocial behavior and an insatiable appetite for "frivolity". Emerging from the excesses of postindustrial Japanese society, the *otaku* are the children of the men and women who sacrificed everything to the gods of "Education," "Consumption," and "Information." Now, disenchanted with modern-day life, the *otaku* in their virtual universe seek to rediscover some form of psychological equilibrium within a society that has lost its points of reference.

Meaning "venerable house", an *otaku* was originally someone so devoted to their pursuit or hobby that they never left home. It has now acquired a perjorative sense for the Japanese, being used to describe someone with no social skills who has nothing better to do all day than play computer games or surf the Internet. Meeting at concerts and manga conventions, the young use it quite happily to describe each other, while Westerners tend to regard the term as less of an insult than the Japanese and more to describe someone who is an obsessive fan of virtual pastimes, or even a geek or a nerd.

Now, almost 30 years since it first appeared, the *otaku* generation is calling the shots. A former "gamer," **Tajiri Satoshi**, developed Pokémon, the celebrated video-game-based media franchise that has generated sales of more than $25 million worldwide. It was **Gainax**, the legendary *otaku*-founded studio, which produced and exploited the phenomenal success of *Evangelion*, the anime (Japanese animated film) packed with references calculated to appeal to the young. One-time pariahs, *otaku* who know how to capitalize on their creative sensibilities are now seen as experts in the content sector of Japanese industry, where the economic stakes have been hugely increased by recognition of the *otaku* subculture. Thanks to the Internet, *otaku* is now accessible all over the world, with millions of international enthusiasts. It has also spread to other areas of youth culture, including fashion, such as "GothLoli" (Gothic Lolita, a blend of punk style and cute little-girl clothing), *cosplay* (costume play) conventions (where fans dress up as video game heroes), and collecting "garage kits" (figurines of anime heroes) or "cels" (paintings on celluloid from cult anime series).

To see something of the world of the *otaku* for yourself, visit Tokyo's Akihabara or Nakano districts. Nakano Broadway is a multistory shopping mall where the original Mandarake store, founded in 1982 and the reference point for everything that the Japanese call *otaku*, is located. The Mandarake group is one of Tokyo's largest *otaku* companies. August is a good month for new enthusiasts to learn more about the culture. Comiket (comic market) is held in August (and December), as is the Wonder Festival, where garage kits are bought and sold.

**Étienne Barral**

Mushiage Bay, Seto Inland Sea

Tsuyama Castle, Kakuzan Park

Japanese sword forging, Bizen Osahune

Okayama Koraku-en, one of the three great gardens of Japan

# Okayama

http://okayama-japan.jp/en/

Protected Edo period merchant town scenery, Bikan Historical District, Kurashiki

Angel Road, Shodoshima Island

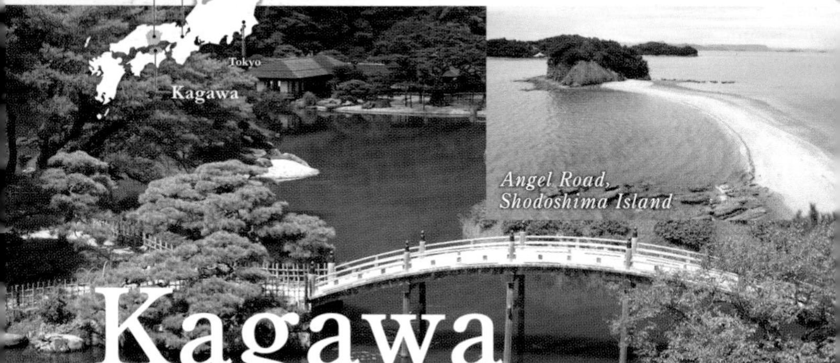


# Kagawa

http://www.pref.kagawa.lg.jp/

Ritsurin Garden, Takamatsu City

Yayoi Kusama " Red Pumpkin "
Photo:Osamu Watanabe ,Naoshima Island

Chichu Art Museum
Photo:FUJITSUKA Mitsumasa ,Naoshima Island

# Administration and Economy

**Japan was shaped by a long tradition of monarchy and strict hierarchies. After WW II, however, remarkable and lengthy political stability followed with the conservative Liberal Democratic Party majority. The bursting of the financial bubble in the early 1990s ended rapid economic growth, resulting in a restructured economy as well as recast political and social realms. Summer 2009 then brought great change in Japan, with Yukio Hatoyama leading the Democratic Party in a landslide victory. The DPJ finance minister Naoto Kan succeeded him the following June; he in turn was succeeded by Yoshihiko Noda in summer 2011.**

### Political parties

Japan has a wide spectrum of political parties ranging from the Communist Party (Kyosanto) to the Nationalist Party (Kokuminto), by way of New Komeito, a center-right party associated with the large Buddhist organization Soka Gakkai. Today's power politics mostly involve two large parties: the **Liberal Democratic Party** (LDP, Jiminto), which has been in power almost without interruption since 1955, and the **Democratic Party of Japan** (DPJ, Minshuto), formed in 1996 by the merger between the New Party for Progress (NPP) and elements of the Socialist Party (SPJ).

## POLITICS

### THE POLITICAL SYSTEM

Japan's parliamentary system is similar to that of the UK, with a two-chamber National Diet. The **1946 Constitution** is based on the principles of pacifism and the separation of power, giving sovereignty to the people, as opposed to the Emperor, who is "the symbol of the State and of the unity of the people," but with no political power. Article 9 of the Constitution forbids any acts of war by the State but authorizes the maintenance of a professional army for self-defense. It is 250,000-strong and very well equipped. Since 1990, in the context of renewed cooperation with the US and the threat from North Korea, this self-defense force has been regularly engaged on the international scene in security operations under the UN and in support of the US in Iraq.

Legislative authority is vested in the two houses of the **Diet**, which are elected by universal suffrage. There are 480 representatives (House of Representatives), who are elected for a four-year term, and 250 senators (House of Councillors), half of whose membership is re-elected every three years. Executive power is devolved to the Cabinet chosen by the **Prime Minister**, who is selected from members of the Diet. He has authority to dissolve assemblies but it is difficult to govern without political control over both Houses. **Judicial authority** is independent of both Houses and controlled by a Supreme Court, whose role is to protect the Constitution and exercise judicial review over tribunals and Courts of Appeal. The Japanese make relatively little recourse to the law and the judicial system is underdeveloped. The death penalty is still in force.

### A CHANGING ADMINISTRATION

The administration consists of agencies and ministries, of which the MITI (now METI, the Ministry of Economy, Trade, and Industry), as leader in economic development, plays a central role in the Japanese state. The ineffectual but powerful central administration largely relies on local authorities to implement its policies and is heavily dependent on the private sector.

The substantial police force is supervised by the NPA, the National Police Agency. A network of community police units operating from some 6,500 local substations *(koban)* ensures excellent neighborhood security.

## ECONOMY

Thanks to a period of spectacular expansion from 1955 to 1990, Japan became the **world's second largest economy**, a position which China could assume for 2010. In 2009 its GDP (Gross Domestic Product) reached $5.068 trillion (£3.096 trillion) with an unemployment rate of 5.1 percent.

Highly developed infrastructures make it easy to move around, and with 20 international airports and many seaports, Japan is the springboard for Asia. However, the country has recently suffered two major crises, firstly with the 1973 oil crisis and then the collapse of the "speculative bubble" in the early 1990s. To re-establish its economy and adapt to a changing world, the Japanese government has adopted a policy of low interest rates and a major program of public works.

## ENERGY DEPENDENCE

Japan's fishing industry is one of the world's largest; its plentiful rivers used to irrigate the rice fields and to produce hydroelectricity. Its large and varied forests supply timber for construction. However, the country is heavily dependent on **imports of essential raw materials** and the energy needed for its development. To reduce its dependence on imported fuel, it has turned to nuclear power and 28 percent of the electricity generated now comes from this, compared with around 20 percent in both the US and UK. Japan works hard to save energy in all areas of life and is considered the world's technological leader in this respect.

## RICE AND FISH

The scarcity of arable land suitable for large-scale crop growing has been compensated by the mastery of irrigation techniques developed over the centuries. Rice is the basis of the Japanese diet and **riziculture** still the major crop in half the cultivated land of the alluvial plains, the rest being devoted to high-value crops such as flowers, fruits, or vegetables. Agriculture represents 1 percent of GDP. The island of Hokkaido is today the only region under extensive agricultural cultivation.

**Fish and seafood** form a significant element of the Japanese diet. Japan has developed a strong fishing industry, both coastal and offshore, thanks to the country's fleet of processing vessels. Aquaculture is a growth sector.

However, **Japan is no more than 39 percent self-sufficient in its dietary requirements**, representing a permanent threat for the country in the event of international crisis.

## A GLOBAL ECONOMY

**Industry** (31 percent of GDP) is Japan's strong point and it leads the world in many sectors: shipbuilding, automotive, chemistry, robotics, electronics, semiconductors, viewdata (videotext), bio-industries, and new materials. Japan is **the world's third largest exporter**, almost exclusively in the areas of high value-added products or cultural products such as manga and anime, while importing cheaper products in return. The Japanese economy also benefits from the rapid growth in other Asian economies, especially that of China, which has become a major economic partner.

Thanks to a large balance of payments surpluses, Japan has made significant overseas investments, so becoming a **major financial power**. Nevertheless Japan remains vulnerable to fluctuations in the world economy because of its energy dependence and the lack of resources.

Today, the country seeks to exploit its **capacity for innovation**. The government has focused on robotics, nanotechnologies, information and environmental technology, and Japan's expenditure on research represents 3.5 percent of GDP (US: 2.6 percent/UK: 1.7 percent, OECD 2006 figures), with 70 percent coming from the private sector.

**Bernard Delmas**

# History

**With its position on the western margins of the Pacific Ocean, beyond mainland Asia, Japan's history has been marked by insularity. In spite of centuries of tumult and marked regional contrasts the Japanese archipelago has remained strongly united. Apart from a few years at the end of World War II, it has never been colonized or occupied. This innovative and pragmatic civilization of extremes has been influenced by other countries, however, and now as a modern, industrialized country Japan is resolutely open to the rest of the world.**

## THE MAJOR ERAS

### PREHISTORY

The earliest signs of civilization in Japan date from the **Jomon** era, an 11-million-year period that lasted from around 10,500 to 300 BC. Its people were hunter-gatherers, fishers, and weavers. The development of bartering led to settlement in villages and pottery making. Even before it was applied to the whole period, the term jomon, meaning "cord pattern," was used to describe the decoration of the first pots discovered, the world's oldest. Jars, statuettes, figurines, generally female and often with a swelling belly, are evidence of the role of pottery in ritual practices and daily life. The exuberance of the forms and motifs in those prehistoric times, which vary depending on period and region, reveal remarkable artistry.
During the **Yayoi** era (300 **BC–AD** 300), named after an archeological site near Tokyo, the first wheel-turned pottery was found. This period is also notable for the development of irrigated wet-rice cultivation and cereal culture, while bronze and iron work also became widespread.

### THE KOFUN ERA (3–7C)

The term *kofun* describes the burial mounds raised for members of the ruling class, in which furniture, weapons, and jewelry were buried with the deceased.

*Haniwa "dancers," Kofun era*



Outside the tomb *haniwa* (cylindrical pottery and hollow clay statues) guarded the funerary monuments. The era of these great tumuli marks the beginning of political centralization with the emergence of a state in the Yamato region and the emergence of the clan system *(uji)*. This powerful Yamato polity, south of Nara, would come to dominate nearly all the country—with the exception of the north of the archipelago, home of the Ainu—creating an imperial dynasty whose authority could not be questioned as it was claimed to be of divine origin *(see box p68)*.

### THE ASUKA ERA (592–710)

The dynasty established at Asuka during the Yamato period introduced reforms to Japan, which was transformed by the arrival of Korean and Chinese immigrants to the country, the introduction of new techniques such as the adoption of Chinese written characters, and the domestication of horses. When Buddhism was introduced in the 6C, Japan assimilated Sino-Indian culture. The Empress Suiko (593–628) laid the foundations of an imperial administration based on the Chinese model. Her nephew and heir, the Prince Regent Shotoku Taishi (574–622), proclaimed Buddhism to be the State religion, built temples dedicated to the Enlightened One, and promulgated a "17 Article Constitution." During the reign of Emperor Kotoku (645–54), power was centralized in a series of administrative measures known as the **Taika reforms**, based on the example of China's Tang dynasty. Peasants and their lands were placed under the authority of the Imperial Court. In 663, under the guise of an alliance with the Korean kingdom of Paekche, soldiers of the Yamato empire invaded the Korean kingdoms of Koguryo and Silla, but were wiped out.

## THE NARA ERA (710–94)

In 710, Empress Genmei established a permanent capital at Nara (**Heijo-kyo**), abandoning the custom of changing the location of the Imperial residence after the death of each emperor. Administrative and penal codes were enacted, which were to remain in place for over a thousand years. Techniques learned from Korean craftsmen brought the arts of ceramics, bronze, silk, and architecture to a high level and they were developed into a specifically Japanese art. Imposing Buddhist monasteries such as Horyu-ji, Kofuku-ji, and Todai-ji were also built.

## THE ARISTOCRATIC HEIAN ERA (794–1185)

Founded in 794, **Heian-kyo** ("capital of peace and tranquility"), present-day **Kyoto**, became the seat of the Imperial Court in preference to Nara, the country's former political and religious center. Emperor Kanmu (737–806) ordered this transfer to escape the influence of the Buddhist schools installed at Nara, which instead of devoting themselves to spiritual matters, too often interfered with political issues. The new capital would remain the heart of Japan for more than a thousand years.

Japan now developed its own writing systems (*hiragana* and *katakana*), and this was a golden age for literature. Feminine influence predominated, particularly in literature. With *The Tale of Genji (Genji monogatari)*, Murasaki Shikibu (973–1016) (*see p97*). During the same period, the poetess Sei Shonagon wrote *The Pillow Book (Makura no soshi)*, intimate observations on the lives of her contemporaries.

In this "Florence of the Far East," the Emperor appointed *kanpaku* (senior advisors) responsible for government business, who soon managed to arrogate imperial power to themselves and effectively ruled the country. Chief among the holders of this almost hereditary office were the **Fujiwara** clan, which led to many feuds among the aristocracy while the great landowning monasteries armed themselves to defend both their lands and status.

## THE KAMAKURA ERA (1185–1333)

A troubled period followed. Far from the influence of the court, principalities emerged under the protection of local chieftains. For centuries local warlords struggled for power, weakening central rule. During this period Japan became the battleground for a succession of military conflicts. The powerful chief **Minamoto no Yoritomo** defeated the warrior **Taira clan**, consolidating the supremacy of the Minamoto family. The Emperor in Kyoto awarded the title of **shogun** (military governor) to

### Mythical origins

The earliest Japanese literary work still in existence, the *Kojiki*, compiled in 712, gives an account of the history of Japan and its mythological origins. One of the primary Shinto sources, it recounts the creation of Heaven and Earth. According to Shinto myth, the imperial dynasty that founded the Japanese nation was descended from the radiant sun goddess **Amaterasu**, daughter of Izanagi, who was held to be the direct ancestress of **Jinmu**, first emperor of Japan. Subsequent emperors claimed to be descended from Jinmu, attributing divine origins to the Imperial Dynasty. The myth consecrated the imperial line and gave it political legitimacy.

the Conqueror, who settled at Kamakura in the modern-day prefecture of Kanagawa. During these years new Buddhist trends emerged, including the Zen school of meditation.

The **powerful military caste** owed its fame to *bushido* (the way of the samurai), a chivalrous code of honor and loyalty marked by the practical application of Zen teaching and neo-Confucian precepts such as fidelity to duty and respect for the clan. The warrior class became dominant to the detriment of the Imperial Court, which lost its influence over the State's affairs.

At the end of the 13C the Mongols stepped up their conquest of Asia and Kublai Khan, grandson of Genghis Khan, called on Japan to pay tribute to China, threatening reprisals if they failed to do so. His ultimatum rejected, so he launched an expeditionary force in 1274. The attempt failed but a second invasion was launched in 1281. A fleet of warships carrying over 100,000 men tried to land in Japan.

Repulsed from the Kyushu coastline, the Mongol fleet was caught in a typhoon and destroyed. The Japanese call this wind that saved them *kamikaze*, literally "divine wind."

## THE MUROMACHI ERA (1336–1573)

The history of this unstable period is inextricably complex and characterized by internal struggles. It began in 1336 with the short-lived restoration of Imperial power initiated by Emperor Go-Daigo, who tried to undermine the Kamakura regime with the help of the powerful warlord Ashikaga Takauji (1305–58), a direct descendant of the Minamoto family.

Takauji subsequently turned against Go-Daigo in favor of another emperor (Komyo), who awarded him the title of shogun in 1338. Go-Daigo fled to Yoshino in the north, near Nara, while Komyo set up his court in the Muromachi district of Kyoto. There were therefore **two Imperial Courts**, Go-Daigo's, known as the Southern Court in Yoshino, and that of Komyo, known as the Northern Court, in Kyoto. The rivalry lasted nearly 60 years.

While the first Portuguese and Spanish traders imported gunpowder, the missionaries following in their wake preached the Gospel. In 1549, the Jesuit Francis Xavier introduced **Christianity** to Japan.

## THE AZUCHI–MOMOYAMA ERA (1573–1603)

In this transitional period, general **Toyotomi Hideyoshi** (1536–98) completed the unification of the country initiated by Oda Nobunaga (1534–82) and decided to consolidate his power by attempting to conquer the Korean peninsula and thereafter China. In 1592 and 1597, he sent expeditionary forces to Korea. The Chinese army repulsed the attackers and the Koreans rose against the occupation troops, refusing to accept Japanese sovereignty. Hostilities finally ceased with the death of Hideyoshi, which precipitated a succession crisis that ended with the accession of **Tokugawa Ieyasu** (1542–1616).

## THE EDO ERA (1603–1867)

Although the Emperor nominally ruled from Kyoto, the **Tokugawa Shogunate** established its administrative capital at **Edo** (present-day Tokyo), seat of the military government. Tokugawa Ieyasu consolidated his power by eliminating his rivals, the supporters of the Toyotomi clan. The Tokygawa clan ruled without interruption for more than 250 years, controlling all aspects of political and social life. In 1613, Christianity was banned, Japanese converts persecuted, and the missionaries expelled. Fearing European expansionism, the authorities **closed the country to foreigners**, with the exception of Korean diplomats, a few Chinese merchants, and Dutch traders of the East India Company, who were allowed to operate in the Nagasaki harbor area alone. No Japanese person was permitted to travel outside the empire. The country turned in upon itself but trade was not totally suppressed and this was an era of peace and security, synonymous with **urban expansion** and **tremendous cultural develop-**

Drawing of Commodore Perry landing for peace and trade talks on March 8, 1854

©Bettmann/Corbis

**ment**. Merchants and craftsmen flourished. Many samurai were now out of work, having lost their masters in wars and conflicts; known as *ronin* ("masterless"), some turned to revolt. Japan underwent a demographic explosion. Then Western expansionism threw everything into turmoil. In 1853, a fleet of "black ships" commanded by Commodore Matthew Perry anchored in the bay of Edo and demanded the relaxation of trade restrictions. Fearing a naval bombardment, the Japanese were obliged to abandon their isolationism; the shogunate, forced to sign a treaty of friendship with the Americans, followed by a commercial treaty. Russia, Britain, France, and The Netherlands rushed into the breach and similar agreements were signed, known to the Japanese authorities as **"unequal treaties,"** that gave foreign traders exorbitant customs privileges (from 1895 they were revised after lengthy representation from Japanese diplomats). This coup led to a wave of national protest that was to prove fatal for the Tokugawa regime.

## THE MEIJI ERA (1868–1912)

Forced to abandon its isolation under pressure from Western powers, the insular empire now moved toward modernization with startling speed. Industrial, political, social, and cultural upheavals swept away the power of the shoguns. The **restoration of imperial power** signaled the end of the regime of clans and fiefs. The feudal system was abolished. A **Constitution** was adopted in 1889 and, while it acknowledged the emperor's supreme power and divine right, it also established a parliamentary system with elected representatives. Shinto became the state religion and Buddhism was disestablished. Japan's former ruling elite abandoned their status as warlords to go into battle on the economic front, and the yen became the national currency. In less than 30 years Japan became a great power and joined the ranks of capitalist countries with the watchwords "rich country, strong military." Formosa, now Taiwan, was annexed in 1895 and Korea in 1910.

## THE TAISHO ERA (1912–26)

The initial euphoria following the democratization of politics and society gradually faded but the island empire felt it was on the right track. For many Japanese, the Taisho period also brought changes in their way of life with the development of a popular and urban culture, the opening of leisure parks, and the growth of cinema, radio, and liberal publishing houses. All this continued until the terrible earthquake of 1923, which destroyed much of Tokyo.

## THE SHOWA ERA (1926–89)

In 1926, Hirohito succeeded the Imperial throne. Japan now recognized as a great power by the West, pursued its policy of colonial expansion to the extent of occupying Manchuria (1931) in northeastern China, hungry for its mineral and agricultural wealth. During the 1930s militarists seized control of the government with the aim of making Japan master of Asia. Criticized on the international scene, Japan left the League of Nations in 1933 and a few years later formed an alliance with the fascist regimes of the German–Italian Axis, confident the Soviet Union would remain neutral. **Militarism** and **ultranationalism** led to repression, while propaganda was used to justify expansionism. In 1937, Japan mounted a full-scale invasion of China, launching the second Sino-Japanese War, which later merged into the **Pacific War**, when the bombing of Pearl Harbor on December 7, 1941 prompted the United States to declare war on Japan. Although the Japanese dominated Asia and the Pacific, their defeat by American naval forces at the Battle of Midway in June 1942 changed the course of the war.

Following massive incendiary bombing of Tokyo, the President of the United States, Harry Truman, decided to unleash atomic power against Japan. The first atomic bomb was dropped over Hiroshima on August 6, 1945, killing 140,000 people. Three days later, a second bomb was dropped on Nagasaki, killing 70,000 civilians. These tragedies brought Japan to its knees.

**Jean-Luc Toula-Breysse**

## POSTWAR JAPAN

Few would have guessed that a country with a lower per capita rate of income than Malaya at the end of World War II would have the highest standard of living in the world within 45 years. Yet Japan has astounded the world with its postwar meteoric trajectory, transforming itself from a nation in defeat to one of the most successful economic forces on earth. Japan regained its poise and dug deep to find the resources and national strength to catapult itself to the status of a world economic power. In 1951, Japan's GNP was $14.2 billion—half of West Germany, three times less than Britain and only 4.2 percent of the USA's economy. By 1970, Japan had overtaken every economy in Europe to represent over 20 percent of the US's GNP. In 1975, it was double that of the United Kingdom, and in 1980, reached $1,040 billion—around 40 percent of that of the US. Yet Japan's postwar era is testament to more than just an ability to conjure up impressive digits: it demonstrates a resolute determination to rebuilding—in social and economic terms. Few countries have experienced such extraordinary and rapid changes in daily life, material culture, as well as pecuniary fortunes as it sought to redefine its role in the world.

### The Aftermath of War

After yielding to **American occupation** (1945–52) and a program of demilitarization and democratization, Japan conceded many US demands. This brought significant legal changes to the Japanese family system, providing a woman with legal rights equal to those of her husband in terms of property ownership and divorce.

Daughters were given the right to inherit the same property as sons. Males at the age of 18 and females at the age of 16 were also now able to marry without parental consent. Suffrage proved a popular move that won widespread support. Japan, in turn, negotiated the retention of its Imperial institution. Japan's postwar occupation by the US-led Allied Powers began in August 1945 and ended in April 1952. The American general **Douglas MacArthur** was its first Supreme Commander.

After destroying the remains of Japan's war machine, the US general held crime trials. Over 500 military officers committed suicide immediately after Japan surrendered, while many hundreds more were executed after being found guilty of war crimes. In 1947, a new constitution took effect with MacArthur intent on decentralization and widespread land reform. During the occupation, Japan's media was subject to rigid censorship. Despite this, the transition period was relatively smooth, with good levels of Japanese cooperation with the Allied Powers. In 1952, the **1951 San Francisco Peace Treaty** took effect and occupation ended.

Japan was once again an independent state, regaining its sovereignty, having pledged concord with 48 nations.

### Cultural and Societal Shifts

During American occupation, Japan's various segments of society had sought ways to bolster their own cultural identity against the constantly shifting political and economic contexts of the transition. Postwar shifts in demographics brought great change to the composition of Japanese communities amid immense material influences of Westernization.

Faced with the diluting effect of large-scale migration and social transformation, Japan fought hard to retain its own identity in the face of tremendous cultural change, shunning many outside influences.

### Political Reformation

Rumbles of political wrangling reached boiling point in 1960, prompting a major sea-change in the Japanese political system. The merging of the socialist parties was the catalyst for the joining together of the conservative prewar Liberal and Democratic parties to secure a majority of legislative seats and create the one-and-a-half-party system that dominated Japanese politics for over 30 years.

It prompted widespread unrest and resistance in 1960 with the Liberal Democratic Party (LDP) making numerous high-profile bids to undo occupation-era reforms. Protests against the renewal of the US–Japan Security Treaty (Anpo) followed, along with a labor strike at the Miike coal mines in Kyushu. As a result, the LDP sacked its party leader and promoted an economic "income-doubling" plan—a highly successful initiative with the Japanese populous.

### Facing the World

Winning the bid to host the **Olympics** in 1964 prompted a much-needed construction boom across the country. Redevelopment significantly reshaped not only the landscape but also, in many ways, the psyche and outlook of its people, spawning the famous **bullet train** (Shinkansen), emblematic of Japan's high-tech capabilities and push for modernization. Japan's sleek, high-speed rail system grabbed headlines across the world in the run-up to the Games. The spectacle of the Olympiad presented the Japanese government with a vehicle to showcase around the globe its revitalized postwar image as a peaceful, democratic, and unified nation. Cultural virtues figured prominently in Japan's Olympic publicity package for the Olympics, an ostensibly safe theme that nevertheless was shaped by and contributed to political forces of the time.

This 'Coming Out Party' worked well for Japan, showcasing its remarkable postwar economic development in a glittering event that consigned Tokyo's withdrawal as host of the 1940 Games due to the outbreak of war to history. Twenty-four years later, at a cost of over $3 billion, Tokyo celebrated the 1964 Tokyo Games with 93 participating nations (5,151 athletes) as a proclamation of Japan's post-war reconstruction and emergence as a major political and economic force worldwide. To underline that theme, the final torchbearer was **Yoshinori Sakai**, who was born in Hiroshima the day the city was destroyed by an atomic bomb (August 6, 1945). The Games passed without controversy, heralding Japan's new era of technological-led prosperity.

Cutting-edge architecture won considerable praise from Olympic organizers, in particular the **Budokan**, modeled on age-old Japanese temple traditions, and a magnificent futuristic swimming venue that was hailed "the cathedral of sports" by IOC chiefs. Japan's standing in the world community was further enhanced when Sapporo played host to the 1972 Winter Olympic Games.

## TIME LINE

**10,500–300 BC – Jomon era**. Sedentarism.
**660 BC** Mythical founding of Japan by Emperor Jinmu, descended from goddess Amaterasu.
**300 BC–AD 300** Yayoi era.
**3–7C** Kofun era, burial mounds.
**592–710** Asuka era. Introduction of Buddhism. 1st Constitution.
**710–94** Nara era. Introduction of legal codes.
**794–1185** Heian era. Foundation of the Rinzai Zen school by Eisai (12C).
**1185–1333** Kamakura era.
**1336–1573** Muromachi era. Civil wars and peasant revolts. Catholicism preached by the Jesuit Francis Xavier (1549).
**1573–1603** Momoyama era. Reunification of the country.
**1603–1867** Edo or Tokugawa era. Japan's ancien régime is at its peak; Christianity banned. The country turns in on itself.
**1853–67** Bakumatsu period. The end of the shogunate. Commodore Perry's American fleet forces the country to open to the West (1853).
**1868** Start of the Meiji era. Restoration of imperial rule.
**1889** – Promulgation of the Constitution.
**1894–5** – First Sino-Japanese war.
**1904–5** Russo–Japanese war. Japanese victory in Manchuria.
**1910** Japan annexes Korea.
**1912–26** Taisho era. Tentative democratic advances.
**1914** Japan declares war on Germany.
**1919** Treaty of Versailles: Japan seizes German territories in the Pacific and China. It joins the League of Nations.
**1923** Great Kanto Earthquake (*see p70*).
**1931** Occupation of Manchuria.
**1945** US atomic bombs dropped on Hiroshima (August 6) and Nagasaki (August 9). Japan capitulates unconditionally on August 15, surrenders on September 2.
**1947** New Constitution.
**1952** Japan recovers its independence.
**1956** Japan joins the United Nations.
**1964** First Asian Olympic Games held in Tokyo.
**1972** US restores control of the Okinawa archipelago to Japan.
**1989** Death of Emperor Hirohito. Prince Akihito becomes emperor of Japan.
**1995** Kobe earthquake (Jan 17). Sarin gas attack in Tokyo (March 20)
**2005** Aichi International Exhibition.
**2006** Princess Kiko gives birth to Prince Hisahito, third in line to the throne. Shinzo Abe is elected Prime Minister.
**2007** Yasuo Fukuda becomes Prime Minister.
**2008** Taro Aso succeeds Yasuo Fukuda as the Japanese Prime Minister.
**2009** For the first time in Japanese history, the DPJ (the Democratic Party) wins a victory over the LDP (the Liberal Democratic Party). Yukio Hatoyama is elected Prime Minister.
**22 Jul 2009** Solar eclipse in Japan/Asia.
**2010** Yukio Hatoyama is the fourth Prime Minister to resign in four years. Naoto Kan succeeds him.
**11 Mar 2011** A magnitude 9 earthquake off the coast of Tohoku and the resulting tsunami cause widespread destruction, including substantial damage to Fukushima nuclear power plant.
**30 Aug 2011** –Yoshihiko Noda elected Prime Minister by parliament.

### Economic Climb

Japan's postwar economy is characterized by a 15-year period of high growth, beginning in the mid-1950s, that allowed it to catch up with the developed economies of the USA and Europe. In many ways Japan was haunted by its bilateral agreement as it allowed detractors to suggest that the country's postwar economic climb owed much to the efforts of its former enemy. Certainly, the US did not require Japan to pay war reparations. In fact, by 1951, the US had poured over $2 billion into the Japanese economy. Japan's renouncement of militarism meant that it need only spend a minimal amount on defense (around 1 percent of its GNP), allowing the government to invest more public funds into programs for developing the nation's industries. However, other social scientists point to the tremendous stress this "US help" placed on the Japanese economy. Postwar inflation resulted in a total augmentation of 15,000 percent from 1945 through 1949, with the US imposing three harsh measures: a balanced budget, the suspension of all state loans to industry, and the abolition of all state subsidies. The Yen was set to a favorable rate of 360 for 1 US$ to stimulate export. What is certain, politics aside, is that Japan was in a severely weakened and exhausted state in the aftermath of World War II and that to revive itself as a nation, and to revamp its political and social infrastructure, it required assistance. Most of its cities had been devastated by attack, with 60 percent of Tokyo razed to the ground by Allied firebombing raids. Air attacks had destroyed 30 percent of Japan's industrial capacity.

Bolstered by high rates of personal savings, healthy private-sector facilities' investment, a committed labor force with a strong work ethic, plentiful supplies of cheap oil, innovative technology, and effective government intervention in private-sector industries, Japan reaped the rewards of its swift-growing postwar thrust and cut. It fine-tuned its competitive strength and achieved economic growth based on exports, private-sector facilities' investment, and the successful stimulation of strong domestic demand that powered an industrial explosion in cities nationwide. By 1965 manufacturing had quadrupled in terms of output compared with prewar figures. Dominating the industrial sector were iron and steel, ship building, machine tools, motor vehicles, and electronics. However, this strong and rapid economic growth did take its toll on the environment.

Much like China today, Japan suffered a significant environmental backlash as a result of its thrust for industrialization, sparking strong opposition and protest across the world. As a nation so in tune with its natural landscape—Japan has a strongly-held traditional ethos that balance is achieved in harmony with the cycles of nature—the strength of this ecological criticism came as a shock. Yet, the Japanese government eventually conceded its mushrooming cities had grown at the expense of natural habitat and clean, pure air.

### International Relations

Despite its wealth and position in the world economy, Japan wielded little influence in global politics for much of the postwar period. A dispute over the Soviet occupation of what Japan calls its Northern Territories (the two most southerly islands in the Kurils (Etorofu and Kunashiri) and Shikotan and the Habomai Islands northeast of Hokkaido, which were seized by the Soviet Union shortly after Japan's World War II surrender), saw Japanese residents deported to Japan, leaving 30,000 Russians on the isles. Although this dispute remains unresolved, in 1956 the **Japan–Soviet Joint Declaration** restored diplomatic ties between the two nations, although a formal peace deal remained out of reach because of the territorial dispute. In 1972, then **Prime Minister Kakuei Tanaka** visited the Republic of China, where he expressed a keen consciousness of Japan's responsibility in the war as well as its intent to realize normal relations between the two countries.

The 1980s saw Japan experience its history textbook controversy in which elements of a "regrettable" past were erased from official memory. Notably, at the time of the death of **Hirohito** (the Emperor whose reign spanned wartime and postwar Japan) in 1989, neither the State nor the Emperor had uttered a clear public apology to other Asian countries for colonial rule and wartime aggression.

Events during the mid- and late-1990s, such as difficult relations between Beijing and Taipei, and the 1998 North Korea missile launch, forced Japan to begin taking security issues more seriously. Japan sought to strengthen its military might, participating in the Gulf War in 1991—just at the time when the country was experiencing the dizzying heights of an unprecedented economic boom-time.

### Oil Shock

Just as Japan settled into an easy economic rhythm in the 1970s, President Richard Nixon's decision to unilaterally end fixed currency exchange rates brought with it a reminder of the country's economic vulnerability and dependency on the US market. In 1971, the American administration imposed a 10 percent surcharge on Japanese imports and pressurized the Japanese Government to revalue the yen upward—much to Japan's chagrin. With over 30 percent of its exports with the US, Japan faced an acute economic crisis. The surcharge prompted rapid contingency planning that saw major state projects, such as the new Tokyo airport at Sanrizuka, pushed to the fore. As the country's main source of energy, oil import supply was a priority in the Japanese Government's energy policy. However, oil increased in price from $2 a barrel to $11 in 1973, to $24 a barrel in 1974, to $35 a barrel in late-1979—a nightmare scenario for the energy-strapped nation. This scenario prompted strenuous energy-saving efforts and technological innovations during crises commonly remembered as "oil shock" by the Japanese. As a result, Japan only requires 12,098gal/55kl of crude oil—nearly half the 23,317gal/106kl it once did—to generate 100 million yen in GDP.

### Technological Shifts

Pressures regarding environmental pollution also sparked a shift toward high-tech and service-sector business as Japan moved its heavy and chemical industries offshore.

A succession of political scandals forced Prime Minister Tanaka Kakuei out of office. In 1982, under the leadership of **Prime Minister Nakasone Yasuhiro**, the privatization of certain state-run enterprises was achieved with some success. As a result of the rapid rate of industrialization, only 18 percent of Japan's labor force was employed in the agricultural sector compared with 50 percent in the 1930s. Major changes began to occur in 1961, the year in which the **Agricultural Basic Law** came into force with the aim of structurally reforming the agricultural sector. The changes, however, were ironically for the worse, not the better, as between 1960 and 2005 agricultural production's share of GDP fell from 9 percent to 1 percent, the agricultural working population from 11.96 million to 2.52 million, the proportion of the total working population employed in agriculture from 26.6 percent to 4 percent, and the number of farming households from 6.06 million to 2.85 million. Furthermore, the percentage of elderly farmers in the farming community has increased to over 50 percent and this aging population is a concern.

Today, Japan's food self-sufficiency—once a proud boast of the nation—has dropped below 40 percent. In 2008, the head of Japan's National Agriculture and Food Research Organization (NAFR) launched a slew of new agricultural concepts and technologies aimed at turning round Japan's agricultural fortunes in conjunction with its consumption-based society.

To some extent, programs to revitalize country life in the late-1980s and 1990s rejuvenated Japan's love affair with its rural regions—although there is still a strong desire within many Japanese people to be viewed as thoroughly urban and modern.

### Banking Woes

During the late-1980s, the region accounted for nearly one-half of the world's expansion, so when the full force of Japan's banking crisis dealt its body-blow, the nation was sent reeling into a deep, painful, and prolonged recession. Japan's accelerated program of deregulation and deepening of capital markets without an appropriate adjustment in the regulatory framework were blamed, together with its weak corporate governance and regulatory forbearance. Rapid credit expansion during the 1980s had placed Japan in a fragile position: the bubble had well and truly burst. The 1995 Kobe earthquake and sarin gas attack by religious cult Aum Shinrikyo in Tokyo's subway system compounded the country's woes. Both events came as challenges to the Japanese Government, and all this against a backdrop of a fast-growing population that had seen over 50 million added to the Japanese roll-call since the end of World War II.

### Population Growth

Japan's population density rapidly became a drain on residential space in major cities, with over 330 people per sq km—a figure that quintuples in the context of habitable land, resulting in overcrowding in Japanese cities. As the urban sprawl continued to burgeon, Japan's rural areas suffered depopulation as workers abandoned jobs in farming, fishing, and forestry for the bright lights and salaries of the cities.

Japan also began to emerge as an exporter of culture during the 1980s as a cult audience around the world began consuming manga (comic books), kaiju (monster) movies, anime (cartoons), and other elements of modern Japanese culture. In the early 1950s, US soldiers returning from the occupation became the first exporters of Japanese storybooks, drawings, and artifacts. Subsequently, US troops based in Japan further played their part in sending a steady stream of cartoons and comics back to friends and family at home. In Japan itself, contemporary forms of popular culture became a form of escape from the problems of an industrial world during the 1990s. Around this, the annual **Japan Fantasy Novel Award** was launched in acknowledgment of the rising popularity of this genre.

Japan's overpopulation crisis had been mooted in the 1930s, prompting the passing of a **Eugenics Law** in 1949 that allowed for abortion based on economic necessity. As a result, the fertility rate dropped by around a half but is still expected to exceed 100 million by 2050, according to current United Nations projections. Life expectancy has risen by nearly 30 years since the end of World War II (now 78 for men and 84.6 for women), while infant mortality has dropped to one of the lowest in the world. Maternal mortality is now virtually zero. Japan's postwar demographics also bear testament to the mass migration from the countryside to the cities with over half of the nation's residents living in Tokyo, the Nagoya region, and the Osaka–Kobe area by the mid-1980s.

Central Tokyo was partially destroyed during the war, but rebuilt along established patterns because it retained its role as Japan's commercial hub and government center. Vast housing projects (known as *danchi*) were built around this trio of key metropolitan areas, becoming middle-class enclaves that represented the beginnings of consumer culture and the supposedly less hectic life of suburbia while easing overcrowding. These neat, modern residential zones epitomized the Japanese postwar dream of family prosperity and mirrored the surge in domestic consumer demand for high-tech goods and labor-saving devices.

### Consumerism Takes Hold

By the mid-1960s refrigerators, washing machines, and TVs had all become highly prized must-have items, with demand for cars and air-conditioning high. At staggering speed, "ordinary" Japanese were able to buy these goods, not just long for them, following Prime Minister Ikeda Hayato's pledge to double the average Japanese income within a decade. The average Japanese family consumed 75 percent more in goods and services than its counterparts in the mid-1930s. As society became more affluent, parents began to invest greater income in the education of their children. University became an accepted norm, with over 90 percent of Japanese children graduating from high school by the mid-1970s—a figure that has risen to 97 percent in recent years. Today, Japanese students attend school 5.5 days a week, 240 days a year compared with 180 days in the US. By the 1980s, Japan's new postwar generation was growing up knowing only affluence and social unity. Today, over 90 percent of Japanese describe themselves as "middle class", with the gap between rich and poor in Japan less than that of the USA. By 1981, Japan was the largest producer of motor vehicles, and by 1983 the country produced nearly 30 percent of all motor vehicles in the world. By 1985, Japan had also cornered the world market in electronic cameras, radios, quartz watches, TVs, calculators, VCRs, stereo equipment, computers, silicon memory chips, and genetic engineering. In 1982, 90 percent of all VCRs were made in Japan, and 70 percent of all computers.

Technology companies continue to invest massively in research and development to stay ahead of the world's great innovating nations and modernize their products and production techniques. Furthermore, a combination of demanding consumers and prolonged economic hard times has also taught Japanese companies how to adapt—quickly. As markets ebb and flow, Japan's leading companies have turned understanding consumer habits—and their changes—into a science. Few nations are as precise in anticipating consumer trends as Japan, where new products are created, distribution channels altered, and the basis of competition redefined at the same time as cost-cutting is evaluated. Accounting for 80 percent of consumers' financial assets and income, this segment has continued to grow in one of the most rapidly aging countries, where a more frugal mindset remains a legacy of the prewar era.

### The Post Postwar Era

Conversely, despite a government proclamation in its 1956 Economic White Paper that the "postwar era was over" *(mohaya sengo de wa nai)* many social scientists, including those within Japan itself, still questioned if this is so many decades on. However, on the 60th anniversary of the end of World War II in 2005, Japan could finally lay this period to rest. It was a fundamental watershed in modern Japanese history, signifying the "final end" of the postwar era, denoting a drawing of a line that, in many ways, freed Japan from the burden of its postwar mantel.

Yet the 21C has been tough for Japan, with political turmoil, economic squeezes, and the March 2011 earthquake and tsunami, not to mention the ticking time-bomb of its aging population. Pressurized government ministers were forced to admit that the country faced a potential shortfall of funds necessary to meet the nation's senior citizens' basic needs. Critics slammed Japan's public works projects as an inefficient use of hard-earned tax revenue, while the economy struggled to rise after a decade-long slump. Protestors demanded an end to the immense powers of bureaucrats in favor of a more democratic political system capable of meeting the nation's challenges, citing the 1990s as "Japan's lost years," in reference to its economic underperformance. Though the Japanese government responded to these unprecedented difficulties by introducing wide-ranging reforms, such as non-profit organizations, information disclosure, and judicial reform legislation, there has been widespread call for more.

Also notable is a strong nostalgia for the **Edo Era**, the feudal era preceding the last century-and-a-half of rapid change. Now perceived by many to have offered stability and greater cultural vitality against a modern backdrop of overcrowding, work-related stress, fragmented family structures, and a continued economic slump, this yearning for the past has garnered a bigger voice in recent years. In 2008, Japan headed toward its worst postwar recession as factory output slumped an unprecedented 9.6 percent during the last quarter—the biggest fall since figures were first compiled in 1953. Unemployment surged and households cut spending as the global financial crisis took hold.

Though low by European and US standards, rising crime rates are the subject of much debate on Japanese morning TV, news shows, and newspaper headlines. An influx of foreign gangsters and a series of high-profile murders have further eroded the image of a crime-free Japan.

Another indication of growing dysfunction in Japanese society is the increase in juvenile delinquency, which has grown by 80 percent since 1972. However, four Japanese cities rank with the Safest Top 20 Cities in the World survey (Mercer, 2008), with Japan ranked fifth in the 2008 Global Peace Index.

Despite the challenges of a difficult global economy, Japan continues to face the future with the efficiency and forward-thinking characteristic of a country that has traditionally shown great resilience. It serves as a world leader in environmental awareness and high-tech research and development. Japanese automotive manufacturers are known worldwide not only for producing environmentally-friendly cars, but also for producing them in a way that is ecologically friendly.

Pioneering research ranging from high-speed transportation systems to nuclear energy and nanotechnologies exemplifies the country's dedication to continuing its global competitiveness. A serious view on corporate social responsibility plus a growing non-governmental sector working for alternative ways to create a better society characterizes Japan's approach to the well-being of its people.

# Art and Culture

**Japan's geographical situation at the "Terminus of the Silk Road," as described by French orientalist René Grousset, also made this the end of the road for the ideas, styles, and techniques that, originating in the West, Central Asia, and China, made their way east.**

**Although sometimes sought out and valued by the Japanese for their intrinsic qualities, these imported cultural influences also evolved into their own unique and complex forms, particularly in the visual arts. From earliest forays into cinema to the enormous popularity of manga today, Japan's creativity never ceases to surprise.**

## PAINTING AND SCULPTURE

### PREHISTORY

Although there is evidence of figurative representation dating back to the Paleolithic era, the most impressive examples come from the neolithic or **Jomon era,** noted for its spectacular ritual vases and richly expressive terra-cotta figurines, which probably represent the "goddesses" of a fertility cult.

During the Chalcolithic or **Yayoi era**, the arrival of metalworking from the Asian continent coincided with the appearance of bronze ritual bells, generally decorated with animal motifs or scenes of daily life. The protohistoric **Kofun era** saw a unique phenomenon in the centralization of political power. Built to receive the bodies of great clan chiefs, including those of the future Imperial Family, the often huge tombs of the Kofun era provide lasting evidence of this centralization.

They contain mortuary chambers, sometimes sumptuously decorated with wall paintings and quantities of burial goods, as well as skillfully worked terracotta figures, arranged above or around the mounds, apparently to protect the deceased.

## THE ARRIVAL OF BUDDHISM

Archeological remains and early written sources indicate that cultural exchanges between Japan and the Asian mainland took place from the Yayoi period onward, but it was not until a centralized state emerged toward the **end of the 6C**, coinciding with the adoption of Buddhism, that the **Chinese influence** became significant. The Chinese system became the model for the organization of the Japanese administration, and the Imperial Court and many aspects of its culture. Chinese and Korean influences can be seen in **Buddhist art**, both in architecture and in the layout of monasteries, as well as the statuary that began to flourish from the beginning of the **Asuka era**. Notable among the works of this rich period is Nara's Horyu-ji (7C), the oldest monastery in Japan, which contains the gilded bronze triad of the Buddha Shakyamuni, cast in 623 by the sculptor Tori. In contrast to the severe hieratic style of this early work, the rounded sweetness of the sculpture of the **Hakuho period** reached its apogee with the Miroku Buddha, carved in lacquered wood, in Chugu-ji, Nara, whose expression of gentle contemplation is a high point in Japanese art.

The **Nara era** (also known as Tenpyo in art history) is characterized by the use of new techniques, while the costly dry lacquer technique was abandoned. This era gave rise to some spectacular creations such as Toshodai-ji's bodhisattva, the Fukukenjaku ("thousand-handed") Kannon, more than 16.4ft/5m high (second half of 8C). The use of clay enabled sculptors to achieve finer, more accentuated modeling, as can be seen in the guardian gods of the gates of Horyu-ji (added in 711), whose imposing stature (12.5ft/3.8m), ferocious expressions, and impressive musculature were designed to protect the monastery from evil demons. The Shoso-in, situated in the compound of the "Great Eastern Temple," Todai-ji (751), the construction of which was the most important religious event to take place during the Nara era, was used to house the collection of Emperor Shomu (701–56). It contained more than 4,000 objects brought to Japan from Constantinople, Persia, India, and China via the Silk Road. The Nara era also saw the beginning of the adaptation of Chinese characters to express the sounds of Japanese, which would lead two centuries later to the invention of the Japanese syllabic notation system and the birth of a calligraphic tradition that is now over a thousand years old.

## THE GOLDEN AGE OF CLASSICAL ART

At the end of the 8C, the imperial capital was established at Heian (Kyoto). Liberated from the cultural influence of China, with which the court had broken off all official relations in 894, during the course of the following centuries Japanese culture would distance itself by degrees from Chinese influence to produce an art that was wholly original. This first "golden age" of Japanese art that constituted the **Heian era** was itself subdivided into smaller periods. Until the mid-10C, the large, powerful but severe statues of the Jogan period showed the still-prevalent influence of Chinese Tang art; conversely, the statuary of the **Fujiwara era** is characterized by sweetness of expression and a lightness of touch. This new, specifically Japanese trend would reach its height with the Amida Buddha carved by the sculptor **Jocho**, housed in the temple of Byodo-in (1053) at Uji, near Kyoto.

The Heian period was also a rich one in terms of painting; the mandalas and other works created in an esoteric Buddhist framework are noteworthy. However, it was the emergence of **secular narrative painting** in the 12C that was to be the most important development in pictorial art during this period, a fine example being the illustration of Murasaki Shikibu's famous *Tale of* Genji (Genji monogatari emaki). In the 11C, the climate of religious uncertainty that surrounded the beginning of the "Last Era of Buddhist Law," (the Japanese preoccupation with *mappo*, the pre-ordained collapse of Buddhist Law), gave rise to many devotional practices, including the illumination of copies of canonical texts (sutra), executed with the greatest of care. This decorative trend would culminate during the following century with the creation of sumptuous ensembles of scrolls such as the Lotus Sutra (Heike nokyo) donated by the Heike clan to the Itsukushima Shrine, on Miyashima Island.

## THE MEDIEVAL PERIOD

During the **Middle Ages,** the Emperor remained at Kyoto while the military government established itself first at Kamakura (1185–1333) and then, Muromachi (1333–1573). It was a split that was both symbolic and cultural, stimulating the appearance of new genres and styles that were different from the formalized aesthetic of courtly art, and challenging the Imperial Court's role as arbiter of taste. Influenced by Zen Buddhism, this new art found its most typical expression in portraiture, which may have developed at the Court but was immediately adopted by the ruling clans, who adapted it to their own preference for simple, realistic monochrome painting. A good example is the portrait presumed to be of Minamoto no Yoritomo (1147–99), founder of the Kamakura Shogunate. Attributed to **Fujiwara no Takanobu** (1142–1205) but probably dating from the 13C, this scroll painting is now at Jingo-ji, Kyoto, where it is one of three hanging scrolls designated National Treasures. During this period, portrait painting was also developed by Zen Buddhist monks but the **Kei school**'s revival of Buddhist sculpture is most typical of the period, notably the work of the sculptor **Unkei**, whose painted-wood sculptures of **Muchaku** and **Seshin**, two Indian monks who lived in the 4/5C, can be seen at Kofuku-ji in Nara (1212). There is no attempt at idealization in these portraits, but instead a new, more realistic style is used to convey inner intensity and spirituality.

Although dominated by a total fragmentation of political power and constant wars, the **Muromachi** period was nevertheless artistically fruitful. The **shoguns of the Ashikaga dynasty** were great patrons who collected Chinese art and encouraged painting, which achieved an artistic highpoint in Zen monasteries. It was during this troubled period that the famous Japanese dry landscape gardens first appeared, Ryoan-ji in Kyoto being the best-known example (late 15C). At the end of the 14C, the shogun Ashikaga Yoshimitsu ordered the construction of Kyoto's Golden Pavilion, the ultimate expression of the aesthetic ideal of the time. A century later, the shogun Ashikaga Yoshimasa built the Silver Pavilion as a refuge where he could enjoy moments of calm while the country was being ravaged by brutal civil wars. Yoshimasa also encouraged the development of the Tea Ceremony, a new social ritual that was both spiritual and aesthetic (*see p112*). Influenced by the Song dynasty in China, painting also underwent a revival, notably in monochrome landscape painting. Works imported from the mainland produced a fruitful Japanese reinterpretation by great painters such as **Sesshu** (1420–1506).

The new Japanese works were displayed on large-scale decorative supports, such as screens and sliding panels, in monasteries and the houses of the aristocracy. Large-scale works in monochrome or color followed, illustrating themes such as *Landscapes of Four Seasons* or *Famous Landscapes* and, especially popular, *Views of the Capital and its Districts*, along with the classics of Japanese literature. Coinciding with the use of humorous subject matter in the first popular art form, an ancient precursor of today's manga, painting was elevated to the status of a profession with the success of the **Tosa and Kano Schools of painting**.

## THE MODERN ERA: POPULAR ART AT ITS PEAK

At the beginning of the modern era, the brief **Azuchi-Momoyama period** saw the trend for large decorative works that had begun in the preceding period reach a highpoint with the emergence of great artists such as **Kano Eitoku** (1543–90) and **Hasegawa Tohaku** (1539–1610). The stability of the **Edo era** that followed gave rise to an amazingly rich urban

*Cypress Tree (16C) attributed to Kano Eitoku, Tokyo National Museum*

©Tokyo National Museum

culture. New forms of artistic expression developed simultaneously with the emergence of an urban bourgeoisie.
The leisured merchant classes of the central regions encouraged the growth of the **Rinpa School**, whose greatest exponents, **Honami Koetsu** (1558–1637), **Tawaraya Sotatsu**, **Ogata Korin** (1658–1716), and his brother **Kenzan** (1663–1743), revolutionized the interpretation of Heian artistic themes, while the bourgeoisie in the new cities supported the creation of a **popular art** of great vitality derived from the development of new printing techniques.
This well-known style of **woodblock prints** known as ukiyo-e ("images of the floating world"), focused on three principal areas: portraits of actors and courtesans, landscapes, and the famous "images of spring," which combined social irony with praise of earthly love.
Great artists working in this medium include **Suzuki Harunobu** (active 1756–70), **Kitagawa Utamaro** (1753–1806), **Sharaku** (active 1794–95), **Katsushika Hokusai** (1760–1849), and **Ando Hiroshige** (1797–1858).
Finding its way into Japan via the Dutch merchants who, from 1641, were the only Westerners allowed to live in Japan, European art aroused the interest of some Japanese painters, such as **Maruyama Okyo** (1733–95), whose experiments in the field heralded the coming of a new era.

## MODERNIZATION AND IDEALISM

The ending of Tokugawa domination saw a gradual decline in *ukiyo-e* and the popular culture of Edo, while Buddhist art, lacking its usual supporters, also lost impetus.
Western-style painting (yoga) began to develop in 1876 with the support of the Meiji government. The fresh approach of **Takahashi Yuichi** was typical of this new period. Around 1900, **Asai Chu** and **Kuroda Seiki** popularized a style inspired by the French open-air painters, while bronze commemorative sculpture began to appear in public spaces, significantly transforming the appearance of big cities. However, in reaction to this Westernization, the critic and art scholar **Okakura Tenshin** revitalized Japanese art by advocating a fusion of traditional Japanese and Chinese styles, stimulating the emergence around 1890 of the Nihonga painters, whose most famous exponents were **Yokoyama Taikan** and **Hishida Shunso**.
Calligraphy, pottery, and *ikebana* all struggled to find a place in this new artistic era.

## THE TWENTIETH CENTURY

### An age of choice

The period between 1912 and 1941 was marked by a succession of European-inspired movements: Post-Impressionism with **Yorozu Tetsugoro** and

**Kishida Ryusei**, Dadaism with the **Mavo group**, proletarian realism, the Surrealism of **Koga Harue** and **Kitawaki Noboru**. On the other hand, Cubism and Constructivism made little impact, demonstrating that Japanese assimilation could be selective.

During the 1930s, many forms of creative and artistic expression such as gardening, architecture, and *ikebana* (thanks to **Teshigahara Sofu**, founder of the **Sogetsu School**) underwent a revival, reinventing Japanese traditions in a dialogue with Modernism.

**Yanagi Soetsu** led the movement for the recognition of folk art or mingei ("handicraft art of the ordinary people"), restoring the connections between Buddhism and crafts.

### War and its consequences

World War II saw a period of intense, state-controlled artistic activity. However, although creativity was stimulated, the wartime government's need for propaganda created a demand for realistic paintings celebrating Japan's military triumphs. **Tsuguharu ("Leonard") Foujita** painted many patriotic battle scenes, some of which were seized by the US in 1946.

Memory of the conflict remained vivid for many years. Thousands of funerary or peace monuments and statues of the bodhisattva Kannon, the incarnation of compassion, were erected throughout Japan. The Hiroshima Panels (1950–82), a series depicting the atomic explosions painted by the husband-and-wife team of **Maruki Iri** and **Maruki Toshi**, graphically illustrate the tragedies of Hiroshima and Nagasaki.

In the mid-1950s the **Gutai group** (Yoshihara Jiro, Shiraga Kazuo, Murakami Saburo, and others), pioneered striking works in the Osaka region that broke with tradition by playing with materials and forms in ways that anticipated later happenings, performance, and conceptual art.

### Toward the future

In the 1950s there was a vogue for abstract art in Japan, although the works of **Okamoto Taro** and **Saito Yoshishige** demonstrated that its challenges were as much social or formal as expressionist.

In the 1960s, Pop Art rediscovered Edo culture, thanks to the painter and graphic artist **Yokoo Tadanori** while groups like **Hi-Red Center** (founded in 1963) staged performances critical of the consumer society.

Around 1970 the **Mono-ha movement** (Lee Ufan and Sekine Nobuo) used installations in earth, wood, and rock to "bring things together," allowing the materials to create their own ecology by establishing a relationship between them with little artistic intervention.

**Michael Lucken**

## CONTEMPORARY ART

After a period during which external influences and styles were absorbed into the homegrown scene, the 1980s marked the arrival of Japanese artists internationally. With a surprising freedom of expression, Japanese art moved easily back and forth between the traditional and the invention of a new artistic language.

There are no barriers between culture and subculture, as **Murakami Takashi** (1962–) demonstrates, producing works inspired by manga and the world of the otaku *(see p64 and p87)*, as well as a range of mass-market objects.

### Tradition vs modernity

Kimonos vs ultramodern street fashion, wooden temples vs high-tech structures of glass and steel: tradition and modernity rub together on a daily basis in urban Japan.

Some artists have appropriated age-old traditions by reinventing them, like **Nakagawa Yukio** (1918–) and **Suda Yoshihiro** (1969–), who have reinvented *ikebana* in a radical way.

The works of **Yamaguchi Akira** (1969–) are inspired by prints of the Edo period, with their pale colors and flat perspective, as are those of **Takano Aya** (1976–), depicting modern teenagers often caught in erotic poses.

## Where to see contemporary art in Japan

In Tokyo, galleries in Roppongi, such as the Mori Arts Center, the National Art Center, 21–21 Design Sight, or the MOT (Museum of Contemporary Art) in the Kiyosumi-Shirakawa district—where some of the city's most dynamic and innovative galleries are also found—put on exhibitions sure to please the most demanding contemporary art lover. Japan also offers many different ways of seeing and experiencing contemporary art. Kanazawa's **21st Century Museum of Contemporary Art,** designed by Seijima, exhibits the work of acclaimed contemporary artists from Japan and all over the world. Several regions mount **triennial art exhibitions**, much of the work remaining in place between exhibitions. Created for the 2006 triennial, American artist James Turrell's House of Light is unlike any other in Japan. Newly-built but in the traditional style, you can stay in the house to experience light in a variety of conditions centered around a sky-viewing room where an aperture in the roof can be opened and closed. Inside, channels of light run around the upper parts of the walls, just below the ceilings.

Equally magical, is a stay on the museum island of **Nao-shima** in the Inland Sea (*see p380*). Here, the Benesse Art Site displays site-specific works of art on permanent exhibition, not only inside in the formal exhibition spaces, but outside in the natural surroundings of Nao-shima Island. Opened in the early 1990s by the Benesse Foundation, the facilities include the **Benesse House** (designed by architect Ando Tadao), the Chichu Art Museum, the Art House Project, and Honmura Lounge & Archive.

**Hélène Kelmachter**

### *"Kawaii!"* Cute or weird?

As in everyday life, the fad for all things *kawaii* (cute or childish) also appears in art, reflecting contemporary Japanese society's quest for identity. The sulky faces of the little girls painted by **Nara Yoshitomo** (1959–) present a sweet-sour image of childhood. This "disturbing strangeness" is also found in the doll paintings of **Kato Mika** (1975–), where the precise detail evokes a certain unease. The computer-generated work of **Aoshima Chiho** (1974–) is populated with tied-up or mutilated young girls, evoking a response torn between the appeal of the sparkling colors and the violence represented.

### Japan at bay

A great power whose world image has long been that of a country at the forefront of technology, Japan's experience of the collapse of the "bubble economy" in the 1990s, and the unemployment and insecurity that accompanied it, has been painful. The provocative work of **Aida Makoto** (1965–) reveals the darkest aspects of Japan; his *Shinjuku Castle*, a cardboard palace for the homeless, is a comment on the economic crisis but also an expression of his taste for the absurd. Inspired by clips from newspapers and television programs, the installations and animations of **Tabaimo** (1975–) glide from an ordinary situation into an enigmatic and disturbing event to reveal the dark side of modern Japanese society.

### The menace of catastrophe

The post-World War II generation grew up in a society marked by technological innovation but also by the experience of the atomic bomb. This dual memory is present in the works of **Yanobe Kenji** (1965–), whose *Radiation Suit Uran*, incorporating a shower unit to wash out contaminants, projects us into a science-fiction world inspired by the 1970 Osaka World's Fair.

Another collective fear runs through contemporary art, as depicted in the lithographs of **Motoda Hisaharu** (1973–), where earthquakes evoke apocalyptic visions of Tokyo in ruins, or the installations of **Kawamata Tadashi** (1953–), with monumental, ephemeral projects in wood created on sites under repair or awaiting destruction.

### The poetry of the imaginary

**Kusama Yayoi** (1928–), a member of the postwar Japanese avant-garde noted for her obsessional, hallucinatory art, has influenced some young artists to create dreamlike work in her style. **Nawa Kohei** (1975–) creates extraordinary objects by covering them with glass beads or by filling a space with giant molecular shapes. A dreamlike quality can also be found in the works of **Mori Mariko** (1967–), who combines the technology of three-dimensional images with references to Buddhism. The same blend of technology and Japanese philosophy is employed by **Miyajima Tatsuo** (1957–), whose electronic digital counters tick off the seconds as they pass, evoking the passage of time and the continuity and interconnectedness of the human life-cycle. The work of **Ishigami Junya** (1974–), a mixture of design, architecture, and installation, testifies to the originality, daring, and renewal of the younger generation of Japanese artists.

**Hélène Kelmachter**

## CINEMA

The Japanese were instantly fascinated by the technology of early cinema and in 1898, their first forays into narrative films were made, with adaptations of ghost stories such as *Bake-jizo (Jizo the Ghost)* and *Shinin no sosei (Resurrection of a Corpse)*.

### THE GREAT DIRECTORS

Japanese cinema is firmly linked to notions of the auteur, art, and the essay. By the outbreak of World War II, the first great directors, **Mizoguchi Kenji** (1898–1956) and **Ozu Yasujiro** (1903–63), had already produced a number of major works, including *Sisters of the Gion* (Mizoguchi, 1936) and *An Inn in Tokyo* (Ozu, 1935). In the 1950s, Japan made an impression on the international film scene with the arrival of the young **Kurosawa Akira** (1910–98), who was the first Japanese film director to win a European award for *Rashomon* (1950),

*Tokyo Story (1953) by Ozu Yasujiro*

Shochiku/The Kobal Collection

the story of the same crime reported from the differing points of view of the chief participants.

The film also took the Golden Lion at the Venice Film Festival and made actor **Mifune Toshiro** Japan's first international film star. **Mizoguchi** often revisited subjects dealing with the plight of Japanese women and also triumphed at Venice with *Ugetsu (Tales of the Pale and Silvery Moon after the Rain)* (1953), the story of a potter seduced by the ghost of a noblewoman; it won Venice's Silver Lion for Best Direction. Despite his epic tales of samurai, inspired by the western movies of John Ford and the works of Shakespeare and the great Russian writers, Kurosawa was considered the most Western of the Japanese directors.

**Ozu Yasujiro** had been dead for some years before his work finally became available and recognized outside Japan. His masterpiece, *Tokyo Story* (1953), is the portrait of a widow played by Hara Setsuko, who retains her sense of duty while Tokyo changes all around her.

**Naruse Mikio** (1905–69) was one of the three most prominent Japanese directors of his time, though his work is the least known outside Japan. Like those of Ozu, his films deal with the role of women in the postwar period and feature a number of Japan's greatest actresses.

## GENRE MOVIES

Japan has two production studios that concentrate on genre cinema. **Toei** specializes in films about yakuza (gangsters), the best-known being those by **Fukasaku Kinji** (1930–2003), especially his *Battles without Honor and Humanity* series (1973–4). Toei also acquired an animation studio that has created a large number of TV series and movies, and adapted Japanese comics into animated series, becoming one of the mainstays of anime today. The **Nikkatsu** studio produced the films of **Suzuki Seijun** (1923–), a visually extravagant filmmaker who was eventually dismissed because of his increasingly surreal style. Both Fukasaku and Suzuki have influenced many independent US filmmakers, from Jim Jarmusch to Quentin Tarantino. It's also worth mentioning that director Tim Burton, who is passionate about kaiju (monster movies), is a big fan of the **Toho** studios, producer of the Godzilla series, which launched atomic-trauma science fiction, the best films being directed by **Honda Ishiro** (1911–93), a close friend of Kurosawa Akira.

Nikkatsu was also responsible for a genre called "**roman porno**," a brand of erotic movies that saved the studio from going under and produced three major directors: **Konuma Masaru** (1937–), **Kumashiro Tatsumi** (1927–95), and **Tanaka Noboru** (1937–2006). This genre was a training ground for several young filmmakers, including **Somai Shinji** (1948–2001) and **Kurosawa Kiyoshi** (1955–), before they moved on to mainstream cinema.

## INDEPENDENT FILM

**Wakamatsu Koji** pioneered independent Japanese film production by creating his own production studio in the 1960s. He inspired other filmmakers under contract with the big studios, including **Oshima Nagisa** (1932–) and **Yoshida Yoshishige** (1933–), who were with Shochiku, and **Imamura Shohei** (1926–2006), who worked for Nikkatsu. Along with **Shinoda Masahiro** (1931–), they constitute Japan's New Wave, creating a stir on the international circuit with the political and erotic content of their movies. Imamura Shohei was twice awarded Cannes' Palme d'or, for *The Ballad of Narayama* (1983) and *The Eel* (1997). A number of Oshima Nagisa's films were successful abroad, notably *In the Realm of the Senses* (1976) and *Merry Christmas, Mr Lawrence* (1983), starring the musicians David Bowie and Sakamoto Ryuichi. In 1984, **Miyazaki Hayao** (1941–) wrote and directed *Nausicaä of the Valley of the Wind*, adapting it from his manga series of the same title and in so doing, turned the world of animation upside down. Together with **Takahata Isao** (1935–), who directed *Grave of the Fireflies* (1988), he set up his own animated production company, Studio Ghibli. Other successful directors include **Oshii Mamoru** (1951), creator of Ghost in the Shell (1995), with Production I.G, and **Kon Satoshi** (1963–), director of *Paprika* (2006), with Madhouse. All these directors have shown at Berlin, Cannes, and Venice, while Miyazaki's *Spirited Away* was the first anime film to win an Academy Award, only the second Oscar ever awarded for Best Animated Feature. **Tsukamoto Shinya** (1960–) launched the cyberpunk wave with Tetsuo, while the actor Kitano Takeshi (1947–) replaced Fukasaku Kinji as director of *Violent Cop*, in which he also starred (as Beat Takeshi). **Kitano** has directed and starred in most of his movies, often writing and/or editing them as well. *Hana-Bi* (*Fireworks*, 1997) won the Golden Lion at the Venice Film Festival and *Zatoichi* (*The Blind Swordsman*, 2003), a remake of a cult title from the 1960s and 1970s, was awarded a Silver Lion. The 1990s saw a renewal of Japan's cinematic talent with the arrival of **Kurosawa Kiyoshi**, **Aoyama Shinji** (1964–), **Kawase Naomi** (1969–), **Koreeda Hirokazu** (1962–), **Miike Takashi** (1960–), and **Nakata Hideo** (1961–), all of whose work has been distributed internationally.

Finally, in 2004, a young filmmaker **Ishii Katsuhito** (1966–) made *The Taste of Tea*, a successful synthesis of Ozu Yasujiro's narrative films (themes of domestic life) and contemporary Japanese pop culture. The film launched another wave of movies drawing on both Japan's regional and traditional cultures, and the world of manga and *anime*, including *Memories of Ma-tsuko* by **Nakashima Tetsuya** (1959), a former advertising man who blends manga with the flamboyance of German director Douglas Sirk's melodramas.

**Stephen Sarrazin**

## PHOTOGRAPHY

Japan is well known for being a world leader in camera manufacture and technology, and the Japanese too for their interest in photography. People of all ages enjoy taking photographs, especially at the photogenic *sakura*, cherry-blossom time, while young people spend hours in *purikura*, photo booths, where all kinds of creative effects can be achieved, far removed from the standard passport photo.

### THE FIRST PHOTOGRAPHERS

**Fukuhara Shinzo** (1883–1948) and his brother **Roso** (1892–1946) pioneered photography in Japan and in 1924, founded the Japanese Photographic Society. The brothers were famous for their pictures of landscapes and flowers, hand-tinted in gentle sepia tones. In the 1920s and 1930s, curiosity about Western ideas stimulated photographic experimentation, inspired by avant-garde Europeans such as the Surrealists. During World War II, Japanese photographers worked largely for the imperial government and in the immediate postwar years, for press and publishing companies. The US-born **Ishimoto Yasuhiro** (1921–) introduced American theories and technology to Japan in 1953 when he moved there to live for a period.

### THE GREAT PHOTOGRAPHERS

In line with the spectacular changes that marked postwar Japan, **Moriyama Daido** (1938–) brings a very personal viewpoint to the urban landscape with his off-centered compositions, close-ups, photographs taken on the run or from a moving vehicle, and his atypical subject matter. Working both in color and black and white, and in panoramic or medium format, and in Polaroid, the photographs of **Araki Nobuyoshi** (1940–) are astonishingly diverse. His images of Tokyo are juxtaposed with the still lives or portraits of young girls in sophisticated, erotic compositions and bondage scenes that made him famous. Another master of the nude, **Shinoyama Kishin** (1940–) stylizes bodies to the point of abstraction.

### CAPTURING A MOMENT IN TIME

For **Sugimoto Hiroshi** (1948–), photography is an almost Zen-like act of meditation. The formal beauty and classical perfection of his work, taken in series, is based on concepts of time, the transience of life, and the conflict between life and death.

**Hatakeyama Naoya** (1958–) defies the passage of time in his work by capturing the arrested moment in his photographs of explosions taken in quarries. The poetic style of **Kawauchi Rinko** (1972–), capturing the small details of everyday life, is a meditation on the wonder of the world and the fleetness of the moment. She confers beauty and emotion on the most ordinary of things.

### PHOTO ID

In work that is as surprising as it is original, **Morimura Yasumasa** (1951–) uses photography as a homage to painting. He recreates the works of Western artists such as Manet and Rembrandt by substituting his own face for those of the original subjects. Following in his wake, several young Japanese photographers have explored the theme of identity through self-portraits or by playing with the photographic image.

**Sawada Tomoko** (1977–) puts herself in the picture in school photographs, substituting her own face for every uniformed schoolgirl, or recreates her image *ad infinitum* in photo booth portraits, or photographs herself dressed in costume against different backgrounds. **Yanagi Miwa** (1967) photographs staged scenes and uses compu-

ter manipulation to produce images of places that are at once familiar and yet seem unreal. Artifice and reality merge in her work to give a surreal view of the 21C city.
Japanese galleries specializing in photography include **Taka Ishii** and **Foil** in Tokyo, and **MEM** in Osaka.

**Hélène Kelmachter**

## MANGA

Manga has become increasingly popular worldwide since the international publication of **Otomo Katsuhiro's** *Akira* in the 1990s. Despite its image as a contemporary phenomenon, a type of manga has existed in Japan since the Middle Ages. The Muromachi era (1336–1573) saw the appearance of the first painted scrolls with pictures and calligraphic text. They sometimes featured humorous drawings and caricatures of people and animals engaged in human activity. The term *manga* itself, which means disorderly or clumsy *(man)* drawing *(ga)*, was not coined until much later, when **Katsushika Hokusai**, a master engraver, called the series of grimacing faces which he published between 1814 and 1834, *Hokusai Manga*.

### EARLY MANGA

It was Western illustrators working in Japan at the end of the 19C, such as English artist and cartoonist Charles Wirgman and French cartoonist and illustrator Georges Ferdinand Bigot, who acted as the springboard for the early modern manga. Wirgman launched the satirical magazine *Japan Punch* and Bigot's work appeared in *Toba-e*.
The first modern Japanese manga by **Kitazawa Rakuten** (**Kitazawa Yasuji**) appeared in 1902 in the newspaper *Jiji Shinpo's* Sunday supplement.
It was influenced by the European style, echoing the subject of one of the Lumière brothers' earliest films. A sign of things to come, Japanese cartoon styles would borrow heavily from the cinema for their scenarios, as well as, the way their stories were framed.

### MODERN MANGA

Manga became very popular in Japan during the interwar period, and nearly every newspaper and magazine featured it. Soon, however, the military regime clamped down, censoring all forms of caricature, using the new medium of comic strips to distribute its own propaganda instead, especially to young people.
Manga did not recover until the early 1960s, this time influenced by American comics brought to Japan by the GIs of the occupying Allied forces.
One artist in particular played a leading part in this renaissance: **Tezuka Osamu** (1928–89). Trained as a doctor (although he never practiced), he devoted himself to manga, single-handedly inventing almost all the characteristics of the modern idiom: cinematic framing, big round eyes for hero and heroine, the use of written onomatopoeia to describe sounds, etc.

#### Mangamania

Japanese manga has spread far beyond the realm of the comic book superhero to deal with almost every subject, from war to cookery, polar exploration to porn, and of course science fiction. As a marketing tool, manga is also a way of targeting the sexes at specific ages; the *shojo* genre, aimed exclusively at young girls, is divided into two main subgenres: "Magical Girl," where the heroines use supernatural powers to combat evil, and "Romance," usually involving stories about Prince Charming. For boys, in the *nekketsu* genre, (literally meaning "hot blood,") action characters attempt to outdo each other's exploits, promoting the values of bravery and loyalty. Adult manga and the soft porn *pantsu* genre mean that, once hooked, the publishers are able to hold onto their audience for life.

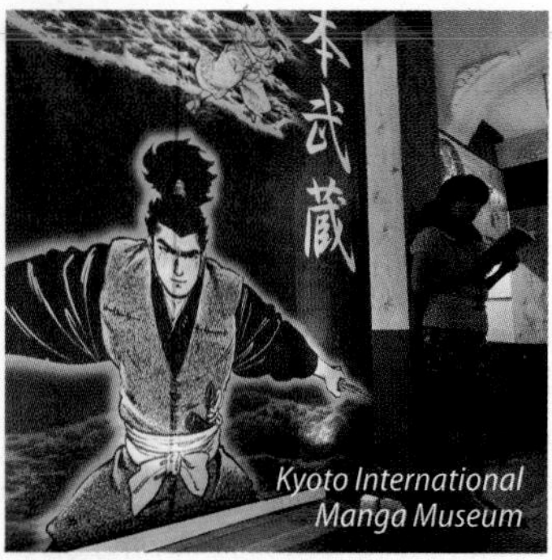

Kyoto International Manga Museum

© Jean-Baptiste Rabouan/hemis.fr

A big fan of Walt Disney (he was said to have seen *Bambi* more than 80 times), Tezuka was equally at home with a camera as with a pencil and in 1963, created the first real hero of Japanese manga, **Tetsuwan Atomu** ("Mighty Atom") known internationally as **Astro Boy**, a small robot boy. The character was phenomenally successful, both on television and in print. During his prolific career, Tezuka published more than 700 works although it was not until 1990, a year after his death, that his status as an artist was officially recognized with a major retrospective organized by Tokyo's National Museum of Modern Art.

## POST TEZUKA

Nowadays the illustrators following in Tezuka's footsteps work in both manga and in animation. Their current leader, **Miyazaki Hayao** (*My Neighbor Totoro, Princess Mononoke,* etc.) has been successful in both genres and is known internationally for his films. On the manga side, new heroes succeeded Astro Boy in the 1970s and 1980s, the best known being **Goldorak** and **Candy**. Both have been hugely successful, not only in Japan but worldwide.
Likewise, creators of manga for adults such as **Otomo Katsuhiro** (Akira) or **Taniguchi Jiro** (Best Scenario Prize at France's Angoulême International Comics Festival for *Harukana Machi-e*) have begun to reach a more discerning audience that values manga as a literary and illustrative art form. But it was the arrival of **Toriyama Akira**'s manga series Dragon Ball in 1993 that really launched "mangamania" internationally. More than 250 million copies have been sold in less than ten years, smashing the record held by *Tintin*, which has sold "only" 200 million over more than 40 years. Manga reaches a wide audience in France, now the biggest consumer of manga after Japan, with more than ten million volumes sold every year.

**Patrick Duval**

# ARCHITECTURE

For many centuries Japan's architecture owed much to foreign influences. While the Kingdom of Paekche (Korea) played a central role, notably with the introduction of Buddhism and the temples associated with it, China provided the initial inspiration for the layout of towns and palaces. Likewise, the architecture of the temples used in Zen Buddhism, introduced in the 12C, was inspired by those created during the Song dynasty. However, the Japanese subsequently devoted centuries to creating its own styles, generally by reworking them to reveal the essence of an indigenous culture. This process of assimilation, well known in Japanese postwar industry, marks the whole of Japan's cultural history. In the 20C, however, this system of appropriating elements from other cultures largely faded out, leaving to the Meiji government the distinction of having presided over the last period during which Japan looked toward European and American inspiration for its architecture. In the second half of the 20C, it was the West that looked to Japan, which enjoyed international acclaim for its modern architecture.

## STAGES OF DEVELOPMENT

As early as the **Yayoi period** (around 500–300 BC), Japanese architecture made ingenious use of wood. Timber was readily available and was used for Buddhist temples, Shinto complexes, and houses for both the elite and ordinary people. Designed to house a spiritual presence *(kami)*, **Shinto shrines** *(see illustration p92)* recreated the physical isolation of the early places of worship using a series of compounds preceded by tall gateways *(torii)*. The innermost sanctuaries are reached after cleansing the hands and mouth at a purification font *(temizuya)*. The shrines are notable for the simplicity of line and the materials used. Secondary structures have double roofs supported by a succession of posts. Only the innermost part of the shrine *(honden)*, raised on pillars, where the *kami* residesis partitioned off. Shrine architecture reached an unparalleled degree of complexity and decoration when shrines began to be dedicated to national heroes such as Tokugawa Ieyasu, whose remains are entombed in the highly elaborate 17C Tosho-gu at Nikko.

In **Buddhist architecture** building complexes were enclosed by walls, into which were set monumental gates *(chumon)*. Buddhist temples consisted of a main building *(kondo)* housing an image of the Buddha, and depending on the size of the temple, a series of auxiliary buildings, including pagodas, inspired by the Indian stupa. Buddhist temples (*see drawing p93*) are differentiated from Shinto temples not only by their roofs with upturned corners, made from tiles or copper rather than thatch or bark, but also through their use of colored lacquer (though color was also used in some Shinto temples). Despite the major earthquakes suffered over the centuries, some very fine Buddhist temples remain in the oldest Japanese cities. For obvious reasons, stone came to replace wood in **defensive architecture**: it was used for the vast foundations surmounted by spiraling walled ramps and keeps, built in a mixture of stone and earth. Himeji Castle in Hyogo prefecture (*see drawing pp94–95 and photograph p366*) is a fine example of a Japanese castle, with many defensive structures and features.

### The Birth Of Modern Architecture

The **Meiji Restoration** marks a turning point in Japanese architecture, when Japan began to adopt Western architectural concepts.

It was a new era of architectural thinking, which led to the spread of a "hard" architecture and the start of new building programs. British architect **Josiah Conder** was appointed by the Meiji government to take up a teaching position, and in less than 20 years, he and his students had designed the buildings that would reflect the status of the new Meiji state (university buildings, ministries, museums) in a wide variety of styles. They included Tatsuno Kingo's Tokyo Station and Bank of Japan, Conder's Iwasaki House (Tokyo), Thomas Waters' Japanese Mint (Osaka), and Katayama Tokuma's National Museums in Kyoto and Nara. All were demonstrably a reprise of all the "neos" once fashionable in Europe.

In continuing its program of modernization during the first third of the 20C, Japan looked toward continental Europe, considered the world leader in Modernist construction techniques and styles. An exception was **Frank Lloyd Wright**, whose Imperial Hotel (1917–22) is partially preserved at Meiji-mura in Magoya. Unlike previously, this was not a "top-down" import from abroad, with study missions or official invitations to foreign professionals (though in 1941, French architect/designer **Charlotte Perriand** was officially invited to advise on industrial design). In general, Japan's acclimatization to the international style came about quite informally, through contact with European architects working in Japan, such as **Bruno Taut** or **Antonin Raymond**, or through Japanese architects making the reverse journey to train at leading European architectural schools and practices. During the 1930s, rampant nationalism led to official rejection of the Modernism introduced by, among others, **Maekawa Kunio** and **Sakakura Junzo**, two former associates of Le Corbusier. The authorities preferred constructions that had no hint of the modern about them apart from their building materials, and the recreation of traditional styles, as in **Watanabe Jin**'s redesign of the Toyko National Museum or the Kabuki-za theater by **Okada Shinichiro** which are typical of the "imperial crown style." A few Modernist buildings that escaped destruction have been relocated to Tokyo's open-air **Museum of Architecture**; they include the house of Maekawa Kunio, who worked in the Tokyo office of Antonin Raymond (St Paul Chapel, Karuizawa), where Modernist principles are translated in wood, and the Koide house by **Sutemi Horiguchi**, combining a thatched roof and Western living spaces.

### The Emergence of Modern Japanese Architecture

The Czech architect **Antonin Raymond,** who had worked in Japan before World War II, was the first Western architect authorized to build during the American Occupation. When he reopened his Tokyo practice in 1948, he introduced new technology developed in the US, utilizing *maruta* (wood blocks used for scaffolding) to reconstruct buildings destroyed by bombing (the Inoue House, Takasaki; St Alban's Episcopal Church, Tokyo). This inexpensive construction system offered an alternative to **Seike Kiyoshi**'s research into prefabricated housing. Raymond was also noted for his passion for reinforced concrete, which influenced **Tange Kenzo** via Maekawa, his one-time collaborator. Some of his buildings can be seen at Takasaki (Gunma Music Center), Nagoya (Nanzan University), and Tokyo (St Anselm's Church).

While modern architecture is gaining ground, the question remains whether there is a modern Japanese architecture. The traditional vs modern debate that began before World War II still revolves around Tange Kenzo. As his Hiroshima Peace Memorial Park (*see p387)* demonstrates, Tange was influenced by Le Corbusier and identified with the Modernists, translating materials and building techniques into structures to which he gave a rare, powerful expressiveness, such as the Yoyogi Stadium for the 1964 Olympic Games, Tokyo.

The break with the tutelary figures of Modernist architecture came with the generation that included **Kurokawa Kisho, Kikutake Kiyonori, Isozaki Arata**, and **Maki Fumihiko**, who were still students when Le Corbusier visited Japan in 1955 (and delivered the drawings for the National Museum of Western Art in Tokyo). It was this genera-

## Kansai International: An Airport in the Sea

Owing to the respective problems of land purchase issues and noise pollution at Narita and Osaka Airports, the Japanese had the astounding idea of building Kansai International Airport on water. This technological exploit called for 20 years of study before the actual works began in 1984 in Osaka Bay. A wall was to be first built on the ocean floor to delineate the future artificial island, reinforced from the outside by a sea wall, to protect the island against typhoons and other natural disasters. Sixty-nine steel chambers were therefore sunk into the ocean floor to form the perimeter of the island, and then, protected by the sea wall, the ground of the future island was built with a layer of fill 98ft/30m thick. Six years later, in 1990, the building of the artificial island 2.5mi/4km long and 6mi/1km wide was completed with another exploit: constructing a bridge 1.86mi /3km long to link the airport to the coast.

Then came a major problem: during construction, the embankment had compressed 27ft /8m, significantly more than the experts had estimated. Unruffled, the Japanese engineers simply came up with another innovation: that of adjustable steel columns to support the terminal building, which could be extended by inserting thick metal plates into their bases. Designed by the Italian Renzo Piano, Kansai International Airport, 1mi/1.7km in length, was on completion the longest airport terminal in the world. Since 1994, flights from the world over have been landing on its single runway that is open 24 hours a day. The airport emerged unscathed from the Kobe earthquake, a victory for its builders, who already plan to build a second, then a third runway.

tion who, during the 1960 International Design Conference held in Tokyo, redefined Japanese architecture with designs that, like those of the avant-garde British group Archigram, broke with the usual concepts relating to infrastructure and architecture. They believed that the city of the future should seem as natural as possible, and its architecture should evolve organically following the cycles of urban growth and decline.
The aim of this **Metabolist movement** (named from the title of a manifesto signed by several of the architects) was the renewal of urban society through its architecture. Few examples were built, however; they include the headquarters of Shizuoka Press (Tange Kenzo) and the Nakagin Capsule Tower (Kurokawa Kisho) in Tokyo, and the Tokoen Hotel and Sado Grand Hotel (Kikutake Kiyonori) at Yonago and Sado.

### Postmodern Metaphors

In the early 1970s, **Isozaki Arata** and **Hara Hiroshi** radically challenged all-out modernization and Japan's unequivocal relationship with the West. Their Postmodernist works offer erudite metaphors for various eras and places that question Japanese identity. While Isozaki wittily combines "collisions" (Ledoux, Michelangelo, and contemporary forms in Tsukuba's Civic Center), Hara builds "multilayered structures" or "atmospheres" influenced by his research into village communities around the world (Kyoto station).

### A New Japanism

The economic reconstruction of the 1960s and 1970s was accompanied by violent destruction of the environment and chaotic expansion of cities. Two masters of residential architecture, **Shinohara Kazuo** and **Ando Tadao,** attempted a spiritual realignment through the domestic environment. Influenced by *minka*, the traditional private residences, Shinohara embraced Japan's chaotic urban condition at the end of the 1970s as a design theme. As carefully conceived works of art, his buildings successively explored tradition and the "savagery of contemporary architecture" (house In Uehara, Tokyo; Tokyo Institute of Technology's Centennial Hall). The younger Ando creates simple, introverted geometric shapes in cast concrete facing toward inner courtyards, using enclosure to establish a human zone and to deflect the surrounding urban chaos. In his own words, "Such things as light and wind only have meaning when they are introduced inside a house in a form cut off from the outside world." His buildings are true acts of "urban guerrillaism," rejecting all contact with an aggressive context (row house in Sumiyoshi, Osaka). Ando's public buildings are equally noted for this approach (Church of the Light, Kobe;

*Times Gallery, Kyoto by Ando Tadao*

## Shinto shrine (Nagare/Honden style)

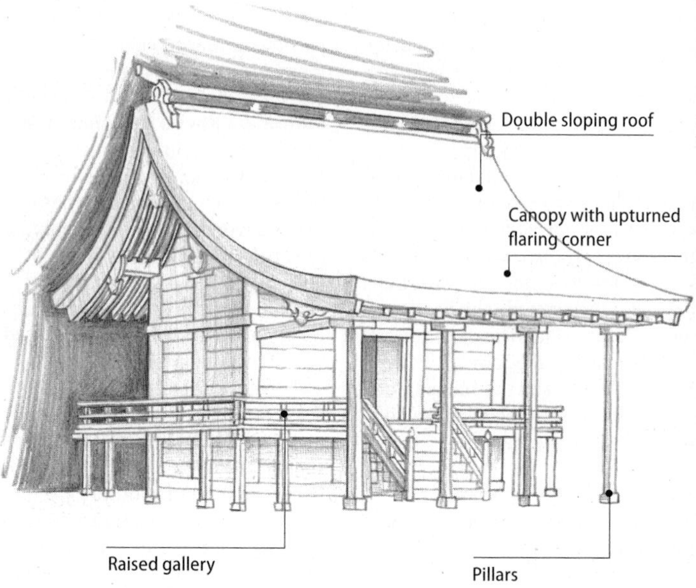


## Shinto complex

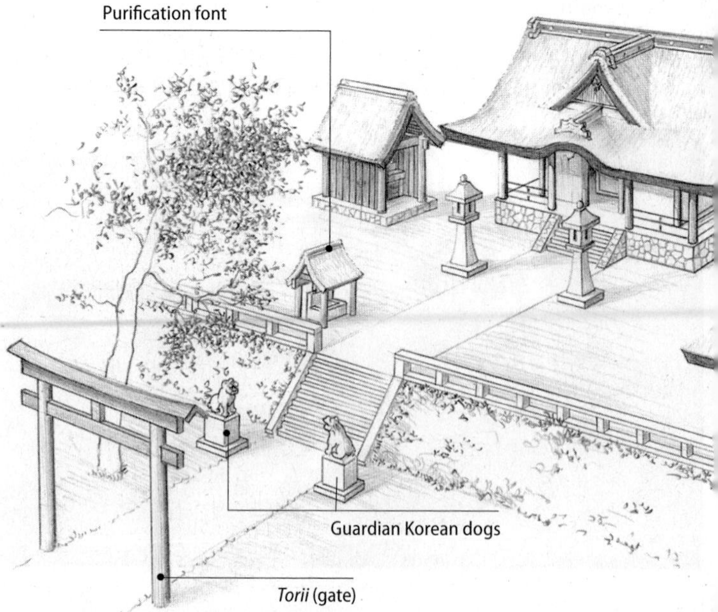

# Zen Buddhist temple

## Facade

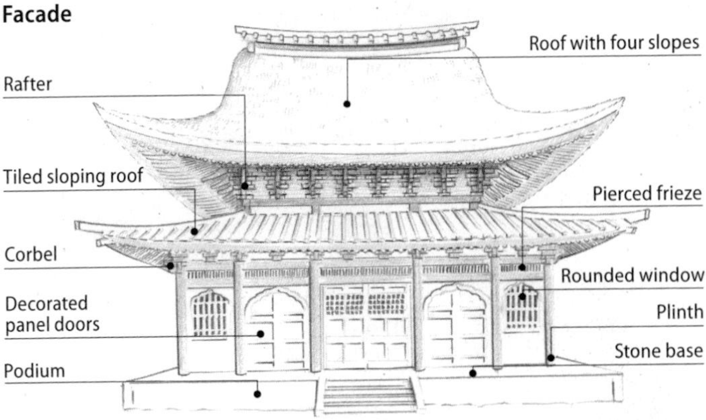


## Cross section

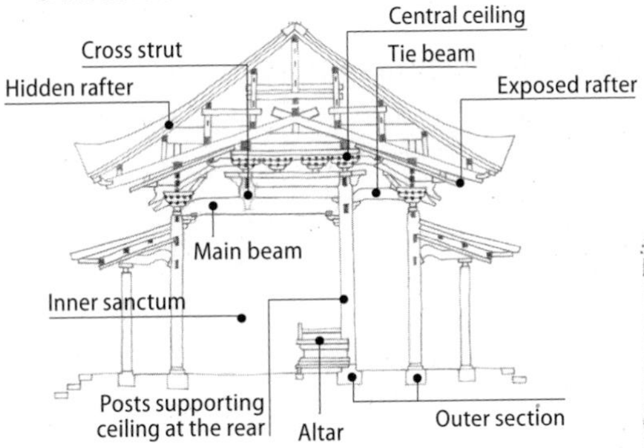


## Five-story Pagoda

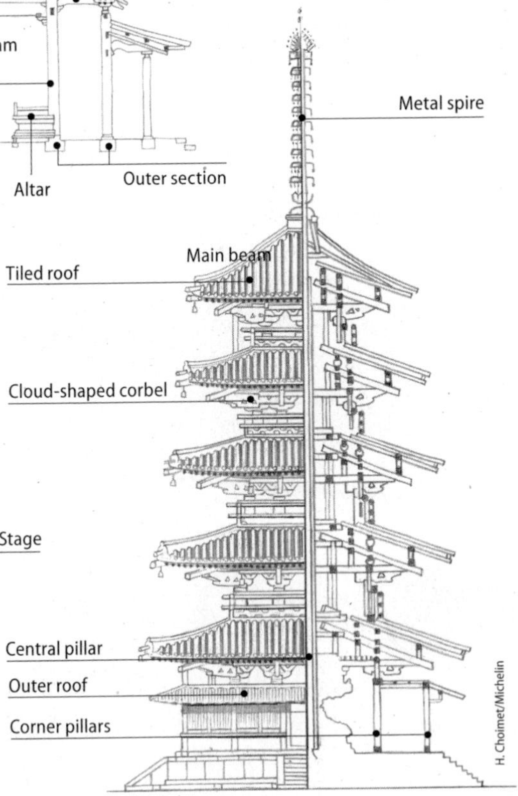


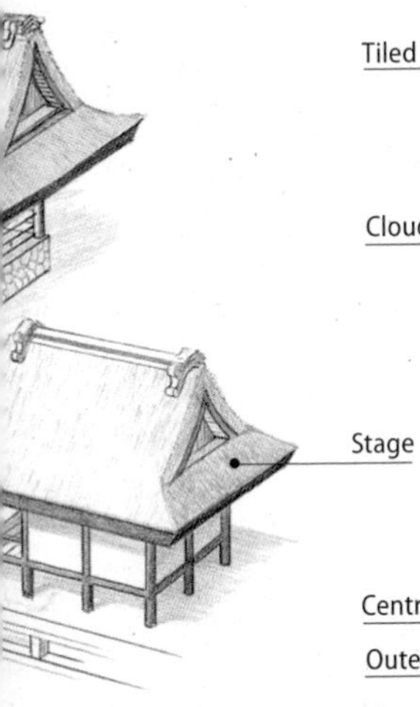


H. Choimet/Michelin

## The Old Eri Family Residence (late-17C) Kagawa Prefecture (Shikoku)

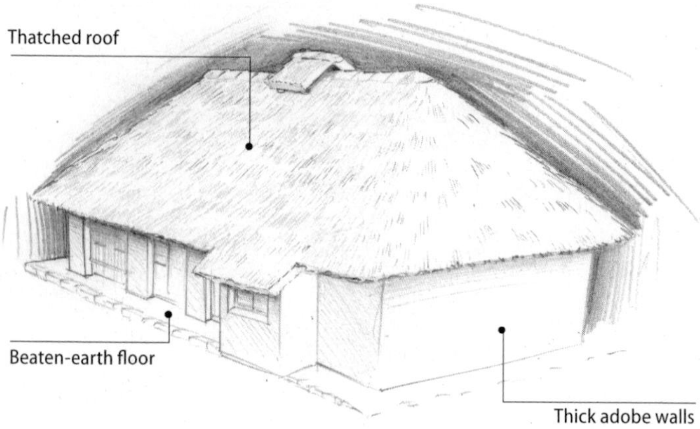


## Himeji Castle (early 17th century)

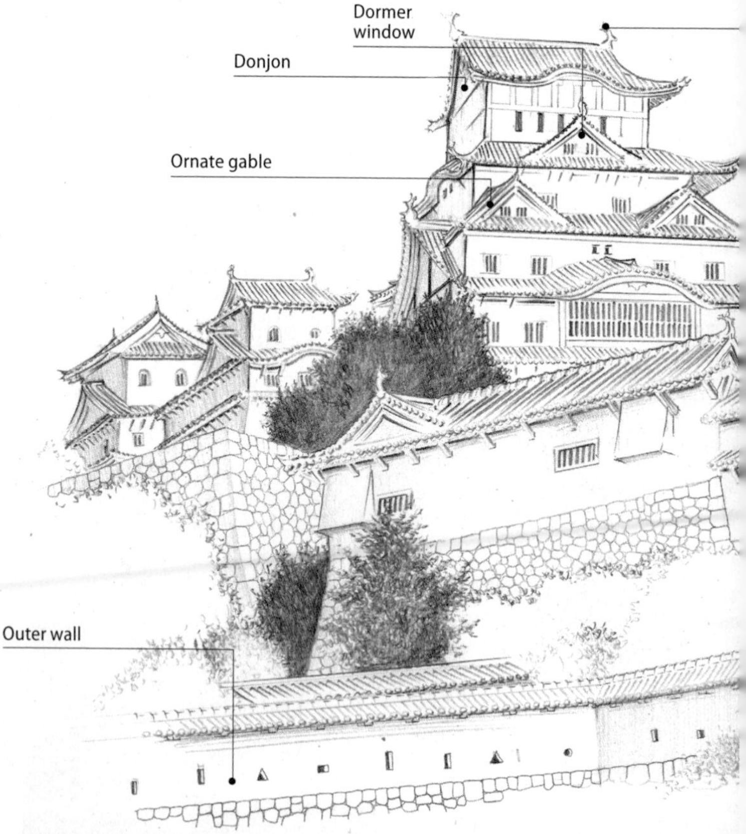

## Shoin-style interior (late-16C)

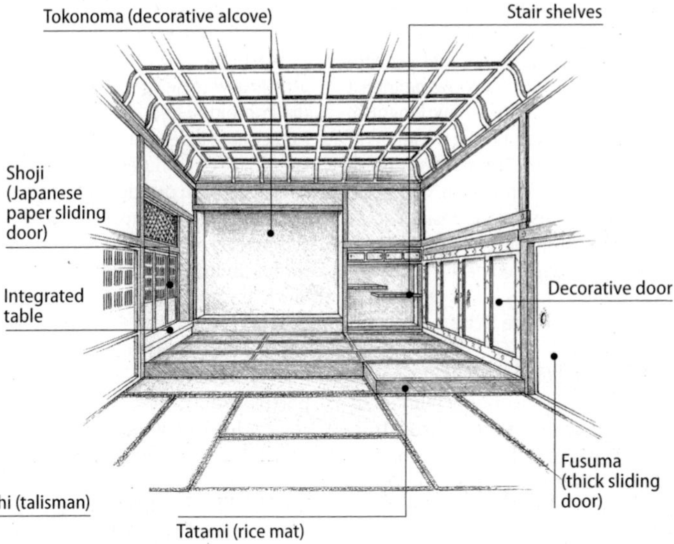


Shachi (talisman)

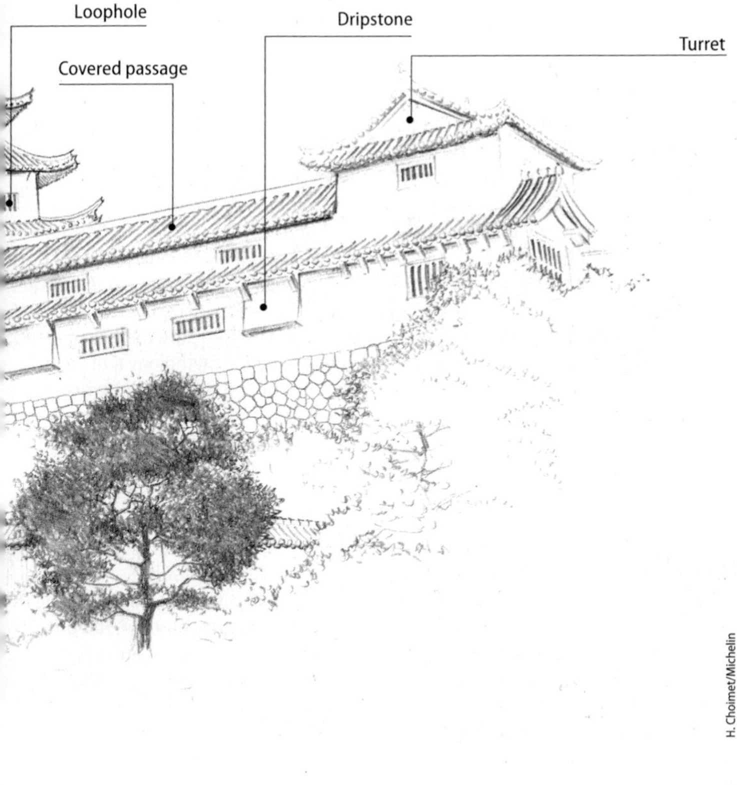


H. Choimet/Michelin

Times Gallery, Kyoto). A generation later, the reading is more referenced. The 1990s work of **Kuma Kengo** (Hiroshige Museum, Tochigi) and **Aoki Jun** (Vuitton store, Tokyo) experiment joyfully with materials and techniques in a mannerist aesthetic, arguing for a new Japanism that aims to reinterpret the traditions of Japanese buildings; **Fujimori Terunobu** (Jinchokan Moriya Museum, Chino), an architectural historian, designs knowingly anachronistic buildings that are hymns to an idealized past.

### Other View of The Urban Environment

During the 1980s and 1990s, the period of the "bubble" economy marked by unbridled speculation and construction, new generations of architects offered other readings of the urban environment. **Takamatsu Shin** thinks of it as a sea to which the only appropriate response is a highly extrovert architecture (Kirin Plaza, Osaka). In the same mode, **Yamamoto Riken** creates rational fragments to house micro communities (Saitama University). In step with this logic of affirmative identity, **Hasegawa Itsuko** designs artificial landscapes (Shonandai Cultural Center, Fujisawa) while, by contrast, **Ito Toyo** aims to combine the physical and virtual worlds of the city. His architecture is transparent, light, and ephemeral (the Sendai Mediatheque). For him and for the younger **Sejima Kazuyo**, the city-dweller is an urban nomad wandering an ever-changing environment (21st Century Museum of Contemporary Art, Kanazawa).

### Urban Subculture

Other talented architects appeared during the 1990s, often noted for their interest in the contemporary urban environment and its manifestations. They include **Atelier Bow-wow, Ban Shigeru, Chiba Manabu, Coelacanth, Mikan, Nishizawa Taira, Takaharu,** and **Tezuka Yui** in the Kanto region, **Abe Hitoshi** at Sendai, **Endo Shuhei** and **Miyamoto Yoshiaki** in the Kansai region, **Murakami Toru** and **Sanbuichi Hiroshi** in Hiroshima, and **Arima Hiroyuki** at Fukuoka.

Finally, thanks to Japan's growing internationalization, its architects increasingly work abroad, such as **Ban Shigeru**, who designed the antenna for the Pompidou Center, Metz, France.

At the same time, many **Western architects** have contributed to Japan's urban landscape with prestigious or fashionable buildings. The most recent include the Swiss firm Herzog & de Meuron (Prada Building, Tokyo), the Netherlands-based MVRDV (Gyre Shopping Center, Tokyo), the French architect Jean Nouvel (Dentsu Building, Tokyo), and the Italian Renzo Piano (Kansai Airport, Osaka).

**Christine Vendredi-Auzanneau**
**Manuel Tardits**

## LITERATURE AND THE PERFORMING ARTS

Although little known in the West, Japanese literature, far from being stuck in the groove of age-old tradition, is constantly renewed by young literary talents. In the performing arts, Noh and Kabuki actors are stars who are adored throughout the whole country, while Japanese music is open to all influences.

## LITERATURE

The oldest Japanese works of literature still in existence are the Kojiki *(The Records of Ancient Matters)* and the Nihon shoki *(Chronicles of Japan)*, written in 712 and 720 respectively. Commissioned by the Court, these texts were the basis for the mythology that grew up around the Imperial Family, who, until 1945, were presented as being in direct descent from the sun goddess Amaterasu *(see also p68)*.

The rules of Japanese poetry were also established in the 8C, in particular the tanka, couplets consisting of 5, 7, 5, then 7 and 7 "sound symbols."

The Manyoshu *(Collection of Ten Thousand Leaves)* is an anthology of 4,500 poems written between the 7C and 8C, which gives a fascinating glimpse of life during the Nara era. It contains poems and prose writings reflecting on war, life-

Yugiri from the Tales of Genji Scroll (12C) attributed to Fujiwara Takayoshi, Gotoh Museum, Tokyo



style, and small domestic dramas. The authors, nearly all anonymous, come from every strand of society.

### The First Novel

An exclusively Japanese literature did not evolve until the Heian period. In fact, until the 9C the Japanese language was written with Chinese characters in a complex system accessible to only a few intellectuals. Around the 900s, the invention of *kana*, a form of syllabic writing, made it possible to write Japanese phonetically, and this did much to democratize literary writing, especially by enabling women to express themselves. Around the beginning of the 11C, **Murasaki Shikibu,** lady-in-waiting at the Imperial Court, wrote **Genji monogatari** (The Tale of Genji), the first true work of fiction in the Japanese language. It skillfully relates the tale of the love life of Genji, a charming, cultivated prince who is nevertheless relatively indifferent to the unhappiness he creates around him. Now considered *the* masterpiece of Japanese literature, it celebrated its millennium in 2008, sparking off various exhibitions and new editions worldwide.

### The Battle Recitals of Medieval Times

Over the following centuries literary output was colored by the interminable clash between two rival clans, the Minamoto and the Taira. This gave rise to many tales of wargenerally oral works carried from village to village by blind monks, who "sang" them, accompanying themselves on the *biwa*, a lute.

### The Refined Literature of The Edo Era

In 1603, the dominance of the Tokugawa Shogunate brought an end to a long, troubled period, bringing a remarkable stability to the country that was to last for nearly three centuries. The themes of war gradually faded from literature, being replaced by those of love and the pleasures of the "floating world" (the urban lifestyle), which also featured prominently in woodblock prints (*see p81*).

**Ihara Saikaku** (1642–93) is unquestionably the greatest novelist of the 17C. His racy, lively style was largely due to his mastery of the haikai form, and although he began his career as a novelist with buke mono (warrior stories) or chonin mono (tales of townspeople), he quickly discovered that demand for his work was much greater when he wrote koshoku mono (amorous or erotic stories) with titillating titles. *The Man Who Lived Only for Love* and *The Life of an Amorous Woman* were huge commercial successes—the first Japanese bestsellers.

### The haiku

During this period of peace when Japan, although closed to the outside world, developed its own artistic rules, poetry—especially the haiku—became a ruling passion. A haiku is a short poem in three metrical phrases of 5, 7, and 5 sound units that, by its brevity, evokes the evanescence of things. **Matsuo Basho** (1644–94) excelled in this deceptively simple art.

Born into a samurai family, Basho (real name Matsuo Munefusa) quickly renounced a life in the military to devote himself to religion and literature. The power of his poems always relies on suggestion rather than description. Emotion comes from the observation of the most ordinary of things, as in this famous haiku:

*Ah! The ancient pond*
*As a frog leaps*
*Sound of the water*

When composing his poems, Basho was guided by two concepts: *wabi*, the notion of simplicity and asymmetry, with a touch of melancholy, and *sabi*, evoking the quest for simplicity and the beauty of things altered by time. In literature as in the other arts, the concept of *wabi-sabi* would become the basis of Japanese aesthetics. This is why Basho remains Japan's most-admired poet today.

### The great novelists of the 18C

Many talented writers of fiction emerged in the 18C, of whom the greatest is incontestably **Ueda Akinari** (1734–1809). His masterpiece, *Tales of Moonlight and Rain (Ugetsu monogatari)*, was brought to the screen by Mizoguchi Kenji.

## Meiji: the Encounter with the West

Japan's opening-up to Western culture toward the end of the 19C, which paradoxically coincided with the Emperor's regaining of power after the 15th Tokugawa Shogun Tokugawa Yoshinobu resigned his position, exerted a profound influence on literature. It ushered in several trends that "imported" from the West, such as the introspective, autobiographical novels of **Shiga Naoya** (1883–1925) or the naturalism inspired by Émile Zola, of which **Shimazaki Toson** (1872–1943) is undoubtedly the best representative.

Short stories in the style of Chekhov, Edgar Allan Poe, or Guy de Maupassant were also popular, with **Akutagawa Ryunosuke** (1892–1927) being the most impressive in this genre. His best-known short story, Rashomon, written in 1915, would provide the film director Kurosawa Akira with the theme of one of his greatest masterpieces. The Akutagawa Prize, Japan's most prestigious literary award for promising new writers, is awarded annually in his honor.

Three Meiji period novelists won international acclaim: **Natsume Soseki** (1867–1916), **Mori Ogai** (1862–1922), and **Nagai Kafu** (1879–1959). The works of Soseki (pen name of Natsume Kinnosuke), such as *I am a Cat* and *Botchan*., deal with many of the very Japanese themes of shame and culpability, the "hero" inevitably being driven to suicide (another major Japanese theme). Mori Ogai's style is even more austere, probably influenced by the author's long sojourn in Germany. Hints of burgeoning patriotism can be detected, together with a strong strain of pessimism.

Nagai Kafu is the only writer not to embrace this tendency, preferring to use themes from the "floating world" of the Edo period in his fiction (*A Strange Tale from East of the River, The Dancer*, etc.)

## From the Postwar Period to Contemporary Literature

During the postwar period, some fine novelists emerged into literary prominence not only in Japan but also internationally. Deeply scarred by Japan's military defeat, they were often nostalgic for the inherited tradition of bushido (the way of the samurai), which they saw as threatened by increasing Westernization. Chief among them was **Dazai Osamu** (1909–48), who published his masterpiece *The Setting Sun* in 1946, while the works of **Tanizaki Junichiro** (1886–1965), including *Diary of a Mad Old Man* and *In Praise of Shadows*, are classics of Japanese literature.

The first Japanese writer to win the Nobel Prize for Literature (1968) was **Kawabata Yasunari** (1899–1972), whose works include *The House of the*

*Sleeping Beauties*, *Snow Country*, *The Sound of the Mountain*, and *The Dancing Girl of Izu*. Another fine writer was **Inoue Yasushi** (1907–91), author of The Hunting Gun and Journey beyond Samarkand, while **Mishima Yukio** (1925–70) was *the* literary personality of the 20C, although his exceptional talent is sadly too often eclipsed by his terrible suicide by seppuku.

Among contemporary writers, the most famous is undoubtedly **Oe Kenzaburo** (1935–), who won the Nobel Prize in 1994. His rather somber style has been profoundly marked by the birth of his brain-damaged son Hikari, who has become a recurring theme in some of his works, such as *A Personal Matter* and *Teach Us to Outgrow Our Madness*.

The literary succession is already assured by a new generation of writers, whose stars include **Murakami Haruki** *(What I Talk About When I Talk About Running)*, **Nakagami Kenji**, **Nosaka Akiyuki**, and **Yoshimoto Banana**; many of their books have been translated into English.

**Patrick Duval**

## THE PERFORMING ARTS

Classical theater in Japan is no dusty relic of the past. Performers of traditional Japanese theatrical arts such as Noh, kyogen, bunraku, and Kabuki are stars today and maintain a vibrant artistic spirit, often handed down through generations, while contemporary innovations such as *butoh*, an avant-garde dance form, often incorporate influences from the traditional performing arts.

### Noh

The classical theater of Japan, combining dance, singing, and music, Noh is characterized by its subtlety and restraint.

It is performed on a square stage with no decor save for a painted backdrop. All-male actors are accompanied by a chorus and musicians. The basic form of Noh was established by the playwright **Zeami** (1363–1443), who codified the rules and revised texts by his father **Kanami** to create the essence of the genre as it is known today. The repertoire overflows with tales of ghosts and demons, warriors and abandoned maidens in epic dramas. The art of Noh has held a fascination for many creative Westerners, including Bertolt Brecht, W.B. Yeats, Samuel Beckett, Benjamin Britten, Peter Brook, Ariane Mnouchkine, and Robert Wilson.

*Kyogen* ("mad words"), also played by male actors, is traditionally performed as an interlude between Noh plays as a counterpoint to the dramatic intensity of the latter. These comic sketches, often containing elements of slapstick or satire, are designed to make the audience laugh about the problems of everyday life.

### Bunraku

Puppet theater, *bunraku*, originated in Osaka during the 17C. It uses stylized puppets to enact stories, the main repertoire being historic sagas, peasant dramas, and legends. Three puppeteers manipulate each large puppet, while the dramatic action is narrated by a chanter accompanied by musicians. The strength of the emotions that the puppeteers manage to convey via these wooden dolls is remarkable.

### Kabuki

Kabuki, the popular, highly stylized form of dance-drama derived from traditional religious and popular dancing styles, was developed in Kyoto in 1603. Created in the early Edo period by a priestess and dancer, **Okuni**, it was first performed exclusively by women, who were often prostitutes. The authorities soon found their choreography too erotic and in 1629 they were banned from the stage and replaced by boys. They too caused scandal and in 1652, the shogunate decreed that only older actors could play Kabuki. To this day, women's parts are played by men known as *onnagata* (*onna* meaning "woman" and *gata* "form"), who manifest the essence of women to a disturbing degree.

Performance skills and secrets are handed down from father to son, or to a nephew or adopted son, if there is no direct male descendant. Kabuki includes partly chanted speeches and naturalistic sound effects. Wooden clappers signal the opening and closing of the

### The influence of Japanese theater abroad

American avante-garde director and playwright Robert Wilson respects and admires Japan's classical theater and the visual language of the Noh plays, drawing upon it for his own work. Eckhard Roelcke described his Tamino in *The Magic Flute* as "a disciplined, Oriental bundle of energy." The robe, painted eyes, and statuesque posture of Wilson's Gurnemanz in *Parsifal* were highly reminiscent of Japanese theatrical figures. English composer Benjamin Britten visited Japan in 1956 and was fascinated by Noh theater, which inspired his three Church Parables. The first of these, *Curlew River*, is based on a **Noh** play, *Sumidagawa (Sumida River)* by Juro Motomasa, although Britten gave it a Christian context and transposed the setting to medieval England. As in Noh theater, all parts are sung by men.

play and cue the actors. Many famous playwrights, including **Chikamatsu Monzaemon** (1653–1724), known as the "Japanese Shakespeare," have written masterpieces for Kabuki actors, with plots borrowed from bunraku, Noh, and kyogen. An ancestor of musical comedy, with its blend of realism, illusion, and symbolism, Kabuki flourished during the second half of the 18C and revolutionized Japanese theater. Characters are identifiable by their highly stylized makeup and costumes. The three characters that make up the Japanese word *kabuki* combine singing (*ka*), dancing (*bu*), and art or skill (*ki*). But kabuki can also mean "extravagant" or "being in the height of fashion."

### Butoh

Long marginalized in Japan, *butoh* is strongly influenced by German Expressionism, the writings of Antonin Artaud ("Theater of Cruelty"), and Georges Bataille. It draws on the depths of the Japanese soul following the traumas of Hiroshima and Nagasaki, combining eroticism and violence, emptiness, and silence in a "dance of darkness." Creator **Hijikata Tatsumi** (1926–86) scandalized with the first performances in the late 1950s. Brought to the West by Ohno Kazuo and the Sankai Juku company, *butoh* is normally performed in white body makeup, with extremely slow and precise movements.

**Jean-Luc Toula-Breyss**

## MUSIC

The Imperial Court's gagaku orchestra, a wind, string, and percussion ensemble, plays in connection with Imperial household duties or rituals, giving only rare public performances. This is Japan's oldest classical music, descended from 8C and 9C Chinese and Korean culture, giving today a glimpse of the early Japanese court's extreme refinement.

Japanese music evolved with the rise of the aristocracy, with roots also in the spoken word and theater.

Heian era (794–1185) courtly life gave way to the 13C–16C feudal culture favoring epic recitation performed by monks wandering from village to village, like European medieval minstrels, accompanying themselves on a **five-stringed lute** or **biwa**. The military elite fostered the birth of Noh (*see p99*), patronizing it until Japan's late-19C modernization.

In the mid-19C, the West forced Japan to open its frontiers and traditional music lost ground in the Western educational system Japan adopted, and lost even more with the resulting huge demand for Western music. Contemporary Japan, with its many auditoriums with excellent acoustics, is an essential stop on international concert or opera company tours. Today an impressive wealth of Western classical music is on offer in Tokyo, and top Japanese musicians, conductors, and composers such as Takemitsu Toru (1930–96 ) or Joe Hisaishi (1950–) have successfully breathed new life into both traditions. Amateurs in Japan have a musical literacy that is quite probably unequaled in the world, while there is also a flourishing instrument-making industry, notably of pianos.

**Michel Wasserman**

# A Way of Life

**For Westerners, one of the great pleasures of visiting Japan is the discovery of the unique aesthetic that infuses all aspects of daily life. It touches everything, from gardening to bathing, from gastronomy to the formal Tea Ceremony—a great passion with the Japanese—and from the mundane to the highly intellectual—testimony to a thousand-year-old tradition.**

## BATHING

The bath *(o-furo)* and the ritual of bathing are absolutely integral to Japanese culture. The Japanese enjoy bathing not simply as a means of relaxation and for the feelings of **well-being** that it stimulates, but also because it perpetuates an age-old tradition. The Japanese passion for cleanliness is also an important factor. The origins of bathing lie in the **Shinto** religion, the animist faith that venerates nature. Before entering the bath, it is important to observe certain rituals, **purifying the body** according to **Shinto rites**, in a reminder never to soil the waters dispensed by the gods.

### THE PLEASURE OF THE BATH

Bathing used to be an activity in which the sexes were not segregated, but when Japan started to open up to the West in the Meiji era, Anglo-American prudishness began to prevail. During the military occupation (1945–52) following Japan's defeat in World War II, the Western Allied Powers ordered the segregation of the sexes in baths, in an attempt to modernize and counter decadence, as they saw it. The owners of some *onsen* (hot springs) had the bright idea of running a cord across the baths in order to keep the sexes apart and respect the new regulations. Nowadays it is still possible in some onsen to reserve an unsegregated private space for family and friends, while fathers sometimes bring their small daughters to baths reserved for men. In practice, the intimacy of nudity abolishes social barriers, although bathers still observe some tacit rules of modesty, such as covering their genitals with a small towel when outside the bath. If using a bath, wash thoroughly under the showers provided before entering the water, making sure to rinse away all soap. Remember that soap should never be used in the baths themselves and long hair must be tied back.

### HOT SPRINGS

From the smallest and most picturesque to the most visited, *onsen* attract more than 151 million people every year. They can be found throughout Japan, situated by the sea, in the mountains, and in both town and country. Thanks to the volcanic nature of the landscape, springs well up from the earth in many places *(see p114 -115)*, some renowned for their healing powers. In 2006, the Ministry of the Environment officially recorded 3,157 *onsen* resorts and 28,154 springs. According to a law passed in 1948, to qualify as an onsen, the water temperature must be at least 77°F/25°C at its source and contain one of 19 minerals designated by the public authorities. Many *ryokan* (traditional inns) pride themselves on having their own springs, and *onsen* are a big draw for Japanese tourists as well as for foreign visitors. One of the oldest and best known is Arima Onsen, north of Kobe *(see p366)*. Said to date back to the 7C, this is where the shogun Toyotomi Hideyoshi (1537–98), accompanied by the distinguished tea master Sen no Rikyu (1522–91), came to recharge his batteries during Japan's feudal era. Arima attracts many Japanese who appreciate the beauty and tranquility of its natural surroundings that are nevertheless within easy reach of the city.

*Onsen* are currently experiencing a boom, but it's not only humans who enjoy bathing in them.

In Tokyo, a large onsen/leisure park has a pool reserved for dogs, which is sometimes also used for racehorses. There are stories of wounded birds being cured, thanks to the healing waters of the onsen, while Japan's macaque monkeys also enjoy relaxing in hot springs, notably at Fukushima in winter.

**Jean-Luc Toula-Breysse**

## The *Onsen* Ritual

Shirahama Onsen, Wakayama
©Wakayama Prefecture/JNTO

In the *onsen* (hot springs) in thermal spas, the ritual is the same as in city sento (public baths). Everyone undresses completely, stowing their clothes and leaving their *yukata* (cotton kimono) in the changing room. They then sit on a small stool and wash and rinse thoroughly with a small cloth in the place set aside for this purpose before entering the bath. Wearing a bathing suit is not permitted, but the more self-conscious can hide behind the small towel provided on entry. It is bad form to enter the water while still dirty, or with soap on the body. In Japan, the bath is not for washing; it is a place for relaxing, relieving stress, and enjoying a moment of repoze: never use soap in a hot bath or spring, make sure you leave it clean, and never put a towel in it. Never empty the bath water on leaving as others will use it after you. The Japanese visit the baths with their family or friends, sometimes with work colleagues, since they can talk peacefully and even drink a cold beer or sake in the boiling water. Often the water temperature is more than 104°F/40°C and can exceed 122°F/50°C, so it's advisable to test the temperature before entering.

## GARDENS

With their passion for gardens, the Japanese have an intimate relationship with nature. In contrast to the Western concept of gardens, where they are seen as places in which nature can be shaped and controlled, in Japan the gardener respects the integrity of the space. For the Japanese, the natural world is populated by a whole host of spirits and, according to Shinto beliefs, communing with nature and the energies of the universe helps to harmonize our relations with the natural world. The creation of gardens is also influenced by the major Japanese faiths and philosophies, Shintoism, Taoism, and Buddhism, chiefly of the Amidist and Zen schools.

### THE ART OF GARDENS

Japanese master gardeners prefer to suggest rather than represent. Working in harmony with the rhythms of seasonal flowering and the color variations of leaves, they respect the impermanence of nature and the natural cycle of life, creating gardens that offer a careful balance between space and content. Like painters, they recompose the reality of the world, the rake across sand replacing a brush across a canvas.

Inspired by Chinese and Korean gardens, the garden as an artform first appeared in the 6C, its popularity spreading during the Heian period, promoted by the aristocracy. The classic manual on the art of the garden, the Sakutei-ki (Records of Garden-Making), thought to have been written during the second half of the 11C, is an invaluable source of information on the principles of creating a Japanese garden.

Many Japanese gardens are designed to integrate the exterior landscape, seen over a wall or hedge, into the background of the garden. As the name suggests, the **shakkei** or **"borrowed landscape" style** incorporates the background landscape into the garden design, as if there were no boundary between them. The gardens of the Katsura Imperial Villa in Kyoto are a perfect example of this technique of assimilating distant elements into what is, strictly speaking, an enclosed space. In the **paradise garden**, the paradise in question is that of Amida, the Japanese name for Amitabha, the principle Buddha of the Pure Land sect of Buddhism. They were a means of visualizing Amida's paradise here on Earth. Typical features are pools dotted with tranquil islets, or encircling a larger island symbolizing man's inner nature. The gardens of the Byodo-in at Uji, near Kyoto are a fine example.

The **tea garden** (*chatei*) is laid out around a pavilion dedicated to the Tea Ceremony (*see p112*). Tea gardens make use of the understated colors of foliage plants and the shade that they create. The rustic character of these small gardens offer an insight into the values of the tea masters, excellent gardeners, and the concept of *wabi* (simplicity and asymmetry) valued so highly by them.

The dry landscape (*kare-sansui*), commonly known as a **Zen garden**, signals a major stage in the evolution of the Japanese garden, following the principles of Zen art: serenity, austerity, asymmetry, simplicity, subtlety, naturalness, and freedom. Zen practitioners used abstract representation to grasp the quintessence of nature. To follow the path of spiritual enlightenment, the gardener-monks freed themselves from all formalism. Hence these gardens reproduce natural landscapes in an abstract way, using rocks, raked sand and gravel, moss, and small shrubs. Water is suggested by the sand and gravel, and the rocks and moss form the landscape features.

A fine example of this genre is attributed to the monk **Muso Soseki** (1275–1351). Tucked away in the northern part of the grounds of the Saiho-ji (Koke-dera-"Moss Temple") in Western Kyoto, is an arrangement of rocks in the shape of a waterfall. The most famous of the dry landscape gardens is **the garden of Ryoan-ji** (Temple of the Peaceful Dragon) in Kyoto, designed in the 15C. It consists of a sea of white sand and 15 rocks arranged in such a way that only 14 are visible at a glance, something that has given rise to many interpretations. To some, it evokes ocean waves surrounding small islands; others see the rocks as mountains peaks floating in mist and cloud. There is no pathway through the stone; it is the ultimate expression of the garden conceived for meditation.

Fashionable during the Edo period, the **strolling garden**, where pools or streams wend their way through a planted landscape, is designed for walking. Paths lead the visitor to discover previously hidden viewpoints, walkways lead over artificial hillocks, while bridges span water. The landscaping frequently echoes celebrated Japanese and Chinese scenery, both real and imagined.

*Dry landscape garden, Ryoan-ji, Kyoto*

In addition to the outstanding gardens in Kyoto are three famous landscape gardens, often described as "The Three Great Gardens of Japan."

They are **Kenroku-en** in Kanazawa *(see p270)*, containing more than 12,000 trees of 150 different species; **Koraku-en** in Okayama *(see pp374–376)*, with maples, cherry trees, bamboos, and Japanese apricots; and **Kairaku-en** in Mito, resplendent in March when the plum trees are in bloom. All three gardens showcase the essentials of Japanesese garden design: a sense of space, formality, serenity, artifice, decorative beauty, and water in abundance. Whatever its style, the Japanese garden is a unique representation of life in miniature beneath an open sky.

**Jean-Luc Toula-Breysse**

## HANDICRAFTS

Japanese folk art is known as *mingei*, from the words *minshu* (people) and *kogei* (craft). Late in gaining recognition in Japan, it was not until the 1920s that, influenced by the distinguished intellectual **Yanagi Soetsu** (1889–1961), folk art took its place alongside the fine arts, which until then were the only arts considered worthy of attention.

Soetsu sparked off the *mingei* movement through his influential book, *The Unknown Craftsman*, encouraging the appreciation of everyday objects whose function may be mundane, but which have a simple beauty.

### BEAUTY IN THE ORDINARY

In *mingei*, the classic distinction that is made between the decorative arts, fine arts, and popular art is no longer valid. The beautiful can be everyday, functional, and anonymous, whatever the material from which it is made.

Japanese craftsmen like to work in paper, silk, and wood, as well as in metal, bamboo, hemp, rice-straw, clay ... a wealth of natural materials with their own intrinsic beauty that the talent of the Japanese artist, respectful of the *kami* living in all natural things, brings out. In the same way, the Japanese style of flower arranging, *ikebana* ("the way of flowers"), aims to pay tribute to nature through its strict rules.

### ARTISTS OR ARTISANS?

In Japan the artist is a craftsman who, rather than attempting to rival the beauty of nature, instead transcribes its beauty into the objects he or she produces. A good example of this is *washi*, the Japanese paper originally used for Buddhist calligraphy, since only its purity was worthy of holy texts. Given the care that goes into the making of a paper initially created to honor first the gods and then the emperors, no Japanese craftsmen working in paper would ever treat it with anything other than the utmost respect. In lanterns, umbrellas, fans, windows, and room dividers, paper plays with light and shadows. It's no accident that it was the Japanese who developed **origami**, the art of folding paper into objects and designs without the use of scissors. The Japanese take great care when unfolding wrapping paper from around a gift, as much care as the person who wrapped it.

### HARD-WON EXPERTISE

Craftsmen reach the pinnacle of their professions after years of practice, improving upon and handing down their techniques to succeeding generations, frequently within the same family. In **pottery**, for example, the techniques for the famous raku (stoneware bowls used in the Tea Ceremony, fired at low temperatures) have been handed down to the present through 14 generations.

Japanese pottery (terra-cotta or glazed stoneware) was initially designed exclusively for domestic use (bowls and dishes), but toward the end of the High Middle Ages (16C), it was adopted by the tea masters, who found sophistication in its extreme simplicity, paying tribute to the honest clay that produced it.

Less fragile than pottery, **wood** is one of the most commonly used materials in Japan. Available in quantity, thanks to the abundance of forests *(Tsee Nature p 114)*, its association with the deities of the forest makes it doubly precious.

**Lacquer** has been used since the Nara period to decorate and protect the most precious woods against humidity. In the maki-e technique developed in the Heian era, gold or silver powder is used as decoration. Other popular materials include bamboo and of course **silk**, which replaced the material made from the inner bark fiber of the mulberry, from which Japanese garments were made in ancient times. In the Nara era, wearing silk was the privilege of the aristocracy and highly sophisticated techniques were employed in weaving and coloring it; in kasuri, for example, used in kimonos or Noh costumes, the threads are dyed before weaving. Finally, **stone**, the most basic of materials, can be carved into lanterns, basins, and sculptures. When patinated by time and eroded by wind and rain, nature adds its own simple finishing touches.

**Philippe Pataud Célérier**

## FASHION
## FROM THE KIMONO …

The history of the kimono goes back nearly a thousand years, reflecting changes in lifestyle and culture, and technical developments in textiles and production.

The kimono is famous for the elegant simplicity of its shape (six bands of the finest silk, hand-painted), its flexibility, and the fact that it suits all sizes, as well as for its sophisticated weaves and rich decoration.

Despite its long history and symbolic role, sales of the kimono declined dramatically after World War II. Women adopted Western dress for everyday life, reserving the traditional costume for great cultural or family occasions, such as the hatsumode (first shrine visit of the New Year), the *Shichi-Go-San* ceremony for children of three, five, and seven on November 15 (when families visit the shrine with children wearing colored kimonos to pray to the gods to keep them safe), graduation ceremonies, weddings, and the Coming of Age ceremony (20 is the age of majority in Japan) on the second Monday in January.

Traditionally, **the cut, colors, and fabric** of the kimono vary according to the occasion, the season, and the age, sex, and marital status of the wearer. But appreciation of the kimono seems to have recently undergone a transformation, with the rise in demand from 20–30-year-olds who, saturated with

### Living National Treasures: Ningen Kokuho

The Japanese have always had a profound admiration for exceptional objects because they represent the peak of what human creativity can achieve and their perfection brings one closer to the supernatural or even the divine. This is chiefly the case with examples of objects introduced into Japan over the centuries, such as the Chinese tea bowl subsequently used by the shoguns. Because of their history, quality, and rarity, they have been classified as "National Treasures" if they are unique, or as "Important Cultural Properties" if only a few examples exist in Japan or elsewhere. Since the Japanese do not distinguish between living and inanimate objects, they have naturally awarded the same honors to exceptional human beings (the *Ningen Kokuho* or Living National Treasures) who are considered the best in their category and who express themselves through the objects they create or the performances they give. Currently Japan has 107 Living National Treasures: 38 individuals and 11 groups in the performing arts (*gagaku*, Noh, *bunraku*, Kabuki, music, etc.), and 44 individuals and 14 groups in arts and crafts (ceramics, textiles, lacquer, metal, bamboo, dolls, paper, etc.) In addition, the Agency for Cultural Affairs (*Bunkacho*) lists 860 works as National Treasures (*Kokuho*) and 9,402 works as Important Cultural Properties (*Juyo Bunkazai*).

**Gilles Maucout**

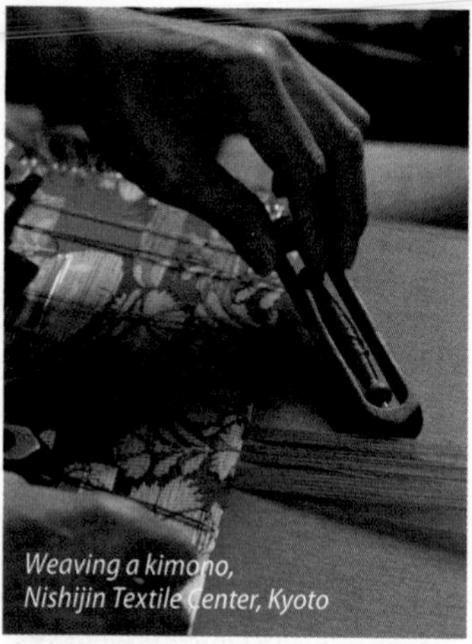

*Weaving a kimono, Nishijin Textile Center, Kyoto*

©Kyoto Convention Bureau / JNTO

Western culture, have delightedly "discovered" their traditional culture and taken up the kimono, wearing it with much more enthusiasm than their parents and on more informal occasions. This new interest is well catered for by websites dedicated to the pleasures and ways of wearing the kimono, since their thoroughly Westernized parents are often not able to show them how it should be worn.

In response to the demand, **kimono shops**, selling secondhand and "vintage" kimonos at knockdown prices have sprung up in Tokyo and Kyoto. They are patronized by foreigners as well as the Japanese because, thanks to its super-simple cut, the kimono can be worn in a contemporary style. **Younger wearers of the kimono** often combine it with Western accessories like necklaces, earrings, designer handbags, and sometimes even high heels. Some young women have gone so far as to wear the kimono with jeans or boots, a style that horrifies the older generation for whom this modern interpretation represents an unacceptable break with tradition. For them, the kimono should only be worn with tabi (little white cotton socks) and geta (wooden clogs) or zori (leather sandals), while the bust should be girdled with a tightly wrapped obi (embroidered silk waistband).

This **mixture of styles**, traditional and contemporary, is particularly noticeable in the fashionable Tokyo districts of Harajuku and Shibuya, although the very chic Ginza Avenue remains traditional. A sign of the times, however, is that you can also find clothes and Western-style handbags made from kimono fabric here. All these trends reflect the evolution of traditional costume and confirm that the "spirit of kimono" remains deeply anchored in Japanese culture.

## ... TO "STREET FASHION"

In accordance with their fresh attitude toward the kimono, young Japanese wear Western clothing with flair and great creativity. While the previous generation followed the rules of French-style fashion to the letter, wearing the classic two-piece suit that was adopted by some as an alternative to the kimono, today's young have taken many liberties, even with already non-conformist Western dress. They have succeeded in inventing a distinctly Japanese version of street fashion, which some foreign designers have reappropriated for their own collections. During the 1970s and 1980s, the celebrated **Issey Miyake** (in 1974, he was the first Japanese designer to combine Japanese and Western style) helped liberate young women from a completely Western style. Ten years later, **Yamamoto Yohji** and **Kawakubo Rei** (Comme des Garçons) challenged Western ideas about the use of color, the construction of garments, body shape, and the sexism of society. These two designers revolutionized fashion, championing conceptual shapes, plainness, and dark colors in place of the "pink, frilly, flowery" trend so much in vogue during the 1960s. **Kawakubo Rei** specializes in "anti-fashion" with austere, asymmetrical shapes.

In reaction to this trend, however, now freed from any hang-ups about Western style or their parents' preoccupations about dress, young Japanese have rediscovered color, frills, and sexy clothing. A feminine, decidedly Japanese style now fills the clothing stores. Greatly influenced by manga, young women want clothes that make them look pretty. The **Lolita style** emerged on the streets of Tokyo with a whole range of specific types: "Gothic Lolitas" wear black lace frills and black makeup for lips and eyes; "Punk Lolitas" sport the same frills but decorated with chains and skulls; "Eros Lolitas" are in lingerie, laced corsets, and boots; "Hime (princess) Lolitas," wear tiaras and layered skirts decorated with roses.

But, despite this exuberance of dress for the young, fashion is still structured in a typically Japanese way. At around 22, the *kawaii* (*see p83)* bag is swapped for a Chanel; at 24, the Armani skirt makes an appearance; at 26, the tailored jacket, and at 28, the trouser suit. In between, young women have learned how to mix styles and origins in their own unique way.

A whole range of Japanese designers, including eco-friendly **Muji (Mujirushi)** and **Uniqlo**, two fashion retailers now branching out worldwide, have made Japan a melting pot in which traditional Japanese delicacy is allied to cutting-edge technological innovation. In their wide variety of styles, ranging from the extreme to the classic, designers are responding not just to the demands of a population that no longer wants one-style-fits-all fashion, but also to the broader quest for freedom that has infused postwar Japan.

**Françoise Moréchand**

## MARTIAL ARTS AND SUMO

Unlike the Chinese martial arts that developed in villages as a defense against attack, the Japanese martial arts are closely linked to the history of samurai or *bushi*, whose exclusive preserve they were for centuries. When it first appeared in the 8C, the word *samurai* was still pronounced *saburai*, from the verb *saburau*, to serve one's master. This ideal of following a code of honor called *bushido* (the way of the samurai) would endure among the warrior class until it disappeared at the end of the 19C.

### THE ORIGIN OF MARTIAL ARTS

The traditional Japanese martial arts developed during the Edo period comprise seven principal skills: the art of the sword *(kenjutsu)*, the art of the spear *(sojutsu)*, the art of using a bow *(archery—kyujutsu)*, combat on horseback *(bajutsu)*, unarmed combat *(jujutsu)*, the use of firearms *(hojutsu)*, and strategy *(hyoho)*. The art of the sword is considered the noblest technique and under the Tokugawa Shogunate, the warrior elite of Japanese society had the right to strike down anyone of a lower class who compromised their honor with no fear of punishment *(kirisute gomen)*.

This warrior mentality remained the ideological basis for the military regime that existed from 1930–45, for whom the practice of martial arts was primarily a way of "serving the emperor" and defending the country. This belief was dramatically illustrated in 1945 at Okinawa (where karate originated) when the inhabitants, short of arms and ammunition, attempted to repulse the US Army with their bare hands.

Following the Occupation, the Allied forces discouraged the teaching of most martial arts and it was not until 1949 that judo, for example, was again permitted, provided that it was run purely on the basis of a democratic sport, having been purged of all references to war and violence. After this, martial arts became completely divorced from the cult of the Emperor and the domination of one social class over another. They became popular sporting disciplines that helped individuals achieve harmony between mind and body, with an emphasis placed on courtesy and respect for the adversary.

Martial arts demand both patience and humility. Learning a martial art involves endless repetitions of kata ("forms"—choreographed patterns of movements) until they can be performed to perfection. Rankings (dan), generally denoted by differently colored belts, classify practitioners according to their skill level. In their still relatively new guise as sports, several martial arts have undergone a real renaissance and some (including judo) have gone on to become Olympic disciplines.

There are **dozens of martial arts** ranging from *jo-jutsu* (combat with a short staff) to *ju-jitsu* (combat with bare hands), along

### The rules of sumo

Sumo rules are simple: it involves pushing an opponent out of the *dohyo*, a clay circle 14.9ft/ 4.55m in diameter surrounded by a rope, or unbalancing him so that some part of his body other than the bottom of his feet touches the ground. There are 70 winning techniques but in general only around 30 are used. The size of the wrestlers is one of the paradoxes of the sport: to compete more effectively, they pack on the weight until they sometimes weigh more than 441lb/200kg. However, this does not prevent them being both supple and fast. In the ring they wear only a *mawashi*, a band of cloth wrapped around the waist and between the legs.

with *tessen-jutsu* (the art of fighting with a *war-fan*—a fan made of iron, designed for combat) or *yabusame* (archery on horseback) but the most popular, in Japan as in the rest of the world, are judo, karate, and aikido, which have existed for less than a century in their modern forms.

### Judo

Derived from *ju-jitsu*, judo (the way of gentleness), was founded by Kano Jigoro in 1882. It is based on a series of throws, rolls, falls, choking techniques, arm locks, and groundwork (changing the position of the body and limbs to gain advantage and control), all designed to immobilize an opponent. Judo became a fully-fledged Olympic sport for men at the Tokyo Olympics in 1964 and for women in 1992.

### Karate

*Karate-do* (the way of the "empty hand") originated in China at the Shaolin Temple toward the end of the 5C. In the 15C, it was adapted and developed by the Japanese of the Ryukyu Islands (Okinawa, *see p510*) in the 15C as a response to a decree banning the inhabitants from carrying weapons. It was popularized by Funakoshi Gichin, himself a native of Okinawa and founder of the Shotokan school of karate in 1938. Modern karate is based on punching, kicking, knee or elbow strikes, and techniques using the flat hand.

### Aikido

Aikido is one of the most recent martial arts. It was developed between 1930 and 1960 by Ueshiba Morihei, who derived it from ancient *ju-jitsu* techniques. In contrast to judo and karate, aikido (the way of vital energy, the *ki*) is not based on attack but on controlling an opponent by utilizing his energy against him. It does not require great physical strength, making it attractive to women, who are taking it up in increasingly numbers.

## SUMO

Sumo is not considered a martial art and is practiced by a small number of wrestlers *(rikishi)*. However, along with baseball, it is one of the most popular sports in Japan, where champions *(yokozuna)* are treated like movie stars. Only outstanding wrestlers achieve this status, however, and it is extremely difficult to make it into the top two divisions *(juryo* and *makuuchi)* that regularly appear in tournaments *(basho)*, and to receive a salary (other wrestlers merely get an allowance). These high-ranked wrestlers *(sekitori)* are also the only ones allowed to wear the *o-icho-mage* hairstyle, a fanlike topknot said to resemble a gingko leaf; it is finally cut off in a ceremony at the end of a wrestler's career.

The **origins of sumo** are almost as old as those of Japan itself, with many of its rituals deriving from Shintoism, such as the throwing of salt into the ring for purification before each bout, the referee's elaborate costume, etc.

Although long the exclusive preserve of Japanese wrestlers, sumo is gradually opening up to foreigners. Hawaiians were the first to break through, during the 1960s and 1970s, and their most famous wrestler Takamiyama even became the first foreign *yokozuna* in the history of sumo. More recently, two Mongolians, **Asashoryu** and **Hakuho**, have held the title.

**Patrick Duval**

## GASTRONOMY
## THE ART OF LIVING

*"Itadakimasu!"* say the Japanese when they sit down to eat. It's often translated as "bon appétit" but in fact means "I humbly receive it" and is an expression of gratitude toward everything that has contributed to the meal. It is addressed firstly to the gods (this is a Shinto custom), then to the animals and vegetables (who have given their lives to feed us), and, finally, to the cook who has assembled all these ingredients in a nourishing, appetizing dish. In another sense, *"itadakimasu"* has the even more precise meaning of "I take your honorable life," recalling the expression *"inochi o itadakimasu,"* used by samurai in olden times when they killed a peasant.

Now, however, although they continue to pronounce this formula three times daily, most Japanese are ignorant of its etymology. Nevertheless, it demonstrates a special relationship with food, with particular attention paid to the products and labor that have gone into the meal. And so, contrary to "bon appétit," which is entirely centered on the simple pleasure of consuming a quantity of food, *"itadakimasu"* seems more like an apology to nature for taking something from it to satisfy a natural need.

In fact, Japanese cooking is an unassuming cuisine, rather more moderate or indeed ascetic than indulgent. For instance, consider the meaning of the word *kaiseki*. Initially a simple hot stone that monks applied to their stomachs to calm hunger pangs, *kaiseki* then came to signify a light repast served before the Tea Ceremony. Today it is used to describe the most sophisticated kind of Japanese banquet.

"Good cooking," said French food writer Curnonsky, "is when things taste of what they are." No definition can better apply to Japanese cooking since it is not so much a question of making foods tasty by adding sauces or combining them with other ingredients as **bringing out the flavor** of each ingredient by different cooking processes. Another challenge is to get the most out of every ingredient so as to **limit the waste** of resources. In fact, Japanese cooking is a **digestible** and **well-balanced** cuisine that aids health and long life; for the past 20 years the Japanese have held the world record for **longevity**.

## A LONG HISTORY

The history of Japanese cookery goes back to the Yayoi era (300 BC–AD 300), during which **rice** cultivation was developed, new styles of pottery and bronze appeared, and conservation techniques of drying or fermentation evolved, leading to the brewing of **sake** and later, the making of **miso**.

During the Nara (8C) and Heian (9–12C) periods, Japan came under Chinese influence. The first dairy products appeared, such as **raku**, a sharp, liquid, cheese-like nutrient. Vinegar and salt also date from this period. Zen Buddhism was introduced in the Kamakura era (1185–1333) and its influence was significant: *shojin* is a Buddhist term meaning "to distance oneself from distractions, purify the body, and prepare oneself with ardor."

**Shojin cuisine** became popular and remains one of the main props of Japanese cuisine. The Muromachi and Momoyama periods (from around the 14C until the end of the 16C) saw the appearance of **soy sauce, sugar**, and **konbu seaweed**, three elements essential to the "Japanese taste." Then, owing to the development of a technique for drying bonito (skipjack tuna; *katsuo bushi)*, **dashi** was invented and still features prominently in Japanese gastronomy.

During the same period, the *Nanban* (literally "Southern barbarians," meaning the Portuguese) introduced fried food into Japan, which soon developed into **tempura** (meat, fish, or vegetables deep-fried in batter). At the end of the 16C, the Tea Ceremony had reached such a pitch of sophistication (inspired by the master Sen no Rikyu) that a special cuisine, **kaiseki ryori**, was created to go with it. Under the influence of Buddhism (the monks of that time were essentially vegetarian), meat consumption was in theory punishable by death.

Later on, from the beginning of the Meiji era (1868), many dietary prohibi-

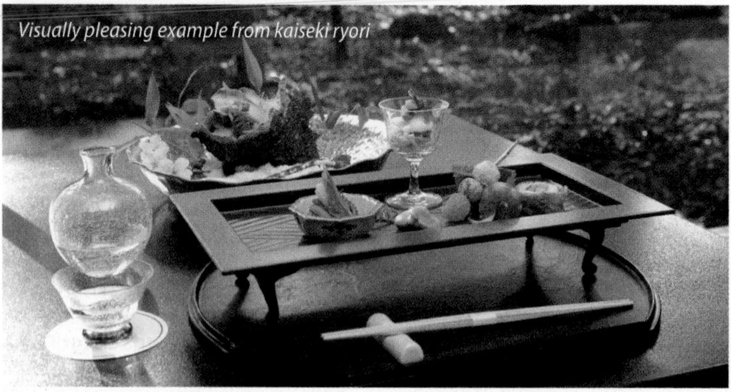

*Visually pleasing example from kaiseki ryori*

© JNTO

tions disappeared. The Emperor publicly praised the benefits of red meat and Western influence led to an influx of new products. They remain well segregated, however, and restaurants often specialize in one type of cooking: sushi, *tonkatsu* (breaded pork), tempura, *yakitori*, and so on.

## TYPES OF CUISINE

### Nabemono: Japanese fondue

Nabemono means "cooking pot" and sukiyaki is the best-known dish in this style of cooking. It consists of thinly sliced beef cooked in a broth called warishita, a mixture of mirin, sake, soy sauce, and sugar. Each mouthful is then dipped in raw egg and eaten with accompaniments such as shiitake and enoki mushrooms, Chinese cabbage, chrysanthemum leaves, tofu, and, finally, thin transparent noodles called shirataki. Shabu-shabu is another dish made with the same basic ingredients, but with a different broth.

### Sashimi, sushi: raw fish

As Japan is surrounded by sea, fish has always played a big part in the national diet, even if the consumption of meat has nowadays overtaken it. On the other hand, eating raw fish has now become popular in many other countries, with sushi bars springing up everywhere. For example, in 2008 there were more than 800 "sushi bars" in a city such as Paris.

The traditional method of preparing raw fish is first to debone it, then serve it either as sashimi—simply sliced and dipped in shoyu (soy sauce)—or as nigiri—a slice of fish is placed on a mound of rice lightly flavored with vinegar and sweetened—or as maki sushi—that is, placed on a bed of rice laid over nori (seaweed), rolled into a cylinder, and then sliced in pieces. Between bites, the palate is cleansed with strips of ginger marinated in vinegar.

Moriawase, an assortment of raw fish, whether sashimi, nigiri, or chirashi (where the fish is served on a bed of white rice) generally comprises one or two red fish such as tuna or bonito; white fish such as sea bass or bream; raw or cooked shrimp; cuttlefish; mackerel; and Japanese omelet.

Seasonal fish or shellfish, sea urchins, or eel may also be ordered, and the selection can be varied not only according to the season but also to the appetite and budget of the client. A good choice is an omakase menu, the chef's selection of the best of the day's products. The platter will also contain wasabi, a fiery grated green root.

### Monks' Cookery

**Shojin** cuisine, introduced to Japan in the Edo period, originated with the meager meals of Zen Buddhist monks and from Chinese *fucha* cooking. It uses only vegetables, seaweed, dried fish, or miso. Natural ingredients ensure a balanced diet. Some temples, notably at Kyoto or Kamakura, offer visitors the opportunity to experience it.

**Kaiseki** is a branch of *shojin* cuisine adapted at the end of the 16C to accompany the Tea Ceremony. It involves a succession of elaborately arranged small dishes, whose formal beauty is an aesthetic experience. It is served in *ryotei* (luxury restaurants) or in *ryokan* (traditional inns).

### The Way of the noodle

Noodles originated in China and are now one of the most popular dishes in Japan, especially with the young, who eat them at home or at the office in the form of Cup Noodle (a Japanese brand of dehydrated instant noodles). Noodle restaurants are also very popular.

There are three main kinds of noodles: **soba**, made with buckwheat flour and eaten hot or cold, also have a symbolic value as soba means "nearby" and it is the custom for those who move house to offer a packet to their new neighbors. A specialty of the island of Shikoku, **udon** are wheat noodles, served in a broth with beef, pork, or deep-fried shrimp. **Ramen** are also wheat noodles, thinner than udon and served in big bowls of stock, or sautéed (yakisoba) with squid and vegetables.

### Tempura: fritters

This dish of Portuguese origin is a variant of the fritters cooked in Mediterranean regions. Vegetables, shrimp, or fish are dipped in a batter of water, egg, and flour, then dropped in boiling oil. The chef's skill lies in making a coating retaining the product's taste and a warm center. Tempura is served immediately and eaten hot. A tempura menu consists of several batches, eaten with a pinch of salt (sometimes mixed with powdered matcha), lightly dipped in a sauce of soy and grated white radish (daikon), or sprinkled with lemon juice. At the end of the meal a large fritter made with shrimp, scallops, and herbs is served with rice, accompanied by a broth, miso soup, or tea.

### Hot-plate Cuisine

Hot-plate cooking or **teppanyaki** is popular in the US, which is why chefs who specialize in it are sometimes called Japanese "cowboys," especially since a well-known chain, Benihana, has popularized this kind of cooking by adding a touch of showmanship (the chef juggles with the food). Here the cook simply grills pieces of beef, shrimp, scallops, or vegetables in front of the client, then sprinkles them with lemon juice or flames them (sometimes with sake). Another hot-plate specialty, **okonomiyaki**, originates from Hiroshima. Okonomi means "as you like it" and yaki means "grilled." It involves a pancake filled with a choice of meat, vegetables, or seafood. The pancake is cooked on both sides and then coated with a sweet brown sauce to which dried seaweed or a few flakes of dried tuna may be added.

### Breaded Dishes

**Tonkatsu**, breaded deep-fried pork, is the Japanese interpretation of a Western dish, the cutlet; pronounced Japanese-style this first became katsu-retsu, then ton (pork) katsu. Introduced into Japan around 1890, it has been popular since the 1930s. Pork fillets or sirloin are dipped into an egg and flour batter, then coated with breadcrumbs and fried in oil. The dish is served with a salad of finely chopped cabbage, white rice, and a tonkatsu sauce, made with vinegar, condiments, and vegetables, which can be either mild (amakuchi) or a bit spicier (karakuchi). The pork and rice may also come in a bowl, with egg and grilled onions (**katsudon**). Alternative versions are made with shrimp (**ebifurai**) or oysters (**kakifurai**).

### Unagi: grilled eel

Rich in proteins, vitamin A, and calcium, eel is usually eaten in summer. In specialist restaurants, recognizable by the character "う," they are delivered live. The chef arranges them on little bamboo skewers before barbecuing or steaming them, or both methods successively. Presented on a bed of white rice in a lacquered box, the eel is anointed with a sweet sauce, the recipe for which (always a secret) varies from one restaurant to another. It can be spiced up to taste with a pinch of sansho, the ground dried leaves of the prickly ash tree.

© Francisco Po Egea/AGE/Photononstop

## The Tea Ceremony

The Tea Ceremony *(cha-no-yu)* or *sado*, (the way of tea), is sometimes wrongly seen in the West as a simple feminine pastime, like one of those cultural activities adopted by geishas for tourists in search of the exotic. This is a complete mis-interpretation of an activity that for centuries was a spiritual discipline central to the warrior class that ruled the country. Today it remains an important element of Japanese culture and the Japanese spirit.

### Origin and context

Between the 10C and the 14C, China's intellectual and artistic influence radiated throughout Asia. Buddhism, calligraphy, painting, architecture, poetry, pottery, the cultivation of bonsai, and flower arranging were all taken up by aristocratic Japanese. The cultivation and culture of tea were imported from China by the monk **Eisai** (1141–1215) and a brew of powdered dried leaves (*matcha*), used to banish sleepiness during meditation sessions in Zen temples. Next, the monk **Ikkyu** (1394–1481) brought to Japan the already established Chinese custom of serving notables with bowls of green tea in the temple's ceremonial halls. Tea leaves were ground to a fine green powder, placed in a bowl (the *chawan*) into which hot water was poured, then the brew was mixed with the aid of a small bamboo whisk (the *chasen*). The tea ceremony became the prerogative of the ruling classes and remained so until the end of the 19C and the fall of the feudal regime.

### Skewered Chicken

**Yakitori** (literal meaning "grilled bird") consists of bite-sized pieces of chicken glazed with a soy-based sauce sweetened with sugar and *mirin*, then grilled on skewers.

Salt and sauce can be added, if desired. Prepared in front of the client, the skewers are served when ready and may be seasoned with *shichimi togarashi* (a condiment made with Cayenne pepper, orange peel, and five other spices). *Yakitori* first originated during the Meiji period, being made from restaurant leftovers recovered by small traders and sold from street stands. Much later, during the 1960s, the importation of chicken from America made *yakitori* one of Japan's most popular dishes.

Along with sushi, it is also the most widely exported. In Japan a *yakitori* meal also includes vegetables and sometimes even beef or pork, while rice is served at the end of the meal, shaped into a ball and grilled *(yaki onigiri)*, sometimes wrapped in *nori* (seaweed).

**Patrick Duval**

## WARRIORS AND SCHOLAR MONKS

Between the 14C and the end of the 19C, China and Japan closed themselves to the rest of the world and each developed an individual culture derived from the foundations of Buddhism and Confucianism. In addition to Shinto, Japan's ancestral faith, the samurai class adopted Zen Buddhism because of the moral virtues it espoused. The tea pavilion became a sacred place to the warrior elite, encouraged in this by the Zen monks who gravitated to them. So, we read about the general **Kawamori Yoshishige**: "He defended the castle of Kishikawa and personally decapitated 208 persons ... He was also an excellent tea master ..."

In due course three important people departed from Chinese influence to make the tea ceremony truly Japanese. **Murata Shuko** (1422–1502) reduced the size of the pavilion, creating the *soan* style: a room spread with four or five tatami mats, where objects of varying origins combined in a purely Japanese style. The tea ceremony accordingly became more intimate, moving from its conventional hierarchic framework. A century later, **Takeno Joo** (1504–55) returned to Zen basics by introducing greater austerity in space and materials used. Finally, **Sen no Rikyu** (1522–91) determined the context of the ceremony, including the passage of guests via the *roji* (a garden marking the transition from the external world to the pure world of the tea pavilion) and the symbolic purification on the *tsukubai* (a stone basin in which to rinse fingers and mouth). He also separated the tea pavilion from the main residence, obliging guests to crouch to enter through the *nijiriguchi,* a small opening that compelled the greatest lord to great humility.

The esthetic of *wabi* (simplicity) was born: it would mark the Japanese psyche forever.

### The Tea Pavilion

While the Chinese tea pavilion (four pillars supporting a roof) is largely open, the Japanese pavilion is hermetically closed in upon itself. All the elements—the morning-gathered flower *(chabana)*, the filtered light on the *shoji*, and the utensils necessary for the ceremony—give the impression of a microcosm where emptiness gives meaning to fullness. In this setting, the master can prepare the tea, his measured movements showing the degree of expertise and precision that he has attained. To achieve this, the brain, breath, and abdomen (the *hara*) need to be perfectly coordinated in a discipline common to all the martial arts (from which comes the term *sado* or "the way of tea").

## THE JAPANESE SPIRIT

Harmony, respect, purity, and serenity are the four fundamental principles involved in the tea ceremony. Nevertheless, while developing the modest tea pavilion, the samurai went much further, forging throughout more than four centuries what would become Japan's great strength: study, concentration, continuous practice, precision of gestures, a sense of detail, determination, and abnegation. All qualities that the Japanese would subsequently put to use in many other situations far removed from the context of the tea ceremony.

**Gilles Maucout**

### Tetsubin and kama

Tetsubin are cast-iron pots, used in feudal times to boil water for tea. There is a distinction to be made between the kettle with a handle, which was set on the fire or hung above it, and the kama, a round pot, generally without handles but with a lug on each side into which a metal handle can be inserted, used exclusively to heat the water in tea ceremonies. In each case these utensils were not used as teapots in the way they are used in Europe. In Japan, teapots are generally made of porcelain, even today.

# Nature

**The Japanese archipelago's geography is one of the world's most contrasted and varied, shaping the character of its inhabitants, who have had to adjust to a difficult environment. It consists of about 3,500 islands and islets lying in a north-to-east chain, extending over 1,864mi/3,000km between latitudes 45° and 25° north.**

## A GREAT SEAFARING COUNTRY

The landmass is modest: 95 percent of Japan's 145,947sq mi/378,000sq km is taken up by the four main islands of Kyushu, Shikoku, Honshu, and Hokkaido. However, if territorial seas are included—the Exclusive Economic Zones (EEZ) that extend 200 nautical miles (230mi/370.4km) out from the coastline—the country achieves an area of 1.7 million sq mi/4.5 million sq km. If Japan's 20,505mi/33,000km of coastline are taken into account, its world ranking for area jumps from fiftieth to sixth.

## A MOUNTAINOUS REGION

Between its northern and southern poles (Hokkaido and Okinawa), Japan's climatic and environmental range varies from the subtropical mangrove region to the resinous subpolar tip, passing through innumerable zones of broad-leaved trees (oak, beech, dogwood, magnolia, maple), resinous trees (*Cryptomeria japonica*), and cherry trees (*Prunus*) of the temperate zones of Honshu, the large central island.

The sea gives the archipelago its heavy rainfall, two-thirds of the country getting ove r59in/1.50m of rain annually. Around two-thirds of the Japanese landmass is forested (186 tree types and 4,500 plant varieties), but only one-fifth is habitable because about 70 percent is mountainous. In fact, slopes with an incline of 15 percent or greater form three-quarters of the country.

## THE PLAINS

Japan has very little arable land (only 16 percent of the territory). The rich, cultivable plains benefit from their volcanic origins. The plain of Kanto, in the Tokyo region, once the largest in Japan (around 5,791.5sq mi/15,000sq km), is now the world's largest conurbation, with around 30 million inhabitants. Urban development and hyper-industrialization have progressively encroached on these plains.

## NATURAL DANGERS

In addition to its many mountains, Japan also has numerous volcanoes. The country's highest mountain, the celebrated Mount Fuji, is in fact a volcanic cone 12,388ft/3,776m high, which has been dormant since the 18C. More than 260 volcanoes have been identi-

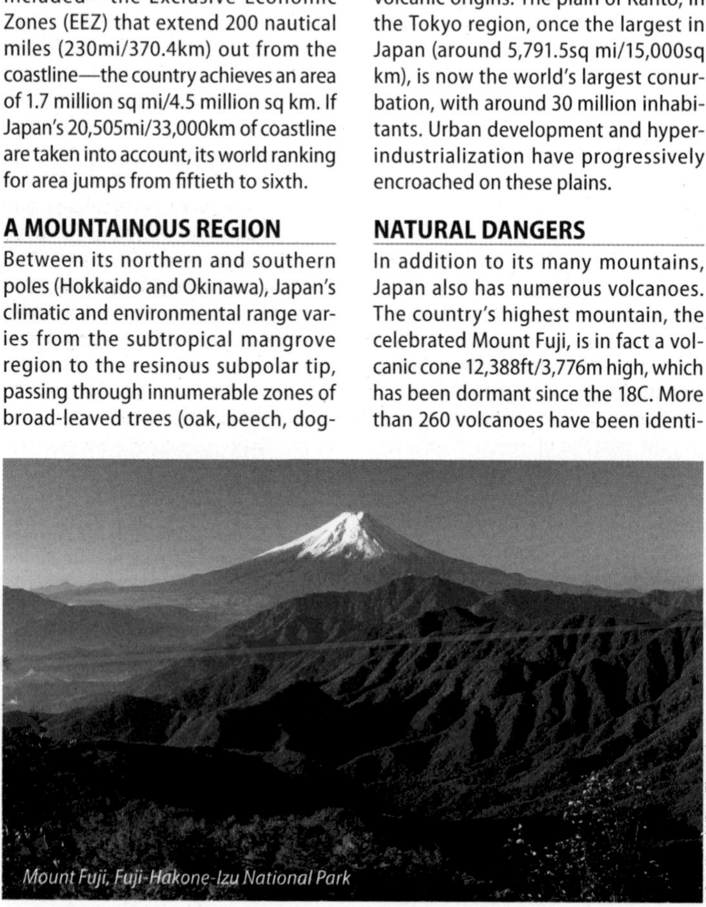

*Mount Fuji, Fuji-Hakone-Izu National Park*

fied in Japan, of which around a hundred are active, comprising 10 percent of the world's active volcanoes. This volcanic activity is due to the fact that the earth's crust is influenced by the "Pacific ring of fire." The Japanese archipelago, situated at the confluence of the Eurasian, Amurian, Pacific, and Philippine Plates, is regularly shaken by these tectonic forces, leading to often devastating earthquakes. The most disastrous killed 140,000 people in 1923, more than 5,500 were killed in Kobe in 1995; then the 2008 earthquakes in Iwate and Miyagi fortunately claimed only a few victims in these less-populated regions, although on a scale comparable to that of Kobe. Most recently, however, was what has already come to be known as the Great East Japan Earthquake: 9.0 on the Richter scale, it unleashed a huge tsunami on Japan's eastern coastline on 11 March 2011. It was the most powerful earthquake to ever hit Japan and one of the five most powerful earthquakes recorded worldwide, leaving over 15,000 dead and 8,000 missing across 18 prefectures.

## AN UNFRIENDLY HABITAT

The Japanese have adapted to this unfavorable natural habitat: the inhospitable slopes mean using irrigated rice cultivation, divided into plots to employ the rural population. Livestock farming is proscribed for lack of pasture, harmonizing with Buddhist principles forbidding slaughter of animals.

For heavy, humid seasons, Japanese architecture has sliding doors to permit currents of air. Faced with earthquakes or heavy snowfalls in the north, they build with wood: abundant, flexible, and lighter than stone, and more resistant to frost. They have learned how to draw hot-water springs (onsen) from boiling, menacing volcanoes, facilitating hygiene, moments of serenity, a place for sociability, and union with nature. And, to combat the lack of usable space, they have enlarged the coastal strips. Conversely, multiple techniques have been developed to control and circulate or dam their plentiful water supply.

### The "back of Japan" and the "front of Japan"

Although Japan's central region is situated in a temperate zone, the mountainous spine that divides it in two throughout almost its entire length experiences some striking contrasts: in winter cold, damp winds blow from the northwest, bringing heavy snowfall on the side facing the Sea of Japan, known as the "back of Japan" (Ura Nihon). On the other side of the Japan Alps, the Pacific coastline or "front of Japan" (Omote Nihon) is much sunnier in winter, but rainy in summer. Tropical air masses from the southwest mount toward the north, bringing monsoon rains (baiu) in June, followed by tropical cyclones in September.

## A RURAL EXODUS

This mastery over Japan's weather and limited space has downsides: coastlines have been overdeveloped and often vandalized. Urban modernity has accelerated the rural exodus. Today three-quarters of the Japanese population lives in towns and cities.

A quarter of the population lives in the Tokyo region alone, which is 2 percent of the territory. Increasingly, sophisticated techniques sometimes overlook the natural dangers. Nuclear power stations proliferate, in defiance of the ever-present seismic threat.

As a result of the numerous dangers the Japanese have always faced, there is still a great emphasis upon collective functioning and coordination, and upon efficiency and exactitude (railway announcements state that a train will arrive at 11.01, for instance). Animistic beliefs remain because no matter how sophisticated the technological world may become. it will never measure up to the chaos that underlies it, and these beliefs give them hope.

**Philippe Pataud-Célérier**

*Prada Building by Herzog & de Meuron, Aoyama, Tokyo*

# DISCOVERING JAPAN

# TOKYO AND SURROUNDINGS

**Much has been written about this enormous metropolis and its sprawling suburbs, its inhabitants sometimes likened to ants scurrying around a vast nest. Tokyo is much more than this, however, even if it is slowly but surely encroaching upon the outskirts of other towns, just as it did upon Yokohama, the country's second city, only 15.5mi/25km from the capital. Including the city center, the suburbs, and the agglomeration of neighboring towns that have also been absorbed, Tokyo is in fact the largest conurbation in the world, extending across Japan's largest plain (2,702.7sq mi/7,000sq km) in the heart of the Kanto region.**

## Highlights

1. The superb collection of **Tokyo National Museum** (p131)
2. The breathtaking view from Roppongi's **Mori Arts Center Gallery** atop the Mori Tower (p146)
3. People watching on **Harajuku Bridge** on a shopping trip, (p157) and (p159)
4. Tranquil **Meiji-jingu** shrine, (pp159–160)
5. Day trips to peaceful **Nikko** and cosmopolitan **Yokohama**, (p201) and (p186)

## The region today

Kanto region is Japan's most densely populated, with 41.5 million inhabitants. With seven prefectures on only 8.6 percent of Japan's total surface area, it holds a third of the country's population and the seat of the central government as well; it is no surprise that is also the nation's most economically productive.

## Administrative organization

The Japanese archipelago is made up of eight regions, spread over the four main islands. From north to south they are: Hokkaido (30,502.1sq mi/79,000sq km); the regions of Tohoku, Kanto, Chubu, Kansai (or Kinki), and Chugoku on the main central island of Honshu (87,645.2sq mi/227,000sq km); Shikoku (6,949.8sq mi/18,000sq km); and Kyushu (14,286.8sq mi/37,000sq km). These regions are themselves divided into 47 prefectures.

- **Population:** 41.5 million.
- **Michelin Map:** Opposite, principal sights map B3.
- **Location:** Situated in Honshu, the largest of the archipelago's islands, **Kanto** now includes the metropolitan prefecture of Tokyo *(to)* (12.5 million inhabitants), plus six other prefectures *(ken)*: Chiba (6 million inhabitants), Ibaraki (3 million), Tochigi (2 million), Gunma (2 million), Saitama (7 million), and Kanagawa (8.5 million). In the neighboring region of Chuba are the prefectures of Shizuoka (*see Izu Peninsula pp224–229)* and Yamanashi (*see Mount Fuji pp214–223)*.
- **Kids:** An afternoon in the futuristic part of Yokohama; walking the Izu Peninsula's trails and then an *onsen*; a stroll beneath the Japanese cedars in Nikko.
- **Timing:** A good balance would be to spend at least a week in Tokyo, then one day in Yokohama; two days in Kamakura; one day for the Hakone region; two days for Mount Fuji; three days for the Izu Peninsula to take advantage of the *onsen*; and three days to enjoy the special natural and cultural heritage offered in Nikko.
- **Don't miss:** Nikko, Kamakura, Shuzenji.

## TOKYO AND SURROUNDINGS

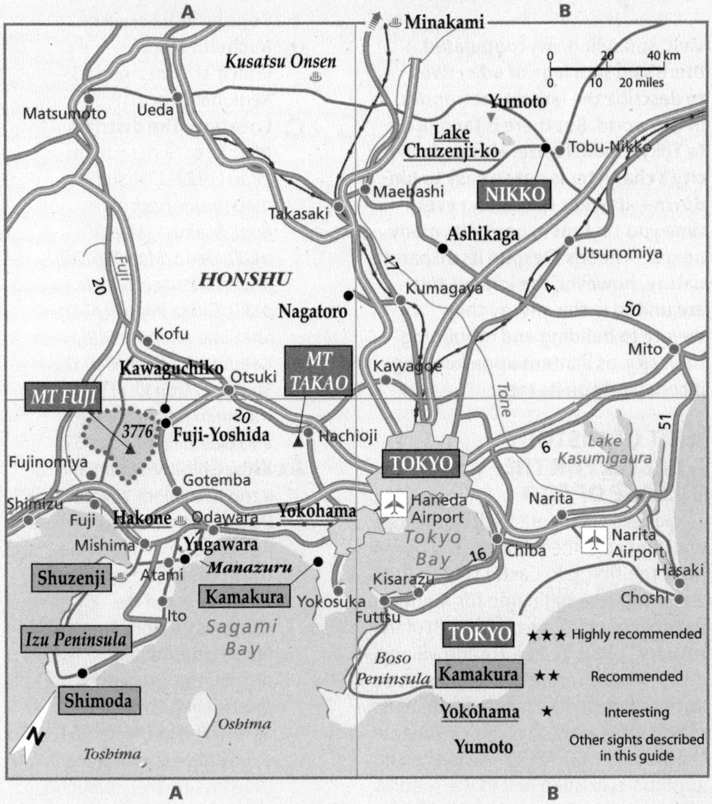


© 2009 Cartographic data Shobunsha/Michelin

With good infrastructure and a large workforce, supported by the best universities in the country funded by financial institutions ever keen to establish their headquarters close to the seat of power, Kanto additionally has the highest regional GDP in Japan. Perhaps more surprising is that less than an hour's train ride from this hyper-industrialized area are regions with very different identities, whether it be Kamakura (Kanagawa prefecture), the great city of temples and gardens, the glittering lakes of the Izu Peninsula, or Nikko (Tochigi prefecture), the sepulchral beauty of which shimmers under a lofty canopy of ancient Japanese cedars.

*Skyscrapers of Shinjuku with Mount Fuji in the background*

©Y. Shimizu/JNTO

# Tokyo★★★東京

**Vast, sprawling, overpopulated... there's no shortage of adjectives to describe the largest metropolis in the world. But there is far more to Tokyo than its size, although the city's character is not so easy to pin down—it needs redefining every time you set foot in one of its many neighborhoods. Despite its disparate nature, however, the inhabitants are united in the energy they devote to building and rebuilding their city, as if intent upon keeping it constantly on its toes.**

## A BIT OF HISTORY

### A CASTLE FOR THE VILLAGE OF EDO

Tokyo didn't really put itself on the map until the end of the 15C, when Ota Dokan built the first Edo Castle (1457); until then, Edo (the old name for modern-day Tokyo, which means "mouth of the estuary,") had been a fishing village. While almost certainly occupied since ancient times—the name of one of its districts, Yayoi-cho, has come to denote the period 3C BC–AD 3C—it had had no autonomy, existing first in the shadow of Nara and then of Kyoto. Following the assassination of Ota Dokan, the castle took on new significance.

Toyotomi Hideyoshi (1536–98), having just brought peace to Kanto, entrusted the province to his chief lieutenant, **Tokugawa Ieyasu** (1542–1616). Ieyasu chose Dokan's castle as his residence, continuing its fortification as the region was still unstable. Victory at Sekigahara (1600) assured him of total supremacy over a Japan that was still in the process of unification.

### THE SHOGUNATE MILITARY GOVERNMENT AND THE *DAIMYO*

Three years later, Edo became the seat of the shogun's military government *(bakufu)*. A town grew up beneath the castle *(jokamachi)*, gravitating toward Ieyasu's centralized power base. In fact, the *daimyo* were routinely obliged to

- **Population:** 13 million.
- **Michelin Map:** Principal Sights map B3 – Regional Map p119.
- **Location: The districts of Tokyo:** General map *(Map I p122–123)*, subway map *(inside back cover flap)*, Asakusa *(Map IV p127)*, Ueno *(Map IV p127)*, Imperial Palace *(Map II p137)*, Ginza *(Map III p142)*, Shinjuku *(Map V p 148)*, Kagurazaka *(Map VI p152)*, Shibuya *(Map VII p155)*, Harajuku *(Map VIII p158)*, and Odaiba *(Map IX p163)*.
- **Kids:** Ghibli Museum and a trip to explore Yoyogi Park at the weekend; the futuristic town of Odaiba.
- **Don't miss:** The temple of Senso-ji and the Kappabashi-dori; Ameyoko Market; the Yanaka district; the Chuo-dori; the Tsukiji fish market; an evening at the Kabuki or in Shibuya; Akihabara ("Electric Town"); Jinbocho, the book-selling district; Harajuku Bridge and Yoyogi Park; Shibuya junction; Shinjuku station morning commute; an evening at Kabuki-cho. **Shrine**: The Meiji-jingu. **Architecture**: The skyscrapers of Nishi-Shinjuku; Tokyo International Forum; the National Art Center; haute couture and prêt-à-porter houses of Omotesando, Ginza. **Museum**: The Tokyo National Museum; the Edo-Tokyo Museum; the National Museum of Modern Art; 21–21 Design Sight; the Mori Art Museum; the Metropolitan Museum of Photography.

live close to it, a relationship to the shogunate that shaped the town

## A CONTINUALLY GROWING SEAT OF POWER

The way towns and cities were organized in Asia thus began to change. The city began to develop its structure from the **center**, with the *bakufu* organizing and allocating districts by social class, according to their relationship with the central power: great lords were located closest to the shogunate, followed by warriors, clerics, merchants, etc. As the elected representatives were not great in number, the center of the city was considerably less populated (*see Imperial Palace pp136–139)* than the **outlying areas**, which were packed with people from all social levels.

This distribution of people—which reflected a political and later a social order, but did not take into account the criteria of town planning—had many consequences that are still visible today. Diverse urban areas formed in the outskirts, as lively as they were distant from a centralized authority, which was strict, discriminatory, and moralizing.

These new suburbs, called Shinjuku, Asakusa, and Ryogoku, prospered through the system of *sankin kotai* (*see box p125)*.

### Earthquakes and violence

One hundred and forty thousand people missing, 300,000 houses destroyed ... at the time of the Great Kanto Earthquake, fire was the main scourge. In 1923, it was all the more destructive because it struck at lunchtime, just as food braziers were glowing red in the streets. The lower part of town, with its densely packed wooden buildings, was reduced to ashes. Fire broke out in hundreds of places across the city and rumors began to circulate: the Koreans living in Tokyo were accused of trying to take revenge on Japan for the occupation of their country. Vigilante groups were formed and 6,000 Koreans disappeared. Whether this was due to the earthquake or the ensuing violence that followed it, the exact cause of many of the deaths was never clearly established.

From that time onward, far from both the seat of power and residential districts (like Yamanote on the slopes of Musashino Terrace in Western Tokyo) the lower part of the city, Shitamachi expanded, incorporating sprawling

## SUGGESTED INTINERARIES IN THREE DAYS:

**Day 1:** Senso-ji Temple (Kaminari-mon, Nakamise-dori); Ueno Park picnic, Edo-Tokyo Museum; evening Kabuki;
**Day 2:** Sushi for breakfast at fish market, then Ginza, Chuo-dori, Imperial Palace Garden, Shinjuku (Shinjuku Gyoen first), Kabuki-cho and Golden Gai late afternoon and Tokyo Metropolitan Government night view of city; **Day 3:** Omotesando, Harajuku, Meiji Shrine; Shibuya (crossroads, little streets), Roppongi Hills early evening, night view from Tokyo Tower.

## IN SEVEN DAYS:

**Day 1:** Morning: Asakusa; Ueno Park lunch, zoo for children; Tokyo Dome City late afternoon; **Day 2:** Morning: Ryogoku Kokugikan, Kiyosumi-teien; afternoon: Edo-Tokyo Museum, Tokyo National Museum; evening: Kabuki;
**Day 3:** Sushi for breakfast at fish market, then day at Yokohama (port, Chinatown); **Day 4:** Morning: Imperial Palace East Garden, glimpse of palace; Shinjuku; **Day 5:** A day in Kamakura;
**Day 6:** Omotesando, Harajuku, Meiji Shrine; Shibuya (crossroads, little streets), Roppongi Hills early evening, Mori Tower night view; **Day 7:** For kids: Ghibli Museum and Inokashira-koen or Odaiba (can replace Yokohama Day 3).

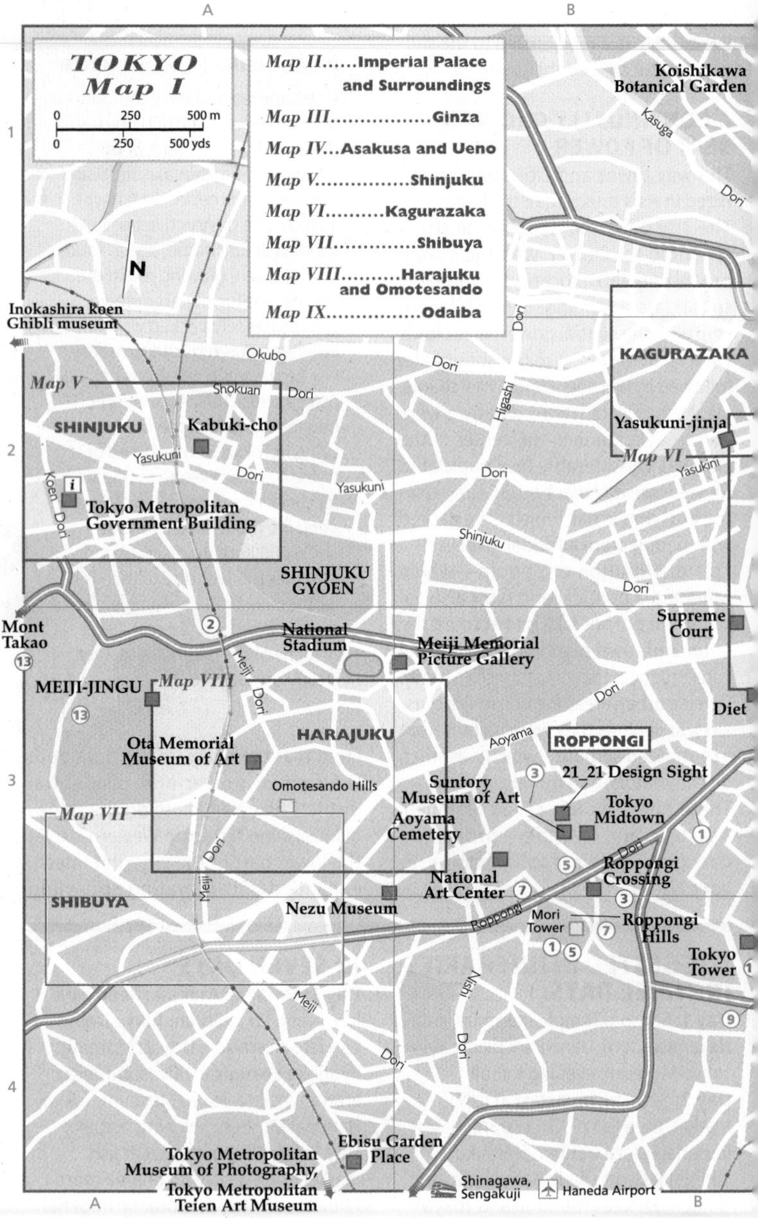


"pleasure districts" (Yoshiwara, north of Asakusa, was at that time the largest of these in Asia). With such attractions, the city grew. Large numbers of unaffiliated samurai mingled with merchants and craftsmen. Despite the disasters that regularly afflicted it—the terrible fire of Meireki destroyed 60 percent of the city in 1657—by the time of the eighth shogun Tokugawa Yoshimune (1684–1751), Edo already had almost a million inhabitants.

## THE MEIJI ERA TO World War II

The opening of diplomatic and commercial relations with the United States

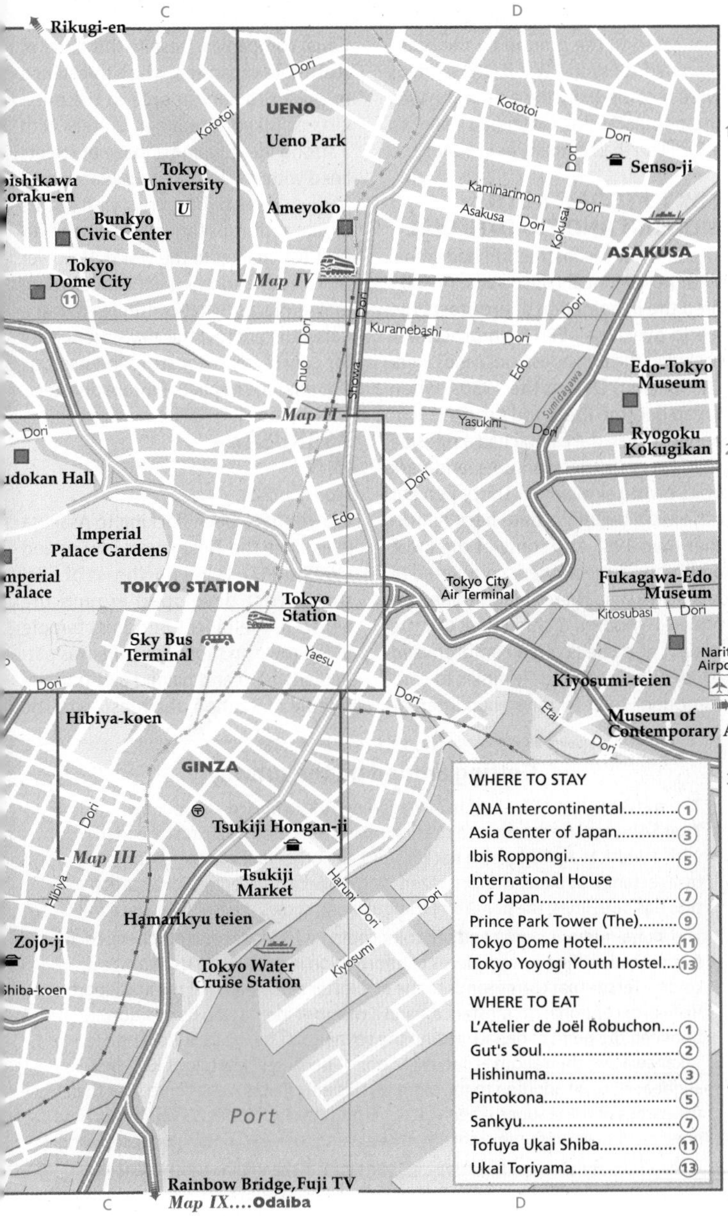




precipitated the fall of the Tokugawa shogunate. On September 13, 1868 in the Meiji era, Edo became the **capital of Japan**, Tokyo—literally, "the capital of the east"—while Kyoto remained the capital of Kyoto prefecture. Influenced by the West, Tokyo underwent a process of modernization and rationalization. The residences of the *daimyo* were pulled down and replaced with the official buildings required by the Emperor for the new Imperial Palace. Ginza was the first district to be Westernized.

The earthquake of 1923 flattened Tokyo (*see box p121*), and it had only just been rebuilt when a quarter of the city was razed to the ground by the bombing raids of World War II (102 air raids were recorded). By the end of the war, the population of Tokyo had fallen to 3.5 million (half as many as in 1940).

### TOKYO TODAY, BOTH MODERN AND TRADITIONAL

The time for reconstruction had come. With no historical constraints, the city fired the imagination of architects the world over. The 1964 Olympic Games provided the first boost, but funds were still lacking. During the 1980s, when Japan became the world's second economic power, the capital had a ringside seat. Every district wanted a landmark of its own: a skyscraper. Thirty percent of Tokyo's buildings date back no further than 1985 and some of the most ambitious projects were completed in less than a year. There are some fine examples of modern architecture, but the impact of these is often compromised by identical-seeming "temples to consumption" built by renowned international companies. Despite this flurry of real estate expansion, which threatened to push ordinary people to the outskirts of Tokyo, a number of areas with a strong identity and a maze of streets lined with low-roofed houses and small gardens remain. The very stylish district of Ginza still rubs shoulders with the largest fish market in the world. However much Tokyo adorns itself with dazzling masterpieces, what continues to fascinate is its energy; the city's propensity for constantly reconstructing itself, as if to limit the impact of future disasters.

## ASAKUSA★★
## 浅草

*Map IV p127.*

Crowds have been flocking to Asakusa ever since the Tokugawa (Edo) period (1603–1867). Lying northeast of Edo, the district developed around the Senso-ji, the oldest Buddhist temple in the town. In those days, life was particularly hard and paying a visit to the temple of Kannon, the most altruistic

### Getting around on the subway

**The network** has 13 lines: nine managed by **Tokyo Metro** and four by **Toei Subway**. The entrance to the first nine is indicated by a circular panel with a white M against a blue background; the other four can be recognized by a rectangular panel with a stylized gingko leaf in the center. For a station that has both lines, the panel is rectangular and shows the front view of a train.

The alpha-numeric signs combine color coding with letters and numbers. Each station is identified by two pieces of information in addition to its name and color: a **letter** that corresponds to the first letter of the name of the line (apart from in exceptional circumstances) and a **number** identifying its position between the point of departure and the terminus. "Change at Shirokane-Takanawa and then alight at Tameike-Sanno" becomes "Change at I03, then alight at N06." In addition to the fact that this information is easier to spot than the names of the stations when you're in the subway, this allows you to work out how much of your journey remains, by referring to the ascending or descending order of the numbers. A voice also announces the upcoming station and all connections in English. A subway map is available at all stations.

Websites: www.tokyometro.jp (Tokyo Metro network) and www.kotsu.metro.tokyo.jp (Toei network). The website www.tokyo-subway.net enables you to plan an itinerary and calculate the price and journey time.

*The addresses in the guide give details of the nearest station, to enable you to quickly find your bearings on the subway map.*

Note: in the guide, subway station names spelt with an "n" before consonants (e.g. Jinbocho) are spelt with an "m" on the map (e.g. Jimbocho).

*For price information about tickets and passes, see Addresses p169.*

### Expenditure and revenues

Under the Tokugawa shogunate, the *daimyo* had certain obligations. They had to spend at least 10 days a month in Edo (a system known as *sankin kotai*) and build a residence near the castle in proportion to their means. When they went away, they were required to leave their families behind as hostages. In this way the shogunate could keep the power and finances of the *daimyo*, who became indebted to the city's merchants, in check. Rice formed the basis of the economy, with a *koku* of rice (the amount judged sufficient to feed one person for a year) being the equivalent of 5 bushels (around 50 gallons/185 liters). The samurai in the service of the shogun received a wage calculated in *koku*. Rice brokers, the *fudasashi*, stored rice belonging to the *daimyo* for a fee and also provided loans at interest rates that were often very high.

of the deities associated with mercy and compassion (*see box p126*), was a wise course of action. However, the goddess would not have proved so popular had it not been for some other factors: first, Asakusa was on the route to Yoshiwara, the famous red-light district (*see box p129)*, and secondly, in the mid-19C the shogun authorities had driven Kabuki—a form of theater they considered too outrageous to be performed in the center of the city—to the outskirts of town. The result was that the actors who were to play the roles of women *(onnagata)* invaded Asakusa to learn their trade from the courtesans of Yoshiwara. The range of pleasures on offer changed with the times. Cinemas, funfairs, archery ranges (which sometimes became brothels), theaters, striptease joints, and cafes—Asakusa was quick to learn from the West various ways of keeping customers happy. In the Meiji era Asakusa even became one of the famous *sakariba*, entertainment districts that gave the Japanese some respite from the rigid and class-divided straitjacket of society. Artists, intellectuals, and writers (Kawabata wrote his *Chronicles of Asakusa* in 1929) strolled happily through the crowded district where "all trembling desires are laid bare," regardless of class.

Bombing during World War II reduced Asakusa to ashes. The district was rebuilt, but still with narrow streets and low-roofed houses huddled around the temple, and the same daily influx of crowds still hungered for pleasure. Twenty million people now visit Asakusa's temple (Senso-ji) every year. Worshippers and tourists rub shoulders with schoolchildren wearing brass-buttoned uniforms.

The smallest children wear round hats made of felt or straw, the smiles on their lips often sparkling with the crumbs of *sembei* (crunchy rice crackers) or the sugar of *kaminari-okoshi* (Japanese sweet crackers).

*3min from Asakusa station.*

The imposing **Kaminari-mon★**, "Thunder Gate," (the two characters are printed on the huge, red paper lantern) marks the entrance to the Senso-ji.

Flanking its two red pillars, the gods of thunder *(Raijin on the left)* and wind *(Fujin on the right)* are charged with frightening away demons *(kimon)*.

Once through the gate, the **Naka mise-dori** pedestrian avenue lined with stands and paper lanterns overflows with *omiyage* (small souvenirs), the sale of which was prompted by priests anxious to find the means to restore their temple.

Today's visitors can choose from combs, yukata, fans, and papier mâché masks (*see Addresses – Shopping pp174–175)*.

On the left, just before a second large gate *(Hozo-mon)* leading to the Senso-ji, overlooked by a five-story **pagoda★** (rebuilt in 1973), is the hiding place of the very secret garden of **Denbo-in★**, attributed to Kobori Enshu, great master gardener of the 17C *(visit by appointment only; ✆03-3842-0181)*.

Sanja Matsuri at Asakusa-jinja

© JNTO

## Senso-ji★★ 浅草寺

*Map IV C2.*

This temple, the oldest one in the city, was founded in the 7C by two fishermen who, according to legend, happened to net a small golden statue of Kannon that had been lying in the Sumida River. Few parts of the 17C central building escaped destruction in World War II. The current building dates from 1958 and is of limited interest, except perhaps to see people at prayer in front of the incense burner (*see box p128*).

To the right of the **main temple★** stands the Shinto shrine **Asakusa-jinja**, erected in 1649 and also known as Sanja-sama (Shrine of the Three Guardians), dedicated to the two fishermen and the head of the village who supported them. The **Sanja Matsuri** one of the most popular festivals in the city, takes place here every year during the third weekend of May. Two million people join the crowd of around a hundred *mikoshi* (portable shrines) that are paraded through the streets (*see photo above*).

## Hanayashiki 浅草花やしき

*Map IV C2.*

*Next to Senso-ji. Open Wed–Mon 10am–6pm. ¥900 (additional charge per attraction).*

This amusement park, now a bit old-fashioned, is one of the last examples of the kind of fairground activities popular in the entertainment world of old Asakusa.

## Sumida-koen Park 隅田公園

*Map IV C2.*

On either side of the Sumida River between the Azuma and Sakura Bridges, Sumida Park comes to life when the cherry blossom trees are in flower, and for the great annual firework display

### Heads – Kannon

Kannon is the female manifestation of the asexual Hindu god Avalokitesvara, whose name means "Lord who looks from on high," that is, who looks down with compassion. And this god is not short of pity, for on the way to becoming a Buddha he paused on the path of enlightenment to give aid to others. Kannon is often represented with 10 heads on top of her own—she is all seeing—and a body covered in 1,000 hands to illustrate her infinitely welcoming nature. In China, Kannon is Guang Yin, goddess of pity and fertility. She even went on to become a famous brand name: Canon.

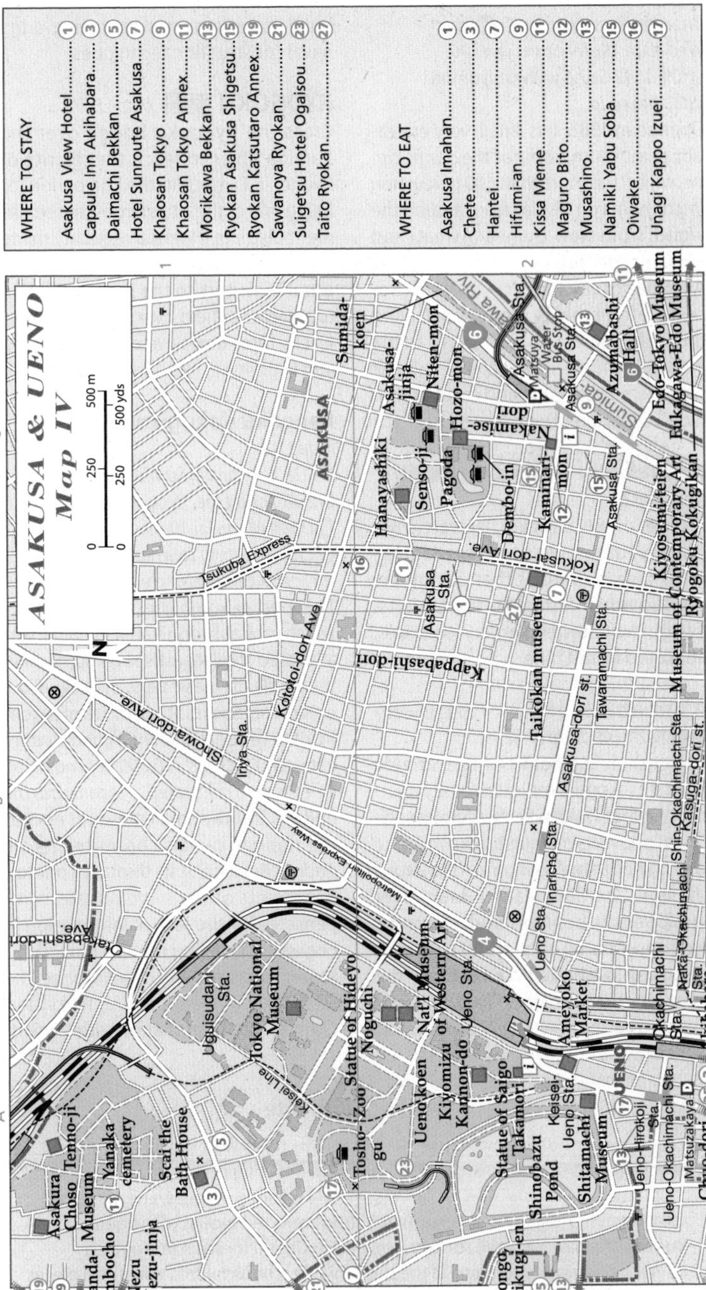




*(hanabi taikai)* on the last Saturday in July. One of the most spectacular in Tokyo, the display has been held since the Edo period.

**Drum Museum** 太鼓館 *Map IV C2. 2-1-1 Nishiasakusa. Access to the Museum is through the Miyamoto Unosuke Shoten, famous Japanese* *drum makers since 1861. Open Wed–Sun 10am–5pm. ¥300. 03-3842-5622. www.miyamoto-unosuke.co.jp.*

Opened in 1988, this small, very educational museum *(some of the drums can be played)* has more than 600 percussion instruments on display from around the world: from New Guinea (Asmat) and Vanuatu, to Africa.

All types of Japanese drum are represented, from the *tsuzumi* (a small hand drum shaped like an hour-glass) to the *oke-daiko* with a shell made of strips of wood joined together and covered with hide and fastened with ropes.

### Kappabashi-dori★ かっぱ橋通り

*Map IV B2.*

A street of specialist kitchenware wholesalers, from ovens to those famous resin dishes (*mihon*) that customers drool over in Japanese restaurants. A large choice of items at very low prices, imported from China.

### Azumabashi Hall★ アサヒビール吾妻橋ホール

*Map IV C2.*

Located on the banks of the Sumida River, the Asahi Beer Hall is easily identified: a large golden flame sculpture "flickers" above its opaque black tomb-like walls. The "flame" is intended to evoke the light, golden head of Asahi beer just after it's been poured. However, weighing no less than 300 tons and designed in a blaze of publicity by the creative French designer Philippe Starck, it could only be erected in position after builders had resorted to cutting-edge naval construction techniques.

## RYOGOKU 両国

*Map I D2/3.*

Cross the Ryogoku Bridge over the Sumida River to reach the district of Ryogoku. Famous in the Edo period for being one of the city's largest entertainment districts (Hokusai regularly made sketches of what went on), nowadays it attracts visitors to the sumo wrestling tournaments held over a period of two weeks, three times a year in January, May, and September *(see Address Book p 174)*.

### Ryogoku Kokugikan 両国国技館

*Map I D2.*

*1-3-28 Yokohami, Sumida-ku. Subway E12, JR Sobu Line, Ryogoku station. Open Mon–Fri 10am–4.30pm. Closed during tournaments except for spectators. No charge.*

The sport of Sumo wrestling, *see p174* which probably originated in China, was allocated the largest sports stadium in the whole of Asia in 1909: the Kokugikan or National Sports Stadium. It's often difficult to get seats *(entry charge varies between ¥500 and ¥50,000 depending on whether you are seated or standing in the gallery)*, but the small museum next to the stadium can also be visited *(see Address Book p175)*. Its display of photos, handprints of the *sumotori*, etc, compensates for the lack of information in English. On leaving the museum, don't forget to taste some *chanko-nabe*, the tasty stew of chicken, tofu, leeks, and Chinese cabbage that provides wrest-

### Dealing with fate

Leaning over the huge bronze censer, passers-by try to waft the healing virtues of the incense fumes toward them, even if it might sting their eyes a little. Students write their wishes for success on little wooden plaques, and give small offerings *(ema)* signifying "horse image" (the preferred mount of the gods). Businessmen attach small stickers *(senjafuda)* with their own name or their company's onto the columns of the shrine, while schoolchildren take small pieces of paper *(omikuji)* out of a wooden box and impatiently unfold them to read their fortune. The luckiest ones will find the *daikichi* (extremely lucky) or *kichi* (very lucky) characters written there. Those not so lucky will have *shokichi* (a bit lucky) or worse, *kyo* (bad luck). In the latter case the paper will be strung up by a thread to be soaked by the rain and battered by the wind.

## Yoshiwara

North of Asakusa, Yoshiwara (now called Senzoku), was a pleasure district for three centuries (1657–1957). Unable to ban prostitution (many bachelors were living in Edo at that time), the shoguns decided to contain it. The red-light district developed its brothels into premises where pleasure was elevated to an art form reputed to be of the subtlest kind, depending on the status of the courtesans. Etiquette was to be obeyed and this evolved its own rules, much like the art of war or that of the Tea Ceremony. In the middle of the 18C there were more than 7,000 girls in the district, some of them of few means, for the art of love was purely a matter of survival for the many peasant girls recruited into the trade. A temple was even dedicated to them: Nagekomi-dera ("where bodies are discarded").

© Universal History Arc/age fotostock

*Ukiyo-e (c1810) by Kikukawa Eizan showing the pleasure district of Yoshiwara*

lers with their daily supply of calories to maintain muscle and bulk. Most restaurants are run by retired sumo wrestlers.

## Edo-Tokyo Museum★★

江戸東京博物館 *Map I D2.*
*1-4-1 Yokohami, Sumida-ku. Subway E12, exit A4, JR Sobu Line, Ryogoku station.* ◯*Open Tue–Sun 9.30am–5.30pm (Sat 7.30pm).* ◉*¥600.*
*www.edo-tokyo-museum.or.jp.*
The style of this imposing building, erected on pillars, brings to mind both a traditional rice loft and a pair of *geta* (wooden clogs). It houses a fascinating museum that tells the history of the city from the Edo period to modern-day Tokyo *(allow at least 2hr to visit its 322,917.3sq ft/30,000sq m space, which starts on the 6th floor).*
The full-scale replica of **Nihonbashi Bridge** (◉*see p141*) leads into the colorful world of the Edo period. Models (like the one of the impressive residence of the daimyo Matsudaira Tadamasa) and full-scale reconstructions of districts, commercial buildings, workshops (a printing workshop), and a Kabuki theater show

how the city planned by Tokugawa Ieyasu (1542–1616) evolved. By the 18C it already contained around a million inhabitants, 60 percent of whom were men.

## Museum of Contemporary Art★★ 東京都現代美術館

*Map I D3 off map.*
*4-1-1 Miyoshi, Koto-ku. 10min walk from Subway E14, exit A3 or 15min from Subway T13.* ◯*Open Tue–Sun 10am–6pm.* ◯*Closed twice a year for 2 weeks (change of exhibition) so it's advisable to phone.* ◉*¥500 (entry charge varies for special exhibitions).* ☏*03-5245-4111.*
*www.mot-art-museum.jp*
As well as the special exhibitions, a permanent collection covering the last 50 years of 20C art can also be seen: Gerhard Richter, Roy Lichtenstein, David Hockney, Frank Stella, Julian Schnabel, and many Japanese artists such as Yoshihara Jiro, Funakoshi Katsura, and Kusama Yayoi. Although only 150 works—out of the 3,800 kept in the museum—are shown in rotation, the entire collection can be viewed on screen in the museum's audio-visual library.

### Fukagawa-Edo Museum★
深川江戸資料館 *Map I D3.*
*1-3-28 Shirakawa, Koto-ku. 10min walk from the previous museum. Subway Z11, E14. Open 9.30am–6.30pm. Closed 2nd & 4th Mon of the month. ¥300.*
A fine reconstruction of the Fukagawa district—a network of wooden workshops, warehouses, and dwellings—which flanked the left bank of the Sumida River in the 19C. One of its streets leads down to the port.

### Kiyosumi-teien Garden★
清澄庭園 *Map I D3.*
*3-3-9 Kiyosumi, Koto-ku, less than 218.7yd/200m from the previous museum. 2 stops S of Ryogoku on the Oedo Line, Subway E14, exit A3. Open 9am–5pm. ¥150.*
This magnificent, little-known garden from the Edo period is worth a detour, particularly in spring when the azaleas create a blaze of color on the little hill overlooking the pond. Its banks are dotted with beautiful stones from all four corners of Japan.

## UENO AND SURROUNDINGS★★★
上野 *Map IV p 138.*
Ueno district is famous for its park. Built on a plain and slightly elevated, it was the object of many a *daimyo's* desires in the past. When the Tokugawa family took control, some fine buildings were constructed, such as the Kanei-ji temple built by Tenkai, advisor to the first Tokugawa shogun.
Only the beautiful five-story pagoda remains today; the rest were destroyed during the Meiji Restoration, when the Emperor and the Tokugawa clan struggled for power. Every April, Japanese crowds come to picnic in the park under the thousands of flowering cherry treestheir beautiful blossom a reminder that things, by their very nature, are transitory.
Ueno is also home to a number of museums with permanent collections, which hold special exhibitions.

## UENO PARK★ 上野公園
*Map IV A1/2.*
*Subway G16, H17, exit 6/7, Keisei Line, Keisei-Ueno station or JR Ueno station, Park exit. Allow a full day.*
The biggest park in Tokyo (210 acres/85ha) is the oldest public garden in Japan. The tour begins with the museums *(JR Ueno station, Park exit)* and finishes at the statue of Saigo Takamori a short distance away from Keisei-Ueno station. If you're short of time, make a point of seeing the **Hon-kan** and the **Gallery of Horyu-ji Treasures** in the Tokyo National Museum.

### National Museum of Western Art★
国立西洋美術館 *Map IV A2.*
*Open Tue–Sun 9.30am–5.30pm (Fri 8pm). ¥420.*
Designed by the Swiss architect Le Corbusier, this museum was opened in 1959 to house the collection of Matsukata Kojiro (1865–1950), a naval construction entrepreneur who made his fortune during World War I. He assembled an exceptional collection of Impressionist art, much of it acquired in Paris. Sadly, a great deal was destroyed during World War II, when works stored in Britain were destroyed by fire and those left in Japan by Allied bombing.
A few pieces remain, including some of the most important: Rodin sculptures, paintings by Monet, Gauguin, Denis *(Young Girl with a Hen)*, and Gustave Moreau's magnificent *pietà*. Having celebrated its 50th anniversary in 2009, the museum's renovated framework now houses an expanded collection from the Renaissance to World War II, but the Impressionist paintings remain the keystone of this collection.

### Statue of Noguchi Hideyo
野口英世像 *Map IV A2.*
*A few hundred yards from the previous museum (right exit). ¥600.*
Opposite the Science Museum, the statue of this eminent Japanese bacteriologist (his portrait has been printed on ¥1,000 notes since 2004), has been erected in honor of the man who discovered the pathogenic agent for syphilis in 1911.

## Tokyo National Museum★★★

東京国立博物館 *Map IV A1.*
*Open Tue–Sun 9.30am–5pm (Apr–Nov Fri 8pm; Apr–Sept Sat–Sun 6pm), last admission 30min before closing.* *¥600 for the 5 buildings of Hon-kan, Heisei-kan, Toyo-kan, Horyu-ji Homotsu-kan, and Hyokei-kan (supplement for special exhibitions). www.tnm.go.jp.*

The oldest (1872) and largest museum in Japan *(around 110,000 pieces, 87 National Treasures)* is set in five main buildings around the main entrance.

**Hon-kan★★★** – The central building, which is also called the Japanese Gallery, is as well stocked as a miniature Smithsonian or Tate: 23 galleries are located on two floors, covering the Jomon period to World War II. Begin on the **second floor** with the Jomon culture and move on to an introduction to Buddhism in Japan (6C), painting and calligraphy from the National Treasures, art of the Court (Heian era), Zen art (Kamakura and Muromachi periods), Tea Ceremony art, Samurai armor, everyday objects, etc. The galleries with paintings and some of the major works are particularly worth visiting: **Akasagarbha★★★**, *the peacock king*, **the Sixteen Arhats** of the Heian era, **Bodhidharma beneath a pine tree** from the Kamakura era, the **Jigoku Zoshi★★**, the *Handscroll of Buddhist Hells*. The **Gaki Zoshi★★★**, the *Scroll of the Hungry Ghosts* (Heian era), is particularly unmissable, a mythical oriental counterpart to the works of Bosch or Bruegel. Ike no Taiga's **Chinese landscape★★★** (18C) is delightful (*see photo below*). Room 8 looks at the two main movements in calligraphy: **Oieryu** (used by the court nobles), a traditional Japanese movement that developed independently from the Heian era onward, and **Karayo**, which was initially linked to Chinese ideograms but then evolved, developing a formal, more abstract, and creative approach better enabling it to reflect the personality and creativity of the calligrapher. **Karayo** became very popular among followers of Confucianism, Zen (Buddhist) priests, poets, and artists. Rooms 9 and 10, devoted to Noh and Kabuki masks, *ukiyo-e* (prints), and to fashion (textiles, kimonos, etc.) of the Edo period are a welcome digression into the world of Japanese art. Ceramic items, sabers, and lacquerware complete this vast collection.

**Heisei-kan★** – *Located behind the Hon-kan and linked to it by a corridor.* Displayed on the ground floor is a large array of archeological objects, mainly proto-Japanese, from 30000 BC to the 19C. It includes superb **Dotaku★★★** (Yayoi period) bronze bells decorated in relief with scenes of everyday life, magnificent

Chinese Landscape *by Ike no Taiga (18C), Tokyo National Museum*

**Haniwa★★★** terra-cotta funeral figurines (Kofun period, 6C) and the famous **dogu★★★**, terra-cotta "clay dolls," probably linked to the cult of fertility (late Jomon, 1000–300 BC). Special exhibitions are held on the floor above.

*As you retrace your steps toward the main door you cross the Hyokei-kan (open only for special exhibitions).*

**Gallery of Horyu-ji Treasures★★★** – *Just behind the Hyokei-kan.*
In 1878 the Horyu-ji temple of Nara, a masterpiece of the Asuka era, donated more than 300 objects to the Imperial Household. Since 1999, these pieces—most of which date from the 7C—have been displayed in a building worthy of their splendor, designed by the architect Taniguchi Yoshio (1937–) who is best known for his redesign of New York's Museum of Modern Art (MoMA).
At the **entrance** you can admire one of the most remarkable objects of the collection: the **kanjoban★★★** (7C). This openwork gilt bronze banner was once used for Buddhist ceremonies. In the **second gallery** there is a beautifully presented group of 48 bronze statues of the Buddha (7C). The **Seated Nyorai★★★** and the **Bodhisattva in half-lotus position★★★** (Asuka period) are exceptionally delicate (*see photo, below*).
A number of these pieces, such as the magnificent **Buddha Triad★★★** (6C), were produced in Korea during the period of the Three Kingdoms and then imported into Japan. These pieces had a determining influence on the Japanese imagination, which at the time—the Buddha was not long known in Japan—was searching for a way to depict Buddhist iconography.
Each Buddha has a fine *kohai*, halo, encircling the head. The **third gallery** contains **gigaku★★★** masks (among the oldest in Japan) made of camphorwood, paulownia, or painted ramie. They are said to have been used during the spectacles that preceded the Buddhist ceremonies copied from the Korean kingdom of Paekche during the first half of the 7C. **Galleries 4** and **5** contain wooden, lacquer, and metal objects (shrines, sutra boxes, bows, *inro*, small medicine boxes). In the **last room (6)** there is a very valuable **illustrated biography★★★** of Shotoku (574–622), the Prince Regent who turned Japan into a Buddhist state. These 10 screen paintings by Hatano Chitei (1069, Heian period) depict episodes from the Prince's life and were originally in the *Eden* (Hall of Paintings), in the *To-in*, the eastern precinct of Nara's Horyu-ji temple. In the interests of preservation they are not on permanent display.

*Bodhisattva in half-lotus position (7C), Tokyo National Museum*



**Toyo-kan★** – The Asian Gallery (excluding Japanese art), displayed over three floors, is devoted to art and archeology from Egypt to China. **First floor:** sculptures from India (Mathura Head of Buddha, 2C), Pakistan (Gandara Seated Buddha), and China; Egyptian and South east Asian archeology. **Second floor:** Chinese archeology. **Third floor:** Korean and Central Asian archeology. *Gallery closed for renovation until April 2012.*

**Tosho-gu★★** 上野東照宮 *Map IV A1*
*In Ueno Park, at the end of the main avenue joining the National Museum of Western Art. Open 9am–6pm (summer); 9am–4.30pm (winter). ¥200.*

Built by Tokugawa Lemitsu in memory of his grandfather **Tokugawa Ieyasu** (1542–1616), founder of the Tokugawa shogun dynasty (1603–1867), this Shinto shrine, built in 1627 and enlarged in 1651 to house shogun relics, has miraculously escaped the various natural and man-made disasters that have afflicted Tokyo. Don't miss the magnificent Chinese-style gate *(kara-mon)*.
The two dragons on either side are the work of the great left-handed sculptor **Hidari Jingoro** (1594–1634) *(see Nikko p201)*. The doors and columns are entirely covered in gold leaf. Inside there are beautiful sculpted ceilings above painted walls—the work of **Kano Tanyu** (1602–74), the most distinguished painter of the Kano School *(see box p299)*.

## The nagaya

*Nagaya*, literally "long, narrow houses," gave structure to the lower town of Shitamachi, and particularly to the narrow streets and alleyways *(roji)* that fed into its main thoroughfares. There were two kinds of row house, depending on whether they faced the street *(omote nagaya: front nagaya)* or a small interior courtyard *(ura nagaya: back nagaya)*.
As the latter could not be used for commerce they were occupied mainly by poor tenants, whose main activity, as Philippe Pons recounts in his book *From Edo to Tokyo*, was "selling the tenants' excrement to local peasant farmers for use as fertilizer."

## Ueno Zoo 上野動物園 *Map IV A1*

*Open Tue–Sun 9.30am–5pm. ¥600. From the temple above, take the Aesop footbridge. You will see a five-story pagoda, the last trace of the Kanei-ji temple built for the Tokugawa family, brought here in 1957. The temple was burned down during the Meiji Restoration. www.tokyo-zoo.net/zoo/ueno.*
Japan's oldest zoo (1882) is still open for business, although a sad episode during World War II nearly put an end to it. Figuring that the zoo would be bombed, releasing the animals into the streets to terrorize the inhabitants, the Japanese army demanded that they all be killed. The staff begged for a reprieve or to be allowed to relocate the animals, but were refused and so the animals were poisoned (the elephants refused their food and died of starvation).
The zoo currently has 2,600 animals across 464 species, including its star attractions: a giant panda and a Sumatran tiger.

## Shinobazu Pond 不忍池 *Map IV A2*

A wildlife protection area that is part of Ueno Park actually consisting of three ponds. A strip of land forms a causeway across the lotus beds for which Shinobazu Pond is famous to a tiny man-made island on which sits **Benten-do**, a 17C temple (rebuilt in 1958) dedicated to Benten, goddess of the arts, the sciences, and wisdom.

## Kiyomizu Kannon-do

清水観音堂 *Map IV A2.*
*South of the Shinobazu Pond (with Hasu Pond on the right), heading toward* ***Kiyomizu.***
A pale imitation of the Kiyomizu in Kyoto *(see p 305)*, this temple, also called Kenei-ji in reference to the Kanei period (1624–44) in which it was built, was initially constructed in 1631 at the highest point of Ueno Park (Suribachi-yama). Its founder, the high priest Tenkai, superintendent of the Tendai Buddhist school, intended it to protect the northern gate of Edo Castle *(now the Imperial Palace)*, a key point vulnerable to attack.
At the end of the 17C, however, it was transferred to its current location and dedicated to **Senju Kannon**, the deity with a thousand arms *(see box p126)*, whose statue can only be seen in February. The faithful also pray to **Kosodate Kannon**, protector of childbearing women. Women whose prayers for fertility have been granted must offer a doll to the goddess to compensate for the real child that they have taken from her. These dolls are cremated on September 25 every year in a special ceremony.

### Statue of Saigo Takamori 西郷隆盛像 *Map IV A2.*

*About 109yd/100m SW of Kiyomizu temple. Call in at the Ueno Royal Museum to check on the special exhibitions program.*

Saigo Takamori (1828–77) was the last of the samurai warriors. At first a fervent advocate of the Meiji revolution, he distanced himself from it once he realized that the Emperor's modernization plans deprived the samurai of their status. He committed *seppuku* (ritual suicide) after defeat at the famous "Satsuma Rebellion" in 1877 (*see p486*), but was rehabilitated by the Emperor in 1891; his statue shows him wearing a *yukata*—a man's kimono. In 2003, his story was retold in Edward Zwick's film *The Last Samurai* (with Tom Cruise).

### Shitamachi Museum★ 下町風俗資料館 *Map IV A2.*

*2-1 Ueno-Koen, Taito-ku, at the SE corner of Shinobazu Pond. Subway: Ueno or Ueno-Okachimachi. Open Tue–Sun 9.30am–4.30pm. ¥300.*

This fascinating museum recreates the district of Shitamachi as it was from the end of the Edo period to the Taisho era, before it was destroyed in the 1923 earthquake (*see box p121*), and then again in World War II bombing raids. The ground floor is the old house of a manufacturer and wholesaler of *hanao*, cloth straps that fastened *zori* (sandals) and *geta* (wooden clogs) to the feet. In the 1920s, when it was common practice to change the color and design every season, *hanao* workshops lined the banks of the Sumida River, each selling around 1,000 straps per day.

The term *Kara-Koro* describes the sound of clogs shuffling along the ground. There is also a shop that sold *dagashi* candies, literally "second-class candies for children of modest means," and a workshop, manufacturing *dayoka* copper, essential for making and repairing teapots, water containers, and gutters. The pieces of orange peel hanging on the walls dispelled the bad smells from the drains, which at that time ran down the center of the street. On the first floor are some historical documents and an array of traditional toys.

## AMEYOKO MARKET★

アメヤ横丁 *Map IV A2.*

*JR Ueno station, Hiroko-ji exit, 109yd/100m from the other side of the Chuo-dori. Open 10am–7pm. www.ameyoko.net.*

Anything from shoes to smoked herring can be bought in this bustling market alongside the rail line. Its eclecticism originates in the black market that developed here to meet the needs of a destitute population after World War II. Peasant farmers made candies *(ame)* from sweet potatoes, a rare but inexpensive commodity, to sell to passers-by, hence "candy sellers' alley" was born. *"Ameya-yokocho"* eventually became *"Ameyoko."*

## YANAKA DISTRICT★★ 谷中

*Map IV A1.*

*Subway C15, JR Yamanote Line or Keisei Line, Nippori station.*

Nature still manages to triumph over the concrete of the city in this peaceful district, where it's pleasant to stroll among temples and wooden houses surrounded by wild grasses. This well-preserved and tranquil environment (there are few cars) escaped the flames of the Great Fire of Meireki in 1657, the earthquake of 1923, and the bombing raids of 1945.

*On leaving Nippori station (Yamanote Line) either take* ***Yanaka-Ginza*** *street (west exit), full of family-owned stands selling senbei, tofu, and other treats, or head for the Tenno-ji (south exit) and cross the tree-lined avenue of Yanaka Cemetery to reach the other sites within walking distance.*

### Yanaka Cemetery★★

谷中霊園 *Map IV A1.*

A vast cemetery lined with gravestones polished like pebbles on the seashore. Famous for its cherry blossom in April, it has a section dedicated to the Tokugawa clan—the last of the shoguns, **Tokugawa Yoshinobu** (1837–1913) is buried here.

Yanaka Cemetery

## Asakura Choso Museum★★

朝倉彫塑館 *Map IV A1.*
*7-18-10 Yanaka.*
*Closed for works until 2013.*

The building housing the museum was the studio and residence of sculptor **Asakura Fumio** (1883–1964), the father of modern Japanese sculpture. His bronzes, particularly, studies of cats, have a feline fluidity. There's a fine **view** of the district from the rooftop garden and a charming small Japanese garden in the central courtyard.

## Scai the Bathhouse

スカイ・ザ・バスハウス *Map IV A1.*
*Kashiwayu-ato, 6-1-23 Yanaka. Open Tue–Sat noon–7pm. No charge. www.scaithebathhouse.com.*

This ancient public bathhouse (200 years old) has been turned into a contemporary art gallery displaying often quite daring works that are changed regularly. Around 109yd/100m away is the **Shitamachi Museum Annex** (*open Tue–Sun 9.30am–4.30pm; no charge)*, with displays on the traditional culture of the Shitamachi, a working-class neighborhood, where you can also see inside an early 20C liquor house.

## Rikugien Garden★★ 六義園

*Map I C1 off map.*
*6-16-3 Honkoma-gome, Bunkyo-ku.*
*Subway N14. Open 9am–5pm. ¥300.*

A gorgeous garden created in 1702 by Yanagisawa Yoshiyasu, *daimyo* and official of the fifth shogun and a cultured man of letters, who designed it in 88 scenes inspired by Japanese poetry.

## AKIHABARA DISTRICT

秋葉原 *Map IV A2 off map.*
*Subway H15, JR Akihabara station.*

From the southern point of Ueno Park the Chuo-dori drops down to Ginza. On the way it crosses more than 0.6mi/1km of Akihabara, an electronic paradise nicknamed "Electric Town," which attracts technology geeks.

The first washing machines appeared here in the 1950s, succeeded by the latest in television sets, microwave ovens, tape recorders, game consoles, computers, etc. Each decade brings its own novelties, such as the very popular (and unique!) ramen (noodle soup) distributor, for which there is a very long line.

Akihabara's discount stores sell all kinds of electronic and electrical goods, drawing the young in their thousands, particularly the *otaku* (*see p 64*).

Every weekend cosplayers from Harajuku (*see p64*) strut the main street *(Showa-dori)* dressed in the costume of a favorite character from a graphic novel or anime (Japanese animated film), and sometimes re-enact their favorite scenes.

## KANDA-JINBOCHO DISTRICT

神田神保町 *Map IV A1 off map.*
*Subway I10, Z07, exit A2.*

The *Jinbocho* book district, known as the "book town" of Japan, has around 160 bookshops and book stands selling some 10 million books on every subject under the sun, and not just in Japanese—foreign literature, including some out-of-print material, can also be found here. For those who think that even the smallest bookstore still contains more ideas of worth than have been presented in the entire history of television, nosing around here is a real pleasure, despite or perhaps even because of the casual disorder. (*See our reading selection pp 20–23.)*

## IMPERIAL PALACE AND SURROUNDINGS★★

皇居 *Map II p 146.*

"Although Western cities have a 'center that's always full' where the values of their civilization (churches, offices, banks, department stores) jostle together, the city I refer to (Tokyo) presents a wonderful paradox: it certainly does have a center, but that center is empty. City life goes on around a place which is both inaccessible and indifferent, a residence hidden by greenery, protected by moats, inhabited by an Emperor who's never seen, or rather, in reality by who knows who," wrote Roland Barthes (*Empire of Signs*, Éditions Skira 1970). Although this 249.6 acre/101ha "empty" space is surprising in such a crowded city, its first use was as the **Tokugawa** seat of power for almost three centuries. In the place where the gardens now stand, from the fortress over which a 164ft/50m keep once towered, political and social order was imposed across Japan. Since then most of the fortifications and grand buildings have been destroyed in wars. Behind the moats, in the western part of the garden, the Imperial residence has been rebuilt and remains discreetly concealed behind a wall of trees and stone ramparts. Housing the Emperor and his family, it is closed to the public except on December 23, the Emperor's birthday, and New Year's Day, when the Japanese arrive in droves. Part of the palace grounds are accessible, however, given over to public parkland. According to Eastern tradition, an empty area is also the space in which all things can exist, and a little empty space is what the people of Tokyo, crammed into their vast city, certainly need.

### IMPERIAL PALACE★ 皇居

*Map II A2.*
*Subway C10, exit 6.*

Surrounded by outer walls, ramparts, and moats, the first Edo Castle was built in 1457 by Ota Dokan (1432–86) to dominate the Bay of Tokyo and the Kanto plain. When Tokugawa Ieyasu took over the castle, which had fallen into ruin after the assassination of Ota, he took on the task of enlarging it. With a sturdy keep that looked down over all

*Boating on the Imperial Palace's north-eastern moat—Chidorigafuchi*

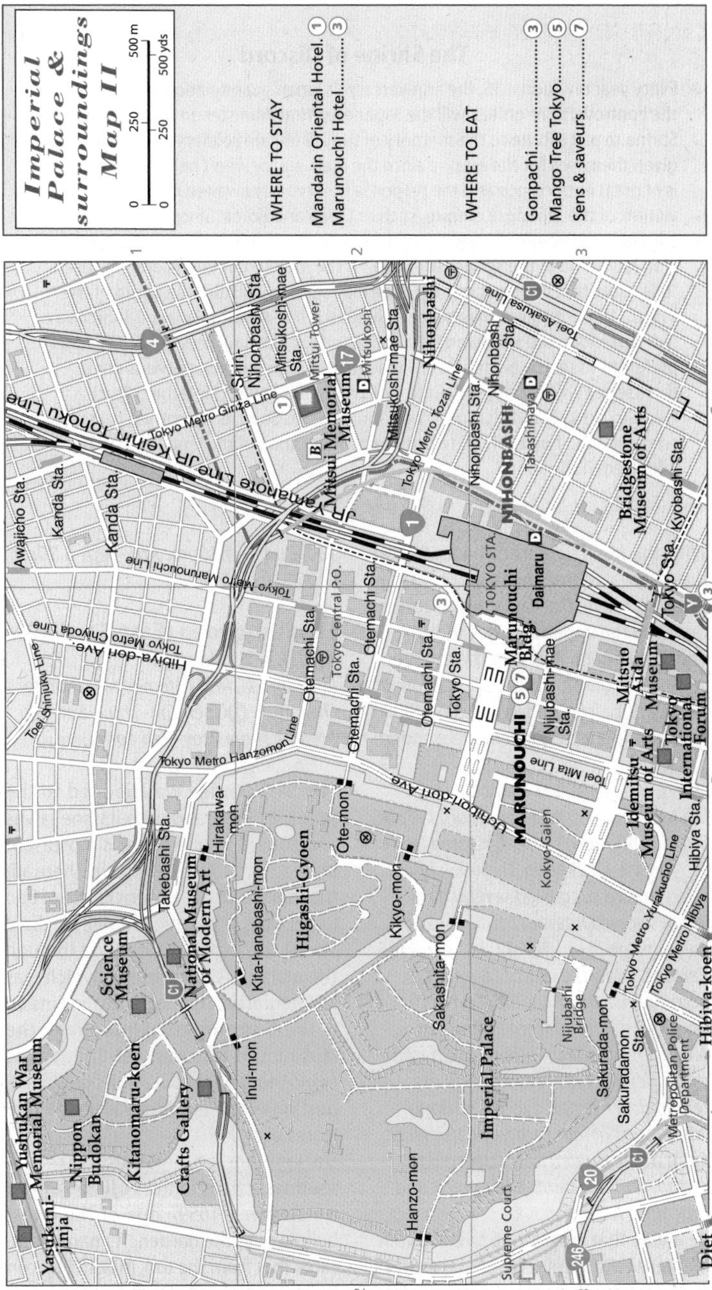




parts of the city, the castle was tangible evidence of the power of the shogunate. As the city's need for defenses increased (waterways, levees, urban fortifications, strengthening of part of the estuary bank below the castle, etc.) it became the driving force behind its construction and development (see A Bit of History p120).

## The Shrine of Discord

Every year on August 15, the anniversary of Japan's capitulation in World War II, the controversy reignites: will the Japanese Prime Minister go to the Yasukuni Shrine to pay tribute to the memory of the 2.5 million soldiers who have given their lives for the empire since the Meiji era, or won't he? The question is of great importance and the response is nervously awaited by the principal victims of the Japanese empire, such as China and Korea. Since 1978, 14 war criminals have been discreetly admitted into the shrine. "We must accept all who have died in the service of Japan," is the monks' comment, adding that a "dead soul that does not rest in peace may seriously disturb the world of the living." This argument may have persuaded Prime Minister Koizumi Junichiro (who attended the shrine on many occasions), but his successor, Abe Shinzo, preferred to send a potted tree. Subsequent prime ministers have aligned themselves with Emperor Akihito, who himself followed his father's lead: Hirohito actually put a stop to the pilgrimages as soon as he learned that war criminals who had claimed to be acting in the name of the Emperor had been admitted to the shrine.

With the Meiji Restoration (1868) and the removal of the Imperial Court from Kyoto to Tokyo, the castle was transformed into the Imperial Palace (Kokyo). The bombing raids of World War II reduced it to rubble, but in 1968, it was rebuilt exactly as before, and in the early 1990s further Imperial residences were added.

### Visit to Imperial Palace

*Open Mon–Fri 8.45am–noon, 1–5pm, Sat–Sun 10am–1.30pm. Closed Dec 28–Jan 4 & Jul 21–Aug 31. No charge. Reservations suggested several days in advance via Internet http://sankan.kunaicho.go.jp or 03-3211-11 ext. 3485. Persons below the age of 18 must be accompanied by an adult. A passport and a permit (print from Internet or request by phone and then collect from the Imperial Household Agency) are required. Arrive at Kikyo-mon 10min before start of tour (subway C10, exit 6; 5min walk). Guided tour restricted to certain parts (75min). Audioguide and brochures in English.*

Be aware that areas open to the public are very restricted. The elegant **Nijubashi** area with its two bridges across the moat is accessible. You can also hire a boat on the north-eastern moat *(Chidorigafuchi)*, which is very popular when the cherry trees are in blossom *(10min walk from Subway Z05; open Mar–Nov Tue–Sun 1–4.30pm, Apr–Sept 5.30pm; ¥500 for 30min).*

### Higashi-gyoen (East Garden)★

皇居東御苑 *Map II B2.*

*Subway C11, M18 (Otemachi station for Ote-mon). Open Tue–Thu & Sat–Sun 9am–4.30pm (Nov–Feb 4pm). No charge (with token).*

The East Garden was opened to the public in 1968, and with its fine lawns and some 250,000 trees, is a pleasant place to stroll. Also to be found here are the remains of the ancient castle of Edo (outer walls of imposing square blocks of stone). The best way to enter is through the main gate **(Ote-mon)**, which was an integral part of the castle. Just inside is the **Sannomaru Shozokan**, the Museum of the Imperial Collections *(no charge)*, which exhibits only a tiny portion of the Imperial family's 8,000 works of art.

On leaving the museum, take the southwest path to the **Fujimi-Yagura** watchtower (1659), one of the finest buildings in the garden. Its name indicates that from the top, Mount Fuji can be seen in the distance. Before arriving at the Kitahanebashi-mon *(north west gate)* that leads to Kitanomaru-koen, visit the Imperial Music Hall, which hosts *gagaku* concerts twice a year—for a privileged few *(see p105)*.

## KITANOMARU-KOEN PARK

北の丸公園 *Map II A1*

*3-1 Kitanomaru-koen. Subway T08, exit 1B.*

The most attractive feature of this park is that it is home to a number of museums.

### National Museum of Modern Art★★ 国立近代美術館

*Map II A–B1.*

*Open Tue–Sun 10am–5pm (Fri 8 pm). Museum ¥420, Crafts Gallery ¥200. www.momat.go.jp.*

This museum houses a good round-up of Japanese art from the Meiji period to the 1980s. Of the 9,000 pieces held here, a selection of 300 is displayed at any one time. A few artists are worthy of special attention: Tomioka Tessai (1836–1924), Yorozu Tetsugoro (1885–1927), Kishida Ryusei (1891–1929), and Kitaoka Fumio (1918–2007).

A few hundred yards away the **Crafts Gallery** contains craft exhibitions of limited interest except for the red-brick building itself (1910, former headquarters of the Imperial Guard).

### Nippon Budokan 日本武道館

*Map II A1.*

*Subways S05, Z06, T07.*

This Japanese martial arts hall, inspired by the Horyu-ji temple in Nara, was built for the 1964 Olympic Games. It also serves as a venue for large music concerts. The Beatles taped *Live at Budokan* in 1966, Deep Purple recorded here for *Made in Japan* in 1972, while *Bob Dylan at Budokan* was released in 1978.

### Yasukuni-jinja★ 靖国神社

*Map II A1.*

*3-1-1 Kudankita, Chiyoda-ku, turn E when leaving Kitanomaru Park, behind the Nippon Budokan. Subway Z06, T07. www.yasukuni.or.jp.*

Past the statue of Omura Masujiro (1824–69), founder of the modern Japanese army, an avenue lined with gingko trees and stone lanterns leads to a door made of cypresswood *(Shin-mon)* decorated with 16-petal chrysanthemums, the Imperial family's emblem. Founded in 1869, the Yasukuni-jinja **shrine complex** contains the Yushukan War Memorial Museum, recognizable by the Zero fighter plane on display. Behind the central hall *(haiden)* is the principal shrine *(honden)*, and behind this is the Reijibo Hoan-den, where the names of those who have died fighting on behalf of the Emperor to whom the Yasukuni ("Restful country") Shrine is dedicated are inscribed by hand on Japanese paper.

### Yushukan War Memorial Museum 遊就館

*Map II A1.*

*3-1-1 Kudankita Chiyoda-ku.*

*Open daily 9am–5pm. ¥800.*

Japan's oldest museum (founded in 1882, rebuilt and renovated in 2002) is dedicated to military history. Its 20 or so rooms are spread over two floors.

The first room evokes the spirit of the samurai, while in the rest souvenirs and photos of war heroes honored at Yasukuni (*see box opposite*) are displayed. Visitors from the West may feel that the displays are selective, resisting pressure from foreign powers who challenge the idea that Japan was simply defending its interests and was forced into war by the West.

### Tokyo Station 東京駅

*Map II B2.*

Built in 1914, this red-brick station did not escape the bombing raids of World War II, but it was rebuilt almost exactly as before except for some alterations necessary to accommodate the new high-speed Shinkansen trains.

## MARUNOUCHI DISTRICT

丸の内 *Map II B3.*

As you leave the station heading west *(toward Miyuki-dori)*, you are immediately confronted with so many tower blocks you get the feeling that here, the elevator must be the most common mode of transport. Most of these buildings bear the name Marunouchi ("within the castle walls"), which refers to a space historically reserved for the most powerful *daimyo*. By building here, they demonstrated their loyalty to the shogun, and for his part he was able to keep a close eye on their growing power. When Tokyo became the capital city, it was natural for government buildings to take over this area. Destroyed by fire in 1872, the land was then bought by the Mitsubishi company, at the request of the Emperor. Since then, Mitsubishi has developed the land, in so doing defining and shaping the district. The Marunouchi Building, affectionately known as "Maru-Biru" *(www.marubiru.jp)*, is its flagship.

Built on 36 floors, this luxury complex of offices, shops, and restaurants offers wide **views** over the city *(see Addresses p175)*. The area's business identity has been enriched with a cultural dimension. The **Mitsubishi Ichigokan Museum** (open *Mon–Fri 10am–8pm, Tue and Sat–Sun 10am–6pm, admission depends on exhibition*) is a copy of the first red-brick building to be constructed in this district (built in 1894 by the British architect **Josiah Conder**, *see p 89*, and demolished in 1968).

Under the aegis of its director Takahashi Akiya, a specialist in French art, it is dedicated to 18–20C modern art. It opened in April 2010 *(Marunouchi 2, Choyoda ward)* with an exhibition, "Manet and Modern Paris," in collaboration with the Musée d'Orsay.

## Tokyo International Forum★★

東京国際フォーラム

*Map II B3.*

*3-5-1 Marunouchi, Chiyoda-ku. Subway Y18, JR Yurakucho station. Open 8am–11pm. www.t-i-forum.co.jp.*

This arts and conference center, opened in 1997, is notable for its long-flowing lines. The 226,042sq ft/21,000sq m atrium is topped by a **huge glass roof★★★** shaped like an inverted ship. At a height of almost 196.8ft/60m, linked iron arches repeat across its 738.2ft/225m length with the regularity of waves on water. The "hull," ribbed with cables and crossed by slightly sloping, tensioned walkways, is supported by just two columns, one at either end. This billion-dollar gem, built at a time when the yen was advantageously low, was designed by Rafael Viñoly, an American architect of Uruguayan origin, born in 1941.

The Forum has seven auditoriums of different sizes *(Hall A has 5,000 seats!)* and 34 conference rooms. It also houses the Oedo Antique Market every first and third Sunday in the month. Every year, it receives a total of more than 20 million visitors. At first basement level *(Forum B1)*, the **Mitsuo Aida Museum★** *(open Tue–Sun 10am–5.30pm; ¥800)* has been exhibiting the calligraphy of the poet Mitsuo Aida (1924–91) since 2003.

His work was influenced by a philosophy stamped with great humanity, inherited from his mentor Yakai Tetsuo, a great Zen monk of the Sodo sect.

## Idemitsu Museum of Arts★★

出光美術館 *Map II B3.*

*Teigeki Bldg, 9th floor, 3-1-1 Marunouchi, Chiyoda-ku. Subway Y18. Open Tue–Sun 10am–5pm (Fri 7pm). ¥1,000. www.idemitsu.co.jp/museum/english.*

This museum, created in 1966 by the founder of the Idemitsu oil company, is renowned for its temporary exhibitions. The main collection includes some fine pieces of Japanese (porcelain from the Hizen area of Kyushu, masterpieces by the artist Sengai, etc.) and Western art, including the world's largest private **Georges Rouault** (1871–1958) collection over 400 works, with the astounding *Miserere*.

## Hibiya Park 日比谷公園

*Map II A–B3 off map.*

*Subway C09.*

This first Western-style garden, opened in 1903, covers the site of an ancient *daimyo* residence, close to Edo Castle. Renowned for its tulips, in September it also has displays of chrysanthemums, the Imperial family's emblem.

East of the garden, on the other side of the administrative district *(Kasumigaseki)*, is the **Diet** *(Kokkai)* or Japanese Parliament *(Subway: Kokkaigijido-mae)*. The building, inspired by the Neo classical style of the US Capitol, was completed in 1936. Made of reinforced concrete and granite, it is dominated by a central tower with a pyramid-shaped roof. The Diet comprises two chambers: the House of Representatives and the House of Peers.

When not in session, the latter is open to the public (open Mon–Fri 9am–4pm; 03-5521-7445; www.sangiin.go.jp).

## NIHONBASHI 日本橋

*E of Tokyo station (Yaiesu central exit).*

### Nihonbashi Bridge日本橋

*Map II C2.*
*NE of Tokyo station on Chuo-dori. Subway G11, A13.*

The "Bridge of Japan" *(Nihonbashi)*, the point zero from which all distances in the country are measured, was built of wood in 1603 by Tokugawa Ieyasu. The current version (1911) is made of stone.

### Mitsui Memorial Museum★

三井記念美術館
*Map II C2.*
*7 F Mitsui Main Building, 2-1-1 Nihonbashi Muromachi, Chuo-ku. Subway G12. Open Tue–Sun 10am–5pm. ¥800. www.mitsui-museum.jp.*

Since 2005, this museum, *(entered through the atrium of the Nihonbashi Mitsui Tower,)* has been housed in the main building of the Mitsui group, established in the 17C. It displays in rotation items accumulated by the Mitsui family over a period of 400 years: kimonos, tea containers, etc. Six of the museum's 3,700 objects are National Treasures. Mitsui, today a well-known and powerful conglomerate, achieved its first commercial success manufacturing sake and selling fabric. In the Meiji period Mitsui diversified into banking and became one of Japan's principal banks.

*Remember to visit the Mandarin Oriental Hotel as you leave (see Addresses p175).*

### Bridgestone Museum of Art★★

ブリヂストン美術館 *Map II C3.*
*1-10-1 Kyobashi, Chuo-ku, S of Nihonbashi Bridge going down Chuo-dori to where it meets Yaesu-dori. Subway T10, G10. Museum: open Tue–Sat 10am–8pm, Sun 10am–6pm. Georgette Tearoom: open 11am–6pm. ¥800. www.bridgestone-museum.gr.jp.*

A collection of Western and Japanese work from the Meiji period onward, assembled by Ishibashi Shojiro, founder of the tire and rubber company, Bridgestone (*ishi* = stone, *bashi* = bridge). On display are some fine sculptures (Rodin, Bourdelle, Despiau, Maillol) and paintings: Manet's *Masked Ball at the Opera* (1873), Van Gogh's *Windmills on Montmartre* (1886), and two Rouault oils on paper. The Japanese paintings include pieces by Oka Shikanosuke (1898–1978).

## GINZA★★ 銀座

*Map III p 142.*

The "place where silver is minted" (after the mint that was established here in the time of Tokugawa Ieyasu) is now also the one where it is spent. You only have to walk down the main shopping street **Chuo-dori** to see how true that is. Just as on Fifth Avenue or Bond Street, it is lined with stores owned by the biggest names in fashion and luxury goods—Armani, Louis Vuitton, Cartier, Chanel, etc.—all vying for space, and at the top end of the real estate market, the prices are sky-high. Ginza's street plan is unusually regular and its buildings have an architectural coherence that is also unusual for Tokyo, thanks to British architect Thomas Waters, who was tasked with the redesign following the area's destruction by fire in 1872. Under Waters' direction, brick-paved streets lined with brick buildings made their first appearance. Meeting up socially in Ginza was thus made easy and it became a fashionable area in which to be seen.

The first department stores started to appear on street corners, but the earthquake of 1923 (see p121) and then World War II brought destruction to the area again. The most recent rebuild has retained Waters' uniformity and coherence, though the buildings are now made of stone, concrete, iron, and glass. Ginza remains a popular place to stroll and go window shopping, retaining its reputation for elegance and sophistication.

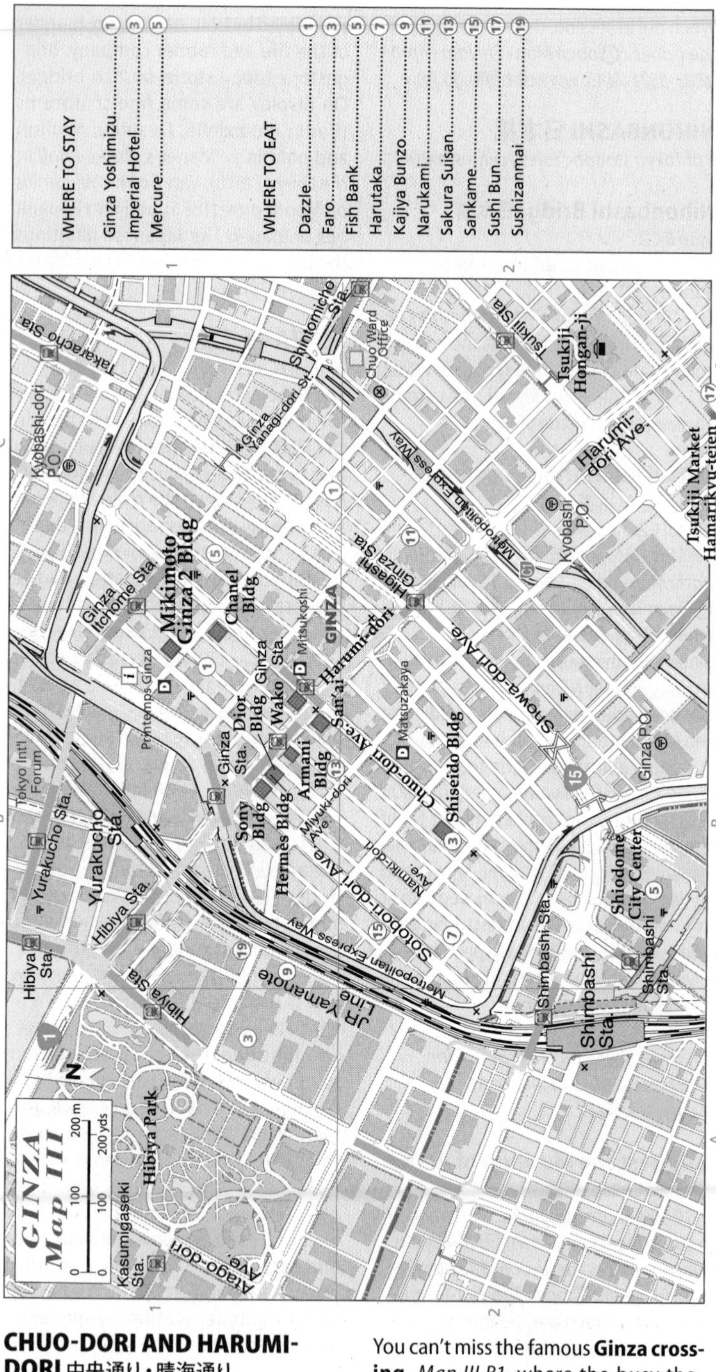




## CHUO-DORI AND HARUMI-DORI 中央通り・晴海通り

*Map III B1/2.*
*Subway G09, M16.*

You can't miss the famous **Ginza crossing,** *Map III B1,* where the busy thoroughfares of **Chuo-dori**, also called **Ginza-dori** *(running north–south)* and

### In the footlights

During the Edo era (1603–1867), many theaters staged Kabuki performances. The largest of these was in Ginza. But the art—very popular for its frequent caricatures of the shogun—experienced varying fortunes. Never entirely prohibited, it was nevertheless moved out of Ginza toward Asakusa in 1841 before it returned, updated and refined by the official canons, in the Meiji era. Thus in 1899 the National Theatre (*Kabuki-za, now closed*) opened its doors on Kobikicho, which is now Ginza 4-chome. The venue dominated Japanese theater for 20 years before being completely destroyed in 1921, in a fire caused by a short circuit. Only partially rebuilt, it was destroyed again in the 1923 earthquake. The theater eventually reopened in 1925. Its façade of concrete and steel had echoes of the Nara (8C) and Momoyama (16C) architectural styles. On May 25, 1945 American bombing raids reduced it to ashes. It was rebuilt for the third time in 1951 (*see also Addresses p177*).

**Harumi-dori** *(east–west)* intersect. There's a large building on every corner of Chuo-dori. **Wako★** *Map III B1*, one of the oldest *depato* (a term derived from "department store") in Ginza, occupies one of the corners. Its clock tower is a landmark—the first was erected in 1894, but was destroyed in the 1923 earthquake. It was rebuilt in 1932, along with the present department store building. Close by, the entrance to the prestigious **Mitsukoshi** department store is via the basement, where the excellent food hall is located; the store entrance is directly connected to the subway. The upper floors are filled with expensive, high-quality goods. Towering over the Ginza crossing is the tall, cylindrical **San-ai** building, whose every neon-lit floor offers a different cocktail of cultures and fashion. The **Cafe Doutor** occupies the first two levels. Its prime location looking out over the crossing makes the cafe a popular but rather expensive venue, but it's great for people —and car—watching.

*Harumi-dori going west and toward Hibiya Park.*

The **Dior Building★★**, *Map III B1*, designed by award-winning architects Sejima and Nishizawa, working jointly as SANAA, has a smooth façade illuminated with thousands of fiber-optic lights at night. The highest tower in the district is the 12-story **Armani/Ginza Tower★**, designed by the Italian couturier in 2007 in collaboration with the architect Massimiliano Fuksas. Its glass façade refects the sky and the surrounding buildings. Lights in the shape of leaves positioned along vertical strips of light cascade down the façade resembling bamboo. Inside is a bar-lounge, a restaurant, and the world's first Armani Spa. A short distance away the **Hermès Building★★★** *Map III B1* occupies an area of 64,583.5sq ft/6,000sq m on 15 floors. The mosaic-style façade, designed by the Italian Renzo Piano, is made up of 13,000 glass blocks (four together are exactly the same size as a Hermès headscarf), creating a "magic lantern" inspired by the glass house built by Pierre Chareau in Paris in the 1920s. On the top floor contemporary art exhibitions provide a stark contrast to the building's clean lines (*no charge*). There's even a small Japanese-style roof garden, though it is closed to the public.

The **Sony Building** *Map III B1*, opened in 1966, is close by; inside, elegant spiral staircases unwind to reveal floor after floor of the latest technological wizardry *(www.sonybuilding.jp)*.

*Harumi-dori, going east and toward Tsukiji market.*

### Tsukiji Jogai Market★★

築地場外市場 *Map I C3.*
*5-2-1 Tsukiji, Chuo-ku. Subway E18, exit A2. Open Mon–Sat 5am–1pm. Closed public holidays. www.tsukiji-market.or.jp or www.shijou.metro.tokyo.jp. Entry to the tuna auction sale*

Tuna auction in Tsukiji Jogai Market

*is prohibited to tourists between 5am and 6.15am and limited to 140 people/ day in two groups.* *Avoid high-heeled shoes, handbags, flash photography.*

The largest fish market in the world makes for a dizzying spectacle: every day 52,000 people (specialist fish merchants, wholesalers, customers) and 32,000 vehicles go in and out of this market, crisscrossed with alleyways as far as the eye can see. Fish of all kinds (fresh, frozen, processed, dried) arrive from all corners of the earth: mackerel, bonito, horse mackerel, sardines, Guam and Mediterranean tuna, coho salmon from Chile, turtles from Kyushu, shrimps from India, octopus from Africa, etc. Every day 2,500 tons of 450 different products (about 600,000 tons per year) pass through Tsukiji, which literally means "recovered land." The land at the mouth of the Sumida River had to be reclaimed to house the fish market, which had been destroyed by the 1923 earthquake after standing for three centuries in the Nihonbashi district.

Today the market is facing a new future: for health and safety reasons, and real estate issues, the government plans to move the market to Koto Ward's Toyosu district by 2012. The Mayor finds the market's presence in this, Tokyo's most chic district, increasingly incongruous. The Democrat majority opposes the project as the proposed site, formerly belonging to a gas company, is heavily polluted, and may block the 2011 finance law if the Mayor persists in wishing to move the market.

Stroll round the outdoor market, where you can enjoy a breakfast of raw fish in one of the many restaurants.

*On Chuo-dori going north toward Kyobashi.*

Two blocks from **Wako**, the dark façade of the **Chanel Building★** *Map III B1* is the first to catch the eye. The largest store on the Chuo-dori with 10 floors has double walls of dark glass that produce a quilted effect. With thousands of white dots (the brand's logo), the façade by American architect Peter Marino, suggests Chanel's signature tweed fabric. When night falls, 700,000 LEDs outline the latest Lagerfeld innovations on its walls. The ninth floor is occupied by gastronome Alain Ducasse's restaurant **Beige** (Coco Chanel's favorite color). On the opposite side of the street is the **De Beers Ginza Building★★**.

Designed by Japanese architect Mitsui Jun, the twisted curve of the front of the building gives the appearance of being caught in time, as it undulates like seaweed with the ebb and flow of the tide. Nearby, the façade of the **Mikimoto Ginza 2 Building★★★** *Map III B1*, (designed by Ito Toyo), is pink despite its cladding of steel. The walls are punctuated with windows of an irregular shape, positioned randomly so that the effect is of a Swiss cheese. The company's founder, Mikimoto Kokichi, was the first to adapt an existing production technique to make cultured pearls (*see p244*). The sumptuous interior houses a restaurant and a tearoom (*see Addresses p177*).

*On Chuo-dori going S toward Shiodome.*

The giant **Shiseido Building**★★ *Map III B2*, housing this Japanese cosmetic giant's headquarters, is the work of Catalan architect Ricardo Bofill. The façade of red-brick-colored panels conceals two restaurants on the upper floors with fine panoramic **views**. There is an art gallery in the basement (*open Tue–Sat 11am–7pm, Sun 11am–6pm; no charge*).

### Hamarikyu-Teien Garden★

浜離宮恩賜庭園 *Map I C4.*
*1-1 Hamarikyu-teien, Chuo-ku. Subway E19, G08. Open 9am–4.30pm. ¥300.*
Situated beside Tokyo Bay, the distinctive characteristic of this garden is that the water level in the lake fluctuates with the tide. There are beautiful banks of peonies in spring. It offers a delightful green interlude after the skyscrapers of Shiodome and is a typical example of a *daimyo* garden from the Edo era.

*You can exit the garden on one of the Sumida River water buses.*

*If you wish, you can go straight to the section on Tokyo Bay (Odaiba) p 162.*

## ROPPONGI★

六本木
*Map I B3/4, p120.*
The name Roppongi ("six trees") comes from the tree ideogram in the name of each of the six *daimyo* who used to live here. Today, the area has a bad reputation, not least because of its nightlife, still closely associated with the American base established here after World War II. *Gaien Higashi-dori* is lined with neon signs and bars patroled by insistent touts. It's a disorientating place, perhaps even more so for Japanese than for the Westerners who come here in droves. Architecturally, the tale of woe is less comprehensive, even though the huge mall, created by Mori Minoru just as the economic bubble was bursting, feels like an overheated department store.
Things have improved considerably since 2007, however, with the creation of new buildings like the National Art Center and 21_21 Design Sight, developed around architecturally and conceptually bold spaces. The six trees have finally borne good fruit. The "art triangle," as it has already been dubbed (*which includes the Mori Tower Museum*), is certain to open up a new future for Roppongi.

## ROPPONGI HILLS★★

六本木ヒルズ
*Map I B4.*
*6-10-1 Roppongi, Minato-ku.*
*Subway H04, exit 1C or E23, exit 3.*
*Stores: open 11am–9pm with exceptions.*

### Mr Satoh's Formula

Mr Satoh, who runs the Shigeyoshi restaurant (*see Addresses p183*), develops a mischievous twinkle in his eye when you ask to see the following day's menu. He has no idea what it will be and says: "It's been the same thing every morning for years" until he comes back from the Tsukiji fish market, where he's known as the "white wolf", who wanted to be a sea fish: "What I cook depends on what I find, but I only find what I'm looking for." And what Mr Satoh is looking for is very simple: "The best seafood. Quality is not just about the freshness of the fish, it's about what's in season. You can't just fish for anything, anywhere, and at any time. This morning, for example, they put some turtles they'd caught off Kyushu on one side for me. They're only available for about two weeks in the year. I took four, which will make a tasty soup for four people, no more."

Tokyo City View, Mori Tower, Roppongi Hills



*Restaurants: open 11am–11pm. www. roppongihills.com.*
The inventory of this vast city complex, 17 years in the making, is rather conventional: offices, shops, gardens, esplanades, walkways, movie theaters, etc. However, the unconventional can be found here too, such as the monster spider, arching its legs over Roku-Roku Plaza. A metaphor for urban life? A symbol of the **Mori Art Museum**, rising 885.8ft/270m above sea level? No, it's just *Maman* (mother), according to its creator, the sculptor Louise Bourgeois.

## Mori Tower★★ 森タワー

*Map I B4.*
It's hard to miss the Mori Tower—54 floors designed by American architects Kohn Pedersen Fox. The unusual entrance, called the Metro Hat, funnels you through two turns of a spiral staircase to the actual tower entrance.

### Tokyo City View★★

*Open daily 10am–11pm, Fri–Sat 1am. ¥1,500 including Mori Art Museum. www. roppongihills. com.*
On the 52nd floor of the tower a circular atrium, 984.3ft/300m in circumference and 36ft/11m high, provides a jaw-dropping 360-degree panoramic **view** over the city. It is magical by day *(with Mount Fuji visible to the west on a clear day)*, and stunning at night.

On the same floor is the **Mori Arts Center Gallery** (*open daily 10am–8pm, Tue 5pm; entry charge varies with exhibition; 03-5777-8600)* and on the floor above, the **Mori Art Museum★★** (*open daily 10am–10pm, Tue 5pm; ¥1,500 including Tokyo City View).* Temporary exhibitions based on the current issues of contemporary art follow each other in rapid succession. Some are the Tokyo leg of large international exhibitions put on jointly by different museums.

## Tokyo Tower★ 東京タワー

*Map I B4.*
*4-2-8 Shibakoen, Minato-ku.*
*Subway E21, H05, I06. Open 9am–10pm. Main Observatory ¥820, Special Observatory supplement of ¥600. www.tokyotower.co.jp.*
Built in 1958 and 1092,5ft/333m high, it resembles the Eiffel Tower in Paris but painted red and white (to be visible from the air). The tower is a relay station for the transmission of more than 20 television channels and includes, among other things, restaurants, an aquarium, and a waxworks museum.

## Zojo-ji★ 増上寺

*Map I C4.*
*4-7-35 Shibakoen. Subway E21.*
*www.zojoji.or.jp/en.*
The Zojo-ji Buddhist temple lies in Shiba Park, west of the Tokyo Tower.

Founded in 1393 and transferred to this site in 1598, when the shogun Tokugawa Ieyasu settled in Edo, it was damaged in the bombing raids of 1945.
It was rebuilt in the 1970s, except for the large gateway at the entrance, the Gate of Triple Deliverance (from anger, stupidity, and greed), **Sangedatsu-mon★**, which had escaped the bombs. Dating from the Edo era (1622), the gate is the oldest wooden structure in Tokyo.

## TOKYO MIDTOWN★
東京ミッドタウン
*Map I B3. Subway E23, exit 8. www.tokyo-midtown.com.*
Lawns, gingko biloba, and camphor trees wend their way through this complex of six buildings dominated by the **Midtown Tower**, basking in the glory of its new record height of 813.6ft/248m. With a huge glass-and-steel canopy outside and gently sloping ramps winding through greenery-filled spaces inside, four floors of luxury goods and 50 or so bars, cafes, and restaurants are waiting to be explored (*open 11am–midnight).* On the second floor Joël Bruant's restaurant looks out over Hinokicho Park.

### Suntory Museum of Art★★
サントリー美術館
*Map I B3.*
*9-7-4 Akasaka, Minato-ku. Open Wed –Sat 10am–8pm, Sun–Mon 10am–6pm. Entry charge varies with exhibition. www.suntory.jp/sma*
Remodeled in April 2007 by Kuma Kengo as part of this new building complex, the museum houses a permanent collection of 3,000 exhibits (lacquerware, Satsuma ceramics, textiles, and Noh costumes), displayed alongside temporary exhibitions organized in association with the major museums of the world. Themes of the temporary exhibitions range from the relationship between French and Japanese art to haute couture (Kosode kimonos) in the Edo era.

*Turn to your right on leaving the museum. There's an excellent **view** over Hinokicho Park from the terrace, the location of 21_21 Design Sight.*

### 21_21 Design Sight★★
トゥーワン・トゥーワン・デザインサイト
*Map I B3.*
*9-7-6 Akasaka, Minato-ku. 1min walk from Tokyo Midtown, Subway E23, exit 8. Open Wed–Mon 11am–8pm. ¥1,000. www.2121designsight.jp*
Built in 2007 and designed by Ando Tadao, the high priest of modern architecture, this building squats on the ground like a crumpled black origami insect. The aim of the design center *(18,298.6sq ft/1,700sq m on two levels)* is to rediscover and reinterpret the objects and events of everyday life through a prism of highly innovative design—21/21 is a play on 20/20 vision—via thought-provoking exhibitions (four annually). Fashion designer Issey Miyake is one of its directors.

### National Art Center★★
国立新美術館 *Map I B3.*
*7-22-2 Roppongi, Minato-ku. Subway C05, exit 6 or H04, exit 4a. Open Wed–Mon 10am–6pm (Fri 8pm). Entry charge varies with exhibition. www.nact.jp/english.*
The National Art Center of Tokyo is a powerful tool in the service of contemporary culture and art, a small $290 million jewel in Tokyo's crown. This 525ft/160m long façade of undulating glass is one of the last works of Kurokawa Kisho (1934–2007), who was at the forefront of Japan's architectural renaissance. He also designed the famous Nagakin capsule tower in Ginza. The **art center building★★** was opened in 2007 and has 150,694.7sq ft/14,000sq m of exhibition space. The biggest art gallery in the world, it is also the first in Japan to have no permanent collection. Inside are 12 rooms of at least 10,764sq ft/1,000sq m (and two of 21,527.8sq ft/2,000sq m), three conference areas, an art library, three cafes, shops, and the Paul Bocuse brasserie at the top of one of the two inverted cones that give the building's glass frontage an unusual shape.

## SHINJUKU★★ 新宿
*Map V p148.*

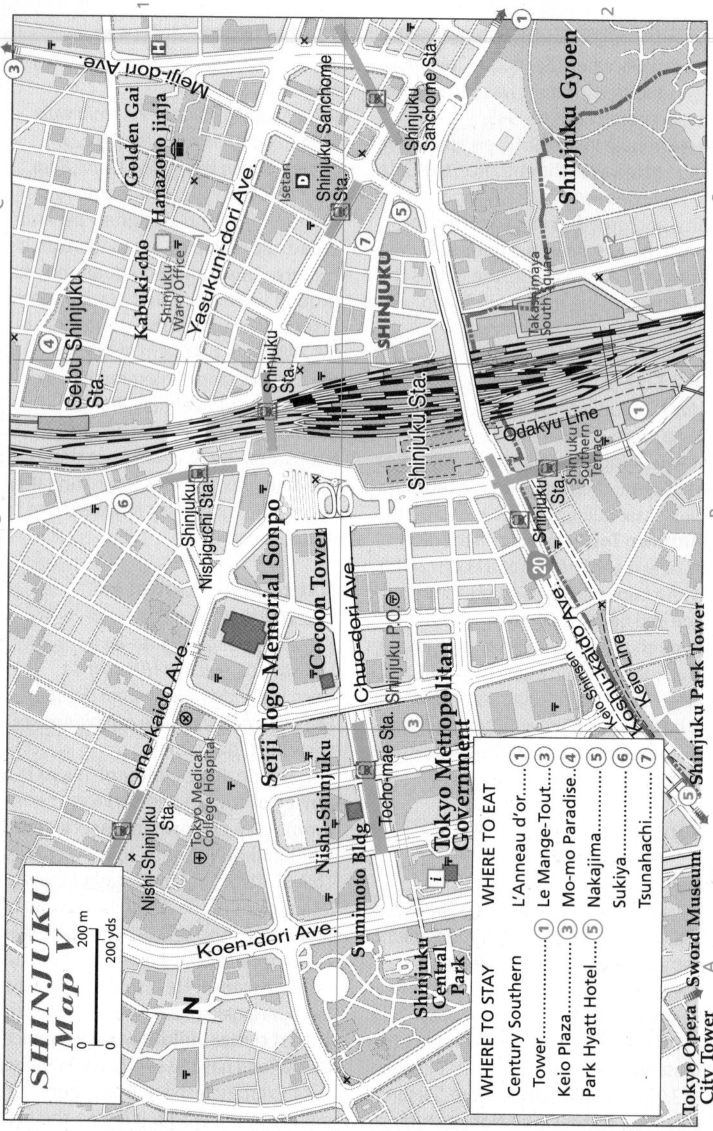




Asphalt now covers *Koshu-kaido-dori*, one of the five principal highways that radiated out across the Japanese landscape in the Edo era. Shinjuku was then owned by the lord Naito, a vassal of Tokugawa Ieyasu. In the midst of all the skyscrapers, it's difficult to imagine the "new villages" *(shinjuku)* that once stood on this marshy ground and profited from merchants on their way to Koshu *(now Yamanashi prefecture)*. The popular tearooms at staging posts along the road offered a range of illicit pleasures. As the district grew, so too did its seamy reputation, which it was never to lose.

The building of a railway station in the late 19C facilitated the movement of goods and Yokohama took the opportunity to increase its silk exports. Shinjuku expanded further, and as it was barely touched by the 1923 earthquake, so did its population. A liberal spirit reigned, and Shinjuku became a social and cultural melting pot where people and ideas mixed freely, attracting all kinds at the margins of society, along with poets and writers who continued to flock here after World War II.

In the 1970s Shinjuku was redeveloped. The western part was subject to a radical zoning plan (the business district), while the eastern end was filled with restaurants, love hotels, peep-shows, massage parlors, and *pachinko* (gaming parlors). Today, to the west of the station (**Nishi-shinjuku**) is a forest of skyscrapers in which more than 300,000 *salarymen* (office workers) go about their business; while to the east (**Higashi-shinjuku**) is Kabuki-cho, the pleasure district. In the station square sandwiched between the two, small street traders and *yatai* (food stands) tempt the *salarymen* in their lunch break, while *office ladies* hurry by in stiletto heels.

Contemporary Shinjuku is a densely populated, major entertainment and administrative district, with the busiest train station in the world.

## WEST SHINJUKU 西新宿

Around 30 or so of the buildings in this forest of skyscrapers are more than 328ft/100m high. Most of them have an observation deck at the top.

*5min from station, west exit.*

### Seiji Togo Memorial Sonpo Japan Museum of Art★ 損保ジャパン東郷青児美術館

*Map V B1.*
*42 F Sonpo Japan Headquarters, 1-26-1 Nishi-Shinjuku. Open Tue–Sun 10am–6pm. ¥1,000.*

This museum belongs to the Yasuda insurance company, renamed Sonpo in 2002. It is housed on the 42nd floor of the Sonpo company building. If you're not familiar with the name, think back to the record auction price achieved at Christie's on March 30, 1987, when the Yasuda Fire & Marine Insurance Co. bought Vincent Van Gogh's *Sunflowers* for 5.3 billion yen. In so doing the company created for itself a worldwide "low budget" publicity campaign. The follow-up was less than triumphant, however, as the company ran out of funds.

### Shinjuku Station

Two and a half million passengers travel on the station's 5,000 overland and subway trains every day. Many stations *(run by different companies)* and lines *(both subway and overland)* feed into this dizzying whirl "where people scurry backward and forward on a thousand practical errands, from the train to the store, from clothes to food, and where a train can run right up to a shoe store" wrote Roland Barthes (*Empire of Signs*, Éditions Skira, 1970). The phenomenon has its roots in the numerous black market centers that flourished in the stations of Tokyo after the war. Shinjuku was the first of these.

Today the foundation has 650 pieces, including many masterpieces, displayed in rotation: Van Gogh's *Sunflowers* (1888), *L'Allée des Alyscamps* (1888) by Gauguin, *Pommes et Serviette* (1879) by Cézanne, and *Nostalgia* (1959) by Togo Seiji (1897–1978) an important Japanese artist, whose own works *(around 200)* feature in the foundation's permanent display. There is an attractive **view** from the museum.

### Tokyo Metropolitan Government★★★ 東京都庁

*Map V A2.*
*2-8-1 Nishi-Shinjuku. Subway E28. North Tower observatory: Open daily 9.30am–11pm. Closed 2nd & 4th Mon of the month. South Tower observatory: Open daily 9.30am–5.30pm. Closed 1st & 3rd Tue of the month. No charge. Large Tourist Information Center on ground floor (open daily 9.30am–6.30pm; 03-5321-3077).*

This building, designed by Japanese architect **Tange Kenzo** (*see box p162*), has the look of a Western-style Gothic cathedral and stands out among the other skyscrapers. The observatories situated in its towers (797ft/243m) provide excellent **views** over Shinjuku. Also referred to as Tokyo City Hall, or "Tocho" for short, its vast dimensions accommodate some 13,000 government workers. A short distance south of the city hall is the **Shinjuku Park Tower** (771ft/235m). The **Park Hyatt Hotel** occupies floors 39–52 (*see Addresses p179*).

### Sumitomoto Building★
### 新宿住友ビル

*Map V A2.*
*2-6-1 Nishi-Shinjuku, Shinjuku-ku. Subway E 28.*

Rising 689ft/210m, the Sumitomoto Building has an atrium running its entire height. A number of relatively inexpensive restaurants are on the 49th to 52nd floors, most with a beautiful **view★** of Tokyo and neighboring skyscrapers; there is a curious WWII history museum as well.

### Cocoon Tower★★
### モード学園コクーンタワー

*Map V B1.*
*1-7-2 Nishi-Shinjuku, Shinjuku-ku. Subway E 28.*

The Japanese agency Tange inaugurated this tower in 2008. At 666ft/203m it is the second tallest building for education after the University of Moscow and contains a fashion school. Recognizable for its unusual white aluminum and blue glass design, its immense crisscross pattern recalls a cocoon.

### Tokyo Opera City Tower
### 東京オペラシティタワー

*Map V A2 off map.*
*3-20-2 Nishi-Shinjuku-ku. Subway E29, exit A2, Keio New Line, Hatsudai station, east exit. www.operacity.jp/en.*

Ten minutes or so to the southwest is Shinjuku's third highest tower *(767.7ft/234m)*. This 54-floor multiplex contains offices, restaurants, and shops, as well as six theaters, the magnificent **Tokyo Opera City Concert Hall**, a contemporary art gallery (*open Tue–Sun 11am–9pm; ¥1,000*), and the highly innovative **NTT Intercommunication Center** (*open Tue–Sun 10am–6pm, Fri 9pm; ¥800; www.ntticc.or.jp*) displaying works combining robotics and new technology. The **New National Theatre** *(behind the tower)* stages opera, ballet, and modern dance performances.

### Sword Museum 刀剣博物館

*Map V A2 off map.*
*4-25-10 Yoyogi, Shibuya-ku. Keio New Line, Hatsudai station 03-3379-1386. Open Tue–Sun 10am–4.30pm. ¥525. English language brochure.*

The sword *(katana)* reflects the spirit of the samurai warrior. The blade and the soul were held in equal esteem, so both the steel of the sword and the character of the samurai had to be well tempered. There is a fine collection of *tsuba* or saber guards, from rudimentary early examples to later models embellished to show the social standing of their owner.

### Golden Gai, "Streets of Gold"

In postwar Shinjuku, which had been completely razed to the ground, a small district sprung up, constructed from recycled material supplied partly by GIs, who were all the more eager to help since these little shacks provided shelter for the *only*, Japanese girls who acted as both concubines and madams. When the Treaty of San Francisco ended the American occupation in 1951, the district went into decline, but the 1958 law prohibiting prostitution brought a new departure. Modest rents attracted unconventional figures (artists, transvestites, etc.), who were aware of the irony in naming this poverty-ridden district "Streets of Gold." Filmmakers, photographers, and writers (Oshima Nagisa, Imamura Shohei, Araki Nobuyoshi, Tanaka Komimasa) all came to recharge their batteries in its 300 bars. Today, no more than 60 of these establishments remain, far fewer than the legions of developers with plenty of ideas for the real estate.

Kabuki-cho at night

© SeanPavonePhoto/Bigstockphoto.com

## EAST SHINJUKU 東新宿

*From JR Shinjuku station, east Kabuki-cho exit, take the wide Yasukuni-dori.*

### Kabuki-cho★★ 歌舞伎町 *Map V C1*

*Subway M08, JR Shinjuku station, east exit.*

In the early 1950s, an association campaigning for the reconstruction of Shinjuku, which had been largely destroyed by World War II bombs, wanted to build a theater for Kabuki performances. Although the project failed for financial reasons, the district adopted the name, along with the uninhibited character of the sort historically associated with actors. Today, neon signs invite you into a shady world of massage parlors, gaming rooms, saunas, host clubs for men and women (*see box opposite*), and karaoke. All desires are catered for. Japanese men in particular appreciate the social interludes that these venues provide, where nothing is taboo and they can discuss any subject. Office ladies, on the other hand, seek to be the object of kind attention.

### Golden Gai★★

新宿ゴールデン街

*Map V C1.*

*Subway M08, JR Shinjuku station, east exit.*

Sandwiched between Kabuki-cho and the Hanazono shrine, the best time to visit this district is at night. Golden Gai is a small, compact area lined with bars. Squeezed in on top of one another, some of the bars can barely accommodate six people and are not very welcoming to tourists, but if you can get in, as the door slams shut, you will probably find yourself in rather gloomy surroundings.

There are some exceptions however, like *La Jetée*, a bar named after the 1962 French short film and owned by a movie fan. Next to the Golden Gai, the Shinto **Hanazono-jinja** is a fitting place to come and pray to the god of business, no matter what that business may be—so you may occasionally come across one or two Yakuza there. Every year, the **Tori no ichi Festival** is held at the shrine.

Dating back to the Edo era, it takes place in November on the day of the Rooster *(tori)* in accordance with the old Chinese lunar calendar. You can buy lucky charms called *kumade* ("bamboo rake") to help bring good fortune in the year to come. A **Flea Market** is held the first Saturday and third Sunday of the month.

### The rise of the host club

In the early evening, men and women go looking for a little company in one of Kabuki-cho's 150 hostess or host clubs. Women-only clubs are expanding rapidly, the flip side of a Japanese society that can be chauvinistic. The young men, or hosts, charged with entertaining them are identified by their long, bleached-blond hair. Their pictures are displayed in the front window or outside by touts, or they themselves have to approach passers-by.

The reputation of a host rests on his kindness, consideration, and humor, everything a client may need after a stressful day at work. Of course, the more she drinks, the more the host earns. Any resemblance to the tea houses where Kabuki actors charged rich women for their company is, of course, purely coincidental.

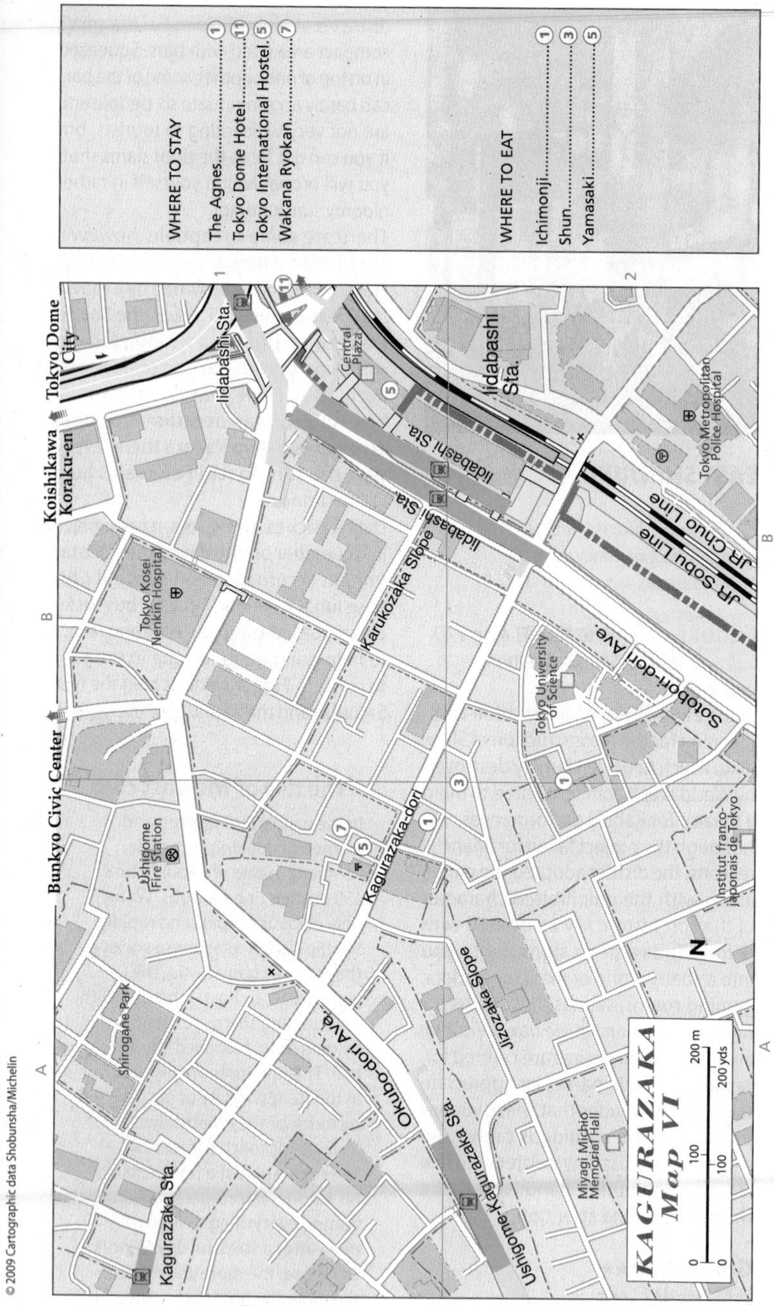


**Shinjuku Gyoen National Garden★★★** 新宿御苑 *Map V C2. 11 Naito-cho, Shinjuku-ku, NW Okido Gate. 5min walk from Subway M10, 10min walk from JR Yamanote Line, Shinjuku station. Open Tue–Sun 9am–4pm. ¥200. www.env.go.jp/garden/shinjukugyoen/english.*

This garden *(1433.3 acre/58ha)*, once owned by the *daimyo* Naito, a feudal lord of the Edo era (*see p69*), has been managed by the Imperial Household Agency since 1906. Next to a Japanese stroll garden is a landscaped English garden and in the southeastern corner, a French-style garden set around an avenue of plane trees. Near the Okido Gate, a tropical greenhouse shelters some 2,000 plants.
The Shinjuku Gyoen is where the Prime Minister holds his *hanami*, a garden party to view *(mi)* the blossom *(hana)* of the cherry trees in spring. In the fall, the chrysanthemums are in bloom and the maple trees blaze a glorious scarlet.

## KAGURAZAKA★ 神楽坂

*Map I and VI opposite.*
This area lies to the northwest of the Imperial Palace gardens. During the Edo era, it was a renowned pleasure district and, like most of the hills overlooking the lower town, was frequented by aristocratic members of society.
Geishas and tea houses attracted lords and rich merchants. *Nomiya*, traditional stands selling sake, were plentiful. Then, as Shinjuku developed, Kagurazaka gradually faded from view.
Today, the daytime atmosphere is still quiet and sleepy, but numerous restaurants bring it to life at night, creating the district's own particular charm.
On the main street, Kagurazaka-dori, you may hear the clatter of wooden *geta* as there are still some geisha houses in the area today.

### Tokyo Dome City★

東京ドームシティ *Map I C1.*
*1-3-61 Koraku, Bunkyo-ku. Subway M22, N11. www.tokyo-dome.co.jp/e.*
This entertainment complex includes: a **baseball stadium** *(sometimes nicknamed "Big Egg")*, which opened in 1988 with a capacity of 55,000; a museum (*open Mar–Sept 10am–6pm, Oct–Feb 10am–5pm; ¥500*); an ***onsen*** *(LaQua: open 11am–9am next day; from ¥2,565)*; a **hotel** (Tokyo Dome Hotel); an **amusement park** (*open 10am–10pm; ¥1,000)* with hair-raising rides not for the faint-hearted! Plus restaurants, shops, and a bowling alley. If baseball interests you you can check the results at www.npb.or.jp/eng.

### Bunkyo Civic Center

文京シビックセンター *Map I C1.*
*1-16-21 Kasuga, Bunkyo-ku. Subway M22, JR Chuo Line, Suidobashi station.*
*Open 9am–9.30pm.*
The 25th floor *(344.5ft/105m)* has a 330-degree observation deck (*no charge)* and a number of restaurants with panoramic **views**.

### Koishikawa Koraku-en Garden★★ 小石川後楽園

*Map I C1.*
*1-6-6 Koraku, Bunkyo-ku, entrance other side of Tokyo Dome. Subway E06.*
*Open 9am–5.30pm. ¥300.*
Created in the early Edo era, this Japanese garden is one of the oldest in Tokyo. It's a "strolling garden" (*see p103*), reproducing in miniature well-known Chinese and Japanese landscapes. Dotted with waterfalls and stone bridges, it is particularly beautiful when the plum trees are in blossom. Visit preferably in winter to avoid the noise from the nearby amusement park.

## SHIBUYA★ 渋谷

*Map VII p155.*
Shibuya is similar in some ways to Shinjuku. At its heart is an enormous crossroads lined with giant screens, beneath which hundreds of thousands of people scurry backward and forward, without ever bumping into each other.
In Shibuya, courtesy is perhaps less a demonstration of mutual respect than a practical way of making sure you don't hit someone.
There are, in fact, countless pedestrian walkways; some of them go round the crossroads, while others run across it—diagonally.
Shibuya owes this frenetic activity to the fact that its two private rail companies, Tokyu and Seibu, create a particularly high footfall around the station. Each is competing with the other for consumers

Shibuya crossroads

© Jose Fuste Raga/age fotostock

and takings. While youngsters head for Fashion Community 109 or the movie theaters in the Bunkamuara arts complex owned by the Tokyu Corporation, others prefer the Parco and Seibu department stores of its competitor. Both companies also own offices, shops, restaurants, cafes, hotels, etc. This district of southwest Tokyo, which also adjoins the surprising Ebisu district, can easily play host to some 750,000 people a day. They also say that stiletto heels are always one step ahead in Shibuya and you can well believe it when you hear them clicking their way rhythmically along the streets.

## AROUND THE STATION

The most popular place to meet is near the statue of the dog **Hachiko★** *Map VII B2,* to whom there is a sad story attached. Every evening, Hachiko would wait for his master, a professor at the University of Tokyo, at the station exit. One day the professor didn't return, having died of a heart attack.

The dog returned to the station every day to wait for his master until he himself died some 10 years later. The tale of Hachiko's loyalty spread throughout Japan. A bronze statue was erected in his memory, though the *yakitori* vendors, who befriended the dog and fed him every day, were soon forgotten.

### Bunkamura★

東急文化村

*Map VII A2.*

*2-24-1 Dogenzaka, Shibuya-ku. 7min walk from Shibuya station, Hachiko exit. Open daily 10am–7pm (Fri–Sat 9pm). www.bunkamura.co.jp.*

Located just behind its proprietor, the Tokyu department store at the end of Kamura-dori, this vast arts center displays a relaxed eclecticism: concert hall, theater *(Cocoon)*, opera house *(Orchard Hall)*, and movie theater follow on from each other on six floors.

An excellent art gallery and some temporary exhibitions complete the picture. You can also enjoy a coffee at the Deux Magots *(open 11am–11.30pm)* or sample a selection of wines in its wine lounge *(open 5pm–midnight)*. Every year since 1991 the Deux Magots in Bunkamura has awarded a literary prize, like its namesake in Paris.

### Toguri Museum of Art

戸栗美術館

*Map VII A1.*

*1-11-3 Shoto, Shibuya-ku. Shibuya station, Hachiko exit. Open Tue–Sun 9.30am–5.30pm. ¥1,000. www.toguri-museum.or.jp.*

Oriental porcelain from Japan, China, and Korea makes up this museum's collections. The pieces were brought together by its founder, the businessman Toguri Toru, to combat the cultural erosion threatening postwar Japan. The so-called Hizen porcelain (a former region of Japan covering what are now the prefectures of Saga and Nagasaki), is particularly well represented in this collection of 7,000 pieces, which also includes 4,000 calligraphy manuscripts and old pictorial works.

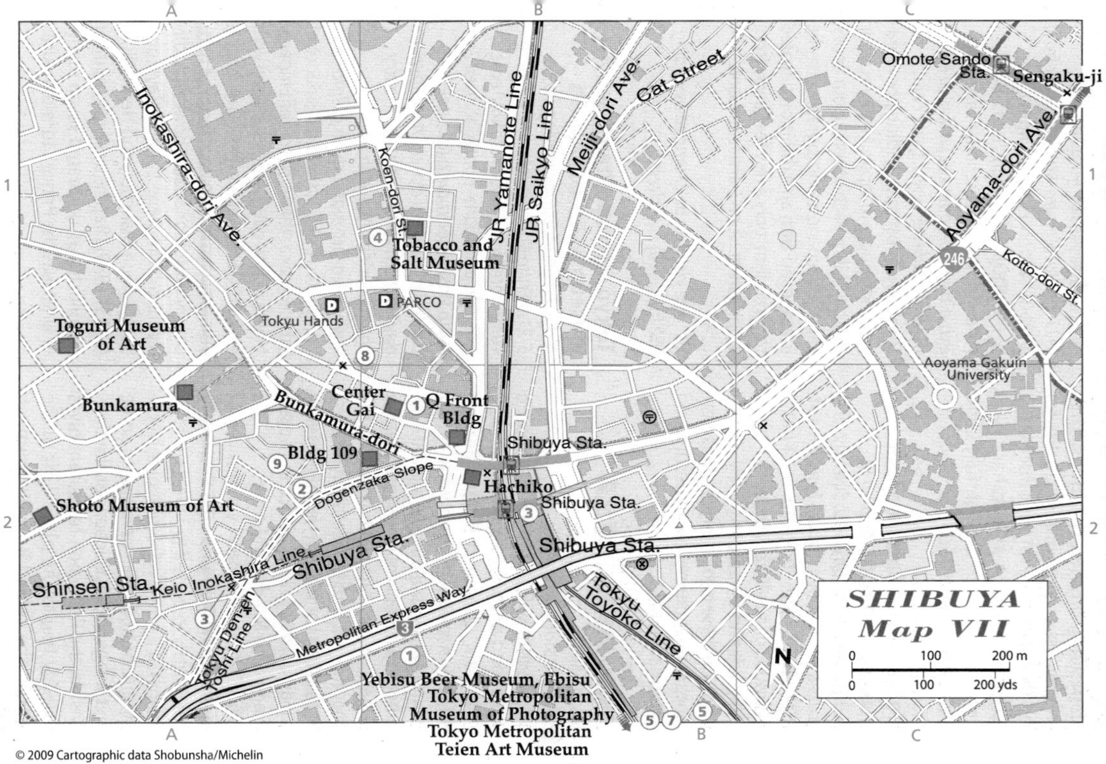




WHERE TO STAY

Cerulean Tower.................. 1
Shibuya Excel Hotel Tokyu. 3
Shibuya Tobu Hotel............ 4
Tokyu Stay Shibuya Shin-Minamiguchi........ 5

WHERE TO EAT

Coco ichibanya CurryHouse Coco........... 1
Hatago.............................. 2
Legato.............................. 3
Okina.............................. 5
Sugawara.......................... 7
Sweets Paradise................ 8
Watami.............................. 9

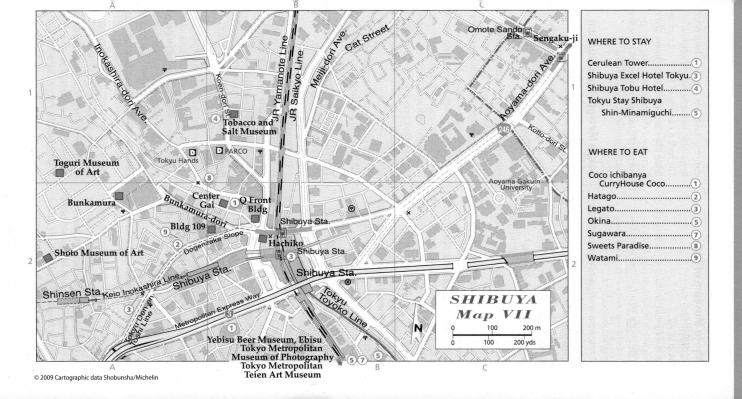

### Shoto Museum of Art
松濤美術館
*Map VII A2.*
*2-14-14 Shoto, Shibuya-ku. 5min walk from Keio Inokashira Line, Shinsen station. Open Tue–Sun 9am–5pm. ¥300. www.city.shibuya.tokyo.jp/eng/shotomoa.html.*
A museum with paintings, sculptures, etc., offering a very eclectic program, depending on the exhibitions. They are no less original or high quality for all that, and give an introduction to great artists such as Nakahara Nantenbo (1839–1925), a delightfully ironic Zen painter.

### Tobacco and Salt Museum
たばこと塩の博物館 *Map VII B1.*
*1-16-8 Jinnan, Shibuya-ku. Subway Z01, exits 6 & 7, Shibuya station, Hachiko exit. Open Tue–Sun 10am–6pm. ¥100. www.jti.co.jp/culture/museum.*
Why salt and tobacco?
Because these forbidden pleasures were once state monopolies. Interesting and informative.

## EBISU DISTRICT 恵比寿
*Map I A4.*
*JR Ebisu station, east exit.*
A moving walkway several hundred feet long with the expressive name "Skywalk" goes up to **Yebisu Garden Place**. A plaza fringed with rather uninteresting buildings is topped with a huge glass roof, looking somewhat like an enormous cartoon bubble, for the incongruous but familiar sight it covers is that of a Louis XIII-style château with an astonishing resemblance to Captain Haddock's Moulinsart Castle.
This "made in Japan" version is just a replica (although a French château was nearly exported to Japan, stone by stone). It's now a reflection of the economic bubble that gave rise to some extravagant constructions at the time. Inside, the Robuchon restaurant gives a lively feel to the place. Left of the castle, the **Yebisu Beer Museum**, *off map (4-20-1 Ebisu, Shibuya-ku; open Tue–Sun 10am–6pm; no charge)* has logically taken its place on land once belonging to the Sapporo brewery. The tour is not one of the most memorable *(the story of the development of the brand and the manufacturing process)*, but the photography museum alone *(see below)* justifies a visit to Ebisu.

### Tokyo Metropolitan Museum of Photography★★
東京都写真美術館 *Map I A4.*
*1-13-3 Mita, Meguro-ku. 7min walk from JR Ebisu station, east exit, right of the castle. Open Tue–Sun 10am–6pm (Thu–Fri 8pm). Entry charge varies with exhibition. Combined ticket for all exhibitions available. www.syabi.com.*
One of the most outstanding photographic exhibitions in Japan. Highly eclectic themes follow each other on four floors. Early 20C Japanese photography may be juxtaposed with an exhibition devoted to surrealism, only a few feet away from a portrait of Henri Cartier-Bresson.

*The visit can be extended by adding the following two sites:*

### Tokyo Metropolitan Teien Art Museum★ 東京都庭園美術館
*Map I A4 off map toward Meguro*
*5-21-9 Shiro Kanedai, Minato-ku. JR Yamanote Line, Meguro station, east exit. Open 10am–6pm. Closed 2nd & 4th Wed of the month (but open if public holiday and closed the following day). Garden ¥200, Museum: entry charge varies with exhibition. www.teien-art-museum.ne.jp/info.*
Completed in 1933, the old residence of Prince Asaka, the husband of Emperor Meiji's eighth daughter, is stamped with early-20C European artistic influences. This Art Deco mini-palace is now a temporary exhibition space showcasing different talents: René Lalique, Raymond Subes, Léon Blanchot, and Henri Rapin (1873–1939). Rapin, a French painter and illustrator, decorated seven rooms in what was the Prince's former house.

### Sengaku-ji 泉岳寺

*Map I B4 off map toward Shinagawa*
*2-11-1 Takanawa, Minato-ku. From Meguro station, take the JR Yamanote Line to Gotanda station, then the Toei Asakusa Line to Sengakuji subway station, exit A2, 218.7yd/200m W. Open Apr–Sept 7am–6pm; Oct–Mar 7am–5pm. Adjoining museum: open 9am–4.30pm (Oct–Mar: 4pm). ¥500.*

A visit to this temple, founded by Tokugawa Ieyasu in 1612, gives an introduction to one of the best-known historical events of 18C Japan, the suicide by *seppuku* of 47 *ronin*—samurai who had lost their leader. The *ronin* avenged the death of their overlord, the Lord of Ako, whom the shogun had condemned to death by *seppuku* for responding to an insult.

After they had executed their master's opponent they gave themselves up to the shogun authorities. The sentence was pronounced and all but one of the *ronin* were in turn condemned to death by *seppuku*, a sentence they carried out one after the other without blinking. They are now reunited in this temple with their lord Asano Naganori. The name and age of each *ronin* is written on each tomb; the youngest was 15 years old, the oldest 77. On December 14, the anniversary of the event, the Japanese flock here in large numbers to pay tribute.

## HARAJUKU★ 原宿

*Map VIII p158.*
*Allow a full day.*

A mix of all the quirkiest things in Tokyo, Harajuku has many attractions: wide and narrow streets dotted with unusual boutiques; social and cultural activities that draw tourists and sociologists from around the world to the area around Harajuku Bridge; and, since the sacred rarely exists far from the profane, adjoining the bridge is the Meji-jingu Imperial Shrine, one of the most venerated Shinto shrines in Tokyo. For those who prefer to be alone, there are two areas for retreat right next to each other: Yoyogi Park, one of the largest green spaces in Tokyo, and Aoyama Cemetery, amid the little edifices erected to its 100,000 residents.

### HARAJUKU★ 原宿 *Map VIII.*

*JR Yamanote Line, Harajuku station, Takeshita-dori or Harajuku Bridge exits.*

The bustling pedestrian street that drops down in front of the station is **Takeshi-dori**. This is to Tokyo what Carnaby Street was—and to some extent still is—to London. The outfits hanging on mannequins outside the shops are as welcoming as scarecrows, with zippers for smiles and punk Mohawks on shaved heads redder than a *torii*. Black leather with studs sticking out far enough to hang a pair of handcuffs on hangs above generously-cut white blouses with high

### On Harajuku Bridge

Every weekend young girls between the ages of 15 and 20—sometimes older—gather here, dressed up (or dressed down) according to whichever particular subculture they have espoused: *visual rock* (the rock group look), *cosplay* (*costume for playing*, manga or *anime* characters), *Gothic Lolita* ("lolitas" exhibiting a lust for life—or death), *Kogal* (California-style shiny blondes with miniskirts and fake lashes), etc. Their motivations vary—some do it for fun, others to be seen without being recognized (makeup and masks confer relative anonymity), some just to break social and dress codes obtained since the times of the Tokugawa.

Some do it to look like their avatars, the self-representations they have chosen to develop in the virtual world and the only identity in which they recognize themselves. They have also recently taken to strolling up and down the main street in Akihabara, another Tokyo district with the nickname "Electric Town" (*see p135*). Are Harajuku girls set to become avatars themselves, this time in the real world, a world that is no less real?

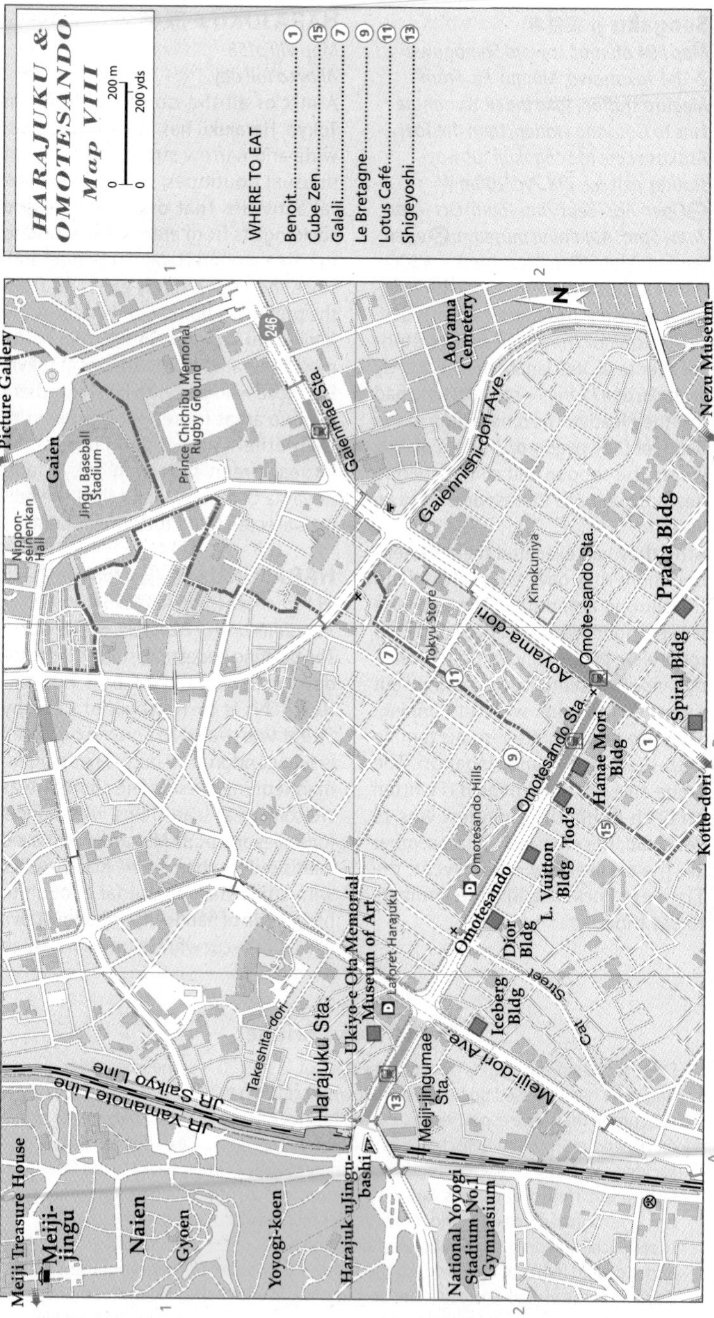




collars over tiny, checked skirts. This is a fashion world for adolescents, from out and out "gothic" to little pink boots and fluorescent bras intended for the helium-inflated chests sported by manga heroines. It's a tourist's dream.

Continuing beyond Meiji-dori, you will come across a maze of quieter alleyways, where a riot of explosive colors radiates across four walls (both inside and out): it's the Design Festa Gallery (*see Addresses p184*).

## Harajuku Bridge 原宿橋

*Map VIII A1/2.*
*Bear right on leaving the station 109yd/100m to Harajuku Bridge.*

Go at the weekend on a fine Saturday afternoon. You'll find a small, shady-looking group of people there. Girls with white faces, turquoise eyelids, and brows decorated with safety pins parade about on the bridge. Others, whose arms have a biscuity pallor, are dressed in underskirts, lace, and crinolines; with the starched movements of the Victorian era, they attach themselves to tourists for as long as it takes for a photograph.

The boldest, "lolitas," in bright-red shorts and with piercings from chin to eyebrow, flip you off provocatively, sometimes seeming to raise their fingers high enough to reach a passing cloud (*see box p157*).

*Bear right on the other side of the bridge to go to the shrine.*

## Meiji-jingu★★★ 明治神宮

*Map VIII A1.*

The Meiji emperor Mutsuhito and his wife, the empress Shoken, are honored at this Shinto shrine. Although recent, it's one of the holiest shrines and no stranger to politics (*see box below*).

The 173-acre/70ha park around the shrine is divided into two estates about 0.6mi/1km apart: the inner estate in the east (Naien), which is by far the more interesting, and the outer estate in the west (Gaien), which can also be accessed from the north side of Aoyama Cemetery at the end of the round trip.

**Naien★★★** 内苑 *Map VIII A1.*
*Subway C03, JR Harajuku station.*

At the end of a wide earth and gravel cutting through a dense forest, a huge portico carved out of a 1,500-year-old cypress tree 39.4ft/12m tall rises up. Before you enter the sacred area of the shrine, make your way along the narrow path on the left through a cluster of trees to the **Gyoen** garden (*open 9am–4.30pm; ¥500*), a beautiful side attraction filled with luxurious vegetation. There's an iris garden at one end of the pond designed by the Emperor for his wife.

The sanctuary was built with public funds in memory of the Emperor, and Japanese people from every province donated 130,000 trees to the enterprise. Destroyed in World War II, it was rebuilt in 1958 according to the original plans. Sparseness and simplicity turn this structure, with its copper-tiled roof, into a striking homage to the surround-

### Politics and religion

The founder of the shogunate, Tokugawa Ieyasu, is honored in a Shinto-Buddhist shrine, while Emperor Meiji has a purely Shinto shrine. Does this represent a difference of nature or just of extent? The man who led the modernization of Japan between 1868 and 1912 decreed Buddhism and Shintoism should be officially separated. His intention was that Shinto, the only indigenous religion, should once again be the only religion of the Japanese people. When this shrine was dedicated to the Emperor eight years after his death, Shintoism became the state religion. The Emperor was the sovereign leader of Japan and also the living representation of the descendants of the Shinto gods who created the country (*see box p62*). However, in 1945 the defeat of Japan sounded the death knell of Shintoism as the state religion. The Emperor, whom the Japanese still call *Tenno*, he "who comes from above," also lost his divine origins—but not his popularity. To get an idea of this, you only have to be at the shrine around New Year.

ing natural world, a world to which the Emperor was not insensitive, as is evident in the traditional short poems *(waka)* that he used to write: "Look and learn from the rocks, hollowed out by drops of water." *(They are recorded in the tiny scrolls that you can pick up for ¥100.)* Farther north, the Meiji Treasure House displays family objects in rotation.

**Gaien** 外苑 *Map VIII C1.*
*Subway G03, JR Line, Sendagaya station.* The avenue lined with gingko trees leads to the **Meiji Memorial Picture Gallery** *(open 9am–5pm; ¥500).* The different stages of the Emperor's life are displayed in 80 wall paintings (mainly of historical interest).

### Yoyogi Park
代々木公園 *Map VIII A1/2.*
One of the biggest parks in Tokyo is also one of the most original in terms of both the informal and formal activities that take place here: sports competitions, festivals, rock concerts—both improvised and planned—dance displays of all kinds, etc. They turn the area into a highly colorful space that is rendered deafening by police sirens, rockers, and *takenokozuku* (literally "young bamboo shoots," meaning street dancers), particularly on Sundays, and is considered much too noisy by the local people. The two **Olympic stadiums** of the Yoyogi National Stadium, designed in 1964 by Tange Kenzo, mark the edge of the park.

## OMOTESANDO★ 表参道
*Map VIII B2.*
Nicknamed the Champs-Élysées or Kings Road of Tokyo, Omotesando literally means "the main road leading to the shrine." Just before you get to the crossroad with the cylindrical tower of **La Foret** store on the corner with Meiji-dori, take a detour via the Ota Museum on the left, up by the Altera Plaza.

### Ukiyo-e Ota Memorial Museum of Art★ 太田記念美術館
*Map VIII A2.*
*1-10-10 Jingumae, Shibuya-ku.*
*Subway: C03, exit 3. Open Tue–Sun 10.30am–5.30pm. Closed from 27 to end of month for change of exhibitions and Dec 12–Jan 2. ¥700. www.ukiyoe-ota-muse.jp.*
More than 12,000 woodblock prints *(ukiyo-e)* spanning the Edo era form the basic collection of this small museum established by Ota Seizo (1893–1977), a former insurance company director. All the great masters are here: Utamaro, Hokusai, Hiroshige, Toyoyuni, Toyaharu, Monorobu, and Harunobu.

*Continue to walk down Omotesando-dori.*

Past the **La Foret** crossroad, the sidewalk to the right of this wide avenue shaded by zelkova trees is lined with big brand names (Dior, Chanel, Louis Vuitton, etc.). On the left, at the foot of the Omotesando Hills, is the property developer Mori's new complex, **Omotesando Hills**, designed by Ando Tadao. The complex—a shopping mall, some stylish apartments, and boutiques with clean lines—attracted a great deal of press coverage when it was built in 2006. It replaced a *Bauhaus* housing block—Dojunkai Aoyama—built to rehouse some of the people of Tokyo after the 1923 earthquake.
Although luxurious in scale, the complex is about as much use as a piece of fine machinery, oiled and all set for the art of living, when all it really has to do is satisfy marketing needs dictated by big international brands. This "packaging" architecture covers an overwhelming emptiness, and the area has lost all trace of the customs and lifestyle once typical of the Showa era. On the other side of the road are six floors of paradise for children, **Kiddyland** *(6-1-9 Jingumae; closed for works until summer 2012).* Soft toys and state-of-the-art technology have been neighbors here for 50 years.
Beyond the **Chanel** store, the **Oriental Bazaar** *(open 10am–7pm)* displays boxes overflowing with Japanese souvenirs and a small (rather disappointing) antiques section. Finally, sparkling in the light at the end of Omotesando-

Omotesando

© Photo Japan/age fotostock

dori, are the glass cubes of the **Hanae Mori Building**, named after the fashion designer Mori Hanae. These, too, were designed by Tange Kenzo (in 1978)—Omotesando's first piece of original architecture!

## AOYAMA 青山

*Map VIII B–C2.*

The Aoyama district is no exception to the rule: ready-to-wear and haute couture stores line the sidewalks with their amazing architecture.

Have a look at the **Spiral Building**★ by Maki Fumihiko *(Map VIII B2)* on Aoyama-dori. Inside are shops and exhibitions. The building is characterized by a somewhat asymmetrical façade with a huge spiral ramp inside. On Minami Aoyama-dori the stores of Issey Miyake, Comme des Garçons (Kawakubo Rei), Prada, **Tod's**★★ (Mitsui Jun), **Cartier** (Bruno Moinard), and fashion designer Yamamoto Yohji *(5-3-6 Minami Aoyama)* follow on from each other.

The most remarkable of these is the **Prada Building**★★★ *Map VIII C2*, designed by the Swiss architects Herzog & de Meuron (2001 Pritzker Architecture Prize winners), who also designed the famous Bird's Nest stadium for the Beijing Olympic Games.

The walls of its six floors are made up of lozenges of blue glass supported in a netting of steel, giving the appearance of quilted fabric. It's particularly worth seeing by night.

### Nezu Museum★ 根津美術館

*Map VIII C2 off map.*

*6-5-1 Minami-Aoyama. Subway: Omote-sando or Minami-Aoyama 6-Chome bus stop. www.nezu-muse.or.jp.*

It was established over 40 years ago by Nezu Kaichiro, who had spent a lifetime collecting calligraphy, sculptures, ceramics, textiles, and archeological materials from Asia.

The museum contains high-quality pieces, like the collection of Chinese bronzes dating from the Shang (1700 BC–1050/25 BC) and Zhou (1050/25 BC –256 BC) dynasties.

### Aoyama Cemetery★★ 青山霊園

*Map VIII C2.*

*Subway: G02, G03*

More than 100,000 tombs fill the Aoyama (Japanese for "blue mountain") Cemetery. Opened in 1872, it covers an area of some 279,861.7sq ft/26,000sq m. Its prestigious occupants include Inukai Tsuyoshi, a prime minister assassinated in 1932, and Shiga Naoya (1883–1971), a modern novelist known for writing stories in the first person, inserting material from his personal life into a fictional framework. The ashes of the famous dog **Hachiko** (see p154) are also buried here next to his master, Professor Ueno Eisaburo. It is worth noting that of all the *gaijin bochi* (cemeteries for foreigners), this is the biggest. In particular there are some tombs here belonging to French foreign office representatives.

Darren Anderson/MICHELIN

## Architecture in evolution

**Tange Kenzo** (1913–2005) graduated from Tokyo University with a degree in architecture and engineering. When he joined the practice of Maekawa Kunio, a pupil of the great master Le Corbusier, Tange was influenced by the use of reinforced concrete, a material, particularly appropriate in the reconstruction of postwar Japan, where the use of flammable wood was severely restricted. In 1949, he won a competition to design the Peace Memorial Park and Atomic Bomb Museum in Hiroshima, launching his career. He was one of several architects to join the Metabolist movement (*see p91*), which aimed to lay the foundations of an architecture that could adapt to a permanently growing urban organism, even if it meant creating sprawling structures that encroached on both sky and sea. His projects flourished in the "Tokyo 1960" development plan, and in 1987, his reputation was sealed when he won the Pritzker Architecture Prize.

## ODAIBA★ お台場

*Map IX p163.*

This **artificial island** in Tokyo Bay was reclaimed for development 20 years ago. Money was pouring in at the time and there was a building project on every acre in the capital. Its name comes from the "cannon batteries" *(odaiba)* that the shogun installed in the 19C as protection against foreign invasion. However, this defense didn't prevent the American Commodore Perry's "black ships" from mooring in the bay in 1853 to request and require that the country be opened up to them.

Since then, the wheels of change have turned ever faster. A metaphor perhaps for this garish modernity is the giant Ferris wheel, parading its technicolor attractions over the Odaiba complex of museums, shopping malls, gaming parlors, luxury hotels, etc. You can get to the bay by computer-controlled train, and waves of tourists spill out of the monorail into this world of leisure, which seems to have expanded to fill the dimensions of the outsize architecture specifically designed to tell us it can fulfill our expectations. For better or worse, you'll never be bored, and don't forget the kids!

From Shinbashi an automated train, the **Yurikamome monorail★★** *(every 5min)*, loops round the seafront buildings before disappearing over Rainbow Bridge. It then goes on to serve the sites described below. If you want to stop off in several places it's better to get a 1-day Open Pass for ¥800; you can also take the Rinkai Line.

### Rainbow Bridge★

レインボーブリッジ *Map IX A1.*

Walk across the bridge, almost 1,968.5ft/600m long and 416.6ft/127m at its highest point, to explore this futuristic district. From Tokyo, access to the bridge (*open Apr–Oct 9am–9pm, Nov–Mar 10am–*

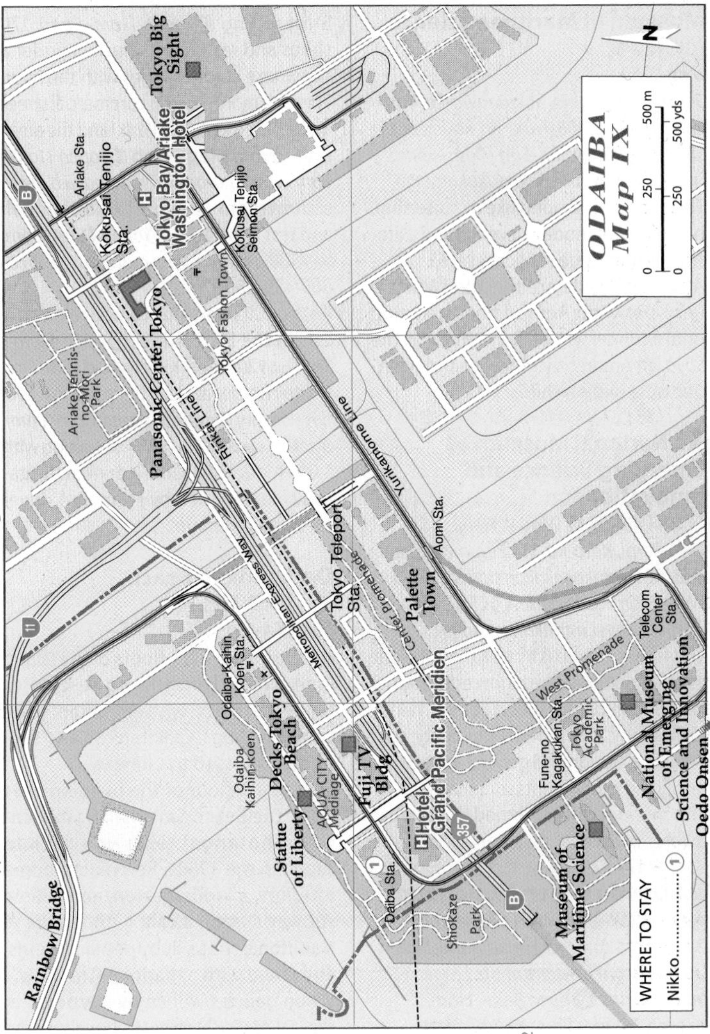




*6pm;* *closed 3rd Mon of the month; no charge)* is via an elevator near Shibaura-Futo monorail station.

## Fuji TV Building★★

フジテレビ本社ビル

*Map IX A1/2.*

*Subway U07, Daiba station.* *Open Tue–Sun 10am–6pm.* *¥500.*

This building, which looks as though it's made out of a giant construction set, was designed by Tange Kenzo (*see box p162*) in 1996, to be the Fuji TV headquarters. On the seventh floor is a hanging garden and on the 25th, a viewing platform (*open Tue–Sun 10am–6pm;* *¥500*).

A Statue of Liberty replica, borrowed from Paris, was set on the shore in 1998 for the Year of France; it was returned to Île des Cygnes in 2000, when the Japanese had their own made.

### Museum of Maritime Science
船の科学館

*Map IX A2.*
*3-1 Higashi-Yashio, Shinagawa-ku. Yurikamome Line U08, Fune-no-kagakukan station. Open Tue–Sun 10am–5pm. ¥700. www.funenokagakukan.or.jp.*
The museum, shaped like a cruise ship, has excellent models *(level 3F)* and a life-size ship's bridge replica*(level 6)*.
At the quayside are the *Yotei Maru*, a ferry between Aomori and Hokkaido until a tunnel was built in 1988, and the *Soya*, an Antarctic icebreaker and scientific observation ship.

### National Museum of Emerging Science and Innovation
日本科学未来館 *Map IX A–B2.*
*2-41 Aomi, Koto-ku. Yurikamome Line U08, Fune-no-kagakukan station. Open Wed–Mon 10am–5pm. Closed Jan 1. ¥500. www.miraikan.jst.go.jp.*
This fine structure is as well thought-out as its exhibitions. The highly educational level 3F exhibitions show robotics, nanotechnology, and superconductivity; particle acceleration and general science are on 5F, and experiments sometimes on 7F. The museum gives a broad, somewhat involved overview that is never dull.

### Ooedo Onsen Monogatari
大江戸温泉物語 *Map IX A2 off map.*
*2-57 Aomi, Koto-ku. Yurikamome Line U09, Telecom Center station. Large indoor baths: open 8am–11am. ¥2,900 (6pm–2am, ¥2,000; after 2am ¥1,700).www.ooedo.jp/english. No tattoos.*
The numerous baths *(indoor, outdoor, sand bath, etc.)* immerse you in the Edo era. Well-kept, pleasant, and unusual.

### Palette Town
パレットタウン *Map IX B2.*
*Yurikamome Line: U10, Aomi station.*
This multifaceted complex includes a **giant Ferris wheel** 328ft/100m in diameter *(open 10am–10pm; ¥900)*, the Zepp Tokyo concert hall *(capacity 2,700)*, and a shopping mall, **Venus Fort,** designed like an 18C Italian city. In this rather B-list setting *(open 11am–9pm)*, 170 shops and restaurants beckon under a sky whose color changes with the hour. There's a more modest commercial street in the basement *(Sun Walk)* and the amazing **Toyota Mega Web** *(open 11am–9pm; no charge; www.megaweb.gr.jp)*, a showroom with an exhibition hall and test drive area *(open 11am–8pm; ¥300; reservations required 0070-800-489-000)*.
Both adults and kids can drive electric cars in the E-com ride *(open 11am–8pm; ¥200)* and Kids Hybrid Ride One *(no charge)* areas. The historical section, History Garage *(open 11am–9pm)*, displays classic cars (1950–70), along with 3,000 model cars. Grab a drink at the Italian cafe designed by Formula 1 driver Alessandro Nannini.

### Decks Tokyo Beach
デックス東京ビーチ

*Map IX A-B.*
On the 6th and 7th floors of the Island Mall, **Little Hong Kong** re-creates Chinese streets, with restaurants and souvenir shops. Children can also take photos, dressed as Chinese.
On the 4th floor of the building next door, the Beach Side Mal, **Daiba Ichome Shotengai** takes you back to Japan in the 1950s. Re-created home interiors, a kindergarten, and even a subway station await, with streets of traditional shops lit by paper lanterns, enlivened with a marionnette show.
Video gamers will enjoy **Joypolis**, in the last of the three decks buildings; the Sega amusement park is on three levels *(unlimited pass: ¥3500 for adults, ¥3500 for under age 14)*.

### Tokyo Big Sight 東京ビックサイト
(東京国際展示場) *Map IX C1.*
*Yurikamome Line U11, Kokusai-Tenjijo-Seimon station.*
Japan's largest exhibition center *(861,112.8sq ft/80,000sq m)* rests on four enormous feet shaped like inverted pyramids. At the entrance is a giant steel-and-plastic sculpture of a saw, buried in the ground, as if cutting through it.

### Panasonic Center Tokyo

パナソニックセンター東京 *Map IX C1. 2-5-18 Ariake, Koto-ku. Yurikamome Line U12, Ariake station. Open Tue–Sun 10am–6pm. No charge. www.panasonic.co.jp/center/tokyo/en.* Four-story technological showcase for the company.

## EXCURSIONS

### MITAKA

### Ghibli Museum★★

三鷹の森ジブリ美術館
*Map I A2 off map.*
*Allow 1hr30min, including the journey.*
*1-1-83 Shimorenjaku, Mitaka-shi.*
*JR Chuo Line, Mitaka station, south exit (20min from Shinjuku station), then loop bus, stop 9 (5min, ¥300 round trip).*
*Open Wed–Mon 10am–6pm.*
*Entry every 2hr by reservation only. www.ghibli-museum.jp. In Japan reserve tickets in advance at Lawson stores (0570-084-633) and then collect ticket within 3 days (¥1,000). As the museum is small, a maximum of 2,400 tickets is allocated daily.*
Delightful tour of Hayao Miyazaki's former studio. The highly talented cartoonist founded the Ghibli studio after the successful film adaptation of his manga *Nausicaa of the Valley of the Wind* (1984); *Porco Rosso* (1992), *Princess Mononoke* (1997), *Spirited Away* (2001), *Howl's Moving Castle* (2004), etc. followed.

### KICHIJOJI★

### Inokashira-koen★

井の頭公園
*5min by foot from Kichijouji station on the JR Chuo line or Tozai subway line, south exit; or 5min by foot to right on leaving Ghibi Museum, at far SE of the park.*
Around a lake crisscrossed by swan-shaped pedalcraft and small boats, walks are pleasant here with spring's cherry blossoms or Fall's scarlet foliage. A small temple in the park is home to Benzaiken, the vengeful goddess of love, said to have enchanted the lake so that lovers crossing it will separate.
Peddlars sell crafts on the shores at weekends. Take the children to the park's zoo and aquarium, before buying them a *kakigori* (shaved ice with syrup) at the entrance in summer.

### Mount Takao★★★ 高尾山

*Map I A3 off map.*
*Allow half a day, including the journey. 31mi/50km W from Tokyo in Hachioji city. Depart platform 3, Keio Line, Shinjuku station to Takaosanguchi station. (50min, ¥370). www.keio.co.jp/english/local/takao.html.*
Mount Takao, 1,968.5ft/600m high, is in Hachioji city *(Tokyo urban area)*, southeast of the Kanto foothills. There are seven different hiking trails. No.1, the Pilgrim Trail, takes you to the summit *(allow 1hr40min for 2.4mi/3.8km)* past Yakuo-in temple *(to pray for good fortune)*. The chairlift *(Sanroku station)* or cable car *(Kiyotaki station)* shortens the distance by a third *(¥900 round trip)*. Forests of 100-year-old cedars, beech trees, and wild flowers on the ascent in different seasons. Fine **view** of Tokyo, and of Mt. Fuji in good weather.
A firewalking festival takes place annually on the second Sunday in March in which hermit monks and others of the Shugendo faith walk barefoot over burning sticks as a purification rite.

### Tsukuba Research Center

産業技術総合研究所つくばセンター
*55min by train north of Tokyo.*
*Take JR Joban line and get off at Arakawaoki-Namiki-2-chome and change for the Kanto bus.*
*5min by foot.*
The Japanese government research organization is in a pleasant, campus-like setting; interesting for technology and natural sciences lovers alike.
**Geology Museum** 地質標本館
This museum in the center *((029) 861 3750; 9.30am–4.30pm, closed Mon and 28 Dec–4 Jan; free)* has many models, terrain cross-sections, stones, fossils, and a fascinating panorama of the Earth's history focusing on Japan and its volcanoes. Nearby a science exhibition (**Science Square Tsukuba**) presents numerous technological innovations and robots, including a realistic T.Rex.

## Theme Parks in Japan

Japan has a strong cultural identity, yet has so enthusiastically embraced foreign-inspired *tema paku* (theme parks) that it is now boasts dozens of superb attractions. An established and growing form of entertainment in Japan today, they can make for a fantastic family day out, with four of the best-known being:

**Tokyo Disneyland Resort**, comprised of Tokyo Disneyland and DisneySea Park *(Urayasu City, Chiba, just outside Tokyo; www.tokyodisneyresort.co.jp/en/)*. **Tokyo Disneyland** is huge (115 acres/46ha) and easy to explore with its circular plan, internal train, and Fastpass to avoid lines. Main Street is roofed for year-round temperature control. Dining establishments tend to favor classic American fast-food, while souvenir shops focus on Mickey. **DisneySeaPark** is next door, its seven themed "ports of call" presenting tales of the sea around the central Mount Prometheus landmark. There are rides, shops, restaurants, live shows and the Fastpass, but since the target audience includes adults as well as children, alcohol is available; illuminations make it romantic by night.

**Sanrio Puroland** *(Tama New Town, west of Tokyo; www.puroland.co.jp/english)* is a fairly small indoor theme park with Hello Kitty and friends in performance around the central "Friendship Tree"; seven main attractions, five themed eateries and Japan's largest Sanrio store guarantee total immersion in Nippon *kawaii*! As the site is accustomed to foreign visitors, there is plenty of information in English. A good choice for small children (those who certify birthdays are fêted on-stage). A full-scale outdoor version of Sario Puroland has been opened near Beppu in Oita City on the southern island of Kyushu *(www.sanrio.co.jp/english/harmony)*. **Harmonyland** has twelve main attractions, and four eateries ranging from fast food to a more formal restaurant.

**Universal Studios Japan** *(Osaka; www.usj.co.jp/e)*. This park brings movie magic to life. Resembling the Orlando version, nine areas contain nineteen attractions, 45 themed restaurants and shops, featuring characters like Snoopy, Shrek and the Sesame Street cast. Many attractions indoors and an Express Pass system to avoid lines. Particularly popular with Asian visitors.

Opening hours and entrance fees vary, so plan your visit in advance by checking the theme parks' websites before you set off. Full travel details are also available here.

*Sanrio Puroland*

# PRACTICAL INFORMATION

## USEFUL INFORMATION

**Tourist Offices** – Tokyo Tourist Information Center, *1 F Metropolitan Government Bldg no. 1. Subway E28, JR Shinjuku station, west exit. Open 9.30am–6.30pm. ℘03-5321-3077. www.tourism.metro.tokyo.jp.*

**Foreign Tourist General Information Center** (TIC JNTO), *10 F Tokyo Kotsu Kaikan Bldg, 2-10-1 Yuraku-cho, Chiyoda-ku. Subway Y18, exit A8 (Map III B1). Open 9am–5pm. Closed Jan 1 (tel. only). ℘03-3201-3331. www.jnto.go.jp.* The TIC JNTO has a **Welcome Inn Reservation desk**, which will find you reasonably priced accommodation in Tokyo and throughout Japan. Members of the hotel network undertake not to exceed the following rates: *¥8,000/Single and ¥13,000/Double for at least two-thirds of the year. Reservations to be made in person or at www.itcj.jp/en.*

If you're planning to visit the museums, save money by purchasing a **Grutt Pass** *(¥2,000)*, which gives free or discounted entry to 66 museums and art galleries in Tokyo. Inquire at the ticket office of one of the participating museums, which includes all the largest ones.

**Bank/Foreign Exchange** – Citibank, *1 F Ote Center Bldg, 1-1-3 Otemachi, Chiyoda-ku. Subway M18, exit C9. Open Mon–Fri 9am–3pm. ATM 24hr. ℘03-3215-0051.* Citibank ATMs accept Western cards. There are branches in Ginza, Shibuya, Aoyama, Shinjuku, etc.

**Post Office** – Tokyo Central Post Office, *Otemachi branch office, Otemachi Bldg, 1F, 1-6-1 Otemachi, Chiyoda-ku, Subay T09, M09 (Map II, B3) ℘03-3284-9650, Mon–Fri, 9am–9pm.*

**Emergency Services/Health** – Fire Service *(24hr; ℘119 or 03-3212-211)* gives information in English. The Tokyo government's Himawari hospitals information service offers a foreign language information service for the capital's medical services *(open 9am–8pm; ℘03-5285-8181; www.himawari.metro.tokyo.jp/qq/qq13enmnlt.asp)* and also an emergency translation service for difficulties in comprehension on admission to hospital *(open 5pm–8pm; ℘03-5285-8185).* The Amda Service International Medical Information Center provides the addresses of multilingual doctors throughout the whole of Japan. *Open Mon–Fri 9am–5pm. ℘03-5285-8088. http://amda-imic.com.*

**Pharmacy** – American Pharmacy, *Marunouchi Bldg, B1F, 2-4-1 Marunouchi, Chiyoda-ku – Subway M17, C10 (Map II, B2). ℘03-5220-7716.*

## TRANSPORTATION

**BY PLANE** – **Narita International Airport** – *℘0476-34-8000 (flight information). www.narita-airport.jp.* Located almost 43.5mi/70km E of Tokyo, it has two terminals with a free transfer shuttle between them. Terminal 1 Tourist Information Center *(open 9am–8pm; ℘0476-30-3383).* Terminal 2 Tourist Information Center *(open 8am–8pm; ℘0476-34-5877).*

**Haneda Airport** – *℘03-5757-8111 (domestic flight information), www.tokyo-airport-bldg.co.jp.* The airport is located 12.4mi/20km S of Tokyo on an island facing the bay at the mouth of the Tama River *(Map I B4 off map).* Most domestic flights arrive at Terminals 1 and 2. Flights from Paris, Seoul, Hong Kong, Beijing, and Shanghai arrive at the International Terminal. Terminal 1, Tokyo Tourist Information Center *(open 9am–10pm; ℘03-5757-9345).*

Trains run between Narita and Haneda *(1hr 45min, ¥1,560).* The same journey costs ¥3,000 by Limousine Bus and takes about 1hr15min.

**From Airport to Central Tokyo** – Each terminal has a station in the basement, Airport Terminal 2 station, and Narita Airport station. From Narita, the Narita Express (N'EX) run by JR East *(www.jreast.co.jp)* leaves almost every 30min *(8am–7pm)* or every hour throughout the rest of the day. It connects to Tokyo station *(53min, ¥2,940)*, Shibuya *(1hr14min, ¥3,110)*, Shinjuku *(1hr20min, ¥3,110)*, and Ikebukuro *(1hr21min, ¥3,110).* Note, only the first three cars go to Shibuya and Shinjuku. If you have time and want to save money, choose the **rapid train** that goes to Tokyo station *(1hr30min, ¥1,280).* The **Skyliner Airport Express** run by Keisei *(www.keisei.co.jp)* stops at Nippori station *(36min, ¥2,400)* and Keisei-Ueno station *(41min, ¥2,400; departure about every 40min).* This is the fastest and most practical way to travel if staying in the Ueno Park area. Both stations are connected to the Yamanote Line, which serves the main stations. Slower but also cheaper *(¥1,000)*, the **Limited Express**, also run by Keisei, takes 1hr7min to Nippori and 1hr11min to Ueno; departure every 20min. Remember, if you take the train, you will need to add the price of a taxi fare, or at least a subway ticket, to get to your exact destination.

**The Limousine Bus Company** (*www.limousinebus.co.jp*) takes passengers from the arrivals hall (Terminals 1 and 2) to a number of hotels in central Tokyo. This door-to-door service is reserved for the best hotels only. Tickets (about ¥3,000) can be purchased from desks at the passport control exit. Bags are labeled and stowed by an efficient member of staff. The Limousine Bus is good for travelers with heavy suitcases who are staying in a hotel on the bus route, or one situated within a short walking distance. (Departure every 5–30min). The Limousine Bus also goes to Shinjuku station *(min. 1hr30min)* and Tokyo City Air Terminal (T-CAT) *(www.tcat-hakozaki.co.jp)* NE of downtown Tokyo *(55min, ¥2,900)*, which connects to Suitengumae station on the Hanzomon Line *(SubwayZ10)*. The steady traffic between the airport and the T-CAT ensures that timetables can generally be met *(it can get more difficult after the T-CAT)*. Departure every 10min.

**BY TAXI** – *℘04-7634-8755.* A journey from the airport to the wards of Bunkyo, Chiyoda, and Chuo costs around ¥19,000, and ¥21,000 to Shinjuku, Shibuya, or Minatosix times as much as a Limousine Busand no faster!

**From Haneda** – departure of the **Tokyo Monorail** every 5–10min *(www.tokyo-monorail.co.jp)* to Hamamatsucho station on the Yamanote Line *(20min, ¥470)*.

A Limousine Bus to downtown Tokyo costs between ¥900 and ¥1,200, and a taxi about ¥8,000.

**BY TRAIN** – Tokyo has four main stations connected to the JR Yamanote Line. The Shinkansen from the west *(Osaka, Kyoto)* arrives at Tokyo station *(Map I C3)* in the central downtown area or at Shinagawa, 3.7mi/6km SW *(Map I B4 off map)*. From the north *(Nagano, Akita etc.)*, the train usually terminates at Tokyo station. Some trains go on as far as Ueno, 2.5mi/4km NE *(Map I C1)*.

*For more information, visit the website www.hyperdia.com.*

**BY BUS** – Long-distance buses (Highway Bus, in Japanese ***Kosoku Bus***) arrive at the major stations on the Yamanote Line *(Tokyo station, Shinagawa, Shibuya, Shinjuku, and Ikebukuro)*. They are 20–50 percent cheaper than the train. Prices can vary significantly between companies. For Nagoya, several buses a day with the **Keio**, **Meitetsu**, and **JR Tour** and **Orion Tour** companies *(6hr30min/7hr, ¥3,500–¥6,400)*.

For Kyoto, departure of **JR Kanto Bus** and **JR Nishinihon Bus** several times a day *(day and night) (8hr, ¥6,000–¥8,000)*. For Osaka, departure with several companies such as **JR Bus Kanto**, **Nishinihon JR Bus**, **Kiokyu**, **Hankyu**, **Seibu** or **Kintetsu** several times a day) *(about 8hr, ¥5,000–8,600)*. For Hiroshima, departure of **Odakyu**, **Hiroden**, and **JR Kanto Bus**, **Chugoku JR Bus**, **Chugoku Bus** *(12hr, ¥11,600 –12,000)*.

*For more information, visit the website* ***www.bus.or.jp***.

**BY BOAT** – Setting off from Tokushima *(Shikoku)* with the **Ocean Tokyu Ferry** company *(1 boat per day, 18hr, ¥9,750 without couchette, ¥19,140 first class)* or at Kitakyushu *(same company, 1 boat per day, 34hr, ¥14,470 without couchette, ¥28,210 first class)* boats land at the port of Ariake in Odaiba *(Map IX C1)*. From there, buses run to the Shin-Kiba subway station *(Subway Y24)*. Alternatively, the Yurikamome Line *(nearest station Kokusai-Tenjijo-Seimon)* runs over the Rainbow Bridge and stops at Shimbashi *(Subway A10, G08)*. Another alternative is the Rinkai Line, which runs to Shinjuku.

## GETTING AROUND TOKYO

Tokyo has no street names. Unlike the Western system used the world over, where a street has either a name or a number, the streets here, with the exception of a few large avenues *(dori)* remain nameless. So, how do the people of Tokyo get about and orient themselves in such a huge, densely populated, and complicated city? It would appear to be impossible and yet it works quite well, thanks to a naming system based on the land registry.

In addition to the name of the ward, to which the suffix *ku* and the district are added, **the address is usually made up of a string of three numbers** (2-11-3 Ginza, Chuo-ku): the first number corresponds to that of a chome, the subdivision of a district with several blocks; the second refers to the block; the third relates to the construction date of the building, not its position in relation to the buildings in front of, or behind it on the site. Therefore no. 3, for example, can be next to no. 17 or no. 8. So, the same address can also be written 11-3 Ginza, 2-chome, Chuo-ku. On most buildings a metal plate inscribed with the numbers *(all three or just the last two)*, is fixed to the telegraph posts or the street light.

Although postal workers and the police are able to find their way around easily, when Tokyo residents venture into unknown territory they can find orienting themselves almost as difficult as foreigners. And although armed with street plans and GPS navigation devices, taxi drivers don't always arrive at their destinations. Visitors may therefore find themselves hopelessly lost, in which case the best advice is to approach a friendly policeman installed in one of the many police substations *(koban)* often found in strategic positions.

## HOW TO GET AROUND

**BY SUBWAY** – Although it's easy to get lost in the streets of Tokyo, everything is simpler below ground, thanks to the impeccable alpha-numeric signs that combine color coding with letters and numbers. These coordinates make it easy to work out how much of your journey remains, depending on whether the numbers are in ascending or descending order. A voice also announces the next station and all connections in English. Admiration for the subway system only increases upon the discovery that almost all stations are equipped with immaculately clean, free toilets and storage lockers. **The network** has 13 lines, nine run by **Tokyo Metro** *(www.tokyometro.jp)* and four by **Toei Subway** *(www.kotsu.metro.tokyo.jp) (see map inside back cover)*. The entrance to the first nine is indicated by a circular panel with a white "M" against a blue background; the other four can be recognized by a rectangular panel with a stylized gingko leaf in the center. For a station served by both lines, a rectangular panel shows the front view of a train. A **subway map** is available at all stations.

*To work out an itinerary and calculate the price and journey time visit the website www.tokyo-subway.net.*

**A day ticket** on the nine Tokyo Metro lines costs ¥710, ¥1,000 to include the four Toei lines, and ¥1,580 with the Toei buses and the Japan Railways Company (JR) network in addition. If you plan to use the subway often over a period of several days, it's better to buy an **IC Card (PASMO, Suica)**, which are rechargeable and valid only for the Tokyo Metro and the Toei lines. There's no prospect of savings here, as the card is debited by at least ¥160 per journey; however, it does save the need to buy tickets until the credit runs out. *Half fare for children 6–12yrs on any ticket.*

To buy a ticket for each journey there are ticket machines that accept coins or notes. The minimum ticket price is ¥160, but it goes up to ¥300 in proportion to the distance traveled. Summary tables show the prices for each station. When these are only written in Japanese, as is quite often the case, pay the minimum *(¥160)* and then pay an additional amount if the ticket is refused at the exit. Fare adjustment machines are provided for this purpose. Insert the ticket and the machine will calculate the amount owing and print a new ticket once the additional

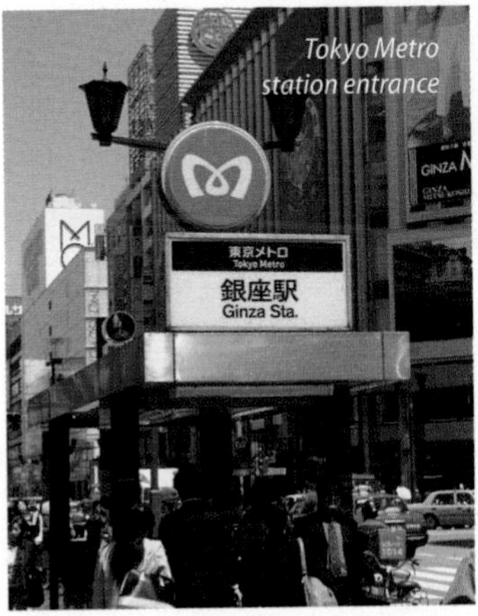

Tokyo Metro station entrance

©JNTO

amount has been paid. Attendants on duty can also provide assistance.

*Strangely for such a large, bustling city, the subway closes at around 12.30am.*

**BY JR** – The **Yamanote Line**, which makes a loop around the center of Tokyo *(about 1hr)*, is a good method of transport and its elevated track also provides an opportunity to see the city. *(The minimum price for a ticket is ¥130)*. At the exit the same price adjustment system is applied as in the subway. A JR ticket is not valid for the subway, so watch out for journeys that combine both. The JR also uses the Chuo Line that runs from Tokyo station to Shinjuku and then out to the suburbs as far as Mount Takao in the west. The Sobu Line *(from Chiba in the east to Mitaka in the west)* serves the same stations as the Chuo Line, crossing the downtown area.

**The Tokyo Free Kippu** *(¥1,580)* is valid for 1 day in the subway, on the buses, and the JR inside Tokyo.

**BY BUS** – Unlike the subway, buses, with few exceptions, display their destination in kanji. Polyglots and the adventurous pay ¥200 per ticket for any distance.

**BY TAXI** – *The first 1.2mi/2km costs ¥710 and each additional 0.6mi/1km around ¥310. Fares increase by 20 percent between 11pm and 5am*. Taxis can prove practical for short distances and are essential after 12.30am, when the subway closes. Tokyo has a taxi fleet of 50,000 cars. Don't be surprised when the rear doors open automatically to let you in and close automatically, too.

In view of the difficulties that some taxi drivers have in finding the correct destination, it's better to be able to point it out on a map. Without a map, it's a good idea to ask for an easily identifiable place (subway, department store etc.) near your final destination and finish the journey on foot, to save you time.

**BY BICYCLE** – The citizens of Tokyo are keen cyclists. They prefer to ride on the pavement, weaving in and out of pedestrians, umbrella held aloft when it rains. A ring of the bell indicates to other cyclists that they are about to overtake. Some districts such as Ueno, Yanaka, and Asakusa are particularly suitable for cycling, while many hotels rent bikes out by the day for a modest sum *(¥200 per day, depending on hotel)*.

**Cycle Rental** – *Sumida Park, near the Sumida Park water bus kiosk, Asakusa. Subway G19. Open 6am–8pm. ¥200 per day.*

**BY BOAT** – The boats of the **Tokyo Cruise Ship Company** *(www.suijobus.co.jp)* sail between Asakusa *(Azuma Bridge)* and Odaiba along the Sumida River. There are different trips to choose from. One departs from Asakusa and stops at Hamarikyu-teien *(35min, ¥720)*. In spite of the sprawling concrete buildings that frequently line the banks, boat trips have the advantage of providing another vantage point from which to see the city. From Hinode Pier, 5min walk from Hamarikyu, boats go on as far as Odaiba *(4 stops)*.

# ADDRESSES

## FOOD & DRINK

In a city with every culinary temptation imaginable, some of which come at a very high price, it is possible to eat for very little outlay in the cheap restaurant chains *(Yoshinoya, Sukiya, Tenya)*. These offer a bowl of rice with meat and a choice of miso soup, fish, salad, etc. *(¥400–600)*. *Conbini*—Japanese convenience stores *(open daily 24hr)*, such as 7-Eleven, Lawson, and AM/PM—have sandwiches *(about ¥120)*, ***onigiri*** (rice balls wrapped in a dried seaweed leaf, with a variety of fillings; *¥90 and ¥130)*, soups, and precooked dishes. Every ***conbini*** has a microwave oven and hot water for soups. Department stores (Mitsukoshi, Matsuya) usually have basement food departments and sell *bento* at a reasonable price.

## NIGHTLIFE

**Metropolis** *(www.metropolis.co.jp)*, a weekly English language publication, is useful for finding out what's on. Free copies are distributed in cafes, restaurants, and hotels. Another useful source of information is the website ***www.realtokyo.co.jp*** for cultural events in the capital. For clubbers, visit ***www.clubbers-house.net***, which lists around 100 clubs.

**Cinemas** – There are numerous movie theaters. For programs and times, look in Metropolis *(see earlier)*, which has a handy map that locates the different cinemas. *Average price per seat: ¥1,800.*

**National Theatre of Japan** – *See Imperial Palace Addresses p175.*

**Tokyo Takarazuka Theater** – *1-1-3 Yuraku-cho, Chiyoda-ku. Subway C09, H07. ¥3,500–10,000. 03-5251-2001. http://kageki.hankyu.co.jp.* Highly colorful revue that was started in 1914 in Takarazuka *(near Osaka)*, mixing musical comedy, opera, and dance. The actresses—and there are only actresses—are very popular. *¥3,500-11,000.*

## SPORT AND LEISURE

**Helicopter Flight** – **Helicopter Cruising**, *14 Chidori, Urayasu, Chiba City. Subway T18, then taxi (15min), JR Keiyo Line, Maihama station, then taxi (5min). Off map. 01-2088-8910 (reservations). www.excel-air.com.* Two round trips at 9pm *(15min, ¥10,500 or 20min, ¥14,800)*, 1 round trip at sunset *(15min, ¥9,500)*, 2 round trips 2hr before sunset *(5min, ¥3,900 or 15min, ¥8,500)*. Children half price, discounts for over-60s.

**Origami** – **International Origami Center**, *1-7-14 Yushima, Bunkyo-ku. Subway C12. Open Mon–Sat 9.30am–6pm. www.origamikaikan.co.jp.* Open since 1859. The center offers free lessons; beginners welcome.

**Tea Ceremony** – **Imperial Hotel** *(see Where to Stay p 176). Open Mon–Sat 10am–4pm. Closed first 2 weeks of Aug. Lesson lasts 20min (¥1,500). Reservations: 03-3504-1111.*

**Sado Kaikan**, *3-39-17 Takadanobaba, Shinjuku-ku. Subway T03, JR Takadanobaba station (Map 1, A1). Mon–Thu 10am–3pm and 6pm–9pm. Lesson lasts 1hr (¥2,000). Reservations 03-3361-2446.*

**Ikebana** – **Ohara School**, *5-7-17 Minami-Aoyama, Minato-ku. Subway G02, C04, exit B1, or B3. 03-5774-5097. www.ohararyu.or.jp/english/lesson.html.* English classes: Wed 10am–12pm, Thu 10am–12pm, 1.30–3.30pm. ¥2,500, with flowers ¥1,500–2,500. Just observing – ¥800. *Reserve a day in advance.*

# ASAKUSA AND UENO

## USEFUL INFORMATION

### ASAKUSA

**Asakusa Tourist Information Center** – *2-18-9 Kaminarimon, Taito-ku. Subway A18, G19. Open 9.30am–8pm. 03-3842-5566.*

### UENO

**Tokyo Tourist Information Center** – *Keisei Line, Ueno station, opposite ticket office in station (Map IV A2). Open 9.30am–6.30pm. 03-3836-3471.*

## TRANSPORTATION

### ASAKUSA

**BY BOAT** – **Tokyo Cruise Ship Company**, *by Azuma Bridge. Subway A18, exit 4. Open 10am–5pm. Departs every 30–40 min. www.suijobus.co.jp.*

## STAY

### ASAKUSA

**Khaosan Tokyo**
**カオサン東京ゲストハウス** *2-1-15 Kaminarimon, Taito-ku. Subway G19 (Map IV C2). 03-3842-8286. www.khaosan-tokyo.com. 8 rooms, 2 dormitories.* Giving the legendary name of the globetrotters' Khaosan Road in Bangkok to this street in Tokyo says a lot for the ambitions of the place: to give a warm welcome to world travelers at a modest price and in modest comfort. Roof terrace overlooking the Sumida River. Supplement for sheets *(¥200)* on the first night. *Free Internet access.*

**Khaosan Tokyo Annex**
**カオサン東京ゲストハウス・アネックス** *2-2-5 Higashi-Komagata, Sumida-ku. Subway G19, exit 4, A18, exit A2b (Map IV C2, off map). 03-5856-6560. www.khaosan-tokyo.com. 70 beds in rooms and dormitories.* On the opposite bank of the Sumida River, the annex has more rooms than its parent hotel. It's also closer to Bar 23 *(open 7pm–2am)*, where Khaosan clients can find drinks at prices designed to encourage consumption *(¥333)*, and plenty of opportunities for meeting people and enjoying discussions into the small hours.

**Taito Ryokan 台東旅館** *2-1-4 Nishi-Asakusa, Taito-ku. Subway G18, exit 3 (Map IV B2). 03-3843-2822. www.libertyhouse.gr.jp. 9 rooms.* A small, dilapidated hotel with internal wood fittings worn shiny and ravaged by time, plus tired furniture. This *ryokan* is low-budget and unpretentious. The young manager, a well-informed English-speaker, has a relaxed, even casual approach. *Shared showers*.

**Hotel Sunroute Asakusa** ホテルサンルート浅草 *1-8-5 Kaminarimon, Taito-ku. Subway G18 (Map IV C2). ℘(03) 3847 1511. www.sunroute.jp.* This business hotel with no special charmis still well-placed to explore Asakusa. Small, well-equipped, soundproof rooms. No breakfast, but available in the restaurant in the same building.

**Ryokan Asakusa Shigetsu** 旅館浅草指月*1-31-11 Asakusa, Taito-ku (Map IV C2). ℘03-3843-2345. www.shigetsu.com. 33 rooms.* Hidden away in a narrow street near the temple of Senso-ji and the busy Nakamise-dori, this ryokan *(with both Japanese and Western-style rooms)* is a peaceful haven. The hearty and varied breakfast is a real treat *(not included)*. Two *o-furo* upstairs with **views** over the Senso-ji temple pagoda. Free Internet access.

**Asakusa View Hotel** 浅草ビューホテル*3-17-1 Nishi-Asakusa, Taito-ku. Subway G19 (Map IV C2). ℘03-3847-1111. www.viewhotels.co.jp/asakusa. 337 rooms.*High above the Asakusa district, yet itself not very tall, the Asakusa View Hotel is like the man—who, by the way, is charming—who ruins the elegance of his smart black suit by wearing white socks. A few errors in taste, which take nothing away from its charm. The sixth floor, built around a garden, has Japanese-style rooms.

**UENO**

**Capsule Inn Akihabara** カプセルイン秋葉原 *6-9 Akihabara, Taito-ku. Subway G14, H15, JR Akihabara station (Map IV A2, off map). ℘03-3251-0841. www.capsuleinn.com. 224 capsules.* A mixed-sex capsule hotel with five floors reserved for men and three for women. The capsules, 28 per floor, are in double layers. Women are prohibited from the upper layer as, according to the proprietor, they may fall when climbing the ladder, being unable to withstand a night of drinking as well as the men. On arrival, leave your shoes at reception and you will be given a pair of skyblue pajamas. Panties, shorts, socks, shirts, and vests can also be provided.

**Sawanoya Ryokan** 澤の屋旅館 *2-3-11 Yanaka, Taito-ku. Subway C14, exit 1 (Map IV A1, off map). ℘03-3822-2251. www.sawanoya.com. 12 rooms.* An entire family greets you when you arrive: the grandmother looking after her two grandchildren, the grandfather, the mother and father running back and forth between kitchen and bedrooms. The clientele is mainly international. Ninety nationalities have passed through in the last 25 years, 30 percent of whom have returned—the sign of a good place. Ask for the key if you plan to come back after 11pm. 2 rooms with private bathroom. Free Internet access, bicycle rental *(¥200 per day)*, coin laundry.

The **Homeikan Ryokan** has three buildings on Hongo hill: Daimachi, Honkan, and Morikawa.

**Daimachi Bekkan** 鳳明館台町別館 *5-10-9 Hongo, Bunkyo-ku. Subway M21, E08 (Map IV A2, off map). ℘03-3811-1186. www.homeikan.com. 31 rooms.* Built in 1950, this establishment has real character. The floors in the lobby and corridors are made of black pebbles *(nachi ishi)* that shine as though they've been polished, and stumps of polished wood *(keyaki)* break through here and there. Every bedroom is decorated differently, with tree trunks embedded in the walls. There is a pond in the garden where carp doze. The "economy" bedrooms are not so charming, with lino floors and walls that show less care for detail. Private family bathroom on ground floor and two more in the basement. Free Internet access, coin laundry.
On the hillside the **Honkan** is the only ryokan listed as an Important Cultural Property. The 25 rooms mainly accommodate groups.

**Morikawa Bekkan** 鳳明館森川別館 *6-23-5 Hongo, Bunkyo-ku. Subway N12 (Map IV A2, off map). ℘03-3811-8171. www.homeikan.com. 33 rooms.* Next to a Buddhist temple, which looks strangely like a church, and an old, wooden, three-story house. Just below Daimachi Bekkan. The *o-furo* are worth a visit for the coral and fish frescoes on the walls.

**Ryokan Katsutaro Annex** 旅館勝太郎 *3-8-4 Yanaka, Taito-ku. 15min walk from Ryokan Katsutaro. Subway C15, exit 2 (Map IV A1, off map). ℘03-3828-2500. www.katsutaro com. 17 rooms.* Established in 2001 near a very busy pedestrian shopping street and the Yanaka Cemetery, this ryokan still feels new. Its elegant façade of small gray bricks is indicative of its whole image: smart, serious, modern, and comfortable. If you plan to arrive back late at night, ask for the access code. Free Internet access, bicycle rental *(¥200 per day)*, coin laundry.

**Suigetsu Hotel Ogaisou 水月ホテル鴎外荘** *3-3-21 Ikenohata, Taito-ku. Subway C14, exit 2 (Map IV A2). 03-3822-4611, www.ohgai.co.jp. 126 rooms.* Just behind the zoo, this hotel is composed of three buildings set around the house and garden of the novelist Mori Ogai, whose name alone seems to attract Japanese clients. The ambience aims to be traditional *(Japanese bedrooms, but some Western-style too)*, and the staff wear becoming kimonos. Two *o-furo* and one room for the Tea Ceremony.

## EAT

### ASAKUSA

**Maguro Bito まぐろ人浅草本店** *1-5-9 Asakusa, Taito-ku. Asakusa station (Map IV C2). 03-3844-8736. Open 11am–10pm.* A *kaiten-sushi* (conveyor belt sushi) with a constant turnover of customers, as is clear from the welcome greeting *(Irashaimase)* of its chefs, echoed by all the staff. Exceptionally good quality for the price. Good variety of fish. Dishes color-coded by price, from ¥120 to ¥560 for *awabi* (abalone). Atmosphere guaranteed.

**Namiki Yabu Soba 並木藪蕎麦** *2-11-9 Kaminarimon, Taito-ku. Subway G19 (Map IV C2). 03-3841-1340. Open Fri–Wed 11am–7.30pm.* Established in a small house squeezed between two large, modern buildings, this restaurant has been serving noodles since 1913. You can sit on tatami mats on the left or chairs on the right. Mini menu in English, which tells you how to eat noodles correctly *(served both hot and cold)*.

**Oiwake 浅草追分** *3-28-11 Nishi-Asakusa (Map IV C2). 03-3844-6283. Open Mon–Sat 6–11.30pm.* A small *izakaya* that livens up considerably when the serving staff grab the *taiko* (drums) or the *shamisen* (traditional stringed instrument).

**Asakusa Imahan 浅草今半** *3-1-12 Nishi-Asakusa, Taito-ku. Subway G18 (Map IV C2). 03-3841-1114. Open 11.30am–9.30pm.* Located on one corner of Kokusai Street, the restaurant sets out its stall by hanging an ox head outside. They claim to offer high-quality meat here, vserved in a *shabu-shabu* (a type of savory hotpot or stew) or a *sukiyaki*. *Menu in English*.

### UENO

**Chete チェテ***5-4-14 Yanaka, Taito-ku. Subway C15, exit 1 (Map IV A1). 03-3823-7890. Open 11am–11pm (lunch noon–3pm).* A tiny cafe with a few tables crowded together. One on a tatami mat looks as though it's part of a window display. For a quick snack or just a drink. More or less bilingual menu. In Swahili *chete* means "market," and you can just about buy anything from the adjoining store from here (jewelry, shoes, clothes).

**Kissa Meme 喫茶めめ** *5-2-29 Yanaka, Taito-ku. Subway C15 (Map IV A1). 03-3821-9118. http://kissameme.jugem.jp. Open weekends only 10am–11pm.* You are requested to take off your shoes on the steps outside before you go into this old wooden house with its cozy interior. Tatami mats, dressers, piano, and lots of old LPs: Astrud Gilberto, Oscar Peterson, John Coltrane, etc., and some classical pieces. For a reasonable price you can have three bowls of differently flavored rice (seasonal vegetables, black sesame, walnut, and curry) followed by dessert. Tea is extra.

**Musashino とんかつ武蔵野** *2-8-1 Ueno, Taito-ku (Map IV A2). 03-3831-1672. Open noon–8pm.* A traditional *tonkatsu* (deep-fried, breaded pork cutlets) restaurant serving high-quality meat.

**Hantei はん亭** *2-12-15 Nezu, Bunkyo-ku. Subway C14, JR Nippori Station (Map IV A1). 03-3828-1440. Open noon–11pm.* This restaurant, in a large wooden house, is renowned for it *kushiage*: skewers of meat, fish, and vegetables coated with breadcrumbs. The touch of originality is at the end of the little pointed sticks served in pairs: scallops, lotus roots, ginger, potato tofu, etc., all served with rice, soup, and tea.

**Unagi Kappo Izuei 鰻割烹伊豆栄***2-12-22 Ueno, Taito-ku. Subway G15 (Map IV A2). 03-3831-0954. Open 11am–9.30pm.* This restaurant is well known to anyone who likes eels. Those who've never tried them can have their first taste here, where the fish is mainly grilled and served with a slightly spicy house sauce made from a secret recipe.

**Hifumi-an 一二三庵** *4-2-18 Sendagi, Bunkyo-ku. Subway C15, exit 2 or JR Nishi-Nippori station, exit 1 (Map IV A1, off map). 03-5832-8677. www.hifumi-an.com. Open Tue–Sun 6–10.30pm. Reservations required (in English by email).* In this beautiful house, a young chef treats a maximum of 15 people to an individually prepared, highly sophisticated evening meal. Each unique menu comprises about 10 dishes: appetizer, clear soup, ***sashimi***, a slow-cooked dish, salad, rice, soup, small marinated vegetables, fruit, Japanese dessert, and tea. It's possible to attend a cooking course here and eat what you've cooked afterward.

## TAKING A BREAK

### ASAKUSA

**Kamiya Bar 神谷バー** *1-1-1 Asakusa. 03-3841-5400. Open Wed–Mon 11.30am–10pm.* . The first Western bar to open in Tokyo. Has regular customers. Try the ***denki bran***, a turbo-charged brandy cocktail (gin, wine, curaçao, and brandy).

**Kappabashi Coffee 合羽橋珈琲** *3-25-11 Nishiasakusa, Taito-ku. Subway G18. 03-5828-0308. Open 8am–8pm.* An elegant place that naturally attracts sophisticated young people who love fine patisserie.

### UENO

**Cafe – Bousingot ブーサンゴ** *2-33-2 Sendagi, Bunkyo-ku. Subway C15. 03-3823-5501. Open Wed–Thu & Mon 1–8pm, Fri–Sat 1–10pm, Sun 1–7pm. www.bousingot.com.* Cafe bookstore where you can sip, among other things, mint diabolo, cappuccino, Corona, and French table wines. Decor is 1960s–70s, jazzy atmosphere.

**Patisserie – Nezuno-Taiyaki 根津のたいやき** *1-23-9-104 Nezu, Bunkyo-ku. Subway C15, exit 1. Open Wed–Thu & Sat–Mon 10.30am until stock sold out (early afternoon).* Hayashi Shozo has been preparing ***taiyaki*** (small cakes shaped like a fish and stuffed with ***anko***, a red bean paste), which are the delight of the neighborhood for some time. He has enjoyed international recognition since 1996, when the United States Ambassador wrote to congratulate him, declaring that here he had found the true heart of Japan. The long queue marks out the place.

## SHOPPING

### ASAKUSA

**Bunsendo 文扇堂** – *Nakamise-dori. Open 10.30am–6pm. Closed one Mon per month. 03-3844-9711.* The great fan specialist.

**Kurodaya 黒田屋** – *1-2-5 Asakusa. Open Tue–Sun 11am–7pm. 03-3844-7511.* This store, which has been open since the end of the 19C, is particularly well known for its small figures made of paper.

**Miyamoto Unosuke 宮本卯之助** – *6-1-15 Asakusa.Open Mon–Sat 9am–6pm. 03-3874-4131.* The taiko specialist, essential for all percussion enthusiasts. Lessons by request.

**Sukeroku 助六** – *Nakamise-dori. Open daily 10am–6pm. 03-3844-0577.* A small store specializing in handmade miniature dolls and stages. Good quality.

### KANDA-JINBOCHO

**Bookshops – Isseido Shoten 一誠堂書店** *1-7 Kanda Jinbocho, Chiyoda-ku. Open Mon–Sat 10am–6.30pm (public holidays 6pm).* Without doubt the most prestigious bookshop for ancient and rare books in Japanese and Western languages (arts, archeology, literature, religion, etc). Also prints, printed books, ancient Western maps, etc.

**Ohya Shobo 大屋書房** – *1-1 Kanda Jinbocho, Chiyoda-ku, facing Yasukuni-dori. Open Mon–Sat 10am–6pm. Closed public holidays. 03-3291-0062 or 03-3295-3456. www.ohya-shobo.com.* Bookshop and gallery of Japanese books from the Edo and early Meiji eras; ancient Japanese maps, ***ukiyo-e*** prints from the Edo and Meiji eras.

**Hara Shobo 原書房** – *2-3 Kanda Jinbocho, Chiyoda-ku, facing Yasukuni-dori, but after the Jinbocho junction going up toward Yasukuni temple. Open Tue–Sat 10am–6pm. Closed public holidays. 03-5212-7801. www.harashobo.com.* Gallery of Japanese ukiyo-e prints, Edo and Meiji era and 20C.

**Yamada Shoten 山田書店** – *Yamada Bldg, 1st & 3rd floors, 1-8 Kanda Jinbocho, Chiyoda-ku. Open Mon–Sat 10am–6.30pm. 03-3295-0252. www.yamada-shoten.com.* Gallery of ukiyo-e prints from the Edo, Meiji, and Taisho eras, modern engravings; and prints.

Sumo at Ryogoku Kokugikan

© Christian Kober/age fotostock

## SPORT AND LEISURE

### RYOGOKU

**Sumo** – *Kokugikan, 1-3-28 Yokoami, Sumida-ku. Subway E12, JR Sobu Line, Ryogoku station (Map I D2).* The stadium hosts 3 sumo tournaments a year *(2 weeks in Jan, May, & Sept)*. Tickets go on sale 1 month before the start of the competition. On the day, cheaper seats at the back of the terraces are put on sale *(¥2,100)* from 8am at Kokugikan. The contests begin at 10am, but the best only enter the lists from 4pm. An adjoining museum displays a large number of objects *(open Mon–Fri 10am–4.30pm; no charge)*.

If you would like to go to a sumo training session, the **Tokitsukaze** stable *(heya)* welcomes visitors. *(3-15-4 Ryogo-ku, Sumida-ku; JR Sobu Line, Ryogoku station, Map I D2; from 7am–10pm.*

# IMPERIAL PALACE

## USEFUL INFORMATION

**Post Office/Withdrawals** – *Tokyo Central Post Office, 2-7-2 Marunouchi, Chiyoda-ku. Open Mon–Fri 9am–9pm, Sat, Sun & public holidays 9am–7pm. ✆03-3284-9500. ATM 24hr daily.*

## STAY

**Mandarin Oriental Hotel マンダリン・オリエンタル東京** *2-1-1 Nihonbashi Muromachi, Chuo-ku. Subway G12, exit 7 (Map II C2). ✆03-3270-8800. www.mandarinoriental.co.jp/tokyo. 157 rooms.* The latest Tokyo luxury hotel; amazing glass lobby on the 38th floor. Served by the Limousine Bus Company. **Michelin Guide Tokyo Yokohama Kamakura 2011 Selection**.

**Marunouchi Hotel 丸ノ内ホテル** *1-6-3 Marunouchi, Chiyoda-ku (Map II B2). ✆03-3217-1111. www.marunouchi-hotel.co.jp. 204 rooms from ¥46,400.* Opposite Tokyo station, contemporary makeover in 2004. **Michelin Guide Tokyo Yokohama Kamakura 2011 Selection**.

## EAT

**Gonpachi 権八 (G-Zone),** *1-2-3 Ginza, Chuo-ku. Subway G10, exit 3, A12, exit A4 (Map II B3 off map). ✆03-5524-3641. Open 11am–3.30am.* Beneath the rail line, the Gonpachi is spacious with prompt service of *soba* (buckwheat noodles), rice, and kebabs; shares space with **La Bohême** (Italian), **Zest Cantina** (Mexican), and **Monsoon** (Asian).

**Mango Tree Tokyo マンゴツリー東京** *35 F Marunouchi Bldg, 2-4-1 Marunouchi, Chiyoda-ku (Map II B3). ✆03-5224-5489. Open 11am–4pm, 5–11pm.* On the 35th floor, delicious Thai buffet and all you can eat *(¥2,700 at lunchtime)*. Elegant presentation.

**Sens et Saveurs サンス・エ・サヴール** *35 F Marunouchi Bldg, 2-4-1 Marunouchi, Chiyoda-ku. Subway M17, JR Tokyo station (Map II B3). ✆03-5220-2701. Open 11am–10pm.* Tokyo on the Mediterranean with the Pourcel brothers, superb and on the 35th floor with a **view** of the Imperial Palace.

## NIGHTLIFE

**Molecular Bar** モラキュラーバー – *Mandarin Oriental Hotel (see Where to Stay). ℘0120-806-823. Open 6–10pm.* Set back from the Oriental Lounge, 12 chairs around a bar, behind which a chef prepares snacks. Count on ¥14,000 for over 20 hors d'oeuvres with cocktail, beer, wine or coffee.

## SPORT AND LEISURE

**Bus Trip** – *Sky Bus Tokyo, counter on ground floor of Mitsubishi Bldg, opposite Tokyo station, Marunouchi south exit (Map II B3).* Departs every hour *(10am–6pm, ¥1,200)* for a 45min trip around the Imperial Palace on board a double-decker bus.

**National Theatre of Japan** 国立劇場 – *4-1 Hayabusa-cho, Chiyoda-ku, next to the Supreme Court. Subway Z05, Y16 (Map II A3). Reservations ℘05-7007-9900. www.ntj.jac.go.jp. Kabuki, bunraku, Noh*, and *kyogen* performances. Audioguide hire, *¥1,500–12,000.*

# GINZA

## STAY

**Ginza Yoshimizu** 銀座吉水 *3-11-3 Ginza, Chuo-ku. Subway A11, H09 (Map III C1). ℘03-3248-4432. www.yoshimizu.com. 12 rooms.* A gem of a *ryokan* in a district where there are now hardly any. Established in 2003, the Yoshimizu is easy to spot in the street because of its openwork door with bamboo plants on either side. Impeccable rooms with generous bathrooms. A warm welcome. On the top floor two *o-furo* are open all night. The organic breakfast is delicious.

**Imperial Hotel** 帝国ホテル *1-1-1 Uchisaiwai-cho, Chiyoda-ku. Subway H07, C09 (Map III A1). ℘03-3504-1111. www.imperialhotel.co.jp. 1,057 rooms.* The first Imperial Hotel opened in 1890. American architect Frank Lloyd Wright replaced it with a larger, oriental-style building, which survived the Great Kanto Earthquake on the very day it opened in 1923. It was damaged in the war, and was finally demolished in 1968, to be replaced two years later. Located on the edge of Hibiya Park, the hotel provides services worthy of its glorious past. **Michelin Guide Tokyo Yokohama Kamakura 2011 Selection**.

**Mercure** メルキュールホテル銀座東京 *2-9-4 Ginza, Chuo-ku. Subway Y19, exit 11, G09, H08, exit 13 (Map III C1). ℘03-4335-1111. www.accorhotels.com. 208 rooms.* Ideally located in downtown Ginza, the Mercure exudes discreet French charm, covering its walls with black-and-white prints of the country. A skillful use of space optimizes the somewhat limited area available in the carefully decorated rooms. Attentive staff.

## EAT

The area around the rail line between Shinbashi and Yurakucho stations is full of cheap restaurants, mainly of the type that serve *yakitori-ya* (grilled chicken skewers), some with tables and benches outside. You really are spoilt for choice.

**Kajiya Bunzo** 鍛冶屋文蔵日比谷店 *1-7-13 Uchisaiwai-cho, Chiyoda-ku. Subway Y18 (Map III B1).* Beneath the rail line, which you can sometimes hear rattling. Go for the traditional room at the back, first removing your shoes, which are put away in a store. Good range of *nabe* (one-pot dishes), *sashimi* (raw fish), and *yakitori*. A remote control handset is used to call the serving staff.

**Narukami** 鳴神 *4-13-3 Ginza, Chuo-ku. Subway A11 (Map III C2). ℘03-6226-4360. Open 10am–8pm (Sat–Sun 6pm).* A charming place just a short distance from the Kabuki-za Theater. Sophisticated and friendly. Lunch menu (sushi, *udon* noodles, pastries). It's also a tearoom.

**Sakura Suisan** さくら水産・銀座三丁目店 *B2 F Ginza Sunny Bldg, 3-4-16 Ginza, Chuo-ku. Subway G09 (Map III B1). ℘03-3561-3671.* "Always the same lowest price" is the restaurant's slogan, displayed next to a leaping fish. Order by checking boxes on an incomprehensible form. You can trust to luck, but there are columns for sashimi, grills, tempura, salads, and snacks. Popular, with quite low prices, but probably not the lowest.

**Sushi Bun** 鮨文 *5-2-1 Tsukiji, Chuo-ku (Map III C2 off map). ℘03-3541-3860. Open Mon–Sat 6am–2.30pm. Closed holidays. Inside the fish market.* This stand is not to be missed if you like raw fish, for it's unrivaled. *(Some other good addresses can be found on the website www.tsukijigourmet.or.jp).* Set menus from ¥2,625.

**Sushizanmai** すしざんまい・有楽町店 *2-1-3 Yuraku-cho, Chiyoda-ku. Subway Y18 (Map III B1). 03-3500-2201. Open 24hr.* Beneath the rail line. After 1am there are still five cooks busy behind the counter and food orders coming in thick and fast. There's no set time for sushi.

**Dazzle** ダズル *9 F Mikimoto Ginza 2, 2-4-13 Ginza, Chuo-ku. Subway G09 (Map III B1). 03-5159-0991. www.huge.co.jp. Open 5.30pm–midnight.* Located at the top of the magnificent Mikimoto Building, this restaurant really lives up to its name. One is indeed "dazzled" by the splendor of the decor. The wine store, sitting inside a glass tower that dominates the room, is an impressive sight, as are the dishes: grilled fillet of sea bass with a white butter saffron sauce, sautéed foie gras, not to mention the desserts…

**Faro** ファロ資生堂 *10 F Shiseido Bldg, 8-8-3 Ginza, Chuo-ku. Subway G09 (Map III B2). 03-3572-3911. Open Mon–Sat 11.30am–11pm. Closed public holidays.* An Italian restaurant on the penultimate floor of the Shiseido Building. A formal head waiter sets the tone, but the food is delicious. The dessert cart has a dizzying selection: panna cota, tiramisu, *zuppa inglese* (custard-based sponge cake), etc. *Lunch menu ¥3,800.* **Michelin Guide Tokyo Yokohama Kamakura 2011 Selection.**

**Fish Bank** フィッシュバンク東京 *41 F Shiodome City Center, 1-5-2 Higashi-Shinbashi, Minato-ku. Subway E19 (Map III B2). 03-3569-7171. Open 11.30am–11.30pm.* In an elegant space on two levels, with a spectacular **view** of Rainbow Bridge, you can enjoy fish and seafood subtly prepared according to traditional French recipes adapted to local tastes. *Lunch menu ¥1,300-1,800.*

**Harutaka** 青空（はるたか） *3 F Kawabata Bldg, 8-5-8 Ginza, Chuo-ku (Map III B2). 03-3573-1144. Open 5pm–midnight.* Opened by a sushi master, this restaurant offers seafood products of unrivaled freshness, chosen with great care at the Tsukiji fish market every day. A subtle experience in a well-kept, minimalist setting. **Michelin Guide Tokyo Yokohama Kamakura 2011 Selection.**

**Sankame** 三亀 *1 F KN Bldg, 6-4-13 Ginza, Chuo-ku (Map III B2). 03-3571-0573. Open every day except Sun and holidays, noon–2pm, 5–10pm.* Kansai cooking has been given pride of place at the Sankame since 1946, but when in season you can also have Hokkaido sea trout marinated in sake, salted grilled eel, or the amazing matsutake mushrooms. *Sampling menu at lunchtime: ¥1,750.* **Michelin Guide Tokyo Yokohama Kamakura 2011 Selection.**

## TAKING A BREAK

**Wako Chocolate Salon** 和光チョコレートサロン – *4-5-5 Ginza, Chuo-ku. Subway G09. 03-5250-3135. Open 10.30am–7.30pm (Sun 7pm).* Runs the length of the Wako building annex. Golden sunlight flickers over the brown paneling and caresses the chocolates and pastries. The nougatine parfait is more than perfect. Coconut macaroons and ice creams, *around ¥1,300.*

**Mikimoto Lounge** ミキモトラウンジ – *3 F Mikimoto Ginza 2, 2-4-12 Ginza, Chuo-ku. Subway G09. 03-3562-3134. Open 11am–7.30pm. May be closed Wed.* There are splendid treats to be enjoyed in this Mikimoto outlet: panna cota with asparagus, strawberry millefeuilles, coconut and banana sponge. *Allow about ¥1,300 for a pastry and ¥1,000 for tea and ¥600 for coffee.*

## SHOPPING

**Ginza Antique Mall** アンティークモール銀座 – *1-13-1 Ginza, Chuo-ku. Subway Y19. Open Thu–Tue 11am–7pm. www.antiques-jp.com.* On three floors, mixed antiques, where the worst items rub shoulders with the best, sometimes with surprisingly good results. Prices quite high. Feel free to bargain.

## LEISURE

**Kabuki-za Theater** 歌舞伎座 – *4-12-5 Ginza, Chuo-ku. Subway H09 (Map III C2). www.kabuki-za.co.jp. Currently closed for renovations.*

# ROPPONGI

## USEFUL INFORMATION

**Bank/Foreign Exchange** – **World Currency Shop**, *Roppongi Hills, 6 F West Walk (Map I B4). Open Mon–Fri 11am–7pm, Sat–Sun 2pm–5pm. 03-5413-9722.*

## STAY

**Asia Center of Japan ホテルアジア会館** *8-10-32 Akasaka, Minato-ku. Subway G04, Z03, E24, exit 4 (Map I B3). 03-3402-6111. www.asiacenter.or.jp. 173 rooms.* Not far from the Roppongi district, this recently-built hotel at the top of a hill offers simple accommodation in a calm and comfortable environment, and at a very reasonable price.

**Ibis Roppongi** アイビスホテル六本木 *7-14-4 Roppongi, Minato-ku. Subway H04, exit 4a, E23, exit 7 (Map I B3). 03-3403-4411. www.ibis-hotel.com. 182 rooms.* Night owls will appreciate the fact that they can walk back here after scouring the clubs and bars of Roppongi. Somewhat restricted space probably won't bother them unduly.

**International House of Japan 国際文化会館***5-11-16 Roppongi, 5-chome, Minato-ku. Subway N04, exit 4, E22, exit 7 (Map I B4). 03-3470-4611.www.i-house.or.jp.* A fine building that reopened in April 2006, *(10min walk from the Mori Tower).* Traditional garden surrounding a building inspired by Le Corbusier in the 1950s. Hi-tech furniture. Serious and sophisticated: You must be proposed by a member to be able to stay here.

**ANA Intercontinental** ANA インターコンチネンタルホテル東京 *1-12-33 Akasaka, Minato-ku (Map I B3). 03-3505-1111. www.anaintercontinental-tokyo.jp. 844 rooms.* Attractive hotel occupying floors 7–35 of a 37-floor tower. The comfortable rooms are elegant and smart—some have beautiful **views** of the Imperial Palace, the Tokyo Tower, and Roppongi Hills. **Michelin Guide Tokyo Yokohama Kamakura 2011 Selection**.

**The Prince Park Tower Tokyo** ザ・プリンス・パークタワー東京 *4-8-1 Shibakoen, Minato-ku. Subway E21, Akabane-bashi exit, I05, exit A4 (Map I C4). 03-5400-1111. www.princehotels.co.jp/parktower. 673 rooms.* Rising up in the middle of a green space, the tower looks like a rocket on its launching pad. Near the Prince Hotel, built by Tange Kenzo, the Zojo-ji, and the Tokyo Tower. From the upper floors, there's a **view** over Tokyo Bay and Rainbow Bridge. Served by the Limousine Bus Company. **Michelin Guide Tokyo Yokohama Kamakura 2011 Selection**.

## EAT

**Pintokona** ぴんとこな *Roppongi Hills, Metro Hat, B2 F, Hollywood Plaza, 6-4-1 Roppongi, Minato-ku. Subway H04, exit 1C, E23, exit 3 (Map I B4). 03-5771-1133. Open 11am–11pm.* The sushi dishes move along a conveyor belt on the counter. You just reach out and help yourself; they're color-coded according to price. There's a hot water tap on the counter for making your own tea, which you can also order.

**Sankyu** 燦糺 (さんきゅう) *1 F Roppongi Shinsei Bldg, 3-1-18 Nishi-Azabu, Minato-ku. Subway H04 (Map I B3). 03-5771-6201. Open 6pm–4am, Sun 5–11pm.* You leave your shoes outside before going into this rustic settng, which you will find at the end of a gravel passage. Australian or Japanese beef *(wagyu)* takes pride of place, the latter significantly more expensive, as its reputation requires. But the meat, marbled with fat, is delicious.

**L'Atelier de Joël Robuchon** ラトリエ・ドゥ・ジョエル・ロブション *2 F Roppongi Hills Hillside, 6-10-1 Roppongi, Minato-ku. Subway H04, exit 1C, E23, exit 3 (Map I B4). 03-5772-7500. Open 11.30am–11pm.* Clean lines in a softly-lit red and black interior. Sophisticated, yet relaxing. Extremely subtle dishes. This is the restaurant of an artist. Service is charming and efficient too. **Michelin Guide Tokyo Yokohama Kamakura 2011 Selection**.

**Hishinuma** 菱沼 (ひしぬま) *B1 F Axis Bldg, 5-17-1 Roppongi, Minato-ku (Map I B3/4). 03-3568-6588. Open 11.30am–2pm, 5.30pm–9pm.* "Serving society through good eating" is the motto of chef Hishinuma Takayuki, who is as devoted to his clients, both great and small, as he is to his culinary creations: vegetarian *kaiseki* dishes inspired by the West, grilled meats, etc. *Set menus from ¥3,400 at lunchtime and ¥12,000 in evenings.* **Michelin Guide Tokyo Yokohama Kamakura 2011 Selection**.

**Tofuya Ukai Shiba** とうふ屋うかい *4-4-13 Shiba-Koen, Minato-ku (Map I B4). 03-3436-1028. www.ukai.co.jp/shiba. Open 11am–10pm.* At the bottom of the Tokyo Tower, this is a charming *ryotei* surrounded by a 71,041.8sq ft/6,600sq m garden with an Art Nouveau touch from the Edo era. You will enjoy unforgettable tofu and some seasonal dishes here.

## NIGHTLIFE

**Toho Cinemas** TOHO シネマズ – *Roppongi Hills, Keyakizaka Complex, 6-10-2 Roppongi, Minato-ku. Subway H04, E23.* The biggest movie theater complex in Tokyo. *All-night screenings at weekends.*

**Bar** – **Agave** アガヴェ *B1 F Clover Bldg, 7-15-10 Roppongi, Minato-ku. Subway H04 (Map I B3). Open Mon–Thu 6.30pm–2am, Fri–Sat 6.30pm–4am. Closed Mon, if public holiday. ☏03-3497-0229.* Go for some Mexico, and switch tequila for sake. 400 different kinds od sake at Agave, named for the plant used to make the powerful alcohol.

**Clubs** – The nightclubbing trend may be to swap the dancefloors of Roppongi for those of Shibuya, but it doesn't change the fact that there are still more clubs here and foreigners come in large numbers.

**NewLex Edo** ニューレックスエド – *B1 F 3rd Goto Bldg, 3-13-14 Roppongi, Minato-ku. Subway H04, E23. Open Sun–Wed 10am–5pm, Thu 9am–5pm, Fri, Sat, & day before public holidays 8pm–5am. ☏03-3401-1661. www.newlex-edo.com.* Formerly the Lexington Queen, for 20 years, models and international rock and movie stars have met up here, along with a crowd of mainly Japanese girls dazzled by their glamor.

**Gaspanic Club 99** ガスパニッククラブ **99** – *B1 F, 3-15-24 Roppongi, Minato-ku. Subway H04, E23. Open from 9pm. ☏03-3470-7190.* A place where supply and demand meet—foreigners keen to strike up an acquaintance with the Japanese and vice versa, and the music doesn't really matter. Of its type, you can't do better. It's the Roppongi guarantee!

## SHINJUKU

### USEFUL INFORMATION

**Tourist Office** – *Tokyo Tourist Information Center, 1 F Metropolitan Government Bldg no. 1. Subway E28, JR Shinjuku Station, W exit (Map V A2). Open 9.30am–6.30pm. ☏03-5321-3077. www.tourism.metro.tokyo.jp.* Guided tours to different districts in several languages, inc. English. *(depart Shinjuku; (min. 5 persons); Mon–Fri 1pm, min age 20; reserve at center or website).*

### STAY

**Century Southern Tower** 小田急ホテルセンテュリーサザンタワー *2-2-1 Yoyogi, Shibuya-ku (Map V B2). ☏03-5354-0111. www.southerntower.co.jp. 375 rooms. From ¥27,920.* **Views** of Mt. Fuji and east and west Tokyo from 20th floor; panoramic maps in rooms. Standard comfort. **Michelin Guide Tokyo Yokohama Kamakura 2011 Selection.**

**Keio Plaza** 京王プラザホテル *2-2-1 Nishi-Shinjuku, Shinjuku-ku (Map V B2). ☏03-3344-0111. www.keioplaza.co.jp. 1,440 rooms.* Shinjuku's first skyscraper, owned by Keio Rail. Panoramic **views**, outside pool, sumptuous rooms. Luxury hotel of 13 restaurants and 8 bars. **Michelin Guide Tokyo Yokohama Kamakura 2011 Selection.**

**Park Hyatt Hotel** パークハイアット東京 *3-7-1-2 Nishi-Shinjuku, Shinjuku-ku. Subway E28 (Map V A2). ☏03-5322-1234. www.parkhyatttokyo.com. 177 rooms.* Luxurious hotel of *Lost in Translation* fame. Served by the Limousine Bus Company. **Michelin Guide Tokyo Yokohama Kamakura 2011 Selection.**

Skyscrapers of West Shinjuku at night

## EAT

**Sukiya すき屋西新宿店**
*Sentoku Building 7-10-16 Nishi Shinjuku (Map V, B1). Open 24 hrs.* Fast-food chain offering *gyudon* (bowl of rice topped with beef); unbeatable prices *(¥230 – 700).*

**Tsunahachi 天ぷら新宿つな八総本店**
*3-31-8, Shinjuku, JR Shinjuku station (Map V C2). 03-3352-1012. Open 11am10.30pm.* Long famed for its tempura, you can choose from prawn, fish, mushroom and lotus root for a few yen. *Spawned smaller Tsunahachi in Tokyo and elsewhere.*

**Mo-mo Paradise**
モーモーパラダイス *Humax Pavilion Shinjuku Kabuki-cho 8F 1-20-1 Kabuki-cho, Shinjuku-ku (Map V C1). Seibu Shinjuku station, JR Shinjuku station East exit. Subway M08. 03-3208-0135. Open 4pm11pm (11.30am11pm SatSun). English menu.* Shabu-shabu chain restaurant *(meat and vegetable dishes dinners cook in sauces)*; all you can eat within 90 mins for ¥1,980.

**Le Mange-Tout ル・マンジュ・トゥ**
*22 Nandomaci, Shinjuku-ku. Ushiogome-kaguraka station on the Oedo Line from Shinjuku. 03-3268-5911. Open Mon–Sat 6.30–9pm.* A rigorous, francophile chef, who speaks French too, having spent some time in Alsace, Tani Noboru's inventive dishes are a carefully prepared blend of French and Japanese expertise. *One single menu with 15 dishes; ¥12,600.* Friendly welcome and atmosphere. Unfortunately, the wines don't always match up. **Michelin Guide Tokyo Yokohama Kamakura 2011 Selection.**

**L'Anneau d'Or ラノー・ドール**
*B1 F Yotsuya Sun Heights, 4-6-1 Yotsuya, Shinjuku-ku (Map V C2, off map). 03-5919-0141. Open Thu–Tue, 12pm–3pm, 6.30–10.30pm (Sat–Sun, 6pm–10.30pm).* "The most important thing is the aroma: if the aroma is good, the taste will also be good," says this French restaurant's talented chef. An absolute must is poached egg served with a truffle and foie gras sauce. **Michelin Guide Tokyo Yokohama Kamakura 2011 Selection.**

**Nakajima 新宿割烹・中嶋**
*B1 F Hihara Bldg, 3-32-5 Shinjuku, Shinjuku-ku (Map V C2). 03-3356-4534. http://www.shinjyuku-nakajima.com. Open Mon–Sat, 11.30am–2pm, 5.30–10pm.* The grandfather was an expert chef in his time, but now it's his grandson's turn to take up the reins with a Kansai menu that changes according to the time of year and includes an excellent *kaiseki, (only ¥800 on the set lunch menu).* **Michelin Guide Tokyo Yokohama Kamakura 2011 Selection.**

## NIGHTLIFE

North of Shinjuku park *(Subway M09, exit C8)*, **Shinjuku Nichome** is the gay quarter of the capital, with a profusion of bars in a small area.

**New York Bar ニューヨーク バー** – *52 F Park Hyatt Hotel (see Where to Stay). 03-5323-3458. Open 5pm–midnight (Thu–Sat 1am).* If you can't stay in the Hyatt, have a drink there, listening to jazz while enjoying the stunning **view**.

## SHOPPING

**Bookshop – Kinokuniya 紀伊國屋書店・新宿本店** *Takashimaya Times Square, Annex Building, 5-24-2 Sendagaya. Open 10am–8pm. Closed one Wed per month.* A branch of the original, long-established bookstore at 3-17-7 Shinjuku-ku *(open 10am–9pm),* where postwar intellectuals gathered and which has now become an institution. *Foreign language books and magazines on the seventh floor.*

**Flea Market – Hanazono-jinja**, every Sun except when ceremony at temple.

# KAGURAZAKA

## STAY

**Tokyo International Hostel**
東京国際ホステル*Central Plaza 18F, 1-1 Kagurakashi, Shinjuku-ku. JR Sobu Line, Iidabashi station, west exit (Map VI B1). 03-3235-1107. www.tokyo-ih.jp. 33 dormitories.* There are certainly better hostels in Tokyo, but they're a lot more expensive. The hostel occupies the 18th and 19th floors of a high-rise building with a shopping mall and restaurants below. There are fine views, and the JR Sobu Line is just over the bridge.

**Wakana Ryokan 旅館和可菜***4-7 Kagurazaka, Shinjuku-ku. Subway Y13, E05. JR Sobu Line, Iidabashi station, west exit (Map VI A1). Opposite Zenkoku-ji temple, 1st left after Le Bretagne restaurant on the left, then 1st right. 03-3260-3769. 3 rooms.* Almost undetectable in the confusion of alleyways in Kagurazaka, this ancient ryokan, run by a woman of no less venerable an age, plunges you into the Japan of times past. If you long for some peace and tranquility put your bags down here, on a tatami mat. No private bathrooms.

**Tokyo Dome Hotel** 東京ドームホテル *1-3-61 Koraku, Bunkyo-ku. Subway M22, N11, JR Chuo Line, Suidobashi station, east exit (Map VI B1 off map). 03-5805-2111. www.tokyodome-hotels.co jp. 1,006 rooms.* Built entirely of glass by Tange Kenzo, the hotel looks down over the Dome to which it owes its name and the roller coasters that thread their way through the LaQua amusement complex. Rooms are spacious and elegant. The **view** becomes interesting above the 10th floor. The hotel gets full when there's a baseball match in the Dome. Served by the Limousine Bus Company.

**The Agnes** アグネスホテル・アンド・アパートメンツ東京*2-20-1 Kagurazaka, Shinjuku-ku. Subway Y13, T06, exit B3, JR Sobu Line, Iidabashi station, west exit (Map VI A–B2). 03-3267-5505. www.agneshotel.com. 56 rooms.* A charming hotel, popular with the French and English. Opulent rooms in pastel tones, some with balconies; also apartment suites with kitchenette. **Michelin Guide Tokyo Yokohama Kamakura 2011 Selection**.

## EAT

**SHUN** 神楽坂SHUN本家 *L.V Annex 1 F 3-2-36 Kagurazaka, Shinjuku-ku. 03-3269-0560. www.kagurazaka-shun.jp. Open Mon–Fri 5–11.30pm, Sat, Sun and Bank Holiday 5–11pm.* The clean lines and soft light give this ***izakaya*** a charming feel. Eight small dishes served as a set menu ***(eight dishes, whatever the seasonal menu, special or soba noodles)*** or à la carte. You can eat **fugu** (sashimi) here. Also at 4-2-5 Kagurazaka, Shinjuku-ku; 03-3266-0089; open–11pm.

**Ichimonji** 懐石・一文字 *3-6 Kagurazaka, Shinjuku-ku (Map VI A1). 03-5206-8223. Open noon–2pm, 6–9pm.* A sophisticated space in which to enjoy the best of kaiseki cuisine. The chef, Kazuhiko Hirose, worked for 13 years as a Tea Ceremony master. *Set lunch menus ¥8,000 to 16,000.* **Michelin Guide Tokyo Yokohama Kamakura 2011 Selection**.

**Yamasaki** 山さき *2 F Fukuya Bldg, 4-2 Kagurazaka, Shinjuku-ku (Map VI A1). 03-3267-2310. Open 6pm–10pm. From ¥7,350.*Only four modest tables here for Mika Yamasaki, a chef well-versed in the technique of preparing ***nabe*** (one-pot dishes), including ***negima nabe***, tuna ***(setoro)*** cooked in a soup and eaten with seaweed, Japanese parsley, etc. *(Oct–Apr).* **Michelin Guide Tokyo Yokohama Kamakura 2011 Selection**.

## TAKING A BREAK

**Cafe – Mugimaru2** むぎまる2 *5-20 Kagurazaka, Shinjuku-ku. JR Sobu Line, Iidabashi station. Open Thu–Tue, noon–9pm. 03-5228-6393. www.mugimaru2.com.* Cozy little cafe for a tea or coffee and a ***manju*** (a red bean-filled cake).

## NIGHTLIFE

**Bar – Iseto** 伊勢藤 *4-2 Kagurazaka, Shinjuku-ku. JR Sobu Line, Iidabashi station. Open 5pm–9pm. 03-3260-6363.* A sake bar from a different era. Dimly-lit wood-paneled interior. Low tables or tatami, meditative atmosphere. Some small nibbles.

# SHIBUYA

## STAY

**Shibuya Tobu Hotel** 渋谷東武ホテル *3-1 Udagawa-cho, Shibuya-ku. Subway Z01 (Map VII B1). 03-3476-0111. 197 rooms.* Halfway between Yoyogi Park and Shibuya station. Good quality/price ratio and a good compromise between green space and urban bustle.

**Tokyu Stay Shibuya Shin-Minamiguchi** 東急ステイ渋谷・新 南口 *3-26-21 Shibuya, Shibuya-ku. JR Shibuya station, New South exit (Map VII B2). 03-5466-0109. www.tokyustay.co.jp. 150 apartments.* Tokyu Stay offers modern apartments of different sizes *(from 161.5sq ft/15sq m to 366sq ft/34sq m)* with a fully-equipped kitchen (microwave, electric hot plate, fridge) and washing machine. Inside, everything is neat and tidy. It's a good solution for long-term stays. Breakfast is available at Jonathan's, the basement-level bar outside the hotel. There are quite a few Tokyu Stay hotels in Tokyo, including a second one in Shibuya and three others in fairly central districts *(Shin-Nihonbashi, Higashi-Ginza, and Yotsuya).*

**Shibuya Excel Hotel Tokyu** 渋谷エクセルホテル東急 *Shibuya Mark City Bldg, 1-12-2 Dogenzaka, Shibuya-ku. Subway G01, Z01, JR Shibuya station (Map VII B2). 03-5457-0109. www.tokyuhotelsjapan.com/en/TE/TE_SHIBU/index.html. 229 rooms.* Just up from the station and the big Shibuya junction, the hotel rises up, slender and white. The cozy, elegant rooms are simply decorated islands of calm amid Shibuya's turmoil. To the north there's a fine **view** over Yoyogi Park, Meiji-jingu, and the high-rise buildings of Shinjuku on the horizon. Served by the Limousine Bus Company.

**Cerulean Tower** セルリアンタワー東急ホテル *26-1 Sakuragaokacho, Shibuya-ku (Map VII B2). 03-3476-3000. www.ceruleantower-hotel.com. 411 rooms.* Outside its stature is impressive. Inside the splendor is a wonder to behold: carpets are so thick and soft that you risk twisting your ankle with every step. Fine **views**, mainly to the north toward Shinjuku. Served by the Limousine Bus Company. **Michelin Guide Tokyo Yokohama Kamakura 2011 Selection.**

## EAT

**Coco ichibanya Curry House Coco** カレーハウスCoCo壱番屋 *Yokota Building, 24-10 Udagawa-cho (Map VII B2). 03-5459-0460. Open 24 hrs.* This chain restaurant has various Japanese curries; choose amount of rice and spice – low prices *(¥400-900).*

**Sweets Paradise** スイーツパラダイス *Chitose kaikan, 13-8, Udagawa-cho, Shibuya-ku (Map VII A1). 03-3463-8525. Open 11am–10pm. ¥1,400 (buffet 1 ½hrs).* This sweet shop looks the part with its pinks, reds, oranges, and rounded shapes. There are: cakes, fondants, tiramisùs, syrups, ice creams, chocolate, tarts, jellies: all you could wish for at the buffet. Curry and pasta for those wanting a real meal.

**Tamawarai** 玉笑 *Kohga Bldg, 4-23-8 Ebisu, Shibuya-ku. JR Ebisu station, east exit and moving walkway (below Franco-Japanese restaurant near Yebisu Garden Place) (Map VII A2 off map, Map 1 A4). 03-3443-513. Open Tue–Sun 11.30am–9.30pm.* The red sienna walls and polished parquet wooden floors create a warm atmosphere. On the menu, delicious hot and cold *soba* noodles, different types of tofu and tempura, all served in low, gentle tones, but there may be a wait.

**Watami** 和民・渋谷道玄坂店 *5F, Dougenzaka Center Building, Dougenzaka 2-29-8 (Map VII A2). 03-5456-6027. Open Sun–Thu 5pm–3am, Fri–Sun and eve of holidays 5pm–5am.* This restaurant chain's discreet ambiance is the setting for enjoying unusual dishes made with organic ingredients. Try the house specialty: ***tetsunabe gyoza*** *(¥313),* a pot of Japanese ravioli. *English menu.*

**Hatago** 旅籠・道玄坂店 *B1 F, 2-28-5 Dogenzaka, Shibuya-ku. Subway G01,Z01 (Map VII A2). 03-5428-3574. Open 11.30am–11pm.* A quiet, basement restaurant on Dogenzaka. Decoration is faux bamboo and hammered iron screens. The menu mainly offers *soba* noodles. Chestnut ice cream on the dessert menu is a delightful surprise. A good choice of *shochu* (a distilled rice, barley, or sweet potato beverage).

**Legato** レガート *15 F E. Space Tower, 3-6 Maruyama-cho, Shibuya-ku. Subway G01, Z01 (Map VII A2). 03-5784-2120. Open Mon–Fri 11.30am–midnight, Sat–Sun 5.30pm–midnight (bar until 4am).* A hundred or more large bulbs dangle from the ceiling. Gently reflected in the dark red hangings and copper plates on the walls, they bathe the room in a twilight glow. In front of the ovens, the beret-clad cook, blends the tastes of East and West. If you don't want to eat, you can just have a drink and enjoy the scene.

**Sugawara** すがわら *2-19-12 Ebisu-Minami, Shibuya-ku (Map VII B2, off map). 03-3793-0281. Open 6.30–11pm, closed Sat–Sun.* Owned by a charming couple, this small restaurant offers seasonal dishes in generous portions: grilled fish, seafood salad with wild vegetables, mushrooms, etc.

**Okina** 翁 *B1 F Five Annex, 1-3-10 Ebisu-Nishi, Shibuya-ku (Map VII B2, off map). 03-3477-2648. Open 6–10pm.* This traditional restaurant has specialized in *soba* for eight generations. The fresh buckwheat noodles are served with a sauce made from a secret recipe and three varieties of dried *bonito*. **Michelin Guide Tokyo Yokohama Kamakura 2011 Selection**.

## NIGHTLIFE

**Bars – Mary Jane 渋谷メアリージェーン** *2 F Fuji Shoji Bldg, 2-3 Sakuragaoka-cho, Shibuya-ku. Subway G01, Z01. Open noon–11pm (Fri–Sat midnight). ☏03-3461-3381.* Things have aged a bit here since 1972. Sip a whisky or tea, and listen to the jazz collection of the owner, who has actually published an anthology. Excellent cheesecake.

**Volontaire ボロンテール** – *6-29-6 Jingumae, Shibuya-ku. Subway C03 (on Meiji-dori, not far from Omotesando). Open noon–1am. ☏03-3400-8629.* Tiny and unusual, bar on 1st floor of sloping building. Room only for a bar, a few stools, and hundreds of vinyls.

**Clubs** – Some of the best clubs in town are not in Roppongi, but in Shibuya. Well-informed clubbers will immediately approve of them.

**La Fabrique de Tokyo ラ・ファブリック** – *B1 F Zero Gate Bldg, 16-9 Udagawa-cho, Shibuya-ku. Subway G01. ☏03-5428-5100.* Modeled on La Fabrique de Paris. More specifically, you can lunch here on the same *flammekueche* as in the Bastille *(open 11am–6pm)*. Dine *(open 6–11pm)* and dance to house, electro, and jazz *(open 11pm–5am)*.

**Womb ウーム** – *Studio Arias, 2-16 Maruyama-cho, Shibuya-ku. SubwayG01. Open Thu from 10pm, Fri–Sat from 11pm, Sun from 2pm. ☏03-5459-0039.* The most prestigious DJs and crowds jostle here, mostly at weekends. Mainly techno and house music. ID required.

**Club Asia クラブエイジア** – *1-8 Maruyamacho, Shibuya-ku. Subway G01. Open only for events. ☏03-5458-2551. www.clubasia.co.jp.* The club that gave Shibuya its noble rhythms. Techno, hip-hop, and trance music.

# HARAJUKU

## STAY

**Tokyo Yoyogi Youth Hostel 東京代々木ユースホステル** *3-1 Yoyogi Kamisono-cho, Shibuya-ku. Subway C02 (Map I A3). ☏03-3467-9163. www.jyh.gr.jp/yoyogi. 60 rooms.* Backing onto the forest surrounding the Meiji-jingu and in the middle of the Olympic Center, this hostel has only austere, individual rooms. Non-members pay a supplement. Key deposit required.

## EAT

**Cube Zen キューブ・ゼン** *1 F Gate Square Bldg, 5-2-14 Jingumae, Shibuya-ku. Subway C04, exit A1 (Map VIII B2). ☏03-5464-3331. Open 6–11pm.* The blinds dividing the main room and the mezzanine into compartments create an intimate atmosphere. A large variety of appetizers (eel's liver tofu, for example) and dishes prepared over hot stones *(ishiyaki)*. The pumpkin cake encourages mastication rather than meditation. You ring a bell to call the waiter. *Menu in English.*

**Gut's Soul ガッツ・ソウル・代々木店** *3F, Oshiro Building, 1-32-1 Yoyogi, Shibuya-ku. ☏03-3320-1452. Open 11am–3pm, 5pm–11.30pm Sat–Sun.* Barbecue in all-you-can-eat formulas from ¥1,280 to ¥3,000 by type of meat and accompaniments, and all-you-can-drink option. Great for meal with friends; diners cook their own meat and vegetables on a grill in the middle of the table.

**Le Bretagne ル・ブルターニュ・表参道店** *3-5-4 Jingumae, Shibuya-ku. Subway C04, exit A2 (Map VIII B2). ☏03-3478-7855. www.le-bretagne.com. Open Mon–Sat 11.30am–11pm, Sun 11am–10pm.* Would you like to be in Finistère on the other side of the world? Le Bretagne serves buckwheat pancakes, crêpes, cider, Calvados, etc. You can almost believe you are there.

**Lotus Cafe カフェ・ロータス** *4-6-8 Jingumae, Shibuya-ku. Subway C04, exit A2 (Map VIII B2). ☏03-5772-6077. www.heads-west.com. Open 10am–4am (Fri–Sat 4am).* The solemnity of the concrete is in stark contrast to the pink and purple, colors no doubt chosen to evoke the lotus flower. Very smart, designer decor. On the menu: pasta, risotto, pizza, meats. *Menu in English.*

**Galali ガラリ** *3-6-5 Jingumae, Shibuya-ku. Subway G03, exit 3 (Map VIII B2). ☏03-3408-2818. www.gala-e.com. Open 5.30pm–4am (Sat, Sun, & public holidays 11pm).* Coming from Omotesando, the restaurant is at the end of a dead end, on the left after the Protech cycle shop. Soft lighting sets off the wood inside. On the counter, made out of two solid beams, 12 sorts of salt are lined up ready to be taken with sake, tequila-style. Delicious sashimi served on a bed of ice. Don't leave without tasting the green-tea ice cream.

**Benoit** ブノワ *10 F La Porte Aoyama, 5-51-8 Jingumae, Shibuya-ku. Subway C04, exit B2 (Map VIII B2). ✆03-6419-4181. www.benoit-tokyo.com. Open 11.30am–10.30pm.* The Tokyo Benoit, like the one in Paris, is under the leadership of Alain Ducasse. Chic Mediterranean cuisine in an environment that is bright, but lacks warmth.

**Shigeyoshi** 重よし *1 F Co-op Olympia, 6-35-3 Jinjumae, Shibuya-ku. Subway C03 (Map VIII A2). ✆03-3400-4044. Open noon–1.30pm, 5.30–10pm. Closed Sun.* The chef always chooses the best seasonal produce. For those who love raw fish, this is the best restaurant in the capital. Note the number of covers is limited. **Michelin Guide Tokyo Yokohama Kamakura 2011 Selection**.

## TAKING A BREAK

**Cafes – THC (Cafe Liberté)** カフェリベルテ *THC Bldg, 6-16-23 Jingumae, Shibuya-ku. JR Harajuku station (Map VIII A2). ✆03-5778-2083. www.tokyohipstersclub.com.* On the 2nd floor of a cube-shaped concrete building is a cafe with a small, green terrace *(individual dishes ¥1,000, lunch ¥1,300).Menu in English.*

**Cafe-hairdresser – Cafe Nalu** ナルーカフェ *1 F MM Bldg, 4-9-2 Jingumae, Shibuya-ku. Subway C04 (Map VIII B2). ✆03-5786-1781.* An example of the cafe-hairdresser formula, very fashionable in Harajuku. On the ground floor you take tea; in the basement, you have your face done.

**Cafe-gallery – Watarium** ワタリウム *3-7-6 Jingumae, Shibuya-ku. Subway G03 (Map VIII B1). ✆03-3402-3001.* Built by Mario Botta, this is an art gallery, art bookstore, stationery store, and cafe. Take your pick.

**Japanese Patisserie – Torindo** 桃林堂 *3-6-12 Kita-Aoyama, Minato-ku. Subway G02 (Map VIII B2). ✆03-3400-8703. 10am–8pm (Wed 9pm).* Traditional pastries, preserved fruits, and vegetables (ginger, carrot, lotus, mushroom, and celery). All delightful to look at, and all delicious.

## NIGHTLIFE

**Clubs & Bars – Bar Shizen** シゼン *2 F, 2-28-5 Sendagaya, Shibuya-ku. JR Harajuku station. Open Mon–Fri 6–10.30pm, Sat–Sun 7pm–2am. ✆03-3746-1334.* The bar is owned by a fashion designer. During the day it's a store where his creations are displayed. At 7pm they're put to one side and hey presto, it's a bar with some fine bottles of wine!

**Le Sang des Poètes – La boîte noire Bldg** ルサンデポエット *4 F, 2-3-26 Jingumae, Shibuya-ku. Subway G03. Open Tue–Sat 6pm–1am, Sun 3–10pm. Closed Mon & public holidays. ✆03-5751-5598.* This tiny bar is on the top floor of a narrow black building, almost invisible at night but for the name in red neon lights. Access is via an external spiral staircase. The intimate atmosphere seems popular with locals.

**The Camel** ザキャメル – *2-5-1 Nishi-Azabu, Minato-ku. Subway G02. Open Mon–Thu & Sun 11.30am–midnight (Fri–Sat 2am). ✆03-3498-1217.* The small lights dangling in the window promise a light, relaxed atmosphere. Beer, cocktails, shochu, plum brandy, wine. Simple, inexpensive dishes (rice, pasta, etc.) if you want a light meal.

**Jazz Club – Blue Note Tokyo** ブルーノート東京 *6-3-16 Minami-Aoyama, Minato-ku, along Kotto-dori and left at Papas Cafe. Subway C04, exit B3. Open Mon–Sat 5.30pm–1am, Sun & public holidays 5pm–12.30am. Reservations suggested. ✆03-5485-0088.* An ever-increasing reputation guaranteed by the greatest American and European artists. *Concert prices start at ¥7,000.*

## SHOPPING

**Design Festa** デザイン・フェスタ – *3-20-18, Jingumae, Shibuya-ku. www.designfesta.com. Open 11am–8pm.* In this store a dozen rooms on several floors display the craziest experiments: whether successful or useless, they're a joyful tribute to creativity, and it does you the world of good.

# ODAIBA

## TRANSPORTATION

### GETTING AROUND ODAIBA

**On the Yurikamome monorail** – *See p162.*

**BY FERRY** – Less futuristic than the Yurikamome Line, it's nevertheless a spectacular way to approach Odaiba. Asakusa–Odaiba (Odaiba Kaihin-koen station): *out 10.10am, 1.20pm & 3.20pm, return 12.10pm, 2.15pm exc. 2nd Tue & Wed in month (exc. Aug). 50–60min. ¥1,520.*

View of Mount Fuji from Mount Takao
©Yasufumi Nishi/JNTO

**Hinode Pier–Odaiba** (Odaiba Kaihin-koen station): *out 10.10am–4.45pm, return 10.45 am–5.15pm. ¥460.*

**Hinode Pier–Odaiba** (Palette Town and Tokyo Big Sight): *Wed–Sun exc. public holidays. Out 10am–5pm (some services do not go via Palette Town and stop at Tokyo Big Sight); return 10.35am–5.35pm (departs from Tokyo Big Sight), 1.25am–5.25pm (departs from Palette Town). ¥400.*

**Hinode Pier–Odaiba** (Museum of Maritime Science): *Wed–Mon. Out 10am, 1pm & 3pm, return 12.30pm, 2.30pm & 4.30pm. ¥400.*

## STAY

**Nikko ホテル日航東京** *1-9-1 Daiba, Minato-ku (Map IX A2). 03-5500-5500. www.hnt.co.jp. 452 rooms*. Convenient for Haneda Airport and Tokyo Disney Resort, this Odaiba hotel is two minutes walk from the nearest metro station and shopping mall. For a magical experience, especially if you are in the market for a little romance, bear in mind that the Nikko describes itself as the "balcony of Tokyo". One look at the truly breathtaking **views** it has to offer over Tokyo Bay and the Rainbow Bridge, and you'll understand why. A real fairytale moment. **Michelin Guide Tokyo Yokohama Kamakura 2011 Selection.**

# AROUND TOKYO

## EAT

### NAKANO

**Budoka 武道家** *Nakano station, Higashiguchi, 985ft/ 300m to the right on Nakano-dori. 03-3229-9390. 11am–3pm, 4pm–11pm.* Having had a moment to enjoy the delightful Ghibli Museum, you will find that this little ramen restaurant, just two stations after Kichojoji, is well worth a stop. It is easy on the budget too, offering a dish of ramen for only ¥700, followed by all the rice you can eat for only ¥50, to dip in the soup. Ask at the counter for the delicious *koime* flavor of soupyou will find it makes for an especially satisfying lunch.

### MOUNT TAKAO

**Ukai Toriyama うかい鳥山** *3426 Minami-Asakawa. Takaosanguchi station (Map I A3, off map). 04-2661-0739. Open 11am–8pm, Sun 11am–8.30pm.* Free shuttle buses between Takaosanguchi station and the restaurant a few miles away. Composed of several traditional thatched roof houses, it nestles beneath the foliage of a lush valley near Mount Takao. The exquisite food is elegantly presented, putting the ideal finishing touch to a walk on Mount Takao.

# South of Tokyo★★

- **Population:** Yokohama: 3,704,626, Kamakura: 172,017.
- **Michelin Map:** Principal Sights Map B3 – Regional Map p119.
- **Location:** 15.5mi/25km south of Tokyo, Yokohama is the principal city in Kanagawa prefecture. Kamakura is 15.5mi/25km farther south, 31mi/50km from Tokyo.
- **Kids:** The **view** from the Landmark Tower and a visit to *Nippon Maru*.
- **Timing:** Allow a full day, leaving Tokyo early in the morning and finishing with dinner in the Chinese quarter, returning late evening.
- **Don't miss:** In Yokohama, the Yamate district and the garden of Sankei-en; Chinatown and its temple in the early evening. In Kamakura, the temples and shrines, particularly in Kita-Kamakura early in the morning.

**Although the cities of Yokohama and Kamakura are relatively close geographically, situated 15.5mi/25km and 31mi/50km south of Tokyo respectively, they are surprisingly different to each other. This distinction can be traced back to their diverse histories. In the course of establishing early relations with the West, Yokohama built the largest industrial port in the country, while some eight centuries earlier, Kamakura, witnessed the creation of Japan's first military government. Hence, while Yokohama is a large cosmopolitan city with a sprinkling of western buildings and a substantial foreign community, Kamakura is a small, quiet town with many historic shrines and temples.**

## YOKOHAMA★ 横浜

**A Bit of History** – Yokohama really started to flourish after the Treaty of Kanagawa was signed in 1854 (*see box opposite*). Five years later, the port was opened and its seafront area divided, one section being reserved for foreigners, while the second, the Japanese area, divided into five districts called Yokohama-cho. A century and a half later (it celebrated its 150th anniversary in 2009), Yokohama is the largest port in the country *(60,000 cargo boats per year)* and the second largest city, with a population of 3.6 million. Located closed to Tokyo, it's now part of the Tokyo conurbation. The *salarymen* who commute from Yokohama into the capital each day are too numerous to count and the Chinese community here is the largest in Japan, yet Yokohama has lost nothing of its original character.

Although the city is constantly changing, the museums are a constant reminder of its identity. Being a port, the presence of a Maritime Museum is not unusual, but the Silk Museum may seem a little out of kilter until you realize that silk is the commodity on which the city built its fortune. Yokohama was quick to learn from Western models of modernity.

A walk across town will reveal how its physical character changes, from the picturesque late-19C houses nestling on Yamate hill, to Minato Mirai 21, with its futuristic, forward-looking architecture. Yokohama can be divided into four homogeneous districts: **Yamate** ("The Bluff"—a hill), where many foreigners once resided; **Kannai**, the historic port and central, government district; **Chinatown**; and **Minato Mirai 21**, the futuristic face of Yokohama.

### YAMATE AND MOTOMACHI DISTRICT★★ 山手・元町

*Map B2 off map. 2min walk from Ishikawa-cho station, south exit.*

**Motomachi**, an elegant shopping street that developed when Westerners settled in this residential district, leads to Yamate hill on the southeast side of the downtown area. At the northeast end of the street a wooded promontory marks the beginning of the Yamate district. From there, paths wind up the hillside to **Harbour View Park**, which offers an excellent **view** over the port and the bay. Nearby, you'll find the Yokohama British House and the **Foreigners' Cemetery** *(open Tue–Sun 10am–5pm)*, where 4,500 people representing some 40 different nationalities are buried. Note that some of the tombs are not without a touch of humor or *post mortem* professional loyalty—a former railway engineer, Edmond Morel, for example, has a headstone shaped like a train ticket. As you stroll along the road running beside the cemetery *(Yamate-Hon-dori)*, you'll see a dozen or so houses, some of them resembling small, English country-manor residences that occupy pride of place amid charming gardens, evidence of the arrival of Westerners in the late-19C. Most were rebuilt after the 1923 earthquake and now seven of them house temporary exhibitions and small museums full of atmosphere. The **Tin Toy Museum** *(open 9.30am–6pm; ¥200)* has more than 3,000 small-scale models dating from 1890 to 1960. The **Yamate Museum** *(open 11am–4pm; ¥150)*, built in 1909, is the only house that remained intact.

Also worth seeing in the nearby Italian Garden is the **Diplomat's House** and **Bluff 18 Ban-Kan**. There is also a museum dedicated to tennis—the **Yokohama Yamate Museum of Tennis**. The first tennis court in Japan was installed in **Yamate Park** in 1876.

*From here you can head forward to Chinatown on the other side of the Nakamura River.*

### The Treaty of Kanagawa

Commodore Perry's fleet moored in Edo Bay in July 1853. The US naval officer was carrying a letter from the American President, requesting that the shogun of Edo open up diplomatic and commercial relations between the two countries. On March 31, 1854, the Japanese signed the Treaty of Kanagawa with the United States. It brought an end to the political isolationism observed by Japan since 1637. Not only was the treaty to have a profound impact on Japanese society, it was also to discredit the shogun government in the eyes of its vassals, who were divided on which path to follow. The modernization sought by the Meiji state was under way. It proved fatal to shogun authority.

## Sankei-en★★ 三渓園

*Map B2, off map.*
*58-1 Sannotani Honmoku, Naka-ku. From JR Negishi station, bus 58, 99, 101, Honmaku stop, then 5min walk, or Minato Mirai bus 8. Open 9am–5pm. ¥500. www.sankeien.or.jp.*

Until 1906 the "third valley" (or "Sankei-en") was the property of a silk merchant, Hara Tomitaro. This traditional Japanese-style garden *(43.2 acre/17.5ha)* is divided into two areas: the external garden, which includes a three-tier pagoda, brought from the Tomyo-ji temple in Kyoto (1475), and a traditional house from the Hida region (the famous gassho-zukuri with roofs "like hands joined in prayer," *see p250*); and the internal garden, with a beautiful pavilion dating to the beginning of the Edo era (the *Rinshunkaku*).

However, it's not the buildings but the garden itself, shaped into a variety of evocative, sweet-smelling landscapes, that attracts some 500,000 visitors a year. *Visit early in the morning, if possible.*

## KANNAI DISTRICT 関内

*Map B2.*

Kannai literally means "inside the barrier," as there used to be a barrier separating the houses occupied by foreigners from the municipal administrative buildings occupied by the Japanese.

YOKOHAMA

Ramen Museum

WHERE TO STAY

| Navios Yokohama | ① |
| New Grand Hotel | ③ |
| Oimatsu Ryokan | ⑤ |
| Royal Park Hotel | ⑦ |
| San-Ai Yokohama | ⑨ |
| Yokohama Hostel Village | ⑪ |

WHERE TO EAT

| El Ella | ① |
| Kisoji | ③ |
| Ootoya | ⑤ |
| Q's Dinner | ⑦ |
| Rinka-en | ⑨ |
| Seiko-Enn | ⑪ |

© 2009 Cartographic data Shobunsha/Michelin

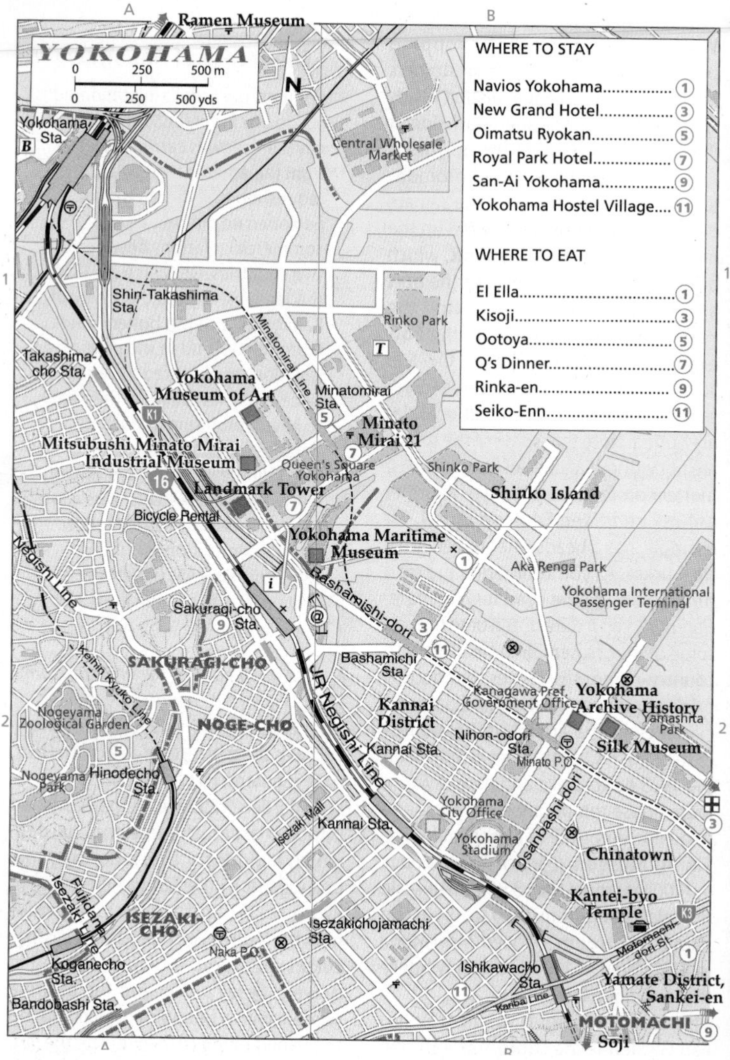

## Yokohama Archives of History
横浜開港資料館

*Map B2.*

*3 Nihon-Odori, Naka-ku.* ○*Open Tue–Sun 9.30am–5pm.* ⊚*¥200.*

This museum, a must for anyone interested in the moment when not just Yokohama but also the whole of Japan opened up to the outside world, is housed in the building where the Treaty of Kanagawa was signed. With more than 200,000 historical pieces dating from the Edo era through to the beginning of the Showa era, it provides a fascinating glim-

pse back in time with the aid of maps, models (ships, buildings, etc.), newspapers of the day, prints, photographs, postcards, and miscellaneous objects.

Since most of the official archives disappeared in the 1923 earthquake or the 1945 bombing raids, the fact that this collection has been assembled is all the more remarkable. In the reading room you can see copies of early Japanese newspapers.

The tree in the inner courtyard is said to be a descendant of the tabunoki incense tree that features in most contemporary

### Japanese silk aids France

In the middle of the 19C the Second French Empire's economy was based on a textile industry that was a world leader in silkworm-breeding and the silk trade. However, between 1855 and 1860, two infections—nosema disease and flacherie—threatened to ruin France's silk industry. The French representative in Edo confirmed that the Japanese silkworm industry was able to compensate for the shortages in France. The archipelago became a much sought-after partner, and continued to be so until the early 20C. From 1860 onward, Duchesne de Bellecourt helped to establish the first merchants from Lyon in Nagasaki and Yokohama. Louis Bourret set up a spinning activity in the international concession of Yokohama. Raw silk from Japan, which was of better quality than silk from China, enabled the silk manufacturers of Lyon to maintain their premier position in the world silk trade.

depictions of the arrival of Commodore Perry and his men.

## Silk Museum シルク博物館

*Map B2.*

*Silk Center, 2F, 1 Yamashita-cho, Naka-ku, not far from the Yokohama Archives of History. Subway: Kannai. Open Tue–Sun 9am–4.30pm. ¥500. www.silkmuseum.or.jp.*

Despite its rather outdated presentation, this museum explains the history of silk and how it is made, from silkworm to the creation of a kimono. It takes between 3,000 and 9,000 silkworm cocoons to make a kimono, depending on size, complexity of design, the fullness of the sleeves, and accessories (*obi* [sash], etc.); each cocoon provides around 4,265ft/1,300m of raw silk. You will also find out how the port of Yokohama became so important for the silk trade. Finally, temporary exhibitions compare the different silk production of other countries: Laos, Uzbekistan, etc.

## CHINATOWN★★ 中華街

*Map B2.*

*To reach Chinatown from the Silk Museum, walk down Osanbashi-dori (10min walk). Subway: Motomachi-Chugakai. www.chinatown.or.jp.*

Like many of the world's ports, Yokohama has a Chinese community: the city was one of the first Japanese ports to open up commercially, and this, together with the subsequent dynamism of its commercial activities, was attractive to those Chinese forced to flee political upheavals in their own country. Another factor was that, not used dealing with the Japanese, Western merchants used *compradore* as interme-

*Chinatown*

© Tibor Bognar/Photononstop

diaries. These were natives of Shanghai who, following the Treaty of Nanking in 1842, aided Western traders in China. This activity developed over the years as Yokohama's influence spread and is today supported by China's rise in strength in international relations.

Chinatown is now a small, prosperous district that attracts impressive numbers of people to its 200 or so restaurants every weekend. In the middle of its narrow, bustling streets, the **Kantei-byo** Chinese temple *(open daily 9am–7pm; no charge)*, richly decorated under its three baroque and rococo-style roofs, shimmers and gleams like a finely-cut ruby with thousands of golden lights shining beneath a bestiary of dragons and octopuses. It's dedicated to Guan Yu, a military hero and former Han general, recognizable by his red face. Deified as the god of war, he now guarantees his popularity with the people by also protecting the temple's riches.

## MINATO MIRAI 21★★
## みなとみらい21

*Map B1.*

*JR Sakuragicho station.*

The solid, but futuristic-looking **Landmark Tower★★** *A1*, is the landmark of Yokohama's equally futuristic seafront. Measuring some 971ft/296m, the tower houses one of the highest observation decks *(Sky Garden)* in Japan

*Landmark Tower*

© Luciano Lepre/Tips/Photononstop

*(895.7ft/273m)* and probably one of the fastest elevators; it shoots skyward at a speed of 2,460.6ft/750m per min so that you reach the Sky Garden in 40 seconds! *(open Jul–Sept Sun–Fri 10am–9pm, Sat 10am–10pm; ¥1,000)*. Close by is the inevitable shopping mall, the **Landmark Plaza,** with an interesting bookshop *(Yurindo)* on the fifth floor.

### Mitsubishi Minato Mirai Industrial Museum

三菱みなとみらい技術館 *Map A1.*

*Behind the Landmark Tower, cross Keyaki-dori. Open Tue–Sun 10am–5.30pm. ¥300. www.mhi.co.jp/e_museum.*

"To help young people launch themselves into the future more successfully" are the words chosen by Mitsubishi to explain the opening of this museum in 1994 on its former industrial site. Its six themed areas *(Space, Ocean, Transport, New Technology, etc.)* take the visitor into a 3D virtual world. The simulated helicopter flight is one of the most popular attractions.

### Yokohama Museum of Art

横浜美術館

*Map A1.*

*3-4-1 Minato Mirai, Nishi-ku, opposite the previous museum. Subway: Minato-mirai. Open Fri–Wed 10am–6pm. ¥500. www.yaf.or.jp.*

This impressive museum of modern art and photography, designed by architect Tange Kenzo (*see p 162*), hosts top-quality temporary exhibitions, with a few recurring themes such as the beautiful sculptures by Isamu Noguchi (1904–88), who worked in the studios of Brancusi.

### Yokohama Maritime Museum★

横浜マリタイムミュージアム

*Map A–B2.*

*Opposite the Landmark Tower. Open Tue–Sun 10am–5pm. ¥600, including Nippon Maru.*

The museum is right next door to the *Nippon Maru* moored at quay no.1, a truly beautiful sight when her sails are hoisted. The lack of information in English makes a visit to the main museum rather frustrating. Topics cover the history of the Japanese Merchant Navy and include a fine collection of models.

The visit continues on board the **Nippon Maru★** *(where there is English labelling)*, which served as a training ship for 50 years, but has formed part of the museum since 1984. The entire ship is open to be explored.

## YOKOHAMA ENVIRONS

### Soji-ji★ 總持寺 *B2 off map.*

*2-1-1 Tsurumi, Tsurumi ward. 6min walk from JR Keihin Tohoku Line, Tsurumi station, west exit. Open Tue–Sun 10am–4pm. www.daihonzan-sohjiji.or.jp. Small booklet in English.*

The main headquarters of the Soto sect and one of the principal Zen schools in Japan *(see box p195)*, this temple has 40 or so buildings, mostly constructed in the early 20C. Built in 1966, the spectacular Daisodo, the Great Hall of the founders, has a floor covered in 1,000 tatami mats.

Two hundred monks live in Soji-ji, a vibrant community where the youngest are tasked with cleaning the floor of the corridor *(Ichimonji Roka)* twice a day, while practicing *zokin-gake*.

This involves running nonstop to the end of the corridor—a distance of 1,968.5ft/600m—while polishing the floor with a cloth wrapped around the arms; breath control in difficult postures is an integral part of Zen discipline.

Try not to miss the Room of the Purple Clouds *(Shi-untai)*, a reception room with panels painted by the best artists of the Taisho era (1912–26), reserved for important visitors.

### Ramen Museum

新横浜ラーメンミュージアム

*A1, off map 2-14-21. Shin-Yokohama, Kohoku. Subway: Shin-Yokohama. Open 11am–11pm. ¥300.*

In a replica Tokyo street from the 1960s learn about the history of ramen *(pronounced lamen)*, wheat noodles from China. You can also sample different qualities and regional varieties.

## KAMAKURA★★ 鎌倉

*Map p193.*

Surrounded by mountains on three sides, the only escape route from this town *(population 173,000)* is across a steel blue sea fringed with dark sand. Was it the limited horizon that compelled the population of this ancient village of storehouses *(kura)* and scythes *(kama)* to build more than 60 religious buildings? The answer lies in an all-too-obvious paradox: it was precisely the military society created by the 12C shogunate and the *bushi* (warrior) way of life that turned Kamakura into a breeding ground for Zen Buddhism. The town is one hour's journey from Tokyo and a paradise for surfers in Sagami Bay.

**A Bit of History** – Kamakura, the capital city of **Minamoto no Yoritomo** (1147–99), the first Kamakura shogun, forcefully entered the history books in 1192. The city even secured a place in the wider history of Japan, although the Kamakura era (1192–1333) was a relatively short period (only 141 years) in the eyes of the shogunate, which endured for centuries. When Yoritomo died, his direct descendants (his son Yoriie was assassinated) were ousted one by one by the Hojo, the seigneurial family of Taira ancestry. The Hojo promptly seized the reins of power and ruled as regents *(shikken)*. For more than a century, nine Hojo *shikken* ruled in turn, pulling the strings of power that supposedly rested in the hands of shoguns chosen from the descendants first of the Fujiwara and then of the Imperial princes.

During the same period (in 1274 and 1281), Japan was twice almost taken over by the Mongols in invasions repelled at high cost by a warrior class that considered itself subsequently poorly rewarded. Their discontent forced Emperor Go-Daigo (1288–1339) into forming a coalition aimed at restoring Imperial power.

With the aid of Ashikaga Takauji (1305–58), the descendant of a loyal vassal of Yorimoto, Kogen (the puppet Emperor installed by the Regents) was driven

Bamboo forest, Hokoku-ji

© JNTO

from Kyoto. Upon this, the lord Nitta Yoshisada (1301–38), Go-Daigo's most charismatic asset, conquered Kamakura. In 1333, the Kamakura era came to an end, when warlord Nitta Yoshisada sacked the town to re-establish Imperial rule.

*Allow at least 2 days for visiting the town.*

## CENTRAL DISTRICT

### Tsurugaoka Hachiman-gu★

鶴岡八幡宮 *B1.*

*15min walk from Kamakura station, east exit. Open 6am–8.30pm. ¥200. No charge.*

Three large *torii* (gates) mark out the attractive **avenue of cherry trees★** *(Wakamiya-oji)*, which extends for almost 4,921.3ft/1,500m to this important Shinto shrine. The trees were planted at Yoritomo's request to honor the *kami* and thus improve his wife's chances of conceiving.

The shrine was founded in 1063 by Yoriyoshi (grandfather of the Minamoto clan) in tribute to Emperor Ojin Himegami. It was moved by Yoritomo to the center of Kamakura, which had been occupied by the future shogun in 1180 *(see box p194)*. Most of the buildings were rebuilt in the Momoyama era, and then again in 1823. Yoritomo's wife, Masako, designed the three bridges that lead to a vast esplanade where you will find the **maidono** or dance pavilion, famous for once having reverberated under the feet of Shizuka, Yoshitsune's mistress. Shizuka was forced to dance to make her reveal the hiding place of her lover to Yoshitsune's half-brother, Yorimoto. Thirsting for absolute power, Yorimoto forced Yoshitsune and his entire family to commit *seppuku*. In the upper part of the shrine at the top of the steps, the *kamino miya* is home to the Tsurugaoka Hachiman-gua **National Treasure Museum** *(open Tue–Sun 9am–4.30pm; ¥200)*. It contains objects of worship and *mikoshi* (portable shrines). The shrine's annual celebration is on September 15, followed by an archery contest on horseback *(yabusame)* on the 16th.

### Hokoku-jia★★★ 報国寺

*Map C2.*

*2-7-4 Jomyo-ji. Bus 23 from Kamakura station, 6th stop, Jomyo-ji. Temple and Garden: Open 9am–4pm, Meditation Pavilion: Open Sun 7am–10.30am. ¥200.*

This Zen temple belongs to the Kencho-ji temple of the Rinzai sect. It was founded in 1334 by Tengan Eko (1273–1335) to honor the memory of Ashikaga Ietoki, grandfather of Ashikaga Takauji.

Apart from some beautiful **sculptures of the Buddha★★** (14C) executed by sculptor Takuma Hogen and others *(in the central building and annex)*, the temple's attraction lies mainly in its **forest of bamboos★★**, which includes some 2,000 moso bamboos, the largest species of this woody plant. *Matcha* tea is available in the adjoining pavilion *(¥500)*.

### Sugimoto-dera★★

杉本寺

*Map C2.*

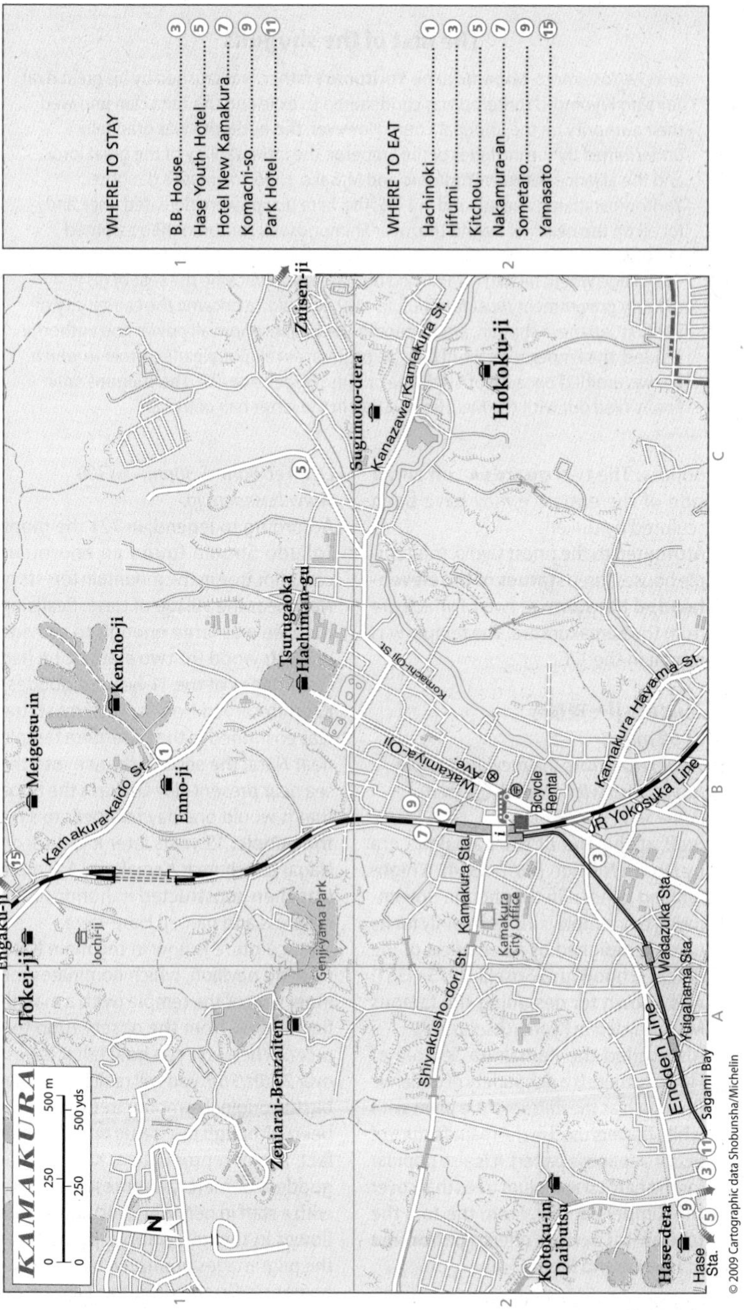


*On Kanazawa Kamakura St., 10min walk back toward Kamakura. Open 8am–4.30pm. ¥200.*

The oldest temple in Kamakura (734) is accessed via a magnificent flight of worn, moss-covered steps flanked by white flags bearing the name of the

### The first of the shoguns

In 1159, Yoshimoto, **Minamoto no Yoritomo**'s father, was crushed by his great rival Taira no Kiyomori. Yoritomo was condemned to exile and the Taira clan imposed their authority on the Imperial Court. However, this authority was gradually undermined by the intrigues of the Emperor, the intractability of the great lords, and the alliance between Yoritomo and Masako, Hojo Tokimasa's daughter. Yoritomo initiated a revolt and in 1185, the Taira troops were defeated once and for all on the beach of Danno Ura, near Shimonoseki. Yoritomo then assumed the title of *sei i taishogun* ("generalissimo who subdues the barbarians") and the village where he had established his base camp became the seat of his first military government *(bakufu)*. Thus, in 1192, Kamakura became the capital city of the first Japanese shogun, a commander-in-chief in whom all power and authority resided; the Emperor retained only his position as religious leader, a role to which he was entitled because of his divine origins *(see box p195)*. The shoguns only finally died out with the Meiji Restoration in the latter half of the 19C.

donors. The two **guards★** on either side of the entrance may have been sculpted by Unkei.

Attributed to the priest Gyoki, this temple houses three **statues of the eleven-headed Kannon★★**, two of which are from the Kamakura era. The temple was rebuilt in the 17C.

## Zuisen-ji★ 瑞泉寺

*C1 off map.*

*20min walk from the previous temple (signposted with arrows). Open 9am–5pm. ¥200.*

Built at the end of the Kamakura era by Do-un Nikaido (1267–1334), a high-ranking general in the shogun government, this temple is visited mainly for its garden, designed by a Zen priest of the Rinzai schoolMuso Soseki (1275–1351) was known for designing the famous Moss Garden in Kyoto *(see p 314)*.

Also called the Kamakura Temple of Flowers, there is a rich variety of endemic flora such as the *mitsumata*, a plant with white flowers used in the manufacture of *washi* (Japanese paper). It is also popular for the narcissi and plum trees that cover the Kimpei-san hill. From the top, the **Ichiran-tei** pavilion offers a **panorama** of Hakone and Mount Fuji.

## HASE DISTRICT 長谷

## Hase-dera★★ 長谷寺

*Map A2.*

*3-11-2 Hase. 5min walk from Hase station. Open Mar–Sept 8am–5pm; Oct–Feb 8am–5.30pm. ¥300. www.hasedera.jp.*

According to legend, in 721 the monk Tokudo Shonin found an enormous camphor tree in the mountain forests of Nara near the village of Hase. Realizing the tree was large enough to provide enough wood for two statues, he had two images of the 11-headed goddess Kannon carved from it. The first statue was enshrined in the Hase-dera temple near Nara; the second thrown into the sea near present-day Osaka in the hope that it would one day reappear to save the people. 15 years later it did so, on Nagai beach near Kamakura. A temple was then constructed in honor of the goddess and named Hase-dera.

The sculpture is now in the main **Kannon-do** pavilion, which dominates the inner part of the temple (with a magnificent **view** from the observation terrace). When you see how tall it is *(just over 29.5ft/9m)*, you will realize just how big the original camphor tree must have been, although the statue on show is, in fact, a later reproduction. Kannon, the goddess of mercy, is represented here with a staff in her right hand and a lotus flower in the leftsymbols, perhaps, of the pilgrimages prompted by her reappearance. On the right the **Amida-do** houses the seated statue of Yakuyoke, who guards against evil spirits. The golden statue, almost 9.8ft/3m high, was paid for by Yoritomo. On your way back, don't miss the **jizo-do** where Fukuju Jizo

*Kannon-do, Hase-dera*

© Bertrand Gardel/hemis.fr

(the *jizo, or* bodhisattva, of happiness) is enshrined. The temple is surrounded by thousands of small stone *jizo*. A little farther down, the **Benten-Kutsu** cave is dedicated to the goddess of the sea.

## Kotoku-in and Daibutsu★

高徳院・鎌倉大仏

*Map A2.*

*Going N from the Hase-dera. Open Apr–Sept 7am–6pm; Oct–Mar 7am–5.30pm. ¥200.*

When Yoritomo's wife ordered the construction of a large statue of the **Buddha**★★ *(Daibutsu)* at this Buddhist temple, she modeled it on the great, gilt bronze statue of the Vairocana Buddha of the Todai-ji in Nara. Five years later, the wooden statue was destroyed by a typhoon. In 1252, it was replaced by this 125-ton bronze statue, 37.1ft/11.31m high, which was originally covered in gold leaf. The *jobon-josho mudra*—hands with upturned palms—allows the highest level of enlightenment to be achieved, which is evident when you gaze into its half-closed eyes, which are almost 3.3ft/1m across.

## Zeniarai-Benzaiten★★

銭洗弁財天

*Map A1.*

*Follow the arrows from the previous temple (20min walk). Open 8am–5pm. No charge.*

An unusual and atmospheric place, with just the *torii* (gates) set into a rocky wall to betray its existence to the outside world.

### Simplicity and subversion

**Zen**, the Japanese form of *Chan* (the Chinese school opposed to all forms of indoctrination and religious creeds, instead concentrating on direct experience and what comes from within), was brought to Japan from China by two monks of the **Tendai** Buddhist school. The first monk, **Eisai** (1141–1215), founder of the **Rinzai** branch, advocated an experimental approach to meditation, blending humor, paradox, and physical and mental challenges in the form of beatings and riddles *(koan)*. The second monk, **Dogen** (1200–53), author of the *Fukanzazengi (General Recommendations Concerning the Practice of the Way)* established the **Soto** school, which teaches the *zazen* seated method of meditation. The aim of both is to lead the pupil to the *satori*, the awakening. These simple practices were encouraged by the shogun authorities because they were contrary to the way the Emperor exercised religious authority. Although of divine origin, the Emperor relied on complex rituals to raise him above the uneducated and therefore ignorant masses.

Passing through the gates leading into a tunnel, you emerge in a large, open space carved out of the rock containing a beautiful shrine. At the back of a hidden cave there's a lovely freshwater spring, which, according to legend, the serpent goddess Ugajin revealed to the shogun Minamoto Yoritomo on the day of the serpent, in the month of the serpent, in the year of the serpent. From the cave, you can rush off to pray at one of the many small altars dedicated to the goddess, and also to the goddess of wealth. The tradition is that if you wash your coins in the water (and even your notes, drying them carefully in the curling fumes of the incense burners), your money will be doubled.

## KITA-KAMAKURA 北鎌倉

### Engaku-ji★★ 円覚寺 *B1 off map.*

*5min walk from Kita-Kamakura station. Open Apr–Oct 8am–5pm; Nov–Mar 8am–4pm. ¥300.*

Kamikaze, which literally means "divine wind," was the name given to the typhoons that destroyed the Mongolian fleet on its way to invade Japan. Later, the name was adopted by Japanese pilots, who carried out suicide attacks toward the end of World War II. This Zen temple was built by Hojo Tokimune (1251–84), the eighth regent *(shikken)* and military governor of Kamakura, to pay tribute to the Japanese and Mongolians who perished during the two invasion attempts of the Mongolian chief Kublai Khan in 1274 and 1281. It contains examples of both *kato mado* (bell-shaped windows) and *sankarado* (wooden latticework), two characteristic features of Zen temples. Though badly damaged in the 1923 earthquake, most of it was later rebuilt.

The main attraction is the **Reliquary** *(Shari-den)*, which is reputed to contain a tooth of the Buddha.

Karate enthusiasts may also like to pay a visit to the tomb of Funakoshi Gichin (1868–1957), the founder of this martial art (*see p108*).

### Tokei-ji★★★ 東慶寺 *Map B1.*

*273yd/250m from Kita-Kamakura station and 5min walk from Engaku-ji, back down Kamakura-kaido. Open Mar–Oct 8.30am–5pm; Nov–Feb 8.30am–4pm. ¥100. www.tokeiji.com.*

Following the death of her husband, Hojo Tokimune, Kakusan-ni withdrew from the world as tradition demanded of a widow. This withdrawal was, however, into the temple that she founded after her husband's death. Thus it was that in 1285, one of the first Japanese nunneries appeared. Although women had few rights, the Tokei-ji managed to obtain extraterritorial status with legal privileges from the shogun government, in particular the right for a woman to divorce her husband provided she had lived in the temple for three years. As a result it became known as the "Divorce Temple." The privilege lasted until the Meiji reforms of 1873, when women were granted the right to divorce.

Walking in the **garden**★★ of this Buddhist temple is a real delight. The cherry,

Engaku-ji

View of Tokei-ji
© JTB/Photoshot

apricot, and peach trees, peonies, and irises all form a wonderful picture at different times of year. The **Treasure House★** *(Matsugaoka Hozo) (open Tue–Sun 10am–3pm)* contains a fine wooden statue of **Sho Kannon Bosatsu Ryuzo★★**. Its clay halo *(do-mon)* was made using a mold engraved with floral designs, a technique that was unique to Kamakura.

There are also some fine **Darumas** *(round, hollow dolls with no arms or legs, representations of Bodhidharma, the founder of Zen)* by the priest Hakuin (1685–1768), as well as the famous **Mikudari-han**, which literally means "three and a half lines": divorce letters given to wives by husbands signifying their agreement to the divorce. A copy was also registered in the temple.

## Meigetsu-in★★ 明月院 *Map B1.*

*5min walk from Tokei-ji. Open Jun 8.30am–5pm; Jul–May 9am–4pm. ¥300.*

Meigetsu-in, the "Bright Moon Hermitage," was founded in 1160 by Yamanouchi Tsunetoshi as a place of rest for the soul of his father, Toshimichi, who died in the Battle of Heiji (1159) while fighting the Minamoto and Taira clans. The site was taken over by Hojo Tokiyori (1227–63), fifth regent of Kamakura, who turned it into a Buddhist temple when he retired. A **dry landscape garden** and beds of irises can be seen through the round doorway of the main building. The tombs are hollowed out of the rock walls, thus leaving space outside for meditation.

## Kencho-ji★★ 建長寺 *Map B1.*

*10min walk from the Meigetsu-in via Kamakura-kaido. Open 8.30am–4.30pm. ¥300.*

Founded by the regent Hojo Tokiyori, this temple bears the name of the period (Kencho, 1249–55) in which it was completed. The first and biggest Zen temple in Kamakura, it was built by the priest Rankei Doryu, a Chinese master who came to Japan to teach Zen.

The complex used to have almost 50 secondary temples, but only a dozen or so remain. Of particular interest is the *bonsho* **temple bell**, cast in 1255 and now classified as a National Treasure. On the other side of the San-mon *(gate)* are **juniper trees** over 700 years old.

The *Butsuden* (Buddha hall) contains an unusual image of the **Jizo Bosatsu,** protector of criminals. The *Hatto* (lecture hall) ceiling was painted by Koizumi Junsaku. The pond was designed by Muso Soseki (1275–1351) in the shape of the ideogram for "spirit."

## Enno-ji★ 円応寺

*Map B1.*

*Opposite Kencho-ji.*

*Open 9am–4pm. ¥200.*

The main feature of this small temple is the statue of Enma *(Yama in Sanskrit)*, the Hindu god of death and hell, more than 750 years old, with a fierce expression. There is also a fine selection of bodhisattvas made of clay.

## YOKOHAMA PRACTICAL INFORMATION

### USEFUL INFORMATION

**Tourist Offices** – **Sakuragicho station** *(A2) (open 9am–7pm)*, **Yokohama station** *(open 9am–7pm)*, and **Shinyokohama station** *(Open 10am–6pm)*. All have information in English.

**Bank/Foreign Exchange** – **Citibank**, *Yokohama station (A1). Open 9am–3pm.* Currency exchange, travelers checks, etc.

**Post Office/Withdrawals** – *1-1 Sakuragi-cho (A2). Open 9am–6pm. ATM at entrance and post office services on 3rd floor.*

**The Bluff Medical and Dental Clinic** – **Medical Clinic**, *82 Yamate-cho, Naka-Ku (B2), ℘045-641-6961. Open 9am–5pm. English-speaking doctors.*

### TRANSPORTATION

**BY TRAIN** – **Yokohama Station** *(A1)* – Take the subway to Sakuragicho station and Minato Mirai 21 central district. Two lines link the Tokyo airports to Yokohama: the Narita Express Line departs from Narita *(90min, ¥4,180)* and the Keihin-Kyuko Line departs from Haneda *(20min, ¥470)*. The Tokaido Line *(28min, ¥450)*, Yokosuka Line *(31min, ¥450)*, and Keihin Tohoku Line *(40min, ¥450)* all depart from Tokyo station.

**BY BUS** – **Limousine Bus Company** – Departs from Narita International Airport *(90min, ¥3,500)* and Haneda Airport *(30min, ¥560)*.

### GETTING AROUND

**ON FOOT** – Follow the **Kaiko Promenade** linking the main downtown sites – *a harborside route indicated by circular plaques set in the ground.*

**BY SUBWAY** – There are two subway lines: blue *(connecting Shonandai Station to Azamino Station)* and green *(connecting Nakayama Station to Hiyoshi Station)*. Allow ¥200–530 depending on distance.

**BY TRAIN** – Local trains *(Tokyu-Toyoko and JR Negishi Lines)* are quicker and cheaper than the subway.

**BY BUS** – **Akai-Kutsu** tourist buses are recognizable by their red-and-yellow retro design. Regular departures from Sakuragicho station for main tourist sites *(¥100). Stations are announced in English.*

**BY BICYCLE Rental** – *Opposite the Landmark Tower (A1). Open 10am–5pm. ¥500 per day.* Near Yokohama Renga, Bashyamichi, Nihonmaru. *¥800 per day.*

Specialist cycle shop near Yamashita Garden. *Small sports cycle ¥1,000 per 3hr.*

## KAMAKURA PRACTICAL INFORMATION

### USEFUL INFORMATION

**Tourist Office** – *Kamakura station (B2). Open Apr–Aug 9am–5.30pm; Sept–Mar 9am–5pm. ℘0467-22-3350.*

### TRANSPORTATION

**BY TRAIN** – **Kamakura Station** *(B2)* – *From* Tokyo station, Yokosuka Line *via* Yokohama station *(55min, ¥890)*. From Yokohama station, Yokosuka Line *(30min, ¥230)*. For Shimoda, Yosuka Line, Ofuna station, change for Limited Express Odoriko.

### GETTING AROUND

**BY TRAIN** – From Kamakura, Enoden Line for Hase *(5min, ¥190)* and Yokosuka Line for Kita-Kamakura *(5min, ¥130)*.

**BY BUS** – Numerous buses for the main temples depart from Kamakura station.

**BY BICYCLE** – Hase and Kita-Kamakura are only 15–20min by bicycle from Kamakura. *Bicycle rental at Kamakura station (B2). ¥500 per hour or ¥1,500 per day.*

# ADDRESSES

## STAY

### YOKOHAMA

**Yokohama Hostel Village ヨコハマホステルヴィレッジ新栄館** *1 F Sanwa Building, 3-11-2 Matsukage-cho, Naka-ku (B2). 045-663-3696. http://yoko-ham.hostelvillage.com/ja. . 60 rooms.* In the former dockland and workers' district of Kotobuki, rooms vacated by migrant and retired workers have been transformed into a hotel. ***Rooms are small, but clean; kitchen and coin laundry area, and roof terrace***. Down-to-earth atmosphere guaranteed.

**Navios Yokohama ナビオス横浜** *2-1-1 Shinko, Naka-ku (B2). 045-633-6000 www.navios-yokohama.com. 135 rooms.* A standard hotel with all modern conveniences. Ideally located, not far from Minato Mirai 21.

**Oimatsu Ryokan ホテル老松***22 Oimatsu-cho, Nishi-ku (A2).* 5min walk from Hinodecho station. *045-231-2926. 26 rooms.* A simple ryokan in a quiet area. An unusual place to find in Yokohama, but note that the owners are not comfortable with Englishyou'll need a phrasebook.

**San-Ai Yokohama Hotel 三愛横浜ホテル***3-95 Hanasaki-cho, Naka-ku (A2). 045-242-4411. www.sanaih.co.jp. 81 rooms.* A former ryokan renovated in Western style, in a quiet street. One of the rare places with reasonable prices in the Minato Mirai 21 area. Charming **view** of the garden from the dining room.

**New Grand Hotel ホテルニューグランド***10 Yamashita-cho, Naka-ku (B2). 045-681-1841. www.hotel-newgrand.co.jp. 400 rooms.* Built after the 1923 earthquake to symbolize the rebirth of the town, the New Grand, its Rainbow Ballroom, and ostentatious luxury are part of local history. All the biggest names have stayed here, from McArthur to Chaplin.

**Royal Park Hotel 横浜ロイヤルパークホテル** *2-2-1-3 Minatomirai, Nishi-ku (A1). 045-221-1111. www.yrph.com. 603 rooms.* Between the 52nd and 67th floors of the Landmark Tower, the rooms of the Royal Park Hotel all have a breathtaking **view**. Superb space and nautical-style portholes in the shower room. Also, try the wonderful sushi at the Shikitei (68th floor) and the Tea Ceremony in a refurbished bedroom. Magic! **Michelin Guide Tokyo Yokohama Kamakura 2011 Selection.**

## EAT

**Ootoya 大戸屋** *Minatomirai business square Bldg, 1F. 3-6-4 Minatomirai, Nishi-ku (A2). 045-681-6256. Open 10am–10pm.* . Portions of sushi, fritters, grilled meat or fish, eaten sitting at the counter.

**Q's Dinner クイーンズダイナ** *Tower A, Queen's Square , 2-3-8 Minatomirai, Nishi-ku(A–B1). 045-682-0109. Open 11am –11pm.* Plethora of small stands, with food from around the world to sustain yourself without hurting the purse. *Soba* (buckwheat noodles), barbecued items, pizza, dim sum, curries, etc.

**El Ella エルエラ** *1 F, 3-132 Motomachi, Naka-ku (B2). 045-661-1688. Open 11am–10pm.* Choice of Italian or French cuisine—try veal à l'orange or clam soup with pesto in a lively environment.

**Seiko-Enn 生香園本館***5-80 Aioi-cho, Naka-ku (B2). 045-651-5152. Open 11.30am–9.30pm.* Cantonese food in a charming, traditional setting.

**Kisoji 木曽路・馬車道店***B1F, 4-55 Ohta-cho, Naka-ku (B2). 045-664-2961. Open 11.30am–11pm.* Kisoji, the best of the roadside diners. Lunchtime ***kaiseki*** menu with excellent quality/ price ratio and in the evening, ***shabu-shabu*** (beef hot-pot) with ***gomadare*** (sesame sauce). Another option is to try some ***kishimen*** (noodles from Nagoya).

For Chinese food enthusiasts, Yokohama's **Chinatown** has a huge choice of restaurants, all on any Tourist Office map. For Cantonese cooking, **Heichinro** and **Manchinro** are essential. For spicier Sichuan cooking, try the **Shei Shei**. Shanghai specialties like *dazha xie*, tasty crabsat **Jo Gen Ro**; and Beijing food at **Tourin**, **Kaseiro**, and **Anrakuen**.

**Rinka-en 隣花苑** *52-1 Sannotani Honmoku, behind Sankei-en (B2 off map). 045-621-0318. Open noon–7pm. Reservations required.* The former 14C residence of a Shinto priest attached to an Izu temple, the house was moved to Yokohama and now gives a rare insight into Izu architecture of the time. They serve first-class ***sankei soba***, the recipe of which has been passed down from generation to generation. An unforgettable culinary experience right next door to the *garden of Sankei-en*. **Michelin Guide Tokyo Yokohama Kamakura 2011 Selection**.

## NIGHTLIFE

**Bars** – **Chinatown** is one of the liveliest areas in the evening. If you want a more male-oriented, very Japanese atmosphere, try the many *izakaya* in **Noge-cho** *(open 6pm–1am)*. And in **Motomachi-dori** you will find a trendier area, popular with tourists.

## SHOPPING

**Bashamichi-dori** *(B2)* – Window shopping and *izakaya* in this street *(michi)* of the two wheels *(basha)*, a reference to the time when foreigners still rode down it in stagecoaches.

**Motomachi** *(B2)* is also a popular shopping street with tourists.

**Aka Renga Park** – *Minato Mirai 21 (B2)*. An old silk warehouse converted into a shopping mall and cultural center.

**Isetatsu** いせ辰 – *184 Yamate, Naka-ku. Open 10am–6pm*. Traditional paper and postcards.

## STAY

### KAMAKURA

**Hase Youth Hotel 鎌倉はせユースホステル** *5-11 Sakanoshita.* 3min walk from Hase Station *(A2 off map). 0467-24-3390. www1.kamakuranet.ne.jp/hase_yh.* . *1 Japanese room, 2 dormitories.* A small, wooden inn opened three years ago by a delightful couple.

**Komachi-so** 小町荘 *2-8-23 Komachi (B2). 0467-23-2151.* . *4 rooms.* A small, quiet guesthouse run by an elderly lady who has lived there since 1957. *O-furo* (bath) and Japanese-style rooms.

**B.B. House** B・Bハウス *2-22-31 Hase (A2 off map). 0467-25-5859. 5 rooms.* A white house near the beach, for female guests only. Peaceful, with plenty of greenery. Japanese-style rooms.

**Hotel New Kamakura ホテルニュー鎌倉** *13-2 Onarimachi (B2) 0467-22-2230.* . *26 rooms.* Just behind the station in a quiet square turned over to parking. Small, but very pleasant Japanese-style rooms. The new wing is more comfortable but the rooms are more expensive.

**Park Hotel 鎌倉パークホテル** *33-6 Sakanoshita (A2 off map). 0467-25-5121. www.kamakuraparkhotel.co.jp. 46 rooms.* A little way from the town center, the Park Hotel offers comfortable rooms and a *rotenburo* (open-air bath) with a **view** over the ocean. Very attentive staff. **Michelin Guide Tokyo Yokohama Kamakura 2011 Selection**.

## EAT

**Nakamura-an** 中村庵 *1-7-6 Komachi-dori (B2). 0467-25-3500. Open Fri–Wed 11.45am–5pm.* . Soba noodles are a specialty, prepared on the spot by a skillful cook. Very popular.

**Sometaro** 染太郎 *3-12-11 Hase (A2). 0467-22-8694. Open 11am–10pm.* . Calm, wood-paneled room, where the owner settles you before huge hot plates to order your choice of *okonomiyaki* (Japanese pancake).

**Yamasato** 山里 *321 Yamanouchi (B1). 0467-22-2156. Open 10.30am–5pm.* . Close to Meigetsu-in, charming restaurant with bamboo-encircled terrace. On the menu: soba, udon noodles; tea, pastries, too.

**Hachinoki** 鉢の木本店 *Kencho-ji entrance(B1). 0467-22-8719. Open Tue–Sun 11am–4pm.* Opened 41 years ago and attached to the temple, was two annex near Meigetsu-in. Ideal to discover Zen cuisine. **Michelin Guide Tokyo Yokohama Kamakura 2011 Selection.**

**Hifumi**日文（ひふみ）*2-9-62 Yuigahama (B2). 0467-22-8676. Open Tue–Sun 11.30am–9pm. Kaiseki* cuisine with seafood and local specialties.

**Kitchou** 帰蝶 *93-25 Nikaido (C1). 0467-22-1071. Open Tue–Sun 11.30am–10pm.* . Pretty restaurant with tatami and low tables, offering sophistication and culinary delights: miniature tofu and pumpkin, fish balls, etc.

# North of Tokyo

**The mountainous region of Nikko is so enchanting that as long ago as the 8C, it attracted the attention of influential priests. Protected by the imposing Mount Nantei, Nikko is dotted with the shrines and temples that arose out of the many forms of worship practiced in the "light of the sun," (as Nikko translates in Japanese). As Nikko was regarded as a holy place rich in *kami*, the first of the shoguns decided to build his mausoleum here. The result was the most beautiful mausoleum in Japan *(Tosho-gu)*, dazzling everyone who visits it. In 1999 UNESCO designated the shrines and temples of Nikko a World Heritage Site.**

- **Population:** Nikko: 15,254; Ashikaga: 159,670.
- **Michelin Map:** Principal Sights Map B2, Regional Map p119.
- **Location:** Tochigi prefecture, 87mi/140km from Tokyo.
- **Kids:** The avenue of *Jizo statues*. If possible, visit May 17 and 18 for the **Yabusame Ceremony**, when a procession of 1,000 warriors follows an archery display given from horseback *(see p206)*.
- **Don't miss:** Taiyu-in and Tosho-gu; an evening at the Takai-ya restaurant.

## NIKKO★★★ 日光

*Map p203.*

The main road to the shrines of Nikko takes you over the Shin-kyo bridge, a delicately arched structure coated in vermilion lacquer that crosses over the Daiya River.

### Shin-kyo Bridge★ 神橋

*B1.*

*Open 8am–5pm. ¥300.*

In 767, the Buddhist priest **Shodo Shonin** (735–817) and his disciples were intent on exploring Mount Nantai, but were held back by the tumultuous waters of the Daiya River. In answer to their prayers the god Jinja Daio appeared with two snakes, one red and one blue, which entwined above the river to form a bridge. The stone sign **Gejo Ishi** *(gejo means "to set foot on")* at the entrance to the bridge *(span of 88.6ft/27m)* is a reminder that only the shoguns and the Emperor were once allowed to use it.

It took its current form when it was rebuilt in 1636 during the reign of the third Tokugawa shogun. In 1907, it was rebuilt again (in the same design) after it had been washed away by a flood, and strengthened with *torii* (gate).

### Kosugi Hoan Museum of Art 小杉放庵記念日光美術館 *B1.*

*Open Thu-Tue, 9.30am–5pm (last admission 4.30pm). ¥700.*

Works by the talented painter Kosugi Hoan (1881–1964) are displayed here. Kosugi is known particularly for the logo-style tiger roundel (Tora no Maki, the "Shotokan tiger") that he designed for the cover of the first book to be written about karate by the "father of modern karate" Funakoshi Gichin *(see p108)*.

## THE TEMPLES

*Rinno-ji, Tosho-gu, Futarasan, and Taiyu-in are on the same site N of the Shin-kyo Bridge. A combined ticket (¥1,000) allows you to visit all these temples and shrines except for the Treasure Museums of Rinno-ji and Tosho-gu, and the corridor leading to the tomb of Ieyasu with the sculpture of the Sleeping Cat (¥520).*

### Rinno-ji★★ 輪王寺 *B1.*

*On the left after the sacred bridge at the top of the road, this is the first temple at the entrance to the site. Open Apr–Oct 8am–5pm; Nov–Mar 8am–4pm. ¥400 (when not included in a combined ticket).*

Shodo Shonin found the mountainous region of Nikko to be so pure that he felt it a fitting place for the god Kannon. The same year in which he succeeded in crossing the Daiya River, he founded the first place of worship in Nikko: the Shironryu-ji (the temple's original name), which was built a short distance from the sacred bridge. After the monk Tenkai (1536–1643), patriarch of the Tendai-shu *(sutra of the Lotus)* Buddhist sect, set about revitalizing the temples in the vicinity, the temple was renamed Rinno-ji and became a model for around 15 other Buddhist temples with the same name in the region.

Once past the large copper sculpture of the Shodo priest, you enter the largest temple in Nikko, listed in the architectural canons of the Tendai sect (a rarity in itself). The **Sanbutsu-do★**, or "Room with the Three Buddhas," houses an enormous statue of **Amida-nyorai★** (the Buddha Amitabha or "Buddha of infinite Light"). Popular for his compassion, this Buddha is flanked by **Senju Kannon** (the goddess with a thousand hands) *(see box p 126)* and **Bato Kannon** (the goddess with a horse's head, protector of the animal kingdom and banisher of bad humor), two of the 33 forms that Kannon is said to assume. It is also in this hall that the rice-eating ceremony, **Gohan Shiki**, takes place, intended to ward off bad luck.

Opposite the temple the **Treasure Museum★** *(open 9am–5pm; ¥300) B1* displays selections from its Buddhist heritage in rotation: 6,000 objects, the oldest of which date back to the Nara era. The **Shoyo-en stroll garden★★**, created in the Edo era, is a miniature version of the landscape of Lake Biwa near Kyoto. Most enjoyable.

### Tosho-gu★★★ 日光東照宮 *B1.*

*Behind the Rinno-ji.*

*Open Apr–Oct 8am–5pm; Nov–Mar 8am–4pm. ¥1,300 (when not included in a combined ticket).*

Access to the largest shrine in Nikko is via the Sennin Ishidan, "the stone staircase of the 1,000 men." At the top is an impressive *torii★* (gate), made of granite from Kyushu (1618). This is the most imposing of the gates to be built during the Edo era. Its *shimenawa* (rice-straw rope indicating a sacred place, used for ritual purification) has been removed because of safety concerns as the weight of the rope *(661.3lb/300kg)* posed a threat to the *torii*. To the left of the *torii* is the **five-story pagoda★**. Built in 1650, it was destroyed in 1815 and rebuilt three years later. Its central pillar, which is 23.6in/60cm in diameter and 98.4ft/30m high *(the whole tower is 118ft/36m in height)*, is suspended by chains from beams on the fourth level. In the event of an earthquake, floating free at the bottom, the pillar helps maintain the pagoda's equilibrium.

The animals depicted on the first level represent the 12 signs of the zodiac. The symbol of "three hollyhocks" *(not really hollyhocks, but wild ginger)* inside a black circle *(Mitsuba aoi)* is the Tokugawa clan crest.

## Tokugawa Ieyasu, protector of the north

Before he died the shogun Ieyasu (1542–1616) left specific instructions for his burial: "Bury me at Mount Kuno (Shizuoka prefecture) for the first five years after my death. Then build a small shrine at Nikko, in which you will place me as a god. I will then become the protector of Japan." The Emperor Go-Mizuno-o deified the first shogun of Edo as Tosho Daigongen, "The great spirit that lights up the East." Ieyasu chose the Nikko site for its position, north of Edo (now Tokyo—a direction in which all evil spirits gathered and so considered unlucky). It was Ieyasu's intention to defend the north like a *tenno*, a celestial guardian of altars. This proved a successful strategy—the Tokugawa shogunate of 1603 brought a stability to Japan that was to last until 1868, when the last shogun Tokugawa Yoshinobu was forced to step down.

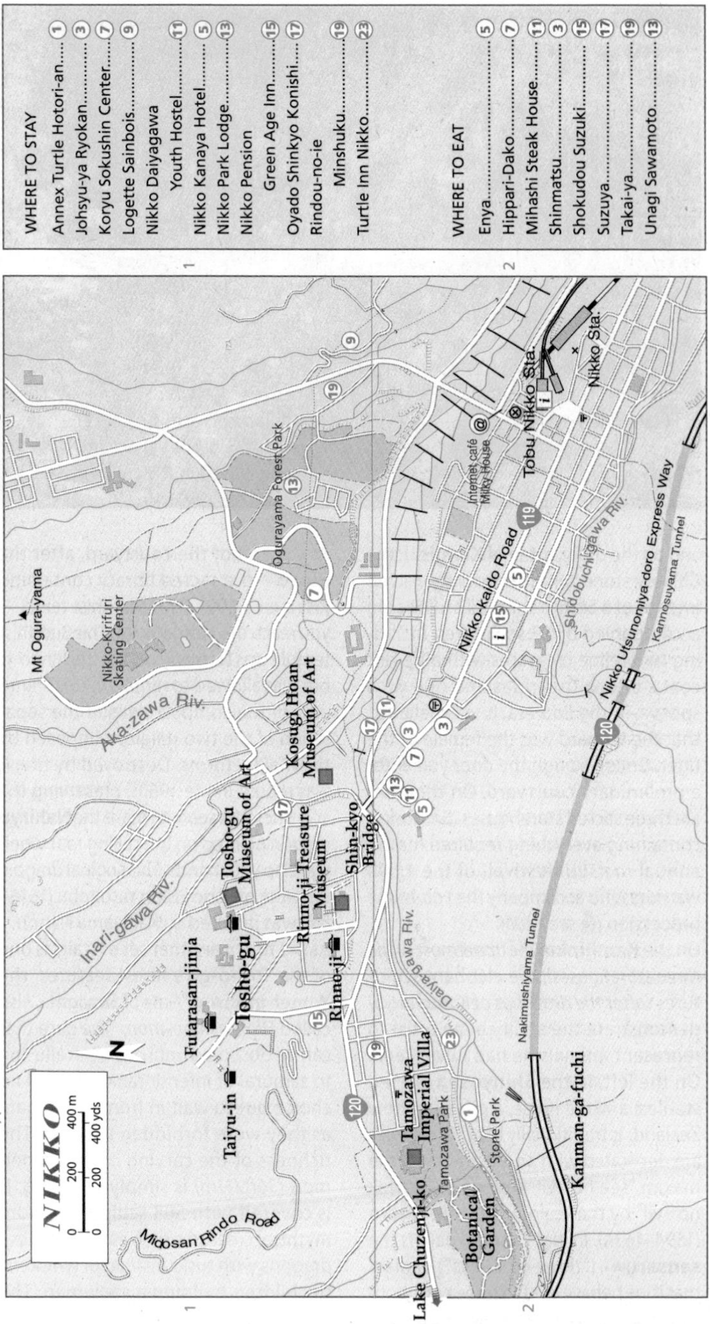




Another stone staircase leads to the **Omote-mon★**, the entrance to the main precincts of the shrine. This gate is a good example of how Buddhist and Shinto architectures have sometimes been combined in one structure: on one side are the **ni-oh** guardians, protectors of the Buddhist pantheon *(see opposite)*

*Detail of Yomei-mon, Tosho-gu*

and on the other, a pair of **Karajishi**, the Chinese stone lions that mark the sacred interior of a Shinto shrine. The lions are accompanied by 82 sculptures, including two feline creatures with different coats, one with stripes and one with spots—in the Edo era, it was believed that the leopard was the female of the tiger. Once through the door you enter a preliminary courtyard. On the right are three sacred storehouses (**Sanjinko**) containing everything required for the annual *matsuri* (festival) of the 1,000 warriors who accompany the *yabusame* procession (*see p206*).

On the **Kamijinko** *(the uppermost of the three storehouses)*, the elephant sculptures *(after the drawings of Kano Tanyu)* demonstrate the ability of an artist to represent animals he had never seen. On the left, in the **Shinyosha** (sacred stables) a white horse, a gift from New Zealand, is traditionally kept. The stables are decorated with an illustration of the maxim "see no evil, hear no evil, speak no evil" by the sculptor **Hidari Jingoro** (1594–1634). In eight carved panels the **sansaru**★ ("three monkeys") explain that if we behave like the three wise monkeys Mizaru *(see no evil)*, Kikazaru *(hear no evil)*, and Iwazaru *(speak no evil)*, we too will be spared evil—three principles that are important in the Tendai Buddhist tenet.

At the end of the courtyard, after the **Rinzo**—the sacred library containing just over 6,000 sutra (Buddhist texts)—you reach the **Yakushi-do**. This Buddhist temple was formerly part of the Rinno-ji, but was allowed to remain in this Shinto part of the complex despite the separation of the two religions imposed by the Meiji reforms. Destroyed by fire, it was rebuilt in the 1960s, preserving the acoustics that seem to make the **Nakiryu** dragon painted on the ceiling roar when you clap your hands. The original dragon, the work of Kano Eishin Yasunobu (1616–85), was restored by Katayama Nanpu.

At the top of another set of stairs is one of the Tosho-gu's finest features, the **Yomei-mon**★★, "Gate of Sunlight." Also called *Higurashino-mon*, "the gate that can be observed until dusk," an allusion to samurai of inferior rank who had no choice but to wait in front of the gate as they were forbidden to enter. The richness of the carving of the Yomei-mon *(36ft/11m)* is simply stunning. It is covered with 508 sculptures, from mythical creatures such as *iki* (Japanese dragons with tusks instead of whiskers) to children building a snowman. The gate is supported by 12 white columns. One of the sculptures is upside down, a gesture made by the artists to show the gods that they were not competing with them. It was common for Buddhist buildings to be erected with three tiles, quite deliberately, missing from a roof, since perfection was seen as the beginning of decline. In a medallion on one of the central columns, you can see some **tigers★**. As you pass through the gate, look up to see two **dragons★** on the ceiling, one facing the sky, looking in eight directions and the other turned toward the earth and its four directions. They were painted by **Kano Tanyu** (1602–74), the Tokugawa shogunate's preferred artist *(see box p299)*.

Once through the Yomei-mon, you enter another courtyard containing the sacred storage hall. The **Shinyosha** is used to store the three **mikoshi★★**, portable shrines dedicated to Tokugawa Ieyasu, Toyotomi Hideyoshi, and Minamoto no Yoritomo. In 1636, their weight had to be reduced from 2,469.2lb/1,120kg to 1,763.7lb/800kg to help the 55 bearers who carried the shrines in ceremonies. Inside, on the ceiling, are three depictions of **bodhisattvas★**, some of the most beautiful in Japan.

At the north end of the courtyard, the beautiful **Kara-mon★** Chinese gate dating from 1617 *(three of the seven divinities of good luck are carved on its west face)* leads to the main shrine, the **Honsha**. This is made up of the **Haiden** *(hall of worship)*, the **Ishinoma** *(the chamber of stones, formerly the corridor)*, whose main function is to link the world of humans (the Haiden) to that of the gods, the **Honden**. The Honden is the shrine's most sacred building as one of its three small rooms *(closed to the public)* houses the Nainaijin, the kami of Ieyasu, Toyotomi, and Yoritomo.

If you don't visit the Honden, head past the Haiden to the corridor leading to Tokugawa Ieyasu's mausoleum. On the way you'll pass the **Treasure Museum** *(¥500)*, where precious objects belonging to the Tosho-gu are displayed. The entrance to the corridor is famous for the **Nemuri neko★**, carved beneath the lintel—*The Sleeping Cat*, attributed to the sculptor Hidari Jingoro (1594–1634), with a small sparrow to one side. This unlikely pairing symbolizes the desire for peace that Tokugawa

### An ostentatious silence

Although Tokugawa Ieyasu wanted a modest shrine, in 1634 his grandson Tokugawa Iemitsu started to build the biggest mausoleum in Japan. As Ieyasu had been deified after his death, his grandson wished to give him a setting befitting this immortality. No expense was spared therefore in the construction of this Momoyama-style building with Baroque highlights—140,000 trees were felled and 5,173 sculptures created. Fifteen thousand craftsmen were employed from start to finish over a period of 17 months. The cost in today's money is estimated to be $330 million dollars.

Ieyasu expressed for his country before his death. After climbing around 200 steps, you will find his tomb at the end of a stone footpath and surrounded by magnificent Japanese cedars.

## Tosho-gu Museum of Art★

日光東照宮美術館 *B1.*

*Behind the Tosho-gu.*

*Open 9am–5pm. ¥800.*

In 1928, the high priest in charge of the Choyokakuthe Tosho-gu's admin-istrative officesassembled talented artists such as Nakamura Gakuryo, Katayama Nanpu, and Arai Kanpo, working under the direction of Yokoyama Taikan (1868–1958), to complete the decoration of the offices. Now housing a museum, among the 150 works displayed are the **Old Pine Tree**, a drawing by Arai, and the **Camelia** by Katayama.

## Futarasan-jinja★

二荒山神社 *A1.*

*W of Tosho-gu. Open Apr–Oct 8am–5pm; Nov–Mar 8am–4pm.*

*Temple ¥200 (when not included in a combined ticket); Garden ¥200.*

Founded by the priest Shodo Shonin in 782, this shrinerebuilt in 1610has a fine **Honden★** (main hall) in the Momoyama style. It was constructed in 1619 by the

### Agyo and Ungyo

The first sound we make in life, with the mouth wide open, is "ahhhh." The last sound, with the lips closed, is "ummmm." Sanskrit tradition put these two sounds together to form the sacred sound "Om or Aum," which Buddhism adopted. The two **ni-oh** statues that are found at the entrance to Buddhist temples in Japan are guardians and protectors—Agyo, is always represented with an open mouth, making the first sound *(Ah)* and his partner, with closed lips, the last one *(Um)*. The two divinities thus symbolize the beginning and the end of all things; perhaps a thought to guide our steps as we enter a sacred place.

second shogun Tokugawa Hidetada (1579–1632), and is dedicated to Okuninushi no Mikoto, one of the mythical founders of Shintoism (*see p159*), and the divine spirits of the surrounding mountains.

The three portable shrines built in 1617 and kept in the **Shinyosha★** (sacred storage hall) are dedicated to the kami of Mount Nantai *(8,156.2ft/2,486m)*, Mount Nyotai *(8,146.3ft/2,483m)*, and Mount Taro *(7,769ft/2,368m)*, symbolizing father, mother, and child respectively. Three ancient **black pines** *(kouyamaki)*, which according to legend were planted by the monk Kukai, capture many visitors' imagination, along with the old bronze lantern called the **ghost lantern**. It bears sword *(katana)* marks, causedaccording to legendby duelists who crossed swords with ghosts attracted by the light. Historians, however, merely suggest sword cuts dealt by the guards to chase away the flying squirrels attracted by the oil of the lamps.

The **Yayoi Matsuri** *(a parade of flower-covered floats from the different districts of Nikko)* takes place each year (April 13–17 ) within the shrine complex.

### Yabusame

Twice a year during the Nikko Festival, a *yabusame* ceremony is held at the lower end of the Tosho-gu shrine. The participants have to shoot three targets placed along a track with a bow and arrow, while galloping by on horseback. *Yabusame* is neither a sport nor a martial art but a religious ritual, the aim of which is to delight the gods with a display of skill and power of concentration.

## Taiyu-in★★ 家光廟大猷院

*Map A1.*

*Opposite the Futarasan. Open Apr–Oct 8am–5pm; Nov–Mar 8am–4pm. ¥550 (when not included in a combined ticket).*

Tokugawa Iemitsu (1604–51), who was deeply respectful of his grandfather, the first of the shoguns, declared: "I shall serve Ieyasu even after my death." And with a similar regard for *his* ancestor, Iemitsu's successor, the fourth shogun Tokugawa Ietsuna, decided to build Iemitsu's mausoleum, not looking southwest, as tradition required, but to the north so that he could face Tosho-gu, where his grandfather lay.

The **Nioh-mon** (gate), the first stage on the path to the mausoleum, is guarded by the famous *ni-oh (see box above)*. The second gate, or **Niten-mon★**, is the most impressive in Nikko. The Gate of the Two Gods (Niten), it is dedicated to **Jikokuten** and **Koumokuten**. The former, Guardian of the East, carries a sword. The Guardian of the West carries a paintbrush and an unrolled scroll. The back of the gate is flanked by the divinities **Raijin**, god of lightning, with a drum and drumsticks, and **Fujin**, god of the wind, carried in a bolster-shaped bag on his shoulder.

Once through the gate you arrive at two towers, one with a bell in it *(shoro)*, and the other a drum *(koro)*, a musical yin and yang that sound in turn above the 33 lanterns lining the path. This leads first to the **Yasha-mon★**, a magnificent, ornamental gate with a dominant motif

of peonies (the symbol of prosperity) and then to the **Kara-mon**, a Chinese-style gate *(Kara)*.
The mausoleum is a short distance from here, but first you reach the **Haiden★** (hall of worship). Inside, **140 dragons** decorate a ceiling the size of 64 tatami mats; on the wall near the entrance is a painting of a **Chinese lion**, the work of the brothers Kano Tanyu and Eishin. The main hall, the **Honden**, is dazzling. Amid the splendor, flying dragons roar, one up toward the sky *(shoryu)* and the other down toward the earth *(koryu)*, under the impassive eye of a phoenix painted on the latticework ceiling.
After the Honden is the amazing white and gold gate **Koka-mon★**, of Ming inspiration. The gate is closed as it leads to the Okunoin *(closed to the public)*, the sacred place where Iemitsu, the third shogun of the Tokugawa dynasty, lies. He died in Ueno (north Tokyo) and was brought here to his final resting place.

## WEST OF THE TOWN

### Kanman-ga-fuchi Walk★★

憾満ガ淵 *Map A2.*

*This lovely walk begins at Stone Park behind the Hotori-an Hotel.*

Joining the Daiya River, known here as the Kanman-ga-fuchi Abyss because of the geological phenomenon caused by lava from Mount Nantai, you reach a magnificent row of **Jizo statues★★** (bodhisabbva) below the attractive cemetery. Continue walking to the Dainichi Bridge, which takes you to the other side of the river.

### Tamozawa Imperial Villa★

日光田母沢御用邸 *Map A2.*

*8-27 Hon-cho. Open Wed–Mon 9am–4.30pm. ¥500. Signs in English.*

This summer residence of the Imperial family was built around the first residence of the Tokugawa Kishu clan, transported from Edo in 1872. A great technical feat, its 106 rooms, linked by corridors, are all on one level. Created originally for Prince Yoshihito (the future Emperor Taisho), the villa had been used by three emperors up to 1947.
The splendid **garden★**, which originally encompassed a botanical garden, is also open to the public.

## EXCURSION

### Chuzenji-ko★ 中禅寺湖

*Map A2, off map.*

*18.6mi/30km NW of Nikko.*

*From Nikko (JR and Tobu Nikko stations), bus no. 2, 1, 11 (50min) to Chuzenji-ko. Add 30min for Yumoto. Allow ¥1,100 (Single) to Chuzenji-ko, ¥1,650 (Single) for Yumoto, unless you have a Tobu Pass (**See Addresses p210**).*

Once you have passed the famous "hill with 48 bends" on this stunning mountain road, make a stop at the Akechi-daira cable car *(¥710 round trip)* for a **view** over Lake Chuzenji and the **Kegon**

View of Chuzenji-ko and Kegon Falls

**Falls★**, the finest in Nikko, at a height of 318.2ft/97m.

The lake shores are lined with beautiful **villas**, built soon after 1899, when the Imperial authorities granted permission for foreigners to travel freely in Japan. Particularly worth visiting is the one owned by the Italian Embassy, designed by the architect Antonin Raymond, who came to Japan to assist Frank Lloyd Wright in the construction of the Imperial Hotel *(see p176)*.

Once past the lake you can opt to cross the Senjogahara plateau to **Yumoto** ("the source of hot water") and its small lake Yunoko. This *onsen*, with nine hot water springs, is one of the most highly regarded in the region.

## ASHIKAGA 足利

*Map p119.*
*About 50mi/80km NE of Tokyo.*
*Take the Ryomo express train on the Tobu Isesaki Line (every 15min) from Tobu Asakusa station (Tokyo) to Ashikaga-shi station (1h30min, ¥1,940).*

Ashikaga is set in beautiful natural surroundings and has some important cultural sites. To the north it is overlooked by Mount Ashio, while to the south are expanses of fertile fields.

### Ashikaga Gakko (Ashikaga School) 足利学校跡

*10min by taxi from Ashikaga-shi station. ¥400, various opening times.*

Ashikaga School, a National Historic Site, played an important role in Japan's educational history. The date of its foundation is uncertain, but school books *(now National Treasures)* were provided by Uesugi Norizane in the Muromachi era (1336–1573). In 1550, over 3,000 students studied Confucianism, divination, and Chinese medicine here.

It closed in 1873.

### Banna-ji 鑁阿寺

*10min by taxi from Ashikaga-shi station, close to Ashikaga Gakko. Open Mon–Sat. ¥400.*

A National Treasure, this Buddhist temple belonging to the Shingon sect consists of seven historic buildings. The shrine, founded in 1196 (in the Kamakura era) by the lord Ashikaga Yoshikane, contains a large image of the god Dainichi (inherited from the Minamoto clan). Toward the end of his life Ashikaga Yoshiyasu, cousin of Minamoto no Yoritomo (founder of the Kamakura shogunate) withdrew to Mount Koya *(see p 340)* to become a monk, subsequently returning to Ashikaga. Acknowledged as one of the three founders of the Shingon sect, Ashikaga Yoshiyasu is still revered by Shingon monks.

### Kurita Museum 栗田美術館

*15min by taxi from Ashikaga station. Open Mon–Fri 9.30am–5pm, Sat–Sun & public holidays until 6pm. ¥1,550.*

This gallery contains the world's largest collection of Imari and Nabeshima porcelain and ceramics, made during the Edo era (1603–1867) by the Hizen Nabeshima clan.

The first porcelain to be produced in Japan, Imari was exported to the West and throughout Asia by the Dutch East India Company. The gallery is set in a garden full of flowers and foliage, with some Japanese-style houses.

### Orihime Shrine 織姫神社

*15min by taxi from Ashikaga station.*

Ashikaga was long famous for its textile industry. In tribute to textile workers of the past, volunteers from the town built a Shinto temple in 1937, located on a hill with splendid **views** over the Kanto plain. In 2004, it was classified as an Important Cultural Property.

### Ashikaga Flower Park あしかがフラワーパーク

*10min by taxi from Ashikaga station, opposite the Kurita Museum. Open 9am–6pm. ¥600, but charges vary according to the month.*

A park covering an area of 430,556sq ft/40,000sq m, with a wide variety of flowers according to the season.

Famous for its magnificent wisteria arbors, one of which is 2,624.7ft/800m long, it also has azaleas, hydrangeas, and water lilies.

## SAITAMA AND GUNMA PREFECTURES
## 埼玉県と群馬県

One or two days in these two prefectures north of the capital provides a radical change in setting: unspoiled natural landscapes, mountains close to 6,500ft/2,000m high, wild flora and fauna, as well as hot springs *(onsen)* to relax body and spirit.

Escapees from the capital are numerous here on weekends, especially in the fall, but no matter what season, you will enjoy the typically Japanese atmosphere to be found here.

### Nagatoro 長瀞

*From Ikebukuro station, take the Seibu line to Kaminagatoro (2h, ¥1,210 via Seibu Chichibu for certain trains).*

**Saitama Museum of Natural History**

*200m/650ft left on leaving Kaminagatoro station. Open Tue–Sun 9am–4.30pm (5pm Jul–Aug). ¥200.*

This museum has a unique way of presenting mountain flora and fauna: stuffed animals to be "touched gently", four mountain scenes containing local species, re-created dinosaurs, and a giant shark all await you.

You can take a nice **excursion** along the river from the museum. On coming to the beach, continue up the shopping street to Nagatoro station, where you can rent bikes *(electric: 4h, ¥1,500; 8h, ¥2,500)* to cross the city and, for experienced cyclists, continue to the top of Mt Hodo *(20min, or 45 min by foot).*

On your way back down, stop at **Hodosan-Jinja★** shrine to the left. Recently repainted, the brilliantly-colored sculptures decorating the walls are worth seeing. *Continue down the street, turn left at the large torii and take the second street on the right. After the bridge, turn left and you will see* **Hozenji** *on your right.* This little country temple is home to a wall sculpture of dragons which still have their original colors, if a little aged. Heading back to Tokyo, don't forget to keep an eye out for the old steam locomotive in the train station.

### Minakami 水上

*165km/102mi from Tokyo by the Kan-Etsu Express Way or by the JR Shonan-Shinjuku line (Shinjuku station), then the Shinkansen Tokyo–Niigata via Omiya (90min, ¥5,350), stop at station JR Jomo-Kogen.*

Skiing, trekking, rock-climbing, rafting, canoeing, and *onsen* (hot springs): MInakami offers numerous invigorating activites in a natural setting, a three-hour drive from the capital. The town extends over a vast stretch of land along the Tonegawa River, on which four dams were built to supply water to Saitama and Tokyo prefectures' 30 million inhabitants. The impressive mountain relief of Tanigawa-dake rises to the northwest. No fewer than 18 ***onsen*** surge to the surface in this town, hence the great number of

*River cruise, Nagatoro*

© JTB/Photoshot

*ryokan* and *minshuku* (family-run lodgings) of all kinds.

**Tanigawa-dake★**
*By route 291 or 55min by bus from Joma-Kogen station.*
The trip to Tanigawa-dake has to be made to fully appreciate the site6, 486ft/1,977m. A cable-car *(8am-5pm, 9am Jan–Apr; ¥2,000 round trip)* takes visitors to 4,265ft/1,300m; experienced walkers can then rally at the peak (*5h round trip*) or return by foot to the valley; several ski trails are open in the winter season.

**Takumi no sato**
*West of JR Jomou-kougen station, reached by route 17. English map available at the Tourist Office.*
The village layout partly dates from the Edo era: Avenue Shukuba was then on the Mikuni road, via which gold from Sado Island *(see p276)* was taken back to Tokyo. Today it is a nice walk among the craftmen's shops, restaurants, and farms. Don't miss going as far as Tainei-ji, from the Kamakura era (12C–14C).

## Kusatsu Onsen 草津温泉
*Map p119.*
*About 3hr45min from Shinjuku station by direct JR Express Bus.*
*www.kusatsu-onsen.ne.jp/foreign.*
*About 140km/87mi from Tokyo.*
Kusatsu is one of most popular *onsen* in Japan because of the quality and abundance of its waters *(7,039gal/32,000l)*. Although its exact date of foundation is unknown, the locality is mentioned in the tales of Yamato Takeru no Mikoto (a legendary hero of the 2C) and Gyoki (8C Buddhist priest). We also know that Minamoto no Yoritomo, the first shogun (12C), often visited to relax at Kusatsu. Soldiers came here to bathe their wounds during the Civil Wars of the 16C, but when trouble broke out, Shingen Takeda—one of the most powerful *daimyo* of the time—closed the public baths for safety reasons.
It was the German academic Erwin von Bälz (1849–1913), invited by the Meiji government to teach in the Faculty of Medicine in Tokyo, who recognized the medicinal benefits of the waters in Kusatsu and promoted them outside Japan. In winter the spa also has a ski slope.

## NIKO PRACTICAL INFORMATION

### USEFUL INFORMATION

**Tourist Offices – Tobu Nikko Station** *(C2). Open 8.30am–5pm. English spoken.*

**Tourist Information Center** – *591 Gokoumachi. Open 9am–5pm. ✆0288-53-3795. Large information center with Internet access (¥50 per 15min).*

**Post Office/Withdrawals** – *896-1 Nakahatsuishi-cho. Open Mon–Fri 9am–7pm, Sat–Sun 9am–5pm. ATM.*

### TRANSPORTATION

**BY TRAIN** – **JR** and **Tobu Nikko Stations** – *S of town center (2min walk apart) (C2).* From Tokyo *(Asakusa station)*, several direct trains per day on the Tobu Line *(1hr50min, ¥2,620 or 2hr30min, ¥1,320 depending on trains)*. If you want to use a JR Pass you must take the JR Utsunomiya Line *(Yamabiko or Nasuno trains)* from Tokyo station to Utsunomiya *(50min, ¥4,800), then the JR Nikko Line (1h20min, ¥4,920)*. From Shinjuku station *(Tokyo)*, regular trains to Utsunomiya *(1hr45min, ¥1,890)*. Once at Utsunomiya, departure every 20–40min for Nikko *(45min, ¥740)*. If you want to get to Niigata (point of departure for Sado, *see p278*) you will have to go back through Tokyo *(Omiya)*.

### GETTING AROUND

**ON FOOT** – The Nikko temples can be visited on foot. *The stations are 20min walk from the Shin-kyo Bridge.*

**BY BUS** – Terminals at the **JR** and **Tobu Nikko** stations. Regular services for the temples and hotels dotted along the main street.

**Passes** – Several passes available, including the **World Heritage Pass**, which includes the train between Tokyo *(Asakusa)* and Nikko, and the use of Tobu buses and trains to Nikko and surrounding areas plus entrance to three temples *(¥3,600 for 2 days)*. Or the Tobu Bus Free Pass costs **¥2,000/ 2 days, if you stay in**

Nikko or ¥3,000, if you add an excursion to Lake Chuzenji *(Chuzenji Free Pass)*.

## SAITAMA AND GUNMA PREFECTURES PRACTICAL INFORMATION

### USEFUL INFORMATION

**Minamaki Tourism Association**
Tobu Nikko Station *(C2)*. *0278-62-0401. www.enjoy-minakami.jp/eng. Open 8.30am–5pm. English spoken.*

**Minamaki Town Office, Tourism and Commerce division** *2min from the station. 0278-62-2111. www.tourism-minakami.com.*

## ADDRESSES

### STAY

#### NIKKO

**Johsyu-ya Ryokan 上州屋旅館** *911 Nakahatsuishi-machi (B2). 0288-54-0155. www.johsyu-ya.co.jp. 8 rooms.* This ryokan offers both Japanese and Western-style rooms. A central location, warm welcome, and plenty of charm at a modest price.

**Nikko Daiyagawa Youth Hostel** 日光大谷川ユースホステル *1075 Nakahatsuishi-machi (B2). 0288-54-1974. 4 dormitories (24 beds). ¥3,300/person.* A simple hostel between the temples and the town center, run by an English-speaking, ecologically-minded couple.

**Nikko Park Lodge** 日光パークロッジ *2828-5 Tokorono (C1). 0288-53-1201. www.nikkoparklodge.com. 4 rooms, 3 dormitories (4 beds each).* Lots of charm and good ideas—*o-furo*, Internet, yoga classes, vegetarian dinners—at this country house set in parkland. *Shuttle service to and from the train station.*

**Rindo-no-ie Minshuku** 民宿りんどうの家 *1462 Tokorono (C1). 0288-53-0131. www.3ocn.ne.jp/~garr/Rindou.htm. 4 rooms.* A bit out of the way in the east of Nikko, charming rooms with gentian-blue tones *(rindou)* in a family house.

**Annex Turtle Hotori-an** アネックスタートル・ほとり庵 *8-28 Takumi-cho (A2). 0288-53-3663. www.turtle-nikko.com. 11 rooms.* A cozy version of the Turtle Inn *(see below)*, of which this is the annex. The ryokan offers rooms on the peaceful river bank, a wonderful *onsen*, and a pleasant lounge area.

**Koryu Sokushin Center** 日光市交流促進センター *2845 Tokorono (C1). 20min walk from the station. 0288-54-1013. 14 rooms.* A new hotel reminiscent of a summer vacation camp. Both Japanese and Western-style rooms.

**Logette Sainbois** ロヂテ・サンボア *1560 Tokorono (C1). 0288-53-0082. www.sanboa.com. 9 rooms. 15min walk from the station and 30min from the temples.* Plenty of charm in this small chalet, where the mistress of the house weaves cloth with a piano in the background. *O-furo. Arrival and departure transfers provided.*

**Turtle Inn Nikko** タートル・イン・日光 *2-16 Takumi-cho. Direct bus from the station, Sogokaikan-mae stop, 5min walk (A2). 0288-53-3168. www.turtle-nikko.com. 10 rooms.* For 35 years the Turtle and its energetic owners have pulled out all the stops for a cosmopolitan, backpacking clientele. Peaceful, interesting rooms.

**Nikko Pension Green Age Inn** 日光ペンショングリーンエイジイン *10-9 Nishisando (A1). 0288-53-3636. 9 rooms.* This huge, half-timbered house offers cozy rooms with comfortable beds. *Ideal location at the start of the temple area.*

**Oyado Shinkyo Konishi** お宿・神橋小西 *1030 Kamihatsuishi (B1–2). 0288-54-1101. www.nikko-konishiya.com. 21 rooms.* Enormous ten-tatami sized rooms in this charming ryokan, where you dine looking out over the garden. Very central location.

**Nikko Kanaya Hotel** 日光金谷ホテル *1300 Kamihatsuishi (B2). 0288-54-0001. www.kanayahotel.co.jp. 71 rooms.* One of the oldest hotels in Japan, with everything designed to appeal to the discerning eye. A choice of **French** cuisine in the dining room, sushi in the **Japanese** restaurant, or **curry** in the Maple Leaf.

### EAT

**Hippari-Dako** ひっぱりだこ *1011 Kamihatsuishi (B2). 0288-53-2933.*

Open *10am–8pm*. A small room with tables and walls covered with visiting cards. Tasty dishes at modest prices: ***teriyaki*** grilled in a soy sauce marinade, ***yaki soba*** noodles, curried ***udon*** noodles, etc.

**Shokudou Suzuki 食堂すずき** *581-2 Gokomachi (B2). 0288-54-0662. Open Thu–Tue, 11.15am–2.30pm, 5.15–9pm.* Italian, Chinese, Korean, and Japanese cuisine. Ideal for those who can't make up their mind.

**Shinmatsu 新松** *934-1 Nakahatsuishi-cho (B2). 0288-54-0041. Open Thu–Tue 11am–3pm, 5.30–11pm.* Three low tables alongside the counter and an owner, as discreet as she is efficient, busy preparing vegetable tempura, sea bream sashimi, etc.

**Suzuya 鈴屋** *2315-1 Yamauchi (behind the Kosugi Hoan Museum of Art) (B1). 0288-53-6117.Open 11am–3pm.* Specialty of ***soba***, ***udon***, and ***yuba*** (dried bean curd) seasoned with ***sansho***, a local plant used to spice up the dishes.

**Unagi Sawamoto うなぎ・澤本** *1019 Kamihatsuishi-machi (B2). 0288-54-0163. Open 11.30am–1.40pm, 5–6.40pm.* Eel has the place of honor in this family-owned restaurant 5min from the Shin-kyo Bridge. A variety of carefully prepared set meals.

**Mihashi Steak House みはしステーキハウス** *1115 Kamihatu Ishimachi (B2). 0288-54-3429. Open 11.30am–8pm.* The best steak in Nikko! *Full menu or meat by weight.*

**Restaurant Enya レストラン日光えんや** *443 Ichiyamachi (C2). 0288-53-5605. Open Tue–Sun 11am–11pm.* Steaks, skewers, and ***shabu-shabu***. A welcoming restaurant that also has some excellent beers.

**Takai-ya 高井屋** *4-9 Hon-cho (A1–2). 0288-53-0043. Reservations required.* You will certainly have a unique experience if you manage to reserve a table in this unusual establishment, run by the Takai family since 1805. In the kitchen is "monsieur le chef," with a fantastic talent for blending new flavors, like smoked trout marinated for three days in salted water, or rolls of yuba with ***wasabi*** (grated horseradish). In the restaurant is "madame," elegant in both mind and body, a contemporary geisha as fascinating to listen to as she is to watch.

You will be the only guests in the dining room, which looks out over a wonderful garden—in order to look after their guests they receive very few. So, relax in the pauses between the whispering of the ***shoji*** (screens), listen to the croaking of the green frogs in the garden.

## TAKING A BREAK

**Tearoom – Yuzawaya 湯沢屋** *946 Shimohatsuishi-machi (B2). Open 11am–5pm. 0288-54-0038.* Two tables decorated with pan hooks from a sunken hearth ***(irori)*** and a rustic decor. Enjoy the green tea with stuffed rice cakes.

## SHOPPING

**Craft Store – Utakata うたかた** *925 Nakahatsuishi (B2). Open 10am–6pm (winter 5pm). 0288-53-6465.* Kimonos, ***obi***, ***tabi*** (traditional Japanese socks), and superb fabrics are sold in this charming boutique.

## STAY

### ASHIKAGA

**Hotel Wakasa ホテルわかさ** *2374-2 Daimondori Ashikaga-shi Tochigi-ken, just beside Banna-ji. www.wakasa-h.co.jp/facilities.htm.* A well-kept business hotel, reasonably priced and ideally located near *Ashikaga Gakko,* Japan's oldest university.

**New Miyako Hotel ニューミヤコホテル本館** *4254-1 Minami-cho Ashikaga-shi Tochigi-ken, just beside Ashikaga-shi station. www.newmiyakohotel.co.jp/honkan.html.* A clean and convenient business hotel next to *Tobu Ashikaga-shi station.* **View** over the Watarase River from the 9th-floor restaurant.

## STAY

### SAITAMA AND GUNMA PREFECTURES

**Ryokan Tanigawa 旅館たにがわ** *next to Tanigawa onsen, Minakami. 0278-72-2468. 35 rooms.* Beautiful, recently-built traditional-style ryokan. Western or Japanese rooms, ***onsen*** integrated into ***rotenburo.***

## EAT

**Hanamizuki 囲炉里庵 花水木** *499 Nagatoro. 0494-66-1113. 11am–2pm, 5pm–8pm, by reservation.* This charming restaurant with its river **view** serves delicious udon *(zuriageudon)* and grilled fish. You eat in a private room, around a square hearth cut in the ground, where the food is cooked. You can also eat in the other, less expensive wing of the restaurant: **Iwazakura**.

# Mount Fuji★★★
# 富士山

**"A wise man climbs Mount Fuji once. A madman climbs it twice." If this saying still holds true, the reason is not so much the difficulty of the walk up the mountain as the number of climbers with whom you share the privilege of reaching the highest summit in Japan … in single file! For Westerners, such is the myth of the mountain, a potent symbol of Japan and all things Japanese, that climbing it is as inevitable as it is unforgettable. As far as the Japanese are concerned, Mount Fuji is still a sacred mountain, revered for at least 12 centuries and visited every year by 17 million people. As close to perfection in shape as it is possible to get, its snowcapped peak has graced millions of images across the world.**

- **Population:** Hakone 12,632.
- **Michelin Map:** Principle Sights Map B3 – Regional Map p119.
- **Location:** Hakone, 62.1mi/100km from Tokyo in Kanagawa prefecture; Mount Fuji, 55.9mi/90km from Tokyo in Yamanashi prefecture.
- **Kids: Tenzan Open-Air Spa**, the **Museum of the Little Prince**, and the **Hakone Checkpoint**.
- **Timing:** Allow two days.
- **Don't miss: The Hakone Open-Air Museum**; the **Itchiku Kubota Art Museum** at Kawaguchi Lake; the **Mishima Yukio Museum** for enthusiasts of his work *(Lake Yamanaka)*.

## THE HAKONE REGION★

Part of the **Fuji-Hakone-Izu National Park**, the region embodies all Japan's most characteristic geographic traits—volcanoes, small lakes, thermal springs, and, where lava has not made the soil too impermeable, verdant forests. As a result Hakone's *onsen* (hot springs), which are only just over one hour from Tokyo, are among some of the finest in Japan.

## THE HAKONE LOOP

### Tenzan Onsen★ 天山湯治郷

*Hakone-Yumoto, 546.8yd/500m after the Okada Hotel. No charge for transfer from Hakone-Yumoto bus station. Open 9am–10pm. ¥1,200. Bathing essentials not supplied.*

One of the largest thermal bath complexes in Japan. Indoor and outdoor baths with

Mount Fuji viewed from Kawaguchiko

© Franck Guizou/hemis.fr

different water temperatures. Sauna and massage rooms for head-to-toe massage.

### Hakone Open-Air Museum★★
彫刻の森美術館

*Electric train from Hakone-Yumoto to Chokoku-no-Mori station. Open 9am–5pm. ¥1,600. www.hakone-oam.or.jp.*

This open-air museum, which celebrated its 40th anniversary in 2009 (and in its day the first of its kind), is a pleasant surprise. Stroll through the grounds and discover the sculptures that stand out superbly against the natural backdrop. The exhibition centers around 120 contemporary sculptures *(Henry Moore, Niki de Saint Phalle, etc.)* and one pavilion is dedicated to Picasso.

### Museum of the Little Prince★ 星の王子さまミュージアム

*909 Sengokuhara. Electric train to Gora, then Tozan Bus to the museum. Open 9am–6pm (last admission 5pm). ¥1,500. www.tbs.co.jp/l-prince.*

Readers of the much-loved children's book *The Little Prince* by Antoine de Saint-Exupéry (written in the Bevin House on Long Island, New York) will enjoy this museum. The models and reconstructions of characters from the book are a little Disney-esque in style.

### Owaku-dani Valley★★ 大涌谷

*From Gora station, funicular tram to Souzan (9min), then cable car to Owaku-dani station, 1st stop. ¥820 with Hakone Free Pass, otherwise ¥1,470 round trip.*

It takes eight minutes to rise from 2,431.1ft/741m to 3,425.2ft/1,044m, from where you can look down on the "valley of hell," Owaku-dani. The valley appeared around 3,000 years ago following a volcanic eruption that shook Kamiyama *(4,717.8ft/1,438m)*. The legacy of the eruption is a brown, ravaged volcanic landscape with active sulfur vents and tendrils of steam from the hot springs. Incidentally, the smell of sulfur was classified by the Environment Ministry as one of the 100 most common smells in Japan. Try local specialty *kuro tamago*, eggs that

Owaku-dani Valley

© Kate Holdsworth/iStockphoto.com

turn black when immersed in one of the boiling springs *(6 eggs ¥500)*.

### Lake Ashi Cruise 芦ノ湖

*From Owaku-dani take the cable car to Togendai (2 stops, ¥1,020 one-way journey). At the exit follow the crowd of visitors going to the pier a bit farther down. Open Mar 20–Nov 23. 9.30am–5pm. ¥970 for one-way journey.*

Cruise boats leave Togendai and cross the waters of this large lake *(11.2mi/18km long)* to Hakone-Machi. It's an uneventful crossing, but the **views** of Mount Fuji are splendid.

### Narukawa Art Museum
成川美術館

*Very close to Hakone-Machi pier. Open 9am–5pm. ¥1,200.*

An exhibition of contemporary Japanese artists of varying degrees of talent. Perhaps the finest picture is provided by the magnificent panoramic **view** to be enjoyed from the cafe. A small collection of Noh masks.

### Hakone Checkpoint★
箱根関所

*Walk N around Lake Ashi (about 15min). Open 9am–4.30pm. ¥500.*

A reconstruction of one of the checkpoints put in place by the Tokugawa shoguns to function during the Edo era.

The checkpoint at Hakone was set up in 1619 and was the first of 53 control points on the Tokaido road (the eastern road linking Edo to Kyoto). As well as checking the credentials etc. of the men who passed through with their weapons, and taxing goods, checkpoints were used to prevent women from leaving Edo. This enabled the shogun to exert pressure on the *daimyo*, who thus had to leave their families behind in their residences near the capital. This system requiring alternate attendance in the lords' domain and at Edo *(sankin kotai)* enabled the shogun to suppress the power and wealth of his vassals (*see p120)*. The careful reconstruction was six years in the making and gives a detailed picture of daily life at a checkpoint.

### Old Tokaido road★★ 旧東海道

*Opposite the checkpoint, the avenue of cedars leads to the old Tokaido road.*

The cedar trees planted along the Tokaido road were no doubt intended to provide shelter for travelers of high rank, particularly the shoguns. Those who had been newly promoted also took this road to the capital, Kyoto, in order to receive their honor from the Emperor. The protocol changed with the reign of Tokugawa Iemitsu when it became the Emperor's responsibility to send an emissary bearing the Imperial mandate to Edo. A stretch of around 1.2mi/2km of this **cedar-lined avenue★★** still exists. Along the way, try an *ama-sake* (sweet, mild drink) at the Amazake-chaya (*open 7am–5.30pm)*, a rustic-style tea house, where the samurai used to stop off on their journeys.

### The Tokaido road as seen by Hiroshige

For an impression of the beauty of the land- and seascapes crossed or skirted by the Tokaido road, study one of the famous series of prints by the great artist Hiroshige Ando (1797–1858): *The Fifty-Three Stations of the Tokaido Road*, executed between 1832 and 1834. The series received such critical and commercial acclaim that in the following years, the artist produced other series devoted to the country's most beautiful landscapes, in particular *Thirty-Six Views of Mount Fuji* (1852 and 1858) and *One Hundred Famous Views of Edo* (1856–8).

### Hakone Shrine★ 箱根神社

*Moto-Hakone, back along the lake heading NW. No charge.*

The shrine's beautiful bright red *torii* (gates) set in the waters at the edge of Lake Ashi stand out from across the water contrasting with the background of greenery. Standing at the end of a magnificent **avenue of cypress trees★★**, this shrine, built in 757, is one of the oldest in Kanto.

## EXCURSIONS

### Yugawara 湯河原

*About 30km/17mi from Hakone – easy access by JR train, Odoriko Express from Tokyo station.*

100km/62mi from Tokyo in Kanagawa prefecture, this town is known for its thermal spas, referred to in 7C literature. Though near Hakone, Yugawara has preserved a peaceful authenticity. Heading up the Fujiki River you come to Oku-Yugawara, a forest with a sprinkling of traditional ryokan, where many Japanese writers drew inspiration: Shimazaki Toson, Natsume Soseki, and Akutagawa Ryuhnosuke amongst others.

### Manazuru Peninsula 真鶴

*About 82min via JR Tokaido from Tokyo station, or from Yugawara station by bus or JR.*

It is a pleasant stroll along the coast or in the old forest here. The sea resort, the old castle ruins, the little port and the beach at Kotogahama all contribute to making this an enjoyable place to stay. Don't miss the sunrise that draws many Japanese on the first day of the New Year.

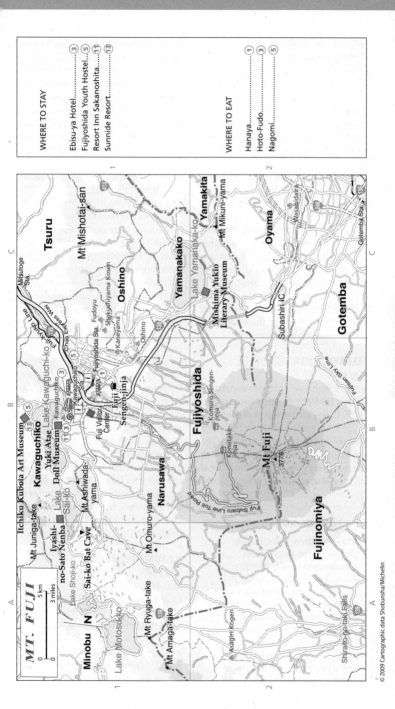

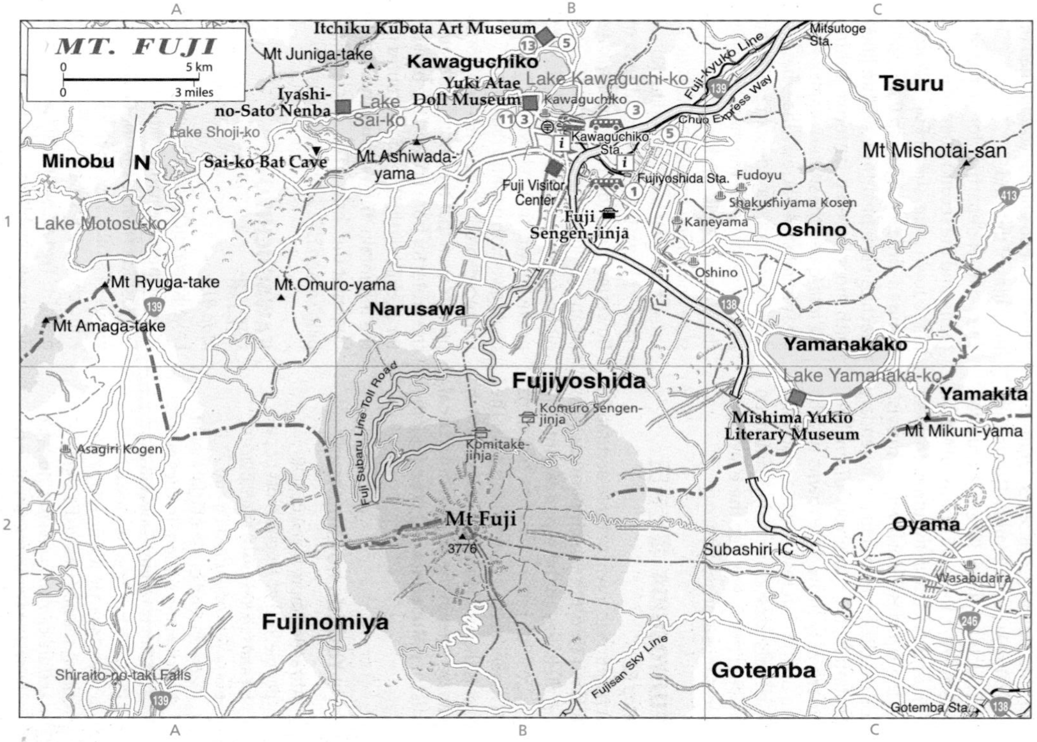


© 2009 Cartographic data Shobunsha/Michelin

WHERE TO STAY

- Ebisu-ya Hotel.................... 3
- Fujiyoshida Youth Hostel... 5
- Resort Inn Sakanoshita...... 11
- Sunnide Resort.................. 13

WHERE TO EAT

- Hanaya.............................. 1
- Hoto-Fudo......................... 3
- Nagomi.............................. 5

## MOUNT FUJI★★★

富士山 *Allow 2 days.*

The sight of the perfect peak of Fuji-san set against a vivid blue sky never fails to enthrall, wherever it is viewed—and it is visible from just about everywhere—from either Yamanashi *(the north face)* or Shizuoka *(the south face)* prefectures. The summit of the volcano is permanently covered in snow and at an altitude of 12,388.5ft/3,776m, it is the highest peak in Japan. Due to their destructive nature (the last eruption was in 1707), the *kami* (spirits) of Mount Fuji are treated with the utmost respect by the Japanese. However, for the visitor, the closer you get to this legendary mountain, the more your disenchantment may grow. The towns nearby are of little interest and the mountain itself gets crowded with those intent on making the ascent. Yet, there are some pleasant surprises, too.

### FUJIYOSHIDA 富士吉田

*Map B2.*

A pilgrimage town, or more accurately, a town through which pilgrims pass on their way to the top of Mount Fuji, Fujiyoshida retains two fine buildings as reminders of its prosperous past. The first is the **Oshi lodging house**, which can be seen in the **Fujiyoshida Local History Museum**★ *(open 9.30am–5pm; ¥300)*. Each town would send a group of pilgrims *(fujiko)* to Mount Fuji under the protection of the *oshi*, the priest responsible for the spiritual and material guidance of the pilgrims on the sacred heights of the mountain. Depending on its financial situation, a town would shoulder either the entire cost of constructing an *oshi* lodging house or share it with other towns. By the end of the Edo era, Fujiyoshida had up to 82 inns of this kind.

The point of departure for all the pilgrims, and the second point of interest in the town is the shrine **Fuji Komuro Sengen-jinja**★★ *(open 9am–5pm)* reached via a beautiful avenue lined with moss-covered lanterns. Behind the *torii* (gates) the shrine complex—an area of almost 24.7 acres/10ha—has put down its roots alongside some stunning ancient cedar trees. The main building, the Honden, built in the Momoyama style and dating from the 17C, is dedicated to several *kami,* including Konohana sakuya hime, the goddess of flowering trees (derived from *sakuya* meaning "flowering cherry tree"). The highly fertile goddess was required to prove her worth by showing that she could give birth during a raging fire. This unprecedented act gave her additional powers from that time on: she became the protector from fire and the facilitator of child birth. One of the routes up the mountain, the **Fujinomiya Trail**, begins at the shrine. The official climbing season is in July and August.

### KAWAGUCHIKO★

河口湖

*Map B1.*

Lake Kawaguchi on the edge of the town of the same name and not far from Fujiyoshida *(1.9m/3km)*, has excellent **views** of Mount Fuji. In spring its flowering cherry trees are a photographer's delight. Two museums also make the detour worthwhile.

#### Kawaguchiko Muse Museum★★

河口湖ミューズ館 (与 勇輝館)

*Map B1.*

#### Yoshida no Himatsuri

Attracting more than 200,000 people, one of Japan's most popular *matsuri* (festivals) takes place every year on August 26 and 27. It marks the end of the official Mount Fuji climbing season. Torches over 9.8ft/3m tall light 1.2mi/2km of the main trail from the town of Fujiyoshida. On the first day *(Chinkasai)*, the gods leave the shrine and are carried in *mikoshi* (portable shrines) and *mikage* (a shrine in the shape of Mount Fuji) to the house of rest of the gods *(Otabisho)*. On the second day *(Susuki)*, they are returned to the shrine.

*Kawaguchiko-Ohashi Bridge.*
*Open 9am–5pm. ¥600.*
This small museum displays dolls made by Atae Yuki (born 1937), who has revived the craft of doll making in Japan. Made out of cotton fabric, many of his creations are modeled on Japanese children and are hauntingly beautiful; he is particularly skilled in creating their expressions. Atae Yuki's dolls have been exhibited worldwide.

### Itchiku Kubota Art Museum★★★ 久保田一竹美術館

*Map B1.*
*2255 Kawagushi, Fujikawaguchiko, 25min by bus or 15min by taxi from Kawaguchiko station. Open Apr–Nov Thu–Tue 9.30am–5.30pm; Dec–Mar Thu–Tue 10am–5pm. ¥1,300.*
This unique and original museum is dedicated to the great textile artist Kubota Itchiku (1917–2003). The central building, a pyramid-shaped structure framed by 16 ancient cypress trees, contains displays of large-scale contemporary kimonos. These "things to wear"—the meaning of "kimono"—which each take an average of two years to make, weigh three or four times more than a regular kimono. Each thread has been produced with a dyeing technique *(tsujigahana)* used between the 14C and 17C. The whole work, called "Symphony of Light," is made up of 80 kimonos inspired by the theme of the four seasons *(only 30 are displayed at any one time)*. The new wing, inspired by Gaudi, houses a collection of Tombodama glass pearls from Mesopotamia dating back 3,500 years. In the garden, a waterfall and tearoom complete your visit.

## AROUND LAKE SAIKO 西湖

*Map A–B1.*
The eruptions of Mount Fuji over thousands of years have considerably altered the appearance of the landscape. Of the 80 caves in the area, the **Saiko Bat Cave** *(open 9am–5pm; ¥300)* is the largest, reaching a depth of 1,246.7ft/380m.

*From the cave, take the Retro Bus to the N of Lake Sai (10min).*

### Iyashi-no-Sato Nenba いやしの里根場

*Map B1.*
*2710 Saiko-Nenba, Fuji-Kawaguchiko.*
*Open 9am–5pm. ¥200.*
*www.fujisan.ne.jp/iyashi.*
Destroyed by a typhoon in 1963, this **traditional village** with a population of 235 was rebuilt in 2003 to revive some specialist skills that were in danger of being lost. Of the 40 houses that make up the village, just under 20 have been rebuilt with thatched roofs in the shape of a warrior's helmet *(kabuto-zukuri)*, a skill which today very few craftsmen are still practicing.

*Itchiku Kubota Art Museum*
Itchiku Kubota Art Museum

### Koshu, a purely Japanese wine

Although famous for its fruits (persimmons, apples, grapes), Yamanashi prefecture was the birthplace of the country's wine industry and is becoming increasingly recognized for its Koshu (the old name for Yamanashi) vines. Although grown in Japan since the 8C BC (probably introduced from the Caucasus via the silk routes), the vines only started to be cultivated on a scale in 1877 after the establishment of the region's first viticultural society. Grapes are grown in the Katsunuma Valley in southeast Yamanashi and today provide 25 percent of Japanese wine. An unstructured dry white, slightly acidic with the aroma of lemons, it has recently been exported to Europe for the first time. Grace Wine, set up in 1923 and one of Japan's largest winemakers *(there are now 90 in Yamanashi prefecture)*, produces 250,000 bottles per year and its Grace Koshu has recently been acclaimed by critics. *For full information visit the website of the Japanese amateur wine association: www.jp-wine.com/en.*

Traditional crafts are on display in some of the houses, including pottery, weaving, doll making, and incense making (using powdered charcoal mixed with plum syrup to produce its characteristic fragrance).

## AROUND LAKE YAMANAKA

山中湖 *Map C1/2.*

Situated at an altitude of 3,215.2ft/980m, the largest *(8.4mi/13.5km long)* and highest lake in the region is very popular in summer, particularly with the citizens of Tokyo, who use it for all kinds of watersports. Adjacent to the lake, in a wooded area (*part of the Bungaku no Mori park)*, are museums dedicated to the famous writer Mishima Yukio and influential author and journalist Tokutomi Soho. Work by the poet Tomiyasu Fusei is also displayed.

### Mishima Yukio Museum (Bungakukan)★★

三島由紀夫文学館 *Map C2.*

*5min from Bungaku-no Mori Koen bus stop. ¥300.*

This museum is bursting with original documents and memorabilia of the great Japanese writer Yukio Mishima. You can also see the desk at which he used to work. Yukio Mishima's major works, such as *Confessions of a Mask*, are on display.

## ASCENT OF MOUNT FUJI★★

富士登山 *Map B2.*

*Climbing is authorized only between Jul 1 and Aug 31. Take suitable clothing—the temperature is only 41°F/5°C at the top.*

Mount Fuji is divided into 10 *gome*, or stations—the first, *Ichi-gome*, at 4,610ft/1,405m, the second, *Ni-gome*, at 5,236.2ft/1,596m, up to 12,388.5ft/3,776m. Most climbers go straight to the fifth station, *Go-gome (7,562.3ft/2,305m)*, by bus on one of the many services that depart from Kawaguchiko, Fujinomiya, and Gotenba stations. The journey of 18.6mi/30km takes 50–60min.

The traditional ascent on foot, the **Fujinomiya Trail**, starts at the Fuji Sengen-jinja. *Allow around 5hr to reach the fifth station (then a further 3hr30min to get to the top)*. There are several routes to Go-gome from the bottom of the mountain. On the north face, the Lake Kawaguchi side, you can take the Sengen or Funatsu Trails; on the south face, the Shizuoka side, the Fujinomiya Gotenba Trail *(which is quite difficult)*, or the Subashiri Trail.

From the fifth station there are just two trails via the north or south face. At the eighth station, the north- and south-face trails meet. *Allow a 5–6hr walk from the fifth station (around another 4,593.2ft/1,400m of uneven terrain)*. The Japanese generally set off at around 11pm *(or 8pm from the first station)* to reach the summit just before dawn *(5am in summer)*. At the top it takes about 1hr to walk around the crater *(2,624.7ft/800m)*. Allow 2hr to descend to the fifth station again.

## HAKONE PRACTICAL INFORMATION

### USEFUL INFORMATION

**Tourist Office** – *Hakone-Yumoto station. Open 9am–5pm. ✆0460-85-8911.* Excellent information in English.

**Post Offices/Withdrawals**– Odawara Higashi Post Office *(open 8am–9pm)*, Yumoto Post Office (*open 9am–5.30pm)*, and Hakone-Gora Post Office *(open 9am–5.30pm).*

### TRANSPORTATION

**BY TRAIN** – The **Hakone Free Pass**, *valid for 2 or 3 days*, covers almost all journeys departing from Shinjuku *(round trip)* and discounts for some sites. Allow ¥5,000 *(2 days)* and ¥5,500 *(3 days)*; www.odakyu.jp/english.

From **Tokyo station**, regular departure of the JR Shinkansen *(35min, ¥3,130)* and the JR Tokaido *(1hr35min, ¥1,450).* From **Shinjuku station** *(Tokyo)*, regular departures on the Odakyu Line *(about 1hr30min, ¥850).* On arrival at **Odawara station**, allow 20min by bus *(¥360)* for Hakone-Yumoto, 40min for Moto-Hakone *(about ¥1,150).*

**BY BUS** – **Odakyu Express Bus** – 24 buses per day from Shinjuku station *(2hr10min, ¥2,150).*

### GETTING AROUND

**BY BUS** – **Hakone Tozan Bus** and **Izu-Hakone Bus** have regular connections to main sites.

**BY ELECTRIC TRAIN** – Practical and picturesque for sites between Hakone-Yumoto and Gora *(between Hakone-Yumoto and Gora ¥390 per ticket).*

## MOUNT FUJI PRACTICAL INFORMATION

### USEFUL INFORMATION

**FUJIYOSHIDA** – **Tourist Office** – *Fujiyoshida station (B1). Open 9am–5pm. ✆0555-22-7000.* Maps and detailed explanations.

**LAKE KAWAGUCHI** – **Tourist Offices** – *Fujikawaguchiko General Tourist Information, Kawaguchiko station (B1). Open 8.30am–5.30pm. ✆0555-22-7000. Maps and detailed explanations.*

**Fuji Visitor Center** – *6663-1 Funatsu (B1). Open 8.30am–5pm. ✆0555-72-0259. Information center for Mount Fuji.*

**BY TRAIN** – From Tokyo (Shinjuku station), the Azusa Line goes to Otsuki *(65min, ¥1,280 or ¥900 by Limited Express).* At Otsuki, continue on the Fuji-Kyuko Line to Kawaguchiko *(B1). (50min, ¥1,110).* The bus from Tokyo, however, is much more practical.

Hakone Tozan Railway

© Kanagawa Prefecture/JNTO

**BY BUS** – Regular departures for Fujiyoshida *(B1)* and Kawaguchiko *(B1)* from Tokyo *(Tokyo or Shinjuku stations) (2hr, ¥1,700)*. If you arrive from Mishima, take the Express Fuji Bus from Mishima to Kawaguchiko *(2hr20min, ¥ 2,130)*. You may have to change at Gotenba.

## GETTING AROUND

**BY TRAIN OR BUS** – 2 buses per hour to Kawaguchiko, but the train is better *(5min, ¥210)*. From Kawaguchiko station, the 1930s-style **Retro Bus** tours the major sites *(¥1,000 per day)*.

**BY BICYCLE** – *Available at some hotels.* Practical for getting to Kawaguchiko.

# ADDRESSES

## STAY

### HAKONE

**Fuji Hakone Guest House**
**富士箱根ゲストハウス**
*912 Sengokuhara. ✆0460-84-6577. www.fujihakone.com. 14 rooms.* Both youth hostel *(minimum service)* and guesthouse, the Fuji welcomes travelers from all over the world. *Onsen, rotenburo*, Internet, kitchen, and lounge. Best of all, a delightful, energetic couple involved in a thousand things.

**Moto-Hakone Guest House**
**元箱根ゲストハウス**
*103 Moto-Hakone. ✆0460-83-7880. 5 rooms.* 10min from Lake Ashi, a miniature version of the Fuji Hakone Guest House with the same people in charge, but guests are welcomed by an English-speaking friend. Pleasant and convenient.

**Choraku-so Nakaji Ryokan**
**長楽荘中路旅館** *525 Kowakidani. ✆0460-82-2192. 4 rooms.* A charming *ryokan* close to the *Open-Air Museum*. The owner, whose energy is impressive at 80 years old, decorates the rooms with her calligraphy.

**Kiritani Hakone-so 桐谷箱根荘**
*1320-598 Gora. ✆0460-82-2246. 24 rooms.* On the heights of Gora, a superb villa with an annex at the side, transformed into a ryokan. Splendid **view** of the mountain. Onsen and tatami-floored dining rooms. A very attractive place.

**Takumi-no-yado Yoshimatsu**
**匠の宿・桂松** *521 Hakone-Machi. ✆0460-83-6661. www.hakone.co.jp. 19 rooms.* A superb *ryokan* enhanced by an internal garden and a magnificent *onsen*. The rooms have clean lines and a *rotenburo* from where you can admire Mount Fuji on the horizon as you bathe.

**Fujiya Hotel 富士屋ホテル** *359 Miyanoshita. ✆0460-82-2211. www.fujiyahotel.co.jp. 155 rooms.* Flower Palace, Kikka-so, Forest Lodge, Restful Cottage—the Fujiya and all its buildings make a veritable museum, blending architectural eclecticism with a colorful history. A 1hr guided tour of this must-see temple will enable you to learn more, and follow in the footsteps of Einstein, Charlie Chaplin, and the Emperors of Japan.

### MOUNT FUJ

### FUJIYOSHIDA

**Fujiyoshida Youth Hostel 富士吉田ユースホステル** *2-339 Shimo-Yoshida Hon-machi (B1). ✆0555-22-0533. 30 beds. ¥600.* A small hostel in an old town house, run by an attentive and welcoming family.

### KAWAGUCHIKO

**Resort Inn Sakanoshita**
**リゾートイン坂の下** *454 Funatsu (B1). ✆0555-72-2193. 8 rooms. Reservations required.* A large, clean, brightly-lit house owned by a charming couple (natives of Mount Fuji). Rooms with tatami, terrace, and barbecue. Quiet and convenient.

**Ebisu-ya Hotel**
**プチホテルエビスヤ** *3647 Funatsu (B1). ✆0555-72-0165. 10 rooms.* An imposing white building with red roof tiles just near the exit to Kawaguchiko station. Japanese-style rooms with a **view** of Mount Fuji.

**Sunnide Resort**
**サニーデ・リゾート** *2549-1 Oishi (B1). ✆0555-76-6004. www.sunnide.com. 28 rooms, 28 cottages.* This old villa, once the property of a famous Kyushu nobleman, has **views** of Mount Fuji and Lake Kawaguchi. The complex includes a ryokan, a renowned restaurant, and 28 hillside cottages.

**YUGAWARA**

**Ryokan Fukiya ふきや** *398 Miyakami Yugawara-machi Ashigarasimo-gun. 0465-62-1000.* Ryokan with refined architecture and decor. Seven types of thermal baths in various settings.

**MANAZURU**

**Shotokumara しょうとく丸** *1162-1 Manazuru Manazuru-machi-Ashigarashimo-gun. 0465-68-1611.* Breathtaking sunrises and sunsets from the rooms. Fish and shellfish caught that morning.

## EAT

**HAKONE**

*Note that few restaurants open in the evening as most ryokans serve an evening meal.*

**Gyoza Center 餃子センター** *1300-537 Gora. 0460-82-3457. Open 11.30am–8pm.* A welcoming atmosphere in which to try ravioli filled with pork, vegetables or ***natto*** (fermented soy beans). There are 13 varieties to choose from altogether, accompanied by miso soup. Try the place next door too: the *Honfa*, a Chinese restaurant.

**Hatsuhana はつ花本店** *635 Hakone-Yumoto. 0460-85-8287. Open Thu–Tue 10am–7pm.* A famous heroine of last century, Hatsuhana, saved her sick husband by serving him ***soba*** noodles with yam paste. It happened in Hakone, in this very house, which has been full ever since. Most popular dish: ***teijo soba*** with yam paste.

**Akatsuki-tei 暁亭** *In the Hakone-Yumoto Hotel, 97 Yumoto-chaya. 0460-85-7330. Open 11.30am–9pm. Reservations required.* A magnificent wooden building surrounded by a garden. Dining rooms with clean lines and ultra-sophisticated ***kaiseki*** cooking.

**MOUNT FUJ**

*Around Mount Fuji the evening meal is usually eaten in the hotel or ryokan.*

**FUJIYOSHIDA**

**Hanaya はなや** *6-9-1 Kamiyoshida (B1). 0555-22-2507. Open 10.30am–3.30pm.* Specialty ***teuchi udon***, thick handmade wheat noodles, eaten in soup cold, or with a hot stock.

**KAWAGUCHIKO**

**Hoto-Fudo, Kawaguchiko-Minami-ten ほうとう不動河口湖南店** *1672-2 Funatsu (B1). 0555-72-5011. Open Mon–Fri 10.30am–4pm, Sat–Sun & public holidays 10.30am–7pm.* A rustic place with tatami mats and large tables, where ***hoto*** (hot pot of ***udon*** noodles with vegetables and mushrooms) is served.

**Nagomi 和（なごみ）** *2719-114 Kawaguchi-Fuji (B1). 0555-76-6390. Open 11am–10pm.* A small room with tatami and a **view** of Mount Fuji, where you can try out some rather sophisticated dishes—pickled herring with soy beans, seafood salad, etc.

**MANAZURU**

**Shirako 割烹 しらこ** *1-5-15 Dohi Yugawara-machi-Ashigarasimo-gun. 0465-63-6363. 11.30am–2pm, 6pm–10pm.* A small Japanese restaurant close to the station, offering delicious fish meals. Breakfast set menus between ¥1,575 and ¥2,415.

**Harlequin Bis エルルカン ビス** *744-49 Miyakami - Yugawara-machi - Ashigarasimo-gun. 0465-62-3633.* Charming setting in a cluster of bamboo. French cuisine with a Japanese twist.

## TAKING A BREAK

**Tearoom – Toge-no-chaya 峠の茶屋** *2494 Kawaguchiko (B1). Open 11am–8pm. 0555-76-8388.* Toge-no-chaya is a branch of Tenka-jaya at Kawaguchiko, which was visted by Dazai. Toge-no-chaya does not seem to have had his visit as it is relatively new..

## SHOPPING

**Craft Store – Rokuro-Kobo-Katase ろくろ工房かたせ** *103 Oshiba, Moto-Hakone (next to the Moto-Hakone Guest House). Open 10am–4pm. 0460-83-6405.* For 60 years Mr Katase has been making ***kokeshi*** dolls *(see box p 417)*. Some are classical in style, others surprisingly contemporary. There are dolls to suit all tastes and purses *(¥3,500–250,000)*. An avant-garde ambassador of ***kokeshi***, Mr Katase likes to talk to his dolls.

# The Izu Peninsula★★
# 伊豆半島

**The Izu Peninsula is featured in Yasunari Kawabata's short story *The Izu Dancer* (1925) about a girl on a walking tour of the peninsula, which brings to life the beauty of the area. While it is true that in the 1920s the peninsula was accessible only along a network of winding tracks—trains did not yet service the whole area—the region was nonetheless already attracting visitors, particularly from nearby Tokyo, who would come to recharge their batteries beside the glittering lakes carved directly out of the volcanic landscape. The area has been developed since then and Highway 414 winds its way across the peninsula and the famous Loop ("spiral") Bridge. Nevertheless, Izu has managed to avoid large concrete developments and has kept its traditional, old-style Japanese hotels.**

- **Population:** Shimoda: 25,396, Shuzenji: 16,328.
- **Michelin Map:** Principal Sights Map B3, Regional Map p119.
- **Info:** See Addresses.
- **Location:** Shizuoka prefecture, about 62mi/100km from Tokyo.
- **Kids:** The Wakano-ura and Chikurin no Komichi walks.
- **Timing:** Allow three days to enjoy the *onsen*.
- **Don't miss:** Once won't hurt; if you want to do something crazy, the memory of Arai Ryokan in Shuzenji will stay with you for ever (*see p229*).

## SHIMODA★★ 下田

Shimoda is an ancient site going back to prehistoric times. Indeed, a great many remains from the Joman period have been found within the city limits. The town's history, however, revolves around the fact that under the terms of the Shimoda Treaty, signed on May 25, 1854 by Hayashi Daigaku, the plenipotentiary ambassador of the shogun government, and Commodore Matthew C. Perry of the American Navy, its port became accessible to Western powers. Despite its interesting history, it is Shimoda's physical beauty that puts it on the tourist map. Situated at the southern end of the peninsula, which until recently was only accessible by boat, Shimoda's trump card is a magnificent bay, with

*Shirahama Beach, Shimoda*

almost tropical vegetation whose tangled roots cling to rugged contours. Nearby Mount Fuji has been on occasion a particularly noisy neighbor.

## EAST OF SHIMODA

### Nesugata-yama★ 寝姿山

*Take the cable car opposite Izukyu Shimoda station (1min). Open 9am–5pm. ¥1,200 round trip.*

Start by tackling Mt. Nesugata, thus named because its shape is reminiscent of a reclining woman. From the top *(656.2ft/200m)*, you can enjoy a beautiful **view** over the town and bay.

### Bay Stage Shimoda
ベイ・ステージ下田

*Walk along the Inouzawa River toward the port bay area, 15min from the station.*

This concrete building overlooking the bay hosts a museum covering the history of the Izu Peninsula and the town of Shimoda *(open 9am–5pm; ¥500)*. Below there is a colorful **fish market** each Sunday morning *(open 8am–11am)*. Have lunch in one of the cheap eateries next door *(open 9am–1.30pm; ¥1,500)*.

### Gyokusen-ji★★ 玉泉寺

*40min walk from the station along the bay (or bus no. 10, ¥160). Open 8.30am–5pm. ¥300, museum ¥400.*

This Zen temple housed the first American Consulate for three years, before it was relocated to Tokyo. A small museum displays a collection of personal objects *(china, glasses)* belonging to Consul Harris, visited by former president Jimmy Carter in 1979. Also noteworthy are a few daguerreotypes left behind by a Russian sailor and photographer, one of the first to use this photographic process invented in 1837.

Above the temple, two small cemeteries face each other: one American and one Russian. They contain the tombs of young sailors who were killed when a typhoon struck the *Diana*, Russia's Admiral Putyatin's vessel, who was on a diplomatic mission to Japan. More unusual is the **milk monument**, commemorating the first official drinking of cow's milk in Japan—in the early 19C milk was still unknown as a drink to the vast majority of Japanese.

## FROM MAI MAI-DORI TO THE PORT

### Hofuku-ji★ 宝福寺

*Mai Mai-dori, 10min from the station. Open 8am–5pm. ¥300.*

Visitors to this temple come mainly because of its small museum and one of the tombs it contains. Both invoke the memory of **Okichi Saito** (1841–90).

At the age of 16, after two years of training to become a geisha, Okichi was forced by the shogun to become a *rashamen* ("sheep," the name given to Japanese women who took Westerners as lovers). It was thought that her great beauty would be an additional asset in the negotiations being undertaken with the US Consul General to Japan, Townsend Harris (1804–78), who was attempting to open up Japan to foreign trade.

After the treaty was signed and Harris had been assigned to other missions, Tojin Okichi, "Okichi the foreigner" as she was now called, was ostracized by the community and began a life of wandering and alcoholism that finally ended when she drowned in the Inouzawa River. As no one claimed the body, a priest at Hofuku-ji gave her a burial, and in so doing unwittingly ensured the temple's popularity (he was in fact banished for this action). Kenji Mizoguchi, one of the first filmmakers to be interested in Okichi, made *Tojin Okichi (Mistress of a Foreigner)* in 1930. Since then, endless tributes have been paid to the woman who was so tainted and ultimately destroyed by her association with a foreigner in the service of her country.

### Namako Kabe★ なまこ壁

*10min walk E of the temple toward the Inouzawa River.*

The walls of the 13 traditional houses that remain here are clad with flat tiles, the joins sealed with rounded seams of white plaster said to resemble sea slugs (*namako* in Japanese). The advantage of arranging the tiles in a diamond-shaped cross-hatched pattern is that it doesn't allow water to collect (causing mold and damp), and the plaster helps with resistance to fire. A costly program of restoration *(2 million yen per house)* is in progress.

### Shimoda History Museum★★

下田開国博物館

*Continue along Mai Mai-dori.*
*Open 8am–5pm. ¥1,000.*

This fascinating museum traces the development of the town after its encounter with Commodore Perry.

A diorama shows how the port had to be adapted to meet the new steam ships' requirements for water and coal, steam ships having been previously unknown to the Japanese.

It also shows how a typhoon that destroyed the Russian vessel commanded by Admiral Putyatin enabled the Russians and the Japanese to cooperate, providing each with an opportunity to learn and develop naval construction methods.

### Ryosen-ji★★ 了仙寺

*At the junction of Mai Mai-dori and Perry Road, 5min from the History Museum and 15min from the station (bus no. 6, ¥160). Open 8.30am–5pm. ¥500; visit with English commentary (5 people or more) ¥1,000. www.izu.co.jp/~ryosenji/eigo.html.*

It was in this temple on May 25, 1854 that the shogun's ambassador Hayashi Daigaku and Commodore Perry signed the Treaty of Peace and Amity that was to lead to the opening of the port of Shimoda. The adjoining Museum of Treasures, run by the ebullient monk Daiei Matsui, contains more than 3,000 original documents relating to this period. It's also fun to see how Japanese artists represented the "foreign devils" who invaded their shores in the 19C. Today the temple is known as the "Hall of Opening the Nation."

### Choraku-ji★ 長楽寺

*Perry Road, 10min from Ryosen-ji.*
*Open 8am–5pm. No charge.*

The Peace Treaty between Russia and Japan was signed in this temple on October 15, 1854. Today, it's a charming, flower-filled place with a small museum *(¥500)* displaying a few historical souvenirs and cultural objects.

From the temple, stroll along Perry Road and the narrow canal lined with picturesque houses to discover the bust of Perry and the **Anchokuro**, the restaurant once run by Okichi Saito after Townsend Harris returned to America.

A few traces of the original restaurant still remain inside; you can then continue on to the port.

### Port and Wakano-Ura Walk★★

下田港・和歌の浦

This pleasant walk goes round the port and then follows the shore as far as the aquarium. The path loops round a hill, where Shimoda Park is located.

## SHUZENJI★★ 修善寺

This small town was established during the Heian era. The monk Kukai (774–835), later known by the name of **Kobo Daishi**, founded the temple of Shuzen-ji after he discovered the Tokko no yu hot spring.

The town of Shuzenji developed around the temple, which took on a new historical significance with the exile of **Minamoto no Yoritomo** to the Izu Peninsula in the 12C.

It was here that the man who would become the first shogun of Japan met his wife, Masako, daughter of his enemy Hojo Tokimasa. After Minamoto no Yoritomo's death, it was here too that his son Yoriie was assassinated—with the complicity of Masako—by the man who became regent, Hojo.

Overcome with remorse, Masako had the temple of Shuzen-ji dedicated to her son. From then on the town became associated with this dramatic story worthy of a Shakespearean tragedy, as well as for its excellent hot springs. The range of fine hotels frequented by top writers, especially during the Meiji Period of 1868–1912, adds to the overall appeal of the town and has put it firmly on the tourist map; celebrated authors who came here to enjoy the waters and draw literary inspiration include Ryunosuke

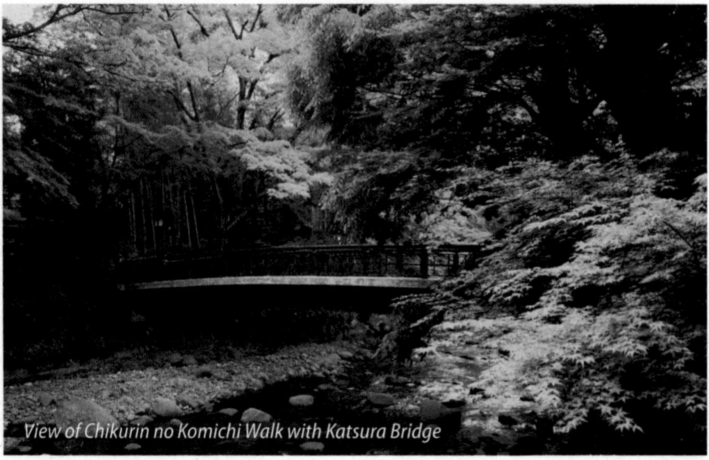

View of Chikurin no Komichi Walk with Katsura Bridge

Akutagawa, Yasunari Kawabata, Yasushi Inoue, and Natsume Soseki.
Soseki (*I am a Cat*) in particular came to Shuzenji to undergo treatment at the hot springs for serious stomach ailments. Indeed, it was during this stay at Shuzen-ji Temple that his illness took a turn for worse and his life hung by a thread; fortunately, the crisis passed, and in gratitude and joy for his return to the land of the living, he authored innumerable *haiku* and Chinese-style kanshi verses as he recovered at Shuzenji Temple.
He wrote the following famous haiku 10 days after the crisis when he was finally able to swallow a little gruel:

Spring trickling,
into the heart,
the taste of porridge.

### Chikurin no Komichi Walk★★ 竹林の小径

*From Kaede Bridge to Katsura Bridge along the river of the same name (around 218.7yd/200m).*
Beside the Katsura River just past the bridge is a small pavilion that shelters the famous **Tokko no yu *onsen***, which, according to legend, appeared when Kobo Daishi struck a rock here with his *tokko* (ritual Tantric staff). The monk is said to have been touched by the sight of a child washing his father's diseased back with cold water. Since then the temperature has been a soothing 105.8°F/41°C.

### Shuzen-ji★★ 修禅寺

*Opposite Tokko no yu. Open 8.30am–4pm. Museum ¥300.*
The Buddhist temple around which the story of Shuzen-ji—from Kobo Daishi to the death of Yoriie Minamoto—has

### The death mask

In 1203, Minamoto no Yoriie, 21-year-old son of the first shogun, was forced to seek refuge in the temple of Shuzen-ji; he had plotted against his maternal grandfather, the regent Hojo Tokimasa, who had removed him from power. One year later, Yoriie was assassinated. He was supposedly poisoned as he unwittingly immersed himself in a bath filled with lacquer. His contorted features are said to have been carved into this death mask that was sent to his mother. Okamoto Kido (1872–1939), a talented exponent of the *torimonocho* or detective novel, turned the legend into the play *Shuzenji Monogatari* (1908) popularizing this tragic story: It was staged both at the Kabuki-za of Tokyo in 1911, and in Paris in 1927.

Shuzen-ji



evolved has experienced many ups and downs (the main hall has burned down on several occasions). When Hojo Soun (1432–1529) financed its reconstruction in the 15C, he placed the shrine under the protection of his cousin, the priest Ryukei Hanjoi, who belonged to the Soto Zen sect. So the temple, maintained first by the Shingon sect founded by Kukai in 807, then by the Rinzai sect from 1275, finally came under the jurisdiction of the Soto sect from 1489. It was destroyed in 1863 and rebuilt under the profoundly pro-Shinto and anti-Buddhist Meiji era. Dating from the first period is the sculpture of the **Dainichi Nyorai★★** (the cosmic Buddha to whom the temple is dedicated), in Sanskrit Vairocana: "He who spreads light all around." The cosmic Buddha is the central figure of Shingon, the "True Word" in Japanese. Sculpted by Jikkei, it was commissioned by Masako for her son's seventh birthday. There are also beautiful Buddhist paintings on display, a saddle in mother-of-pearl, and of course the famous **red mask** with distorted features (*see box p227*) in the adjoining **museum★**.

### Shigetsu-den★★ 指月殿

*Opposite the Shuzen-ji. Cross the Katsura River and follow the signs.*

In this small temple constructed entirely of wood, the oldest temple on the Izu Peninsula (13C), Minamoto no Yoritomo's wife Masako created a sutra library (Buddhist texts) to appease her son's soul and to protect her own, since her complicity in his murder was undeniable. Next to the temple, in Genji Park at the bottom of Shikayama hill, the grave of **Minamoto Yoriie** (1182–1204) was restored in 1703 to commemorate the 500th anniversary of his death.

## IZU PENINSULA PRACTICAL INFORMATION

### USEFUL INFORMATION

**SHIMODA – Tourist Offices – Shimoda Municipal Tourist Association**, *1-4-27 Shimoda, in front of the station. Open 10am–5pm. 0558-23-5593.*

**Shimoda International Exchange Club** – *0558-22-3166. Voluntary tourist guide association.*

**SHUZENJI – Tourist Office – Izu Municipal Tourist Association**, *Shuzenji section 838-1, at exit to village, opposite post office. 0558-72-2501.*

### TRANSPORTATION

**SHIMODA**

**BY TRAIN** – From Tokyo or Shinjuku station, Odoriko or Superview Odoriko *(2hr50min, about ¥6,800)* to Shimoda station. Or Shinkansen to Atami, then change for the train to Shimoda.

*Sit on the left on the train from Tokyo to enjoy the view over the sea and the Izu coastline.*

**BY BICYCLE Rental** – **Noguchi Rent-A-Cycle**, *1-3-14, Shimoda. 3min walk from the station. Open 9.30am–6pm. ¥2,000 per day.*

**SHUZENJI**

**BY TRAIN** – From Tokyo, direct trains Odoriko *(2hr, ¥4,080)* or change at Mishima for Shuzenji station. For Nagoya, Izuhakone Sunzu Line to Mishima, then Shinkansen Hikari *(1hr20min, ¥8,060)*.

**BY BUS** – From Shimoda to Kawazu, train then bus from Kawazu to Shuzenji *(12 per day, 1hr30min, ¥1,650)*.

# ADDRESSES

## STAY

### SHIMODA

**Ryokan Nansuiso 旅館南水荘** *1-21-17 Higashi-Hongo. 0558-22-2039. 6 rooms. Reservations through the Tourist Office.* Light, spacious rooms with **views** over the Shimoda canal and the flowering cherry trees. *Onsen.*

**Yamane Ryokan やまね旅館** *1-19-15 Shimoda. 0558-22-0482. 9 rooms. Reservations through the Tourist Office.* In the town center, a well-kept *ryokan* run by an endearing, elderly couple who don't speak much English.

**Shimoda Bay Kuroshio 下田ベイクロシオ** *4-1 Kakisaki. 0558-27-2111. www.baykuro.co.jp. 40 rooms.* Although the outside isn't up to much, there's a magnificent **view** from the bay windows of this *ryokan*, which has all modern conveniences.

**Kanaya Ryokan 金谷旅館** *114-2 Kochi. 10min by taxi from Shimoda. 0558-22-0325. http://homepage2.nifty.com/kanaya. 10 rooms, annex 3 rooms.* One of the finest *ryokan* in Japan, established in 1866. Kawabata makes reference to it in his books and the superb staircase was immortalized during the filming of *The Izu Dancer.*

### SHUZENJI

**Shuzenji Youth Hostel** 修善寺ユースホステル *4279-152 Shuzenji. 2.5mi/4km in the hills above the town, bus no 6 toward Nijinokyo, "Newtown exit" stop. 0558-72-1222. 16 dormitories. ¥3,800/person.* A large, white building in the heart of nature. Peaceful and basic.

**Arai Ryokan 新井旅館** *70 Shuzenji. 0558-72-2007. http://arairyokan.net/english. 25 rooms.* If you get the chance to spend the night in one ryokan, this is one of the finest in Japan. Built in 1872, the hotel is a model of refinement and architectural subtlety, much of it listed, the 7C baths are outstanding. There are even organized visits for nonresidents. A museum displays a sample of its 700 pieces in rotation. *Prices ¥24,300–73,650/person, breakfast and dinner inc. Spa: ¥150.*

**Yagyu-no-Sho 柳生の庄** *1116-6 Shuzenji. 0558-72-4126. www.yagyu-no-sho.com. 15 rooms.* The Yagu, a samurai family famous for being martial arts instructors to the Tokugawa shoguns, have created a perfect temple. No detail is left to chance—flowers are arranged by a great Ikebana professional in an *onsen* surrounded by roses. Adjoining *kendo dojo* (training school for fighting with bamboo swords).

## EAT

### SHIMODA

**Kiyu 亀遊** *1-10-18 Shimoda. 0558-22-8698. Open 11am–10pm.* A pleasant restaurant serving grilled fish, abalone sautéed in butter, and tempura.

**Uo-Suke 魚助** *1-6-8 Shimoda. 0558-27-3330. Open Wed–Mon 11.30am–3pm, 5.30–10pm.* Bar or stylish dining room upstairs, where you can try the Shimoda specialty: *kin-medai*, "fish with golden eyes".

### SHUZENJI

**Bokunenjin 朴念仁** *3451-40 Shuzenji. 0558-73-0073. Open Thu–Tue 11am–3pm. Closed 3rd Thu of the month.* Splendid **view** from the bay window of the nearby enormous bamboo plantation. the *soba* noodles, which are tasty enough, leave you wanting more.

**Matsuba Jyaya 松葉茶屋** *4281-41 Shuzenji. 0558-72-0576. Open Wed–Mon 10.30am–8pm.* The specialty is *kamameshi*, rice with vegetables served in a cast-iron pot.

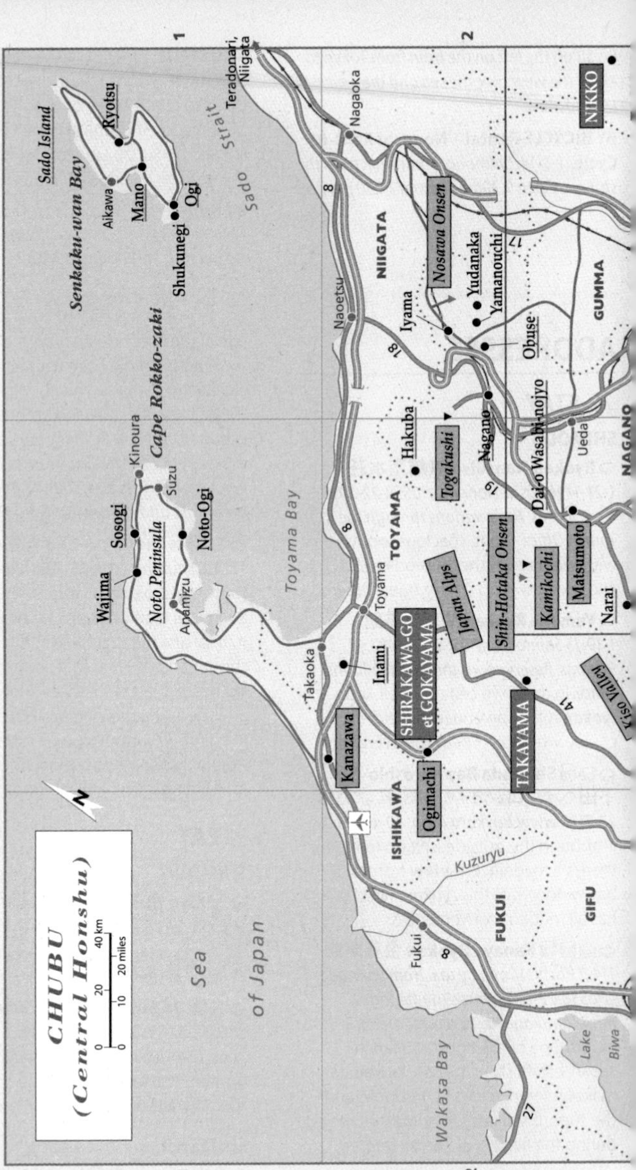


**At the center of Japan, with the mega-cities of Tokyo to the east and Kyoto to the west, the Sea of Japan sea northward, and the Pacific Ocean southward, Chubu is dominated by the spectacular peaks of the Japan Alps and offers a wide choice of terrain and tourism possibilities. Popular for its ski trails, hot springs, and hiking trails, the region is a mix of great urban centers *(Nagoya, Niigata, Nagano)*, cities of history and art *(Takayama, Kanazawa)* and quaint rural villages nestling in narrow valleys. The ancient Nakasendo Road constructed during the Edo era today still crosses the region.**

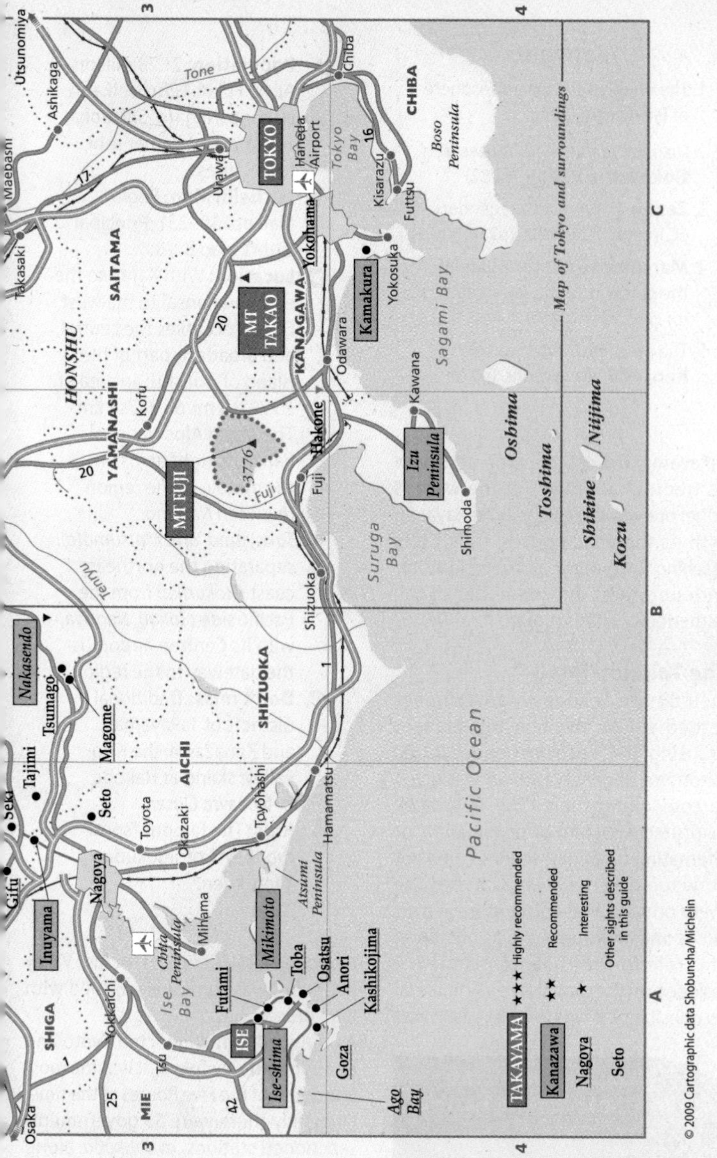


## A land of contrasts

Considered Japan's "rice basket", the northern region called Hokuriku is a strip of land squeezed between a steep mountain range and the Sea of Japan. Snow-laden in winter, hot and humid in summer, this region is an industrial fiefdom and a place where traditional craftsmanship and sites have been preserved. The peaks of the Japan Alps National Park in the center of Honshu, which are among the highest in the country, often exceed 9,843ft/3,000m. The region's urban centers also have distinct identities: Nagoya, the fourth largest city in Japan, gave birth to Toyota Industries, whereas Nagano hosted the 1998 Winter Olympic Games. Cities like Kanazawa, once peopled with samurais and geishas, Matsumoto with its castle,

# CENTRAL HONSHU (CHUBU)

## Highlights

1 The deeply spiritual atmosphere of **Ise-jingu** (p242)

2 Distinctive thatched houses of **Gokayama Valley** (p252)

3 **Zenko-ji**, home of a legendary 6C image of Buddha (p254)

4 **Matsumoto Castle**, guarding the gateway to the Japan Alps for centuries (p259)

5 The aesthetic perfection of **Kenroku-en** gardens (p270)

- **Population:** 21.78 million – Aichi, Fukui, Gifu, Ishikawa, Nagano, Niigata, Shizuoka, Toyama, and Yamanashi Prefectures.
- **Michelin Map:** Region Map pp230–231 Principal Sights Map B2/3.
- **Location:** With Kanto to the east and Kansai to the west, Chubu occupies the central, and broadest, part of the island of Honshu: an area of 25,783sq mi/66,777sq km. The Japan Alps National Park cuts right across the middle of the region *(between Nagano, Takayama, and Matsumoto)*, separating the northeast coast *(Hokuriku)* from the Pacific side *(Tokai)*. Nagoya, with its Centrair airport, is the gateway to the region.
- **Don't miss:** Traditional districts of Takayama and Kanazawa; the Kiso valley; skiing at Hakuba or Nozawa *Onsen*.
- **Kids:** The famous "snow monkeys" of Jigokudani Yaen-koen.

Takayama, the city of carpenters with its traditional houses at the water's edge, or even the village of Gokayama, with its thatched houses, their roofs reaching the ground, all leave the visitor with unforgettable memories of the authenticity of this region.

### The Tokaido Road

In 1603 the Tokugawa government settled at Edo. While in appearances granting the *daimyos* (feudal lords) autonomy, in reality priority was given to controlling them. The Tokugawa instituted a system of *sankin-kotai*, or alternating residency, so they could not grow too rich: the *daimyos* had to live every other year at Edo, and leave their wives and children there as hostages. This rule forced them to maintain a residence in the capital, a heavy financial responsibility. It was for this reason that the Tokaido Road, crossing the Kiso Valley in Chubu, was continually busied with long processions of travelers.

As the road that connected Kyoto and Edo (modern-day Tokyo), it was the most important of the Five Routes of the time. Originally there were 53 government-sanctioned stations, or *shukuba*, along the Tokaido, where weary travelers could stop for food and lodging. This number was in reference to the 53 Buddhist teachers the youth Sudhana visited in his quest for enlightenment, as recounted in early Chinese and Japanese writings, such that the Tokaido Road was a metaphor for his spiritual journey. These *shukuba* were later immortalized by the great *ukio-e* master Hiroshige in his series *The Fifty-Three Stations of the Tokaido.*

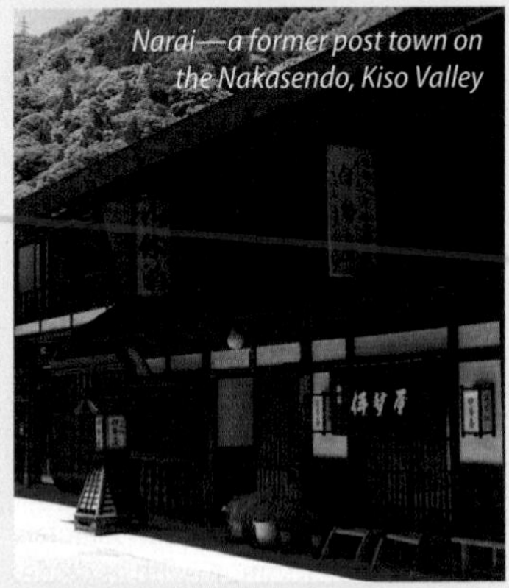

*Narai—a former post town on the Nakasendo, Kiso Valley*

# Nagoya★
# 名古屋

**The prosperous city of Nagoya, the fourth largest in Japan, and the stronghold of the Toyota empire, has established itself as one of the most powerful engines of Japanese economic growth. From weaving looms to automobiles, by way of porcelain and *pachinko* (the pinball game was invented here), the city was the cradle of Japanese industrial capitalism at the beginning of the 20C. A hundred years later, it is well on its way to becoming the country's second industrial hub. Badly damaged by air raids during WW II, Nagoya was recast in the Toyota company mold, a grid pattern of wide boulevards designed for cars straddled by walkways for pedestrians. Although hardly a magnet for tourists, this gray, sprawling metropolis is not lacking in leisure activities or places to visit, including an interesting castle, an important shrine, and a first-class aquarium. Of the towns in the surrounding area, possible destinations for excursions are Inuyama and Gifu, where cormorant fishing is practiced in summer.**

- **Population:** 2,262,185 (Greater Nagoya: 8.5 million) – Aichi Prefecture.
- **Michelin Map:** Principal Sights Map B3; Regional Map p231.
- **Location:** Nagoya is on the Pacific coast, 223.7mi/360km west of Tokyo and 115.6mi/186km east of Osaka. Most of the city stretches eastward from its vast central station, where the JR lines *(Shinkansen and others)*, the Meitetsu and Kintetsu private lines, buses, and subways all converge. The Sakura-dori subway line leads 2.2mi/3.5km to the east, to Hisaya-odori Park, location of Nagoya TV Tower. The downtown area is here, in particular the Sakae district, center of the city's nightlife. The castle is farther north; the harbor and Atsuta-jingu to the south.
- **Kids:** The port area has a number of entertaining and educational attractions.
- **Timing:** Allow one day for the city and two days for its surrounding area.
- **Don't miss:** Tokugawa Art Museum and Port of Nagoya Public Aquarium; Inuyama Castle; watching cormorant fishing at Gifu or Inuyama *(in summer)*.

## SIGHTS

### Around JR Nagoya Station

Virtually a city within a city, the central station of Nagoya, also known as Meieki, is used by more than a million passengers a day. Built in 1999, it is the largest station in the world in surface area *(15.8sq mi/41sq km)*, and is teeming with shops, restaurants, and hotels. Above it are the two white **JR Central Towers** *(803.8ft/245m high)*, while below are nearly 3.7mi/6km of underground shopping arcades. Proudly ignoring the economic downturn, the surrounding area has seen an explosion of new building: **Midland Square** *(810.4ft/247m)* in 2006, in front of the central exit from the station, was joined in 2007 by the **Lucent Tower** *(590.6ft/180m)* to the north, with its slightly curved outline; then in 2008, on the south side, by the startlingly innovative **Spiral Tower** *(557.7ft/170m)*. All these skyscrapers have **panoramic** bars and restaurants at the top, which are best at night.

### Noritake Garden ノリタケの森

*10min walk N of the station. Subway: Kamejima. Open Tue–Sun 10am–5pm. ¥500.*

### Pachinko fever

Lined up in serried ranks, like bees in a hive, the solitary *pachinko* players are glued to their machines amid the flashing lights and incredible din of the pachinko parlors. Invented in Nagoya in the 1930s, *pachinko* is now ranked third in the Japanese leisure economy, after restaurants and tourism. Japan has some 18,000 *pachinko* parlors, equipped with 5 million machines. Nearly a quarter of all Japanese—students, white collar workers, housewives, retired people—are said to play regularly, many of them addicts who spend whole days frittering away their wages. Being only just within the law (with a few exceptions, gambling is forbidden in Japan), *pachinko* is often accused of benefiting organized crime and the North Korean regime, which is said to control the considerable revenue behind the scenes.

A center of ceramic production for centuries, the Nagoya region is today responsible for almost 90 percent of the exports of Japanese porcelain, of which the Noritake company, founded in 1904, is the country's biggest manufacturer. The site of the company's first factory is now a museum displaying some fine old pieces in Art Deco style, and also houses a studio where you can see demonstrations of the techniques of painting on porcelain, which are still used today. There is a shop on the way out.

**Toyota Commemorative Museum of Industry and Technology** トヨタテクノミュージアム産業技術記念館

*546yd/500m N of Noritake Garden. Subway: Kamejima. Open Tue–Sun 9am–4.30pm. ¥500.*

The largest company in Japan and the world leader in automobile manufacture, the car giant Toyota owes its growth to an original and highly successful system of production based on the avoidance of the three forms **waste**

## USEFUL INFORMATION

**Tourist Offices** – *In Nagoya station (open 9am–7pm; 052-541-4301) and the Oasis 21 complex, outside Sakae subway station (Open 10am-8pm; 052-963-5252).*

**Nagoya International Center** – *1-47-1 Nagono, Nakamura-ku, 3F Kokusai Center Bldg, on Sakura-dori. 7min walk from Nagoya station. Open Tue–Sun 9am–7pm. 052-581-0100.* Information in English (newspapers, TV), internet access.

## TRANSPORTATION

**BY PLANE** – **Centrair** – Nagoya International Airport is situated on an artificial island in Ise Bay, 21.7mi/35km to the S, linking Chubu with other Japanese regions and international destinatons. The Meitetsu private train line connects the airport to Nagoya station *(30min, ¥870).*

**BY TRAIN** – **Nagoya Station** – Many Nozomi or Hikari Shinkansens to Kyoto *(40min, ¥44,930)*, Osaka *(1hr25min, ¥6,180)*, and Tokyo *(2hr, ¥10,580)*. Limited Express trains to and from Nagano *(2hr50min, ¥6,620)*, Matsumoto *(2hr, ¥5,870)*, Takayama *(2hr30min, ¥5,870)*, and Kanazawa *(2hr55min, ¥6620)*.

**BY BUS** –**From Tokyo** – 4 buses per day *(2 during the day and 2 at night)* with the companies **Keio**, **Meitetsu**, and **Orion Tour** *(6hr30min/7hr, ¥3,000–6,400)*. There are also buses to Kyoto and Osaka.

## GETTING AROUND

**BY SUBWAY** – Very practical, with 6 lines serving the city. Tickets ¥200–320. There is a day pass *(¥850), which also includes the bus. Signs in English.* **By Bus** – The **Me-guru** tourist bus leaves every hour *(weekends every 30min)* from the bus terminal opposite Nagoya station *(Level 2F)* and serves the city's main tourist attractions, including the **Castle** and **Tokugawa Art Museum**, apart from the harbor. *¥200 per journey or ¥500 for a 1-day pass.*

*(muda, mura, muri)* that was perfected by its founder Toyoda Sakichi in the 1920s. He began by making the first sewing machines in Japan before investing in the burgeoning automobile industry. The museum, which occupies the former Toyota factory, traces the history of the business, from its beginnings to the present day.

### Nagoya Castle★ 名古屋城

*Subway: Shiyakusho.*

*Open 9am–4.30pm. ¥500.*

Originally a fortified town on the Tokaido road linking Edo and Kyoto, Nagoya grew up around its castle, built in 1612 on the orders of the shogun Tokugawa Ieyasu for his ninth son Yoshinao. The citadel included a five-story keep, its roof proudly adorned with two gold dolphins *(kinshachi)*. The residence of the Owari branch of the Tokugawa until 1868, it was one of the best-preserved castles in Japan, but was unfortunately destroyed by bombs in 1945. The 151ft/46m-high **keep** was rebuilt in 1959 in a faithful replica of the original, including the gold dolphins, although it is now made of reinforced concrete and an elevator takes you to the top, from where you can enjoy a fine **view** of the city. The old wooden buildings of **Honmaru Palace**, which once stood beneath the keep, should be entirely rebuilt by 2018. This palace once housed, among other things, the magnificent Kano School painted screens and *fusuma* currently exhibited on the first floor of the keep. To the east, the former castle grounds are home to the beautiful **Ninomaru Garden**, which is particularly attractive when the cherry trees are in blossom. You can see a Tea Ceremony in the pavilion.

### Tokugawa Art Museum★★ 徳川美術館

*Subway: Ozone, exit 3, 10min walk S.*

*Open Tue–Sun 10am–5pm. ¥1,200.*

Located in a former private residence dating from the 1930s, this museum houses the family treasures of the Owari branch of the Tokugawa shoguns, especially those bequeathed by Tokugawa Ieyasu and his son Yoshinao. The collections, displayed in rotation, comprise more than 10,000 pieces, some 60 of which are classified as either National Treasures or Important Cultural Properties. Among them are many samurai helmets, swords and pieces of armor, lacquerware, pottery, and other instruments connected with the Tea Ceremony, calligraphic scrolls and precious screens, and costumes and masks from the Noh theater. The museum also displays a number of reconstructed interiors from Nagoya Castle, but its greatest treasures are the 12C **painted scrolls**★★★ *(emaki)* illustrating the *Tales of Genji*, the masterpiece of Japanese literature *(see p97)*. These fragile works are only on public show for one week a year: in the fall. For the rest of the year, they are replaced by facsimiles and video images.

### Atsuta-jingu★ 熱田神宮

*3.1mi/5km S of the downtown area.*

*Subway: Jingu-Nishi, then 5min walk E.*

*No charge.*

Dedicated to the sun goddess Amaterasu (here called Atsuta-no-Okami), Atsuta-jingu is, after those of Ise and Izumo, the **third most venerated shrine in Japan,** visited by 9 million worshippers every year. Quite close in its architecture to Ise Shrine, it was rebuilt in 1955 after having burned down during the war. According to the old chronicles, Atsuta-jingu was founded in the year 86 to house the sword of Amaterasu's brother, the *kami* (Shinto deity residing in trees, rocks and other natural phenomena) Susano-o. It was thanks to this magic sword, known as *Kusanagi-no-tsurugi* (Grass-Cutting Sword), and as legendary in Japan as Excalibur in Britain, that Prince Yamato-takeruthe son of the 12th Emperorwas able to defeat his enemies. It is one of the Three Sacred Treasures symbolizing the legitimacy of the imperial throne, along with the jewel in the Imperial Palace in Tokyo and the mirror in **Ise Shrine** *(see p242)*. Hidden away in the main temple, it cannot be seen by mere mortals, who have to make do with the **Treasure Hall** *(open 9am–4.30pm; ¥300)* displaying old paintings, *bugaku* (dance) masks, pottery, and sword blades. At the entrance to the wooded g**rounds**—a pleasant oasis of greenery—stands a magnificent, giant camphor tree dating from the 11C.

### Nagoya Port★ 名古屋港

*Subway: Nagoyako, exit 3, then 7min walk.*

Founded a century ago, this is one of the country's largest industrial ports. It stretches to the south of the city over a vast area partly reclaimed from the sea. Part of the port has been developed for tourists and includes a number of **attractions**.

**"Fuji" Antarctic Museum** – *Open Tue–Sun 9.30am–5pm. ¥300.* Now at anchor in a dock in the port, this oceanographic vessel was involved in a number of Antarctic expeditions between 1965 and 1983—328ft/100m long, and weighing 5,200 tons, it could break up to 31.5in/80cm of ice. Life inside the ship is realistically reconstructed, with costumed mannequins in the machine rooms, canteen, officers' mess, infirmary, and dormitories, and a moving floor as if at sea. A small museum traces the history of Japanese exploration in the South Pole.

**Port of Nagoya Public Aquarium**★★ – *Open Dec–Mar Tue–Sun 9.30am–5pm; Jul 21–Aug 31 9.30am–8pm. Rest of the year 9.30am–5.30pm. ¥2,000.*

Opened in 1992 and enlarged in 2001, this is one of the largest aquariums in Japan, and probably the best. Its high-tech wizardry is extremely impressive, as well as admirably educational. The concept is that of an ocean voyage from the Sea of Japan to the Antarctic, by way of the Great Barrier Reef in Australia. Among the high points of the visit are: a hologram showing how land mammals evolved into cetaceans 50 million years ago; an artificial beach where sea turtles lay their eggs; a pool of 140 penguins, with snow falling as if on an ice floe; the enchanting underwater ballet of a shoal of 20,000 sardines; an Imax theater.

## EXCURSIONS

### Seto 瀬戸

*12.4mi/20km NE of Nagoya. From Sakae-machi station (in front of the Sakae subway station), take the Meitetsu-Seto Line to Owari-Seto station (35min, ¥470).*

In the 12C, Seto was the great center of Japanese **ceramics**. Its potters adapted Chinese forms to Japanese tastes, thus creating a specifically national style and establishing such a strong association between the town and the production of ceramics that the word *setomono* (objects from Seto), came to be used as the generic term for all ceramics, pottery, porcelain, and earthenware. Today, the town *(population 132,000)*, twinned with Limoges in France, is trying to give a new impetus to an industry that has been in decline but still employs a third of its population. As techniques have evolved, new applications have been found to take advantage of ceramics' insulating properties—it is now used in the components for cell phones, computers, and semiconductors. The town has several museums, as well as many workshops, where visitors can try their hand at pottery.

**Seto Gura Museum** – *Open 9am–6pm. ¥500.* This large complex near the station, *(on the other side of the river)* was built for Expo 2005, held in Aichi prefecture. On three floors, it presents a large-scale reconstruction of Seto before the war, when the porcelain industry was still working at full stretch. There are old coal-fired ovens, trams, and period houses. The museum traces the history of Seto ceramics over the past 13 centuries. In the tearoom, you can choose a cup for your green tea from a collection of valuable pieces.

### Inuyama★★ 犬山

*15.5mi/25km N of Nagoya. From Nagoya station, take the Meitetsu Line to Inuyama station (35min, ¥540). Tourist office in the station (open 9am–5pm; 0568-61-600). For the castle, get off at the next station (Inuyama-yuen), farther N of the town, near the Kiso River.*

This sleepy little town on the banks of the Kiso River, in the northwest of Aichi prefecture, has the oldest castle in Japan. Its picturesque alleyways, temples, and shrines, and the nearby Meiji-mura are well worth a day's excursion. From June to September, demonstrations of **cormorant fishing** take place every evening from 5pm on the Kiso River. Visitors can watch while dining on board flat-bottomed boats (*reservations 0568-61-0057; see also Gifu, p 239*).

**Inuyama Castle★★** 犬山城 –
*15min walk W of Inuyama-yuen station. Open 9am–4.30pm. ¥500; including garden ¥1,200.*
Designated a National Treasure, the castle stands on a small hill, from where it commands a magnificent **view** of the Kiso River, Mount Ena, and Nobi Plain. It was built in 1537 by Oda Yojiro Nobuyasu, the uncle of Oda Nobunaga, the first man to unite the whole of Japan. Its white keep, in the squat, sober Momoyama style *(four floors, 62.3ft/19m)*, surrounded by a balcony and topped by an elegant roof with curved, turned-up edges, has miraculously survived civil wars, fires, and earthquakes. Inside, a rough-hewn central pillar, shiny with the patina of centuries, supports the whole structure. Belonging to the Naruse clan until the Meiji era, the castle was once surrounded by pavilions and turrets, which have not survived.
At the foot of the castle hill stretches the elegant Japanese garden of **Uraku-en**★ (*open Mar–Nov 9am–5pm, Dec–Feb 9am–4pm; ¥1,000, tea ¥500*) planted with maples, camellias, and bamboo. There are several tea houses including the **Jo-an**★, designated a National Treasure. This tiny pavilion, made of adobe and rice paper, is no bigger than three tatami mats—its sober simplicity is true to the spirit of austerity associated with the world of tea. It was Oda Nobunaga's younger brother, the warlord Oda Uraku (1547–1621), who, on retiring to devote himself to his passion for tea, built this small pavilion in the precincts of the Kennin-ji in Kyoto, in 1618. It was moved here in 1972.

Inuyama Castle
© JNTO

The small **Karakuri-kan museum** (*on Honmachi, the street to the S of the castle; open 9am–5pm; ¥100*), which displays wooden puppets from the Edo period, is a real delight. At weekends, the last puppetmaker in the town comes here to give demonstrations.

**Meiji-mura★** 博物館明治村
*5.6mi/9km E of Inuyama.*
*Bus (every 30min, journey time 20min, ¥410) from Inuyama station. Open Mar–Oct 9.30am–5pm; Nov–Feb 9.30am–4pm. ¥1,600.*
This open-air museum, located in a 247-acre/100ha park, gathers together 65 public and private buildings dating from the Meiji era (1868–1912), scattered around a lake. The brick, stone, or painted wooden buildings come from Nagasaki and Kobe, and include offices, a Kabuki theater, banks, gothic churches, and villas with Victorian turrets. There are also some steam locomotives and old trams dating back to the time when Japan was fascinated by all things Western.
Not to be missed are the façade and lobby of Tokyo's **Imperial Hotel**, designed by Frank Lloyd Wright in 1923. He also designed the furniture used in the mezzanine cafe.

## Tajimi 多治見

*23.6mi/38km NE of Nagoya.*
*From Nagoya station, JR Chuo Honsen Line to Tajimi station (40min, ¥650).*

Like Seto, this town *(population 100,000)* specializes in **ceramics**, and there are a number of museums, kilns, and workshops open to visitors. The best known is the studio of **Kato Kobei**★★ *(10min by bus from the station, Minami Ichinokura stop; open 10am–5pm; museum ¥300, pottery workshop ¥3,000; 0572-22-0509)*. Housed in a magnificent Edo period residence, it showcases the works of the Kato family, potters for seven generations, and in particular those of **Kato Takuo**, father of the current master, whose output, strongly influenced by ancient Persian art, earned him the title of Living National Treasure. The unusual **Sakazuki Art Museum is** 984ft/300m away *(open Wed–Mon 10am–5pm; ¥400)*, and is devoted to sake cups. More than 1,500 cups of all styles and periods are on display. During the Meiji era, Tajimi produced almost 80 percent of the sake cups in Japan. The upper floor has cups for the Tea Ceremony, made by the principal Living National Treasures of Japanese pottery.

## Seki 関

*31mi/50km N of Nagoya.*
*Bus from Nagoya station (every hour, 1hr10min).*

The capital of Japanese **sword** *(katana)* manufacturing, this little town has been producing the country's finest blades for eight centuries. During the Muromachi era (1338–1573), Seki had nearly 300 master swordsmiths, providing weapons for the greatest samurai in Japan. Today, there are still 18 of them, licensed to make 24 swords a year each. The rest of the town has been converted to the production of kitchen knives, razors, and scissors. To visit a forge, reservations are required from the town's Tourist Office *(0575-23-7704)*.

**Seki Swordsmith Museum** *(Seki Kaji Denshukan) – 5min walk from the station. Open Wed–Mon 9am–4.30pm. ¥200.*
This museum focuses on the history and techniques of sword making in Seki and development of the cutlery industry.

## Mino★ 美濃

*24.8mi/40km N of Nagoya and 12.4mi/20km from Gifu. 1hr30min by bus from Nagoya station.*

Famous since the 8C for the production of traditional Japanese *washi* **paper**, this small town (population 24,000) retains a historic center dating from the early Edo period (17C). Its two parallel main streets are lined with superb merchant houses; to demonstrate their wealth, merchants added lavish *udatsu (*earthenware roof struts*)*, like those on the **Imai family residence** *(open 9am–4.30pm; ¥800)*, a former *washi* paper wholesaler (now a museum), or the **Kosada house**, an old sake brewery. A festival of *washi* paper lanterns is held each year on the second weekend in October.

## Gifu★ 岐阜

*21.7mi/35km N of Nagoya. 25min by train on the JR Tokaido Line (¥450) or 30min on the Meitetsu Line (¥540). Tourist office (open 9am–6pm) on Level 2 of the JR station.*

Formerly a staging post on the Nakasendo road linking Edo and Kyoto, Gifu grew up beside its castle, south of the Nagara River. An earthquake in 1891 and the air raids of 1945 destroyed much of the town's heritage, but it still produces quality handicrafts and attracts crowds of tourists in the summer to watch the cormorant fishing.

**Gifu Castle** – *From the station, take the bus to Gifu-koen-mae park. A cable car (¥1,050 round trip) goes up to the Castle. Open 9am–5pm (summer,* ***viewpoint*** *accessible until 10pm); 9.30am–6.30pm (winter); Golden Week: 10.30am–4.30pm. ¥200.*
Gifu-jo was built as a fort in 1203 at the top of Mount Kinka *(formerly Mount Inaba; 1,079ft/329m)*, but fell into the hands of Oda Nobunaga's clan in the 16C, and was finally destroyed in the early 17C. This modern reconstruction of the castle is worth a visit for the lovely **view** over Nobi Plain—on a clear day, you can see all the way to Nagoya.

## Fishing, Gifu-style

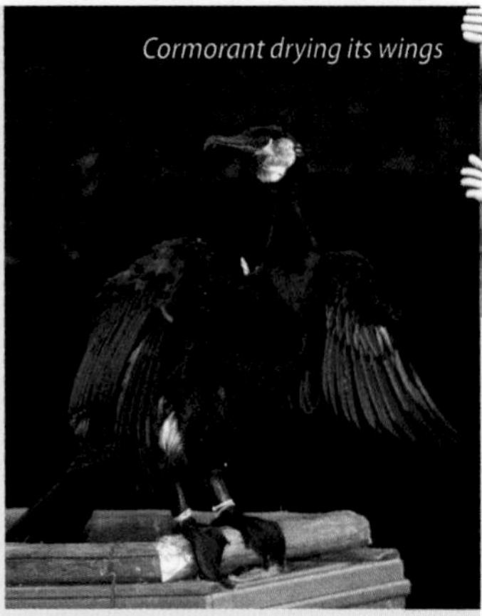
*Cormorant drying its wings*
© Frantisek Staud/Alamy

Gifu's major attraction, cormorant fishing *(ukai)*, goes back 1,300 years. Now practiced by just six families, fathers hand down to sons the privilege granted by the Imperial Household Agency, the fish caught at the season's start being served at the Emperor's table.
The long, wooden fishing boats set off at nightfall, the light of burning braziers hanging from the front attracting the fish. Two assistants navigate while the *usho*, the master fisherman, stands handling his team of 10 to 12 cormorants like a puppetmaster, ensuring the ropes never tangle; traditionally he wears a black linen cloth and a hat, a navy blue kimono, and a skirt of braided rice straw. The trained birds, held on lashes, dive and capture in their beaks small, shiny fish similar to trout, called *ayu*. Metal rings on the cormorants' necks prevent them from swallowing their prey.
He regularly pulls a bird out of the water and squeezes its neck until it regurgitates the *ayu*. "There is nothing cruel about this technique," says Yamashita Tetsuji, one of the master fishermen of Gifu. "The cormorant can still swallow the smaller fish. The bird is treated like a member of the family."
The fishing itself does not last long, but is preceded by the enjoyable ritual of families or groups of friends kneeling on tatamis in the boats moored on the shore, eating picnics washed down with generous quantities of beer and sake, while waiting for the show to start.
The fishing season lasts from May 11 to October 15. It takes place every evening from 6pm, unless there is heavy rain or the moon is full, in the clear waters of the Nagara River *(1.2mi/2km north of Gifu station, near Nagara-bashi bridge)*.

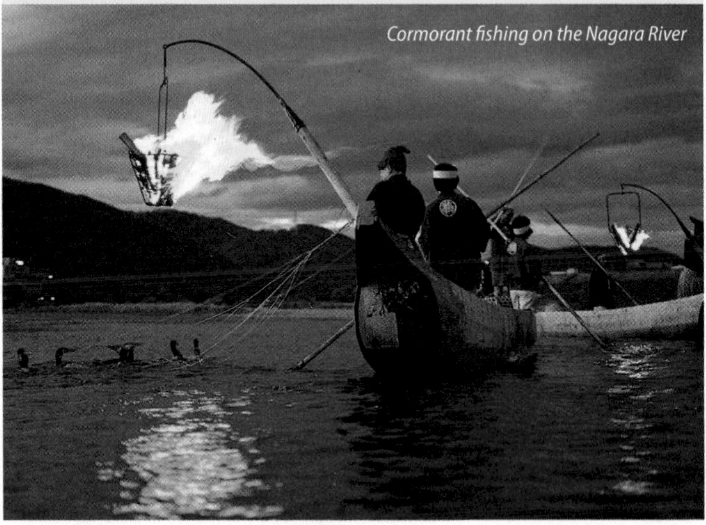
*Cormorant fishing on the Nagara River*
© JNTO

**Ozeki Lantern Factory** – *1-18 Oguma-cho, 6mi/1km S of Gifu-koen. ℘058-263-01-11.*
Gifu's specialties are oil-paper umbrellas *(wagasa)* and *washi* paper or silk paper lanterns *(chochin)*, hand mounted on a slender framework of bamboo.
For more than a century, this workshop has been producing the best lanterns in the town and has more than 600 examples on display, some painted with landscapes or traditional patterns, others with more contemporary designs by Isamu Noguchi.

*From the station, bus no. 11 goes to the boarding area from where viewing boats embark to closely shadow the fishing boats.*

*Tickets are available from the office on the dock and in the nearby hotels. ¥3,300 for a trip of about 2hr, ¥6,000 including dinner on board. Reservations suggested: ℘0582-62-0104.*

# ADDRESSES

## STAY

### NAGOYA

**Hotel Palace Nagoya** ホテルパレス名古屋 *3-10-6 Taiko, Nakamura-ku. ℘052-452-7000. www.palace-nagoya.jp. 105 rooms.* This hotel is good value for money. *A courtesy bus is available to its patrons.*

**Nagoya Flower Hotel Part II** 名古屋フラワーホテル *5-6 Takehashi, Nakamura-ku. ℘052-451-2200. www.flowerhotel.co.jp. 79 rooms.* This is a well-maintained *business hotel* that has the advantage of being located conveniently near the station.

**Ryori Ryokan Kinsuiso** 料理旅館・金翠荘 *1-28-14 Chikusa, Chikusa-ku. Subway: Fukiage. ℘052-731-8156. www.e-ryouri.com. 12 rooms.* This lovely, 100-year-old ryokan is a haven of peace at attractive prices.

### INUYAMA

**Inuyama International Youth Hostel** 犬山国際ユースホステル *162-1 Aza-Himuro, Tsugao, 1.2mi/2km from Inuyama-yuen station. ℘0568-61-1111. www.inuyama-iyh.com. 29 rooms.* A model of its kind. *From ¥3,300/person.*

**Meitetsu Inuyama Hotel** 名鉄犬山ホテル *107-1 Kitakoken. ℘0568-61-2211. www.m-inuyama-h.co.jp. 124 rooms.* Inuyama's flagship hotel, at the foot of the castle. *A wide range of prices.*

## EAT

### NAGOYA

**Yabaton** 矢場とん本店 *3-6-18 Osu, Naka-ku. Subway: Yabacho. ℘052-252-8810. www.yabaton.com.* Open *Tue–Sun 11am–9pm.* Pork is the specialty of the house. The *miso-katsu, (pork steaks topped with miso sauce)*, are divine.

**Azuma Zushi Honten** 東鮓本店 *1-5-21 Sakae, Naka-ku. ℘-052-231-3141. Open Tue–Sun 10.30am–9pm.* The quality of its sushi has been recognized since 1869. A relaxing place to go on a Sunday, with a nice **view** of the garden.

**Hourai-Ken** あつた蓬莱軒・神宮店 *2-10-26 Jingu, Atsuta-ku. ℘052-682-5598. www.houraiken.com. Open Wed–Mon 11.30am–8.30pm.* For 80 years, this restaurant has been serving the legendary *hitsumabushi*, a dish of eels in *teriyaki* sauce.

**Torigin Honten** 鳥銀本店 *3-14-22 Nishiki. ℘052-973-3000. www.torigin.co.jp. Open 5pm–midnight.* The specialty is the Nagoya *Cochin* chicken, served in every way possible: from the spurs to the comb, grilled or raw.

### TAJIMI

**Coupe du Cinnamon** クープ・ドゥ・シナモン *In Ichinokura, next to Sakazuki Art Museum. ℘0572-21-3353. Open Wed–Mon 11am–5pm.* This friendly Italian taverna serves delicious pizzas baked in wood-fired ovens.

### INUYAMA

**Restaurant Narita Neuf Okunuratei** フレンチ創作料理なり多 *395 Higashi-Koken. ℘0568-65-2447. Open 11am–12pm. Closed 1st Mon of the month.* This splendid Edo period house (1842) once belonged to a kimono merchant. The chefKazuo Naritatrained with French chefs, hence the cuisine is a fusion of Franco-Japanese: Marseilles-style bouillabaisse side by side with filet mignon à-la-Narita.

# Ise-shima★★
# 伊勢・志摩

**The Ise-Shima National Park covers most of the Shima Peninsula. The town of Ise is famous for the Ise Shrine, the most sacred building in Japanese Shintoism, dedicated to the sun goddess Amaterasu, mythical ancestor of the Imperial dynasty. An unusual feature of this shrine is that it is torn down and rebuilt every 20 years. A UNESCO World Heritage Site since 2004, it attracts more than 6 million visitors a year. The peninsula is home to other historic sites such as the two "wedded rocks," the Meoto-iwa. The town of Toba is famous for its female free-divers, the *ama*, and its cultured pearls. Farther south, along the magnificent jagged coastline of Ago Bay, is a multitude of islands, inlets, and promontories.**

- **Population:** Ise town: Population 96,003 – Mie Prefecture.
- **Michelin Map:** Principal Sights Map B3 – Regional Map p231.
- **Location:** The town of Ise is located 62mi/100km south of Nagoya ; its main station is Ise-shi *(Kintetsu and JR lines)*. Ise-jingu is divided into two large shrine compounds: the Geku, *(10 minutes' walk from the station)*, and the Naiku, *(3.7mi/6km farther on)* which can be reached by bus. The Kintetsu Line continues to Toba and then Kashikojima on Ago Bay.
- **Timing:** Ideally allow two days, including a night in Toba.
- **Don't miss:** The Naiku Shrine; the *ama* divers near Toba.

## BACKGROUND

**A mythical origin** – Ise Shrine, and more particularly the Naiku, is believed to house the sacred mirror of the sun goddess Amaterasu, which is, with the sword and the jewel, one of the Three Sacred Treasures of the imperial throne.

A symbol of Amaterasu, the mirror is a reminder of the time when the gods lured her from the cave into which she had shut herself (in protest at her brother's actions), by arousing her curiosity. Amaterasu gave the mirror to her grandson Ninigi when he descended to rule the earth. It then passed to Jinmu, the first Japanese Emperor, the goddess's great-great-grandson.

According to the old chronicles, worship of Amaterasu was originally celebrated in the Imperial Palace, but was then transferred to Ise by Yamatohime, daughter of the 11th Emperor Suinin, in the year 4. But the actual date of Ise's foundation is more likely to have been later, somewhere around 478.

**Imperial links** – Ise Shrine has always been closely associated with the Imperial dynasty. An imperial princess has held the office of high priestess of Ise *(Saio)* since ancient times.

The present holder is Emperor Akihito's sister, Ikeda Atsuko. Although today Shintoism and the State are officially separated, Ise remains a place where religion, national sentiment, and politics are inextricably linked. The Emperor has a strong connection with Ise-jingu. For example, on his official travels, he is careful never to sit with his back turned to the shrine. In his palace in Tokyo, he symbolically grows rice and sends an envoy to Ise once a year to present the harvest to the goddess Amaterasu.

In actual fact, it must be said that the popularity of Ise originates less In the Imperial worship than It does in the fact of the great pilgrimages, which developed In particular from the 16C onward. During the Edo period (1603–1867), they attracted millions of the faithful

### Ancient and modern

Every 20 years since the 7C, the two shrines of Ise have been demolished and rebuilt in their original form. A number of explanations have been put forward as to the origin of this costly ritual known as *Shikinen Sengu*, including the Shinto emphasis on rituals of purification and regeneration. Perhaps the fact that 20 years is about the time that their thatched roofs would normally last plays a part, or it may be that it is a way of ensure building techniques are passed on from one generation to the next. Whatever the answer, eternally renewed and yet always the same, Ise Shrine embodies both the ephemeral and the eternal. The next rebuilding ceremony will take place in 2013.

## ISE 伊勢

### ISE-JINGU★★★ 伊勢神宮

The Grand Shrine of Ise comprises two large compounds containing an inner shrine, the Naiku, and an outer shrine, losethe Geku. In addition, there are more than 100 small shrines scattered throughout the town and the surrounding area. A tour of the shrines normally starts with the Geku, but the Naiku is the more interesting of the two.

#### Naiku★★★ 内宮

*From Ise-shi station, follow the main street S for 109yd/100m until you reach the stop for bus no. 11. From there, take bus nos. 51 or 55 (15min, ¥410). Open dawn–dusk. No charge.*

The inner shrine, *(also called Kotai-jingu, and dedicated to Amaterasu)* lies in a forest of giant cedars, camphor trees, and cypresses that covers 13,591 acres/5,500ha. Visitors enter via the 328ft/100m-long **Uji Bridge** over the clear waters of the Isuzu River. This bridge is also rebuilt every 20 years. The path turns right and leads across a landscape garden to the **Temizuscha**, a pool where the faithful wash their hands and mouth, a symbol of the purification of both body and mind. Others perform their ablutions on the river bank.

The members of the Imperial household and the clergy have special halls, the **Saikan** *(purification hall)* and the **Anzaisho** *(hall for visitors from the Imperial household)*, between the great gates *(torii)* that mark the entrance to the sacred precinct. A wide stone staircase then leads to the edge of the inner sanctum, which only the Emperor, the Empress, and religious dignitaries are allowed to enter.

The crowd has to be content with looking on from behind a fence at the the white silk curtain concealing the entrance. It is a simple rectangular, wooden building, raised on piles, with a thatched roof and two crossed beams at either end known as *chigi*. Beside the building is an empty space marked out by white pebbles indicating where the old shrine was, (and where the next one will be built in 2013, for the 62nd time). As many as 10,000 trees more than 200 years old are needed to rebuild the Naiku and the Geku.

**Oharai-machi**★ – During the Edo period, the pilgrimage to Ise was so

### USEFUL INFORMATION

**Tourist Offices** – In **Ujiyamada station** at **Ise** *(Kintetsu Line)*, 5min from **Ise-shi** station *(open 9am–5.30pm; 0596-23-9655)*, and at the entrance to the **Geku** *(open 8.30am–5pm; 0596-28-3705)*.

### TRANSPORTATION

**BY TRAIN** – Two lines link **Nagoya** and **Ise-shi** station: **Kintetsu** *(1hr25min, ¥2,690)* and **JR** *(1hr25min, ¥2,450)*. The same lines go on to Toba, but only the Kintetsu Line continues to **Kashikojima** and **Ago Bay**. From **Ise-shi**, the Kintetsu Line also connects with **Kyoto** *(2hr)* and **Osaka-Nanba** *(1hr45min)*.

**BY BUS** – The **CAN Bus**, which leaves from Ise-shi station, serves the Ise sites (**Geku, Naiku), Futami**, and **Toba** *(1-day pass ¥1,000)*.

popular that it gave rise to a number of pleasure districts in the surrounding areas, where dances and purification rituals also took place. "There is so much business going on here that the noise is tremendous," a Japanese author wrote as early as the 17C. "Money flows like water, without a moment's pause." The area of bustling streets on the approach to the Naiku is called Oharai-machi. They are lined with traditional businesses, tea houses, restaurants, and shops selling local handicrafts.

### Geku★★ 外宮

*5min walk from Ise-shi station. From the Naiku, take the bus back to the stop before the station. Open dawn–dusk. No charge.*

Officially known as Toyouke Dai-jingu, the outer shrine is dedicated to Toyouke-no-omikami, goddess of agriculture and industry, protector of harvests and the home.

Symbolically, it is she whose task it is to offer Amaterasu and the other *kami* the sacred food that the priests of Ise leave twice a day, morning and evening, in the Mike-den *(a pavilion behind the Gosho-den, the principal shrine)*. This is also closed to the public, who have to remain behind a fence. Like the Naiku, the Geku is rebuilt every 20 years in identical style, give or take a few details, exhibiting the same bare, primitive style regarded by the Japanese as the height of beauty and purity.

## EXCURSIONS

### FUTAMI★ 二見

*4.3mi/7km E of Ise (see map pp230-231). 10min by JR train to Futaminoura station.*

This small seaside resort, which grew up in the 1920s near Ise Shrine, Meoto-iwa, is famous for its "wedded rocks".

### Meoto-iwa★ 夫婦岩

*15min walk E of the station.*

These two much-photographed rocks lie just offshore. They are associated with Izanagi and Izanami—according to Japanese mythology, the creators of the Japanese archipelago and parents of Amaterasu. The larger "male" rock is 329.5ft/9m in height and has a small *torii* (gate) on the top. It is connected to the "female" rock *(height 13ft/4m)*, by a *shimenawa*, a rope of braided rice straw used to mark out a sacred space in the Shinto religion *(see photo below)*. The rope is 98.4ft/30m long and is replaced by priests three times a year *(May 5, Sept 5, & Dec 25)*, in a ceremony accompanied by singing and drumming. From May to July, and notably during the Summer Solstice on June 21, you can see the sun rise between the two rocks and even glimpse the silhouette of Mt. Fuji in the distance.

Meoto-iwa

### The mermaids of Toba

Gathering seaweed, sea urchins, abalones, lobsters, and oysters from the seabed, the *ama* are "daughters of the sea." Up until the 1960s, they would dive bare-chested, dressed in nothing but a loincloth, with ropes on their ankles connected to tubs bobbing on surface, acting both as floats and containers for the catch. But the tradition, handed down from mother to daughter, is in decline, and today it is mostly older women wearing one-piece bathing suits who carry it on, (the average age is 67). The strongest can go down as far as 65.6ft/20m and hold their breath for 2 minutes. As soon as they surface and lift their heads out of the water, they give a curious whistle to decompress the air in their lungs. A native of Osatsu, Nakamura Yasuko, now in her sixties, has been diving since the age of 15. "The white tunics we wear ward off sharks and make it possible for us to be seen in case of accident. It's a profitable profession, but it means spending hours in cold water. Our daughters are not as tough as we were, they all dream of a different life."

**Hinjitsukan** – *On the seafront, 218.7yd/200m before the rocks. Open 9am–4.30pm. ¥300.*
This majestic wooden building, dating from 1887, was where the Imperial Family and important state dignitaries would stay when they visited Ise Shrine. They would relax here and sometimes bathe in the sea. Now a museum, the building is notable for its large *(120-tatami)* hall and a beautiful, traditional garden.

## TOBA★ 鳥羽

*5mi/8km SE of Futami. From Futami, JR Line (10min, ¥200). From Ise, Kintetsu Line (16min, ¥320) or JR Line (¥230). Tourist office at the station exit (open 9am–5pm).*
A small, very tourist-oriented port town *(population 23,000)*, Toba is the world center for cultured pearls, most of them produced by the Mikimoto company. The region's rocky coastline, with its many small coves and rocky inlets, is also famous for its female divers, the *ama*, who for centuries have plunged into the sea here without the aid of breathing apparatus to collect seaweed, shellfish, and crustaceans.

### Mikimoto Pearl Island★★ ミキモト真珠島

*5min walk from the station. Open 9am–4.30pm. ¥1,500.*
It was on this small island facing Toba harbor that Mikimoto Kokichi (1858–1954), known as "the pearl king," became the first person in the world to produce cultured pearls. The technique involves introducing a parasite into the shells of young oysters.
Harvested after around four years, 1 percent of them will have produced perfect pearls.
There is a **museum** on the island that explains the process and displays jewelry and works of art made out of pearls, and, from April to November, tourists can see demonstrations of pearl fishing by *ama* divers.

### Toba Aquarium★ 鳥羽水族館

*In the harbor, just opposite the island. Open Apr–Oct 9am–5pm; Nov–Mar 9am–4.30pm. ¥2,400.*
Among the 850 varieties of marine and freshwater creatures in this aquarium is a group of seals and sea lions that give regular shows, much to the delight of children. The aquarium also contains flat-nosed dolphins from Ise Bay, manatees, sturgeons, dugongs, Amazonian pirarucu, and other unusual sea creatures.

### Toba Sea-Folk Museum 海の博物館

*2.5mi/4km S of Toba. Bus no. 72 (25min), Umi no hakubutsukan stop. Open 9am-5pm (4.30pm Dec-Mar). ¥800.*
This museum contains around 40 traditional fishing boats from the villages on the peninsula and explains

the fishing methods, traditions, and beliefs of the local seagoing people, especially the *ama* divers of Ise, whose practices go back nearly 2,000 years.

### Osatsu★ 相差（おおさつ）

*9.3mi/15km S of Toba. Mie Kotsu bus (Kuzaki Line, 35min) to Osatsu stop. Lunch ¥3,500; tea and snack ¥2,000. Reservations required. ✆0599-33-7453.*
A small harbor in a rocky inlet, this is home to one of the main communities of *ama* on the Shima Peninsula. A wooden hut near the shore, where the divers go to rest and warm themselves after they come out of the water, has been converted so that the tourists can meet them and chat while getting a taste of the day's catch.

### Ago Bay★ 英虞湾

*15.5mi/25km S of Toba. Kintetsu Line to the terminus at Kashikojima (29min, ¥960).*
This magnificent bay is the center for Japanese pearl cultivation. Just offshore lies a string of small wooded islands.
**Bay Cruises** – *Opposite Kashikojima station. 3 times daily. 50min round trip. ¥1,400. ✆0599-43-1048.*
From **Kashikojima**★ harbor, a tourist boat cruises the bay, allowing visitors a close-up view of the oyster beds in the pearl farms.
**Yokoyama Observatory**★ – *2.5mi/4km N of Kashikojima. Kintetsu Line to Shima-Yokoyama station, then 30min walk.*
Perched at an altitude of 492ft/150m, the observatory provides a **panoramic view** of Ago Bay. There is a small information center for visitors (*open 9am–4.30pm*); also walks in the nearby woods.

## ADDRESSES

### STAY

#### ISE

**Hoshidekan** 星出館 *2-15-2 Kawasaki. Ise-shi station. ✆0596-28-2377. www.hoshidekan.jp. 10 rooms.* On the edge of the Kawasaki Kaiwai district, once called "the kitchens of Ise," this splendid ryokan also has a lovely garden.

**Town Hotel Ise** タウンホテル伊勢 *1-8-18 Fukiage. Ujiyamada station. ✆0596-23-4621. 20 rooms.* A business hotel with functional rooms. *English spoken.*

#### FUTAMI

**Nishokan** 日章館 *537-1 Futamicho-e. 10min walk from the station. ✆0596-43-5000. 10 rooms.* A friendly place by the sea, not far from the **Meoto-iwa rocks**. Japanese rooms and *o-furo.*

#### TOBA

**Road Inn Toba** ロードイン鳥羽 *1-63-11 Toba. ✆0599-26-5678. www.greens.co.jp. 52 rooms. A classic business hotel.*

**Ryokan Kaigetsu** 旅館海月 *1-10-52 Toba. ✆0599-26-2056. www.kaigetsu.co.jp. 13 rooms.* A beautiful, friendly 120-year-old ryokan. *English spoken.* Excellent fresh seafood.

#### AGO BAY

**Shima Kanko Hotel** 志摩観光ホテル *Kashikojima, Ago-cho, Shima-shi, near Kashikojima station. ✆0599-43-1211. www.miyakohotels.ne.jp. 152 rooms.* A huge hotel overlooking the bay. *Attractive prices.*

### EAT

#### ISE

**Daiki** 大喜 *2-1-48 Iwabuchi. ✆0596-28-0281. Open 11am–9pm.* A highly regarded restaurant, with reasonable prices. Try the ***tekone-sushi***, a traditional fish dish (steamed rice topped with flaked *bonito*). For those on more generous budgets, there is a set ***kaiseki*** menu, for which reservations are required.

**Nakamura** 中むら *12-14 Honmachi, just outside the entrance to the Geku. ✆0596-28-4472. 11am–4pm.* Since the Edo period, this inexpensive eating house has been serving bowls of Ise ***udon***, thick white noodles cooked in a dried bonito stock, to pilgrims visting the shrine.

#### MATSUSAKA

**Wadakin** 和田金 *1878 Nakamachi. 8min walk from the station. ✆0598-21-1188 Open 11.30am-8pm.* Located 6.2mi/10km north of Ise, the town of Matsusaka produces some of Japan's best beef, very much equal to famous Kobe beef. An institution dating from the Meiji era, they have their own ranch. You will receive a princely welcome. Try the ***sukiyaki*** menu, a real treat.

# Takayama★★★
# 高山

**Surrounded by mountains that rise to over 9,842.5ft/3,000m, this "mini alpine Kyoto" seems frozen in time. Thanks to its old districts dating from the Edo period, with their wooden houses, sake breweries, antique shops, temples, and shaded shrines, this small city has character and atmosphere. As the former capital of Hida province, Takayama was famous for its carpenters, who built the opulent merchant houses in the town and also helped to build the temples of Kyoto. However crowded with tourists it gets, especially at weekends, Takayama is well worth a visit. In the surrounding area, the villages of Shirakawa-go and Gokayama have both been designated World Heritage Sites because of their *gassho-zukuri*, old thatched houses with sloping roofs where several generations live together.**

- **Population:** 101,191 – Gifu Prefecture.
- **Michelin Map:** Principal Sights Map B2 – Regional Map p 230.
- **Location:** In the north of Gifu prefecture, 112mi/180km from Kanazawa, 102.5mi/165km from Nagoya, and 105.6mi/170km from Nagano, Takayama is on a plateau at an altitude of 1,903ft/580m, surrounded by peaks more than 9,842.5ft/3,000m high. The old quarter of Sanmachi is 15 minutes' walk to the east of the railway station, on the right bank of the Miya River. Most of the city's attractions are within walking distance and well signposted in English.
- **Timing:** Allow two days in Takayama, and two more for Shirakawa-go and Gokayama. If you plan to stay in the valleys, make reservations in advance.
- **Don't miss:** A leisurely stroll in the Sanmachi district, looking at the craft shops and lingering in the morning markets; staying in a farmhouse in Shirakawa-go or Gokayama.

## BACKGROUND

**The city of carpenters** – Poor in agricultural resources but rich in wood for building, Takayama was renowned for its skilled carpenters, considered the best in Japan. Unable to pay the taxes in rice and cloth imposed by the Emperor, the villagers would leave for several months a year to work in the capital, Heian *(now Kyoto)*, where they built temples and palaces. On their return, they would put the knowledge they had acquired to good use, building houses and temples in their own city. These skills have been handed down from father to son to the present day. Not only was Takayama enriched by frequent contact with Kyoto, after 1692 (when it was placed under the direct control of the shogunate, which appointed its governor) it also maintained close ties with Edo.

**A place of harmony** – A former fortified town, Takayama's castle was destroyed by the Tokugawa in 1695. The grid-style layout, inspired by Kyoto, was divided between the samurai quarter near the Enako River, the temple quarter on the slopes of Higashiyama, and the merchants' quarter on the bank of the Miya River. It is this latter area, known as Sanmachi, with its 17C wooden buildings, that attracts visitors today. Neatly aligned one after the other, the merchant houses run the length of the narrow streets.
One or two stories high, they have gently sloping roofs ending in wide canopies, and façades with dark wooden doors and latticework. The whole effect is one of harmony and coherence. Close by are

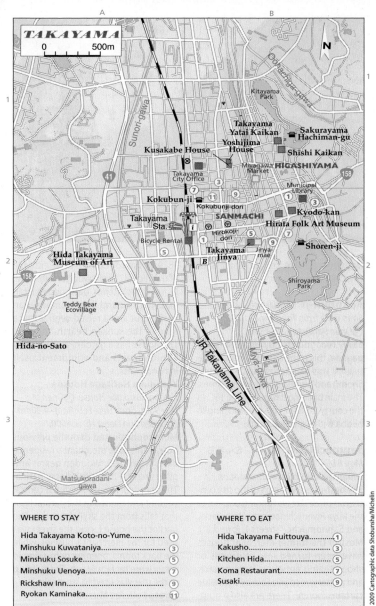

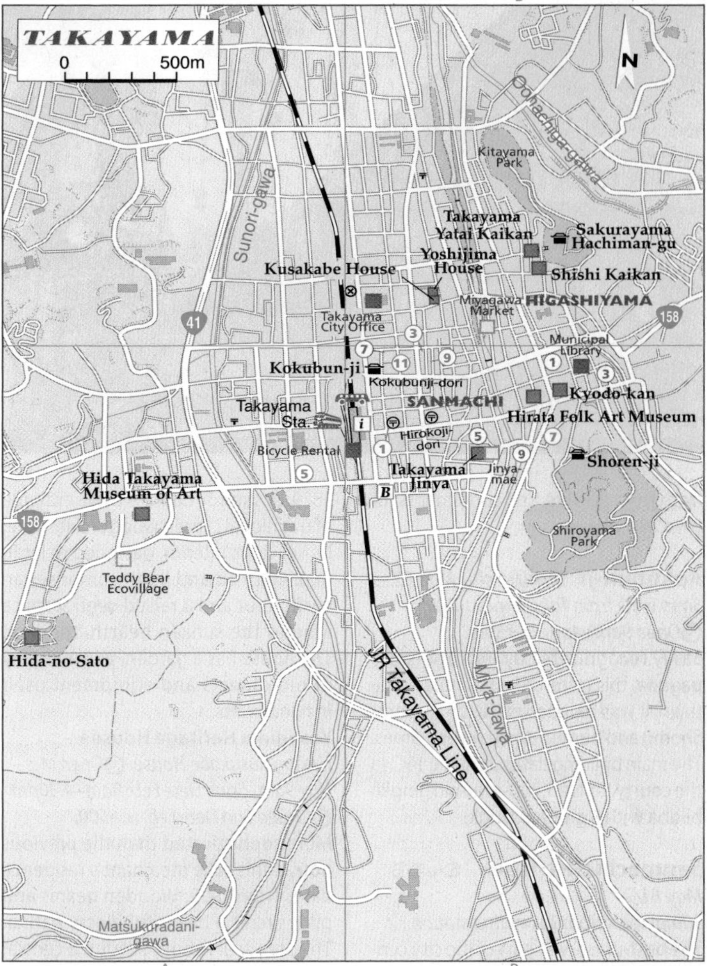


WHERE TO STAY

- Hida Takayama Koto-no-Yume ............ 1
- Minshuku Kuwataniya ............ 3
- Minshuku Sosuke ............ 5
- Minshuku Uenoya ............ 7
- Rickshaw Inn ............ 9
- Ryokan Kaminaka ............ 11

WHERE TO EAT

- Hida Takayama Fuittouya ............ 1
- Kakusho ............ 3
- Kitchen Hida ............ 5
- Koma Restaurant ............ 7
- Susaki ............ 9



canals that were used for washing clothes and as a source of water for quenching fires, and into which winter snow could be cleared away.

Geography has kept the area somewhat isolated, allowing Takayama to develop something of its own culture over the past 300 years

## SIGHTS

### Miyagawa Market 朝市 *B1 & B2.*

*Along the Miya River to Sanmachi and on the square in front of the Takayama-jinya.* *Open 6am–noon.*

Farming women from the surrounding area have been coming to these two markets at dawn to sell vegetables,

*Street in Sanmachi District, decorated for the Tanabata Matsuri in July*

© Y. Shimizu / JNTO

fresh fruit, flowers, and condiments for over 200 years.

### Kokubun-ji 飛騨国分寺 *Map B2.*

*5min walk from Takayama station. Open 9am–4pm. ¥300.*

Easily recognizable by its three-story pagoda, this is the oldest temple in the town. It was founded in 746 by Emperor Shomu and burned down several times. The main building dates from the 16C. In the courtyard is a 1,200-year-old gingko biloba with a gnarled trunk.

### Sanmachi District★★ さんまち

*Map B1/2.*

*10min walk from Takayama station.*

The best-preserved part of the city centers on three streets running parallel to the Miya River: Ichinomachi, Ninomachi, and Sannomachi *("streets 1, 2, and 3")*. Most of the former merchant houses have been turned into museums or shops selling antiques, lacquerware, and pottery, recognizable by their blue curtains *(noren)*. There are also a number of sake breweries, which can be identified by the balls of cedar needles hanging in the entrances. Visitors are always welcome for a tasting.

**Kusakabe Heritage House★** – *Shimo-Ninomachi. Open Mar–Nov 8.30am–5pm; Dec–Feb 8.30am–4.30pm. ¥500.*

The former residence of a pawnbroker and silk merchant, rebuilt after a fire in 1879, this sturdy house is a fine example of traditional cypresswood architecture. Its spacious interior, designed to let in maximum air and light, comprises an earth floor and a raised central space around the sunken hearth, the *irori*. The house has a garden, and a display of old objects and equipment used in handicrafts.

**Yoshijima Heritage House★** – *Next to Kusakabe House. Open Mar–Nov 9am–5pm; Dec–Feb: 9am–4.30pm. Closed Sun Dec–Feb. ¥500.*

More sophisticated than the previous house, this sake merchant's residence dates from 1908. Wooden beams and pillars have a beautiful glossy patina. The stairwell is built around a central column and bathed in the natural light that falls from the skylight above. The part of the house facing the street was used for the merchant's busines, while the back rooms, opening onto a simple patio, were for family use. The building at the rear was used to store sake.

**Hirata Folk Art Museum★** – *39 Kami-Ninomachi. Open 9am–5pm. ¥300.*

Set in a large, plain house built in 1897, which belonged to a merchant family that sold candles and ointments, this museum conveys an idea of daily life in a middle-class home of the Edo period, with its display of household utensils, mirrors, lacquerware, toilet requisites, toys, etc.

## USEFUL INFORMATION

**Tourist Office** – Opposite Takayama station entrance *(B2). Open Apr–Oct 8.30am–6.30pm; Nov–Mar 8.30am–5pm. ℘0577-32-5328. www.hida.jp.*

## TRANSPORTATION

**BY TRAIN** – From Tokyo, Kyoto, or Osaka, the simplest route is via Nagoya, from where the Limited Express Hida leaves every hour *(2hr30min, ¥5,360).*

**BY BUS** – Bus station on the left as you come out of the JR station *(B2), ℘0577-32-1688.* 3 buses per day to Kanazawa, at 9.50am, 12.50pm, and 3.50pm *(3hr, ¥3,300). Reservations necessary.*

## GETTING AROUND

**BY CAR** – Taking the car will be much more practical than going by bus for exploring Shirakawa-go and Gokayama. There are several car rental companies around the station, including **Eki Rent-A-Car** *℘0577-33-3522* and **Nippon Rent-A-Car** *℘0577-34-5121. You can return the car in Kanazawa.*

**Kyodo-kan★** –
*75 Kami-Ichinomachi. Open 8.30am–5pm. ¥300.*
This small museum, housed in a former 19C sake brewery, traces the history of Takayama through a collection of documents, handicrafts, and objects of archeological, ethnographic, or religious interest.

### Takayama Yatai Kaikan★★

高山屋台会館 *Map B1.*
*178 Sakura-machi, in the NE of the city. Open 8.30am–5pm (9am–4.30pm Dec–Feb). ¥820.*
This large hall is used to display in rotation four of the 23 large, colorful floats *(yatai)* used in the city's festivals—the Sanno Matsuri on April 14 and 15, and, the Hachiman Matsuri on October 9 and 10 (*see p 26*). The others are stored in warehouses in the downtown area. Dating from the 17C and 18C, the floats are richly decorated with gleaming lacquer, gilt, and mother-of-pearl inlays. Lanterns and drapes, and mechanized figures sitting on top of the floats complete the overall highly elaborate effect. In the adjoining exhibition hall is a large-scale model (1:10) of the Tosho-gu shrine at Nikko.

### Shishi Kaikan★ 獅子会館 *MapB1.*

*53 Sakuramachi, near the previous museum. Open 8.30am–5pm (9am–5pm Dec–Mar). ¥600.*
More than 800 lion masks used in the traditional dances in Japanese festivals are exhibited in this small museum. The purpose of the dances is to purify the path of the procession before the altars bearing deities pass along it. More interesting are the short, but amusing shows of *karakuri* puppets, wooden automata dating from the Edo period. They sit on top of the floats while their operators, concealed below, make them perform acrobatics to the sound of drums and flutes.

### Higashiyama District 東山

*Map B1.*
*10min E of Sanmachi. Allow for a 1hr walk.*
The atmosphere in the temples and shrines district is calm and soothing. You can follow a 2.2mi/3.5km-long trail that takes in the main buildings, set in lush vegetation. Some of the temples contain fine statues.

### Takayama Jinya★★ 高山陣屋

*Map B2.*
*1-5 Hachikenmachi, in the S of Sanmachi. Open Mar–Oct 8.45am–5pm; Nov–Feb 8.45am–4.30pm. ¥420. Ask at the entrance for a guided tour in English (40min, no charge).*
Originally the residence of the Kanamori clan, this building served as the regional government office for Hida when the province was directly controlled by the Tokugawa shoguns, from 1692 to 1868.

The only surviving building of its kind in Japan, it was used as a courthouse and as a tax collection center. The great courtroom is reached through an imposing door and a narrow vestibule. Ordinary people had to kneel behind a barrier and make their appeals to the authorities in the dark. Close by was a room used for torture! The rest of the building lodged the *daikan* (local governor), his distinguished guests, and the staff. To the south were the great storehouses for rice, wood, and other produce collected in tax, which was a heavy burden on the peasants in this poor, mountainous province, giving rise to frequent revolts.

### Hida Takayama Museum of Art★★★ 飛騨高山美術館 *Map A2.*

*1.2m/2km to the SW of Takayama station, in the direction of Hida-no-Sato. From the bus station, bus from stop 6 or free shuttle bus (a London Bus from the museum). Open 9am–5pm. ¥1,300.*
Created by a wealthy and enthusiastic collector, Tetsuya Mukai, this museum houses a collection of beautiful **European Art Nouveau** glassware, furniture, and glass pieces by Tiffany, Lalique, Daum, and Gallé. Several rooms are devoted to the great masters of European decorative art in the pre-World War I period: Louis Majorelle, Charles Rennie Mackintosh, the Vienna Secessionists. The highlight of the collection has to be one of Lalique's **glass fountains** (1932) that once adorned the traffic circle on the Champs-Élysées in Paris.

### Hida-no-Sato★★ 飛騨の里 *Map A2*

*1.6mi/2.5km to the SW of Takayama station. 10min walk from the previous museum. From the bus station, bus from stop 6 (10min, ¥200). Open 8.30am–5pm. ¥700.*
In a small wooded valley beside a lake, this open-air museum contains a folk village of some 30 farmhouses, mostly dating from the 18C and 19C. They are large traditional rural houses or *minka*, with wide roofs of thatch, bark, or shingle and well-preserved interiors. In the center of the main room is an *irori*, a hearth hollowed out of the beaten-earth floor, around which the family would gather. The rooms and storehouses display farming tools and everyday objects that give a glimpse of life in the mountain villages. In some of the houses, people can be seen working at traditional crafts like ceramics, dyeing, weaving, and cabinetmaking. For those who don't have time to visit Shirakawa-go and Gokayama, this museum is a good way of discovering the famous *gassho-zukuri* (*see Ogimachi, below*).

## EXCURSIONS

### SHIRAKAWA-GO★★★
白川郷

*49.7mi/80km NW of Takayama (see map p 230-231). From Takayama bus station, buses leave 8 times daily for Ogimachi, the main village in the valley (50min, ¥2,400). There are also buses 2 times daily linking Ogimachi and Kanazawa (1hr15min, ¥1,800).*
Tucked away in the heart of the mountains, the villages of Shirakawa-go are scattered about amid forests and paddy fields on the banks of the Sho River, which also flows through the adjoining valley of Gokayama. For centuries, Shirakawa-go and Gokayama were "lost valleys," cut off from the world by snow during the winter.
Due to their isolation, they developed a particular way of life based on a system of mutual cooperation between neighboring families. In 1995, both valleys were designated UNESCO World Heritage Sites, thanks to their *gassho-zukuri*, traditional three- or four-story wooden houses. Their triangular thatched roofs slope at an angle of 60 degrees to withstand the heavy snow in winter. These giant farmhouses could accommodate up to 30 people from several generations of the same family; most are still lived in. Up until the 1970s, the attics were used for breeding silkworms and storing mulberry leaves, whose fibers were used to produce *washi* paper. Until the 19C, the region also manufactured gunpowder. Today, its main industry is tourism. The crowds who flood in during the day, especially

Gassho-zukuri houses in Shirakawa-go

© JTB/Photoshot

at weekends, tend to somewhat spoil the magic of the place, which is best appreciated by spending a night here.

### Ogimachi★★ 荻町

*Map available at the Tourist Office where the buses park (open 8.30am–5pm).*

This well-preserved village on the east bank of the Sho River *(population 600)* has 60 *gassho-zukuri,* most dating from the 19C, and nearly half of them still inhabited. Each *gassho-zukuri* is surrounded by a plot of land containing paddy fields and kitchen gardens.

The thatched roofs are completely replaced every 30 years, but thanks to all the villagers pitching in and helping, this only takes a day.

On the last Sunday in October, the whole village is hosed down in a spectacular fire prevention exercise. Start your visit by climbing to the **Shiroyama Tenbodai** viewpoint *(15min walk on a path to the NE)*, which offers an overall **view**★★ of the village. You will see how the houses are neatly arranged parallel to the river, aligned north to south to limit their exposure to bad weather.

**Wada House**★ – *In the N of the village. Open 9am–5pm. ¥300.*

This house dates from the 18C and is the largest *gassho-zukuri* in Ogimachi. It belonged to the wealthy family that once ran the village and still live in it. Note the soot-blackened roof structure above the central hearth. The upper floors, which were used for breeding silkworms, have exhibits of period equipment. Observe the ingenious way in which the beams and pillars are held together, not with nails or screws but with ropes, which allow the structure to yield and sway slightly under the pressure of the snow and wind without breaking.

### An explosive recipe

With little land available for rice cultivation, the villagers of Shirakawa-go and Gokayama made maximum use of the meager resources available to them. Having to spend the long winters in their farmhouses, they bred silkworms, feeding them on mulberry leaves. They made use of everything they could: the fibers of the mulberry tree were used to produce paper; the silk worms' excrement stored in the ground, along with that of humans, to ferment until nitrate was obtained, and the nitrate was then mixed with charcoal and sulfur to make gunpowder. The products they made—silk, paper, and gunpowder—were then carried on men's backs across the mountains to trade in Takayama and Kanazawa.

**Myozen-ji**★ – *At the foot of the mountain to the E. Open 9am–5pm. ¥300.*
A Buddhist temple of the Jodo Shinshu sect, the temple bell is sheltered beneath a fine thatched roof. The vast *gassho*-style lodging adjoining the temple contains a display of everyday rural objects.

**Hachiman-jinja** – *5min walk farther S.*
This Shinto shrines, surrounded by a cedar forest-houses the village's guardian deity. To the east of the complex, the **Doburoku Matsuri Hall** *(open 9am–5pm; ¥300)* contains displays about the festival that takes place in mid-Oct. *Doburoku* is an unrefined sake with a fruity taste. Visits end with a tasting.

**Gassho-zukuri Minkaen**★ – *In the S of the village, on the west bank of the river. Open 8.40am–5pm (9am–4pm Dec–Feb). ¥500.*
Twenty-five *gassho-zukuri* farmhouses from a nearby village, threatened with being swallowed up by the building of a dam in 1967, were moved into this open-air folk museum, which gives a good idea of traditional life in the area. Craft demonstrations are given in some of the houses and it is possible to take part in dyeing or weaving workshops, or to try making *soba* (buckwheat noodles).

## GOKAYAMA★★★ 五箇山

*N of Shirakawa-go, on Route 156. From Ogimachi, a bus leaves 4 times daily for the villages of Suganuma and Ainokura (50min) and the JR station at Takaoka (1hr45min from Ainokura), from where a train can take you back to Kanazawa (30min).*

Ainokura, Gokayama
©JTB/Photoshot

This enchanting valley, adjacent to Shirakawa-go, has several hamlets scattered along the Sho River, each with its splendid *gassho-zukuri*. Less accessible than Shirakawa-go, Gokayama gets around half as many visitors. A rustic calm pervades the thatched houses, which double as inns, where you eat your dinner around the hearth. At night, the only sound is the croaking of frogs.

### Suganuma★★ 菅沼

*Route 156, 12.4mi/20km from Ogimachi (30min by bus).*
Situated on a terrace above a bend in the river, Suganuma *(population 40)* proudly guards its nine surviving *gassho-zukuri*. Two of them house the **Folk Museum** *(open 9am–4pm; ¥300)*, which showcases the valley's past activities, including the making of gunpowder.

**Iwase House**★★ – 1.9mi/*3km upriver of Suganuma. Open 9am–5pm. ¥200.*
The Iwase family will show you around this magnificent *gassho*-style house, the largest of its kind in Japan *(five floors, 85.3ft/26m long, 42.7ft/13m wide, and 49.2ft/15m high)*, dating from the end of the 16C.

**Murakami House**★★ – *Kamigachi, 3.1mi/5km downriver from Suganuma. Open 9am–5pm. ¥300.*
This *gassho-zukuri* was built in 1578 and is the oldest in Japan. The family living here will make you tea and sing you a folksong by the fire.

### Ainokura★★ 相倉

*6.2mi/10km from Suganuma. Buses stop at the junction 547yd/500m below the village. Map available at the information office in the car park, which is higher up (open 8.30am–5pm).*
The main village in Gokayama, situated on a plateau overhanging the Sho River, contains 20 *gassho-zukuri*. It is almost identical in appearance to Ogimachi, but the atmosphere is more tranquil. Several of the farmhouses have been turned into

*minshuku* and, if you want to relax after a hike in the forest, there are a number of *onsen* nearby.

**Folk Museum** – *Open 8.30am–5pm. ¥300.* This museum, housed in two *gassho-zukuri*, showcases the history and traditions of the valley, including the period in the 12C when it was used as a refuge by the surviving samurai of the Taira clan (*see p 68*). Folk costumes and instruments, handicrafts, and *washi* paper from the region are also on display.

# ADDRESSES

## STAY

### TAKAYAMA

**Minshuku Kuwataniya** 民宿桑谷屋 *1-50-30 Sowamachi. 5min walk from the station (B2). 0577-32-5021. www.kuwataniya.com. 13 rooms.* A good, very friendly *minshuku.*

**Minshuku Uenoya** 民宿上野屋 *95 Kaminino-machi (B2). 0577-32-3919. www4.ocn.ne.jp/~uenoya. 5 rooms.* A simple, friendly minshuku with Japanese-style rooms.

**Hida Takayama Koto-no-Yume** おやど・古都の夢 *6-11 Hanasato-cho (B2). 0577-32-0427. www.takayama-koto.co.jp. 20 rooms.* An oasis of refinement 55yd/50m from the station. Very good prices for such a superb ryokan.

**Minshuku Sosuke** 民宿惣助 *1-64 Okamoto-cho (A2). 0577-32-0818. www.irori-sosuke.com. 13 rooms. Lodging with half-board.* A fine building, but expect a slightly cool welcome.

**Rickshaw Inn** 力車イン *54 Suehiro-cho (B2). 0577-32-2890. www.rickshawinn.com. 10 rooms.* A lovely place. The owner, the English-speaking and outgoing Eiko, is a mine of information.

**Ryokan Kaminaka** 旅館かみなか *1-5 Hanaoka-cho (B2). 0577-32-0451. www9.ocn.ne.jp/~kaminaka. 13 rooms.* A welcoming family guesthouse surrounded by a lovely garden. *English spoken.*

### SHIRAKAWA-GO

**Gassho-no-yado Yokichi** 合掌の宿・よきち *351 Ogimachi. 05769-6-1417. 5 rooms.* Beautiful traditional house serves copious portions of tasty regional dishes. *O-furo* for private use.

**Magoemon** 合掌乃宿・孫ェ門 *360 Ogimachi, on the river bank, near the bridge. 05769-6-1167. 6 rooms.* Lovely, traditional thatched building; communal bathroom. Big meals served around *irori*; a storyteller relates local legends after dinner.

**Tousuke-no-yu Fujiya** 藤助の湯ふじや *Hirase Onsen, 8mi/13km from Ogimachi. 05769-5-2611. www.tousuke-fujiya.com. 11 rooms.* Refurbished former *gassho-zukuri* on Sho River, now an legant, luxurious ryokan.

### GOKAYAMA

**Yomoshiro** 民宿・与茂四郎 *395 Ainokura, in the center of the village. 0763-66-2377. 5 rooms.* Family gassho-zukuri, also a rustic inn; communal bathroom. Grilled trout, tempura, carp sashimi; vegetables served convivially around the central hearth. There may be traditional folk music after dinner.

## EAT

### TAKAYAMA

**Koma Restaurant** 独楽 *1-6 Hanaoka-cho (B1/2). 0577-34-6488. Open Wed–Mon 11am–9pm.* A *teppanyaki* restaurant, where *okonomiyaki* are made and shared, watched by the mischievous but friendly two female owners. *Menu in English.*

**Hida Takayama Fuitouya** いろり茶屋冬頭屋 *45 Kami-ichi-no-machi (B2). 0577-32-0404.* Excellent cuisine centered on regional products *(meat, vegetables, ferns)* served in a 100-year-old setting.

**Kitchen Hida** キッチン飛騨 *1-66 Honmachi (B2). 0577-36-2911. Open Thu–Tue.* The famous Hida beef is served here in all kinds of ways.

**Kakusho** 角正 *2-98 Baba-cho (B2). 0577-32-0174. Open 11.30am–8pm.* Six pavilions dotted around a magnificent garden. Meals based around the kind of vegetarian food that used to be the preserve of monks.

**Susaki** 料亭州さき *4-14 Shinmei-cho (B2). 0577-32-0023. Reservations required.* A dozen seasonal dishes, ceremoniously presented. Eating here is a thoroughly sensual experience, and has been for more than 200 years.

# The Japan Alps★★
# 日本アルプス

**Along with steep gorges and deep forests, the Japan Alps National Park, in the center of Honshu, contains the highest peaks in the country after Mount Fuji, many of them more than 9,842.5ft/3,000m. The area's many excellent ski resorts have the advantage of also possessing hot springs, where visitors can relax after a day's skiing. Nagano, made famous by the 1998 Winter Olympics, grew up around its ancient temple, Zenko-ji, which attracts more than 6 million visitors a year. In a lofty mountain setting at 1,942ft/592m above sea level, the city of Matsumoto has one of the finest castles in Japan. Hiking enthusiasts will enjoy the nearby alpine trails of Kamikochi or, farther south, the lovely Kiso Valley. It was through this valley that the Nakasendo ("the road through the central mountains") passed, linking Edo (now Tokyo) and Kyoto inland, just as the Tokaido road connected them along the coast.**

- **Population:** Nagano: 379,620, Matsumoto: 229,068.
- **Michelin Map:** Principal Sights Map B2 Nagano Prefecture – Regional Map p230.
- **Location:** Nagano is 143mi/230km from Tokyo and 115.6mi/186km from Niigata. Matsumoto is 43.5mi/70km from Nagano, 60mi/97km from Takayama, and 118mi/190km from Nagoya. Shinano JR trains cross the region from north to south, from Nagano to Nagoya via Matsumoto and the Kiso Valley. The ski resorts and mountain villages are served by buses, but some roads are closed during winter.
- **Timing:** Allow two days to visit the sights of Nagano and Matsumoto, and two extra days for a trip into the countryside.
- **Don't Miss:** Zenko-ji in Nagano; Nozawa *Onsen*; Matsumoto Castle; hiking at Kamikochi or between Tsumago and Magome.

## NAGANO★ 長野

This modern city in the north of the prefecture, *1hr 40min from Tokyo by Shinkansen*, is surrounded by numerous ski resorts, all about an hour away by bus. Occupying the basin of the Shinano River, Nagano grew up in the 13C, around the vast Zenko-ji, the city's temple and main attraction.

### Zenko-ji★★★ 善光寺

*1.2mi/2km N of Nagano station. 30min walk along Chuo-dori or 15min by bus (¥100). Open 4.30am–4.30pm (summer); 6am–4pm (winter). ¥500.*

A place that all Japanese dream of visiting at least once in their lives, the Zenko-ji is the largest temple in Japan after the Todai-ji in Nara (*see p331*). Surrounded by a bustling religious district, it is also very lively—there is almost a fairground atmosphere on Nakamise-dori, the great avenue leading to the shrine, lined with temple lodgings for pilgrims, abbey residences, and a large number of shops, which spill over onto the adjoining streets. Buses regularly disgorge streams of tourists eager to see the temple.

**A mythical beginning** – Legend relates that the temple was founded in order to house a statue of Amida *(the Buddha of the Western Paradise)*, offered as a gift to Emperor Kinmei from Korea in 552, when Buddhism was introduced into Japan. The statue was thrown into a canal after an epidemic, but was retrieved by a poor peasant named Honda Yoshimitsu, who took it back to his native village and built an oratory for it in 602. By 670, this had become a temple, which grew in size and popularity during the Kamakura era, a time when the cult of Amida was spreading throughout Japan. As the temple has burned down on several occasions, the current structure, built between 1707 and 1726, is the 11th reconstruction.

**A temple of tolerance** – A vast complex, with many subsidiary temples, Zenko-ji has a number of unusual aspects. Firstly, it welcomes both the Jodo and Tendai sects, which take it in turns to hold services. Secondly, unlike other Japanese temples, it has always been open to women. Indeed, an abbess is in charge of the Jodo branch. Finally, the layout is unique: the temple runs from north to south, with Mount Omine, symbol of the Western Paradise, behind it. Many believers have built mausoleums at the foot of the mountain in the hope of future rebirth.

**Visit** – A long, paved ramp climbs gently upward, past the 30 or so temple lodgings where visitors can stay. It leads through the gate of **Nio-mon** *(rebuilt in 1918)* and guarded by two impressive deities, past a row of guardian *jizo (bodhisattvas)*, to the monumental, two-story **San-mon**★ (1750), which is open to visitors. The avenue finally comes out onto a broad esplanade, where the **Hondo**★★, the two-story main hall, is located.

## USEFUL INFORMATION

**NAGANO**

**Tourist Office** – In the JR station. *Open 9am–6pm. ☏026-226-5626.*

## TRANSPORTATION

**BY TRAIN** – From Tokyo, the Shinkansen Asama leaves every 20min *(the most direct route, 1hr35min, ¥7,460)*. From Nagoya, reckon on 2hr50min and ¥6,620. To Matsumoto, the most direct route is the JR Shinonoi Line *(1hr7min, ¥1,110)*. For Kanazawa, JR Shinetsu Line to Noetsu, then Limited Express Hakutaka *(4hr, ¥6,410)*.

**BY BUS** – *Terminal opposite the station (west exit), in the West Plaza.* From Tokyo, leave from the Shinjuku Highway Bus Terminal *(3hr40min, ¥4,000)*.

This huge building, designated a National Treasure, is made from approximately 60,000 lengths of wood and has a roof of cypress bark. At the entrance to the vast, tatami-covered hall is a wooden statue of **Binzuru**★★★, a disciple of Buddha said to be able to cure physical ailements—so many worshipers have touched it for help over the years that the features of the face have been worn away. At the far end, on the west side, a richly decorated altar contains the statue around which the temple grew up: the **Ikko Sanzon**, a golden triad

*Nakamise-dori, street leading to Zenko-ji*

©Nagano Prefecture/JNTO

### Dawn ceremony

To see a small part of the ritual life of a Japanese temple, attend a morning service at Zenko-ji *(check on times the day before).* It is celebrated by the high priest or priestess, who blesses the heads of the kneeling worshipper as he or she passes. Shaven-headed monks in scarlet silk robes makes their way in procession to the altar and kneel before it. Clouds of incense drift about the room while readings of sacred texts alternate with hypnotic chanting. When the gong sounds, a curtain in front of the altar is lifted to reveal a golden phoenix on a bright-red background. The second curtain reveals the reliquary containing the sacred statue. The priest pretends to open the chest, without in fact doing so. In accordance with tradition, the Buddha has to remain hidden.

depicting Amida flanked by the two *bosatsu,* Kannon and Seishi sharing one halo. The statue is kept hidden away in a reliquary—not even the priests are allowed to see it—but a replica is shown to the crowd at a ceremony that takes place every seven years.

To the right of the altar, a staircase leads to a dark underground corridor, where worshippers grapple for a metal key mounted in the right-hand wall directly beneath the sacred statue, which is supposed to open the gates of paradise to them.

### M-Wave Nagano Olympic Memorial Arena エムウェーブ

*3.1mi/5km to the NE. From the station, take a bus (stop 1) in the direction of Yashima, get off at the M-Wave-mae stop (20min, ¥260). Open Sept–Mar 10am–11.30pm. ¥2,100 including hire of skates.*

A colossal covered arena *(787.4ft/240m long and 393.7ft/120m wide),* with a speed-skating track built for the 1998 Olympic Games. There is a small **museum** about the Olympics. Skaters venturing onto the rink will have great fun here, though.

## EXCURSIONS

### Obuse★ 小布施

*9.3mi/15km NE of Nagano.*

*Nagano Dentetsu Line to Obuse station (20min, ¥750). Map and bicycle rental at the Tourist Office on the way into the center of town (open 9am–5pm).*

The main claim to fame of this small town *(population 12,000)* is that it was the place where the artist **Katsushika Hokusai** (1760–1849), the master Japanese printmaker, chose to settle during the last years of his life. He bequeathed many works to the town.

Obuse also has a number of small **museums** on various themes: bonsai, lamps, antique pottery, etc. There are some fine vineyards and chestnut groves in the area surrounding the town—chestnut-flavored ice cream and confectionery are its specialty.

**Hokusai-kan Museum★★** – *10min walk SE of the station. Open 9am–5pm. ¥500.* Apart from 30 or so prints, the main attractions of this museum devoted to Hokusai (and his followers) are the great master's original works, which include ink drawings and *kakejiku* (wall scrolls). His genius lay in being able to capture the essence of a movement or the beauty of a kimono-clad courtesan in just a few strokes. The museum's exhibits also include ceiling panels and two festival floats decorated by the artist.

**Takai Kozan Museum** – *55yd/50m from the previous museum, at the end of the street. Open 9am–5pm. ¥300.*

Takai Kozan (1806–83), a wealthy Obuse merchant, was not only Hokusai's patron and friend, but also one of his pupils. His darkly ironic works depict demons and ghosts, ugly-looking fantasy creatures inspired by the traditional representation of the Buddhist hells.

**Gansho-in** – *30min walk E of the station. Open 9am–5pm. ¥300.* A Buddhist temple of the Soto sect, founded in 1472. Its ceiling bears a stunning phoenix painted by Hokusai.

### Yudanaka★ 湯田中

*21.7mi/35km NE of Nagano. Nagano Dentetsu Line to Yudanaka station (45min, ¥1,230).*

An *onsen* resort in the district of Yamanouchi, Yudanaka nestles in a gorge of the Yokoyu River, below the ski resort of Shiga Koken. Most visitors come here to see the **wild monkeys** bathing in the mountain's hot springs.

**Jigokudani Yaen-koen**★ – *From the station, bus to Kanbayashi Onsen, then 30min walk along the trail. Open Apr–Oct 8.30am–5pm; Nov–Mar 9am–4pm. ¥500.*

A popular subject for amateur photographers, the colony of 200 or so macaques living near this pool in the monkey park visit regularly for an invigorating dip in the hot water as relief from winter temperatures. Unfortunately, their presence is not entirely natural as the park keepers put food out for them. The surroundings are not so natural either, spoiled by concrete and electric cables, but this is still a unique opportunity to see the mischievous monkeys playing and running about, oblivious to the presence of humans.

### Nozawa Onsen★★ 野沢温泉

*28mi/45km NE of Nagano. JR Iiyama Line to Togari-Nozawa-onsen station (1hr, ¥740), then bus (9 per day, 15min, ¥300). From the east exit of Nagano station, there are also buses that go direct to the station (3 per day, 1hr15min, ¥1,400). Information office in the middle of the village (open 9am–5.30pm; 0269-85-3155).*

Although at a relatively low altitude *(5,413.4ft/1,650m)*, Nozawa *Onsen*'s skiing area is excellent, thanks to the quality of its snow. Catering for both ski enthusiasts and families, the resort has retained the feel of an old-fashioned mountain village, with its cobbled lanes echoing to the clogs of vacationing Japanese on their way to the baths. There are 13 public baths *(no charge)* in the village— a good way to relax after an energetic day's skiing.

**Skiing area** – *Open Dec–Apr. ¥4,600 for a 1-day pass.* Compact and easily reached, Nozawa Onsen has 31mi/50km of ski slopes, two cable cars, and 22 chairlifts. If you ski from top to bottom you will be descending 3,560ft/1,085m, and the longest slope is 6mi/10km. Downhill skiing, cross-country skiing, ski jumping, snowboarding, the resort can cater for all ski forms and levels, and there is also a children's club.

**Public Baths** – *Open 6am–11pm. No charge (bring your own towel).*

The most popular of the baths is **Oh-yu**★★, housed in a fine wooden building, looking rather like a temple, in the middle of the village. Not far away is the hot spring **Ogama**, where the water is 176°F/80°C—so hot the villagers can boil their food in it and the craftsmen use it to soften the vine shoots with which they make toys. ***Onsen* Kenkokan** *(W of the village; open Wed–Mon 10am–7pm; ¥1,500)* offers more comfort with several baths, a sauna, gym, steam room, jacuzzi, etc. Last, but not least, there is **Arena** *(N of the village; open Thu–Tue 10am–9pm; ¥1,500)*, a large, covered swimming pool with whirlpools, waterslides, a spa, and a sauna.

**Japan Museum of Skiing**★ – *At the foot of the slopes. Open Wed–Mon 9am–4pm. ¥300.* Housed in a building shaped like a church, this museum covers the history of skiing in Japan and the 1998 Winter Olympics at Nagano, several events of which were hosted by Nozawa *Onsen*. Portraits of the resort's stars are also on display—despite the village's small population of just 4,200, it has produced no fewer than 15 Olympic champions over the years.

### Togakushi★★ 戸隠

*12.4mi/20km NW of Nagano. From Nagano station (stop 7, outside the Zenko-ji exit) bus nos. 70 and 71. Take the aptly named Togakushi Birdline Highway as far as the Chusha-Miyamae stop (12 per day, 1hr, ¥1,360).*

Nestling in the midst of a magnificent cedar forest, at an altitude of 3,937ft/1,200m, this alpine village *(pop-*

Cedar tree trail to Togakushi Okusha

©Nagano Prefecture/© JNTO

*ulation around 5,000)* welcomes skiers in winter, and hikers from the end of April. Popular hiking destinations are three shrines, all within a relatively short distance: the **Hokosha**★ *(lower shrine)*, the **Chusha**★ *(middle shrine)*, and the **Okusha**★ *(upper shrine)*. In the Middle Ages, Togakushi was a major center for Shugendo, an ascetic cult whose practitioners, were warrior monks *(yamabushi)* who lived like hermits in the mountains. They are also said to have been skilled in the *ninja* arts of espionage, illusion, and assassination. The village is also known for its bamboo handicrafts and its *soba*, noodles made from buckwheat harvested in the mountain pastures, and eaten hot or cold in the many restaurants along the main street of the village.

**Togakushi Folk Museum** – *15min walk uphill from the bus stop, opposite the fork leading to the Okusha. Open end Apr–mid Nov, 9am–5pm. ¥500.*

The museum tells the story of the *ninja* warriors through displays featuring weapons, clothes, and photographs, and explains their techniques. The **Ninja Village for Children** next door is a maze-like building filled with traps, hidden doors, and secret staircases *(Fri–Wed, 9am–5pm*

**Okusha-jinja** – *45min walk.*

A mountain **trail**★★ leads through a forest of ancient cedars to this shrine hidden away on the side of Mount Togakushi. According to legend, this was where the rock that sealed the cave into which Amaterasu had withdrawn when offended by brother, was removed and tossed away by the *kami* Amenotajikarao, who, in so doing, created the mountain.

## Hakuba★ 白馬

*37mi/60km to the W.*

*From Nagano station (stop 6, east exit), buses for Hakuba station every hour (1hr, ¥1,400). Hakuba is also connected by train to Matsumoto (1hr, ¥2,700). Tourist office at the station exit (open 8.30am–5pm; 0261-72-2279).*

Winter and summer alike, the resort of Hakuba (population 10,000) is a paradise for outdoor sports enthusiasts. At the heart of the Japan Alps, surrounded by towering peaks, it hosted the downhill, super-giant slalom, Nordic skiing, and ski jumping events in the Nagano Winter Olympics. Popular with young people, it offers some of the best skiing in Japan, as well as some pleasant *onsen*. During the summer season, the activities switch from skiing to hiking, climbing, camping, mountain biking, rafting, canoeing, canyoning, golf, fishing, and parascending.

**Skiing area** – *Open Dec–early May. ¥4,300 for a 1-day pass to Happo-One.*

There are seven resorts linked by bus, including the central resorts of Happo-One, Hakuba 47, and Goyu-Toomi. **Happo-One**★ is at the foot of the mountains, just five minutes by bus from the station. The slopes cater for all levels of skier and snowboarder, and rise to a height of 6,007ft/1,831m. There are 13 slopes *(including a superb 1.9mi/3km slalom slope)* and 31 ski lifts.

**Hakuba Ski Jumping Stadium** – *At Happo-One. Open Apr–Nov 8.30am–4.30pm; Dec–Mar 9am–3.30pm. ¥500.*

Built in 1992, there are two ski jumps—one normal hill *(length 295ft/90m)* and one large *(394ft/120m)*. Take an elevator to the top of the slope to get an impressive "ski-jumper's eye view."

## MATSUMOTO★★ 松本

Spread out across a valley framed by the snowy peaks of the Japan Alps, Matsumoto is a major crossroads at the heart of Chubu. It is an attractive city, with a great deal of charm and a relaxed atmosphere. Originally called Fukashi, it developed in the 16C as a fortified town around the castle that still stands proudly at its center.

Designated a National Treasure, the castle has the oldest wooden keep in Japan. Farther south, the old merchant quarter of Nakamachi is full of fine storehouses from the Edo period, in stark contrast to the modern architecture of the **Matsumoto City Museum of Art** and the **Japan Ukiyo-e Museum**.

## USEFUL INFORMATION

**MATSUMOTO**

**Tourist Office** – Outside the station. *Open 9.30am–6pm. ✆0263-32-2814. www.city.matsumoto.nagano.jp.*

**Post Office/Withdrawals** – *2-7-5 Chuo. Open Mon–Fri 9am–4pm. ATM open Mon–Fri 8.45am–9pm, Sat–Sun 9am–7pm.*

## TRANSPORTATION

**BY TRAIN** – **Matsumoto Station** – From Nagano, JR Shinonoi Line *(1hr12min, ¥1,110)*. From Nagoya, the most direct train is the Limited Express Shinano (Wideview) *(2hr, ¥5,870)*.

**BY BUS** – **Matsuden Bus Terminal,** *opposite the station, below the ESPA store.* 4 buses per day to Takayama: at 7.50am, 11.10am, 1.50pm, 5.10pm *(2hr20min, ¥3,100)*.

### Matsumoto Castle★★★ 松本城

*15min walk NE of the station. Open 8.30am–4.30pm. ¥600 including museum. Guided tour in English available, no charge.*

Many Japanese castles are merely restorations or reconstructions based on an original. Not so Matsumoto, which is a fascinating example of a fortified "flatland" castle *(hira-jiro)*, one of the best-preserved in the country, still imbued with the smoke and clamor of pastbattles. Set in the heart of the city, it is surrounded by three deep moats filled with still water, where carp and swans swim lazily. Because of its black color, it is known as "Crow Castle", in contrast to the White Heron Castle in Himeji (*see p366*). The history of the site begins in 1504, when the region was dominated by a small fortress built by the Ogasawara clan. In 1582, Toyotomi Hideyoshi (1536–98) gained control, and installed his loyal supporter, Ishikawa Kazumasa, who remodeled the building

*Matsumoto Castle with a view to the surrounding mountains*

© John Warburton-Lee/Photononstop

and added the great keep (1593), the castle's finest building.

Built in a period of unrest, Matsumoto Castle was designed above all for defense. Many of its features are familiar from medieval castles in Europe: moats, huge walls, walkways, narrow staircases, projecting galleries, and arrow slits, all designed to make it impregnable. The biggest difference is that the building is of wood and not stone. The sober elegance of the dark-wood of the keep may be aesthetically appealing, but from a military point of view it presented an easy target for the flaming arrows of attackers. However, potential assailants would still have to get past the three successive enclosures that once sheltered the lord's palace and the living quarters of his 1,200 samurai.

**Visit** – The keep stands on an artificial rise in the middle of a wide moat. The smooth convex walls of its stone base fall almost sheer to the water.

Access is by a delightful vermillion-colored bridge. Seen from outside, the 98.4ft/30m-high main tower appears to have five floors with flat roofs enlivened by triangular pediments, more rounded and ornate on the south side. Once inside, it can be seen that there are in fact six floors, including a dark, low-ceilinged secret third floor, where the samurai would assemble in case of siege.

The keep is flanked by two secondary towers, to the southeast and northeast, linked by an elevated corridor. Visitors to the upper floors can see the forest of thick, rough-hewn wooden pillars that bear the weight of the structure. The display cases contain a collection of old firearms: rifles, muskets, mortars, and arquebuses. From the top floor, reached by a narrow staircase, there is a **panorama** of the mountains. In the ceiling is a small shrine dedicated to a goddess who prevents fires. The tour ends with the *tsukimi-yagura* turret, added in 1636, and used as a pleasure pavilion from which to view the moon. It is surrounded by a bright-red lacquered balcony.

**Japan Folklore Museum** – *Open 8.30am–4.30pm. Entry included in castle ticket.*

On the way out of the castle you will find this museum, which contains a model of the fortified town as it was at the time of the Tokugawa shoguns (17C and 18C), as well as swords and armor. The city's folk traditions are also represented in a collection of dolls, a specialty of Matsumoto.

## Nakamachi District★ 中町

*10min walk S of the castle. Walk down the big, tree-lined avenue called Daimyo-dori as far as the Metoba River.*

To the left, on either side of the river are the two attractive streets of Nawate-dori and Nakamachi-dori, lined with former storehouses *(kura)* from the Edo period. Their tiled roofs and thick walls decorated with black and white latticework were designed to protect the merchandise. Today, most have been turned into cafes, *soba* (noodle) restaurants, art galleries, and trendy boutiques. On Nakamachi-dori, **Nakamachi Kura Shikku-kan** *(open 9am–10pm; no charge)* displays local crafts. Nearby, in the small **Geiyu-kan** theater *(performances Sun & public holidays 1.30pm and 3pm; ¥700)*, you can listen to old songs accompanied by the *shamisen* (three-stringed instrument) while enjoying a green tea.

## Matsumoto City Museum of Art 松本市美術館

*5min walk SE of Nakamachi, on Ekimae-dori. Open Tue–Sun 10am–5pm. ¥800.*

Opened in 2002, this museum shows the work of local artists, including the calligraphy of Kamijo Shinzan, the landscapes of Tamura Kazuo, and the colorful, avant-garde creations of Kusama Yayoi, one of the most famous living artists in Japan.

## Japan Ukiyo-e Museum (JUM)★★ 日本浮世絵博物館

*1.9mi/3km W of the station. 10min by taxi (¥1,500) or by Dentetsu Kamikochi Line (platform 7), Oniwa stop (6min, ¥170), then 15min walk. Open Tue–Sun 10am–5pm. ¥1,050.*

Although not easy to reach, housed in an ultra-modern building, this museum is definitely worth a visit as it contains the vast collection of the Sakai family. Among Matsumoto's richest merchants and patrons during the Edo period, over five generations the Sakai family collected more than 100,000 prints, paintings, screens, and old books, making it the largest private collection of its kind in the world, though displayed here in relatively small rooms. The *ukiyo-e* ("images of the floating world") woodblock prints are displayed in three-monthly rotation, in subdued lighting because of their fragility. Depsite this, their rare beauty still shines through. The collection includes many masterpieces by Utamaro, Hiroshige, Hokusai, and Sharaku. *An English-language brochure is available.*

## EXCURSIONS

### Daio-Wasabi Farm★

大王わさび農場

*9.3mi/15km NW of Matsumoto. Access by train, JR Oito Line to Hotaka (25min, ¥320), then 15min by bicycle (rental outside the station, ¥200 per hour). Open 8.30am–5.30pm (summer); 9am–4.30pm (winter). No charge.*

This is the largest *wasabi* plantation in Japan, 37 acres/15ha of fields irrigated by spring water from the mountains. (*Wasabi* is a strong-tasting radish, whitish-green in color.) There are stands selling an endless variety of products made with *wasabi*: biscuits, tea, chocolate, ice cream, and milk shakes.

### Kamikochi★★ 上高地

*31mi/50km W of Matsumoto. Matsumoto Dentetsu Line to Shin-Shimashima (30min, ¥680), then bus (1hr15min, ¥2,000). Kamikochi can also be reached by bus from Takayama (1hr30min, ¥2,000). Cars have to park in the car park at Nakanoyu, which is 5mi/8km from Kamikochi and linked to it by shuttle bus. Open late Apr–mid-Nov. The information center (open 9am–5pm) at the bus station provides a free guide (in English) to hikers.*

Situated on the banks of the Azusa River in a deep valley at 4,921ft/1,500m above sea level, this mountain resort set amid stunning scenery is one of the great centers for hiking and climbing in the Japan Alps National Park *(Chubu-Sangaku)*. On any day in high season, hundreds of hikers set off to tackle its tallest peaks: **Hotaka-dake** *(10,466ft/3,190m)* and **Yariga-dake** *(10,433ft/3,180m)*. Kamikochi itself consists of a mere handful of hotels and shops, and entry by car is prohibited. It is possible to make a day excursion to Kamikochi from Matsumoto or Takayama, but if you spend the night here, then you can set off on a hike early the next morning before the crowds arrive.

**Azusa-gawa Valley★** – Two easy, well-signposed circuits *(2hr round trip)* follow the Azusa River in a loop, starting from the Kappa-bashi suspension bridge, near the bus station. The first, which goes south, leads to **Taisho-ike**, a lake formed in 1915 when the Yake-dake volcano erupted and partly blocked the Azusa River. On the way back, cross Tashiro-bashi and see the statue of Walter Weston *(see box p261)* on the left bank. The other loop, going north, runs along the right bank as far as Myojin-bashi. Cross the bridge for a view of the picturesque **Myojin-ike★** and the ring of snowy peaks reflected in its clear waters.

### An alpine missionary

The development of Kamikochi as a tourist center owes a great deal to the Reverend Walter Weston (1861–1940), an English missionnary and amateur mountaineer, who climbed the peaks of the region and popularized mountaineering as a sport in Japan. Although he didn't coin the term "Japan Alps," Weston was responsible for putting the area on the mountaineering map in 1896, publishing *Mountaineering and Exploration in the Japanese Alps.*

### The secret of lacquerware

Lacquer *(urushi)* is a resin extracted from the sumac shrub. It is applied in thin layers, which are sanded down and polished between each coat. The number of layers determines the ultimate quality of the object—Kiso lacquerware can have anything up to 18 layers. The color is obtained by incorporating natural (charcoal, cochineal) or chemical (iron oxide, mercury sulfate) pigments. Kiso lacquerware is of several types: *roiro* (shiny black, like the surface of a mirror), *shunkei* (wood coated a light red, so that the grain is visible), and *tsuishu* (a mixture of colors, with mother-of-pearl inlays, giving an impressive, multicolored marbled effect).

## Shin-Hotaka *Onsen*★★ 新穂高温泉

*43.5mi/70km W of Matsumoto.*

*Bus from Matsumoto (2hr, ¥2,800) or from Takayama (1hr20min, ¥2,400).*

This thermal spa, with its many hot springs, is famous for having the longest cable car ride in Asia *(¥2,800 round trip)*, taking visitors up to 7,073.5ft/2,156m on the 9,544ft/2,909m-high Mount Nishi-Hotaka.

From there the **panoramic view**★★ over the Japan Alps is simply breathtaking. From the point where the cable car drops you off on the mountain, it's a three-hour hike back to Kamikochi.

## KISO VALLEY★★ 木曽谷

In the south of Nagano prefecture lies this heavily wooded valley, which forms a natural route across the Japan Alps. The Kiso River runs through the valley for around 43.5mi/70km. When the Tokugawa were in power (1603–1867), two main roads linked the shogun's capital Edo (present-day Tokyo) with the Imperial capital, Kyoto. The first, the Tokaido road, ran along the Pacific coast. The second, the **Nakasendo**, crossed the mountains between Matsumoto and Nagoya, and followed the Kiso Valley. Eleven of the road's 69 stations or post towns grew up along the valley, places where the *daimyo* (feudal lords). Forced to visit Edo regularly to pay tribute to the shogun, could stop off on their journey. At that time, it took three days to travel through the valley compared with a few hours by car or train today. Part of the 17C paved road is still visible in places.

### Kiso-Hirasawa★ 木曽平沢

*021.7mi/35km S of Matsumoto.*

*Access by the JR Chuo Line (45min, ¥570).*

During the Edo period, this town, set among vineyards, acquired a reputation throughout Japan for the quality and beauty of its lacquerware *(see box above)*, prompting many travelers on the Nakasendo road to stop here. Today, the tradition continues, and the village and its surrounding area contains, around 200 specialist workshops employing approximately 900 people, including around 60 master lacquerers. The main street is lined with shops selling china, boxes, containers, tables, furniture, screens, and panels of lacquered wood.

**Kiso Center for Arts and Crafts** – *15min walk N of the station. Open Wed–Mon 9am–5pm. No charge. 0264-34-3888 (reservation mandatory).*

Both shop and museum, this large gallery displays the work of some 50 lacquerers. You can even try your hand at lacquering *(reservations required; ¥1,500).*

### Narai★ 奈良井

*3.1mi/5km S of Kiso-Hirasawa.*

*Next station on the JR Chuo Line.*

Consisting of a single street 0.6mi/1km long, this former post town on the Nakasendo, halfway between Kyoto and Edo, still has some fine old two-story wooden houses with wide canopies and openwork façades. Now a protected site, the village *(population 800)* is almost identical to Tsumago and Magome, but has the advantage of being far less crowded. Spend the night in one of its small inns and feel as if you are stepping back in time a century or two. It also specializes in making small lacquered combs.

**Nakamura House** – *10min walk S of the station.* ○*Open Tues–Sun 9am–4.30pm (3.30pm in winter).* ⊜*¥200.*

A superb example of a traditional Edo period house, with a central hearth *(irori)* and garden at the rear. It once belonged to a rich merchant who dealt in combs—the shop occupied the part of the ground floor facing the street.

## Tsumago★ 妻籠

➋ *56mi/90km S of Matsumoto. JR Chuo Line to Nagiso station (2hr, ¥1,450), then a bus (10min, ¥300). Tourist Office in the middle of the village (*○*open 8.30am–5pm; ✆0264-57-3123).*

Hemmed in by mountains, this former post town on the Nakasendo was abandoned after the opening of the Chuo railway and the main road in 1911. After decades of neglect, having miraculously escaped the sweeping modernization of the 1960s and 1970s, it was deemed the ideal candidate for a makeover as a tourist destination.

As in Narai and Magome, electricity cables, TV aerials, and telephone lines were buried or hidden, and the wooden houses of the Edo period restored and turned into museums, restaurants, inns, and shops selling handicrafts and souvenirs. A long, paved street *(pedestrian only)* cuts through the town. At one end is an old wooden noticeboard on which the shogun's edicts used to be displayed.

During the Edo period, the cypress forests of the Kiso Valley were closely guarded since they provided the wood used to build castles, temples, and national shrines. The town's inhabitants were forbidden on pain of death to cut down even the smallest tree.

There are three places of interest along the main street, all in close proximity (○*open 9am–5pm; ⊜combined ticket ¥700*).

**Tsumagojuku Honjin** – ⊜*¥300 (¥700 with the Wakihonjin Okuya).* This inn was an official stopping place for *daimyo* (feudal lords) on their way to Edo. The building is divided into two areas: a fine, spacious dwelling for the feudal lord and his men, and another smaller and plainer for the Shimazaki family, who ran the village. It was meticulously restored in its entirety in 1995.

**Wakihonjin Okuya** – ⊜*¥600 (¥700 with the Tsumagojuku Honjin).* An imposing, two-story cypresswood building, with a delightful moss garden; it also served as a halt for passing samurai. It was rebuilt in 1877 and welcomed the Meiji Emperor on a brief stay in the region.

**Rekishi Shiryokan** – *9am–5pm – ⊜¥600.* This local history museum next to the Okuya displays lacquerware, as well as, models and photographs of Tsumago, before and after its restoration.

🥾 **Trail from Tsumago to Magome**★ – *5mi/8km (2hr30min walk). Baggage forwarding service Jul 21–Aug 19 daily; Mar–Nov weekend only. Leave baggage before 11.30am at the Tourist Office in Tsumago, pick up from 1pm at the Tourist Office in Magome.* ⊜*¥500 per item.*

A rural trail that makes its way beneath cypresses, past small waterfalls and hamlets bright with flowers in the summer months. At 2,625ft/800m, the trail crosses a pass before descending once again to the village of Magome, from where there is a magnificent view of the surrounding mountains.

## Magome★ 馬籠

➋ *56mi/90km from Nagoya. Wideview Shinano express train to Nakatsugawa (50min, ¥2,940), then bus (30min, ¥540). Tourist office in the village (*○*open 9am–5pm; ✆0264-59-2336).*

Situated on a hillside facing west, the village stretches along a steep, but lovely stone-paved street lined with souvenir shops, restaurants, and *minshuku*. The restored buildings recreate the atmosphere of a post town in the Edo period. There is a small **Folk Museum** halfway along the street (○*open 9am–4.30pm; ⊜¥300*), showcasing village traditions and crafts. In the lower part of the village is a beautiful **mill wheel**—the peasants grind buckwheat and hull rice.

**Yubunesawa Resort** – *1.9mi/3km S of Magome. Free shuttle bus every hour 9.50am–11.50am and 1.50pm–4.50pm.*

*Open 10am–10pm reception; closes at 8.30pm). ¥1,500.*
Fed by the hot springs of Mount Ena, this vast aqua spa complex has both indoor and outdoor baths, pools with water massage, two swimming pools with waterslides, etc. An ideal place to soothe tired muscles after a hike.

# ADDRESSES

## STAY

### NAGANO

**Comfort Hotel Nagano** コンフォートホテル長野 *1-12-4 Minami-Chitose. 026-268-1611. www.choice-hotels.jp. 76 rooms.* A well-maintained business hotel 3min walk from the JR station. Excellent value for money.

**Shimizuya Ryokan Chuokan** 清水屋旅館中央館 *49 Daimon-cho. 026-232-2580. 8 rooms.* A friendly, family-run ryokan in a superb 130-year-old house.

**Fuchino-bo** 淵之坊 *462 Motoyoshi-cho, in front of the entrance to the Zenko-ji. 026-232-3669. 6 rooms.* Magnificent *shukubo* (temple lodging) from the Edo period. Spacious Japanese rooms and divine vegetarian cuisine.

**The Saihokukan Hotel** 犀北館 *528-1 Agatamachi. 026-235-3333. www.saihokukan.com. 89 rooms.* An old hotel, opened in 1890, and somewhat extravagantly refurbished with marble columns. The Japanese restaurant is immaculate.

### YUDANAKA

**Uotoshi Ryokan** 魚敏旅館 *2563 Sano, Yamanouchi. 6min walk from Yudanaka station, after Sakae Bridge. 0269-33-1215. www.avis.ne.jp/~miyasaka. 8 rooms. From ¥7,980 (in winter prices can drop to ¥1,050, kotatsu, (low table with a heat lamp underneath), included with room).* A simple, family guesthouse with a magnificent cypresswood *onsen. English spoken.*

### NOZAWA *ONSEN*

**Pension Schnee** ペンション・シュネ *Near the Hikage cable car. 0269-85-2012. 12 rooms – from ¥9,500, with additional ¥1,000 late Dec and early Jan; breakfast ¥1,400.* A pretty chalet below the ski slopes, run by a lovely family of former Olympic champions. Western rooms. Copious breakfast with homemade jams.

**Haus St Anton** ハウス・サンアントン *Ooyudouri, Nozawa-onsen-mura. 0269-85-3597. 20 rooms.* This pleasant, small, Tyrolean-style chalet is run by a former Olympic skiing champion. *Some rooms have private bathrooms.*

**Ryokan Sakaya** 旅館さかや *9329 Nozawa-onsen-mura. 0269-85-3118. www.ryokan-sakaya.co.jp. 29 rooms.* This elegant ryokan has a wonderful *onsen*. Delicious *shabu-shabu* (Japanese meat fondue). Unforgettable.

### TOGAKUSHI

**Gokui Lodge** 宿坊・極意 *3354 Togakushi. 5min walk from the Chusha bus stop. 026-254-2044. www.egokui.com. 8 rooms (breakfast and dinner included).* Superbly located in a 400-year-old former *shukubo* (temple lodging) adjoining the Chusha temple. Friendly service and exquisite food.

### HAKUBA

**Yamano Hotel** 山のホテル *Happo-One, opposite the Olympic Ski Jumping Stadium. 0261-72-8312. www.hakuba-yamanohotel.com. 24 rooms.* Looking rather like a Swiss chalet, this hotel is close to the ski slopes and has comfortable, modern Japanese and Western rooms. *Natural spa. English spoken.*

### MATSUMOTO

**Super Hotel Matsumoto Ekimae** スーパーホテル松本駅前 *1-1-7 Chuo. 0263-37-9000. www.superhotel.co.jp. 71 rooms.* A business hotel 218.7yd/200m from the station. Nothing out of the ordinary, but certainly the best value in the city.

**Marumo Ryokan** まるも旅館 *3-3-10 Chuo. 0263-32-0115. 8 rooms.* A friendly, family guesthouse. *O-furo* for private use.

**Jonokura** 城之蔵 *2-1-17 Chuo. -0263-31-8711. 13 rooms.* Well-maintained hotel with comfortable rooms and discreet, friendly service.

### KAMIKOCHI

**Nishi-Itoya Mountain Lodge** 西糸屋山荘 *Kamikochi, Azumi, W of the Kappa Bridge. 0263-95-2206. Open Apr 25–Nov 14. www.nishiitoya.com. 38 rooms, 1 dorm (for 8). Lodging with half-board.*

**SHIN-HOTAKA *ONSEN***

**Hotel Hotaka** ホテル穂高 *About 109yd/100m from the cable car. 0578-89-200. www.okuhi.jp. 49 rooms.* This large complex compensates for a lack of personality with a splendid open-air *onsen* with **views** of the mountains. *Breakfast and dinner included.*

## KISO VALLEY

**NARAI**

**Iseya** 民宿伊勢屋 *388 Narai, Shiojiri-shi. 0264-34-3051. www.oyado-iseya.jp. 10 rooms – ¥7,600 – breakfast and dinner included.* This friendly ***minshuku*** occupies a fine Edo-period house on the main street, with an ornamental garden.

**TSUMAGO**

**Fujioto** 旅館藤乙 *Near the Wakihonjin Okuya. 0264-57-3009. 10 rooms.* A lovely ryokan, one of the most comfortable in the village, with a splendid garden. Good-quality meals.

**Koushinzuka** 民宿こおしんづか *25min walk from the village, on the trail to Magome (bus stop just outside). 0264-57-3029. 4 rooms – ¥11,000.* Old-style ***minshuku*** with calm, rustic atmosphere. Dinners around central hearth.

**MAGOME**

**Tajiyama** 但馬屋 *Main street. 0264-59-2048. 10 rooms – ¥16,800 – breakfast and dinner incl. Minshuku* in traditional house. Rustic, but pleasant. *Communal bathroom; copious meals.*

## EAT

**NAGANO**

**Bikura** 欅屋びくら *10 F West Plaza Bldg, 1355-5 Suechiro-cho. 026-264-7717. Open 4.30–11pm.* This restaurant has one of the most unusual settings in the city, at the top of a building opposite the west exit of the station. Eclectic Japanese and Western cuisine.

**Motoya** そば処・元屋 *587-3 Daimon-cho. 026-232-0668. Open Wed–Mon 11am–2.30pm.* A popular—and always packed—restaurant specializing in the *soba* for which Nagano is famous.

**Yayoiza** 弥生座 *503 Daimon-cho. 026-232-2311. Open 11.30am–8.30pm.* Opened in 1847 and something of an institution. Regional dishes like ***shabu-shabu***, based around the famous Nagano beef.

**MATSUMOTO**

There are several 100-year-old eateries on **Nawate-dori,** selling sweet potato (**Mimatsuya**, *open 8.30am–7pm*), *soba* (**Benten Honten**, *open Fri–Wed 11am–6pm*), and pastries (**Sweet**, *open 8.30am–5pm*).

**Kura** 蔵 *1-10-22 Chuo. 0263-33-6444. Open Thu–Tue 11.30am–10pm.* Open since 1963 and located over three stories in a former fish canning factory, this restaurant offers such unusual dishes as ***basashi*** (horsemeat sashimi), ***hachinoko*** (bee larvae), as well as simple sushi.

## KISO VALLEY

**NARAI**

**Tokkuriya** 徳利屋 *516 Narai, Shiojiri-shi. 0264-34-2189. 11am-4pm and evenings with reservation.* One of village's oldest houses. Meals around hearth. Local cuisine. *Lunch menu at ¥1,680.*

## SPORT AND LEISURE

**Evergreen Outdoor Center** エヴァーグリーン・アウトドアセンター – *Happo-One. 0261-72-3066. www.evergreen-hakuba.com.* Run by a cheerful Canadian, the center offers a full range of sporting activities, both in summer and winter: cross-country or off-piste skiing, kayaking, rafting, mountain biking, climbing, etc.

## EVENTS AND FESTIVALS

**NOZAWA *ONSEN***

The **Dosojin** fire festival on Jan 15 includes one of the three best firework displays in Japan.

## SHOPPING

**Handicrafts – Belle Amie**, ベラミみむら人形店 *3-7-23 Chuo, Matsumoto, Open Mon–Sat 9am–7pm. 0263-33-1314.* This shop-workshop-museum has been producing all kinds of high-quality regional dolls for over 50 years.

# Kanazawa★★
# 金沢

- **Population:** 453,127 – Ishikawa Prefecture.
- **Michelin Map:** Principal Sights Map B2 – Regional Map p230.
- **Location:** Kanazawa is on the northeast coast of Honshu, 93mi/150km from Takayama and 155mi/250km from Nagoya, and occupies a narrow plain between the Sea of Japan and the Japan Alps National Park, at the gateway to the Noto Peninsula. This sprawling city stretches southeast of the JR station, between the Asano and Sai Rivers. Its center is located around the Kenroku-en and the castle grounds, which can be reached by bus from the station. Farther south, the shopping area of Katamachi, near the Korinbo department store, is the liveliest part of the city. In the west is the old samurai quarter of Nagamachi and to the south of the Sai-gawa, the Teramachi temple quarter. In the northeast of the city, across the Asano-gawa, is the geisha quarter of Higashi Chaya.
- **Timing:** Allow two days to see the city.
- **Don't miss:** The Kenroku-en; the 21st Century Museum of Contemporary Art; the Nagamachi and Higashi Chayamachi districts.

**In the 17C, Kanazawa was one of the most powerful feudal cities in Japan. In terms of wealth, artistic influence, and size of population, it could more than hold its own with the great capitals of Europe at the time. Like Kyoto, it escaped the bombing of World War II, so, although it also has its fair share of modern architecture, the samurai and geisha quarters, with their winding alleys and little wooden houses topped with glazed tiles, are preserved intact. Famous for the Kenroku-en, one of the three most beautiful gardens in Japan, as well as its fine cuisine, richly varied handicrafts, Noh theater, and museums, Kanazawa is definitely *iki*—tasteful, refined, and distinguished. For a pleasant excursion outside the city, the Noto Peninsula, with its jagged coastline, will plunge you into a rural Japan of wild beauty and sleepy fishing villages, where the pace of life is far gentler.**

## A BIT OF HISTORY

Kanazawa, which literally means "golden marsh," is said to derive its name from a stream where the region's peasants once found deposits of gold. In the 16C, the city was ruled as an autonomous fiefdom by a Buddhist sect until it was seized by Maeda Toshiie, a vassal of the shogun Toyotomi Hideyoshi, in 1583. A castle was built and the small town was transformed into a powerful feudal city over which the Maeda clan would rule for three centuries.

*Gold leaf*



The vast, fertile, wooded region of Kaga *(now Ishikawa prefecture)*, which they

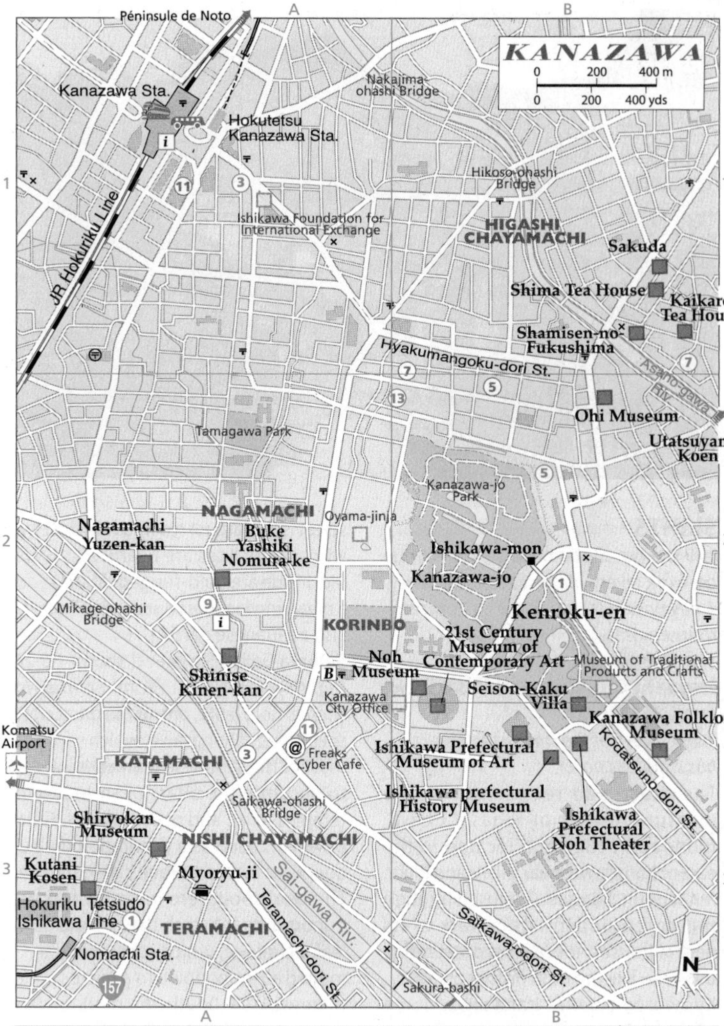


| WHERE TO STAY | |
|---|---|
| Apa Hotel Kanazawa Nomachi | 1 |
| Hotel Hinodeya | 3 |
| Kanazawa Hakuchoro Hotel | 5 |
| Minshuku Ginmatsu | 7 |
| Minshuku Yamadaya | 9 |
| Murataya Ryokan | 11 |
| Sumiyoshi-ya Ryokan | 13 |

| WHERE TO EAT | |
|---|---|
| Cafe Hakucho | 1 |
| Genzaemon | 3 |
| Kotobukiya | 5 |
| Omicho Market | 7 |
| Unkai | 11 |



controlled, made them so prosperous that they became the country's second most powerful family and, rather like the Medici in Italy, became patrons of the arts. Porcelain and pottery, silk dyeing, gold leaf, lacquerware, and the Noh theater all flourished under their patronage, and remain local specialties today.

Higashi Chayamachi District

© Kanazawa City/JNTO

## SIGHTS

From the JR station, an excellent bus network *(every 15min, ¥200 per journey, 1-day pass ¥500)* tours the city's main tourist sights.

### Higashi Chayamachi District★

ひがし茶屋街 *B1.*

*1.2mi/2km E of the station. Ashiba-cho bus stop (bus no. 6).*

The grace and refinement of the pleasure district of Higashi Chaya, founded in 1820 and located in the east of Kanazawa, near the Asano River, remains unchanged. Glimpsed through the dark wooden latticework of its geisha houses, it is a closed, secretive universe, like the Gion district of Kyoto. Known as *geigi* in Kanazawa, some 50 geisha still practice their profession in the city, entertaining clients with poetry recitals, Tea Ceremonies, elegant conversation, and song and dance accompanied by the *shamisen*. Two geisha houses on Higashi Chaya-gai can be visited:

**Shima Tea House★** – *Open 9am–6pm. ¥200.* The luxurious interior of this well-preserved former tea house on two floors has *shamisen*, combs, games, and kitchen utensils on display, as well as superb pieces of lacquered wooden furniture.

**Kaikaro Tea House★** – *Open 9am–5pm. ¥700.* On the other side of the street is the largest tea house in the city, whose pure lines are nearly 200 years old. Inside are gold-fringed tatamis and a gleaming lacquered staircase. There is also a Japanese garden.

**Sakuda** Gold & Silver Leaf Shop – *1-3-27 Higashiyama. Open 9am–6pm. No charge.* Gold leaf is one of the great craft specialties of Kanazawa, which supplies most of the Japanese market. It is used to decorate the altars of shrines and temples, fans, and other objects. Gold powder is used as a decoration on lacquerware in a technique called *maki-e*. The workshop here gives visitors an opportunity to watch the *kinpaku* gold leaf technique, which consists of hammering an ingot down to a microscopic thinness (1/10,000th of a mm). Gilded screens are displayed on the upper floor and there is a shop selling various gilded objects (lacquerware, pottery, chopsticks, lotions containing specks of gold, etc). 1hr workshop on gold-leaf gilding possible (¥500).

**Shamisen-no-Fukushima** – *Open 10am–4pm. Closed weekends & public hols. No charge.*

In this 100-year-old shop, the Fukushima family makes superb *shamisen*, the three-stringed, long-necked lutes used by the geisha. The sound box is made of ebony, sandalwood, or oak, and covered in snake- or catskin.

## USEFUL INFORMATION

**KANAZAWA**

**Kanazawa Tourist Information Center** – *To the right of the east entrance to the JR station (A1), east exit. Open 9am–7pm. ✆076-232-5555. www.kazanawa-kankoukyoukai.gr.jp.* The **Association of Voluntary Guides**, based in the Tourist Information Center *(open 10am–6pm; reservations suggested; ✆076-232-3933/5555), provides English-speaking guides for free.*

**Ishikawa Foundation for International Exchange** – *Rifare Bldg, 1-5-3 Honmachi (A1). 5min walk from the central station. Open Mon–Sat 9am–6pm. ✆076-262-5931. www.ifie.or.jp.* A library on the third floor, with foreign newspapers and free internet access *(open 9am–6pm).*

**Post Office/Withdrawals** – *Korinbo Post Office (A2). ATM open Mon–Fri 7am–11pm, Sat 9am–9pm, Sun 9am–7pm.*

**WAJIMA**

**Tourist Office** – In the bus terminal. *Open 8am–7pm. ✆0768-22-6588.* Only a little information in English.

## TRANSPORTATION

### GETTING TO AND FROM KANAZAWA

**BY PLANE** – **Komatsu Airport**, *located 18.6mi/30km SW of Kanazawa (A3 off map).* 11 flights per day from Tokyo (Haneda) *(1hr, ¥22,000).* A Limousine Bus *(1hr, ¥1,000)* connects the airport with the city center. There is also 1 flight per day from Tokyo *(Narita)*, 1 flight per day from Sapporo, 1 flight per day from Sendai, 2 flights per day from Fukuoka, and 1 flight per day from Okinawa.

**BY TRAIN** – **JR Station** *(A1)* – To and from Nagoya, 8 trains per day by the Limited Express Shirasagi *(2hr54min, ¥6,620).* By Shinkansen, 21 trains per day *(2hr30min, ¥7,800).* From Takayama, allow *2hr30min and ¥4,820.* 39 trains per day to and from Tokyo *(3hr53min, ¥12,710).* To Anamizu *(Noto-hanto)*, JR Nanao Line to Nanao, then Noto Railway *(2hr10min, ¥1,940).*

**BY BUS** – *Bus terminal outside the station (A1). Open 7.20am–8pm.* 11 buses per day to Wajima *(2hr, ¥2,200)*, 6 buses per day from Tokyo *(7hr30min, ¥7,840)*, 10 buses per day from Nagoya *(4hr, ¥4,060).*

### GETTING AROUND KANAZAWA

**BY BUS** – The easiest way for tourists to get around is to take the Kanazawa Loop Bus *(every 15min 8.30am–6pm, 1-day pass ¥500)*, which makes a circuit of the city's tourist attractions. Buses leave from the east exit, platform 1, of the JR station. Alternatively, take one of the three Flat Bus routes *(departures from platform 11, ¥100 per journey)* or see the city by night with the Light-up Bus *(Sat only, until 8.50pm).*

**BY BICYCLE** – There are several rental companies around the station, including **JR Kanazawa Station Rent-A-Cycle**, on the left when you come out of the west exit *(open 8am–8.30pm, ¥1,200 per day or ¥200 per hour).*

### GETTING TO AND FROM WAJIMA

**BY BUS** –Wajima Eki-mae bus terminal. For Sosogi, 8 buses per day: *7.15am–7.10pm (40min, ¥740).* For Kanazawa, 11 buses per day *5.55am–7.10pm (2hr, ¥2,200).*

### GETTING TO AND FROM NOTO-OGI

**BY PLANE** – **Noto Airport**, located 62mi/100km NE of Kanazawa. 2 flights per day from Tokyo (Haneda) *(1hr, ¥22,000).*

**BY TRAIN** – From Anamizu station only. For Kanazawa, Noto Railway to Nanao, then JR Nanao Line *(2hr10min, ¥1,940).*

**BY BUS** – For Anamizu, buses leave every hour *(1hr25min, ¥2,200).* From Sosogi, take the bus along the lovely coast road, via Sosogi-Kinoura *(40min, ¥800)*, Kinoura, Rokugo-zaki, the thermal baths at Yoshigaura, to Suzu *(60min, ¥890)*, and finally, Ogi.

### Ohi Museum★

大樋美術館 *Map B2.*
*2-17 Hashiba-cho. 8min walk from Higashi Chaya, Hashiba-cho bus stop (bus no. 7). Open 9am–5pm. ¥700.*
Ohi pottery *(named after a village in the suburbs of Kanazawa)* is quite similar in style to the raku pottery of Kyoto on which it is based *(see p 298)*. It was introduced into Kanazawa in 1666 by the Chozaemon family, who arrived as part of the entourage of a master of the Tea Ceremony invited by Maeda Tsunanori. The same family has continued the tradition ever since—the current master is **Ohi Chozaemon Toshiro**, the tenth generation and a highly regarded artist, whose works can be found in many Japanese and foreign museums. Shaped by hand, without a potter's wheel, Ohi ware is characterized by its black or amber glaze, obtained by slow firing, and is intended specifically for the Tea Ceremony. With its pure forms, rough surfaces, and monochrome colors, it embodies the essence of the Japanese concept of *wabi-sabi*: simple, austere beauty.

### Kanazawa Castle Park

金沢城公園 *Map B2.*
*Open Mar 1–Oct 15 7am–6pm; Oct 16–Feb 28 8am–4.30pm. No charge.*
The residence of the powerful Maeda lords for 14 generations, from 1583 to 1869, Kanazawa Castle was ravaged by fire in 1759, and again in 1881. All that remains of the original building is the monumental gateway, the **Ishikawa-mon**★, built in 1788, in the southeast of the grounds. Its fine wrought-iron work is a reminder of this historic feudal city's former greatness. Work has been going on to rebuild the castle since 1997. The first part of the reconstruction was completed in 2001: the former arsenal, the Gojukken Nagaya, flanked by two turrets, the Hishi Yagura and Tsuzuki Yagura *(open 9am–4.30pm; ¥300)*. Great care was taken to ensure only traditional methods of construction were used, with no nails or screws. Raised on a stone base, the walls are made of bamboo latticework filled in with adobe and covered in several layers of plaster.

### Kenroku-en★★★ 兼六園 *Map B2.*

*Kenrokuen-shita bus stop (bus no. 9). Open Mar 1–Oct 15 7am–6pm; Oct 16–Feb 28 8am–4.30pm. ¥300.*
Considered one of the three most beautiful gardens in Japan, alongside those of Mito and Okayama, Kenroku-en *(28.2 acres/11.4ha)* attracts more than 2 million visitors a year. Created in 1676, and enlarged and improved by successive generations of Maeda lords, it once formed the outer grounds of Kanazawa Castle. Its name, meaning "garden of six

Irises in bloom in Kenroku-en in early summer

©Kanazawa City / JNTO

21st Century Museum of Contemporary Art, Kanazawa
Housed in a round, glass-clad building that makes no distinction between front and back, Kanazawa's 21st Century Museum of Contemporary Art is, in keeping with its design concept, "open like a park to the surrounding community." The facility was designed by world-renowned architects SEJIMA Kazuyo + NISHIZAWA Ryue / SANAA.
The city where tradition meets modernity
KANAZAWA
Kenrokuen Garden
Considered one of Japan's three great gardens, Kenrokuen embodies an historical and cultural heritage that first began to coalesce during the 17th century. Visitors can enjoy the beauty of the changing seasons against a backdrop of traditional Japanese landscape garden design.
JAPAN
KANAZAWA
TOKYO
OSAKA
NAGOYA
KANAZAWA
Ishikawa
Niigata
Toyama
Komatsu-airport
Gokayama
Nagano
Gifu
Shirakawa-go
Takayama
Fukui
http://www.kanazawa-tourism.com/
Shirakawa-go (Gifu)
Idyllic Spring Scenery
Takayama (Gifu)
Traditional Streetscape
Gokayama (Toyama)
Fantastic Winter Illumination

combined elements," refers to the six attributes it is said to possess: spaciousness, seclusion, artifice, antiquity, water, and panoramas—although, to escape the crowds and fully appreciate these qualities, it is best to go early or at the end of the day. Ponds, streams, waterfalls, artificial hills, groves, rocks, paths—everything in the Kenroku-en has been carefully designed to create aesthetic perfection. In addition, unlike many other gardens in Japan, the **views** are not spoilt by ugly buildings in the background.

Like all great landscape gardens, its atmosphere and colors change with the seasons and flowering times: plum trees in the spring, cherry trees in April, azaleas in May, and irises in the summer mists (*see photo p270*).

Chrysanthemums and the purple of the maples mark the advent of the Fall, while in winter, branches of pines are supported by ropes tied to pillars to stop them from breaking beneath the weight of the snow.

**Visit** – At the edge of Kasumi Pond is the famous **Kotoji-toro**, a stone lantern supported on two long legs that resemble the bridge of a *koto* (the Japanese zither). In the southeast, beside Hisago Pond, stands the **Yugao-tei Tea House**, built by Kobori Enshu in the 17C. Look out for the oldest fountain in Japan, powered by an ingenious system based on the differing water levels of two ponds. Last but not least, you can try a *matcha* tea (*¥700*) in the Shigure-tei Tea House.

**Seison-kaku Villa**★ – *5min SE of Kenroku-en. Open Thu–Tue 9am–4.30pm. ¥700.*

This magnificent residence adjoining the garden was built in 1863 by Maeda Nariyasu for his mother. Beneath a curved roof of cypress shingles, the house is an elegant succession of tatami rooms with finely decorated sliding doors inlaid with rare Dutch colored glass.

## Ishikawa Prefectural Museums 石川県立美術館

*Map B2/3.*
*5min walk SE of Kenroku-en, near Seison-kaku Villa.*

These small museums are not exceptional but are worth a visit if you have the time.

**Kanazawa Folkloric Museum**
*Open Fri–Wed 9am–4.30pm. ¥300.*
Examples of the crafts for which Kanazawa is famous (Kutani ceramics, Kaga Yuzen dyed silk, lacquerware, gold leaf), along with the tools and techniques used to produce them. There are regular demonstrations.

**Ishikawa Prefectural History Museum** *Open 9am–4pm. ¥350.*
The collections and displays in this museum, housed in three brick buildings of a former military arsenal, date from the beginning of the 20C and recount the story of the Ishikawa region from the Jomon period to the present day.

*21st Century Museum of Contemporary Art*

**Ishikawa Prefectural Museum of Art** – *Open 9am–5pm. ¥300.* Among the finest pieces in the collection, all dating from the period of the Maeda lords, are precious scrolls, lacquerware, Kutani porcelain, and old kimonos. There are also a number of contemporary works by artists living in the Ishikawa region.

**Ishikawa Prefectural Noh Theater** *Open Tue–Sun 9am–10pm. ¥200.* This theater has continued the traditions of the Kaga Hosho school of Noh since the Edo period. Performances are given at 1pm on the first Sunday of every month except August, and the second Sunday in April and September. On other weekends you may come across a rehearsal.

## 21st Century Museum of Contemporary Art★★ 金沢２１世紀美術館

*Map B2/3.*

*Hirosaka (bus no. 10) or Korinbo (bus no. 15) bus stops. Open Tue–Sun 10am–6pm (Sat–Sun 8pm). ¥350.*

Although only opened in 2004, Kanazawa's Museum of Contemporary Art is already considered a major player in its field, showing the work of Japanese and foreign artists of international caliber. This vast, circular glass building created by architects Sejima Kazuyo and Nishizawa Ryue, places the emphasis on light and movement. Split into a series of zones *(gallery, theater, children's workshops, media laboratory, library)*, the museum is intended to be accessible to everyone and inspires a sense of playful discovery. Among the works on permanent display are installations by the American James Turrell, Frenchman Patrick Blanc, Britons Anish Kapoor, Damien Hirst, and Tony Cragg, the Italian Francesco Clemente, and Argentinian Leandro Erlich.

The museum often has artists in residence. Its collections, which include not only art but also handicrafts, design, fashion, and films, make a conscious attempt to keep abreast of new forms of expression emerging around the world.

Noh Museum



## Noh Museum 金沢能楽美術館

*Map B2.*

*Next to the previous museum, near Kanazawa City Hall. Open Tue–Sun 9am–5pm (9.30am–5pm in winter). ¥300.*

Noh theater flourished in Kanazawa under the patronage of the Maeda clan during the Edo period. The local Kaga Hosho school popularized this classical Japanese opera well beyond the samurai class for which it was traditionally reserved. Since Noh was so deeply rooted in the hearts of the city's inhabitants, it was able to survive the abolition of feudalism and the warrior clans. This small museum explains the structure of Noh performances and displays a precious collection of **kimonos** and **masks** worn by the actors.

## Teramachi District 寺町

*Map A3.*

*20min walk S of Kenroku-en. Jusangen-machi or Hirokoji bus stop (bus no. 13).*

On the opposite bank of the Sai River, the tranquil quarter of Teramachi contains no fewer than 70 temples a reminder of the 15C when the city was a Buddhist principality. To counter their influence, the temples were moved away from the castle into this area, which marked the city limits at the time.

**Myoryu-ji★** *Open 9am–4pm. ¥800. Visit by guided tour (40min) only. Reservations required. 076-*

Buke-yashiki Nomura-ke

© Kanazawa City/JNTO

*241-0888. Tour is in Japanese, but a brochure in English is provided.*
Maeda Toshitsune used this temple as a secret hiding place in the 17C. Also known as the temple of the Ninja, it is a dizzying labyrinth crammed full of ingenious traps, secret passages, and concealed rooms designed to catch possible attackers unaware. There are no fewer than 29 staircases connecting its 23 rooms and corridors. From the outside, this temple-fortress seems to have only two floors.
Once inside, it can be seen that there are in fact four, plus three intermediate levels. According to one legend, there is also a tunnel underneath the well, linking it to Kanazawa Castle.

## Nishi Chayamachi District

にし茶屋街 *Map A3.*
*5min walk W of Teramachi, on the other side of Minami-odori.*
Along with the Higashi Chaya area, this was Kanazawa's second pleasure district. Although smaller in size, it is still home to five pretty tea houses *(ochaya)* with openwork sliding doors, presided over by some 20 geisha.

**Shiryokan Museum**
*Open 9am–5pm. ¥200.*
The interior of this tea house has been reconstructed, including the room where the geisha would entertain customers to the sound of the *shamisen* (flute).

**Kutani Kosen**★ – *15min walk to the SW, following the rail line. Open 9am–4.30pm. No charge.*
A pottery kiln with displays of traditional Kutani porcelain, characterized by its bright colors and floral patterns. Visitors can also try their hand at painting on pottery *(from ¥1,050).*

*Back in the city center, walk through the Katamachi district, the focus for the city's shopping and nightlife, then, after the Korinbo department store, turn W toward Nagamachi.*

## Nagamachi District 長町

*Map A2.*
*5min walk from Korinbo bus stop (bus no. 15).*
The former samurai quarter of Nagamachi, with its beautiful cobbled alleys that wind between low walls of ocher cob, old canals, and sumptuous residences, has been preserved. It plunges the visitor into the atmosphere of former feudal times.

**Buke-yashiki Nomura-ke**★★ – *1-3-32 Nagamachi. Open Apr–Sept 8.30am–5.30pm; Oct–Mar 8.30am–4.30pm. ¥500.*
This luxurious samurai residence, built entirely of dark brown wood, belonged to Nomura Denbei Nobusada, one of Maeda Toshiie's closest associates in the 16C. Twelve generations of the Nomura family lived here until the Meiji era, enriching

the house with a delightful ornamental garden, including a miniature waterfall. The *Jodan no ma*, the art rooma later additionhas magnificent latticework and carved caissons of mahogany, ebony, and cypresswood.

**Shinise Kinen-kan★** – *Open 9.30am–5pm. ¥100.*

Originally in the south of the city, this former Chinese herbalist's shop, founded in 1779, was moved to the entrance of the Nagamachi district and turned into a museum. The shop with its pharmacy cabinets is on the ground floor, on the side facing the street (the rear part comprises private quarters and a garden).

**Nagamachi Yuzen-kan** – *In a modern building near Chuo-dori in the western part of the district. Open 9am–noon, 1–5pm. ¥350.*

This workshop showcases the techniques for making traditional Kaga Yuzen dyed silk. Visitors can try wearing a kimono *(¥1,000)* or painting on silk *(¥4,000)*.

## Omicho Market★

近江町市場 *Map B1*

*10min walk from the station. Musashigatsuji bus stop (bus no. 18). Open Mon–Sat 8am–6pm.*

There are hundreds of stands selling fruits and vegetables, fish and other foodstuffs in this covered market that is nearly 300 years old. A feast for the senses, the maze-like market also houses a number of small, inexpensive eating houses serving seafood and sushi (*see Address Book p 277*).

EXCURSION

## NOTO PENINSULA★

能登半島

North of Kanazawa, the Noto Peninsula is regarded by many Japanese as a place where the frenetic pace of modern life has still not taken hold. One of its fishing villages was the setting for director Imamura Shohei's film *Warm Water Under a Red Bridge*, in which a disillusioned Tokyo dweller, having divorced his wife and lost his job, rediscovers enjoyment of life. In fact, the eastern coast is highly urbanized, and only the western part of the peninsula has remained rural and traditional, with its wild natural beauty and rugged coastline.

### Wajima★ 輪島

*81mi/130km NE of Kanazawa.*

A small fishing port *(population 31,000)* on the northwest coast of the peninsula, Wajima is one of the area's principal attractions. Its main claim to fame is the highly regarded lacquerware *(Wajima-nuri)* and its lively **market★**, in full swing every morning *(open 8am–noon; closed 10th & 25th of the month)*. Both tourists and villagers flock to the 100-odd stands, which sell not only seafood and dried fish, but also a vast array of lacquerware. The female fish vendors hail customers in loud, cheeky voices. Continuing north along the main street *(Asaichi-dori)*, you will reach the **harbor**, where fishermen calmly mend their nets oblivious to the big black crows circling overhead.

**Wajima Shikki Kaikan★** – *15min walk SW of the market, next to Shin-bashi bridge, which crosses the Kawarada River. Open 8.30am–5pm. ¥200.*

Over 5,000 lacquerware objects made by the 170 members of the Wajima Association of Lacquerers are on display here. There are also shops selling lacquerware. *Prices range from ¥8,000 to ¥50,000 for a soup bowl.*

*Wajima lacquerware*

© JNTO

Depending on the process used, it may take up to 120 applications over six months to produce a bowl. The museum on the first floor exhibits superb lacquerware items, some more than 400 years old. You may sometimes be able to watch craftsmen at work, who will explain their techniques.

**Kiriko Kaikan**★★ – *20min walk E of the station or 5min by bus, Tsukada stop. Open 8am–5pm. ¥600.*
This exhibition hall has a collection of some of the finest *kiriko*—giant, colored paper lanterns—that are paraded during Wajima's festivals to attract the attention of the gods. Some are almost 49ft/15m high. A video of the festivals is also shown.

**Soji-ji**★ – *Monzen, 15.5mi/25km SW of Wajima on Route 249 (45min by bus). Open 9am–5pm. ¥400.*
Founded in 1321, this magnificent temple was one of the main bases of the Soto school of Zen Buddhism until it was destroyed by fire in 1898. Subsequently restored, it still has some superb buildings containing interesting Buddhist statues. The temple has a room where visitors can take part in a session of zazen meditation *(¥700; reservations required; 07680-42-0005).*

## Sosogi★ 曽々木

*10.6mi/17km E of Wajima (40min by bus).*

The magnificent **coast road**★ runs past terraced paddy fields of Senmaida and the jagged inlets of the coastline battered by the fierce waves of the Sea of Japan. The small village of Sosogi has two interesting houses with thatched roofs that once belonged to the Tokikuni family, descended from Taira Tokitada, one of the survivors of the Taira clan, who took refuge here. The **Shimo Tokikuni-ke,** or "low house" *(10min walk from the bus stop; open Apr–Nov 8.30am–5pm, Dec–Mar 8.30am–4pm; ¥600),* was built in 1590, and has a fine garden.
The nearby **Kami Tokikuni-ke,** or "high house" *(open as above; ¥500)* was built at the beginning of the 19C for another branch of the same family.

### Cape Rokugo-zaki

*15.5mi/25km to the NE.*

Once beyond Sosogi, the road leads past a succession of undulating hills and sheer cliffs until it reaches Roguko-zaki Cape, the farthest point on the peninsula.
There are several hiking trails near the lighthouse, which are particularly pleasant in summer.

## Noto-Ogi★ 能登小木

*15.5mi/25km S of Sosogi.*

Protected by a deep fjord, Noto-Ogi is mainly worth a visit for its magnificent **bay**, filled with deep-sea fishing boats, with rows of lamps suspended above their decks. Squid fishing by lamplight is in fact quite common in Japan—not surprising when you consider that the Japanese consume more squid than any other nation in the world.

# ADDRESSES

## STAY

### KANAZAWA

**Hotel Hinodeya** ホテルひので屋
*2-17-25 Honmachi (A1). 076-231-5224. www.hinodeya.info. 20 rooms. ¥500.* Well maintained, comfortable and practical *business hotel,* a few minutes from the JR station (east exit).

**Minshuku Ginmatsu** 民宿銀松
*1-17-18 Higashiyama. Hashibacho bus stop (B1). 5 rooms. ¥1,000. Restaurant.* This simple, clean *minshuku* is located in the attractive Higashiyama district.

**Minshuku Yamadaya** 民宿山田屋
*2-3-28 Nagamachi (A2). 076-261-0065. 5 rooms.* Simple rooms in a lovely old house near the information office in the historic quarter of Nagamachi.

**Murataya Ryokan** 村田屋旅館
*1-5-2 Katamachi (A3). 076-263-0455. www.murataya-ryokan.com. Closed Jan 30–Mar 1. 11 rooms. Western: ¥500; Japanese: ¥800 (reservations required).* This friendly ryokan *(the lady of the house speaks English and will shower you with information)* is ideally situated for an evening out.

**APA Hotel Kanazawa-Nomachi** アパホテル金沢野町 *2-4-22 Nomachi (A3). 076-280-8111. www.apahotel.com/hotel/hokuriku/09_kanazawa-nomachi. 100 rooms.* This hotel in the Nishi Chaya district *(2min walk from Nomachi* *station)* provides comfortable rooms at reasonable prices. One of the least expensive in the APA chain, which has five other hotels in the city.

**Sumiyoshi-ya Ryokan** 旅館すみよし屋 *54 Jukken-machi (B2). 076-221-0157. www.sumiyoshi-ya.com. . 12 rooms.* A lovely ryokan in a spectacular building.

**Kanazawa Hakuchoro Hotel** 金沢白鳥路ホテル *6-3 Marunouchi (B2). 076-222-1212. www.hakuchoro.com. 85 rooms ¥1,500.* A beautiful hotel dating from the beginning of the 20C, close to **Kenroku-en**, with a magnificent *onsen* and a lovely Japanese garden.

## WAJIMA

**Wajima Station Hotel** 輪島ステーションホテル *19-1-50 Kawai-machi, just on the left as you come out of the station. 0768-22-0177. 34 rooms. ¥780.* Friendly *business hotel*.

**Hotel Koushuen** ホテル高州園 *2-31-6 Tsukada-machi. 0120-23-2432. www.koushuen.co.jp. 132 rooms. Lodging with half-board.* This huge hotel complex overlooking the coast offers a vast range of services in the basement. Bar and karaoke available after nightfall. Friendly service. Japanese and Western rooms.

## SOSOGI

**Minshuku Yokoiwa-ya** 温泉民宿・横岩屋 *Ku-2, Sosogi, machi-no-machi. 0768-32-0603. www.wajima.gr.jp/yokoiwaya/. 7 rooms – breakfast and dinner included.* Ideally located by the sea. *O-furo.*

## NOTO-OGI

**Noto-Isaribi Youth Hostel** 能登漁火ユースホステル *Yo 51-6, Ogi, Noto-cyo Housu-gun. 8min walk from the Ogi-kou bus stop. 0768-74-0150. www2.plala.or.jp/isaribi0150. . 5 dormitories – ¥8,400. ¥630, dinner ¥1,000.* A lovely hostel owned by a friendly fisherman.

**Hyakuraku-so** 百楽荘 *Hyakura Kusou. 30min walk from the disused station of Tsukumo-wan-Ogi to the top of the hill overlooking the bay. 0768-74-1115. www.100raku.com. 25 rooms.* This unusual ryokan overlooks the superb Tsukumo Bay. A tunnel takes you 98.4ft/30m down to sea level, where there is a wonderful *onsen*. You can also go fishing and diving.

# EAT

## KANAZAWA

Fish and seafood reign supreme in Kanazawa. The city makes something of a specialty of *kaiten-zushi*, those restaurants where plates of sushi revolve on a conveyor belt.

**Cafe Hakucho** 白鳥 *2-48 Kenroku-machi (B2). 076-261-6314. Open Thu–Tue 9am–6pm. .* A pleasant little restaurant located a few minutes from the Katsura-zaka exit of **Kenroku-en**. Simple dishes: fish, grilled oysters, etc.

**Omicho Market** 近江町市場 *Open Mon–Sat 8am–6pm. Two kaiten-zushi,* **Okura** *(10.30am–8pm) and* **Omicho Ichiba-Zushi** *(10.30–6.30pm, Fri, Sat–9pm, Sun 11am–4pm).* The *kaiten-zushi* are supplied by some 170 stands and eateries selling vegetables, fish, and seafood (cod, b ream, shrimp, crab). Freshness is guaranteed. The choice is yours!

**Unkai** 雲海 *ANA Crown Plaza Hotel Kanazawa, 16-3 Showamachi (A1). 076-224-6111. Open 11.30am–2.30pm, 5–9.30pm.* Next to a Japanese garden on the fifth floor of the ANA Hotel, this restaurant offers refined cuisine in an elegant setting.

**Genzaemon** 源左ェ門 *5-3 Kigura-machi (A3). 076-232-7110. Open Mon–Sat 5pm–midnight.* A 50-year-old restaurant well known for the freshness of its fish. The friendly, twinkly-eyed owner, Hayashi, is always happy to share a drink.

**Shamojiya** しゃもじ屋 *3, Jukken-machi (B2). 076-264-4848. Open Mon–Sat 11.30am–2pm, 5–10pm.*

This restaurant is best known for its *sashimis*—not surprising, given how close it is to the market.

**Kotobukiya** 壽屋 *2-4-13 Owari-cho. Musashigatsuji bus stop (B2). 076-231-6245. Open 11.30am–2pm, 6–7.30 pm.* For 150 years and four generations, this venerable institution has been serving *shojin ryori*, highly refined vegetarian dishes in the purest Buddhist tradition. The restaurant is often booked for funerals.

## NOTO-OGI

**Asaichi-shokuza Kaizen** 朝市食座・海膳 *At the end of Asaichi-dori, at the corner of the market street. t0768-23-1842. Open 11am–2pm. Closed 10th & 25th of the month. .* On the first floor of a shop selling local produce. Fish, seafood: everything is fresh.

# Sado Island★ 佐渡島

**Sado is popular among the Japanese as a place where both nature and traditions have been preserved. During the Middle Ages, it was the island to which aristocrats and samurai defeated in power struggles would be sent into exile. But Sado turned a curse into an asset. Given those sent into exile were often highly cultured, they stimulated the island's artistic life, which has flourished ever since. Among the most notable were Emperor Juntoku (1197–1242), the monk Nichiren (1222–82), and Zeami (1363–1443), one of the creators of Noh, a form of theater still widely practiced here, with no fewer than 34 stages scattered throughout the island. Sado is also famous for its *Bunya Ningyo* puppets, and for the Kodo drummers, who have superstar status in Japan. In the 17C, the island experienced a gold rush, and artists and noblemen were replaced by thousands of convicts sent to work in the mines, a backbreaking activity that went on for more than three centuries. Today, Sado mainly attracts city dwellers in search of a little of the old Japan, as well as hikers who like to camp in summer in its flower-strewn fields or near the rocky capes used as a refuge by migrating birds.**

- **Population:** 62,733 – Niigata Prefecture.
- **Michelin Map:** Regional Map p230.
- **Location:** 34mi/55km off Niigata, in the Sea of Japan, Sado Island covers an area of 331sq mi/857sq km, which makes it the sixth largest island in the country. It consists of two mountain ranges with a broad rice-growing plain in the middle, hence the characteristic "S" shape. The island's capital, Ryotsu, is connected to Niigata by ferry and hydrofoil. The other notable town is Mano, on the west coast. Ogi, in the south of the island, is where ferries from Naoetsu land. A bus network serves the main points on the island, but runs a reduced service from November to March.
- **Kids:** A *Bunya Ningyo* puppet show.
- **Timing:** Allow two days to tour the island. Renting a car at Ryotsu harbor will make getting about a lot easier.
- **Don't miss:** The Earth Celebration, in August; the gold mine at Sado Kinzan.

## SIGHTS

### RYOTSU★ 両津

The main harbor town of Sado, Ryotsu is, logistically, the most convenient point of entry to the island, but it is not the most attractive place.

### Sado No-gaku-no-sato Museum 佐渡能楽の里

*Minamisen Line, bus no. 2 toward Sawata, Nogaku-no-sato stop (10min).* *Open 8.30am–5pm. ¥800.*

This small museum displays interesting masks and costumes from the Noh theater. More unusual is the show by robotized puppets mechanically executing the movements of a Noh performance.

### Futatsu-game and Ono-game★★ 二つ亀・大野亀

*From Ryotsu, Uchikaifu Line bus to Washizaki (about 1hr).*

These two superb rocky sites, linked by a footpath, are in the northeast tip of the island. The name of the first means "two turtles," because of its natural shape. There is also a popular **beach** here. Inevitably, given the size of the

## USEFUL INFORMATION

### TOURIST OFFICES

**Ryotsu** – *On the ground floor of the Kisen Ferry Terminal. Open Jul–Aug 7am–6pm; Sept–Jun 7.30am–5.30pm. ☏0259-23-3300. www.mijintl.com.*

**Ogi** – *On the ground floor of the Marine Plaza Bldg. Open 9am–5pm. ☏0259-86-3200.*

## TRANSPORTATION

### RYOTSU

**BY TRAIN** – From **Tokyo to Niigata**, Shinkansen Toki *(1hr45min, ¥10,270)*. Limited Express Hokuetsu or Hakutaka from Kanazawa to Naoetsu *(2hr, ¥5,550)*, JR Shinetsu Line from Nagano to Naoetsu *(1hr33min, ¥1,280)*. For Sendai (*see p269*), Shinkansen Max Toki from Niigata to Omiya *(Saitama)*, then Shinkansen Yamabiko *(3hr20min, ¥18,970)*.

**BY BOAT** – From **Niigita**, boats leave every hour for Ryotsu *(2hr30min by ferry, ¥2,320; 1hr by jetfoil, ¥6,220)*. From Naoetsu, about 1 or 2 boats per day for Ogi: *7am–4.20pm (2hr40min, ¥2,530)*.

### MANO

**BY BUS** – The sites E of Mano are all along the route of the Minamisen bus line: *www.mijintl.com.*

**Bicycle Rental** – At the Tourist Office. *Open May–Oct 8.30am–5pm. Closed the rest of the year. ¥1,100 per day. ☏0259-55-3589.*

### OGI

**Bus Terminal** – Buses leave from just behind the post office, not far from the Tourist Office.

### GETTING AROUND THE ISLAND

**BY BUS** – The island has no rail network, but is served by 15 bus lines, each with a different color: *www.mijintl.com.* **Unlimited pass** *¥2,000 for 2 days.*

**BY TAXI** – **Okesa Taxi**, at the ferry terminal in Ryotsu. Ask for Akinori Tari, who speaks English and looks after his customers very well *(¥4,500, ☏090-3403-5626)*.

**BY CAR** – Several rental companies at Ryotsu ferry terminal *(all about ¥7,000/day, plus ¥20/km and cost of gas)*.

second *(548ft/167m)*, the locals believe that, like all unusual natural sites, it houses a deity. On the path between the two sites, you pass **Sai no kawara**, a natural cave containing hundreds of *jizo* statuettes, symbolizing the children who make their last stop here on their way to heaven.

*Ono-game rocks*

© JNTO

### The drums of Sado

Kodo is a world-famous group of percussionists based near the small village of Ogi. Every year, around August 18, the group organizes the Earth Celebration at Ogi, a kind of Japanese Woodstock vibrating for three days to the sound of the *taiko*, large traditional drums once used for religious ceremonies and village festivals. Sado has, in fact, preserved a rich musical heritage. There are a number of festivals throughout the year involving songs and folk dances, such as the *okesa* and *onidaiko*, accompanied by *ondeko* drums ("demon drums"), intended to chase away evil spirits and ensure a plentiful harvest.

## MANO★ 真野

*16mi/26km W of Ryotsu on Route 350 (45min by Minamisen Line bus).*

The town of Mano, near the bay of the same name, the most sheltered on the island, is surrounded by sites of historical and religious interest, and also has a good **beach** .

### Konpon-ji★ 根本寺

*In front of the bus stop. Open 8am–5pm. ¥300.*

This temple is one of the 44 principal centers of the Buddhist sect founded by the monk Nichiren. Its fine buildings, with their impressive thatched roofs, are arranged around a pleasant garden.

### Myosen-ji 妙宣寺

*5min walk W of the Konpon-ji. Open 9am–4pm. No charge.*

Two generations of carpenters are said to have worked on this five-story pagoda *(78.7ft/24m in height)* before its completion in 1825. The first disciple of the Buddhist monk Nichiren, Nittoku Abutsubo, is believed to have founded the shrine in 1221.

### Kokubun-ji 国分寺

*2.5mi/4km walk from Myosen-ji along the footpath.*

The oldest temple on Sado. The present building dates from 1679, but excavations have revealed foundations laid in 741 by Emperor Shomu.

### Sado Rekishi-Densetsukan Museum 佐渡歴史伝説館

*1.9mi/3km walk from Kokubun-ji, on the same path. Open 8am–5.30pm. ¥700.*

Similar to the one in Ryhotsu, this museum also uses robots, this time to illustrate the region's history, but is distinguished by the fact that they are modeled on characters drawn from the island's own past.

### Sado Kinzan★ 佐渡金山

*1305 Shimo-Aikawa. From Mano, Ogi Line bus to Sawata, then Nanaura-Kaigan Line to Aikawa. From there, another 43.7yd/40m walk to the gold mine. In summer, buses go directly to the site. Open Apr–Oct 8am–5pm; Nov–Mar 8.30am–5pm. ¥800.*

This gold mine dates back to 1601 and remained in use until 1989. During its 380-odd years as a working mine, 80 tons of gold have been extracted from its 248.5mi/400km of galleries. More than half went to stoke the public finances of the Tokugawa Shogunate. The mine's educational **museum** uses robots to explain the various extraction processes. The system for pumping spring water to supply the upper galleries is particularly ingenious.

## OGI★ 小木

*10.6mi/17km SW of Mano (50min by Ogi Line bus).*

The gateway to the southwestern part of the island, with its maritime links to Naoetsu, Ogi *(population 3,000)* was the port through which gold products were exported to Edo between the 17C and the 19C. A rather sleepy place today, the town comes to life every year for the great **Earth Celebration** *(Aug 18–20, www.kodo.or.jp)*, featuring the Kodo *taiko* drums. Another big draw for tourists are the **Tarai-bune**, large wooden tubs used by the village women as boats to collect seaweed and abalones. *For the modest sum of ¥450, wearing their traditional costume, the women will take you out in their boats for a trip around the harbor.*

### Sadokoku Ogi Folk Museum★ 佐渡国小木民俗博物館

*To the W of Ogi on Route 45. Shukunegi Line bus (11min). Open 8.30am–5pm. Closed Dec–Feb Sat–Sun. ¥500.*
This museum displays various relics from the island's past, including a fine reconstruction of a ship from the Edo period. A former school from the 1920s adjoining the museum houses thousands of everyday objects used by the islanders.

### Shukunegi 宿根木

*0.9mi/1.5km from the previous museum.*
In a village known for its shipyards, it is not surprising to find in its narrow streets some fine 100-year-old houses built of planks taken from disused boats. One of them, the **Seikuro house**, is open to the public *(open 9am–4pm, and 8.30am–5pm in Jul–Aug; ¥400)*. Not far from it, on a street corner, is a triangular house shaped like a boat.

## ADDRESSES

### STAY

**RYOTSU**

**Green Village Youth Hostel** グリーンヴィレッジ・ユースホステル*750-4 Niibo Uriuya. Uryuya bus stop, going S from Ryotsu. 0259-22-2719. www.e-sadonet.tv. 6 roomsfrom ¥3,200 in dormitory and ¥4,100 in room.* Lovely youth hostel with Japanese rooms.

**Sado Seaside Hotel** 佐渡シーサイドホテル*80 Sumiyoshi. 20min walk from the harbor. 0259-27-7211. www.sadovira.on. arena.ne.jp. 13 rooms. Dinner ¥1,575.* A useful hotel situated between the spa and the beach. Japanese rooms and *o-furo. Free internet access. English spoken.*

**Kunimi-so Minshuku** 民宿国見荘 *750-4 Niibo Uryuya. Uryuya bus stop, going S from Ryotsu. 0259-22-2316. 11 rooms.* This remarkable, traditional *minshuku* is more than 400 years old. Its owner, Honda Yohachiro, who has turned part of his house into a theater, will be glad to give you a short demonstration of his *Bunya Ningyo* puppets. The first puppets, which appeared in the 16C, are believed to have derived from balls of cloth that the monks fixed to a handle and struck on the floor to emphasize the sacred verses of Buddhism.

**MANO**

**Itoya** 伊藤屋
*278 Mano-Shinmachi, in the heart of Mano, on the main road. 0259-55-2019. www.itoyaryokan.com. 16 rooms. Restaurant open 11am–10pm (breakfast and dinner included).* This gorgeous ryokan, just 218.7yd/200m, from the beach offers good-quality service and facilities.

**OGI**

**Ogi Sakuma-so Youth Hostel** 小木佐久間荘ユースホステル
*Carry along the Shukunegi road, until you reach the Shell service station, then take the road on the right (30min walk, about ¥1,000 by taxi). 0259-86-2565. Closed Oct–May. 5 rooms¥7,200. ¥630. Restaurant.* A Japanese house adapted to American style. *O-furo.*

**Kamome-so** かもめ荘
*11-7 Ogi. 5min walk from the harbor. 0259-86-2064. 12 rooms.* The *onsen* at this well-maintained, modern ryokan are superb and also open to non-residents *(open 10am–9pm; ¥350). O-furo.*

**Hana-no-Ki** 花の木
*78-1 Shukunegi. 7min by car from the harbor. 0259-86-2331. 5 rooms.* Restaurant. This exquisite ryokan is a sensual experience, a dream of stone and wood, and traditional Japanese screens. Dinners are sumptuous *(between ¥3,500 and ¥5,000)*: specialties include *zuwai-gani* (crab). Pottery classes available. *You can arrange to be picked up from the jetty.*

### EAT

**RYOTSU**

**Tenkuni** 天國
*206 Ryotsu-Minato. 0259-23-2714. Open 11.30am–10pm.* Simple, copious Japanese food. One of the most popular restaurants in Ryotsu.

**MANO**

**Toki** 登貴
*743-2 Mano-Shinmachi. t0259-55-2147. Open Mon–Sat 11.30am–9.30pm—by reservation.* This friendly *izakaya* serves all kinds of fish and seafood, depending on the catch of the day.

# KYOTO AND KANSAI

**Kansai is one of the most popular of Japan's regions, and for several reasons, not least its exceptional geographical location. Covering 12,740sq mi/33,000sq km *(11 percent of Japan)*, it lies at the center of the Japanese archipelago open to three bodies of water: the Sea of Japan to the north, the Pacific Ocean to the south, and the Inland Sea facing the island of Shikoku; despite the region's mountainous relief, these three seas are interconnected by convenient land "corridors" made up of plains *(Osaka, Wakayama)* and basins *(Kyoto, Nara, Shiga)*. Kansai is also the cradle of Japanese civilization.**

## Highlights

1. 1,001 statues of Kannon at Kyoto's **Sanjusangen-do**, (p295)
2. Peaceful Moss Garden of **Saiho-ji**, (p315)
3. The collection, setting, and structure of the **Miho Museum**, (p320)
4. Wandering **Nara**'s parkland, (p329)
5. The shrines of **Kumano Kodo**, (pp346-349)

## Japan: past, present, and future

In the 8C, first Nara and then Kyoto were adopted as the Imperial capital, Kyoto remaining so for a thousand years. Their golden age is well represented in their cultural heritage, both cities having mercifully been spared serious damage from earthquakes. Containing as it does the cities of Kobe, Kyoto, and Osaka, Kansai is also the country's second most important economic region.

Home to one-fifth of the Japanese population and well-positioned geographically, the region has great potential in terms of its commercial and port facilities (though Kansai International Airport was not opened until 1994) and is now a major IT, manufacturing, and scientific center: Kansai Science City, built on the slopes of the Keihanna Hills and straddling the prefectures of Kyoto, Osaka, and Nara, is destined to play a vital role in the 21C. Thus the region is not only a big draw for tourists, but also attracts increasing numbers of Japanese to service its dynamic economy.

- **Population:** 24 million.
- **Michelin Map:** Regional Map p283 — Principal Sights Map B3.
- **Location:** Kansai *(or Kinki)* is the "province of the west"; Kanto is the "province of the east," as the regions west and east of the famous Tokaido road connecting Kyoto and Tokyo in the Edo period. Kansai is in southern Honshu, covering 12,740sq mi/33,000sq km divided into five *ken* (prefectures): Mie, Shiga, Hyogo, Nara, and Wakayama, and two *fu* (urban prefectures): Kyoto and Osaka.
- **Kids:** Boat trip on the Hozu River at Arashiyama; Shirahama beach; the Nachi waterfall at Kumano with overnight stay in a *shukubo* (temple lodging); the International Manga Museum in Kyoto; the Philosopher's Path.
- **Timing:** Given 8 days, spend 3 in Kyoto, 1 in Nara, 1 in Ise, 1 day on Mount Koya, 1 night at Osaka to sample nightlife, and the last day in Kobe for Himeji Castle *(itinerary of about 167.8mi/270km, starting from Kyoto; can be combined in part with JR Kansai Pass)*.
- **Don't miss:** Kyoto, Himeji Castle, Nara, Ise, Mount Koya, and Kumano Sanzan shrines.

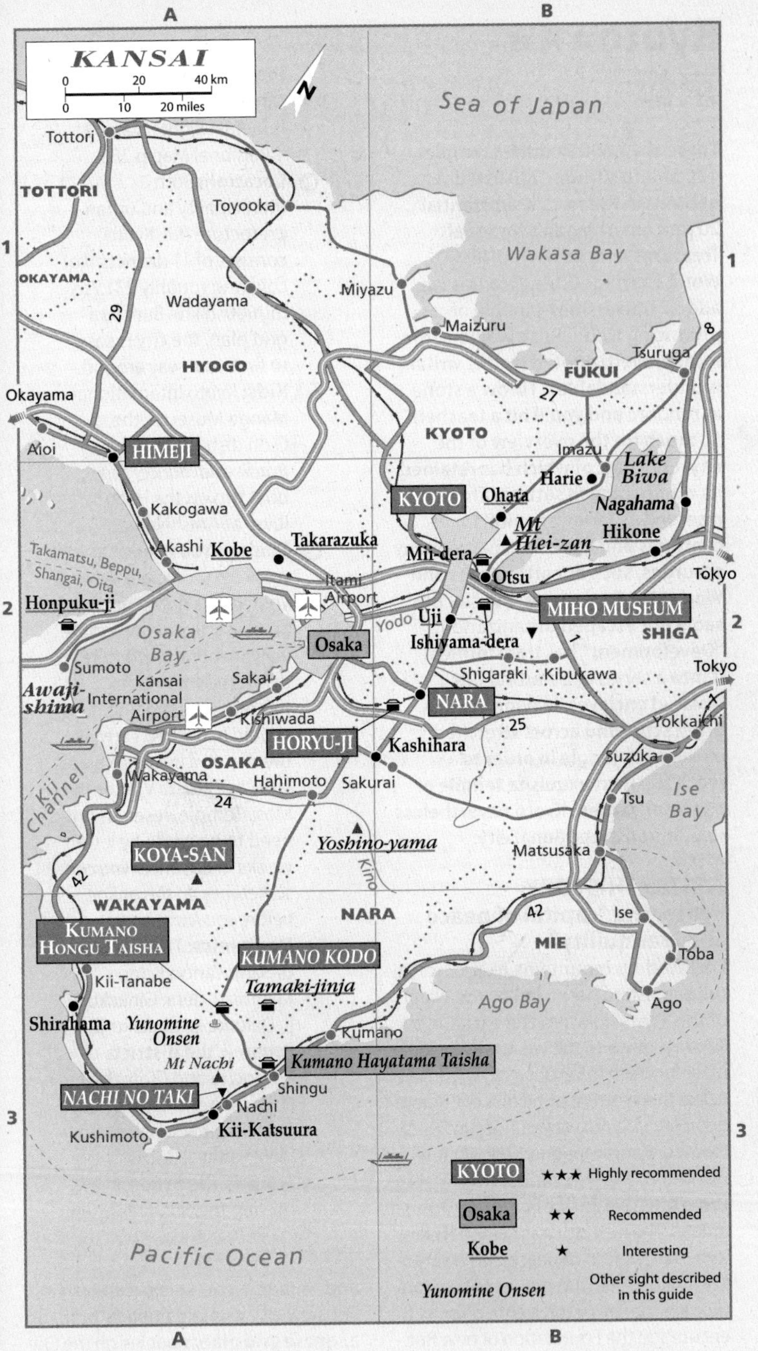
KANSAI
0 20 40 km
0 10 20 miles
N
Sea of Japan
Wakasa Bay
Tottori
TOTTORI
Toyooka
OKAYAMA
Wadayama
Miyazu
Maizuru
29
HYOGO
FUKUI
Tsuruga
8
27
Okayama
Aioi
HIMEJI
KYOTO
Imazu
Harie
Lake Biwa
KYOTO
Ohara
Nagahama
Kakogawa
Mt Hiei-zan
Hikone
Akashi
Kobe
Takarazuka
Mii-dera
Otsu
Tokyo
Takamatsu, Beppu, Shangai, Oita
Itami Airport
MIHO MUSEUM
Honpuku-ji
Yodo
Uji
SHIGA
Osaka Bay
Osaka
Ishiyama-dera
Sumoto
Shigaraki
Kibukawa
Tokyo
Awaji-shima
Kansai International Airport
Sakai
NARA
Kishiwada
25
Yokkaichi
HORYU-JI
Kashihara
Suzuka
Kii Channel
Wakayama
OSAKA
Hahimoto
Sakurai
Tsu
Ise Bay
24
Yoshino-yama
KOYA-SAN
Kino
Matsusaka
42
WAKAYAMA
NARA
42
Ise
KUMANO HONGU TAISHA
MIE
KUMANO KODO
Toba
Kii-Tanabe
Tamaki-jinja
Ago Bay
Ago
Shirahama
Yunomine Onsen
Kumano
Mt Nachi
Kumano Hayatama Taisha
Shingu
NACHI NO TAKI
Nachi
Kii-Katsuura
Kushimoto
KYOTO ★★★ Highly recommended
Osaka ★★ Recommended
Kobe ★ Interesting
Yunomine Onsen Other sight described in this guide
Pacific Ocean
A
B
1
2
3

# Kyoto★★★
# 京都

**There are 1,600 Buddhist temples, 400 Shinto shrines, 200 listed gardens in Kyoto … a substantial 20 percent of Japan's National Treasures, and 20 or so UNESCO World Heritage Sites. If to this we add 37 universities capable of producing Nobel Prize winners, the local proverb quoted by this writer is understandable: "Throw a stone at random and you'll hit a teacher!" So much for the overview of the city, only part of which has retained its original green setting. Though it served as Japan's capital for 11 centuries and has been spared many scourges, such as earthquakes and World War II bombing, the city has sadly not escaped urbanization. "Development" has transformed it into a series of beautiful but isolated enclaves, leaving visitors often scurrying across stretches of concrete jungle in order to reach the next exquisite temple or peaceful garden. Kyoto nevertheless remains an exceptional city.**

- **Population:** 1,466,957.
- **Michelin Map:** Principal Sights Map B3 – Regional Map p 283.
- **Location:** Both municipality and urban prefecture *(fu)*, Kyoto consists of 11 districts *(ku)* covering roughly 231.7sq mi/600sq km. Built to a grid plan, the city is easy to find your way around.
- **Kids:** Kyoto International Manga Museum; the Gion district; an *odori (traditional dance) show*; boat trip on the Hozu River at Arashiyama.
- **Timing:** You need at least a week to appreciate Kyoto, if your visit is not to become an obstacle race. Alternate walks around the different districts with visits to temples. The more famous should be visited early in the day and in some cases, such as Katsura Villa or the Moss Temple, reservations need to be made by letter weeks in advance *(you can sometimes do this online before you leave home)*.
- **Don't miss:** The **temples** of Sanjusangen-do, Kiyomizu-dera, Ginkaku-ji, Daitoku-ji, Kinkaku-ji, Ryoan-ji; the **districts** of Pontocho and Gion; the Philosopher's Path. On the outskirts: Katsura Imperial Villa, Saiho-ji (Moss Temple), the Byodo-in at Uji, and the Miho Museum.

## A BIT OF HISTORY

### Kyoto, the "capital of peace and tranquility"

Enclosed by mountains to the north, the Yamashiro basin, fed by the waters of the Kamo-gawa to the east and the Katsura-gawa to the west, was an ideal place in which to lay out a city according to the then current principles of Chinese geomancy. Kyoto was founded in 794 by Emperor Kanmu (reigned 781–806), who wanted to free his capital (Nara) from the excessive influence of Buddhist monks. The new city was named **Heian-kyo**, the "capital of peace and tranquility." To counter the power of the Nara monks, the Emperor went so far as to encourage the Foundation of new Buddhist sects, with doctrines introduced by two monks who have since become legendary: Saicho (767–822) and Kukai (774–835), founders of the Tendai-shu and Shingon-shu sects respectively. The new city was laid out *(like Nara)* on a **square grid plan** modeled on the Chinese Tang dynasty capital of Chang'an *(now Xian)*.

Once the Imperial Palace had been erected facing the inauspicious north,

Ho-do, Byodo-in, Uji



temples and shrines were built to protect the different entrances to the city: **To-ji** and **Sai-ji** to the south, **Kamigamo-jinja** in the northwest, and **Enryaku-ji** (founded by Saicho on Mount Hiei in 788) to the northeast.

## An aristocratic crossroads of art and religion

The new Japanese capital enjoyed its heyday during the Heian period (794–1185), and began to develop its own national style after the fall of the Tang dynasty (907). Heian-kyo then became a great aristocratic crossroads of the arts and religion under the aegis of the **Fujiwara** family. By introducing a regency system, with the role of regent being passed from father to son, the Fujiwara were able to retain power until the end of the 12C (*see box, below*). This continuity of power fostered Kyoto's cultural development, as can be seen from the Byodo-in erected in the south of the city. As a result, the Chinese style of painting was superseded by the Yamato style, better suited to the movable features of Japanese buildings (sliding panels, screens, etc.). As the cult of Amida gained ground, a suitable way of representing the Buddha had to be found, one worthy of "this Buddha of infinite light," and so the technique of *kirikane* (gold leaf decoration) came to dominate sacred iconography. The Fujiwara family prospered but toward the end of the 12C, they could not prevent the growing influence of the Taira clan over Emperor Go-Shirakawa (1127–92). There was increasing rivalry in the cor-

### Sessho and sekkan – the Fujiwara regents

The Heian era (794–1185), also known as the Fujiwara period, reflects the dominance of the Fujiwara family, which became powerful through its influence, alliances, and marriages with members of the Imperial Family, a process that culminated in the creation of the new role of regent. **Fujiwara no Yoshifusa** (804–72) became *sessho*, "regent for an Emperor while still a minor," to Seiwa (850–80), who was just eight years old when he became Emperor in 858. **Fujiwara no Yoshifusa**'s son, **Fujiwara no Mototsune** (836–91), strengthened the family's power, and in 884 introducing the position of *kanpaku*, or regent for Emperors who had already attained their majority, including Yozei, Koko, and Uda. This new hereditary office, which gave the Fujiwaras full powers, was referred to as *sekkan*, a contraction of *sessho* and *kanpaku*.

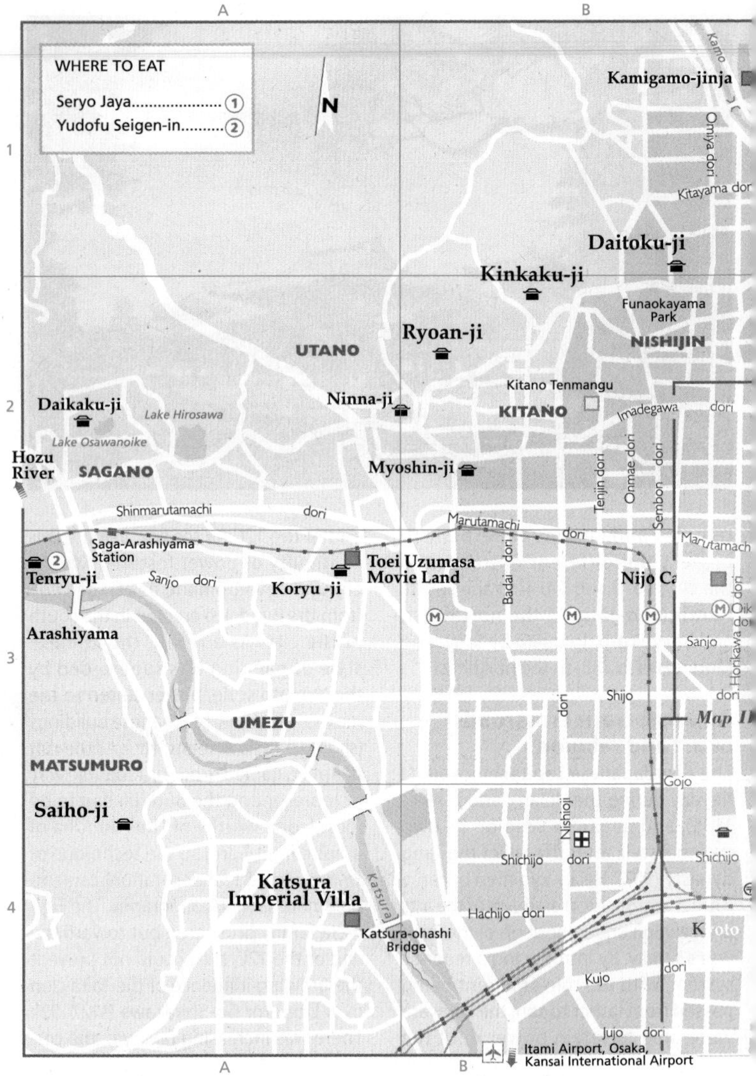


ridors of power and open warfare eventually broke out between the Taira and Minamoto clans. This led to the first decentralized shogunate at Kamakura (see box p194).

## Higashiyama—The culture of the "Eastern Mountains"

During the Kamakura period (1185–1333) Kyoto became less important. It was not until the Ashikaga shoguns, descendants of the Minamotos, came to power that Imperial rulers returned to the city. The Ashikaga era (1333–1573), also known as the Muromachi era *(named after the district of Kyoto where the shoguns lived)*, was one of the most flourishing for the arts. The **Golden Pavilion** *(Kinkaku-ji)* was built during the rule of the third shogun **Ashikaga Yoshimitsu** *(1358–1408)*.

But this period, though innovative, was followed by years of chaos in which rivalries between feudal lords led to the terrible Ten Years' War: *Onin no ran* (1467–77).

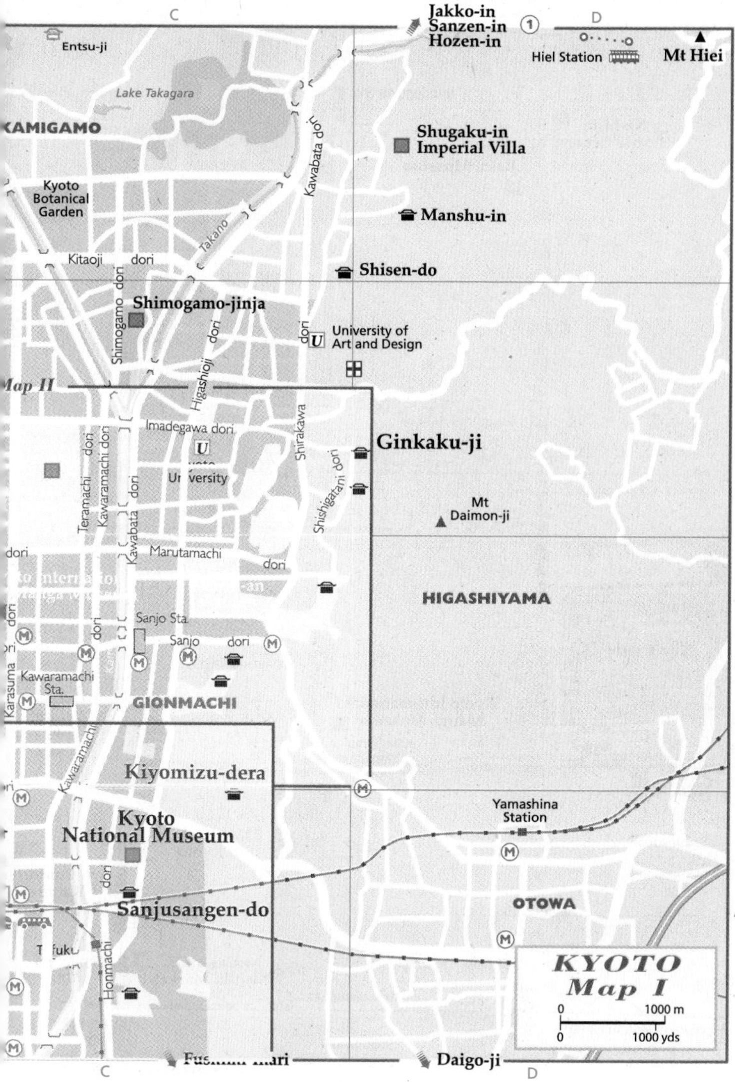




The war reduced Kyoto to ashes, but eventually a new artistic and philosophical movement began to gain strength, inspired by the eighth shogun of the *bakufu* of Muromachi: **Ashikaga Yoshimasa** (1443–96). Retiring to the Eastern Mountains *(Higashiyama)*, **Ashikaga Yoshimasa**, perfected a form of meditation pared down to essentials by Zen Buddhism, of which the **Silver Pavilion**, Ginkaku-ji, became the prototype structure (*see p303*).

The aristocracy was won over to an ascetic lifestyle, at once in harmony but also in conflict with the turmoil of the period, which was softened or sublimated by cultural pursuits such as the formal Tea Ceremony *(cha-no-yu)*, the art of creating dry landscape gardens (in which the spirit is nourished rather than the physical senses), or the pleasures of flower arranging *(Ikebana)*. When Yoshimasa died, Kyoto lapsed into anarchy. Everything was affected, even "The Way of the Warrior," the Samurai code.

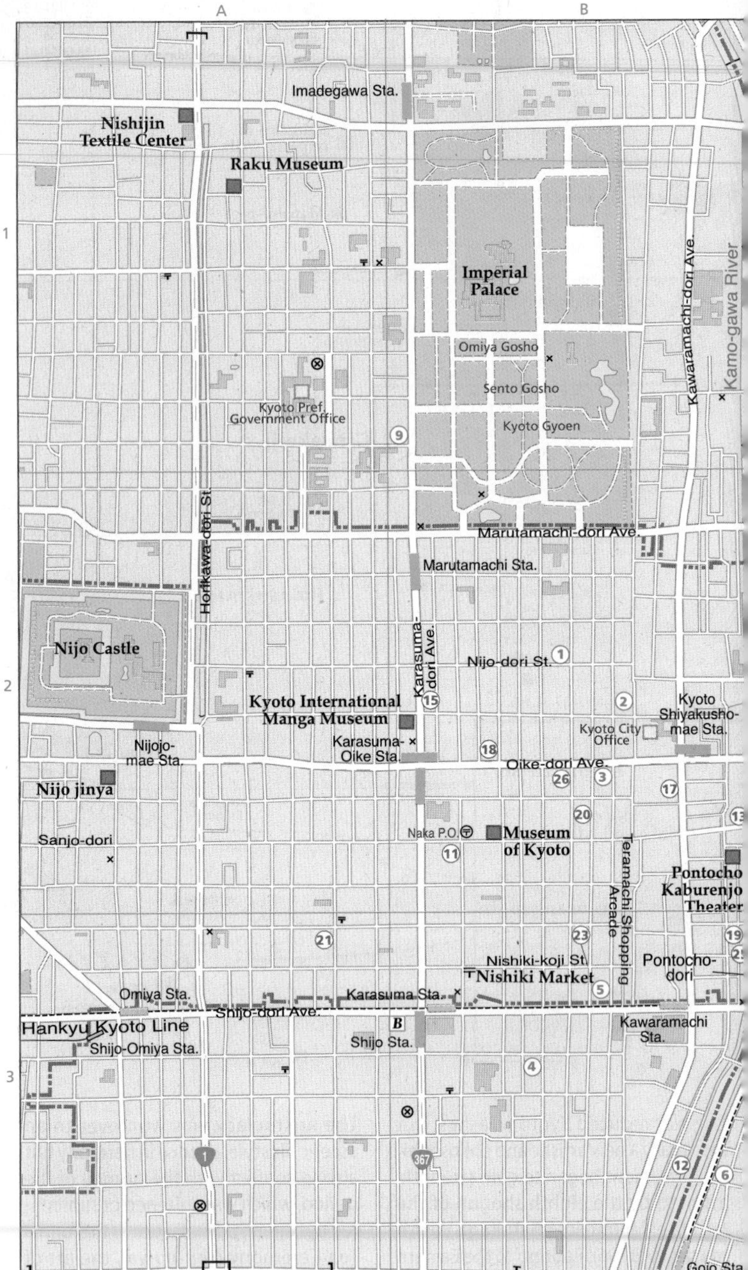


For the military leader **Oda Nobunaga,** who established his headquarters in the neighboring region of Gifu, it was necessary to re-establish authority over Kyoto. In 1573, **Oda Nobunaga** finally drove the last shogun of the Ashikaga dynasty from the Imperial capital.

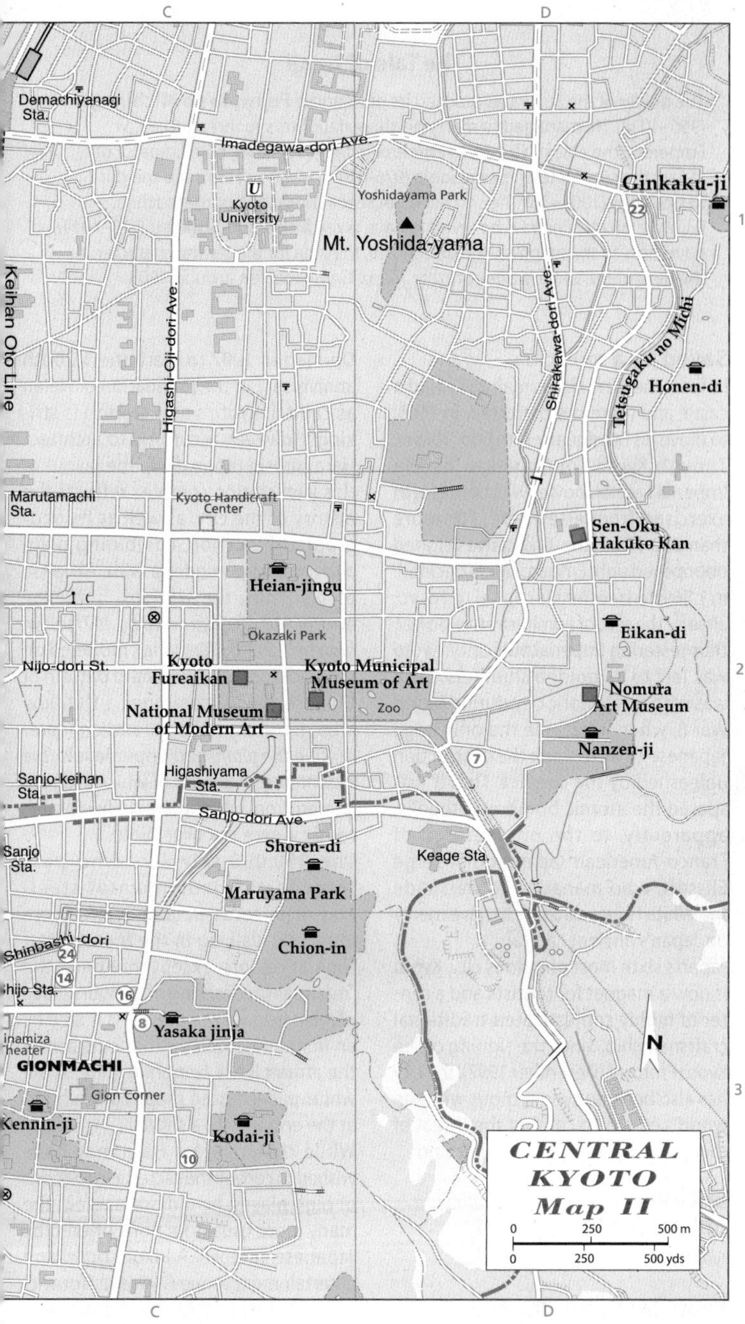




Once established in his power base, Nobunaga began to build the castle of Nijo, but was assassinated soon after (1582), leaving his lieutenants, **Toyotomi Hideyoshi** and **Tokugawa Ieyasu,** the task of completing and transforming it into an aristocratic residence *(shoin-zukuri)*.

### The Tale of Genji

The power of the Fujiwaras reached its peak under **Fujiwara no Michinaga** (966–1028). He managed to marry his three daughters to three successive Emperors: the eldest, Shoshi, to Emperor Ichijo (980–1011), 66th Emperor of Japan; the second to Emperor Sanjo (976–1017), Ichijo's cousin; and the third to Go-Ichijo (1008–36), the son her elder sister Shoshi had borne to Ichijo. Fujiwara no Michinaga is believed to have given **Murasaki Shikibu** (973–1014), governess to the empress-consort Shoshi, the idea for the central character: the hero of the *Genji monogatari* or *Tale of Genji,* written around 1008.

### Saved by a miracle

In fact, the new shogun already had a castle and therefore preferred, in 1603, to move his headquarters to Edo *(Tokyo).* Though Kyoto continued to be the Imperial capital, power was henceforth exercised from elsewhere. For more than 250 years, the Tokugawa reigned unopposed until Emperor Meiji decided, in 1 869, to transfer his capital to Tokyo, already the seat of administrative power, thus restoring Imperial authority. Kyoto was left to its golden slumbers. Luck was with this historic city during World War II, when it became the only large Japanese city to escape the destruction unleashed by the conflict. That it was spared the atomic bomb was thanks, apparently, to the intervention of Franco-American Japanologist Serge Elisséff, who managed to persuade the White House advisors to have mercy on Japan's ancient capital.

Japan's sixth most populous city, Kyoto is now a magnet for tourists and a center of highly sophisticated traditional craftsmanship. Since the signing of the Kyoto Protocol (December 1997), the city has also become synonymous with the world's efforts to combat the threat of climate change and global warming.

## SIGHTS

## AROUND THE STATION

*Allow 2 days.*

### Kyoto Station★ 京都駅

*Map III B2.*

*Don't overlook Kyoto's excellent Tourist Office on the 9th floor. Open 10am–6pm. Closed 2nd & 4th Tue of the month & Dec 29–Jan 3.*

Opened in 1997 to mark the 1,200th anniversary of the foundation of Heian as capital, Kyoto's new station is striking. However, according to architect Hara Hiroshi (born 1936), the layout of this vast station complex reflects the history of the city, as well as its geographical location, combining plain and mountains under a wide expanse of sky. Thus, the station's immense atrium *(88.6ft/27m wide by 197ft/60m high by 1,542ft/470m long)*, modeled on the traditional checkerboard pattern of Chinese towns, combines a flat, low area *(the entrance to the station representing the plain)* and upper levels *(the mountains)* at the top of which is a roof garden, from where there is a fine **panoramic view**★ out over Kyoto.

The 250,000 travelers who pass through this monumental steel-and-glass construction each day are implicitly walking in the footsteps of their ancestors, except that here, the "mountain," consisting of 16 floors *(three of them below ground level)*, is scaled by an immense escalator that cuts across the atrium like a *kamishide* (one of the white-paper zigzag shapes often hung at the entrance to a shrine).

While the architect Hara may have wished to convey the sacred associations of high places, he did not neglect the many more usual functions offered by Japanese stations. A luxury hotel and entertainment venue *(900 seats)* form its right wing, while the Isetan department store with its array of shopping arcades and restaurants, always full to capacity, occupy the opposite side.

## To-ji★★ 東寺 *Map III A2/3.*

*15min walk SW of the station. Kintetsu Line, Toji station or bus nos.202, 207, 208. Open 9am–4.30pm. ¥500.*

When the capital was relocated to Heian-kyo in 794, the "Temple of the East" was immediately erected to protect this key point of the new town. The work was entrusted to the monk Kukai, who, at the beginning of the 9C, introduced from China the teachings of the Buddhist Shingon-shu ("True Word") sect. Placed under the jurisdiction of Kukai in 823, the To-ji quite naturally became (with Kongobu-ji on Mount Koya, *see p343*) the main center for the dissemination of this new esoteric form of Buddhism. The most noticeable structure is of course the five-story **pagoda**★★, the highest in Japan at 187ft/57m. It was rebuilt in the 17C, as were most of the buildings in the temple precincts. To the south, the main hall, or **kondo**★ (1599), houses the triad of **Yakushi Nyorai**★★ (*see box right)*. In the **kodo**★, the lecture hall, there is a large sculpted **mandala**★★ consisting of the tutelary figure of the solar Great Buddha, **Dainichi Nyorai**, surrounded by 21 satellite statues arranged in groups: Buddhas *(Nyorai)*, bodhisattvas *(bosatsu)*, and, third in the hierarchy of Buddhist divinities, the five *Myo-o*, or "kings of magic knowledge." In the center stands **Fudo Myo-o**★, "the immutable one"—the defender of Buddhist law is always depicted with a straight sword *(tsurugi)* and a cord.

*On the 21st of each month, a charming flea market (antiques, secondhand items, old kimonos) is held in the square in front of the To-ji.*

### The Buddha of Healing

Yakushi Nyorai can be recognized by the small pot of medicine he carries in his left hand. He is in fact the only Buddha depicted holding an object. The pot he holds normally has 12 facets, representing the 12 redemptive tasks Yakushi undertook to fulfill in order to become a Buddha. His right hand sketches out the *mudra* (gesture) of "the dispelling of fear." The skilled Buddha of Healing is always accompanied by an even number of servants, such as the divinities Nikko ("Sunlight") and Gakko ("Moonlight"). His is an important role since his task is to cure, day and night, the deadliest of diseases: ignorance, the source of all our desires and the cause of humanity's suffering.

## Nishi Hongan-ji★ 西本願寺

*Map III A1/2.*

*10min walk NW of the station. Bus nos.9, 28, 205, 206, 207. Open 6am–6pm (summer); 5.30am–5.30pm (winter). No charge.*

A modest temple was first built in the mountains to the east of Kyoto around the mausoleum of Shinran Shonin (1173–1262), founder of the Jodo Shin-shu sect (*see box p296)*. In 1591, after various changes of fortune, the mausoleum was transferred to its present location when land was given to the sect by Toyotomi Hideyoshi, a man always on the lookout for popular support. The **San-mon**★ *(main gate, 1645)* of Nishi Hongan-ji (Western Temple of the Original Vow) leads straight into the **Hon-do (main hall**, 1760). It houses statues of Amida, Prince Shotoku, and the monk Honen. The prayer hall has sliding panels decorated with phoenixes and peacocks painted by artists of the Kano School. Farther south, the **Daishi-do**, the founder's hall (1637), houses a seated statue of Shinran Shonin.

## Higashi Hongan-ji★ 東本願寺

*Map III B1/2.*

*5min walk from Nishi Hongan-ji. Bus nos. 5, 26, 57, 101. Open Mar–Oct: 5.50am–5.30pm; Nov–Feb: 6.20am–4.30pm. No charge.*

A counterpart to Nishi Hongan-ji *(Western Temple)*, Higashi Hongan-ji *(Eastern Temple of the Original Vow)* was built as a result of a handover of power complicated by sibling political rivalry. On the death of the chief abbot Kosa (1543–92), responsibility for the temple, which

generally devolved on the eldest son, passed to his third son, as Kosa and Toyotomi Hideyoshi had decided. Ten years later, Japan's new strongman, Tokugawa Ieyasu, in turn donated a plot of land, but this time to the eldest son, who had not yet received anything. As a result, in 1602 the Higashi Hongan-ji was erected

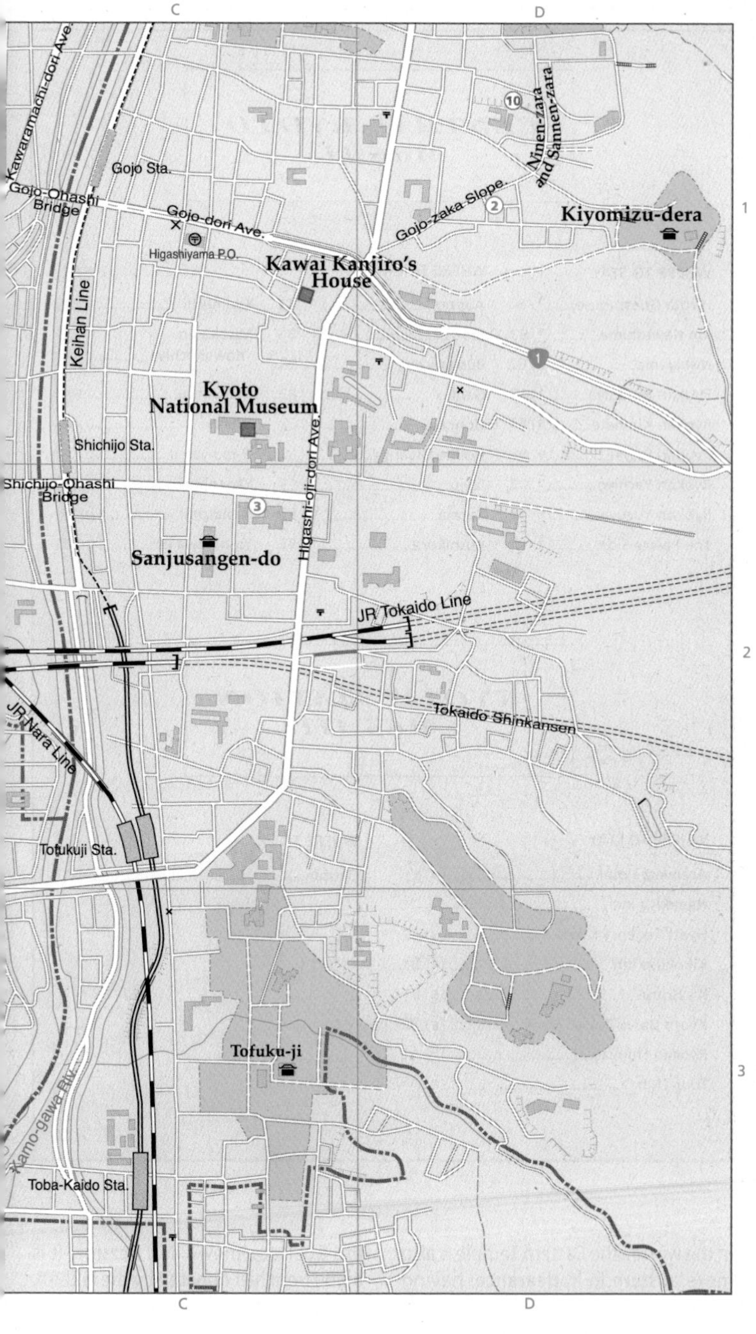




to the east of the Nishi Hongan-ji. With the backing of the shogun, this temple became the new headquarters of the Jodo Shin-shu sect and the mausoleum of Shinran Shonin was transferred here. More imposing than its rival the Western Temple (the founder's hall, **Goei-do**★, is one of the largest all-wooden buildings

## *CENTRAL KYOTO Map II*

| WHERE TO STAY | | |
|---|---|---|
| Hirota Guesthouse | 1 | B2 |
| Inn Kawashima | 4 | B3 |
| Nishiyama | 2 | B2 |
| Ryokan Hiiragiya | 3 | B2 |
| Ryokan Kinmata | 5 | B3 |
| Ryokan Sawai | 6 | B3 |
| Ryokan Yachiyo | 7 | D2 |
| Ryokan Yuzuya | 8 | C3 |
| The Palace Side | 9 | B1 |

| WHERE TO EAT | | |
|---|---|---|
| Aunbo | 10 | C3 |
| Bio-Tei | 11 | B2 |
| Bussaracan | 12 | B3 |
| Ganko | 13 | B2 |
| Gonbe | 14 | C3 |
| Honke Owariya | 15 | B2 |
| Izuju | 16 | C3 |
| Kerala | 17 | B2 |
| Kushikura | 18 | B2 |
| Kyomachi | 19 | B3 |
| Misoka-an Kawamichiya | 20 | B2 |
| Mukadeya | 21 | A3 |
| Omen | 22 | D1 |
| O-mo-ya | 23 | B3 |
| Yagenbori | 24 | C3 |
| Yamatomi | 25 | B3 |
| Yoshikawa Inn | 26 | B2 |

## *KYOTO STATION Map III*

| WHERE TO STAY | | |
|---|---|---|
| Aranvert Hotel | 1 | B1 |
| Hanakiya Inn | 2 | D1 |
| Hyatt Regency Kyoto | 3 | C2 |
| Kikokuso Inn | 4 | B1 |
| K's House | 5 | B1 |
| Kyoto Dai-ni Tower Hotel | 6 | B2 |
| Ryokan Shimizu | 7 | A1 |
| Tour Club | 8 | A1 |

| WHERE TO ERAT | | |
|---|---|---|
| Okutan | 10 | D1 |

in the world), the Eastern Temple is also more austere in appearance, having burned down on numerous occasions. The present structure is as recent as 1895. Strolling along the corridor connecting the Goei-do with Amida Hall, you will see a glass case displaying one of the ropes used to raise the beams of the Goei-do. Known as a **kezuna**, it is made from hair donated by the faithful. The largest rope *(15.7in/40cm in diameter)* is 32.8ft/10m long and weighs a ton.

*Now walk through the little Shosei-en garden and cross the Kamon River, heading SE.*

## Sanjusangen-do★★★

三十三間堂 *Map III C2.*
*15min walk E of the station. Keihan Line, Shichijo station. Bus nos. 100, 206, 208.*
*Open Apr–Nov 15 8am–5pm; Nov 16–Mar 9am–4pm. ¥600.*

Founded in 1164 by the charismatic warlord Taira no Kiyomori (*see p194*), this temple dates from 1266, its predecessor having been burned down in 1249. The first surprise is its sheer size: the main room is 393.7ft/120m long. This partly explains the temple's name, since the room is divided into 33 bays *(san ju san)*. Nor is this a random numberas the goddess of mercy, Kannon *bosatsu* to whom the temple is dedicatedchanged form 33 times to rescue mankind. The second surprise is a veritable forest of statues, shimmering like a magnificent brass orchestra as you walk past them in the semidarkness. Under the gaze of the visitor, the **1,001 statues of Kannon**★★★ seem to stare back in return, each with a slightly different expression beneath its gilded exterior (*see photo below*). With the exception of the 124 dating from the original foundation of the temple, they were carved by the best artists of the Kamakura period, such as **Unkei** and his son **Tankei**. Head of the renowned Kei-ha Buddhist school, Tankei also masterminded the immense statue of **Kannon with 11 heads** *(9.8ft/3m high)* presiding over the center of the building. While this group of 1,001 statues is an amazing sight *(80 artists are said to have worked on them over more than a century)*, the sculptural quality of each of the **28 divinities**★★★ arrayed at their feet *(Kamakura period)* is no less impressive. These deities are of Hindu origin. Guardians of the goddess of mercy, they wear intimidating expressions. The realism and vivacity of their features, and the intensity of their inlaid crystal eyes is striking. Look out for Naraen-Kengo *(Nayarana in Sanskrit)*, Karura *(Garuda)*, Mawara-nyo *(Maha-bala)*, Missha-kong *(Vajra-pani)*, and the elderly Basu-sennin *(Vasu)*.

### The Development of Carved Wooden Statues

The "joined-block" construction for wooden statues, *yosegi-zukuri*, as seen at Sanjusangen-do, is still rudimentary: only the upper limbs are sculpted separately before being affixed to the main statue, carved from a solid block of wood. It was not until the sculptor **Jocho** *(whose oldest works date from 1022)* that sculptors in wood began to create statues by assembling a number of carved wooden blocks using mortise and tenon joints. Jocho's best-known work is the Amida Buddha at Byodo-in in Uji (*see box p319*).

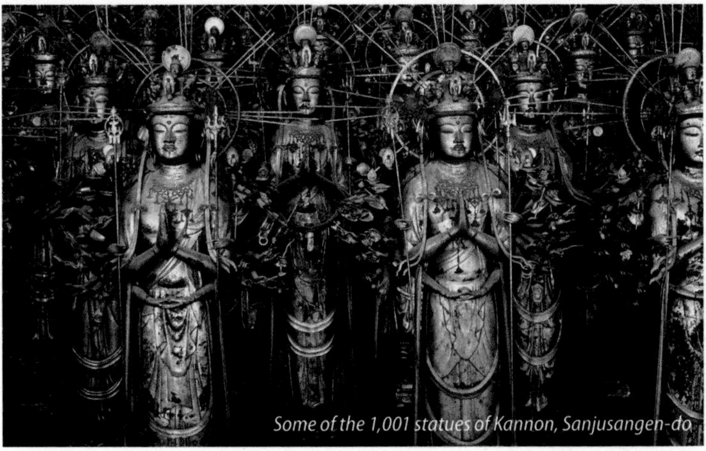

*Some of the 1,001 statues of Kannon, Sanjusangen-do*

## Pure Land and True Land Buddhism

**Amida**, the Japanese pronunciation of the Sanskrit Amitabha, "infinite light," and of Amitayus, "eternal life," was the name adopted by the monk Dharmakara after he had refused enlightenment for himself, unless he could bring nirvana to anyone who appealed to his name. This *bodhisattva*, who became a Buddha under the name of **Amitabha**, is one of the most popular in the Great Vehicle *(one of the two main schools of Buddhism)*. The paradise offered by his branch of Pure Land Buddhism is easily accessible: the worshipper simply needs to recite the Nembutsu: *"Namu Amida butsu"* ("In the name of Amida Buddha"). From the dozen or so sects spawned by Amida, two main streams emerged: the Jodo-shu or "Pure Land" school, founded by Honen Shonin (1133–1212), also known by his posthumous name of Enko Daishi, and the "True Pure Land" school or **Jodo Shin-shu**, established by Shinran Shonin (1173–1262). Their differences are less to do with doctrine and more about power struggles, to which not even the Pure Land sect proved immune.

*An archery contest involving more than 600 competitors is held annually on the nearest Sunday to January 15 on the veranda of Sanjusangen-do.*

## Kyoto National Museum★★★

京都国立博物館 *Map III C1.*
*Same access as for Sanjusangen-do.*
*Special exhibitions:* ◷*Open Tue–Sun 9.30am–6pm (Fri 8pm).* ⊶*Permanent exhibitions hall and collection closed for renovation until 2013.* ◉¥500 *(supplement for special exhibitions). www.kyohaku.go.jp.*

The reforms introduced by Emperor Meiji (1868) were the inspiration for this monumental red-brick building. Architecturally, the Kyoto National Museum *(formerly the Imperial Museum)* reflects the foreign influences welcomed by Katayama Tokuma, the Emperor's official architect. Pediments, terraces, and rooflines suggest the Baroque.

The irony is that the museum was inaugurated in 1897 with the intention of protecting Kyoto's cultural and architectural heritage, which were threatened by the Emperor's modernization program. A similar concern lay behind the foundation of the national museums in Tokyo and Nara.

The main building is reserved for temporary special exhibitions *(consistently of a high standard)*. The museum's permanent exhibits (⊶ *closed for renovation until 2013)* are divided into eight individual collections: Archeology, Ceramics, Sculpture, Painting, Calligraphy, Textiles, Laquerwork, and Metals. The 120,000 items are exhibited in rotation, but some masterpieces are always on show.

In room 4, you can admire a magnificent Chinese funerary statue: **Lady of the Palace Holding a Pekinese★★** *(Tang dynasty, 8C)*. Gallery 5 is dominated by four gigantic kings guarding each of the cardinal points. The most important, **Tamon-ten Vaisravana★★★** *(late Heian period, 11C)*, has the task of defending the northern gate, the one most exposed to malevolent spirits according to Chinese geomancy. He therefore holds himself upright, impassible and menacing, while the other guardians are more relaxed and dressed in flowing garments. His attributes include a *stupa* (votive tower symbolizing Buddhism) in his left hand and a *halberd* (two-handed pole weapon) grasped in his right.

This room also houses some fine wooden sculptures of **Jizo Bosatsu★★** *(Heian period, 9C)*, a popular divinity devoted to helping the suffering.

Among the collections of **paintings★★** *(galleries 8 to 12)*, which span the Heian and Edo periods, are works by Sotatsu, an exponent of the more narrative and typically Japanese *Yamato-e* style of illustration, which emerged during the Heian period. Two of the museum's masterpieces are portraits on *kakemono* (hung scrolls, literally "the thing which hangs") by Fujiwara Takanobu (1142–1205) of the leaders of the rival clans during the Kamakura period: **Minamoto no Yoritomo**★★★ (1147–99) and **Taira no Shigemori**★★★ (1138–79) (*see box p194*). With its stark geometrical composition, the latter exhibits the dark asceticism of a *raku*. Painted on a roll of paper, the **Gaki-zoshi**★★★ *(Heian period, 12C)* depicts hungry ghosts *(gaki)*, a rare subject in Japanese painting, treated here with ethereal vivacity. Eight panels depicting the world of birds and flowers in each of the four seasons★★, originally from Daisen-in temple, are one of the major works of **Kano Motonobu** (1476–1559) (*see box p299*). Descending from the heavens on a peacock encircled in clouds, the **Mayura Vidyaraja**★★ is a silk painting of Chinese provenance *(Song dynasty, 11C)*, from Ninna-ji temple. Finally, **room 14** has some magnificent **kosode**★★, forerunners of the modern kimono, with narrow openings for the hands at the ends of the sleeves.

## Kawai Kanjiro's House★

河井寛次郎記念館 *Map 1 C4, Map 3 C1. 10min walk N of the National Museum. Keihan Line, Gojo station. Bus nos.100, 202, 206, 207, Umamachi stop. Open Tue–Sun 10am–5pm. Closed Aug 10–20 & Dec 24–Jan 7. ¥900.*

A visit to the workshop of Kawai Kanjiro (1890–1966), one of the world's greatest potters, includes a tour of the *machiya* (*see box p298*) where he lived. The interior is beautifully furnished.

# THE CENTER

*Allow a full day for this itinerary, which starts with the Imperial Palace and ends in the Pontocho district in the early evening.*

## Imperial Palace★ 京都御所

*Map II B1/2.*
*Subway: Imadegawa or Marutamachi (Karasuma Line). Bus nos.10, 59, 93, 102, 201, 202, 203, 204. Visit by guided tour (1hr) only Mon–Fri at 9am, 11am, & 1.30pm for the Kyoto Gosho; 11am & 1.30pm for the Sento Gosho. No charge. A permit must be obtained at least 30min beforehand (but better to get it the day before) from the Imperial Household Agency (open Mon–Fri 8.45am–noon, 1–5pm), located in the park N of the main entrance on Karasuma-dori. The Agency also issues permits for Katsura and Shugaku-in Imperial villas (see p312 and 302). Passport required. Reservations can be made via the Internet at http://sankan.kunaicho.go.jp.*

At the heart of the Imperial Park *(210-acre/85ha)*, a popular green space in the center of the city, lies the **Kyoto Gosho**, the Imperial Palace, its sheer size evident from the surrounding wall. The various buildings of the Palace, past which a terse guide urges you at the double, are set in grounds of 24.7 acres/10ha—a visit to the Imperial Palace is not the most enriching of experiences! Originally erected in 794 1.2mi/2km west of its present site, time and again the Palace rose phoenix-like from its ashes *(16 fires between 960 and 1227)*. Finally, in 1788 it was decided to transfer it to this location, an area thought—wrongly, as it turned out—to be much safer. The present version dates from the end of the 19C, reproducing the palace as it was in the golden age of Japanese civilization during the **Heian period**. Of the various buildings

### Aoi Matsuri, May 15, 10.30am

Initially a purification rite to guard against bad harvests, the **Hollyhock Festival** is now more a commemoration of the Heian era. The slow, rather formal procession departs from the Central Palace and heads for the first shrine built in Kyoto-Kamigamo-jinja. At the halfway point, a halt is called at its twin shrine of Shimogamo. The hollyhock, with its protective properties, emblem of the Tokugawas, should not be confused with the *wasabi* (Japanese horseradish), better known for its culinary virtues.

### Machiyas

Referred to by the locals as *unagi-no-nedoko*, or "eel beds," these town houses *(machiya)* are typical of old Kyoto. The front of the *unagi-no-nedoko* generally serves as a shop, behind which the rest of the building extends
This long, narrow layout is due to the fact that tax was calculated not on floor area but on the length of street frontage. A string of several workshops may therefore share a single shop window. A courtyard garden lets in light and the buildings are often raised on supports so that air can circulate beneath. Very few have survived.

before which the guide calls a halt, the **Shodaibunoma**★, or courtesans' salon, consists of a hall divided into three rooms arranged hierarchically, reflected in the paintings that adorn the doors and sliding panels *(fusuma)* of each. Thus the **Tiger**, **Stork**, and **Cherry Tree** rooms were occupied by courtesans of progressively lower rank. In the Palace's main pavilion, the **Shishin-den**, is the room where the Taisho and Showa Emperors were crowned. Of special interest is the next pavilion, the **Seiryo-den**, once the Emperor's residence.
At the end of your visit, the peaceful **Oike no niwa garden**★ provides a welcome moment of calm.

*Go due W along Naka-Dachiuri from Karasuma-dori, keeping to the west side of the Imperial Palace.*

## Raku Museum★★ 楽美術館

*Map II A1.*
*84 Aburahashizemu, Nakadachiuri, Kamigyo-ku. 10min walk from the Imperial Palace or Imadegawa subway station (Karasuma Line). Open Tue–Fri 10am–4pm. ¥800. www.raku-yaki.or.jp.*
This small museum stands next door to the home of the Raku family. It was opened in 1978 by the 14th generation of this family of ceramic artists. Austere as the tea bowls on display, the building houses some magnificent pieces ranging from the earliest *raku* made by Chojiro *(born 16C)* to those of Raku Kichizaemon *(born 1949, 15th generation)*.
The method of production *(rapid firing followed by accelerated cooling)*, was first used at the beginning of the Momoyama period. The simplicity and austerity of these thick-walled, rustic-looking bowls immediately appealed to those who, like Ashikaga Yoshimasa (*see p286*), wished to transform the Tea Ceremony into an occasion for meditation.

*From Raku Museum, walk up the busy Horikawa-dori, which runs at right angles as far as the SW corner of Imadegawa and Horikawa-dori. Allow roughly 15min.*

## Nishijin Textile Center

西陣織会館 *Map II A1.*
*Subway: Imadegawa (Karasuma Line), then 10min walk. Bus nos. 9, 12, 59, 101, 102, 201, 203, stop 1min walk away. Open 9am–5pm. No charge. www.nishijin.or.jp/eng/eng.htm.*
A branch of the powerful Hata clan arrived in this district 1,500 years ago, bringing new agricultural techniques and a knowledge of silkworm breeding, a lucrative industry and one of the reasons why Emperor Kanmu *(reigned 781–806)* moved his capital to Kyoto. Nowadays, this former workshop and exhibition center, located in the weavers' district of Nishijin, explains various weaving techniques. Fashion shows are also held to display the finished products *(9.30am–3.30pm)*. You can buy or hire all kinds of kimonos, or have yourself photographed in a kimono of your choice.

## Nijo Castle★★ 二条城 *Map II A2.*

*10min walk SW of the Imperial Palace. Subway: Nijojo-mae (Tozai Line). Bus nos. 9, 12, 50, 101. Open 8.45am–4pm. Closed Tue in Dec, Jan, Jul, & Aug. ¥600. Display panels and audioguides in English.*
Erected by Ieyasu, the first Tokugawa shogun in 1603, the year Edo (Tokyo) became the administrative capital of Japan, this castle was the symbol of

**Tokugawa** power for some 15 generations until 1867, when the last shogun abdicated. It was then taken over by the Imperial Government, (which made it its headquarters). It now belongs to the municipality of Kyoto.
The beginning of the 17C saw the end of the Momoyama period, and with it, the ostentatious splendor in which Toyotomi Hideyoshi (1536–98) had so delighted. His successor, Tokugawa Ieyasu, also wished to display his power over the newly-unified country, but had to find a more discreet way, aware absolute power tends to be opposed not openly but in secret. Constructed in the style of a *shoin-zukuri*, or aristocratic residence, though unsuited to siege warfare, this castle was by no means defenseless.
Once through the richly sculpted and gilded **Kara-mon**★ *(Chinese gate)*, you are inside **Ninomaru Palace**★★, designated a National Treasure.
The 30 or so rooms cover an area of 32,292sq ft/3,000sq m.
Some of the decoration is outstanding: majestic *tokonoma* (alcoves), *chigai-dana* (staggered shelves) of extreme delicacy, coffered ceilings embossed with brightly colored motifs, and *fusuma* (sliding panels) painted by artists of the Kano School (*see box above*).
Behind these gilt partitions, however, are concealed countless alcoves, once occupied by guards ready to spring forth at the slightest creaking of **"nightingale floors"** sensitive to the footsteps of even a ghost. The beautiful **garden**★ with its lake and rocks is attributed to the great landscape designer Kobori Enshu (1579–1647).

## Nijo jinya★ 二条陣屋 *Map II A2.*

*5min walk S of the castle on Omiya-dori. Visit by guided tour (1hr) only in Japanese; non-Japanese-speakers are asked to bring a bilingual companion), Thu–Tue at 10am, 11am, 2pm, & 5pm. ¥1,000. Reservations required. 075-841-0972.*
This inn was built in the 17C to accommodate visiting *daimyo* (feudal lords). As they demanded the highest levels of security, the building had to be proofed against threats of all kinds. Behind the inn's reinforced, fireproof walls, a maze of corridors serves 24 cunningly constructed rooms. Secret passages, trapdoors, hidden stairways, false ceilings, and "nightingale floors" (*see above*) make this historic inn a fascinating place to visit.

*15min walk E in the direction of Karasuma-dori via Oike-dori.*

## Kyoto International Manga Museum★

京都国際マンガミュージアム
*Map I C3 and Map II B2. Oike-agaru, Karasuma-dori, Nakagyo-ku. Subway: Karasuma-Oike, exit 2. Bus nos.15, 51, 65 (Kyoto city) or nos. 61, 62, 63 (Kyoto bus), stop near Karasuma-Oike. Open Thu–Tue 10am–6pm. Last admission at 5.30, delayed closing depending on season. ¥500. www.kyotomm.com.*
This museum, established in 2006 in a former primary school dating from the late-19C comes as a wonderful surprise. It is as playful as its subject: manga, a word invented in the 19C by master printmaker Hokusai (1760–1849), which

### The Kano School

This school of professional painters was in existence for eight generations, replacing the monks who, until that time, had carried out the commissions of the shoguns. The founder, **Kano Masanobu** (1434–1530), excelled in a monochrome decorative style based solely on black ink. During the Momoyama period, gold leaf was introduced by Kano Eitoku (1543–90), which greatly appealed to Toyotomi Hideyoshi. His grandson, Kano Tanyu (1602–74), became official painter to Tokugawa Ieyasu *(decorating, for example, Nijo Castle)*. The realistic style he adopted, featuring herons and peacocks against a background of gold leaf, snow, or cherry blossom, celebrated nature.

translates as "derisory image" (*see Understanding Japan p56*).

Around 50,000 mangas fill a whole wall of shelving 459ft/140m long. In the basement is an archive of 15,000 items covering the history of manga to the present day. On the first *(ground)* floor, former students of Kyoto's famous Seika University are busy creating new manga, while the next floor is used for permanent exhibitions featuring stories and drawings *(174 plates depicting maiko, apprentice geisha, are on display)* and temporary exhibitions. In one small classroom, you can listen to the storyteller Yassan *(3 performances per day)* as he demonstrates the early illustrated stories that *kamishibai* used to hawk from one village to another in the paniers of their bicycles. There were once 50,000 of these peddlers in Japan, but they gradually disappeared with the advent of television.

*10min walk SE. Go down Karasuma-dori as far as Sanjo-dori on your left.*

### Museum of Kyoto

京都文化博物館 *Map II B2.*

*Sanjo-Takakura, Nakagyu-ku. 5min walk from Karasuma-Oike subway station or Karasuma station (Hankyu Line). Open Tue–Sun 10am–7.30pm. ¥500. www.bunpaku.or.jp.*

With its fine red-brick façade facing Sanjo-dori, this municipal museum *(not to be confused with the Kyoto National Museum, see p296)* is proof of how important the **Sanjo-dori** road was at the beginning of the Edo period.

It was originally the only way of reaching Sanjo Bridge across the Kamo River and then the Tokaido road. Inside the museum, the city's history *(from its foundation in the Taisho period, some 11 centuries ago)* is illustrated by fine models. A lack of information in English makes things difficult to understand, though the museum does have a volunteer English-speaking guide.

The museum also has its own fascinating **cinema** *(3rd floor)* and regularly organizes special exhibitions. On the first *(ground floor)*, a reconstructed street of shops, "Roji Tempo," dating from the end of the Edo period, connects the museum to an ultramodern annex, where you can have a meal or snack and buy souvenirs *(traditional craft items)*.

## PONTOCHO AND SURROUNDINGS★ 先斗町

*Map II B–C2.*

*Allow the latter part of an afternoon and spend the evening on the terrace of one of Pontocho-dori's countless restaurants. The lunch hour is the best time to visit Nishiki market.*

### Nishiki Market★ 錦市場 *Map II B3*

This pedestrianized, covered street, the "belly of Kyoto," is packed with stands selling many of the ingredients of traditional Kyoto cuisine: wild vegetables, spices, dried fish, and Uji tea. It is popular with gourmets and fans of traditional crafts. Good-quality cutlery, crockery, etc. is also on sale. (*see Addresses p325*). It runs into Teramachi Arcade.

Nishiki Market

©Y. Shimizu/JNTO

### Teramachi Arcade 寺町通

*Map II B2/3.*

Another rather run-of-the-mill, large shopping arcade that extends from one side of Shijo-dori to the other. Some stores specialize in fashion for the young, but there are also some old shops *(bookshop, stationer's)* and a print workshop *(Nishiharu)*, where you are welcomed by one of Japan's great experts in the field of *ukiyo-e* (woodblock prints). The quality of the goods on sale is matched by the courtesy of the owner *(see Address Book p 326)*.

*Return to Shijo-dori and head E toward the Kamo River. On the sidewalk to the right are the entrances to two of Kyoto's largest stores:* ***Takashimaya*** *and* ***Hankyu****. Pontocho-dori is the first lane on your left, just before Shijo-bashi.*

### Pontocho-dori★ 先斗町通

*Map II B2/3.*

Running parallel with the Kamo River, this lane lined with small wooden houses is barely 6.6ft/2m wide and gets very crowded at night. Popular since the early 18C on account of its many *ochaya* (geisha tea houses), today it is the bars, restaurants, and *izakaya* (bars serving food and drink) that attract visitors. On the east side are pleasant terraces *(open May–Sept)* lit by lanterns reflected in the river. Though the Pontocho-dori★ caters for tourists, the level of service is variable *(refer to the Address Book p 321, rather than selecting an establishment at random)*.

At the end of the Pontocho-dori, you will see the façade of **Pontocho Kaburenjo Theater** *(Map II B2)*. Every year since its opening in 1895, the theater has presented the **Kamogawa Odori** or "Dance of the Kamo River" *(see Addresses p326)*, one of Kyoto's most successful geisha festivals. *To extend your visit, follow the Takasegawa Canal, where the bars are much more free and easy.*

## EAST OF THE CENTER: AROUND HEIAN-JINGU

*Allow a morning or afternoon.*

### Heian-jingu★ 平安神宮

*Map II C2.*

*Keihan Line, Sanjo station. Bus nos. 5, 32, 46, 57, 100, Kyoto Kaikan Bijutsukan-mae stop. Open Mar–Oct 8.30am–5.30pm; Nov–Feb 8.30am–4.30pm. Shrine no charge; garden ¥600.*

This Shinto shrine was erected in 1895 to mark the 1,100th anniversary of the city. Standing in the north part of Okazaki Park, it is a 5:8 scale replica of the Gosho, the former Imperial Palace built in the Heian period in the 8C.

It is dedicated to the Emperor Kanmu, founder of Kyoto, and Komei, the last sovereign to reside there. The height of the ridge of the impressive *torii* (entrance gate) is the same as the water level of Lake Biwa. Behind the shrine, the **garden**★ is notable for its cherry trees, irises, and maples.

### Kyoto National Museum of Modern Art★

京都国立近代美術館 *Map II C2.*

*Subway: Higashiyama (Tozai Line). Bus nos. 5, 32, 46, 57, 100, Kyoto Kaikan Bijutsukan-mae stop. Open Tue–Sun 9.30am–5pm (Apr–Oct Fri 8pm). ¥420.*

The permanent collections of this important museum consist of paintings in the (typically Japanese) **Nihonga style** by artists such as Nishiyama Suisho (1879–1958) and Hirota Tatsu (1904–90). There are also works in the **Yoga style** (the term used for the Western painting style first practiced in the Meiji period) by such artists as Kuroda Jutaro (1887–1970), Suda Kunitaro (1891–1961), Kishida Ryusei (1891–1929), and of course **Foujita** (1886–1968), including a wonderful **Reclining Nude**★★★ dating from 1937.

Ceramic works by Kitaoji Rosanjin (1883–1959) are exhibited alongside some of the 420 items created by the prolific Kawai Kanjiro (1890–1966, *see p297)*. These are complemented by works from Western artists including Piet Mondrian *(see Katsura Imperial Villa p312)*, Max Ernst, Matisse, and Odilon Redon, who is represented with a magnificent *Youthful Buddha* (1905).

The museum also has a fine **photographic collection** (Ansel Adams, Alfred Stieglitz).

### Kyoto Municipal Museum of Art 京都市美術館 *Map II C2.*

*Immediately opposite the National Museum of Modern Art. Open Tue–Sun 9am–5pm. ¥400.*

This museum's collections consist principally of works by local artists from the Meiji Restoration era to the present day. Takeuchi Seiho, Tamioka Tessai, and Asai Chu are three of the diverse artists represented.

### Fureaikan (Kyoto Museum of Traditional Crafts) 京都伝統産業ふれあい館 *Map II C2.*

*5min walk from the preceding museums, in the basement of the Miyako Messe, opposite Heian-jingu. Open 9am–5pm. No charge.*

This museum is devoted to traditional craftsmanship, with the emphasis on the history of technology.

## THE NORTHEAST

*Allow a morning or afternoon.*

### Shimogamo-jinja★

下鴨神社 *Map I C2.*

*Keihan Line or Eizan Line, Demachiyanagi station. Bus nos. 4, 205, Shimogamo-mae stop. Open 6am–6pm. No charge.*

Founded in the 6C by Emperor Kinmei *(and rebuilt in the 19C)*, Shimogamo is one of Kyoto's oldest shrines and has a twin, Kamigamo, in the northwest of the city *(see box p308)*. Shimogamo-jinja is dedicated to the mountain god and his wife, the river goddess, who are lavishly honored here in the heart of a large park fed with water from the Kamo-gawa. A magnificent tree-lined avenue provides the setting for the spectacular *yabusame* (mounted archery contest) that accompanies the **Aoi Matsuri** *(see box p297)* each year in mid-May.

### Shisen-do 詩仙堂 *Map I C1.*

*Eizan Line, Ichijoji station, then 15min walk. Bus no. 5, Ichijoji-sagarimatsu-cho stop, then 5min walk E. Open 9am–5pm. ¥600.*

Now a Zen temple belonging to the Soto sect, this villa was founded in 1631 by the poet Ishikawa Jozan (1583–1672), who had been expelled by Shogun Tokugawa. It has a remarkable **garden**★. Defying the convention of the time, the poet combined dry landscape, tea garden, and stroll garden features *(see p103)*.

### Manshu-in★ 曼殊院 *Map I D1*

*30min walk N of Shisen-do. Bus no.5, Ichijoji-shimizu-cho stop, then 20min walk. Open 9am–5pm. ¥500.*

Originally sited on the northern slope of Mount Hiei, this temple was relocated here during the Edo period and rebuilt with a number of different *shoin* (pavilions). The influence of Katsura Villa is evident in its rooms, which feature some very fine *fusuma* (sliding panels) painted by Kano Eitoku (1543–90), for the Tiger Room, and Kano Tanyu (1602–74), for the waterfalls of the main pavilion. Of later date, the Bamboo and Peacock Rooms were decorated by Ganku Kishiku (1756–1839). In the **dry landscape garden**★ outside, a magnificent **five-needle pine** *(Pinus pentaphylla)* rises from a bed of painstakingly raked white sand. It has stood on its tiny green island for more than 400 years.

### Shugaku-in Imperial Villa★★

修学院離宮 *Map I D1.*

*20min walk N of Manshu-in. Eizan Line, Shugaku-in station, then 20min walk. From Kyoto station, bus no. 5, Shugakuin Rikyu-michi stop (1hr20min), then 15 min walk E. Visit by guided tour (1hr15min) only Mon–Fri at 9am, 10am, 11am, 1.30pm, & 3pm. No charge. You need to obtain a permit in advance from the Imperial Household Agency (see p297). Minors not admitted. Passport required.*

Lying at the foot of the Higashiyama mountain chain, the Imperial villa derives its name from the old Shugaku temple, which it replaced in the 16C. Three villas were built here by order of the shogun as a vacation residence for the retired Emperor Go-Mizuno-o (1596–1680).

Consisting of a number of pavilions, they are laid out on different levels in a fine 69-acre/28ha park. Following the itinerary, the lower villa *(Shimo no chaya)* is reached first, followed by the middle villa *(Naka no chaya)*, where one of the pavilions, the **Kyaku-den**, has a magnificent **kasumidana**★★ (shelves arranged to represent mist or clouds against a background of painted panels), and some very cedar doors decorated with chariots *(hoko)* and carp. Proceed then to the upper villa *(Kami no chaya)*, by far the most interesting. The first of its two pavilions, the **Rinun-tei**, "the pavilion near to a cloud," has a clear **view**★ over the Yokuryuchi pool, in the middle of which rises a majestic tea pavilion, the **Kyusui-tei**.

## THE EAST: THE PHILOSOPHER'S PATH AND SURROUNDINGS

*Allow a full day.*

The Tetsugaku no Michi, or **Philosopher's Path**★ *Map II D1*, which takes its name from the monks who for centuries walked this way pursuing their meditations, is one of the parts of the city you can really enjoy on foot. The path follows a small canal shaded by weeping willows and cherry trees.

### Ginkaku-ji★★★ 銀閣寺 *Map II D1.*

*Bus nos. 5, 17, 32, 100, 102, 203, 204, Ginkakuji-michi stop. Open Mar–Nov 8.30am–5pm; Dec–Feb 9am–4.30pm. ¥500.*

The Silver Pavilion is of course reminiscent of the Golden Pavilion (*see p308*). Built a little later, it lacks in ostentation what it gains in modesty. Ashikaga Yoshimasa (1435–90), eighth shogun and grandson of Yoshimitsu (*see p286*), built his **Silver Pavilion** on a much smaller scale than that of his ancestor. The shogun was then living a far more modest lifestyle. He had just introduced the Higashiyama culture: the culture of the Eastern Mountains, named for the topography of this part of Kyoto, where he lived. It was rooted in a form of Zen philosophy inspired by *wabi-sabi* (refinement in simplicity), of which the Tea Ceremony *(cha-no-yu)* is the fullest expression. Yoshimasa is said to have played a key role in the development of the Tea Ceremony, which was transformed from an everyday activity into a formal ritual. The first such ceremony is believed to have been held in a small

*Ginkaku-ji*
© Christian Goupi/age fotostock

room just a few feet square *(chashitsu)* in the middle of this garden. The room is said to have been designed by Zen-ami (1386–1482), a gardener belonging to the *eta* (outcast) caste, who were regarded with distaste by the Zen masters. Redesigned on many occasions, the **garden**★★ consists of two parts. The first combines *Kogetsudai*, cones of sand designed to reflect the moon's rays, and *Ginsadan*, long strips of alternately rough and smooth sand. The second, hugging the hillside *(with pine trees, a small lake, and rocks)*, draws its inspiration from the **moss garden** (*see p315*) that a century before had influenced the garden of the Golden Pavilion.

### Honen-in 法然院 *Map II D1.*

*10min walk S of Ginkaku-ji, on the left of the canal. Open 9am–4pm. No charge.*

This modest temple is approached via a magnificent avenue of *momiji* (maples), *sugi* (cedars), *shidare-zakura* (weeping cherries), *tsubaki* (camellias), and *Fuji musume* (clematis). To your right, on the hillside, a small cemetery shelters the tomb—marked by a tree planted between two stones—of **Tanizaki**, author of *In Praise of Shadows*.

The temple has a small, dry landscape garden. It is dedicated to the founder of the Buddhist Jodo-shu sect, the monk **Honen** (1133–1212), (*see box p296*). A small hall houses temporary special exhibitions.

## Sen-Oku Hakuko-kan★

泉屋博古館 *Map II D2.*
*20min walk back down the Philosopher's Path. Turn right when you come to the Otoyo-jinja shrine, then take the first path on your left. 24 Shimomiyanomae-cho, Shishigatani. Subway: Marutamachi (Karusma Line), then bus no. 93 or 204. Open Tue–Sun 10.30am–5pm. ¥730. www.sen-oku.or.jp.*
This collection of 3,000 items acquired by the Sumitomo family is exhibited in rotation in a minimalist setting. The highlights are some **Chinese bronzes**★★ from the Shang and Zhou dynasties (17C bc–ad 453). The museum also possesses some fine mirrors dating from the Han (202 bc–ad 220) and Tang (618–907) periods, some Ming (1368–1644), and Qing (1644–1911) dynasty paintings, plus a few works by the painter Shi Tao (1642–1707). The visit ends with a collection of **Noh masks**★★ and costumes (16C and 18C), and a pleasant **garden**.

## Eikan-do★ 永観堂 *Map II D2.*

*Roughly 10min walk S of Sen-Oku Museum. Bus nos.5, 32, 57, 100. Open 9am–5pm. ¥600. www.eikando.or.jp/english.*
This Buddhist temple, first of Shingon then of Jodo allegiance *(see box p296)*, bears the name of the monk Eikan (1033–1111), whose real name was Yokan. He devoted his life to the poor and infirm and built a hospital in the temple precincts. Eikan found his vocation after meeting Amida, an event depicted in the sculpture **Mikaeri Amida Nyorai**★, *Amida Looking Over His Shoulder.*
The Buddha *(Nyorai)* is said to have revealed himself to Eikan while he was saying his prayers. The figures in the sculpture are shown in a pose that was very innovative for the time. There is also a fine silk painting: **Yamagoshi Amida**★, *Amida Appearing Behind the Mountains.* This vertical scroll *(a National Treasure)* depicts Amida receiving a dying man and guiding him toward the Pure Land Western Paradise, a major theme in Buddhist iconography.
The temple complex is popular in the Fall on account of its **gardens**, when the leaves of the maples turn red and gold. To the rear is a pagoda, from which there is a fine **view** of the city.

## Nomura Art Museum

野村美術館 *Map II D2.*
*2min walk S of Eikan-do, on the right. Open Tue–Sun 10am–4.30pm. Closed Jun 15–Sept 15 & Dec 15–Mar 15. ¥700.*
This museum is devoted to the Tea Ceremony and all its trappings. It was founded by wealthy businessman Nomura Tokushichi (1878–1945), who made his fortune in stockbroking, banking, and insurance.

## Nanzen-ji★★ 南禅寺 *Map II D2.*

*5min walk S of Eikan-do. Subway: Keage (Tozai Line). Bus nos.5, 57. Open Mar–Nov 8.40am–5pm; Dec–Feb 8.40am–4.30pm. Hojo garden ¥500, San-mon ¥500, Nanzen-in ¥300.*
This temple was originally a villa built for Emperor Kameyama (1249–1305). Toward the end of his life the Emperor became the disciple of a great Buddhist teacher, and in 1291 the villa was converted into a temple. The Zen Temple of the South *(Nanzen-ji)* became the headquarters of the Rinzai sect, whose teachings were introduced to Japan in 1191 by the Chinese monk Eisai *(see boxes p195).*
Destroyed during the terrible Onin War (15C), it was largely reconstructed in the 17C, along with the triple gate **San-mon**★ with its ceiling painted by artists of the Kano School. Once through the San-mon, the **Hojo seiryo-den**★★★ is the most important pavilion. Its two rooms *(Dai-hojo and Ko-hojo)* have been designated a National Treasure on account of their sliding panel *(fusuma)* paintings. The *24 Paragons of Filial Piety* and the celebrated **Mizunomi no Tora**★★, *Tiger Drinking Water,* were painted by Kano Eitoku (1543–90) and Kano Tanyu (1602–74) *(see box p299).* The **Zen garden**★ attached to the *hojo*, known as the Leaping Tiger Garden, is a fine example of a *kare-sansui* (dry lands-

Terrace of Kiyomizu-dera overlooks the whole city

cape garden), laid out by Kobori Enshu. An imposing massif of rocks and plants, supposed to recall the tiger painted by Tanyu, stands out boldly between the gravel and a white wall.
Of the secondary temples set in the 27-acre/11ha wooded park surrounding Nanzen-ji, **Nanzen-in**★, comprising a mausoleum *(last resting place of the Emperor Kameyama)* and a fine 14C landscaped garden, is hidden away behind a magnificent Meiji period **aqueduct** (1890).
South of the San-mon, **Tenjuan**★ is flanked by a fine dry landscape garden. **Konchi-in** (*open 8.30am–5pm; ¥400*), located southeast of the gate and just outside the temple enclosure, boasts a garden by Kobori Enshu. A stork and tortoise are symbolized by two facing groups of rocks.

## THE EAST: FROM KIYOMIZU TO MARUYAMA PARK

*Allow a full day, starting early in the morning for a quiet stroll around Kiyomizu-dera.*

### Kiyomizu-dera★★★ 清水寺

*Map I C3/4 and Map III D1.*
*Bus nos.100, 202, 206, 207, Kiyomizu-michi or Gojozaka stop, then 10min walk. Open 6am–6pm (summer 6.30pm). ¥300.*
Consisting of seven pavilions, including a bell tower *(shoro)* and a **pagoda** *(sanjunoto)* built at different levels on the slopes of Higashiyama, this site is notable for its main **temple** and the **Otawa waterfall**.
Founded in 798 by the monk Enchin *(and last rebuilt in the 17C under the patronage of Tokugawa Iemitsu)*, the "Temple of Clear Water" *(Kiyomizu-dera)*, rises from a tall wooden platform built on piles *(roughly 65.6ft/20m high)*. Providing a breathtaking **view** over Kyoto, this **immense terrace**★ has also seen its share of tragedy: in the Edo period, it was popularly believed that those who jumped and survived would see their dreams come true. The temple treasury houses an 11-headed statue of Kannon (*see p295*) that is put on display every 33 years *(the number of her reincarnations)*. Lower down the mountainside, the **Otawa-no-taki** is famed for its sacred waters, celebrated regularly with processions.

*Go back down from the temple, then take the stairway on the right.*

### Ninenzaka and Sannenzaka

二年坂・三年坂 *Map III D1.*
The **Sannenzaka** ("Three-year Slope") is the favored route of pilgrims who have been staying at Kiyomizu-dera.
A cobbled street lined with old wooden town houses, it is a reminder of the Higashiyama culture (*see Silver Pavilion p303*). There are shops selling the famous local Kyo-yaki (or Kiyomizu-yaki) pottery used for the Tea Ceremony *(cha-no-yu)*,

*Float at the Gion Matsuri*

© Q. Sawami / JNTO

## Gion Matsuri

This spectacular festival, which goes on throughout July, culminates in a great parade on the 17th, which has its origins in a procession to ward off the plague of 869. Thirty or so floats, decorated with flowers and brightly colored fabrics (*see photo, right*), process through the streets of Gion from the Yasaka-jinja, to the sound of drums and flutes. The evening before, the streets are lit with lanterns and filled with crowds.

and antique dealers, souvenir shops, and restaurants now occupy this predominantly tourist-orientated district disdainfully overlooked by the remains of an ancient Buddhist temple complex: the four-story **Yasaka**★ pagoda. This is to your left, in a street at right angles to the **Ninenzaka** ("Two-year Slope"), which takes over from Sannenzaka and runs alongside the **Ryozen Kannon** memorial. This immense concrete statue *(78.7ft/24m high)* is a monument to the Japanese who lost their lives in World War II. The Ninenzaka then becomes the **Higashiyama Path** or Nene Street, deriving from the nickname of the female founder of the Kodai-ji temple, to which it leads.

### Kodai-ji★★ 高台寺 *Map II C3.*

*15min walk from Kiyomizu-dera and 10min from Gion. Bus nos. 100, 202, 206, 207, Higashiyama-yasui stop. Open Apr–Nov 9am–4.30pm; Dec–Mar 9am–4pm. ¥500.*

Kita no Mandokoro (Nene to her friends) founded this temple after the death of her husband, Toyotomi Hideyoshi, with the intention of retiring and becoming a Buddhist nun, a practice common among high-ranking noble women. A subtemple of the Kennin-ji, Kodai-ji was famed for its beauty. Having been burned down a number of times, it has unfortunately lost much of its former glory. The few pavilions that remain intact nevertheless are reminders of the original splendor, in particular **Kaisan-do**, the founder's hall, which was decorated by artists of the Kano and Tosa schools.

The mortuary chapel, **Otama-ya**★, dedicated to the *daimyo* Toyotomi Hideyoshi, has some fine Momoyama period *maki-e* (lacquerwork items with incrustations of precious materials, in this case gold). The **garden**★★, created by landscape designer Kobori Enshu (1597–1647), is another of the site's attractions.

On leaving Kodai-ji, make a slight detour by taking one of the streets that climb up the hillside to reach the entrance to **Kyoto's cemetery**. From the top there is an interesting **view**★, with the shapes of the tombs and buildings merging to create an unusual harmony.

*Now return to the Higashiyama Path. A popular route, bordered by flowering cherry trees in spring and red-leaved maples in the Fall, it runs alongside Maruyama Park.*

### Maruyama Park and Yasaka-jinja★ 円山公園・八坂神社 *Map II C3.*

This is east Kyoto's green lung. Covering some 25 acres/10ha, its fresh and fragrant lawns are dotted with rare tree species, including a wonderful **flowering weeping cherry**★ *(shidare-zakura)*. Stands selling postcards and all kinds of wares line the main path leading due west to **Yasaka-jinja**★. The shrine funds the important annual festival, **Gion Matsuri**, which is held in July *(see box above opposite)*. The entrance to the shrine's enclosure is marked by an immense scarlet stone *torii* (gate), facing Shijo-dori.

*547yd/500m NE of the park, you arrive at Chion-in.*

**Chion-in★** 知恩院 *Map II C3.*
*Keihan Line, Shijo station or Sanjo station. Bus nos.12, 46, 100, 201, 202, 203, 206, Chionin-mae stop.*
*Open Mar–Nov 9am–4.30pm; Dec–Feb 9am–4pm. ¥400.*
This temple was built in the 13C next to the mausoleum of Honen, founder of the Jodo school *(see box p 296)*, to which Chion-in belongs. Once through its colossal gate, the **San-mon**★, you reach the **Mieido**★ on the north side of the courtyard, the most important of the temple buildings and dedicated to Honen, as can be seen from the central statue, thought to be a self-portrait. A walkway to the east connects the pavilion to the **Amida-do**, the hall of Amida Buddha, venerated by the Jodo sect. A second walkway to the north leads to the monks' assembly hall, with access to the guest rooms to the east: one large (**Ohojo**) and one small (**Kojoho**). Rebuilt in the 17C, like most of the pavilions on this site, they are decorated with fine **paintings**★ by artists of the Kano School. The **garden** was designed by Kobori Enshu. Honen's mausoleum stands on the hillside, east of the Mieido.

**Shoren-in★** 青蓮院 *Map II C2*
*5min walk N of Chion-in. Subway: Higashiyama (Tozai Line). Bus nos. 5, 46, 57, 100, Jingu-michi stop. Open 9am–4.30pm. ¥500.*
Though burned down in a serious fire in the 19C, Shoren-in still has some fine features: a 700-year-old **camphor tree**, some **paintings** of the celebrated Kano and Tosa Schools, and in particular, the magnificent **gardens**★ laid out by Soami and Kobori Enshu.

*5min walk from Maruyama Park, heading SE.*

## GION DISTRICT★★ 祇園周辺

*Map II C3.*
*Keihan Line, Shijo station. Bus.nos. 12, 46, 100, 201, 202, 203, 206, 207.*
Kyoto's most famous *hanamachi* (literally "flower town") or geisha district has lost some of its lustre. During its golden age in the first half of the 19C, more than 3,000 geisha worked here in some 700 *ochaya (Tea Houses)*. Mizoguchi's film *A Geisha/Gion Festival Music (see box below)* portrayed it with realism.
Though spoiled by mass tourism, the district is still fascinating. **North of Shijo-dori**, the **Shinbashi** district is a warren of romantic cobbled streets bordering the canal. The willow-shaded **Shirakawa-dori**★ has some venerable *ochaya* and *okiya* (geisha houses), where *maiko* (trainee geishas) come and go in their *pokkuri* (high-soled clogs).
South of the main street, **Shijo-dori**, turn into **Hanami-koji**★, which runs at right angles to it. On the corner is Gion's most famous *ochaya*: **Ichiriki**, recognizable by its red panels. If you want to meet a geisha, you need an introduction and must be prepared to spend several hundred thousand yen. On Hanami-koji, the **Gion Kobu Kaburenjo Theater** *(Gion Corner)* provides a cursory glimpse of the geisha's traditional arts.

*The street then descends toward Kennin-ji.*

### A Geisha (Gion Festival Music)

Directed in 1953 by Mizoguchi Kenji, this film tells the story of a girl who in order to escape her drunkard father decides to become a *maiko* in the red-light district of Kyoto. Miyoharu, a celebrated geisha, takes Eiko under her wing and trains her in the sophisticated arts of her trade. All goes well until the day she is required to satisfy the lusts of a government official in order to help a bankrupt industrialist. It's the only thing she has not been taught, but the one thing she will have to face if she wishes to continue in her profession. A quasi-documentary made just after World War II.

**My name is "Foumi-Hanan," maiko, trainee geisha**

*Geiko's exquisite attire*

"I come from Chiiba, my name is now Foumi-Hanan ('Wealth, beauty, intelligence')." Just 13 when she decided to become a *maiko*, Foumi-Hanan was one of the 100 "apprentices of the art of entertainment" now active in Japan's former capital. "When I finished secondary school, I left for Kyoto. I was just 15." Her figure, deportment, devotion to tradition, fierce determination to learn the traditional arts (*shamisen*, *koto*, singing…), and the consent of her parents soon convinced an *okasan*, head of one of Kyoto's geisha houses, to take her on and train her. "I immediately learned the Kyoto dialect," a prerequisite for continuing her training. "It took me two years, but the apprenticeship to become a *geisha* may last up to five, all paid for by my *okasan*. At the end of this first stage, I shall be allowed to paint my bottom lip red. It is not until I become a full geisha or *geiko* (of whom there are 100 or so in Kyoto) that I shall also be able to paint my upper lip. Then I shall be ready to show my *okasan*'s clients all she has taught me."

**Kennin-ji★** 建仁寺 *Map II C3.*
*Open 10am–4.30pm. ¥500.*
This is one of Japan's oldest **Zen temples**, founded by the monk Eisai (1141–1215). The Gate of the Imperial Messenger *(Chokusi-mon)* and the adjacent small **Zen garden** are well worth a visit.

## THE NORTHWEST

*Allow at least 1 day. This itinerary takes in a number of exceptional sites in a fairly limited area.*

**Kamigamo-jinja★** 上賀茂神社
*Map I B1.*
*Bus nos. 4, 46, 67, Kamigamo-jinja-mae stop. Open 8am–4pm. No charge. A special tour in English (30min) includes a Shinto purification ceremony and a visit to the temple treasure hall. Daily 9.30am–4.30pm. ¥500. Reservations suggested. 075-781-0011.*
A UNESCO World Heritage Site, Kyoto's oldest shrine is in a splendid location. Covering 163 acres/66ha, its precincts are overlooked by the sacred mountain of Ko-yama. The complex consists of more than 30 religious buildings, the main one surrounded by two waterways. Dedicated to the god of thunder, who regularly hurls lightning bolts on the Ko-yama, it was originally founded in the 7C. The shrine became the main center of worship in Heian-kyo, *(now Kyoto)*, when Emperor Kanmu (reigned 781–806) made the city his new capital. It was therefore important in the spiritual genesis of Kyoto, as can be seen from the annual **Aoi Matsuri** *(see box p297)*. Passing through the first *torii* (gate), you reach the shrine via a long avenue *(sando)* shaded by cedar trees. Behind the second *torii*, two cones of sand with purifying properties ward off evil spirits. On the top of each are set two pine needles, commemorating the thunderbolt which split a pine tree in two on the day the shrine was consecrated. After crossing the Neigibashi (a second stage of purification), pilgrims arrive at the main building *(honden)*.
Reconstructed for the seventh time in 1863, it is still modeled on the original structure built in the Heian period, a golden age for the arts, and has been a model for shrine architecture ever since *(see box opposite)*.

**Daitoku-ji★★★ 大徳寺**
*Map I B1.*
*Bus nos. 12, 101, 102, 204, 206, Daitokuji-mae stop. Open Mar–Nov 9am–5pm; Dec–Feb 9am–4.30pm. Ryogen-in ¥350, Zuiho-in ¥400, Daisen-in ¥400, Koto-in ¥400. Allow a morning or afternoon.*
This immense enclosure is as quiet as a graveyard. The complex was built by monk Daito Kokushi of the Rinzai sect at the request of Emperor Go-Daigo (1288–1339). Only four of the 22 buildings are open to the public.
If you enter by the south gate of the monastery *(Kitaouji-dori)*, the first building you reach is **Ryogen-in**★ (1502), with a *hojo* (abbot's living quarters) flanked by five wonderful **gardens**. The oldest of them, the **Ryogin-tei**, was designed by Soami.
Adjacent to it is the **Totekiko**, Japan's smallest dry landscape garden. A hundred yards farther on, on your left, **Zuiho-in**★ has fine gardens designed by Shigemori Mirei (1896–1975). His avant-garde concepts are always beautifully attuned to the enigmatic abstraction of these Zen creations. The Garden of the Cross, however, bears witness to the conversion to Christianity of its former owner, the *daimyo* Otomo. Farther north, **Daisen-in**★★ *(the most visited of the temples)* is strikingly beautiful but less peaceful. It was built in 1509 by Kogaku Shoko, who was also an excellent gardener.

## Shinto shrines: two styles, one purpose

The style of **Kamigamo-jinja** with its gently curving lines *(roof projecting beyond the wall)* marks a radical break with the straight lines of the Nara period. It is characteristic of 80 percent of the 80,000 surviving Shinto shrines, the remainder being similar to the **Ise Shrine**, whose double roof is secured by a ridge beam weighted down with 10 ridge billets, with extended barge boards ending in crossed finials at either end. Though constructed differently, both shrines are dismantled and reconstructed every 20 years *(Ise)* and every 21 years *(Kamigamo)*. A vast 15.5 tons of cyprus bark are needed to reconstruct the roof of Kamigano-jinja *(the next rebuild is due in 2015)*. Shrines are rebuilt as part of the belief in the renewal of nature.

The **fusuma**★★ (sliding panel) paintings by Soami, Kano Motonobu, and Kano Yukinobu (15C and 16C) are beautiful. The pavilion is surrounded by three **dry landscape gardens**★★★, reproducing in three dimensions the characteristic black-and-white style of *sumi-e* paintings (ink and wash), framed here

*Dry landscape garden of Daisen-in, Daitoku-ji*

Kinkaku-ji

©travelif/iStockphoto.com

by black-fringed walls. The northeastern garden *(created by Soami or Kogaku)* is divided by a partition wall and opens onto a cascade of white gravel, leading in turn to a sand pathway. The flow of the path is a metaphor for life—as it negotiates the obstacles it encounters, it is transformed into a powerful river: proof once our problems have been overcome, we can look to the horizon *(symbolized here by a boat)* and lose ourselves in the sea of eternity. Returning southwestward *(turn off when you get to the bell of the tower on your right, then take the first alley on your left just after the Zuiho-in)*, where at the end of a magnificent, tree-lined pathway you will discover **Koto-in**★. Founded in 1601 on the orders of Hosokawa Tadaoki (1563–1645), a great warrior who fought under Toyotomi Hideyoshi, this temple is a haven of peace.

## Kinkaku-ji★★★ 金閣寺

*Map I B2.*

*From Daitoku-ji, bus nos.12, 101, 102, 204, 205 (10min); from Kyoto station, bus nos. 101 and 205; from Keihan Line, Sanjo station, bus nos. 12 and 59, Ryonji-mae stop. Open 9am–5pm. ¥400.*

Set amongst luxuriant greenery reflected in the waters of a lake *(the Mirror Pond)*, at first glance the **Golden Pavilion** looks like a mirage. But the crowds approaching in serried ranks, cameras at the ready, soon remind us that this is a World Heritage Site, with all its attendant disadvantages. Yoshimitsu (1358–1408), third shogun of the Ashikaga dynasty, relinquished power in 1397 to become a monk under the name of Rokuon, and went on to build the Golden Pavilion. Its name, Kinkaku-ji, derives from the fact that the two upper stories are clad in gold leaf. This retreat *(the first (ground) floor is reserved for meditation and the upper floor houses Buddhist relics)* stands in the vast Rokuon-ji temple enclosure, modeled on the stroll garden of the Moss Temple.

As **Ashikaga Yoshimitsu** was a great devotee of Zen philosophy, it is not surprising that his pavilion was converted into a temple after his death. For several centuries, the pavilion *(though not all the buildings of the Rokuon-in temple)* miraculously escaped the ravages of Kyoto's civil wars, in particular the devastating fire of the Onin War (1467–77) caused by Ashikaga Yoshimasa's successor *(founder of the Silver Pavilion)*. It did, however, go up in flames in 1950, when a mentally disturbed monk set fire to it, which, six years later, prompted Mishima to write *The Temple of the Golden Pavilion*.

The pavilion was subsequently rebuilt. Its **first level** is in the style of an aristocratic dwelling of the Heian period *(shinden-zukuri)*; the **second** in the style of a samurai residence, with the roof curving slightly upward like a saber; the **third** and **last** is in the *karayo* style of Zen temples. The roof is dominated by a Chinese phoenix, an appropriate symbol since the bird is believed to rise from its own ashes.

**Ryoan-ji★★★** 龍安寺 *Map I B2.* *From Kinkaku-ji (allow 30min to walk about 0.9mi/1.5km) or Sanjo station (Keihan Line) bus no. 59, Ryoanji-mae stop. Open Mar–Nov 8am–5pm; Dec–Feb 8.30am–4.30pm. ¥500. Arrive early or late in the day to avoid the crowds and to see how the shadows transform the view of the garden in the morning and late afternoon.*

Almost everything that can be said about this Zen garden has been said, to the point where the Buddhist temple for which it was created, the **Temple of the Peaceful Dragon**, is almost forgotten. It was founded in 1473 by one of the most powerful feudal lords of the time, Hosokawa Katsumoto, vassal of the Shogun **Ashikaga Yoshimasa**, the founder of the Silver Pavilion. Knowing he had not long to live, he decided to build it and retire there with the monks. He did indeed die in the year the temple was built, too soon to meditate overlooking the Zen garden.

The garden is said to have been designed by the painter/gardener Soami (1472–1525) at the end of the 15C. Rectangular in shape, 80ft/25m from east to west and 33ft/10m from south to north, the **garden**★★★ is boxed in by three clay walls. On a finely raked surface of white sand, 15 rocks *(divided into five groups)* are carefully arranged on a bed of moss, posing a perpetual *koan*, or riddle, for the Zen Rinzai School. What did the artist have in mind? Does the sand suggest the sea? Why can you only see 14 rocks at any one time?

**Ninna-ji★** 仁和寺 *Map I A–B2.* *15min walk SW of Ryoan-ji. Keifuku Kitano Line, Omuro station. Bus nos.8, 10, 26, 59; Omuro Ninnaji stop. Open 9am–4.30pm. ¥500; including museum visit ¥800.*

This temple was originally the Omuro Gosho palace, the Imperial Palace of the Omuro district. Begun by Emperor Koko, it was completed by his son, Emperor Tenno (867–931), who became a monk and retired there. The palace was then converted into a temple for the Buddhist Shingon sect, with monks chosen exclusively from the ranks of the Imperial Family until the time of the Meiji Restoration. The present buildings date from the 17C. One of its emblems is the **Niomon** (the gate of Ni-oh Ungyo and Agyo). Built by Tokugawa Iemitsu, it is one of the three great gates located around Kyoto. Among the temple's notable sights are the **kondo** *(a National Treasure)*, the **five-story pagoda**★ *(108.3ft/33m high)*, and two magnificent **gardens**★: a *kare-sansui (dry landscape)* garden on the south side and a second, featuring a pond and a bridge *(chisenkaiyushiki)*, to the north.

**Myoshin-ji★** 妙心寺 *Map I B2.* *15min walk SE of Ninna-ji. Keifuku Kitano Line, Myoshinji station. Bus nos. 10, 26, Myoshin-ji-mae stop. Open 9am–5pm. ¥500 (separate charge for each temple). Zen courses available in English. www.myoshinji.or.jp/english/index.html.*

This 776-acre/310ha complex is the headquarters of the Myoshin-ji school of the Buddhist Rinzai sect, which has more than 3,000 temples throughout Japan. Founded in 1338 by Kanzan Egen with the support of Emperor Hanazono, it comprises a central temple and 46 secondary temples. From the first, you can view the **Yokushitsu**★, an ingenious wooden structure (1656) used by the monks for bathing, with an area that could be transformed into a steam room. The **Hojo**, the Abbot's quarters, and the **Hatto**, the Dharma hall, house some magnificent *sumi-e* (ink and wash paintings) by Kano Tanyu (1602–74). From a height of 66ft/20m, the intense black eyes of the **dragon**★★ painted on the ceiling of the Hatto seem to follow you around *(the dragon plays a protective role)*. Of the three secondary temples open to the public, the **Keishun-in, Daishin-in,** and **Taizo-in**★★ *(open 9am–5pm; ¥500)*, the latter is the most interesting. It houses a masterpiece known as **Hyonenzu**★★, *Catching a Catfish with a Gourd*, painted by Josetsu. This Japanese painter of Chinese origin (1405–23) is regarded as the founder of the Zen art of *sumi-e* ("the way of black ink"), a monochrome technique used to promote Zen philosophy. The temple has a magnificent **garden**★★ *(often not too busy)* dating from **the** Muromachi period (1336–1573). It was designed by the great master Kano Motonobu (1476–1559) at the very end of his life. And if you have not yet found the answer to Josetsu's riddle about catching a catfish with a gourd, take a close look at the shape of the pond. Rather gourd-like, perhaps?

*Leave this complex by the north gate and return to Ryoan-ji, a pleasant walk of about 20min.*

### Koryu-ji★★ 広隆寺 *Map I A3.*

*Keifuku Arashiyama Line or JR Sagano Line, Uzumasa station. Bus nos. 11, 75, 91, 93. Open 9am–5pm (winter 4.30pm). ¥700.*

Dating from 1165, the **kodo**★ *(lecture hall)* of this temple is one of Kyoto's oldest buildings. It houses a 9C statue of Amida, Buddha of the Pure Land (*see box p296*). At the back of the *kodo*, the **taishido**, dedicated to **Shotoku Taishi** (574–622), displays a statue of this celebrated prince who drew up the *Jushichijo no Kenpo*, or "Constitution in 17 Articles." This charter promised social harmony through the new religion of Buddhism, which the Prince was instrumental in spreading throughout Japan. Shotoku Taishi is said to have given the founder of Koryu-ji the magnificent statue that has been displayed ever since in the **Reiho-kan** (treasure hall).

It depicts the **Miroku Bosatsu**★★★ (*Maitreya* in Sanskrit), the Buddha who is to arise several million years after his master, Amida Buddha, and lead human beings to final enlightenment. Dating from the first half of the 7C and finely carved in red pine, the statue's enigmatic smile under half-closed eyes radiates sweetness and serenity.

## THE SOUTHWEST

*Allow half a day for each site.*

### Katsura Imperial Villa★★★

桂離宮 *Map I A4.*

*20min walk from Katsura station (Hankyu Line), or, from Kyoto station, bus no. 33, Katsurarikyu-mae stop, then 8min walk. Visit by guided tour (1hr) only Mon–Fri 9am–3.30pm. No charge. You need to obtain a permit in advance from the Imperial Household Agency (see p297). Minors not admitted. Passport required.*

West of the station, the garden and Imperial villa of Katsura were commissioned by Prince Toshihito (1579–1629) and his son Prince Toshitada (1619–62). A number of graceful *shoin* (pavilions), completed in 1664, are arranged

*Katsura Imperial Villa*

## USEFUL INFORMATION

**Tourist Offices** – **Kyoto Tourist Information for Foreigners**, *Kyoto Station Bldg, 9F, access from Isetan department store (Map III B2). Open 10am–6pm. Closed 2nd & 4th Tue of the month & Dec 29 – Jan 3. ℘075-344-3300.* On level 9 of Kyoto station, a mine of information about the city. *Maps and brochures in English.* Small foreign-language library. *Ask for the free Kyoto Visitor's Guide, which lists events and places of interest.*

**Kyoto City Tourist Information** – *Kyoto Station, 2F, main hall. Open 8.30am–7pm. ℘075-343-6655.* Another option if **Tourist Information for Foreigners** is closed.

**Kyoto SGG Club** – *Kyoto Station, Shinkansen Hachijo-guchi exit. Open 10am–4pm. ℘075-861-0540. www.eonet.ne.jp/~kyotosgg.* Enjoy the services of an English-speaking guide free of charge *(apart from transport costs and meals, which you are expected to cover).* Book a week in advance with the SGG.

**JTB Sunrise Center** – *Higashi Shiokoji-cho, Shimogyo-ku. ℘075-341-1413. www.jtbgmt.com/sunrisetour.* Bus tours of Kyoto, and also of Nara, Osaka, Ise, Himeji, etc., with an English-speaking guide.

**Johnnie Hillwalker** – *2A1401 Mukaijima New Town, Fushimi. ℘075-622-6803. http://web.kyoto-inet.or.jp/people/h-s-love. Guided walks, in English, every Mon, Wed & Fri, leaving at 10.15am from Kyoto station (5hr).* The program includes temples, shrines, gardens, historic districts, and craft workshops.

**Bank/Foreign Exchange** – ATMs accepting foreign cards are available at post offices, in particular the Central PO *(see below).*

**Citibank** – *Shijo-dori, between Karasuma and Muromachi (Map II B3). International ATMs 24hr.*

Some *conbini* (convenience stores) also have international ATMs, in particular the **7-Eleven** chain.

**Post Offices/Withdrawals** – **Central Post Office**, *main exit from Kyoto station, west side (Map III B2).* In the south wing of the building, a post office counter is open 24hr.

**Nakagyo Post Office**, *corner of Sanjo-dori and Higashi-Notoin (Map II B2). ATMs.*

**Health** – **International Community House**, *2-1 Torri-cho, Awataguchi, Sakyo-ku. ℘075-752-3010.* Will provide details of an English- or French-speaking doctor.

## TRANSPORTATION

**BY PLANE** – **Kansai International Airport (KIX)** – *(Map I B4 off map). ℘0724-55-2500. www.kansai-airport.or.jp.* The airport has a rail link to Kyoto station via the JR Haruka Line *(every 30min, journey time about 1hr20min, ¥2,980 or ¥3,490 with reservation).* The airport is also served by bus no. 8 *(every 40min, journey time 1hr45min, ¥2,300).* The stop is in front of the Avanti department store by the south exit *(Hachijo)* from Kyoto station. Alternatively, minibuses run by **Yasaka** *(℘075-803-4800)* and **MK Taxis** *(℘075-778-5489)* provide a door-to-door service between Kansai International Airport and Kyoto city center *(¥3,000).* Both companies have desks in the arrivals hall. Book your seat 2 days before departure from Kyoto.

**Itami Airport (ITM)** – *(Map I B4 off map). ℘06-6856-6781.* The airport has a bus link with Kyoto station *(every 20min, journey time 55min, ¥12,800).* The stop is in front of the Avanti department store by the south exit *(Hachijo)* from the station. Minibuses run by MK Taxis also provide a door-to-door service between Itami Airport and Kyoto city center *(¥2,300).*

**BY TRAIN** – **Kyoto Station** – *(Map I C4).* The station is the terminus for Shinkansen *(bullet)*, and JR and Kintetsu trains. **Kawaramachi station** *(Map I C3)* serves the Hankyu Line. The Keihan Line operates out of **Sanjo station** *(Map I C3).* The Shinkansen Hikari departs for Tokyo *(hourly,*

*2hr50min, ¥13,220)*, Nagoya *(hourly, 40min, ¥5,340)*, Hiroshima *(twice a day, 2hr10min, ¥10,990)* and Fukuoka *(twice a day, 3hr20min, ¥15,410)*. For Nara, take the JR Line *(every 30min, journey time 40min, ¥690)* or Kintetsu Line *(Express: every 10min, journey time 45min, ¥610)*. For Kobe, JR Line *(every 10min, journey time 50min, ¥1,050)* or Hankyu Line *(every 10min, journey time 60min, ¥600), changing at* Osaka-Juso. For Osaka, JR Line *(every 10min, journey time 30min, ¥540)*, Hankyu Line *(every 10min, journey time 43min, ¥390)* or Keihan Line *(every 5min, journey time 49min, ¥400)*. For Himeji, JR Line *(every 10min, journey time 1hr30min, ¥2,210)*. For Ise, Kintetsu Line *(hourly, 2hr, ¥5,320)*.

**BY BUS** – **From Kyoto station** *terminus (north side, Map I C4)* JR Dream night bus leaves at 10pm and 11pm for Tokyo station, JR New Dream bus at 10.30pm and 11.30pm for Shinjuku *(Tokyo) (8hr, ¥8,180 S or ¥14,480 R in both cases)*. JR Seishun Dream *(9.10pm, for Tokyo station)* and JR Seishun New Dream buses *(9.10pm, for Shinjuku)* cost only ¥5,000 *(¥9,500 R)*, but are less comfortable. For Fukuoka, the Keihan night bus leaves Kyoto station *(south side, in front of the Avanti department store)* at 10pm *(10hr, ¥10,500)*.

## GETTING AROUND KYOTO

**BY SUBWAY** – The network consists of two lines: Karasuma Line (north–south) and Tozai Line (east–west), which intersect at Karasuma-Oike station. Convenient for moving quickly around the city center, but not very useful for visiting the more out-of-the-way temples. Trains run 5.30am–11.30pm. *Tickets cost ¥210–¥340, depending on distance*.

**BY TRAIN** – Several lines serve city destinations. The Hankyu Line runs southwest from Kawaramachi-Shijo station to Katsura Villa, and northwest into the Arashiyama district. Arashiyama is also served by the Keifuku Line, from Shijo-Omiya station, and by the JR Sagano Line, from Kyoto station. The northwest of Kyoto is served by the Eizan Line. *To find your way around the labyrinth of Kyoto station, ask for a detailed plan.*

**BY BUS** – A dense network of bus routes enables you to get to almost all the temples and places of interest. *Buses run 7am–9pm, and some until 11pm*. The same fare *(¥220)* applies for any destination within the "white" zone, which covers almost the whole of Kyoto. A **bus route map**, with explanatory notes, can be obtained from Kyoto Tourist Information and from the information office at the main bus terminal, opposite the entrance to Kyoto station.

Buses do not arrive at regular intervals and are sometimes stuck for hours in traffic. Make longer trips by subway or train, then take a bus for the final leg of the journey.

**Passes** – A **City Bus All-day Card** *(¥500)* allows you unlimited bus travel for 1 day. A **Traffica Kyoto Card** *(¥3,000)* is valid for buses

around the lake, along with a platform from which to watch the moon rise. Raised on delicate wooden piles, they are slightly staggered to form a "flying geese" configuration. Their minimalist façades combine dark-wood with the white paper of sliding doors and windows, forming geometrical shapes. The stroll garden (*see p103*) (and some of the pavilions) are attributed to architect and gardener Kobori Enshu.

### Saiho-ji (Moss Temple)★★★

西芳寺 (苔寺) *Map I A4.*

*From Katsura, Matsuo station (Hankyu Line), from Kyoto Station, bus no. 28, Matsuotaisha-mae stop, then 15 min walk W. Visit by appointment only, applications to be made in writing (in English) at least 7 days beforehand to the Saiho-ji Temple, 56 Kamigaya-cho, Matsuo, Nishikyo-ku, Kyoto 625-8286. State the name and address of*

and subway trains, entitling you to travel amounting to ¥3,300. The cards can be purchased at bus and subway station ticket offices. A **Kyoto Sightseeing Card** *(¥1,200 for 1 day or ¥2,000 for 2 days)* is valid for buses and subway trains, and also entitles you to reductions for some temples and museums. A **Kansai Thru Pass** allows you unlimited travel on all subway lines, trains *(apart from the JR network)*, and regional buses (Kyoto, Osaka, Kobe, Himeji, Nara, and Koya-san) for 2 days *(¥3,800)* or 3 days *(¥5,000)*, as well as reductions at many places of interest. It can be purchased at the Kyoto Station Bus Information Center and at Kansai International Airport *(http://www.surutto.com/index.cgi)*.
A **JR Kansai Pass** is valid for between 1 day *(¥2,000)* and 4 days *(¥6,000)* on the JR Kansai network, excluding Shinkansens *(bullet trains)*.
A **JR Sanyo Pass** allows you to travel for 4 days *(¥20,000)* or 8 days *(¥30,000)* on the JR Kansai network and also on Shinkansens *(apart from the Nozomi)* between Kyoto and Fukuoka (Hakata). These two passes can be purchased at JR stations on presentation of your passport.
**BY TAXI** – Taxis will carry up to 4 people and there are usually plenty of them. The fare is around ¥660 for the first 1.2mi/2km, then ¥100 every 0.3mi/500m. If you plan to spend all day visiting temples, involving a lot of walking, they are handy for the short distances between the temple complexes.
**Doi Taxi** *(℘090-9596-5546; www3.ocn.ne.jp/~doitaxi)* has an English-speaking driver. Similar service from Yasaka Taxi *(℘075-842-1212)*.
**BY BICYCLE** – **The most practical way to get around the city is by bicycle.** Apart from the steep hills to the east, the terrain is flat, sloping slightly from north to south, and you can ride unimpeded on the wide pavements of the city's avenues. Also make the most of the fine cyclepath that runs north–south along Kamo River.
**Bicycle Rental** – **Kyoto Cycling Tour Project**, *109yd/100m W of the Central Post Office, near the APA building. From ¥1,000 per day. ℘075-354-3636. www.kctp.net.* There are several other rental outlets around town. The association also organizes some enjoyable guided bicycle tours *(3–7hr)*, which show Kyoto off the beaten track. **Budget Inn**, *295 Aburanokoji-cho, Aburanokoji, Shichijo-sagaru, Shimogyo-ku, .3mi/500m NW of Kyoto station. Open 8am–9.30pm. ℘075- 344-1510. www.budgetinnjp.com. This hotel rents out bicycles for ¥800 per day.* **Bol.cycle Shop**, *685 Sakaimachi, Anekohji-sagaru, Nakagyo-ku, near Yoshikawa restaurant. ℘075- 221-5333. One central address, bicycle rental by the hour (¥105 per hour).*
If you are staying more than a week in Kyoto, you might even consider buying a second-hand bike. *¥3,000 for basic models, ¥5,000–7,000 for the more sophisticated.*

---

*each visitor (minors not admitted), the date you would like to visit (suggest alternatives), and include a stamped addressed envelope with your address in Japan for the reply. ¥3,000. Guided tour (2hr).*
The **Moss Garden** is enchanting, especially after the rains of May and June. Designed in 1339 by Buddhist monk Muso Soseki (1275–1351) on the site of a monastery dedicated to Amida Buddha (which had itself replaced an older villa belonging to Prince Shotoko), the Moss Temple *(better known as Koke-dera)* is laid out on two levels.
The **lower garden**, showing Heian influence, is arranged around a lake; the **upper garden**, clinging to the hillside, mimics the bed of a rocky cascade. This was the first Zen garden and has since influenced many others, such as the gardens of the Golden and Silver

*Moss Garden, Saiho-ji*

Pavilions. Interestingly, the 120 varieties of moss for which it is now famous did not grow here until the Meiji period, when the garden fell into neglect.

## THE SOUTHEAST

*At least a full day, depending on your pace.*

### Tofuku-ji★★ 東福寺 *Map III C4.*

*Keihan Line or JR Nara Line, Tofukuji station, then 10min walk SE. Open 9am–4pm. ¥400 (supplement for Hojo ¥400). www.tofukuji.jp.*

Headquarters of the Rinzai school of Zen Buddhism, this temple was built in 1236 by the monk Enni under the guidance of Kujo Michiie (1193–1252), *sessho* (regent) for Emperor Chukyo (1221). This great statesman of the Kamakura period wanted to build a vast edifice modeled on the Todai-ji and Kofuku-ji temples in Nara—Tofuku-ji is a combination of the two names. Although destroyed by fire on numerous occasions—in the Meiji period, it even lost its Buddha hall *(butsu-den)*—this temple has many interesting features: the **Tsuten-kyo**★★, a bridge set in a magnificent forest of maples; the **San-mon**★★, a gate with a majestic half-hip roof, decorated with sculptures of the Buddha and 16 *arhats* (sages) carved by Teicho on the first floor. Listed as a National Treasure, this is the oldest-surviving Zen gate in Japan (13C). Within the enclosure, the meditation room *(zendo)*, toilets *(tosu)*, and bathroom *(yokushitsu)* date from the Muromachi period (14C). The **Hojo**★ (abbot's quarters) is nevertheless the highlight, not on account of its age *(it was reconstructed in 1890)*, but because of the way it is laid out: unusually, it opens on every side onto a magnificent **garden**★★, creating some interesting juxtapositions.

The western garden, for instance, consists of splendid mosses and is counter-balanced on the south side by a dry landscape garden with seven cylindrical stones representing the constellation of the Great Bear. Blending the Zen simplicity of the Kamakura period with the geometrical abstraction of modern art, it was designed in 1945 by **Shigemori Mirei** (1896–1975), a leading exponent of the movement to revitalize the art of the Japanese garden.

### Fushimi-Inari Taisha★★

伏見稲荷大社 *Map I C4 off map.*

*Keihan Line or JR Nara Line, Fushimi Inari or Inari station, then 5min walk E. Open all year round. No charge. Be sure to wear good shoes; site offers many food options.*

The central shrine is one of over 30,000 Inari shrines in Japan, and one of the most unusual places of worship in the whole of the country. A path wends its way for approximately 2mi/4km up the hillside to the shrine, passing through hundreds of vermilion **torii**★★ (gates). Ukanomitama no Mikoto (better known as Inari) is the tutelary goddess of rice, Japan's staple cereal. It is therefore perhaps easy to understand why, ever since the 8C, the Japanese have been seeking Inari's favor by erecting *torii* branded with their names. Since rice attracts rodents, it is also logical that at intervals along the tunnel created by the gates, there are small stone statues of foxes, predators of the rodents, including one with the key to a rice granary in its jaws, a metaphor for its protective role. Nowadays, peasant farmers imploring the goddess for bumper crops have been superseded by those seeking greater wealth.

**Daigo-ji★★** 醍醐寺 *Map I D4, off map.*
*Subway: Daigo (Tozai Line), then 10min walk E. Open 9am–5pm. ¥600.*
This famous temple of the Shingon school is now a UNESCO World Heritage Site. At the top of Mount Kasatori, the Buddhist monk Shobo, better known by his posthumous name of Rigen Daishi (832–909), discovered a spring with life-giving powers. He built a monastery dedicated to the goddess Kannon (874), which expanded over several levels until the 13C. Seriously damaged in the civil wars, the complex was rebuilt at the end of the 16C on the orders of Toyotomi Hideyoshi (1536–98).
Access to the lower temple, or **Shimo Daigo,** is via the Kamahura period (13–14C) **Nio-mon**★. A number of buildings occupy the enclosure: the main hall *(kondo)*, the lecture hall *(kodo),* and the treasure hall. But it is the **five-story pagoda**★ that really catches the eye. Intended for Emperor Daigo (897–930), but not completed until 951, it is one of the oldest in Japan. Inside *(generally closed to the public)*, its precious mandalas *(designs of concentric circles)* painted on wood are indicative of the earliest art forms of tantric Buddhism. It is a 45-minute walk from the Nio-mon along the path to the upper temple, or **Kami Daigo**, an architectural masterpiece from the Momoyama period, rebuilt in 1606 on the orders of Toyotomi Hideyoshi. There is also opportunity to drink the famous "life-giving" waters. On the way back down to the lower temple, you will see *(immediately opposite the Nyo gate)* the former residence of the principal of Daigo-ji: the **Sanpo-in**★, which literally means "House of Three Treasures" (Buddha, Dharma, Sangha). Its listed buildings open onto a magnificent **tea garden**★★ in the style of the lavish Momoyama era.
The garden combines a tea pavilion, a *kare-sansui* (dry landscape) garden, and *Sakazukushi (moss on a background of white sand)*. It was designed by master gardener Takeda Baishoken, again on the orders of Toyotomi Hideyoshi, who visited the temple to admire the blossoming cherry trees and decided to settle there.
In the spring of 1598, he even organized a cherry-blossom viewing party *(hanami)* for more than 900 guests. Toyotomi Hideyoshi died that same year, and the event is now commemorated in the annual Hideyoshi Hanami Parade on the second Sunday in April *(information from the Tourist Office)*.

## EXCURSIONS

**ARASHIYAMA★** 嵐山 *Map I A3.*
*Allow a morning or afternoon.*
*JR Sagano, Keifuku Line, or Hankyu Line to Arashiyama station. Bus nos.11, 28, 93.*
Popular with tourists, the suburb of Arashiyama is in a beautiful natural setting, although spoilt by the inevitable souvenir shops. **Togetsu-kyo**, literally "the bridge that spans the moon," now has to make do with the Katsura River and is where tourists tend to congregate. Bicycles, rickshaws, and boats are all options to hand for exploring its busy surroundings.

**Tenryu-ji★** 天竜寺 *Map I A3.*
*328yd/300m N of Togetsu Bridge.*
*Open 8.30am–5pm. ¥500.*
Dating from the 14C, the "Temple of the Celestial Dragon," belonging to the Rinzai sect of Zen Buddhism, was almost entirely rebuilt in the Meiji period. The **garden**★, one of the oldest in Japan, was designed by Muso Soseki (1275–1351).
At the end of the garden, through a beautiful forest of bamboo, is the **Okori Sancho** *(open 9am–5pm; ¥1,000)*, the private villa of **Okochi Denjiro**, a 1930s star of samurai films. There is a fine **view**★ of the Kyoto valley.

**Daikaku-ji★** 大覚寺 *Map I A2.*
*From Tenryu-ji, bus no. 28; from Shijo-dori, bus no. 91. Open 9am–4.30pm. ¥500.*
Originally the country retreat of the Emperor Saga, this building was converted into a temple of the Shingon school in 876. The Emperor was a great friend of the monk Kukai, known posthumously as Kobo Daishi, who had introduced from China the "True Word" school of Buddhism, Shingon-shu. The main hall *(shinden)* has some wonderful *fusuma* (sliding panel) **paintings★** by the Kano School.

**Boat Trip on the River Hozu★** 保津川下り *Map I A2 off map.*
*Allow 1hr20min. JR Sagano Line to Kameoka station (the station after Arashiyama). On leaving the station, turn left and head toward Hozugawakudari (10min walk to the pier). The boats take you to a point near Togetsu Bridge and depart 9am–5.30pm every hour. ¥3,900.*
The more adventurous can run the rapids of the Hozu River in a flat-bottomed boat: spectacular, while quite safe in the hands of skilled oarsmen.

## HIEI-ZAN★ 比叡山
*Allow a morning or afternoon.*
*From Sanjo station (Keihan Line), bus nos. 16 and 17; from Kyoto station, bus nos. 18 and 19 to Ohara bus terminal (about 45min).*
Dispatched to China for a year by Emperor Kanmu to seek out new doctrines, the monk Saicho (767–822), returned in 805 with the teachings of the Tendai school. The monastic complex that he founded at Enryaku-ji on Mount Hiei to the northeast of Kyoto became the headquarters of the Tendai sect.

**Ohara★ and Sanzen-in★**
大原・三千院 *Map I D1 off map.*
*From Ohara station, walk E up the path lined with stands selling pickles (the local specialty) following the river (10min). Open 8am–4.30pm. ¥600.*
The main attraction in this small country town, apart from its local specialty of "Ice Kyuri," Japanese cucumbers delicately marinated in "kelp water," is the Sanzen-in, founded by the monk, Saicho. The main hall of the temple houses a valuable statue of Amida Buddha meditating. Behind it is a lovely **garden★** planted with maples and cedars, and full of small *jizo* (bodhisattva) statues. Jizo Bosatsu, who vowed to help alleviate the suffering of all creatures in hell is much-loved throughout Japan.

**Hosen-in★** 宝泉院
*Map I D1 off map.*
*On leaving Sanzen-in, turn right. The Hozen-in temple is just after Shoren-in. Open 9am–5pm. ¥800, including tea.*
A wonderful 700-year-old **pine tree★** graces the garden of this little-visited temple. Inside, the ceiling still bears traces of the blood shed by the 370 samurai, who committed *seppuku* (ritual suicide) after the Battle of Sekigahara (1600), in which General Tokugawa Ieyasu defeated Hideyoshi's son (*see p120*). The ceiling, is in fact, made from the floor of the mighty castle his father, Toyotomi Hideyoshi (1536–98), had built on Fushimi Hill. The castle was destroyed in 1622 and the hill transformed into a peach orchard *(momoyama).*

**Enryaku-ji★** 延暦寺
*Map I D1 – off map.*
*From Ohara, bus nos. 17 and 18 to Yase station (terminus of the Eizan Railway line), from where a cable car (every 30min, journey time 20min, ¥840) takes you to the summit of Hiei-zan. The temple is then a 20min walk. Return via direct bus (every hour, journey time 1hr, ¥800) from the temple to Sanjo station (Keihan Line) and Kyoto station. Open 8.30am–4.30pm. ¥550.*
Little now remains of the large monastic complex built on Mount Hiei by **Saicho** (767–822), one of the patriarchs of the Buddhist Tendai school. Enryaku-ji was the base from which Saicho taught the doctrine ot the Tendai school.
Having become increasingly powerful over the centuries at the expense of its rivals, the complex was finally destroyed

### The Children's Kabuki Festival of Nagahama

For close to 250 years, every year in mid-April magnificently decorated floats parade in Nagaham's streets with a miniature Kabuki troupe: young boy actors aged 5 to 12.

Two and a half centuries ago kabuki existed for children here, but they had no stagehence the idea of floats. Supported by rich families rivaling each other in the pomp and wealth they could display in this manner, the Nagahama festival is today one of Japan's three greatest float parades, as well as one of the only kabuki performances given by children.

The boys undergo two relentless months of training in this traditional art to strive to meet the expectations of both families and instructors. Then, on April 15 and 16, clothed in magnificent costumes and wearing heavy wigs, the boys ceaselessly perform their play over and over on their "traveling art musuem", before an audience of thousands.

*From Kyoto, take the Shinkansen Hikari then Kokuriku Line to Nagahama, via Malbara (45 min, ¥3,470), or from Hikone station take the Tokaido Line to Malbara station, then the Hokuriko Line to Nagahama (20 min, ¥230). Nagahama festival: April 15–16. Museum where floats are warehoused: 9am–5pm. ¥600*

in the 16C by General Oda Nobunaga (1534–82), who captured Kyoto and brought the dominance of the Ashikaga clan to an end. Of the former complex of more than 3,000 pavilions and temples, three principal groups of buildings now remain: the **To-to** to the east, the **Sai-to** to the west, and the **Yokawa** to the north *(of little interest)*. Of the first group, however, don't miss the statues in the **Kokuho-den**★ and the great hall of **Konponchu-do**★, the main building. Of the second group, it is worth seeing the **Shaka-do**★, rebuilt by Hideyoshi, and the **Hokke-do**, for its praying monks.

## UJI★ 宇治

*Allow 3hr, including journey time. 2.5mi/4km S of Kyoto. JR Nara Line to Uji station (30min, ¥230).*

Famous for its green tea, this region also boasts the magnificent Byodo-in, which features on all ¥10 coins.

### Byodo-in★★ 平等院

*Leave the station on the S side, cross the main street, then take the next street on the left. Just before you reach the bridge, turn right into the narrow alley of shops parallel to the river and continue straight on to the temple. Open 8.30am–5pm. ¥600. Visit the Phoenix Hall by guided tour every 20min 9.10am–4.10pm. ¥300.*

Exemplifying the splendor of the Heian period, this former country residence was built by the regent (*sessho*) Fujiwara no Michinaga (966–1028) (*see box p285*), who retired here just before the year 1000 to practice meditation. On his death, his son Yorimichi converted it into a temple dedicated to the Amida Buddha (1052). The central pavilion with its two open wings, represents a bird in flight.

The central hall, or **Ho-do**★★ *(Phoenix Hall)*, houses a National Treasure: a great statue of the **Amida Buddha**★★★ dating from the 11C and ttributed to the monk **Jocho** (*see box p295*).

On the walls are nine color paintings, also of the Amida Buddha descending from the Pure Land *(Western Paradise)* over which he presided, as he had undertaken to receive all the dying who wished to enter his Pure Land, a key concept during the Heian period (794–1185).

The fact that there are nine paintings is an allusion to the number of levels of salvation found in the Pure Land. Created in 2000 by Akira Kuryu, the **museum**★ houses a fine collection of works of art.

In 1994, the temple was added to the UNESCO list of World Heritage Sites.

**Taiho-an★** 市営茶室・対鳳庵

*On leaving Byodo-in, turn right and follow the river for 328yd/300m. Tickets can be purchased at the Tourist Information Center. Open 10am–4pm. ¥500.*

This charming wooden pavilion is an authentic tea house, and was built to teach people the elaborate code of rules governing the Tea Ceremony. The main room is called the *Honseki*; other rooms are the *hiroma-chaseki* and *ritsurei-seki*.

## HIKONE CASTLE★ 彦根城

*Allow a morning or afternoon, including the journey. About 25mi/40km NW of Kyoto. JR Biwako Line to Hikone station (every 20min, journey time 50min, ¥1,100). From the station, about 15min walk up the main street. Open 8.30am–5pm. Castle ¥500, combined ticket including museum ¥900.*

Dominating the east bank of **Lake Biwa** and built between 1603 and 1622 by the warlord Ii Naosuke, Hikone Castle is one of the oldest feudal castles dating from the Edo period. Its keep, moat, and ramparts are well-preserved.

The castle houses a small museum *(collections of armor and Noh theater costumes)*. From the terrace of the **Tenshu**★, which caps the three stories of the keep, there is an uninterrupted **view** over the lake. On the northeast side of the castle, follow the path that is marked out to the **Genkyu-en**★, a beautiful landscaped garden of Chinese inspiration where you can drink Uji green tea.

## HARIE 針江

*Map B2 p283.*

*About 37mi/60km northwest of Kyoto. From Hikone, JR Tokaidohon Line then JR Biwako Line to Shin-Asahi station via Omi-Shiotsu (1h 15 min, ¥1,110). From NIshi Otsu or Heizen-Sakamoto station, take Kosei Line to Shin-Asahi station (30 min, ¥740). From Shin-Asahi station, 15 min walk.*

Not caring for modern water systems, this little village has developed a unique lifestyle: each home has its own spring sheltered in its own shed, or *kabata*, used as both well and kitchen. For ¥1,000, you get a pass to wander around the village and enter the homes indicated by signs to take a look at the *kabata*. *Don't miss the little Shinto shrine in the middle of the village, of course devoted to a water divinity.*

## MIHO MUSEUM★★★ ミホミュージアム

*Allow a morning or afternoon, including journey time. About 12.4mi/20km SE of Kyoto. JR Biwako Line to Ishiyama station (15min, ¥230), then Teisan bus no.150 to the museum (every hour, 9.30am–1.30pm out, 11am–5pm return, journey time 50 min, ¥800). Open Tue –Sun 10am–5pm. Closed Jun 15–Jul 15 & Dec 15–Mar 15. ¥1,000. Before making the trip, check opening dates. 078-82-3411. www.miho.or.jp.*

In complete harmony with the mountainous landscape south of Lake Biwa, this museum, designed by architect Ieoh Ming Pei *(designer of the Louvre Pyramid in Paris)*, takes the visitor by surprise in more ways than one.

On arrival, a small electric vehicle driven by an elegantly dressed hostess takes you through a tunnel to re-emerge after a few hundred yards in front of a building set into the mountainside. Inside, the exhibits *(from the ancient civilizations of Japan, China, the Middle East, and the Greco-Roman world)* are displayed with an elegant simplicity. They include a **Buddhist statue from the Gandhara**★★★ *(modern-day northern Pakistan and eastern Afghanistan)* carved shortly after the reign of King Kanishka I (2C), and a **mosaic of Dionysus**★★ discovering Ariadne on Naxos *(stone tesserae, of 3C or 4C Romano-Syrian origin)*.

The **north wing** features Japanese arts and hosts special exhibitions. It also houses the collection of Koyama Mihoko, founder of the Shinji Shumeikai sect, which believes that the contemplation of art and living in harmony with nature gives meaning and enjoyment to life; the sect now has 300,000 devotees worldwide.

# ADDRESSES

## STAY

*In the high season (Apr–May, mid-Aug, and New Year) some hotels increase their prices by 10–30 percent.*

### AROUND THE STATION

**K's House ケイズハウス京都**
*418 Naya-cho, Dotemachi-dori, Shichijo-agaru (Map III B1). 075-342-2444. www.kshouse.jp. 23 rooms.* Located in a neat yellow house, this hostel with English-speaking staff is a model of cleanliness and friendliness. The dormitories *(¥2,300/person)* and rooms are furnished with wooden beds and air-conditioning. Pleasant lounge, well-equipped kitchen, patio, lockers, Internet access *(¥100/20 min),* and bicycle rental *(¥700 per day).*

**Tour Club ツアークラブ**
*362 Momiji-cho, Shimogyo-ku (Map III A1). 075-353-6968. www.kyotojp.com. 16 rooms and dormitories.* With nearby Japanese garden and tatami lounge, the dormitories *(¥2,450/person, showers upstairs)* and bedrooms (Japanese or Western) with bathrooms *(¥6,990 for double)* are squeaky clean. Internet, bicycle rental, laundry, etc.

**Kyoto Dai-ni Tower Hotel 京都タワーホテル**
*Higashinotoin-dori Shichijo-sagaru, Shimogyo-ku (Map III B2). 075-361-3261. www.kyoto-tower.co.jp. 306 rooms. ¥15,000. ¥1,732.* Only a short walk from the station, ideally placed for getting about by bus, this hotel gets a good write-up from all foreigners. Quality service: the owner is always available to help.

**Ryokan Ohanabo お花坊**
*Higashi Honganji-mae, Shimogyo-ku (Map III B1). 075-371-3688. 12 rooms.* Opposite the Higashi Hongan-ji temple, this traditional wood-built ryokan is clean and pleasant. It has spacious, attractive bedrooms, with or without bathrooms. A vegetarian evening meal or *kaiseki* can be served on request.

**Ryokan Shimizu 京の宿しみず**
*644 Kagiya-cho, Shichijo-dori, Wakamiya-agaru (Map III A1). 075-371-5538. www5.ocn.ne.jp/~yado432. 12 rooms. ¥1,050.* A modern, well-cared-for ryokan in a quiet street. The owners are attentive to your needs and speak English. Cedarwood *o-furo*. Internet, bicycle rental.

**Kikokuso Inn 枳殻荘**
*Kawaramachi, Shichijo agaru, Hitosujime nishiiru (Map III B1). 075-371-7781. www.kikokuso.com. 7 rooms.* Intimate and adorable old-style ryokan, in a house more than a century old. The rooms (only one with a bathroom) are laid out along a wooden veranda overlooking a delightful courtyard garden. There is a picturesque *o-furo* in a rock garden setting. Internet.

**Hyatt Regency Kyoto ハイアット・リージェンシー京都**
*644-2 Sanjusangendo-mawari, Higashiyama-ku (Map III C2). 075-541-1234. www.hyattregencykyoto.com. 189 rooms.* Kyoto's most luxurious Western-style hotel. Restful, sophisticated decor. The Italian and Japanese restaurants are first-class. Be sure to have a drink at the **Touzan bar**, planned by the great interior designer Takashi Sugimoto. *In winter, the fourth night's stay is free.*

### CITY CENTER

**The Palace Side ザ・パレスサイド**
*Karasuma-dori, Shimodachiuri agaru, Kamigyo-ku (Map II B1). 075-415-8887. www.palacesidehotel.co.jp. 120 rooms. ¥1,100.* Sited opposite the Imperial Palace, this hotel offers unbeatable prices. The bedrooms are small, but clean and well equipped, particularly those with a mini-kitchen. *Internet free of charge, coin laundry, and restaurant.*

**Hirota Guesthouse 広田ゲストハウス**
*665 Seimei-cho, Tominokoji-nishi, Nijo-dori, Nakagyo-ku (Map II B2). 075-221-2474. 6 rooms.* An unexpected oasis of calm. At the bottom of the garden, the "cottage" (a former shed) comprises 2 Japanese-style rooms, a bathroom, and kitchen. Ideal for a family or group of friends. The house has 5 bedrooms (*tatami* floors), which share a bathroom. The female owner, a retired guide and interpreter, speaks perfect English. *Bicycle rental.*

**Inn Kawashima 川嶋旅館**
*207-2 Ayano-koji, Yanaginobanba-nishiiru, Shimogyo-ku (Map II B3). 075-351-2089. www5.ocn.ne.jp/~innkawa. 7 rooms. ¥900.* Located in a *machiya* (wooden house) typical of old Kyoto, and in a quiet street, this charming ryokan has rooms arranged around a well-maintained courtyard garden. The owner speaks English and a little French. *The only drawback is that everyone shares just 1 bathroom.*

**Nishiyama ホテル西山**
*Gokoumachi-dori, Nijyo-sagaru, Nakagyo-ku, near Kyoto City Hall (Map II B2). 075-222-1166. www.kyoto-nishiyama.com. 29 Japanese and 3 Western rooms. ¥1,500.* Through the picture windows of this contemporary ryokan, you overlook

a fine inner garden with a **waterfall**. The waterfall can also be viewed from the relaxing *o-furo* in the basement. The rooms are large, attractive, and well laid out, but could do with some redecoration and larger bathrooms.

**Ryokan Hiiragiya 柊屋旅館** *Nakahakusancho, Fuyacho-dori, Anekoji-agaru (Map II B2). ☎075-221-1136. www.hiiragiya.co.jp. 28 rooms. lodging with half-board.* The *nec plus ultra* of Kyoto ryokans. Magnificent, with woodwork polished to a high gloss over the centuries. The place has received many illustrious guests, samurai, politicians, and artists, such as **Kawabata**, a habitué of room no. 16, where he wrote his novels. Sliding panels opening onto heavenly gardens, ancient artifacts worthy of a museum, divine *kaiseki* cuisine served in your room, comfortable futons: everything here is geared toward the repose of the soul. **2011 Michelin Guide Kyoto Osaka Kobe Selection.**

**Ryokan Kinmata 宿・近又** *407 Gokomachi-dori, Shijo-agaru (Map II B3). ☎075-221-1039. www.kinmata.com. 7 rooms. ¥36,750-52,500 /person. lodging with half-board.* Built in 1801, this distinguished ryokan, which has been in the same family for seven generations, still has its superb, original wooden decor and antique furniture. The owners provide sophisticated, delicious-tasting *kaiseki* cuisine. The bedrooms *(tatami floors)* overlooking two courtyard gardens decorated with stone lanterns do not have their own bathrooms, but hot baths can be enjoyed in the cedarwood *o-furo*.

### GION AND KIYOMIZU-DERA

**Hanakiya Inn 花喜屋** *583-101 Higashi-Rokucho-me, Higashiyama-ku, Gojobashi (Map III D1). ☎075-551-1397. www.hanakiya.jp. 3 rooms.* Hidden away in a lane near the Kiyomizu-dera temple, this small family-run B&B comprises 3 Japanese-style rooms opening onto a little courtyard. Guests share a bathroom and lounge with books, coffee, and a computer available.

**Ryokan Sawai 澤食** *4-320 Miyagawasuji, Higashiyama-ku (Map II B3). ☎075-561-2179. www.kyoto-sawai.jp. 7 rooms. ¥700.* In the southern part of Gion, this ryokan is run by a retired university professor of great charm and occupies one of the oldest *ochaya* in the district. A simple, family guesthouse with oddly shaped rooms, creaking floors, and dividing walls affording little privacy *(1 shared bathroom)*. The table d'hôte is excellent.

**Ryoka Yuzuya 柚子屋旅館** *545 Yasaka-jinja, Minami-donari, Gion (Map II C3). ☎075-533-6369. 9 rooms. ¥66,000-72,000. lodging with half-board.* Hugging the slope of a hill in the Yasaka shrine enclosure, this sublime ryokan is one of Kyoto's rarest pearls. Arranged around a tree-shaded patio, the elegant rooms feature antique furniture and, in some cases, cedarwood bathrooms. ***Compared with other luxury ryokan, the prices are affordable. English spoken.***

### NORTH EAST KYOTO

**Ryokan Yachiyo 旅館八千代** *Nanzen-ji, Sakyo-ku (Map II D2). ☎075-771-4148. www.ryokan-yachiyo.com. 20 rooms.* First-class ryokan near the entrance to the Nanzen-ji. The restaurant and its terrace overlook a delightful garden of mosses and azaleas, with a pool in which carp laze. The rooms *(the best are in the older building)* are spacious and beautiful. Guests are pampered by hostesses in kimonos *(nakai-san)*.

### OTSU

**Biwako Hotel 琵琶湖ホテル** *2-40 Hama-machi. ☎077-524-7111.* This hotel on the shores of Lake Biwa has an indoor *onsen* on the fourth floor, and another on the terrace with a beautiful **view** of the lake, especially at night. The restaurant's immense bay windows mean you enjoy a meal overlooking the water.

### MAKINO (BETWEEN HIKONE AND HARIE)

**Prince Hotel Okubiwako Makino 奥琵琶湖マキノプリンスホテル** *Takagihama, Makino, 1 min by foot from Makino JR station. ☎074-028-1111. www.princehotels.co.JP/makino.* This single-level hotel has entirely wood rooms with a chalet feel, offering **views** of the lake. *Private pool and beach.*

## EAT

### CITY CENTER

**Bio-Tei びお亭** *2F corner of Sanjo-dori and Higashi-Notoin (Map II B2). ☎075-255-0086.* Open *11.30am–2pm and 5pm–8.30pm. Closed Mon, Thu evening, Sat noon & Sun and holidaysformulas at ¥840-¥1,260.* Friendly, family bistro consisting of a counter and a few wooden tables. Serves tasty and inexpensive organic (but not vegetarian) dishes: tofu and vegetable salads, chicken curry, soya croquettes, and raw fish sashimi, as well as yogurts, ice creams, and homemade cakes.

**Honke Owariya 本家尾張屋**
*Kurumayacho-dori, Nijo sagaru (Map II B2). ✆075-231-3446. Open 9am–7pm.* Kyoto's oldest noodle restaurant, dating back to 1645; official purveyor to the Imperial Family. Specialties include ***hourai soba*** (noodles with mushrooms, eggs, shrimp, and white radishes) and ***sobazushi*** (noodle sushi). ***Menu in English.***

**Misoka-an Kawamichiya 晦庵・河道屋本店**
*295 Shimohakusan-cho, Fuyacho-dori, Sanjo-agaru, Nakagyo-ku (Map II B2). ✆075-221-2525. Open 11am–8pm.* A charming 300-year-old ***soba*** (buckwheat noodle) restaurant. Their specialty is ***hokoro for two people***, a hotpot of noodles, pieces of chicken, tofu, mushrooms, and vegetables. Also try the delicious ***oyako-nanban***; hot noodles with chicken, egg, and onions. ***Menu in English.***

**Ganko がんこ京都三条本店**
*Sanjo-dori, Kawaramachi higashiiru (Map II B2). ✆075-255-1128. Open 11.30am–11pm.* You can try most local specialties at more than reasonable prices in this large, very lively restaurant.

**Kerala ケララ**
*Kawaramachi, Sanjo-agaru (2nd floor) (Map II B2). ✆075-251-0141. Open 11.30am–9pm.* Excellent Indian food, especially dishes typical of the southern state for which the restaurant is named: shrimp curry, chicken, and vegetables, ***masala dosa*** (spicy Indian pancakes), etc.

**Kushikura 串くら**
*Takakura-dori, Oike-agaru (Map II B2). ✆075-213-2211. www.fukunaga-tf.com/kushikura. Open 11.30am–10.30pm.* Housed in a fine old ***machiya*** with a pleasant **courtyard garden**, this restaurant specializes in succulent ***yakitori*** cooked over a charcoal grill.

**Yamatomi 山とみ**
*Pontocho, Shijo-agaru (Map II B3). ✆075-221-3268. Open Wed–Mon noon–11pm.* Halfway along the Pontocho, on the river side. This welcoming ***izakaya*** benefits from a pleasant **waterside terrace**. The best strategy is to order a number of small dishes such as ***yuba*** sashimis (the skin of soya milk), slices of roast duck, fried tofu, ***teppan age*** (assorted kebabs), grilled chicken wings, etc.

**Bussaracan 仏沙羅館**
*Kiyamachi-dori, Matsubara-agaru (Map II B3). ✆075-361-4535. www.bussaracan.com. Open Thu–Tue 11.30am–10pm.* On fine days, it is a pleasure to eat on the terrace of this Thai restaurant raised up on stilts beside the Kamo River. Sophisticated cuisine and subtle flavors: fried chicken served in a banana leaf, beef curry and coconut milk.

**Kyomachi 京町**
*156 Umenoki-cho, Pontocho-dori, Shijo-agaru, Nakagyo-ku (Map II B3). ✆075-223-2448.* Open *5.30–10pm. Formula at ¥7,500.* A venue ideally located in the middle of Pontocho: delicious local cuisine, such as traditional ***hamo*** (a kind of eel), which you can enjoy on the terrace or indoors, in a tatami room.

**Mukadeya 百足屋**
*Shinmachi-cho, Shinmachi Nishiki-agaru, Nakagyo-ku (Map II A3). ✆075-256-7039. Open Thu–Tue 11am–10pm.* A magnificent ***machiya*** is the setting for this sophisticated restaurant, which serves succulent vegetarian dishes of Zen inspiration and other ***obanzai*** (traditional Kyoto cuisine) specialties.

**O-mo-ya 錦小路**
*Nishiki-koji, Fuyacho agaru (Map II B3). ✆075-221-7500. www.secondhouse.co.jp. Open Tue–Sun noon–8.30pm (Sat–Sun 10.30pm).* Near Nishiki market, in a superb paneled room decorated with ceramics, this restaurant serves Japanese food with a French twist. Set menu in the evening, including a number of starters and tasty little dishes such as cassolette of crème brûlée with cheese, or sea bream with broccoli on a bed of asparagus.

**Yoshikawa Inn 料理旅館・天ぷら吉川** *Tominokoji dori, Oike-sagaru, Nakagyo-ku (Map II B2). ✆075-221-5544. www.kyoto-yoshikawa.co.jp. Open Mon–Sat 11am–8.30pm.* A renowned tempura restaurant in a historic setting. You can eat at the counter or in rush-matted rooms beside the garden.

## GION AND KIYOMIZU-DERA

**Gonbe 権兵衛祇園店**
*254 Kitagawa, Gion-cho (Map II C3). ✆075-561-3350. Open Fri–Wed noon–9pm.* Near Gion, this popular Japanese restaurant prepares succulent dishes of ***soba***, ***udon***, and ***donburi*** (bowl of rice with a topping) with loving care. Its ***tori nanban***, a bowl of noodles with

duck, or *tamago toji*, the same with half a boiled egg, are filling and cheap.

**Izuju 祇園いづ重**
*Corner of Shijo-dori and Higashi-Oiji-dori (Map II C3). 075-561-0019. Open Thu–Tue, 11.30am–8pm.* Behind its unassuming street frontage, which you could easily miss, this sushi restaurant (established in 1892) conceals a delightful old-style dining room decorated with Imari porcelain. It specializes in ***saba sushi*** (square-shaped mackerel sushi), among other varieties.

**Okutan 奥丹**
*340 San-chome, Ninenzaka Kiyomizu (Map III D1). 075-525-2051. Open Fri–Wed, 10.30am–5.30pm.* One of Kyoto's best tofu restaurants, tucked away in a lovely peaceful Japanese garden. Its one specialty is ***yudofu***, a tofu hotpot served with yam soup, rice, and vegetable tempuras *(¥3,175)*.

**Aunbo 阿吽坊**
*Shimokawara-dori, Yasaka-torimaecho sagaru (Map II C3). 075-525-2900. http://blog.aunbo.com. Open Thu–Tue noon–9.30pm.* Two blocks away from the Yasaka shrine, this is one of the best places to try Kyoto cuisine; a small dining room with a really friendly atmosphere. Order the popular ***ichiju sansai*** menu, which includes three seasonal dishes.

**Yagenbori やげんぼり末吉町店**
*Kiritoshi-kado, Sueyoshi-cho, Gion (Map II C3). 075-551-3331. www.yagenbori.co.jp. Open 11.30–11pm.* A place beside the romantic Shirakawa Canal to enjoy typical local dishes: tempura, ***hoba-misoyaki*** (miso, mushrooms, chicken, and grilled onions in magnolia leaves), ***shabu-shabu***. The ***kaiseki*** here *(from ¥7,000)* are more affordable than in the expensive ***ryotei***.

**EAST KYOTO**

**Omen おめん銀閣寺本店**
*Ginkaku-ji, 218.8yd/200m W of the temple, on Shishigatani-dori (Map II D1). 075-771-8994. Open Fri–Wed 11am–9pm.* Near the Silver Pavilion, a restaurant well-known for its ***udon***, wheat noodles served in a vegetable broth with sesame seeds.

**NORTHWEST KYOTO**

**Yudofu Seigenin 西源院**
*13 Goryonoshita-cho, Ryoan-ji, Ukyo-ku (Map I A3). 075-462-4742. Open 10am–5pm.* In Ryoan-ji temple, this restaurant looks out on an enchanting garden and is renowned for its ***yufodu***, tofu hotpot with vegetables and herbs.

**OHARA**

**Seryo Jaya 芹生茶屋**
*Sanzenin, 22 Syorin-in-cho (Map I D1 off map). 075-744-2301. Open 9am–5pm.* On the left of the entrance to Sanzen-in, with a fine ryokan in the garden. The menu is available in English and dishes are displayed in the window. Excellent ***soba*** dishes, mushrooms and rice with bamboo, plus country fare, such as trout and seasonal vegetables.

**OTSU**

**Honke Tsuruki soba 本家鶴喜そば**
*4-11-40 Sakamo. 077-578-0002. Open daily 10am–6pm, closed 3rd Fri of month.* This welcoming restaurant with a magnificent wooden facade offers all kinds of hot and cold ***soba*** dishes and set menus.

**HIKONE**

**Hakkeitei 八景亭**
*Hikone Castle, 3-41 Kinkame-cho, Hikone. 074-922-3117. Reserve in advance.* This inn is in an idyllic setting, in a garden of Hikone Castle; it also offers ***kaiseki*** set menus for lunch *(¥,7,560)* and dinner *(¥8,820)*.

## TAKING A BREAK

**Tearooms and Cafes – Kanoshoju-an 叶匠壽庵** *S of the Philosopher's Path, beside the Nyakuo-ji shrine (Map II D2). 075-751-1077. Open Thu–Tue 10am–4.30pm.* Hidden away behind a bamboo hedge, an authentic, traditional tea house, well away from the tourist cafes on either side of the walk.

**Cafe Efish エフィッシュ** – *Kiyamachi-dori, gojo sagaru (55yd/50m S of Gojo (Map III C1). 075-361-069. Open 11am–10pm.* On the bank of the Kamo River, an attractive designer cafe serving tea, coffee, fruit juices, sandwiches, and cakes. A good place to relax at the end of the day.

## NIGHTLIFE

The bar and nightclub district is on Kiyamachi-dori *(Map II C2/3)*, a street parallel to Pontocho, between Shijo-dori and Sanjo-dori. *Drinks usually cost around ¥500. You may have to pay an entry fee on live-music evenings.*

**Bars – Spanish Harlem Latin Club スパニッシュ ハーレム ラテン クラブ**
*Reiho Bldg, B1F, 2 blocks N of Shijo, W of Kiyamachi, on the bank of the little canal (Map II C3). Open 7pm–2am (Sat–Sun 5am).*

℘075-212-1504. For lovers of latin jazz, salsa, *bachata*, etc. Dancefloor with DJ in attendance, or bands at the weekend.

**A Bar あ・バー** – *On 2nd floor of previous venue (Map II C3). Open 5pm–midnight. ℘075-213-2129.* Surprising, log-cabin decor. Young clientele and relaxed atmosphere in which to enjoy a beer or cocktail.

**Rag ライブスポットラグ** – *5F Empire Bldg, Kiyamachi-dori, N of Sanjo (Map II C2). Open 6pm–4am. ℘075-255-7273.* Bar featuring live music, with regular jazz, rock, blues, funk, and "world music" gigs. Several other bars share the same building.

**Rub-a-Dub ラバダブ** – *Kiyamachi-dori, almost on the corner of Sanjo (Map II C2). Open 7pm–2am (Sat–Sun 4am). ℘075-256-3122.* A tiny basement reggae bar with dancing at the weekend.

**Gael Irish Pub ゲールアイリッシュパブ** – *Ohto Bldg, 2F Nawate-dori, 55yd/50m N of Shijo (Map II C3). Open 5pm–midnight. ℘075-525-0680.* Pub-style venue frequented by an English-speaking crowd.

**Yoramu よらむ** – *Nijo-dori, near Higashi-Notoin (Map II B2). Open Tue–Sun 6pm–midnight. Closed 1st Sun of the month. ℘075-213-1512.* Fabulous sake bar run by an Israeli with an in-depth knowledge of Japan. The drinks list includes some old sakes with incredible lemon, rosé wine, plum, and coffee flavors.

**Zappa ザッパ** – *Takoyakushi-dori, between Kawaramachi and Kiyamachi (Map II B3). Open Mon–Sat 6pm–1am (Sun 6pm–10pm). ℘075-255-4437.* A small bar with a friendly atmosphere at the end of a cul-de-sac, where you can also eat Indonesian delicacies.

## SHOPPING

### SPECIALTY FOODS

**Shichimiya 七味家本舗** – *Corner of Sannenzaka and Kiyomizu-michi (Map I C3). ℘075-551-0738.* Since the days of the samurai, this store has enjoyed a reputation for its peppers and spices, including the famous *shichimitogarashi*, a blend of red pepper and six spices, excellent with meats, cheeses, etc.

**Funahashiya 船はしや** – *Sanjo Ohashi, Nishi-zume (Map II C2). ℘075-221-2673.* Right on the corner of the Sanjo Bridge, on the west bank. Do not miss this old-fashioned store, whose specialty is rice crackers, packaged in attractive wooden boxes or wrapped in handmade paper.

### TEA

**Horaido 蓬莱堂茶舗** – *Teramachi Arcade, N of Shijo (Map II B2/3). ℘075-221-1215. Open daily except 2nd, 12th and 22nd of month,10am–9pm.* This store sells nothing but Uji teas, regarded as Japan's finest, and all the utensils required for the Tea Ceremony, including bowls and teapots.

**Ippodo 一保堂茶舗** – *Teramachi-dori, 22yd/20m N of Nijo-dori (Map II B2). Open 9am–7pm. ℘075-211-3421.* A fine old tea outlet (*sencha, matcha, ujishimizu*, etc.) with a small sitting area for tea-tasting.

### CRAFT ITEMS

**Kintakedo 金竹堂** – *Shijo-dori, W of Hanamikoji-dori (Map II C3). ℘075-561-7868.* Workshop specializing in combs and brooches for Geisha hair arrangements, made of mother-of-pearl, wood, or hornreal collector's items.

**Miyawaki 宮脇賣扇庵** – *Corner of Rokkaku-dori and Tomino-koji (Map II B2). ℘075-221-0181.* Since 1823, Miyawaki has been manufacturing superb fans made of silk, paper, wood, mother-of-pearl, and laquerware, in both folding and non-folding versions.

**Kyukyodo 鳩居堂** – *Corner of Teramachi-dori and Aneya-koji (Map II B2). ℘075-231-0510.* Firm specializing in fragrant incenses (sandalwood, rose, aloes, etc.), incense-burners, calligraphic inks, and brushes. Fine selection of Japanese papers.

**Miura Shomei 三浦照明** – *Shijo-dori, near Yasaka-jinja (Map II C3). ℘075-561-2816.* Store selling traditional and modern rice-paper lanterns, and bamboo, bronze, or stone lamps, in particular those designed by **Isamu Noguchi**.

**Kagoshin 籠新** – *Sanjo-dori, 55yd/50m W of Higashi-Oji (Map II C2). Open Mon 2–6pm, Tue–Sun 9am–6pm. ℘075-771-0209.* Founded in 1862, this firm uses 50 or so varieties of bamboo to make baskets, chopsticks, plates, etc.

### PAPER

**Suzuki Shofudo 鈴木松風堂**– *Yanaginobanba, N of Takoyakushi (Map II B2/3). ℘075-241-3030.* Store specializing in Japanese *washi* papers.

### ANTIQUES/PRINTS

If you enjoy hunting for antiques, explore the streets around **Shinmonzen-dori** *(Map II C3)*, in the Shinbashi district. Good quality.

Of less interest is the **Kyoto Antiques Center, a complex of 20 or so boutiques** *(Teramachi-dori, N of Nijo-dori, Map II B2/3)*. The main **flea market** is held on the 21st of each month at the To-ji temple *(Map III A2/3)*, in the south of Kyoto.

**Nishiharu** 西春 – *Teramachi Arcade, on the corner of Sanjo-dori (Map II B2/3). ℘075-211-2849. Open 2pm6.30pm.* Mr Tohru Sekigawa, the respected owner, receives his customers in a tiny tatami room, where he displays Edo and Meiji period ***ukiyo-e* (wood block prints)**, all with a certificate of authenticity. A real institution.

### FASHION CLOTHING, KIMONOS

**Aizenkobo** 愛染工房 – *Nakasuji Omiya-nishi, Kamikyo-ku. ℘075-441-0355. Open 10am–4pm.* The Utsuki family has made fabrics with natural indigo for 17 generations. In their workshop/boutique are bedspreads, pillowcases, scarves, chemises, and kimonos worked in batik *(shibori)*.

**Kikuya** キクヤ – *Manjuji-dori, between Sakaimachi and Yanaginobanba (Map II B2/3). ℘075-351-0033. Open 9am–6pm.* Store specializing in antique and secondhand kimonos at affordable prices.

**Mimuro** みむろ – *Matsubara-dori, E of Karasuma (Map II B3). ℘012-036-6529.* More than 50,000 different kimonos, displayed on 5 floors.

## ENTERTAINMENT

### DANCE

In spring and fall each year, the geishas and ***maiko*** (apprentice geishas) from Kyoto's five schools put on colorful **dance performances** *(odori)*, appearing in their finest headgear and most dazzling kimonos. They perform several times in the afternoon. Ticket prices range from ¥1,650 to ¥6,000. Detailed information can be obtained from your hotel or a Tourist Office.

The season opens with the **Miyako Odori**, Apr 1–30, at the Gion Kobu Kaburenjo Theater (*Hanamikoji-dori, Map I, C3; ℘075-561-1115)*. The **Kyo Odori** takes place 1st Sat–3rd Sun in April at the Miyagawa-cho Kaburenjo Theater *(Miyagawasuji; ℘075-561-1151)*. The **Kitano Odori** is held Mar 25–Apr 7 at the Kamishichiken Kaburenjo Theater *(Imadegawa-dori, E of Kitano Tenmangu, Map I B2; ℘075-461-0148)*. The **Kamogawa Odori** takes place May 1–24 and Oct 15–Nov 7 at the Pontoncho Kaburenjo Theater *(Pontocho-dori, Map II B2; ℘075-221-2025)*.

The season ends with the **Gion Odori**, Nov 1-10, at the Gion Kaikan Theater *(near the Yasaka-jinja, Map II C3; ℘075-561-0160)*.

You can also attend performances all year round at **Gion Corner** (*Yasaka Hall, Hanamikoji-dori, Map II C3; ℘075-561-119)*. As well as dances by ***maiko***, these sessions *(7pm & 8pm, 1hr, ¥3,150)* include demonstrations of ***Ikebana*** (flower arranging), ***gagaku*** (court music), ***bunraku*** (puppetry), and ***kyogen*** (comic theater). Geared toward passing tourists, these performances give a poor idea of the arts involved.

### THEATER

**Kabuki – Minami-za Theater** 京都四条南座 *Shijo-Ohashi (Map II C3). ℘075-561-1155.* The best place to see Kabuki, and Japan's oldest venue for this form of theater. The country's top actors perform here during the Kaomise Festival, Dec 1–25. At other times, the program is unpredictable. Information can be obtained from the Tourist Office.

**Noh – Kanze Kaikan** 京都観世会館 *Niomon-dori, opposite the Museum of Modern Art (Map II C2). ℘075-771-6114.* Several performances at the weekend *(from ¥2,500)*. You can also attend the **Takigi-Noh** (*℘075-761-3889)*, a performance of Noh theater by torchlight, at the Heian-jingu *(Map II C2). Information: ℘075-771-6114.*

### SENTO

Most ***sento*** (public baths) comprise hot baths, "electric" baths (to relax the muscles), and medicinal-herb baths.

**Hakusan-Yu** 白山湯六条店– *Shinmachi-dori, Rokujo sagaru, 55yd/50m N of the Higashi Hongan-ji (Map III B1). ℘075-351-2733. Open Thu–Tue, 3pm–11pm, ¥410.* Outdoor bath on the women's side, herb bath, sauna, jacuzzi. One of the best in Kyoto.

**Goko-Yu** 五香湯 – *Kuromon-dori, Gojo agaru. ℘075-812-1126. Open Tue–Sun 2.30pm–0.30am (Sun 7am–midnight), closed 3rd Tue in the month.* Another spacious ***sento*** on 2 floors, comprising a large sauna, a jacuzzi, herb baths, and an outdoor bath.

### MEDITATION

**Kennin-ji** 建仁寺 – *S of Gion (Map II C3). ℘075-561-6363. Zazen* sessions available.

**Myoshin-ji** 妙心寺 – *NW Kyoto (Map I B2). ℘075-461-5226.*

**Ryusen-an** 龍泉庵 – *In the Daitoku-ji (Map I B1). ℘075-491-0543. Reservations required.* Popular Zen center.

# Nara★★★
# 奈良

**At the heart of Nara is a beautiful 1,480-acre/600ha park, a wide verdant space with views of the wooded mountains surrounding the city. Around 1,200 deer are allowed to roam freely in the park, venerated as messengers of the gods. Heijo-kyo (as Nara was formerly known) was established at the end of the Silk Road. It was Japan's first permanent capital, a position it occupied from 710 to 784. This marked the beginning of a strong, centralized state, a catalyst for the growth of a national identity. Buddhism, an import from China and Korea, took root here, flourishing under the patronage of successive sovereigns, including four empresses. Walking through the calm streets of Nara today is like skimming the pages of a history book. A cradle of Japanese tradition and literature, this city has never lost its human scale and possesses some of the finest artistic treasures and some of the oldest buildings in the country, including eight UNESCO World Heritage Sites.**

- **Population:** 367,609– Nara prefecture.
- **Michelin Map:** Principal Sights Map B3 – Regional Map p283 – Town Map p334.
- **Location:** Nara, capital of Nara prefecture, is in the north of the prefecture on its only plain, the Yamato. Both Kyoto *(28mi/45km)* and Osaka *(19mi/30km)*, are nearby by train. Nara's relatively small size and grid layout make it easily manageable on foot, apart from the western suburbs. The principal sights are around Nara Park and not far from the Kintetsu and JR stations. The main shopping area is on the main thoroughfare, Sanjo-dori, and the pedestrian arcades to the south of Kintetsu station.
- **Kids:** Children will love feeding special crackers to the **deer** in the park, available everywhere from street vendors.
- **Timing:** A day should be enough to see Nara, by starting early in the morning. Limit yourself to the principal sights around the park (Todai-ji, Nara National Museum, Kofuku-ji, Kasuga Taisha), finishing up with Horyu-ji. For a more thorough, leisurely visit, reckon on spending one night in the city. Avoid weekends, especially in April and May, because of the crowds.
- **Don't miss:** Horyu-ji, the oldest Buddhist temple in Japan; Todai-ji, the largest wooden building in the world; a stroll in the forest around the Kasuga Taisha.

## A BIT OF HISTORY

**The Nara period** – Nara has played a crucial role in Japanese history, having been founded in 710 as the first true capital of the country, under the name Heijo-kyo ("city of peace"). It remained so until the capital was transferred elsewhere in 784. Until 710, the capital had changed with each succeeding monarch because of Shinto traditions concerning death; whenever a monarch died, his palaces were considered impure and had to be destoyed and rebuilt elsewhere. This entailed a costly and destabilizing move with each new monarch and was hardly conducive to the establishment of a well-run state.

To overcome this and perhaps also because the growing influence of Buddhism had swept away the old taboos, the Empress Genmei issued an edict

## USEFUL INFORMATION

**Tourist Offices** – Nara City Tourist Information Center, *23-4 Kamisanjo-cho (B2). Open 9am–9pm. ℘0742-22-3900. narashikanko.jp. There are Tourist Offices at Kintetsu Nara station (B1) (open 9am–5pm), JR Nara station (A2) (open 9am–5pm), and Sarusawa Pond (B2) (open 9am–5pm).* All four branches provide maps, brochures, and information in English.

**GUIDED TOURS** – Nara SGG Club *℘0742-22-5595,* Nara Student Guide *℘0742-26-4753,* Nara YMCA *℘0742-45-5920.* English-speaking volunteer guides. Transportation costs and meals extra. Reservations required at least one day in advance.

**BANK/FOREIGN EXCHANGE** – Most banks are on Sanjo-dori (B2). JP Bank *(Noborioji-cho, next to Nara Linehouse, open Mon–Fri 8am–9pm, Sat–Sun 9am–5pm),* a Japan Post Bank ATM, accepts foreign cards. Other ATMs accepting foreign cards can be found in post offices *(see below).*

**POST OFFICES** – Ogawa-cho Post Office *(JR Nara station, next to Lawson grocery (A2), open Mon–Fri 9am–7pm, Sat 9am–5pm*); and Higashimuki Post Office *(Higashimuki-Kita Shopping District, 218.7yd/200m NE of the Kintetsu station (B1); open Mon–Fri 9am–7pm, Sat–Sun 5pm).*

## TRANSPORTATION

### GETTING THERE

**BY TRAIN** – **Kintetsu Nara Station** *(B1)* – The more central of the two stations. Trains to Kyoto *(every 30min, journey time 33min, ¥610),* Osaka *(Nanba station, every 15min, journey time 40min, ¥540),* and Kansai International Airport via the Nankai Line to Nanba *(every 20min, journey time 1hr10min, ¥1,430).* **JR Nara Station** *(A2)* is in the SW, 10min walk from the center: trains to Kyoto *(every 30min, journey time 40min, ¥690),* Osaka *(Tenno-ji, every 10min, journey time 30min, ¥450),* and Kansai International Airport via Tenno-ji *(1hr20min, ¥1,660).*

**BY BUS** – **Terminai at Nara Kintetsu** *(B1)* and **JR** *(A2)* **stations** – Buses to Kansai International Airport *(every hour, journey time 1hr25min, ¥1,800),* Itami Airport *(about every hour, journey time 1hr, ¥1,440),* Shinjuku (Tokyo) by the Nara Kotsu night bus *(1 per day, 7hr45min, ¥8,400 single or ¥15,120 return),* and Yokohama by the Nara Kotsu night bus *(1 per day, 9hr, ¥7,800 single or ¥14,040 return).*

### GETTING AROUND

**BY BUS** – There are many bus routes crisscrossing the city, and most buses stop at the JR and Kintetsu stations. Bus routes nos.2 and 6 do a complete circuit of the city and the park in a clockwise direction; nos.1 and 5 go counterclockwise. Bus routes nos. 52, 63, 67, 70, 88, and 97 serve the temples in the SW.

**BY BICYCLE** – Practical for getting around the park and Naramachi. Bicycle renta – Nara Eigyosho, *JR Nara station (A2), kiosk opposite the taxi stand. Open 8am–6pm. ¥500 per day. ℘0742-26-3929.*

soon after her accession to the throne in 707, ordering the establishment of a permanent capital and thus putting an end to the Court's wanderings. Built on the model of Chang'an, the capital of the Chinese Han (206BC–220AD) and Tang (618–907) dynasties, Nara's design, later to be adopted in Kyoto, followed a geometrical grid intended to proclaim the glory of a dynasty whose descent from the gods was traced in the *Kojiki*, a book compiled in 712 (describing the creation of the *kami* and Earth). The great temples of previous reigns, such as Kofuku-ji and Yakushi-ji, were moved to Nara while others, such as Todai-ji, were created anew.

The new city comprised palaces, shrines, public buildings, houses, and well-laid roads, covering a square-shaped area of about 6,200 acres/2,500ha, with a population estimated at about 100,000. Thanks to the support of successive emperors, Buddhism flourished here, initiating a period of unprecedented artistic and intellectual richness exemplified by the creation of the great bronze Buddha *(Daibutsu)* of Todai-ji between 747 and 752.

**Thirteen centuries of history** – Over time, the great temples of Nara came to hold ever-greater sway over political life, so the Court decided to counter this by relocating the capital, first to Nagaoka-kyo in 784, and then to Kyoto (Heian) in 794. Nara lost some of its importance and saw its religious pre-eminence challenged by the monks of Enryaku-ji on Mount Heian, who also launched attacks against it. The city was sacked and burned a number of times during the Civil Wars, notably in 1180 and again in 1567, with disastrous consequences for the temples. Nonetheless, they managed to recover from these depredations, being rebuilt and refurbished, first during the Kamakura period and then during the Edo era. The year 2010 marked the 1,300th anniversary of its foundation, including the rebuilding of the former Imperial Palace, in the northwest of the city *(see p297)*.

### Hungry deer

The sacred deer of Nara are in fact Sika deer *(Cervus nippon)*. Their hazelnut-brown coat with white spots turns a dark gray in winter. The mating season is in the fall, and in the spring the hind gives birth to a single fawn, which stays with its mother for six months. Once believed to be messengers of the gods, deer have now been designated National Treasures. Until 1637, killing one was punishable by death. The deer have become so accustomed to being fed by visitors to the park that they follow them constantly, trying to eat whatever comes within their reach, to the extent that plastic wrappers have become the main cause of death among the herd.

## SIGHTS

### AROUND NARA PARK★★

奈良公園 *Map B–C 1/2*

Created in 1880, the vast lawns of Nara Park *(Nara-koen)*, interspersed with ponds, wooded groves, and avenues, lie at the foot of the gently sloping Mount Wakakusa. Herds of **deer**, venerated since ancient times as messengers of the *kami* (the Shinto gods), are allowed to roam freely. Visitors enjoy feeding them little crackers called *shika-senbei*.

*Herds of deer, Nara Park*

**Kofuku-ji★★** 興福寺 *Map 1/2.*
*Tokondo Hall: open 9am–5pm, (last admission 4.45pm). ¥300. Kokuhokan: open 9am–5pm. ¥500. Nanen-do: open on Oct 17 only.*
Built in 669 in Uji, south of Kyoto, then transferred to Nara in 710 by the powerful Fujiwara family, to whom it belonged, this **temple** expanded as its owners gained in influence. In its glory days, from the 8C to the 12C, it covered an area of 129,000sq ft/12,000sqm and comprised some 175 buildings. Despite subsequent damage and reconstruction, it is architecturally one of the few Buddhist structures to have kept its original style, known as the *wayo* style (a purely Japanese style, not influenced by Chinese models).
As the center of the **Hosso School**, one of the many Japanese Buddhist sects, it has a large number of masterpieces in its collections.
Before entering the precinct from the south side, pause to enjoy the **view** of the **five-story pagoda★** reflected in the lake *(Sarusawa-no-ike)*. The pagoda looks light and airy, as if it is about to fly away across the temple compound. Built in 730, it burned down several times *(in 1017, 1060, 1180, 1356, and 1411)*, but was always reconstructed, the last reconstruction dating back to 1426, during the Muromachi period.
At 164ft/50m it is the second-highest pagoda in Japan after that of To-ji, in Kyoto, and one of the great landmarks of Nara.
**Tokon-do★★**, the Eastern Golden Hall, was built in honor of Empress Gensho in 726. Destroyed five times by fire, it was last rebuilt in 1415. With its broad, straight roof, seven bays, terrace and dark interior, it is typical of the 8C. The monks held their ceremonies outside the hall. Yakushi Nyorai, the Buddha of Healing (*see box p291*), was worshipped here, and his large bronze statue (1415) dominates the middle of the hall, flanked by the *bosatsu* Gakko (symbol of the moon) on the right and Nikko (symbol of the sun), left, both dating from the end of the 7C. Figures of celestial guardians and fierce-lookng generals stand at the four corners, defending the faith.
**Kokuhokan★★**, the former refectory of the monks, is now used as the Treasure House. It contains a number of old statues, including a bronze **Buddha's head★★** from 685, depicting Yakushi Nyorai (*see box p291*), all that remains of a statue that once stood in the Tokon-do. Its eyes show a Chinese influence. There is also a **Senju Kannon★★** here, a thousand-armed deity from the Kamakura period (12C) in lacquered and gilt wood, its beauty matched only by an extraordinary 8C three-headed **Ashura★★★** (guardian of the Law) in lacquered hemp, with six arms as long and thin as tentacles.

## Nara National Museum★★
奈良国立博物館 *C1.*
*Open Tue–Sun 9am–5pm (last admission 4.30pm). ¥500. Guided tours (30min) available. No charge.*
Opened in 1895, Nara National Museum houses a major collection of Buddhist art spread over two buildings connected by an underground passageway.
**Old Building**– The main works on display here are Japanese Buddhist sculptures *(galleries 1, 2, 3, and 8 for the bronzes)* from the Asuka to the Kamakura periods, most of which have been left here in trust by the great monasteries of Nara and the surrounding area.
The works are shown in rotation, with displays changing each season. Strikingly realistic statues of monks alternate with grandly meditative Buddhas (Yakushi, Amida, Shaka), graceful *bosatsu* (Kannon, Nikko, Gakko), and fierce-faced protectors. The building also houses Buddhist statues from Gandhara, China, and Korea *(galleries 4 and 6)*, Chinese bronze vases *(galleries 14 and 15)*, and *gigaku* masks *(gallery 7)*.
**Modern Building** – The West Wing houses the permanent collections of paintings, calligraphy, and archeology. Here, too, the display is changed periodically. The East Wing is used for special exhibitions.
At the end of October and beginning of November, the museum displays the magnificent **treasures of Shoso-in★★** (objects brought from the continent via the Silk Road) usually kept at Todai-ji

Middle Gate and Daibutsu-den, Todai-ji



(see below), the origins of which go back to the Nara period.

**Isui-en Garden★** 依水園 *Map C1.*
*Open Wed–Mon 9.30am–4.30pm.*
*¥650.*
Somewhat off the tourist circuit, this traditional garden provides a relaxing interlude from sightseeing. It comprises two gardens dating from the Meiji era: the one on the west side *(turn right after the entrance)* is a stroll garden *(see p103)* laid out around a small pond; its counterpart on the east side uses the "borrowed landscape" *(shakkei—see p102)* of Wakasuka Hill in the background to create an appealing effect of depth.

**Todai-ji★★★** 東大寺 *Map C1.*
*Open Apr–Sept 7.30am–5.30pm; Oct 7.30am–5pm; Nov–Feb 8am–4.30pm; Mar 8am–5pm. Daibutsu-den ¥500, Hokke-do ¥500, Kaidan-en ¥500.*
In 743, Emperor Shomu commissioned an ambitious project: the construction of a building to house what was to be the most colossal bronze statue in the world, the great Buddha of Nara, which was eventually consecrated in 752. Because of the major role it played in the country's religious history, Todai-ji always enjoyed the favor of the Emperors, even after the capital had been moved to Kyoto. The original plan included two seven-story pagodas, now no longer in existence, one on each side of the central building. Twice burned down, in 1180 and again in 1567, Todai-ji was last rebuilt in 1708 on an area two-thirds of its original size. Nearly three million tourists visit the site annually.
At the entrance, visitors pass through the **Nandai-mon★**, the Great South Gate with its five bays and two roofs. Its pillars tower over two impressive wooden statues: the **Ni-oh guardians★★** (1203), made by the sculptors Unkei and Kaikei. One guardian has his mouth open, the other's mouth is closed, symbolizing the beginning and end of life *(see p206)*.
At the end of the avenue is the Great Buddha Hall, the **Daibutsu-den★★**

### The Shuni-e ceremony

The monks of Todai-ji have performed the same ceremony every year for the past 1,200 years: *Shuni-e*, a ritual of repentance in which they confess their sins to the Kannon in the Nigatsu-do. They must purge themselves of the "three poisons": greed, anger, and stupidity, which contaminate their souls and prevent them from seeing the truth. The rituals continue for two weeks at the beginning of March. At nightfall, the monks run along the balcony of the **Nigatsu-do**, waving huge torches and chanting. Finally, they offer sacred water to both the deity and the watching crowd.

(*see photo p331*). Even though the most recent reconstruction has reduced its size and changed its proportions, it remains the largest wooden building in the world (*159ft/48.5m high and 187ft/57m wide*). A fine, eight-sided bronze lantern from 752, decorated with musical *bosatsu*, stands in front of it. Traditionally, the building's central skylight is opened twice a year (*Aug 15 & Dec 21–Jan 1*) to show the people the face of the deity.

The interior reveals the great, gilt bronze statue of **Daibutsu Vairocana**★★, the cosmic Buddha, sitting on a lotus flower in a state of enlightenment. Its enormous height (*50ft/15m*) and weight (*250 tons*) make it the largest bronze Buddha in the world. Created in 751 by the Korean Kimimaro—supposedly aided by 370,000 workers—the work has been restored many times. Only the pedestal is original: the head dates from the 17C. To the left of Daibutsu is Nyoirin Kannon, who grants wishes, and to his right, Kokuzo Kannon, symbol of wisdom.

At the rear is a 1:50 scale model of the original temple. You may also notice a hole in one of the building's pillars, the same size as the Buddha's nostril: it is said that those who manage to slip through it will go to paradise.

*Turn left on the way out and follow the path going E for about 437yd/400m until near the belfry and the vermilion torii.*

Rebuilt in 1667, **Nigatsu-do**★ is a temple supported on piles, resembling a smaller version of Kiyomizu-dera in Kyoto (*see p305*).

There is a fine **view** of Nara from its terrace. Farther south, **Hokke-do**★★, also known as Sangatsu-do, is the oldest building in Todai-ji (*erected in 746, but partially rebuilt in the Kamakura era*). It houses 16 remarkable statues from the Nara period, of which 12 are designated National Treasures. In the middle is a dry-lacquer statue of **Fukukensaku Kannon**★★, its hands joined in prayer, flanked by two beautiful bodhisattvas and a host of celestial guardians with terrifying faces.

About 330yd/300m to the west, on a small hillock on the other side of Daibutsu-den, stands **Kaidan-in**★, in which four precious statues of the celestial kings dating from the Nara period are preserved. Finally, head north, leaving a pond to your left, and you reach **Shoso-in**★, a curious storehouse made of logs and mounted on piles (*closed to public*). It is used to store the ritual utensils for the ceremonies at the Todai-ji, as well as the treasures bequeathed to the temple by Emperor Shomu: thousands of objects (screens, ceramics, masks, fabrics, etc.) brought along the Silk Road from China, India, Persia, and Byzantium. Every year in the Fall, some of these treasures are put on display in the Nara National Museum.

## Kasuga Taisha★★ 春日大社 *C2.*

*Summer: 6.30am–5.30pm; winter: 7am–4.30 pm (varies by visit); special visit: ¥500; museum: ¥400; Shinen: ¥500.*

Located in the eastern part of Nara Park, Kasuga Taisha (*Kasuga Grand Shrine*) lies at the foot of two sacred mountains, Kasuga-yama and Mikasa-yama, once venerated as places chosen by the *kami* to come to earth. Shaded by Japanese cedars, the shrine buildings lie on the edge of a picturesque and well-preserved **primeval forest**★. Founded in 768 (or 710, according to some sources), the shrine's significance in Japanese history is that it housed the guardian deities of the Fujiwara clan. In about the 10C, during the Heian era, it was affiliated to Kofuku-ji, an association that would last until 1868, when Shintoism was separated from Buddhism by the Meiji Restoration.

Kasuga Taisha is famous for its **3,000 lanterns**, donated by the faithful over the centuries. Moss-covered stone lanterns line the main avenue from the great *torii* to the entrance; others, in bronze, hang in the corridors of the buildings. All are lit during the **Mantoro festivals**, which take place twice a year in the shrine (*Aug 14–15 & Feb 3*). The shrine is also notable for its **architecture**★, even though most of

Kasuga Taisha and its wisteria



the buildings are 19C reconstructions. The long and narrow main building has a large thatched and gabled roof.
It integrates well into its surroundings, large red pillars contrasting effectively with the green of the trees and the mauve of the wisteria: the shrine's priestesses wear clusters of wisteria in their hair (*see photo above*). To the west of the shrine, the **Homotsu-den** (treasure hall) displays *bugaku* masks, Noh costumes (*see p99*), and old weapons and armor.

*When you leave the shrine, follow the path on the left, which leads S through the woods. Leaving the forest after about another 875yd/800m, take the road on the right and then 110yd/100m farther on, the street on the left, which leads to Shin-Yakushi-ji, as indicated by a sign.*

### Shin-Yakushi-ji★

新薬師寺 *Map C2.*
*Open 9am–5pm. ¥600.*
Built in 747 at the request of Empress Komyo to thank the god for restoring her husband, Emperor Shomu, to health, this temple was once one of the largest in Nara. The main hall, the only original building, houses a fine 8C **statue**★ depicting Yakushi Nyorai (the Buddha of Healing) (*see box p 291*) accompanied by 12 celestial guardians.

## NARAMACHI★ 奈良町

*Map B2.*
This former merchant quarter stretching south of the Sarusawa Pond, around the temple of Gango-ji, is a maze of tranquil, picturesque little streets lined with *machiya* traditional wooden houses used as shops, workshops, and private dwellings by the same families for generations. Some are now handicraft shops or cafes. The atmosphere is authentically Japanese.

### Naramachi Koshi-no-ie

ならまち格子の家 *Map B2.*
*Open Tue–Sun 9am–5pm.*
*No charge.*
This restored *machiya* typifies the layout of a traditional Nara house: a low façade, a tiled roof, windows protected by wooden latticework, and a long, narrow interior opening at the rear onto a small garden and storehouse.

### Naramachi Shiryokan

奈良町資料館 *Map B2.*
*Open Tue–Sun 10am–4pm.*
*No charge.*
This Edo period *machiya* is a museum housing a varied assortment of objects: porcelain, signs, old coins, and prints. Note the small red-and-white stuffed monkeys hanging from the canopy. They are "substitute monkeys," belonging to the Chinese cult of *koshin*. Each little

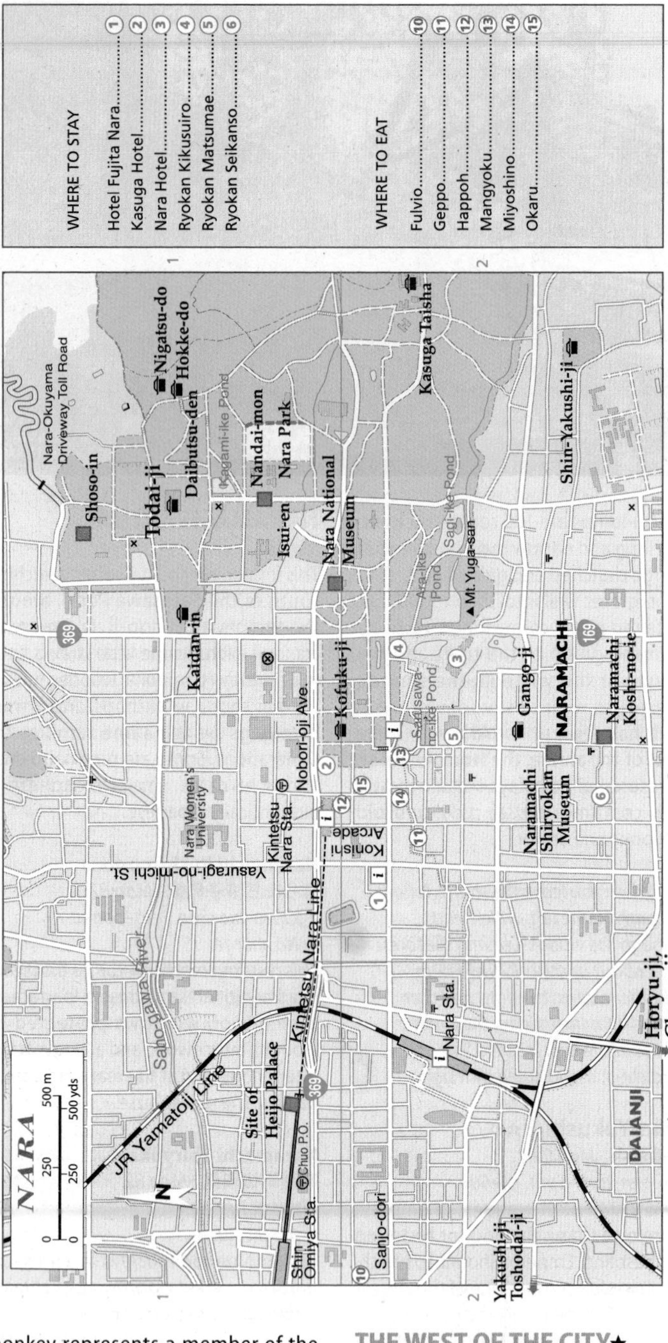




monkey represents a member of the family, whom it is supposed to protect from misfortune and suffering by taking on these problems itself.

## THE WEST OF THE CITY★

### Site of Heijo Palace

平城京跡 *Map A1.*

*From Kintetsu Nara station, take the*

*Kintetsu Line to Saidaiji station, leave by the north exit and walk 10min E.* *Open Tue–Sun 9am–4.30pm (7.30pm Sat–Sun.* *No charge for foreigners on presentation of passport. 1hr English audio-guide (MP3 or iPod/iPad version) downloadable at Heijo Palace website, as well as site plan and numbers associated with commentaries: http://www.1300.jp/foreign/english/kyuu-seki/audio_guide/index.html.*

Situated in the northwest of modern-day Nara, the former Heijo Palace (710–84) covered an area of 320 acres/130ha and was surrounded by a 16ft/5m-high clay rampart with 12 entrances.

Running north to south, this Imperial complex included official buildings where political and religious ceremonies were held, among them the *Dai-goku-den* (audience hall), the *Chodo-in* (ceremonial hall), and the *Dairi* (Imperial residence), as well as offices, shops, workshops, etc.

Each building had its own base, tiled roof, and vermilion laquered pillars. These wooden buildings may have disappeared but the site, which has been occupied exclusively by paddy fields ever since, still conceals potential archeological finds. Excavations have revealed, for example, one of the gardens of the Chodo-in to the east.

The site was chosen for the celebrations to mark Nara's 1,300th anniversary in 2010, and a good deal of reconstruction work has taken place, notably the **Suzaku Gate** (the Great South Gate) and the Imperial audience hall, the **Daigoku-den**.

The **Heijo Palace Site Museum** at the west entrance displays an overview of the site as well as ceramics, tiles, and tablets found during the excavations. On the eastern side, the **Excavation Site Exhibition Hall** houses models of the Imperial residence and the audience hall.

## Toshodai-ji★ 唐招提寺

*Map A2, off map.*
*From the Kintetsu or JR stations, bus nos.63 and 70 to Toshodai-ji stop, or bus nos.52, 97 and 98 to the Toshodai-ji-higashiguchi stop (20min, ¥240).*

*Open 8.30am–5pm.* *¥600. Miedo: open 6 Jun only.* *¥500 supplement.*

Although it has undergone much restoration over the centuries, Toshodai-ji nevertheless remains a harmonious example of Nara-period architecture. A temple belonging to the Ritsu sect, it is the work of Ganjin (688–763), a Chinese monk invited by Emperor Shomu to teach Buddhism in 759. Ganjin had an unusually hard time crossing the Sea of Japan, suffering shipwreck five times, and by the time he reached Japan, he had gone blind.

The **Miedo**, the hall at the far end of the garden, contains a **statue**★ of Ganjin, the oldest lacquered effigy in Japan. Designated a National Treasure, **Kon-do**★★, the temple's principal pavilion, has a colonnade of eight pillars at the front. The interior contains three large, dry-lacquer statues of the Buddhas Yakushi and Rushana, and the *bosatsu* Senju Kannon. Behind the Kon-do is the lecture hall, the **Ko-do**★, with a curved roof, which was originally part of Heijo Palace and contains several valuable statues, including a large 8C **Miroku Bosatsu**★.

### Yakushi-ji★ 薬師寺

*Map A2, off map.*
*10min walk S of Toshodai-ji. Open 8.30am–5pm. ¥800.*

Founded by Emperor Tenmu in 680 and moved to Nara in 718, this temple, the center of the Hosso sect, is one of the oldest and most sacred in the city. Seriously damaged by fire in 973 and again in 1528, it has been entirely rebuilt, apart from the beautiful **To-to**★★, the East Pagoda. Three storys and 111ft/34m high, it appears to have six levels because of the canopies between the floors. The principal hall, the **Kon-do** (1635), houses a large bronze triad of the **Buddha Yakushi**★★ dating from 697 and strongly influenced by the naturalist style of the Chinese Tang dynasty, while the showpiece of the **Toin-do**, or East Hall (1285), is a 7C **Sho Kannon**★ showing Indian influence.

## EXCURSIONS

### HORYU-JI★★★ 法隆寺

*Map A2, off map.*
*From JR Nara station, Yamatoji Line to Horyu-ji station (10min, ¥210), then 20min walk to the N or bus no. 72 (5min, ¥170). Alternatively, from JR or Kintetsu stations, bus no. 52 or 97 to Horyu-ji-mae stop (1hr, ¥760). Open Feb 22–Nov 3 8am–5pm; Nov 4–Feb 21 8am–4.30pm. ¥1,000.*

Located in the town of Ikaruga, 7.5mi/12km southwest of Nara, Horyu-ji, the "Temple of the Flourishing Law," features the oldest wooden buildings in the world. These masterpieces of the Asuka period were built in 607 on the orders of Empress Suiko and Prince Regent Shotoku. Some of the buildings may have been destroyed by a fire in 670 and rebuilt in the 8C. Horyu-ji was the first site in Japan to be designated a UNESCO World Heritage Site.

**Sai-in (Western Precinct)**★★★ – An avenue lined with pine trees leads to **Nandai-mon**, the Great South Gate, which dates from the Muromachi period (14C). Farther on is a much older gate (late 7C), **Chu-mon**★, with bulbous pillars, flanked by two **guardians**★ (Kongorikishi), one of clay (711), the other of wood (12C).

In the middle of the central courtyard is the oldest and most sacred of the buildings, the **Kondo**★★★ or Golden Hall. It contains a triad of **Shaka Nyorai**★★ *(Sakyamuni, the historical Buddha)* from 623, by the sculptor Tori. The almond-shaped eyes, elongated face, the draping of the clothing, and the direct attitude of the sculpture are

*Gojuno-to and Kon-do, Horyu-ji*

strongly influenced by the stone statues of the Chinese Northern Wei dynasty (386–534). The wall paintings depict the Buddhist paradise in the style of the Indian frescoes of Ajanta. Most are replicas, the originals having burned in a fire in 1949.

Beside the Kondo is the **Gojuno-to**★★★, a five-story pagoda probably built in about 700, making this the oldest pagoda in Japan. Each level symbolizes one of the five tantric elements: earth, water, wood, air, and space. The base has clay statues illustrating the life of the Sakyamuni Buddha; the one facing north depicts his ascent to nirvana.

At the far end of the precinct, on the right, is the **Daihozo-den** *(treasure hall)*, which displays several treasures from the Asuka period (7C), including a camphorwood **Kudara Kannon**★★★, a masterpiece of grace and refinement, and the **Tamamushi no zushi**★★★, the altar of Empress Suiko, which is covered in 9,000 iridescent beetle wings.

**To-in (Eastern Precinct)**★ – The main focus here is the **Yumedono**★★, or Pavilion of Dreams (739), where Prince Shotoku received answers to his political and philosophical questions in his dreams. Mounted on a stone podium, this eight-sided building houses a perfectly-preserved 7C gilt wooden statue of **Kuze Kannon**★★ *(statue on view Apr 15–May 15 & Oct 15–Nov 15 only)*.

## Chugu-ji★ 中宮寺 *Map A2, off map*

*Open Mar 21–Sept 30 9am–4.30pm; Oct 1–Mar 20 9am–4pm. ¥500.*

A passageway at the far end of the Eastern Precinct leads to this small temple, founded by Prince Shotoku in honor of his mother in 621. It is worth visiting for its black camphorwood statue of **Miroku Bosatsu**★★★ *(Buddha of the Future)*, seated in a meditation position, a masterpiece of Japanese statuary.

## KASHIHARA 橿原

*A-B2 region map.*

*About 12mi/20km south of Nara. From Kintetsu Nara station, take the Kintetsu Line to Yagi-nishiguchi station via Yamato Saidaiji (45min, ¥430). On leaving the station, turn right, then right again, go straight and turn left after the traditional bridge. After 1,300ft/400m you come to Hanairaka, the Imai-cho cultural exchange center.*

**Hanairaka 華甍**

*Open Tue–Sun 9am–5pm. No charge.*

This great wooden edifice dates from the Meiji period (1903) and is today a tourist center and museum; *you can ask for a plan and brochures on the Imai district and its history.* A model also presents it as it was during the Edo period.

**Imai-cho★ 今井町**

This district, with its rows of 17C traditional houses, brings the day-to-day of the Edo period to life with several dwellings open to the public. Founded by a monk, the trade town of Imai belonged to a Buddhist temple which waged battle against Oda Nobunaga's army in 1570 before surrendering; in exchange, it received the status of autonomous city. It was therefore built based on the plan for the fortified town. The streets are not entirely straight, so that arrows did not reach their targets, and every house facade has at least one iron ring to tie horses to.

The **Imanishi Home** *(Apr 15–May 15 and Oct 15–Nov 15; open Tue–Sun 10am–5pm; ¥400)* dates from 1650 and exhibits the interior of a rich merchant's home.

*From Yaga-nishiguchi station, take the Kinsetsu Line to Kashihara Jingumae station (4min; ¥200).*

**Kashihara-Jingu 橿原神宮**

According to Shinto mythology, this temple was where the first Emperor of Japan, Jinmu, was enthroned. Behind the temple, a little pebbled path that is nice and cool in summer takes you to the summit of Unebi Mountain.

## Yoshino-Yama★ 吉野山

*About 26mi/42km south of Nara. Take the Kintetsu Line from Kashiharajingumae station in Kashihara (55min, ¥460) to Yoshino station. From there, take the cable car to Yoshino-yama.*

Perched at about 3,281ft/1,000m on Yoshino Mountain, this village is famous for its 30,000 cherry trees that bloom for an entire month, which thousands of

Japanese come to admire. Four different areas at different altitudes explain this long blooming season: **Shimonosenbon** *(the 1,000 cherry trees at the bottom)*, **Nakasenbon** *(about 1,000 cherry trees halfway up)*, **Kaminosenbon** *(the 1,000 cherry trees at the top)*, and **Okunosenbon** *(the 1,000 cherry trees behind)*.

Founded by the priest Gyoki in the 8C, then rebuilt in the 15C, **Kinpusen-ji★** *(8am–4.30pm; ¥400)* is the main temple and the biggest in Japan after Todai-ji; it stands about 111ft/34m high. The last great religious waystation before climbing **Mount Omine**, this Buddhist temple also traditionally welcomes women on pilgrimage in the Kii Mountains *(see Kumano Kodo, p346)*, but who could not enter the sacred circle of the peak, reserved for men, where mountain ascetics trained.

Along the main road coming down from the temple, shops, and restaurants jostle with temples, shrines, and other tourist sites. A little after Kinpusen-ji *(on the left)* **Yoshimizu Temple** *(9am–5pm; ¥400)* has beautiful **painted screens**.

2600ft/800m further is **Gunpoen Garden** *(¥300)* in the precinct of a magnificent temple turned into a ryokan; here, the branches of the weeping cherry tree touch the surface of a little stone-edged pond *(see Addresses, below)*.

At the **Hanayagura viewpoint** *(20min by foot)* there is a beautiful **panorama** of the mountain. Nearby, the seven water divinities of the **Mikumari shrine★** *(9am–5pm; no charge)* live side by side in the sanctuary's right wing, in altars flanked on each side by two protective demons turning their backs on those of the altar.

## ADDRESSES

### STAY

**Ryokan Seikanso:** 静観 *29 Higashi-Kitsuji-cho (B2). 0742-22-2670. 9 rooms. ¥700.* A delightful ryokan, built in 1916 around a magnificent inner garden. The friendly owner speaks a little English. The rooms, although slightly faded, are pleasant and well-lit. Try to book one of the six rooms that look out onto the garden *O-furo, internet access, and bicycle rental.*

**Hotel Fujita Nara** ホテルフジタ奈良 *47-1 Sanjo-dori (B2). 0742-23-8111. www.fujita-nara.com. 117 rooms. ¥1,500.* Conveniently located, with friendly, English-speaking staff, bright, clean, soundproofed rooms, two restaurants, and an attractive saloon bar with a **view** of the garden, this hotel is a good choice in the medium-price category.

**Ryokan Matsumae** 旅館 松前 *28 Higashiterabayashi-cho (B2). 0742-22-3686. www.matsumae.co.jp. 21 rooms. ¥800.* A tranquil ryokan, located in a little street not far from Sarusawa Pond. The owner speaks good English. Small, clean rooms with, and without bathrooms.

**Kasuga Hotel** 春日ホテル *40 Noborioji-cho (B1). 0742-22-4031. www.kasuga-hotel.co.jp. 35 rooms – ¥18,900/31,500. Lodging with half-board.* The exterior of the hotel reproduces the architectural style of the wooden buildings of the Tenpyo period (late-8C). The interior has spacious, well-equipped, light-filled Japanese rooms with high-tech equipment. Excellent *kaiseki* cuisine and a superb *o-furo*, with a **waterfall** and **open-air bath** surrounded by rocks and greenery.

**Nara Hotel** 奈良ホテル *Nara-koennai (B2). 0742-26-3300. www.narahotel.co.jp. P. 120 rooms. ¥2,500.* This hilltop hotel near the park, built in 1909, is Western in style apart from the cypresswood façade inspired by the Momoyama period (16C). Many celebrities have stayed here. If you want atmosphere, ask for a room in the older part of the hotel, with their high ceilings, old wall-lights, and fireplaces.

**Ryokan Kikusuiro** 菊水楼 *1130 Takabatake-cho (B2). 0742-23-2001. 16 rooms. Lodging with half-board.* The oldest ryokan in Nara, designated an Important Cultural Property. 150 years ago, it provided accommodation for Buddhist priests; today, the lucky few can dine on divine *kaiseki* food in the company of one of the famous Nara geishas, or sleep in one of its rooms decorated with lacquerware, screens, and precious scrolls. Each room has a *nakai-san* (hostess), who will attend to your every need. *Only half the rooms have bathrooms.*

### YOSHINO

**Chikurin-in-Gunpoen 竹林院群芳園** *Yoshinoyama. Shuttle from Yoshino's Kintetsu station from 2.30pm by reservation. 746-32-8081. www.chikurin.co.jp/e/home.htm. Dinner and breakfast included.* In the center of an immense Japanese garden, this former Buddhist temple turned into a ryokan offers you stunning traditional rooms in an idyllic setting. Very beautiful *rotenburo.*

## EAT

**Miyoshino 三好野** *27 Hashimoto-cho (B2). 0742-22-5239. Open 11am–8.30pm.* This small, family-run cafe on Sanjo-dori specializes in *udon* noodle dishes, many of which (with eggs, beef, tempura, etc.) are depicted on the wall.

**Okaru おかる** *13 Higashimukiminamimati (B2). 0742-24-3686. Open 11am–9pm. ¥1,100.* The best *okonomiyaki* in Nara: savory pancakes stuffed with octopus, squid, pork, leek, or shrimp. The decor is fairly simple, and diners eat either at tables or on tatami mats.

**Fulvio フルヴィオ** *270-10, 4Omiya-cho(A2). 0742-36-5515. www42.tok2.com/home/fulvio. Open Mon–Sat 11am–1.30pm, 6–10pm. ¥1,500/4,500.* A small restaurant, only 3min walk from Shinomiya station. Delicious Italian cuisine concocted by the Japanese chef, Fulvio, who can be seen at the ovens behind the counter. Don't miss the spaghetti in squid ink or the lasagne.

**Happoh 八寶** *22 Higashi-mukinakamachi (B1/2). 0742-26-4834. www.happoh.com. Open 11.30am–10.30pm.* An elegant, restful setting, with music and the gurgling of a **mini-waterfall** in the background; a place to savor tasty, refined Japanese cooking from a varied, inexpensive menu.

**Mangyoku まんぎょく** *9 Ganrinin-cho (B2). 0742-22-2265. Open Tue–Sun 6–11pm.* Located in a small street set back from Sanjo-dori, near Sarusawa Pond, this is a typical old Nara house with lanterns and a hurdle fence. Inside, old furniture, prints, a polished parquet floor, and wooden beams make for a pleasant setting. Good home-style dishes like *nikujaga* (beef stew), steamed chicken, grilled salmon, vegetable platters, and other seasonal food.

**Geppo 月吠** *45 Tsubai-cho (B2). 0742-26-4325. Open Mon–Sat 11.30am–2. 30pm, 5.30pm–11pm. Formulas for lunch ¥750/¥1,500; for dinner ¥3,500/¥6,000.* One of the best restaurants in Nara, tucked away in an alley behind an unassuming wooden door. The chef, Nakatori, a former *butoh* dancer, offers clever Japanese–French fusion cooking. A traditional room at the front, and a modern room at the rear, decorated with contemporary paintings.

### KASHIHARA

**Suian 粋庵** *10min from Yaginishiguchi station, 1-4-35 Imai-cho. 0744-29-3807. Tue-Sun 11.30am–1.30pm and 5pm–10pm.* At the heart of the Imai-cho district, this traditional restaurant with its wooden facade serves good *soba* menus.

## TAKING A BREAK

**Mellow Cafe メローカフェ** – *Axe Unit, 1-8 Konishi-cho (B2). Open 11am–11.30pm. 0742-27-9099.* A trendy cafe with attractive *terra-cotta decor*, located in a shopping complex above the Konishi Arcade. A relaxing place for a drink in the afternoon or early evening; also serves Italian meals.

## SHOPPING

**Handicrafts – Nara Craft Museum ならら工藝館** *1-1 Azemame-cho (B2). Open Tue–Sun 10am–5pm. 0742-27-0033.* This lovely museum in the Naramachi district both displays and sells traditional handicrafts from Nara: wooden dolls, ceramics, laquerware, etc.

**Ink – Kobaien 古梅園** *7 Tsubai-cho, 109yd/100m from the Geppo restaurant. Open Mon–Fri 9am–5pm. 0742-23-2965.* One of the oldest sumi ink factories in the country; the workshops can be visited and the shop sells sticks of colored ink.

**Paper – Akemitori 朱鳥** *1 Hashimoto-cho (B2). Open 9am–8pm. 0742-22-1991.* A shop located in the pedestrian arcade S of Sanjo-dori and specializing in *tenugui*, printed cotton cloth used for making towels and accessories.

**Clogs – Uetomi 上富** *Shimomicado-cho, arcade street connecting Sanjo-dori and Naramachi (B2). Open Fri–Wed 10am–6pm, and some unpredictable closings. 0742-22-2904.* This little shop, one of the oldest in Nara, is packed with handmade *geta* (traditional clogs). *Straps available to order.*

# Koya-san★★★
# 高野山

**Koya-san, the largest grouping of monasteries in Japan, stands at the summit of a densely forested mountain. Almost a thousand Buddhist monks pray and meditate high up in the clear skies. For 12 centuries, Koya-san has been to Japan what Santiago de Compostela is to Europe: a famous center for devotion that attracts around a million pilgrims a year. In times gone by, only the bravest would climb the arduous trails up to the lofty retreat. In spite of its isolation, Koya-san was a powerful religious center in the Middle Ages, housing approximately 1,500 monasteries, of which around a hundred survive today, including 30 temple lodgings *(shukubo)*, offering food and accommodation to travelers. Designated a UNESCO World Heritage Site, along with the other sacred sites and trails on Kii Peninsula, this town—shrouded in mist and incense—gives visitors the opportunity to enter a mysterious, esoteric Japan.**

- **Population:** 4,008– Wakayama Prefecture.
- **Michelin Map:** Principal Sights Map B3 – Regional Map p283
- **Location:** Koya-san occupies a mountainous plateau at an altitude of 2,952.8ft/900m on Kii Peninsula, 52.8mi/85km south of Osaka and 41mi/66km east of Wakayama. From the plain, a cable car will take you up to the station, located 1.9mi/3km north of the town. The main street becomes Route 371 in the direction of Okuno-in, and continues toward the south of the peninsula, connecting with Kii-Katsuura and Kumano Sanzan.
- **Timing:** One day should be enough for a visit, but if you really want to savor the mystical atmosphere, stay overnight. If you wish to visit the Kii Peninsula too, it's advisable to rent a car.
- **Don't miss:** A night in a temple and the dawn ceremony.

## AN OVERVIEW

**A legendary founder** – The history of Mount Koya goes back to 816, when the monk Kukai, known as **Kobo Daishi**, who had studied Buddhism in China, obtained permission from the Emperor to create a hermitage on the mountain. Legend relates that he was led to this isolated site by the Shinto deities of the peninsula. In 832, he founded the first monastery here—Kongobu-ji—in order to preach his new doctrine, Shingon. From that point, Koya-san continued to grow in influence. At its height, in the 15C, it embraced over 1,500 monasteries and 90,000 monks, enjoying the protection of powerful lords.

These monks were also soldiers who were always ready to interrupt their prayers and descend from their entrenched position in the mountains to launch armed raids on the rival monasteries of Kyoto, especially those of Mount Hiei. In retaliation, Koya-san was attacked and burned down on several occasions. To put an end to these constant conflicts, the Tokugawa shoguns decided, in the 17C, to cut off the monasteries' means of subsistence by confiscating their vast estates. This was the beginning of a slow decline.

**Koya-san today** – The life of this tranquil town, a UNESCO World Heritage Site since 2004, is entirely centered on the monasteries, where nearly 1,000 monks devote themselves to prayer and meditation. As elsewhere in Japan, their principal function, for which they are paid, is to perform funeral rites and honor the

### Kukai, a sacred figure

Kobo Daishi, whose real name was Kukai, was born in 774 on the island of Shikoku, which today is dotted with temples dedicated to his memory (see p452). An aristocrat, he studied classical Chinese letters, but left university to become a wandering ascetic. From 804 to 806 he was in China, where he was able to study the Tantric doctrine of Chenyang, which he brought back to Japan, renaming it Shingon.

Honored by the Emperor on his return, he became a spiritual guide to the Court and in 823 was put in charge of To-ji in Kyoto. Nevertheless, he spent most of his life at Koya-san. After his death in 835, many legends spread about his miracles and other exploits. Venerated by the common people as if he were a god, Kukai was also a great humanist, poet, calligrapher, and philosopher, one of the fathers of classical Japanese culture. He is credited, for example, with the invention of the *hiragana* syllabary.

memory of ancestors. But in Koya-san, this activity takes on a different dimension, thanks to the fervent cult surrounding Kobo Daishi since his death. His disciples claim that he is still alive, in a state of meditation *(samadhi)*, waiting for Miroku, the Buddha of the Future. Twice a day, the monks go in procession to his mausoleum in Okuno-in cemetery and take him a meal. The legendary powers of the holy man have also attracted thousands of the faithful to be buried beside him, hoping in this way to be reborn in paradise. Spread throughout the town, the *shukubo* (temple dwellings), maintained by monks, provide accommodation for pilgrims and tourists.

**The Shingon school** – Claiming 12 million followers and 12,000 affiliated monasteries around the world, Shingon Buddhism,the True Word sect, is an esoteric doctrine that states everyone on earth can achieve enlightenment and

## USEFUL INFORMATION

**Tourist Office** – Koya-san Tourist Association, *by the Senjuin-bashi bus stop (B2). Open 8.30am–5pm.* ℘*0736-56-2616. www.shukubo.jp.*

**Bank/Foreign Exchange**– Kiyo Bank, 54.7yd/50m to the left of the post office *(see below)*. *Open Mon–Sat 9am–3pm.*

**Post Office/Withdrawals**– Opposite the Tourist Office. *Open Mon–Fri 9am–3pm.* **ATM** *Open Mon–Fri 9am–6pm, Sat 9am–5pm, Sun 9am–3pm.*

## TRANSPORTATION

**BY TRAIN** – **From Nanba Station in Osaka** – Take the Nankai Koya Line to Gokurakubashi. Four Limited Express trains per day *(1hr25min, ¥1,990)* or Express trains every 30min *(1hr45min, ¥1,230)*.

**From Gokurakubashi**, cable car *(5min)* to Koya-san station, 1.9mi/3km N of the town. Buses go from the station to the center *(10min, ¥280)*.

**GETTING AROUND KOYA-SAN**

The most central bus stop, **Senjuin-bashi**, is at the crossroads on the main street, near the Tourist Office *(B2)*. The town stretches from the **Dai-mon** gate in the west, to **Okuno-in** cemetery in the east. A bus *(every 20–30min)* serves the whole route, but it's just as easy to walk.

If you're only sleeping one night in Koya-san, get the **Koya-san World Heritage Ticket** at Nanba station. This is a 2-day pass that includes, for less than ¥2,780, the Osaka–Koya-san round trip and reduced prices in the town itself. From Kyoto, Nara, or Kansai International Airport. The **Kansai Thru Pass** is also an option.

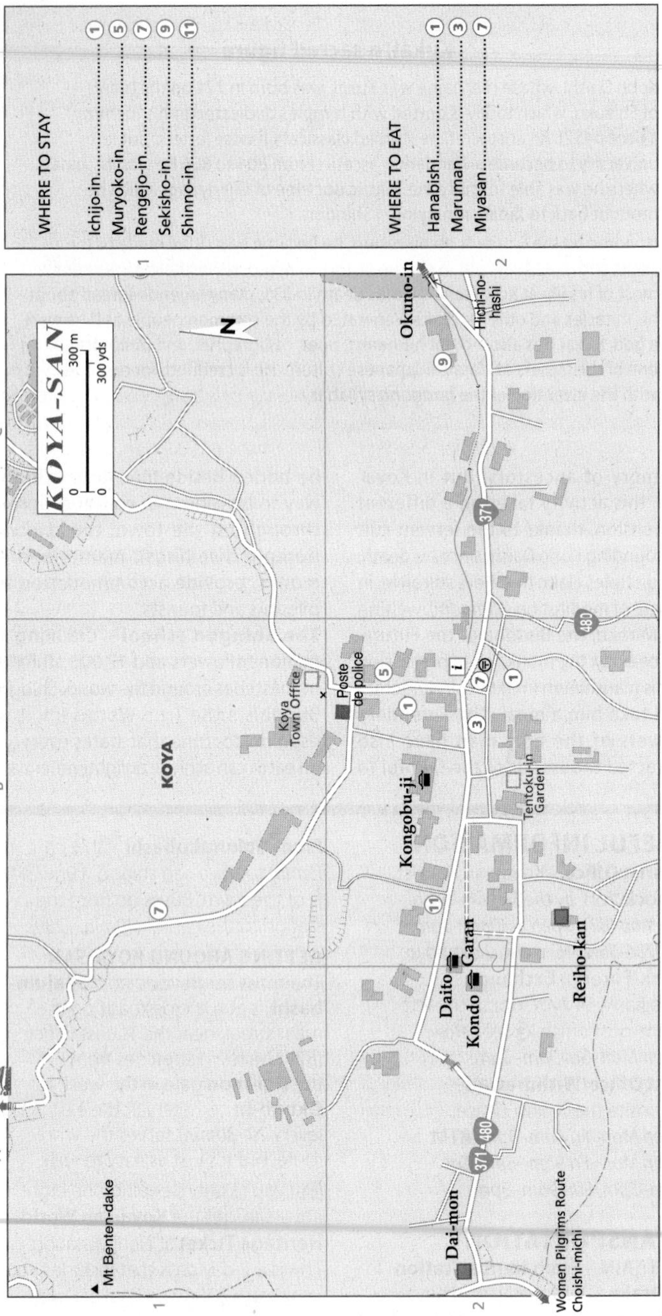




become a Buddha through the endless repetition of mantras (incantations) and the use of *mandalas* (symbolic images) as an aid to meditation.

## SIGHTS

Koya-san occupies a plateau surrounded by eight mountains, which, in the symbolism of Shingon Buddhism, represent the eight petals of the lotus blossom on which the Buddha sits. Koya-san has three great complexes: **Danjo Garan**, **Kongobu-ji**, and **Okuno-in**.

### Konpon Daito★ 壇上伽藍 *Map B2.*

*Open May–Oct 8.30am–5.30pm; Nov–Apr 8.30am–4.30pm. Daito ¥200, Kondo ¥200, Reihokan Museum ¥600.*

The entrance to this sacred precinct, about 328yd/300m to the west of the complex, is through an impressive gate on two floors, **Dai-mon** *(reconstructed in 1705)*, flanked by two guardian deities. The center of Danjo Garan is dominated by **Daito**★, a large, vermilion pagoda 164ft/50m high. The original was built by Kobo Daishi in 816, but the present version dates from 1947. The rather gaudy interior houses a large gilded statue of **Dainichi Nyorai** (the cosmic Buddha) accompanied by four other Buddhas and surrounded by lacquered pillars painted with *bosatsu*.

Just opposite is the **Kondo**★, the principal pavilion, where major religious ceremonies are held. Erected in 819, it was rebuilt for the seventh time in 1932. The central altar in the gilded hall contains a **Yakushi Nyorai** (the Buddha of Healing) *(see box p289)*. Behind the Kondo, is the **Miedo** (1848), an elegant pavilion with a vast, protecting roof of cypress bark, containing portraits of Kobo Daishi with his disciples *(open once a year on Mar 21)*.

**Reihokan Museum**★ – This museum to the south of Danjo Garan, on the other side of a pond, is well worth a visit as it is here that Koya-san's greatest treasures have been preserved since 1939. Its collection comprises several thousand works, of which about 200 are displayed in rotation. Many are designated National Treasures or Important Cultural Properties. The galleries are full to overflowing with sculptures and mandalas (diagrams of the universe), whose style and esoteric symbolism recall Tibetan tantric art: terrifying figures leaping from the flames, benign or grimacing deities. The great wall hangings extolling the Buddha and his various manifestations have the grace and freshness of Renaissance painting and the teeming vividness of medieval altarpieces. Most of the sculptures are in the style of the Heian period: imposing bodies, detailed clothing, fierce or austere faces, and so on.

### Kongobu-ji★ 金剛峯寺 *Map B2.*

*Open 8.30am–4.30pm. ¥500.*

In the center of the town is Koya-san's holy of holies, Kongobu-ji, headquarters of the Shingon sect. The complex comprises administrative buildings, a religious university, and a temple open to visitors. Built in 1593 by Toyotomi Hideyoshi, it has been destroyed and rebuilt several times *(the last time in 1863)*. The main hall, **Ohiroma**★, contains beautiful *fusuma* (sliding panels) by Kano Motonobu, founder of the Kano School during the Muromachi period (16C). The Willow Room, decorated by one of his pupils, was where Hideyoshi's nephew Toyotomi Hidetsugu committed ritual suicide in 1595. At the far end of Kongobu-ji is the largest rock

#### The fire ceremony

At five in the morning, the gong sounds to announce that the service is about to start. The fire ceremony *(goma)* is held in all the temple dwellings at dawn and guests are cordially invited. In the half-light of the shrine, the priest sits down before an altar laden with offerings, bells, and candlesticks, and burns bundles of sticks in a bronze bowl. The fire crackles, burning away illusions and liberating men from their passions. Lined up on either side, sitting on their heels with their eyes closed, the monks chant mantras in low voices. The clouds of incense, the tinkling of little bells, the candlelight reflected on the silk robes: everything about the ceremony is eerie and spellbinding. When the ritual is over, the monks turn back into hosts, washing floors, cleaning rooms, and preparing breakfast.

### Unusual monks

The main function of the monks of Koya-san may be to pamper the souls of the dead, but they also like the good things in life. They are not hermits and in fact lead comfortable lives, open to the outside world. They do not take vows of abstinence or chastity (most are married), and they are not averse, when the opportunity arises, to eating meat, drinking sake, or singing karaoke. All this is a long way from the austerity originally preached by the Buddha. But here it is believed that Buddhism can be a skill, adaptable to the pleasures of modern life without hypocrisy. "For us," says one of the monks, "Buddhism isn't about suffering and renunciation, but about trying to find happiness through spiritual elevation."

garden in Japan, **Banryu-tei**★, whose rocks evoke mountains (some say two dragons) emerging from a sea of clouds. The visit ends with the monastery's huge kitchen, where meals (mainly rice) were cooked for about 2,000 monks.

**Okuno-in**★★ 奥の院 *C2, off map. 30min walk E of village. No charge.*
Okuno-in, the **cemetery**, is unquestionably the most fascinating place in Koya-san. Here, in the bluish shade of age-old Japanese cedars with giant trunks, nearly **200,000 graves** are scattered. Famous names, shoguns, samurai, high priests, and artists lie side by side with ordinary people. Flashy modern gravestones alternate with older, more intimate examples, moving in their simplicity. Some are distinctly comical, such as the cup and the giant rocket, erected by a coffee company and an aeronautics firm respectively, or the monument built by an insecticide manufacturer to beg forgiveness of the ants he exterminated. For all that, many Japanese still regard the possibility of placing their parents' urn under the protection of Kobo Daishi as a huge privilege and an assurance that they will one day be reborn in paradise. Such is the demand for the limited number of plots that prices have become astronomical.

*Flagstoned path, Okuno-in*
© JNTO

From the first sacred bridge *(Ichi-no-hashi)* at the entrance, a **flagstoned path**★★ of 1.2mi/2km, lined with moss-covered stone lanterns, leads through this strange, melancholy undergrowth, amid lichen-eroded gravestones rising in tiers up the slopes. Silence reigns over this city of the dead, occasionally interrupted by the clicking of *geta* (wooden clogs worn by the monks) or the tinkling of bells carried by the white-clad pilgrims. Near the third bridge *(Mimyo-no-hashi)* is a picturesque row of bronze statues, popular deities in scarlet bibs, which visitors sprinkle with water to purify the karma of the dead.

Soon after the bridge, at the top of a flight of 30-odd steps, you will come to **Toro-do**★, the Lantern Hall, the lanterns of which glitter on the ceiling like stars in the night sky. Donated by the faithful, some have been burning for hundreds of years. Behind this building is **Gobyo**★, the mausoleum of Kobo Daishi, who is believed to have been in a state of meditation for nearly 1,200 years. Twice a day, monks come here in procession to offer him not only food, but also fans in summer, heating in winter, new clothes once a year, and so on. To acquire merits and beg favors of the holy man, entire families pray fervently at the mausoleum. Most leave generous offerings.

### WALKS

**Women Pilgrims Route** *A2, off map* – Until 1872, Koya-san, rather like Mount Athos in Greece, was forbidden to women. They were, however, allowed to take the forest trail skirting the eight peaks that surround the basin where the holy city lies. Now well-signposted, the complete circuit takes about 5hr30min, but you can do just part of it and stop to contemplate the many beautiful **views** along the way.

**Choishi-michi** *A2, off map* – Before the cable car was installed at the beginning of the 20C, this 13.67mi/22km trail *(7hr walk)* was the only way to get to Koya-san. It is still much used by pilgrims, especially those who have previously gone around the 88 temples on the island of Shikoku *(see p 452)*. Granite slabs stand every 354.3ft/108m to mark out the path. The trail starts in the plain, at the temple of Jison-in in the village of Kudoyama, one train stop before the terminus of the line to Koya-san. Because of the marked difference in height from bottom to top *(2,296.6ft/700m)*, this walk is only recommended to trail-hardened hikers, unless the downward direction is preferred.

## ADDRESSES

### STAY

#### KOYA-SAN

There are no hotels in Koya-san, only **shukubo** *(temple dwellings)* that provide Japanese-style accommodation. The standard of comfort may sometimes be rudimentary, but there's no denying the charm. Vegetarian meals, included in the price and served in the rooms in the evening and morning, are almost unavoidable. *Advance reservations required.*

**Ichijo-in 一乗院** *Near Kongobu-ji (B2). 0736-56-2214. www.itijyoin.or.jp. 37 rooms.* This temple, gleaming with gold, serves excellent, copious meals. Rooms are comfortable and attractive. The newest—and most expensive—have bathrooms, air conditioning, and internet access.

**Muryoko-in 無量光院** *In the direction of the town hall (B2). 0736-56-2104. 22 rooms.* A friendly, authentic temple. One of the monks is a French-speaking Swiss, who will hold forth passionately about Koya-san. The rooms are fairly spartan.

**Rengejo-in 蓮華定院** *Next to the Tokugawa mausoleum (B1). 0736-56-2233. 40 rooms.* The rooms of the temple have gorgeous sliding panels. The best rooms have a **view** of the garden. *Refined cuisine. Fluent English spoken.*

**Sekisho-in 赤松院** *Near Ichi-no-hashi (C2). 0736-56-2734. 60 rooms.* A temple much-appreciated by tourists, with lovely rooms in the old part. The rooms in the modern annex have private bathrooms, but less character.

**Shinno-in 親王院** *N of the Danjo Garan (B2). 0736-56-2227. 7 rooms.* A small temple, which means you won't run into large groups in high season. A well-preserved old setting, a pleasant *o-furo*, and rooms decorated with attractive *fusuma*.

### EAT

#### KOYA-SAN

The **shukubo** all serve vegetarian food *(shojin ryori)*. The number of dishes varies according to the price of the room, but Koya-san also has a few non-vegetarian restaurants.

**Miyasan 宮さん** *Alley near the central crossroads (B2). 0736-56-2827. Open Mon–Sat 4–10pm.* Students, monks, town employees: the whole of Koya-san rubs shoulders in this tiny, but friendly *izakaya* in the evening. *Menu in English.*

**Hanabishi 花菱** *Next to the post office (B2). 0736-56-2236. Open 11am–6pm.* Koya-san's most chic restaurant. Lovely black decor. Refined *kaiseki* cuisine at reasonable prices, including sushi and, in winter, *yosenabe* (one-pot cooking).

**Maruman 丸万** *Main street (B2). 0736-56-2049. Open 9am–6pm.* A good variety of solid fare (sushi, *tonkatsu*, shrimp fritters, *udon*, curries, etc.). *Quick service. Menus on the window.*

# Kumano Kodo ★★★
# 熊野古道

**After Buddhism was introduced into Japan in the 6C, the Kumano region gradually absorbed the new religion—especially its ascetic practices—giving rise to an extraordinary fusion of Shintoism and Buddhism (the local deities are considered manifestations of Buddhist deities). The three shrines of Kumano Sanzan became a major destination for pilgrimages. Several routes crossing the peninsula converge on the Kumano Hongu Taisha. The most popular, the Nakahechi route, was taken by pilgrims from Kyoto: the 497mi/800km round trip could take anything from 30 to 40 days. Another route, the Kohechi, connected Koya-san and Kumano Sanzan: it was the shortest, but also the most difficult, crossing three passes at an altitude of more than 3,280.8ft/1,000m. Along the routes, a dense network of secondary shrines, called *oji*, gave pilgrims the opportunity to make offerings and perform rituals, and also to rest a little. For some years, Wakayama prefecture has been actively encouraging the revival of these routes, which have been twinned with the Camino de Santiago de Compostela since 1988 and a UNESCO World Heritage Site since 2004.**

- **Michelin Map:** Principal Sights Map A3 .
- **Info:** Travelers interested in exploring the pilgramage routes can obtain information from the Tanabe City Kumano Tourism Bureau, 24-1Nakayashiki-cho, Tanabe. ✆0739-26-9025. www.tb-kumano.jp. *See also* the Wakayama prefecture website: http://kanko.wiwi.co.jp/world/english.
- **Location:** Kumano Hongu Taisha is 250mi/400km south of Kyoto. The JR Kisei line from Wakayama connects Kumano with Shirahama, Kii-Katsuura, Nachi and Shingu.
- **Kids:** Walking the pilgramage routes and Yunomine Onsen.
- **Timing:** Allow a day for Shirahama and Kii-Katsuura, from where you'll leave the next morning after visiting the fish market; a day at Kumano Hongu Taisha and Yunomine Onsen; a day for the pilgramage route and shrines of Kumano Sanzan.

## SIGHTS

### Kii Peninsula★
紀伊半島

*By car, follow the Koya Ryujin Skyline (Route 371), which goes to Kii-Tanabe and Shirahama. At Ryujin Onsen, you can also turn off along Route 425 toward Hongu and Kii-Katsuura.*

*By train, take the Nankai Koya Line to Hashimoto, then the JR Wakayama Line to Wakayama, where you can connect to the JR Kisei Line that runs along the coast, stopping at Shirahama, Kii-Katsuura, Nachi, and Shingu.*

#### Shirahama *Onsen* 白浜温泉

*15min by bus from JR Shirahama station. Bicycle rental at the station (open 9am–6pm; ¥500).*

This well-known thermal spa, one of the three oldest in Japan *(the others being Arima Onsen and Dogo Onsen)*, is more than 1,300 years old. Among its other attractions is a splendid white sandy **beach**, rated one of the cleanest and

most pleasant in the whole of Japan. *Bathing from the beginning of June to the end of September.*
**Sakino-yu** – *Open Thu–Tue 8am–5pm (summer 7pm).* *¥300.* Located 0.6mi/1km south of the beach, this public bath has a delightful open-air pool at the edge of a rocky shore.

### Kii-Katsuura 紀伊勝浦

*49.7mi/80km from Shirahama (1hr20min by train).*
Nestling in a magnificent but unfortunately somewhat built-up bay, Kii-Katsuura is one of the principal tuna fishing ports in Japan. The **tuna market** held here every morning at dawn can hold its own against Tsukiji fish market in Tokyo (*see p143*).
The Hotel Urashima, on the island opposite the harbor, has a lovely *rotenburo* (outdoor hot-spring pool) open to visitors (*see Addresses p349*).
*From Kii Katsuura, take the JR Kisei Line to Nachi station (5min; ¥140) or the bus from Kii-Katsuura to the Daimon-zaka Chushajo-mae stop (20 min, on the hour from 6am–6pm; ¥410).*

## Kumano Sanzan★★★ 熊野三山

The Shinto worship of nature is well represented by Kumano Sanzan, the three sacred shrines of **Kumano Hongu**, **Kumano Hayatama**, and **Kumano Nachi**, at the tip of the peninsula. During the Middle Ages this region was identified with the Buddhist paradise of the Pure Land. Pilgrims flocked here from Kyoto along old, paved routes (*kumano kodo*) that cut through the steep mountainsides and dense forests.
**Kumano Nachi Taisha★★** 熊野那智大社– *30min by bus from Kii-Katsuura station. Open 8am–5pm. Museum ¥300, waterfall ¥300.*
A perfect embodiment of the Shinto worship of natural forces, the majestic waterfall **Nachi no Taki**★★ has been venerated since ancient times, drawing ascetics who come to be purified in its icy waters. It stands out, 436.4ft/133m high, like a long, white veil against the dark green vegetation. A fine example of the fusion of Buddhism and Shintoism, a Buddhist pagoda, Seiganto-ji, lies close to the shrine and its little museum.
From the shrine, it is possible to walk back down *(2hr)* to Nachi station along **Daimon-zaka**★★, an old path of mossy stones that winds its way through a forest of imposing cedars. It will give you a good idea of the pilgrimage trails that criss-cross the peninsula.
**Kumano Hayatama Taisha★** 熊野速玉大社– *15min walk from Shingu station. Shrine: Open 5.30am–6pm. Nocharge. Shinpokan (Treasure Hall): open 9am–4pm. ¥500*
Resplendent in vermilion, the shrine is dedicated to **Hayatama**, the Shinto god of the life force, later associated with **Yakushi Nyorai**, the Buddha of Healing (*see box p291*). Rebuilt in 1894, it houses a large number of votive objects. To the south, a sloping flight of steps leads down to a sacred rock, **Gotobiki-iwa**, where the deities of Kumano are said to have "landed."
**Kumano Hongu Heritage Center★** 世界遺産 熊野本宮館– *Buses go to Hongu from the JR stations of Shingu (10 buses daily, 1h20min – Kumano Kotsu, Nara Kotsu, and Meiko buses) and Kii-Tanabe (5 buses daily, 2h). 100-1 Hongu, Hongu cho. Open 9am–5pm. www.city.tanabe.lg.jp/hongukan/en.*
Facing Kumano Hongu Taisha Shrine, the Kumano Hongu Heritage Center has exhibitions on the UNESCO World

### Kumano Mandalas

Painted on paper with inexpensive ink, about 40in/100cm high and 60in/150cm wide, easy to transport, mandalas serve for religious visualization in order to teach. The Kumano Bikuni, itinerant nuns, promoted the Kumano pilgrimage with these paintings, where each object and character has a story. Historically, only the Nachi shrine possesses mandalas, dating from the 16C and 17C. In 2007, Tanaka Shigezo, the renowned Japanese painter, prepared the mandalas for the Hongu and Hayatama shrines.

*Kumano Hongu Taisha*

© Tanabe City Kumano Tourism Bureau/JNTO

Heritage listed Sacred Sites and Pilgrimage Routes in the Kii Mountains. The Wakayama World Heritage Center permanent exhibition in particular presents Kumano mandalas—absolutely not to be missed.

### Kumano Hongu Taisha★★★

熊野本宮大社 – *Facing the Kumano Hongu Heritage Center.* ○*Open 8am–5pm.* ⊜ *No charge; Treasure Hall: ¥300.*
At the top of the long staircase in the shade of cryptomeria trees can be seen the Hongu Shrine to the divinity Ketsumiko, later equated with the Buddha Amida. In 1889, the building was carried off by a flood; hence it was moved to here, west of its original location on a bank of the Kumano River, where giant *torii* stand. At the entrance to the site, are banners with its emblem: a crow (*yatagarasu*), whose three feet symbolize the heavens, the earth, and humanity. This shrine is over 800 years old, one of the oldest in Japan. The use of natural, unfinished materials creates harmony with the surrounding forest. Instead of nails and bolts, complex joinery fits pieces of wood together, reinforcing the impression of coherency. The beautiful arched roof is covered with cypress bark and decorated with bronzes, as well as rounded wooden blocks and crossed beams pointing skyward. Peering between chinks in the fencing reveals the sacred corridor under the pavilion's verandas, specific to the Kumano style: it was here that monks went to devote themselves to meditation, prayer, and sutras, and where they sometimes even communed with the Divine.

### Oyunohara 大斎原 – *10min by foot from Kumano Hongu Heritage Center.*
The Oyunohara clearing, the original site of the Kumano Hongu Shrine, is reached by the **O-Torii★★**, an immense steel arch about 111ft/34m high. Legend says the Kumano divinities came down to earth as moons in a great oak in the clearing, rendered sacred. At first only a purified space for rituals and offerings, with Buddhist influence the clearing gradually became a shrine of several pavilions. It was only after the great 1889 flood that the sacred clearing, a place of nature worship for over 2,000 years, returned to its natural state. During festivals, the great portal is lit at night, creating a magic atmosphere to bring man closer to the Kumano divinities.

🥾 From Hongu, a pleasant trail through woods and paddy fields *(1hr walk)* leads to the small, hot-spring village of **Yunomine Onsen**, where you can spend the night.

**Yunomine *Onsen*** 湯の峰温泉

In a valley, the village of Yunomine has one of Japan's longest-known hot springs, discovered 1,800 years ago and closely bound to the Kumano pilgrimage. The inhabitants boil vegetables and eggs *(which can be purchased in local shops)* in a public *onsen*, the **Yuzutsu**, along the stream crossing the village. A little further and by reservation, you can bathe *(30min; 2 persons max)* in the **Tsuboyu★**, a little stone basin fed by underground water at 195°F/90°C, in a wooden shed. The curative waters give pilgrims a brief moment to soothe both body and soul.

*From Yunomine Onsen, take the Ryujin bus to Hosshinmon-oji (35min).*

**Hosshinmon-oji★** 発心門王子

To reach the sacred space of Kumano Hongu Taisha, pilgrims achieve various levels of spiritual awakening before rebirth in the pure earthly paradise of Kumano. Hoshinmon-oji is one of the physical stations marking these ritual steps in mortal reincarnation and one of the five principal *oji* (secondary shrine of Kumano).

From Hoshinmon-oji, a section of the **Nakahechi pilgrimage★★** route alternates with ground mountain **panoramic views** and quaint village roads, views of terraced tea plantations, and restful forest paths. After the **Fushiogami-oji** viewpoint, from which **Oyunohara Island** can be seen surrounded by mountains, the road takes you to Kumano Hongu Shrine. Don't miss this walk, but take a companion, and maps from the hotel or a Tourist Information Center.

## EXCURSION

### Mount Tamaki 玉置山

*From Totsukawa Onsen, about 30min by taxi or by hotel bus to the Tamaki-jinja parking lot from which the path leads.*

*A guide is necessary in the mountains: ask about one at your hotel.*

At dawn from the top of the sacred mountain of Tamaki *(3,530ft/1,076m)*, clouds can be seen enveloping the **Kumano Mountains**. It is a sight worth getting up early to see at sunrise, reached by a 20min walk on paths shaded by giant cedars.

Near the summit, **Tamaki-jinja★** *(8am–5pm; ¥300)* rises among thousand-year-old trees and sacred sites; a deified tree, 3,000 years old, protects the shrine. *Rooms are available for pilgrims wishing to spend the night near the summit.*

# ADDRESSES

## STAY

### KII-KATSUURA

**Hotel Nakanoshima** ホテル中の島
*On Nakanoshima Island facing the port, free shuttle every 15–30min from 5.30am–10pm. 0735-52-1111. www.hotel-nakanoshima.jp/english/index.html.* This large complex occupies the entire island; beautiful traditional rooms with balcony and **view** of the sea. Very good cuisine, **Olympic pool**, and superb outdoor and indoor *onsen* overlooking the sea. Private *onsen* by reservation *(¥210 for 50min).*

**Hotel Urashima** ホテル浦島
*On the island opposite the harbor. 0735-52-1011. www.hotelurashima.co.jp. 800 rooms.* Served by shuttle, this concrete colossus has some great assets: *2 swimming pools* and *6 onsen*, including a fantastic one in a sea cave.

### YUNOMINE *ONSEN*

**Adumaya Ryokan** 旅館あづまや
*122 Yunomine, Hongu cho ipponbashi. 0735-42-0012. www.adumaya.co.jp.* In the heart of the Kumano forest, this ryokan offers traditional rooms, simple and welcoming, and excellent cuisine steamed in the *onsen*. Relax in the indoor wooden bath, or outside in a stone *onsen* among trees. The charming owner offers *bento* for eating on the pilgrimage routes.

### MOUNT TAMAKI

**Hotel Subaru** ホテル昴
*From the Shingu JR station via Kumano Hongu Taisha Shrine (Hongu Taisha mae), Nara Kotsu bus to Totsukawa Onsen (45min, ¥2,050), then shuttle to hotel (by reservation). 0746-64-1111.* This superb hotel at the mountains' feet has 7 indoor and outdoor *onsen*, as well as a pools fed by the same spring. An old hand-run cable car carries visitors a little way up the mountain.

# Osaka★★
# 大阪

**When greeting each other, Osakans don't say *"Konnichiwa"* but *"Mokari makka?"* (literally, "Making any money?"). Osaka has always been a city of merchants. With its harbor, and its many canals ideal for transporting goods, it was even, in the 16C, the principal trading center in Japan, and was known as "the kitchen of the nation"—hence its tradition of hospitality, zesty dialect (Osaka-ben), and wonderful food. Osakans are extrovert, enterprising, and hedonistic, and love eating well and going out. Osaka's *mizu shobai* nighttime entertainment industry is a teeming maelstrom of neon lights, pachinko halls, karaoke joints, Ferris wheels, bars, hostess clubs, and "maids cafes"—all places to unwind from the stresses of living in Japan's second megalopolis, an urban monster full of underground shopping malls and futuristic skyscrapers. Where Kyoto and Nara are windows onto an age-old Japan, Osaka is a vibrant showcase of the latest contemporary trends.**

- **Population:** 2,644,581 (Greater Osaka: 17 million) – Osaka Prefecture.
- **Michelin Map:** Principal Sights Map B3 – Regional Map p283.
- **Location:** Osaka, on a bay on the Inland Sea, 24.9mi/40km from Kyoto and 20.5mi/33km from Kobe, is served by Kansai International Airport, located on an artificial island to the south. The sprawling city comprises: the north, Kita-Umeda, spreading around JR Osaka station, the commercial heart of Osaka and an area of skyscrapers and big stores; the south, Minami, from Nanba station via the Dotonbori Canal to the Shinsaibashi district, Osaka's nightlife district, full of restaurants and bars. Farther east is the castle area; to the southeast, the area around Tenno-ji; and finally, to the west, Osaka Bay. Note that the Shinkansen arrive at Shin-Osaka station, 5min by subway north of JR Osaka station.
- **Kids:** Head for Osaka Bay: the aquarium, the Ferris wheel, and Universal Studios Japan.
- **Timing:** Two days should be enough to see the main sights. Obtain a comprehensive map of the city, and use the subway and trams for moving around.
- **Don't miss:** Dotonbori by night; the view from the observatory of Umeda Sky Building; a *bunraku* puppet show (*see p357*).

## A BIT OF HISTORY

**A city of water** – The founding of Osaka goes back to the 3C. The city, then called Naniwa, grew up around its port. Emperor Kotoku even made this his capital from 645 until his death in 654. Naniwa established commercial and diplomatic ties with Korea and China, and was instrumental in the spread of Buddhism in Japan, through the temple of Shitenno-ji, built in 593. The inhabitants built many canals and bridges to facilitate the transportation of goods and strengthen the city's vocation as a commercial center.

**"The pantry of Japan"** – Things really took off toward the end of the 16C, when the shogun Toyotomi Hideyoshi—the man who unified Japan—built his castle here. The city grew in prosperity in the 17C, when it was the hub of Japanese agricultural output, supplying rice to the new capital Edo and becoming known as "the granary of the nation." The wealthy merchants of Osaka became patrons of literature and theater, especially Kabuki and *bunraku* (*see p357*), the latter having been created in Osaka. In the 19C, the city specialized in textiles, the electrical industry, and manufactured products. Until the 1920s, Hanshin—the great coastal industrial area in which Osaka played the pivotal role—remained the economic engine of the country.

**Tokyo's rival** – A prime target for American bombs, Osaka was almost razed to the ground during World War II, then rebuilt to a modern blueprint. In 1970, it was the site of the first Universal Exposition to be held in Asia. Already the third largest commercial port in the country, Osaka's ambition to become a major player in pan-Asian trade came a step closer to fruition with the opening in 1994, of Kansai International Airport.

### Japanese Innovation

The economic capital of Kansai, a region with a Gross Domestic Product greater than that of Canada or Spain, Osaka is a place where many inventions first saw the light of day: instant noodles, prefabricated houses, automated ticket machines, moving walkways, vacuum-packed meals, Walkmans, utility knives, calculators, etc. Several multinationals also started out in Osaka, such as Matsushita (Panasonic), Sharp, Sanyo, Glico, and Suntory. And among the celebrities born in Osaka are the two biggest stars of contemporary Japanese architecture, Tange Kenzo and Ando Tadao.

## SIGHTS

## THE NORTH (KITA-UMEDA)

The main terminus for bus, subway, and public and private train lines, this bustling urban crossroads is crammed with big stores *(Daimaru, Hanshin, Hankyu, Bic Camera, Herbis Plaza)*, underground shopping malls *(Whity Umeda, Diamor Osaka)*, and an endless labyrinth of footbridges and pathways. It doesn't take long for the newcomer to get lost in this huge concrete jungle, where the skyscrapers vie for space. Huddling in the shadow of these giants of glass and steel are narrow streets packed with eateries and *izakaya*, bars where you can have a quick meal at the counter. By day, Kita is the ideal place for shopping and having fun at the same time: a good example is the trendy shopping complex **Hep Five** (*open 11am–11pm; last admission 10.15pm; ¥1400-¥2200) Map I B1*, which has a giant whale in its atrium and an impressive 347.8ft/106m-high Ferris wheel on the roof.

**Umeda Sky Building★** *Map I A1, off map. Observatory: Open 10am–10.30pm. ¥700.*

To the west of Hankyu Umeda station, an underground passageway leads to this futuristic building built in 1993 by the architect Hara Hiroshi.

This "city in the sky" consists of twin towers joined, at a height of 567.6ft/173m, by a circular terrace, the **Floating Garden Observatory**, which offers a stunning 360-degree **view★★**.

The sight is especially bewitching at night, when the city is all lit up. But beware: the glass elevator that takes you up to the top is not recommended for anyone who suffers from vertigo.

## THE CENTER AND THE WEST★

The island of Nakano-shima, sandwiched between the Dojima and Tosabori Rivers, is home to an interesting museum. Farther west, the castle grounds, with its cherry trees, are a pleasant place for a stroll.

### Museum of Oriental Ceramics★ 東洋陶磁美術館

*Map II B1 off map.*
*5min N of both Yodoyabashi and Kitahama subway stations. Open Tue–Sun 9.30am–5pm. ¥500.*

This museum, founded in 1982, has one of the largest collections of ceramics in the world: some 2,700 rare items

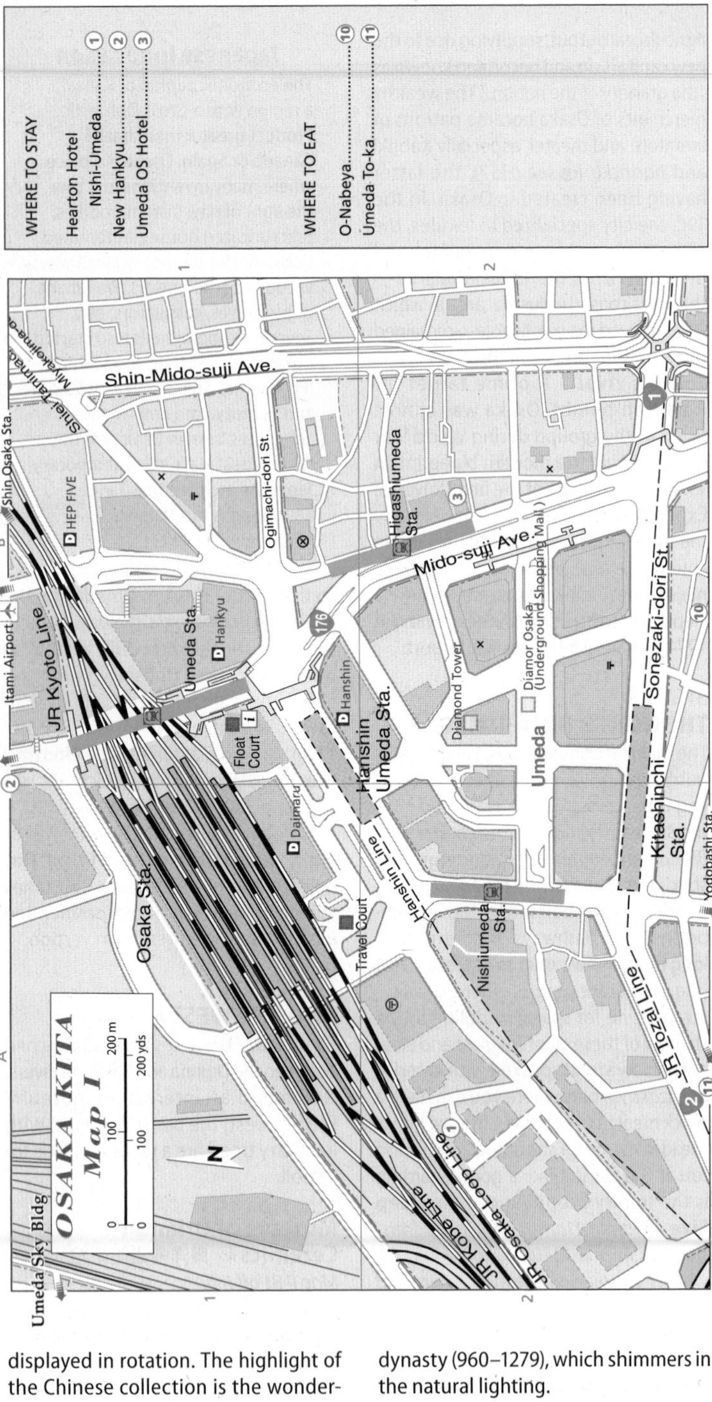




displayed in rotation. The highlight of the Chinese collection is the wonderful **celadon★** (pottery) from the Song dynasty (960–1279), which shimmers in the natural lighting.
There are also ceramics from Korea, and, to a lesser extent, Japan.

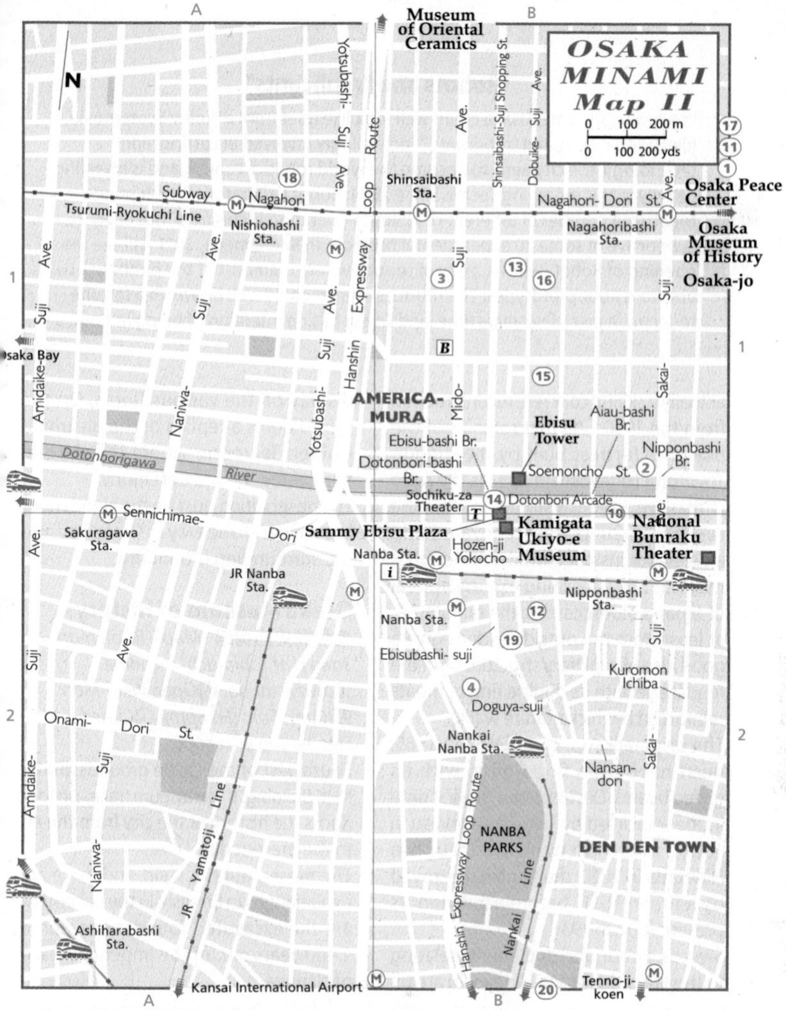


WHERE TO STAY

- Carpe Diem ..... (1)
- Kaneyoshi Ryokan ..... (2)
- Nikko Osaka ..... (3)
- Swissôtel Nankai Osaka ..... (4)

WHERE TO EAT

- Chibo ..... (10)
- Hyotan Taiko-en ..... (11)
- Jiyuken ..... (12)
- Kani Doraku ..... (14)
- Kichiyoshi ..... (13)
- Ma-Nabeya ..... (15)
- Nishiya ..... (16)
- Sora ..... (17)
- Vrai de Vrai ..... (18)
- Watami ..... (19)
- Zuboraya ..... (20)



## Osaka Castle★ 大坂城

*Map II B1 off map.*
*15min W of Tanimachi 4-chome subway station. Open 9am–5pm. ¥600.*
Surrounded by attractive grounds planted with plum and cherry trees, the canopied roofs of Osaka Castle rise against a background of towering skyscrapers. It's a striking contrast, but somewhat deceptive, as the keep is

## Robots and "replicants"

In a few years' time, Osaka could well look like a set from a Ridley Scott movie, filled with robots and "replicants." Increasingly involved in cutting-edge technology, the city aims to become the world robotics capital, and is investing heavily in this emerging sector. Since 2004, Robot Laboratory, which brings together a number of different companies operating in this field, has been supportive of some 20 experimental projects. In Kita-Umeda, 2011 will see the opening of RoboCityCore, a city of robots, where members of the public will be able to try out prototypes. The robotics market could well be worth a fortune to Japan in just a few years time, and Osaka has no intention of being left out.

actually a skillful concrete reconstruction from the 1930s. All that remains of the powerful fortress built by the shogun Toyotomi Hideyoshi in 1583 is the base of massive, irregular stones. In 1997, the castle was completely renovated and an elevator installed inside. Although it may not have anything like the appeal of Japan's oldest castles, the building—at least from the outside—does give a good idea of a military structure from the feudal age with its double ring of moats reinforced by thick granite walls.

The original keep, completed in 1585, must have cut a fine figure, with its gilded beams. Destroyed for the first time in the attack led by Tokugawa Ieyasu in 1615, it was rebuilt by his heir Tokugawa Hidetada in 1620, then again destroyed by a fire in 1665, before achieving its present form in 1931.

Swords, armor, and documents relating to the life of Toyotomi Hideyoshi are on display on the various floors. On the third floor is a replica of the gleaming Golden Tearoom, where the shogun performed the Tea Ceremony.

The observation post on the eighth floor has a **view** all the way to Osaka Bay and the surrounding mountains.

### Osaka Museum of History

大阪歴史博物館 *Map II B1 off map. 3min N of Tanimachi 4-chome subway station. Open Wed–Mon 9.30am–5pm (Fri 8pm). Closed Dec 28–Jan 4. ¥600.*

Southwest of the castle grounds, in the NHK Building, this museum traces on four floors the history of the city from the 4C to the present day.

The presentation is vivid, and there are explanations in English. In the basement are the excavated foundations, some 1,400 years old, of the Imperial Palace of Naniwa.

*Dotonbori at night*

## Osaka International Peace Center 大阪国際平和センター

*Map II B1, off map.*
*5min W of Norinomiya subway station.*
*Open Tue–Sun 9.30am–5pm. ¥250.*
In the southeast of the castle grounds, 10 minutes' walk from the Museum of History, Osaka International Peace Center commemorates the victims of the aerial bombardment of the city during World War II, and of the atom bombs dropped on Hiroshima and Nagasaki. With its detailed displays of the horrors inflicted during the conflict, the center aims to instill in future generations a genuine desire for peace.

## THE SOUTH (MINAMI)★

An entertainment district if ever there was one, Minami is a kind of Japanese Las Vegas: picturesque, noisy, and fascinating, a vast leisure and pleasure zone stretching from Nanba station in the south to the Honmachi district (north), packed with restaurants, bars, theaters, fairground attractions, and amusement arcades beneath an incredible array of neon lights, gaudy signs, and giant screens on the sides of buildings.

### Around Dotonbori★★ 道頓堀

The epicenter of this visual anarchy is the pedestrian thoroughfare of **Dotonbori**★★ *Map II B1* and its adjoining canal, where all the lights in Osaka seem to be concentrated. The area has to be seen at night, lit up by its iconic signs: giant crabs with moving pincers, inflatable *fugu* fish, kitsch red dragons, and Glico's running man. Glico, a company producing candy and cookies, has had that same sign above the bridge, **Ebisu-bashi** *Map II B1*, since 1919, and has since become one of the most famous visual landmarks in the city. Around the bridge there is a constant parade of fun-loving teenagers in "interesting" outfits, their bags and cell phones covered in badges, soft toys, and other *kawaii* (cute) accessories (*see p107*).

Here and there, you'll see *yatai* (food stands) selling an Osakan specialty, *takoyaki*: small octopus fritters.

**Dotonbori Gokuraku Shotengai**– *Open 11am–11pm. ¥315.*
This live replica of the streets of Osaka in the Taisho era *(1912–26)*, on the fifth floor of Sammy Ebisu Plaza, has a host of stands selling chicken skewers, *okonomiyaki*, rice with curry and noodles. There is also a street of fortune tellers.

**Ebisu Tower** *Map II B1– Closed to the public.* This building to the north of the canal is topped by a dizzying Ferris wheel, not round but between an oval and a rectangle.

**Kirin Plaza** *Map II B1– Open 11am–8.30pm. No charge.*
This modern building created by Takamatsu Shin houses a brewery, a restaurant, and a fashionable gallery space.

**Hozen-ji Yokocho**★ *Map II B2* – South of Dotonbori, this narrow paved street, with its faded charm, leads to the little temple, Hozen-ji, lit by attractive paper lanterns. It is dedicated to the goddess Mizukake Fudo, whose moss-covered statue is sprinkled with water by passers-by hoping for good luck.

**Kamigata Ukiyo-e Museum** *Map II B2 – Open 11am–8pm. ¥500.*

### Fashion fun in Amerika-mura★

The Amerika-mura district, known as Ame-mura, is a bohemian village to the west of Shinsaibashi, famous for its boutiques selling youth-oriented ethnic and trendy clothing. Originally, US Army surplus was sold in this area, hence the name. The replica of the Statue of Liberty on top of one of the buildings is a useful landmark. A mini-capital of informal *fashion*, where hip designers have their showrooms, Ame-mura is equally full of cafes, bars, and discos. At weekends, there's a constant wild procession of *fashionistas* with hair dyed in Day-Glo colors or done up in beehives, Gothic Lolitas in outrageous miniskirts, punks with piercings, and leather-jacketed rockers with pompadours.

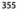

## USEFUL INFORMATION

**Tourist Offices** – **Osaka Visitors' Information Centers**, *open 8am–8pm. www.tourism.city.osaka.jp. 3F Shin-Osaka (Map I B1 off map). ℘06-6305-3311. Osaka-Umeda, Mido-suji exit, under footbridge near bus station (Map I B1). ℘06-6345-2189. 1F Tennoji (Map II A2 off map). ℘06-6774-3077. Nanba station, exit 24 (Map II B2). ℘06-6211-3551.*

**Guided Tours** – **Osaka SGG Club**, *Osaka Visitors' Information Center, Nanba station. ℘066-631-9116.* English-speaking volunteer guides. Transportation and meals extra.

**Bank/Foreign Exchange**– **Citibank**, *Midosuji Diamond Bldg, 2-1-2 Nishi-Shinsaibashi (Map II B1). ATM 24hr.* **Sumitomo Mitsui**, *Hankyu-Umeda station, in the basement (Map I B1). Open Mon–Fri 9am–9pm, Sat–Sun 10am–5pm.* This bank exchanges most currencies and also has an international ATM *(open 7am–11pm).*

**Post Office/Withdrawals** – ATMs in all post offices, including the Central Post Office. **Central Post Office**, *Osaka-Ekimae no. 1 bldg, 1-3-1 Umeda, south exit from the JR station (Map I A2). 24hr.* Exchange service *(open 9am–6pm)* and international ATM *(open 24/7, Sun 8am–midnight).*

## TRANSPORTATION

**BY PLANE** – **Kansai International Airport (KIX)** – *℘0724-55-2500. www.kansai-airport.or.jp.* Japan's second biggest airport is on an artificial island, 31mi/50km SW of Osaka. Connections to 75 cities in 31 countries. Tourist Information Center (TIC), *℘0724-566-025. 8.30am–8.30pm, Nov-Mar: 9am–9pm, exchange bureau, and international ATM in arrivals hall.*

**From Airport to Center** – **By train** *(station on level 2F)*: trains to Nanba station with Nankai Airport Line *(every 20min, trip 40–45min, ¥890–¥1,390 ),* Tennoji with JR Kansai Airport Line *(every 20min, trip 50min, ¥1,760),* Tennoji with the JR Haruka Line *(every 30min, trip 40min, ¥1,760),* Osaka station with the JR Kansai Airport Line *(every 30min, trip 70min, ¥1,160)* and Shin-Osaka with JR Haruka Line *(every 30min, trip 50min, ¥2,470).* **By bus**: buses to Nanba station *(every 30min, trip 45min, ¥1000)* and Osaka station *(every 20min, trip 50min, ¥1,500).*

**Itami Airport (ITM)** – *℘06-6856-6781.* Located 6.2mi/10km N of Osaka, the city's second airport is connected to some 30 Japanese cities.

**From the Airport to the Center** – **By train:** Osaka Monorail to Hotarugaike, then transfer to the Hankyu Hotarugaike Line for Umeda *(20min, ¥420).* **By bus**: buses to Nanba station *(every 20min, journey time 25min, ¥620)* and Osaka station *(every 15min, journey time 25–30min, ¥620).*

**BY TRAIN** – **Shin-Osaka** Station *(Map I B1 off map)* – Shinkansen to Tokyo *(2hr50min, ¥13,240),* Hiroshima *(1hr30min, ¥9,080),* and Fukuoka *(2hr45min, ¥14,590).*

**Osaka-Umeda** Station *(Map I B1)* – Trains to Kobe with the JR Line *(every 3min, journey time 20–35min, ¥540),* the Hankyu Line *(every 10min, journey time 30min, ¥310),* or the Hanshin Main Line *(every 10min, journey time 30min, ¥310)*; trains to Kyoto with the JR Line *(every 10min, journey time 30min, ¥540)* or the Hankyu Line *(Kawaramachi, every 5min, journey time 45min, ¥390)*; trains to Nara with the JR Yamatoji Line *(every 20min, journey time 45min, ¥780).*

**Yodobashi Station** *(Map I A2 off map)* – Trains to Sanjo with the Keihan Line *(every 5min, journey time 52min, ¥400).*

**Nanba Station** *(Map II A–B2)* – Trains to Nara with the Kintetsu Line *(every 5min, journey time 35min, ¥540).*

**BY BUS** – **Umeda Terminus** *(Map I B1)* and **Nanba** Terminus (OCAT, at JR Nanba, *Map II A2*) – *www.bus.or.jp.* Buses to Tokyo *(8hr, ¥4,500–6,000),* Hiroshima *(5hr, about ¥5,000),* Nagasaki *(10hr, about ¥11,000),* and many other cities.

**BY BOAT** – **Nanko Ferry Terminal** – *www.optc.or.jp.* Boats to Shikoku: Kochi *(9hr, ¥4,500),* Matsuyama *(9hr, ¥6,300)*; to Kyushu: Shinmoji *(12hr, ¥6,700),* Beppu *(13hr, ¥8,800),* and Miyazaki *(13hr, ¥10,400).*

**GETTING AROUND OSAKA**

**BY SUBWAY** – Osaka Municipal Transportation Bureau, *06-6582-1400. www.kotsu.city.osaka.jp.* The best way to get around Osaka. *Subway lines are open 5am–midnight every day and tickets cost ¥200–300 (depending on distance).* The network has 9 lines, plus the circular JR Osaka Loop Line.

**Pass** – A **One-Day Pass** *(¥850, ¥600 on Fridays and the 20th of every month)* gives unlimited travel on the subway *(but not JR trains)* for 1 day.

**JR Kansai Pass** – *1 day (¥2,000) to 4 days (¥6,000).* Valid on the JR network in Kansai, and the Haruka Shinkansens.

**Kansai Thru Pass** – *2 days (¥3,800) or 3 days (¥5,000).* Unlimited travel on all subways, trains (excluding JR network), and buses in the region (Kyoto, Osaka, Kobe, Himeji, Nara, and Koya-san).

**Osaka Unlimited Pass** – *1 day (¥2,000) or 2 days (¥2,700).* Unlimited travel on subway, free or reduced-price entry to most museums and other attractions. On sale in Tourist Offices.

**BY TAXI** – Average trip, ¥2,000. Use **MK** Taxi—lowest fares. *06-6452-4441*

This little museum of prints is located in a yellow house on the west side of Hozen-ji. The production of prints, linked to the Kabuki Theater, flourished in Osaka during the Edo period *(17C and 18C)*. Some 30 original works are on display.

**National Bunraku Theater★** *Map II B2* – Traditional puppet shows, presented by Master Yoshida Minosuke III, a Living National Treasure and his company *(see Addresses/Nightlife p360)*.

## Shinsaibashi 心斎橋

The long avenue called **Mido-suji** has wide sidewalks planted with ginkgo. Many of the big **luxury brand** names have stores here. Running parallel with it to the east, the **Shinsaibashi-suji** shopping arcade *Map II B1* houses a host of shops, and, in the basement, the largest underground mall in western Japan: **Crysta Nagahori**.

## Nanba District 難波 *Map II B2.*

East of Nanba station, the covered mall **Doguya-suji** specializes in kitchen utensils and china. Knives, saucepans, tableware: there's a bit of everything here, even those wax models of dishes displayed in Japanese restaurant windows. A short distance away is **Kuromon Ichiba** *Map II B2,* the largest market in Osaka, about 656.2yd/600m of stands selling fruit, vegetables, fish, and other foodstuffs. To the south, the **Den Den Town** district *Map II B2* has a string of stores selling electrical and electronic equipment at bargain prices.

*Bunraku performance*

©JNTO

## Tennoji Park 天王寺公園

*Map II B2, off map.*

This park near Tennoji station includes a zoo, a botanical garden, and the Municipal Museum of Art. Other sites are located nearby.

**Osaka Municipal Museum of Art** 大阪市立美術館 – *Open Tue–Sun 9.30am–5pm. ¥300.*

This 1930s building houses a large collection of Japanese and Chinese artworks ranging from the 12C to the 19C, including some fine *maki-e* (gilded lacquerware). There are also temporary exhibitions.

**Shitenno-ji** 四天王寺 – *Open 8.30am–4pm. ¥200–¥700 depending on rooms visited.*

To the northeast of the park, this temple was built in 593 by Prince Shotoku and would be the oldest in Japan if it hadn't been flattened by bombs in 1945. The reconstruction, although faithful to the original, is unfortunately made of concrete, not wood.

**Shinsekai** 新世界 – These few streets, with their old-fashioned, downmarket atmosphere, lie beneath the 338ft/103m-high Tsutenkaku Tower. Built in 1956 and modeled on the Eiffel Tower, it was the symbol of the postwar reconstruction of Osaka.

**Spa-World★** スパワールド *– Subway: Dobutsuen-mae. 10am–10pm (Sat 4am). ¥2,400–3,000.*

Spread over six floors, this vast bathing complex attracts thousands of visitors a day. Each bath has a different theme: Roman baths, Turkish baths, Finnish saunas, Balinese spas, etc. You will also find a swimming pool with water slides, open-air baths, a gym, water sports, massage parlors, etc.

## Osaka Bay★ 大阪湾

*Map II A1 off map.*

The ultra-modern harbor district *(Tenpozan)* has many attractions.

**Osaka Aquarium Kaiyukan★★** 海遊館*– Subway: Osakako. Open 10am–8pm. ¥2,000.* An army of uniformed hostesses greets you at the entrance to this aquarium devoted to the marine life of the Pacific Ocean. The star of the show is a huge whale shark, but you will also see an incredibly large sunfish, sea otters, king penguins, rays, dolphins, seals, turtles, and tropical fish. Kaiyukan is one of the largest aquariums in the world, with a collection of some 580 marine species. The main tank measures 190,699 cubic ft/5,400 cubic m, and contains 11,000 tons of water.

**Suntory Museum★** サントリーミュージアム – *Closed to the public.*

The work of architect Ando Tadao, this impressive concrete, glass, and steel building formerly hosted exhibitions of painting and photography.

**Tenpozan Ferris Wheel** 天保山大観覧車 – *Open 10am–9.30pm. ¥700.* At a height of 367.5ft/112m, this is one of the largest Ferris wheels in the world. It affords a magnificent **view** over Osaka Bay and the coast as far as Kobe. *From Tenpozan pier, a boat (¥600) will take you to Universal City.*

**Universal Studios Japan** ユニバーサル・スタジオ・ジャパン – *From JR Osaka station, Yumesaki Line to Universal City station (10min). Open 9am–7pm. ¥6100.* Modeled on its American counterpart and much-loved by Japanese families, this theme park features 17 attractions inspired by famous Hollywood blockbusters such as *Spiderman, Jaws, E.T., Jurassic Park,* and *Terminator*, as well as a plentiful supply of restaurants.

## EXCURSION

### Tezuka Osamu Manga Museum★ 手塚治虫記念館

Situated in **Takarazuka★**, 30 minutes by train from Osaka on the Hankyu Line, the **Tezuka Osamu Manga Museum★** (*open Thu–Tue 9.30am–5pm; ¥500*) is devoted to the work of the famous *mangaka* Tezuka Osamu (*see p87*). There is also a library, and an animation workshop that will delight the kids.

# ADDRESSES

## STAY

**Carpe Diem カルペ・ディエム** *3-1-14 Nakahama, Joto-ku. (Map II). 06-6961-0444. www.carpediem-osaka.jp/jp/index.htm. 4 rooms, ¥10,000/¥13,000. Reservations required.* Located E of the castle, this lovely residence has three pavilions in a magnificent garden. The first has a communal bathroom, dining room, and kitchen. The second is a hostel, with 3 rooms separated by paper sliding doors. The last, with 1 room *(the "Tea Ceremony room")* and its own washbasin and toilet, can accommodate up to 5 people.

**Hearton Hotel Nishi-Umeda ハートンホテル西梅田** *3-3-55 Umeda, Kita-ku. Subway: Nishi-Umeda (Map I A2). 06-6342-1111. www.hearton.co.jp. 471 rooms.* This big, ocher-colored building near JR Osaka station houses a clean, modern hotel with efficient service. The rooms are cozy and soundproofed. *most look out onto the rail tracks).*

**Kaneyoshi Ryokan かねよし旅館** *3-12 Soemon-cho. Subway: Nipponbashi (Map II B1). 06-6211-6337. www.kaneyosi.jp. 15 rooms. ¥1,575.* This friendly, modern ryokan, ideally located beside **Dotonbori Canal**, has clean, bright, spacious rooms.

**Umeda OS Hotel 梅田OSホテル** *2-11-5 Sonezaki, Kita-ku. Subway: Higashi-Umeda (Map I B2). 06-6312-1271. www.oshotel.com. 283rooms. ¥1,600.* A luxurious, but reasonably priced, hotel in a big concrete tower in the south of Umeda. Comfortable soundproofed rooms with good facilities *(some of them non-smoking).*

**New Hankyu 新阪急ホテル** *1-1-35 Shibata, Kita-ku. Subway: Umeda (Map I A–B1). 06-6372-5101. www.hankyu-hotel.com. 922 rooms.* This huge, top-class hotel, directly connected with Osaka-Umeda station, has spacious, quiet rooms with all modern conveniences, as well as shops, bars, and restaurants. *Airport shuttle from the main entrance.*

**Hotel Nikko Osaka ホテル日航大阪** *1-3-3 Nishi-Shinsaibashi (Map II B1). 06-6244-1111. www.hno.co.jp. 640 rooms. ¥2,400.* One of the finest hotels in the downtown area, located in an imposing 32-story tower near Shinsaibashi subway station. A vast, elegant lobby, English-speaking staff who will attend to your every need, and immaculately clean rooms with contemporary decor in warm colors. *Swimming pool, sauna, bars, restaurants, and airport shuttle.*

**New Hankyu 新阪急ホテル** *1-1-35 Shibata, Kita-ku. Subway: Umeda (Map I A–B1). 06-6372-5101. www.hankyu-hotel.com. 922 rooms.* This huge, top-class hotel, directly connected with Osaka-Umeda station, has spacious, quiet rooms with all modern conveniences, as well as shops, bars, and restaurants. *Airport shuttle from the main entrance.*

**Swissôtel Nankai Osaka スイスホテル南海大阪** *5-1-60 Nanba, Chuo-ku. 06-6646-1111. www.swisshotel.com. 548 rooms.* In the heart of the Nanba district, this luxurious hotel can offer you rooms with an impressive **view** of the city, as well as a superb **Olympic pool**.

## EAT

**Osaka** is a food lover's paradise. The choice is incredibly varied and almost never disappointing. The city's motto: eat till you drop!

**Jiyuken 自由軒** *3-1-34 Nanba. Subway:Nanba or Nipponbashi (Map II B2). 06-6631-5564. Open Tue–Sun 11.20am–8pm.* This restaurant in the Nanba Center shopping mall south of Dotonbori is famous for its curried rice. Try the *meibutu carry*, a dish of saffron-flavored rice with beef and onions.

**Watami 和民南海難波駅前店** *Near Namba station, 3F Nanba Chowa Bldg, 12-30 Nanbasennichimae, Chuo-ku (Map II - B2). 06-6644-3605. Open Sun–Thu, 4pm–2am, Fri–Sun and eves of holidays 4pm–4am.* This chain restaurant, with its wood interior of nooks and crannies, offers all kinds of imaginative organic dishes. Ask for the house specialty: *tetsunabe gyoza* (¥313), a pot of Japanese ravioli.

**Chibo 千房道頓堀店** *1-5-5 Dotonbori. Subway: Nipponbashi (Map II B1/2). 06-6212-2211. www.chibo.com. Open Mon–Fri 11am–11pm, Sat–Sun 11am–2am.* The specialty of this five-story restaurant is one of Osaka's most popular: *okonomiyaki*, a pancake stuffed with cabbage and meat, cooked on a hot plate, then drenched in okonomiyaki sauce. On the top floor is "President Chibo," a steak house.

**Ma-Nabeya MA-なべや (まあ、なべや)** *Fuku Building – Shinsaibashi, 4F, 2-8-26 Higashi-Shinsaibashi. Subway: Shinsaibashi or Nagahoribashi (Map II B1). 06-6212-4130. www.ksnetwork.com. Open 5pm–midnight.* A stylish *tabehodai* (all-you-can-eat) restaurant for a fixed price; eat as much as you like for 90min.

Feast on beef *shabu-shabu* (fondue) or *sukiyaki* (cooked on a hot plate).

**O-Nabeya 大鍋や** *1-9-24 Sonezaki-shinchi, Kita-ku. Subway: Kitashinchi (Map I B2). 06-4796-3225. www.o-nabeya.com. Open Mon–Sat 5pm–5am.* A friendly restaurant specializing in ***oden*** (eggs, vegetables, and fishcakes) and ***kushikatsu*** (meat coated in breadcrumbs and deep-fried on skewers). ***No English menu or English-speaking personnel.***

**Sora 空** *1-10 Shimo Ajihara-cho, Tennoji-ku. Subway: Tsuruhashi, exit 6, first street on the right (MapII B1, off map). 06-6773-1300. www.yakinikusora.jp. Open Wed–Mon, 4pm–midnight (Sat–Sun, 5pm–midnight).* One of the best Korean restaurants in Osaka, in the heart of Tsuruhashi's maze of little streets. Good choice of grills, with ***kimchi*** (spicy pickled cabbage).

**Zuboraya づぼらや新世界本店** *2-5-5 Ebisu-higashi, Naniwa-ku. Subway:Ebisucho (Map II B2, off map). 06-6633-5529. www.zuboraya.co.jp. Open 11am–11pm.* On corner of street to Tsutenkaku Tower; giant ***fugu***-shaped lanterns outside. ***Fugu***, a white fish that can release a deadly poison if prepared incorrectly, is thehouse specialty: fugu in sushi, sashimi, croquettes, fritters, and so on.

**Hyotan Taiko-en 太閤園・割烹瓢箪** *9-10 Amajima-cho, Miyakojima-ku (Map II B1, off map). 06-6356-1111. Open 11.30am–10pm.* Opposite the Fujita Museum of Art and N of Osaka Castle, the restaurant in the garden of Taiko-en is located beside a pond, the perfect setting for a ***kaiseki*** meal. ***Lunch formula ¥3,500.***

**Kani Doraku かに道楽本店** *1-6-18 Dotonbori. Subway:Nanba or Nipponbashi (Map II B1). 06-6211-8975. Open 11am–11pm.* This restaurant in the pedestrian section of Dotonbori is easily identified by the giant crab on the front. Crab is the house specialty, caught in the cold waters of Hokkaido, and cooked in sushi, ***nabe***, tempura, and ***kanisuki*** menu at ¥5,460.

**Kichiyoshi 吉よし** *1-3-32 Shinsaibashi-suji. Subway: Shinsaibashi or Nagahoribashi (Map II B1). 06-6244-4147. Open 5pm–3am.* A lovely restaurant serving traditional cuisine. Interesting set-price combination menus (tempura, sashimi, ***yakitori***, ***nabe***).

**Nishiya にし屋** *1-8-18 Higashi-Shinsaibashi. Subway: Shinsaibashi or Nagahoribashi (Map II B1). 06-6241-9221. Open 11am–11pm (Sun, 9.30pm).* Built of wood, like the old ***sukiya***-style tea houses, this restaurant specializes in ***udon*** (wheat noodles). Try the ***kitsune udon***, noodles served in a soup, with leek, fried tofu, and meat or dried fish.

**Umeda To-ka 梅田燈火** *2-5-28 Sonezaki-shinchi, Kita-ku. Subway: Nishi-Umeda, exit 9 (Map I A2). 06-6345-8118. Open 5pm–1am.* A trendy restaurant in a private garden. Contemporary decor with a tropical theme and creative Japanese cuisine. Dishes include sea bream with sake or lotus roots, shrimps with taro, lobster croquettes, etc.

**Vrai de Vrai/Chez Hiro ヴレ・ド・ヴレ / シェ・ヒロ** *1-24-8 Shin-machi, Nishi-ku. Subway: Yotsubashien or Nishiohashi (Map II A1). 06-6535-7807. Open Tue–Sun 11.30am–2pm, 6–10pm. . ¥1,500/¥6,000.* French cuisine by Japanese chef Hiro. Excellent beef stew. Eat inside, in an intimate setting, or on the little terrace bordered by olive trees.

## NIGHTLIFE

**Minami** is the epicenter of Osaka's nightlife, with hundreds of bars and clubs on Dotonbori, and in Shinsaibashi and Amerika-mura. The buzz is incredible.

**Bilboard Live ビルボードライブ** *Awe Bldg B1F (Map I A2) – 06-6342-7722 – shows at 6.30pm and 9.30pm.* An institution in Osaka, with the greatest names in jazz, soul, funk, and world music.

**The Cellar セラー** – *Shin-Sumiya Bldg, 2-17-13 Nishi-Shinsaibashi. Open 6pm–2am. 06-6212-6437.* A cozy basement pub in the heart of Amerika-mura. Live jazz and rock bands at weekends.

**Theater– National Bunraku Theater 国立文楽劇場** *12-10 Nipponbashi, 1-chome. Shows at 11am & 4pm. 06-6212-2531.* ***Bunraku***, the Japanese puppet theater, was created in Osaka at the end of the 17C. This theater built in 1984 presents shows for 3-week periods in Jan, Apr, Jul, and Nov. ***Audioguide in English.***

## EVENTS

**Tenjin Matsuri** *(Jul 24–25)*: Osaka's most spectacular festival, including a procession to the Tenman-gu shrine, a night parade of boats on the Okawa River, and a closing fireworks display.

# Kobe★
# 神戸

**From the Chinese quarter, little Nankin, the aromas of Peking duck and *dim sum* fill the air. Old-fashioned street lamps and a large Bavarian-style house with a weathervane on top rub shoulders with a synagogue, a mosque, and a Jain temple in the European district. With its fine houses perched on hills overlooking the sea, Kobe—like Yokohama and Nagasaki—is a port with a strongly exotic feel. The city had links with China a thousand years ago, and was one of the first to open up to the West at the beginning of the Meiji era. American and European merchants and sailors imported their own culture and customs: fashion, jazz, movies, steaks *(the famous Kobe beef)*, and pastries. Hit by a terrible earthquake in 1995, Kobe has risen from the ashes, a modern city gradually reclaiming land from the sea. Heavily built-up as it is, it's still a pleasant city to walk around in, and at night, when its lights are reflected in the bay, the view is picture-postcard romantic. Last, but by no means least, a visit to Kobe is highly recommended, thanks to the proximity of the finest castle in Japan: Himeji Castle.**

- **Population:** 1,550,406 (Greater Kobe: 3 million) – Hyogo Prefecture.
- **Michelin Map:** Principal Sights Map B3 – Regional map p283.
- **Location:** Kobe extends along a narrow coastal strip, 20.5mi/33km from Osaka and 46.6mi/75km from Kyoto, sandwiched between the sea and Mounts Maya and Rokko. A large thoroughfare, Flower Road, crosses the city from Shin-Kobe station *(where the Shinkansen arrive)*, to the harbor in the north. The liveliest area is around Sannomiya, the main station, where the ordinary (local) JR trains arrive. From there, pedestrian malls lead southwest to the Chinese quarter of Nankin-machi. To the north of the railway, at the foot of the hills, is the European quarter of Kitano. It's easy to get around Kobe on foot, and there are plenty of street signs in Roman letters.
- **Kids:** Maritime Museum; in summer, head for Suma Beach *(see Addresses p370)*.
- **Timing:** Allow an afternoon and evening in Kobe, then a visit to Himeji the next morning. *The Kobe City Loop Bus makes getting around easy.*
- **Don't miss:** Himeji Castle.

## BACKGROUND

**A cosmopolitan flavor** – The name Kobe is said to derive from Kamibe, "guardians of the gods," after the Ikuta-jinja shrine, founded in the year 201. As early as the Nara period, the city had links with China. Thanks to its trading connections, the port grew, adopting the name Hyogo in the 13C. In 1868, at the beginning of the Meiji era, Kobe was one of the first five ports authorized to trade with the outside world, bringing Japan's two centuries of isolation to an end. Many Westerners settled in Kobe, first near the harbor, then in the Kitano district, where they built sumptuous residences. It was this period that gave Kobe its cosmopolitan flavor, and its reputation as an economic powerhouse—the reason why it was heavily bombed at the end of World War II.

**A city reborn** – Devastated by the Hanshin earthquake of January 17, 1995 *(see box p364)*, the city has been entirely rebuilt and has recovered much

### Foreigners in Kobe

Approximately 45,000 foreigners live in Kobe, from more than 100 different countries. The four largest communities are the Koreans (23,700), the Chinese (12,500), the Vietnamese (1,300), and the Americans (1,280).

of its economic dynamism. The fourth largest merchant port in Japan, it has a major industrial park built on land reclaimed from the bay *(more than 2,471 acres/1,000ha)*, as well as a large foreign population, numbering 45,000.

In addition, many foreign multinationals, such as Nestlé and Procter & Gamble, have their Japanese headquarters in Kobe. Expatriates enjoy the city for its relaxed pace, nightlife (including jazz clubs), hot springs *(Arima Onsen)*, and biannual fashion shows *(the Kobe Collection)*.

## SIGHTS

## THE CENTER AND THE BAY

The area around Sannomiya station *(B1)* and Motomachi station *(B2)* is where the big stores and shopping arcades can be found. As you descend toward the harbor, you come to the **Old Foreign Settlement** *(B2)*, between Flower Road and Meriken Road ("street of Americans"). This is where foreigners lived before they settled on the Kitano hills farther north. The district is dotted with Western-style buildings from the end of the 19C and the beginning of the 20C, such as the former American consulate (1880), now a cafe.

### Kobe City Museum★★

神戸市立美術館 *Map B2.*

*Open Tue–Sun 10am–5pm (Fri 7pm).* *¥200.*

Housed in a former bank (1935) in neo-Classical style with Doric columns, the City Museum showcases cultural exchanges between Asia and the West. One of the highlights of its collections is the rare series of **Nanban paintings**★★ from the 16C and 17C. These works, on screens and scrolls, are inspired by the European Renaissance art introduced by the missionaries. Some vividly depict the arrival of Portuguese ships (the word *nanban* means "southern barbarians").

Unfortunately, they are so fragile that they can only be displayed for 40 days a year *(end Jul–early Sept)*. For the rest of the time, visitors have to be content with facsimiles, and the other rooms showcasing the archeology and history of Kobe.

### Nankin-machi (Chinatown)

南京町 *Map A–B2.*

On the other side of Meriken Road, a big gate adorned with dragons marks the entrance to Kobe's Chinatown. More modest in size than the Chinatowns of Yokohama or Nagasaki, it is a small but teeming enclave of a few streets.

A host of restaurants vie for your attention, with brightly colored signs, the shouting of touts, and the enticing smells of cooking. This is a pleasant area to stroll in at night, when the shops are all lit up.

### Around the Harbor

**Meriken Park** *Map B2* – Meriken Road leads straight to the wharf, where foreign ships once unloaded their cargo. On the east side of the park, part of the wharf hit by the 1995 earthquake has been deliberately left in a damaged state: the only trace of the earthquake still visible today.

**Kobe Maritime Museum** *Map B2 – Open Tue–Sun 10am–5pm. ¥500, (or ¥900 with Port Tower).*

The roof of this modern building, made of steel tubes, is designed to resemble the slender prow of a ship. The museum's collections follow the maritime history of Kobe. They include some interesting model ships, among them a 29.5ft/9m replica of *HMS Rodney*, the flagship that led the first Western flotilla into Kobe harbor in 1868, and a scale model, adorned with precious stones, of the *Oshoro Maru*, one of the first Japanese sailing ships.

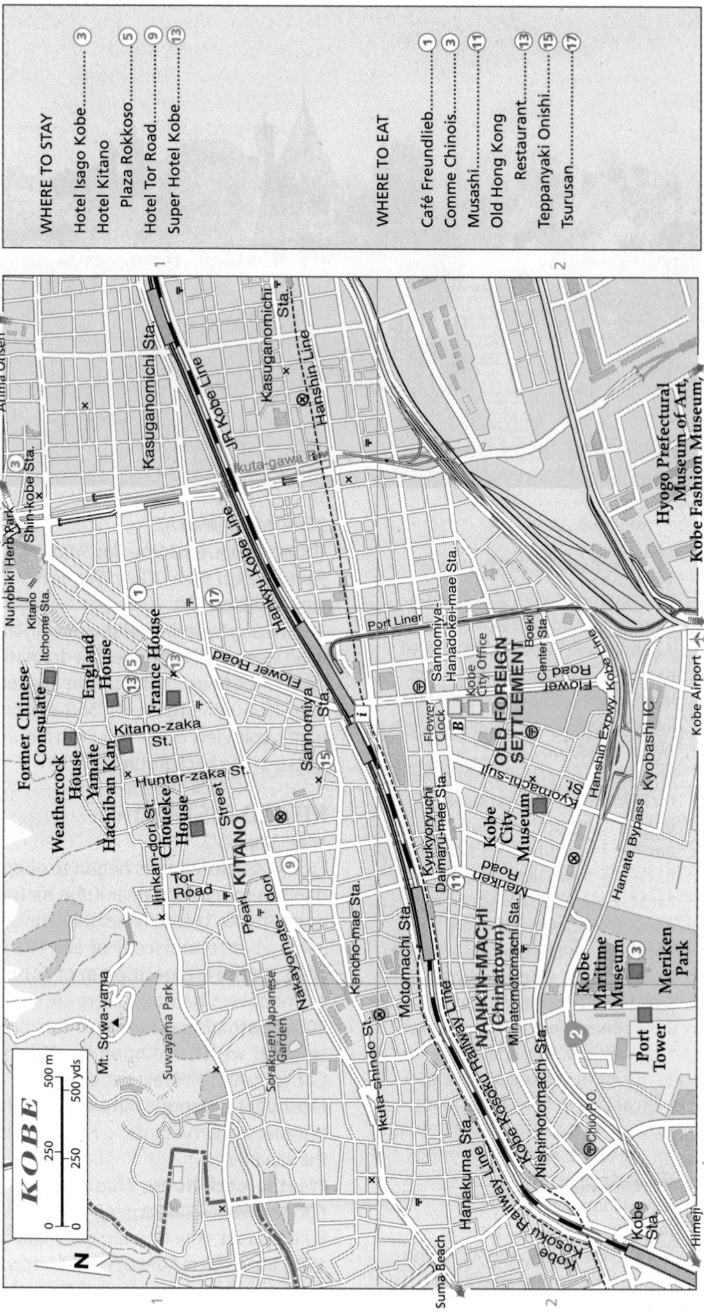


© 2009 Cartographic data Shobunsha/Michelin

The museum also houses **Kawasaki Good Times World**, a high-tech interactive space run by the Kawasaki company, manufacturer of motorcycles, ships, trains, and aircraft, which started in Kobe. Among many other attractions is the flight simulator, giving visitors the experience of piloting a helicopter.

*Weathercock House and the view over the city of Kobe*



## The Kobe Earthquake

On January 17, 1995, at 5.46am, a massive earthquake of magnitude 7.2 shook the Kobe region with all its power. The hypocenter in fact lay near the harbor, along a fault line that crosses the strait between Awaji Island and Kobe.

The shocks, which were remarkable for involving an exceptional degree of vertical movement *(up to 3.3ft/1m in places)*, brought buildings down like houses of cards. A mere 20 seconds were enough to leave 6,424 dead, tens of thousands of wounded, and 100 billion dollars' worth of damage. The much-criticized late arrival of the Emergency Services forced the panic-stricken inhabitants to mount the rescue operation themselves with whatever was to hand. This disaster was a trauma for the whole nation, shattering the myth of Japan's preparedness for earthquakes.

In addition, no provision had been made to help the survivors. Today, despite new laws having been introduced, nearly a quarter of Japanese detached houses still do not conform to earthquake prevention standards.

**Port Tower** *Map A2 – Open Mar–Jun &Oct–Nov 9am–9pm;Jul–Sept 9am–10pm; Dec–Feb 9am–7pm. ¥600.*
An amazing hyperboloid structure in latticed steel, the Port Tower is a dramatic sight when lit up at night. From the top (354.3ft/108m), there is a 360-degree panoramic view of the bay, with Mount Rokko in the background.

## KITANO DISTRICT★

北野 *Map B1/2.*
From 1887, foreigners began to abandon the concession near Kobe harbor and settle in this hilly neighborhood, somewhat reminiscent of San Francisco. Kitano is a microcosm of Kobe's cosmopolitan heritage; there are some 30 *ijinkan* (houses of foreign merchants), some of which are open to visitors, Catholic and Protestant churches, a mosque, synagogue, and even a Jain temple. All very exotic ... at least to the Japanese.

**Weathercock House** *Map B1 – Open Wed–Mon 9am–6pm. ¥300.*
Built by a wealthy German merchant in 1909, this brick residence is best-known for the weathervane on its roof. It must be said that the interior is only moderately interesting, a patchwork of Biedermeier furniture and Art Nouveau decoration with a few mock-Gothic touches.

**Choueke House★** *Map B1 – Open Wed–Mon 9am–5pm. ¥500.*
A kind of English country house, with a lovely garden to match. Of the *ijinkan* that are open to visitors, Choueke House is the only one still lived in by its owner, a Syrian businessman named Mr Choueke. His personal collection includes oriental objects and Nanban prints from the end of the 19C.

**Yamate Hachiban Kan★** *Map B1 – Open Apr–Oct 9am–6pm; Nov–Mar 9am–5pm. ¥500.*
*A curious cross between* a Tudor mansion and a Japanese pagoda, this residence houses several bronzes by Rodin, Bourdelle, and Renoir, and a few fine Buddhas from Thailand and Gandhara. If you're in the mood, you can also visit French, English, Danish, Dutch, and Austrian houses, the former Chinese and Panamanian consulates, and so on. A ticket giving you admission to several of the houses is available *(¥2,000–3,500)*.

### Nunobiki Herb Park

布引ハーブ園 *Map C1, off map.*
*The Shin-Kobe Ropeway leaves from just behind the Shin-Kobe Oriental City building. Open 9.30am–5pm (Sat & during the summer 8.30pm). ¥1,200 round trip.*
This herb garden on Mount Rokko *(altitude 1,312.3ft/400m)*, to the north of Kitano, is mainly of interest for the **view★**, especially stunning at night, when the whole vast Kobe-Osaka conurbation is spread out below like a carpet of light.

## THE EAST OF THE CITY

### Hakutsuru Sake Brewery Museum 白鶴酒造資料館 *Off Map.*

*From Sannomiya station, take the Hanshin Line to Sumiyoshi station, then 5min walk to the S. Open Tue–Sun 9am–4.30pm. No charge.*
The Nada district, near the coast, is famous for its many sake breweries. In fact, it is the leading center for sake production in Japan: more than a quarter of the bottles sold in the country originate here. Sake has been made here for nearly 700 years.

#### Legendary beef

The pampered Kobe cattle are regularly massaged with sake, listen to Mozart, and have beer added to their water. The result is an exceptional marbled beef, soft as butter, which melts in the mouth. The meat contains a higher than normal percentage of unsaturated fat (therefore low in cholesterol), which is distributed in, rather than around, the muscle, creating the marbling. However, the prices are astronomical. In theory, the label "Kobe beef" is exclusive to a single breed of cattle (*wagyu*) raised locally. In reality, the cattle are often raised elsewhere (the island of Kyushu, ranches in California, and Australia, for example) before being sent to Kobe for slaughter. Only Matsusaka beef comes anywhere close to matching the quality of Kobe.

Some of the breweries may be visited, including this one—accommodated in a former storehouse with a nice smell of straw and old wood. The museum uses life-size models to explain the various stages of the production process. Video and brochures are available in English. *A free tasting concludes the visit.*

### Hyogo Prefectural Museum of Art★ 兵庫県立美術館

*Map C2, off map.*
*From Sannomiya station, take the Hanshin Line to Iwaya station, then 8min walk S. Open Tue–Sun 10am–6pm. ¥500.*
Built in 2004 by the architect Ando Tadao, this impressive concrete building on the seafront has a fine collection of works by 20C Japanese and international artists.
These include sculptures by Henry Moore, Giacometti, Arp, and Brancusi, and Western-style canvases by two well-known Japanese painters, **Koiso Ryohei** and **Kanayama Heizo**. There are also temporary exhibitions.

Himeji Castle

© JNTO

## Disaster Reduction and Human Renovation Institution★
人と防災未来センター

*C2 off map.*
*328yd/300m from the Hyogo Museum of Art, following the main road W.*
*Open Tue–Sun 9.30am–5.30pm (Fri–Sat 7pm). ¥600.*

The somewhat offputting name conceals a highly instructive museum devoted to the terrible earthquake of 1995.

A film on a giant screen simulating the quake, followed by a life-size reconstruction of devastated streets, give visitors the feeling that they are watching the event live. The presentation is so realistic it's hard not to come out feeling shaken.

## Kobe Fashion Museum
神戸ファッション美術館

*C2 off map.*
*Hanshin Line to Uozaki station (or JR Sumiyoshi station), then Rokko Line monorail to Island Center station, then 2min walk from SE exit. Open Thu–Tue 10am–6pm. ¥500.*

This museum is the only interesting attraction on Rokko Island. The collections in this futuristic building *(which resembles a spaceship)*, include dazzling kimonos, rare fabrics, and precious brocades, along with classic dresses by Dior, Cardin, and Yves Saint-Laurent.

Curiously, the museum completely overlooks today's great Japanese couturiers.

## Arima *Onsen* 有馬温泉

*C1 off map.*
*Bus from Sannomiya station (1 or 2 per hour) or subway to Tanigami station, then change for the Kobe Dentetsu Line to Arima Onsen (35min). Alternatively (although it takes longer), take the cable car to Mount Rokko, which links to the Arima cable car.*

Located on the other side of Mount Rokko, Arima is one of the three oldest hot springs in Japan, mentioned as early as 631 in the *Nihon shoki*. Overrun with tourists, the resort is a succession of inelegant hotel complexes, but there are still several public baths, as well as a few intimate ryokan to stay in.

EXCURSION

## HIMEJI★★★ 姫路

This town *(31mi/50km west of Kobe)* is well worth seeing for its wonderful feudal castle, designated a National Treasure and a UNESCO World Heritage Site. The grounds round off the visit nicely.

### Himeji Castle★★★ 姫路城 *Map B1.*

*15min walk from Himeji JR station. Open Jun–Aug 9am–5pm; Sept–May 9am–4pm. ¥600. English-speaking volunteer guides are sometimes available: ask at the ticket office. The castle is under renovation until Mar 2014, while remaining open for visits.*

One of the great masterpieces of Japanese architecture, Himeji Castle

## USEFUL INFORMATION

**KOBE**

**Tourist Office** – Kotsu Center Bldg, *1F at the south exit of Sannomiya station (B1). Open 9am–7pm. ✆078-322-0220.*

**Bank/Foreign Exchange** – **Citibank**, *Imon Bldg, behind the Flower Clock, next to the Shell station (B2). ATM 24hr.* For foreign exchange, Sumitomo Exchange Corner, *2F Sannomiya station (B1).*

## TRANSPORTATION

**KOBE**

**BY TRAIN** – **Sannomiya Station** *(B1)* – The more central of the two stations, served by JR, Hankyu, and Hanshin Lines. **Osaka-Umeda**: JR Line *(25min, ¥390)* or Hanshin and Hankyu Lines *(29min, ¥310)*. **Kyoto**: JR Line *(50min, ¥1,050)* or Hankyu Line *via* Osaka-Juso *(60min, ¥600)*. **Nara**: JR Line to Osaka, then Yamato JR Line *(80min, ¥1,210)*. **Himeji**: JR Rapid *(40min, ¥950)*.

**Shin-Kobe Station** *(C1)*, farther north, has frequent Nozomi Shinkansen for Kyoto *(30min, ¥2,730)*, Hiroshima *(1hr10min, ¥9,230)*, Fukuoka (Hakata) on the island of Kyushu *(2hr15min, ¥ 13,760)*, and Tokyo *(2hr50min, ¥14,470)*.

**HIMEJI**

**BY TRAIN** – **Himeji Station** *(A3)* – The simplest way to Himeji is to take the JR Rapid from Kobe *(40min, ¥950)*, Osaka *(1hr, ¥1,450)*, or Kyoto *(1hr30min, ¥2,210)*. From Kyoto, if you have a JR Pass, it's better to take the Shinkansen *(45min)*.

**GETTING AROUND HIMEJI** – The castle is 15min from the station: keep walking straight ahead. You can also get there by bus (**Loop Bus**, *every 15/30min, ¥100*) or ask at the tourist information desk for a free bicycle for the day (highly practical for sightseeing in the area around the castle).

is known as the White Heron Castle *(Shirasagi-jo)*. Its graceful outlines *(a central five-story keep surrounded by three smaller bastions)* and white plaster walls resemble a bird taking flight *(see photo opposite)*. Built on a hill in the middle of a vast plain, this impregnable fortress is a model of the art of defense: a labyrinth of moats, ditches, and traps, fan-shaped ramparts, loopholes *(sama)*, projecting parapets, and passages leading nowhere, all designed to keep attackers at bay. But Himeji was also, and above all, a symbol of the shogun's prestige, hence the beautiful swooping curves of its roofs, a little like waves on the ocean. Because it is in an excellent state of preservation, the castle has featured in a large number of period films, including Kurosawa Akira's *Ran* (1985).

**History** – In spite of all its defenses, the castle has never been fought over in its four centuries of existence. It stands on the site of an older fort, built in 1346 by Akamatsu Sadanori. Toyotomi Hideyoshi seized it in 1577 and enlarged it to make a strategic fortress, around which a town began to grow. After the Battle of Sekigahara (1600), Tokugawa Ieyasu entrusted the castle to his son-in-law Ikeda Terumasa, who expanded it to its present form between 1601 and 1609. Control of the complex subsequently passed to a number of clans, who added various buildings and turrets. Slightly damaged by air raids in 1945, its wooden structure was entirely refurbished and strengthened between 1956 and 1964.

**Visit** – **The route, marked with arrows** *(about 2hr)*, leads through a maze of doors, staircases, and corridors to a vast courtyard planted with cherry trees and pines *(nishi-no-maru)*, where the lord, his family, and his vassals had their quarters. Next follows the main enclosure *(honmaru)*, where the **central keep** *(tenshukaku)* is to be found. The 151ft/46m-high tower, designed both as a watchtower and a final bastion in case of attack, has five floors plus a base of irregular stones held together by lime-based cement.

The roof combines triangular peaks *(chidori-hafu)* and curved gables *(kara-hafu)*. At the very top are two *shachi-hoko (a mythical animal with the head of a tiger and the body of a fish)*, 6.6ft/

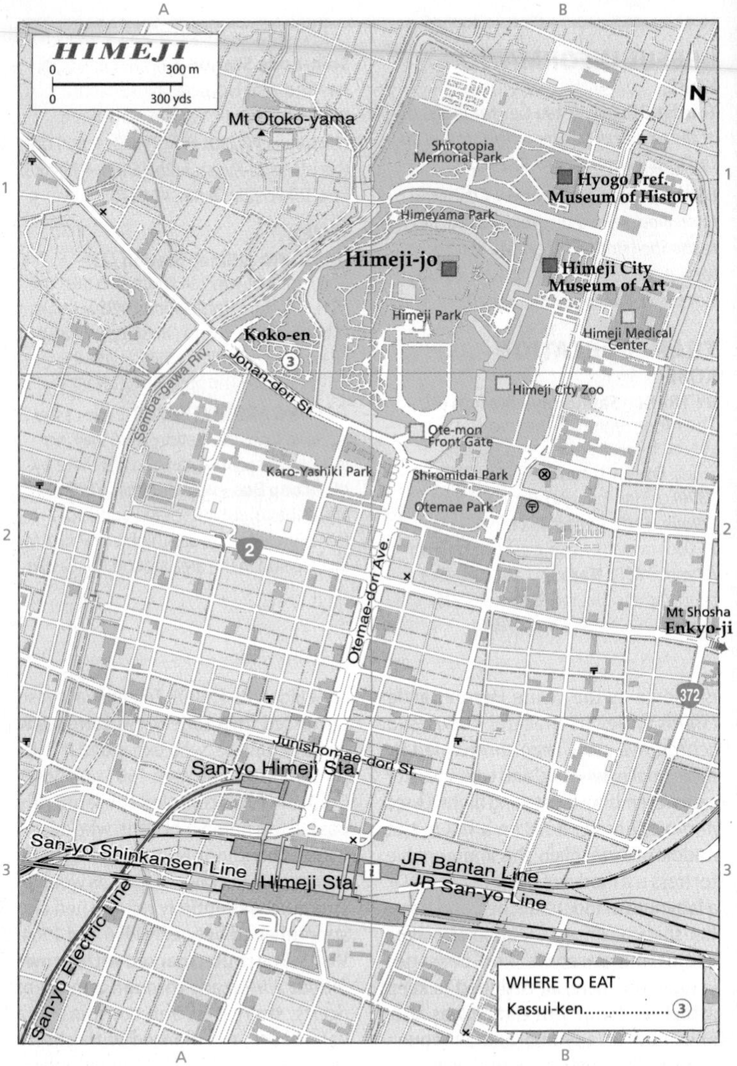




2m high. Inside, a series of dark, narrow staircases leads to the top, from where there is a clear **view** of the town. Note the massive cypresswood pillars, the bases of which are 3.1ft/95cm across. The oldest is 780 years old. *Collections of armor, swords, and rifles are on display on the different floors.*

## Around the Castle

**Koko-en★** *Map A1 – Open 9am–4.30pm (summer 5.30pm). ¥300.*
These eight delightful gardens, modeled on the gardens of the samurai residences of the Edo period, date from 1992. One of them, **Cha-no-niwa**, has a tea house.

**Himeji City Museum of Art★**
*Map B1 – Open Tue–Sun 10am–4.30pm (summer 5.30pm). ¥200.*
This small brick building houses a fine collection of Impressionist and modern paintings, including works by Corot, Courbet, Monet, Matisse, Derain, and Delvaux. The annex displays works by Japanese artists from the 19C through the present day.

**Hyogo Prefectural Museum of History** *Map B1 – Open Tue–Sun 10am–4.30pm. No charge.*
Designed by the architect **Tange Kenzo**, this museum showcases the history of Japanese castles, with scale models of 12 castles in Japan that have kept their original structure. There are also a few antiquities, including some Buddhas.

**Engyo-ji★** 圓教寺 *Map B2 off map. From the stop outside the station, bus no. 6 or 8 to Shosha cable car (25min). After the cable car ride (5min, ¥900 round trip), there is another 30min walk. Open 8.30am–5pm. ¥300.*
This temple complex *(Tendai sect)* on **Mount Shosha** *(to the north of Himeji)* romantically combines Buddhist art with nature. Lined with maples, cherry trees, and statues of the thousand-armed goddess Kannon, the trail leads to Daiko-do, a pavilion where some scenes from the movie *The Last Samurai* were shot.

## EXCURSION
## AWAJI-SHIMA 淡路島

*A2 region map.*
Between Honshu and Shikoku, the island of Awaji has two major works by architect **Ando Tadao**: the **Awaji Yumebuta Hotel** and the **Honpuku Temple**.

**Awaji Yumebutai** 淡路夢舞台
*2 Yumebutai, Awaji-shi. Hotel from ¥14,000/person for Japanese room (four persons) and ¥30,000 for a double room. 070-974-1111.*
This vast complex includes an international conference center, hotel, and a memorial to the victims of the 1995 earthquake. Designed by Ando Tadao, the **Tea Ceremony house** hidden in a cylindrical labyrinth of clear water and stones, the outdoor **echo chamber** with the roof plunging down in its middle, the **amphitheater** with its play of water and lights, and the **chapel** lit by the cross cut into its ceiling are all worth a visit—unless you prefer to contemplate the stepped **water curtain** or the shell paving. Built over the great hole left after earth was moved from the island to construct the artificial island for Kansai Airport *(see p90)*, Awai Yumebutai's pure lines are Ando Tadao's symbols for rebirth and rebuilding.

**Honpuku-ji★** 本福
*20min by foot from Higashiura Bus Terminal. Open 9am–5pm. ¥300.*
Two concrete walls hide everything but the roof of the temple, itself an eliptical pond. A staircase heads downward in its middle, among multi-colored water lilies *(flowers open in the morning)*. At the bottom, the rounded walls and predominant red color gives the room a closed, secret feel, emphasized when a ray of sunlight hits the statue of Buddha *(4pm in summer, 3pm in winter)*. In heading up the stairs to go out, the sky fills your field of vision, like the last homage to the purity of the lines that architect Ando Tadao designed for the temple in 1991.
*You can continue S to the island of Shikoku (see p452).*

# ADDRESSES

## STAY

### KOBE

**Super Hotel Kobe**
スーパーホテル神戸 *2-1-11 Kano-cho (B1). 078-261-9000. www.superhotel.co.jp. 80 rooms.* A simple, reasonably priced *business hotel*. The rooms are small, but clean and well equipped.

**Hotel Isago Kobe**
ホテルいさご神戸 *4-3-7 Kumochi-cho (C1). 078-241-0135. www.isago.co.jp. 28 rooms.* An excellent little hotel, combining Japanese tradition and modernity. Cozy but elegant Japanese and Western rooms, tactful service, top-quality food.

**Hotel Kitano Plaza Rokkoso**
ホテル北野プラザ六甲荘 *1-1-4 Kitano-cho (B1). 078-241-2451. www.rokkoso.com. 49 rooms.* A lovely hotel, renovated in light beige tones. Clean, quiet rooms, most with an attractive **view**.

**Hotel Tor Road**
ホテルトアロード *13-1-19 Nakayamate-dori (B1). 078-391-6691. www.hoteltorroad.co.jp. 78 rooms.* A very cozy establishment. The rooms on the 9th and 10th floors are decorated in typically English style. Other rooms are more standard, but equally well maintained.

## EAT

### KOBE

**Cafe Freundlieb** カフェ・フロインドリーブ *4-6-15 Ikuta-cho (C1). 078-231-6051. Open Thu–Tue 10am–7pm.* Lodged beneath the nave of a former Lutheran church, this German tearoom serves good salads, sandwiches, and pastries.

**Musashi** とんかつ・武蔵 *2F Newmoto Bldg, 1-7-2 Motomachi-dori (B2). 078-321-0634. Open Thu–Tue 11am–7.30pm.* Established in 1939, this restaurant specializes in *tonkatsu*, pork cutlets, pork fillets, and shrimps in breadcrumbs.

**Comme Chinois** コム・シノワ *2F Kobe Kaiyo Hakubutsukan (Kobe Maritime Museum) (B2). 078-332-7675. Open Thu–Tue.* Elegant restaurant serving sophisticated French-Asian cuisine.

**Old Hong Kong Restaurant** 老香港酒家北野店 *2-1-5 Kitano-cho (B1). 078-222-1556. Open 11.30am–9pm.* There is delicious Cantonese cooking to be had here, in this house in Kitano furnished in the style of 1930s Hong Kong.

**Teppanyaki Onishi** 鉄板焼 大西 *3F Kitano Phoenix Bldg, 1-7-16 Nakayamate-dori (B1). 078-332-4029. Open Tue–Sun.* This is an excellent *teppanyaki* restaurant *(the food is cooked on a hot plate)*: the famous Kobe beef to be had here, flavored with brandy, is just about as tender and juicy as anyone could ever wish for. This, together with the friendly atmosphere, makes for a pleasant experience.

**Tsurusan** 鶴参 *3-2-10 Ninomiya-cho (C1). 078-251-1987. Open Wed–Mon 5–10.30pm.* This is known as a good, reliable restaurant. It also has the reputation for serving the finest of the famous Kobe beef that is to be had.

### HIMEJI

**Kassui-ken** 活水軒 *68 Honmachi (A1). 079-289-4131. Open 9.30am–5pm.* The great attraction of this restaurant nestling in the gardens of Koko-en is the heavenly **view** of a waterfall and a small pond. It serves Himeji's specialty, grilled conger eel as well as noodle and rice dishes. Arrive early to avoid the lunch crowds, or drop in for an afternoon drink.

## NIGHTLIFE

Kobe is famous for its jazz venues. *Sets start between 6.30pm and 10pm.*

**Sone** ソネ – *1-24-10 Nakayamate-dori, W of Kitano-zaka (B1). 078-221-2055.*

**Satin Doll** サテンドール神戸三宮店 – *2F Bacchus Bldg, 1-26-1 Nakayamate-dori, W of Kitano-zaka (B1). 078-242-0100.*

## SPORT AND LEISURE

**Boat Rides** – **Naka Pier Terminal**, in front of Port Tower *(A2). 078-360-0884. About 50min, ¥1,000.* Try to come at night, when it is at its best.

**Beaches** – In summer, Kobeans flock to the lovely **Suma Beach** *(A2 off map)*, 20min by train to the E of Kobe *(Suma station)*. Nearby is **Akashi Kaikyo Bridge**, the longest suspension bridge in the world *(12,831.3ft/3,911m)*, linking the Kobe region with Awaji Island.

**Nada sake factories** – Free visits and 10-minute explanatory film in English; *tasting*.

**Kiku-Masamune Sake Brewery Museum** 菊正宗酒造記念館 – *1-9-1 Uozaki-Nishimachi, Higashinada-ku. 078-854-1029. Open 9.30am–4.30pm.*

**Kobe Shu-Shin-Kan Brewery** 神戸酒心館 – *1-8-17 Mikagetsukamachi. 078-841-1121.Open 10am–6pm by reservation;* and its restaurant **Sakabayashi** *(11am–2.30pm and 5pm-10pm).*

### HIMEJI

**Nadagiku Sake Brewery** 灘菊酒造– *121 1-chome Tegara, 5min by taxi from Himeji station. 079-285-3111. Closed 31 Dec–3 Jan.* This famous brewery was founded in the Meiji period in 1910 by the Kawaishi family. It is possible to have a tour in English by making a reservation in advance.

### AWAJI-SHIMA

**Matsuho no Sato *Onsen*** 松帆の郷– *3570-77 Iwaya, Awaji-shi, Hyogo-ken. 079-972-5311. Open 11am–9pm. ¥700.* There are a great many baths to be enjoyed in this *onsen*: baths to stretch out in, baths with bubbles, others with the water in cascades, and a beautiful **view** of the bridge.

# WESTERN HONSHU (CHUGOKU)

**Chugoku occupies the southwestern tip of the island of Honshu. Its name, literally meaning "middle country," harks back to the time when Japan was divided into the near country (Kingoku), the middle country (Chugoku), and the far country (Ongoku)—relating to their distance from the capital, which was first Nara, then Kyoto. Mountainous and heavily forested, the Chugoku mountain chain running across the center splits the region into two quite distinct areas: San-in, in the north, and San-yo, in the south.**

- **Population:** 7.8 million – Okayama, Hiroshima, Yamaguchi, Shimane, and Tottori Prefectures.
- **Michelin Map:** Principal Sights Map A–B3.
- **Location:** At the western tip of the island of Honshu, Chugoku covers an area of approximately 12,239.4sq mi/31,700sq km. The three principal cities in the region are Hiroshima, Okayama, and Tottori. A Shinkansen Line runs the length of the San-yo coast, from Kobe to Kyushu, while the JR San-in Line runs along the north coast.
- **Timing:** Allow four days for San-yo and an equal amount of time for San-in. If possible, do a circular tour that takes in both.
- **Don't miss:** The shrines of Miyajima and Izumo; Peace Memorial Park in Hiroshima; Koraku-en in Okayama; Adachi Museum in Matsue; the Ohara Museum in Kurashiki; the dunes of Tottori; Iwami Ginzan Silver Mine.

### Highlights

1. The gardens of **Koraku-en**, beautiful in any season (p374-376)
2. Modern art on **Naoshima** (p380)
3. Pausing for commemoration and meditation at **Hiroshima's A-Bomb Dome** (p384)
4. An early-morning visit to the **Tottori** sand dunes (p392)
5. Shopping for pottery in the workshops of **Hagi** (p399)

## The Region Today

San-in ("the shady side of the mountain") faces the Sea of Japan, looking toward Korea and Russia. The terrain is somewhat inhospitable, with only a few narrow, lowland areas into which rivers flow. Nature reigns supreme and the climate is harsh with snowy winters and rainy summers. From the sand dunes of Tottori to the samurai quarters of Hagi, life in Chugoku moves at a slow pace. The old traditions are respected in all aspects and walks of life, whether praying in the shrines that cling to mountainsides, bathing in the sleepy seaside onsen resorts, or working in the kilns, where pottery has been fired for over 300 years, or in the sake breweries handed down from father to son. Foreign travelers, a rare sight here, are always treated with great hospitality.

*Edoya, Jokamachi District, Hagi*

©JTB/Photoshot

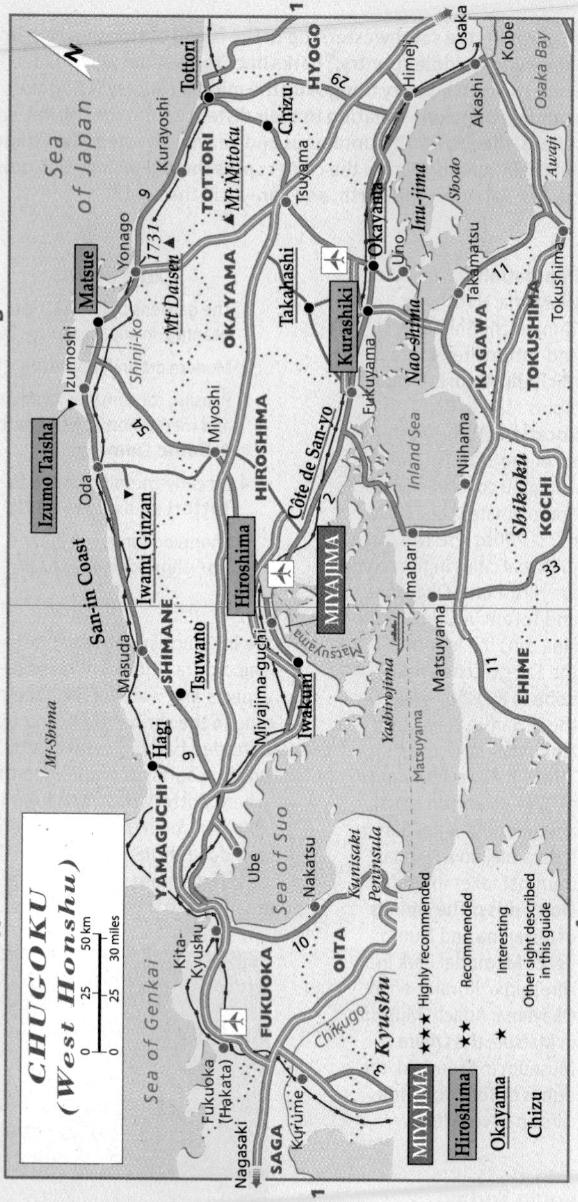




In complete contrast, San-yo ("the sunny side of the mountain") has a milder climate and is more urban and industrial in nature, especially along the Setouchi coast *(Okayama, Hiroshima, Yamaguchi)*, home to major steelworks. The dynamic city of Okayama has built its prosperity on agriculture, wood, textiles, and trade. Hiroshima, rebuilt after the terrible atomic attack of 1945, is today a thriving metropolis. However, the region is also an area of great natural beauty, with an indented coastline of channels, inlets, and bays looking out over an endless string of islands floating on the great blue expanse of the Inland Sea (Seto Naikai).

# The San-yo Coast★: Okayama★
# 山陽：岡山

**One hour by Shinkansen from Osaka, Okayama is the gateway to Chugoku and, via the Great Seto Bridge *(8mi/13km)* over the Inland Sea, also to the island of Shikoku. Wedged between the sea and the mountains, this commercial hub lies at heart of an historic region *(the old kingdom of Kibi)* with a mild, sunny climate ideal for fruit farming. Although the city itself is not especially attractive, it is well worth a visit for the wonderful Koraku-en, one of the most beautiful stroll gardens in Japan. It is also a useful base for exploring the surrounding area: Kurashiki, a picturesque merchant enclave from the Edo era with its well-preserved old houses; the small island of Naoshima, devoted to contemporary art; and the town of Takahashi, with its elevated castle. And if you want to sample the charms of the countryside, nothing beats a bicycle ride on the Kibi Plain.**

- **Population:** 695,765 – Okayama Prefecture.
- **Michelin Map:** Principal Sights Map B3 – Regional Map p372.
- **Location:** Okayama is a medium-sized city on the shores of the Inland Sea, 100mi/161km from Hiroshima, 111.8mi/180km from Osaka, and 44.7mi/72km from Takamatsu. The downtown area lies between the station to the west and the Asahi River to the east. It is here, around Koraku-en and the castle, that the museums are concentrated. The commercial district, with its luxury boutiques and department stores, is close to the river, but the area around the station is much livelier at night.
- **Kids:** Renting a villa (*see box p374)* is a sound option if you're going as a family. In the summer, take advantage of the lovely beaches on the island of Naoshima. And don't miss the unusual Japan Rural Toy Museum in Kurashiki.
- **Timing:** Allow two days: one for Okayama and Kurashiki, another for the island of Naoshima or, alternatively, Takahashi, and Kibi Plain.
- **Don't miss:** A stroll in Koraku-en; the Ohara Museum in Kurashiki.

## SIGHTS

All the main sights are a stone's throw from JR Okayama station, but you can also hop on a tram for part of the way.

### Yumeji Art Museum★

夢二郷土美術館 *Map C1.*
*To the N of Koraku-en, in front of the main entrance. Open Tue–Sun 9am–5pm. ¥700.*

The artist **Takehisa Yumeji** (1884–1934), a native of Okayama, was one of the leading lights of the Romantic movement during the Taisho era (1912–26). Sometimes called the Japanese Toulouse-Lautrec, he shared the French artist's desire to make his art more accessible to the people by producing posters and prints. But whereas Toulouse-Lautrec gave an unflinching picture of the Bohemian life of Montmartre, including its prostitutes, Yumeji preferred to depict slender young women with delicate features—*bijin-ga* (elegant beauties)—in traditional kimonos, embodying a certain ideal of purity. His work, employing a number of different media (ink, pastels, charcoal, watercolors, etc.) reveals a self-taught artist with a fresh style, who combined

*Koraku-en in winter, Okayama Castle in the background*

©Okayama-ken Kanko Renmei/JNTO

strong lines with muted colors, and tried to achieve a blend of some elements of Japanese tradition with the modern Western trends that were inescapable in Japan at the beginning of the 20C.

**Koraku-en★★★** 後楽園 *Map C1*
*Main entrance by Tsurumi Bridge, in the NW, or through the south gate, opposite the castle. Open Apr–Sept 7.30am–6pm; Oct–Mar 8am–5pm. ¥350, combined ticket with the castle ¥520, with the castle plus Hayashibara Museum ¥670.*
*Stands in Koraku-en sell oniwa-soda-chi* bento, *takeout meals that match the garden's seasonal colors (¥1,500), to eat in the open air, weather permitting.*

**Rural villas**

Okayama prefecture runs five international villas reserved for foreign tourists, including two restored former farmhouses in the mountains and two modern villas by the sea. Each one can accommodate up to 10 people *(there is a fully equipped kitchen)*, but they can also all be booked together too. The rents are affordable, and bicycles and CD players are available.
*Information: www.international-villa.or.jp.*

Situated on an island in the middle of the Asahi River, once only accessible by boat *(there are now three bridges)*, this exceptional garden was created in 1700 by the *daimyo* of Okayama, Ikeda Tsunamasa. Anxious to have a place near his castle where he could relax, receive guests, and practice riding and archery, he spent no less than 14 years perfecting the garden. Today, Koraku-en is considered one of the three finest gardens in Japan, the others being Kairaku-en in Mito and Kenroku-en in Kanazawa. *(see p270)*.
It is not exceptionally large *(32 acres/13ha)*, but it is beautiful, varied, and in flower throughout the year, changing color with the seasons. A *kaiyu* (stroll garden) *(see p103)*, it is filled with wide lawns, hills, ponds, and tea houses, with paths winding in between, as well as a 2,100ft/640m-long stream of pure water, making the garden pleasantly cool in summer. Although since the Meiji era the former fields and rice paddies have been replaced by lawn, there is still a working tea plantation. The plums *(ume)* gathered in the garden are used to make a sweet wine called *umeshu*.
Every January 1 and 3, to celebrate the New Year, the Japanese cranes that are raised here are released to fly over the garden—with a wingspan of nearly 9.8ft/3m, they are a spectacular sight.
**Visit** – *From the main entrance, in the N, turn right and walk counterclockwise.*

The first building is **Enyo-tei**, the main pavilion, from where the lord enjoyed the view of the garden and its "borrowed landscape" *(shakkei—**see p 102)* of Mount Misao in the background. Behind the pavilion is a small **Noh theater**, reconstructed after the war. Farther down, a superb weeping cherry

## USEFUL INFORMATION

**OKAYAMA**

**Tourist Office** – *Okayama station (A1) Open 9am–6pm. ℘086-222-2912.*

**Okayama International Center** – *2-2-1 Hokan-cho (A1). Open Mon–Sat 9am–5pm. ℘086-256-2914.* Information on the prefecture and city of Okayama.

**KURASHIKI**

**Tourist Office** – *Kurashiki-kan, 1-4-8 Chuo. Open Apr–Oct 9am–6pm; Nov–Mar 9am–5.15pm. ℘086-424-1220.* In the heart of the Bikan district. Practical and friendly.

**NAOSHIMA**

**Tourist Office** – *In Miyanoura harbor. Open 9am–5pm. ℘087-892-2299. www.naoshima.net.*

## TRANSPORTATION

**OKAYAMA**

**BY PLANE** – **Okayama Airport** *(A1 off map)* – 9 flights per day to Tokyo *(1hr10min, ¥30,200)*, 1 flight per day to Sapporo *(1hr50min, ¥46,200)*. There is a shuttle to and from Okayama station *(30min, ¥680)*.

**BY TRAIN** – **Okayama Station** *(A1/2)* – The city is served by Shinkansen (Sanyo Line). Trains every 20min to Tokyo *(3hr20min, ¥15,850)*, Kyoto *(1hr30min, ¥7,330)*, and Hiroshima *(34min, ¥5,350)*. For the island of Shikoku, take the JR Seto-Ohashi Line *(1hr, ¥1,470)*.

**GETTING AROUND** – **NAOSHIMA**

**Getting to and from Naoshima** – *See p380.*

**BY BUS** – From the harbor, regular shuttle buses do a circuit of the island, stopping at Honmura, Benesse House, and Chichu Art Museum *(¥100)*.

**BY BICYCLE** – 1–2hr to go round the island. Bicycle rental at **Cycle Plaza**, Nogami, JR station west exit. *31-6 Motomachi, ¥100/hr, ¥500/day, 7.30am–7pm (Sun 8am–6pm).*

tree droops over **Kayo Pond** *(Kayo-no-ike)*, which is fed by a waterfall. In summer, a myraid of big white lotuses bloom here. In the middle of the water sits a huge granite rock, *(24.6ft/7.5m high and with a circumference of 65.6ft/20m)*. It was moved here three centuries ago, having been cut into 90 pieces to make it easier to transport. As you continue, you pass the remains of the **jetty** where the *daimyo* moored his boat when coming from the castle, now covered by a thicket of bamboo. Just after the south gate is the little **Renchi-ken** tea house, where you can enjoy some tea while contemplating the view. Climb **Yuishin Hill** for a magnificent **view**★★ of the garden, particularly impressive in May, when the azaleas are in bloom. At **Sawa Pond** *(Sawa-no-ike)*, the largest in the garden, look for carp swimming between the small islands covered in green pines and white sand. Farther south is the **Ryu-ten** pavilion, and nearby a stream running over a bed of colored pebbles that leads to fields of irises, in bloom in June. In the eastern part of the garden, near **Kako Pond** (Kako-no-ike) and its waterfall, are groves of plum and cherry trees. After pausing in front of a patch of land planted with rice and lotuses, look north to see row upon row of **tea plants.**

*Leave by the south gate of the garden, then cross the footbridge to get to the castle.*

### Okayama Castle★ 岡山城

*Map C2.*

*Open 9am–5pm. ¥300.*

Built by the daimyo Ukita Hideie in 1597, Okayama Castle is also known as *U-jo*, "Crow Castle," because of its black wooden walls. Black was synonymous with strength and sobriety, white with wealth and splendor. The one exception here is the gilded *shachi* (mythical fish protecting the building from fire) at the corners of the roofs. A flatland castle *(built on a plain)*, it is protected on the east side by the Asahi River. Unfortunately, the castle die not withstand the bombing of World War II and in 1966, was rebuilt in reinforced

concrete. The engineers even installed an elevator in the keep.
The interior houses objects *(armor, swords, lacquerware)* that belonged to the Ukita and Ikeda clans. Apart from the stone base, the only part of the castle that is now original is the **Tsukimi turret** in the northwest corner of the enclosure.

### Hayashibara Museum of Art★
林原美術館 *Map C2.*
*5min walk from the castle. Open Tue–Sun 9am–5pm. ¥300.*
Formerly located within the castle grounds, this building belonged to the Ikeda clan before being bought by Hayashibara Ichiro, a wealthy industrialist, who, in 1964, turned it into one of the first private museums in Japan. It houses an extensive collection, displayed in rotation, of more than 10,000 items from ancient Japan, including **kimonos**★ from the Noh theater of the late Muromachi era, a **screen**★★ decorated with a view of Kyoto in the 18C, as well as armor, swords, lacquerware, and paintings in ink inherited from the Ikeda family.

### Okayama Orient Museum
オリエント美術館 *Map B1/2.*
*15min walk from the station. Open Tue–Sun 9am–5pm. ¥300.*
Housed in a big, concrete building, this museum of Middle Eastern art and archeology was created in 1947, thanks to a donation from a wealthy Okayama businessman. It contains some 5,000 items, mostly from the **ancient Persian empires**. Its two floors are arranged around a large, central patio containing a marble fountain reminiscent of the courtyard of an early caravanserai. The works are displayed in chronological order: prehistoric hunter-gatherers, the rise of cities, and ancient empires, Persia and Greece, Islamic civilization. Among the finest pieces is a bas-relief from the Assyrian royal palace of Nimrod *(Iraq, 9C bc)*, a funerary bas-relief from Palmyra *(3C bc)*, fragments of Roman mosaics from Syria *(5C)*, and glazed pottery from Iran *(13C and 14C)*.

## EXCURSIONS
## TAKAHASHI★ 高梁
*A1 off map.*
*31mi/50 km NW of Okayama. Access by train on the Hakubi Line (55min, ¥820).*
A small town hemmed in by mountains and surrounded by paddy fields, Takahashi has a well-preserved historic quarter 0.6mi/1km north of the station, centered on a street called Ishibiya-cho, which is lined with merchant and samurai houses from the Edo period. Some are open to visitors, such as **Buke Yashiki-kan** *(open 9am–5pm; ¥300)*, which has about 10 rooms, a garden, and a storehouse at the rear, where armor is displayed. On the same street, the Rinzai Zen temple **Raikyu-ji** *(open 9am–5pm; ¥300)* has a gorgeous **dry landscape garden**★ designed in 1604 by the famous architect, gardener, and tea master Kobori Enshu (1579–1647). Its borders of raked sand combining rocks and azalea groves stand out gracefully against the borrowed landscape *(shakkei)* of Mount Atago. But, although not easy to reach, Takahashi's main point of interest remains its castle.

### Bitchu-Matsuyama Castle★
備中松山城
*3mi/5km N of the station. Access by bus (30min, ¥400), taxi, or on foot.*
*Open 9am–5pm. ¥300.*
Perched high on Mount Gagyu, at an altitude of 1,410.8ft/430m, this fortress is the highest in Japan. The original structure, built in 1240, was enlarged at the beginning of the 16C at the time of the Sengoku wars. After the Meiji Restoration, the castle was forgotten until the town undertook to restore it in the 1950s. The small (two-story) **keep** was rebuilt in wood. From the castle terrace, there is a lovely **view** of the river below and the surrounding mountains.

## KURASHIKI★★
倉敷
*15.5mi/25km W of Okayama.*
*15min by train on the JR Sanyo Line.*
An obligatory stop on the San-yo road between the Inland Sea and the northern regions, this merchant town

Bikan Historical District, Kurashiki

© Okayama-ken Kanko Renmei / JNTO

prospered, thanks to the rice and textile trades. Enjoying the status of a free port, linked to the sea by canals, it became so rich that it was placed under the direct supervision of the shogunate during the Edo period. Kurashiki *(population 470,000)* is currently the largest center for production of jeans in Japan. Located 875yd/800m to the south of the station, the **historical district of Bikan**★★, with its storehouses and romantic canals lined with weeping willows, has retained its old character *(see photo above)*. Today, its many art museums, restaurants, ryokan, and handicraft shops make it a lively tourist center. *Boat rides on the canals (20min, ¥300) are available Mar–Nov Tue–Sat 9.30am–11.30am, 1–4pm.*

## Ohash House 大橋家住宅

*3-21-31 Aichi, at the entrance to the Bikan district. Open Tue–Sun 9am–5pm. ¥500.*

The Ohashi family built its fortune in the 18C on salt and rice. Because of the influence it exerted, it was given permission by the shogunate to build this residence in 1796. The wide front door leads to an open space separating the house from the street: a style theoretically reserved for the samurai class. The original house had more than 25 rooms, and about 30 people lived here, including servants. The interior is typical of the houses of rich Kurashiki merchants. with tatami rooms at the front, for business and for entertaining guests, and private rooms at the rear. On the upper floor, an attic was used for storing the family's possessions (kimonos, china, scrolls). At the far end of the garden is a storehouse that has been turned into an exhibition hall.

*Cross the avenue called Chuo-dori to get to the main canal of Bikan, where the principal museums can be found.*

## Ohara Museum of Art★★
大原美術館

*Open Tue–Sun 9am–5pm. ¥1,000.*

In 1930, Ohara Magosaburo, who had made his fortune in textiles, created a museum to display his **collection of Western art**, one of the finest in Japan. Located on the right *(west)* bank of the canal, the building has a colonnaded façade like a Greek temple, a copy of the entrance to the Royal Museum in Ghent, Belgium. The museum's **Main Gallery** showcases Western sculptures and paintings, including a comprehensive survey of the various French and European movements at the beginning of the 20C: Barbizon school, school of Paris, Impressionists and post-Impressionists, Nabis, Fauves, Symbolists, and academic painters. Highlights include a vibrant Monet *Waterlilies* (1906), a magnificent Gauguin from the Tahitian period (1892), and an *Annunciation* by El Greco (late 16C), as well as works by Renoir, Toulouse-Lautrec, Pissarro, Puvis de Chavannes, Modigliani, Matisse, and Foujita.

### A family of art patrons

Ohara Ken-Ichiro, director—and grandson of the founder—of the Ohara Museum of Art, traces the history of the collection: "My grandfather Magosaburo was a cotton baron but also a philanthropist, who among other things founded the hospital in Kurashiki. When it came to art, his first interest was Eastern art of the past, but then his friend, the artist Kojima Torajiro, introduced him to Western painting. Between 1912 and 1923, Kojima made several trips to Paris, Belgium, Germany, and Switzerland to buy modern paintings for Magosaburo, visiting Monet's studio at Giverny and Matisse's studio in Paris. At the time, very few Western works could be seen in Japan. Magosaburo's one wish was to enlighten the Japanese public by showing his collection. The works acquired during that period form the kernel of the museum's holdings. My father Soichiro added artists belonging to the Mingei movement, and modern European, American, and Japanese art. I myself continue to buy a great deal of contemporary art."

Among the postwar artists represented are Fautrier, Soulages, Pollock, and De Kooning. Sculptures by Rodin, Bourdelle, and Henry Moore are on display in the garden. At the far end, the museum's **annex**, built in the style of a traditional Kurashiki storehouse, is devoted to modern and contemporary Japanese artists such as Fujishima Takeji, Koide Narashige, Aoki Shigeru, Kumagai Morikazu, Kishida Ryusei, and Yasui Sotaro. The **Craft Art Gallery** displays the work of some of the leading artists of the Folk Art or *Mingei* movement (*see p 104*). The Chinese Room in the adjoining **Asiatic Art Gallery**, (just before the exit) houses, among other works, a fine stone Buddha of the Northern Wei Dynasty (386–534).

*Continue S along the same bank.*

## Kurashiki Museum of Folkcraft
倉敷民芸館

*Open Tue–Sun 9am–4.45pm. ¥700.*
Opened in 1948, this museum is housed in a former rice *kura* (storehouse) typical of Kurashiki, with whitewashed cob walls with black tiles. It is the largest museum of popular Japanese handicrafts after the one in Tokyo. The collection comprises about 15,000 items *(displayed in rotation)*, most of them ordinary objects made by anonymous artisans. The prime objective is to demonstrate the beauty in everyday objects, but also to support local craft traditions.

## Japan Rural Toy Museum★
日本郷土玩具館

*Open 9am–5pm. ¥400.*
No fewer than 5,000 toys on display and 40,000 in store. Children of all ages will love this colorful museum with its dolls, automata, lucky charms, wooden or papier mâché *(hariko)* animals, and figures, kites, miniatures, and games from across Japan. There are some rare items from the Edo period in display cases on the ground floor and the attic. The museum has a little shop selling the ubiquitous *maneki-neko* (cats with raised paws) and Daruma dolls (lucky figurines of Buddhist origin).

*Walk back along the canal and cross the little bridge opposite the Tourist Office. Carry straight on, then turn right onto Honmachi-dori.*

## Honmachi-dori 本町通り

This narrow lane is lined with picturesque traditional houses, with roofs of silver-gray tiles and whitewashed walls adorned with wooden latticework, attractive old shops, sake breweries, cafes, and galleries. To the south of the street, **Ivy Square**formerly the site of a textile milltoday accommodates more restaurants, shops, and cafes, as well as the **Memorial to Kojima Torajiro** (*open Tue–Sun 9am–5pm; ¥500*), an Impressionist painter who helped Ohara Magosaburo to build his collection (*see box above*).

## NAOSHIMA★ 直島

*From Okayama, take the JR Seto-Ohashi Line to Chayamachi, then the Uno Line to Uno (50min, ¥570). The ferry terminal is opposite Uno station. The ferries (13 per day, 20min, ¥280) arrive at the harbor of Miyanoura. Ferries also link Miyanoura with Takamatsu, on the island of Shikoku (5 per day, 50min, ¥510).*

A little island tucked away among a hundred others in the Inland Sea, halfway between Okayama and Takamatsu, Naoshima *(3.1sq mi/8sq km, population 3,470)* is a unique place, an attempt to blend contemporary art with a well-conserved natural environment, to combine the preservation of the past and avant-garde artistic enterprise.

Once a sleepy island of fishing villages, Naoshima emerged from anonymity in 1992, when the Benesse Group chose it to establish a museum of contemporary art doubling as a hotel. The architect **Ando Tadao** was given the task of designing this highly original complex. Since then, the project has been enlarged, and the island has become very fashionable.

### Benesse House★ ベネッセハウス

*In the south of the island. Access by island shuttle bus, on foot, or by bicycle. Open 8am–9pm. ¥1,000.*

The architect **Ando Tadao**, well known for his sober, minimalist concrete buildings (*see box p351*), has succeeded brilliantly in matching the museum's architecture with its natural environment. Nestling amid the vegetation, the various sections of the building hug the contours of the land, rising in stages, interspersed with greenery, to the top of a hill overlooking the sea. The works on display were all produced specially for these surroundings. They are not numerous, but all are shown in a way that enhances them, whether Bruce Nauman's neon lights blinking in the middle of a vast cylindrical space, Iannis Kounellis's wall of lead, Richard Long's stone and wood circles, or Yasuda Kan's monumental pebbles.

What makes Benesse House so unique is that it is also a hotel, with rooms featuring contemporary works by artists such as Sol LeWitt, Thomas Ruff, Christo, and Keith Haring. A small monorail *(for guests only)* leads to the **Oval**, a structure in the center of which is an ornamental pond.

There are additional rooms in two annexes built in 2006, one of which has a restaurant and leads onto the beach. The grounds of the house are also dotted with installations. Notable among them is Kusama Yayoi's huge pumpkin, plumped down on a jetty facing the sea like a child's toy forgotten by a giant.

### Chichu Art Museum★ 地中美術館

*20min walk from Benesse House or by island shuttle bus. Open Mar–Sept Tue–Sun 10am–6pm; Oct–Feb 10am–5pm. ¥2,000.*

### BETTING ON CONTEMPORARY ART

The success of the Naoshima experience launched 20 years ago by the president of the Benesse correspondence and education publishing group in the realm of contemporary art has created dynamic redevelopment based on contemporary art, which is extending to the other islands of the Inland Sea. In 2010 *(Jul–Oct)* the first **Setouchi International Art Festival "100-Day Art and Sea Adventure"** was launched. Intended to be a triennial event, this first year included 75 international artists (including Christian Boltanski, Mariko Mori, and Olafur Eliasson) were called upon to create projects on the seven islands (Naoshima, Teshima, Megijima, Ogijima, Shodoshima, Oshima, Inujima, and Takamatsu port). One of the important aspects of the triennial is to involve the local inhabitants, in order to highlight their cultural heritage.

*Further information at www.setouchi-artfest.jp (in English)*

Buried beneath the slope of a hill overlooking the islands and former saltmarshes of the Inland Sea, the Chichu Museum, opened in 2004 and again the work of Ando Tadao, is an unsettling space.
It houses only a small number of works, but they benefit from a very theatrical presentation, in which visitors are led on a journey that is sensory, intellectual, and emotional. Along with the sequence of Monet *Waterlilies* are contemporary site-specific instalations by James Turrell and Walter de Maria.

### Art House Project★★
家プロジェクト

*Village of Honmura. Access by island shuttle bus, on foot, or by bicycle. Open Tue–Sun 10am–4.30pm. ¥1,000 for six installations, or ¥400 for one. Reservations required 2 days in advance for the Kinza site.*
*A brochure in English, available in the village, lists the various sites to visit.*
Honmura, in the west of the island, had its hour of glory in the 17C and 18C. Situated on the maritime trading route between the island of Shikoku and the ports on Honshu, the village became a pirate den, led by the Takahara family. There are still some fine traditional houses that can be seen from that time, in dark wood with heavy gray-tiled roofs. In 1998, in collaboration with the Benesse Foundation, the municipality began to renovate some of them to accommodate contemporary art installations.
The temple **Minami-dera**★, for example, has been restored by James Turrell and provides an interesting visual experience for visitors, while **Kadoya**, more than 200 years old, accommodates the light installations of Miyajima Tatsuo.

### Inu-jima 犬島
*7.5mi/12km N of Naoshima. Museum (10am–4.30pm) ¥1,000 by reservation only. 086-947-112. www.inujima-ap.jp. 45min ferry (n) from Naoshima (¥4,000 round-trip, reserve at least 4 days ahead).*

**Momotaro the hero**

According to a legend from the Edo period, the little boy Momotaro was found floating down a river in a giant peach by an elderly couple. He set off to fight the cannibal demons of the island of Onigashima, on the Inland Sea. On the way, he befriended a dog, a monkey, and a pheasant, who all helped him to defeat the ogres.

Like many islands in the Inland Sea, Inu-jima *(0.20sq mi/0.54sq km, population 55)*, housed a copper refinery (*seirensho*), no longer in use. Once again thanks to the Benesse Foundation, this vast brick shell has now been transformed into an unusual **museum**, with a cafe and a bookshop.
A work by the artist Yanagi Yukinori is currently on display, while others are being instaled. As with Naoshima, an arts festiva, lthe Setouchi International Art Festival (*see box opposite*) was held in 2010.

## KIBI PLAIN 吉備平野
*Bicycle route begins 9.3mi/15km E of Okayama. Take JR Kibi Line to Bizen Ichinomiya station (11min, ¥200), where bikes can be rented. They can be dropped off on arrival at Soja station. From there, you can get back to Okayama, or take the JR Hakubi Line to Takahashi.*
The Kibi Plain Bicycle Route is a specially designed trail across the Okayama countryside, scattered with remains dating back to the old kingdom of Kibi *(4–5C)*. Places of interest along the way include the **Kibitsu-jinja**, a shrine built in 1425 and dedicated to Prince Kibitsuhiko, the inspiration for the legend of Momotaro (*see box p 381*); **Tsukuriyama-kofun**, an imposing 5C burial mound; and the **Bitchu Kokubun-ji** and its five-story pagoda, near Soja.

# ADDRESSES

## STAY

### OKAYAMA

**Matsunoki Ryokan** まつのき旅館 *19-1 Ekimoto-cho (A2). ℘086-253-4111. www.matunoki.com. 59 rooms.* An unassuming ryokan located behind the station. Japanese and Western rooms. *Excellent value for money.*

**Excel Okayama** エクセル岡山 *5-1 Ishizeki-cho (B2). ℘086-224-0505. www.excel-okayama.com. 89 rooms.* A *business hotel* ideally located near the castle and the museums. Small, but functional rooms.

**Okayama Plaza Hotel** 岡山プラザホテル *2-3-12 Koraku-en (C1). ℘086-272-1201. www.oplaza-h.co.jp. 84 rooms.* A chain hotel with all modern conveniences, close to Koraku-en.

**Hotel Granvia** ホテルグランヴィア岡山 *1-15 Ekimoto-cho (A2). ℘086-234-7000. www.granvia-oka.co.jp. 328 rooms.* The rooms are well maintained and beautifully decorated. There are 11 banqueting rooms and restaurants. A real must.

### KURASHIKI

**Kurashiki Ivy Square** 倉敷アイビースクエア *7-2 Honmachi. ℘086-422-0011. www.ivysquare.co.jp. 161 rooms.* This red-brick building from the end of the 19C, a former courthouse converted into a cotton mill in 1899, is now a charming hotel.

### NAOSHIMA

**Minshuku Okada** 民宿おかだ *199-1 Tsumiura-cho. ℘087-892-3406.* ⊠. *4 rooms.* Conveniently located between Benesse House and the village of Honmura, this little guesthouse is run by a delightful couple.

**Naoshima Furusato Umi-no-ie Tsutsuji-so** 直島ふるさと海の家つつじ荘 *352-1 Naoshima-cho. ℘087-892-2838. 4 rooms, 10 yurts (40 beds). Closed Dec 31 and Jan 1.* Very close to the beach. The yurts are air-conditioned, a bit spartan, but pleasant. *Showers in adjacent trailers.*

**Benesse House Museum** ベネッセハウス *Gotan-ji. ℘087-892-2030. www.naoshima-is.co.jp. 65 rooms.* Rooms on the upper floor of the museum, with a **view** of the Inland Sea, and free admission to the museum. A unique—but expensive—experience.

## EAT

### OKAYAMA

**Toritetsu** とり鉄岡山錦町店 *3-101 Nisikimati-cho (A2). ℘086-235-3681. Open 5pm–midnight (Fri, Sat, and eve of public holidays 4am).* A small *yakitori* restaurant with a young, trendy vibe.

**Toriyoshi** 鳥好駅前本店 *5-8 Honmachi, Okayama station (A2). ℘086-233-5810. Open 4pm–midnight.* This popular place is a tavern, where the waitresses bustle about between huge wooden tables. Oysters in vinegar, sashimi, tempura, etc.

**Art Dining Musashi** アートダイニング武蔵 *1-7-18 Nodaya-cho (A2). ℘086-222-3893. Open 11am–2pm and 5pm–10pm.* A good place for gourmets. In Mar and Apr, try the *sawara* sashimi: *sawara* is a Spanish mackerel from the Inland Sea.

### KURASHIKI

**Taisyotei** 大正亭 *2-14 Honmachi. ℘086-422-8100. Open 11am–10pm.* The specialty is the sardine-based *matsuri* sushi.

**Mingeijaya Shinsui** 民芸茶屋新粋 *11-35 Honmachi. ℘086-422-5171. Open Mon–Sat 5–10pm. Oden* (hot pot) is served from behind a wooden counter.

### NAOSHIMA

**Yamamoto Udon** 山本うどん店 *2526-1 Naoshima-cho, next to the Mitsubishi Materials Co-op. ℘087-892-4072. Open Mon–Sat 10am–4.30pm.* A popular udon restaurant.

**Saryo Oomiyake** 茶寮大三宅 *Honmura, Naoshima-cho. ℘087-892-2328. Reservations required.* French and Japanese cuisine in one of the island's oldest houses *(1600)*.

# The San-yo Coast★: Hiroshima★★

# 山陽：広島

**Some people visit the city out of a sense of duty, while others prefer to avoid the experience for fear of finding it too upsetting, but nobody can be indifferent to Hiroshima, whose greatest claim to fame, sadly, is that it was struck by the first atomic bomb in August 1945. Within just a few seconds, the explosion had turned the center of the city into a wasteland.**

Today, only the charred framework of the A-Bomb Dome remains to bear witness to the nuclear inferno. Hiroshima's martyrdom was a turning point in the history of the world: Mankind now has the means to destroy itself, which is why the city is so determined to deliver a warning to future generations, through its Peace Memorial Park. But like a phoenix reborn from its own ashes, Hiroshima has also looked to the future and today it is a dynamic city, the largest in Chugoku, with an active port and a vibrant nightlife. A couple of miles away, the island of Miyajima has one of the most famous **views** in Japan: the *torii* (gate) of the Itsukushima Shrine, which appears to float in the water just offshore. The little town of Iwakuni, once a samurai stronghold, has a well-preserved and picturesque wooden bridge.

- **Population:** 1,173,940 – Hiroshima Prefecture
- **Michelin Map:** Principal Sights Map A3 – Regional Map p372.
- **Location:** Situated on the Inland Sea, 99.4mi/160km from Okayama and 174mi/280km from Fukuoka, Hiroshima occupies the delta of the Ota River, which divides the city into several islands. It is easily covered on foot, or, failing that, by tram. The JR station is to the east of the downtown area and Peace Memorial Park to the west.
- **Kids:** Some of the images and eyewitness accounts presented in the Peace Memorial Museum may be disturbing for younger children, but Miyajima, with its deer and walking trails, should appeal to the whole family.
- **Timing:** You can visit Hiroshima and Miyajima in one day, but it's more sensible to allow two days. Reckon on spending one night in Hiroshima and the other on Miyajima.
- **Don't miss:** Peace Memorial Park; the island of Miyajima.

## BACKGROUND

**A strategic base** – Hiroshima was founded in 1589 by the feudal lord Mori Terumoto, who built his castle on the largest of the islands formed by the branches of the Ota River—hence the name of the city (*Hiro* means "large" and *shima* "island"). It expanded during the Edo period, and became industrialized soon after the Meiji Restoration. During the First Sino–Japanese War (1894–1895), the Imperial High Command was based here and in the 1930s, the armaments industry became established in the area. Hiroshima Bay, including the naval center at Kure, became the principal military base in the west of Japan. During World War II, Hiroshima was a strategic base maintaining the land defenses of southern Japan.

**August 6, 1945** – Under the code name "Manhattan Project," the Americans had been secretly working on an atomic bomb since 1942. In September 1944, the decision was taken to use it against Japan. A first test took place on July 16, 1945, in the desert of New Mexico. Four days later, the American high command drew up a list of targets: Hiroshima, Nagasaki, Kokura, and Niigata. In the early hours of the morning of August 6, 1945, the B-29 bomber *Enola Gay* took off carrying a 4-ton uranium-235 bomb nicknamed *Little Boy*. By dawn, the skies were clear over Hiroshima, and the city was chosen as the target. The bomb, dropped at 8.15am, exploded 1,903ft/580m above the ground, directly over Shima Hospital in the heart of the city. Immediately, the sky was split by a flash of light and a terrifying explosion. A mushroom-shaped cloud rose over the horizon and the sky turned black. The explosion, equivalent to 15,000 tons of TNT, instantly razed the city to the ground. Of the 350,000 inhabitants and military personnel present at the time of the attack, 80,000 people were immediately killed.

In the following weeks, another 60,000 died, and 92 percent of the city's buildings were completely destroyed. Eyewitness accounts by survivors describe nightmarish visions: wounded people with disfigured faces and mutilated bodies staggering through the rubble like sleepwalkers, their clothes in tatters; others, horribly burned, screaming with thirst as they lay dying. Little known at the time and long suppressed by the American authorities, the secondary effects of radiation were equally terrifying: loss of hair, anemia, internal bleeding, fever, and infections. Subsequently, many of those exposed to radiation died of cancer, leukemia, and other diseases. Still today, we have every right, when confronted with these horrors, to wonder about the military purpose and moral validity of unleashing such a weapon on a civilian population.

**Capital of peace** – There were many who believed that the city would never come back to life and that it would be at least 75 years before any plants could be grown there again. Nevertheless, the population managed to rebuild it quite quickly, and in 1949, Hiroshima was proclaimed a City of Peace by the Japanese parliament. Reconstructed on a grid plan, the new city regained its pre-eminence in the region and its economic dynamism. Hiroshima may now look like any other Japanese city, but it has not forgotten its past, and continues to honor the memory of its dead through museums, annual ceremonies, and other initiatives for peace.

## SIGHTS

### A-Bomb Dome★

原爆ドーム *Map A1.*

*15min by tram from Hiroshima station.*

Facing Aioi Bridge and the Motoyasu River, the A-Bomb Dome *(Genbaku Domu)* is one of the few structures to have withstood the atomic blast but still be standing. Designed by the Czech architect Jan Letzel in the European style and erected in 1915, it was the Industrial Promotion Hall. All that remains now—left as a reminder of this catastrophic event—is the blackened metal structure, some twisted girders, and ruined walls. The surrounding buildings were destroyed but because the bomb exploded almost vertically above it, the dome was not entirely destroyed. In December 1996, it was designated a UNESCO World Heritage Site. To prevent it from collapsing, it

### *Hibakusha*, the open wounds of the A-bomb

Known as *Hibakusha* in Japanese, the survivors of the atomic bomb today number, officially, 266,500. One of them, Mito Kosei, is a volunteer guide in Hiroshima. He was still in his mother's womb when exposed to radiation: "Since 1957, *Hibakusha* like me have been entitled to free medical treatment, but many are ashamed of their condition and prefer not to identify themselves." In addition to their physical suffering, the *Hibakusha* were for a long time covertly discriminated against. Regarded as contaminated and contagious, they felt themselves to be undesirables, people who had lost their humanity.

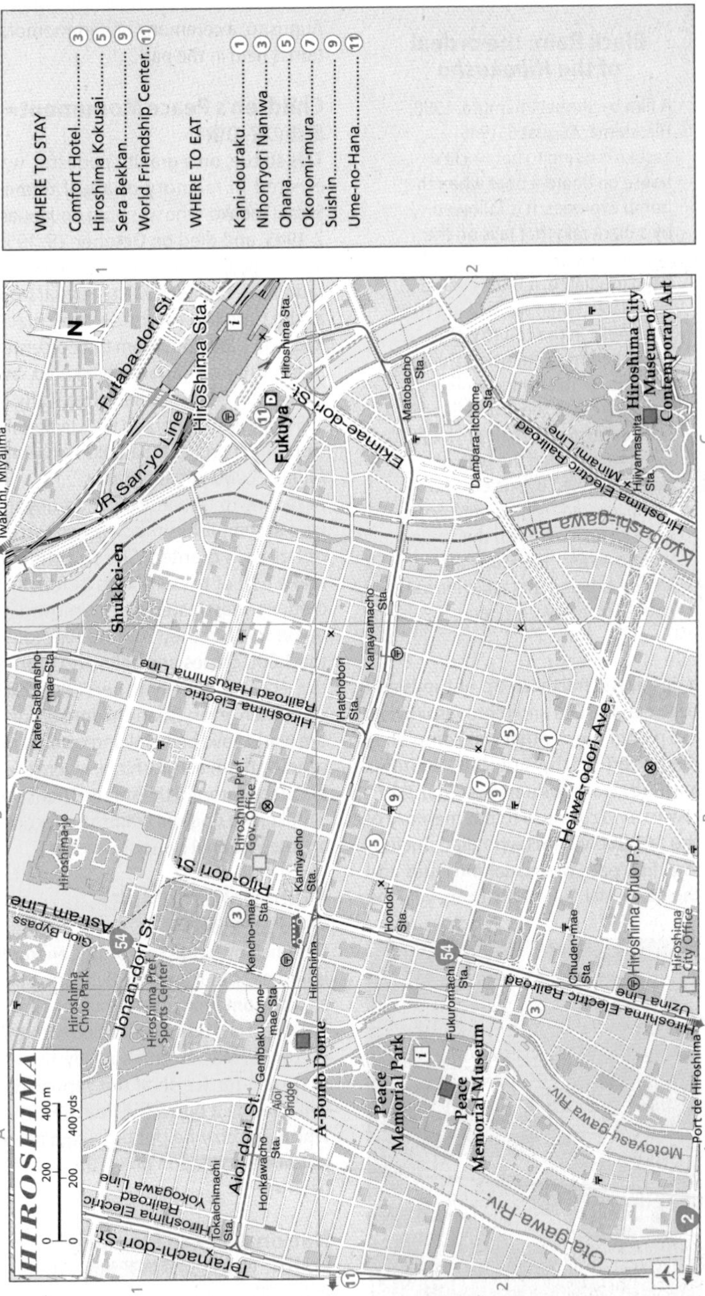




has had to be strengthened on several occasions, notably in 2002.

*Cross the river to the park, which is opposite.*

## Peace Memorial Park★★

平和記念公園 *Map A2*

Created in the 1960s by Tange Kenzo and planted with camphor trees and oleanders, the park covers 29.7 acres/12ha.

### Black Rain: the ordeal of the *Hibakusha*

A film by Shohei Imamura, 1988. Hiroshima, August 6, 1945. Yasuko is going to her uncle's house on board a boat when the bomb explodes; it is followed by a black rain that falls on the passengers. Unaware she has been irradiated, it is only some years later, when she is living peacefully in the country, that death begins to stalk her. Through the story of this young woman, the film tells of the ordeal lived by all ***Hibakusha***: to their physical suffering is added the pain of being shunned by society and being labeled "contagious". Some went so far as to bring their own lives to an end, to escape the shame of being that which Japan could not forgive: a victim.

It lies at the northern tip of the island between the Ota and Motoyasu Rivers, in a part of the city that was completely destroyed by the bomb. It includes a number of monuments *(fountains, towers, and columns)* to the memory of the 140,000 victims who died, including the Peace Memorial Museum and the Memorial Cenotaph. Every year, on August 6, a ceremony of commemoration is held in the park.

*A-Bomb Dome with the Peace Memorial Park in the background*

©JNTO

## Children's Peace Monument★
原爆の子の像

This statue, on a granite pedestal, was erected in memory of a girl named Sasaki Sadako, who was born on January 7, 1943, and died on October 25, 1955, at the age of 12 of leukemia caused by radiation. Sadako was two years old at the time the explosion took place, and was 1.2mi/2km from the epicenter. Most of her neighbors were killed, but she emerged unscathed. Tragically in 1954, she was diagnosed with leukemia. Hoping to recover, Sadako set about folding 1,000 origami cranes.

According to Japanese tradition, anyone who accomplishes this task will see his or her wish granted. She had time to make 644 of these cranes before she died. Her classmates were so moved by her story that they continued folding the 1,000 cranes and collected money to erect a monument to her (1958). Ever since then, every year, children around the world have been folding cranes and sending them to Hiroshima, where they are placed around the statue. Thanks to Sadako, the origami crane has become an international symbol of peace.

## Memorial Cenotaph
原爆死没者慰霊碑

Designed by Tange Kenzo, the Cenotaph is in the form of an arch. Beneath it lies a tomb containing the names of all the victims of the bomb, inscribed with the epitaph: "May all the souls here rest in peace, for we shall not repeat the evil." Beside it burns the **Peace Flame**, which will only be put out when every last nuclear weapon on earth has been destroyed.

## National Peace Memorial Hall★ 国立広島原爆死没者追悼平和祈念館

*Open Mar–Nov 8.30am–6pm (Aug 7pm); Dec–Feb 8.30am–5pm.*
*No charge.*

To the right of the cenotaph, this gray marble-and-glass building built in 2002, again the work of Tange Kenzo, honors the memory of the victims of the bomb by presenting the full horror of Hiroshima. In the circular central hall, a fountain marks ground zero, its water having the symbolic function of soothing the souls of those who died thirsty. A 360-degree image shows the devastated city after the catastrophe. In the basement, computers show video testimonies and films shot at the time. The archives contain about 100,000 eyewitness accounts, all of them very moving. A wall screen displays the names and photographs of the dead.

### Peace Memorial Museum★★

広島平和記念資料館 *Map A2.*
*Open Apr–Jul 9am–6pm; Aug–Nov 8.30–6pm; Dec–Mar 9am–4.30pm. ¥50. Audioguide available in English (¥300). Guided tours available, or meet a hibakusha (see box opposite). 082-541-5544.*

Also designed by Tange Kenzo, this harrowing museum shows the consequences of the atomic explosion through a large collection of photographs and objects that belonged to the victims. One of the two buildings displays a very realistic reconstruction of the ruins after the cataclysm, with terrible waxwork figures and genuine remnants of the tragedy: tattered clothes, melted bottles, vitrified tiles, twisted girders, and clocks with their hands frozen at 8.15am. The mechanism of the A-bomb and the damage caused by it are meticulously described, as well as the suffering endured by the population. There is also an informative overview of Hiroshima before and during the war, tracing the course of events leading up to the bombing, and attempting to explain why the city was chosen as a target by the US army. Japanese militarism and its own many atrocities do not go unmentioned, nor does the fact that, among the victims, there were many Koreans and Chinese who had been working in the city as forced laborers. The American viewpoint, depicting Hiroshima as a "necessary sacrifice" to hasten the end of the war is also called into question: could it be that the United States was also trying to beat its rivals, the USSR, to domination of the region? The last section of the museum uses charts and scale models to show the current state of the world's nuclear arsenal, emphasizing the threat that the arms race poses to the future of mankind, and Hiroshima's commitment to peace.

### Shukkei-en★ 縮景園 *Map B–C1.*

*Kaminobori-cho. 20min walk NE of Peace Memorial Park. Open Apr–Sept 9am–6pm; Oct–Mar 9am–5pm. ¥250.*

This small garden *(10 acres/4ha)* was designed in 1620 by the local *daimyo* Asano Nagaakira. It is situated close to the Kyobashi River, from which it draws the water for its pretty central pond. The pond itself was modeled after the West Lake in Hangzhou, China, former capital of the Southern Song dynasty (1127–1279). Wiped out by the A-bomb, Shukkei-en was rebuilt in 1951 from the original plans. Since then, the trees have had time to reach their adult height, shielding the park from its urban surroundings. The garden contains miniaturized versions of some of the country's most famous landscapes—the main hill, for example, symbolizes Mount Fuji, and the pond, with its many small islands, evokes the Inland Sea.

### Hiroshima City Museum of Contemporary Art

広島市現代美術館 *Map C2.*
*1-1 Hijiyama-koen. Hijiyama-shita tram stop, Line 5. Open Tue–Sun 10am–5pm. ¥360.*

Erected in 1989, this circular building set around a central open space *(agora-style)* is situated in Hiyajima Park on top of a hill planted with cherry trees. It was designed by the architect Kurokawa Kisho, who is associated with the Metabolist movement (see p91) and also designed the National Art Center in Tokyo. In addition to temporary exhibitions, there is a permanent collection of works by postwar Japanese and foreign artists, including a number from China and Korea.

## USEFUL INFORMATION

**Tourist Offices** – In Hiroshima station *(C1)* *(open 9am–5.30pm)* and Peace Memorial Park *(A2)* *(open 9.30am–6pm; 082-247-6738).*

In Hiroshima and Chugoku, get the **Seto Inland Sea Welcome Card**, free from Tourist Offices, which gives visitors 20 percent reductions to places of interest, etc.

## TRANSPORTATION

**BY PLANE** – **Hiroshima Airport** – *25mi/40km E of center (A2 off map).* Flights to Tokyo *(1hr20min, ¥30,900)*, main Japanese cities. **Limousine Bus** *(1hr, ¥1,300).*

**BY TRAIN** – **Hiroshima Station** – Hiroshima is on the Tokyo-Osaka-Hakata Shinkansen Line. To Fukuoka *(Hakata)*, the journey takes 1hr15min and costs ¥8,700. *(To Shin-Osaka, 1hr30min, ¥9,950; to Tokyo, 5hr, ¥18,050).*

## EXCURSIONS

### MIYAJIMA★★★ 宮島

*From Hiroshima station, JR Sanyo Line to Miyajima-guchi (every 10min, journey time 25min, ¥400). Ferries for the island from the pier facing the station (10min, ¥170). Last boat returns at 10.14pm.*

Miyajima has been a sacred Shinto site since ancient times. With a surface area of 11.6sq mi/30sq km, it is forbidden either to be born or to die here, so there is no maternity hospital or cemetery on the island. The unusual feature of its main attraction, the beautiful **Itsukushima Shrine**, is that it is partly built in the sea. At high tide, the shrine appears to be floating on the water. The **view** of its great red *torii*, set in the water a short distance offshore, is one of the most famous in Japan.

**Miyajima's** mountains, forests, beaches, hiking trails, and freely roaming deer make it a favorite with families. The island was designated a UNESCO World Heritage Site in 1996.

#### Itsukushima Shrine★★★
厳島神社

*5min walk from the ferry terminal.* *Open Mar–mid-Oct 6.30am–6pm; mid-Oct–Feb 6.30am–5.30pm.* *¥300.*

Built on piles within a rugged bay, the shrine of Itsukushima is a superb example of how a man-made structure can blend in with its natural surroundings. Rated one of the three most beautiful **views** in the whole country *(with* ***Matsushima****,* *see p408**, and* ***Amano Hashidate****)*, thousands of visitors come here every year to admire this classically beautiful building. According to tradition, the shrine dates from 593.

However, most of the buildings were not erected until the Heian period (in the *shinden* style used for aristocratic residences) by Taira no Kiyomori (1118–81), head of the Taira clan and governor of the region, who made Itsukushima his palace. Restored and enlarged several times, notably in 1556, the shrine is dedicated to the three daughters of the god Susano-o, of whom the eldest, Itsukushima, is the goddess of the sea.

The famous **"floating" torii**★★★ about 656ft/200m offshore was rebuilt in 1875. Made of vermilion-lacquered camphorwood, it is 52.5ft/16m high. The fact that it stands offshore is thought to relate to the sacred nature of the island: ordinary people were not allowed to set foot on it and had to approach by sea, through this gate, in order to get to the temple. It is possible to walk to the *torii* at low tide, when the sea floor is exposed and strewn with fragments of shell. The *torii* blazes with color in the evening sunset like a vast Japanese ideogram, and more subtly after nightfall, when lit by the moon.

The shrine itself comprises several buildings linked by pontoons and verandas, including the hall of worship (**haiden**), the pavilion of offerings (**heiden**), and the main hall (**honden**). On the jetty facing the bay is the oldest **Noh theater stage** in Japan (16C). The **treasure house**, in a pavilion a little apart from the other buildings (*open 8am–5pm; ¥300)*, includes a number of objects *(sacred scrolls, weapons, musical instru-*

*ments, masks, fans)*, offerings from the Taira, and others over the centuries. At the rear of the building is the **Tahoto**, a two-story pagoda.

### Daisho-in★★ 大聖院

*5min walk along the path that rises to the E of the shrine. Open 8am–5pm. No charge.*

This colorful temple at the foot of Mount Misen houses an eclectic collection of Buddhist statues and popular deities. All the traditional paraphernalia of temples are here: a stone staircase with a row of prayer wheels in the middle, a pool with carp, and porticos. From the terrace, there is a fine **view** of Miyajima.

### Senjokaku 千畳閣 (豊国神社)

*On the hill to the N of the shrine. Open 9am–4pm. ¥100.*

Built by Toyotomi Hideyoshi at the end of the 16C, but never completed, this huge camphorwood temple is the largest building on the island, with a surface area of 857 tatami *(Senjokaku means "hall of one thousand mats")*. It is dominated by an elegant five-story **pagoda, Gojuno-to**★, which dates from 1407.

### Miyajima History and Folklore Museum★ 宮島歴史民俗資料館

*5min walk to the W of the shrine. Open Tue–Sun 8.30am–5pm. ¥300.*

Housed in a fine 19C merchant house with a garden, this museum displays a large number of everyday objects from the Edo period, notably a giant rice spoon, reproductions of which can be found in most shops on the island.

### Mount Misen Observatory★ 弥山展望台

*20min walk to the cable car in Momijidani Park, then 15min by cable car (open 9am–5pm; ¥1,800 round trip) to Shishiiwa, and, finally, 20min walk to the top.*

With an altitude of 1,739ft/530m, this is the highest point on the island. From the terrace of the observatory, there is a spectacular **view**★★ of the shrine and the other islands of the Inland Sea.

#### Generations of bridge building

Ebizaki Kumetsugu is the head carpenter of Kintai Bridge, like his father before him, and so on all the way back to 1673. Every 30 years, he and his team have the task of partly rebuilding the bridge using Japanese cypress wood *(hinoki)*. "Everything is done by hand. We rely on our own experience and don't calculate anything by computer. The hardest thing is to anticipate how the wood will react over time, how it will withstand bad weather. The most recent rebuilding work was in 2004. With the quantity of wood that we used, we could have built 50 houses."

The mountain, which has preserved its luxuriant primeval forest where monkeys and deer roam freely, has some pleasant hiking trails.

## IWAKUNI★ 岩国

*25mi/40km SW of Hiroshima. Trains every 15min on the Sanyo Line (45min, ¥740). From Iwakuni station, there is a shuttle bus service to Kintai Bridge (15min, ¥240).*

This town *(population 150,000)* is located at the mouth of the Nishiki River, in Yamaguchi prefecture. Its principal attraction is a fine five-arched wooden bridge.

### Kintai Bridge★★ 錦帯橋

*Open 8am–5pm. ¥300, combined ticket with the cable car and castle ¥930.*

In 1673, Kikkawa Hiroyoshi, *daimyo* of Iwakuni, tired of seeing the bridges over the Nishiki River washed away every rainy season, ordered a Chinese-style bridge to be built, with humpback arches resting on solid stone pillars able to withstand floods. Thanks to the skill of the local carpenters, the elegant Kintai Bridge stood proudly for almost three centuries until it was brought down by a typhoon in 1950: it was reconstructed in identical form three years later. Until the

Meiji Restoration, the use of the bridge was reserved for noblemen and samurai, the common people having to cross the river by boat.
Known as the "Brocade Sash Bridge" because of the curtain effect produced by its five arches, it is 16.4ft/5m wide and 633.2ft/193m long. It is a fine example of the effectiveness of traditional building techniques, with not a single nail being used (*see box p389*). Its arches rise to a height of 36ft/11m above the river.

*On the other side of the bridge, head for the cable-car station.*

### Iwakuni Art Museum★
岩国美術館

*Open Mar–Nov Fri–Wed 9am–5pm; Dec–Feb Fri–Wed 9am–4pm. ¥800.*
Located in the town's old samurai quarter, this museum has a fascinating collection of weapons, helmets, and armor. The upper floors display *maki-e* (gilded lacquerware), ceramics, paintings in the classic *yamato-e* style, and some lovely screens from the Edo period.
Opposite the museum, in a small **vivarium** (*open 9am–5pm; ¥100*), you can see the **white snake of Iwakuni**, a rare variety of red-eyed albino snake. *The town has the only specimens in the world of this fast-disappearing species.*

### Iwakuni Castle 岩国城
*Access by cable car (every 20min, ¥540). Open 9am–4.45pm. ¥320.*
Standing at the top of Shiroyama, the castle is a concrete reconstruction dating from 1962. The original was built in 1608 by the local lord, Kikkawa Hiroie, and destroyed seven years later by the shogun Tokugawa Iemitsu.
The ruins of the old castle can still be seen some 164ft/50m away, those responsible for the reconstruction having evidently preferred to move it to the edge of the hill.
The interior is of no great interest, but the position offers a good **view** of the town below and on a clear day, the islands of the Inland Sea.

## ADDRESSES

### STAY

**World Friendship Center**
ワールドフレンドシップセンター
*8-10 Higashi Kan-on (A2, off map). 082-503-3191. http://wfchiroshima.net. 6 rooms – ¥3,900/person – breakfast included.* Small guesthouse run by American pacifist association founded in 1965. The rooms are bright and pretty. English classes, and opportunities to meet A-bomb survivors.

**Comfort Hotel**
コンフォートホテル広島
*3-17 Komachi (A2). 082-541-5555. www.choicehotels.com. 282 rooms. Breakfast included.* A charmless, but functional chain hotel close to Peace Memorial Park.

**Sera Bekkan 世羅別館**
*4-20 Mikawa-cho (B2). 082-248-2251. www.yado.to. 35 rooms.* One of the few traditional ryokan in the heart of Hiroshima. *O-furo* on the top floor.

**Hiroshima Kokusai**
ひろしま国際ホテル *3-13 Tatemachi (B2). 082-248-2323. www.kokusai.gr.jp. 74 rooms.* This hotel in the heart of the city has fully-equipped rooms and a wide range of restaurants, including **Geishu** for sophisticated local meals and **Tonfon** for Chinese cuisine.

### EAT

**Ohana** お花 *3-4 Nagarekawa-cho (B2). 082-545-7555. Open 5pm–midnight.* A lively *izakaya*; eat at the counter.

**Okonomi-mura** お好み村
*5-13 Shin-tenchi (B2) Open 11am–10pm.* . Try the *okonomiyaki*: a stuffed pancake.

**Suishin** 酔心 *6-7 Tatemachi (B2). 082-247-4411. Open 11.20am–10pm.* Specializing in *kamameshi* and *donburi*.

**Kani-douraku**
かに道楽広島店 *7-4 Nagarekawa-cho (B2). 082-244-3315. Open 11am–11pm.* Crab *(kani)* in every form possible.

**Ume no Hana** 梅の花
*11 F Fukuya Bldg, Hiroshima station (C1). 012-017-2066. Open 11am–10pm.* Soybean-based dishes.

**Nihonryori Naniwa** なにわ
*6 F Rhiga Royal Hotel Hiroshima (B1). 082-228-5919.* Highly sophisticated *kaiseki* dinner.

# The San-in Coast
# 山陰

**A tour of the San-in coast in the north of Chugoku, on the shores of the Sea of Japan, is a journey into *Ura-Nihon*, the hidden Japan. Well away from the main tourist routes, it is a wild, thinly-populated region, where age-old traditions are still respected. It is full of stunning landscapes, fascinating cultural sites, delightful onsen, and old feudal towns steeped in history, and there are plenty of open-air activities to enjoy too.**

- **Population:** Tottori: Population 210,259, Matsue: Population 202,310 Hagi: Population 56,901 –Tottori, Shimane, and Yamaguchi prefectures.
- **Michelin Map:** Principal Sights Map A–B3 – Regional Map p372.
- **Location:** On the shores of the Sea of Japan, the San-in coast comprises Tottori and Shimane prefectures, and the northern part of Yamaguchi prefecture. Tottori is 88.2mi/142km from Okayama; Matsue is 75.8mi/122km from Tottori, and 136.7mi/220km from Hagi.
- **Kids:** A camel ride or cart ride on the Tottori dunes; in Matsue, Vogel Park, and a boat trip on the castle moats.
- **Timing:** Allow a minimum of four days, stopping over at Tottori, Matsue *(two nights)*, and Hagi. If you have a car, stop at Misasa Onsen, Kaike Onsen, or Yunotsu Onsen. Most towns and places of interest can be reached with the JR San-in Line, which runs along the coast, or failing that, the local bus network. Always check when the buses are running, as some only run at weekends or during the summer.
- **Don't miss:** Tottori sand dunes; Adachi Museum of Art near Matsue; the shrine of Izumo Taisha; Iwami Ginzan Silver Mine; the old streets of Tsuwano; the pottery kilns and Uragami Museum in Hagi.

## TOTTORI★ 鳥取

Famous for its vast sand dunes, part of the San-in Coast National Park, this large port city at the mouth of the Sendai River is fairly unremarkable in itself, but its mountainous hinterland, especially Daisen-Oki National Park, is full of fine temples, pleasant *onsen*, and many opportunities for hiking.

### Tottori Folkcraft Museum
### 鳥取民芸美術館

*651 Sakae-machi. 5min walk NE of Tottori station. Open Thu–Tue 10am–5pm. ¥500.*

Lodged in a small, wooden merchant house from the Edo period, this museum is affiliated to the Mingei movement, which aims to promote traditional crafts. Its collection comprises nearly 5,000 objects illustrating the Japanese concept of *wabi-sabi* (finding beauty in simple, used, imperfect things), among them some lovely Japanese and Korean pottery, old furniture, kimonos, bamboo utensils, etc.

### Kannon-in Garden 観音院庭園

*162 Uemachi. 10min to the E of Tottori station by public minibus (¥100). Open 9am–5pm. ¥600, including a matcha tea tasting.*

Commissioned in the 17C by the feudal lord Ikeda Mitsunaka, this garden was designed by a pupil of the famous landscape gardener Kobori Enshu, and

Tottori sand dunes

© Tottori Prefecture / JNTO

modeled on the tea gardens of Kyoto. It includes a small, rock-strewn hill and a fine pond in the center of which are two small islands representing the turtle and the crane *(symbols of longevity)*. It also benefits from a superb "borrowed landscape" in the background, completely free of urban development.

### Jinpukaku Mansion 仁風閣

*2-121 Higashi-machi. 10min NE of Tottori station by public minibus (¥100). Open Tue–Sun 9am–5pm. ¥150.*
Located at the foot of Kyusho Hill, where Tottori Castle once stood, this immaculately white European-style residence was built in 1907. The first mansion in the town to have electricity and a telephone, it played host to Prince Yoshihito *(the future Emperor Taisho)* whenever he stayed in the region. The interior houses a few items of imported European furniture. At the rear, there is a pleasant Japanese garden and a large lawn.

### Tottori Sand Dunes★★ 鳥取砂丘

*3.1mi/5km N of the city. From Tottori station, bus every 20min to Sakyu Kaikan stop (30min, ¥360). Camel rides and cart rides are available throughout the year. From Apr to Nov, there are opportunities for sandsurfing, parascending, and hang gliding. Details on all these activities from the Sand Pal Tottori Information Center at the Sakyu Kitaguchi stop just before the dunes, 0857-20-2231.*
These yellow and brown sand dunes are unique in Japan and stretch along the coast for 9.9mi/16km, reaching a width of 1.2mi/2km in places. Some of the dunes reach a height of 295.3ft/90m. They were created tens of thousands of years ago by sediment carried out to sea by the Sendai River, then pushed back to shore by the marine currents. Their changing shapes, and the interplay of light and dark as they shift in the wind, recall the most beautiful Saharan landscapes *(see photo left)*. In winter, covered with a thin white blanket of snow, the effect is quite surreal. The dunes are home to a major center for research into agriculture in dry environments. Set back from the coast are vast plantations of shallots, the largest in Japan.
The best time to visit the dunes is early in the morning, when the amazing shapes created by the wind during the night are revealed. It is dangerous to swim near the dunes; a safer alternative is **Uradome Beach** *(3.1mi/5km to the east)*. Also from Uradome, you can take a boat trip *(Mar–Nov, 40min, ¥1,200)* along the jagged coastline with its magnificent caves and pine-covered islands. To the west of Tottori, 7.5mi/12km away, is **Hakuto Beach**, popular with surfers and windsurfers.

## EXCURSIONS

### Chizu 智頭

*18.6mi/30km S of Tottori. JR Inbi Line to Chizu station (30min, ¥2,010).*
Perched at an altitude of 984.3ft/300m, near the source of the Sendai River, this delightful little town *(population 10,000)* was a large forestry center during the Edo period. Five minutes' walk from the station is **Ishitani House** *(open Thu–Tue 10am–5pm; ¥500)*, an impressive 40-room residence that once belonged to a wealthy Chizu merchant. Lord Ikeda of Tottori would stop here whenever he made his biennial journey to Edo to pledge allegiance to the shogun.

## USEFUL INFORMATION

**TOURIST OFFICES**

**Tottori** – Information booth in the station. *Open 9.30am–6pm. ℘0857-22-3318.*

**Matsue** – Outside the JR station. *Open 9am–6pm. ℘0852-21-4034.*

**Hagi** – Office next to Higashi-Hagi station. *Open 9am–noon, 1–5pm. ℘0838-25-3145.* There is another office at Hagi station in the south.

## TRANSPORTATION

**TOTTORI**

**BY TRAIN** – **To and from Okayama**, Inbi Line Express *(5 per day, 1hr50min, ¥5,080).*

**To and from Matsue**, JR San-in Line *(6 per day, 1hr30min, ¥4,700).*

**MATSUE**

**BY TRAIN – To and from Okayama**, Limited Express Yakumo *(7 per day, 2hr40min, ¥6,070).* **To and from Tottori**, JR San-in Line *(6 per day, 1hr30min, ¥4,700).* **To and from Hagi**, JR San-in Line via Masuda *(4 per day, 3hr30min, ¥6,700).* **To and from Hiroshima**, Limited Express to Hamada *(1hr25min)*, then bus *(2hr).*

**HAGI**

**BY TRAIN** – **To and from Matsue**, JR San-in Line via Masuda *(4 per day, 3hr30min, ¥6,700).*

**To and from Hiroshima**, via Nagatoshi and Asa *(4 per day, 3hr30min, ¥7,430).*

**To and from Fukuoka (Hakata)**, via Nagatoshi and Asa *(4 per day, 4hr, ¥6,380).*

**BY BUS** – **Hagi Bus Center**, located downtown. Regular buses to Shin-Yamaguchi *(Hagi-go Bus, 1hr30min)* and Hiroshima *(4hr).*

The massive roof is supported by imposing cedarwood pillars, and there is a delightful garden at the rear. Another place worth a visit, also on the main street, is the **Suwai sake brewery**, dating from 1859, where you will be able to taste a wonderfully light and fragrant *daiginjo-shu* (sake made with polished rice milled to at least 50 percent).

### Mount Mitoku★ 三徳山

*25mi/40km W of Tottori. JR San-in Line to Kurayoshi station, then bus (every hour, 40min) to Mitoku-san. The last bus coming back leaves at 3pm (1hr30min round trip, ¥600). The difficult upper part of the trail is only for adults in good physical condition, and is impassable in rainy or snowy weather.*

The 2,949.5ft/899m-high Mount Mitoku *("Mountain of the Three Virtues")* is a former shrine of the Buddhist Tendai sect used during the Heian era (794–1185) as a school and retreat for monks. A series of stone staircases leads first to **Sanbutsu-ji**, the main temple, surrounded by 1,000-year-old cedars. The Treasure Hall is open to visitors (*open 8am–5pm; ¥400).* Behind it, a steep path takes you through the luxuriant vegetation to **Monjudo**, perched on a precipice from where there is a splendid **view** of the valley. The climb continues, with the help of creepers and chains for the very steep walls before you reach a rocky ridge and at last see **Nageiredo**★★, a 12C temple built into a rift in the cliff and designated a National Treasure. How this building was erected on such a vertiginous site remains a mystery.

**Misasa Onsen** 三朝温泉 – This town on the road between Kuroyashi and Mount Mitoku has been known for almost 1,000 years for its hot springs, believed to have rejuvenating powers because of their high radium content. There are a dozen ryokan dotted along the river, as well as a free public *rotenburo* (outdoor hot-spring pool).

### Mount Daisen★ 大山

*From Tottori, JR San-in Line to Yonago station (1hr, ¥3,480), then bus (every hour, 50min, ¥700) to Daisen-ji.*

Reaching a height of 5,672.6ft/1,729m, this massive extinct volcano rises directly from sea level. From a distance, it resembles Mount Fuji. In winter, its snowy slopes attract skiers and snowboarders, replaced by hikers when spring arrives. Getting to the top, from the temple of Daisen-ji, takes about five hours both ways. The whole region is part of **Daisen-Oki National Park**. The forest vegetation turns flame-red in the Fall.

**Daisen-ji Temple 大山寺** – *Open Apr–Nov: 9am–4pm. ¥300.*
From the bus stop in the village, in front of the Tourist Information Center, cross the river to reach the lovely cedar-lined avenue that leads to the temple. Founded in 718, it was an active center of the Tendai sect until the 16C, and at its height boasted nearly 3,000 monks. Unfortunately, most of the buildings were destroyed in successive fires, leaving only a small part of the original complex. To the left of the temple, a path leads to the **Ogamiyama Shrine**, an integral part of the temple before the separation of Buddhism and Shintoism in the Meiji era.

**Kaike Onsen 皆生温泉** – *3.1mi/5km N of Yonago station, access by shuttle bus (20 min – ¥280).* This hot-spring resort, full of big seaside hotels, is famous for its waters, rich in mineral salts and calcium, bubbling up directly from beneath the sand.

**Yonago Waterbird Sanctuary 米子水鳥公園** – *20min by bus from Yonago station. Open Apr–Oct: 9am–5.30pm; Nov–Mar:7am–5.30pm (Sat–Sun and holidays 8.30am). ¥300, children no charge.*
This lagoon attracts the largest concentration of migrating birds in Japan during the winter. More than 75,000 varieties winter here, including whistling swans from the Siberian tundra.

## MATSUE★★ 松江

Known as the "water city" because of its many canals, Matsue stands by the sea, where Nakaumi lagoon and Lake Shinji meet. A former feudal stronghold, capital of Izumo province *(now Shimane prefecture)*, this pleasant city is a mine of cultural and historical treasures, such as its castle, one of the best-preserved in the country. Matsue also prides itself on having been the adopted home of the writer **Lafcadio Hearn** (1850–1904), the author of many books on Japan, who became a Japanese national under the name Koizumi Yakumo *(see box opposite).*

*On presentation of a passport, foreign tourists get reductions of 30–50 percent on admission prices to museums and tourist attractions in the city and its surroundings. To get around, rent a bicycle at the station or use the Lakeline Bus (every 20min, ¥200 per journey or ¥500 per day), which does a circuit of the principal sights.*

### Matsue Castle★ 松江城

*1.2mi/2km N of Matsue station. Open Apr–Sept 8.30am–6.30pm; Oct–Mar 8.30am–5pm. ¥550.*
The dark silhouette of the keep of Matsue Castle rises in the center of a hill surrounded by moats. Built in 1611 by the *daimyo* Yoshiharu Horio, it is a fine example of military architecture—although it never came under attack—and one of the best-preserved in Japan. Six storys high *(98.4ft/30m)*, it has a wooden framework adorned with gables and roofs that turn up at the ends. Inside, documents, scale models, weapons, and armor trace the history of the city. When you get to the top, don't miss the 360-degree **view** over Matsue and its surroundings, Lake Shinji, and Mount Daisen.

### Horikawa Sightseeing Boat 堀川遊覧船

*Castle entrance. Open spring and fall 9am–5pm; winter 4pm; summer 6pm. Trip: 50min. ¥1,200, child ¥600.*
The castle moats, known as *Horikawa*, are linked to a network of canals that were once used for transporting goods. This pleasant tour in a flat-bottomed boat, steered by an often-talkative boatman, will take you beneath bridges and past banks fringed with cherry trees and willows. It's a good way to soak up the relaxed atmosphere of the city.

### Buke Yashiki 武家屋敷

*10min walk N of the castle.*
*Open 9am-4.30pm. ¥220.*
Situated midway along Shiominawate-dori, a beautiful street lined with Edo period houses, this samurai residence dating from 1730—the largest in Matsue—once belonged to the Shiomi, a medium-ranking military family in the service of the Matsudaira lords. The grand appearance of the front gate contrasts with the Spartan sobriety of the interior, which still contains furniture and domestic objects.

### Meimei-an 明々庵

*In a little street to the N of Buke Yashiki.*
*Open 9am–5pm (depending on season). €400.*
This superb tea house, with its curved thatched roof, was built in 1779 in the garden of the residence of one of his vassals by the feudal lord Matsudaira Fumai, the seventh of that name, a respected master of the Tea Ceremony. Restored and moved here in 1966, it regularly attracts experts in the art of tea. You can have *matcha* tea served *here (¥400)*, though without the ceremony.

### Lafcadio Hearn Memorial Museum and Old Residence

小泉八雲記念館・旧居

*Near Meimei-an, on Shiominawate-dori.*
*Museum: Open Apr–Sept 8.30am–6.10pm; Oct–Mar 8.30am–5pm. ¥300.*
*House: Open 9am–4.30pm. ¥350.*
*Closed Dec 16–29, Jan 1.*
Although the writer Lafcadio Hearn spent barely 15 months in Matsue, where he taught English in the city's high school, it was this city that sparked his love of Japan—he recorded his impressions of it in *Glimpses of Unfamiliar Japan.*
The museum has a large collection of his letters and manuscripts, as well as objects recalling his life in Japan. Next door is the house where he lived, unchanged since his departure, and with a pretty garden. The writer's great-grandson still lives in Matsue, where he teaches literature at the university.

### Japanophile Lafcadio Hearn

Born in 1850 to an Irish father and a Greek mother, the writer and journalist **Lafcadio Hearn** was a tireless globetrotter (London, New York, Canada, Martinique). But it was in Japan, where he arrived in 1890, that he found his spiritual home. In Matsue, he met and married a samurai's daughter, converted to Buddhism, and took Japanese citizenship under the name Koizumi Yakumo. Appointed Professor of English Literature at the University of Tokyo, he taught there until his death in 1904, and published several books on Japanese culture, myths, and folklore, becoming a true link between Japan and the West.

### Tanabe Art Museum 田部美術館

*Next to Lafcadio Hearn Memorial Museum. Open Tue–Sun 9am–5pm. ¥600.*
This museum devoted to the Tanabe clan displays objects amassed by the family over 25 generations. Most are related to the Tea Ceremony, especially ceramics, but the collection also includes calligraphy, paintings, prints, and other antiques.

### Shimane Prefectural Art Museum★ 島根県立美術館

*On the lake shore, 5min walk from Matsue station. Open Wed–Mon 10am–6.30pm. ¥300 (¥1,150 with temporary exhibition).*
This futuristic, light-filled building has a permanent collection of modern and contemporary Japanese and Western artworks, and also holds temporary exhibitions. There are works on the theme of water, sculptures on wood, photographs, and many prints, including Hokusai's famous *Views of Mount Fuji*, and Hiroshige's series on the Tokaido road. Visit toward evening, as this is an ideal place to see the romantic **sunset**★ over Lake Shinji.

Garden in Adachi Museum of Art

©Adachi Museum of Art/JNTO

## EXCURSIONS

### Matsue Vogel Park

松江フォーゲルパーク

*7.5mi/12km W of Matsue. Take the Ichibata tram line from Matsue Shinjiko Onsen station to Vogel Park station (15min). Open Apr–Sept 9am–6.30pm; Oct–Mar 9am–5pm. ¥1,500.*

Created in 2001 on the shores of Lake Shinji, midway between Matsue and Izumo, this theme park has four huge **tropical greenhouses** containing a richly colored abundance of irises, fuchsias, orchids, and begonias. The park also houses some 80 varieties of exotic bird. Children love feeding the toucans, watching demonstrations of falcons in flight, and seeing penguins from the Cape. Beside a duck pond is a small restaurant serving *soba* (buckwheat noodles).

### Adachi Museum of Art★★

足立美術館

*1.42mi/20km S of Matsue. JR San-in Line to Yasugi station (15min), from where a free shuttle bus serves the museum (15min). Open Apr–Sept 9am–5.30pm; Oct–Mar 9am–5pm. ¥2,200.*

In 1970, Adachi Zenko (1899–1990), a business tycoon who made his fortune in Osaka, built this museum to display his collection of modern Japanese art in his native region. He also set about creating, with a team of gardeners, a remarkable **Japanese garden**★★★, which the American magazine *Journal of Japanese Gardening* has rated *the most beautiful garden in Japan (ahead of the garden of the Katsura Imperial Villa in Kyoto)*. The garden covers an area of 40.8 acres/16.5ha and has four different sections: a dry landscape garden, a moss garden, a pond garden, and a white gravel and pine garden, with the wooded ridge of the mist-shrouded mountains in the background. Visitors are not admitted to the garden, but have to look at it through the windows of the museum, which nevertheless effectively frame the **views**. Works by various Japanese artists are on display, notably **Yokoyama Taikan** (1868–1958), and are changed with the season.

### Izumo Taisha Shrine★★

出雲大社

*21.7mi/35km W of Matsue. Ichibata tram line from Matsue Shinjiko Onsen station to Izumo-Taisha-mae station (1hr, ¥790). Open 6am–8pm. No charge.*

The great shrine of **Izumo Taisha**, also called Izumo Oyashiro, is the second most important Shinto shrine in Japan after Ise (*see p 242*). It is dedicated to the *kami* Okuninushi, god of the earth and the harmony of nature, agriculture, and medicine, who is said to bring happiness and harmony to human relationships, especially marriage, which is why the shrine attracts a lot of young women who wish to get married. To begin a prayer here, clap your hands not twice, as is usual, but four times to draw the deity's attention not only to you, but also to your loved one.

Izumo Taisha is said to be the oldest shrine in Japan and is known to have existed since at least the 7C. The area where it stands was once an island, separated from the coast by a sound that has since been filled in by alluvial deposits. Most of the existing buildings, however, date from 1874, and the main building from 1744 *(apparently its 25th reconstruction).*

The main shrine is surrounded by a rectangular double fence. It is accessed via an avenue of pines twisted by the wind, then through the **O-torii**, the largest shrine gate in Japan, adorned with a huge sacred rope of rice straw *(shimenawa)* 42.7ft/13m long and weighing 3 tons. The **Honden** *(main hall)*, some 78.7ft/24m high, stands on a raised platform. This is typical of the architectural style known as *taisha-zukuri,* the oldest style used for shrines, characterized by a roof of cypress bark with a double slope and curved canopies, and an imposing front staircase on piles. Its proportions are fairly modest in comparison with the previous building dating from the Heian period, which, with a height of 157.5ft/48m, was then the largest wooden building in Japan, ahead of Todai-ji in Nara.

### A divine gathering

Throughout Japan October is called "the month without gods" *(kanna-zuki)*, except in Izumo, where it is labeled "the month of the gods" *(kami-arizuki)*. According to legend, in October all the *kami* gather together at Izumo Taisha. Arriving by sea, they are greeted with much pomp and ceremony by the shrine's priests.

**Shimane Museum of Ancient Izumo** – *To the right of the shrine. Open 9am–6pm. Closed 3rd Tue of the month. ¥600.* Opened in 2007, this museum traces the history of the region of Izumo. Relics unearthed by archeological excavations *(bronze bells and swords, pottery, funerary objects)* are on display. A 1:10 scale model gives an idea of how the shrine looked 1,000 years ago, when it stood on high piles and was reached by a huge 358ft/109m-long staircase.

**Hinomisaki** – *6.2mi/10km along the coast road. There are regular buses (35min).* This magnificent cape to the northwest of Izumo, watched over by a **lighthouse** dating from the beginning of last century, attracts many walkers. Visitors can climb to the top of the lighthouse *(open 9am–4.30pm; ¥200)* to see the **view**. On the left, a trail runs along the coast, which leads, after 0.6mi/1km,

Izumo Taisha Shrine

© Tibor Bognár/age fotostock

to a small harbor, where the 400-year-old **Hinomisaki Shrine** lies hidden.

### Iwami Ginzan Silver Mine★
石見銀山

*48mi/77km W of Matsue. JR San-in Line to Oda-shi station (1hr, ¥1,100). From there, there are regular buses to the village of Omori (30min, ¥560), at the entrance to the site. Open Mar–Oct 9am–5pm; Nov–Feb 9am–4pm. ¥400.*

A UNESCO World Heritage Site since 2007, the former Iwami Ginzan Silver Mine was at its production peak in the 16C and 17C.

It is estimated that at that time 38 tons of pure silver were being extracted each year—one-third of all the silver produced in the world. Much of the ore was transported to the coast to be turned into small oval bars, which were used as currency in trade, first with Korea and China, then with Europe.

The mining region of Iwami Ginzan played a major role in the economic expansion of Japan—several hundred shafts were sunk here—with mining villages, a network of roads, and commercial ports. The whole area was under the direct control of the Edo shogunate.

Today, it is possible to visit the **Ryugenji Mabu★** deposit, situated at an altitude of 1,968.5ft/600m, where you can explore a 512ft/156m-long underground gallery shored up by wooden planks. The working conditions in the dark, damp tunnels were harsh and the life expectancy of the miners barely exceeded 30. The site is 35 minutes' walk from the pretty village of **Omori**, where you can visit a small **mining museum** *(open 9am–5pm; ¥500)*. The nearby 18C stone temple **Rakan-ji** *(open 9am–5pm; ¥500)* contains statues of the 500 *rakan* (disciples of the Buddha), who watch over the souls of dead miners.

**Yunotsu Onsen** – *6.2mi/10km from Iwami Ginzan along a descending trail (3hr hike).*

Nestling in a deep valley, this little port, which once used to export the silver ore, is linked to the mining area by a flagstoned path that winds through the woods. Its old-fashioned atmosphere, hot baths, ryokan, and tranquil cafes are all good reasons to stop here.

*From Yunotsu, take the JR San-in Line to either Matsue or Hagi.*

## HAGI★ 萩

*Map p 372.*

A former feudal town hemmed in between the hills and the sea, Hagi has preserved its old samurai quarter intact. The modern world seems to have bypassed this sleepy little town with an Edo-period atmosphere. In spring, the scent of orange flowers rises from the orchards.

The town is also famous for its kilns, making *hagi-yaki* ceramics, with their milky, pink-beige coloring. It played a vital role in the revolutionary movement of the Meiji era, which, in 1867, brought down the shogunate, restored the Emperor, and opened the country to the West.

*Don't get off at JR Hagi station but at Higashi-Hagi farther east, which is the more central of the two. On the way out of the station, there are several bicycle rental shops—bikes are a practical way to visit Hagi. Alternatively, buses (every 30min, ¥100) do a circuit of the town.*

### Teramachi, Jokamachi, and Horiuchi Districts★
寺町・萩城城下町・堀内

The town center of Hagi lies to the west of Higashi-Hagi station, on the island formed by the delta of the Abu-gawa and farther west still is the site of the former Hagi Castle. It is reached through the **Teramachi district**, famous for its many small temples. To the north is **Kikugahama Beach**, with its exceptionally clear waters.

**Shizuki-koen** – *Open 8am–6.30pm (winter 4.30pm). ¥210.*

This park lies on the former site of Hagi Castle, of which only the outer walls and inner moats remain today. Built by the Mori clan *(the local lords)* in 1604, it was demolished in 1873 during the Meiji

Restoration. From the castle ruins, a 20-minute walk will take you to the top of Shizuki Hill *(469ft/143m)*.

**Horiuchi** – The district at the foot of the castle was where high-ranking samurai, such as the Kuchiba, the Suu, the Masuda, and the Fukuhara, had their residences. Protected by long, rough walls of whitewashed cob, the houses of the aristocrats still retain their Edo period wooden entrances.

The **Hagi Museum**, built in 2004 in the style of the neighboring old buildings *(open 9am–5pm; ¥500)*, traces the history of the city.

**Jokamachi** – Farther east is this quarter that housed samurai of lower rank and wealthy merchants. The best preserved residences are on two streets that run parallel: Edoya and Kikuya.

Among these is **Kikuya House** *(open 9am–5pm; ¥700)*, built by a powerful merchant family in 1604, which has a lovely garden. Around it are arranged the living quarters, the kitchens, and the storehouses, where period objects and utensils are on display.

The nearby **Ishii Tea Bowl Museum** *(open Thu–Tue 9am–noon, 1–4.45pm; ¥500)* has a collection of *chawan* (tea bowls) produced in Hagi.

Farther north, the **Kumaya Museum of Art** *(open Tue–Sun 9am–5pm; ¥700)* displays objects that once belonged to the wealthy Kumaya family, including a large number of ink paintings and objects relating to the Tea Ceremony.

## Hagi Uragami Museum★★

山口県立萩美術館浦上記念館

*S of Jokamachi, on the other side of the canal. Open Tue–Sun 9am–5pm. ¥300 without temporary exhibition.*

In a spacious modern building dating from 1996, designed by the architect Tange Kenzo, this museum has an excellent collection of nearly 5,000 *ukiyo-e ("images of the floating world" prints from the Edo period)*, among them Hokusai's famous *Thirty-six Views of Mount Fuji*, including *The Great Wave off Kanagawa*and portraits of Kabuki actors by Sharaku, and courtesans by Utamaro. The museum also houses a large collection of Korean and Chinese ceramics and porcelain. The first floor is used for temporary exhibitions.

## Around Shoin-jinja 松陰神社

*10min walk S of Higashi-Hagi station. Open 8.30am–5pm. No charge.*

This shrine is dedicated to the memory of **Shoin Yoshida** (1830–59), one of the leaders of the Meiji Restoration. A poor samurai, he led a brief, tragic life, and was beheaded at the age of 29 for rebelling against the authority of the shogun. While under house arrest toward the end of his life, he founded a private school, **Shoka-sonjuku**. The shrine preserves this just as it was: a small building open to the elements, with modest tatami rooms and paper windows, where the master preached the spirit of resistance and the idea of nationhood to his pupils.

### The Miwa, a great dynasty of potters

The potteries of Hagi owe their reputation to the quality of their *chawan*, the bowls used in the Tea Ceremony. According to the saying, "*Ichi* Raku, *ni* Hagi, *san* Karatsu," the *raku*-style is the ideal pottery to use for the Tea Ceremony, followed by the pottery from Hagi, and finally that from Karatsu. What makes Hagi ceramics special is their porous glaze, which allows the tannin from the tea to seep through its cracked surface, so that the pastel tones—pink or ivory—of the stoneware take on a slightly beige hue as the bowls age. The process was introduced by the Koreans around 1600. Today, Hagi has many kilns and pottery workshops, some of them open to visitors. Born in 1910, **Miwa Jusetsu** is the eleventh generation of a family of potters and one of the most famous in Hagi. Designated a Living National Treasure, he has worked hard to revive the art of ceramics. His tea bowls fetch several million yen. His son, **Miwa Kazuhiko**, has taken a more avant-garde approach, veering away from the utilitarian context.

Several future prime ministers of the Meiji era and founders of modern Japan, including Prince Ito Hirobumi, father of the Constitution, were oncepupils at the school.

**Toko-ji** – *Open 8.30am–5pm. ¥300.* Five minutes' walk along the river to the east of the shrine, at the foot of a wooded hill, is this late-17C temple, in the style of a Chinese pagoda, dedicated to the lords of the Mori clan. Behind it, an avenue lined with 500 stone lanterns leads to a mausoleum housing five of the family's tombs.

## EXCURSION

### Tsuwano★ 津和野

*40.4mi/65km NE of Hagi. Direct bus (Bocho Bus, 1hr45min, ¥2,130) or train via Masuda (2hr35min, ¥1,620). Tourist Information Center on the way out of the station (open 9am–5pm).*

A former fortress town huddling deep in a valley, the charming Tsuwano (population 8,800) can still claim its atmospheric old streets, lined with well-preserved samurai houses and picturesque sake breweries. A canal full of colorful carp and fringed with irises runs alongside the main thoroughfare, Tonomachi-dori.

**Catholic Church** – *Main street. 7min walk from the station. Open 7.30am–5.30pm. No charge.* A Catholic church with tatami floors; remove your shoes. Built in 1931 in tribute to Jesuit missionary St Francis Xavier and the 36 Japanese Christians martyred here for refusing to renounce their faith in 1868.

**Taikodani Inari Shrine** – *10min walk farther S. Open 9am–4pm. No charge.* Perched on the side of a hill, this shrine is one of the sacred sites of Inari, the Shinto deity of harvests and trade, whose messenger is a fox (*kitsune*). It was built in 1773 and modeled on the Fushimi-Inari in Kyoto. Access to the shrine is through a long tunnel of 1,045 vermilion *torii* (gates).

**Tsuwano Castle** – A chairlift *(15min, ¥450)* leads to the top of the hill, and the remains of this 1325 building. From here, there is a magnificent **view★** of the valley.

A **steam train**, the *SL Yamaguchi-go (Golden Week & Jul–Aug daily, Mar–Nov weekends only; 2hr; ¥1,620)*, does a daily round trip between Shin-Yamaguchi and Tsuwano. From Shin-Yamaguchi, you can connect to the Shinkansen Line for Hiroshima on the San-yo coast *(see p383)* or Fukuoka *(see p 472)* on the island of Kyushu *(about 40min)*.

## ADDRESSES

### STAY

**TOTTORI**

**Shiitake Kaikan Taisuikaku**
**しいたけ会館・対翠閣** *1-84 Tomiyasu. 0857-24-8471. www.taisuikaku.com. 24 rooms – from ¥11,700/person half-board.* Simple, excellent ryokan, 5min walk S of the station; 4 Western rooms with bathroom, and a lovely communal *o-furo* for the Japanese rooms.

**Hotel New Otani**
**ホテルニューオータニ鳥取**
*2-153 Ima-machi. 0857-23-1111. www.newotani.co.jp. 136 rooms – from ¥20,790.* A comfortable, well-maintained, Western-style business hotel opposite the station. *Reduced prices for tourists.*

**Kansui-tei Kozeniya**
**観水庭こぜにや** *651 Eiraku onsen-cho. 0857-23-3311. www.kozeniya.com. 25 rooms – from ¥12,750, breakfast included.* Elegant modern ryokan, 10min walk NE of the station; Japanese and Western rooms, with and without bathroom, around ornamental pond. Indoor and outdoor *onsen*.

**AROUND TOTTORI: MISASA ONSEN**

**Izanro Iwasaki 依山楼岩崎**
*By the river. 0858-43-0111. www.izanro.co.jp. 77 traditional and Western rooms - from ¥18,000/person for 2-person room, breakfast and dinner included.* Behind large building is a ryokan magnificently situated amid gardens and waterfalls. *12 different baths, all wonderful.*

**MATSUE**

**Tokyu Inn 松江東急イン**
*590 Asahimachi. 0852-27-0109. www.tokyuhotels.co.jp. 181 rooms – from ¥15,300. ¥1200.* A basic, practical *business hotel* opposite the station.

**Ohashikan 大橋館**
*40 Suetsugu Honmachi. 0852-21-5168. www.ohashikan.jp. – 21 rooms – from ¥13,000, breakfast and dinner included.* This ryokan, run by an American, is near the main bridge. Spacious rooms and a pleasant onsen. Good local cuisine.

**Naniwa Issui なにわ一水**
*63 Chidori-cho. 0852-21-4132. www.naniwa-i.com. 26 rooms – ¥20,100/ person.* Elegant ryokan in the Shinjiko Onsen district, in east Matsue, enjoys a romantic **view** of the lake. Well-equipped rooms, some with Western-style beds. *A magnificent onsen.*

### AROUND MATSUE: IWAMI GINZAN

**Nogawaya Ryokan**
旅館のがわや *30 Yunotsu-cho, Yunotsu. 0855-65-2811. www.nogawaya.com. 10 rooms – from ¥21,500, breakfast and dinner included.* An authentic, friendly ryokan with an onsen.

### HAGI

**Senshunraku**
萩焼の宿千春楽 *467-2 Kikugahama Horiuchi. 0838-22-0326. http:// senshunraku.jp. 12 rooms – from ¥15,000/ person, breakfast and dinner included.* This ryokan in the center of town, facing Kikugahama Beach, has a pleasant garden and a number of baths, some covered, some open-air. Japanese and Western rooms. *Good seafood cuisine.*

**Hagi Honjin 萩本陣**
*385-8 Tsubaki Higashi. 0838-22-5252. www.hagihonjin.co.jp. 108 rooms – from ¥15,000, breakfast and dinner included.* Situated E of Higashi-Hagi station, this large ryokan is one of the finest in the city and has huge, luxurious rooms, both Japanese and Western. A superb onsen and, best of all, a ***rotenburo*** on the top of a hill, reached by a private monorail.

## EAT

### TOTTORI

**Daizen Izakaya**
**居酒屋鳥取大善**
*715 Sakae-machi, at the entrance to the shopping mall, on the N side of the station. 0857-27-6574. Open 11am–midnight.* The owner speaks English. The menu includes sushi, ***katsudon*** (bowl of rice with pork), assorted tempura, and ***yakiniku*** (grilled meat). *Good choice of local sakes.*

**Takumi Kappo たくみ割烹店**
*652 Sakae-machi. 0857-26-6355. Open 11am–2pm; 5pm–10pm. Closed 3rd Mon of the month.* Lovely wood-paneled room in Tottori Folkcraft Museum. Try the beef ***shabu-shabu***, crab sushi, and other local specialties. *Menu in English.*

### AROUND TOTTORI: CHIZU

**Mitaki-en みたき園**
*1.2mi/2km from the village. 0858-75-3311. Closed Dec–Mar. Lunch by reservation only.* In a mountain forest near a waterfall; the roof is in cedar bark, tatami room heated by ***irori*** (sunken hearth). The ***sansai-ryori*** is wonderful food. *Menus from ¥2,500.*

### MATSUE

**Yakumo-an 八雲庵**
*308 Kitabori-cho. 0852-22-2400. Open 10am–3.30pm.* This lovely restaurant, housed in an 18C former samurai residence on Shiominatawe-dori, near Buke Yashiki, has a tranquil garden with a carp pond. The ***soba*** and ***udon*** noodles are made on the premises.

**Minami 庭園茶寮みな美**
*14 Suetsugu Honmachi. 0852-21-5131. Open 11.30am–3pm; 5.30pm–8pm.* This elegant restaurant in a lakeside ryokan near Matsue Oashi Bridge serves sea bass in parcels ***(suzuki-yaki)*** and steamed rice with bream ***(tai-meshi)***. You can also book a private tatami room for a more elaborate ***kaiseki*** meal. *Menu from ¥1,680.*

### AROUND MATSUE: IWAMI GINZAN

**Shinyu Cafe 震湯カフェ内蔵丞**
*On the main street of Yunotsu. 0855-65-4126. Open Fri–Wed 11am–5pm.* An ideal place for a coffee or a light meal, in an old wooden house full of character. The owner speaks English and arranges guided tours.

### HAGI

**Ajiro 懐石料理あじろ**
*68 Minami-katakawatyu. 0838-22-0010. Open 11am–2pm; 5pm-10pm.* The seasonal ingredients are always fresh, the sashimi and tempura delicious, and the presentation very elegant, with Hagi ceramics. *Lunch formulas from ¥2,100; dinners from ¥2,320.*

**Nakamura なかむられすとらん**
*394 Hijiwara. 0838-22-6619. Open 11am–2pm; 5pm–8pm.* This restaurant is in the center of Teramachi. Although slightly old-fashioned, it is popular for its seafood specialties, especially sea urchins ***(uni)*** and fresh sashimi. *From ¥1,575.*

# NORTHERN HONSHU (TOHOKU)

**Tohoku, the northeastern part of Honshu, is the largest region in Japan after the island of Hokkaido, one of the original homelands of the Ainu. The Japanese regarded the chilly periphery of their archipelago as a hostile, backward region, to be entered reluctantly and with caution.**
**The marginalized Tohoku was so remote from the centers of power *(Nara, Kyoto, Edo)*, which had been refined over 1,000 years by the culture of court etiquette that it became the refuge of social misfits and the disinherited, *eta* (outcasts), and *yamabushi* (nomadic hermits). Basho, author of *Oku-no-Hosomichi* (The Narrow Road to the Deep North), visited the area and recollected: "Dozing on my pillow—Reveries—The moon in the distance—The smoke of tea."**

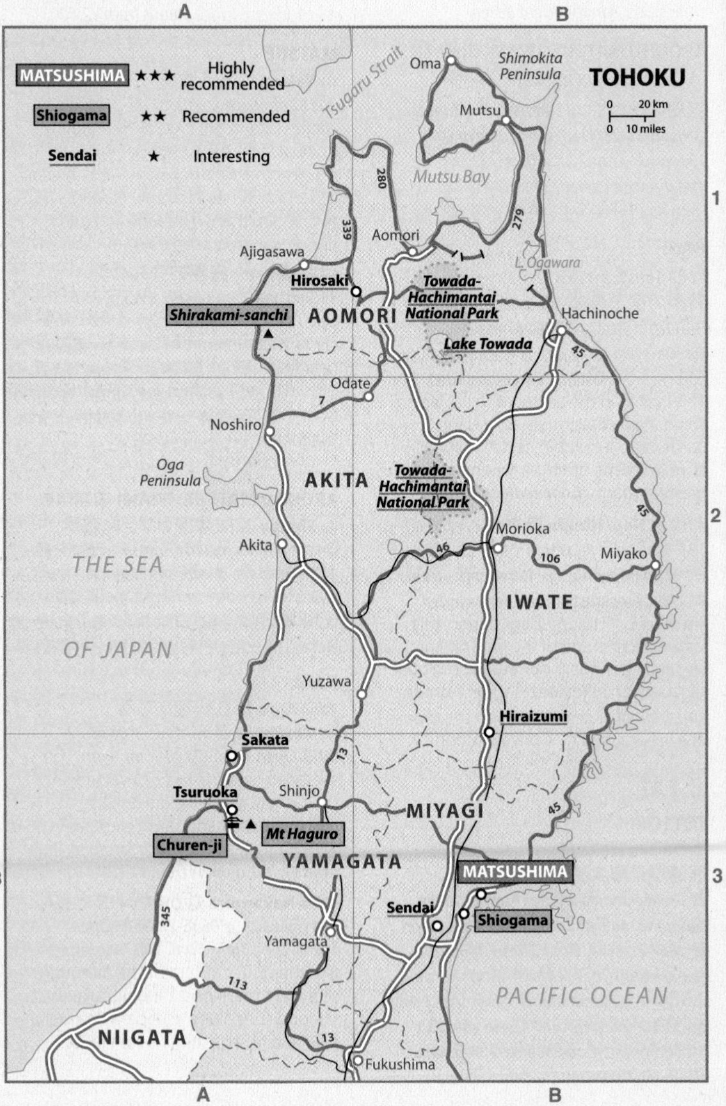

- **Population:** 10 million.
- **Michelin Map:** Principal Sights Map B–C2.
- **Location:** Tohoku is 25,869sq mi/67,000sq km in 6 prefectures: **Fukushima** *(5,322sq mi/13,783sq km, pop. 2 mil)*; **Miyagi** *(2,649sq mi/6,861sq km, pop. 2.4 mil)*; **Yamagata** *(3,601sq mi/9,326sq km, pop 1.2 mil)*; **Iwate** *(5,899sq mi/15,278sq km, pop. 1.4 mil)*; **Akita** *(4,483sq mi/11,612sq km, pop. 1.2 mil)*, and **Aomori** *(3,713sq mi/9,617sq km, pop. 1.5 mil)*.
- **Kids:** Sendai City Museum: Date Masamune's armor; Shiogama fish market; a boat trip around Matsushima Bay; Tsuruoka: Churen-ji temple; **Anzu**; a stroll in the Shirakami-sanchi forest.
- **Timing:** 1 day, Sendai; 1 day, Matsushima; half day, Shiogama; 3 days, Tsuruoka; 3–4 days for Hirosaki area.
- **Don't miss:** Mt Haguro; Oirase Gorge, Lake Towada; Shirakami-sanchi mountains. **Festivals**: Apr cherry-blossoms *(Hirosaki)*; Neputa Matsuri *(Hirosaki)*, Aug 1–7; Tanabata Matsuri *(Sendai)*, Aug 6–8.

### Highlights

1. Sailing amid stunning scenery of **Matsushima Bay** (p408)
2. **Historic Zuigan-ji**, founded more than 10,000 years ago, (p408-409)
3. The opulent golden hall of **Konjiki-do** at Chuson-ji (p409)
4. "Living Buddha" mummified monk of **Churen-ji** (p413-415)
5. Rich and unique biodiversity in the forests of **Shirakami-sanchi** (p421)

### In touch with today

Three centuries ago the region's severe climate and austere landscape appealed to this monk-poet. Since then, the bay of Matsushima has been singled out as one of Japan's three most scenic **views**, Tohoku is no longer isolated, while Sendai is a dynamic university city. The Shirakami mountain range is on the UNESCO World Heritage Site list and the Shinkansen connects Tokyo-Sendai in under two hours.

Today Tohoku offers visitors some of the most spectacular scenery to be found in Japan. The western coast's Snow Country (*Yukiguni*) has some of the world's most impressive snowfall figures (compared with the much more temperate east coast); travelers may enjoy great skiingwith a relaxing trip to a hot spring to warm up!

### Tsunami and Earthquake of March 11 2011

On March 11 2011 the eastern coast of Tohoku was hit by a 9.0 magnitude earthquake causing fires, landslides, a tsunami, and flooding, plus extensive building and infrastructure damage, including at the Fukushima Daiichi nuclear facility. Much of the area is beginning to recover and relief and reconstruction efforts are underway in the coastal areas. Trains are operating under temporary timetables, while buses have resumed their usual schedules. At the time of writing, many sights and businesses have reopened, and most of these have resumed their usual operating hours; nevertheless, please confirm opening hours before you travel to avoid disappointment and check with local Tourist Offices as to events and festivals. Regularly updated information is availble at www.jnto.go.jp/eng.

# Sendai★ and surroundings★★★ 仙台

**Like many provincial cities, Sendai owed its influence to a strong overlord. While the all-powerful Tokugawa shogunate united the country by eliminating their rivals, the *daimyo*, General Date Masamune (1566–1636), managed to impose his authority over the Miyagi region, later extending it throughout Tohoku and building a castle at Sendai, from which to rule his territories. Sendai has prospered ever since; although totally destroyed during WW II, it was rebuilt and its technical universities now attract outstanding students. Town planning has made the "city of universities and schools" as equally well known as "Mori no Miyako,"—"the city of trees"—in particular for its zelkovas *(elms imported from the Caucasus)*. It is the ideal starting point for a trip around Matsushima Bay.**

- **Population:** 1,040,164.
- **Michelin Map:** Principal Sights Map B2.
- **Location:** Sendai is 231.8mi/373km north of Tokyo. It is the regional capital of the prefecture of Miyagi (population 2.4 million), bounded by the Pacific Ocean to the east, Fukushima Prefecture to the south, that of Yamagata to the west, Akita to the northwest, and Iwate to the north.
- **Kids:** Take a **boat** from Shiogama to reach Matsushima.
- **Timing:** Allow a half-day for Sendai and Shiogama, and a full day for Matsushima.
- **Don't miss:** Matsushima Bay; the auction at Shiogama fish market; an evening at Robata in Sendai; a trip to the Entsu-in temple *(Matsushima)*.

## SIGHTS

The city developed alongside the Hirose River, overlooked by Sendai Castle, before extending east of this natural frontier. The eastern districts are divided by main arteries, the largest being Aoba-dori and **Jozenji-dori**★ *B1*, famous for its September Jazz Festival *(2nd weekend)*, December lights and **Mediatheque**★ *(open Tue–Sun 9am–10pm) B1*, whose innovative architecture by Ito Toyo is daringly built around a still tubular lattice structure that glows artificially from within. The western districts, by contrast, are home to parks, museums, and universities.

## WEST OF THE CITY CENTER

### Zuiho-den★★ 瑞鳳殿 *Map B2.*

*Zuihoden iriguchi. 15min from JR Sendai station by Loople Bus. Open 9am–4.30pm. ¥450.*

This mausoleum was built for Date Masamune in the year after his death *(see box p407)*. It was inspired by Nikko's famous Tosho-gu shrine, built between 1634 and 1636, which became the model for all *daimyo* in search of postmortem splendor *(see p202)*. Destroyed during the 1945 bombings, it was rebuilt almost identically during the 1970s, with concrete replacing the original wood. A short distance from the temple a path leads to tombs of Date's descendants and followers.

### Sendai City Museum★★

仙台市博物館 *Map A2.*

*26 Kawauchi. 10min by Loople Bus from the mausoleum (Museum/International Cente bus stop). Open Tue–Sun 9am–4.45pm. ¥400. English audio-guide (no charge).*

This impressive historical museum was opened in 1961, thanks to the gift of some 10,000 objects from the heirs of Sendai's founder, Date Masamune. Among the

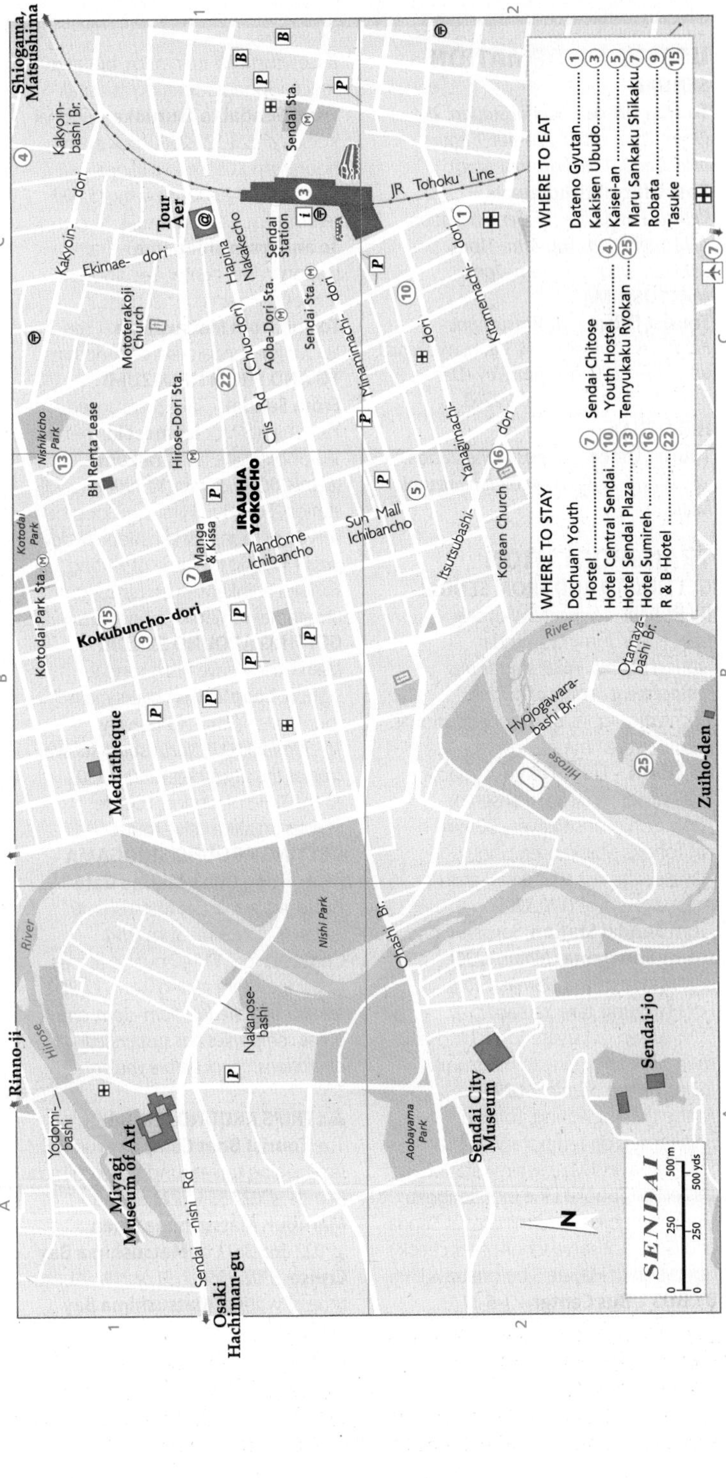


© 2009 Cartographic data Shobunsha/Michelin

## USEFUL INFORMATION

**SENDAI**

**Tourist Office** – *Sendai Station, 2F, (9am–7pm; ✆022-224-4069; hours after Dec 2011 to be announced).*

**Post Office/Withdrawals** – *Central Post Office, 1 F, Sendai Station. ATM open Mon–Thu 7am–11pm, Sat 9am–9pm, Sun 9am–7pm.*

**MATSUSHIMA**

**Tourist Office** – *JR Matsushima--Kaiganeki, daily 9am–4.30pm, weekends and Jan–Oct 9am–5pm, Nov–Dec 8.30am–5pm. ✆022-354-2263.*

**HIRAIZUMI**

**Tourist Office** – *Opposite the station. ✆0191-46-2110. www.town.hiraizumi.iwate.jp.*

## TRANSPORTATION

**GETTING TO AND FROM SENDAI**

**BY PLANE** – Airport SW of city, train every 30min to Sendai Station *(25min, ¥630; shuttle bus replacement at time of writing).* Domestic flights, but no international flights at the time of writing.

**BY TRAIN** – From **Tokyo**, Yamabiko Shinkansen, Max Shinkansen or Hayate Shinkansen every 30min (JR Tohoku Shinkansen Line). Hayate is fastest *(1hr40min)* and most expensive *(¥10,390).*.

From **Sendai Station**, Senseki Line serves **Shiogama** *(16min, ¥230)* and **Matsushima** *(25min, ¥400).*

For Hiraizumi, take Yamabiko 47 Shinkansen or Hayate 5 to Ichinoseki, then JR Tohoku Line to Hiraizumi *(62mi/100km, 50min, ¥4,390).*

At the time of writing, Tohoku Shinkansen on temporary timetable; Shiogama and Matsushima stations served by Tohoku Line (not Sengoku Line); Yamabiko 47 terminates at Sendai and does not serve Ichonoseki; check operation of Hayate 5 before traveling.

**BY BUS** – **Bus Center** – *1-6-31 Aobachuo. ✆022-261-533.* Long-distance bus for Aomori, Tokyo *(6hr, ¥6,200)*, Nagoya, etc. Buses cost half train price, but take much longer. Operating as usual.

**From Sendai to Tsuruoka** – Shonai Kotsu *(✆023-522-2600)* bus every hour from 7.05am to 8.55pm *(2hr30min, ¥ 2,900 one-way, ¥5,400 return)*; operating as usual.

**To and from Shiogama** – Train station in city center. See above for Sendai train connections.

**To and from Matsushima** – See above for Sendai train connections.

**TO AND FROM HIRAIZUMI**

**From Sendai** – Take Shinkansen Yamabiko 57 for **Ichinoseki**, then JR Tohoku Line for **Hiraizumi** *(62mi/100km, 55min, ¥4,190).* From JR station, Run-Run Hiraizumi loop bus serves all tourist destinations *(1-day pass ¥300).* At the time of writing, Tohoku Shinkansen on temporary timetable; Yamabiko 57 not in service.

**GETTING AROUND SENDAI** – Main buses leave from Sendai station. **Loople Bus** covers main tourist sites *(9am–4pm, every 15–30min, ¥600). North-south subway crosses the city (ticket ¥200–¥350).* At the time of writing, Loople Sendai on alternative route.

**GETTING AROUND SHIOGAMA** – From **Shiogama's Marine Gate Building**, ferries for Matsushima every 30min 9am–5pm *(1hr).* Cheapest fare ¥1,140 but no access to bridge. Sightseeing boat *(¥2,200; temporary schedule 9am–3pm; one of the companies has suspended operations: check before you go).*

**TRIPS AROUND THE BAY** – The **Tourist Boat Company** runs a sightseeing trip around Matsushima's islands *✆022-354-2233. See also* **Marubun Matsushima Kisen** *✆022-365-3611*, or **Matsushima Bay Cruise** *✆022-354-2191 or 2192.* At the time of writing, **Matsushima Bay Cruise** intends to resume service by early Aug 2011; the other two companies are operating as usual, with some itineraries suspended.

unique exhibits is Date Masamune's famous armor, including the helmet thought to have served as a model for the costume of the darkest character in *Star Wars*, Darth Vader, along with souvenirs of the journeys to Christian lands made by Hasekura Tsunenaga (1571–1622), *daimyo* of Sendai. As well as opening up new trading routes, he sought to meet Pope Paul V in Rome at the very time when the shogunate was banishing Christianity from Japan.

### Sendai Castle 仙台城跡 *Map A2.*

*Tensyudai Aoba-ku. Museum: open 9am–5pm. ¥700. Computer-generated film with English-language headsets.*
Date's castle was destroyed by bombing in 1945 and nothing remains except a stone turret and a few remnants dispersed around the terrace that so splendidly overhangs the city. Built on the heights of Mount Aoba, the site remains a strategic point overlooking the gorge and river. Interesting, small museum.

### Miyagi Museum of Art

宮城県美術館 *Map A1.*
*34-1 Kawauchi-Motohasekura. 15min walk from the castle. Open Tue–Sun 9.30am–5pm. ¥800 general admission, ¥300 permanent exhibition.*
Opened in 1981, the museum's core collection features Japanese art from the Meiji era to modern times. In addition to work by Japanese artists such as Sato Churyo, **Takahashi Yuichi**, and Matsumoto Shunsuke, it also displays some work by major overseas artists such as Kandinsky, **Klee**, and sculptor Barry Flanagan.

### Daruma at Matsushima

This rather tubby papier mâché figure is Daruma, better known as Bodhidharma, founder of Zen. Before he founded the Buddhist school, he meditated for a long time, nine years. Nine also being the number of months of a pregnancy, which explains why he is red, the color of placenta. Unlike a newborn child, however, Daruma woke to find his legs and arms had shriveled away—matter had become pure spirit. Daruma is popular in Matsushima because he lived in the temple of Zuigan-ji. Traditionally, Daruma dolls are sold with the eyes left unpainted, the better to "define" your wishes. The left eye is painted in when making a wish, the right one when it has been fulfilled.

## NORTH OF THE CITY CENTER

### Rinno-ji★ 輪王寺

*Map A1, off map.*
*Mount Kitayama. 15min from JR Sendai station by bus nos. 13, 14, 24. Open 8am–5pm. Temple no charge, garden ¥300.*
As a simple castle was not enough to defend Sendai, Date had temples and shrines built to protect the city from evil spirits. Erected in the north of the city, the Buddhist temple of Rinno-ji was intended to guard what was considered by the Japanese to be the most inauspicious compass point. The **garden**★ is the highlight of the visit.

### Date Masamune

One of Japan's most eccentric warlords, he was nicknamed "the one-eyed dragon" on account of the eye he lost through a childhood illness.
He compensated for an unattractive physique, however, by the elegance of his armor. Date, which means "Dandy," epitomizes the style of the Japanese feudal overlords, all-powerful and with great presence and charisma.
He fought alongside Toyotomi Hideyoshi and then Tokugawa Ieyasu, before retiring finally to the Tohoku region.

### Osaki Hachiman-gu★★

大崎八幡宮 *A1 off map.*
*Hachimangu-mae. 15min from JR Sendai station by bus nos. 10 or 15. Open 8am–5pm. No charge.*
Construction of this shrine was ordered by Date Masamune, who wanted to establish the guardian deities of his castle here. Built in 1607 on the top of a hill, it is a fine example of the architecture of the Momoyama era (1573–1603). Its flamboyant **porch** and also the **coffered ceiling**★★ decorated with 55 brightly colored hand-painted flowers relieve the handsome austerity of gold and black lacquer. Every year throughout January 14, during the **Dontosai Matsuri,** a long procession of scantily clad men files past on the way to burn their New Year decorations in front of the Hachiman shrine.

## EXCURSIONS

### SHIOGAMA★★ 塩竈

Located around 18.6mi/30km northeast of Sendai, Shiogama is best known for its large tunafish market, which supplies Tokyo's best restaurants. The town is also the ideal starting point for reaching Matsushima by boat.

### Fish market★★ 塩釜魚市場

*Higashi-Shiogama. Allow 10min from Shiogama by taxi (about ¥1,000). Tuna auction 5min from the market.*
This lively market, which employs nearly 400 people, has four sections *(deep-sea fish, small fish, salted fish, and other seafood products such as dried seaweed)*. There is a small restaurant where you can sample most of the produce sold on the stands. Miyagi specialties include *hoya* (sea anemones, increasingly studied in the fight against Alzheimer's), *shako-ebi* (texture and taste of shrimp), the famous Matsushima *kaki* (oysters), and tuna, sold at the special tuna market where auctions take place daily between 7am and 8am.

### Shiogama-jinja★★ 塩釜神社

*Ichimori-yama, on the city's highest point. Open 9am–6pm. www.shiogamajinja.jp.*
Rebuilt in the 17C, this shrine with asymmetric roofs in the *Nagare-zukuri* style is actually made up of three buildings *(Ugu, Sagu, Betsugu)*, each dedicated to one of the three local deities responsible for Tohoku's well-being. Of these, **Shiotsuchi-Oji no kami**, housed in the Betsugu, is by far the most important. As protector of fishermen and all who live by the sea, she taught the locals how to extract salt from seawater, a technique integral to the process of preserving food in brine, which became widespread in Japan. She also protects pregnant women, which raises the question of a link between salt and pregnancy—*shio* means salt, but it also signifies the tide. There is also a Japanese saying that births occur during an incoming tide when the moon is high in the heavens, its roundness perhaps evoking the fullness of pregnancy.
There is a small **museum** with various exhibits linked to salt production and inshore fishing methods.

### MATSUSHIMA★★★ 松島

Located 25mi/40km northeast of Sendai, Matsushima Bay, the "island of pines", contains more than 260 islands. "Ah Matsushima ah! A-ah Matsushima ah! Matsushima ah!" as the poet Basho summed it up in a celebrated *haiku* that will undoubtedly be quoted to you.

### Zuigan-ji★★★ 瑞巌寺

*91 Matsushima Aza-Chonai. Open 8am–4.30pm (Mar and Oct, 8am–4.30pm; Jan and Dec, 8am–3.30pm; Apr–Sep, 8am–5pm). ¥700.*
This cultural complex was constructed in the Heian era (828) and belonged to the Tendai Buddhist sect before being transformed into one of the many Zen temples that sprang up in the Kamakura era (*see p 68*). It fell into obscurity in the 15C, but owed its renaissance to Date Masamune. In 1604, the powerful *daimyo* needed an aristocratic residence not far from Sendai. Like Nijo Castle *(Kyoto)*, completed by Tokugawa Ieyasu at the beginning of the 17C (*see p 298*), although it was remodeled elegantly, it was not left defenseless.

Kano School gilding and painting decorate the *fusuma* (sliding panels), while the corridors are laid with "nightingale floors" *(uguisubari)*—planks that squeak like birds to betray the steps of intruders. Date transported the best carpenters and sculptors from Kyoto and Wakayama to work on the cedars *(sugi)* brought directly from Mount Kumano. Highlights of a visit include the **Jyodan no ma**★, a room reserved exclusively for the warlord, the **Kairo**★, a corridor with Chinese-style doors *(karato)* with magnificently carved lintels *(ranma)*, and the **Kuri**★, a Zen kitchen remarkable for its massive, high roof structure.

Outside, a handsome cedar walk leads to a steep cliff face dotted with statues and small caves that the hermit monks used for meditation.

## Entsu-in★★ 円通院

*67 Matsushima Aza-Tyounai. Open 8am–5pm. ¥300. It may be possible to lunch at Ungai by making a reservation: 022-353-2626 (Apr–Nov 8.30am–5pm; Dec–Mar 9am–4pm).*

*At the time of writing Ungai was closed, due to reopen by Oct 2011.*

If you are fortunate, you may be able to visit this temple with Harukaa Zen monk, who is the daughter of the senior monk. Haruka is one of only two women to have been admitted to the rank of monk in the Tohoku region.

Entry is by the garden of "great sorrow," through a moss garden and then a dry landscape garden. Representing the bay of Matsushima, it is composed of rough, streaked, and smooth stones, respectively referring to birth, apprenticeship, and accomplishment—the three stages of life. The path is bordered by maples, azaleas, and camellias, and leads to the **Sankeiden**★★, the mausoleum of Mitsumune, the grandson of Date Masamune, who died aged 19 in Edo Castle, probably by poisoning. Suspicion fell on the Tokugawa family, since, with a gift for military strategy, at some point he would have posed a threat for the shogunate, already barely able to hang onto its political power. In this small, magnificently decorated shrine can be seen the hopes the Date clan had cherished for this promising grandson. A statute of Mitsumune riding a white horse stands out against walls and corbelling skillfully overlaid in sparkling gold. He is accompanied by statutes of seven faithful retainers, who committed *seppuku* when he died. Above the right- and left-hand doors are painted a rose and a narcissus with white petals respectively. Symbolizing Rome and Florence, and testifying to the visit made by Tsunenaga to the Pope on Date's orders *(see p 407)*, these two flowers so detestable to the Tokugawa *(all allegiance to Christianity being severely punished by the shogunate)* were not rediscovered until 1945, nearly 300 years after the tomb was built in 1646. Exit by way of the pretty rose garden before tasting *shojin*, vegetarian cuisine, on the tatamis of the meditation pavilion *(Hon-do)*.

*Return to the bay.*
*Around 219yd/200m.*

## The Bay★

On a crescent of land overlooking the bay you will find the **Kanran-tei**★ tea house *(56 Miyajiken, a short distance from the pier at 53 Aza-chonai; open 8am–5pm; ¥200; Apr–Oct 8.30am–5pm, Nov–Mar, 8.30am–4.30pm; scheduled for normal operation by Oct 2011)*. This "place to view the ripples on the water" offers a splendid **view** of the bay. Its doors in the *shoin-zukuri* style are embellished with beautiful paintings by Kano Sankaru (1559–1635). Left of the Kanran-tei, the islet of **Godaido**★ *(scenery unaffected by the Mar 11 tsunami)* has a small temple hall *(open to the public every 33 years, next opening in 2039)* in Momoyama style, rebuilt in 1609 by Masamune. The prefix "Go" *("five" in Japanese)* refers to the statues of the five Buddhist guardians kept in the temple; they represent the *Mikkyo*, a term designating the "secret teachings" of Japan's **Shingon** or **Tantric** Buddhism. A **red footbridge** *(Fukuura-bashi; bridge currently closed)* connects the islet of

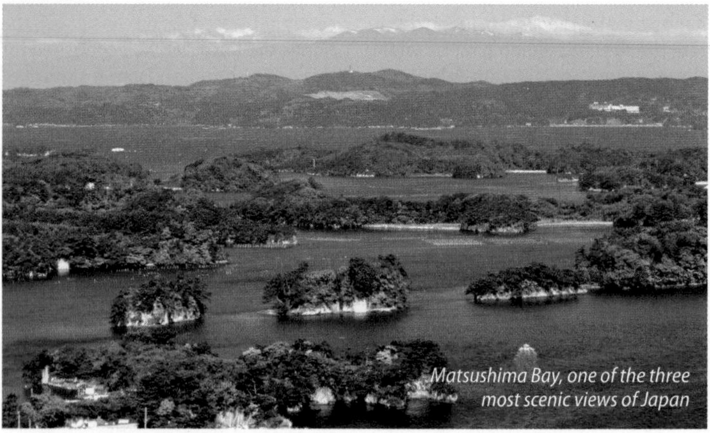

*Matsushima Bay, one of the three most scenic views of Japan*

© JNTO

**Fukuura**★ *(scenery unaffected by the Mar 11 tsunami)* to the shore. It is a botanical reserve, where some 250 plant species have been recorded *(open Mar–Oct 8am–5pm, Nov–Feb 8am–4.30pm; bridge toll: ¥200, no charge for park admission; scenery unaffected by the Mar 11 tsunami).* Facing Fukuura, the **Date Masamune Wax Museum** *(Matsushima Kaigan, on the seafront walkway opposite; open daily 8.30am–5pm; ¥1,000)* exhibits 25 dioramas detailing his life, plus a gallery of famous Tohoku personalities.

## The Most Beautiful Views over the Bay★★★

*Sokanzan and Ogitani are within walking distance of the ferry terminal. The two other sites are a taxi ride away (about ¥600).*

In the center of the city *(on the other side of the Takagi River, 10min walk from Takagimachi station)*, the 210ft/64m-high **Matsushima tower** offers a splendid panorama over the bay. **Shintomi-yama***(scenery unaffected by the Mar 11 tsunami)*, a small hill behind the Wax Museum, is an ideal place to view the sunset. The park of **Saigyo Modoshi no matsu**★★ *(scenery unaffected by the Mar 11 tsunami)* literally, "the pine tree that compelled Saigyo to depart from Matsushima," commands one of the finest viewpoints over the bay, while **Ogitani**★★ *(on N45 coming from Sokanzan; scenery unaffected by the Mar 11 tsunami)* and **Sokanzan**★*(scenery unaffected by the Mar 11 tsunami)*, "the hill with two views" *(from where you can see Shiogama and Matsushima Bay in one panoramic view)*, are two popular observation points.

## HIRAIZUMI★ 平泉

This small town's claim to fame is due to the **Fujiwara** family (see box p285), who made it their political and cultural capital from the 12C. The Fujiwara became prosperous thanks to the exploitation of the huge gold mine at Mutsu, east of Oshua region now located between the prefectures of Fukushima and Aomori. However, the wealth and power of the Fujiwara also led to the fall of Hiraizumi by bringing down upon it the implacable military strength of Yoritomo, the first of the shoguns.

Hiraizumi was razed to the ground and today shows few traces of its former luster, save for the Chuson-ji temple whose beauty draws visitors from all over the world, and is UNESCO World Heritage listed. Built respectively in the north and south of Hiraizumi, the Chuson-ji and Motsu-ji were intended to protect the town against evil spirits.

### Chuson-ji★ 中尊寺

*About 1mi/1.6km N of Hiraizumi station. 10min by bus from the JR station (Run-Run Bus in front of the station's Tourist Information Center). Open Apr–Oct 8am–5pm; Nov–Mar 8.30am–4.30pm. ¥800.*

This temple was founded in 850 by the priest Jikaku Daishi (794–864) as a satellite to the temple of Enryaku-ji at Mount Hiei *(north of Kyoto)* (ⓒ *see p318)*. Affiliated to the Tendai Zen Buddhist sect, it came under the rule of the powerful Fujiwara family, who expanded the site with more than 40 temples. However, the Fujiwara's rivalry with the intractable shogun **Minamoto no Yoritomo** (1147–99) (ⓒ *see box p194*) spelled the end of Chuson-ji. It was destroyed and rebuilt several times, and all that remains today is the **Kyozo** *(the sutra repository)* and the **Konjiki-do★★★**. Built in 1124, this Golden Hall is entirely covered in gold leaf inlaid with mother-of-pearl imported from Okinawa. Images of animals emerge among beautiful mosaics, while the mummified bodies of four generations of the Fujiwara family lie behind the sculptured peacocks on the lower level of the altars.

## Motsu-ji 毛越寺

*About 0.4mi/700m S of Hiraizumi station. 5min by bus from the JR station (Run-Run Bus in front of the station's Tourist Information Center).* ◷*Open Apr 5–Nov 4 8.30am–4.30pm. Rest of the year 8.30am–5pm.* ◎*¥500.*

Like Chuson-ji, the Motsu-ji was built in the 9C by the priest Jikaku Daishi. In the 12C, this monastic complex included more than 50 pagodas and some 500 dwellings for priests and other temple associates, again testifying to the power of the Fujiwara family. Before it was reduced to ashes in a great fire in 1226, the richness of the central pavilion was unequaled in Japan. The original buildings have never been rebuilt but their foundations are laid out in the **Gokuraku-jodo★**, a Heian-style garden, intended to represent the paradise of the Pure Land Buddha.

On the fourth Sunday in May, the *gokusui-no-en* takes place on the banks of the Yarimizu stream that winds through the garden; it's a recreation of an elegant, aristocratic country outing such as took place during the Fujiwara era. The participants write *waka* (traditional poems) and throw them into the stream.

## Genbikei★ 厳美渓

*From Hiraizumi, take the train to Genbikei station. The gorge is a 5min walk from the river. There are many bus services from Ichinoseki station. Flat-bottomed boat trips (90min) through the gorge.* ◷*Open Apr–Oct 8.30am–4.30pm; Nov–Mar 9am–3pm.* ◎*¥1,500.*

The tumultuous waters of the Iwaigawa cut through the gorge over nearly 1.2mi/2km of waterfalls, hot-water springs, and gnarled outcroppings. It's one of **Japan's Top 100 Scenic Beauty Sites**, according to the inevitable official classification.

# ADDRESSES

## 🛏 STAY

### SENDAI

#### ⌂ Dochuan Youth Hostel
道中庵ユースホステル *2-3-7 Onada Taihaku-ku (C2 off map).* ✆*022-247-0511.* ⊠. *10 rooms, dormitories.* 5mi/8km S of Sendai, easy by JR Taishido. Ryokan-style place with wood *o-furo* and internet access.

#### ⌂ R & B Hotel
R&B ホテル仙台広瀬通駅前 *2-6-37 Aoba-ku, Hon-cho (C1).* ✆*022-726-1919. nttbj.itp.ne.jp. 203 rooms.* ⊡. Functional, but charmless rooms in *business hotel*.

#### ⌂ Sendai Chitose Youth Hostel
仙台千登勢ユースホステル
*6-3-8 Aoba-ku, Odawara (C1).* ✆*022-213-8001, fax* ✆*022-265-7551.* ⊡. *13 rooms.* Charming inn, inner garden with shrine. Internet, bicycle rental, coin laundry.

#### ⌂⌂ Hotel Central Sendai
ホテルセントラル仙台
*4-2-6 Chuo, Aoba-ku (C2).* ✆*022-711-4111. www.hotel-central.co.jp. 97 rooms.* Former ryokan, now *business hotel*. A warm welcome; *3min from the station.*

#### ⌂⌂ Hotel Sumireh ホテル菫会館
*1-13-5 Ichibancho, Aoba-ku (B2).* ✆*022-222-8100. www.10.ocn.ne.jp/sumireh. 18 rooms.* Flowery, tasteful Japanese or western rooms; fun owner, with a dozen cats.

#### ⌂⌂⌂ Tenryukaku Ryokan
旅館天龍閣 *22-20 Otamayashita (B2).* ✆*022-222-9957. www.tenryukaku.com. 26 rooms.* Beautiful ryokan at foot of Zuiho-den; dining room overlooking Hirose River—ideal for **Tanabata Festival fireworks**.

**MATSUSHIMA**

**Resort Inn Matsushima** リゾートイン松島 *17 Matsushima-aza Sanjyukari. 022-355-0888. http://www.resort-inn.jp. 29 rooms.* Slightly out of town, a rare budget hotel. Bay **views**.

**Hotel Matsushima Taikanso** ホテル松島大観荘 *Inuta Matsushima. 022-354-5214. www.taikanso.co.jp. 239 rooms.* Luxury establishment with very comfortable rooms.

**HIRAIZUMI**

**Genbikei Itsukushi-en** 厳美渓いつくし園 *15 Minamitakinoue, Genbi-cho, Ichinoseki-shi. 5min walk from Genbikei station. 191-29-2101. www.itsukushien.co.jp. 48 rooms. Lodging with half-board.* Ryokan overlooking Genbikei gorge.

## EAT

**SENDAI**

**Dateno Gyutan** 伊達の牛たん本店 *4-10-11 Chuo Aobaku (C2). 022-722-2535. Open 11am–10pm.* The head chef is a master and a great friend of French chef Joël Robuchon.

**Kakisen Ubudo** かき鮮 海風土 (うぶど) *Located in Sendai station's sushi restaurant strip (C1). 022-212-2340. Open 10am–10.30pm.* One of the best sushi restaurants in Sendai.

**Tasuke** 味 太助本店 *4-4-13 Ichiban-cho (B1). 022-225-4641.* Try the local specialty, *gyutan*; charcoal-grilled beef tongue.

**Maru Sankaku Shikaku** まる・さんかく・しかく *4-3-7 Ichiban-cho (B1). 022-222-1471. Open 11.30am–11pm.* Grilled fish, sashimi, and vegetables in season.

**Kaisei-an** 開盛庵 *1-2-21 Ichiban-cho (B2). 022-266-2520. Open 11.30am–9pm.* Restaurant serving *unagi* (eel) for 126 years. Reservations required on second and third floors.

**Robata** 元祖・炉ばた *2-10-28 Kokubun-cho (B1). 022-266-0897. Open 5am–10pm.* A celebration of Japanese style. Seating is at a U-shaped bar around the open hearth.

**MATSUSHIMA**

**Matsushima Sakana (Fish) Market** 松島さかな市場 *4-10 Fugendo. 022-353-2318. Open 8am–5pm; second floor only; first floor to open soon.* Upstairs in the fish market; freshness guaranteed.

**Aji-dokoro - Santori Chaya** 味処・さんとり茶屋 *24-4-1 Senzui. 022-353-2622. Open Thu–Tue 11.30am–10pm, open holidays.* The only restaurant offering fresh oysters all year round, Santori also specializes in *sokadon*.

**Shunkai** 旬海 *51-2 Aza-chonai, behind the Japanese tea house. 022-353-4131. Open 11.30am–9pm (by reservation in evenings from Dec–Apr).* One of the few local restaurants open in the evening. Grilled fish, sashimi, and *soba* noodles.

## NIGHTLIFE

**SENDAI**

**Kokubun-cho** is Sendai's nightlife quarter and also that of the whole of Tohoku. Its tangle of streets is filled with bars, restaurants, *pachinko*, and massage parlors. A touch of France can be found at **Gulp Down Cafe** *(2-1030 Fox Bldg, 3 F, 6pm–1am)*; Middle Eastern ambience at **Sindbad** *(Explaza 1F, 2-2-22 Kokubun-cho, 5pm–5am)*.

## SHOPPING

**SENDAI**

**Culinary Specialties** – **Kanezaki Kamaboko** 鐘崎 *3-5-16 Ichibancho, S of Manga & Kissa. Reduced business hours of 10am-6pm at time of writing.* Specializes in **sasakamaboko**, a fish, shrimp, or ham cake eaten as a snack.

**Ocha-Igeta** 井ヶ田 *7-23 Ichibancho, S of Manga & Kissa, next to Kanesaki Kamaboko. Open 10am7.30pm. Matcha* green tea and elegant cakes.

**Crafts** – **Tsutsumi-no-Ohinakkoya** つつみのおひなっこや *2-10-10 Tsutsumimachi. Open 9am–5pm. 022-233-6409.* Sato is one of the last makers of **tsutsumi**, charming small painted terra-cotta dolls. Family museum, shop, and doll-making *(Daruma)* workshop *(reservations required)*.

## EVENTS AND FESTIVALS

**SENDAI**

**Tanabata Matsuri** – A summer celebration *(Aug 6–8)*. Sendai's streets fill with 1,500 bamboo poles bearing decorations floating in the wind; fireworks the evening before the festival.

**Dontosai Matsuri** – Every year on Jan 14, a large procession of men, clad only in white loin cloths, gather, at the Hachiman Temple to burn New Year decorations and pray for a prosperous year.

# Tsuruoka and surroundings★ 鶴岡

**Situated at the foot of a volcanic, mountainous region bordering the Sea of Japan, Tsuruoka benefits from a favorable natural environment. This peaceful little provincial city is not without attractions and is the ideal starting point for a tour of the "Dewa Sanzan," the three sacred mountains so dear to the famous *yamabushi* hermits *(see box p 416)*. Less than 18.6mi/30km away, Sakata—Yamagata prefecture's second major city—has a number of museums with cutting-edge modern architecture.**

- **Population:** Tsuruoka: 145,820; Sakata: 95,264.
- **Michelin Map:** Tsuruoka: Principal Sights Map B2.
- **Location:** In Yamagata Prefecture *(pop 1.2 million)*, **Tsuruoka** is bound by Mount Chokai to the north, the sacred Dewa mountains to the east, the Asahi mountain chain in the south, and the Sea of Japan to the west. **Sakata** is about 18.6mi/30km northwest of Tsuruoka.
- **Kids:** A trip to Mount Haguro and a night in its *shukubo*.
- **Timing:** Allow a full day for Tsuruoka and the environs, and another day for Sakata.
- **Don't miss:** Churen-ji and Mount Haguro in the Tsuruoka region; the Honma Museum of Art and the Domon Ken Museum of Photography at Sakata.

## SIGHTS

### Chido Museum★ 致道博物館

*10-18 Kachushin-machi. 5min walk from Tsuruoka City Hall, 10min by taxi from Tsuruoka station. Open 9am–4.30pm. Closed Dec 28–Jan 4. ¥700.*

Just west of Tsuruoka Park, formerly dominated by **Sakai Castle** *(the seat of one of Yamagata's leading families)*, this museum comprises various buildings that were transferred here and turned into mini museums on Tsuruoka's history and culture. Chido Museum was launched during the 1950s by the influential Sakai family, owners of the park.

The collection includes two magnificent buildings from the Meiji era: the **first district administrative center**★ *(former Nishitagawa District Office)*, dominated by a clock tower (1881), and the **first police station**★ (1884), with an exhibition of historical documentation on the region. These buildings were originally commissioned by the prefectural governor who, after the prefectures were created in 1871, took over regional responsibility for the Meiji government's policy of encouraging Western architectural styles. The **farm**★ *(former Shibuya family home)*, with its curved, thatched roof in *kabuto-zukuri* style (shaped like a samurai helmet), is an example of a traditional rural dwelling.

The **Folklore House**★ *(Mingu no kura)* is home to an interesting ethnographic museum devoted to fishing-related topics. Note the commemorative steles designed to appease the souls of caught salmon. The highlight of the visit is the Sakai family's **Japanese garden**★★, one of the finest in Tohoku. It is next to a rather special tea house, which has two openings *(one is more usual, since darkness helps the meditation required for the Tea Ceremony)*. In fact, this tea house also served as a work room, specifically as a place for doing calligraphy.

## EXCURSIONS

### Churen-ji★★ 注連寺

*Bus from Tsuruoka station (50min, ¥980 RT). Alight at Oami bus stop. Open May–Oct 8am–5pm; Nov–Apr 9am–4pm. ¥500.*

### One prayer, three gods

Gas-san, Haguro-san, and Yudono-san, collectively known as **Dewa Sanzan**, are the three sacred mountains of Yamagata prefecture *(formerly Dewa province)*. Each has a precise significance. Haguro-san symbolizes prosperity in the present life, Gas-san the world of the dead, and Yudono-san that of reincarnation and rebirth. For nearly 1,500 years, these three mountains have been venerated by pilgrims who would willingly climb them all, if not for the fact that heavy snows make the ascents of Gas-san *(6,509ft/1,984m)* and Yudono-san *(4,934ft/1,504m)* impossible. The Gosai-den temple on Haguro-san, which is lower *(1,358ft/414m)* and therefore accessible all year round, has therefore come to represent the spirits of all three mountains. Gas-san was featured in a novel by Mori Atsushi, who won the Akutagawa Prize in 1973.

The big attraction in this temple, built in the time of Kobo Daishi, is the **mummy**★★ of the monk Tetsumonkai Shonin (1768–1829), who auto-embalmed himself during his lifetime through drastic fasting and practices of mortification. To become a living mummy, a monk would eat only nuts and seeds for 1,000 days, and for a further 1,000 days, only bark and pine roots *(mokujiki)*. Following these two stages, the monk would drink a tea made from the sap of the urushi tree. This toxic substance, generally used to make lacquer, would preserve

## USEFUL INFORMATION

**TSURUOKA**

**Tourist Office** – *Tsuruoka Tourist Information Center, 1-1 Suehiro Machi, in Tsuruoka railway station. Open 9.30am–5.30pm; 10am–5pm (winter). ℘0235-25-7678. www.t-town.jp/kanko.*

**Taxi Companies** – *Shoko Hire Co. ℘0235-22-0055, Hire Center Co. ℘0235-22-5155.*

**SAKATA**

**Tourist Office** – *In the railway station. Open 9am–5pm. ℘0234-24-2454. www.sakata-kankou.gr.jp.*

**Sakata Tour Guide** – *℘0234-24-2233. About ¥1,000 for 1hr.*

## TRANSPORTATION

**BY TRAIN – Getting to and from Tsuruoka. JR Tsuruoka Station** – *℘0235-22-0055.* From **Tokyo**, take the Joetsu Shinkansen to Niigata *(90min)*, then the Inaho Express for Tsuruoka *(110min)*.

From **Sendai**, take the Senzansen Line to Yamagata *(70min)*, then the Uetsu Line for Tsuruoka *(2hr10min)*.

**Getting to and from Sakata**

From **Tsuruoka** to **Sakata** *(17.4mi/28km)*, trains around every 30min. JR Uetsu Line *(36min, ¥480)* or Limited Express Inaho 1 *(19min, ¥1,690)*.

From **Sakata** to **Hirosaki** *(157.2mi/253km)*, allow 4hr and ¥12,500 by the Limited Express Nihonkai or 3hr36min and ¥6,910 by the JR Uetsu Line.

**BY BUS – Getting to and from Tsuruoka. Tsuruoka Bus Terminal** *(Shoko mall) – ℘0235-24-4455.* From Tsuruoka to Sendai *(generally every hour 7.20am–7.20pm, 2hr35min, ¥5400 RT)*. From Tsuruoka to Sakata *(JR station)*, 9 per day *(50min, ¥800)*.

**Getting to and from Sakata**

**Sakata Bus Terminal** – To Sendai, usually every hour: 6.05am–6.30pm.Journey time around 3–4hr, depending on timetable *(¥3,100 Single, ¥5,800 Return)*.

**GETTING AROUND SAKATA**

Bicycles can be rented from the Tourist Information Center in Sakata station *(open 10am–5pm; no charge)*. A tourist map with various cycle routes is available in English.

**Run-Run Buses** serve the city's tourist sights for an all-in fare of ¥100.

the body while warding off flesh-eating maggots. Finally, the monk would retire to meditate in an underground chamber connected to the surface by a bamboo breathing tube until death intervened. If his body did not decompose after death, he would become a *sokushinbutsu* (there are 16 in Japan), someone who achieved nirvana while still living.

The temple's **coffered ceilings**★, painted during the 1980s, are also interesting. In the modern manga style, painted by Atsushi and Kubo, they are intended as charms designed to protect the roof from fire. Before leaving the temple, take a look at a magnificent **wooden bell**★ hanging in the entrance. Made in the Meiji era, its name, *wani-guchi*, means "crocodile's mouth."

### Mount Haguro★★ 羽黒山

*From Tsuruoka station take the bus in the direction of Mount Haguro, terminating at the summit (50min, ¥1,050). Or get off at the foot of Mount Haguro and hike up (5,577ft/1.7km, 1hr). www.dewasanzan.jp/info.*

Haguro-san, Gas-san, and Yudono-san (*see box above*), are the sacred sites of Shugendo (*see box p416*), an ancient belief system dating from the 7C, which combines Shinto and Buddhist beliefs. Along with Omine-san (in the Kii Peninsula, *see p344*), these mountains are the most sacred sites for the *shugenja*, the followers of Shugendo. The path up the mountain to its summit at 1,358ft/414m includes 2,446 stone steps that take an hour to climb. It follows a magnificent **trail**★★★ lined with hundreds of cedars, many 350 to 500 years old, and takes you past a superb **five-story pagoda**★★ boasting five symmetrical roofs, 98.4ft/30m in height. The pagoda is surrounded by more cedars, **Cryptomeria japonica**, including the 1,000-year-old "grandfather of cedars," and is the oldest pagoda in Tohoku. It was constructed by Tairo no Masakado during the Heian era (937), although thought to have been rebuilt in 1400. Unusually, there are no other shrines in this sacred place as many were destroyed during the Meiji reforms that separated Shintoism and Buddhism. Just before the summit, you can visit—or even stay in—the **shukubo Saikan**★★ (monks' lodgings, *see Address Book p 417*). Reconstructed in 1697, it is the sole survivor of 30 monasteries destroyed during the Meiji era, although between times, this building was turned into a Shinto shrine. At the summit is the **Gosaiden**★★, a temple with an impressive thatched roof *(6.9ft/2.1m)*. Its shared Buddhist and Shinto influences make it one of the rare examples of architectural syncretism to have escaped the Meiji fury. Perhaps it was protected by the Gosaiden, guardian of the spirits of the three mountains (*see box opposite*).

### SAKATA★ 酒田

Sakata owes its prosperity to its geographical situation at the heart of the trading routes along the western coast of Japan. The city was a transit port for *kitamae bune* (large cargo vessels that plied the Sea of Japan from Osaka to Hokkaido) and during the Edo period (1603–1867) became Japan's second port after Sakai *(near Osaka)*.

Tucked into the mouth of the Mogami River that empties into the Sea of Japan, it is also the port from which the many commodities produced in the region were shipped out *(especially to Kyoto)*. They included rice and sake, and other commodities such as the lucrative virgin safflower oil, one of the vegetable oils richest in polyunsaturated acids, formerly used as a dye. It is not surprising, therefore, that the city still bears traces of its prosperous merchants, including the old, but still influential **Honma** family, without whom Sakata would probably not be what it is today,

#### A Bit of Advice

Tsuruoka is celebrated in Japan for producing what are considered the country's most delicious—and costliest—soybeans. Legend has it, they are so good that a feudal lord of the Sakai clan had his retainers bring him some every day.

### Shugendo and Yamabushi

Practitioners of Shugendo, the sect whose goal is the search and attainment of the way *(do) to* divine spiritual powers *(gen)* through ascetic practices *(shu)*, are known as *shugenja* or *yamabushi* ("one who lies in the mountains"). Living an ascetic life in Japan's mountainous regions, many go to Mount Haguro to make solitary retreats, during which they subject themselves to feats of endurance such as *nanibushi*, when the yamabushi retires to a cave to inhale the irritant fumes of peppers or meditates for several days under a waterfall. Most of the rites remain a secret, however. *Yamabushi* can be recognized by their costume, unchanged for more than 1,000 years; it includes the *hangai*, a hat woven from cypress wood, and the *horagai*, "conch shell of the Law," used to signal to each other of their presence in the mountains.

one of the most attractive cities in the Yamagata prefecture.

*Apart from the two museums (of Art and Photography) 3.1mi/5km SW of Sakata station (around 20min by bus), the tourist highlights are all close to each other. A good way of getting around is by bike: bicycles are available on loan free of charge at Sakata station (open 10am–5pm). The most logical route for a half-day tour is: Honma Museum of Art, Somara (see below), the Honma Residence, Sankyo Rice Warehouse, and then return to Sakata station.*

## Honma Museum of Art★

本間美術館

*7-7 Onari-cho, Sakata-shi. 5min walk from Sakata station. Open Thu–Mon, 9am–5pm (Jul–Aug: 6.30pm); Nov–Mar 9am–4.30pm). Closed Dec 22–Jan 7. ¥900. www.homma-museum.or.jp.*

In 1947, the Honma family opened the first private Japanese museum. Originally focused on objects from the Sakai family, over time the collection was enlarged to reflect the region's culture. Variously themed temporary exhibitions *(from early to contemporary art)* are in a **recent building** at the entrance to the garden, and in the **Seienkaku**★ at the end of the garden, a handsome wooden buildingthe former summer residence of the Sakai overlord. It was built in 1813, at the same time as the **Kakubu-en garden**★★. Typical of stroll gardens *(see p103)* that flourished in the great cities of the time, it is a harmonious grouping of pools, islets, artificial hills, rocks, and lanterns.

Here is also the **studio of Ito**, an artist-potter making Tea Ceremony bowls, known as *Honmayaki*, after a technique developed by Honma Yusuke, a former museum director. Each weighs exactly 21.2oz/600g, for a perfectly weighted bowl in the hand. It's not usually possible to visit the studio. Honmayaki is sold in the museum shop.

## Honma Residence★★

本間旧本邸

*Around 0.7mi/1.2km from Sakata station (5min walk). 7min by Run-Run bus from Sakata station (¥100), Nakamachou stop. Open Mar–Oct 9.30am–4.30pm; Nov–Feb 9.30am–4pm. ¥700.*

Thanks to its wealth, reputed to have made the Honma a far more powerful clan than most *daimyo* in Tohoku, this merchant family's residence has a unique feature. Built in 1768 by the Honma family, it also provided a residence for the Sakai overlord during his regional inspection tours. As a result, it combines a Shoin-style exterior worthy of a samurai with an elegant interior appropriate to a merchant. This unusual division of a common space is reflected in every detail of the house. The quality of the wood, the decoration, and even the height of the floor change when you move from one part of the house to another. The house is proof of the social hierarchy prevailing under the Tokugawa.

## Sankyo Rice Warehouse

山居倉庫

*Sankyo-machi 1-1-20, 1mi/1.6km from Sakata station (20min walk). Take the shuttle bus (Run-Run Bus) from the JR station (8min, ¥100), Sankyo Higashi-cho stop.*

Built in 1893 by a rice merchant, these 12 wooden warehouses along the bank of the Niida River are shaded by large zelkova trees protecting them from summer sun and icy winter winds, keeping the rice at the ideal temperature. Still in use today, three of them now perform other functions.

The first building is now the **Shonai Rice Historical Museum** (*open 9am–4.30pm; ¥300*). The 11th, **Hana no Yakata**, has been turned into a museum on the history and culture of Sakata (*open 9am–6pm; ¥300*). Highlights include the works of Tsujimura Jusaburo, a famous maker of dolls and puppets. The 12th warehouse, **Sachi no Yakata**, currently serves as a Tourist Information Center and souvenir shop selling local products (*open 8.30am–5.30pm*). There's also a cafe with a zelkova-shaded terrace, as well as the Hokotei restaurant. *Bicycle rental available.*

*Cross the Mogami River and Kyoden. The two museums are about 109yd/100m from each other.*

## Domon Ken Museum of Photography★★

土門拳記念館

*3mi/4.8km from Sakata station. 20min by bus (Sakata City bus) from the station (¥100), Domon Ken stop. Open Tue–Sun 9am–4.30pm. ¥420.*

A native of Sakata, Domon Ken (1909–90) was one of the great masters of photographic realism. With an endowment of 70,000 photographs, this museumthe first photographic museum in Japanis devoted to his work. The building appears to float on a manmade lake. It was designed by Taniguchi Yoshio, the famous Japanese architect best known for his redesign of New York's Museum of Modern Art several years later.

## Sakata Museum of Art★

酒田市美術館

*Open Nov–Apr Tue–Sun 9am–5pm, Dec–Mar. ¥520.*

This hillside museum opened in 1997. Ikehara Yoshiro's building is a triumph, merging with the surrounding garden, Mount Chokai area, Mogami River, and city of Sakata. Works by painter Morita Shigeru (1907–2009) and sculptor Takahashi Tsuyoshi (1921–91), the museum's two major permanent collections, are less impressive.

# ADDRESSES

## STAY

### SAKATA

**Sakata Tokyu Inn 酒田東急イン** *1-10-20 Saiwai-cho, Sakata. 234-26-0109. 94 rooms. ¥13,500– ¥1,000.* Adequate *business hotel*, facing Sakata JR station.

### HAGURO-SAN

**Mount Haguro Saikan** 羽黒山斎館（羽黒山参籠所 *Take bus from Tsuruoka for Haguro. 10min from Hagurosantyo bus stop. 0235-62-2357. http://templelodging.com. 300 beds. Half-board. ¥7,350 per person, two meals.* 300-year-old shukubo (temple lodging).

## EAT

### TSURUOKA

**Al Checciano** アル・ケッチァーノ *83 Ichirizuka, Shimoyamazoe. 0235-78-7230 - 11.45am–2pm and 6pm–9pm. Reserve for specialty menu, ¥8, 500.* Japanese and Italian cuisine.

### SAKATA

**Sakata Fish Market** さかた海鮮市場 *10min by bus from Sakata station (¥150), Koto stop.* In port district, fish stands on ground floor *(open 8am–6pm)*, restaurants above. Tobishima restaurant is good value *(open 7am–7pm)*.

**Somaro 相馬楼** *Maikozaka 1-2-20 Hiyoshi-cho. 10min by bus from Sakata station (¥150), Kotobukicho stop. 234-21-2310. www.somaro.net. Open Thu–Tue 10am–5pm (Dec–Feb 5pm).* Magnificent, unique house; traditional food and maiko singing and dancing *(performances around 2pm; entry and dancing ¥1,000; ¥700 for admission without dancing; ¥3,504 bento)*.

# Hirosaki★
# 弘前

**Spared the damage suffered by other cities during World War II, unlike Aomori which was razed to the ground, Hirosaki has many attractions, such as the thousands of ancient cherry trees surrounding the castle that are the pride of the city every spring. This rural region is Japan's leading apple producer and an important university center. Along with the other *daimyo*, the Tsugaru clan, who ruled the city from the 17C onward, lost their high office in the Meiji era. However, taking advantage of the drive toward modernization and higher education under the Meiji reforms, they sent family members to study in Tokyo, who greatly benefited the city upon their return.**

- **Population:** 167,717.
- **Michelin Map:** Principal Sights Map B2.
- **Location:** Hirosaki is in Aomori prefecture, 37mi/60km northwest of Lake Towada.
- **Kids:** Neputa-mura and the Oirase Gorge; a stroll in the beech forests of the Shirakami mountains.
- **Timing:** Allow a full day for Hirosaki, two days for the Lake Towada region, and another two days for the Shirakami mountains.
- **Don't miss:** Cherry-blossom time in April; the Hirosaki Neputa Matsuri, held August 1–7; lunch at Suimeiso and dinner at Anzu.

## SIGHTS

Hirosaki grew up around its castle, protected by Shinto shrines to the north and Buddhist temples to the southwest. Bounded to the west by Mount Iwaki, the city sprawls over the flat land to the east, where the railway station is located.

### Hirosaki Castle 弘前城

*Bus to Hirosaki, Shiyakusyomae stop.*

Completed in 1611, the castle was occupied by generations of the Tsugaru clan until the Meiji era, but apart from moats and ramparts, little remains of it today except five gates designated Important Cultural Assets.

The castle keep was rebuilt in 1810 and has now been turned into a small historical **museum** *(open 9am–5pm; ¥300)*, which dominates the 121-acre/49ha **public park**★, famous throughout Japan for the flowering of its 2,600 cherry trees. At the end of April, crowds of people descend to picnic beside the moats, an event often filmed by Japanese television.

## USEFUL INFORMATION

**HIROSAKI**

**Tourist Office** – *At the station central exit. Open 8.45am–6pm. ☎0172-83-3000. English spoken.*

## TRANSPORTATION

**BY TRAIN** – **From Hirosaki** to **Towada** – Take the Limited Express train Tsugaru 98 to Misawa, then the Towada Kankou Dentetsu to Towada-shi *(79mi/127km, 2hr30min, ¥4,470)*.

**From Hirosaki** to **Shirakami** – Take the Limited Express train Kamoshika to **Futatsui** *(46.6mi/75km, 1hr, ¥ 2,890)*. From Futatsui, take the bus to **Fujisato** *(9.3mi/15km, every hour 11am–4.15pm, around ¥450)* or a taxi *(about ¥4,500)*. At Fujisato, get off at the **Shirakami-sanchi World Heritage Conservation Center** to pick up information on visiting Shirakami-sanchi.

**BY BUS** – Long-distance buses arrive at the terminal behind Joppal department store west of the station.

## SOUTH OF THE CASTLE

### Fujita Kinen Teien★
藤田記念庭園

*8-1 Kami Shirogane-cho, on the park's southern edge. Open Tue–Sun 9am–5pm (closed winter). ¥300.*

This Japanese garden was created in 1919 by Fujita Kenichi (1873–1946), one of Japan's most successful businessmen. Within its 26,312sq yd/22,000sq m area, you will find a **traditional Japanese house** with a floor made from *yakusugi* (ancient pines from Yakushima), an **archeological hall** *(displaying exhibits dating back to the pre-Jomon era)*, a pavilion for the Tea Ceremony, and a somber Taisho era dwelling with a magnificent **veranda**★.

### Zenrin-gai★ 禅林街

*15min walk S from the previous site.*

Thirty-three temples *(recalling the number of reincarnations undergone by the goddess Kannon)* flank this peaceful "Buddhist way" leading to the Tsugaru family temple of Choso-ji.

At the start is an octagonal tower *(the shape is unusual in Japan)* called the **Sazaedo**★, built in 1839 by a local merchant in memory of those who died in two terrible famines—the Tenmei (1783) and Tenpo (1833–1839). Inside, the corridor is decorated with images of Kannon's reincarnations.

At the end of the avenue stands the **Chosho-ji**★ *(open 9am–4pm; ¥300)* with its majestic gate, the **San-mon**★★, 52.5ft/16m high, built in 1629 by Nobuhira, the second Tsugaru overlord. The Chosho-ji contains 500 small statues of the disciples of Buddha.

*Float in the Hirosaki Neputa Matsuri*

©Aomori Prefecture/JNTO

## NORTH OF THE CASTLE

*Opposite the park, due N.*

### Nakacho Historic Quarter★
仲町

The people who served the *daimyo* lived in this district until the Meiji Reformation. Several houses are open to visitors: the **Iwata House**★ *(31 Wakado-cho; open Jul–Oct Tue–Wed, Fri–Sun 10am–6pm; no charge)* shows how a samurai family lived. The **old Ishiba shop**★ *(88 Kamenoko-machi; open 9am–5pm; ¥100)* was trading during the Edo period and is still open today.

*Make for the NW side of the park.*

### Neputa-mura 津軽藩ねぷた村

*61 Kamenokomachi, at the NE corner of Hirosaki Castle's park. Open 9am–5pm. ¥500.*

#### Mysterious *kokeshi*

The earliest *kokeshi* (traditional wooden dolls) appeared in Tohoku at the end of the 19C. Their origin is unclear and open to various interpretations, especially since the word is spelled in *hiragana* (syllables) and not in the conventional *kanji* (characters). Explanations include: a doll with a head in the shape of a poppy seed; souvenirs sold by local artists to passing tourists who frequented the onsen, for whom the doll's cylindrical shape would be a reminder of the massage-tables; or votive dolls designed to appease the souls of dead babies. In past periods of food shortage, newborn children or the youngest female child would sometimes be killed so the rest of the family could survive.

A center containing workshops devoted to the many local crafts and customs of the Aomori region northeast of Hirosaki, such as dolls *(kokeshi, see box p419)*, pottery, lacquer, *shamisen*, tea houses, etc. The highlight is the **Hirosaki Neputa-no-Yakata Museum**★, containing the highly decorative festival floats that bear large illuminated screens or giant fans used during the famous Hirosaki festival, the **Neputa Matsuri**. The word *neputa* derives from *neputee* or "drowsiness" in the local dialect, referring to the farmers' custom of placing giant lanterns along the river bank in order to keep them awake when they were returned late from a hard day's work.

## EXCURSIONS

### Towada-Hachimantai National Park★

十和田八幡平国立公園

Towada Park and the Hachimantai plateau *(205,098 acres/83,000ha)* together constitute one of northern Japan's most beautiful National Parks. To reach it, take the train to Towada-shi *(see Addresses p421)*, then the bus in the direction of Lake Towada. Get off at the Ishigido stop and continue on foot along the road runing beside the river that meanders through the stunning **gorge of Oirase**★★ to Nenokuchi, on the edge of Lake Towada *(2hr40min, 5mi/8km)*. This is a popular walk with the Japanese, some of whom bring along paints and easel. There are spectacular **waterfalls** at **Kumoi** and **Choshi** *(5.6 tons of water falling per second)*.

A short distance from Nenokuchi's JR bus terminal, is **Lake Towada**★, where you can take a boat trip to Yasumiya *(50min, ¥1,500)*. The boat runs between the two headlands of **Nakayama** and **Ogura** that project into the southern part of this ancient craterlake, one of the largest in Japan at 1,315.6ft/401m above sea level. You can also go canoeing, notably with the dynamic North Village team *(http://www.novi.jp/access.html)*, promoters of the "slow life", who are currently setting up on the shores of the lake.

### Shirakami-sanchi★★

白神山地

*Get off at the World Heritage Conservation Center (Fujisato) (see opposite page) for practical information regarding visiting Shirakami-sanchi—weather, etc. The site itself is 13.7mi/22km (45min) from here.*

Shirakami-sanchi is a mountainous area covering 321,237 acres/130,000ha and straddles the border between the prefectures of Akita and Aomori. Their slopes covered in forest, the mountains here are 328–3,937ft/100–1,200m above

**UNESCO Natural Heritage Sites**

**Yakushima**, **Shirakami-sanchi, Shiretoko** and the **Ogasawara Islands** are the four Japanese sites designated by UNESCO as World Natural Heritage Sites *(the first two in 1993, Shiretoko in 2005 and Ogasawara in 2011)*. This classification seeks to safeguard sites that are of outstanding natural importance. The other 11 Japanese sites listed are designated as of cultural importance.

*Shirakami-sanchi*

©Yasufumi Nishi/JNTO

sea level. The central area of around 42,008 acres/17,000ha has been designated a Natural Heritage Site by UNESCO. Remote and inaccessible from urban centers, the site comprises a unique **beech forest** virtually untouched by man. Its Siebold beeches represent the last remaining large area of the great primary forests that once cloaked the slopes of Japan's northern mountains. The leaves of the trees trap rainwater, which then trickles down the trunks to the forest floor, forming pockets of water that sustain a whole ecosystem. The region is home to more than 500 plant species and a wide variety of animals, including around 15 species of large mammal, such as the Japanese serow *(a type of goat-antelope)* and the Japanese **black bear**.
Eighty-four species of bird have also been recorded, including **golden eagles**, green and black woodpeckers, and over 2,000 insect species.

### Shirakami-sanchi World Heritage Conservation Center (Fujisato)

白神山地世界遺産センター藤里館
*15min by bus from Futatsui. Fujisato Ranger Office, Satokori 63. Open Wed–Mon 9am–5pm. No charge. 185-79-3001. www.unep-wcmc.org/sites/wh/shira.html.*
The Center *(957sq yd/800sq m in area)* provides comprehensive information on the fauna and flora of this Natural Heritage Site, the first in Japan to obtain international listing.
You'll learn how bonsai growers love the Japanese beech *(Fagus crenata)*, which is famous for its property of marcescence *(leaves that dry during fall, but remain on the tree throughout winter, finally dropping when the new buds open in spring)*. An adjacent room displays the work of local artists, some of them well-known, such as the talented **Hirano Shoji.**
*As Shirakami is difficult to access, a visit is best accompanied by a ranger, who has a thorough knowledge of the wood's ecosystem and its wildlife. There are also some well-signposted pedestrian trails.*

## ADDRESSES

### STAY

**HIROSAKI**

**Route Inn Hotel**
ホテルルートイン弘前駅前
*5-1 Ekimae-cho, Hirosaki. 0172-31-0010. www.route-inn.co.jp. 48 rooms.* . Opened in 2008, this hotel in the famous Route Inn chain is a short distance from the station, close to the post office. Modern, practical, and comfortable, it is popular with the region's *salarymen*.

**TOWADA**

**Hotel Towada-so**
ホテル十和田荘
*16, Towada, Okuse, Towada. 0176-75-2221. 236 rooms.* Huge hotel complex situated on the lakeside *(facing the Nakayama promontory)*, offering many facilities with a wide range of prices.

**FUJISATO (SHIRAKAMI-SANCHI)**

**Hotel Yutoria Fujisato**
ホテルゆとりあ藤里
*Kamiyunosawa, Fujikoto, Fujisato-machi, Yamamoto-gun, Akita. Bus or taxi from the station (about 5.6mi/9km).* Lodging with half-board. *0185-79-1070.* This hotel has many facilities *(swimming pool, onsen, boutiques, restaurant)* and is an ideal location for visitors to Shirakami-sanchi. *A few minutes from the upper reaches of the Shirakami-sanchi World Heritage Conservation Center.* Western-style rooms.

### EAT

**HIROSAKI**

**Suimeiso** 翠明荘
*69 Motodera-machi, Hirosaki. 0172-32-8281. www.suimeiso.co.jp. Open Tue–Sun 11am–2pm, 5–10pm.* Lunch in this 1895 *shoin-zukuri* style house is a memorable experience. Elegant wood paneling and a well tended Japanese garden.

**Anzu** 郷土料理店・杏
*44-1 Oyakata-amchi, Hirosaki. 172-32-6684. Open 5pm–midnight. Shamisen concerts 7.30–9.30pm.* This welcoming *izakaya* features experienced *shamisen* students, who play every evening.They are among the best in Japan. Simple, tasty cooking.

**"In the ideal geography of the Japanese, Hokkaido is a blank space. Most Japanese in their forties have never been there, will never go there, and would be hard pressed to express an opinion about it. For them, this land has no prestige because it has almost no history..." That was written 30 years ago by the Swiss travel writer Nicolas Bouvier in his *Japanese Chronicles*. The land does, however, have a memory, a powerful one, even if it has been recorded by a people who, although they may not have a language of their own, certainly have a unique history—the Ainu. Toward the end of the 19C, the Meiji government decided to launch a full-scale colonization of Hokkaido ("road to the northern sea"). Between 1887 and 1922, 2 million Japanese immigrants flocked to these vast landscapes, bringing with them their culture, agricultural methods, and herds of cattle.**

### Highlights

1. The festival atmosphere during **Yuki Matsuri** ice sculpture competition *(p424)*
2. **Shiretoko Goko** in the Fall, (p438)
3. **Goryokaku** fortress (pp440–441)
4. View from **Mount Hakodate**, (p445)
5. Walks in the densely forested wilderness of **Lake Akan**, (p449)

- **Population:** 5.9 million.
- **Michelin Map:** Principal Sights Map B–C1.
- **Location:** The great northern island *(30,317sq mi/ 78,521sq km, about 20 percent of the total landmass of Japan)*, 932mi/1,500km from Tokyo, is surrounded by the Pacific Ocean, the Sea of Japan, and the Sea of Okhotsk. It is separated from Honshu by the Tsugaru Strait.
- **Kids:** The Sapporo Snow Festival *(Yuki Matsuri)*.
- **Timing:** One day in Sapporo, another in Otaru, and two days for Noboribetsu and its surroundings.
- **Don't miss:** The National Parks *(Daisetsu-zan, Shiretoko)*; Noboribetsu Onsen *(especially Dai-ichi Takimoto-kan)*; Shiretoko Peninsula as a whole; Shiraoi Ainu Museum.

## Pristine National Parks

"It is Japan, but yet there is a difference somehow," wrote explorer Isabella Bird in the 19C. Indeed, the history of Hokkaido reaches further back than the rest of Japan; the expressive terra-cotta figurines of the ancient Jomon era were found here. Over the centuries pioneers, farmers, disgraced samurai, and gold prospectors came to this remote land with its harsh climate, thick forest, and icebound coasts. Rice cultivation developed in the west, and cattle ranching in the north and east, carving new landscapes out of what are still vast areas of forest *(70 percent of the island)*. In 1972, the Winter Olympics at Sapporo *(the first held outside Europe or the United States)* not only put Hokkaido on the map in

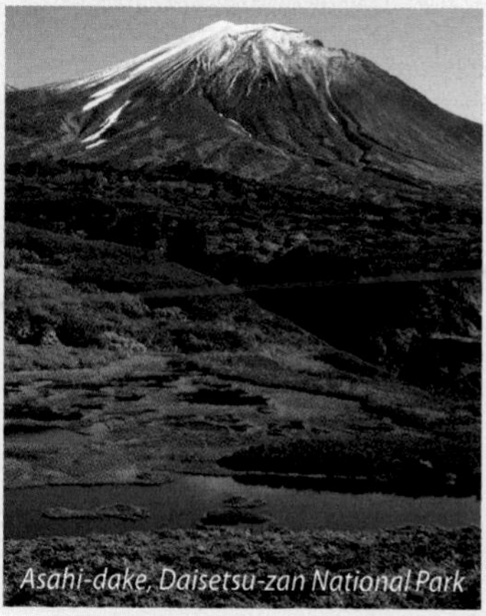
*Asahi-dake, Daisetsu-zan National Park*

©JTB/Photoshot

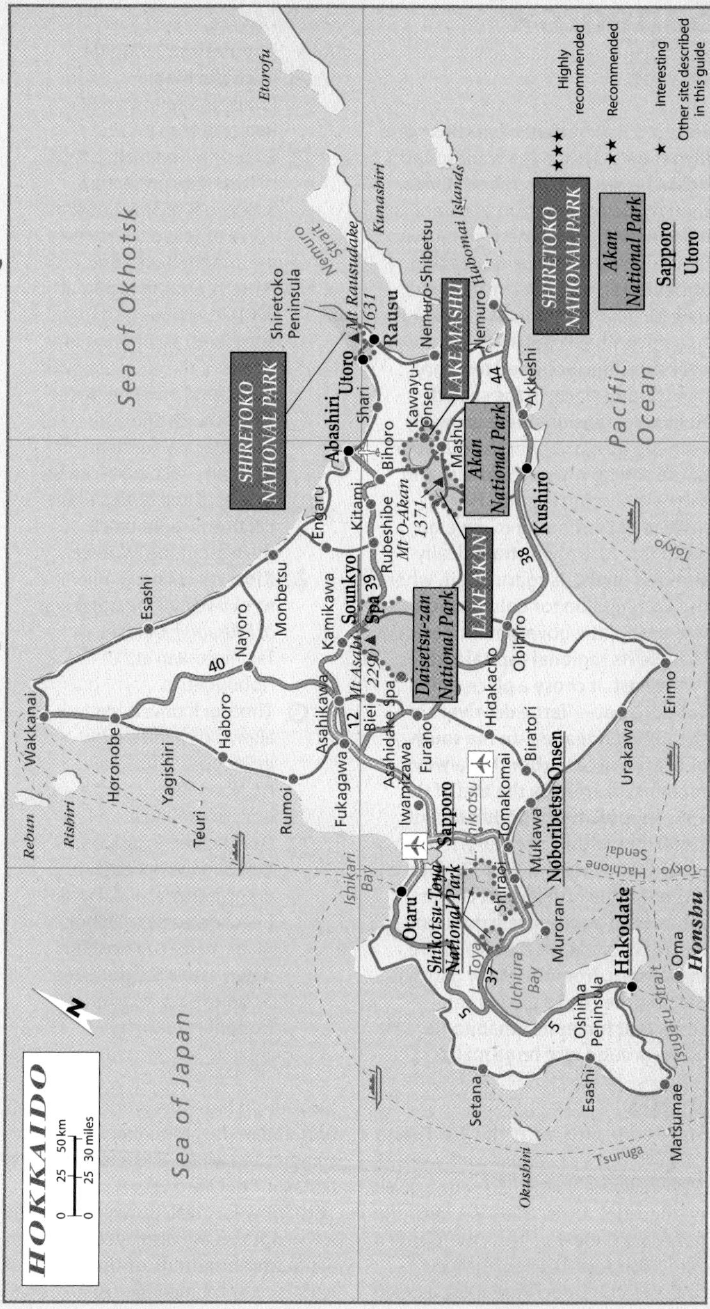




terms of winter sports, they also aroused a new interest among the Japanese. Ever since, the Japanese have been coming to the archipelago's largest island in huge numbers *(nearly 50 million every year)*, aware that its natural heritage *(no fewer than six National Parks)* is now their greatest asset.

# Sapporo★
# 札幌

**Sapporo is a modern city, whose grid layout owes less to the traditional urban layout imported from China than to the pragmatism of colonizers influenced by the American farmers invited to Japan to introduce new agricultural methods. In 1868, the new Meiji government was anxious to gain as much control as possible over this Ainu-occupied territory, particularly since, in the sea off Hokkaido, tensions were growing with the Russians over the question of the sovereignty of Sakhalin and the neighboring islands. Hence instead of continuing to develop Hakodate, the town strategically situated on the Tsugaru Strait, where the Commission for Colonization was based, the government decided to build its regional capital farther to the east. It chose a place called Sat poro pet—"large dry river" in the Ainu language—to the south of Otaru Bay, a harbor that always remains ice-free. By the end of the 19C, Sapporo had a population of 2,600, but within a century, it had grown to nearly 2 million. Today, although the fifth largest city in Japan is an aggressively modern metropolis, nature is everywhere in Sapporo, from the many gardens dotting the city to the winter snow that forces its inhabitants underground into huge malls.**

- **Population:** 1,925,504.
- **Michelin Map:** Principal Sights Map B1–Regional Map p423.
- **Location:** The main city of Hokkaido prefecture, Sapporo is 655mi/1,054km north of Tokyo. The streets are arranged on a grid pattern, around blocks of 328ft/100m by 328ft/100m, numbered according to the points of the compass, with the central point being the TV Tower *B2*. The address of the Botanical Gardens, for example—N3 W8—can be read as: three blocks to the north and eight blocks to the west of the TV Tower.
- **Kids:** Yuki Matsuri *(one week a year at the beginning of February)*; Dai-ichi Takimoto-kan at Noboribetsu.
- **Timing:** If time is limited, allow a day and a night in Sapporo, and a day for Noboribetsu and its surroundings.
- **Don't miss:** Sapporo's Yuki Matsuri in February is unforgettable, and should be followed by a "Genghis Khan" barbecue washed down with a Sapporo beer, or some *bata-kon* ramen; Noboribetsu *Onsen*.

## SIGHTS

Start your visit with the **TV Tower** *(295.3ft/90m) B2, 15min walk from JR Sapporo station*. Built in 1957 and modeled on the Eiffel Tower, there is a beautiful panoramic **view** of the city *(open 9am–10pm; ¥700)* from the top.

To the west is **Odori Park** *A–B2*, a green artery through the city, 344.5ft/105m wide by 0.9mi/1.5km long (*odori* means "large street"), originally intended as a firebreak between the municipal buildings and the residential areas to the south, which were prone to frequent fires. Today, the park is crowded in both summer and winter, and is famous for its fantastic **Yuki Matsuri**★★★.

This Snow Festival, at which gigantic ice sculptures are displayed, has been attracting hundreds of thousands of visitors every February *(see photo p428)* since the 1950s. Some of the sculptures can weigh more than 700 tons.

## NORTH OF ODORI PARK

*Near the corner of Tokei-dai-dori.*

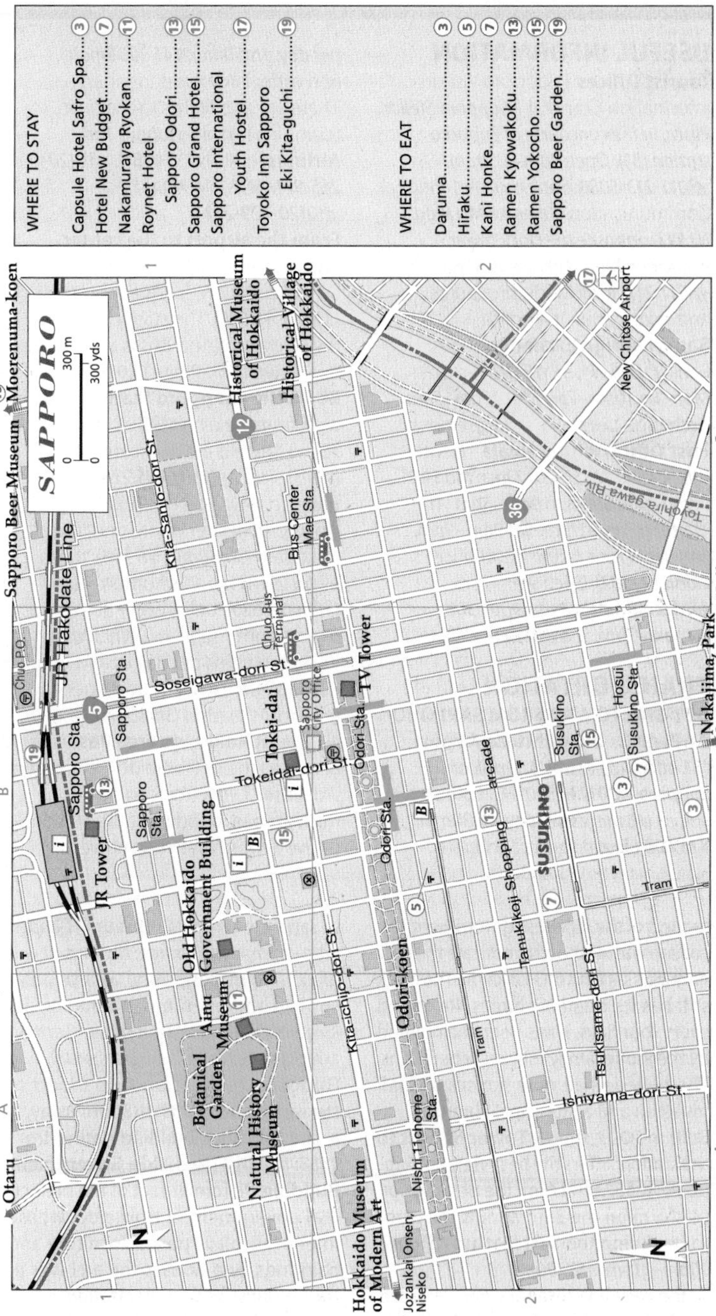




The clock tower **Tokei-dai** *B1* (*open daily 8.45am–5pm; closed Jun–Oct 4th Mon of the month, Nov–May every Mon; ¥200)* was erected in 1876 by Americans from Massachusetts as part of the drill hall of the former Sapporo Agricultural College. The first of its kind in Japan, run by three American teachers at the

## USEFUL INFORMATION

**Tourist Offices** – Sapporo Visitors Information Corner, ***1 F Sapporo Stellar Place, in the concourse of Sapporo station (B1). Open 9am–5.30pm.*** ***☏011-213-5088.*** Sapporo International Communication Plaza, ***3 F MN Bldg, N1 W3, opposite the clock tower (B1). Open Mon–Fri 9am–5.30pm.*** ***☏011-211-3678.*** Maps, brochures, and information in English.

**Bank/Foreign Exchange** – Hokkaido Bank, ***Odori W4, S1 W5*** *(B2)*. ***Open Mon–Fri 10am–7pm, Sat 10am–5pm.*** Exchange bureau in the basement.

**Post Office/Withdrawals** – Central Post Office, ***N6 E1*** *(B1)*. ***Open Mon–Fri 9am–8pm, Sat–Sun 9am–5pm.*** *ATM* ***Mon–Fri 7am–11pm, Sat 9am–9pm, Sun 9am–7pm.*** Odori Post Office, ***Odori W2 (B2). Open 9am–7pm.*** *ATM Mon–Fri 8.45am–9pm, Sat 8.45am–7pm, Sun 8.45am–5pm.*

## TRANSPORTATION

**GETTING TO AND FROM SAPPORO**

**BY PLANE** – **New Chitose Airport** *(C2 off map) – 23mi/37km SE of Sapporo,* *☏0123-23-0111*. Flights to Tokyo ***(46 flights per day, 1hr30min, ¥33,600 Single)***, Osaka ***(19 flights per day, 1hr50min, ¥41,300 Single)***, and other large cities in Japan. There are also flights to the main towns in Hokkaido ***(about 1hr)***.

**Airlines** – JAL, N2 W4 ***(B1). ☏0120-255-971***. ANA, N4 W4 ***(B1).*** *☏0120-029-222*.

**From the airport to the center** – The quickest route is by train to JR Sapporo station. Trains every 20min ***(35min, ¥1,040)***. The station is below the arrivals lounge. Buses are cheaper but slower ***(1hr20min, ¥1,000)***.

**BY TRAIN** – **Sapporo Station** – ***10min walk from the center (B1)***. To and from Tokyo, there is a daily ***Hokutosei*** (sleeper train) ***(16hr, ¥25,270)***. Many trains to towns on Hokkaido: 11 Hokuto trains per day to and from Hakodate ***(3hr30min, ¥8,590)***; trains every 20min to and from Otaru ***(30min, ¥620)***; trains every 30min to and from Asahikawa ***(1hr30min, ¥4,680)***; 6 trains per day to and from Kushiro ***(4hr, ¥9,120)***; 4 trains per day to and from Abashiri ***(5hr30min, ¥9,640)***.

The **JR Hokkaido Free Pass** gives access to the JR Hokkaido network for 7 days ***(¥23,400)***. You can book one from abroad, or buy it at the station or the airport when you arrive.

request of the Japanese government, the college was intended to educate the new migrants settling on Hokkaido. The clock still has its original chimes. Rewound every four days, it has been maintained by the Inoue family for two generations. The college hall now houses a small museum and a municipal library.

Built in 2003, the **JR Tower** *B1* next to the station, offers the best **views** of Sapporo. At 567.6ft/173m, the observation platform on the 38th floor is the place to be during the Yuki Matsuri *(open 10am–11pm; ¥700)*.

To the east of the station (*7min by bus*) is the **Sapporo Beer Museum** *C1 off map*, a red-brick building dominated by a tall chimney bearing the pole-star symbol. The former Sapporo brewery, the first in Japan and now a museum ***(open 9am–6pm; no charge; tastings at end of exhibition: costs vary)***, is a popular spot in the evenings, thanks to its large restaurant with a quasi-German atmosphere (*see Addresses p433*).

Opposite the station *(two blocks to the west)*, about 328yd/300m away, is a fine red-brick building dating from 1888: the **Old Hokkaido Government Building** *B1*, former seat of the prefectural government of Hokkaido, whose interior displays period furniture and paintings, and houses the archives of the Commission for Colonization.

*Continue W for about 547yd/500m.*

**BY BUS** – **Sapporo Station Bus Terminal** – *On the left as you come out of Sapporo station (B1).* **Chuo Bus Terminal**, *Odori E1 (B1).* Buses are often a cheaper and faster way of getting around Hokkaido than trains. 5 buses per day to and from Hakodate *(5hr, ¥4,680)*, 9 buses per day to and from Toyako Onsen *(2hr40min, ¥2,700)* and Abashiri *(6hr, ¥6,210)*, and 11 buses per day to Noboribetsu Onsen *(2hr30min, ¥1,900)*.

**GETTING AROUND SAPPORO**

**ON FOOT** – The downtown area is easily manageable on foot. If it's rainy or too cold, use the Pole Town underground mall between Odori and Susukino.

**BY SUBWAY** – There are three lines covering the city, the most useful being the Nanboku Line *(in green)*, which links Sapporo station with Susukino and Nakajima-koen. *Tickets start from ¥200 per journey.* A day pass costs ¥800 *(¥500 at weekends)* and a **subway + bus + tram pass** ¥1,000. The **Sapporo-Otaru Pass** *(¥1,500)*, on sale from the JR offices at the station, covers the subway and the JR Sapporo-Otaru Line.

**BY BUS** – From May to Oct, from Sapporo station, tourist buses make continuous circuits of the city, stopping at the principal sights *(one journey ¥200; day pass ¥750). Departures every 30min, 9am–5pm.* Chuo Bus, *℘011-231-0500.* The same company also runs day excursions to Niseko, Lake Shikotsu, Otaru, Furano, and Biei.

**CAR RENTAL** – Nippon Rent-A-Car, N6 W3, *north exit from the JR station, near the Crest Hotel (B1). ℘011-746-0919. 24hr.* Nissan Rent-A-Car, *1 F Asty 45 Bldg, N4 W5, opposite the Royal Century Hotel (B1). Open 8am–10pm. ℘011-231-4123.*

**BICYCLE RENTAL** – Rent-A-Cycle Sapporo, *105 Keihoku Village, N2 E2 (B1). Open 8.30am–5pm. ¥1,000 per day. ℘011-223-7662.*

**OTARU**

**BY TRAIN** – Station in the center of the town. To and from Sapporo, trains every 20min *(30min, ¥620)*.

**NOBORIBETSU**

**BY TRAIN** – Station 5mi/8km S of the center. To and from Sapporo, take the JR Chitose Line *(69.6mi/112km, 2hr15min, ¥2,100). About ¥1,600 for a taxi into the town.*

*Yuki Matsuri*

## Botanical Gardens★

北大植物園 *A1.*

*N3 W8, 547yd/500m SW of Sapporo station.* ◷*Open Apr 29–Nov 23 Tue–Sun 9am–4pm.* ◉*¥400.*

Completed in 1886, these Botanical Gardens cover 32 acres/13ha and were originally intended to help the migrant farmers understand their new homeland, with its harsh sub-Arctic temperatures. They include an **arboretum** (*elms, conifers, maples*), an **alpine garden**, a 13,993sq-ft/1,300sq-m greenhouse (*mainly orchids*), and an **ethnobotanical section listing** 180 species of plant used by the Ainu for food, medicine, clothes, and transportation. The **Ainu Museum**★, located just inside the entrance to the garden, has exhibits of clothes made from elm bark, women's sealskin dresses, and many ritual objects such as the skulls of bears and turtles.

A rare **13-min ethnographic film**★★★ made in 1935 shows the ritual slaughter of a bear in a ceremony known as the *iyomante*—the bear's spirit returns to the land of the gods, so that the deities who had temporarily appeared disguised as bears to answer the needs of men could again manifest themselves in this form that provided meat and fur.

The poisoned arrows used to kill the bear during this ceremony are soaked in *torikabuto* (a kind of aconite of the *Ranunculaceae* family)—a poison itself considered a deity, whose role is to persuade the bear to accept the invitation of the god of fire. Young bears were always spared because the gods residing in them are not yet able to escape by their own means. The **Natural History Museum**, about 109yd/100m inside the garden, contains displays of stuffed animals, including the unusual Japanese flying squirrel. *Continue W for about 547yd/500m.*

## Hokkaido Museum of Modern Art★ 北海道立近代美術館

*A2 off map.*

*N1 W17. Subway: Nishi-Juhachome (Tozai Line), exit 4, then 5min walk N.* ◷*Open Tue–Sun 9.30am–5pm (Jul–Sept Fri 7.30pm).* ◉*¥450.*

The collection, numbering around 4,300 items in its entirety, is displayed in rotation and is divided into three categories: Hokkaido artists from the Meiji period onward, modern and contemporary Japanese artists, and artists from around the world. This last section concentrates on paintings from the School of Paris, along with Art Nouveau and Art Deco, and includes Pascin, Kisling, Soutine, **Chagall**, Rouault, Foujita, **Tiffany**, Lalique, and **Gallé**.

The great Hokkaido female artist **Kataoka Tamako**, who was born in Sapporo in 1905 and died in 2008 at the age of 103, is also represented. She was an exponent of the technique known as *nihon-ga* (literally, "Japanese-style painting").

## SOUTH OF ODORI PARK

The nightlife district of **Susukino** *B2 (Subway: Susukino)* lies between blocks S3 and S7, and is full of the usual features of Japanese cities at night: karaoke clubs, pachinko parlors, hostess bars, and so on. By day, you can enjoy some fresh air in **Nakajima Park** *B2 off map (15min walk farther S, or Nakajima-koen subway station, after Susukino)*. It has a number of facilities, including a sports center, an astronomical observatory, a pond, and Japanese garden, a **tea house** (*dating from the 17C, commissioned by the tea master Kobori Enshu and brought here from Honshu*), the **Hokeikan** guesthouse (*where members of the Imperial Family have stayed*), and the **Sapporo Concert Hall (Kitara)**. The hall's innocuous exterior conceals a magnificent 2,008-seater, **arena-style auditorium**★★, much-admired for its acoustics, with a great organ built by French company Alfred Kern.

## AROUND THE CITY

### Historical Village of Hokkaido★ 北海道開拓の村

*C1 off map.*

*9.3mi/15km E of Sapporo. Nopporo Forest Park. From Sapporo station, train to Shin-Sapporo (20min), then bus (10min to Shinrin-Koen stop) or taxi (about ¥1,000).* ◷*Open May–Sept*

*Tue–Sun 9am–5pm; Oct–Apr Tue–Sun 9am–4.30pm. ¥830.*
Visitors can gain an impression of what life was like in the early days of the island's colonization in this open-air museum. It has around 60 meticulously reconstructed buildings representing the Meiji and Taisho eras, divided into four areas *(town, farm, fishing village, and mountain village)*. In summer, you can get around the museum's site *(133.4 acres/54ha)* in a horse-drawn cart, or in winter on a sleigh *(¥270)*.

### Historical Museum of Hokkaido★ 北海道開拓記念館

*C1 off map.*
*Nopporo Forest Park. 5min walk from the Historical Village. Open Tue–Sun 9.30am–4.30pm. ¥500. Audioguide in English ¥120.*
This huge museum is organized chronologically, covering everything from the morphogeographical beginnings of the island 2 million years ago to its colonization and the most recent economic developments. We learn, for example, how, in the 7C, the Satsumon culture laid the foundations for what would become the Ainu culture and how, from the end of the 12C, the first Japanese shogunate gradually began to encroach upon their daily lives.
At that time, the *wajin* (the name given to migrants from Honshu) were settling en masse in the southern part of Hokkaido *(called Ezochi until 1869)*, almost overwhelming the indigenous population, the Ezo, who rebelled for the first time in the middle of the 15C. The Meiji period, the high point of the island's colonization, is brought to life with archive material and documents.

### Moerenuma Park★

モエレ沼公園 *C1 off map.*
*About 6.2mi/10km NE of Sapporo. Subway: Kanjodori-higashi (Toho Line), then bus no. 69 or 79 to Moere-Koen Higashiguchi, the east entrance to the park (25min). Open 7am–10pm. No charge.*
Designed by the Japanese-American sculptor **Isamu Noguchi** (1904–88), this 467-acre/189ha park is almost a sculpture in its own right. It opened in 2005, but was completed Noguchi's death and was conceived as part of a vast project to surround the urban area of Sapporo with a green belt, and was built on a site originally earmarked for an immense waste treatment plant. This ground, "plowed into a landscape of dreams," in the sculptor's own words, has seen the flowering of some often-spectacular geometric constructions, such as the Tetra Mound, the Play Mountain, and Mount Moere, which looks rather like a pre-Colombian monument redrawn by Mondrian.

## EXCURSIONS

*25mi/40km NW of Sapporo.*
*See map p421.*

### OTARU 小樽

This city *(population 140,000)* also functions as Sapporo's port and has the advantage of being ice-free throughout the year. Otaru built its fortune on two different kinds of business: herrings and banking. During the Meiji era, to capitalize on the island's economic development, it was chosen by the Bank of Japan as the location for its Hokkaido branch. Its importance increased after Japan's adoption of the gold standard, when it was entrusted with buying the gold mined on Hokkaido.
The gold bolstered the central bank's reserves, thus ensuring the viability of the yen and guaranteeing its international credibility. Otaru thus became the Wall Street of northern Japan.

### The town

On leaving the station, take the Chuo bus to Mount Tengu *(12min, ¥210)*, and the foot of the **Otaru Tenguyama Ropeway**. The cable car *(open 9.30am–9pm, summer10pm; ¥1,000 round trip; winter: 9am–9pm, summer: 9.30am–9pm, 10pm in Aug)* rises to an altitude of 889ft/271m in a few minutes. A small museum devoted to skiing *(no charge)* is a reminder that Otaru is popular as a winter sports resort. The slopes of Mount Tengu were chosen to host some

### The Ainu, recognition at last

The Ainu settled in the northern parts of Japan *(Tohoku, Hokkaido)* before the Jomon era (10,000–300 BC), and also on Sakhalin and the Kuril Islands. The colonization of Hokkaido, launched by the Meiji government in 1869, sealed the fate of these hunter-gatherers with their animistic beliefs. Discriminated against and stigmatized for their hirsuteness, the Ainu were forced to become Japanese in order to survive, losing their language, culture, and land in the process. Although their claims finally drove the Japanese Parliament to pass a law in 1997 for the promotion of Ainu culture, it was not until June 6, 2008 that the Japanese Parliament finally unanimously recognized them as an indigenous group "with its own language, religion, and culture."

of the events in the Sapporo Winter Olympics in 1972. Another room has a display of around 700 masks of **Hananade Tengu**—a Japanese folk deity with a red face and very long nose.
From the **observatory**★, there is a magnificent **view** of the town and its harbor.

*From the station, walk down the main street (Chuo-dori), then turn right when you reach the Temiya Line railway track. 8min walk.*

**Otaru City Art Museum** *(1-9-5 Ironai; open Tue–Sun 9.30am–5pm; ¥300)*
Works by many of the artists connected with the town, such as Nakamura Zensaku (1901–83), a native of Otaru, whose Hokkaido landscapes can also be seen in many of Japan's major museums.
Nearby is the **Otaru City Museum of Literature** *(open Tue–Sun 9.30am–5pm; ¥300)*.
Otaru's two most important literary figures are **Ito Sei** (1905–69), famous in Japan for translating *Lady Chatterley's Lover* and **Kobayashi Takiji** (1903–33), who wrote about the working classes and whose most important book, *Kanikosen (The Factory Ship)*, is still relevant today. The story of sailors on a fishing boat who rebel against their working conditions actually became a bestseller among Japanese youth faced with increasingly uncertain employment prospects in 2008.
Walk back toward the central avenue until you come to **Unga Plaza,** where you will find a selection of local products—cookies, sake, etc.—in the oldest storehouse in Hokkaido *(open 9am–6pm, summer 9pm)*, renovated in the Taisho style.
The nearby **Otaru Museum** *(open 9.30am–5pm; ¥300)* showcases the history of the city, especially through its herring industry (50 years ago, it produced close to 1,000 tons compared with one-third of that today). Then walk along the magnificent **Otaru Canal**, which is always very lively, but especially after nightfall. End your tour of Otaru with a visit to the glassblowers' district to the east of **Sakaimachi-dori**. You will find the **Kitaichi Glass Factory** and its **Museum of Venetian Art** *(open 9am–6pm; ¥700)*.
This local craft has its origins in the old practice of fishing by lamplight, which is how the Otaru fishermen used to catch anchovies.

*From Otaru, return to Sapporo, then take the JR Chitose Line to Chitose (25.5mi/41km, 40min, ¥810).*

## SHIKOTSU-TOYA NATIONAL PARK★
支笏洞爺国立公園

Founded in 1949, this park encompasses many important sites, including **Lake Shikotsu**, **Noboribetsu**, **Lake Toya**, and the seething **Usu volcano** (*see map p423*).

**Lake Shikotsu★** 支笏湖
*From JR Chitose station, take the south exit. From stop no. 3, bus every hour 8.50am–4.50pm (allow 45min, ¥900).*

Riding around the Lake Toya, Shikotsu-Toya National Park

©Hokkaido Tourism Organization/JNTO

*You can also rent a bicycle (open 9am–5pm, ¥300 per day) and reach the lake along the cycle trail (allow 2hr). Information from the Tourist Office at Chitose station, 2 F Pewre Chitose. 012-27-7331.*

Shikotsu, *("large pool" in Ainu)*, is a crater-lake formed 40,000 years ago by the collapse of the upper part of the cone after a volcanic eruption. What makes it unusual is that the lake never freezes, even in winter, thanks to the fact that its waters reach a depth of 1,191ft/363m in places, giving the lake a constant temperature of 38.5°F/3.6°C.

The **Visitor Center** *(open 9am–5.30pm, winter 4.30pm)* provides maps and information on hiking trails around the lake. With so many mountains to climb, enthusiasts could easily stay for a week. Mount Eniwa *(4,330.7ft/1,320m)*, for example, was used for downhill events at the Sapporo Winter Olympics in 1972. There are also many waterfalls and hot springs, and, at 1,873.4ft/571m above sea level, the emerald-green Lake Okotanpe. Sticking to the simplest route, allow around two hours to hike around the lake, making sure you visit the famous moss cave mentioned in all the leaflets.

*From Chitose, take the Limited Express Suzuran to Noboribetsu Onsen (43.5mi/70km, 45min, ¥3,040).*

## Noboribetsu Onsen★
登別温泉

*5mi/8km N of JR Noboribetsu station. About ¥1,500 for a taxi.*

Lying at the foot of Hiyoriyama, 656.2ft/200m above sea level, this hot-spring resort is one of the most famous on Hokkaido. Noboribetsu, which comes from *Nupurupetsu*"dark, cloudy river" in Ainujustifies its name with the 10,000 tons of muddy, sulfurous water welling up every day from this *jigoku-dani* ("hell valley"), stoked by a seething volcano. The quality and great mineral variety of these thermal waters are what gives this resort its current reputation. First developed in the Taisho era (1912–26), it takes pride in now having the most impressive *onsen* in Japan.

**The *onsen*** – Most Japanese tourists paddle about in the *onsen* of their hotels, but for an entrance fee, you can use some of them without being a resident. The Tourist Office *(60 Noboribetsu Onsen-cho; open 10am–4pm)*, located midway along the main thoroughfare of this little resort, will give you a list. The most spectacular—and the most expensive—is **Dai-ichi Takimoto-kan**★, located at the far end of the resort *(open 9am–5pm)*. For ¥2,000, you will gain entrance to a large *onsen* complex *(53,820sq ft/5,000sq m)* divided into 30 pools composed, unusually, of seven waters with different mineral properties

*(sodium bicarbonate, naturally hydrated sodium sulfate, ferrous sulfate, etc.).*
To fully appreciate the waters that well up from the ground here at temperatures ranging from 122°F/50°C to 194°F/90°C, follow one of the paths that lead to an observation platform. After a walk of less than 15 minutes from the Tourist Office you will be able to look down on the whole spectacular **Hell Valley**.
In another 20 minutes you will arrive at the hot-water lake **Oyu numa**, but you would be advised to skip a visit to the bear parks, where the conditions in which they are kept are upsetting and unworthy of the Ainu culture.

*From Noboribetsu station, take the JR Muroran Line to Shiraoi (11.8mi/19km, 20min, ¥350).*

**Shiraoi Ainu Museum★**
アイヌ民族博物館
*2-3-4 Wakasusa-cho, Shiraio-gun. Open 8.45am–5pm. ¥750. 15min walk from the station. Traditional dancing every hour 9.15am–4.15pm. Lunch available (Ainu menu ¥1,000). www.ainu-museum.or.jp/english/english.*
This reconstruction of an Ainu village, on the shores of Lake Poroto, is owned, promoted, and managed by the Ainu, who wish to present their culture in the best light. The curator, Kitahara Jirotahimself an Ainuis one of the leading experts on Ainu culture. The village comprises a museum, botanical garden, cowshed, and five *cises*traditional houses in which women go about their everyday activities. Inside the houses there are always two fires: one to warm the house and to cook and dry fish, and another used for rituals, always positioned close to a window. *Performances of singing and dancing are given regularly.*

*From Noboribetsu, take the JR Muroran Line to Toya station, via Higashi Muroran (33mi/53km, 1hr10min, ¥1,040).*

**Lake Toya★** 洞爺湖
This crater-lake, covering a surface area of 27sq mi/70sq km, is at an altitude of 272.3ft/83m. The Usu volcano lies on its southern rim. It erupts not just from the top, but also through vents at its base, as it did in 2000.
This unpredictability has resulted in a very uneven landscape with a constantly seething layer of magma not far below the surface. The **Volcano Science Museum★** *(15min by bus from Toya station, then 2min walk from the Lake Toya bus terminal)* explains about Usu, one of the most active volcanoes in Japan *(open 9am–5pm; ¥600).*
A number of excursions are available, depending on the volcano's mood. The most popular involves taking the cable car *(open May–mid-Oct 8.15am–5.30pm, mid-Nov–mid-Mar 9am–4pm, rest of the year times vary; ¥1,450)* from Sanroku station *(15min from the bus terminal by Donan Bus)* to Showa Shinzan.

## ADDRESSES

### STAY

**SAPPORO**

**Capsule Hotel Safro Spa**
スパ・サフロ *S6 W5 (B2). 011-531-2233 (reception for men) or 011-531-2424 (reception for women). www.safro.org. 84 capsules, men and women separated.* Capsule hotel in the heart of the nightlife district. *Access to an excellent spa in the same building.*

**Hotel New Budget**
ホテルニューバジェット札幌
*S3 W6 (B2). 011-261-4953. www.new.budget.com. 161 rooms.* Unbeatable prices at this *business hotel* in Susukino. Service is cut to the minimum: almost everything can be bought from vending machines. *Rather cramped rooms.*

**Sapporo International Youth Hostel**
札幌国際ユースホステル *6-5-35 Toyohira-rokujo (C2 off map). Subway: Gakuenmae (Toho Line), exit 2. 011-825-3120. www.youthhostel.or.jp/kokusai. 35 rooms/dorms.* 10min by subway from the downtown area; excellent for a limited budget. Ultra-clean dormitories *(4 beds)* and rooms. Unmarried couples cannot share private rooms. *O-furo* or private showers upstairs; coin laundry.

**Nakamuraya Ryokan**
中村屋旅館 *N3 W7 (A1). 011-241-2111. www.nakamuraya.com. 25 rooms.* Comfort and an authentically Japanese

atmosphere at this ryokan opposite the entrance to the Botanical Gardens.

**Roynet Hotel Sapporo Odori ロイネットホテル札幌大通** *S2 W4 (B2). 011-208-0055. www.roynet.co.jp. 200 rooms.* Comfortable Western rooms at reasonable prices.

**Toyoko Inn Sapporo Eki Kita-guchi 東横イン札幌駅北口** *N6 W1 (B1). 011-728-1045. www.toyoko-inn.com. 357 rooms.* Large hotel near the station *(exit 16).* Well-equipped rooms with Internet access.

**Sapporo Grand Hotel 札幌グランドホテル** *N1 W4 (B1). 011-261-3311. www.grand1934.com. 562 rooms.* The oldest hotel in Hokkaido (1934) impresses with its size *(3 buildings)*, many restaurants, and plentiful staff. *Spacious rooms.*

**NOBORIBETSU ONSEN**

**Kashoutei Hanaya 花鐘亭はなや** *134 Noboribetsu-onsen. 0143-84-2521. www.kashouteihanaya.co.jp. 16 rooms. Restaurant.* Close to Noboribetsu *onsen*, this ryokan is one of the town's most enchanting, with a fine *rotenburo; ¥8,550 per person, ¥12,750 half-board.*

## EAT

**SAPPORO**

Apart from seafood, beer, and ramen (Chinese noodles) cooked with butter and corn, Sapporo is famous for its "Genghis Khan," a delicious mutton and vegetable barbecue. Note very few restaurants open in the evening as most visitors dine in their hotels.

**Ramen Kyowakoku 札幌ラーメン共和国** *10 F Esta Bldg, N5 W2 (B1). 011-209-5031. Open 11am–10pm.* On the top floor of the shopping mall, eight stands serving noodles from Hokkaido's different regions. Friendly retro ambience, with red lanterns and old posters.

**Ramen Yokocho 元祖ラーメン横丁** *S5 W3 (B2). Open 11am–2pm.* A tiny, but famous street in Susukino, lined with noodle houses. .

**Daruma だるま本店** *S5 W4 (B2) 011-552-6013. Open 5pm–3am (Fri–Sat, 5am, Sun 1am).* Unpretentious restaurant on a narrow street, run by three lively ladies. It's hard to find: look for the sign showing a bald, bearded Genghis Khan. Excellent "Genghis Khan" barbecue.

**Hiraku 開（ひらく）** *2 F President Matsui Bldg, S1 W5 (B2). 011-241-6166. Open Mon–Sat 5–11pm.* Restaurant specializing in oysters (hot or cold), *soba noodles*, sushi, and seasonal dishes. Try the oyster stew.

**Sapporo Beer Garden サッポロビール園** *N7 E9 (C1) 0120-150-550. Open 11am–10pm.* This restaurant occupies the former Sapporo brewery. A giant beer vat sets the tone; visitors come here to feast on "Genghis Khan" barbecue and beer, and Viking sushi and crab menus.

**Sushizen すし善・円山店** *N1 W27 (A2 off map). 0111-644-0071. Open Tue–Sun 11am–2pm, 6–10pm.* This restaurant has been in business for nearly 40 years. The lunch menu, including raw fish dishes, is excellent. *Pricier and more formal in the evenings.*

**Kani Honke かに本家札幌駅前本店** *N3 W2 (B2). 011-551-0018. Open 11.30am–11pm.* Part of a restaurant chain specializing in Hokkaido crab, with branches all over Japan. Try a delicious *kaiseki* meal of royal crab, snow crab, or spider crab taken straight from the tank.

**OTARU**

**Masazushi 政寿司本店** *1-1-1 Hanazono, Sushiya-dori. 013-4-23-0011. Open Wed–Mon, 11am–10pm.* Otaru's great sushi restaurant. People even come from Sapporo to try its famous snow crab. *Unmissable.*

## NIGHTLIFE

**Discotheques – Booty ブーティ** *S7 W4 (B2). 011-521-2336. Open Fri & Sat only, 9pm–4am. No charge. Drinks about ¥500.* The only club in Japan owned by a Frenchman, Sébastien Pons, who doubles as a DJ. The music is funk, hip-hop, R & B, rap, and reggae. Relax in the lounge bar on the first floor. *Sapporo's trendiest club.*

**Bars – Hallstairs ホールステアーズ** – *Open 11pm–3am.* A basement bar where the decor is black and the atmosphere "alternative." Relaxing atmosphere, with rock, soul, and jazz.

**Bar Habana ハバナ** – *Open 6pm–3am.* Colorful bar upstairs in the Tanuki-koji mall, where you can sip Mojitos and Cuba Libres while salsa, meringue, and bachata play.

**Jersey Bar ジャージーバー** – *Open 6pm–1am. 0111-242-4335.* Irish pub much-loved by both expatriates and locals.

**Rad Brothers ラッドブラザーズ** – *Open 6pm–6am.* Very lively. A young crowd, and good music.

# Daisetsu-zan National Park ★★
# 大雪山国立公園

**In the heart of Hokkaido, Daisetsu-zan is the largest National Park in Japan. Its 888sq mi/2,300sq km encompass a number of volcanic peaks, such as Mount Tomuraushi, Mount Tokachi, and Mount Asahi, which reaches an altitude of 7,513ft/2,290m. The "Roof of Hokkaido" is known as Kamui Mintara ("playing field of the gods") by the Ainu. Gorges, cliffs, waterfalls, lakes, and hot springs wreathed in steam draw the crowds, both in summer and winter, to these luxuriant foothills in one of the most impressive mountain ranges in Japan.**

- **Population:** Asahikawa 348,153.
- **Michelin Map:** Principal Sights Map C1 – Regional Map p423.
- **Location:** Asahikawa is 87mi/140km east of Sapporo.
- **Kids:** A walk on Mount Asahi, the cable car to Kuro-dake, and a night at the youth hostel to take advantage of its magnificent *rotenburo*.
- **Timing:** You will need at least one day to take advantage of the hiking opportunities afforded by Sounkyo and Mount Kuro. Spend the night in the park itself so that you can soak lazily in an *onsen* as evening falls.
- **Don't miss:** Sounkyo Gorge; a walk on Mount Asahi.

## SIGHTS

### ASAHIKAWA 旭川

*There is a well-stocked Tourist Information Center in the right wing of the station on the way out (open 9am–5.30pm). English spoken.*

The second largest city on Hokkaido lies at the confluence of the rivers flowing down from the Daisetsu-zan massif. Visitors to the National Park can rent their winter sports equipment here. Asahikawa's claim to fame is as the home town of writer Inoue Yasushi (1907–91), whose novel *The Hunting Gun* has been translated into many languages. A small museum stands on the site of his birthplace, the **Inoue Yasushi Memorial Hall** *(Shunko 5jo-chome; open Tue–Sun 9am–5pm; ¥200)*. It is located to the northeast of the station, on the opposite side of the Ishikari River, which can be reached on foot along the town's main thoroughfare, Heiwa-dori. On the west side of the river, near the Asahi Bridge, is the **Kawamura Kaneto Ainu Memorial Hall** *(open summer 8am–6pm, winter 9am–5pm; ¥500)*, devoted to the culture of the Ainu.

*Sounkyo, take bus no. 3 outside the station (1hr50min, ¥1,950) or a train (JR Sekihoku Line) to Kamikawa station (31mi/50km, 1hr10min, ¥1,040). From Kamikawa, take the Dohoku Bus (3min walk from the station) to Sounkyo terminal (30min, ¥800).*

### SOUNKYO★ 層雲峡

Regarded as the northern gateway to Daisetsu-zan National Park, this small hot-spring resort sits at an altitude of 2,198ft/670m at the foot of Kuro-dake, near the area's most beautiful waterfalls. You can relax in one of the resort's many *onsen* or in the **Kuro-dake no yu** public bath *(open 10am–9pm; ¥600)* in the

## TRANSPORTATION

**BY TRAIN – From Sapporo –** Take the Limited Express Super Kamui to **Asahikawa** *(87mi/140km, 1hr20min, ¥4,880).*

heart of the village. The bus terminal, post office, and Tourist Information Center *(open 11.30am–5pm)* are close by, on the opposite bank of the river.

### Kuro-dake★ 黒岳

*Allow half a day. Take good shoes and warm clothes.*

Take the cable car *(open 8am–4.30pm, summer 6am–7pm, with variations by month; ¥1,850 round trip)* to Kuro-dake station *(altitude 4,265ft/1,300m)*, which has a fine observation point on its roof *(no charge)*. Food and equipment for winter hiking are available. A chairlift 218.7yd/200m from the cable car exit takes 15 minutes *(schedule varies by season; ¥600 round trip)* to reach the seventh station of Mount Kuro *(altitude 4,987ft/1,520m)*. Reckon on an hour's walk, then follow the steep trail that leads to the summit *(6,509ft/1,984m); (about 1hr30min)*. The alpine vegetation is especially colorful in the Fall. There is a beautiful **panoramic view**★★ from the summit—you can see the peaks of Keigetsu-dake *(6,358ft/1,938m)*, Ryoun-dake *(6,972ft/2,125 m)*, and Hokuchin-dake *(7,362ft/2,244m)*.

### Sounkyo Gorge★★ 層雲峡

*15.5mi/25km downhill from the center of Sounkyo. Allow 40min walk to the most spectacular waterfalls, or 15min by bike. Bicycle rental at the Northern Lodge Hotel, about 55yd/50m above the public baths (¥1,000 per day).*

Winding for nearly 15mi/24km along the magnificent Daisetsu-zan mountain range, the Soun gorge *(kyo)* is a spectacular sight, especially the **Ryusei and Ginga waterfalls**★★ *(295.3ft/90m and 393.7ft/120m high respectively)*, which hurtle down the rocky cliffs

For a view of both falls, take a trail that starts at the rear of the car park and climbs through the forest to emerge after a walk of 15 minutes at a wonderful **panorama**★.

*From Asahikawa station, take bus no. 4 to Asahidake Onsen. Direct buses leave at 9.10am, 12.40am, and 3.30pm between Jun 15 and Oct 15, and at 9.10am or 2.10pm between Oct 16 and Mar 31 (1hr10min, ¥1,320).*

### Asahi-dake★★ 旭岳

A young volcano, Asahi-dake is the highest peak in the Daisetsu mountain range, which stretches for over 31mi/50km, and includes a number of peaks above 6,562ft/2,000m. The rocky faces of Mount Asahi, often wreathed in cloud, are steep, but the lovely Sugatami plateau nearby is more accessible. Toward the end of the day, head for the small resort of Asahidake Onsen. It has many hot springs, the most attractive of which are in the open air in an enchanting alpine setting.

### Sugatami Region★★ 姿見

*The easiest way to reach the plateau (altitude 5,249.3ft/1,600m) is by cable car (open summer 9am–4pm, 6am–5.30/6.30pm, ¥1,800 round trip; ¥2,800 in summer, 10min). The alternative is a fairly steep and difficult hike (2hr).*

Various walks are possible from the point where the cable car drops you off, either accompanied with a guide *(English-speaking guide available)* or without. There are a number of observation points along the walking trails where you can see plants *(alpines such as chinguruma and rhododendron)* and animals *(brown bear, red squirrel, rabbit, pika)*, and bubbling pools—a reminder, as are the wisps of smoke that rise up from the ground here and there, that the volcano is still very active. The peak can be reached in about two hours, depending on the weather.

## ADDRESSES

### STAY

**SOUNKYO**

**Sounkyo Youth Hostel**
層雲峡ユースホステル *Sounkyo Onsen, Kamikawa-cho. 5min walk from cable car. 01658-5-3418. www.youthhostel.or.jp/sounkyo. Open May–late Oct by season 12*

*rooms/dorms.* Lovely building. Some English spoken—unusual for Sounkyo.

**ASAHIDAKE *ONSEN***

**Shirakabo-so Youth Hostel**
大雪山白樺荘ユースホステル
*Daisetsuzan Shirakabaso in Asahidake Onsen, Higasikawa-town. 0166-97-2246. http://park19.wakwak.com/~shirakaba/english.html. 20 rooms/dorms. ¥760. Lodging with half-board.* Our favorite place to stay in this resort. *English spoken.*

**EAT**

**Yumoto Ginsenkaku Hotel**
湯元銀泉閣 *Sounkyo Kouenmachi. 011-209-5031. Open 11am–10pm.* One of the few restaurants open all year, the menu has some pleasant surprises.

# Shiretoko National Park ★★★ 知床国立公園

- **Population:** Abashiri: 40,507.
- **Michelin Map:** Principal Sights Map C1 – Regional Map p423.
- **Location:** The peninsula lies in the northeast of Hokkaido. Sapporo to Abashiri: 220.6mi/355km; Abashiri to Utoro: 47.8mi/77km; Utoro to Rausu: 18.6mi/30km.
- **Kids:** A boat trip beside the cliffs.
- **Timing:** Allow at least three days.
- **Don't miss:** The five lakes trail *(Shiretoko Goko)*; Kamuiwakka Falls.

**The Shiretoko National Park (*shiretoko* means "the end of the earth" in the Ainu language) covers the northern half of this 40.3mi/65km-long peninsula shaped like a finger pointing toward the Sea of Okhotsk. Founded in 1964, the park has a surface area of 149sq mi/386sq km. Still virtually unspoilt, at its center is a volcanic ridge culminating in Mount Rausu *(5,449.5ft/1,661m)*, with, to the north, the slightly lower peaks of Mount Lo *(5,128ft/1,563m)* and Mount Shiretoko *(4,114ft/1,254m)*. Covered in coniferous forests, their slopes end in sheer cliffs dropping down to the sea, which is sometimes covered with ice. Brown bears wander in the park, which has been attracting increasing numbers of tourists, mostly Japanese, especially since 2005 when Shiretoko was designated a UNESCO World Heritage Site because of the interaction between its marine and terrestial ecosystems.**

## SIGHTS

### ABASHIRI 網走

*Allow half a day.*

Situated 230.5mi/371km to the east of Sapporo, the climate of this port town *(population 40,000)* is harsh and its landscape inhospitable. As the fresh water of the Armour River flows into the Sea of Okhotsk, the northernmost of Japan's seas, diluting its salinity, ice forms more easily.

As a consequence, the sea is blocked by ice from January to April. It perhaps comes as no surprise to learn that there is a prison here—where political prisoners were sent during the Meiji era. Abashiri is the starting point for tourists exploring the lagoon before rushing on to Shiretoko National Park.

#### Abashiri Prison Museum★
博物館網走監獄

*15min S of the station by bus no 2. Open 8am–6pm. ¥1,050.*

## TRANSPORTATION

**BY PLANE – Memanbetsu Airport –** ✆0152-74-3115. Planes from Sapporo *(5 flights per day, 45min, ¥21,400)*, Tokyo *(5 flights per day, 1hr40min, ¥41,200)*, and Osaka *(2 flights per day, 2hr10min, ¥48,400)*. The Abashiri bus connects the airport with Abashiri *(30min, ¥880)* and Utoro *(depending on season, 2hr30min, ¥3,000)*.
**BY TRAIN – From Sapporo –** 4 Okhotsk Limited Express trains per day to Abashiri *(5hr30min, ¥9,640)*, then 9 trains per day to Shari *(40min, ¥810)*, the station closest to Shiretoko National Park (25mi/40km).
**BY BUS – From Sapporo –** 9 buses per day to Abashiri *(6hr, ¥6,210)*. From there, you can get a bus to Utoro *(May–Oct 4 per day, 1hr30min, ¥2,300)*, but buses to Otori are more frequent from Shari *(8 per day in summer, 5 per day in winter; 50min, ¥1,490)*.

**From Utoro** – Buses *(7 per day in summer, 4 per day in winter, 30min)* serve Shiretoko Nature Center, Iwaobetsu, and the five lakes *(Shiretoko Goko)*. From Jun 15 to Oct 15, 1 bus per day links Utoro with Rausu via the Shiretoko Pass *(1hr, ¥1,310)*. From mid-Jul to mid-Sept, the shuttle bus linking Shiretoko Nature Center with Kamuiwakka Falls leaves every 20min *(50min, ¥1,180)*.
**BY CAR – Car Rental – At the airport or outside Abashiri station**: Nippon Rent-A-Car ✆0152-74-4177, Nissan Rent-A-Car ✆0152-74-3785. There is another branch of Nippon Rent-A-Car at Shari station ✆0152-23-1090.

The Japanese Alcatraz was for criminals, but those who opposed or rejected the political reforms imposed by the Meiji Emperor were also sent here.
What made conditions for the prisoners all the more unbearable was that the jail was unheated. The museum is housed in the old prison buildings. The suffering of their daily life is illustrated with waxwork figures. The prison was moved to a new location and building in 1984.

### Okhotsk Ryuhyo Museum★
オホーツク流氷館
*5min walk from the Abashiri Prison Museum. Open 8am–6pm. ¥520.*
To get an idea of what the conditions are like in winter in this part of Japan, the visitor puts on a woollen coat similar to those worn by the Ainu, and enters a room where the temperature does not exceed –4F. The experience continues with a look at what are known here as "sea angels" or *Clione limacina*.
These small, translucent, orange mollusks share with the phytoplankton living beneath the ice floes the distinction of being the first link in the food chain.

### Hokkaido Museum of Northern Peoples★
北海道立北方民族博物館
*5min walk from Okhotsk Ryuhyo Museum. Open Tue–Sun 9.30am–4.30pm. ¥450.*
This museum demonstrates how the northern peoples classified as "Arctic," whether hailing from Siberia, northern Europe, or North America, were able to develop ways of life adapted to extreme conditions (a harsh climate, sparse vegetation, the Polar night, etc.). Among these, of course are, the Ainu. The striking thing that emerges from this fine ethnographic collection is how much the cultures of such very different people have in common.

## SHIRETOKO NATIONAL PARK★★ 知床国立公園
*Allow at least 2 days.*
*This park, probably the wildest on Hokkaido, comes with a number of warnings. Always make your presence known, such as by wearing a small bell around your neck. Brown bears can be dangerous, particularly if surprised and especially females with their young. Be particularly cautious in the Fall when they are more active. You are also*

Kamuiwakka-no-taki

©JTB/Photoshot

*advised not to enter the park in the early morning or at dusk, and not to go alone. It is advisable to hire a Japanese guide, especially if you are planning a long excursion, such as to Cape Shiretoko.*

On your right *(4.3mi/7km before Utoro)*, you will see the spectacular 262.5ft/80m-high **Oshinkoshin no taki**★, a waterfall considered one of the hundred most beautiful in Japan. From the little port of Utoro, huddled at the foot of this enormous rock, a coast road follows the western side of the park until a left fork leads to Shiretoko Nature Center, Shiretoko Goko *(the five lakes)*, and Kamuiwakka Falls.

## Shiretoko Nature Center

知床自然センター

*3.1mi/5km from Utoro. Open 8am–5.40pm (summer); 9am–4pm (winter). No charge.*

Unfortunately, there is little information in English available on the local flora and fauna in this center. You will have to be content with the splendid **aerial views** of the peninsula in the documentary film shown every hour *(¥500)*. Rausu Visitor Center *(open 9am–5pm)*, on the other side of the park, also has little information in English. Just behind the center, a circular trail leads to **Furepe no taki**★, a **waterfall** that gushes down the cliff and plunges into the Sea of Okhotsk.

## Shiretoko Goko★★ 知床五湖

*9.3mi/15km from Utoro. Open 7.30am–6pm.*

A 1.9mi/3km hiking trail *(about 1hr walk)* will take you around the five lakes, along fragrant paths and buttressed footbridges over swamps. When you look up, startled by the sound of a deer or a fox emerging from a bamboo grove, the leaves of the maples, flaming red in the Fall, will enchant you.

## Kamuiwakka-no-taki★★

カムイワッカ湯の滝

*6.2mi/10km from Shiretoko Goko along a dirt track. Barred to cars from Jul 15 to Sept 15, when you will have to take the shuttle bus from Utoro (see Address Book p434). From the bus stop, about 30min walk.*

This hot-spring area is dominated by a mass of hot water cascading from pool to pool, much to the delight of the Japanese. Don't forget a swimming costume and non-slip shoes, necessary to negotiate the series of smaller falls in order to get to this waterfall.

## East of Utoro ウトロ

*After the fork, Route 334 crosses the mountainous ridge of the peninsula and then descends to Rausu, a small port on the west coast. Note there is no access to Shiretoko Pass (2,493.4ft/760m) in winter, and sometimes even up until mid-June because of the snow.*

Climbing **Rausu-dake** *(5,449.5ft/1,661m)* is only for experienced hikers. For a less testing climb, take the trail from Utoro. It is not signposted but is easy to spot and begins behind Chinohate Hotel in Iwaobetsu (*open Jun–Oct only, about 8hr round trip*). Walking back down to Rausu is not advisable (*5hr walk*) because of snow patches and the risk of getting lost; it's better to take the bus back to JR Shiretoko Shari Station.

## ADDRESSES

### STAY

**ABASHIRI**

**Business Ryokan Miyuki** ビジネス旅館みゆき *S4 W4. 0152-43-4425. 13 rooms.* On the main street, 10min walk from the station; small family-run ryokan. Basic, but acceptable. *O-furo.*

**Hotel Shimbashi** ホテルしんばし *1-2-12 Shinmachi. 0152-43-4307. 42 rooms.* Decent hotel, not especially attractive but conveniently located opposite the station.

**Abashiri Central Hotel** 網走セントラルホテル *S2 W3. 0152-44-5151. www.abashirirooms.com.96 rooms.* A stylish and very comfortable hotel in the middle of town.

**UTORO**

**Iwaobetsu Youth Hostel** 知床岩尾別ユースホステル *5mi/8km from Utoro, toward Shiretoko Goko. 0152-24-2311. iwaobetsu@sirius.ocn.ne.jp. 10 dormitories (8 beds).* Hostel in the middle of the countyside; a useful base for hikers who want to climb Rausu-dake. It also organizes sea-kayaking excursions. *Spartan dormitories and meals.*

**Shiretoko Campsite** 国設知床野営場 *On the hill, behind the Hotel Prince. 0152-24-2722. Closed Oct 1–Jun 19.* For properly equipped campers, a well-kept campsite amid the trees, with toilets and sinks. No showers, but you can wash in the adjoining Yuhidai no yu Onsen *(¥400).*

**Guesthouse Lantan** ゲストハウス・ランタン *At the entrance to the village, on the left. 0152-24-2654. 12 rooms.* Easy to spot because of the surfboards at the entrance. Friendly wooden guesthouse with pleasant Japanese rooms (and a light-filled dining room). *O-furo.*

**Hotel Kifu Club** ホテル季風クラブ知床 *At the exit from the village, on the right. 0152-24-3541. 15 rooms.* Lovely wooden house with large picture windows and a chimney. Spacious rooms with **views** of the sea, fine cuisine, a vast *o-furo*, and two *rotenburo. The owner can arrange walks to see the bears and deer.*

**Iruka Hotel** いるかホテル *At the entrance to the village, just after the large rock on the left. 0152-24-2888. www.ikura-hotel.com. 13 rooms.* Cozy hotel with pretty blue decor and clean, small rooms (both Japanese and Western), a *rotenburo,* and a pleasant terrace facing the sea. *The owner arranges excursions to see the bears and dolphins, as well as ice diving.*

**RAUSU**

**Hotel Sakaeya** ホテル栄屋 *In the center, near the harbor. 0153-87-2171. 13 rooms (from ¥6,300/person).* Hotel with comfortable rooms at reasonable prices.

### EAT

**ABASHIRI**

**Kiyomasa** 鮨 *S3 W2. 0152-61-0003. Open Wed–Mon, 5pm–midnight.* Sushi restaurant with plain decor. Sushi can be made to order by the chef or chosen from the conveyor belt.

**Torihiro** 鳥ひろ *S3 E1. 0152-45-5150. Open Mon–Sat, 5–11pm.* Restaurant serving delicious charcoal-grilled *yakitori*. Friendly atmosphere.

**UTORO**

**Cafe En** 知床カフェ・えん *On the main street, on the left after the bridge. 0152-24-3122. Open 11am–11pm.* A pleasant second-floor room with oak tables. At lunchtime, there's a *shake teishoku* menu (grilled salmon, soup, salad) or *hambagu* steak.

**Cafe Fox** カフェ・フォックス *On the ferry quay, closed Nov–Apr. 0152-24-2656. Open 6am–6pm.* Unpretentious eatery, practical for take-out picnics.

**Ikkyuya** 一休屋 *Opposite the bus station, next to the bridge. 0152-24-2557. Open 11am–6pm.* A family-run restaurant specializing in *donburi* (bowls of rice) garnished with *ikura* (salmon eggs), sea urchin, and raw salmon.

**Kani-no-ya** 知床かに乃屋 *On the left as you approach the harbor. 0152-24-2671. Open 11am–11pm.* An excellent *kaiten-sushi* (conveyor belt) restaurant in the orange building next to the Dai-han-so store. Fine seafood cuisine.

# Hakodate and around ★ 函館

**With wide avenues following the lines of the coast, an old merchant quarter with an East-meets-West atmosphere, churches and temples of all confessions, a rocky headland reaching toward the island of Honshu and overlooking the city, offering Japan's most beautiful panoramic views to be seen by night—with all this, Hakodate lives and breathes the sea. An appealing, pleasant city, it is proud of its beautiful monuments including a citadel that could have been designed by French military architect Vauban, and is today a superb park. Hokkaido's leading port, its fish market is busy in the early hours as the first boatloads arrive. You can enjoy a treat in the restaurants surrounding the recently refurbished docks. The area around Hakodate offers numerous opportunities for excursions, from old towns and villages to beautiful natural sites.**

- **Population:** 294,065.
- **Michelin Map:** Principal Sights Map B1, Regional Map p423.
- **Info:** ℘0138-23-5440, 9am-7pm Apr–Oct, to 5pm Nov Mar; closed Dec 31 and Jan 1 (Hakodate) or ℘0138-27-3333, 9am 7pm Apr Oct, to 5pm Nov-Mar; closed Dec 31 and Jan 1 *(Motomachi)*.
- **Location:** Hakodate is about 198mi/320km from Sappororo and 422mi/680km north of Tokyo.
- **Kids:** Try on costumes from the 1900s at the Former Hakadate Ward Public Hall.
- **Timing:** Give yourself two days to get a sense of the city, which is bigger than it first appears, and to walk up Mount Hakodate.
- **Don't miss:** The slopes of Motomachi; the panoramic view from Mount Hakodate, especially by night; tasting sushi for an authentic Japanese breakfast, early in the morning at the fish market.

## SIGHTS

### Goryokaku★ 五稜郭跡

*43-9 Goryokaku-cho. Tramway stop Goryokaku Koen Maie, then 15min walk. ℘0138-51-4785. Tower open Apr 21-Oct 20, 8am-7pm. ¥840 (children ¥420). Free admission to the park.*

The fortress of Goryokaku was built in 185764 to protect the port opened to Westerners in 1854. Designed by architect Ayasaburo Takeda, its five-branched star design takes inspiration from European "Vauban" forts and was the first Western-style fort in Japan. This not only limited the number of blind spots where cannon could not fire, but also created many more gun emplacements than on a traditional Japanese fortress.

Its bastions, turned into gardens, are especially pleasant in springtime when the **cherry trees** are in blossom or in the autumn when the leaves turn brilliant colors. The moats, dry or filled with water, create beautiful perspectives against the hand-hewn stonewalls. In 2010, a re-creation of the Ezo Governor's Palace gave additional cachet to the site. During a visit, the observation tower, that more than anything recalls an airport control tower, may seem slightly out of place.

Nevertheless, the museum presentation of the historic events is interesting and the **view**★★ to be had at the top, at 351ft/107m, is quite simply spectacular. Moreover, the majesty of the citadel is heightened by the rocky headland of Hakodate overlooking the straits.

Open-air plays about the town's history are performed by 500 amateurs in July and August.

**Hakodate Museum of Art**
道立函館美術館 *37-6 Goryokaku. Open TueSun 9.30am5pm. ¥170. 0138-56-6311.*
This modern building is home to 19C and 20C Japanese art collections. Rodin's statue of Balzac is here, as well as, works by Bourdelle and Renoir. Interesting temporary exhibitions are also organized.

## The Port Area★

Hakodate's busy port is a place of both local everyday life and vestiges of the past. Early birds can enjoy octopus sushi at the "Asal-chi" fish market close to the station *(open from 5am)*. Its some 300 shops are a cheery, colorful show. Just behind the station, the *Mashu Maru*, the last ferry linking Hakodate and Aomori before the Seikan tunnel opened, has been turned into a museum.
Head along Avenue Tomoe Ohashi to Mount Hakodate. Even if it is difficult to enter it, the wholesale fish market is worth a look.
Adjacent are the old docks. All along the sea are the red-brick façades of the old warehouses with their pretty Meiji pediments. They have been converted to contain a multitude of souvenir shops within an entire panoply of products that Japanese tourists adore. The numerous restaurants as well as the Jiyu fish market *(open all day)* make the docks the liveliest place in town. Behind the docks, city side, the former post office built in 1911 is also home to a great many restaurants and shops. A visit to the Kahei Takadaya *(13-22 Suehiro; Wed–Mon, 9am–6pm; 0138-27-5226; ¥300)* is a chance to see the inside of a **strongbox-house★** with its thick shutters. You will come across these houses several times when visiting the Motomachi district. Hakodate owes much to this great merchant, Kahei Takadaya, born at the end of the 18C; he is credited with the significant development and thriving of both the city and its port. The house is home to interesting objects recalling the life of this great benefactor.

**Motomachi★★** 元町坂

*Take the tramway to its terminus, Hakodate Dokku-Maie station; then head up Avenue Uomi-Zaka to the Foreign Cemetery.*

**Foreign Cemetery** 外人墓地
Overlooking the sea in a calm, serene setting, one reaches the cemetery where foreigners have been laid to rest by taking little streets running between early residences. Different sections are set aside for the Chinese, Orthodox Russians, Christians, Protestants, and Catholics. The surprising nature of the place recalls that the city of Hakodate has been open to the rest of the world since 1854.

*Retrace your steps until you come to Koryu-ji temple.*

**Koryu-ji★** 高龍寺
*21-11 Funami-cho. Open 9am–5pm. 0138-23-0631.*
This temple is unquestionably the most beautiful in Hakodate. Unpainted, built of wood, one can feel a certain spirituality. Although settled in this location in the early 18C, it was founded in the early 17C. Destroyed by a fire during an attack on the city (1868) by the Imperial forces, it was rebuilt between 1900 and 1911. The **imposing gates**, abundantly carved with lions, dragons, and phoenix, give onto the courtyard, where the main building stands. To the right, behind the curious gallery fitting into the terrain, there is a charming **garden** planted with pines and azaleas. Among the interesting artworks belonging to the temple, there is a representation of Buddha on his deathbed, painted by Hakyo Kazizaki in 1811.

*Take the next first street on your right after the temple. On the hillside's flank, on the slopes of Mount Hakodate, it will take you to*

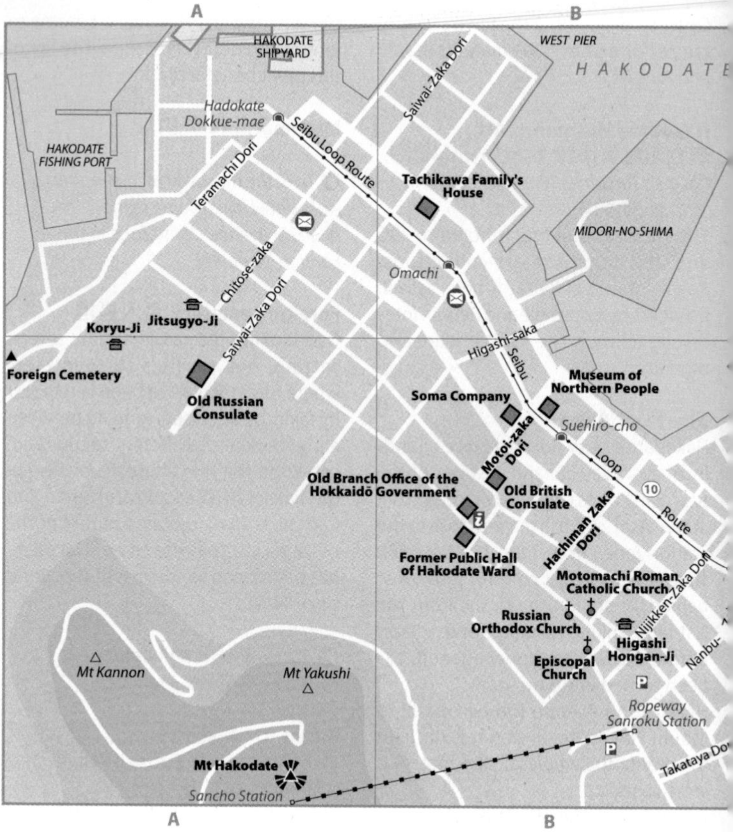


*the district surrounding the town hall and containing the churches.*

### Jitsugyo-ji 実行寺

Located in a pleasant garden, the temple is surrounded by an immense **cemetery** containing a bilingual French-Japanese commemorative monument. It relates the disembarkation of the French in 1855, recorded by the monk Matsuo Nichiryu, whose statue overlooks the setting.

*Take Saiwai Zaka slope, heading up and right, to pass in front of the former Russian Consulate (1908), a vast edifice of wood and brick; its advanced state of deterioration makes it impossible to visit. Then head downward to the left of Tokiwa Zaka slope to the bottom.*

### Tachikawa Family's House 太刀川家

Notice the pretty, slightly curved green façade of this old home belonging to a rich Meiji era family. Today it contains a rather nice cafe (*open Tue–Sun 10am–6pm; 0138-22-0340*).

*Now take the boulevard until you come to Yayoi Zaka slope. Notice on the corner the impressive 1930 façade of the old Nishi police station.*

### Museum of Northern People★ 北方民族資料館

*21-7 Suehiro-cho. Open Apr–Oct 9am–7pm, Nov–Mar 9am–5pm. ¥300 (children ¥150); ticket combined with Kahei Takaday Museum (¥500). 0138-22-4128.*

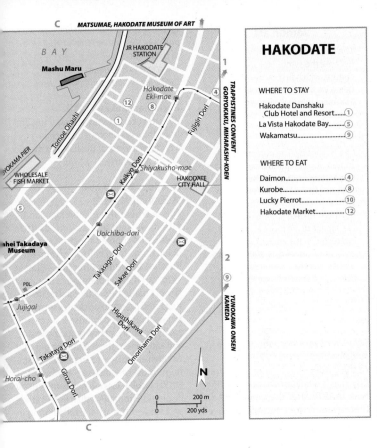

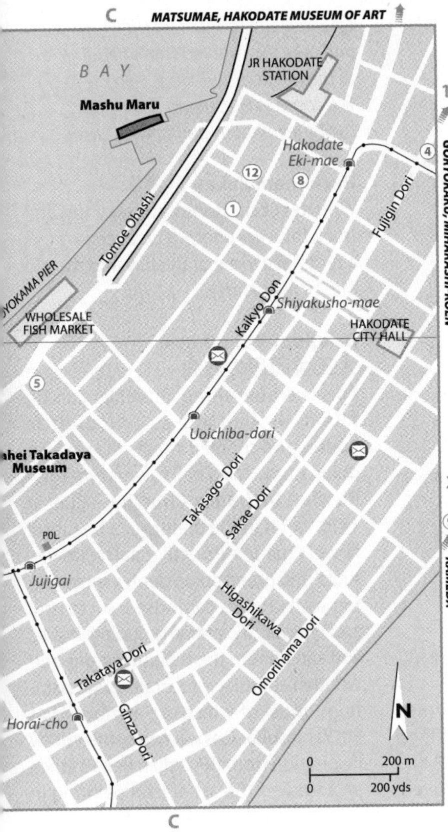

## HAKODATE

**WHERE TO STAY**

Hakodate Danshaku
  Club Hotel and Resort......①
La Vista Hakodate Bay.........⑤
Wakamatsu..............................⑨

**WHERE TO EAT**

Daimon....................................④
Kurobe.....................................⑧
Lucky Pierrot.........................⑩
Hakodate Market..................⑫

© 2011 Cartographic data Shobunsha/Michelin

---

This interesting museum bears witness to Ainu culture. Among the exhibits are beautiful costumes, jewelry, and paintings.

### Motoi Zaka★ 基坂

There is a majestic **view** of the Hakadate City Hall. Notice at the corner and imposing green building bearing the name of the **Soma Company★**, built in 1913.

### Old British Consulate
### 旧イギリス領事館

*33-14 Motomachi.* ◎*Open Apr–Nov 9am–7pm, Dec–Mar 9am–5pm.* ◎*¥300 (children ¥150).* ℘*0138-27-8159.*
Built in the 1930s in a style more Portuguese than English, this residence stands in the middle of a very pleasant garden. It is home to a small **museum** and **tearoom**.

▷ *Now cross Motomachi Park.*

### Old Branch Office of the
### Hokkaido Government
### 旧北海道庁函館支庁庁舎

*12-18 Motomachi.* ◎*Open Apr–Nov 9am–7pm, Dec–Mar 9am–5pm.* ◎*¥200 (children ¥100).* ℘*0138-27-3333.*
This harmonious building, built in 1909, stands out owing to a peristyle of which the four tall, slender columns are surmounted with Corinthian capitals embellished with a carved pediment. Inside, a fascinating **museum** traces the history of **photography** and exhibits a few old cameras.

### Former Hakodate Ward Public
### Hall★★ 旧函館区公会堂

*11-13 Motomachi.* ◎*Open Apr–Oct*

### Jomon art

The Hakodate figurine *(dogu)* has become the symbol for Jomon culture, which first came into being on the island of Hokkaido. Magnificently well-preserved, it is one of the world's most beautiful vestiges of the prehistoric era. A copy can be seen in the Hakodate City Hall lobby. The numerous Jomon objects found bear witness to a certain mastery of the arts, with real finesse in their execution. With a great many sites throughout northern Tokoku and Hokkaido, the Japanese are more and more interested in the ancient Jomon civilization. Indeed, in 2009 Japan requested classification on the UNESCO World Heritage list for all these sites; the procedure is not yet yet concluded.

*9am–7pm, Nov–Mar 9am–5pm. ¥300 (children ¥150). 0138-22-1001.*

At the gardens' high point, the former City Hall is a beautiful wooden edifice built in 1910 after the great 1907 fire that ravaged the city and destroyed 12,000 homes. In yellow and blue, its balconies, columns, and small windows overlook the bay.

The first floor of this long building is surmounted with a sloping roof ending in two imposing triangular pediments. The façade is broken up into three porches on the ground floor; there is a charming loggia on the first floor.

The inside smells pleasantly of waxed wood, and consists of a series of salons furnished in the style of the early 20C. In the large room on the first floor, panels *(in Japanese)* relate the contributions of various foreign countries to the history of Hakodate.

There is a **superb view★★** of the bay and city from the balcony. After having finished your visit, you may perhaps run across Japanese dressed in costumes dating from 1900, unless you wish to try one on yourself *(hire possible from mid-Apr–end Dec).*

*Leave the former City Hall, turn right, and take the cobbled street heading to the religious buildings district. You will come to Hachiman Zaka slope, then the religious buildings quarter.*

**Hachimam Zaka★ 八幡坂**

With its cobblestones, streetlamps, and trees, this very photogenic avenue offers a birds' eye **view** of the bay and the old *Mashu Maru* ferry.

**Religious Buildings★**
**大三坂周辺の教会**

This is where three churches can be found, nestled in a setting of little houses and cobbled streets from which onion domes and bell towers emerge.

**Russian Orthodox Church★** – Built in 1916, this is in the middle of a beautiful flowery garden. Its octagonal belltower, roofs, and green onion domes surmounted with crosses comprise a successful and typically Byzantine grouping. Inside, you can admire the beautiful icons and wooden altarpiece decorated with paintings, most of which are attributed to Rin Yamashita. This woman painter drew inspiration from the Italian Renaissance and studied the art of icon painting in St. Petersburg (*photographs are not authorized inside).*

**Motomachi Roman Catholic Church** – Preceded by a small forecourt and dominated by a square belltower ending in a tower with an octagonal spire, the Catholic Church also dates from the early 20C. The **interior★** is in the Neo-Gothic style, abundantly decorated, its rib-vaulted ceiling painted blue, and sprinkled with little golden stars.

The Daisan Zaka and Cha-Chaa slopes are on a smaller scale and more intimate. The modern, strange white cruciform of the **Episcopal Church** stands out over the trees.

*Take the street that heads out opposite the Catholic Church and that runs along the buildings of the Hongan-ji temple. Then turn left and head down Nijukken-Zaka slope.*

**Higashi Hongan-ji 東本願寺**
*Nijukken-Zaka slope.*
*Open 9am–5pm.*
Of imposing proportions,Higashi Hongan-ji was built in the early 20C. It is the first reinforced concrete temple to be built in Japan; hence the impressive size of its tiled roof. The interior remains rather traditional, with an especially beautiful coffered ceiling.
Nearby, you can see a German-style half-timbered house; it is home to a butcher's shop making delicious Carl Raymon sausages. They recall once again the Western presence in Hakodate.

**Mount Hakodate★ 函館山**
*19-7 Motomachi. Cable car operates Apr 26–Oct 31, 10am10pm; Nov 1–Apr 25, 9pm. One way ¥650 (children ¥320), round trip ¥1,160 (children ¥590). 0138-23-3105.*
Symbol of the city, Mount Hakodate culminates at an altitude of about 1,000ft/334m, advancing majestically into the Tsugaru detroit. Originally volcanic, the sea has beaten its black rock to form tall cliffs shrouded in rich vegetation. Numerous walking paths criss-cross it, offering beautiful **views**. The Senjojiki plateau is best to enjoy these wild seascapes.
The cable car takes you quickly to the mountaintop, from where there is an extraordinary **panoramic view★★★**, of Hakodate, lovely by day or night.

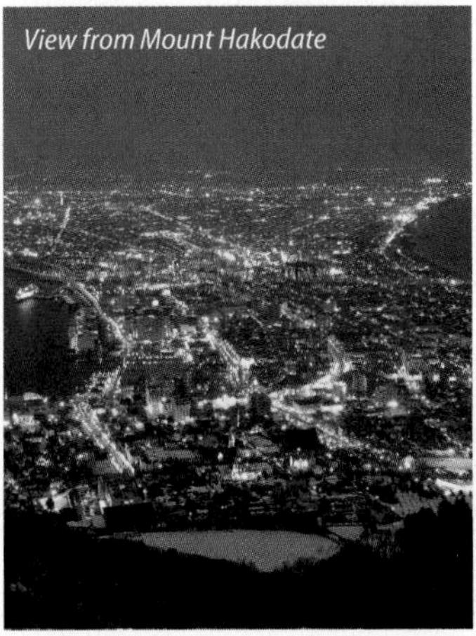
View from Mount Hakodate
©Hokkaido Tourism Organization/JNTO

Though it can get crowded, in 2009 it was the favorite tourist destination among Japanese travelers, ranking before Kyoto!

**Yunokawa Onsen 湯の川温泉**
*Tramway, Yunokawa Onsen stop.*
A spa district is developing to the west of the city, with numerous hotels and-Japanese baths. There is a good **view** of Mount Hakodate from the beach. At night in the open sea, the lights of fishing boats track down squid dancing on the water.

**Miharashi-Koenn 見晴公園**
*Miharashi Koen Dori. 0138-40-3605.*
This park on the heights was created by the Iwafune family at the end of the Meiji era. The only large park on the island of Hokkaido, it is magnificent, especially in spring and in the Fall, a favorite with amateur photographers. The former summer pavilion is a beautiful wooden construction, offset by its setting in a little Japanese garden.

**Trappistines Convent**
**トラピスチヌ修道院**
*346 Kamiyunokawa-cho. Bus from the station or Yunokawa tramway terminus, Trappistine Iriguchi stop, then 10min walk. Access to park and museum only. Open daily 9am–5pm. 0138-57-3331.*
Founded by eight French Trappists in 1898, it is now home to about 60 nuns. The brick buildings are not very interesting, but Asian tourists find the statue of Archangel St. Michael or the re-created Lourdes cave, in the park, very exotic. It is also possible to enjoy a pretty **view** of the city, and its surroundings and to take a look at the exhibit on the Cistercian Order.

## EXCURSIONS

**Kameda Peninsula 亀田半島**
Kameda Peninsula offers superb landscapes. Route 278 runs along the ocean and leads to **Mount Esan**, a volcano still active; its base is covered with azaleas in springtime. **Cape Esan**, turned into a park, overlooks the sea. The road then

heads through the verdure toward Minamikayabe, then Ofune, both important sites in Jomon civilization. In Ofune, the **archaeological museum** exhibits many objects unearthed at archaeological digs (*open Nov 13–Apr 19, 9am–5pm*). From Shikabe, you reach **Lake Onuma★**. The grim mass of the Komagatake volcano dominates the beautiful landscape. The lake surroundings offer a multiplicity of **sports activities**: skiing, hiking, golf, etc. The lake comprises 126 large and small islands. Further to the south, **Nanae** is a ski area with a marvelous **view** of Hakodate.

### Matsumae 松前

*Bus directly from Hakodate station.*
This pretty little town was the first in Hokkaido to welcome a clan from Honshu, the Matsumae feudal lords who bestowed their name on the place in 1604. It has numerous parks, their paths edged with **cherry trees**.
The **castle** stands out, with its two-story keep. Rebuilt in 1854, it was again rebuilt in 1949, following a fire. It is home to an interesting **history museum**. It is also possible to visit **Matsumae han Yashiki**, a re-created Edo period Village, as well as the **district of the five old temples**, which contains 55 graves of members of the Matsumae clan.

## ADDRESSES

### STAY

**Hakodate Danshaku Club Hotel & Resort Hakodate 男爵倶楽部** *22-10 Otemachi. 0138-21-1111. www.danshaku-club.com.* Next to the fish market; high-tech design rooms.

**La Vista Hakodate Bay ラビスタ函館ベイ** *12-6 Toyokawa. 0138-23-6111. www.hotespa.net/hotels/lahakodate. 356 rooms.* Right in the center *of town, beautiful modern rooms, lovely view.*

**Wakamatsu 割烹旅館 若松** *1-2-27 Yunokawa. 0138-21-1 111. www.wakamatsuryokan.com. 29 rooms.* Very beautiful hotel in traditional ryokan style. Nice view of the sea and Mount Hakodate.

### EAT

**Hakodate** is known for its seafood and fish. The squid (ika) is prepared in 1,000 different ways including fine slices in delicious sushi. Another specialty is a bowl of savory noodles (*ramen*). You'll find a great many restaurants in the lively **old docks district**, and **around the station**. The Motomachi district, on the other hand, is rather dead.

**Hakodate Market 函館朝市** Here, you can enjoy fish specialties that are easy on the wallet. Try especially the ***kaisen-don***, a bowl of rice topped with fish pieces.

**Daimon 大門** *Near the station. Open 5pmmidnight, and at lunchtime in season.* This little district has developed around two small pedestrian streets, with about 30 small restaurants with outside dining. You have the pick of sushi, *yakitori*, *ramen*, *tempera*, etc.

**Lucky Pierrot ラッキーピエロ** *The most central one is south of the old docks. Tramway stop: Jujigai Open 10am–12.30am.* Japanese fast food chain. Varied, generous hamburgers at unbeatable prices.

**Kurobe くろ兵衛** *8-23 Wakamatsu. 0138-22-7147. Open Mon–Fri 5pm–10pm, closed weekends and holidays.* Grilled chicken, in every form, in a nice and friendly setting.

**Asari Honten 阿さ利本店** *10-11 Hourai. 0138-23-0421. Open Thu–Tue 11am–10.30pm.* In an old house near the religious buildings quarter and the departure point for the cable car *(about 1,968ft/600m)*. You will be welcomed in small rooms, where you will be served ***sukiyaki***, a delicious dish of thin slices of beef dipped in egg yolk, served with vegetables.

### TAKING A BREAK

**Péché Mignon ペシェ・ミニヨン** *1-2 Nogi. 0138-31-4310. Open Thu–Tue 10am–7pm.* In a calm street in the Yunokawa district. The chef concocts small marvels, including the divine Mont Blanc pastry.

# Akan National Park ★★
# 阿寒国立公園

**With its volcanoes, mountain lakes with clear waters and hot springs, Akan National Park offers tourists magnificent excursions. With the wide, open skies and immense horizons, no matter the time of year, the beauty of the landscapes, is always impressive. Nature here is completely unspoilt: night skies sparkle with a thousand stars, cranes skim across the heavens and bears are never far away, as is indicated by the numerous forest signs warning walkers out for a stroll!**

**Michelin Map:** Principal Sights Map C1, Regional Map p423.

**Info:** (0154) 673 200, Mon–Sun 9am–6pm

**Location:** Akan is located southwest of Hokkaido and about 248mi/400km from Sapporo.

**Kids:** Take the kids on a fishing trip at Lake Akan; or to the Akan International Crane Center to see hundreds of these beautiful Japanese birds in flight.

**Timing:** Give yourself about three days.

**Don't miss**: Akan Lake and the climb up the volcanoes; the Akankohan and Kawayu *onsens*; the panoramic views of Lake Mashu.

## SIGHTS

### Lake Kussharo★★ 屈斜路湖

35mi/57km in circumference, the largest lake on the island of Hokkaido is also the second-largest in Japan; it lies in a former gigantic crater. Its maximum depth reaches 387ft/118m; the center is occupied by the immense island of Nakajima, *(about 7.5mi/12km in circumference)*, the den of a local monster called Kusshi. His silhouette, which strangely enough recalls that of the Scottish "Nessie", can be seen on the beach at Sunayu to the delight of both children and adults.

### Kawayu Onsen★ 川湯温泉

This major spa resort, a bit off the beaten track, is a good base for exploring the lakeshore. There are numerous paths accessible from the Tourist Office or from the **museum** devoted to sumo Taiho Koki that weave between the wisps of steam in a pretty, wooded environment. There are a good many *ashiyu* (hot foot baths) found regularly along the way.

### Sunayu 砂湯

This popular beach has one interesting characteristic: if you dig into the sand, hot water springs forth! There is also a beautiful **view**★ of the lake from the old wooden jetty here.

### Wakoto Peninsula★★ 和琴半島

Accessible by foot, bike or car, this is also a popular place but it's worth going out of your way to visit the *onsen*: a basin very simply dug and set into the shore of the lake. Don't forget to bring a towel. The winter, when there are fewer tourists, you would think that you are alone in the whole world. Those who are not faint of heart can then remove their clothes to head for the hot water, to contemplate the frozen lake among the wisps of steam rising around them. Be careful: the water in the basin is very hot, a bit nearer to the lake the water is closer to warm. To warm up or just to relax, you can then take the footpath running 1.5mi/2.5km along the point.

### Mount Iou★ 硫黄山

The road between Kawayu Onsen and the train station crosses vast extents of moors spotted here and there with azaleas; it runs alongside the mountain continually shrouded in the mist. It then comes to Mount Iou, a fair-sized volcano *(1,883ft/574m)*, which they say sleepswith one eye open. The Ainu call it Atosanupuri, the "naked mountain".

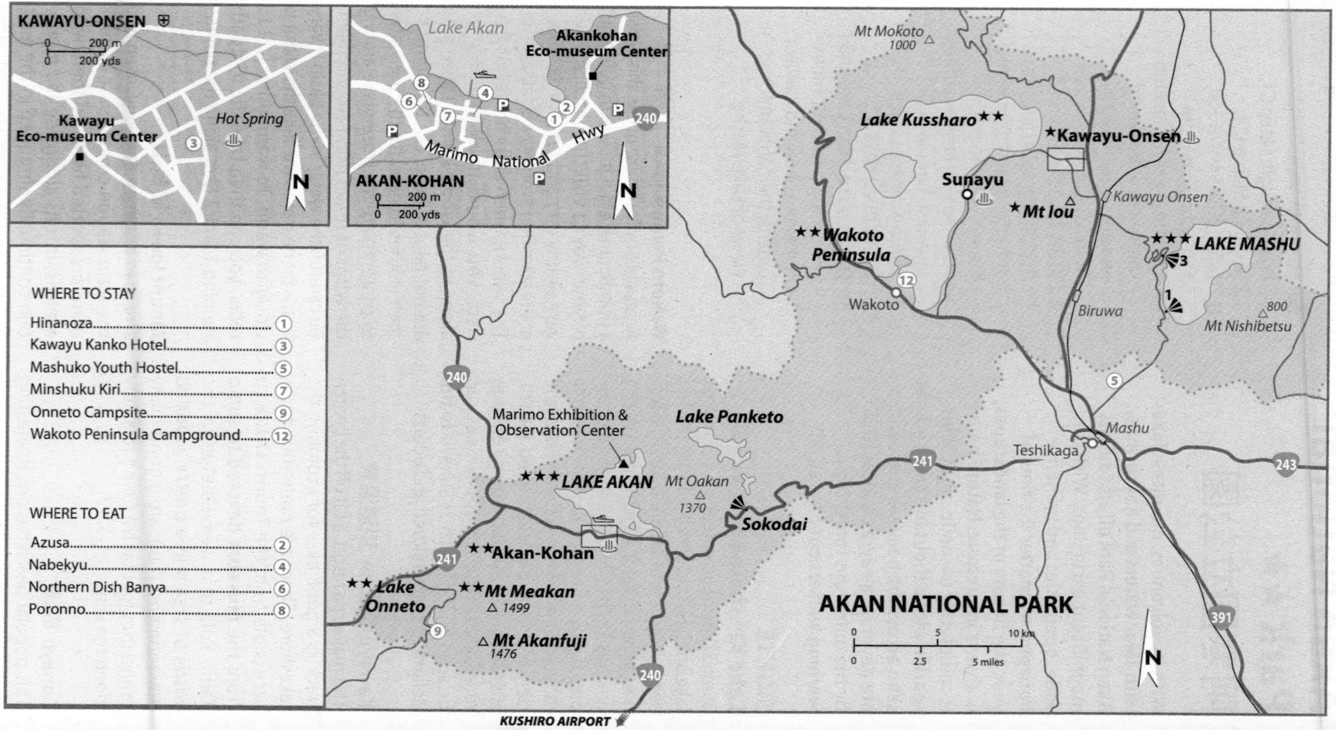

© 2011 Cartographic data Shobunsha/Michelin

**KAWAYU-ONSEN** ⊕

Hot Spring

Kawayu
Eco-museum Center

**AKAN NATIONAL PARK**

10 km

5 miles

**AKAN-KOHAN**

Akankohan
Eco-museum Center

Lake Akan

Marimo National HWY

**WHERE TO STAY**

| | |
|---|---|
| Hinanoza | ① |
| Kawayu Kanko Hotel | ③ |
| Mashuko Youth Hostel | ⑤ |
| Minshuku Kiri | ⑦ |
| Onneto Campsite | ⑨ |
| Wakoto Peninsula Campground | ⑫ |

**WHERE TO EAT**

| | |
|---|---|
| Azusa | ② |
| Nabekyu | ④ |
| Northern Dish Banya | ⑥ |
| Poronno | ⑧ |

**LAKE MASHU**

Mt Nishibetsu 800

Kawayu Onsen

**Kawayu-Onsen**

**Mt Iou**

Biruwa

Mashu

Teshikaga

**Sunayu**

*Lake Kussharo*

Mt Mokoto 1000

Wakoto

**Wakoto Peninsula**

*Lake Panketo*

**Sokodai**

Mt Oakan 1370

Marimo Exhibition &
Observation Center

**LAKE AKAN**

**Akan-Kohan**

**Mt Meakan** △ 1499

**Mt Akanfuji** 1476

**Lake Onneto**

KUSHIRO AIRPORT

Beyond the parking lot, the earth is white, deserted, overrun with a rare yellowish-colored plants emerging here and there amid the wisps of vapor and small geysers of boiling water. The strong odor of sulfur smells like rotten eggs from childhood science classes! *Access is regulated and it is strongly recommended not to go beyond the safety barriers.*

*Now continue on Rt. 52, which gradually zigzags its way up to Lake Mashu.*

## Lake Mashu★★★ 摩周湖

This lake, overlooked by Mount Mashu, occupies the crater of a volcano. Of a circumference of 12mi/20km and a total depth going beyond 656ft/200m, it makes a strong impression with its stark slopesalmost cliffsdropping straight down to the clear waters. It is not possible to go all the way around the rim, but there are three observation towers that also make it possible to admire its beauty, albeit from afar.
The first, **observation tower no. 3★★**, offers a **view** made even more beautiful by the fact that it is possible to see the sea in the distance. Then comes **observation tower no. 1★★**, where the birds'-eye **view** onto the lake is impressive. It is only regrettable that the place is so popular and paced with souvenir shops, restaurants, etc.

*Head back down to Mashu Onsen and take Rt. 241 to Akan, which gradually rises through the forest.*

At the location known as **Sokodai★** *(parking lot with toilets, to the left of the road by taking a path that heads upward)* there is a wonderful **view** of Lake Panketo. As you drive along the weaving roads you will catch sight of the imposing mass of **Mount Akan** and in the distance, of **Mount Meakan**.

## Lake Akan★★★ 阿寒湖

Dominated by the haughty mass of the volcano, you'll find here magnificent flora and fauna, and experience absolutely unforgettable walks. To make it a little easier to get across the lake's 16mi/26km circumference, numerous boats leave from Akan Onsen so that you can discover the treasures the area has to offer. Serious nature lovers can go fly-fishing along the banks, the waters of the lake not being too deep.

### Akan-kohan★★ 阿寒湖畔

The pleasant spa resort of Akanko Onsen (阿寒湖温泉) is home to numerous hotels and auberges, some of them with rather high standing, and all in the wooded setting of the lakeside. Visitors will be attracted or aggravated by the extremely tourist-oriented nature of the place, although it must be admitted this brings a certain liveliness. Once again, there are a great many **foot-baths** along the streets of the small town.
**The lakeside★** – There is a track that takes you around the lake, a pleasant thing to do at sunrise. Beyond the landing stage, you can take the park's natural paths to discover numerous hot springs. You will also see a great many animals such as squirrels and birds in their natural habitat.
**Eco-museum★** – *Akankohan Eco Museum Center, 1-1 Aknko Onsen. Wed–Mon 9am–5pm. No charge.* The floor of the museum reproduces an **aerial view** of the region. The modern and educational presentation shows the various animal species living in Akan.
**Maeda Ippoen Foundation** Near the museum, a lovely chalet-like stone house with a 1950s design is home to the Maeda Ippoen Foundation. This important dignitary of the Meiji era, who loved Akan deeply, passed that love of the forest onto his family. His daughter-in-law, Mitsuko, established the foundation in 1983. She manages close to 16sq mi/4,000ha of the forest, especially the west bank of the lake, with a view to restoring the forests the way they were three centuries ago. A great deal of planting has been done, especially to re-establish the balance between conifers and leafy trees. Mitsuko also aims to protect the trees from the deer fond of nibbling on the bark.

*Mount Akan and Mount Akanfuji viewed from the Lake Onneto*

**Ainu Kotana★** This Ainu village lies at the end of a large street of shops with about 36 homes, containing about 200 people. It has the look of a large sloped square surrounded by souvenir shops and restaurants. Tall totems stand at the center. At the high end of the village, the large communal house, *onne-chisse*, offers **performances**. In the back, it also has an arena for night performances to close the Ainu market.

**Boating excursion on the lake★★**
Pleasant cruises make it possible to visit the island of Churu; there is a small aquarium there with algae shaped like balls, called *marimo*.
The boat can also make a stop at the landing stage, the departure point for climbing up Mount Akan *(count on about 5hr30min to head up and a good 2hr to come back down; medium difficulty)*.
From the summit there is a beautiful **panoramic view★★** of the lake and the mountains towards Mount Akan.

### Lake Onneto★★ オンネトー湖

Baptized the "lake of five colors", it lies in a landscape of great beauty, edged with fir trees overlooked by the smoking shape of Mount Meakan. A signposted path runs along its eastern edge. After about 50min you will come to the **Yunotakia Falls★** *(164ft/ 50m high)*, the waters are at a temperature of about 110°F. A basin has been dug and arranged to make it possible to bathe there.

### Mount Meakan★★ 雌阿寒岳

This young volcano going back about 20,000 years produces gas eruptions, the last one going back to 1959. Two thousand years ago a second crater, Mount Akanfuji, grafted itself onto the southern side of the Mount. There are two paths leading to Meakan's summit. The first one, that you will encounter in coming from Akan, after the Nonaka *onsen*, is easier; it takes about 2hr to climb to the top. The other path, at the far end of the lake, can take up to 3hr of walking. At an altitude of 4,918ft/1,499m, the **view** from the top is splendid. The volcano still being active, it would be foolhardy to go into the crater. You can then retrace your steps or head back down to Akan-kohan, which takes about 3hr.

## EXCURSIONS

### Akan International Crane Centre 阿寒国際ツルセンター

*23-40 Akan, 40min south of Akan. Open 9am–5pm. ¥400, children ¥200. ℘0154 66-411.*

Heading in the direction of Kushiro and its airport, Route 240 gradually heads downward into a large cultivated valley, where the landscapes recall Europe. Looking up, you will see hundreds of Japanese

cranes. A special center has been created to allow them to find food in the winter. The show *(Nov–Mar)* the birds put on in the snow, battling sometimes with eagles to save their food, is very beautiful. Many amateur photographers crowd here to attend the performance.
The little **museum** will tell you everything you ever wanted to know about Japanese cranes.

### Kushiro 釧路

The town of Kushiro has a pleasant, modern port with many facilities. In the surrounding area, Kushiro Shitsugen National Park is an immense marshland that can be crossed by train.

## ADDRESSES

### STAY

**AKAN**

**Onneto Campsite**
オンネトー国設野営場 *Moashoro, Ashoro-cho, 0.12mi/200m from the far end of Lake Onneto. ℘0156-25-2141. Open May–end Oct.* Simple level of comfort, but splendid, peaceful site.

**Minshuku Kiri** 民宿 桐 *4-3-26 Akanko Osen. ℘0154-67-2755. http:/www10.plala.or.jp/kiriminsyuku. 9 rooms.* In the main street facing Emerald Hotel, on the first floor of a souvenir shop. Good food, warm welcome; very nice *onsen*.

**Hinanoza** 鶴雅別荘 鄙の座 *2-8-1 Akanko Onsen, Akan-cho. ℘0514-67-3050. www.hinanoza.com. 25 rooms.* This magnificent ryokan-like hotel is a unique experience. Wonderful **view** of lake from the rooms.

**KUSSHARO**

**Wakoto Peninsular Campground**
和琴半島湖畔キャンプ場 *Wakoto-hanto kyanpu-jo.* On the shores of Lake Kussharo, facing Mount Wakoto, ideally located campsite with a restaurant; *¥400/person per night.*

**Mashuko Youth Hostel**
摩周湖ユースホステル *Take the Bihoro/Kawayu bus from the JR Mashu station to the Youth Hostel Maie. ℘0154-82-3098.* Very nice youth hostel; *a shuttle bus can come and get you at the JR station; ¥3,950 with youth hostel card.*

**Kawayu Kanko Hotel**
川湯観光ホテル *1-2-30 Kawayu-onsen, Teshikaga-cho. ℘015-483-2121. 26 rooms.* Very beautiful traditional hotel at the *Kawayu Onsen* resort.

### EAT

**AKAN-KOHAN**

**Nabekyu** 奈辺久
*4-4-1 Akanko Onsen. ℘0154-67-2607. http://www.lake-akan.com/nabekyuu/Index.htm. Open 11am–3pm, 6–9pm.* Restaurant offering nice fish specialties.

**Azusa** あずさ *1-5-8 Akanko Onsen. ℘0154-67-2474. Open 11am–midnight.* For a quick and economical dinner; mostly meat dishes.

**Poronno** ポロンノ *4-7-8 Akanko Onsen. ℘0154-67-2159. 10am–9.30pm.* Discover Ainu specialties. Delicious, spicy yukku curry.

**Northern Dish Banya**
北国の味番八 *4-7-6 Akanko Onsen. ℘0154-67-2316. 11am–3pm and 8pm–midnight.* Simple, but great quality: local specialties with wild onions and grilled fish.

### TAKING A BREAK

**Pan de Pan** パンデパン
*1-6-6, Akanko Onsen. ℘0152-67-4188. www.tsuruga.com/pandepan. 8.30am–6.30pm.* European-inspired pastries in a lively, colorful setting.

### ACTIVITIES

**Boat trips** – **Akan Sightseeing Cruise Company** *1-5-20 Akanko Onsen. ℘0154-67-2511. www.akankisen.com.* Tour of the lake *(11mi/18km)* with a stop on the island to visit *marimo* museum. Ferries *(1hr25min, ¥1,850, children ¥960).* Motorboat rentals *(1 price: ¥4,500/person).*

**Procession** – **Torch procession** nightly with **Ainu songs and dances**. 8.20pm from Marimukan parking lot to Ainu village. 9pm: show in the open-era theater *Jun 1–Nov 30; adults ¥1,000; children ¥500).*

**Festival** – 3 days in early October, the Ainu celebrate the colorful **Marimo Matsuri**.

# SHIKOKU

**Smallest and least populated of the four main Japanese islands, Shikoku was divided into four provinces—hence its name: *shi* (four) and *koku* (lands)—which became Ehime (Matsuyama), Kagawa (Takamatsu), Tokushima, and Kochi prefectures. For centuries, difficult accessibility kept it off the great trade routes of the Inland Sea reaching out to China and Korea.**

### Highlights

1. Lounging on a secluded beach on sleepy **Hon-jima** (p458)
2. A dip at **Dogo Onsen**, one of the oldest in Japan (p460)
3. Exploring the historic town of **Ozo**, in remote Ehime-ken (p462)
4. Kayaking down the **Oboke Gorge** in the Iya Valley (p463)
5. Browsing for fresh produce and local crafts at **Kochi market** (p467)

## Shikoku Today

Shikoku is linked to the main island of Honshu by a system of three long bridges mostly used by those taking buses along the old Shikoku Temple Pilgrimage route, in the footsteps of Buddhist sage Kobo Daishi (774–835). Somewhat neglected, this still relatively unspoilt island hides quaint temples and villages, beautiful verdant mountains, and rice paddies.

*Kazura-bashi, Iya Valley, Tokushima*



- **Population:** 4,160,000 – Ehime, Kagawa, Tokushima, and Kochi Prefectures.
- **Michelin Map:** Regional Map p453—Principal Sights Map A–B3.
- **Location:** South of Honshu and east of Kyushu, Shikoku covers 7,258.7sq mi/18,800sq km. The island's highest peak is Mount Ishizuchi *(6,502.6ft/1,982m)* in Ehime prefecture. The rail network has three main lines: the JR Yosan Line, *(leaving Okayama to run west along the coast from Takamatsu to Matsuyama)*, the JR Dosan Line, *(transversing the island from Takamatsu to Kochi via Oboke)*, and the JR Kotoku Line, *(along the eastern coastline from Takamatsu to Tokushima)*.
- **Kids:** Head for the Pacific coast, with Katsurahama Beach and Kochi whale-watching cruises.
- **Timing:** About 3 days in Matsuyama and Takamatsu; a week for the complete Takamatsu–Kotohira–Iya Valley–Kochi–Cape Ashizuri–Uchiko–Matsuyama tour.
- **Don't miss:** Dogo Onsen in Matsuyama; the Ritsurin-koen garden at Takamatsu; the Iya Valley countryside; the Cape Ashizuri cliffs; one or more of the island's sacred temples.

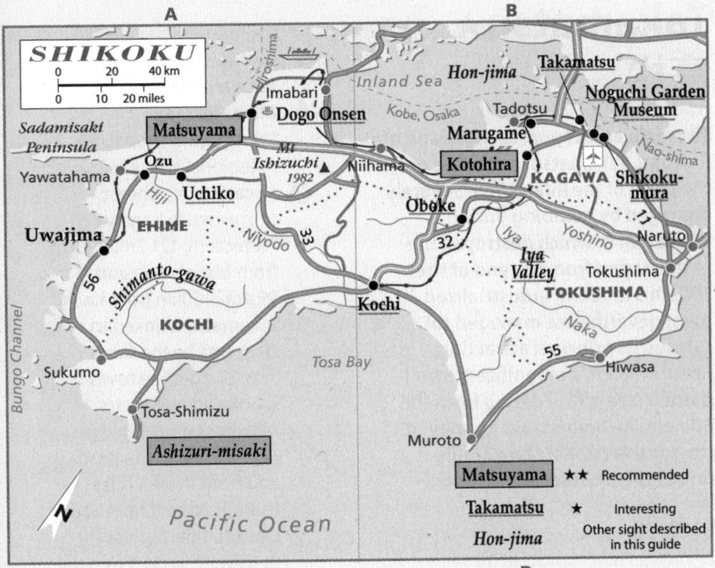



It also offers many leisure pursuits: hiking, rafting, bathing, ocean boating trips, etc. The steep mountains inland are among western Japan's highest, stretching east to west to separate Shikoku in two. A narrow coastline northward edged by the Inland Sea *(Seto Naikai)* has always been in flow with surrounding civilization, making it the most populated, developed part of the island; its main towns are Takamatsu eastward and Matsuyama to the west. The Inland Sea's peaceful, sunny shores and mild climate are ideal for growing olives, peaches, and citrus fruits right across the scattering of small islands here.

Rain is much more prevalent in the south, where the Pacific's waters are warm and fish abundant. While the coast is often struck by typhoons, vegetation is lushly subtropical with bamboo, banyans, camellias, and palm trees.

There are only a few isolated fishing villages, meaning the natural environment has been preserved along the coast, where promontories carve out delightful bays.

*Dogo Onsen Honkan, Matsuyama*

# Takamatsu★ 高松

**The main access port to the island of Shikoku, Takamatsu is situated on the coast of the Inland Sea. Severely damaged by bombing during World War II, which destroyed the castle dating from the end of the 16C, this modern, industrialized town nevertheless managed to salvage its principal attraction, Ritsurin-koen, a magnificent stroll garden *(see p 103)* dating from the Edo era. An hour's train journey to the southwest, Kotohira Shrine is one of the most sacred in Japan.**

- **Population:** 338,358 – Kagawa Prefecture.
- **Michelin Map:** Principal Sights Map B3 – Regional Map p453.
- **Location:** Northeast of Shikoku in Kagawa Prefecture, 121.2mi/195km from Matsuyama and 99.4mi/160km from Kochi, Takamatsu is linked to Okayama by the Great Seto Bridge. The town is quite sprawling; its railway station is in the north, close to the port, and from there a busy thoroughfare, Chuo-dori, leads to the south as far as Ritsurin-koen. From the port, boats serve the island of Nao-shima *(see p 380)*.
- **Timing:** One day is enough for a visit to Takamatsu. An extra day would allow you to explore the surrounding countryside, Kotohira, or perhaps the islands.
- **Don't miss:** Ritsurin-koen; Konpira-san; the local specialty, *sanuki udon*, wheat noodles.

## SIGHTS

*You can rent bicycles at the station to get around the town. Otherwise, take the local JR line trains or those of the Kotoden Line.*

### Ritsurin-koen★★★ 栗林公園

*Map A3.*
*1.6mi/2.5km S of JR Takamatsu station (30min walk). Train to JR Ritsuin-koen-kitaguchi station or Kotoden Risturin-koen station. Bus nos. 9 or 10. Open Apr–May & Sept 5.30am–6.30pm; Jun–Aug 5.30am–7pm. Rest of the year, hours vary. ¥400.*

Backing onto Mount Shiun-zan to the west, whose wooded peak forms a natural backdrop to the vista, this stroll garden *(kaiyu)* extends over an area of 39.5 acres/16ha *(185.3 acres/75ha, including the mountain)*. Designed in 1625 by Ikoma Takatoshi, the feudal lord of the province, it was enlarged and embellished over a period of 100 years until 1745, by five generations of the Matsudaira, who inherited the fiefdom.

Ritsurin-koen



Sandy paths wind their way among a string of ponds full of colored carp; small valleys alternate with low hills in an undulating landscape. Lakes are dotted with islands studded with strangely shaped rocks and artistically distorted black pines, whose twisted branches suggest dragons, or cranes in flight. The park contains some 160 types of trees and flowers that change with

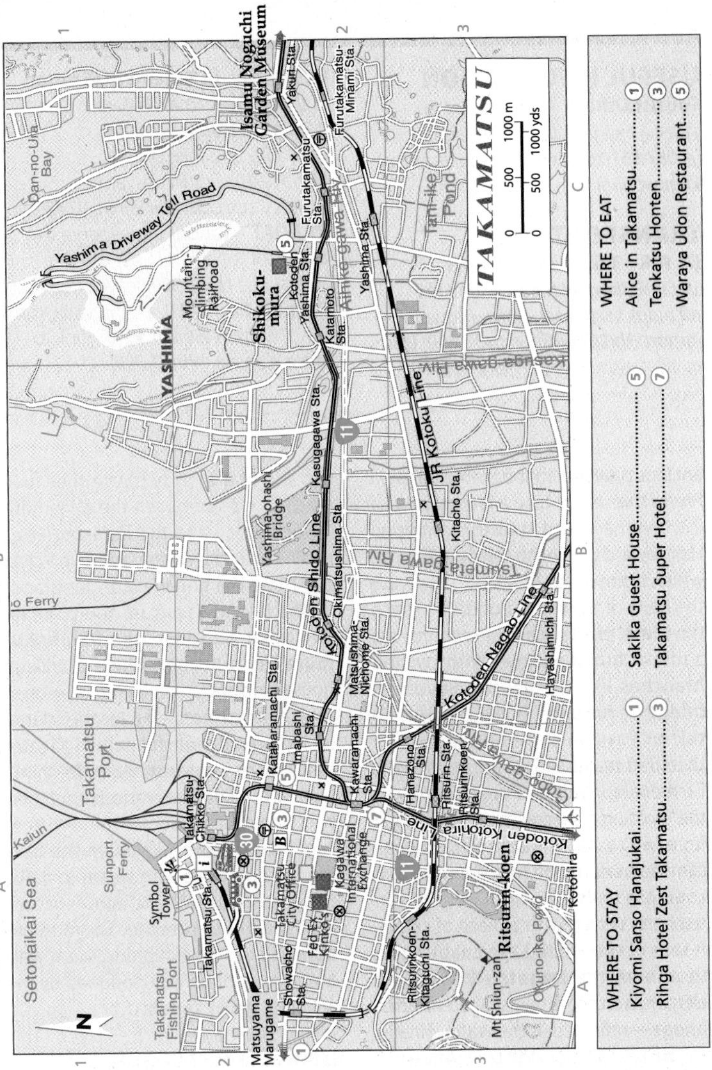




the seasons: camellias, plum trees, and magnolias in winter; cherry trees, wisteria, and rhododendrons in spring; iris, lilies, and lotus in summer; desmodiums and maple trees in the Fall. This harmonious blend of panoramas, landscapes, and buildings is a masterpiece of the art of the Japanese garden.

**Visit** – **Round trip** *(1hr) leaving from the East Gate. Another possibility is to start from inside the North Gate.*

Just beyond the East Gate, to the right, the **Sanuki Folkcraft Museum** *(open 8.45am–4.30pm; no charge)* contains displays of regional furniture and traditional craft items, including colored kites. Sanuki is the name of the

## Did you know?

The town of Takamatsu is one of the main centers for the cultivation of **bonsai trees** in Japan, particularly pines—it supplies 80 percent of Japan's pine bonsai. The main nurseries are at Kinashi, 3.7mi/6km south of the town center.

## USEFUL INFORMATION

**Tourist Office** – At JR Takamatsu station exit *(A2). Open 9am–5pm. ℘087-851-2009. www.city.takamatsu.kagawa.jp/kankou.*

## TRANSPORTATION

**BY AIR** – **Takamatsu Airport** – *10.6mi/17km S of the JR station (A3 off map).* Flights for Tokyo *(Haneda airport, 1hr20min, about ¥29,000)* **Bus** to JR station *(every hr, 45min, ¥740).*

**BY TRAIN** – **JR Takamatsu Station** *(A2)* – To Okayama, JR Marine Liner *(55min, ¥1,470).* To Osaka, go to Okayama and take Shinkansen Hikari *(2hr, ¥6,910).* For Matsuyama, Limited Express Ishizuchi *(2hr15min, ¥7,420).*

**BY BOAT** – Various ferries serve the islands of the Inland Sea. The one for Nao-shima *(see p 380)* leaves from **Sunport Ferry** *(A1)*, a 5min walk from the JR station *(50min, ¥510).* Link to Kobe (Kansai) *(4hr, ¥1,800).*

ancient province that became Kagawa Prefecture. Next, take a left in front of the Commerce and Industry Promotion Hall, toward the **South Garden** *(Nantei)*, which is the best preserved. Following the bank of the North Pond, you reach the **black pine path**★★ *(Hako-matsu)*, a row of brooding trees with twisted branches like candlabras. Beyond a bridge *(to the right)*, is the **Higurashi-tei**, or "Pavilion of the Setting Sun," a thatched tea house dating from 1898. Farther along is the **Kikugetsu-tei**★★, the "Holding the Moon" tea house dating from 1640, where the lords of Matsudaira came to perform the Tea Ceremony and compose *haikus*. You can drink green tea here, served with a piece of candy. A tour of the South Lake enables you to admire the **Engetsu-kyo**★ —an elegant, crescent-moon-shaped wooden bridge—reflected in the water. Finally, the **Hiraiho**★ offers the best **view** over the park. The less stylized **North Garden** *(Hokutei)* is set around two lakes: the **Fuyosho**, where lotus grows in profusion, and the **Gunochi**, where the lord used to hunt ducks.

### Shikoku-mura★ 四国村 *Map C2.*

*3.1mi/5km E of the center of Takamatsu. 10min walk from JR Yashima station or 5min walk from Kotoden Yashima station (Shido Line). Open Apr–Oct 8.30am–5pm; Nov–Mar 8.30am–4.30pm. ¥800.*

The volcanic plateau of **Yashima**, which rises to an altitude of 961.3ft/293m, was the site of a bloody battle that took place in 1185 between the Minamoto *(or Genji)* clan and the Taira *(or Heike)*, ending in defeat for the latter. On a clear day there is a fine **view** of the islands of the Inland Sea from the plateau. The **open-air museum of Shikoku-mura** lies at its foot, where 33 village houses and ancient buildings have been reassembled from all over the island, including a delightful Kabuki theater built by the peasants of Shodo-shima during the Edo era, various thatched huts where they squeezed the juice from sugar cane and broke down the bark of mulberry trees with steam to make paper *(washi)*, a mill, and houses occupied by lighthouse keepers. The museum also includes an exhibition room with a small indoor garden designed by the architect **Ando Tadao**.

### Isamu Noguchi Garden Museum★

*イサム・ノグチ庭園美術館 Map C2. 5mi/8km E of the center of Takamatsu. 3519 Mure, Mure-cho. 10min by taxi from JR Yashima station or Kotoden Yashima station. By appointment only Tue, Thu & Sat at 10am, 1pm, & 3pm. Guided tour (1hr). ¥2,100. ℘087-870-1500. www.isamunoguchi.or.jp*

Talented American-Japanese sculptor and designer **Isamu Noguchi** (1904–88) divided his time between two studio-residences: one in New York and one situated here, at Mure, an area once inhabited by stone-cutters and now

### A Myriad of Islands

Many of the Inland Sea's islands are uninhabited, while others are well-known and rich with legend; Megi-jima, for example, the "island of ogres" off the Takamatsu coast, is supposedly where the little hero Momotaro slayed a demon. The largest island, Shodo-shima, recalls the Mediterranean with its olive groves and mock Greek temples. The most interesting, however, is **Awaji-jima**, on the Naruto Strait, between Shikoku and Kansai. *Ningyo joruri* puppet theater *(936-3 Fukurahei, 079-952-0260, 9am–5pm, performances daily except when troupe is exceptionally absent)* has been performed here for over 500 years. The island is also the main producer of incense, supplying 70 percent of the Japanese market. It is said this fragrant material was discovered accidentally in the 16C by Awaji fishermen. Having found pieces of dark wood in debris a storm washed ashore, they were amazed at the enchanting scent it gave off when burned. They proclaimed it a miracle, and took it to the Emperor, thereby bringing about creation of the Japanese incense craft known today.

absorbed by the galloping urbanization of Takamatsu. The studio, formerly a sake brewery during the Edo era, contains various bronzes and stone sculptures. Other examples of his work, some of them unfinished, are scattered about the garden. Influenced by Brancusi as much as by the Zen spirit of the Japanese gardens, Noguchi carved thick granite monoliths, contrasting rough and polished surfaces, and sharp angles with feminine curves. On a grassy incline, stones form a sacred circle around the sculptor's tomb, symbolized by a sculpture in the form of an egg.

## EXCURSIONS

### KOTOHIRA★★ 琴平

*A3 off map.*

*18.6mi/30km SW of Takamatsu.*

*Access by train (1hr) on the JR Dosan Line (¥830) or Kotoden Line (¥610).*

The main attraction of this small town is the Kotohira-gu Shrine, more usually called **Konpira-san**★★, built at the top of the steep-sided Mount Zozu at a height of 1,709.3ft/521m. It is dedicated to *kami* Omono-nushi, protector of sailors and fishermen. A famous place of worship since the 11C, it receives four million pilgrims every year. The entire complex was originally dedicated to Konpira Daigongen, a Shinto-Buddhist deity likened to Kunbhira, the crocodile god of the sacred waters of the Ganges. Following the separation of religions during the Meiji Restoration, in 1878 the shrine was rededicated solely to the Shinto divinity.

To reach the main temple, you must climb 785 stone steps. Shaded by cherry and other trees, the way is lined with stands selling candy, stone lanterns, and votive tablets. Just before the top, be sure not to miss the **Shoin**★★ *(open 8.30am–5pm; ¥800)*, the old reception hall, built in 1660, which houses a collection of fine *fusuma* painted by Maruyama Okyo (1733–95): tigers, herons, flowers, and birds, and Chinese sages in mountain landscapes. Climb a few steps higher to see the Shrine of the Rising Sun, **Asahi no Yashiro** (1837), dedicated to the goddess Amaterasu, which has finely sculpted roof timbers. More steps lead to the **Hongu**, the main hall, and to the **Ema-do**★, where there is an exhibition of marine objects, models of boats, and votive plaques. From there, the remaining 583 steps lead to the Okusha, the inner sanctuary.

**Kanamaru-za**★ – *At the foot of the hill. Open 8.30am–5pm. ¥500.*

During the Edo era, there were many theaters, markets, lotteries, and sumo contests to entertain the pilgrims. Built in 1835, the **Kabuki theater** is the oldest in Japan. Inside, go backstage to see the ingenious wooden mechanism used to rotate the scenery. Occasional performances are held during the season *(Apr–mid-May)*.

## MARUGAME 丸亀

*A2 off map.*
*18.6mi/30km W of Takamatsu.*
*Access by train (25min) on the JR Yosan Line (¥540).*

This port *(population 110,000)* lies at the foot of one of the stretches of the Great Seto Bridge. South of the railway station, a 15min walk away, the **Marugame-jo** *(open 9am–4.30pm; ¥200)*, its castle built at the end of the 16C, is one of the rare examples to have retained its original wooden keep. This fan-shaped building sits on top of an artificial, 164ft/50m-high mound.

At the port, a 10min walk north of the station, the small **Uchiwa no Minato Museum** *(open 9.30am–5pm; no charge)* is dedicated to the traditional paper fans *(uchiwa)* that are manufactured in Marugame—the town produces 90 percent of the national production.

### Hon-jima 本島

*6.2mi/10km off the coast from Marugame. It is linked to the port by 9 ferries per day (20min, ¥1,150 round-trip, last boat back at 7.30pm). Bicycle rental in front of the ferry dock.*

The main island of the seven Shiwaku islands, Hon-jima *(2.7sq mi/7sq km, population 650)* used to be a hideout for pirates *(wako)*, who scoured the Inland Sea. Eventually recruited by the shoguns, from the end of the 16C up to the Meiji era they served as customs officers, collecting a tax on maritime traffic heading for Osaka.

The island's main village, **Kasashima**, still has the ancient customs house from the Edo era. Nowadays, the majority of the population is retired. With its many wooden houses from the Edo and Meiji eras, the island has a timeless feel. Hidden away, too, are some remote sandy beaches.

## ADDRESSES

### STAY

**Sakika Youth Guest House**
高松さきかユースゲストハウス
*6-9 Hyakken-cho (A2). 087-822-2111. 21 rooms–¥5,145/person.* Youth hostel offering the best value for money in the town.

**Takamatsu Super Hotel Kin-en-kan**
スーパーホテル高松禁煙館
*1-4-12 Kanko-dori (A2). 087-897-9000. www.superhotel.co.jp. 68 rooms.* Typical *business hotel,* practical and comfortable. Another Super Hotel offers the same services in the shopping arcade *(1-1 Tamachi).*

**Rihga Hotel Zest Takamatsu**
リーガホテルゼスト高松 *9-1 Furujin-machi (A2). 087-822-3555. 122 rooms. www.rihga.com/ index.html.* Good hotel, more luxurious than the former two, located in the center of Takamatsu. It has 3 restaurants.

**Kiyomi Sanso Hanajukai**
喜代美山荘花樹海
*3-5-10 Saiho Cho (A2 off map). 087-861-5580. hanajyukai.co.jp. 48 rooms.* Superb hotel built in a small forest area. Its **panoramic** day room and great onsen provide unequaled **views** over Takamatsu Bay.

### EAT

**Waraya Udon Restaurant**
うどんのわら家 *At the entrance to Shikoku-mura museum (C2). 087-843-3115. Open 10am–7pm.* Very popular and cheap country-style restaurant specializing in *sanuki udon* (noodles made from wheat flour).

**Tenkatsu Honten 天勝本店**
*At the west end of the Hyogo-machi arcade (A2). 087-821-5380. Open 11am–10pm (Sat–Sun 9pm).* This sushi restaurant (in the *ikesu category*, where the fish are caught as you watch) has enjoyed an unrivaled reputation since 1866!

**Alice in Takamatsu**
アリス・イン高松 *Symbol Tower (A2). 087-823-6088. Open 11.30am–10.30pm; lunch menu from ¥1, 500.* Nestling 495.4ft/151m up in the highest tower in Shikoku, this gastronomic restaurant "floats" over a port surrounded by the blue of the beautiful Inland Sea. Lunch is sophisticated: marinated sea bass, gratin of shellfish, carrot consommé, etc.

# Matsuyama★★ 松山

**The lively main town of Shikoku, Matsuyama, has grown up around a superb castle perched on the top of a hill. Situated at the center of the great Temple Pilgrimage route, the town itself boasts seven temples, including the eminent Ishite-ji. But the main local attraction has to be a visit to the delightful baths at Dogo Onsen, one of the oldest thermal spas in Japan, which, apart from steam, also exudes a delightful old-fashioned atmosphere.**

- **Population:** 525,051 – Ehime Prefecture.
- **Michelin Map:** Principal Sights Map A1 – Regional Map p453.
- **Location:** The town is on a plain in the island's northwest, 121mi/195km from Takamatsu. The JR station is 547yd/500m to the west of the castle. Dogo Onsen, 1.2mi/2km to the east of the center, is served by trams, as is the whole of the town. The ferry port is 6.2mi/10km to the north, at Takahama.
- **Kids:** Take a trip on the *Botchan Ressha*, the little steam train.
- **Timing:** One day is all you need to see the places of interest, unless you choose to stay and relax at Dogo Onsen.
- **Don't miss:** The castle; a bath at Dogo Onsen.

## SIGHTS

### Matsuyama Castle★★ 松山城

*10min walk E of the JR station. Take the tram from Kencho-mae or Shinonome-guchi, then the cable car or chairlift (¥500 round trip). Open 9am–4.30pm. ¥500.*

The castle at Matsuyama is undoubtedly among the finest in Japan because of its impressive position on the slope of a hill at a height of 433ft/132m, with spectacular **views**★ overlooking the town and the Inland Sea. The warlord Kato Yoshiaki began construction of the castle in 1602. Twenty-six years later, a five-story fortress and other palatial buildings, enclosed by walls had been built halfway up the hill.

Below the castle lay the fortified town, surrounded by moats; the western part was inhabited by samurai and the eastern part by craftsmen and tradesmen; the temples were situated to the north. Since then, like many castles Matsuyama-jo has undergone various reconstructions.

The main keep, destroyed by lightning in 1784, was restored as a three-story building in 1854. Further work was also carried out in 1968 and 1986 in order to restore it to its original style, employing only techniques and materials used in its original construction (no nails or concrete).

Having passed through the **Tonashi-mon**, you emerge onto a wide plateau planted with cherry trees. Inside the keep is a large collection of sabers, armor, ancient documents, objets d'art, painted panels, and pieces of calligraphy that belonged to the feudal lords Kato, Gamo, and Matsudaira.

*Walk back down the hill by the path on the west side, behind the castle.*

**Ninomaru Shiseki Teien** – *Open 9am–4.30pm. ¥100.*
At the bottom of the hill, this garden occupies the site of the old feudal palace, which burned down in 1872. The remains of the old palace walls now enclose a rock garden and pools into which a waterfall cascades.

**Bansui-so** – *3min walk from Ninomaru Shiseki Teien. Open Tue–Sun 10am–6pm. ¥800.* To the south, at the foot of the castle hill, this impressive villa was

**Did you know?**

Matsuyama is proud of being the capital of the **haiku** a short, yet meaningful poem consisting of 17 syllables. Born in the town, the poet Masaoka Shiki (1867–1902) revitalized and modernized this traditional form of poetry, of which Basho (1644–1694) is acknowledged as the great master.

built in the French neo-Classical style in 1922 by Count Hisamatsu Sadakoto, 15th lord of the Castle. Today it serves as an annex to the Ehime Prefectual Art Museum and displays Japanese 20C art.

### Dogo Onsen★★ 道後温泉

*1.2mi/2km E of Matsuyama. Tram Line 5 (¥150) or the Botchan Ressha train (¥300). Open 6am–11pm.*

The atmosphere in this small onsen is relaxed; people using the spa wander around the hotels and souvenir shops in *yukata* (cotton kimonos). Dogo Onsen is one of the oldest in Japan. Its alkaline springs *(108°F/42°C)* are even mentioned in the *Nihon Shoki* (*Japanese Chronicles*, 720) and have been visited by many Emperors and eminent historical figures. The baths also feature in writer Natsume Soseki's novel *Botchan* (1906), set in Matsuyama and read by nearly all Japanese schoolchildren. Virtually everything at the onsen is still as it is described in this largely autobiographical work, beginning with the small steam train imported from Germany in 1887: the **Botchan Ressha**. It has only recently been put back into service and renamed in his honor.

Arriving at the square where the tram station is located—also now restored—visitors are greeted by a large clock, **Botchan Karakuri**, erected in 1994. Small mechanical figures enact scenes from the novel at each quarter hour, accompanied by music. Close by is a foot bath *(ashiyu)*, where tired feet can be soothed in its thermal waters. A shop-lined arcade leads to the baths.

**Dogo Onsen Honkan** ★★★ – Constructed in 1894, this large and rather surreal wooden building looks like a cross between a Japanese castle and a seaside villa, with its mix of pagoda-style roofs, colonnades, balconies, paper lanterns, glass windows, and paper partitions. At the top is a turret bearing the figure of a white heron, recalling the onsen's mythical origin. The building served as the bathhouse in the film *Spirited Away* by the Japanese director Miyazaki Hayao. At the reception desk you can obtain a leaflet in English listing the prices and how to use the onsen.

Decorated with beautiful mosaics, there are two baths *(single sex)* and four rates: the **Kami-no-yu** *("Bath of the Gods")* is the cheapest and most popular, with a communal changing room *(bath ¥400, bath and light meal of tea and rice crackers ¥800)*. The **Tama-no-yu** ("Bath of the Spirits") is a little more intimate *(bath ¥1,200, bath and light meal served in a private room on the 3rd floor, ¥1,500)*. The second floor of the building houses a display of objects linked to the baths or to the Tea Ceremony, and some ancient examples of calligraphy. You could also take the guided tour of the **Yushinden** (*open 6.30am–9pm; ¥250*), baths reserved for the Imperial Family that were still in use until 1950. On the third floor is a room dedicated to Natsume Soseki. Finally, in a modern annex 1min walk away from the shopping arcade is the **Tsubaki-no-yu**, "the Camellia Bath," which is very popular with local retired people (*open 6am–11pm; ¥360*). It is worth noting that most of the ryokan in Dogo Onsen have their own baths.

### Ishite-ji★ 石手寺

*0.6mi/1km E of Dogo Onsen. 15min walk from the tram station, or bus nos. 2 or 8 in the direction of Oku-Dogo (¥160). Open 24hr. No charge.*

Of the 88 temples of the Shikoku Temple Pilgrimage, Ishite-jithe 51stis the most impressive and the most famous. It is also the most-visited after Zentsu-ji, near to Kotohira, where Kobo Daishi grew up. Constructed during the Kamakura era, around 1330 *(its origin goes back to the 9C)*, it contains some beautiful, Chinese-style architecture. Of

## A Thousand-Year-Old Pilgrimage

For 1,000 years, pilgrims *(henro)* traversed the island of Shikoku in a clockwise direction, in the search for enlightenment. Easily recognized by their white clothing, conical straw hats, sticks, and little bells, today's pilgrims make the same journey as the one made by the famous monk **Kukai** in the 8C *(known posthumously as Kobo Daishi)*, founder of the Buddhist Shingon school. They stop at each of the island's 88 sacred temples, 88 being the number of sins that the Shingon doctrine proclaims a man must cleanse himself of before he can achieve beatitude. The route in fact includes 89 temples because from temple 88 *(Okubo-ji)* pilgrims must complete the loop by revisiting temple 1 *(Ryozen-ji)*. On foot it takes two months to walk the 745.6mi/1,200km route, but these days many of the 100,000 pilgrims that come here annually travel by car or in air-conditioned tourist buses.

particular note are the Ni-mon, a gate with a floor built above it, the belfry, and a three-story pagoda.

## EXCURSIONS

### UCHIKO★ 内子

*25mi/40km S of Matsuyama.*

*Access by train (1hr) on the JR Yosan Line (¥740). Bicycle rental at Uchiko station (open Thu–Tue 9am–4pm).*

In the early years of the Meiji era, this little town of 20,000 inhabitants began specializing in the production of vegetable wax *(moku-ro)*.

Derived from the berries of the sumac tree *(urushi)*, it is used to make candles, polish, cosmetics, pencils, and medical ointments, and also for waterproofing the traditional paper umbrellas. Uchiko is also the birthplace of Oe Kenzaburo, who won the Nobel Prize for Literature in 1994.

The center of the town is a 15min walk from the station. Worth seeing is the splendid **Yokaichi Street**★, a charming, flower-filled, 0.6mi/1km-long main road lined with delightful houses from the Edo era, old candle makers still in business, a sake brewery, a tea house, and various souvenir and craft shops. The **Uchiko-za**★ *(open 9am–4.30pm; ¥300)* the local Kabuki theaterbuilt in 1916 and faithfully restored, presents *bunraku* shows in August. You can visit the auditorium *(650 seats)*, the backstage areas, and the basement, with its complex machinery for changing the scenery, made entirely from wood. Uchiko still has several wax merchants' residences dating from the Edo era,

## USEFUL INFORMATION

**Tourist Offices** – At JR Matsuyama station *(open 8.30am–5.15pm; 089-931-3914)* and at the foot of the mechanical clock at Dogo Onsen *(open 8am–8pm)*. To contact English speaking volunteers, *089-921-3708.*

## TRANSPORTATION

**BY AIR – Matsuyama Airport** – 3.7mi/6km W of the town *(bus every hour from the JR station, 20min)*. Flights for Tokyo *(1hr20min, ¥28,600)*, Osaka *(50min, ¥15,200)*, and also Nagoya, Fukuoka, and Okinawa.

**BY TRAIN – To and from Takamatsu** – JR Yosan Line *(2hr28min, ¥5,500)*.

**To and from Okayama** – JR Yosan Line *(3hr, ¥6,830)*.

**To and from Kochi** – via Tadotsu *(4hr20min, ¥10,380)*.

By Boat – Links to **Hiroshima** *(1hr in speed boat, ¥6,300; 2hr40min by ferry, ¥2,700)*, **Kobe** *(about 8hr30min, ¥6,100)*, **Osaka** *(9hr, ¥5,500)*, **Beppu,** and Oita. To go to the port *(Matsuyama Kankoko)*, take the Sightseeing Port Limousine Bus from the tram station at Dogo Onsen *(25min, ¥600)* or from Matsuyama station *(25min, ¥450)*.

particularly the **Kami-Haga-tei** *(open 9am–4.30pm; ¥400)*, built in 1894 by the Hon-Haga family, where you can see a typical Japanese interior of the time, a collection of buildings connected with the manufacture of wax, and a small museum.

## Ozu 大洲

*About 8mi/13km from Uchiko by Rt. 56; 15min by the JR Yosan train line, Iyo Ozu stop.*

Like its neighbor Uchiko, Ozu grew in the late-Edo era around the manufacture and trade of wax extracted from plants. It is today still a good example of a town that developed at the foot of a castle. The street of Obanahan-dori bears witness to this period, with well-preserved former merchant homes on the left and former samurai homes to the right. There are also a few early residences in neighboring streets.

The late-19C **Garyu Sanso villa★** was built by the Jokos, a successful family of merchants; it alone makes a visit to Ozu worthwhile *(open 9am–5pm; ¥500; brochure in English)*. The villa's sober interior – inspired by the Imperial villa of Katsura in Kyoto – shows extreme refinement in every detail. At the far end of the mossy garden there is a pavilion on piles, overlooking the Hiji River; every summer, traditional cormorant fishing takes place here.

The **castle** in the town was rebuilt in 2004, following an original 17C model, and with early techniques using no nails or concrete. The various phases of reconstruction are presented in the four-story dungeon. On the top floor there is a beautiful view over the town and river *(9am–5pm; ¥500)*.

## Uwajima 宇和島

*17mi/28km from Ozu by Rt. 56. 45min by the Yosan JR train line taken to the terminus.*

An elegant three-story **castle★** overlooks the town and its port. This is one of 12 castles in the country having preserved their original structures, designed in the late-16C by the famous architect **Todo Takatora** (15561630), who also built the castles in Ozu, Kyoto, and Edo. There is a stunning **panoramic view** of the town from the top floor *(open 9am4pm; ¥200)*.

The Date clan administrated the town for 250 years, Tokugawa Ieyasu having first entrusted the stronghold to Date Hidemune, Masamune's son, in 1614.

The **Tenshaen** garden *(Tensya Koen; open 8.30am4pm; ¥300)* bears witness to the family's great wealth. Created in 1866 by Date Munetada, the clan's seventh daimyo, this decorative garden is especially beautiful in April, when wisteria and irises are in bloom. The central pond, with its ornamental stones, as well as **Harusame Tei** *(calligraphy pavilion)* and **Sen-nen en Kan** *(Tea Ceremony house)*, all make this a remarkable place.

# ADDRESSES

## STAY

**Matsuyama Youth Hostel**
松山ユースホステル *22-3 Dogo-Himezuka. 10min from Dogo Onsen train stop. 089-933-6366. 8 rooms, 14 dormitories.* One of Japan's best youth hostels. *O-furo.*

**Hotel Patio Dogo**
ホテルパティオ・ドウゴ *20-12 Yuno-machi, Dogo Onsen. 089-941-4128. www.patio-do.co.jp. 101 rooms – from ¥14,700 – ¥750.* Charming, mid-category hotel.

**Dogo Kan 道後館**
*7-26 Dogo Takocho, Dogo Onsen. 089-941-7777. www.dogokan.co.jp. 90 room – ¥25,455/person half-board.* The resort's most luxurious hotel.

**Obayu Hot Spring** *Hijikawa-cho, Ozu 089-334-2007.* Centuries-old, traditional ryokan; delightful welcome.

## EAT

**Goshiki 五志喜本店** *3-5-4 Sanbancho. 089-933-3838. Open 11am–11pm.* Famous for *goshiki somen*.

**Dogo Bakushukan 道後・麦酒館** *13-20 Dogo-Yunomachi. 089-945-6866. Open 11am–9.30pm. Izakaya* near Dogo Onsen.

# The Iya Valley★
# 祖谷渓

**Hidden among the high mountains at the center of the island of Shikoku, the Iya Valley is one of the most isolated regions of Japan. Dotted with cottages, its slopes covered with maple forests, steep-sided gorges, and ancient vine bridges spanning emerald-green torrents, the effect is very picturesque.**
**Due to its inaccessibility, the valley provided a refuge for the survivors of the Taira clan after their defeat by the Minamoto at the Battle of Yashima in 1185. Swapping the sword for the hoe and scythe, the warriors became farmers and today, many villagers can claim to be descended from ancestors who served at the Court during the Heian era.**
**A rural paradise until the 1970s, the valley was disrupted by economic development, with the construction of buildings, roads, car parks, and water courses; a frenzied round of concrete-laying that affected agriculture and spoilt the beauty of the countryside. Despite that, Iya remains a haven of peace, where you can enjoy many outdoor activities, from rafting to hiking.**

- **Population:** 5,000 *(Miyoshi District: Population 35,000)* – Tokushima Prefecture.
- **Michelin Map:** Regional Map p453.
- **Location:** The Iya Valley is at the center of Shikoku, 46.6mi/75km west of Tokushima, 37.3mi/60km south of Takamatsu, and 28mi/45km north of Kochi. The Iya, which has its source on Mount Tsurugi *(6,414ft/1,955m)*, follows a course about 37.3mi/60km to the east of the Yoshino River, of which it is a tributary. The JR Dosan Line (Takamatsu–Kochi) serves Awa Ikeda and Oboke, at the entrance to the valley.
- **Kids:** A boat trip through the Oboke Gorge.
- **Timing:** Few buses run in the valley, so if you are short on time, you could rent a car or opt for a day's Bonnet Bus tour *(see p464)*. Otherwise, allow for a two-day stay.
- **Don't miss:** Oboke Gorge; the bridge at Kazura-bashi.

## SIGHTS

### OBOKE 大歩危

*From Awa Ikeda, Route 32 and the railway line follow the course of the Yoshino River right through a spectacular gorge, as far as Oboke, 15.5mi/25km farther south.*

The name of this fairly insignificant small town literally means "Great Dangerous Step," because of the extraordinarily steep-sided aspect of the valley here.

#### Oboke Gorge★ 大歩危峡

*Boats (open 9am–5pm, 30min, ¥1,050) leave the pier at the foot of the Oboke-kyo Mannaka Hotel. 15min walk N of JR Oboke station.*

The result of natural erosion, the spectacular gorges of the Yoshino River run for about 2.5mi/4km between Oboke and Koboke in the hollows of steep chalk cliffs streaked with shale varying in color from gray, black, and red-brown. The dark-green waters of the river are particularly good for rafting and kayaking (see Address Book p 464). Among the thick vegetation covering the banks you can see traces left by wild animals *(woolly macaques, deer)*, as well as huge, evocatively shaped rock formations.

#### Lapis Oboke Museum
ラピス大歩危

*Main road between the site of the gorge and Oboke station. Open 9am–5pm. ¥500.*

### Awa Odori, Japan's biggest festival

The town of Tokushima is famous for its folk dance festival Awa Odori, the most impressive in the country. From August 12 to August 15, during *Bon*, the **Festival of the Dead**, more than 100,000 dancersboth men and women, dressed in brightly colored kimonosparade through the streets to the sound of *shamisen* (three-stringed instrument plucked with a plectrum), drums, brass, and flutes. Kicking up their feet and keeping time with their arms, the dancers move forward maintaining a bewitching rhythm, something like a samba, and chanting *"Ah! Yatosa! Yatosa!"* It is known as the "dance of the lunatics" because the lyrics state: "Whether you dance or not you are mad, so you might as well dance."

This museum offers a geological history of Shikoku and various examples of rocks and crystals from all over the world, including a meteorite from Mars.

### Heike Yashiki 平家屋敷

*Route 45, 2.5mi/4km E of Oboke station. Open 8am–6pm (Nov–Feb 8am–5pm). ¥500.*

This thatched house was originally the residence of Emperor Antoku's doctor, who fled here after the defeat of the Heike in 1185 *(the Emperor commited suicide by throwing himself into the sea)*. The interior has retained its fine timber structure and displays a varied collection of agricultural and craft tools.

## NISHI IYA★★ 西祖谷

Accessible from Oboke or Awa Ikeda, the western part of the Iya Valley *(Nishi Iya)* is the most tourist-oriented. Cut off from the world for a long period, it survived by growing buckwheat, barley, tobacco, and millet.

Despite a scattering of unattractive buildings, it has been reasonably successful in resisting the excessive tide of concrete, particularly along the panoramic route★★ (the old Route 32) that winds over 12.4mi/20km between the hamlets of Nishi Iya and Iya-guchi in the north, in the direction of Awa Ikeda.

Along the way are several **spectacular viewpoints** of the gorges, whose slopes are covered with conifers and wild cherry trees. The statue of the Manneken-pis is a copy of the one in Brussels, built on a rock overlooking a 656.2ft/200m precipice. The nearby Iya Onsen Hotel has a wonderful, open-air onsen on the banks of the river (¥1,500), reached by cable car.

## USEFUL INFORMATION

**Tourist Offices** – In JR Awa Ikeda station *(open 9am–5pm; 0883-72-5865)* and the Lapis Oboke Museum *(open 9am–5pm; 0883-84-1489)*.

## TRANSPORTATION

### GETTING TO AND FROM THE IYA VALLEY

**BY TRAIN** – The Awa Ikeda and Oboke stations are served by the JR Dosan Line. Awa Ikeda is also on the JR Tokushima Line. Trains run to and from **Takamatsu** *(1hr20min, ¥3,270)*, to and from **Kochi** *(50min, ¥3,100)*, and to and from **Tokushima** *(1hr50min, ¥1,580)*.

### GETTING AROUND

**BY BUS** – From JR Awa Ikeda station, round-trip several times daily to Nishi Iya *(Iya Onsen and Kazura-bashi)*. Kazura-bashi and Higashi Iya Apr–Nov several times daily. For Chiiori, take the Oboke bus to Oshima tunnel.

**BY CAR** – Rental for around ¥5,000 per day at JR Awa Ikeda station *(0883-72-0807)* or at Oboke-kyo Mannaka Hotel *(0883-84-1216). Reservations required.*

**BY TOUR BUS** – **The Bonnet Bus**, an little old-fashioned bus, leaves JR Awa Ikeda station at 11.40am, tours the places of interest *(Oboke Gorge, Kazura-bashi, Iya Onsen)*, and returns at 6.20pm *(Mar–Nov; ¥5,200, including boat trip and lunch; reservations required; 0883-72-1231)*.

**Kazura-bashi★** 祖谷のかずら橋
*Route 32, 2.2mi/3.5km NE of Nishi Iya.*
*Open dawn–dusk. ¥500.*
It is this river crossing built from vines, 147.6ft/45m long and 49.2ft/15m above the water, that makes this area famous. It dates from the 12C, when the Taira clan took refuge in the valley. If threatened by possible attackers, the warriors could easily cut the cords of the bridge to block their way. A score of identical bridges onced crossed the river, but only this one and two others farther up the valley have survived. The bridge is remade every three years using the traditional techniques for plaiting the lianas, but is now reinforced with carefully concealed steel cables. The logs that make up the walkway are spaced so that a foot can pass between them, which makes crossing the bridge a little nerve-wracking. There is a small **waterfall** 164ft/50m upstream.

**Chiiori★** ちいおり
*12.4mi/20km E of Oboke station. After Kazura-bashi, continue for about 3.1mi/5km on Route 32 as far as the Oshima tunnel. From there, the road to the right climbs for 3mi/5km (a 90min walk) up to the house. Visit by appointment, Thu-Tue. No charge. 0883-88-5290. www.chiiori.org.*
In the tiny hamlet of Chiiori, "House of the Flute" is a thatched house dating from 1720, bought and restored by the American writer Alex Kerr.
Arriving in the valley in the early 1970s, he was the first to issue an environmental wake-up call. In his book *Lost Japan*, published in 1993, Kerr recounts how, in the process of modernization, the country is gradually disfiguring the environment. Thus, out of Japan's 30,000 streams and rivers only three have escaped the ravages of concrete in some form or other. In the valley, most of the thatched roofs have been replaced by cheaper-to-maintain corrugated iron or industrial tiles. The author founded an association that fights for the valley's ecological preservation. His warning seems to be slowly bearing fruit. Chiiori proudly shows off its ancient architecture, its cedarwood flooring, its *irori* (sunken hearth), and enjoys a **panoramic view** of the valley. Accommodation is available for visitors *(Thu–Mon – dormitory and full board; ¥3,800)*, who must help with the chores.

**HIGASHI IYA★** 東祖谷
More difficult to access than Nishi Iya, the eastern part of the valley *(Higashi Iya)* sees far fewer visitors.

**Ochiai-Shuraku** 落合集落
*Route 439, 11.2mi/18km E of Kazura-bashi.*
The hamlet of Ochiai, with its terraces rising up the mountain slope, planted with rice and tobacco, is thought to have been founded in the Middle Ages by the former samurai-turned-farmers of the Heike clan. Most of the houses date from the Edo era; some of the old-style thatched roofs are under restoration.

**Oku Iya Kazura-bashi★**
奥祖谷かずら橋
*Route 439, 23.6mi/38km E of Kazura-bashi. Open 8am–4pm. ¥500.*
At the foot of Mount Tsurugi *(6,414ft/1,955m)*, the second highest summit on Shikoku , is this pair of vine bridges—the longest and highest nicknamed "the husband" (*Otto no hashi)*, and the smaller one "the wife" *(Tsuma no hashi)*. Reinforced with steel cables, they are rebuilt at intervals.
As with the **Kazura-bashi**, though safe, the bridges can feel rickety when crossing. Farther upstream, you can cross the river in a gondola mounted on a cable and pulled by a rope.

## ADDRESSES

### STAY

**Iyashi-no-Onsenkyo**
いやしの温泉郷 *Sugeoi, Higashi-Iya. 0883-88-2975. www.sobanoyado.jp. 12 rooms, 2 bungalows – from ¥14,850/ person.* On Route 439, right at the end of Higashi Iya, is a welcoming collection of thatched cottages built of wood or stone, offering Japanese or Western rooms.

There is a good restaurant serving soba made on the premises. *A pleasant onsen, with open-air bath.*

**Oboke-kyo Mannaka** 大歩危峡まんなか *15min walk N of JR Oboke station. ℘0883-84-1216. www.mannaka.co.jp. 30 rooms – from ¥12,000.* The Hotel overhanging the Oboke Gorge; comfortable Western and Japanese, high-quality cuisine. Spacious *onsen*.

**Iya Onsen Hotel** ホテル祖谷温泉 *Route 32, Nishi Iya. ℘0883-75-2311. www.iyaonsen.co.jp. 21 rooms – from ¥17,370/person.* Japanese-style rooms and divine *kaiseki* cuisine made with seasonal ingredients. You can also lunch without breaking the bank. *The onsen, at the foot of the gorge, is a pure delight.*

### EAT

The hotels mentioned also have restaurants. Near Kazura-bashi, cheap cafes serve *yakizakana*: river fish grilled on charcoal.

**Senkichi** 仙吉 *Route 45, near to Ikyonoyu Onsen, Nishi Iya. ℘0883-87-2733. Open Apr–Nov Fri–Wed 11am–5pm.* A rustic setting and local cuisine, including the tasty *Iya soba* (buckwheat noodles).

### SPORT AND LEISURE

**Rafting** – Two companies with English-speaking staff organize trips downriver on rafts in the Oboke Gorge, as well as kayaking and canyoning. From *¥6,500 for a half-day.* **Mont-Bell** – *℘0883-76-8110; www.montbell.com.* **Happy Raft** – *℘0887 -75-0500; www.happyraft.com.*

# Kochi and the Pacific Coast★
# 高知・太平洋側

**Separated from the rest of Japan by mountains on one side and the Pacific on the other, the Kochi region has retained its own character and special features, notably its dialect, the Tosa-ben, which was also the name of the province until the beginning of the 17C. Washed over by the warm, fish-laden waters of the Kuroshio Current—the Japanese equivalent of the Gulf Stream—the coast enjoys a warm, humid climate, with the country's highest annual rainfall after Okinawa. Kochi has a glorious castle and a fine botanical garden. The neighboring beach at Katsurahama is considered one of Japan's most beautiful. To the southwest, the coast is carved out of virgin tropical vegetation, as is the Shimanto, claimed to be Japan's last remaining free-flowing river. At the southernmost point of the coast, the waves of the Pacific beat against the spectacular promontories of Cape Ashizuri.**

- **Population:** Kochi: Population 330,078 – Kochi Prefecture.
- **Michelin Map:** Principal Sights Map B3 – Regional Map p453.
- **Location:** South of Shikoku, 87mi/140km from Matsuyama; 99.4mi/160km from Takamatsu, Kochi is on the Pacific. Cape Ashizuri is 93.2mi/150km farther southwest. A wide avenue and tramway run north from the JR station into town.
- **Kids:** Makino Botanical Garden and Katsurahama beach; summer whale-watching cruise.
- **Timing:** 3 days, including travel, for Kochi, the Shimanto River, and Cape Ashizuri. Visit Kochi on Sunday for the market.
- **Don't miss:** The Kochi Castle; the Cape Ashizuri panorama; *katsuo no tataki* (seared bonito), a Kochi specialty.

## SIGHTS

Opposite the JR Kochi station, a major road leads to the south and **Harimaya-bashi** *(about a 10min walk)*, the center of the town. There, tucked away amid some modern buildings, is Harimaya-bashi's small red bridge. Crossing an arm of the river that has now been filled in, it was the scene of a secret lovers' tryst between a Buddhist monk and a young servant-girl in the 19C.

Farther to the north, the **Sunday Market**★ *(Nichi-o-ichi)* has taken place along a stretch of the *Otesuji-dori* (road) for nearly three centuries. Several hundred stands sell the products of the region's farmers, fishermen, and craftsmen—vegetables, fruit, flowers, fish and shellfish, coral artifacts, knives, pottery, etc.—laid out over 0.75mi/1.2km. The Otesuji-dori comes out at the entrance to the castle.

### Kochi Castle★★ 高知城

*15min walk W of Harimaya-bashi. Open 9am–5pm. ¥400.*

Originally built as a prestigious pleasure palace and not simply an austere fortress, Kochi Castle is among the most classically elegant and well-preserved in the whole country. Built in 1603 by the feudal lord Yamanouchi Kazutoyo, it was rebuilt after a fire in 1748. Entry is through the impressive **Ote-mon**★, a gate enhanced by fine ironwork and flanked by thick stone walls.

High on the ramparts, trapdoors and slits in the walls allowed projectiles to be aimed at possible assailants.

> **The market town**
>
> The Sunday market is Kochi's largest and best known but it is not the only one: every day, except Monday, a market is held somewhere in the town, the largest being on Tuesdays and Fridays.

Just beyond the entrance you can see the statue of Itagaki Taisuke, a native of Kochi and founder of the Freedom and People's Rights Movement, which pushed for democracy during the Meiji era. A wide stone staircase leads to the top of the hill *(141ft/43m high)* on which were built the houses of residential lords *(Ninomaru)*.

These were destroyed during the Meiji Restoration in 1873 to make room for a park planted with cherry trees.

The only part to survive was the five-story **keep**★★, which stands in the center of the internal defensive compound *(Honmaru)*. It is reached by a roundabout route, with a staircase that comes to a dead end in an attempt to fool the enemy. From the top there is a lovely **view** over the whole of the town.

### Makino Botanical Garden★ 牧野植物園

*On the hill at Godaisan, 3mi/5km to the E. Buses run from Kochi station (every hour, 20min) to Makino-shokubutsuen-mae. Open 9am–5pm. ¥700.*

Founded 50 years ago by Professor Makino Tomitaro (1862–1957), father

## USEFUL INFORMATION

**Tourist Offices** – In JR Kochi station *(open 9am–5pm; 088-826-3337) and JR Nakamura station (open 9am–5pm; 0880-35-4171).*

## TRANSPORTATION

**BY PLANE** – **Kochi Airport** *6.2mi/10km E of Kochi.* Bus *(every hour, 35 min, ¥700)* from the JR station. Flights for Tokyo *(1hr15min, ¥30,000)*, Nagoya, Osaka, Fukuoka, and Okinawa.

**BY TRAIN** – Kochi is on the JR Dosan Line. Trains run to and from **Takamatsu** *(2hr20min, ¥4,750)* and to and from **Okayama** *(2hr30min, ¥5,590)*.

**BY BUS** – 5 buses daily from **Matsuyama** *(2hr30min, ¥3,500)*. Links also with the other large towns, Shikoku and Honshu.

**BY FERRY** – Ferries for Tokyo and Osaka leave the **port at Kochi**, *(located 15min by tram to the S of the town)*.

### Sumo-dogs

The Kochi region has a long tradition of fighting dogs. The result of cross-breeding (the Inu, an indigenous dog from Shikoku, with western breeds such as bulldogs, German short-haired pointers, or mastiffs), the Tosa is a formidable, short-haired animal of impressive size, with a steely jaw and weighing up to 220.5lb/100kg. Every year, dozens of breeders enter their champions in the tournaments held here. The matches take place in an arena according to rules similar to those governing sumo wrestling. Dogs enter the ring dressed in ceremonial silk costumes. Each bout lasts for about 10 minutes. The first dog to fall to the ground, bark, whine, take three steps back or turn its back on its opponent is the loser. The winner is rewarded with an honorific title, the highest one being, as among the sumo wrestlers, that of *yokozuna*, "Grand Champion."

of Japanese botany, this center for the research into and conservation of plant species includes a museum, a restaurant, and a 14.8-acre/6ha park, with flower-beds and greenhouses full of orchids, hibiscus, lotus, medicinal plants, and bonsai trees—in total there are almost 3,000 varieties of plants.

### Chikurin-ji★ 竹林寺

*Opposite the Botanical Garden.*
*Open 8.30am–5pm. ¥400.*

No. 31 of the 88 sacred temples on the Temple Pilgrimage route, the "Temple in the Bamboo Forest" was founded in 724 by Gyoki, a Buddhist monk. Its five-story pagoda was refurbished in 1970, but the temple contains a lovely **Zen garden** *(designed in the 14C by Soseki)* and some fine statutes from the Heian and Kamakura eras (10–13C) in the **Treasure House**★.

## EXCURSIONS

### Katsurahama★ 桂浜

*7.5mi/12kmi S of Kochi.*
*Bus (every 30min, journey time 35min) from Harimaya-bashi.*

Forming a promontory at the southern end of Urado Bay, the popular **beach**★ at Katsurahaman is long, sandy, and lined with pine trees. On the promenade bordering the beach is a statue of **Sakamoto Ryoma**, a celebrated local hero who rebelled against the shogunate and was assassinated in 1867, aged 32. There is a small museum dedicated to him at the foot of the hill to the west. On the other side of the beach, the **Tosa Token Center** holds contests between Tosa fighting dogs in the tournament season (*open May, Jun, Nov, Jan; Sun 9am–4pm; ¥2,000; ask locally about tournament dates).*

### Shimanto River★ 四万十川

*68.4mi/110km SW of Kochi. Train to Nakamura (1hr40min, ¥4,500). From the JR station, walk to the river, where there are boat trips (50 min, ¥2,000).*

The Shimanto-gawa *(121.8mi/196km)* is claimed to be the **last large free-flowing river in Japan**, unspoiled by dams or concrete dikes. Its clear water is full of *ayu* trout, which the local people fish from the beginning of the summer. The bridges have no parapets so that the floodwaters flow over them rather than washing them away. The sandy islands and banks are covered in dense vegetation, where herons and egrets nest. **Dragonflies** and **fireflies** swoop and flutter everywhere. From Nakamura, a town located near the estuary, you can also rent kayaks in which to paddle upriver.

### Ashizuri-misaki★★ 足摺岬

*93mi/150km SW of Kochi.*
*Train to Nakamura (1hr40min, ¥4,500), then bus to Tosa-Shimizu (1hr), a small fishing port 6.8mi/11km from the cape, which is reached by another local bus.*

At the southern tip of Shikoku, Cape Ashizuri forms a spectacular spur. The base of its steep cliffs, 262.5ft/80m below, is lashed by the foamy waves of the ocean. At the entrance to the site is a bronze statue of **John Manjiro**

Ashizuri-misaki

(1827–98), a prominent local figure and the first Japanese to visit the United States. A path follows the coastline beneath an archway formed by numerous camellias *(in flower Jan–Mar)*.

From the lighthouse, built in 1914, there is a fine **view**★★ over the ocean, where it is sometimes possible to catch glimpses of **turtles**. Near the lighthouse, the **Kongofuku-ji temple 38** on the pilgrimage route was founded in 822 by Kobo Daishi in honor of the thousand-armed divinity Kannon.

The buildings date from 1662. Near the town of **Tatsukushi** *(9.3mi/15km to the west of the cape, as the tide goes out)*, **rock formations** emerge from the seabed looking like the felled trunks of fossilized trees. Close by is an underwater park, where you can climb down an enclosed spiral staircase to the sea floor and watch fish from an observation room.

# ADDRESSES

## STAY

### KOCHI

**7 Days Hotel** セブンデイズホテル *2-13-17 Harimayacho. ☎088-884-7100. www.7dayshotel.com. 80 rooms – ¥7,880.* Very central, charming, stylish business hotel. Rooms small, but well-maintained; copious breakfast; recommended.

**Josei-kan 城西館** *2-5-34 Kamimachi. ☎088-875-0111. www.joseikan.co.jp. 70 rooms – ¥30,000.* Near castle; for the past century, lodgings for the Japanese Emperor when in Kochi.

### NAKAMURA

**Iyashi-no-Sato** 四万十いやしの里 *3363 Shimoda, 5mi/8km from Nakamura. ☎0880-31-5111. 30 rooms – from ¥14,700/person.* Overlooking Shimanto estuary, beautiful, Japanese-style rooms with futon or bed, some with terrace; private *rotenburo*. Pleasant *onsen*.

### ASHIZURI-MISAKI

**Ashizuri Thermae** 国民宿舎足摺テルメ *1433-3 Ashizuri-misaki. ☎0880-88-0301. www.terume.com. 41 rooms - from ¥10,650/person, half board..* In a wild setting facing the sea, and of interest for its extensive thermal spa facilities: swimming pool, sauna, indoor and outdoor *onsens*.

## EAT

**Hirome Ichiba** ひろめ市場*Near to the castle, at the end of the Obiyamachi arcade. ☎088-822-5287. Open 8am–11pm.* This popular covered market has 60 or so cheap eating places serving Chinese dishes and local specialties. Try the *katsuo no tataki*: sashimi of lightly grilled bonito coated with salt and lemon.

**Tosahan** 土佐藩高知本店 *At the start of the Obiyamachi arcade. ☎088-821-0002. Open 11.30am–10pm.* An elegant address, with a decor of dark-wood, where you can enjoy Kochi cuisine, mainly seafood. The lunch menu is reasonably priced.

## SPORT AND LEISURE

**Whale Watching** – Whaling was carried out for nearly 500 years from the villages and towns along this part of the coastline. While the Japanese continue to hunt whales in the North Pacific and Antarctic, whaling has ceased in the waters around Shikoku. Boat trips now provide opportunities to see whales as they pass near to the coast.

The season lasts May–Sept.

Trips *(3hr, ¥5,000)* leave from the port of Kochi *(☎088-842-2850)* or from Cape Ashizuri *(☎0880-84-0723)*.

# KYUSHU

**In the far southwestern corner of the Japanese archipelago is Kyushu, Japan's third largest island. The southern part of the island has a tropical feel, while the north has a more temperate climate. Its many National Parks contain luxuriant forests dominated by holm oaks, camphor trees, bamboos, cedars, and magnolias. A myriad of smaller islands, many uninhabited, are spread out across the East China Sea. The name Kyushu means "nine provinces," referring to the original provinces into which the island was divided before the seven present-day prefectures were created. The island is mountainous, with two volcanic chains meeting in the center at Mount Aso *(5,223ft/1,592m)*.**

### Highlights

1. Futuristic **Fukuoka** urban renewal: **Canal City** and **Hawks Town** (pp473-474 and p475)
2. Stopping for noodles in Chinatown, **Nagaski** (p481)
3. Scaling **Mount Unzen** on the Shimabara Peninsula (pp483-484)
4. Sunset at **Kunimigaoka** (p490)
5. An immersive black sand treatment at **Takegawara Onsen, Beppu** (p506)

- **Population:** 14.7 million – Fukuoka, Kagoshima, Kumamoto, Miyazaki, Nagasaki, Oita, and Saga prefectures.
- **Michelin Map:** Principal Sights Map A3.
- **Location:** To the southwest of Honshu, from which it is separated by a narrow strait of 2,297ft/700m, the island of Kyushu covers an area of 14,454.5sq mi /37,437sq km, slightly less than that of Switzerland. Fukuoka-Hakata, in the north, marks the end of the Shinkansen Line from Tokyo. There are airports at Fukuoka, Oita *(Beppu)*, Nagasaki, Kagoshima, and Kumamoto. JR express trains run between the main cities. JR Kyushu operates a Shinkansen Line between Kagoshima in the south, with Kumamoto and Fukuoka-Hakata.
- **Kids:** Dolphin-spotting on a boat trip from Tsujishima harbour
- **Timing:** Allow at least a week to see the island's main sights.
- **Don't miss:** A bath in the hot sands at Ibusuki and a riverside *onsen* at Kurokawa; Nagasaki Bay and its terraced hills; the Kyushu National Museum in Dazaifu; excursions to the island of Yakushima and Mount Aso.

## A Land of Fire

Kyushu's vast moonlike caldera is one of the largest in the world. Also known as "the land of fire," Kyushu is an area of intense volcanic activity, as demonstrated by the steaming "hells" of Beppu and a multitude of other hot springs, such as Kurokawa Onsen, Ibusuki, and Yufuin. But the sea is never far away, and the jagged coastline forms a striking contrast with the mountains. Thanks to the deep waters of these sinuous bays, great ports such as Kagoshima and Nagasaki grew up here.

Kyushu is the cradle of the most ancient of the Japanese cultures *(Yayoi era, 300BC to 300AD)*. Its proximity to Korea and China made it the main point of contact between Japan and mainland Asia. It was also the point of entry for the first Westerners to visit Japan: the Portuguese who landed on the island in the 16C, followed by the Spanish, British, and Dutch. With the arrival of European missionaries, notably the Jesuit priest St. Francis Xavier, Christianity spread rapidly throughout the island, making many converts. Long persecuted by

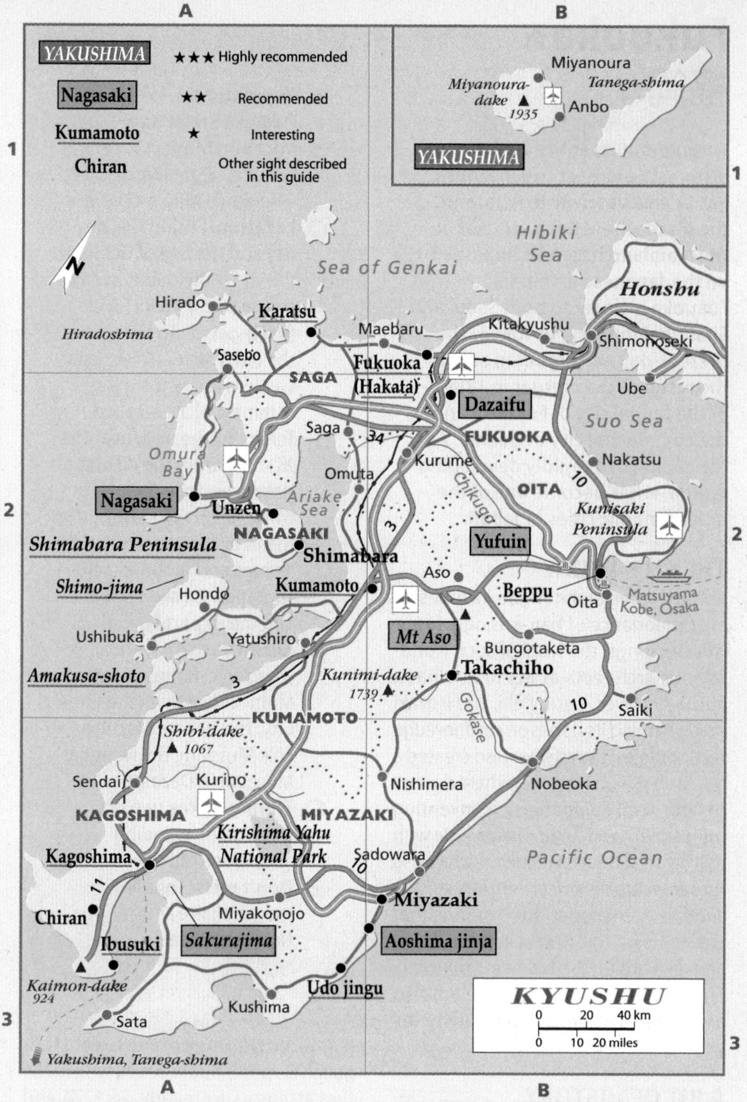



the central government and forced to practice their faith in secret, today the island is dotted with their small mock-Gothic Christian churches. The Korean and Chinese influences gave birth to a rich and varied ceramic art, from the sober pottery of Karatsu to the multi-colored porcelain of Arita and Imari.

In the north the port of Fukuoka, the main entry point by sea, is a thrusting, energetic, aggressively modern city. Farther west, Nagasaki has a more romantic feel, with a mixture of European and Asian influences. Kagoshima, in the south, lies in the shadow of Sakurajima, a volcano as graceful as Mount Fuji in appearance—but when angry, still-spewing clouds of ash into the air. Last, but not least, the island of Yakushima contains a magnificent forest of 1,000-year-old cedars.

Nevertheless, Kyushu is also Japan's fourth economic zone after the main metropolitan areas of Tokyo, Osaka, and Nagoya, accounting for approximately 10 percent of the country's GNP.

# Fukuoka★
# 福岡

**Throughout its entire 2,000-year history, the largest city in Kyushu has been a gateway to Asia, and the place where the culture of the mainland has most impinged on the Japanese archipelago: Fukuoka is closer to both Seoul and Shanghai than it is to Tokyo. The present-day metropolitan area is the result of the merger in 1889 of the feudal city of Fukuoka and the commercial city of Hakata. As the capital of a rapidly developing region, it has become one of the most dynamic cities in Japan.**

- **Population:** 1,457,176 – Fukuoka Prefecture.
- **Michelin Map:** Principal Sights Map A3 – Regional Map p471.
- **Location:** Facing Hakata Bay and the Sea of Genkai, the city is divided down the center by the Naka River *(Naka-gawa)*. To the west, the old quarter of Fukuoka Castle is today the main commercial area, called Tenjin. To the east, near the JR station, are the district of Hakata and the Canal City complex. In the middle, the island of Nakasu is noted for its bars and nightlife. The JR station is called Hakata and the airport Fukuoka.
- **Kids:** The giant Ferris wheel and Robosquare in Momochi; activities at Canal City; the Hakata Machiya Folk Museum; the National Museum in Dazaifu.
- **Timing:** Allow two or three days, including excursions outside the city.
- **Don't miss:** Dinner in a *yatai*; the Kyushu National Museum.

## THE CITY TODAY

Its innovative architecture includes an overabundance of hair-raisingly futuristic buildings, the work of such world-famous architects as Reem Koolhaas, Michael Graves, Cesar Pelli, and Isozaki Arata. Pinning its hopes on cutting-edge technologies, the city has also created a research park by the sea, where dozens of high-tech companies are inventing tomorrow's world. But, side by side with this flashy modernity, Fukuoka has also preserved its historical heritage, and its *yatai*: old-fashioned food stands that are set up on the streets in the evening and dismantled the following morning. These serve simple dishes in a noisy, aroma-filled atmosphere recalling the great, teeming capitals of Asia.

## A BIT OF HISTORY

**Mongolian hordes and the *kamikaze*** – Rice cultivation and techniques for casting iron and bronze were introduced to the north of Kyushu from the Korean peninsula more than 2,000 years ago. From there, they spread throughout Japan. By the 6C, Dazaifu, the regional capital *(later moved to Fukuoka)*, was maintaining diplomatic relations with the Chinese Sui dynasty (581–618). In the Middle Ages, Nanotsu—the old port of Fukuoka—became one of the most prosperous in Japan.

It aroused the envy of the Great Mongolian Emperor Kublai Khan, who made two attempts to invade, in 1274 and 1281, raising one of the largest armies in history consisting of 150,000 soldiers and 4,400 ships.

The Japanese were massively outnumbered, relying on their modest fortifications built along the shoreline to repel the invading hordes. Defeat seemed inevitable, until the area was providentially hit by a typhoon that destroyed the invaders' fleet and forced them to retreat. The Japanese called it *kamikaze*, the "divine wind" that saved Japan.

## SIGHTS

*The Fukuoka Welcome Card, available from Tourist Offices, offers overseas visitors reduced prices to tourist attractions, hotels, and restaurants.*

### Shōfuku-ji 聖福寺

*15min walk from JR Hakata station, or 5min walk from Gion subway station. No charge.*

This is the oldest Zen temple in Japan, founded by the monk Eisai *(who also introduced tea to Japan)* on his return from China in 1195. The fine wooden building with its double roof *(closed to the public)* has, as is so often the case in Japan, been destroyed and rebuilt several times over the centuries. Only the garden is open to the public.

### Kushida-jinja 櫛田神社

*10min walk from Gion subway station. Museum: Open 10am–5pm. ¥300.*

A beautiful and very old *gingko biloba* tree marks the entrance to this shrine founded in 754 *(the present buildings date from 1587)*, which is also the starting point every summer for the spectacular Yamagasa Matsuri *(see box above)*.

A small **museum** displays the huge, richly decorated floats that are carried during the festival.

### Hakata Machiya Folk Museum★ 博多町屋ふるさと館

*Opposite the shrine. Open 10am–5.30pm. ¥200.*

The collections of this museum, devoted to the traditional culture and lifestyle of Hakata, are displayed in a number of restored merchants' houses from the Taisho era (1912–26). There are faithful reconstructions of shop interiors from the beginning of the century, and regular demonstrations of local crafts: doll making, silk weaving, the making of spinning tops. There is also a 20min video about the Yamagasa Matsuri.

### Canal City Hakata キャナルシティ博多

*10min walk W of JR Hakata station.*

Almost a city within a city, this huge American-style shopping mall opened in 1996 and covers an area of

### Yamagasa Matsuri

Every year for the past 700 years, from July 1 to 15, this colorful festival in Fukuoka culminates in a furious race between teams of 26 men, representing the different districts of the city. Each team has to carry a float weighing almost a ton over a 3.1mi/5km course in a specified time, while the spectators throw water over them as they pass. The contestants run dressed in a simple costume consisting of a *shimekomi* (or *fundoshi*), the loincloth worn by sumo wrestlers (so their legs and buttocks are exposed), a light cotton jacket bearing the insignia of their team, and sandals made of rice straw.

## USEFUL INFORMATION

**Tourist Office** – In Hakata station. *Open 8am–8pm. 092-431-3003.* An association of volunteers offers guided tours in English *(092-733-5050; www.welcomefukuoka.or.jp)*.

## TRANSPORTATION

**BY PLANE – Fukuoka Airport** – Two subway stops from JR Hakata station *(5min, ¥250)* on the Fukuoka Airport Line. From Tokyo, departures almost every hour, between 6.30am and 8.10pm *(about 1hr25min, ¥33,000)*.

**BY TRAIN – Hakata Station** – From Tokyo, the fastest train is the Shinkansen Nozomi *(5hr30min, ¥22,120)*, but it does not accept the Japan Rail Pass. The JR Pass can be used on the Hikari trains, but you will have to change at Shinosaka or Okayama *(6hr)*. The **JR Kyushu Pass** gives access to the whole of the JR network in Kyushu for 5 days *(¥16,000)*.

### A Young Geisha

Umeka ("plum fragrance"), 21-years-old, is one of the 25 geishas still practicing her profession in the traditional tearooms and restaurants of Fukuoka. As entertainers specializing in the traditional arts, geisha are far removed from the skimpily-dressed hostesses who work in some bars. "In the old days, the geisha had a protector *(danna)* to whom they granted their favors, but that isn't the case today," says Umeka. A native of Fukuoka, she began her apprenticeship when she left high school. "I never imagined how hard it would be, for a modern girl like me, to learn and become accustomed to the profession. It's very demanding, on both an artistic and personal level. We work every night, so it's impossible to go out with friends or have a family life."

2,583,338.5sq ft/240,000sq m near the Naka-gawa. Part of this river has been diverted to form an **artificial canal** that flows through the middle of a central atrium; huge jets of water erupt from the canal at regular intervals. The mall also houses a **13-screen multiplex cinema**, hotels, a **variety theater**, and hundreds of **boutiques**, **restaurants**, and **gaming halls**. Street performances and concerts take place throughout the day.

## Asian Art Museum★★

福岡アジア美術館

*7F–8F Riverain Center Bldg. Subway: Nakasu-Kawabata, exit 6. Open Thu–Tue 10am–8pm. Closed Dec 26–Jan 1, Closed Wed. ¥200.*

Situated within a large, light-filled modern building, opened in 1999, this museum is the first in the world to be entirely devoted to modern and contemporary Asian art, bringing together some 2,300 works by painters and sculptors from India, China, Myanmar, Malaysia, Thailand, the Philippines, Pakistan, and of course Japan. There are no statues of Buddha here—the museum displays original and unusual works, sometimes humorous or eccentric, sometimes based on folk and ethnic traditions, and always of high quality.

As well as the work of already-celebrated artists such as **Nam June Paik**, **Zhang Xiaogang**, and **Jamini Roy**, there are temporary exhibitions by young artists in residence, as well as a triennial exhibition of contemporary art.

## Nakasu and Tenjin 中州・天神

**The island of Nakasu** in the middle of the Naka-gawa comes to life after nightfall, when its neon lights cast colored reflections on the water, and thousands of *salarymen* (office workers) converge on the area, sitting shoulder to shoulder on the wooden benches of the *yatai* (mobile foodstalls), devouring bowls of noodles or *yakitori*, washed down with sake. Farther west, the **Tenjin** area is a shopper's paradise, full of fashionable boutiques and department stores. The **ACROS building**, designed by Emilio Ambasz, dates from 1995. Its south side bears a spectacular terraced garden.

## Momochi district★

シーサイドももち

*1.9mi/3km NW of the center. Subway: Nishijin (Kuko Line), then 15min walk to the N.*

The ultramodern district of Momochi is built on land reclaimed from the sea.

**Fukuoka Tower** – *Open Apr–Sept 9.30am–10pm; Oct–Mar 9.30am–9pm. ¥800.* The tower is 767.7ft/234m high and covered in 8,000 sheets of mirror glass. At 403.5ft/123m, its observation deck has magnificent **views**★ over the city.

**Robosquare** – *2nd floor of the TNC TV tower, behind Fukuoka Tower. Open 10am–7pm. Closed 2nd Wed (not Jan, Jul, Aug) and Dec 31–Jan 2. No charge.*

A hundred robots are on permanent display—some in humanoid form.

**Fukuoka City Museum** – *5min walk S. Open Jul–Aug Tue–Sat 9.30am–7pm,*

*Sun 9.30am–5pm. Rest of the year Tue–Sun 9.30am–5pm. Closed Dec 28–Jan 4. ¥200.* Among its exhibits are a **gold seal★** given to the city in the year 57 by a Chinese Emperor of the Han dynasty (206 BC–AD 220).

**Sky Dream giant wheel** – *In the Marinoa leisure complex in the west. Subway: Meinohama, then 10min walk. Open noon–10pm. ¥800.* This is the largest Ferris wheel in Japan and the third largest in the world at a height of 394ft/120m. A sensational ride is guaranteed!

**Hawks Town** – *Farther east. Subway: Tojin-Machi, then 10min walk.*
Built on land reclaimed from the sea, Hawks Town contains the futuristic **Fukuoka Yahoo! Japan Dome**, home to the Fukuoka SoftBank Hawks baseball team, and the **JAL Resort Sea Hawk Hotel** designed by the architect Cesar Pelli, the atrium of which houses a spectacular tropical jungle.

## EXCURSIONS

## DAZAIFU★★ 大宰府

*9.3mi/15km SE of Fukuoka. From Nishitetsu Fukuoka station in Tenjin, take the Nishitetsu Omuta private train line and change at Futsukaichi (30min, ¥390). Tourist Office and bicycle rental outside the station.*

### Dazaifu Tenman-gu★
### 大宰府天満宮

*5min walk N of the station.*
*No charge.*

A beautiful arched bridge over a pond leads to this shrine, founded in 905. The present building, in Momoyama style (1586), is listed as a National Treasure. It was erected in memory of Sugawara-no-Michizane (845–903), a famous scholar, poet, and minister, who lived at the court of Kyoto before falling into disgrace and being exiled to Dazaifu. After his death, he was deified as a *kami* (god) of literature and calligraphy under the name **Tenman Tenjin** (or Tenman-gu). Shrines dedicated to him can be found all over Japan. Every year, thousands of students hoping to pass their exams come here to pray to his statue. The shrine's pleasant garden contains thousands of Japanese plum trees *(ume)*; there is a festival every year on February 25 to celebrate their blossoming.

### Kyushu National Museum★★★ 九州国立博物館

*Adjoining the shrine. Open Tue–Sun 9.30am–4.30pm. ¥420.*
Opened in 2005 and designed by Kikutake Kiyonori, the museum is an architectural curiosity in itself, with its gigantic blue titanium roof *(525ft/160m long by 262.5ft/80m wide)* that undulates like a wave, and its wide plate-glass windows reflecting the surrounding forest. The light-filled interior is vast. The newest of the national museums, after those in Tokyo, Kyoto, and Nara, it focuses on the history of Japan's cultural exchanges with the rest of Asia. The permanent collections, displayed

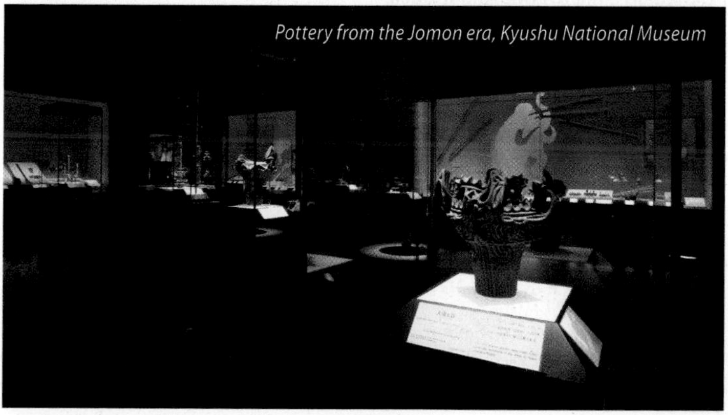
*Pottery from the Jomon era, Kyushu National Museum*

in rotation, are arranged in chronological order, covering prehistoric times and the Jomon era *(room 1)*; the Yayoi and Kofun eras *(room 2)*; the ancient eras of the Nara and Heian *(room 3)*; the Middle Ages: the Kamakura and Muromachi eras *(room 4)*; the modern age, from the Momoyama to the Edo era. The **Ajippa** interactive space on the ground floor allows children to discover Japan's different cultures.

## KARATSU★ 唐津

*31m/50km to the NW.*

*From JR Hakata station, take the Kuko Line to Meinohama (20min, ¥290), then the JR Chikuhi Line to Karatsu (1hr20min, ¥1,110). Tourist Office in the station.*

This seaside town in Saga prefecture (population 134,000) is famous in Japan for its **pottery**. Baked at high temperatures, these Korean-influenced ceramics are covered in either an opaque black or dark brown glaze, or in a white glaze with floral patterns scratched into it. Much in demand by devotees of the Tea Ceremony, they often fetch astronomical prices. Many of the workshops in the town allow visitors to observe the craftsmen working at the furnaces. The furnace **of Nakazato Taroemon★** *(5min walk SE of the station; no charge)*, which has been been in the same family for 14 generations, is probably the most famous. It also includes a gallery.

**Karatsu Castle** – *20min walk N of the station. Open 9am–4.30pm. ¥400.* Perched on a hill overlooking the sea, this castle was built in 1602 by the *daimyo* Terasawa Hirotaka, a vassal of Toyotomi Hideyoshi. Demolished during the Meiji era, it was rebuilt in 1966.

# ADDRESSES

## STAY

**Hakata Riverside Hotel** ハカタ・リバーサイドホテル *4-213 Kami-Kawabata-machi, Hakata-ku. 092-291-1455. http://home.att.ne.jp/orange/rsh/main01.htm. 18 rooms.* Small hotel inside Kawabata arcade. Clean, comfortable; well-located. Some rooms overlook river.

**Wafu Ryokan Kashima Honkan** 和風旅館・鹿島本館 *3-11 Reisen-machi, Hakata-ku. Subway: Gion. 092-291-0746. 27 rooms. Restaurant.* Elegant ryokan built in Taisho era *(1912–26)*. Beautiful surroundings, Japanese rooms, very friendly welcome in English, reasonable prices. *O-furo.*

**Takakura Hotel Fukuoka** タカクラホテル福岡 *2-7-21 Watanabe-dori, Chuo-ku. Subway: Nanawai Line, Nishitetsu Omuta Line, Yakuin station. 092-731-1661. www.takakura-hotel.co.jp. 107 rooms.* Beautiful rooms, impeccable service. Golden Week: fixed prices *(see p10)*.

## EAT

### FUKUOKA

There are many late-night eateries for hungry night-owls, but also try one of the 100 or so street stands, or ***yatai***, along the Naka-gawa.

**Maruyoshi** まるよし *5 Watanabe-dori, Chuo-ku. 090-3196-1920. Open Mon–Sat 7pm–3am. Closed on rainy days.* Try the house specialty of *motsu-nabe*.

**Canal City Hakata** キャナルシティ博多 *1-2-25 Sumiyoshi, Hataka-ku. Open 11am–10.30pm.* Eight restaurants on mall's top floor, serving *ramen* noodles.

**Motsu Ryori Kawano** もつ料理かわ乃・春吉本店 *2-16-8 Haruyoshi, Chuo-ku. 15min walk from Tenjin station. 092-761-2926. Open Mon–Sat 5–10pm.* Fifties-style restaurant serving traditional local dishes. Menu varies, tripe always in season.

**Baramon** 波羅門（ばらもん） *6 F JAL Resort Sea Hawk Hotel Fukuoka, 2-2-3 Jigyohama, Chuo-ku. 092-844-8000. Open 7am–9.30pm.* An *ikesu* restaurant, meaning your fish dinner comes from a tank in the restaurant. *(Mar–Nov only).*

**Sushi Yamanaka** 寿司やま中 *8-8 Watanabe-dori, 2-chome, Chuo-ku. 092-731-7771. Open Mon–Sat 11am–10pm.* Recent sushi bar with gleaming interior design by Isozaki Arata; best fresh fish and seafood.

### DAZAIFU

**Ume-no-hana** 梅の花 *Dazaifu Bessou Shizen-an, next to Dazaifu Tenman-gu. 092-928-7787. Open 11am–10pm.* Superb traditional tofu restaurant. Very reasonable prices.

# Nagasaki★★
# 長崎

**Nagasaki (the "long cape") winds along a long, narrow bay, overlooked by old colonial houses clinging in picturesque fashion to the surrounding hills. As early as the 16C, this natural deep-water harbor was attracting attention from foreign nations—Portuguese galleons and Chinese junks, Jesuit priests and merchant adventurers all made their way here. During Japan's two centuries of isolation *(sakoku)*, from 1641 to 1853, Nagasaki was its only link with the outside word. Thanks to the city's history and its mixture of Eastern and Western influences, Nagasaki today has a discreetly cosmopolitan charm and a large Christian minority, much-persecuted over the centuries. As the victim of the second atomic bomb, like Hiroshima, Nagasaki has its own Peace Park as a poignant reminder of the tragedy. That terrible episode in its history has not stopped the place from being reborn as a lively, modern, port city, fueled by the dynamism of the great Mitsubishi dockyards.**

- **Population:** 429,110 – Nagasaki Prefecture.
- **Michelin Map:** Principal Sights Map A3 – Regional Map p471
- **Location:** Nagasaki stretches along the Urakami River and around a narrow harbor surrounded by steep hills, 68.4mi/110km southwest of Fukuoka. Several tram lines cross the city from the station: 1.5mi/2.5km north of the station is the Urakami district and the Peace Park; 0.6mi/1km to the south lies the Shian-bashi district, noted for its nightlife, Chinatown, and the colonial villas of Glover Garden on the hills.
- **Timing:** Allow two days for the city. From the harbor, you can take a ferry to the Amakusa archipelago, and from there, get to Kumamoto.
- **Don't miss:** The Atomic Bomb Museum; the view from Mount Inasa; a bowl of *chanpon* noodles in Chinatown; Glover Garden.

## A BIT OF HISTORY

**The " Christian century"** – The arrival of Portuguese and Chinese ships in 1571 marked the beginning of the transformation of Nagasaki from a small fishing village to a bustling trading port, and products from China and Europe came flooding in: tobacco, bread, clothes, firearms. Some products, now made in the city, have kept their original Portuguese names, like the famous Nagasaki honey cake, Castella (*kasutera*).

Following in the wake of Spanish missionary Francis Xavier, who preached in Japan from 1549 to 1552, the Jesuit fathers founded hundreds of churches in Nagasaki and in the south of Kyushu. With the aid of books, artistic exchanges, and a growing awareness of Western medicine, Christianity became influential for a brief period, but things soon turned sour. Worried by the widespread influence of the Jesuits, the shogun ordered their expulsion in 1597. It was accompanied by a wave of anti-Christian persecution, culminating in the great Shimabara Rebellion of 1637, when nearly 40,000 peasants, many of them Christian, rose up against the shogunate and were slaughtered. For the next 250 years, Japanese Christians were forced to practice their religion in secret. Today, there are about 30,000 Christians in the city of Nagasaki.

**Dejima, a door half-open** – Less concerned with proselytizing than the Portuguese, the Dutch were able to continue discreetly doing business in Japan.

In 1641, the artificial island of Dejima, in Nagasaki Bay, constructed on the orders of Tokugawa Iemitsu, was allocated as a base for Dutch trading activities. Strictly confined to this island, they remained Japan's only point of contact with the outside world until 1855. When the ban on Dutch books was lifted in 1720, hundreds of students flocked to Nagasaki to study European art and science. With the Meiji Restoration, the city again became a rapidly expanding, cosmopolitan port.

**The atomic bomb**—During World War II, with its many factories producing arms, ships, and planes, Nagasaki was one of the lynchpins of the Japanese military-industrial complex. It was not, however, the main target of the American B-29 bomber that took off from the US base on the island of Tinian in the Pacific on the night of August 9, 1945, three days after the bombing of Hiroshima. But, finding its original target, the industrial center of Kokura (now Kitakyushu), obscured by clouds, the bomber fell back on Nagasaki. Released blindly at 11.02am, the bomb exploded at an altitude of 1,903ft/580m, not over the Mitsubishi steelworks which might have been an expected target, but, by a cruel twist of fate, over Urakami Cathedral, where people were at prayer, celebrating the Western faith for which their ancestors had given their lives. The bomb, *"Fat Boy,"* containing 15.4lb/7kg of plutonium, killed 70,000 instantly and a similar number subsequently died from the effects of radiation. Although 10 times more powerful than *"Little Boy,"* which had struck Hiroshima, the death toll would have been far higher, had the hills around Nagasaki not contained the blast and helped shield the south of the city.

## SIGHTS

### Urakami District★ 浦上

*Map A1.*
*Matsuyamamachi tram stop, Lines 1 and 3.*

A long flight of steps leads up to the esplanade of **Peace Park** *(A1)*. Here, a huge statue points a finger skyward, the direction from which the nuclear cataclysm came on August 9, 1945. Below, a black marble column marks the hypocenter of the explosion. Beside it is what remains of the old **Urakami Cathedral** *(A1)*, which was destroyed by the blast. Built in 1895, it was Japan's largest Roman Catholic cathedral and the largest church in Asia. The present cathedral is a replica of the original red-brick building, with its two towers. It was rebuilt in 1959 on its original site, some 1,640ft/500m northeast of the hypocenter. The statues in front of the cathedral still bear the scorch marks of radioactive fallout. To the north of the new cathedral is the **house of Dr Nagai Takashi** *(open 9am–5pm; ¥100)*, now a small museum commemorating the work of this radiologist (1908–51), who devoted his last years to caring for those affected by radiation sickness before himself succumbing to leukemia.

### The "Hidden Christians"

After the decree of 1614 in which their religion was banned, the 400,000 Japanese Christians had to either renounce or conceal their faith. "The crackdown was brutal," says Father Renzo De Luca, who runs the museum at the 26 Martyrs Memorial. "For more than two centuries, hundreds of Christians who refused to recant were executed on this hill: crucified, burned alive, or hanged." Thousands of others continued to worship in secret, venerating Buddhist figures like the compassionate goddess Kannon, who reminded them of the Virgin Mary—the museum contains a number of statuettes of *Maria Kannon*, their backs marked with concealed crosses. The authorities offered rewards for anyone who would inform on the Christians. Suspects were forced to trample on biblical images in order to prove they were recanting their faith, in a ritual known as *fumie* (*see box The Christians of Amakusa p491*).

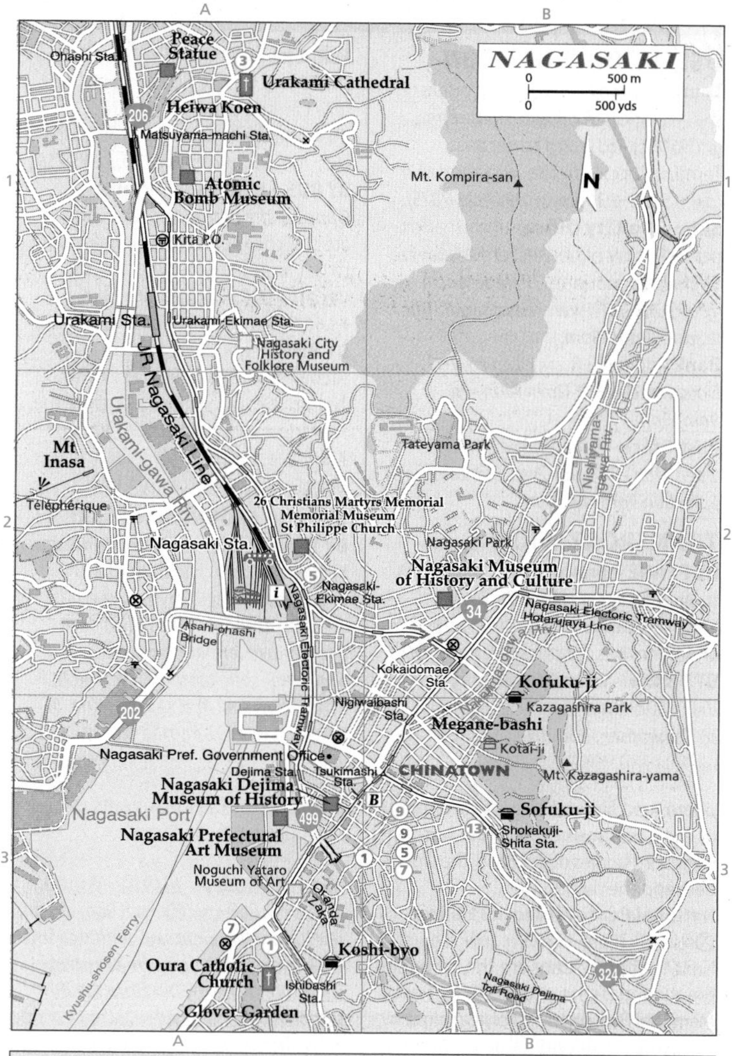


| WHERE TO STAY | |
|---|---|
| ANA Hotel Nagasaki Gloverhill | 1 |
| Nagasaki Catholic Center | 3 |
| Minshuku Fumi | 5 |
| Nagasaki Washington Hotel | 9 |
| Nishiki-so Bekkan | 7 |
| The Hamilton Nagasaki | 13 |

| WHERE TO EAT | |
|---|---|
| Don | 1 |
| Ryotei Kagetsu | 5 |
| Shikairou | 7 |
| Yossou | 9 |



**Atomic Bomb Museum**★★ *A1 – S of the park. Open 8.30am–5.30pm. ¥200.* This moving and informative museum shows scenes of Nagasaki, both before and after the explosion, presenting a vivid picture of the devastation caused by the bomb and an appeal for world peace and nuclear disarmament. The

## USEFUL INFORMATION

**Tourist Offices** – In the concourse of the JR station *(A2) (open 8am–8pm; ℘095-823-3631)* and Kenei Bus Terminal, opposite the JR station *(A2) (open 9am–5.30pm; ℘095-828-7875).*
**Shimbara City Office** – Information center in row of houses left on leaving Shimabara station, *537 Uenomachi. ℘095-763-1111. www.city.shimabara.lg.jp. 8.30am–5pm.*
**Bank** – Juhachi Bank Honten, *1-11 Douzamachi (B3). Open Mon–Fri 9am–3pm.*
**Post Office** – *1-1 Ebisumachi (A2). Open Mon–Fri 9am–7pm, Sat 9am–5pm, Sun 9am–12.30pm.*

## TRANSPORTATION

**BY PLANE** – **From Tokyo** – 16 flights daily to Nagasaki *(2hr, ¥35,800).* Regular shuttles between airport and Kenei Bus Terminal *(55min, ¥800).*
**BY TRAIN** – **To and from Tokyo** – Via Fukuoka, no direct service, *(6hr by Shinkansen, about ¥21,520).* Link for **Fukuoka** by Limited Express Kamome *(1hr50min, ¥4,910).* For Kumamoto, take Limited Express Kamome 2, then change at Tosu for JR Kagoshima Line to Kumamoto *(3hr25min, ¥5,750).*
**BY BUS** – **Kenei Bus Terminal** – *Opposite the JR station (A2).* Buses are the cheapest and simplest way to get around the region. Regular departures for Kumamoto *(3hr, ¥3,600)* and Beppu *(6hr15min, ¥4,500).*
**BY BOAT** – For the Amakusa Archipelago *(see p 491)*, take bus no. 10 from Kenei terminal, opposite the JR station, to Mogi harbor *(30min, ¥160)*, then a ferry to Tomioka, in the island's north *(1hr10min, ¥1,600).*

### GETTING AROUND NAGASAKI

**BY TRAM** – *6.30am–11pm, ¥100/trip, ¥500 1-day pass.* The blue *(no. 1)* or red *(no. 3)* lines run between west *(Akasako terminus)* and east *(Hotarujaya terminus for Line 3, Shokakuji-shita terminus for Line 1).* The yellow *(no. 4)* and green *(no. 5)* lines run north-south in the city's east.

photos and films taken in the aftermath of the catastrophe show the horribly disfigured bodies of the dead, the wounded, and the dying.
**National Peace Memorial Hall**★ – *Open 8.30am–5.30pm. No charge.*
Next to the museum are the twin rectangular glass structures of the Peace Memorial Hall, set in a pool lit at night by 70,000 fiber-optic lights. Below ground, 12 pillars of light symbolize the hope for peace. This is a resource center, displaying both written and video testimonies by survivors. It also houses a cenotaph before which the inhabitants of Nagasaki pray for the departed.

**Lantern festival**

In February, for the Chinese New Year, the streets of Chinatown are lit by some 15,000 colored lanterns. Thousands of people come to see the fireworks, acrobatic displays, demonstrations of martial arts, and the dragon dances.

### Mount Inasa★ 稲佐山 *Map A2.*

*Access by cable car (Open 9am–10pm; ¥700 one-way journey), entrance 5min walk W of the Takaramachi tram stop (Lines 1 and 3), or by bus from the JR station (20min, ¥150).*
From the top of this 1,092.5ft/333m high hill, the **view**★★ of Nagasaki Bay is magical by day or night.

### 26 Martyrs Memorial★

日本二十六聖人記念碑 *Map A2.*
*15min walk from Nagasaki station. Museum: Open 9am–5pm. ¥250.*
This monument was erected on Nishizaka hill in 1962 as a tribute to the 26 Christians—6 Europeans and 20 Japanese—forced to walk from Kyoto to Nagasaki, where they were crucified on February 5, 1597. The martyrs were canonized by the Catholic Church in 1862, by Pope Pius IX. Behind the monument is

a small museum that traces the history of the "hidden Christians" of Nagasaki through sacred objects, relics, etc.

### Nagasaki Museum of History and Culture 長崎歴史文化博物館

*Map B2.*
*5min walk N of Sakuramachi tram stop, Line 3. Open 8.30am–7pm. Closed 3rd Tue of the month. ¥600.*
Opened in 2005, this museum tells the story of Nagasaki and its dealings with the outside world through many objects brought to the city by Portuguese, Chinese, and Dutch mariners.

### Kofuku-ji 興福寺 *B2/3.*

*5min walk from Kokaido-mae tram stop, Lines 3, 4, and 5. Open 8am–5pm. ¥300.*
This Ming-style temple in the Teramachi district was founded by an Obaku Zen monk in 1620. Try a *matcha* tea while looking out over its peaceful garden.

### Megane-bashi 眼鏡橋 *Map B3.*

*Between Kofuku-ji and Nigiwaibashi tram stop, Lines 4 and 5.*
This Chinese-style "spectacles bridge," so-called because of the way its two arches are reflected in the waters of the Nakashima River, dates from 1634 and is the oldest stone bridge in Japan.

### Sofuku-ji★ 崇福寺 *Map B3.*

*Shokakuji-shita tram stop, Line 1 terminus. Open 8am–5.30pm. ¥300.*
At the end of the street of temples stands this flamboyant building, built by the Chinese community of Nagasaki in 1629 and associated with the Obaku Zen Buddhist sect. Chinese sailors worshipped their protecting deity, Masa, here and left behind a statue to him. The second of its three gates *(daiippo-mon)* and the Buddha Hall *(daiohoden)* have been designated National Treasures.

### Chinatown 中華街 *Map B3.*

*Near the Tsukimachi tram stop, Lines 1 and 5.*
Four gates decorated with multicolored dragons mark out Nagasaki's Chinatown. Although smaller than the Chinese districts in Yokohama and Kobe, it is the oldest Chinatown in Japan. It stretches for 218.7yd/200m along a busy street lined with shops and restaurants, which close early. In the 17C, approximately 10,000 of Nagasaki's 60,000 inhabitants were Chinese. Still an energetic and thriving community today, the Chinese have played an important role in shaping parts of the city, influencing its art, architecture, and culinary traditions. Take a break here and try the local specialty, *chanpon*—a soup made with thick noodles and other ingredients (pork or seafood, cabbage, and vegetables).

### Dejima★ 出島 *Map A3.*

*Dejima tram stop, Line 1. Open 9am–6pm. ¥500.*
A small, artificial island in the shape of a fan, built in 1636 to house Nagasaki's European community and restrict the expansion of Christianity. For more than 200 years, Dejima was the only point of contact between Japan and the outside world. When the shogunate expelled the Portuguese, the Dutch were obliged to transfer their trading operations to Dejima. Once a year the Dutch merchants were authorized to leave the island and travel to Edo to pay tribute to the shogun. Just a dozen employees of the Dutch East India Company, all men, lived permanently on the island in one-story wooden houses, their existence enlivened only by occasional visits from prostitutes. While the Dutch traded in gold, silver, ivory, spices, silks, and porcelain, the Japanese were more interested in acquiring Western technological know-how by studying medical and scientific treatises translated from the Dutch.
When Japan opened up again in 1853, the island enclave lost its purpose and the surrounding land was gradually filled in. Today, swallowed up in the general urban sprawl, the site has now become a museum. Over the past 10 years, 10 buildings including warehouses, houses, and a Protestant church, have been rebuilt and furnished in early 19C style. To complete the reconstruction of the original island, there is a proposal to dig a canal around the site.

**Nagasaki Prefectural Art Museum★** 長崎県美術館 *Map A3*
*10min walk S of Dejima. Open Tue–Sun 10am–8pm. ¥400.*
Opened in 2005, this museum is worth a visit, if only for its striking new building with slender lines and vast glass windows reflected in water. The roof terrace *(reached by elevator)* has a fine **view** of the harbor. The group of 500 Spanish paintings *(the largest of its kind in Asia)* bequeathed to the museum by Suma Yakichiro, a former diplomat who lived for many years in Spain, forms the core of the museum's collections. Among the artists represented are **Picasso** (including a superb *Still Life with Pigeon* of 1941), Miró, Dalí, and Goya. The museum also displays paintings by local artists, and temporary exhibitions are often held here.

**Oranda Zaka** オランダ坂 *Map A3.*
*5min walk from Shiminbyoin-mae tram stop, Line 5.*
With the opening up of Japan to the outside world in 1859, foreigners were allowed to leave Dejima and many settled in this residential district. Its gently sloping cobbled streets earned it the name *Oranda Zaka,* or Dutch Slopes *(at that time, all Europeans were still called "Dutch" by the inhabitants of Nagasaki).* The banks and commercial buildings were all located at the bottom of the hill, while Western-style houses, schools, and consulates clung to the hillside itself. Several wooden houses in the district have been restored and contain small museums, including a **photography museum** *(open Tue–Sun 9am–5pm; ¥100),* where you can see a collection of photographs of Nagasaki from the end of the 19C and the beginning of the 20C.

**Koshi-byo** 孔子廟 *Map A3.*
*Ouratenshudo-shita tram stop, Line 5. Open 8.30am–5pm. ¥525.*
This **colorful shrine** at the foot of Higashi-yamate hill was built in 1893 by the Chinese of Nagasaki in honor of Confucius. The **statues** of the master's 72 disciples were a gift from China, which financed the complete restoration of the building in 1980.
Beside it is a small historical **museum** displaying pieces on loan from the National Museum of China and the Palace Museum in Beijing.

**Glover Garden★★** グラバー園
*Map A3.*
*Ouratenshudo-shita tram stop, Line 5. Golden Week & Jul 15–Oct 9 8am–9.30pm. Rest of year 8am–6pm. ¥600.*
It was on this hill overlooking the harbor at the southern edge of the former European concession that a small group of wealthy Westerners lived in the middle of the 19C. The area is now a park and open-air museum in which nine of the elegant, colonial-style mansions have been reconstructed.
The meticulously detailed presentation, interiors, antiques, and family photos evoke the 19C well, despite the crowds and slightly kitsch ambience.

*Start your visit from the top of the hill, reached by moving walkways.*

**Walker House** – Born in England in 1851, Captain Robert N. Walker became involved in the Japanese shipping industry. In 1898, together with Thomas Glover, he went on to set up the first soft drinks factory in Japan *(in Nagasaki),* producing Banzai lemonade and cider, which later became the Kirin Brewery.
**Ringer House** – More opulent than Walker House and built of stone, this house dates from 1865. British businessman Frederick Ringer ran a number of companies, including a tea export business and a gas and electricity company.
**Alt House** – Another British tea merchant, William Alt, lived for three years in this impressive house built in 1864. It has a wide porch and fine veranda supported by Tuscan-style columns.
**Glover House★** – Built in 1859, this is the most imposing of all the mansions. It belonged to Thomas Glover, a Scottish adventurer whose various enterprises included shipbuilding, brewing, and arms dealing. With its four wings forming

### East meets West in more ways than one

During the Meiji era, it was quite common for expatriate European and American businessmen in Nagasaki to "marry" courtesans in order to ensure exclusive rights to their favors, in return for which the women would receive accommodation and money. This somewhat questionable arrangement gave rise to the romantic, fictional character of Madame Butterfly, whose passion for an American officer ends in tragedy when he abandons her. The more mercenary figure of "temporary wife" Madame Chrysanthème, in the story by French writer Pierre Loti, was based on a real person: the young Okane-san, who was Loti's "temporary wife" when he served as a naval officer in Nagasaki. The gentle and beautiful Otaki-san was the companion of German doctor and naturalist Philipp Franz von Siebold, who spent six years on Dejima in the 1820s. Siebold discovered a new species of hydrangea, which he named *Hydrangea otakusa* after Otaki-san.

a cross, it is the oldest European-style wooden residence in Japan. It is known as **"Madame Butterfly's House"** because Glover's wife, a former geisha, is said to have been the inspiration for the story on which Puccini's famous opera was based. Above the house is a statue of the Japanese singer Miura Tamaki (1884–1946), noted for her performance in the role. Toward the exit, in another building, you can see the fabulous dragons and floats used during the Kunchi Festival in the Fall.

### Oura Catholic Church
大浦天主堂 *Map A3.*

*Just outside Glover Garden. Open 8am–6pm. ¥250.*

A wooden mock-Gothic church with fine stained-glass windows. It was built in 1865 by Japanese carpenters under the direction of the French priest Father Petitjean, first bishop of Nagasaki, who helped to restore the Catholic Church's links with the "hidden Christians." The church commemorates the 26 martyrs of 1597.

## EXCURSIONS

### Shimabara Peninsula★
島原半島

*About 37mi/ 60km southeast of Nagasaki.*

The landscapes and volcanic waters of Unzen Amakusa National Park *(Japan's leading National Park, created in 1934)* are a welcome contrast to the city.

### Unzen★ 雲仙

*Access by bus from Nagasaki (from airport or the Nagasaki medical care center stop, 1hr45min) or by Rt. 57.*

For over 300 years this spot at the foot of one of Mount Unzen's craters has been appreciated for the therapeutic virtues of its sulfured waters. They boil up naturally from the ground (at temperatures up to 248°F/120°C), releasing steam and gases that give a certain odor to the downtown area.

As at Beppu (*see p506)* they are called "**hells★**" (*jigoku*) but there is no satanic punishment awaiting the people strolling around the site in their *yukata*! They come to relax in one of the many hotels or ryokan nearby, or to admire the seasonal changes against the backdrop of volcanic reliefs.

Unzen, at an altitude of 2 296ft/700m, also has temperate summers that from the late 19C to WWII many Westerners living in China came to enjoy. Western-style hotels were built to welcome them, and though they have just about completely disappeared, with the exception of the Unzen Kanko Hotel (*see Addresses p484)*, the city has kept several buildings from that period, inspired by European or American architecture.

For this reason the town has a certain charm, also owing to it not having the mass tourism so apparent in resorts like Beppu.

### Mt. Unzen 雲仙岳

*About 4mi/7km from Unzen. Take Rt. 57, then follow the "Nita Pass"* signs.

Mt. Unzen is a volcanic grouping comprised of several cones, including Mounts Myoken *(4,373ft/1,333m)*, Fugen *(4,458ft/ 1,359m)*, and Heisei Shinzan *(4,875ft/1,486m)*; this last was formed during the most recent—and terrible—1991 eruption *(see below)*.
The cable car *(open 8.50am–5pm; ¥1,220 round-trip; go in the morning before the mist forms)* leaving from Nita Pass at 3,510ft/1,070m takes you to the slopes of Mt. Myoken, from where there is superb **panorama★★** of the peninsula from the observation platform, as well as of the Ariake Sea, Amakusa Archipelago, and Heisei Shinzan. Unzen Golf Course, Japan's first opened in 1913, is below. Azaleas cover Mt. Myoken's slopes in spring.

## Shimbara 島原

**Mt. Unzen Disaster Memorial Hall** – *1-1 Heiseimachi, near the ferry terminal. Open daily 9am–6pm. ¥1,000, audio guide in English available.*
An interesting complement to a Mount Unzen excursion, this museum explains volcanism and Japan's various volcano types. It also describes the violent 1991 eruption in detail; 43 people died and several districts of the town were destroyed. Shimbara and the peninsula are part of UNESCO's Geopark program.
**Castle** – The original 17C castle was rebuilt in the 1960s. The museum evokes the Christian era, in the keep *(9am-5.30pm; ¥520)*.
**Bukeyashiki★** – About .5mi/700m from the castle, the samurai district remains authentic, especially Shitanocho Street, with its little water supply canal. Three Edo period residences can be visited.

# ADDRESSES

## STAY

**Minshuku Fumi** 民宿富美
*4-9 Daikoku-machi, near the JR station (A2). 095-822-4962. 5 rooms.* Modest; owners speak a little English. Japanese-style rooms. Communal toilets and bathrooms.

**Nagasaki Catholic Center**
長崎カトリックセンターユースホステル
*10-34 Uenomachi. From JR station, take red bus line to Jyunkan, Catholic Center-mae stop (A1). 095-846-4246. www.e-yh.net/nccyh/index2.htm. 17 rooms, 2 dormitories (16 beds).*
Part youth hostel, Catholic center where Pope John Paul II stayed in 1981.

**Nishiki-so Bekkan**
旅館にしき荘別館 *1-2-7 Nishikoshima (B3). 095-826-6371. 11 rooms.* Small, well-maintained family guesthouse, 10min from Shian-bashi stop. Japanese-style rooms, some with a fine **view** of city.

**Nagasaki Washington Hotel**
長崎ワシントンホテル *9-1 Shinchimachi. 1min from Tsukimachi tram stop (B3). 095-828-1211. www.nagasaki-wh.com. 300 rooms.*
A good hotel at Chinatown entrance.

**The Hamilton Nagasaki**
ザ・ハミルトン長崎 *7-9 Maruyama-machi (B3). 095-824-1000. www.hamilton-gr.jp/nagasaki. 87 rooms.* Quiet, comfortable hotel overlooking Maruyama Park (Shian-bashi); friendly, English spoken.

**ANA Hotel Nagasaki Gloverhill** 全日空ホテルグラバーヒル
*1-18 Minami-Yamatemachi (A3). 095-818-6601. www.ana-gloverhill.co.jp. 217 rooms.*
Very good hotel, 3 restaurants: Japanese, French, and Chinese.

**UNZEN**

**Unzen Kanko Hotel**
雲仙観光ホテル *320 Unzen, Obama machi. 095 773 3234. Room price includes breakfast and dinner.* Hotel from 1910, tastefully modernized. Large rooms, *onsen*.

## EAT

**Shikairou** 四海楼 *4-5 Matsugae-machi (A3). 095-822-1296. www.shikairou.com. Open 11.30am–9pm.* Chinese restaurant in chic Glover Garden district serving *chanpon* (cheap noodle dish) for 4 generations.

**Yossou** 吉宗（よっそう）本店
*8-9 Hamamachi (B3). 095-821-0001. Open 11am–9pm.* Enjoy the famous *mushi-zushi*, a cod and rice-based local specialty.

**Don** 呑 *1 F Mikawa Bldg, 6-4 Motoshikkui-machi (A–B3). 095-829-3788. Open 5–9.30pm.*
Sashimi and grilled fish, whale meat, too.

**Ryotei Kagetsu** 料亭花月
*2-1 Maruyama-machi (B3). 095-822-0191. www.ryoutei-kagetsu.co.jp. Open Wed–Mon noon–10pm. Reservations required.*
Historic location, high-class restaurant; magnificent garden.

# Kumamoto★ and Mount Aso★★
# 熊本・阿蘇山

**A prosperous city during the Tokugawa Shogunate (1603–1867), Kumamoto grew up around its castle facing Shimabara Bay. Perched on a hill and surrounded by high walls, the castle is one of the finest reconstructed examples in Japan. Kumamoto is also known for its beautiful garden, Suizen-ji. There are plenty of opportunities for excursions in the surrounding area. To the south is the Amakusa Archipelago and its spectacular mosaic of small islands, home to the descendants of Japan's "hidden Christians," where churches pop up in surprising fashion from deep inside little rocky creeks. To the northeast stands Mount Aso, the world's largest caldera covered with green meadows, lakes, forests, thermal springs, and smoking craters, their slopes a mass of different hiking trails.**

- **Population:** 677,669 (Prefecture: 1.83 million) – Kumamoto Prefecture.
- **Michelin Map:** Principal Sights Map A3 – Regional Map p471.
- **Location:** Kumamoto is located 68.4mi/110km south of Fukuoka, 105.6mi/170km north of Kagoshima and, going west, 31mi/50km from Aso and 93.2mi/150km from Beppu. A tram line links the JR station and the downtown area 1.6mi/2.5km to the northeast, where you will find the castle, the bus station *(Kotsu Center)*, and the main shopping district.
- **Kids:** A boat trip to see the dolphins at Amakusa; a horse or pony ride in the meadows of Mount Aso.
- **Timing:** Allow two or three days. From Mount Aso, you can continue toward Yufuin and Beppu. From Amakusa, you can get to Nagasaki. Renting a car is a very useful way of getting around the region.
- **Don't miss:** Kumamoto Castle; the caldera of Mount Aso.

## SIGHTS

### Kumamoto Castle★ 熊本城

*10min by tram from the JR station, Shiyakusho-mae stop. Open Apr–Oct 8.30am–5.30pm; Nov–Mar 8.30am–4.30pm. ¥500 (¥640 for a combined ticket with Gyobu-tei). For a guided tour (no charge), see the yellow-jacketed volunteers at the entrance.*

Situated on a hill surrounded by moats and strong stone fortifications, Kumamoto Castle was once deemed impregnable and is now the symbol of the city. Built between 1601 and 1607, under the guidance of the local lord Kato Kiyomasa, this citadel was a model of military engineering for its time. It included a number of defensive innovations in its design—smooth-surfaced, gently curving *(mushagaeshi)* ramparts to prevent attackers from climbing them, projecting parapets, loopholes—and no fewer than 49 towers and 29 gates. Despite these precautions, the castle was besieged and burnt down in 1877, during the Satsuma Rebellion. The keep was restored in 1960, in a similar style to the original, but with a concrete framework. Some of the other buildings have also been rebuilt, restoring at least some of the castle's former splendor.

To reach the main courtyard, you must make your way round a maze of walls, but here you will find the **keep**, flanked by two smaller towers. It contains some interesting exhibits: samurai armor,

### The Satsuma Rebellion

The Satsuma (Kagoshima) Rebellion, led by the warrior Saigo Takamori in 1877, was the last stand of the samurai who rejected the Meiji Restoration and the modernization that would cause the old feudal system to disappear and with it, the loss of their social status and privileges. The rebels laid siege to Kumamoto before being cut to ribbons by an Imperial army that outnumbered them 10 to one. To avoid capture, Saigo committed *seppuku*.

models of the castle, manuscripts, and paintings. To the west of the keep is the **Uto-Yagura watchtower**, the only surviving section of the original castle.

*Walk W across the castle grounds (Ninomaru).*

## Kyu-Hosokawa Gyobu-tei★ 旧細川刑部邸

*Open 8.30am–6pm (summer); 8.30am–5pm (winter). ¥300.*

This 300-year-old residence constructed in the *shoin-zukuri* style (a Chinese-inspired style typical of the houses of high-ranking samurai) was once the property of one of the members of the Hosokawa family, which controlled Kumamoto from 1632 until the Meiji era. With its large porch, it is representative of the aristocratic residences built in that period.

## Kumamoto Prefectural Art Museum★ 熊本県立美術館本館

*In the grounds of the castle. Open Tue–Sun 9.30am–5pm. Museum ¥260, Hosokawa Gallery ¥500.*

In a large brick building, this museum houses a collection of Japanese and Western works from various periods. Buddhist statues and examples of calligraphy can be seen alongside prints, engravings, and watercolors by Renoir, Gauguin, and Picasso.

A new gallery devoted to the **Hosokawa collection**★ displays the works in rotation *(calligraphy, paintings, pottery, armor)* of the Eisei Bunko Museum, Tokyo, where the inheritance of the Hosokawa clan is preserved.

*Retrace your steps to the Shiyakusho-mae tram stop.*

## Suizen-ji Garden★★ 水前寺公園

*Near the Suizen-ji-koen tram stop. Open Mar–Nov 7.30am–6pm; Dec–Feb 8.30am–5pm. ¥400.*

## USEFUL INFORMATION

**Tourist Office** – *In the concourse of the JR station. Open 9am–5.30pm. 096-352-3743.*

## TRANSPORTATION

**GETTING TO AND FROM KUMAMOTO**

**BY TRAIN** – The **JR Hohi Line** links Kumamoto with Aso *(Limited Express 1hr5min, ¥ 2,180)* and Beppu *(3hr10min, ¥4,830)*. Trains run to and from Fukuoka-Hakata *(1hr30min, ¥3,940)*, Kagoshima *(1hr30min, ¥6,510)*, and Nagasaki *(via Tosu) (2hr45min, ¥7,170)*.

**BY BUS** – Kotsu Center bus station *(096-361-5233)* is located downtown, near the Kumamotojo-mae tram stop *(15min by tram from the JR station)*. Regular buses to Nagasaki *(3hr, ¥3,600)*, Aso *(1hr30min)*, Beppu *(3hr40min)*, Kagoshima *(3hr30min)*, and Fukuoka *(2hr)*.

**BY BOAT** – Shin-ko ferry terminal can be reached by bus *(35min)* from the Kotsu Center. Ferries for Amakusa *(4 per day, 75min, ¥2,810)*.

**GETTING AROUND KUMAMOTO**

**BY CAR** – **Renting a car** for the day is an ideal way to explore this area. *Reservations suggested*. At Aso station: Eki Rent-A-Car *0967-34-1001*. In Hondo harbor *(on Shimo-shima)*, Toyota Rent-A-Car *0969-23-0100.*

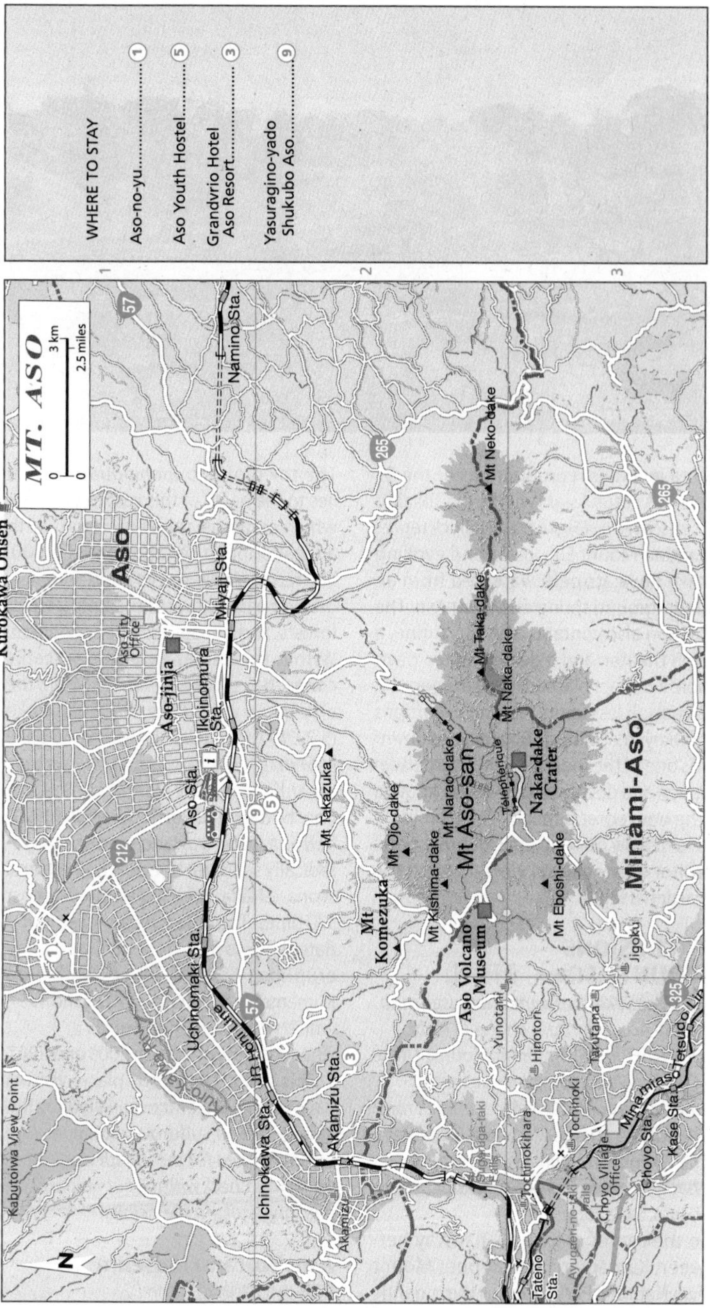


Situated outside the center of the city, this garden was created in 1632 by Hosokawa Tadatoshi. It combines the simple, unadorned style of the tea gardens of the Momoyama era with the grander, more detailed layout of an Edo stroll garden *(see p103)*. Intended as a place of relaxation, its 158-acre/64ha

Suizen-ji Garden

© Luthy Yannick/age fotostock

area includes reproductions of the 53 famous natural sights of the old Tokaido road (see p216), such as a hillock representing Mount Fuji, or a pond evoking Lake Biwa, its pure water fed from an underground spring on Mount Aso. The garden also contains a Shinto shrine, a Noh theater, and a delightful tea pavilion: a perfect place to enjoy a green tea. Although less famous than the gardens of Okayama, Mito, or Takamatsu, Suizen-ji is one of the most beautiful gardens in Japan and deserves to be better known. The one regret is that it is in the middle of a heavily built-up area, depriving the visitor of any natural views beyond the garden itself.

## EXCURSIONS

### MOUNT ASO★★ 阿蘇山

*31mi/50km E of Kumamoto (see map p485). Access by train on the JR Hohi Line (1hr10min–1hr30min). Tourist Office (Open 9am–6pm), bicycle rental, and car rental outside Aso station. From the station, a regular bus service serves the Volcano Museum and the cable car that goes up to Naka-dake crater (daily, 35min, ¥620).*

In the center of Kyushu, halfway between Kumamoto and Beppu, Mount Aso National Park includes the gigantic **caldera** of Mount Aso, formed when the volcano collapsed some 80,000 years ago. With a circumference of 74.5mi/120km, it is among the largest in the world. The town of Aso *(population 30,000)* lies to the north of this vast depression, which contains a dozen villages with a total population of about 100,000. The fertile slopes are covered with lush grazing pastures, terraced fields, lakes, forests, and hot springs used for *onsen*. Within the caldera are five volcanic cones: Naka-dake *(4,941ft/1,506m, the only active one of the five)*, Taka-dake *(5,223ft/1,592m, the highest)*, Neko-dake *(4,619ft/1,408m, recognizable by its craggy peak)*, Kishima-dake *(4,167ft/1,270m)*, and Eboshi-dake *(4,386.5ft/1,337m)*. Classified as a "gray" volcano—one that sporadically sends up hot clouds of ash and scoria—Naka-dake has erupted almost 170 times. The oldest recorded eruption dates back to 553. Closer in time are the eruptions of 1884, when ash fell on Kumamoto, and those of 1933 and 1957, which were equally powerful.

The most recent were in 2005 and 2007. This is still a dangerous place; visitors have been hurt, and even killed, by falling rocks and sulfurous emissions *(not recommended for those with respiratory problems). Check with the authorities if you plan any walks in the vicinity.*

#### Aso Volcano Museum

阿蘇火山博物館 *Map B2.*

*9mi/15km S of Aso along Route 111. Open 9am–5pm (summer); 9am–4.30pm (winter). ¥840.*

This museum presents the geology of the volcano and the surrounding countryside with photos, models, and a short explanatory film. Cameras positioned inside the most active part of the volcano relay its activity live to the musem.

*A map of the hiking trails around the volcano is available from the museum and there are volunteers who can act as guides. Ask at reception.*

**Plain of Kusasenri★** – Beyond the museum stretches this lush, grassy plain. In the distance is Mount Eboshi, reflected in the clear waters of a lake. Children can enjoy pony rides here.
**Komezuka★** – On the road from Aso, stop to climb *(10min)* this small, perfectly shaped volcanic cone, said to resemble an upturned bowl of rice.

## Naka-dake Crater★★

阿蘇中岳東火口 *Map B3.*
*Take the cable car (open 9am–5pm, ¥500) from the terminal 2.5mi/4km W of the museum. Closed in the event of eruptions or emissions of toxic gases. Not recommended for those in poor health.*
An acrid smell of sulfur fills the air, and steam, smoke, and gas rise constantly from this active crater, but the **view** is stunning. At the bottom of the crater, 1,968.5ft/600m wide and 525ft/160m deep, is a dark green acid lake with a temperature close to 608°F/320°C. Around it, a **panorama** of black rocks stretches as far as the eye can see. Concrete bunkers are provided as shelter in case of emergency. Several clearly-signposted hiking trails start from the crater, the best being the one that leads to the top of Takadake *(5,223ft/1,592m)*. From there, you can see the whole of the caldera.

## Aso-jinja 阿蘇神社 *Map B1.*

*Village of Ichinomiya, 3mi/5km NE of Aso. Access from JR Miyaji station.*
This Shinto shrine, dating back nearly 2,000 years, is dedicated to the 12 *kami* of Mount Aso, the most important of whom is Takeiwatatsu, grandson of the mythical Emperor Jinmu, traditional founder of Japan. It is one of the few shrines in the country to have retained its Buddhist gate with two roofs, which dates from 1850.

## Kurokawa Onsen★★ 黒川温泉

*Map C1 off map.*
*18.6mi/30km NE of Aso.*
*Buses running between Kumamoto and Beppu link Aso station and Kurokawa Onsen (4 per day, 1hr, ¥960). From the information office at the car park (open 9am–6pm), you can obtain a map and a pass (¥1,200) to three onsen of your choice.*
Halfway between Kumamoto and Beppu, huddled in a narrow valley, this small village *(population 400)* hugs the Tanoharu River. Exceptionally well preserved, it is

Naka-dake Crater, Mount Aso

one of the most charming thermal sites in the country. Apart from the birdsong and the sound of the river, there is only the clip-clop of the *geta* (wooden sandals) worn by the *yukata*-clad bathers to disturb this tranquil place. There are almost 30 *onsen*, which double as inns, along the banks of the river. They all provide hot baths in the open air, set among the rocks of the river, or in small wooden clearings.

## TAKACHIHO 高千穂

*About 50mi/80km from Kumamoto (2hr, 1hr from Mt. Aso), about 74mi/120km from Miyazaki by Rt 218 (3h). Takachiho–yama summit: 5,164ft/1,574m.*

Belonging to Miyazaki Prefecture, Takachiho is nevertheless closer geographically to Kumamoto and Mt. Aso.

### Takachiho-jinja 高千穂神社

*Next to Miyako bus station.*

A large staircase, slightly off-center to the main building to avoid turning one's back to the altar when coming back down, leads to this Shinto shrine said to be founded 1,800 years ago. Protected by centuries-old trees, there is an atmosphere of great serenity troubled only at night by spectators come to attend the Yokagura given during part of the year in a neighboring building.

### Takachiho Gorge, on the Gokase River 高千穂峡

*About .6mi/1km W of town center; drive along Rt. 218. An English sign-posted trekking path (0.6mi/1km circuit, 30min) overlooks the gorge. It can also be reached by the river, with a rowboat (20min, ¥1000, three persons maximum per boat; 8.30am–4.30pm).*

The Gokase River weaves between two high basalt flows hardened here 120,000 years ago when Mt. Aso erupted. The path takes you first to a sacred pond and then to waterfalls – especially the Manai cascade, the most impressive – as well as whirlpools, rocky masses, and at the narrowest point, three superposed bridges.

### Kunimigaoka 国見ヶ丘

*5min by car heading W of town center, Rt. 218.*

This site, literally called "sea of clouds", is especially impressive at sunset when the clouds cling to the rocky peaks surrounding the town. The **panoramic view★** is impressive; in clear weather it is possible to see as far as the craters of Mount Aso. Three large—and somewhat kitsch—statues recall one of the versions of Shinto mythology according to which Ninigi-no-mikoto, grandson of goddess Amaterasu O-mi kami, came down to earth at Takachiho.

### YOKAGURA, THE DANCE OF THE GODS

Every year, from mid-November after the rice harvest to mid-February, the men of Takachiho dance the generations-old Yokagura, a cycle of 33 masked dances following episodes from Shinto mythology; the full performance lasts an entire night. The rest of the year, only four dances are performed. Over the last 20 years the Yokagura's renown has gone beyond Japan's borders, with performances abroad, particularly at European festivals. Yet it is primarily a community experience—450 men of all generations take turns to cover the performances—as well as, according to one of the oldest members of the troupe, the means for entering into contact with ancestors, thanking them for the harvest and asking for their protection for the future.

In 21C Japan, it's as if this recitation of "the slowly negotiated agreement between a benevolent Heaven and its earthly posterity, and the uninterrupted Imperial ascendancy that bears witness to it" (N. Bouvier) has lost nothing of its power. *Performances mid-Feb–mid-Nov (1hr) at 8pm, Takachiho-jinja, ¥500; from mid-Nov–mid-Feb, about 20 complete performances; contact the Tourist Office ☎098-273-1213.*

### The Christians of Amakusa

Historically, Amakusa was one of the main centers for the growth of **Christianity**, which had been introduced to Japan by Portuguese missionaries. By 1589, the archipelago had 30 churches, a major Jesuit college with its own printing works, and no fewer than 23,000 converts out of a total population of 30,000. After Christianity was banned at the beginning of the 17C, many recanted their faith. Thousands of others were tortured to death. Those who continued to pray in secret to little statues of the Virgin disguised as Kannon later became known as the "hidden Christians" *(see box p 476)*. When religious freedom was restored in 1873, many French missionaries came to settle in these islands, where they rebuilt churches to revive a faith that had, for two and a half centuries, been carried on in secret. Today, almost 10 percent of the population of the island is Catholic (compared with 1 percent in the rest of Japan).

### Ama-no-Iwato jinja 天岩戸神社

*About 5mi/8km E of town center (20min by car or bus from Takachiho Bus Center).*
The shrine was built overlooking the Gokase River, where, according to Shinto mythology, the sun goddess **Amaterasu O-mi kami**, ancestor of the Imperial Family, closed herself into a cave to punish her brother Suzano-no-mikoto, thereby causing continual night. The several attempts the other *kami* made to cause her to come out, which were finally successful, are told in the Yokagura.
After having passed a tall, rough wood *torii*, a beautiful avenue shaded by large trees leads to the shrine. Behind the main building *(accessible only with shrine priest)*, it is possible to make out Amaterasu's cave, in the cliffside on the other side of the river. The oldest building *(left of the entrance)* contains the mirror that is a symbol for the goddess. The path continues by taking the path heading down to the river. After a few minutes it comes to the little Ama-no-Yasukawara shrine in the depths of the cave. All around the shrine and at the river's edge there is a multitude of piled flat pebbles, each one left by a visitor having made a wish.

## AMAKUSA ARCHIPELAGO★ 天草諸島

*46.6mi/75km SW of Kumamoto. From the Kotsu Center, buses (1hr30min, ¥2,180) go to Hondo, the main town of Shimo-shima, which is also served by ferry from Shin-ko ferry terminal in Kumamoto. Tourist Office (open 9am–5pm) and car rental on arrival. There are few buses on the island itself.*
South of Shimabara Peninsula, between Nagasaki and Kumamoto, Amakusa-shoto comprises a string of around 100 islands, the main island being the mountainous Shimo-shima (220sq mi/570sq km), with a jagged coastline.

### Shimo-shima★ 下島

The capital, **Hondo**, a small town of 40,000 inhabitants, is on the northeast coast. It is linked to Kumamoto by a series of five spectacular bridges connecting several of the islands in the strait.
**Sakitsu harbor** – *In the SW of the island, 11.2mi/18km from Hondo.*
At the end of a narrow fjord, surrounded by low mountains, nestles this modest fishing village. There is a small mock Gothic **church** with a steeple and gray-tiled roof, built in 1928. The floor is covered with tatami mats, so you must take off your shoes to enter. Nearby, a statue of the Virgin looks out over a rocky cape at the exit to the bay. Fishermen setting out to sea beg her protection.
**Oea village** – *3.1mi/5km N of Sakitsu along the coast.*
Here, a white **church** stands on a green hill overlooking the sea. Inside, the rib-vaulted ceiling is decorated with bright flowers. It was built and entirely financed in 1933 by Father Garnier, a kindly priest who is still affectionately remembered by the villagers. Below the church, near the cemetery, a statue of the Virgin of Lourdes stands hidden amid the bougainvillea. The nearby

**Rosary Museum** (*open Thu–Tue 8.30am–5.30pm; ¥320*) displays objects related to the Marian cult of the "hidden Christians" and examples of the religious images they were forced to trample underfoot as a sign that they had renounced their faith. The museum also tells the story of the great Shimabara Rebellion of 1637, when 40,000 rebels—Christians and starving peasants—were mercilessly slaughtered by the shogun's troops.

## ADDRESSES

### STAY

**KUMAMOTO**

**Minshuku Ryokan Kajita** 民宿旅館梶田 *1-2-7 Shinmachi. 096-352-4543. 10 rooms*. A friendly family hotel, with public and private *o-furo*.

**MOUNT ASO**

**Aso Youth Hostel** 阿蘇ユースホステル *922-2 Bochu, Aso-shi. 20min walk from the station (B2). 0967-34-0804. 9 dormitories*. Long-established, ideal for a long stay. Private kitchen, etc.

**Yasuragino-yado Shukubo Aso** やすらぎの宿・宿房あそ *1076 Kurokawa, Aso-shi. 15min walk from the station (B1/2). 0967-34-0194. 12 rooms. Lodging with half-board.* Superb traditional *minshuku* run by delightful owners. *O-furo*.

**Aso-no-yu** 阿蘇乃湯 *6 Ozato (B1). 0967-32-1521. www.asonoyu.com. 11 rooms*. A rustic setting, Japanese rooms, and *o-furo*.

**Grandvrio Hotel Aso Resort** 阿蘇リゾート・グランヴィリオホテル *Komezuka-onsen. Taxi from Akamizu station (allow 15min, ¥1,000) (A2). 0967-35-2111. www.aso-hotelresort.com. 180 rooms*. A large, beautiful hotel nestling in the heart of the caldera.

**TAKACHIHO**

**Kaminoya** 民芸民宿 かみの家 *806-5, Mitai, Takachiho-cho, Nichiusuki-gun. 0982-72-2111. www.kaminoya.jp. 8 rooms*. An immaculate *ryokan* in the centre of Takachiho with Japanese-style rooms, though Western beds are available. Generous and delicious meals. The owner is happy to run guests to and from Yokagura performances, as well as supply information on hikes in the local countryside.

**AMAKUSA**

**Amakusa Prince Hotel** 天草プリンスホテル *92 Higashi-machi, Hondo City. 10min walk from the harbor. 0969-22-5136. www.amakusa-prince hotel.jp. 28 rooms*. A comfortable hotel near the harbor.

**Gosoku no Kutsu** 石山離宮 五足のくつ *2237 Shimoda-Kita, Amakusa-machi, Amakusa-shi, about 15mi/25km from Hondo and 7mi/12km from Oe. t 0969 45 3633. www.rikyu5.jp.* Clinging to a hillside in one of the most unspoilt parts of the west coast, this establishment is a real haven of peace. The rooms are in contemporary Japanese-style houses nestled in greenery. Vast, refined, with **views** of both sea and garden.

### EAT

**KUMAMOTO**

**Ohako** おはこ *Turn right when leaving the station, walk 80m. 096-355-2160. Open Mon–Sat.* Excellent, reasonably priced food. Try the *basashi* (horsemeat sashimi).

**Suzunoya** 鈴の屋 *2 F Ryukyu-ya Bldg, Sannenzaka-dori. 096-324-5717. Open 11am–10pm.* A traditional ambience with a hint of modernity. Varied Japanese cuisine.

**AMAKUSA**

**Yakko Sushi** 奴寿司 *By the harbor, next to the Prince Hotel. 0969-23-4055. Open 6–10pm.* Highest quality fish, rice, *wasabi*, etc.

### SHOPPING

**Kumamoto Prefectural Traditional Crafts Center** 熊本県伝統工芸館 – *NW of the castle, Shiyakusho-mae tram stop. Open Tue–Sun 9am–5pm.* A variety of wooden, ceramic, and bamboo artifacts.

### SPORT AND LEISURE

**Boat Trips** – Ikura Club, *Tsujishima harbor, on the N coast of Amakusa. 0969-33-0198.* Several trips a day to see the island's dolphins.

**Horse Riding** – El Patio Ranch *9.3mi/15km N of Aso, along the Yamanami Highway. 0967-22-3861.* Short rides in the parkland of the caldera.

# Kagoshima★ 鹿児島

**The southernmost city on Kyushu, charming, sun-drenched Kagoshima is often compared to Naples, with which it is twinned. Surrounded by purple mountains, it curls around a deep-set bay, in the threatening shadow of the ever-smoking Sakurajima volcano, the local Vesuvius, which regularly spews forth plumes of ash.**
**A former samurai stronghold, for centuries it was controlled by the Shimazu clan, which at a long and therefore safe distance from Edo, could rule the province of Satsuma *(now Kagoshima prefecture)* and the Ryukyu Islands (Okinawa) more or less as it pleased. Chinese and Korean influences, brought here across the sea, have also left their mark on the local ceramics and on the city's culinary traditions, with its emphasis on pork *(especially from black pigs)* and sweet potato. *Shochu*, an alcoholic drink made from sweet potato is a local specialty—there are 120 distilleries in the city! Kagoshima was also Japan's first point of contact with Christianity, when Jesuit priest Francis Xavier arrived on the island in 1549.**
**Another important figure in local history was Marshal Saigo Takamori (1827–77) who, after helping to restore the Meiji Emperor, changed sides and led the Satsuma Rebellion. Kagoshima Bay is bordered on one side by the Satsuma Peninsula, where the *onsen* resort of Ibusuki, popular for its hot sand baths, nestles in an attractive setting.**

- **Population:** 610,820 – Kagoshima Prefecture.
- **Michelin Map:** Principal Sights Map A3 – Regional Map p471.
- **Location:** In the far south of Kyushu, 121mi/195km from Kumamoto and 196mi/315km from Fukuoka, Kagoshima is located on a bay. It has two train stations: Kagoshima, near the harbor, and the main station, Kagoshima-chuo, which is farther south. The downtown area is situated between the two stations, around the Tenmonkan-dori shopping mall, and is served by buses and two tram lines.
- **Kids:** Kagoshima aquarium; Ibusuki beach.
- **Timing:** Allow one day for the city and another for Chiran and Ibusuki. From Ibusuki, jetfoils go directly to Yakushima.
- **Don't miss:** Sakurajima volcano; the sand baths at Ibusuki.

## SIGHTS

From the main station of Kagoshima-chuo, a tourist bus *(every 30min, ¥180 per journey or ¥600 for a 1-day passm*does a circuit of the city's main sights.

### Kagoshima City Art Museum★
鹿児島市立美術館

*15min by bus from Kagoshima-chuo station. Open Tue–Sun 9.30am–5.30pm. ¥200.*

Built on the ruins of Tsurumaru Castle, at the foot of Shiroyama hill, this museum houses the city's modern art collections. Most of the works on display are by local Japanese artists from the end of the 19C and the beginning of the 20C, who were influenced by the great Western schools of the same period.
The Paris-trained painter **Kuroda Seiki** (1856–1924) is well represented. Another room displays an assortment of **European works**, from the Impressionists to the 1950s: Monet, Renoir, Cézanne, Ernst, Matisse, Picasso, Mondrian, Kandinsky, Fautrier.

## USEFUL INFORMATION

**Tourist Office** – Central office in the concourse of Kagoshima-chuo station *(open 8.30am–7pm; ✆099-253-2500)*.

## TRANSPORTATION

**BY PLANE** – **Kagoshima** airport, 18.6mi/30km to the N, can be reached by bus from Kagoshima-chuo station *(every 20min, journey time 50min, ¥1,200)*. Daily flights to Tokyo *(1hr40min, ¥37,700)*, Naha *(1hr20min, ¥24,100)*, Yakushima *(35min, ¥12,750)*, Osaka, Nagoya, Seoul, and Shanghai.

**BY TRAIN** – A **Shinkansen** line links Kagoshima-chuo with Shin-Yatsushiro to the north, where you can change for Fukuoka-Hakata *(2hr30min, ¥9,400)*, Beppu *(4hr30min, ¥11,920)*, Kumamoto *(1hr, ¥6,350)*, and Nagasaki *(via Tosu, 4hr, ¥12,400)*.

**BY BUS** – Long-distance buses leave from the Express Bus Center, outside Kagoshima-chuo station. Regular services to Kumamoto *(3hr30min)*, Oita *(5hr40min)*, Fukuoka *(4hr)*, and Osaka *(11hr40min)*.

**BY BOAT** – **Jetfoils for Yakushima** *(4 per day, 2hr–2hr30min, ¥7,000)* leave from the North Pier in the harbor. Two of them stop at Ibusuki. Regular ferries *(4hr, ¥5,000)* leave from the South Pier. Ferries for Okinawa *(1 per day, 24hr30min, ¥15,200)* leave from Shin-ko harbor, farther south.

A final section is devoted to the decorative arts of Satsuma, ceramics from the Momoyama era (end of the 16C), and crystalware from the end of the 19C.

### Reimeikan (Prefectural Museum of Culture)★

黎明館（鹿児島県歴史資料センター）

*218.7yd/200m walk from the previous museum. Open Tue–Sun 9am–4.30pm. ¥300.*

Also located on the site of the former castle *(the moats and some pieces of wall are all that remain)*, this museum is laid out on three floors and showcases the history of the region from prehistoric times to the Meiji Restoration. The southern part of Kyushu, birthplace of the Jomon civilization some 10,000 years ago, was open to Chinese and Western influences from an early date. It was a powerful feudal fiefdom under the control of the Shimazu clan from the 12C to the 19C.

### Sengan-en★ 仙巌園（磯庭園）

*1.9mi/3km NW of the center. 35min by bus from Kagoshima-Chuo station. Open 8.30am–5.30pm. ¥1,000.*

Also known as Isotei-en, this garden was originally commissioned in 1658 by Shimazu Mitsuhisa, the nineteenth lord of the Shimazu clan, who had a villa constructed here. With its well-tended tropical plants, bamboos, and ornamental pond, it is a beautiful spot, with fine distant **views** of the bay and the smoking cone of Sakurajima. Unfortunately, the immediate view is spoilt by the sight of the main road and the rail tracks in the foreground. Just outside the garden, the collections of the **Shoko Shusei-kan** are housed in what was once the first Western-style factory in Japan, founded in 1855, which produced glassware, ceramics, and weapons. The objects on display come from the collections of the Shimazu family. Behind the museum building, you can visit the workshops and watch the glass-blowers at work.

### Dolphin Port ドルフィンポート

*20min by bus from Kagoshima-chuo station or 10min walk from Kagoshima station.*

This shopping mall stretches along the boardwalk by the harbor. There are plenty of restaurants.

**Kagoshima City Aquarium**★ – *On the North Pier. Open 9am–6pm. ¥1,500.* One of the largest in Japan, this aquarium covers several floors, and provides an excellent introduction, both entertaining and educational, to the tropical marine life of Kagoshima and

### The "house of fireflies"

This small cafe in the center of Chiran has been turned into a museum. Owned by Akihisa Torihama, it is called *Hotaru-kan*, the "house of fireflies". It was here that his grandmother, Tome-san, cooked a last meal for the young kamikaze pilots before they left on their missions. Out of affection for her, they all called her *Oka-san*, "mother." Many secretly entrusted her with letters for their girlfriends or families to escape the military censors. "Contrary to the legend, these young men weren't fanatical patriots who set off full of enthusiasm," explains her grandson. "They weren't even volunteers, but under pressure from society and the high command, they couldn't refuse. Knowing that the war was lost, they thought their sacrifice was pointless. Rather than fanaticism, their letters express their sadness at having to die so young and their sorrow at leaving their loved ones."

Okinawa. The visit ends with a dolphin show in a large pool, which will delight children.

## Sakurajima★★ 桜島

*From the terminal by the North Pier, ferries (every 15min, journey time 15min, ¥150) serve the peninsula. Tourist Office (open 9am–5pm) and bicycle rental beside the ferry terminal. A bus service (every 30min) makes a circuit of the peninsula.*

Sakurajima, to the north of Kagoshima Bay, is one of the most active volcanoes in Japan *(see photo below)*. It consists of three peaks, the highest reaching an altitude of 3,665ft/1,117m. Sakurajima is active more or less constantly, raining ash down on Kagoshima at regular intervals. In a major eruption in 1914, which claimed many lives, the volcano spewed out 3 billion tons of lava that engulfed the surrounding villages and filled in the 1,312ft/400m-wide strait, thus joining what was then an island of 31sq mi/80sq km to Kyushu. Canals, barriers, and basins have been built on its slopes in order to channel the flow of lava and reinforced concrete shelters are intended to provide protection against falling volcanic debris.

On the plus side, the fertile soil is ideal for growing the biggest *daikon* (Chinese radish) in Japan, as well as kumquats and citrons. Its hot springs also draw many tourists.

*Sakurajima viewed from Kagoshima City*

**Yunohira**★ – From the harbor, a road *(2hr walk there and back)* winds between the lava fields and the pine forests to this magnificent **observation point** over the volcano and the bay.

**Furusato Onsen**★ – *On the south coast. Open 8am–8pm. ¥1,500.* Located at the edge of the ocean, the water for this amazing *rotenburo* carved out of volcanic stone comes from a spring at the foot of a large tree, whose strong roots shelter a small Shinto shrine. Men and women bathe here together, dressed in the white *yukata* that are provided to respect the sacredness of the site.

## EXCURSIONS

### Chiran 知覧

*21mi/34km S of Kagoshima.*
*Regular bus service from Kagoshima-chuo station (1hr20min; ¥840).*

A quiet town surrounded by wooded hills and tea plantations, Chiran was one of the 113 fortresses built to protect the feudal lords of Satsuma, and also one of the principal bases from which kamikaze missions set off during World War II (*see box p495*).

#### Bukeyashiki★ 武家屋敷

*Near the center. Open 9am–5pm. ¥500.*

Seven samurai houses dating from the Edo period (mid-18C) stand side by side on a long street lined by a low stone wall. A stream filled with carp flows through a specially-cut channel. All the houses have delightful rock gardens that cleverly incorporate the "borrowed scenery" of the surrounding hills.

#### Peace Museum 知覧特攻平和会館

*1.2mi/2km W of the city. The bus from Kagoshima also stops at the museum. Open 9am–5pm. ¥500.*

During the Battle of Okinawa, toward the end of World War II, most Japanese kamikaze planes took off from Chiran. Almost all the pilots were young men between the ages of 17 and 28. The museum commemorates the 1,036 kamikazes (or *tokkotai*, "special attack units") from Chiran, who committed suicide by flying their fighter planes crammed with explosives directly into American ships. Photographs show them in officer's uniforms, in pilot helmets and goggles. The display cases reveal their poems, letters, and personal belongings.

*From Chiran, buses go to Ibusuki or to Kiire station, where you can catch a train to Ibusuki.*

### Ibusuki★ 指宿

*31mi/50km S of Kagoshima.*
*From Kagoshima-chuo station, JR IbusukiLine (1hr, ¥970).*

This onsen resort at the end of the Satsuma Peninsula has a glorious natural setting, surrounded by white sandy beaches and rocky inlets filled with

*People having volcanic sand baths, Ibusuki*

tropical vegetation; the cone of the **Kaimon-dake** volcano can be seen in the background. Nearby, eels swim in the clear waters of the vast **Lake Ikeda** in the caldera of a former volcano.

### Ibusuki Sunamushi Onsen★★
指宿砂むし温泉

*Sunamushi Kaikan, near the beach. 20min walk from the station. Open 8.30am–noon, 1–8.30pm. ¥900.*

Ibusuki is famous for its volcanic sand baths, reputed to have a beneficial effect on neuralgia, rheumatism, and other aches and pains. The Japanese have been flocking here for three centuries, to be buried up to their necks in sand by elderly ladies, who are dab hands with a shovel *(see photo opposite)*. The steam from the thermal waters beneath the beach heats the sand to a temperature of 131°F/55°C. This steam is full of marine minerals, and the heat speeds up the circulation of the blood, helping to eliminate toxins.

### Satsuma Denshokan Museum★ 薩摩伝承館

*Opposite the Ibusuki Hakusuikan Hotel. 5min by taxi from the JR station. Open 9am–5pm. ¥1,500.*

Opened in February 2007, this superb building, surrounded by water, reproduces the architecture of the Heian era temples, in particular that of Byodo-in in Uji *(see p319)*.

Its collections of Satsuma porcelain—nearly 3,000 pieces assembled by the family of the institution's founder—are unique, and trace the history of these intricately decorated ceramics, which became popular in Europe toward the end of the 19C. The ground-floor rooms display massive *kirande* vases ornamented with multicolored and gilded decorations. The first floor showcases Chinese ceramics, notably masterpieces from the Imperial porcelain of the Song dynasty (960–1279).

### Kirishima Yaku National Park★

*About 40mi/65km N of Kagoshima. From Kagoshima Station take JR Kirishima Line to Kirishima jingu station (45min, ¥1820), then take the bus to Takachiho-gawara to undertake climbing Mt. Takachiko, or take the Yukemuri-go bus (1h, ¥740) to Ebino-kogen, where the lake route begins (trekking).*

Nature-lovers will enjoy an escape to this natural park, its territory including the originally volcanic **Kirishima Mountains**. There is a superb landscape of about 20 mountain peaks, many of them over 3,281ft/1,000m in altitude; crater lakes and plateaus rival each other in beauty. The Spring and Fall are obviously the best seasons for both the weather and for admiring the vegetation, especially the azaleas.

There are several signposted treks of various levels, crisscrossing the territory which was the first in Japan to be recognized as a National Park, in 1934 *(for information on the treks: Takachiho-gazara Visitor Center; 099-557 2505; open 9am–5pm)*.

**Mt. Takachiho** *(5,164ft/1,574m)* stands out among the peaks as having greater importance in Shinto mythology; it was here that Ninigi-no-mikoto, grandson of goddess Amaterasu and therefore ancestor of the current Emperor, is said to have come down to earth to bring rice to Japan.

### Kirishima jingu★

*About 4.3mi/7km S of Mt. Takachiho.*

The sacredness in which Mt. Takachiho is held is explained by the presence of a nearby Shinto shrine. The first shrine was built in the 6C; its founding is mentioned in the oldest official chronicles, the *Kojiki* and the *Nihon shoki* (8C). The current shrine dates from the Edo era and was financed by the 21st Lord of Satsuma. It is literally submerged in a splendid vegetation comprised of centuries-old trees—pines, maples, seizures—some of which are considered sacred. Throughout the year, numerous ceremonies are held in the main building (*honden*) in connection with rice, which recalls the myth; most of them the public is not allowed to attend. The annexed building (*kagura den*) is, however, open to the general public for various ceremonies.

# ADDRESSES

## STAY

### KAGOSHIMA

**Little Asia Guest House** 鹿児島リトルアジア *1-1 Chuomachi. 1min walk from Kagoshima-chuo station, west exit. 099-812-7700. . Restaurant.* Family guesthouse for young travelers. Laundry, bicycle rental, kitchen for residents; owners speak English.

**Hotel Crestia Kagoshima** ホテルクレスティア鹿児島 *2-21-22 Nishida. West exit of Kagoshima-chuo station. 099-813-0055. www.crestia.jp. 82 rooms.* A large, well-maintained, functional *business hotel.*

**Hotel Nakahara Bessou** 温泉ホテル中原別荘 *15-19 Terukunicho, downtown, opposite Chuo Park. 099-225-2800. www.nakahara-bessou.co.jp. 53 rooms.* Well-located, comfortable family.

**Castle Park Hotel** 城山観光ホテル *41-1 Shinshoin-cho. 10min by free shuttle bus from the station. 099-224-2211. www.shiroyama-g.co.jp. 365 rooms.* Kagoshima's finest hotel, at the top of Shiroyama hill, with 4 restaurants.

### IBUSUKI

**Marutomi** 民宿丸富 *5-24-15 Yunohama, near the sand bath. 0993-22-5579. . 7 rooms.* A reasonably priced *minshuku.* Clean, welcoming Japanese rooms (without bathrooms). The annex has a small *onsen.*

**Ibusuki Hakusuikan Hotel** 指宿白水館 *Chirin-no-Sato. 5min by taxi from the station. 0993-22-3131. www.hakusuikan.co.jp. 205 rooms.* Gardens, swimming pool, luxurious rooms *(beds or futons)*, 4 restaurants, huge baths.

## EAT

### KAGOSHIMA

**Arahobana** 新穂花・鹿児島店 *2F Dolphin Port. 099-219-8670. Open 11am–10pm.* Cuisine from the Amami Islands, based on sweet potatoes, pork, seaweed, and chicken broth.

**Ajimori** あぢもり *13-21 Sennichi-cho, near Tenmonkan-dori. 099-224-7634. Open 11.30am–8.30pm.* Old-style restaurant specializing in *kurobuta* and *tonkatsu.*

**Kumasotei** 熊襲亭 *6-10 Sepia-dori, near Tenmonkan-dori. 099-222-6356. Open 11am–10pm.* Private rooms with tatamis, menu in English, local cuisine: *kibinago*, pork *shabu-shabu*, etc.

### CHIRAN

**Taki-an** 高城庵 *In the "samurai street." 0993-83-3186. Lunch only. .* 257-year-old house, for enjoying *soba* (buckwheat noodles) while admiring the garden.

# USEFUL INFORMATION

**Tourist Offices** – In Miyanoura, at the harbor terminal *(open 8.30am–5pm; 0997-42-1019).* In Anbo, in the center of the village, on the main road *(open 8.30am–5pm; 0997-46-2333).* There is another office on the left as you come out of the airport *(open when planes arrive; 0997-4-4010).*

# TRANSPORTATION

*There is no connection between Yakushima and Okinawa; you have to go via Kagoshima.*

**BY PLANE** – The JAC company, a subsidiary of JAL, connects Kagoshima and Yakushima *(5 flights per day, 40min, ¥12,750).* The airport is on the NE coast, halfway between Miyanoura and Anbo, and can be reached by taxi or bus.

**BY BOAT** – The Toppy jetfoil is the most practical way to get to Yakushima from Kagoshima *(5 per day)* and Ibusuki *(2 per day).* The journey lasts between *2hr and 2hr30min* and costs *¥7,000.* The Orita Kisen ferry, which leaves Kagoshima at 8.30am, is slower at *4hr*, and costs *¥5,000.*

### GETTING AROUND YAKUSHIMA

**BY BUS** – A bus makes a circuit of the island every hour in both directions, between **Nagata and Oko no taki, via Miyanoura, the airport, Anbo, Onoaida, and Yudomari.** Another bus connects Miyanoura and Shiratani Unsuikyo. A third goes from Miyanoura to Arakawa Tozanguchi via Anbo and Yakusugi Land.

**BY TAXI** – Several companies operate on the island, including Yakushima Kotsu Taxi *(0997-46-232 or 42-0611).*

**BY CAR** – Reckon on paying between *¥6,000* and *¥10,000* per day to rent a small car. The rental companies are at the airport. **Terada Rent-A-Car** *0997-42-0460.* Matsubanda Rent-A-Car *0997-42-0027.*

# Yakushima★★★
# 屋久島

**Surrounded by coral reefs and often shrouded in mist, much of Yakushima is like a lush primeval forest. The island has a high level of biodiversity and is covered with a subtropical rainforest containing many *sugi*, Japanese cedars, some of the tallest of which are among the most ancient trees in the world. Designated a UNESCO World Heritage Site in 1993, the island is a place of extremes: on the coast the heat is positively tropical, with white sandy beaches, while in the mountains the cold is alpine, with snowcapped peaks in winter. Pentagonal in shape, the island bristles with some 50 mountains that are over 3,280.8ft/1,000m in height. The tallest, Mount Miyanoura *(6,348.4ft/1,935m)*, is the highest peak in southern Japan. The island's craggy contours and tropical latitude combine to give it record levels of rainfall: 157.4in/4m per year on the coast and more than 315in/8m in the mountainous interior. Locals say it rains 35 days in every month! But this drawback is fully compensated by the luxuriant plant life and the enchantment of the dense forest with its numerous trails, which make Yakushima a genuine paradise for hikers.**

- **Population:** 13,541 – Kagoshima Prefecture.
- **Michelin Map:** Principal Sights Map A3 – Regional Map p471.
- **Location:** 37.3mi/60km to the south of Kagoshima, the island has a surface area of 193sq mi/500sq km and a circumference of 83.9mi/135km. The population is concentrated in two urban centers: Miyanoura, the principal town, in the north, and Anbo, in the east. The airport is located halfway between the two. Most boats land at Miyanoura. A road runs around the edge of the island, passing through the small town of Onoaida in the south.
- **Timing:** Allow two or three days. Take a good pair of shoes, warm clothes, an umbrella, and a raincoat for hiking. Avoid Japanese public holidays, when the hotels are full and the trails get too crowded; also June—July (the rainiest season).
- **Don't miss:** Mononoke forest; hiking in Yakusugi Land or, for the more adventurous, Jomon-sugi; the Oko no taki waterfall.

## AN OVERVIEW

**The "Alps of the ocean"** – The result of a volcanic eruption 14 million years ago, Yakushima is distinguished by its highly mountainous terrain.

The island has several peaks that are more than 5,905.5ft/1,800m high, including Miyanoura-dake *(6,348.4ft/1,935m)*, Nagata-dake *(6,187.7ft/1,886m)*, and Okina-dake *(6,102.4ft/1,860m)*, the highest peaks in the whole of Kyushu.

This rugged appearance is echoed on the coasts, especially in the southwest, where rocky cliffs plunge straight into the sea. To the north and east, the shoreline slopes more gently, lapped by the warm waters of the Kuroshio Current, which sustain a large variety of corals and tropical fish.

**An abundance of vegetation** – Forest covers 90 percent of the surface of the island. While the coast basks in a subtropical climate similar to that of Okinawa, the mountain peaks, snow-capped in winter, plunge to temperatures worthy of Hokkaido.

### Wildlife

Yakushima is of interest for its animal life, which is quite different to that in the rest of Japan. Hidden in the island's forests are large colonies of red-faced macaques *(yaku-zaru)* and small wild deer *(yaku-shika)*, each numbering around 3,000. Notable among the 150 species of bird are the Japanese robin (*komadori)* and the Japanese wood pigeon. Last, but not least, the island has 15 species of reptile (including a poisonous snake, the *mamushi*, and several hundred varieties of insect).

The vegetation reflects these differences: near the coast it is tropical *(mangrove swamps, deeply shaded forests of bay trees, camphor trees, camellias, banyans, and fig trees)*, becoming more temperate *(mixed forests of oaks, larches, maples, cypresses, and cedars)*, and finally subalpine *(rhododendrons, mosses, and lichens)* the higher you climb. As the island is a microcosm of all the ecosystems in Japan, the plant life is lush and extremely varied for the surface area: there are nearly 1,900 species and subspecies of plant and flower, many of them endemic to the island, especially in the mountains. The acidity of the soil and the high humidity favor the proliferation of ferns and epiphytes (lianas and mosses), which cover the trunks and branches of the trees.

**Ancient cedars** – Between 1,968.5ft/600m and 5,249.3ft/1,600m, the warm temperate forest is characterized by the abundance of *Cryptomeria japonica* or Japanese cedars *(sugi)*, including many extremely old specimens. Cedars more than 1,000 years old are known as *yakusugi*, and younger trees *kosugi*. Since the soil is relatively poor in nutrients, the trees grow slowly, making their wood exceptionally dense and resistant. Venerated in ancient times, these trees were cut down in large numbers for logging by the Shimazu clan. During the Edo period (1603–1867), they were used to provide the shingles for temple roofs in Kyoto. In 1964, much of the forest was declared a National Park.

## SIGHTS

Buses are infrequent, so if you're in a hurry or simply prefer the comfort of a car, it's a good idea to rent one to get around the island *(see Addresses p498)*.

### Yakushima Environmental and Cultural Village Center

**屋久島環境文化村センター**

*5min walk from Miyanoura harbor.*
*Open Tue–Sun 9am–4.30pm. ¥500.*
This information centerpresents a broad outline of the geography, history, and culture of Yakushima. An *Imax* film, projected on a giant screen, takes you on a dizzying flight over the mountains and ancient forests in the interior of the island. *There's a cafe-restaurant serving meals and Western-style breakfasts.*

### Shiratani Unsuikyo★

**白谷雲水峡**

*7.5mi/12km S of Miyanoura (30min by bus, ¥300).*
At an altitude of 2,624.7ft/800m, this deep ravine conceals a magnificent rainforest of conifers, including many *yakusugi* cedars. Three easy, well-signposted hiking trails *(1hr, 1hr40min, and 3hr)* take you along the Shiratani River, passing some truly ancient trees on the way, including **Yayoi-sugi★**, a 1,200-year-old cedar. The three-hour trail is the most rewarding—it takes you across a hanging bridge and several clear, fast-flowing streams, before reaching the **Mononoke forest★★**, so-named in tribute to the filmmaker Miyazaki Hayao *(see p 85)* who used it as the inspiration for his film *Princess Mononoke*.

### Nagata Inakahama★

**永田いなか浜**

*13mi/21km W of Miyanoura (35min by bus).*
This long beach of white sand near the village of Nagata is ideal for bathing and is also one of the largest nesting sites in the world of the endangered **loggerhead turtles**. Between May and August, as many as 500 turtles at a time come

©Kagoshima Prefectural Tourist Federation/JNTO

per night to lay their eggs on the beach where they were born, 10–20 years earlier. Each female makes two or three trips here per season, each time burying around 100 eggs. Of the young turtles that hatch, only a small number will escape predators. The small **Umigame-kan Museum** in Nagata (*open Wed–Mon 9am–5pm; ¥200*) has information about sea turtles and their life cycle.

## The Southwest Coast★ 南西海岸

*26mi/42km (1hr by car) from Nagata to Yudomari. There are no buses along the forest road.*

**Seibu Rindoh forest road**★★★ – Skirting sheer cliffs down which icy streams tumble, this spectacular narrow road crosses one of the wildest parts of the island. It is not uncommon to come across herds of small deer, or groups of monkeys busy delousing one another, or gleaning berries that have fallen onto the road. Don't feed them or go too close, you may get bitten or scratched.

**Oko no taki waterfall**★★ – *16.2mi/26km from Nagata, 21.7mi/35km (1hr by bus) from Anbo.* From the car park, a path leads along the riverbed to a large natural swimming pool, turquoise in color, fed by water cascading down from a height of 288.7ft/88m with a deafening roar. The waterfall is classified as one of the 100 most beautiful in Japan.

**Hirauchi Kaichu *onsen*** – *40min by bus from Anbo. ¥100. Bring your own towel.* Accessible only at low tide, these pools have been carved out of the rocks by the sea. Bathing is mixed, so the more modest come here at night.

## Yakusugi Museum 屋久杉自然館

*1.9mi/3km from Anbo, on the road to Yakusugi Land. Open 9am–4.30pm. Closed 1st Tue of the month. ¥600.*

This museum traces the long history of logging on the island, especially during the Edo period. It shows how the trunks of trees that have been cut down or are left lying on the ground can regenerate and grow new shoots. A cross-section of a 1,660-year-old tree is also on display. An annex to the museum has exhibits on the crafts that use wood from the cedar tree.

## Yakusugi Land★★ ヤクスギランド

*10mi/16km W of Anbo (40min by bus, ¥300).*

A winding road leads to this **forest reserve** that rises in tiers between the altitudes of 3,280.8ft/1,000m and 4,265ft/1,300m. The forest here contains age-old cedars with thick, gnarled trunks measuring between 16.4ft/5m and 29.5ft/9m in circumference. Forced to survive in difficult conditions, most have developed a complex network of roots in order to gain a foothold in cracks in the rocks. Some of the trees have become intertwined, while others have twisted branches and form a profusion of contorted shapes in the dim light of the undergrowth.

Four hiking trails *(30min–2hr30min)* crisscross the valley. You may have to negotiate some wooden steps and well-secured hanging bridges along the way, but will pass by several superb *yakusugi* (trees), including the 3,000-year-old **Kigen-sugi**★★.

### Jomon-sugi Hiking Trail★★★

縄文杉ルート

*1.9m/3km before Yakusugi Land, follow the right fork. The bus arrives at Arakawa Tozanguchi, the starting point of the trail, at 6.30am and returns at 5pm. About 10hr walk there and back.*

Strating from the small car park, the trail straddles a precipice and then, for the first two hours, follows an old abandoned rail track. After about 50min, you will reach **Kosugi Dani**, a former camp where 500 or so woodcutters and their families lived between 1920 and 1970. The trail then plunges deep into the forest, passing the first ancient tree, **Sandai-sugi**, which is some 500 years old. The next part of the trail is a tough, steep climb, but you can pause for breath at **Wilson Kabu**★, named after the English plant collector Ernest Henry Wilson, who, in 1914, discovered the stump of this giant tree, which had been cut down in 1586. Its cavernous roots form a gaping hole large enough for several people to stand upright.

A little farther along the trail is the ancient 3,000-year-old **Daio-sugi**★ and its companion **Meoto-sugi**★, intertwined like a couple of lovers locked in an eternal embrace. Finally, at an altitude of 4,265ft/1,300m, you reach **Jomon-sugi**★★, an immense giant of a tree that according to legend is 7,200 years old, though in fact it is closer to 2,600.

## ADDRESSES

### STAY

*Always phone in advance for reservations. You will be collected on arrival.*

**MIYANOURA**

**Yaedake Sanso Lodge** ロッジ八重岳山荘 *1.9mi/3km S of Miyanoura, on the Shiratani Unsuikyo road. 0997-42-1551. 8 cottages.* Idyllic, in forest next to the river for swimming and kayaking. The rooms have tatami floors and toilets, but no baths. Meals with other guests in a separate room.

**Seaside Hotel Yakushima** シーサイドホテル屋久島 *On the hill facing the harbor. 0997-42-0175. www.ssh-yakushima.co.jp. 80 rooms.* Comfortable, practical hotel, spacious Western and Japanese rooms, some with a **sea view**. *Outdoor swimming pool in summer.*

**SOUTH OF THE ISLAND**

**JR Hotel Yakushima** JRホテル屋久島 *Onoaida, 9.3mi/15km S of Anbo. 0997-47-2011. www.jrk-hotels.com. 46 rooms.* The best hotel on the island, facing the ocean. Elegant, luxurious Western-style rooms, some with fabulous **views**.

### EAT

*In the evenings, expect to be able to have dinner only where you are staying.*

**MIYANOURA**

**Shiosai** 潮騒 *On the main road, 328yd/300m from the harbor, near the Eneos station. 0997-442-2721. Open Fri–Wed 11am–9pm.* Modest cafe with good traditional cuisine. *Saba-nabe* specialty (mackerel hot pot).

**Yakushima Kanko Center** 屋久島観光センター *On the main road facing the harbor. 0997-42-0091. Open 7am–9pm (summer); 7am–7pm (winter).* Over-large store selling souvenirs and camping and hiking equipment. *A varied menu: try the delicious deer sashimi.*

**ANBO**

**Chaya Hirano** 茶屋ひらの *At Hirano, 3.1mi/5km S of Anbo. 0997-46-2816. Open 11am–3pm.* Delightful restaurant with cedarwood decor.

# Miyazaki
# 宮崎

**With its palm-fringed avenues, peaches, and sub-tropical climate—it's the sunniest place in Japan— Miyazaki draws many Japanese and Korean holiday-makers who come to enjoy watersports and golf here. It is also known throughout Japan as the winter training base for professional sports teams, especially the prestigious Tokyo Yomiuri Giants baseball team.**

- **Population:** Miyazaki Prefecture: 313,224.
- **Michelin Map:** Principal Sights Map A3.
- **Info:** Miyazaki Convention & Visitors Bureau, 3-46 Miyata-cho. ☎985-266100. www.kanko-miyazaki.jp.
- **Location:** On the south-east coast of Kyushu, 130km/80mi from Kagoshima and 175km/108mi from Kunamoto.
- **Timing:** Allow a day.
- **Don't miss:** Shinto shrines along the Nichinan coast.

## A BIT OF HISTORY

The town and its surroundings are part of important episodes in **Shinto mythology**. The two great shrines on the Nichinan coast, standing in a remarkable unspoiled natural setting, alone make a trip here worthwhile. Despite the passing of centuries, they have undeniably preserved a certain mysique.

### Aoshima jinja★★ 青島神社

*About 3mi/5km S of Miyazaki by Rt. 377. From Miyazaki station take bus to Aoshima stop (40min, ¥700) or the JR Nichinan to Aoshima station (25min, ¥270). A bridge links the island to the coast.*

The shrine is in a unique natural setting: an island about 1mi/1.5km across, shaped by erosion some 10- or 15,000 years ago, surrounded by astonishing rocky formations of basalt nicknamed "the giants' washboard" (*Oni-no-sentaku-ita*).

Nestled in a magnificent forest of palm and other centuries-old trees, the shrine is to the divinities Hikohohodemi-no-Mikoto and Toyotamahime.

There is a small **museum** recounting the main episodes of Shinto mythology, with mannequins and explanatory panels (*in English*). The last room is devoted to more contemporary "gods"—the Tokyo Yomiuri Giants baseball players, who come to the shrine to make their wishes during the winter training season in Miyazaki.

### Udo jingu★ 鵜戸神宮

*About 25mi/41km S of Miyazaki by Rt. 220. Take the bus from Miyazaki bus station to the Udo Jingu stop (85min, ¥1,470). Climb the 700 stone steps from the parking lot to reach the shrine.*

This Shinto shrine devoted to the Imperial cult (*jingu*) is on a cliffside at the edge of the sea. After having gone past two gates and two bridges, you come to the entrance to the cave in which the main building (*honden*) blazes with color and decoration. According to Shinto mythology, it is here that the goddess Toyotamahime, daughter of the god of the sea and wife to Hiko-

*Udo jingu*

## TRANSPORTATION

**BY PLANE** – JAL and ANA offer flights from Tokyo Haneda (1hr35min, about ¥33,200) and Osaka (1hr, about ¥21,700) andJAC airline, a subsidiary of JAL, links Miyazaki to Fukuoka (daily on the hour, 45min, about ¥20,000). From the airport to Miyazaki: JR (8min – ¥340)or bus (30min – ¥430).

**BY TRAIN** – **To/from Kagoshima**: Kirishima JR links Kagoshima and Miyazakl stations (2hr15min, ¥4,090); **to/from Beppu**: Dream Nichirin JR night train (1 per day, 4h15min, ¥6,070) or Nichirin JR to Miyazaki (2 per day, 3h15min, ¥6,070).

hohodemiho-no-Mikoto (grandson of Ninigi-no-Mikoto) came to give birth to her son. Although she had asked her spouse not to attend the birth, he could not refrain from entering the cave. He then discovered that Toyotamahime had assumed her original appearance, that of a water dragon (*wani*). Unable to bear the discovery of her secret, she left immediately for the land of the sea, abandoning her son.

Behind the main building (*honden*), the protuberances in the rock are supposed to represent the breasts the goddess left behind to nourish her son, because water sweats from them at certain times of the year. This is why it is a special place of cult for women who are pregnant, breast-feeding, or who wish to have a child.

Below the entrance to the cave, a large rock shaped somewhat like a tortoise is also part of the myth; he is said to have brought the goddess here for the birth and is thought to be still waiting for her return. Little earthenware amulets (undama) are sold in the shrine; men throw them with their left hand, and women with their right, to make wishes; if it reaches the part of the rock marked off with a rope, the wish is thought to come true. Hikonagis-Takeugaya-Fukia-esu-no-Mikoto, the son of the goddess, is the father of Kamuyamato-Iwarebiko-no-Mikoto, better known under the name of Jinmu, the first Emperor of Japan.

## ADDRESSES

### STAY

**Miyazaki Fujin Kaikan YH**
ユースホステル宮崎婦人会館 *1-3-10 Asahi. ℘0985-24-5785. www.jyh.or.jp/english/kyushu/miyazaki/index.html.* 15min walk from the railway station, this pleasant youth hostel has spacious tatami-mat or Western-style dormitories at reasonable rates. There's a 10pm curfew. Japanese breakfast available (¥500) if you order the night before.

**Hotel JAL City Miyazaki**
ホテルJALシティ宮崎 *4-2-30 Tachibanadori Nishi, Miyazaki-shi. ℘0985-25-2580. www.jalhotels.com/domestic/kyusyu/miyazaki/.* P *210 rooms.* Dependable city-centre business hotel 10min walk from the railway station and a 20min taxi ride from the airport.

**Miyazaki Kanko Hotel**
宮崎観光ホテル *1-1-1 Matsuyama, Miyazaki-shi. ℘0985-27-1212. www.miyakan-h.com/english/.* P *370 rooms.* On the north bank of the Oyodo river, this modern hotel has ***onsen*** and ***rotenburo*** facilities, five restaurants serving a variety of international cuisine, bar, tea lounge, shops (florist, bakery, souvenirs) and a spa.

**Sheraton Grande Ocean Resort**
シェラトン・グランデ・オーシャンリゾート *Hamayama, Yamasaki-cho. ℘0985-21-1133. www.seagaia.co.jp/english/hotel/sgor.html.* P *743 rooms.* At the centre of the Phoenix Seagaia Resort, this five-star skyscraper from Sheraton has all the features you'd expect: Japanese and Western rooms, suites, fitness centre with 25m pool and spa; shops, karakoke room, restaurants, bars, non-smoking floor, private ***rotenburo*** (¥500/hour). It's close to the Phoenix Country Club, which has one of Japan's top-three golf courses.

View from Kunimigaoka ★
By air
From Tokyo: 90 mins
From Osaka: 60 mins
From Fukuoka: 45 mins
MIYAZAKI
Japan
Steeped in myth and legend, an unexplored wonderland of scenic landscapes from long ago.
Mikado Shrine December Festival
Takachiho Night Kagura (Shinto dance)
Udo Jingu Shrine ★
Umagase Point
Takachiho Gorge
Aoshima Shrine ★★
http://www.kanko-miyazaki.jp/

# Beppu★
# 別府

**Beppu is a strange sight from the air, its plumes of steam making it look like an industrial zone; yet it is rather a "paradise of hells," the near-boiling waters of the thermal spas being highly regarded by the Japanese. Twelve million people visit every year to enjoy the town's various *onsen*, over 3,000 hot springs pumping out 21 million gal/100 million l of water a day, with baths for every taste: mud baths, sand baths, open-air baths, baths containing iron or clay. Nevertheless, few come here just for a rigorous detox; with the almost hedonistic atmosphere, this is far more a place to relax and make friends. Unfortunately, Beppu has not escaped mass tourism, to the degree that it is nicknamed the "Las Vegas of the *onsen*." If the rustic appeals, opt for neighboring Yufuin.**

- **Population:** 126,355 – Oita Prefecture.
- **Michelin Map:** Principal Sights Map A3 – Regional Map p471.
- **Location:** On the north-east coast of Kyushu, 6.2mi/10km to the north of Oita, where the airport is located. The main sights are in Beppu and Kannawa, 3.7mi/6km north of the station.
- **Timing:** Allow two days.
- **Don't miss:** Takegawara Onsen and Hyotan Onsen.

## SIGHTS

In Beppu, you can easily spend several days going from one bath to another. With the many free public baths, don't forget to take a towel, a *yukata* (light kimono), and soap, as these are not provided.

### Takegawara Onsen★★ 竹瓦温泉

*10min walk SE of the station. Open 8am–9.30pm. Closed 3rd Wed of month. ¥1,000.*

The magnificent well-preserved wooden architecture here immediately transports you to the Meiji era, with its dimly-lit, simple, and old-fashioned interior. Visitors are buried up to the neck in one of the tubs of scorching hot black sand, before rinsing off and taking a quick dip in a hot bath of water, rich in iron.

### Hyotan Onsen★★★
### ひょうたん温泉

*Kannawa district. From the station, take bus no. 33 or 34, and get off at Jigokubaru. Open 9am–1am. ¥700.*

Approximately 2,297ft/700m east of the main bus station of Kannawa, this *onsen* nestles in particularly delightful green surroundings. It includes a sand bath, a *rotenburo* (open-air bath), a gourd-shaped indoor bath *(hyotan)*, a sauna, and a waterfall bath for shoulder massage. Lunch is served, and private *rotenburos* can be reserved for families.

### Kaihin Sunayu★★ 海浜砂湯

*Beside the sea, near Beppu Daikaku station. Open 8.30am–5pm. ¥1,000.*

This sand bath next to the beach is heated by water welling up from the ground. One of the most popular in Beppu, smiling old ladies shovel hot sand over visitors until they are buried up to the neck. The idea is to then remain motionless, and sweat it out for as long as possible.

### Onsen Hoyo Land★
### 別府温泉保養ランド

*Myoban district. From the station, take bus no. 5, 41, or 43 as far as Konya Jigokumae. Open 9am–10pm. ¥1,050.*

Despite its dilapidated appearance, this building contains several wonderful mud baths, including a large, mixed open-air pool, where you can wallow like a hippopotamus to your heart's content. There are also a number of thatched huts *(yu-no-sato)* in the area, where bath salts are made.

**Jigoku Meguri★** 別府地獄めぐり
*Kannawa district. From Beppu station, take bus no. 5, 9, 41 or 43 to the Kannawa bus terminal (20min).* *Open 8am–5pm. Combined ticket for 8 jigoku ¥2,000, or ¥400 each.*
The most impressive of the town's sights are the *jigoku*, pools and wells spitting out water and mud, and belching gas. Some are now mini theme parks, with grotesque statues and caged animals. Try **Umi jigoku** (Sea Hell), a beautiful pool shrouded by vegetation; silica and radium make it a deep cobalt blue. The water is at 208.4°F/98°C and could boil an egg. **Shiraike jigoku** (White Pool Hell) is milky-white, with sulfurous and slightly fetid vapors. Two other "hells" are worth visiting, 1.9mi/3 km to the north *(5min by bus no. 16 or 2)*: ferrous oxide makes **Chi-no-ike jigoku** (Bloos Pool Hell) blood-red, while nearby **Tatsumaki jigoku** (Tornado Hell) spurts its geyser at about precisely every 25 minutes.

## EXCURSION

### YUFUIN★★ 湯布院

*18.6mi/30km W of Beppu. From JR Beppu station, take the JR Kyudai Line (1hr15min) or a bus (1hr, ¥900). Tourist Office (Open 9am–7pm) and bicycle rental outside the station.*
Well-known in Japan (4 million visitors a year) but somewhat neglected by foreign tourists, this thermal spa nestles in a verdant basin at the foot of the majestic Mount Yufu-dake (5,197ft/1,584m). It is home to a good dozen onsen and a myriad of friendly ryokan, each with its own hot baths, along with restaurants, cafes, museums, and art galleries. Nature looms large here and at dawn, the steam rising from **Lake Kirin-ko** wreathes the town in a dreamlike mist.
**Yufuin station** – Designed by Isozaki Arata, this train station is a small gem, traditional in style. It houses an art gallery *(no charge)* and—at the other end of the platform, an *ashiyu*—a thermal foot bath in which to relax. From the station, a **tsuji basha**, (a horse-drawn cart), is available to take families on a pleasant tour of the town *(every 30min 9am–4pm; tour lasts 50min; ¥1,200)*.

## ADDRESSES

### STAY

**Ryokan Sennari** 旅館千成
*2-18 Noguchi-motomachi. 0977-21-1550. www.beppu-sennari.com. 6 rooms.* Less than 2min from station. Service as if in a well-established ryokan. Beautiful garden.

**Yamada Besso** 山田別荘
*3-2-18 Kitahama. 0977-24-2121. www.yamadabessou.jp. 9 rooms.* Beautiful family-run ryokan, Japanese rooms; superb *rotenburo* in the garden.

**YUFUIN**
**Saigakukan** 彩岳館 *2378-1 Kawakami, Yufuin-cho. 0977-44-5000. www.saigakukan.co.jp. 24 rooms.* Pleasant ryokan with unrestricted **view** of Yufu-dake from its *rotenburo*.

### EAT

**Ureshi-ya** うれしや
*7-12 Ekimae-cho. 0977-22-0767. Open Tue–Sun 5.30pm–2am.* Friendly restaurant, moderately-priced menu.

## USEFUL INFORMATION

**Tourist Office – Main exit (east) of station.** *Open 9am–5pm. 0977-24-2838.* There is another office on the corner of Ekimae-dori and Ginza Arcade. *Free Internet access.*

## TRANSPORT

**BY PLANE** – Oita airport is connected to JR Beppu station by bus *(45min, ¥1,450)*. Flights to Tokyo *(1hr40min, ¥31,800)* and other large cities in Japan.

**BY TRAIN** – To and from Fukuoka, **Limited Express Sonic Line** *(1hr50min, ¥5,250)*. For Nagasaki, Ltd Exp. Sonic to Fukuoka, then Ltd Exp. Kamome *(4hr, ¥9,560)*. For Kumamoto, Ltd Exp. Kyushu Odan *(3hr, ¥5,130)*. The same train serves Aso *(2hr, ¥3,940)*.For Miyazaki, Nichirin Ltd Express *(3hr30min, ¥6070)*

**BY BOAT** – Ferries by **Kansai Kisen's Ships** *(0977-22-1311)* to Osaka *(11hr20min at night)* via Matsuyama *(4hr30min)* and Kobe *(10hr)*.

# OKINAWA ARCHIPELAGO

**Also known as the Ryukyu Islands, the 60-odd islands that form the Archipelago are spread out in an arc over more than 621mi/1,000km between the south of Kyushu and Taiwan. The largest, Okinawa-honto, is also the political and economic center of Okinawa Prefecture. Its capital, Naha, contains most of the cultural attractions, several large hotels, and theme parks.**

## Highlights

1. Samplng tasty **Ryuku** *ryori* dishes (p511)
2. The palaces of the **Shuri-jo** complex in Naha (p512)
3. The aquarium at **Ocean Expo Park** (p514–515)
4. Diving in **Manta Ray Scramble** (p518)

- **Population:** 1,383,515 – Okinawa Prefecture.
- **Michelin Map:** Principal Sights Map C2/3.
- **Location:** Around 994mi/1,600km southwest of Tokyo, the East China Sea lies to the east of the Okinawa Archipelago and the Pacific Ocean to the west. The main island, Okinawa-honto, contains Naha, the capital, which has an international airport. Some 186.4mi/300km to the south is the Miyako island group, and 93mi/150km farther southwest, the Yaeyama Islands, including Ishigaki-jima. The climate is subtropical, with an average temperature of 73.4°F/23°C.
- **Timing:** The best time to visit is between October and April. Avoid the typhoon season between June and October, and the main Japanese public holidays *(New Year and Golden Week April/beginning May)*. Three days is the minimum recommended stay.
- **Don't miss:** Ocean Expo Park; Ishigaki, Taketomi, and Iriomote islands. For diving, Zamami, Ishigaki, and Iriomote islands.

## Tropical paradise

More sparsely populated and better preserved are the Yaeyama Islands, which lie farther south: Ishigaki-jima with its splendid bays, the mangrove swamps and wild jungles of Iriomote-jima, and Taketomi-jima, with its stone houses and fields of sweet potato and sugarcane. These are tropical paradises with a real South Seas flavor. Beneath an azure sky, the ocean shimmers emerald and turquoise, while its depths teem with marine life, including colorful fish, manta rays, and whale sharks, and the beaches glitter with fine white sand against a backdrop of tropical vegetation bursting with flowers.

But this picture postcard view is not quite the whole story. For centuries, Okinawa was an independent kingdom with a strong sense of identity. It was also unfortunately the scene of one of the bloodiest battles of WWII, in which a third of the population perished and the local cultural heritage was almost completely destroyed. Even though the islands were ceded back to Japan in 1972 after a quarter of a century of occupation, American military bases remain, and still exert considerable influence on the local economy. The main island has also suffered from the uncontrolled spread of industry and tourism.

Fortunately, the indigenous culture has not entirely given up the ghost. It still survives in old legends and ancestor worship, in the local language, food and crafts *(textiles and pottery)*, and in drum dances and slow songs accompanied by *yup* guitars made from the skin of the *habu*, a poisonous snake found on the islands.

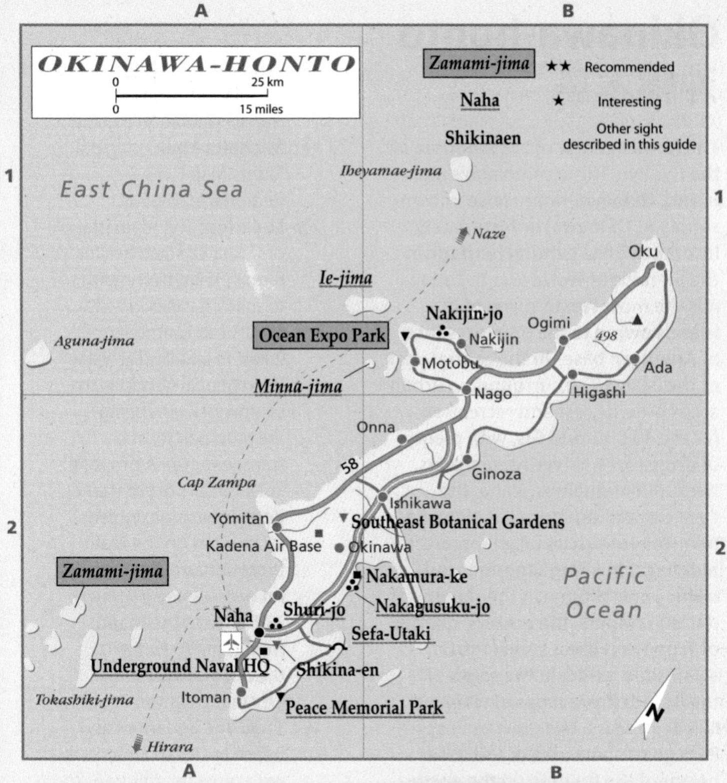

## OKINAWA-HONTO

0 ——— 25 km
0 ——— 15 miles

**Zamami-jima**   ★★   Recommended

<u>Naha</u>   ★   Interesting

**Shikinaen**   Other sight described in this guide

East China Sea

*Ibeyamae-jima*

*Naze*

Oku

*Ie-jima*

**Nakijin-jo**

Ogimi

**Ocean Expo Park**

Nakijin

498

Ada

*Aguna-jima*

Motobu

Nago

Higashi

*Minna-jima*

Onna

Cap Zampa

58

Ginoza

Ishikawa

**Southeast Botanical Gardens**

Yomitan

Okinawa

Pacific Ocean

Kadena Air Base

**Zamami-jima**

**Nakamura-ke**

**Nakagusuku-jo**

**Naha**   **Shuri-jo**

<u>Sefa-Utaki</u>

**Underground Naval HQ**

Shikina-en

*Tokashiki-jima*

Itoman

**Peace Memorial Park**

*Hirara*

© 2009 Cartographic data Shobunsha/Michelin

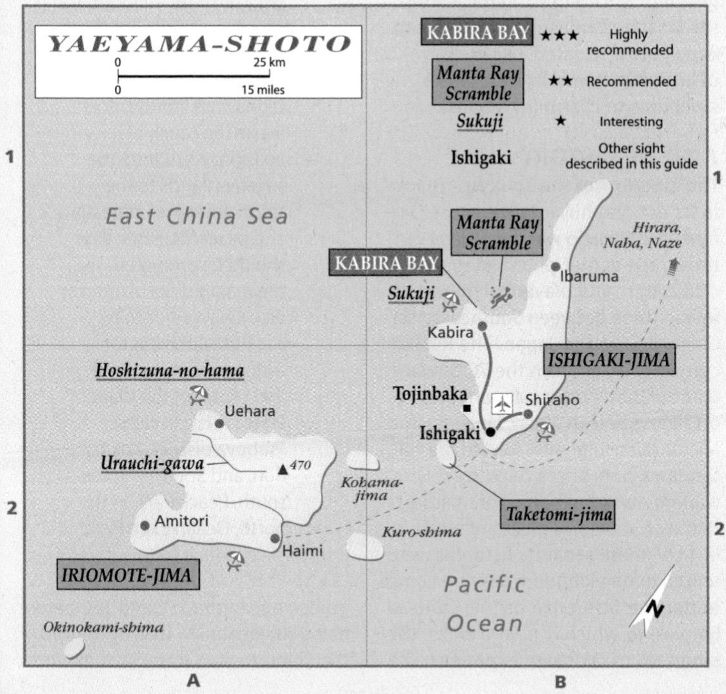

## YAEYAMA-SHOTO

0 ——— 25 km
0 ——— 15 miles

**KABIRA BAY**   ★★★   Highly recommended

**Manta Ray Scramble**   ★★   Recommended

<u>Sukuji</u>   ★   Interesting

**Ishigaki**   Other sight described in this guide

East China Sea

**Manta Ray Scramble**

*Hirara, Naha, Naze*

**KABIRA BAY**

<u>Sukuji</u>

Ibaruma

Kabira

**ISHIGAKI-JIMA**

<u>Hoshizuna-no-hama</u>

Uehara

**Tojinbaka**

Shiraho

<u>Urauchi-gawa</u>   ▲ 470

Kohama-jima

Ishigaki

Amitori

Kuro-shima

**Taketomi-jima**

Haimi

**IRIOMOTE-JIMA**

*Okinokami-shima*

Pacific Ocean

© 2009 Cartographic data Shobunsha/Michelin

# Okinawa-honto
# 沖縄本島

**The former center of the kingdom of the Ryukyu, the archipelago's main island, Okinawa-honto (also known simply as Okinawa) unfortunately lost much of its cultural heritage in the air raids of World War II. Today, it is the most Westernized of the islands owing to the omnipresence of American bases in the central part of the island. The surrounding urban areas provide rest and recreation for the 45,000-odd GIs, with plenty of drugstores, drive-ins, pizzerias, bars, and nightclubs. Naha, the ever-expanding capital, is almost a mini-Tokyo with its tall, ill-assorted buildings, bustling nightlife, and traffic jams. Hidden in the shadow of the skyscrapers, the potters' quarter of Tsuboya is like a survivor from a vanished world. In the south of the island, the ravages of war have left deep scars. The moving Peace Park gives some idea of the sheer horror of the fighting. In the north, the Motobu Peninsula, where Ocean Expo Park is situated, has areas of untouched countryside, plus a sprinkling of charming islands.**

- **Population:** Island: Population 1,100,000, Naha: Population 319,683.
- **Michelin Map:** Principal Sights Map C2/3 – Regional Map p509.
- **Location:** The main island of Okinawa stretches for 84mi/135km from north to south; it varies in width from 3.1 to 12.4mi/5 to 20km. Planes land at Naha International Airport in the southwest, Naha being the principal city and transport hub. A monorail links the airport to the downtown area, which is centered on the main thoroughfare, Kokusai-dori. An expressway *(Highway 330)* crosses the island from Naha to Nago in the north via Okinawa City in the center.
- **Kids:** The aquarium and beach at Ocean Expo Park are a must for children. You can also visit the Southeast Botanical Gardens.
- **Timing:** If your time in Okinawa is limited, don't waste too much of it on Okinawa-honto: the smaller islands to the south are more interesting and peaceful. Three days should be enough to see the main points of interest on Okinawa-honto by car, but watch out for traffic jams in the south and center of the island.
- **Don't miss:** In Naha, Tsuboya district, Kokusai-dori, and Shuri-jo; in the south, Peace Park; in the north, Ocean Expo Park.

## A BIT OF HISTORY

**The kingdom of the Ryukyu** – Thanks to its geographical position, the Okinawa archipelago was, for several centuries, the center of an independent civilization, and played an important role in trade between Southeast Asia, China, Korea, and Japan. The Ryukyu culture evolved from the 7C onward, borne of the different cultural influences of Chinese, Korean, Malay, Japanese, and Micronesian migrants. Toward the 10C, Okinawa-honto was ruled by several warlords, who built a host of small forts that also served as places of worship. In 1429, these separate fiefdoms were united in one kingdom. Having come under the influence of the Chinese Empire, to which it paid tribute, the kingdom of Okinawa experienced a golden age in the 15C and 16C before being subjugated in 1623 by the lord of the Shimazu clan from Satsuma *(now*

## A healthy diet

The likely reason why Okinawans hold the world record for longevity is their low-fat diet, which counters the effects of aging, and protects against cardiovascular disease and cancer. The Okinawan cuisine, considered medicinal by the islanders, consists mainly of rice, soy bean derivatives like tofu, a lot of vegetables, and sea produce, including seaweed, and green tea. The most popular local dish is *chanpuru*, a mixture of tofu, *goya* (a bitter melon, rich in vitamin C), and sautéed meat. *Umibudo,* or "sea grape" is a strange-tasting seaweed shaped like a miniature bunch of grapes. Pork is also common: in fact, every part of the pig is used, from the head to the trotters, in many different dishes including *rafuti*, a stew simmered in ginger, with sugar, soy sauce, and *awamori*, the powerful, local rice-based liquor.

*Kagoshima)* in the south of Kyushu *(see p 491)*. The island nevertheless continued to trade with China until 1879, when it was finally annexed by the Japanese government.

**The Battle of Okinawa** – There have been few more ferocious battles in history. The final phase of the war in the Pacific got underway when American troops landed on Okinawa on April 1, 1945. Although outnumbered, the Japanese had prepared their defenses well, creating a maze of underground tunnels and blockhouses. The slaughter was terrible, involving massive firepower, kamikaze attacks, hand-to-hand fighting, and mopping-up operations with flame-throwers. The fighting lasted 82 days and claimed more than 230,000 lives, including 120,000 of the island's inhabitants. The Okinawans were not only bombarded by the Americans, they were also mistreated by the Japanese soldiers, forced to join the army as auxiliaries or to commit mass suicide so as not to fall into the hands of the victors.

**The military burden** – Although the rest of Japan regained its sovereignty in 1952, the US army retained control of Okinawa, establishing military bases on the island, which would become particularly active during the Korean and Vietnam Wars. In 1972, Okinawa was ceded back to Japan, but Okinawa-honto still has 75 percent of the American troops stationed in Japan, much to the displeasure of the islanders, who feel they get a raw deal from the Japanese central government.

## SIGHTS

### NAHA★ 那覇

The booming capital city of Naha is well on its way to becoming a modern metropolis, with its towering skyscrapers and state-of-the-art monorail. The main street in downtown Naha is the long and lively **Kokusai-dori★** *(pedestrian-only on Sundays)*, which stretches for 1mi/1.6km and is full of souvenir shops, military surplus stores, restaurants, bars, hotels, and shops selling traditional lacquerware. At the east end of the street, opposite the Mitsukoshi department store, is the **Makishi covered market** *(open 10am–8pm)* nicknamed "the kitchen of Naha." Its stands, presided over by spry old ladies known as *anmaa*, display a multitude of colorful fish, vegetables, exotic fruit, and other ingredients typical of the island's cuisine, such as pig's head and dried snake.

### Tsuboya District★ 壺屋

*5min walk SE of Kokusai-dori, at the end of the Heiwa-dori shopping arcade.*

A calm atmosphere prevails in this charming old quarter, with its cobbled streets, workshops, and small craft stores. It has been the center of **pottery** production in Okinawa for more than three centuries. The potters of Tsuboya traditionally produced large jars for storing water, *awamori* (the local rice-based liquor), or miso paste. Today, they mostly make small items for the tourist market: teacups, sake cups, and *shiisa*, the lion-dog figure that the islanders place on the roofs of their houses to

### The priestesses of Okinawa

The old religion of the Ryukyu Islands was based on a belief in *onarigami*, the spiritual superiority of women over men and their greater ability to communicate with the gods. Worship was in the hands of the *noro*, virgin priestesses dressed in white (who may originally have been queens), and oracles were delivered by female shamans called *yuta*. Today many of the islands' older women still maintain ancestor worship, the foundation of the islands' religion. They burn incense and say daily prayers in front of the family altar *(buchidan)*. The *yuta*, who practice both medicine and magic, may also be called on to perform a kind of exorcism: when a person has been deprived of his *mabui* (soul), they aid recovery by invoking ancestors.

ward off evil spirits. The district has a small **Pottery Museum** *(open Tue–Sun 10am–6pm; ¥315)* explaining the history, techniques, and different styles of pottery, both glazed and unglazed.

## Shuri-jo★ 首里城

*1.9mi/3km NE of Kokusai-dori. Monorail to the Shuri terminus, then 15min walk, or bus no. 7 from Kokusai-dori (30min). Open 9am–8.30pm (summer); 9am–6.30pm (winter). ¥800.*

Now designated a UNESCO World Heritage Site, from 1429 to 1879, Shuri-jo was the seat of the independent kingdom of the Ryukyu before being annexed by Japan. This former castle stood on a hill with a **view** of the East China Sea on one side, and the Pacific on the other. It comprised a complex of buildings, including fortifications, palaces, and temples, surrounded by terraced gardens. Combining Chinese and Japanese influences, it mixed elegant, pillared wooden pavilions with solid stone walls and a host of bastions, turrets, and tunnel-like gates cut into the thick granite.

Razed to the ground during World War II, when it was used as the Japanese military headquarters, it was partly rebuilt at the beginning of the 1990s and the restoration is still in progress. Visitors enter through the fine Chinese-style gate, the **Shurei-mon★**, rebuilt in 1958 *(which appears on ¥2,000 banknotes)*, and after going through a further series of gates, including the impressive stone **Kankai-mon**, come out onto the main esplanade, the **Una,** where the King of Ryukyu would hold great ceremonies. It is surrounded by several pavilions, including the **Sei-den★**, the principal hall, with its double roof and wide, colorful porch.

## Shikina-en 識名園

*1.2mi/2km to the E. Bus no. 1 or 5 (20min) to Shikina-en-mae. Open Thu–Tue 9am–5pm. ¥400.*

Built toward the end of the 18C, this garden and its villa were used as a residence by the Ryukyuan Royal Family and their guests, including ambassadors from China. Destroyed during World War II, it was restored in 1975. The general layout of the garden is inspired by that of Japanese stroll gardens *(see p 103)*, with a lake in the middle. The villa, with its red-tiled roof, on the other hand, is typical of the local architecture, while a small stone bridge shows a Chinese influence.

## THE SOUTH★

The southern part of the island, heavily damaged by aerial bombardment, saw most of the fighting during the terrible battle of Okinawa.

It was not only the location of the underground headquarters of the Japanese Navy, but also had a network of caves that were used as shelters by both Japanese soldiers and civilians.

## Japanese Underground Naval Headquarters 旧海軍司令部壕

*Tomigusuku, Route 7, 2.5mi/4km SW of Naha. Bus no. 33, 46, or 101 to Tomigusuku-koen (25min), then 10min walk. Open 8.30am–5pm. ¥420.*

The Japanese Navy established its headquarters beneath the hill on which the former castle of Tomigusuku was built, digging out a vast labyrinth of underground corridors and rooms. Realizing defeat was imminent, Vice-Admiral Ota Minoru and his 4,000 men committed mass suicide on June 13, 1945. Some of the walls still bear the marks of exploding grenades.

### Peace Memorial Park★
平和祈念公園

*Itoman, Route 331, 13.7mi/22km S of Naha. Bus no. 31, 33, 46, or 89 to Itoman (40min), then bus no. 82 to Heiwa-kinen-koen (20min). Open 9am–5pm. ¥500.*

With its peaceful **view** over the south of the island, Mabuni Hill was the scene of the final stages in the Battle of Okinawa. Today it is a moving memorial park, containing a number of monuments in memory of the victims. Rows of marble tablets scattered over the lawns bear the names of the 238,429 people *(Japanese and Americans, civilians, and combatants)* who fell during this episode.

The **Peace Memorial Museum★** *(open Tue–Sun 9am–4.30pm; ¥300)* traces the stages of the battle and presents the poignant testimonies of survivors. While many islanders perished in the American bombardment, many others were victims of the Japanese Army.

**Himeyuri Monument** – *1.6mi/2.5km W of the park, on Route 331. Open 9am–5.30pm. No charge.*

This monument is dedicated to the memory of a group of 219 high-school girls who, having worked as nurses to the Japanese soldiers, committed suicide with their teachers in a cave to avoid capture by the Americans.

### Sefa-utaki★ 斎場御嶽

*Chinen, Route 331, about 12.4mi/20km SE of Naha. Bus no. 38 from Naha (50min). Open 24hr. No charge.*

Part of the Related Properties of the Kingdom of Ryukyu UNESCO World Heritage Site, Sefa-utaki is of major importance to the indigenous religion of Okinawa as a place where worshippers could be closer to *Nirai Kanai*, the utopian paradise where the gods lived. *Utaki* is an Okinawan term for the sacred sites *(groves, rocks, caves, etc.)* where the islanders would communicate with the gods and make offerings to them. According to myth, it was at Sefa-utaki that the goddess Amamikiyo descended and gave birth to the Okinawa archipelago. From the 15C, this was the principal place of worship for the Ryukyuan kings, who came here to celebrate the beginning of harvest. The rites were led by a high priestess known as Kikoe Ogimi, usually the sister or aunt of the King. Altars are scattered amid the foliage of the tropical forest. At the far end of the site, a triangular opening formed by two immense rocky walls leads to the most sacred part of the site facing the island of Kudaka, where the first divine couple settled.

## THE CENTER

It is only when you follow Route 58 across the central part of the island that you fully realize quite how much land *(20 percent of the island)* is occupied by American military bases and camps *(Kadena, Kinser, Hoster, Lester, etc.)*. On one side of the road, behind barbed wire fences, lie airstrips filled with the roar of F-18 Hornets and F-22 Raptors, and neat green lawns and equally neat little houses for the expatriate families. On the other side-stand the houses of the local Okinawans in cramped profusion. The surrounding towns, like Okinawa City, are a depressing succession of fast food joints, military surplus stores, downmarket shops, and seedy bars. The area farther north is a jumble of beach resorts and rather tacky tourist attractions.

### Nakagusuku-jo 中城城跡

*Kitanakagusuku, Route 330, 8mi/13km NE of Naha. Bus no. 23 to Futenma (1hr), then taxi (10min). Open 8.30am–5.30pm (Jun–Sep: 6.30pm). ¥300.*

Standing proudly on a hill 492ft/150m above the sea, this ruined castle was originally built by the Aji clan in the 14C, then enlarged by the local lord Gosamaru in the 15C before finally being destroyed by a rival lord, Awamari, in 1458. Only part of the huge perimeter

### The birthplace of karate

Karate (*see also p108*), which today has 50 million followers, was developed in the former kingdom of the Ryukyu, before spreading to Japan and then the rest of the world. The Okinawan fighting method *te* (bare hand) was a martial art that developed in the 14C under the influence of Chinese boxing, which had been brought to the islands by merchants and sailors from continental Asia. At the beginning of the 17C, when the island was occupied by the Shimazu clan from Kyushu, the Okinawans were forbidden to bear arms. Left without a means of defense, they began perfecting their combat techniques in secret. From 1904, karate began to be taught in Okinawan schools and gradually emerged from the shadows. Today, it is practiced in the many *dojo* (training halls) on the island.

walls remain, but they give a good idea of the size of the original building. From the top of the hill, there is a fine **view** of the island.

### Nakamura-ke 中村家

*10min walk from Nakagusuku Castle. Open 9am–5.30pm. ¥500.*

The residence of the Nakamuras, an important Okinawan farming family, dates from the beginning of the 18C. Protected from typhoons by a row of trees, it's the best-preserved traditional house on the island. It has thick limestone walls and a red-tiled roof on which stands a *shiisa* (the protective lion-dog figure), a stone pigsty, and grain stores raised off the ground to keep them safe from rodents.

### Southeast Botanical Gardens 東南植物楽園

*Okinawa-kita, Route 330, 15.5mi/25km N of Naha. Bus no. 11 to Okinawa-kita (1hr), then 10min by taxi. Open 9am–5.30pm. ¥1,000.*

Popular with families, this botanical garden covering an area of 10 acres/4ha, features a Polynesian lake and a butterfly house. It contains around 100 plant species, 3,000 kinds of tropical flower, and 200 varieties of tree, including a large number of palms and banana trees. A small train takes visitors around the park, much to the delight of children.

## THE NORTH★

The most unspoilt part of the island, North is a mixture of large beaches and hills covered in subtropical forest. Most sights of interest are concentrated in the lush peninsula of Motobu and its garland of islands.

### Nakijin-jo 今帰仁城跡

*Route 115, 13.7mi/22km N of Nago. From Nago, bus no. 65 or 66 (1hr). Open 9am–5pm. ¥400.*

A few ruins on the top of a hill are all that is left of what, in the 14C, was the main fortress of the northern province of Hokuzan, ruled by the local Aji clan before the Ryukyu kingdom was united in 1429. Apart from a walk along the ramparts, not a great deal remains, but the site is noteworthy for its cherry trees, which blossom toward the end of January, and its magnificent **view** of the sea.

### Ocean Expo Park★★ 海洋博公園

*Route 114, 11mi/18km N of Nago. From Naha, express bus no. 111 to Nago (1hr40min), then bus no. 65 or 66 (1hr). Open Mar–Sept 8.30am–7pm; Oct–Feb 8.30am–5.30pm.*

Built on the site of the 1975 World's Fair, whose theme was the oceans and marine life, and which was held in Okinawa, Ocean Expo Park includes the **Okinawa Churaumi Aquarium**, a botanical garden, a museum of Oceanic Culture, a **large beach**, a restaurant, and a historic village. A small electric bus *(¥200)* takes you to the various attractions of the park.

**Okinawa Churaumi Aquarium★★** – *¥1,800.* This spectacular aquarium is the park's main point of interest. The

## USEFUL INFORMATION

**Tourist Offices** – At Naha airport *(open 9am–9pm; ✆098-857-6884)* and in the city, on Okiei-dori, at the corner of Kokusai-dori *(open 10am–8pm; ✆098-868-488)*.

## TRANSPORTATION

**BY PLANE** – **Naha Airport** – 1.9mi/3km to the SW of the city. Access by monorail *(20min, ¥230)* or taxi *(about ¥800)*. Flights to Tokyo *(2hr30min, ¥37,400)*, Osaka *(2hr, ¥31,400)*, Kagoshima *(1hr20min, ¥24,100)*, and most other large Japanese cities. Also flights to Seoul, Taipei, and Shanghai.

**BY BOAT** – **Naha Terminal, Naha Port** – Ferries linking Kagoshima *(1 per day, 24hr 30min, ¥15,200)* with Fukuoka on the island of Kyushu. Ferries to Miyako-jima and Ishigaki-jima. *Access: 10min walk to the N of Asahibashi bus station.*

**Shinko Terminal, Naha Port** – Ferries to Tokyo *(47hr, ¥23,600)*, Osaka, Kobe, Nagoya, and Taiwan. Ferries to Miyako-jima and Ishigaki-jima. Access: bus no. 101 *(25min)* from Asahibashi bus station. **Tomari Terminal, Naha Port** – Ferries to the small islands of Kume and Kerama. Access: bus no. 101 *(20min)* from Asahibashi bus station.

### GETTING AROUND OKINAWA-HONTO IN NAHA

A monorail *(open 6am–11pm, ¥200–290)* crosses the city from the airport to the Shuri district, stopping at Kokusai-dori *(Kencho-mae and Makishi stops)*. City buses *(nos. 1 to 17)* cost ¥200 per journey. A taxi ride costs about ¥600.

**BY BUS** – **Asahibashi Bus Station** – *One monorail stop SE of Kokusai-dori. Buses to the different regions of the island.*

**BY CAR** – Cars can be rented at the airport or in the city, from ¥5,000 per day. **Nippon Rent-A-Car** *✆098-868-4554*, **OTS** *✆098-857-0100*, **Japaren** *✆098-852-1900*.

**BY GUIDED TOUR** – Two companies offer half-day tours of the main places of interest. Reckon on paying about ¥4,800. **Naha Bus** *✆098-868-3750*, **Okinawa Bus** *✆098-861-0083*.

second largest in the world after Georgia Aquarium in Atlanta, USA, it showcases the marine life of the Kuroshio Current that flows past the Archipelago. In the main tank, which holds 264,860cu ft/7,500cu m of water *(the equivalent of three Olympic swimming pools)*, behind a screen of glass 23.6in/60cm thick, visitors can see whale sharks, manta rays, and many other fish. Dolphin shows are held at regular intervals.

**Tropical Dream Center** – *¥670.* This botanical garden contains 2,000 species of orchid and other tropical flowers and fruits in a series of greenhouses.

**Oceanic Culture Museum** – *¥170.* A small museum that attracts fewer visitors than the park's other attractions, it displays objects *(tools, masks, totems, musical instruments, canoes)* from the islands of Polynesia, Melanesia, Micronesia, and Southeast Asia.

**Emerald Beach★** – This superb beach of fine sand, very popular at weekends with families, extends along the bay the north of the park. It is equipped with showers, lockers, deckchairs, and beach umbrellas, and there are lifeguards on hand.

## Minna-jima★ 水納島

*From Motobu harbor, 5 to 8 ferries per day (25min, ¥1,600 Return).*

Within easy reach of the peninsula, this tiny, crescent-shaped island may only be a mere 1.5sq mi/4sq km in area and populated by just a few fishing families, but it is famous for its beautiful **beach★** of fine sand *(equipped with showers and changing rooms)* just by the jetty. Various water sports are on offer, including diving, or you can just laze in the sun. A few stands serve snacks.

**Ie-jima★** 伊江島

*From Motobu harbor, 4 ferries per day (30min, ¥1,330 Return). Bicycle rental at the ferry pier.*

A pretty island *(9sq mi/23sq km)* NW of Motobu Peninsula, Ie-jima is perfect for biking. The north's rocky cliffs, the south's lovely beach, the inland sugar-cane, pineapples, and tobacco is lovely. From the central hill **Gusuku-yama**, *(564ft/172m)* is a splendid **view** of the whole island. Late April over a million water lilies bloom to the north.

## THE NEARBY ISLANDS

**Zamami-jima★★** 座間味島

*From Tomari harbor in Naha, 2 to 4 ferries per day (fast trip: 50min, ¥3,140 or ¥5,970 round-trip; slow trip 2hr, ¥2,120 or ¥4,030). Information Office (Open 8.30am–5.30pm), bicycle, and scooter rental at the harbor.*

Located 18.6mi/30km southwest of Naha, this island paradise in the Kerama archipelago, boasts some superb beaches lapped by turquoise waters and huge coral reefs. It is also famous as a place where **humpbacked whales** can be viewed. Boat trips out to see the whales leave in the mornings from January to March *(2hr30min, ¥5,000)*. **Furuzamami beach★★**, some 15min walk to the east of the harbor, is well equipped, with snorkeling equipment available for hire and trips by sea kayaks also organized. The village of Zamami has several guesthouses for those who would like to spend a night here.

# ADDRESSES

## STAY

### NAHA

**Tatsuya Ryokan**
民宿たつや旅館・那覇店 *1-9-21 Tsuji. 098-860-7422. http://tatsuya.client.jp. 5 rooms.* 15min from Asahibashi bus station, a pleasant, inexpensive family *minshuku* (guesthouse). *English spoken. Free Internet access and bicycles.*

**Hotel JAL City**
ホテルJALシティ那覇 *1-3-70 Makishi. 098-866-2580. www.naha.jalcity.co.jp. 304 rooms.* Brand new hotel offering modern, yet cozy comfort.

### CENTRAL REGION

**Rizzan Sea-Park Hotel**
リザンシーパークホテル谷茶ベイ
*Tancha Bay, Onna Village. 098-964-6611. www.rizzan.co.jp. 558 rooms.* Large resort hotel by sea: 2 pools, 5 restaurants, a spa, shops, and even wedding chapel.

### NORTHERN REGION

**Chisun Resort Churaumi**
チサンリゾート沖縄美ら海
*938 Ishikawa, Motobu-cho. 098-048-3631. www.solarehotels.com. 94 rooms.* Affordable hotel complex facing beach at Ocean Park Expo, with pool.

### ZAMAMI-JIMA

**Joy Joy** ジョイジョイヴィレッジ
*NW of Zamami village. 098-987-2445. 5 rooms.* Small, convivial guesthouse with diving center. Reservations required.

## EAT

### NAHA

**Dao** ベトナム料理ダオ
*In the Mutsumi-bashi market arcade. 098-867-3751. Open 10am–11pm.* A simple little Vietnamese restaurant. Good and inexpensive. *¥500 lunch menu.*

**Nabi-to-Kamado**
ナビィとかまど那覇本店 *2-12-24 Kumoji. 098-863-3177. 5.30pm–6pm.* Stylish *izakaya*, 10min walk from Kokusai-dori, on the avenue alongside the monorail. Okinawan specialties and Japanese dishes, beautifully presented.

### SOUTHERN REGION

**Cafe Curcuma** カフェくるくま
*1190 Chinen, Nanjyo City. 098-949-1189.* Open Wed–Mon *10am–6pm.* Very popular Asian restaurant on hill with lovely garden, magnificent **view**. Organic salads, shrimp curries, pork with sesame, Thai chicken.

### NORTHERN REGION

**Pizza Cafe Kajinhou**
ピザ喫茶花人逢 *1153-2 Azayamazato, Motobu Town. 098-047-5537. Open Thu–Mon 11.30am–6.30pm.* Beautiful traditional house, terraced garden, **sea view**. Pizzas, salads, fruit juices, coffee.

## SHOPPING

### NAHA

**Kakuman** – *1-3-66 Makishi. 098-867-1591.* This Kokusai-dori shop is the oldest selling traditional Okinawan lacquerware.

# Ishigaki-jima★★
# 石垣島

**The gateway to the Yaeyama, the southernmost islands in Japan, Ishigaki-jima is a tropical paradise: an emerald sea, stunning coral reefs, beaches of pure white sand, and cultured black pearls. Unlike Okinawa-honto, the island was largely spared the fighting in 1945 and no American bases are located here. With its stone houses and old temples, it is the perfect place to explore the remains of the ancient culture of the Ryukyu. Head to the small nearby island of Taketomi, where the pace of life slows down even further and you can ride in a cart pulled by buffalo, see traditional weaving looms, fishing nets drying in the sun, and water drawn from wells. Another island barely touched by civilization is Iriomote, with mangrove swamps worthy of the Amazon, and beaches of fine sand. Its mountains, with their impenetrable jungle, are home to the yamaneko, a leopard cat discovered here in 1967 and found nowhere else.**

- **Population:** 46,728.
- **Michelin Map:** Principal Sights Map C3 – Regional Map p509.
- **Location:** 279.6mi/450km from Okinawa-honto and 161mi/260km from Taiwan, the Yaeyama Archipelago consists of 15 islands, including Ishigaki-jima, the principal island, and Iriomote-jima, farther to the west. The city of Ishigaki, with its airport, is in the southwest of Ishigaki-jima.
- **Kids:** A ride in a buffalo cart on Iriomote or Taketomi.
- **Timing:** A stay of at least three days is ideal.
- **Don't miss:** Kabira Bay; a trip up the Urauchi River.

## SIGHTS

### Ishigaki City 石垣市内

The island's one outpost of modern civilization, this town is centered on its harbor and the two shopping malls behind the main thoroughfare. Everything is within walking distance.

**Yaeyama Museum** – *On Yui Road, near the post office. Open Tue–Sun 9am–4.30pm. ¥200.* This small museum has a modest collection of old ceramics, canoes, and examples of the traditional crafts of the islands, including weaving.

**Miyara Donchi** – *10min walk N of the harbor. Open Wed–Mon 9am–5pm. ¥200.* Built in 1819, this house was the residence of the governor of the Yaeyama Islands. Surrounded by a garden, it is notable for its pyramid-shaped roof of red tiles.

**Torin-ji** – *On Yui Road. 15min walk NW of the harbor. No charge.* This Rinzai Buddhist temple dates from 1614. Note the statues of the guardian kings at the entrance.

**Tojin-baka** – 3.7mi/*6km NW of the city, along the coast road. No charge.* This cemetery contains the graves of the Chinese laborers who found refuge on the island in 1852 after rebelling against the crew of the American ship taking them to California. Of the 380 fugitives, 128 were shot or committed suicide.

### Kabira Bay★★★ 川平湾

*12.4mi/20km N of Ishigaki City. Bus (30min, ¥700) from the terminal located on the street just opposite the harbor.*

One of the most beautiful and unspoilt places in Japan, this bay is a true haven, with transparent waters, white sandy beach, and string of small islands just off the coast. The reefs offshore have the largest concentration of corals in Japan—nearly 215 varieties. It is also famous for its cultured black pearls. Bathing isn't really possible, but you can take a trip on a glass-bottomed boat *(30min, ¥1,500).*

## USEFUL INFORMATION

**Tourist Offices** – At the airport *(open 8am–8pm; ✆0980-88-6038)* and in the city, the building opposite the library *(open Mon–Fri 8.30am–5.30pm; ✆0980-82-2809; www.city.ishigaki.okinawa.jp/International)*.

## TRANSPORTATION

### GETTING TO AND FROM ISHIGAKI-JIMA

**BY PLANE** – Ishigaki airport, 1.9mi/3km NE of the city. Buses *(every 20min, journey time15min, ¥200)* or taxi *(about ¥800)*. Daily flights by JTA and ANK to Naha, and by JTA for Tokyo *(3hr30min, ¥61,400)* and Miyako-jima.

**BY BOAT** – Ishigaki harbor, in the downtown area. Ferries 4 times weekly to Naha *(14hr, from ¥6,800)* and 3 times weekly to Miyako-jima *(5hr, ¥1,890)*.

### GETTING AROUND ISHIGAKI-JIMA

**Individually** – From the bus station at the harbor, buses to Kabira, Yonehara, and Shiraho. Car rental *(Nippon, Nissan, Orix)* at the airport, and scooter rental downtown.

**In an Organized Group** – **Hirata Tourism**, in the harbor station *(✆0980-82- 6711)*. Many tours around Ishigaki, Taketomi, and Iriomote.

**Sukuji beach★** – 1.2mi/*2km W of Kabira.* Forming a long crescent of fine golden sand, the beach is equipped with showers, changing rooms, and other facilities.

**Manta Ray Scramble★★** – A few minutes by boat to the west of the Kabira peninsula, this is the best-known diving site in the region due to the huge manta rays that glide through its waters.

## EXCURSIONS

### Taketomi-jima★★ 竹富島

*4.3mi/7km S of Ishigaki. Ferry every 30min (10min; round-trip ¥1,100). Bicycle rental in the village.*

A flat, oval island, only 2.3sq mi/6sq km in area, Taketomi is easily crossed on foot or by bike. Located in the middle of this peaceful retreat *(population 360)*, the village is well-preserved and

*Tranquil streets of Taketomi-jima*

criss-crossed small streets lined with low walls of coral stone, behind which are gardens bursting with hibiscus and bougainvillea.
The houses, of wood or stone, have long roofs of terra-cotta tiles typical of Okinawa, adorned with grimacing *shiisa* (lion-dogs) to ward off evil spirits. Stop at **Mingei-kan** (*open 9am–5pm; no charge*), where the *minsa* belts that young women used to weave for their future husbands are now made.
The island has several fine beaches, notably **Kaiji-hama★** in the southwest. The sand here is known as "star sand" (*hoshizuna*), the grains being formed from the shells of microscopic, star-shaped marine organisms.
**Rides in buffalo carts** (*30min, ¥1,200*) are also available.

## Iriomote-jima★★ 西表島

*19mi/31km SW of Ishigaki.*
*Ferries every hour for Ohara in the S (40min, ¥1,540) or Uehara/Funaura in the N (50min, ¥2,000), the island's two ferry piers. Buses, taxis, and rental of cars, scooters, and bicycles available. The main road goes only about halfway around the island, so some villages are just accessible by boat.*

With a population of around 2,300 within a surface area of 111.6sq mi/289sq km, this mountainous island is one of the last wild regions in Japan—almost 90 percent is covered in dense tropical jungle and mangrove swamps. The coast is surrounded by the largest coral reef in Japan.
Apart from wonderful beaches and diving sites, the island also has many hiking trails, as well as rivers that are negotiable by boat or kayak.
This natural sanctuary is home to some exotic fauna, such as the wild cat of Iriomote, an endemic species of which only about 100 remain.
**Urauchi-gawa★** – Take a motorboat trip (*70min – ¥1,500*) along 5mi/8km of this, the island's principal river, with mangrove trees at its mouth.
Disembark and follow the trail (45min hike) to a beautiful waterfall in which you can bathe.
**Yubu-jima** – A small island off the east coast, with a botanical garden.
Most people visit to enjoy the crossing through shallow water from Iriomote-jima in a **cart pulled by buffalo** (*¥1,300*).
**Hoshizuna-no-hama★** – This fine beach located at the northwest point of the island is famous for its "star sand," made up from the shells of marine protozoa.

# ADDRESSES

## STAY

### ISHIGAKI-JIMA

**Rakutenya Guesthouse 民宿楽天屋** *291 Okawa, Ishigaki City. 0980-83-8713. 10 rooms – ¥3,500/person.* A rustic, but convivial guesthouse in a delightful, old wooden building.

**East China Sea Hotel ホテルイーストチャイナシー** *Facing the harbor, Ishigaki City. 0980-88-1155. www.eastchinasea.jp/Index2. html. 79 rooms.* A comfortable *business hotel* in a centrally located skyscraper. The upper floors are quieter.

**Auberge Kabira おーべるじゅ** *Kabira Bay. 0980-88-2229. www.nikikabira.com. 8 rooms – from ¥32,000 (5% reduction for foreigners).* A charming little hotel by the beach. Western-style rooms with a terrace overlooking the bay. *Spa and sauna.*

### IRIOMOTE-JIMA

**Nilaina Resort ニライナリゾート** *Near Uehara harbor. 0980-85-6400. www.nilaina.com. 3 villas - from ¥23,100.* Close to Hoshizuna beach, stylish and intimate, the hotel has a *diving center* and organizes *canoe trips*.

## EAT

### ISHIGAKI-JIMA

**Rakuza 楽座** *Ayapani mall, Ishigaki City. 0980-88-8100. Open 5–11pm.* A charming *izakaya* located in the pedestrian arcade near the market, with a pink pennant at the entrance. *Local dishes.*

**Yamamoto やまもと** *11-5 Misaki, Ishigaki City. 0980-83-5641. From 5pm until no more meat.* Opposite Shinei-koen, an ideal place to try Ishigaki beef, charcoal-grilled and perfectly tender.

# INDEX

# INDEX

## J



## K

## L



## M

## O



## P

## T

## U

## V



## W



## Y



## Z

# INDEX

## STAY

## EAT

# MAPS AND PLANS

## THEMATIC MAPS



## MAPS AND PLANS

# LEGEND
## Understanding the symbols

| Highly Recommended | Recommended | Interesting |
|---|---|---|
| ★★★ | ★★ | ★ |

## Hotels and Restaurants

**Hotels**
- Up to ¥10,000
- ¥10,000–¥20,000
- ¥20,000–¥30,000
- Over ¥30,000

**Restaurants**
- Up to ¥1,500
- ¥1,500–¥3,000
- ¥3,000–¥8,000
- Over ¥8,000

¥1050 — Price for breakfast
— Breakfast included
P — On-site parking
— Credit cards not accepted

## Symbols in the text

| | |
|---|---|
| | Tourist information |
| | Directions |
| | Hours of operation |
| | Period of closure |
| | Especially for kids |
| | Closed to the public |
| | Entry fees |
| | Also see |
| | A bit of advice |
| | Tours |
| | Hiking trails |
| | By bicycle |
| A2 B | Located on map |

## Maps

### MONUMENTS AND SITES

| | |
|---|---|
| | Sightseeing route with departure point indicated |
| | Ecclesiastical building |
| | Synagogue |
| | Mosque |
| | Wayside cross - Fountain |
| | Fortified walls - Tower - Gate |
| | Historic house, castle - Ruins |
| | Factory / Power plant - Dam |
| | Viewpoint |
| | Viewing table |
| | Fort - Cave |
| | Quarry - Mine |

### PRACTICAL INFORMATION

| | |
|---|---|
| | Tourist information |
| P | Parking - Park and Ride |
| | Tramway - Subway |
| | Railway - Coach station |
| | Overhead cable car |
| | Funicular - Rack railway |
| | Tourist or Steam railway |
| | Post - Covered market |
| | Ferry services: Passengers and cars |
| | Passengers only |

### ABBREVIATIONS AND SPECIAL SYMBOLS

| | | | |
|---|---|---|---|
| i | Tourist information | ⊗ × | Police station |
| B | Bank, Bureau de change | ⊕ ⊤ | Post office |
| U | University | | Temple |
| T | Theater | | Hot spring |
| — | Metro station | | Shop |
| | | | Hospital |

### ADDITIONAL SYMBOLS

| | |
|---|---|
| | Motorway (unclassified) |
| ❶ ❶ | Junction: complete, limited |
| | Pedestrian street |
| | Unsuitable for traffic, street subject to restrictions |
| | Steps |
| | Footpath |
| ③ | Access route number common to Michelin maps and town plans |
| B F | Ferry (river and lake crossings) |
| △ | Swing bridge |

### RECREATION

| | |
|---|---|
| | Oudoor, Indoor swimming pool |
| | Stadium - Racecourse |
| | Marina, Moorings |
| | Trail refuge hut - Hiking trail |
| | Outdoor leisure park/center |
| | Theme/Amusement park |
| | Wildlife park, Zoo |
| | Gardens, park, arboretum |
| | Aviary, bird sanctuary |

LREADY KNOW THE GREEN GUIDE,
FIND OUT ABOUT THE MICHELIN GROUP
MICHELIN
MICHELIN

# The Michelin Adventure

It all started with rubber balls! This was the product made by a small company based in Clermont-Ferrand that André and Edouard Michelin inherited, back in 1880. The brothers quickly saw the potential for a new means of transport and their first success was the invention of detachable pneumatic tires for bicycles. However, the automobile was to provide the greatest scope for their creative talents. Throughout the 20th century, Michelin never ceased developing and creating ever more reliable and high-performance tires, not only for vehicles ranging from trucks to F1 but also for underground transit systems and airplanes.

From early on, Michelin provided its customers with tools and services to facilitate mobility and make traveling a more pleasurable and more frequent experience. As early as 1900, the Michelin Guide supplied motorists with a host of useful information related to vehicle maintenance, accommodation and restaurants, and was to become a benchmark for good food. At the same time, the Travel Information Bureau offered travelers personalised tips and itineraries.

The publication of the first collection of roadmaps, in 1910, was an instant hit! In 1926, the first regional guide to France was published, devoted to the principal sites of Brittany, and before long each region of France had its own Green Guide. The collection was later extended to more far-flung destinations, including New York in 1968 and Taiwan in 2011.

In the 21st century, with the growth of digital technology, the challenge for Michelin maps and guides is to continue to develop alongside the company's tire activities. Now, as before, Michelin is committed to improving the mobility of travelers.

## MICHELIN TODAY

### WORLD NUMBER ONE TIRE MANUFACTURER

- 70 production sites in 18 countries
- 111,000 employees from all cultures and on every continent
- 6,000 people employed in research and development

# Moving
## for a world

Moving forward means developing tires with better road grip and shorter braking distances, whatever the state of the road.

## CORRECT TIRE PRESSURE

RIGHT PRESSURE

- Safety
- Longevity
- Optimum fuel consumption

-0,5 bar

- Durability reduced by 20% (- 8,000 km)

-1 bar

- Risk of blowouts
- Increased fuel consumption
- Longer braking distances on wet surfaces

# forward together
## where mobility is safer

It also involves helping motorists take care of their safety and their tires. To do so, Michelin organises "Fill Up With Air" campaigns all over the world to remind us that correct tire pressure is vital.

## WEAR

### DETECTING TIRE WEAR

The legal minimum depth of tire tread is 1.6mm. Tire manufacturers equip their tires with tread wear indicators, which are small blocks of rubber moulded into the base of the main grooves at a depth of 1.6mm.

Tires are the only point of contact between the vehicle and road.

**The photo below shows the actual contact zone.**

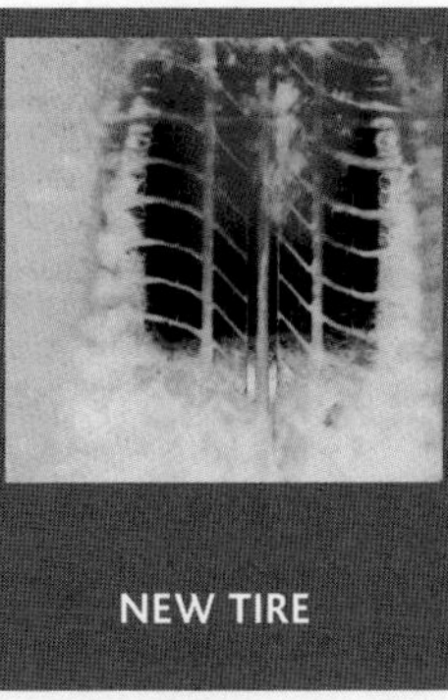

NEW TIRE

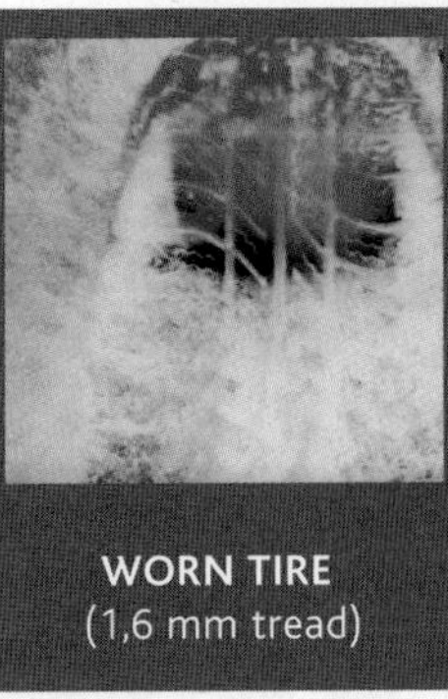

WORN TIRE
(1,6 mm tread)

*If the tread depth is less than 1.6mm, tires are considered to be worn and dangerous on wet surfaces.*

# oving forward

## means sustainable mobility

### INNOVATION AND THE ENVIRONMENT

By 2050, Michelin aims to cut the quantity of raw materials used in its tire manufacturing process by half and to have developed renewable energy in its facilities. The design of MICHELIN tires has already saved billions of litres of fuel and, by extension, billions of tons of CO2.

Similarly, Michelin prints its maps and guides on paper produced from sustainably managed forests and is diversifying its publishing media by offering digital solutions to make traveling easier, more fuel efficient and more enjoyable!

The group's whole-hearted commitment to eco-design on a daily basis is demonstrated by ISO 14001 certification.

Like you, Michelin is committed to preserving our planet.

# Chat with Bibendum

Go to
www.michelin.com/corporate/en
Find out more about
Michelin's history and the
latest news.

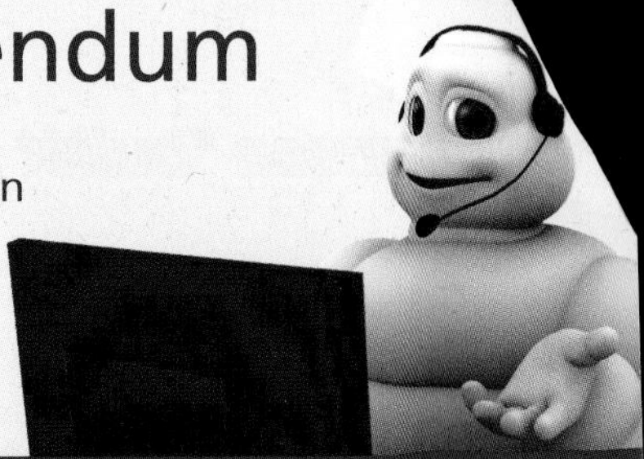

## QUIZ

Michelin develops tires for all types of vehicles.
See if you can match the right tire with the right vehicle...

Solution : A-6 / B-4 / C-2 / D-1 / E-3 / F-7 / G-5

## ...hinkansen "bullet trains"

*Yamagata Shinkansen "TSUBASA"*

*Nagano Shinkansen "ASAMA"*


**Nagano Shinkansen**
*(222.4 km)*
*Train Name: ASAMA*

**Nagano**

*San'yo Shinkansen "HIKARI Rail Star"*

*Tokaido & San'yo Shinkansen "HIKARI"*


**San'yo Shinkansen** *(622.3 km)*
*Train Names: NOZOMI, MIZUHO, HIKARI (incl. HIKARI Rail Star), SAKURA, KODAMA*

**Tokaido Shinkansen** *(552.6 km)*
*Train Names: NOZOMI, HIKARI, KODAM*

*(Tokyo thru Hakata, 1,174.9km)*

**Hakata** **Kokura** **Hiroshima** **Okayama** **Shin-Osaka** **Kyoto** **Nagoya** **Shin-Yokohama** **Shinag**

***Note: There are six types of train services, "NOZOMI," "MIZUHO," "HIKARI," "SAKURA," "KODAMA" and "TSUBAME" c the Tokaido, Sanyo and Kyushu Shinkansen, and the stations at which trains stop vary with train types. The JAPAN RA PASS is only valid for "HIKARI," "SAKURA," "KODAMA" and "TSUBAME" trains, and not valid for any seats, reserved c non-reserved, on "NOZOMI" and "MIZUHO" trains. To travel on the Tokaido, Sanyo and Kyushu Shinkansen, the pas holders must take "HIKARI," "SAKURA," "KODAMA" or "TSUBAME" trains, or pay the basic fare and the Shinkanse express charge to take "NOZOMI" and "MIZUHO" trains.***

*Kyushu Shinkansen "Series 800"*


**Kumamoto**

**Kyushu Shinkansen**
*(288.9 km)*
*Train Names:*
*MIZUHO, SAKURA,*
*TSUBAME*

**Kagoshima-chūō**

Presented by JAPAN RAILWAYS GROUP

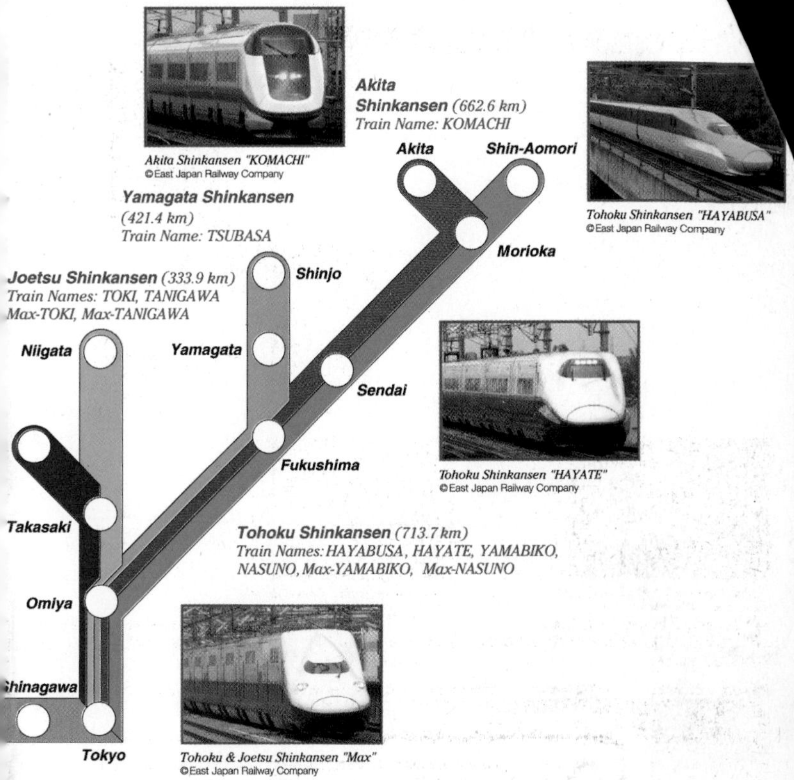


## •Stations in Tokyo area

**that have JAPAN RAIL PASS exchange offices**

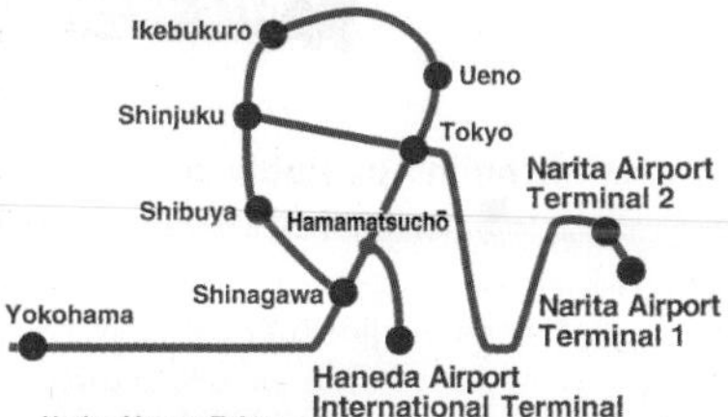


**Narita Airport - Tokyo**
About 60 min. by JR's limited express "Narita Express"
About 90 min. by JR's rapid train

## •Stations in Kansai area

**that have JAPAN RAIL PASS exchange offices**

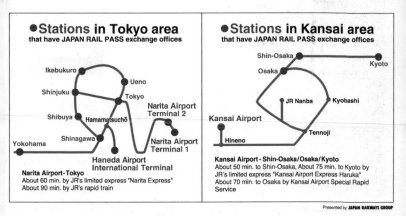

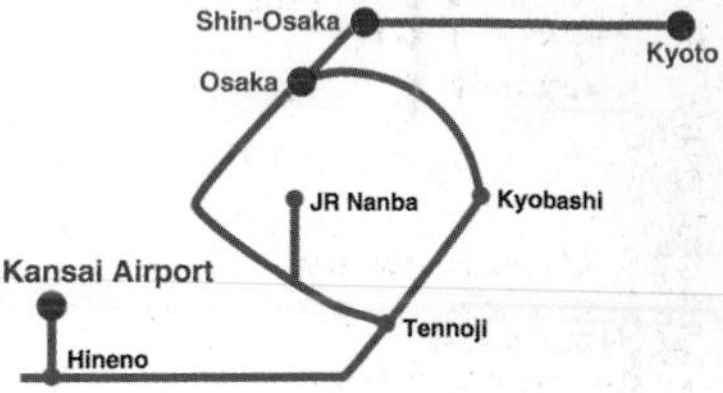


**Kansai Airport - Shin-Osaka/Osaka/Kyoto**
About 50 min. to Shin-Osaka, About 75 min. to Kyoto by JR's limited express "Kansai Airport Express Haruka"
About 70 min. to Osaka by Kansai Airport Special Rapid Service

Presented by JAPAN RAILWAYS GROUP

**Michelin Apa Publications Ltd**
58 Borough High Street, London SE1 1XF, United Kingdom


ISBN 978-1-907099-35-9
Printed: December 2011
Printed and bound in Germany